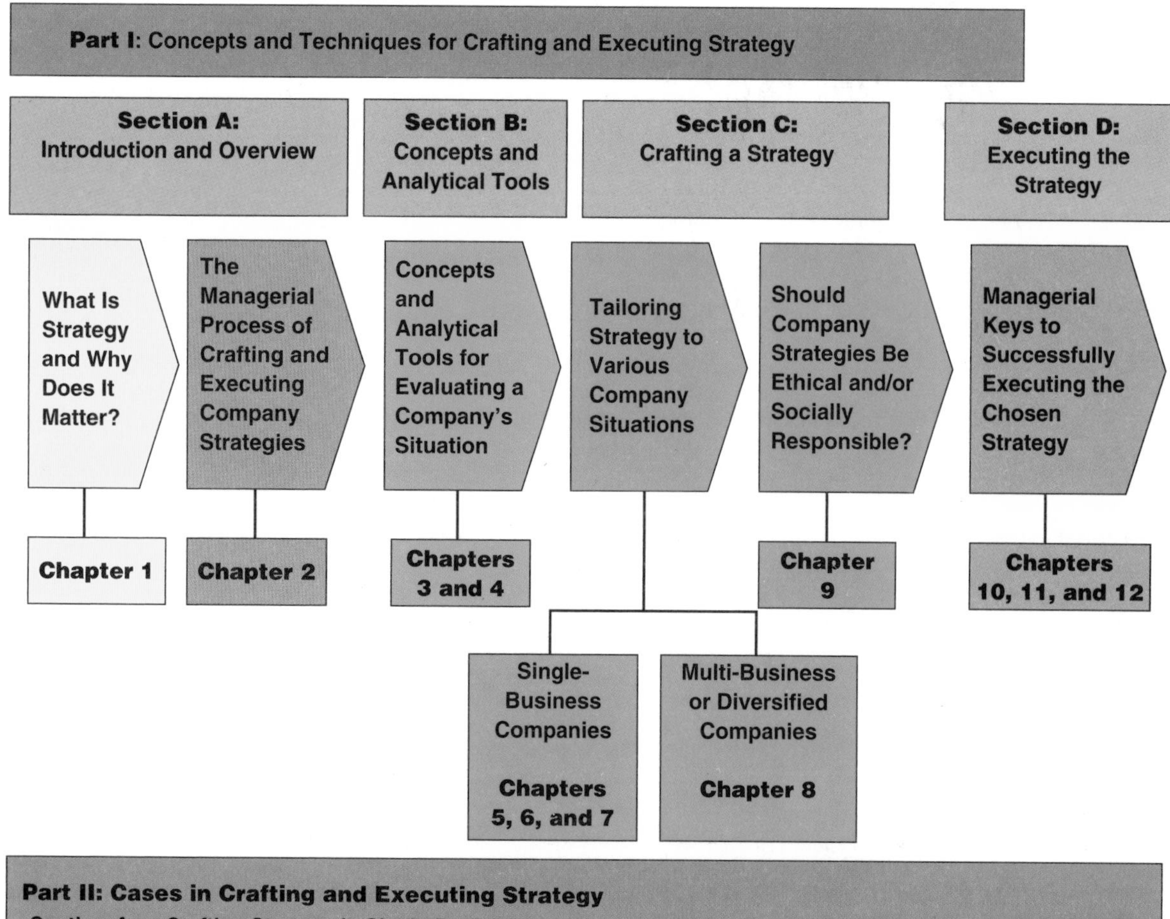

Part II: Cases in Crafting and Executing Strategy

Section A: Crafting Strategy in Single-Business Companies (17 cases)
Section B: Crafting Strategy in Diversified Companies (2 cases)
Section C: Implementing and Executing Strategy (5 cases)
Section D: Strategy, Ethics, and Social Responsibility (2 cases)

Crafting and Executing Strategy

The Quest for Competitive Advantage

Concepts and Cases

Arthur A. Thompson, Jr.
University of Alabama
A. J. Strickland III
University of Alabama
John E. Gamble
University of South Alabama

Crafting and Executing Strategy

The Quest for Competitive Advantage

Concepts and Cases

17TH EDITION

Boston Burr Ridge, IL Dubuque, IA New York San Francisco St. Louis
Bangkok Bogotá Caracas Kuala Lumpur Lisbon London Madrid Mexico City
Milan Montreal New Delhi Santiago Seoul Singapore Sydney Taipei Toronto

CRAFTING AND EXECUTING STRATEGY: THE QUEST FOR COMPETITIVE ADVANTAGE: CONCEPTS AND CASES

Published by McGraw-Hill/Irwin, a business unit of The McGraw-Hill Companies, Inc., 1221 Avenue of the Americas, New York, NY, 10020.

This book is printed on acid-free paper.

4 5 6 7 8 9 0 VNH/VNH 0

ISBN 978-0-07-353042-0
MHID 0-07-353042-5

Vice president and editor-in-chief: *Brent Gordon*
Executive editor: *Michael Ablassmeir*
Developmental editor II: *Laura Griffin*
Editorial coordinator: *Kelly Pekelder*
Senior marketing manager: *Anke Braun Weekes*
Marketing coordinator: *Michael Gedatus*
Senior project manager: *Harvey Yep*
Lead production supervisor: *Michael R. McCormick*
Interior designer: *Cara Hawthorne*
Senior photo research coordinator: *Lori Kramer*
Senior media project manager: *Susan Lombardi*
Cover design: *Jillian Lindner*
Interior design: *Jillian Lindner*
Cover image: *Punchstock*
Typeface: *10.5/12 Times New Roman*
Compositor: *Laserwords Private Limited*
Printer: *RR Donnelley*

Photo Credits: *Chapter 1, p. 4, © Images.com/Corbis, Bek Shakirov; Chapter 2, p. 22, © Images.com/Corbis, Robert Rogers; Chapter 3, p. 54, © Images.com/Corbis, Lael Henderson; Chapter 4, p. 100, © Images.com/Corbis; Chapter 5, p. 138, © Images.com/Corbis, Bruno Budrovic; Chapter 6, p. 164, © Images.com/Corbis; Chapter 7, p. 206, © Images.com/Corbis; Chapter 8, p. 238, © Images.com/Corbis, Christopher Zacharow; Chapter 9, p. 288, © Images.com/Corbis, Sheila Golden; Chapter 10, p. 326, © Images.com/Corbis, Rob Colvin; Chapter 11, p. 356, Images.com/Corbis, David C. Chen; Chapter 12, p. 384, © Images.com/Corbis, Paul Anderson.*

Library of Congress Cataloging-in-Publication Data

Thompson, Arthur A., 1940-
Crafting and executing strategy : the quest for competitive advantage : concepts and cases / Arthur A. Thompson, Jr., A. J. Strickland III, John E. Gamble.—17th ed.
p. cm.
Includes index.
ISBN-13: 978-0-07-353042-0 (alk. paper)
ISBN-10: 0-07-353042-5 (alk. paper)
1. Strategic planning. 2. Strategic planning—Case studies. I. Stickland, A. J. (Alonzo J.) II. Gamble, John (John E.) III. Title.
HD30.28.T53 2010
658.4'012–dc22

2009000710

www.mhhe.com

To our families and especially our wives:
Hasseline, Kitty, and Debra

About the Authors

Arthur A. Thompson, Jr., earned his B.S. and Ph.D. degrees in economics from The University of Tennessee, spent three years on the economics faculty at Virginia Tech, and served on the faculty of The University of Alabama's College of Commerce and Business Administration for 24 years. In 1974 and again in 1982, Dr. Thompson spent semester-long sabbaticals as a visiting scholar at the Harvard Business School.

His areas of specialization are business strategy, competition and market analysis, and the economics of business enterprises. In addition to publishing over 30 articles in some 25 different professional and trade publications, he has authored or co-authored five textbooks and six computer-based simulation exercises that are used in colleges and universities worldwide.

Dr. Thompson spends much of his off-campus time giving presentations, putting on management development programs, working with companies, and helping operate a business simulation enterprise in which he is a major partner.

Dr. Thompson and his wife of 48 years have two daughters, two grandchildren, and a Yorkshire terrier.

Dr. A. J. (Lonnie) Strickland, a native of North Georgia, attended the University of Georgia, where he received a bachelor of science degree in math and physics in 1965. Afterward he entered the Georgia Institute of Technology, where he received a master of science in industrial management. He earned a Ph.D. in business administration from Georgia State University in 1969. He currently holds the title of Professor of Strategic Management in the Graduate School of Business at The University of Alabama.

Dr. Strickland's experience in consulting and executive development is in the strategic management area, with a concentration in industry and competitive analysis. He has developed strategic planning systems for such firms as The Southern Company, BellSouth, South Central Bell, American Telephone and Telegraph, Gulf States Paper, Carraway Methodist Medical Center, Delco Remy, Mark IV Industries, Amoco Oil Company, USA Group, General Motors, and Kimberly Clark Corporation (Medical Products). He is a very popular speaker on the subject of implementing strategic change and serves on several corporate boards.

John E. Gamble is currently Associate Dean and Professor of Management in the Mitchell College of Business at the University of South Alabama. His teaching specialty at USA is strategic management and he also conducts a course in strategic management in Germany, which is sponsored by the University of Applied Sciences in Worms.

Dr. Gamble's research interests center on strategic issues in entrepreneurial, health care, and manufacturing settings. His work has been published in various scholarly journals and he is the author or co-author of more than 30 case studies published in an assortment of strategic management and strategic marketing texts. He has done consulting on industry and market analysis for clients in a diverse mix of industries.

Professor Gamble received his Ph.D. in management from The University of Alabama in 1995. Dr. Gamble also has a Bachelor of Science degree and a Master of Arts degree from The University of Alabama.

Preface

The two standout features of this 17th edition are a much-refined 12-chapter presentation and a fresh, compelling collection of 26 cases. A combination chapters/cases text is eminently suitable for courses where instructors wish to provide students with a foundation in the core concepts and analytical tools of strategic management as a prelude to having them work through a series of case assignments and/or participate in a strategy simulation exercise in which the class is divided into teams of two to five members and each team manages a company that competes head-to-head against companies run by the other teams. Two best-selling state-of-the-art online strategy simulations, *The Business Strategy Game* and *GLO-BUS,* are optional companions for this text—both simulations were created by this text's senior author as a means for instructors to give students *an engaging, learn-by-doing* experience in crafting and executing a strategy and applying the concepts and analytical tools covered in the chapters.

CHANGES, IMPROVEMENTS, AND DIFFERENTIATING FEATURES

As in any substantive revision, the chapter coverage has been trimmed in some areas, expanded in others. The content of two chapters in the prior edition has been condensed into a single chapter in this edition. A new section on strategic leadership has been added. There is important new coverage of corporate and environmental sustainability. As always, much effort has gone into refining the explanations of core concepts and analytical tools, updating and refreshing the examples, and including the latest research findings pertinent to a first course in strategy. At the end of each chapter, you will now find (1) "Assurance of Learning Exercises," which will help you measure student comprehension of the chapter content, and (2) "Exercises for Simulation Participants," which tightly connect the topics covered in the chapters to the issues and decisions that students have to wrestle with in managing their simulation company. However, we have preserved the fundamental character that has driven the text's success over three decades—the chapter content continues to be solidly mainstream and balanced, very much in step with the best academic thinking and contemporary management practice.

Complementing the text presentation is a powerhouse lineup of 26 diverse, timely, and thoughtfully crafted cases. Thanks to the talented efforts of dedicated case researchers in strategic management across the world, we have been fortunate in assembling a set of high-interest cases with unusual ability to work magic in the classroom. Great cases make it far easier for you to drive home valuable lessons in the whys and hows of successfully crafting and executing strategy. Many of the cases in this edition involve high-profile companies, and all are framed around issues and circumstances tightly linked to the content of the 12 chapters, thus giving students a wealth of opportunities to apply the concepts and analytical tools they have read about. We are confident you will be impressed with how well these cases will teach and the amount of student interest they will spark.

And there's an array of support materials in the Instructor Resources package to equip you with enormous course design flexibility and a powerful kit of teaching/learning tools. We've done our very best to ensure that the 17th edition package will work especially well for you in the classroom, help you economize on the time needed to be well-prepared for each class, and cause students to conclude that your course is one of the very best they have ever taken—from the standpoint of both enjoyment and learning a lot.

Differentiation from Other Texts

There are three noteworthy traits that strongly differentiate this text from others in the field:

1. *The coverage of resource-based theory of the firm in the 17th edition is unsurpassed by any other leading strategy text.* RBV principles and concepts are prominently and comprehensively integrated into our coverage of crafting both single-business and multibusiness strategies. In Chapters 3 through 8, we repeatedly emphasize that a company's strategy must be matched *not only* to its external market circumstances *but also* to its internal resources and competitive capabilities. Moreover, an RBV perspective is thoroughly integrated into the presentation on strategy execution (Chapters 10, 11, and 12) to make it unequivocally clear how and why the tasks of assembling intellectual capital and building core competencies and competitive capabilities are absolutely critical to successful strategy execution and operating excellence.
2. *The coverage of business ethics, core values, social responsibility, and environmental sustainability is unsurpassed by any other leading strategy text.* In this edition, we have embellished the highly important Chapter 9, "Ethical Business Strategies, Social Responsibility, and Environmental Sustainability," with fresh content so that it can better fulfill the important functions of (1) alerting students to the role and importance of ethical and socially responsible decision making and (2) addressing the accreditation requirements of the AACSB International that business ethics be visibly and thoroughly embedded in the core curriculum. Moreover, discussions of the roles of values and ethics are integrated into portions of Chapters 1, 2, 10, and 12 to further reinforce why and how considerations relating to ethics, values, social responsibility, and sustainability should figure prominently into the managerial task of crafting and executing company strategies.
3. *The caliber of the case collection in the 17th edition is truly top-notch.* From the standpoints of student appeal, being eminently teachable, and suitability for drilling students in the use of the concepts and analytical treatments in Chapters 1 through 12, the 26 cases included in this edition are the very latest, the best, and the most on-target that we could find. The ample information about the cases in the Instructor's Manual makes it effortless to select a set of cases each term that will capture the interest of students from start to finish.

What to Expect in the 12 Chapters

In preparing the text chapters for this 17th edition, we have strived to hit the bull's-eye with respect to both content and teaching/learning effectiveness. The overriding objective has been to do three things exceptionally well:

- Thoroughly explain core concepts and analytical tools in language that students can grasp. The discussions have been *carefully crafted to maximize understanding and facilitate correct application*—the enterprise of sound teaching is never well served by page-saving succinctness that leaves too much unsaid. And we have deliberately employed a pragmatic, down-to-earth writing style designed to engage students who, for the most part, will soon be practicing managers.
- Provide first-rate examples at every turn. Illustrating the connection and application of core concepts and analytical tools to real-world circumstances correctly is the only effective way to convince readers that the subject matter merits close attention and deals directly with *what every student needs to know* about crafting, implementing, and executing business strategies in today's market environments.
- Incorporate well-settled strategic management principles, recent research findings and contributions to the literature of strategic management, the latest thinking of prominent academics and practitioners in the field, and the practices and behavior of real-world companies—weaving these things into each chapter is essential to keep the content solidly in the mainstream of contemporary strategic thinking.

In addition, we have made a point of highlighting important strategy-related developments that permeate the world economy and many industries—the continuing march of industries and companies to *wider globalization,* the growing scope and strategic importance of *collaborative alliances,* the spread of *high-velocity change* to more industries and company environments, and how *advancing Internet technology* is driving fundamental changes in both strategy and internal operations in companies across the world. There is also coverage of corporate governance; the keys to successful diversification; and how Six Sigma, best practices, benchmarking, proper workforce compensation, and a strategy-supportive corporate culture act to promote operating excellence and effective strategy execution. You'll find up-to-date coverage of the continuing march of industries and companies to wider globalization, the growing scope and strategic importance of collaborative alliances, the spread of high-velocity change to more industries and company environments, and how online technology is driving fundamental changes in both strategy and internal operations in companies across the world.

Organization and Chapter Descriptions The following summaries call attention to the noteworthy features and topical emphasis in the 12 text chapters:

- Chapter 1 is focused directly on what strategy is and why it is important. There are substantive discussions of what is meant by the term *strategy,* the different elements of a company's strategy, and why management efforts to craft a company's strategy tend to be squarely aimed at building sustainable competitive advantage. Considerable emphasis is given to how and why a company's strategy is partly planned and partly reactive and why a company's strategy tends to evolve over time. There's an important section discussing what the term *business model* means and how it relates to the concept of strategy. The thrust of this first chapter is to convince students that good strategy + good strategy execution = good management. The chapter is a perfect accompaniment for your opening-day lecture on what the course is all about and why it matters.

- Chapter 2 concerns the managerial process of actually crafting and executing a strategy—it makes a great assignment for the second day of class and is a perfect follow-on to your first day's lecture. The focal point of the chapter is the five-step managerial process of crafting and executing strategy: (1) forming a strategic vision of where the company is headed and why, (2) the managerial importance of developing a balanced scorecard of objectives and performance targets that measure the company's progress, (3) crafting a strategy to achieve these targets and move the company toward its market destination, (4) implementing and executing the strategy, and (5) monitoring progress and making corrective adjustments as needed. Students are introduced to such core concepts as strategic visions, mission statements, strategic versus financial objectives, and strategic intent. An all-new section underscores that this five-step process requires strong strategic leadership. There's a robust discussion of why *all managers are on a company's strategy-making, strategy-executing team* and why a company's strategic plan is a collection of strategies devised by different managers at different levels in the organizational hierarchy. The chapter winds up with a concise but meaty section on corporate governance.
- Chapter 3 sets forth the now-familiar analytical tools and concepts of industry and competitive analysis and demonstrates the importance of tailoring strategy to fit the circumstances of a company's industry and competitive environment. The standout feature of this chapter is a presentation of Michael Porter's five-forces model of competition that we think is the clearest, most straightforward discussion of any text in the field. Globalization and Internet technology are treated as potent driving forces capable of reshaping industry competition—their roles as change agents have become factors that most companies in most industries must reckon with in forging winning strategies.
- Chapter 4 presents the resource-based view of the firm and convincingly argues why a company's strategy must be built around its resources, competencies, and competitive capabilities. The roles of core competencies and organizational resources and capabilities in creating customer value are *center stage* in the discussions of company resource strengths and weaknesses. SWOT analysis is cast as a simple, easy-to-use way to assess a company's resources and overall situation. There is solid coverage of value chain analysis, benchmarking, and competitive strength assessments—standard tools for appraising a company's relative cost position and market standing vis-à-vis rivals. *An important feature of this chapter is a table showing how key financial and operating ratios are calculated and how to interpret them;* students will find this table handy in doing the number-crunching needed to evaluate whether a company's strategy is delivering good financial performance.
- Chapter 5 deals with a company's quest for competitive advantage and is framed around the five generic competitive strategies—low-cost leadership, differentiation, best-cost provider, focused differentiation, and focused low-cost provider.
- A much-revamped Chapter 6 extends the coverage of the previous chapter and deals with what *other strategic actions* a company can take to complement its choice of

a basic competitive strategy and to employ a strategy that is wisely matched to both industry and competitive conditions and to company resources and capabilities. The chapter features sections on what use to make of strategic alliances and collaborative partnerships; merger and acquisition strategies; vertical integration strategies; outsourcing strategies; and the broad strategy options for companies competing in six representative industry and competitive situations: (1) emerging industries; (2) rapid-growth industries; (3) mature, slow-growth industries; (4) stagnant or declining industries; (5) turbulent, high-velocity industries; and (6) fragmented industries. The concluding section of this chapter covers first-mover advantages and disadvantages, including the first-mover benefits of pursuing a blue ocean strategy.

- Chapter 7 explores the full range of strategy options for competing in foreign markets: export strategies, licensing, franchising, multicountry strategies, global strategies, and collaborative strategies involving heavy reliance on strategic alliances and joint ventures. The spotlight is trained on two strategic issues unique to competing multinationally: (1) whether to customize the company's offerings in each different country market to better match the tastes and preferences of local buyers or whether to offer a mostly standardized product worldwide and (2) whether to employ essentially the same basic competitive strategy in the markets of all countries where it operates or whether to modify the company's competitive approach country-by-country as may be needed to fit the specific market conditions and competitive circumstances it encounters. There's also coverage of the special issues of competing in the markets of emerging countries and the strategies that local companies in emerging countries can use to defend against global giants.
- Our rather meaty treatment of diversification strategies for multibusiness enterprises in Chapter 8 begins by laying out the various paths for becoming diversified, explains how a company can use diversification to create or compound competitive advantage for its business units, and examines the strategic options an already-diversified company has to improve its overall performance. In the middle part of the chapter, the analytical spotlight is on the techniques and procedures for assessing the strategic attractiveness of a diversified company's business portfolio—the relative attractiveness of the various businesses the company has diversified into, a multi-industry company's competitive strength in each of its lines of business, and the *strategic fits* and *resource fits* among a diversified company's different businesses. The chapter concludes with a brief survey of a company's four main postdiversification strategy alternatives: (1) broadening the diversification base, (2) divesting some businesses and retrenching to a narrower diversification base, (3) restructuring the makeup of the company's business lineup, and (4) multinational diversification.
- Chapter 9 provides comprehensive coverage of some increasingly pertinent front-burner strategic issues: (1) whether and why a company has a *duty* to operate according to ethical standards and (2) whether and why a company has a *duty* or *obligation* to contribute to the betterment of society independent of the needs and preferences of the customers it serves. Is there a credible business case for operating ethically and/or operating in a socially responsible manner? Why should a company's strategy measure up to the standards of being environmentally sustainable? The opening section of the chapter addresses whether ethical standards are

universal (as maintained by the school of ethical universalism) or dependent on local norms and situational circumstances (as maintained by the school of ethical relativism) or a combination of both (as maintained by integrative social contracts theory). Following this are sections on the three categories of managerial morality (moral, immoral, and amoral), the drivers of unethical strategies and shady business behavior, the approaches to managing a company's ethical conduct, the concept of social responsibility, the moral and business cases for both ethical strategies and socially responsible behavior, the concept of environmental sustainability, and why every company's strategy should be crafted in an manner that promotes environmental sustainability. The contents of this chapter will definitely give students some things to ponder and, hopefully, will make them far more ethically aware and conscious of why *all companies* should conduct their business in a socially responsible and sustainable manner. Chapter 9 has been written as a "stand-alone" chapter that can be assigned in the early, middle, or late part of the course.

- The three-chapter module on executing strategy (Chapters 10–12) is anchored around a pragmatic, compelling conceptual framework: (1) building the resource strengths and organizational capabilities needed to execute the strategy in competent fashion; (2) allocating ample resources to strategy-critical activities; (3) ensuring that policies and procedures facilitate rather than impede strategy execution; (4) instituting best practices and pushing for continuous improvement in how value chain activities are performed; (5) installing information and operating systems that enable company personnel to better carry out their strategic roles proficiently; (6) tying rewards and incentives directly to the achievement of performance targets and good strategy execution; (7) shaping the work environment and corporate culture to fit the strategy; and (8) exerting the internal leadership needed to drive execution forward. The recurring theme throughout these three chapters is that implementing and executing strategy entails figuring out the specific actions, behaviors, and conditions that are needed for a smooth strategy-supportive operation and then following through to get things done and deliver results—the goal here is to ensure that students understand the strategy-implementing/strategy-executing phase is a make-things-happen and make-them-happen-right kind of managerial exercise that leads to operating excellence and good performance.

We have done our best to ensure that the 12 chapters hit the bull's-eye in covering the concepts, analytical tools, and approaches to strategic thinking that should comprise a senior/MBA course in strategy. The ultimate test of this or any text, of course, is the positive pedagogical impact it has in the classroom. If this edition sets a more effective stage for your lectures and does a better job of helping you persuade students that the discipline of strategy merits their rapt attention, then it will have fulfilled its purpose.

THE CASE COLLECTION

The 26-case lineup in this edition is flush with interesting companies and valuable lessons for students in the art and science of crafting and executing strategy. There's a good blend of cases from a length perspective—over one-third are under 16 pages yet offer plenty for students to chew on; about a fourth are medium-length cases; and the remainder are detail-rich cases that call for more sweeping analysis.

At least 21 of the 26 cases involve companies, products, or people that students will have heard of, know about from personal experience, or can easily identify with. The lineup includes at least 11 cases that will provide students with insight into the special demands of competing in industry environments where technological developments are an everyday event, product life cycles are short, and competitive maneuvering among rivals comes fast and furious. Eighteen of the cases involve situations where company resources and competitive capabilities play as large a role in the strategy-making, strategy-executing scheme of things as industry and competitive conditions do. Scattered throughout the lineup are 9 cases concerning non-U.S. companies, globally competitive industries, and/or cross-cultural situations; these cases, in conjunction with the globalized content of the text chapters, provide abundant material for linking the study of strategic management tightly to the ongoing globalization of the world economy. You'll also find 3 cases dealing with the strategic problems of family-owned or relatively small entrepreneurial businesses and 22 cases involving public companies about which students can do further research on the Internet.

Nine of the 26 cases have accompanying videotape segments—Costco Wholesale, JetBlue Airways, Competition in the Movie Rental Industry, Dell Inc., Panera Bread Company, Competition in Video Game Consoles, Google, Wal-Mart, and Southwest Airlines.

TWO ACCOMPANYING ONLINE STRATEGY SIMULATION EXERCISES: *THE BUSINESS STRATEGY GAME* AND *GLO-BUS*

The Business Strategy Game and *GLO-BUS: Developing Winning Competitive Strategies*—two competition-based strategy simulations that are delivered online and that feature automated processing of decisions and grading of performance—are being marketed by the publisher as companion supplements for use with this and other texts in the field. *The Business Strategy Game* (*BSG*) is the world's leading strategy simulation, having been played by more than 500,000 students at 600+ universities across the world. *GLO-BUS,* a somewhat simpler online simulation introduced in 2004, has been used at more than 150 universities across the world in courses involving more than 50,000 students.

The two simulations are very tightly linked to the material that your class members will be reading about in the text chapters—the senior author of this text is a co-author of both *BSG* and *GLO-BUS.* Moreover, both simulations were painstakingly developed with an eye towards economizing on instructor course preparation time and grading. You'll be pleasantly surprised—and we think quite pleased—at how little time it takes to gear up for and to administer a fully automated online simulation like *BSG* or *GLO-BUS.*

In both *BSG and GLO-BUS,* class members are divided into management teams of one to five persons and assigned to run a company in head-to-head competition against companies run by other class members. In *BSG,* the co-managers of each team run an athletic footwear company, producing and marketing both branded and private-label footwear. In *GLO-BUS,* the co-managers of each team operate a digital camera company that designs, assembles, and markets entry-level digital cameras and upscale, multifeatured cameras. In both simulations, companies compete in a global market arena, selling their products in four geographic regions—Europe-Africa, North America, Asia-Pacific, and Latin America. There are decisions relating to plant operations, workforce compensation, pricing and marketing, finance, and corporate social responsibility.

You can schedule 1 or 2 practice rounds and 4 to 10 regular (scored) decision rounds; each decision round represents a year of company operations. When the instructor-specified deadline for a decision round arrives, the algorithms built into the simulation award sales and market shares to the competing companies, region by region. Each company's sales are totally governed by how its prices compare against the prices of rival brands, how its product quality compares against the quality of rival brands, how its product line breadth and selection compares, how its advertising effort compares, and so on for a total of 11 competitive factors that determine unit sales and market shares. The competitiveness of each company's product offering *relative to rivals* is all-decisive—this is what makes them "competition-based" strategy simulations. Once sales and market shares are awarded, the company and industry reports are then generated and all the results made available 15–20 minutes after the decision deadline.

Both simulations feature a Learning Assurance Report that rates your students' performance on facets of learning included in accreditation standards for most business school programs. Also, at the end of each text chapter is a section containing exercises for simulation participants that require students to use what they have read in the chapter in running their simulation company.

The Compelling Case for Incorporating Use of a Strategy Simulation

There are five *exceptionally important benefits* associated with using a competition-based simulation in strategy courses taken by seniors and MBA students:

- Assigning students to run a company that competes head-to-head against companies run by other class members *gives students immediate opportunity to experiment with various strategy options and to gain proficiency in applying the core concepts and analytical tools that they have been reading about in the chapters.* The issues and decisions that co-managers face in running their simulation company embrace the very concepts, analytical tools, and strategy options they encounter in the text chapters. Giving class members *immediate "learn-by-doing" opportunity* to apply and experiment with the material covered in their text, while at the same time honing their business and decision-making skills, generates solid learning results.
- *A competition-based strategy simulation arouses positive energy and classroom excitement, engages students in the subject matter of the course, is a fun way for students to learn, and steps up the whole tempo of the course by a notch or two—all of which greatly facilitate the achievement of course learning objectives.* The healthy rivalry that emerges among the management teams of competing companies can be counted on to stir competitive juices and spur class members to fully exercise their strategic wits, analytical skills, and decision-making prowess. *Nothing energizes a class quicker or better than concerted efforts on the part of class members to gain a high industry ranking and avoid the perilous consequences of falling too far behind the best-performing companies.* Case analysis assignments

lack the capacity to generate the interest and excitement that occur when the results of the latest decision round become available and co-managers renew their quest for strategic moves and actions that will strengthen company performance. As soon as your students start to say "Wow! Not only is this fun but I am learning a lot," which they will, you have won the battle of engaging students in the subject matter and moved the value of taking your course to a much higher plateau in the business school curriculum. This translates into a livelier, richer learning experience for students and better instructor-course evaluations.

- Because a simulation involves making decisions relating to production operations, worker compensation and training, sales and marketing, distribution, customer service, finance, and corporate social responsibility and requires analysis of company financial statements and market data, *the simulation helps students synthesize the knowledge gained in a variety of different business courses. The cross-functional, integrative nature of a strategy simulation helps make courses in strategy more of a true capstone experience.*
- *Using both case analysis and a competition-based strategy simulation to drive home the lessons* that class members are expected to learn *is far more pedagogically powerful and lasting than case analysis alone.* Both cases and strategy simulations drill students in thinking strategically and applying what they read in your text, thus helping them connect theory with practice and gradually building better business judgment. What cases do that a simulation cannot is give class members broad exposure to a variety of companies and industry situations and insight into the kinds of strategy-related problems managers face. But what a competition-based strategy simulation does far better than case analysis is thrust class members squarely into an active managerial role where they have to take the analysis of market conditions, the actions of competitors, and their company's situation seriously. Because they are held fully accountable for their decisions and their company's performance, co-managers are strongly motivated to dig deeply into company operations, probe for ways to be more cost-efficient, and ferret out strategic moves and decisions calculated to boost company performance. Such diligent and purposeful actions on the part of company co-managers translate into a productive and beneficial learning experience.
- *Use of a fully automated online simulation can reduce the time instructors spend on course preparation and grading papers.* Simulation adopters often compensate for the added student workload of a simulation by trimming the number of assigned cases from, say, 10 to 12 to perhaps 4 to 6, which significantly reduces the time instructors have to spend on case preparation. Course preparation time can be further cut because you can use several class days to have students meet in the computer lab to work on upcoming decisions or a three-year strategic plan (in lieu of lecturing on a chapter or covering an additional assigned case). Lab sessions provide a splendid opportunity for you to visit with teams, observe the interplay among co-managers, and view the caliber of the learning experience that is going on. Furthermore, you can compensate for the added student workload associated with participating in a simulation by cutting back on other assignments that entail considerable grading on your part. Grading one less written case or essay exam or other written assignment saves enormous time. With either simulation,

grading is effortless, requiring only that you enter percentage weights for each assignment in your online grade book.

In sum, *a three-pronged text-case-simulation course model has significantly more teaching/learning power than the traditional text-case model.* Indeed, a very convincing argument can be made that a competition-based strategy simulation is *the single most effective teaching/learning tool that instructors can employ to teach the discipline of business and competitive strategy, to make learning more enjoyable, and to achieve course learning objectives.*

A Bird's-Eye View of *The Business Strategy Game*

The setting for *The Business Strategy Game* (*BSG*) is the global athletic footwear industry—there can be little doubt in today's world that a globally competitive strategy simulation is *vastly superior* to a simulation with a domestic-only setting. Global market demand for footwear grows at the rate of 7–9 percent annually for the first five years and 5–7 percent annually for the second five years. However, market growth rates vary by geographic region—North America, Latin America, Europe-Africa, and Asia-Pacific.

Companies begin the simulation producing branded and private-label footwear in two plants, one in North America and one in Asia. They have the option to establish production facilities in Latin America and Europe-Africa, either by constructing new plants or buying previously constructed plants that competing companies have sold. Company co-managers exercise control over production costs based on the styling and quality they opt to manufacture, plant location (wages and incentive compensation vary from region to region), the use of best practices and Six Sigma programs to reduce the production of defective footwear and to boost worker productivity, and compensation practices.

All newly produced footwear is shipped in bulk containers to one of four geographic distribution centers. All sales in a geographic region are made from footwear inventories in that region's distribution center. Costs at the four regional distribution centers are a function of inventory storage costs, packing and shipping fees, import tariffs paid on incoming pairs shipped from foreign plants, and exchange rate impacts. At the start of the simulation, import tariffs average $4 per pair in Europe-Africa, $6 per pair in Latin America, and $8 in the Asia-Pacific region. However, the Free Trade Treaty of the Americas allows tariff-free movement of footwear between North America and Latin America. Instructors have the option to alter tariffs as the game progresses.

Companies market their brand of athletic footwear to retailers worldwide and to individuals buying online at the company's Web site. Each company's sales and market share in the branded footwear segments hinge on its competitiveness on 11 factors: attractive pricing, footwear styling and quality, product line breadth, advertising, the use of mail-in rebates, the appeal of celebrities endorsing a company's brand, success in convincing footwear retailers dealers to carry its brand, the number of weeks it takes to fill retailer orders, the effectiveness of a company's online sales effort at its Web site, and customer loyalty. Sales of private-label footwear hinge solely on being the low-price bidder.

All told, company co-managers make as many as 53 types of decisions each period that cut across production operations (up to 10 decisions each plant, with a maximum of 4 plants), plant capacity additions/sales/upgrades (up to 6 decisions per plant), worker compensation and training (3 decisions per plant), shipping (up to 8 decisions each plant), pricing and marketing (up to 10 decisions in 4 geographic regions), bids to sign celebrities (2 decision entries per bid), financing of company operations (up to 8 decisions), and corporate social responsibility and environmental sustainability (up to 6 decisions).

Each time company co-managers make a decision entry, an assortment of on-screen calculations instantly shows the projected effects on unit sales, revenues, market shares, unit costs, profit, earnings per share, ROE, and other operating statistics. The on-screen calculations help team members evaluate the relative merits of one decision entry versus another and put together a promising strategy.

Companies can employ any of the five generic competitive strategy options in selling branded footwear—low-cost leadership, differentiation, best-cost provider, focused low-cost, and focused differentiation. They can pursue essentially the same strategy worldwide or craft slightly or very different strategies for the Europe-Africa, Asia-Pacific, Latin America, and North America markets. They can strive for competitive advantage based on more advertising or a wider selection of models or more appealing styling/quality, or bigger rebates, and so on.

Any well-conceived, well-executed competitive approach is capable of succeeding, provided it is not overpowered by the strategies of competitors or defeated by the presence of too many copycat strategies that dilute its effectiveness. The challenge for each company's management team is to craft and execute a competitive strategy that produces good performance on five measures: earnings per share, return on equity investment, stock price appreciation, credit rating, and brand image.

All activity for *The Business Strategy Game* takes place at www.bsg-online.com.

A Bird's-Eye View of *GLO-BUS*

The industry setting for *GLO-BUS* is the digital camera industry. Global market demand grows at the rate of 8–10 percent annually for the first five years and 4–6 percent annually for the second five years. Retail sales of digital cameras are seasonal, with about 20 percent of consumer demand coming in each of the first three quarters of each calendar year and 40 percent coming during the big fourth-quarter retailing season.

Companies produce entry-level and upscale, multifeatured cameras of varying designs and quality in a Taiwan assembly facility and ship assembled cameras directly to retailers in North America, Asia-Pacific, Europe-Africa, and Latin America. All cameras are assembled as retail orders come in and shipped immediately upon completion of the assembly process—companies maintain no finished goods inventories and all parts and components are delivered on a just-in-time basis (which eliminates the need to track inventories and simplifies the accounting for plant operations and costs). Company co-managers exercise control over production costs based on the designs and components they specify for their cameras, workforce compensation and training, the length of warranties offered (which affects warranty costs), the amount spent for technical support provided to buyers of the company's cameras, and their management of the assembly process.

Competition in each of the two product market segments (entry-level and multi-featured digital cameras) is based on 10 factors: price, camera performance and quality, number of quarterly sales promotions, length of promotions in weeks, the size of the promotional discounts offered, advertising, the number of camera models, size of retail dealer network, warranty period, and the amount/caliber of technical support provided to camera buyers. Low-cost leadership, differentiation strategies, best-cost provider strategies, and focus strategies are all viable competitive options. Rival companies can strive to be the clear market leader in either entry-level cameras or upscale multifeatured cameras or both. They can focus on one or two geographic regions or strive for geographic balance. They can pursue essentially the same strategy worldwide or craft slightly or very different strategies for the Europe-Africa, Asia-Pacific, Latin America, and North America markets. Just as with *The Business Strategy Game,* most any well-conceived, well-executed competitive approach is capable of succeeding, *provided it is not overpowered by the strategies of competitors or defeated by the presence of too many copycat strategies that dilute its effectiveness.*

Company co-managers make 49 types of decisions each period, ranging from R&D, camera components, and camera performance (10 decisions) to production operations and worker compensation (15 decisions) to pricing and marketing (15 decisions) to the financing of company operations (4 decisions) to corporate social responsibility (6 decisions). Each time participants make a decision entry, an assortment of on-screen calculations instantly shows the projected effects on unit sales, revenues, market shares, unit costs, profit, earnings per share, ROE, and other operating statistics. These on-screen calculations help team members evaluate the relative merits of one decision entry versus another and stitch the separate decisions into a cohesive and promising strategy. Company performance is judged on five criteria: earnings per share, return on equity investment, stock price, credit rating, and brand image.

All activity for *GLO-BUS* occurs at www.glo-bus.com.

Administration and Operating Features of the Two Simulations

The Internet delivery and user-friendly designs of both *BSG* and *GLO-BUS* make them incredibly easy to administer, even for first-time users. And the menus and controls are so similar that you can readily switch between the two simulations or use one in your undergraduate class and the other in a graduate class. If you have not yet used either of the two simulations, you may find the following of particular interest:

- Time requirements for instructors are minimal. Setting up the simulation for your course is done online and takes about 10–15 minutes. Once setup is completed, no other administrative actions are required beyond that of moving participants to a different team (should the need arise) and monitoring the progress of the simulation (to whatever extent desired).
- Participant's Guides are delivered at the Web site—students can read it on their monitors or print out a copy, as they prefer.
- There are extensive built-in Help screens explaining (1) each decision entry, (2) the information on each page of the Industry Reports, and (3) the numbers presented in the Company Reports. *The Help screens allow company co-managers to*

figure things out for themselves, thereby curbing the need for students to always run to the instructor with questions about "how things work."

- The results of each decision round are processed automatically and are typically available to all participants *15 minutes* after the decision round deadline specified by the instructor/game administrator.
- Participants and instructors are notified via e-mail when the results are ready.
- Schedules for the decision rounds are instructor-determined. Decision rounds can be scheduled once a week, twice a week, or even twice a day, depending on how instructors want to conduct the exercise.
- Following each decision round, participants are provided with a complete set of reports—a six-page Industry Report, a one-page Competitive Intelligence report for each geographic region that includes strategic group maps and bulleted lists of competitive strengths and weaknesses, and a set of Company Reports (income statement, balance sheet, cash flow statement, and assorted production, marketing, and cost statistics).
- Two open-book multiple-choice tests of 20 questions are built into each simulation. The quizzes, which you can require or not as you see fit, are taken online and automatically graded, with scores reported instantaneously to participants and automatically recorded in the instructor's electronic grade book. Students are automatically provided with three sample questions for each test.
- Both simulations contain a three-year strategic plan option that you can assign. Scores on the plan are automatically recorded in the instructor's online grade book.
- At the end of the simulation, you can have students complete online peer evaluations (again, the scores are automatically recorded in your online grade book).
- Both simulations have a Company Presentation feature that enables students to easily prepare PowerPoint slides for use in describing their strategy and summarizing their company's performance in a presentation either to the class, the instructor, or an "outside" board of directors.
- *A Learning Assurance Report provides you with hard data concerning how well your students performed vis-à-vis students playing the simulation worldwide over the past 12 months.* The report is based on eight measures of student proficiency, business know-how, and decision-making skill and can also be used in evaluating the extent to which your school's academic curriculum produces the desired degree of student learning insofar as accreditation standards are concerned.

For more details on either simulation, please consult Section 2 of the Instructor's Manual accompanying this text or register as an instructor at the simulation Web sites (www.bsg-online.com and www.glo-bus.com) to access even more comprehensive information. Using Internet conferencing technology, the simulation authors conduct seminars several times each month (sometimes each week) to demonstrate how the software works, walk you through the various features and menu options, and answer any questions. By all means, please feel free to call the senior author of this text at (205) 722-9145 to arrange a personal demonstration or talk about how one of the simulations might work in one of your courses. We think you'll be quite impressed with the capabilities that have been programmed into *The Business Strategy Game* or *GLO-BUS,* the simplicity with which both simulations can be administered, and their exceptionally tight connection to the text chapters, core concepts, and standard analytical tools.

RESOURCES AND SUPPORT MATERIALS FOR THE 17TH EDITION

FOR STUDENTS

Key Points Summaries

At the end of each chapter is a synopsis of the core concepts, analytical tools and other key points discussed in the chapter. These chapter-end synopses, along with the margin notes scattered throughout each chapter, help students focus on basic strategy principles, digest the messages of each chapter, and prepare for tests.

Two Sets of Chapter-End Exercises

Each chapter concludes with two sets of exercises. The "Assurance of Learning Exercises" can be used as the basis for class discussion, oral presentation assignments, short written reports, and substitutes for case assignments. The "Exercises for Simulation Participants" are designed expressly for use by adopters who have incorporated use of a simulation and wish to go a step further in tightly and explicitly connecting the chapter content to the simulation company their students are running. The questions in both sets of exercises (along with those Illustration Capsules that qualify as mini-cases) can be used to round out the rest of a 75-minute class period should your lecture on a chapter last only for 50 minutes.

A Value-Added Web Site

The student section of the Online Learning Center (OLC) or Web site www.mhhe.com/thompson contains a number of helpful aids:

- Twenty-question self-scoring chapter tests that students can take to measure their grasp of the material presented in each of the 12 chapters.
- A "Guide to Case Analysis" containing sections on what a case is, why cases are a standard part of courses in strategy, preparing a case for class discussion, doing a written case analysis, doing an oral presentation, and using financial ratio analysis to assess a company's financial condition. We suggest having students read this Guide prior to the first class discussion of a case.
- PowerPoint slides for each chapter.
- Study questions for each of the 26 cases in this edition.

Premium Content Delivered at the Web Site

The publisher's Web site for the text has an assortment of offerings that you may find valuable for your course. Purchasing access to our premium learning resources right on the Web site provides students with the following value-added resources—narrated slides and videos, which along with chapter tests, are also available for iPod download to help students prepare for exams.

FOR INSTRUCTORS

Online Learning Center (OLC)

In addition to the student resources, the instructor section of www.mhhe.com/thompson includes a comprehensive Instructor's Manual and other support materials. Your McGraw-Hill representative can arrange delivery of instructor support materials in a format-ready Standard Cartridge for Blackboard, WebCT, and other Web-based educational platforms.

Instructor's Manual

The accompanying IM contains suggestions for organizing and structuring your course, sample syllabi and course outlines (including those with and without use of an accompanying strategy simulation), a set of lecture notes, a copy of the test bank, and comprehensive teaching notes for all 26 cases in this edition.

Test Bank

There is a test bank containing more than 900 multiple-choice questions and short-answer/essay questions. It has been tagged with AACSB and Bloom's Taxonomy criteria.

EZ Test

McGraw-Hill's flexible electronic testing program EZ Test Online (www.eztestonline.com) allows instructors to create paper and online tests or quizzes using the 900-question test bank or the instructor's own questions.

PowerPoint Slides

To facilitate delivery preparation of your lectures and to serve as chapter outlines, you'll have access to approximately 500 colorful and professional-looking slides displaying core concepts, analytical procedures, key points, and all the figures in the text chapters. The slides are largely the creation of Professor Jana Kuzmicki of Troy State University.

Instructor's Resource DVD

All of our instructor supplements are available in this one-stop multimedia resource, which includes the complete Instructor's Manual, Computerized Test Bank (EZ Test), accompanying PowerPoint slides, the Digital Image Library with all the figures from the text and videos accompanying the cases and chapters.

The Business Strategy Game and *GLO-BUS* Online Simulations

Using one of the two companion simulations is a powerful and constructive way of emotionally connecting students to the subject matter of the course. We know of no more effective and interesting way to stimulate the competitive energy of students and prepare them for the rigors of real-world business decision making than to have them match strategic wits with classmates in running a company in head-to-head competition for global market leadership.

ACKNOWLEDGMENTS

We heartily acknowledge the contributions of the case researchers whose case-writing efforts appear herein and the companies whose cooperation made the cases possible. To each one goes a very special thank-you. We cannot overstate the importance of timely, carefully researched cases in contributing to a substantive study of strategic management issues and practices. From a research standpoint, strategy-related cases are invaluable in exposing the generic kinds of strategic issues that companies face, in forming hypotheses about strategic behavior, and in drawing experienced-based generalizations about the practice of strategic management. From an instructional standpoint, strategy cases give students essential practice in diagnosing and evaluating the strategic situations of companies and organizations, in applying the concepts and tools of strategic analysis, in weighing strategic options and crafting strategies, and in tackling the challenges of successful strategy execution. Without a continuing stream of fresh, well-researched, and well-conceived cases, the discipline of strategic management would lose its close ties to the very institutions whose strategic actions and behavior it is aimed at explaining. There's no question, therefore, that first-class case research constitutes a valuable scholarly contribution to the theory and practice of strategic management.

In addition, a great number of colleagues and students at various universities, business acquaintances, and people at McGraw-Hill provided inspiration, encouragement, and counsel during the course of this project. Like all text authors in the strategy field, we are intellectually indebted to the many academics whose research and writing have blazed new trails and advanced the discipline of strategic management. The following reviewers provided seasoned advice and splendid suggestions for improving the chapters in this 17th edition:

Dennis R. Balch	University of North Alabama
Jeffrey R. Bruehl	Bryan College
Edith C. Busija	Murray State University
Donald A. Drost	California State University–San Bernardino
Randall Harris	California State University–Stanislaus
Mark Lewis Hoelscher	Illinois State University
Phyllis Holland	Valdosta State University
James W. Kroeger	Cleveland State University
Sal Kukalis	California State University–Long Beach
Brian W. Kulik	Central Washington University
Paul Mallette	Colorado State University
Anthony U. Martinez	San Francisco State University
Lee Pickler	Baldwin-Wallace College
Sabine Reddy	California State University–Long Beach
Thomas D. Schramko	The University of Toledo
V. Seshan	Pepperdine University
Charles Strain	University of Houston–Downtown
Sabine Turnley	Kansas State University
S. Stephen Vitucci	Tarleton State University
Andrew Ward	University of Georgia
Sibin Wu	University of Texas–Pan American

We also express our thanks to Lynne Patten, Nancy E. Landrum, Jim Goes, Jon Kalinowski, Rodney M. Walter, Judith D. Powell, Seyda Deligonul, David Flanagan, Esmerlda Garbi, Mohsin Habib, Kim Hester, Jeffrey E. McGee, Diana J, Wong, F. William Brown, Anthony F. Chelte, Gregory G. Dess, Alan B. Eisner, John George, Carle M. Hunt, Theresa Marron-Grodsky, Sarah Marsh, Joshua D. Martin, William L. Moore, Donald Neubaum, George M. Puia, Amit Shah, Lois M. Shelton, Mark Weber, Steve Barndt, J. Michael Geringer, Ming-Fang Li, Richard Stackman, Stephen Tallman, Gerardo R. Ungson, James Boulgarides, Betty Diener, Daniel F. Jennings, David Kuhn, Kathryn Martell, Wilbur Mouton, Bobby Vaught, Tuck Bounds, Lee Burk, Ralph Catalanello, William Crittenden, Vince Luchsinger, Stan Mendenhall, John Moore, Will Mulvaney, Sandra Richard, Ralph Roberts, Thomas Turk, Gordon Von-Stroh, Fred Zimmerman, S. A. Billion, Charles Byles, Gerald L. Geisler, Rose Knotts, Joseph Rosenstein, James B. Thurman, Ivan Able, W. Harvey Hegarty, Roger Evered, Charles B. Saunders, Rhae M. Swisher, Claude I. Shell, R. Thomas Lenz, Michael C. White, Dennis Callahan, R. Duane Ireland, William E. Burr II, C. W. Millard, Richard Mann, Kurt Christensen, Neil W. Jacobs, Louis W. Fry, D. Robley Wood, George J. Gore, and William R. Soukup. These reviewers provided valuable guidance in steering our efforts to improve earlier editions.

As always, we value your recommendations and thoughts about the book. Your comments regarding coverage and contents will be taken to heart, and we always are grateful for the time you take to call our attention to printing errors, deficiencies, and other shortcomings. Please e-mail us at athompso@cba.ua.edu, astrickl@cba.ua.edu, or jgamble@usouthal.edu; fax us at (205) 348-6695; or write us at P.O. Box 870225, Department of Management and Marketing, The University of Alabama, Tuscaloosa, Alabama 35487-0225.

Arthur A. Thompson

A. J. Strickland

John E. Gamble

Guided Tour

Chapter Structure and Organization

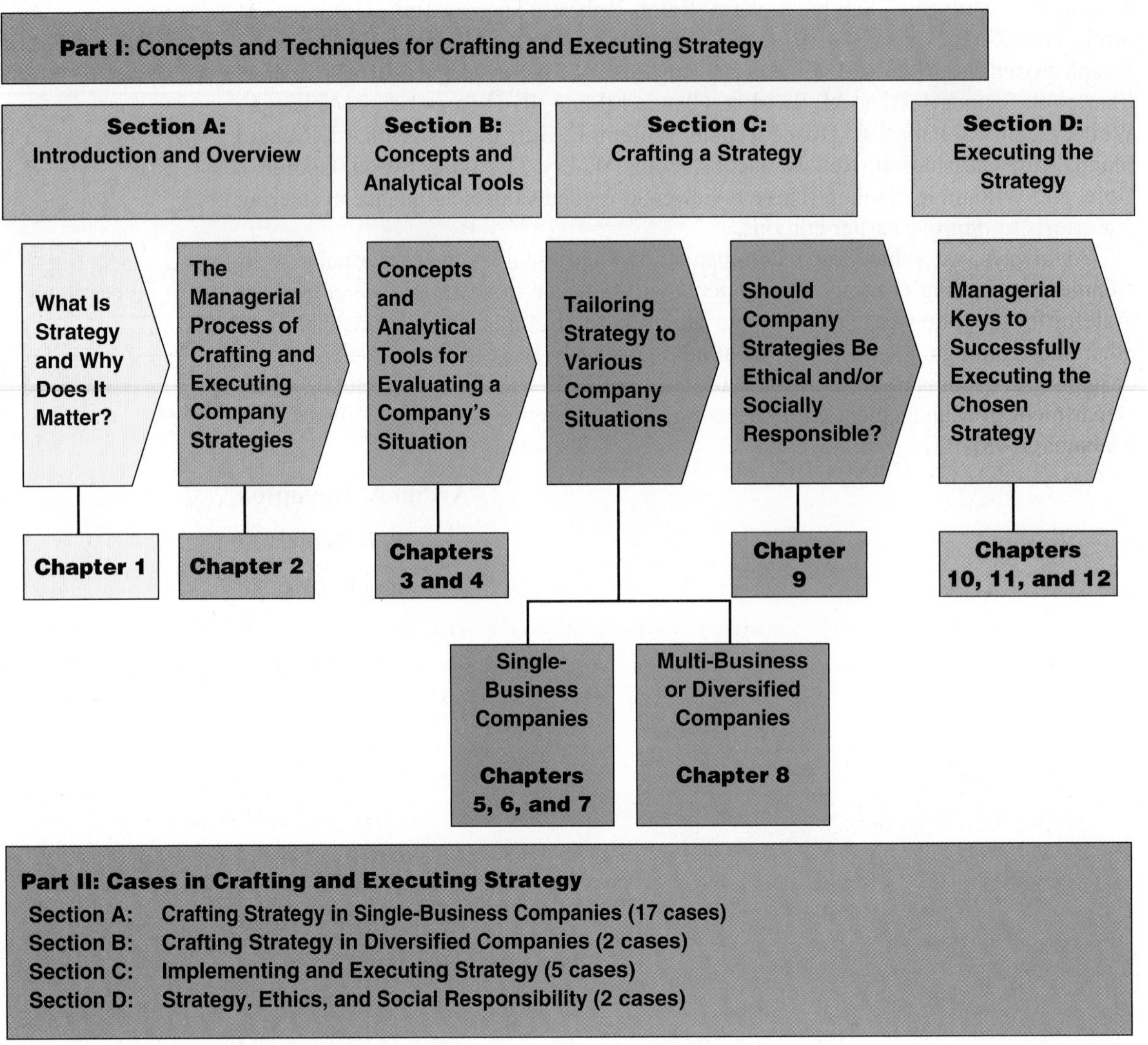

Part I: Concepts and Techniques for Crafting and Executing Strategy
Section A: Introduction and Overview
Section B: Concepts and Analytical Tools
Section C: Crafting a Strategy
Section D: Executing the Strategy
What Is Strategy and Why Does It Matter?
The Managerial Process of Crafting and Executing Company Strategies
Concepts and Analytical Tools for Evaluating a Company's Situation
Tailoring Strategy to Various Company Situations
Should Company Strategies Be Ethical and/or Socially Responsible?
Managerial Keys to Successfully Executing the Chosen Strategy
Chapter 1
Chapter 2
Chapters 3 and 4
Chapter 9
Chapters 10, 11, and 12
Single-Business Companies
Chapters 5, 6, and 7
Multi-Business or Diversified Companies
Chapter 8
Part II: Cases in Crafting and Executing Strategy
Section A: Crafting Strategy in Single-Business Companies (17 cases)
Section B: Crafting Strategy in Diversified Companies (2 cases)
Section C: Implementing and Executing Strategy (5 cases)
Section D: Strategy, Ethics, and Social Responsibility (2 cases)

CHAPTER 1

What Is Strategy and Why Is It Important?

Strategy means making clear-cut choices about how to compete.
—**Jack Welch**
Former CEO, General Electric

A strategy is a commitment to undertake one set of actions rather than another.
—**Sharon Oster**
Professor, Yale University

Without a strategy the organization is like a ship without a rudder.
—**Joel Ross and Michael Kami**
Authors and Consultants

LEARNING OBJECTIVES

1. Understand of the role of business strategies in moving a company in an intended direction, growing its business, and improving its financial and market performance.
2. Develop an awareness of the four most frequently used and dependable strategic approaches for setting a company apart from rivals and winning a sustainable competitive advantage.
3. Learn that business strategies evolve over time because of changing circumstances and ongoing management efforts to improve the company's strategy.
4. Understand why a company's strategy must be underpinned by a business model that produces revenues sufficient to cover costs and earn a profit.
5. Learn the three tests that distinguish a winning strategy from a so-so or flawed strategy.
6. Learn why good strategy making and good strategy execution are the most trustworthy signs of good management.

Managers face three central questions in evaluating their company's business prospects:

- What's the company's present situation?
- Where does the company need to go from here?
- How should it get there?

The question "What's the company's present situation?" prompts managers to evaluate industry conditions and competitive pressures, the company's current performance and market standing, its resource strengths and capabilities, and its competitive weaknesses. The question "Where does the company need to go from here?" pushes managers to make choices about the direction in which the company is headed—what new or different customer groups and customer needs it should endeavor to satisfy and how it should change its business makeup. The question "How should it get there?" challenges managers to craft and execute a strategy—a full-blown action plan—capable of moving the company in the intended direction, growing its business, strengthening its ability to compete, and improving its financial performance.

In this opening chapter, we define the concept of strategy and describe its many facets. We shall indicate the kinds of actions that determine what a company's strategy is, why strategies are partly proactive and partly reactive, and why company strategies tend to evolve over time. We will look at what sets a winning strategy apart from a ho-hum or flawed strategy and why the caliber of a company's strategy determines whether it will enjoy a competitive advantage or be burdened by competitive disadvantage. By the end of this chapter, you will have a pretty clear idea of why the tasks of crafting and executing strategy are core management functions and why excellent execution of an excellent strategy is the most reliable recipe for turning a company into a standout performer.

Each chapter begins with a series of chapter **learning objectives,** pertinent **quotes** and an introductory preview of the chapter's contents.

ILLUSTRATION CAPSULE 1.1
Starbucks' Strategy in the Specialty Coffee Industry

In 2008, Starbucks was the world's leading specialty coffee retailer, with more than 11,000 stores in the United States and approximately 4,500 stores in 43 other countries. Since 2000, the company's sales of ready-to-drink coffee, coffee beans, coffee-flavored products, pastries, and coffee accessories had grown by more than 20 percent annually to reach $9.4 billion in 2007. Its net earnings had increased from $95 million in 2000 to $672 million in 2007.

The company's success and dramatic growth were attributable to its superior execution of an excellent strategy. Starbucks' business strategy was made up of the following elements:

- *Expand the number of Starbucks stores domestically by blanketing metropolitan areas, then adding stores on the city's perimeter.* Starbucks also made its locations readily available to consumers by entering into licensing agreements with food service vendors operating in airports, universities, hospitals, and other places where people congregated.
- *Make Starbucks a global brand by opening stores in an increasing number of foreign locations.* The international expansion effort involved opening company-owned-and-operated stores in some foreign countries, while entering into licensing agreements with reputable and capable local companies in other countries.
- *View each store as a billboard for the company and as a contributor to building the company's brand and image.* Each detail was scrutinized to enhance the mood and ambience of the store, to make sure everything signaled best-of-class and reflected the personality of the community and the neighborhood. The thesis was "Everything matters." The company went to great lengths to make sure the store fixtures, the merchandise displays, the colors, the artwork, the banners, the music, and the aromas all blended to create a consistent, inviting, stimulating environment that evoked the romance of coffee, that signaled the company's passion for coffee, and that rewarded customers with ceremony, stories, and surprise.
- *Broaden in-store product offerings.* Starbucks stores went beyond coffee to include coffee-flavored ice cream, Frappuccino, teas, fresh pastries and other food items, candy, juice drinks, music CDs, coffee mugs, and coffee accessories.
- *Fully exploit the growing power of the Starbucks name and brand image with out-of-store sales.* Examples of such out-of-store sales included the sale of ground coffee and coffee beans in U.S. grocery stores. Starbucks also sold Frappuccino in U.S. grocery and convenience stores through a partnership with PepsiCo and sold coffee-flavored ice creams in grocery stores through a partnership with Dreyer's Grand Ice Cream.
- *Display corporate responsibility and environmental sustainability.* Key social responsibility and sustainability initiatives included purchasing Fair Trade Certified coffees, donating more than $30 million annually to charitable organizations, purchasing paper cups made from recycled materials, and implementing in-store recycling programs.
- *Control the costs of opening new stores.* The company centralized buying, developed standard contracts and fixed fees for certain items, and consolidated work under those contractors who displayed good cost-control practices. The retail operations group outlined exactly the minimum amount of equipment each core store needed so that standard items could be ordered in volume from vendors at 20 to 30 percent discounts, then delivered just in time to the store site from either company warehouses or the vendor. Mod[illegible]esigns for display cases were developed, and the w[illegible] layout was developed on a computer, with soft[illegible] allowed the costs to be estimated as the design ev[illegible]. All this cut store-opening costs significantly and reduced store development time from 24 to 18 weeks.
- *Promote customer-friendly service and enhance store ambience by making Starbucks a great place to work.* Schultz's thesis was that high employee morale would spill over to inject energy, positive vibes, and a feel-good atmosphere into the operations of its stores, thereby making the Starbucks experience more pleasing to patrons.

However, while Starbucks strategy was largely on target, it was far from being set in concrete. In early 2008, co-founder and CEO Howard Schultz announced that Starbucks would slow the pace of store expansion in the U.S. and close 600 of its U.S. stores that were underperforming; over 70 percent of the stores scheduled for closing had been opened since 2006 and were in areas where Starbucks already had a number of other stores nearby. The basic reason why so many new Starbucks stores had failed to reach the expected sales and profit levels had to do with putting stores so close together that they cannibalized each others sales—a number of customers found it more convenient to shop at a newly-opened store rather than go to the nearby store they had previously patronized. Schultz also began launching a series of new initiatives to re-ignite sales at Starbucks stores via new product offerings and actions to wow customers with an even better experience, by offering new products and providing store patrons with an even more intriguing Starbucks' experience.

Sources: Information posted at www.starbucks.com (accessed March 17, 2008 and July 26, 2008); various annual reports and company press releases.

In-depth examples—**Illustration Capsules**—appear in boxes throughout each chapter to expand on important chapter topics, connect the text presentation to real-world companies, and convincingly demonstrate "strategy in action." Some are appropriate for use as mini-cases.

Margin notes define core concepts and call attention to important ideas and principles.

WHAT DO WE MEAN BY *STRATEGY*?

CORE CONCEPT

A company's ***strategy*** consists of the competitive moves and business approaches that managers are employing to grow the business, attract and please customers, compete successfully, conduct operations, and achieve the targeted levels of organizational performance.

A company's **strategy** is management's action plan for running the business and conducting operations. The crafting of a strategy represents a managerial *commitment to pursue a particular set of actions* in growing the business, attracting and pleasing customers, competing successfully, conducting operations, and improving the company's financial and market performance. Thus, a company's strategy is all about *how*:

- *How* management intends to grow the business.
- *How* it will build a loyal clientele and outcompete rivals.
- *How* each functional piece of the business (research and development, supply chain activities, production, sales and marketing, distribution, finance, and human resources) will be operated.
- *How* performance will be boosted.

In choosing a strategy, management is in effect saying, "Among all the many different ways of competing we could have chosen, we have decided to employ this combination of competitive and operating approaches to move the company in the intended direction, strengthen its market position and competitiveness, and boost performance." The strategic choices a company makes are seldom easy decisions, and some of them may turn out to be wrong—but that is not an excuse for not deciding on a concrete course of action.[1]

Figures scattered throughout the chapters provide conceptual and analytical frameworks.

Figure 4.5 Translating Company Performance of Value Chain Activities into Competitive Advantage

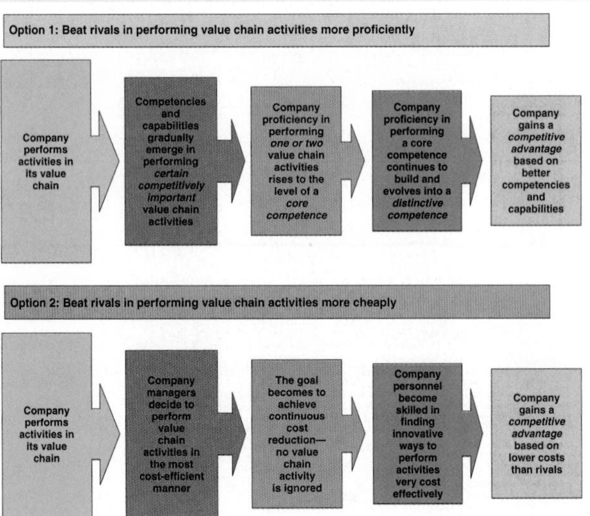
Option 1: Beat rivals in performing value chain activities more proficiently
Company performs activities in its value chain
Competencies and capabilities gradually emerge in performing certain competitively important value chain activities
Company proficiency in performing one or two value chain activities rises to the level of a core competence
Company proficiency in performing a core competence continues to build and evolves into a distinctive competence
Company gains a competitive advantage based on better competencies and capabilities
Option 2: Beat rivals in performing value chain activities more cheaply
Company performs activities in its value chain
Company managers decide to perform value chain activities in the most cost-efficient manner
The goal becomes to achieve continuous cost reduction—no value chain activity is ignored
Company personnel become skilled in finding innovative ways to perform activities very cost effectively
Company gains a competitive advantage based on lower costs than rivals

KEY POINTS

The tasks of crafting and executing company strategies are the heart and soul of managing a business enterprise and winning in the marketplace. A company's strategy is the game plan management is using to stake out a market position, conduct its operations, attract and please customers, compete successfully, and achieve organizational objectives. The central thrust of a company's strategy is undertaking moves to build and strengthen the company's long-term competitive position and financial performance and, ideally, gain a competitive advantage over rivals that then becomes a company's ticket to above-average profitability. A company's strategy typically evolves over time, emerging from a blend of (1) proactive and purposeful actions on the part of company managers and (2) as-needed reactions to unanticipated developments and fresh market conditions.

Closely related to the concept of strategy is the concept of a company's business model. A company's business model is management's story line for how and why the company's product offerings and competitive approaches will generate a revenue stream and have an associated cost structure that produces attractive earnings and return on investment—in effect, a company's business model sets forth the economic logic for making money in a particular business, given the company's current strategy.

Key Points sections at the end of each chapter provide a handy summary of essential ideas and things to remember.

substitute for doing cutting-edge strategic thinking about a company's external situation—anything less weakens managers' ability to craft strategies that are well matched to industry and competitive conditions.

ASSURANCE OF LEARNING EXERCISES

1. Using your favorite Internet search engine, do some research on competitive forces and driving forces that are at work in the snack food industry. Draw a five-forces diagram for the snack food industry and briefly discuss the nature and strength of each of the five competitive forces. Make a list of the driving forces operating in the snack foods industry and draw some conclusions about whether the likely impact of these driving forces on snack foods companies will be favorable or unfavorable.
2. Refer back to the strategic group map in Illustration Capsule 3.1: Who are Toyota's closest competitors? Between which two strategic groups is competition the strongest? Why do you think no automobile manufacturers are positioned in the upper right corner of the map? Which company/strategic group faces the weakest competition from the members of other strategic groups?
3. Using the information provided in Table 3.2 and your knowledge as a casual dining patron, what are the key success factors for restaurants such as Outback Steakhouse or Carrabba's Italian Grill? Your list should contain no more than six industry key success factors. In deciding on your list, it's important to distinguish between factors critical to success in the industry and factors that enhance a company's overall well-being.

EXERCISES FOR SIMULATION PARTICIPANTS

1. Which of the five competitive forces is creating the strongest competitive pressures for your company?
2. What are the "weapons of competition" that rival companies in your industry can use to gain sales and market share? Refer back to Figure 3.4 to help you identify the various competitive factors.
3. What are the factors affecting the intensity of rivalry in the industry in which your company is competing. Use Figure 3.4 and the accompanying discussion to help you pinpoint the specific factors most affecting competitive intensity. Would you characterize the rivalry and jockeying for better market position, increased sales, and market share among the companies in your industry as fierce, very strong, strong, moderate, or relatively weak? Why?
4. Are there any driving forces in the industry in which your company is competing? What impact will these driving forces have? Will they cause competition to be more or less intense? Will they act to boost or squeeze profit margins? List at least two actions your company should consider taking in order to combat any negative impacts of the driving forces.

Value-added **exercises** at the end of each chapter provide a basis for class discussion, oral presentations, and written assignments. Several chapters have exercises that qualify as "mini-cases."

CASE

20 Robin Hood

Joseph Lampel
New York University

It was in the spring of the second year of his insurrection against the High Sheriff of Nottingham that Robin Hood took a walk in Sherwood Forest. As he walked he pondered the progress of the campaign, the disposition of his forces, the Sheriff's recent moves, and the options that confronted him.

The revolt against the Sheriff had begun as a personal crusade. It erupted out of Robin's conflict with the Sheriff and his administration. However, alone Robin Hood could do little. He therefore sought allies, men with grievances and a deep sense of justice. Later he welcomed all who came, asking few questions and demanding only a willingness to serve. Strength, he believed, lay in numbers.

He spent the first year forging the group into a disciplined band, united in enmity against the Sheriff and willing to live outside the law. The band's organization was simple. Robin ruled supreme, making all important decisions. He delegated specific tasks to his lieutenants. Will Scarlett was in charge of intelligence and scouting. His main job was to shadow the Sheriff and his men, always alert to their next move. He also collected information on the travel plans of rich merchants and tax collectors. Little John kept discipline among the men and saw to it that their archery was at the high peak that their profession demanded. Scarlock took care of the finances, converting loot to cash, paying shares of the take, and finding suitable hiding places for the surplus. Finally, Much the Miller's son had the difficult task of provisioning the ever-increasing band of Merrymen.

The increasing size of the band was a source of satisfaction for Robin, but also a source of concern. The fame of his Merrymen was spreading, and new recruits were pouring in from every corner of England. As the band grew larger, their small bivouac became a major encampment. Between raids the men milled about, talking and playing games. Vigilance was in decline, and discipline was becoming harder to enforce. "Why," Robin reflected, "I don't know half the men I run into these days."

The growing band was also beginning to exceed the food capacity of the forest. Game was becoming scarce, and supplies had to be obtained from outlying villages. The cost of buying food was beginning to drain the band's financial reserves at the very moment when revenues were in decline. Travelers, especially those with the most to lose, were now giving the forest a wide berth. This was costly and inconvenient to them, but it was preferable to having all their goods confiscated.

Robin believed that the time had come for the Merrymen to change their policy of outright confiscation of goods to one of a fixed transit tax. His lieutenants strongly resisted this idea. They were proud of the Merrymen's famous motto: "Rob the rich and give to the poor." "The farmers and the townspeople," they argued, "are our most important allies. How can we tax them, and still hope for their help in our fight against the Sheriff?"

Robin wondered how long the Merrymen could keep to the ways and methods of their early days. The Sheriff was growing stronger and becoming better organized. He now had the money and the men and was beginning to harass the band, probing for its weaknesses. The tide of events was beginning to turn against the Merrymen. Robin felt that the campaign must be decisively concluded before the Sheriff had a chance to deliver a mortal blow. "But how," he wondered, "could this be done?"

Robin had often entertained the possibility of killing the Sheriff, but the chances for this seemed

C-362

26 **cases** detail the strategic circumtances of actual companies and provide practice in applying the concepts and tools of strategic analysis.

FOR STUDENTS: An Assortment of Support Materials

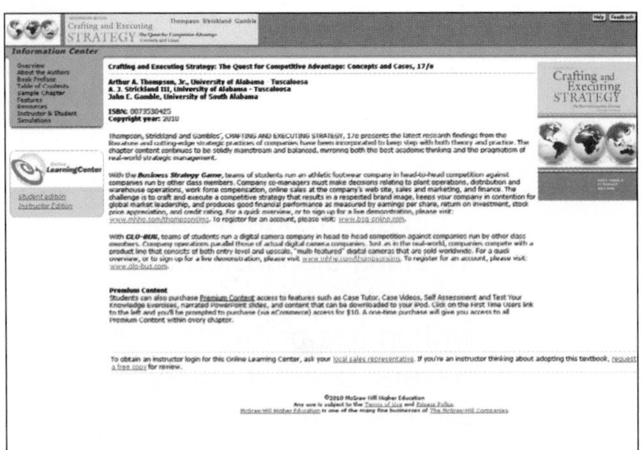

Web site: www.mhhe.com/thompson The student portion of the Web site features 20-question self-scoring chapter tests, a Guide to Case Analysis, and PowerPoint slides for each chapter.

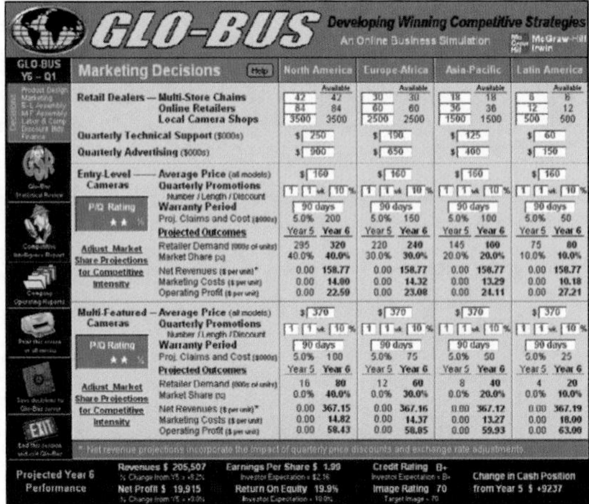

The *Business Strategy Game* or *GLO-BUS* Simulation Exercises Either one of these text supplements involves teams of students managing companies in a head-to-head contest for global market leadership. Company co-managers have to make decisions relating to product quality, production, work force compensation and training, pricing and marketing, and financing of company operations. The challenge is to craft and execute a strategy that is powerful enough to deliver good financial performance despite the competitive efforts of rival companies. Each company competes in North America, Latin America, Europe-Africa, and Asia-Pacific.

Brief Contents

Part One Concepts and Techniques for Crafting and Executing Strategy

Part Two Cases in Crafting and Executing Strategy

Table of Contents

Illustration Capsules

Part Two Cases in Crafting and Executing Strategy

Section A: Crafting Strategy in Single-Business Companies

Crafting and Executing Strategy

The Quest for Competitive Advantage

Concepts and Cases

part one 1

Concepts and Techniques for Crafting and Executing Strategy

CHAPTER 1

What Is Strategy and Why Is It Important?

LEARNING OBJECTIVES

1. Understand the role of business strategies in moving a company in the intended direction, growing its business, and improving its financial and market performance.
2. Develop an awareness of the four most reliable strategic approaches for setting a company apart from rivals and winning a sustainable competitive advantage.
3. Learn that business strategies evolve over time because of changing circumstances and ongoing management efforts to improve the company's strategy.
4. Understand why a company's strategy must be underpinned by a business model that produces revenues sufficient to cover costs and earn a profit.
5. Gain awareness of the three tests that distinguish a winning strategy from a so-so or flawed strategy.
6. Learn why good strategy making and good strategy execution are the most trustworthy signs of good management.

Strategy means making clear-cut choices about how to compete.

— **Jack Welch**
Former CEO, General Electric

A strategy is a commitment to undertake one set of actions rather than another.

— **Sharon Oster**
Professor, Yale University

Without a strategy the organization is like a ship without a rudder.

— **Joel Ross and Michael Kami**
Authors and Consultants

Managers face three central questions in evaluating their company's business prospects:

- What's the company's present situation?
- Where does the company need to go from here?
- How should it get there?

The question "What's the company's present situation?" prompts managers to evaluate industry conditions and competitive pressures, the company's current performance and market standing, its resource strengths and capabilities, and its competitive weaknesses. The question "Where does the company need to go from here?" pushes managers to make choices about the direction in which the company is headed—what new or different customer groups and customer needs it should endeavor to satisfy and how it should change its business makeup. The question "How should it get there?" challenges managers to craft and execute a strategy—a full-blown action plan—capable of moving the company in the intended direction, growing its business, strengthening its ability to compete, and improving its financial performance.

In this opening chapter, we define the concept of strategy and describe its many facets. We shall indicate the kinds of actions that determine what a company's strategy is, why strategies are partly proactive and partly reactive, and why company strategies tend to evolve over time. We will look at what sets a winning strategy apart from a ho-hum or flawed strategy and why the caliber of a company's strategy determines whether it will enjoy a competitive advantage or be burdened by competitive disadvantage. By the end of this chapter, you will have a pretty clear idea of why the tasks of crafting and executing strategy are core management functions and why excellent execution of an excellent strategy is the most reliable recipe for turning a company into a standout performer.

WHAT DO WE MEAN BY *STRATEGY?*

CORE CONCEPT

A company's *strategy* consists of the competitive moves and business approaches that managers are employing to grow the business, attract and please customers, compete successfully, conduct operations, and achieve the targeted levels of organizational performance.

A company's **strategy** is management's action plan for running the business and conducting operations. The crafting of a strategy represents a managerial *commitment to pursue a particular set of actions* in growing the business, attracting and pleasing customers, competing successfully, conducting operations, and improving the company's financial and market performance. Thus, a company's strategy is all about *how*:

- *How* management intends to grow the business.
- *How* it will build a loyal clientele and outcompete rivals.
- *How* each functional piece of the business (research and development, supply chain activities, production, sales and marketing, distribution, finance, and human resources) will be operated.
- *How* performance will be boosted.

In choosing a strategy, management is in effect saying, "Among all the many different ways of competing we could have chosen, we have decided to employ this combination of competitive and operating approaches to move the company in the intended direction, strengthen its market position and competitiveness, and boost performance." The strategic choices a company makes are seldom easy decisions, and some of them may turn out to be wrong—but that is not an excuse for not deciding on a concrete course of action.[1]

In most industries companies have considerable freedom in choosing the hows of strategy.[2] Thus, some rivals strive to improve their performance and market standing by achieving lower costs than rivals, whereas others pursue product superiority or personalized customer service or the development of competencies and capabilities that rivals cannot match. Some opt for wide product lines, whereas others concentrate their energies on a narrow product lineup. Some competitors position themselves in only one part of the industry's chain of production/distribution activities (preferring to be just in manufacturing or wholesale distribution or retailing), while others are partially or fully integrated, with operations ranging from components production to manufacturing and assembly to wholesale distribution or retailing. Some competitors deliberately confine their operations to local or regional markets; others opt to compete nationally, internationally (several countries), or globally (all or most of the major country markets worldwide). Some companies decide to operate in only one industry, while others diversify broadly or narrowly, into related or unrelated industries.

At companies intent on gaining sales and market share at the expense of competitors, managers typically opt for offensive strategies, frequently launching fresh initiatives of one kind or another to make the company's product offering more distinctive and appealing to buyers. Companies already in a strong industry position are more prone to strategies that emphasize gradual gains in the marketplace, fortifying their market position and defending against the latest maneuvering of rivals. Risk-averse companies often prefer "conservative" strategies, preferring to follow the successful moves of pioneering companies whose managers are willing to take the risks of being first to make a bold and, perhaps, pivotal move.

There is no shortage of opportunity to fashion a strategy that both tightly fits a company's own particular situation and is discernibly different from the strategies of rivals. In fact, a company's managers normally attempt to make strategic choices about the key building blocks of its strategy that differ from the choices made by competitors—not 100 percent different but at least different in several important respects. A company's strategy stands a better chance of succeeding when it is predicated on actions, business approaches, and competitive moves aimed at appealing to buyers in ways that set the company apart from rivals and at carving out its own market position. Simply copying successful companies in the industry and trying to mimic their market position rarely works. Rather, there needs to be some distinctive element to the strategy that draws in customers and produces a competitive edge. Carbon-copy strategies among companies in the same industry are the exception rather than the rule.

For a concrete example of the actions and approaches that comprise strategy, see Illustration Capsule 1.1, which describes Starbucks' strategy in the specialty coffee industry.

Strategy and the Quest for Competitive Advantage

The heart and soul of any strategy are the actions and moves in the marketplace that managers are taking to improve the company's financial performance, strengthen its long-term competitive position, and gain a competitive edge over rivals. A creative, distinctive strategy that sets a company apart from rivals and yields a competitive advantage is a company's most reliable ticket for earning above-average profits. Competing in the marketplace with a competitive advantage tends to be more profitable than competing with no advantage. And a company is almost certain to earn significantly higher profits when it enjoys a competitive advantage as opposed to when it is hamstrung by competitive disadvantage. It's nice when a company's strategy produces at least a temporary competitive edge, but a **sustainable competitive advantage** is plainly much better. What make a competitive advantage sustainable as opposed to temporary are actions and elements in the strategy that cause an attractive number of buyers to have a *lasting preference* for a company's products or services. Competitive advantage is the key to above-average profitability and financial performance because strong buyer preferences for the company's product offering translate into higher sales volumes (Wal-Mart) and/or the ability to command a higher price (Mercedes-Benz), thus driving up earnings, return on investment, and other measures of financial performance.

CORE CONCEPT

A company achieves ***sustainable competitive advantage*** when an attractive number of buyers prefer its products or services over the offerings of competitors and when the basis for this preference is durable.

Four of the most frequently used and dependable strategic approaches to setting a company apart from rivals, building strong customer loyalty, and winning a sustainable competitive advantage are:

1. *Striving to be the industry's low-cost provider.* Wal-Mart and Southwest Airlines have earned strong market positions because of the low-cost advantages they have achieved over their rivals and their consequent ability to underprice competitors. Achieving a cost-based advantage over rivals can produce a durable competitive edge when rivals find it hard to match the low-cost leader's approach to driving costs out of the business. While United Airlines, Delta Airlines, US Airways, and Northwest Airlines have moved in and out of bankruptcy, Southwest Airlines' proficient execution of its low-cost strategy—which includes point-to-point routes, no-frills service, and efficient ground operations—has yielded profits for 35 consecutive years.

ILLUSTRATION CAPSULE 1.1
Starbucks' Strategy in the Specialty Coffee Industry

In 2008, Starbucks was the world's leading specialty coffee retailer, with more than 11,000 stores in the United States and approximately 4,500 stores in 43 other countries. Since 2000, the company's sales of ready-to-drink coffee, coffee beans, coffee-flavored products, pastries, and coffee accessories had grown by more than 20 percent annually to reach $9.4 billion in 2007. Its net earnings had increased from $95 million in 2000 to $672 million in 2007.

The company's success and dramatic growth were attributable to its superior execution of an excellent strategy. Starbucks' business strategy was made up of the following elements:

- *Expand the number of Starbucks stores domestically by blanketing metropolitan areas, then adding stores on the city's perimeter.* Starbucks also made its locations readily available to consumers by entering into licensing agreements with food service vendors operating in airports, universities, hospitals, and other places where people congregated.
- *Make Starbucks a global brand by opening stores in an increasing number of foreign locations.* The international expansion effort involved opening company-owned-and-operated stores in some foreign countries, while entering into licensing agreements with reputable and capable local companies in other countries.
- *View each store as a billboard for the company and as a contributor to building the company's brand and image.* Each detail was scrutinized to enhance the mood and ambience of the store, to make sure everything signaled best-of-class and reflected the personality of the community and the neighborhood. The thesis was "Everything matters." The company went to great lengths to make sure the store fixtures, the merchandise displays, the colors, the artwork, the banners, the music, and the aromas all blended to create a consistent, inviting, stimulating environment that evoked the romance of coffee, that signaled the company's passion for coffee, and that rewarded customers with ceremony, stories, and surprise.
- *Broaden in-store product offerings.* Starbucks stores went beyond coffee to include coffee-flavored ice cream, Frappuccino, teas, fresh pastries and other food items, candy, juice drinks, music CDs, coffee mugs, and coffee accessories.
- *Fully exploit the growing power of the Starbucks name and brand image with out-of-store sales.* Examples of such out-of-store sales included the sale of ground coffee and coffee beans in U.S. grocery stores. Starbucks also sold Frappuccino in U.S. grocery and convenience stores through a partnership with PepsiCo and sold coffee-flavored ice creams in grocery stores through a partnership with Dreyer's Grand Ice Cream.
- *Display corporate responsibility and environmental sustainability.* Key social responsibility and sustainability initiatives included purchasing Fair Trade Certified coffees, donating more than $30 million annually to charitable organizations, purchasing paper cups made from recycled materials, and implementing in-store recycling programs.
- *Control the costs of opening new stores.* The company centralized buying, developed standard contracts and fixed fees for certain items, and consolidated work under those contractors who displayed good cost-control practices. The retail operations group outlined exactly the minimum amount of equipment each core store needed so that standard items could be ordered in volume from vendors at 20 to 30 percent discounts, then delivered just in time to the store site from either company warehouses or the vendor. Modular designs for display cases were developed, and the whole store layout was developed on a computer, with software that allowed the costs to be estimated as the design evolved. All this cut store-opening costs significantly and reduced store development time from 24 to 18 weeks.
- *Promote customer-friendly service and enhance store ambience by making Starbucks a great place to work.* CEO Howard Schultz's thesis was that high employee morale would spill over to inject energy, positive vibes, and a feel-good atmosphere into the operations of its stores, thereby making the Starbucks experience more pleasing to patrons.

However, while Starbucks' strategy was largely on target, it was far from being set in concrete. In early 2008, co-founder and CEO Schultz announced that Starbucks would slow the pace of store expansion in the U.S. and close 600 of its U.S. stores that were underperforming; over 70 percent of the stores scheduled for closing had been opened since 2006 and were in areas where Starbucks already had a number of other stores nearby. The basic reason why so many new Starbucks stores had failed to reach the expected sales and profit levels had to do with putting stores so close together that they cannibalized each other's sales—a number of customers found it more convenient to shop at a newly opened store rather than go to the nearby store they had previously patronized. Schultz also began launching a series of new initiatives to re-ignite sales at Starbucks stores via new product offerings and actions to wow customers with an even better experience, by offering new products and providing store patrons with an even more intriguing Starbucks experience.

Sources: Information posted at www.starbucks.com (accessed March 17, 2008, and July 26, 2008); various annual reports and company press releases.

2. *Creating a differentiation-based advantage keyed to such features as higher quality, wider product selection, added performance, value-added services, more attractive styling, technological superiority, or unusually good value for the money.* Successful adopters of differentiation strategies include Johnson & Johnson in baby products (product reliability), Harley-Davidson (outlaw image and distinctive sound), Chanel and Rolex (luxury and prestige), Porsche and BMW (engineering design and performance), and Amazon.com (wide selection and convenience). Differentiation strategies can be powerful so long as a company is sufficiently innovative to thwart clever rivals in finding ways to copy or closely imitate the features of a successful differentiator's product offering.
3. *Focusing on serving the special needs and tastes of buyers comprising a narrow market niche.* Prominent companies that enjoy competitive success in a specialized market niche include eBay in online auctions, Best Buy in home electronics, McAfee in virus protection software, Starbucks in premium coffees and coffee drinks, Whole Foods Market in natural and organic foods, and The Weather Channel in cable TV.
4. *Developing expertise and resource strengths that give the company competitively valuable capabilities that rivals can't easily match, copy, or trump with substitute capabilities.* FedEx has developed a resource-based competitive advantage through its superior capabilities in next-day delivery of small packages. Walt Disney has hard-to-beat capabilities in theme park management and family entertainment. Dell's build-to-order manufacturing capabilities in computer hardware have consistently allowed it to earn healthy profit margins while offering businesses and consumers competitive prices. Ritz-Carlton and Four Seasons have uniquely strong capabilities in providing their hotel and resort guests with an array of personalized services. Very often, winning a durable competitive edge over rivals hinges more on building competitively valuable expertise and capabilities than it does on having a distinctive product. Clever rivals can nearly always copy the attributes of a popular or innovative product, but for rivals to match experience, know-how, and specialized competitive capabilities that a company has developed and perfected over a long period is substantially harder to duplicate and takes much longer.

The tight connection between competitive advantage and profitability means that *the quest for sustainable competitive advantage always ranks center stage in crafting a strategy.* The key to successful strategy making is to come up with one or more strategy elements that act as a magnet to draw customers and that produce a lasting competitive edge over rivals. Indeed, what separates a powerful strategy from a run-of-the-mill or ineffective one is management's ability to forge a series of moves, both in the marketplace and internally, that set the company apart from its rivals, tilt the playing field in the company's favor by giving buyers reason to prefer its products or services, and produce a sustainable competitive advantage over rivals. The bigger and more sustainable the competitive advantage, the better are the company's prospects for winning in the marketplace and earning superior long-term profits relative to rivals. Without a strategy that leads to competitive advantage, a company risks being outcompeted by stronger rivals and/or locked into mediocre financial performance. Hence, company managers deserve no gold stars for coming up with a ho-hum strategy that results in ho-hum financial performance and a ho-hum industry standing.

Figure 1.1 Identifying a Company's Strategy—What to Look For

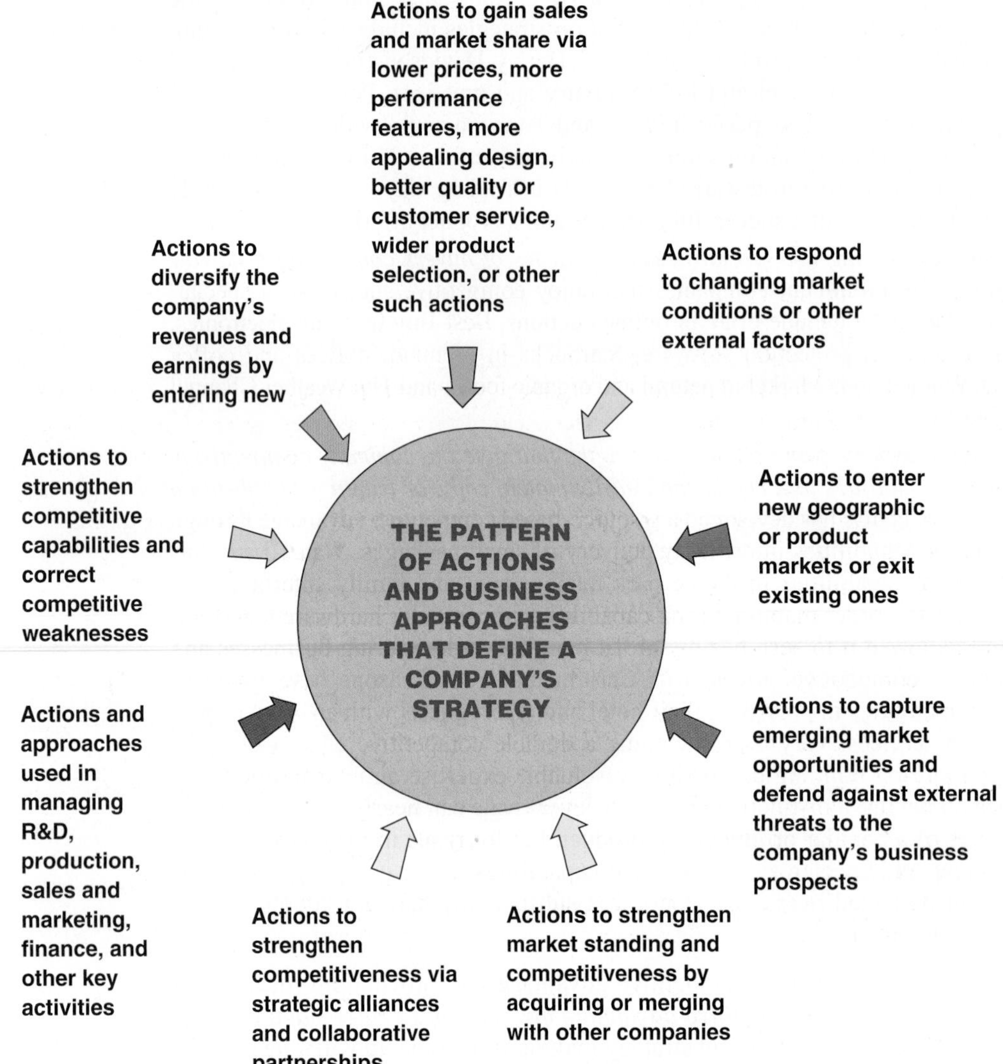

Identifying a Company's Strategy

The best indicators of a company's strategy are its actions in the marketplace and the statements of senior managers about the company's current business approaches, future plans, and efforts to strengthen its competitiveness and performance. Figure 1.1 shows what to look for in pinpointing the key elements of a company's strategy.

Discovering what strategy a company is employing entails researching the company's business approaches and actions in the marketplace. In the case of publicly owned enterprises, the strategy is often openly discussed by senior executives in the company's annual report and 10-K report, in press releases, and in information posted on the company's Web site. To maintain the confidence of investors and Wall Street, most public companies have to be fairly open about their strategies. Company executives typically lay out key elements of their strategies in presentations to securities analysts (the accompanying PowerPoint slides are usually posted in the investor relations section of the company's Web site) and stories in the business media about the company often include aspects of the company's strategy. Hence, except for some about-to-be-launched moves that remain under wraps, there's usually nothing secret or undiscoverable about a company's present strategy.

Why a Company's Strategy Evolves over Time

Regardless of where a company's strategy comes from—be it the product of top executives or the collaborative product of numerous company personnel—it is unlikely that the strategy, as originally conceived, will prove entirely suitable over time. Every company must be willing and ready to modify its strategy in response to changing market conditions, advancing technology, the fresh moves of competitors, shifting buyer needs and preferences, emerging market opportunities, new ideas, and mounting evidence that the strategy is not working well. Thus, *a company's strategy is always a work in progress.*

CORE CONCEPT
Changing circumstances and ongoing management efforts to improve the strategy cause a company's strategy to evolve over time—a condition that makes crafting a strategy a process, not a one-time event.

Most of the time a company's strategy evolves incrementally from management's ongoing efforts to fine-tune this or that piece of the strategy and to adjust certain strategy elements in response to unfolding events. But, on occasion, major strategy shifts are called for, such as when a strategy is clearly failing and the company faces a financial crisis, when market conditions or buyer preferences change significantly, or when important technological breakthroughs occur. In some industries, conditions change at a fairly slow pace, making it feasible for the major components of a good strategy to remain in place for long periods. But in industries where industry and competitive conditions change frequently and sometimes dramatically, the life cycle of a given strategy is short.[3] For example, companies in industries with rapid-fire advances in technology like medical equipment, electronics, Internet retailing, and wireless devices often find it essential to adjust one or more key elements of their strategies several times a year, sometimes even finding it necessary to reinvent their approach to providing value to their customers.

A company's strategy is shaped partly by management analysis and choice, and partly by the necessity of adapting and learning by doing.

But regardless of whether a company's strategy changes gradually or swiftly, the important point is that a company's present strategy is always temporary and on trial, pending new ideas from management, changing industry and competitive conditions, and any other new developments that management believes warrant strategy adjustments. Thus, a company's strategy at any given point is fluid, representing the temporary outcome of an ongoing process that, on the one hand, involves reasoned and creative management efforts to craft an effective strategy and, on the other hand, involves ongoing responses to market change and constant experimentation and tinkering. Adapting to new conditions and constantly learning what is working well enough to continue and what needs to be improved are consequently normal parts of the strategy-making process and results in an evolving strategy.

A Company's Strategy Is Partly Proactive and Partly Reactive

The evolving nature of strategy means that the typical company strategy is a blend of (1) proactive decisions to improve the company's financial performance and secure a competitive edge, and (2) as-needed reactions to unanticipated developments and fresh

Figure 1.2 A Company's Strategy Is a Blend of Proactive Initiatives and Reactive Adjustments

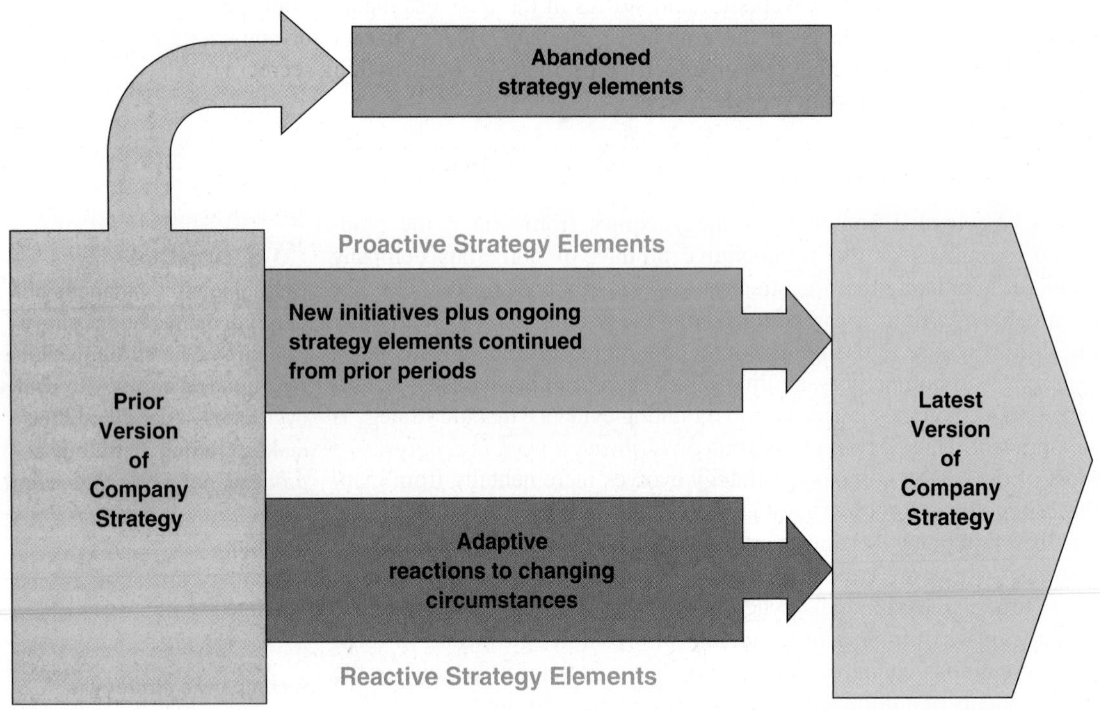

market conditions—see Figure 1.2.[4] The biggest portion of a company's current strategy flows from previously initiated actions and business approaches that are working well enough to merit continuation and newly launched initiatives aimed at boosting financial performance and edging out rivals. This part of management's action plan for running the company consists of its *proactive strategy elements.*

But managers must always be willing to supplement or modify all the proactive strategy elements with as-needed reactions to unanticipated developments. Inevitably, there will be occasions when market and competitive conditions take an unexpected turn that call for some kind of strategic reaction or adjustment. Hence, a portion of a company's strategy is always developed on the fly, coming as a response to fresh strategic maneuvers on the part of rival firms, unexpected shifts in customer requirements and expectations, fast-changing technological developments, newly appearing market opportunities, a changing political or economic climate, or other unanticipated happenings in the surrounding environment. These adaptive strategy adjustments form the *reactive strategy elements.*

As shown in Figure 1.2, a company's strategy evolves from one version to the next as managers abandon obsolete or ineffective strategy elements, settle upon a set of *proactive/intended strategy elements,* and then adapt the strategy as new circumstances unfold—an ongoing process that results in a strategy that is a *combination* of proactive and reactive elements.

STRATEGY AND ETHICS: PASSING THE TEST OF MORAL SCRUTINY

In choosing among strategic alternatives, company managers are well advised to embrace actions that can pass the test of moral scrutiny. Just keeping a company's strategic actions within the bounds of what is legal does not mean the strategy is ethical. Ethical and moral standards are not governed by what is legal; rather, they involve issues of right versus wrong and of duty—what one *should* do. A strategy is ethical only if (1) it does not entail actions and behaviors that cross the line between "should do" and "should not do" (because such actions are unsavory, unconscionable, or injurious to other people or unnecessarily harmful to the environment), and (2) it allows management to fulfill its ethical duties to all stakeholders—owners/shareholders, employees, customers, suppliers, the communities in which it operates, and society at large.

CORE CONCEPT

Ethics go beyond legality; to meet the standard of being ethical, a strategy must entail actions that can pass moral scrutiny in the sense of not being shady, unconscionable, or injurious to others or unnecessarily harmful to the environment.

Admittedly, it is not always easy to categorize a given strategic behavior as definitely ethical or definitely unethical; many strategic actions fall in a gray zone in between. Whether they are deemed ethical or unethical hinges on how high one sets the bar. For example, is it ethical for advertisers of alcoholic products to place ads in media with a largely underage audience? (In 2003, growing concerns about underage drinking prompted some beer and distilled spirits companies to agree to place ads in media with an audience at least 70 percent adult, up from a standard of 50 percent adult.) Is it ethical for an apparel retailer attempting to keep prices attractively low to source clothing from foreign manufacturers who pay substandard wages, use child labor, or subject workers to unsafe working conditions? Many people would say no, but some might argue that a company is not unethical simply because it does not police the business practices of its suppliers. Is it ethical for the makers of athletic uniforms, shoes, and equipment to pay coaches large sums of money as an inducement for the coaches to use the manufacturer's products in their sport? (The compensation contracts of many college coaches include substantial payments from sportswear and sport equipment manufacturers; the teams subsequently end up wearing the uniforms and using the products of these same manufacturers.) Is it ethical for pharmaceutical manufacturers to charge higher prices for life-saving drugs in some countries than they charge in others? (This is a fairly common practice that has recently come under scrutiny.) Is it ethical for a company to turn a blind eye to the damage its operations do to the environment (even though its operations are in compliance with current environmental regulations)—especially if it has the know-how and the means to alleviate some of the environmental impacts by making relatively inexpensive changes in its operating practices?

Senior executives with strong ethical convictions are generally proactive in linking strategic action and ethics; they forbid the pursuit of ethically questionable business opportunities and insist that all aspects of company strategy reflect high ethical standards.[5] They make it clear that all company personnel are expected to act with integrity, and they put organizational checks and balances into place to monitor behavior, enforce ethical codes of conduct, and provide guidance to employees regarding any gray areas. Their commitment to conducting the company's business in an ethical manner is genuine, not hypocritical lip service.

Ethical misconduct, corporate misdeeds, and fraudulent accounting practices all entail substantial downside risk. Aside from just the embarrassment and black marks that accompany headline exposure of a company's misbehavior, the hard fact is that many customers and many suppliers are wary of doing business with a company that engages in sleazy practices or that turns a blind eye to illegal or unethical behavior on the part of employees. They are turned off by unethical strategies and unbecoming conduct—rather than become victims or get burned themselves, wary customers will quickly take their business elsewhere and wary suppliers will tread carefully. Moreover, employees with character and integrity do not want to work for a company whose strategies are shady or whose executives lack character and integrity. The damage that unethical strategies and behavior can do to a company's reputation and overall business is substantial. Besides, immoral or unethical actions are plain wrong.

THE RELATIONSHIP BETWEEN A COMPANY'S STRATEGY AND ITS BUSINESS MODEL

CORE CONCEPT

A company's *business model* explains the rationale for why its business approach and strategy will be a moneymaker. Absent the ability to deliver good profitability, the strategy is not viable and the survival of the business is in doubt.

Closely related to the concept of strategy is the concept of a **business model**. A company's business model is management's story line for how the strategy will be a moneymaker. The story line sets forth the key components of the enterprise's business approach, indicates how revenues will be generated, and makes a case for why the strategy can deliver value to customers and create a profit for the company.[6] A company's business model thus identifies the basis for why its strategy will result in enough revenues to cover costs and realize a profit.

The nitty-gritty issue surrounding a company's business model is whether the chosen strategy makes good business sense from a moneymaking perspective. Why is there convincing reason to believe that the strategy is capable of producing a profit? How will customers be served? How will the business generate its revenues? Will those revenues be sufficient to cover operating costs? The concept of a company's business model is, consequently, more narrowly focused than the concept of a company's strategy. A company's strategy *relates broadly to its competitive initiatives and action plan for running the business* (but it may or may not lead to profitability). However, a company's business model zeros in on *the principle business components by which the business will generate revenues sufficient to cover costs and produce attractive profits and return on investment.* Absent the ability to deliver good profits, the strategy is not viable, the business model is flawed, and the business itself will fail.

Companies that have been in business for a while and are making acceptable profits have a proven business model—because there is hard evidence that their strategies are capable of profitability. Companies that are in a start-up mode or that are losing money have questionable business models; their strategies have yet to produce good bottom-line results, putting in doubt their story line about how they intend to make money and their viability as business enterprises.

Magazines and newspapers employ a business model based on generating sufficient subscription and advertising revenue to cover the costs of delivering their products to readers. Cable TV companies, mobile phone providers, satellite radio companies, and broadband providers also employ a subscription-based business model. The business model of network TV and radio broadcasters entails providing free programming to audiences and then charging advertisers fees based on audience size. Wal-Mart has perfected the business model for big-box discount retailing—a model also used by The Home Depot, Costco, and Target. Gillette's business model in razor blades has involved selling the razor at an attractively low price and then making money on repeat purchases of razor blades. Printer manufacturers like Hewlett-Packard, Lexmark, and Epson have pursued much the same business model as Gillette—selling printers at a low (virtually break-even) price and making large profits on the repeat purchases of printer supplies, especially ink cartridges. Illustration Capsule 1.2 discusses the contrasting business models of Microsoft and Red Hat.

WHAT MAKES A STRATEGY A WINNER?

Three questions can be used to distinguish a winning strategy from a so-so or flawed strategy:

1. *How well does the strategy fit the company's situation?* To qualify as a winner, a strategy has to be well matched to industry and competitive conditions, a company's best market opportunities, and other aspects of the enterprise's external environment. At the same time, it has to be tailored to the company's resource strengths and weaknesses, competencies, and competitive capabilities. Unless a strategy exhibits tight fit with both the external and internal aspects of a company's overall situation, it is likely to produce less than the best possible business results.

CORE CONCEPT

A winning strategy must fit the enterprise's external and internal situation, build sustainable competitive advantage, and improve company performance.

2. *Is the strategy helping the company achieve a sustainable competitive advantage?* Winning strategies enable a company to achieve a competitive advantage that is durable. The bigger and more durable the competitive edge that a strategy helps build, the more powerful and appealing it is.
3. *Is the strategy resulting in better company performance?* A good strategy boosts company performance. Two kinds of performance improvements tell the most about the caliber of a company's strategy: (*a*) gains in profitability and financial strength and (*b*) gains in the company's competitive strength and market standing.

Strategies that come up short on one or more of the above questions are plainly less appealing than strategies passing all three test questions with flying colors. Additional criteria for judging the merits of a particular strategy include (1) the degree of risk the strategy poses as compared to alternative strategies and (2) the degree to which it is flexible and adaptable to changing circumstances. These criteria are relevant and merit consideration, but they seldom override the importance of the three test questions posed above.

Managers can also use the same questions to pick and choose among alternative strategic actions. A company evaluating which of several strategic options to employ can size up how well each option measures up against each of the three questions. The strategic option with the highest prospective passing scores on all three questions can be regarded as the best or most attractive strategic alternative.

ILLUSTRATION CAPSULE 1.2
Microsoft and Red Hat: Two Contrasting Business Models

The strategies of rival companies are often predicated on strikingly different business models. Consider, for example, the business models for Microsoft and Red Hat in operating system software for personal computers.

Microsoft's business model for making money from its operating system products is based on the following revenue-cost-profit economics:

- Employ a cadre of highly skilled programmers to develop proprietary code; keep the source code hidden so as to keep the inner workings of the software proprietary.
- Sell the resulting operating system and software package to personal computer (PC) makers and to PC users at relatively attractive prices (around $75 to PC makers and about $100 at retail to PC users); strive to maintain a 90 percent or more market share of the 150 million PCs sold annually worldwide.
- Keep costs on the front end (in developing the software) fixed; set the variable costs of producing and packaging the CDs provided to users at only a couple of dollars per copy—once the break-even volume is reached, Microsoft's revenues from additional sales are almost pure profit.
- Provide a modest level of technical support to users at no cost.
- Keep rejuvenating revenues by periodically introducing next-generation software versions with features that will induce PC users to upgrade the operating system on previously purchased PCs to the new version.

Red Hat, a company formed to market its own version of the open-source Linux operating system, employs a business model based on sharply different revenue-cost-profit economics:

- Rely on the collaborative efforts of volunteer programmers from all over the world who contribute bits and pieces of code to improve and polish the Linux operating system. The global community of thousands of programmers who work on Linux in their spare time do what they do because they love it; because they are fervent believers that all software should be free (as in free speech); and, in some cases, because they are anti-Microsoft and want to have a part in undoing what they see as a Microsoft monopoly.
- Collect and test enhancements and new applications submitted by the open-source community of volunteer programmers. Linux's originator, Linus Torvalds, and a team of 300-plus Red Hat engineers and software developers evaluate which incoming submissions merit inclusion in new releases of Red Hat Linux—the evaluation and integration of new submissions are Red Hat's only up-front product development costs.
- Market the upgraded and tested family of Red Hat Linux products to large enterprises and charge them a subscription fee that includes 24/7 support within one hour in seven languages. Provide subscribers with updated versions of Red Hat Linux every 12–18 months to maintain the subscriber base.
- Make the source code open and available to all users, allowing them to create a customized version of Linux.
- Capitalize on the specialized expertise required to use Linux in multiserver, multiprocessor applications by providing fees-based training, consulting, software customization, and client-directed engineering to Red Hat Linux users. Red Hat offers Linux certification training programs at all skill levels at more than 60 global locations—Red Hat certification in the use of Linux is considered the best in the world.

Microsoft's business model—sell proprietary code software and give service away free—is a proven money maker that generates billions in profits annually. On the other hand, the jury is still out on Red Hat's business model of selling subscriptions to open-source software to large corporations and deriving substantial revenues from the sales of technical support, training, consulting, software customization, and engineering to generate revenues sufficient to cover costs and yield a profit. Red Hat's fiscal 2007 revenues of $400 million and net income of $60 million are quite meager in comparison to Microsoft's.

Sources: Information posted at www.microsoft.com and www.redhat.com (accessed May 6, 2008).

WHY ARE CRAFTING AND EXECUTING STRATEGY IMPORTANT?

Crafting and executing strategy are top-priority managerial tasks for two very big reasons. First, there is a compelling need for managers to proactively shape, or craft, how the company's business will be conducted. A clear and reasoned strategy is management's prescription for doing business, its road map to competitive advantage, its game plan for pleasing customers and improving financial performance. High-achieving enterprises are nearly always the product of astute, creative, proactive strategy-making that sets a company apart from its rivals. Companies don't get to the top of the industry rankings or stay there with imitative strategies or with strategies built around timid resolutions to try to do better. And only a handful of companies can boast of strategies that hit home runs in the marketplace due to lucky breaks or the good fortune of having stumbled into the right market at the right time with the right product. So there can be little argument that a company's strategy matters—and matters a lot.

Second, a *strategy-focused enterprise* is more likely to be a strong bottom-line performer than a company whose management team does not take its strategy making responsibilities seriously. There's no escaping the fact that the quality of managers' strategy making and strategy execution has a highly positive impact on revenue growth, earnings, and return on investment. A company that lacks clear-cut direction, has vague or undemanding performance targets, has a muddled or flawed strategy, or can't seem to execute its strategy competently is a company whose financial performance is probably suffering and whose business is at long-term risk. The chief executive officer of one successful company put it well when he said:

> In the main, our competitors are acquainted with the same fundamental concepts and techniques and approaches that we follow, and they are as free to pursue them as we are. More often than not, the difference between their level of success and ours lies in the relative thoroughness and self-discipline with which we and they develop and execute our strategies for the future.

Good Strategy + Good Strategy Execution = Good Management

Crafting and executing strategy are thus core management functions. Among all the things managers do, nothing affects a company's ultimate success or failure more fundamentally than how well its management team charts the company's direction, develops competitively effective strategic moves and business approaches, and pursues what needs to be done internally to produce good day-in, day-out strategy execution and operating excellence. Indeed, *good strategy and good strategy execution are the most trustworthy signs of good management.* Managers don't deserve a gold star for designing a potentially brilliant strategy but failing to put the organizational means in place to carry it out in high-caliber fashion. Competent execution of a mediocre strategy scarcely merits enthusiastic applause for management's efforts either. The rationale for using the twin standards of good strategy making and good strategy execution to determine whether a company is well managed is therefore compelling: *The better conceived a company's strategy and the more competently it is executed, the more likely that the company will be a standout performer in the marketplace.*

Throughout the text chapters to come and the accompanying case collection, the spotlight is trained on the foremost question in running a business enterprise: What must managers do, and do well, to make a company a winner in the marketplace? The answer that emerges, and that becomes the message of this book, is that doing a good job of managing inherently requires good strategic thinking and good management of the strategy-making, strategy-executing process.

The mission of this book is to provide a solid overview of what every business student and aspiring manager needs to know about crafting and executing strategy. This requires exploring what good strategic thinking entails; presenting the core concepts and tools of strategic analysis; describing the ins and outs of crafting and executing strategy; and, through the cases that have been included, helping build skills both in diagnosing how well the strategy-making, strategy-executing task is being performed in actual companies and in prescribing actions for how the companies in question can improve their approaches to crafting and executing their strategies. At the very least, we hope to convince you that capabilities in crafting and executing strategy are basic to managing successfully and merit a prominent place in every manager's toolkit.

As you tackle the following pages, ponder the following observation by the essayist and poet Ralph Waldo Emerson: "Commerce is a game of skill which many people play, but which few play well." If the content of this book helps you become a more savvy player and equips you to succeed in business, then your journey through these pages will indeed be time well spent.

KEY POINTS

The tasks of crafting and executing company strategies are the heart and soul of managing a business enterprise and winning in the marketplace. A company's strategy is the game plan management is using to stake out a market position, conduct its operations, attract and please customers, compete successfully, and achieve organizational objectives. The central thrust of a company's strategy is undertaking moves to build and strengthen the company's long-term competitive position and financial performance and, ideally, gain a competitive advantage over rivals that then becomes a company's ticket to above-average profitability. A company's strategy typically evolves over time, emerging from a blend of (1) proactive and purposeful actions on the part of company managers and (2) as-needed reactions to unanticipated developments and fresh market conditions.

Closely related to the concept of strategy is the concept of a company's business model. A company's business model is management's story line for how and why the company's product offerings and competitive approaches will generate a revenue stream and have an associated cost structure that produces attractive earnings and return on investment—in effect, a company's business model sets forth the economic logic for making money in a particular business, given the company's current strategy.

A winning strategy fits the circumstances of a company's external situation and its internal resource strengths and competitive capabilities, builds competitive advantage, and boosts company performance.

Crafting and executing strategy are core management functions. Whether a company wins or loses in the marketplace is directly attributable to the caliber of that company's strategy and the proficiency with which the strategy is executed.

ASSURANCE OF LEARNING EXERCISES

1. Go to www.redhat.com and check whether the company's recent financial reports indicate that its business model is working. Is the company sufficiently profitable to validate its business model and strategy? Is its revenue stream from selling training, consulting, and engineering services growing or declining as a percentage of total revenues? Does your review of the company's recent financial performance suggest that its business model and strategy are changing? Read the company's latest statement about its business model and about why it is pursuing the subscription approach (as compared to Microsoft's approach of selling copies of its operating software directly to PC manufacturers and individuals).
2. Go to www.bestbuy.com, click on the investor relations section, and explore Best Buy's latest annual reports and 10-K filings to see if you can identify the key elements of Best Buy's strategy. Use the framework provided in Figure 1.1 to help identify the key elements of Best Buy's strategy. What type of competitive advantage does Best Buy seem to be pursuing?
3. Given what you know about the specialty coffee industry, does Starbucks' strategy as described in Illustration Capsule 1.1 seem to be well matched to industry and competitive conditions? Does the strategy seem to be keyed to a cost advantage, differentiating features, serving the unique needs of a niche, or developing resource strengths and competitive capabilities rivals can't imitate or trump (or a mixture of these)? How has Starbucks' strategy evolved (or failed to evolve) in recent years? What is there about Starbucks' strategy that can lead to sustainable competitive advantage?
4. On December 15, 2003, Levi Strauss & Company announced it would close its two last remaining apparel plants in the United States to finalize its transition from a clothing manufacturer to a marketing, sales, and design company. Beginning in 2004, all Levi's apparel was to be produced by contract manufacturers located in low-wage countries. As recently as 1990, Levi Strauss had produced 90 percent of its apparel in company-owned plants in the United States employing over 20,000 production workers. With every plant closing, Levi Strauss & Company provided severance and job retraining packages to affected workers and cash payments to small communities where its plants were located. Still, these communities struggled to recover from the loss of jobs associated with Levi Strauss's plant closings; many of the former Levi Strauss employees who took new jobs found it difficult to match their previous levels of compensation and benefits. Does Levi Strauss's strategy to outsource its manufacturing pass the moral scrutiny test? Is it ethical for a company to close plants employing over 20,000 workers and shift production to low-wage-paying contract manufacturers in foreign countries? Why or why not?

EXERCISE FOR SIMULATION PARTICIPANTS

This chapter discusses three questions that must be answered by managers in organizations of all sizes. After you have read the Participant's Guide or Player's Manual for the strategy simulation exercise that you will participate in this academic term, you and your co-managers should come up with one- or two-paragraph answers to the following three questions prior to entering your first set of decisions. While your answer to the first of the three questions can be developed from your reading of the manual, the second and third questions will require a collaborative discussion among the members of your company's management team about how you intend to manage the company you have been assigned to run.

1. Where are we now? (Is your company in a good, an average, or a weak competitive position vis-à-vis rival companies? Does your company appear to be in sound financial condition? What problems does your company have that need to be addressed?)
2. Where do we want to go? (Where would you like your company to be after the first five decision rounds? By how much would you like to increase total profits of the company by the end of the simulation exercise? What kinds of performance outcomes will signal that you and your co-managers are managing the company successfully?)
3. How are we going to get there? (Which of the basic strategic and competitive approaches discussed in Chapter 1 makes the most sense for your company to pursue? What kind of competitive advantage over rivals do you intend to try to build?)

CHAPTER

2

Leading the Process of Crafting and Executing Strategy

LEARNING OBJECTIVES

1. Grasp why it is critical for company managers to think long and hard about where a company needs to head and why.
2. Understand the importance of setting both strategic and financial objectives.
3. Recognize that the task of crafting a company strategy draws on the entrepreneurial talents of managers at all organizational levels.
4. Understand why the strategic initiatives taken at various organizational levels must be tightly coordinated to achieve companywide performance targets.
5. Become aware of what a company must do to achieve operating excellence and to execute its strategy proficiently.
6. Understand why the strategic management process is ongoing, not an every-now-and-then task.
7. Learn what leadership skills management must exhibit to drive strategy execution forward.
8. Become aware of the role and responsibility of a company's board of directors in overseeing the strategic management process.

If you don't know where you are going, any road will take you there.

—Cheshire Cat to Alice
Lewis Carroll, Alice in Wonderland

If you can articulate a vision that makes people passionate, there are so many amazing things you can do.

—Dr. Sophie Vandebroek
Xerox Corporation

How can you lead if you don't know where you are going?

—George Newman
The Conference Board

Crafting and executing strategy are the heart and soul of managing a business enterprise. But exactly what is involved in developing a strategy and executing it proficiently? What are the various components of the strategy-making, strategy-executing process? To what extent are company personnel—aside from top executives—involved in the process? In this chapter we present an overview of the managerial ins and outs of crafting and executing company strategies. We give special attention to management's direction-setting responsibilities—charting a strategic course, setting performance targets, and choosing a strategy capable of producing the desired outcomes. We also explain why strategy making is a task for a company's entire management team and discuss which kinds of strategic decisions tend to be made at which levels of management. The chapter concludes with a look at the roles and responsibilities of a company's board of directors in the strategy-making, strategy-executing process and how good corporate governance protects shareholder interests and promotes good management.

WHAT DOES THE STRATEGY-MAKING, STRATEGY-EXECUTING PROCESS ENTAIL?

The managerial process of crafting and executing a company's strategy consists of five interrelated and integrated phases:

1. *Developing a strategic vision* of where the company needs to head and what its future product/customer/market/technology focus should be.
2. *Setting objectives* and using them as yardsticks for measuring the company's performance and progress.
3. *Crafting a strategy to achieve the objectives* and move the company along the strategic course that management has charted.
4. *Implementing and executing the chosen strategy efficiently and effectively.*
5. *Evaluating performance and initiating corrective adjustments* in the company's long-term direction, objectives, strategy, or execution in light of actual experience, changing conditions, new ideas, and new opportunities.

Figure 2.1 displays this five-phase process. Let's examine each phase in enough detail to set the stage for the forthcoming chapters and give you a bird's-eye view of this book.

PHASE 1: DEVELOPING A STRATEGIC VISION

Very early in the strategy-making process, a company's senior managers must wrestle with the issue of what direction the company should take. Would a change in the company's present product/market/customer/technology focus likely improve the company's market position and future prospects? Deciding to commit the company to follow one

Figure 2.1 The Strategy-Making, Strategy-Executing Process

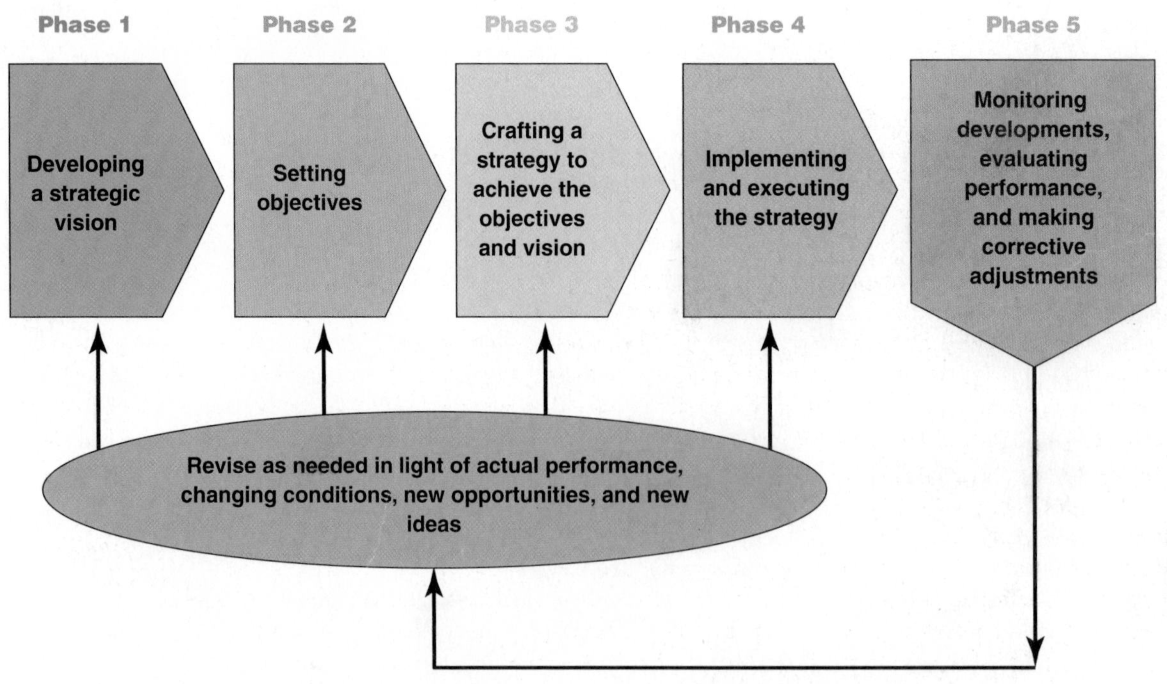

Table 2.1 Factors to Consider in Deciding on a Company's Future Direction

External Considerations	Internal Considerations
• Is the outlook for the company promising if the company sticks with its present product/market/customer/technology focus and strategic direction? • Are changes under way in the competitive landscape acting to enhance or weaken the company's prospects? • What, if any, new customer groups and/or geographic markets should the company get in position to serve? • Are there any emerging market opportunities the company ought to pursue? • Should we plan to abandon any of the markets, market segments, or customer groups we are currently serving?	• What are our ambitions for the company—what industry standing do we want the company to have? • Will our present business generate sufficient growth and profitability to please shareholders? • What resource strengths does the company have that will aid its ability to add new products/services and/or get into new businesses? • Is the company stretching its resources too thin by trying to compete in too many product categories or market arenas, some of which are unprofitable? • Is the company's technological focus too broad or too narrow?

direction versus another pushes managers to draw some carefully reasoned conclusions about whether and how to modify the company's product/market/customer/technology focus and long-term direction. A number of factors need to be considered in deciding where to head and why such a direction makes good business sense—see Table 2.1

Top management's views and conclusions about the company's direction and future product/customer/market/technology focus constitute a **strategic vision** for the company. A strategic vision delineates management's aspirations for the business, providing a panoramic view of "where we are going." A strategic vision thus points an organization in a particular direction, charts a strategic path, and molds organizational identity. A clearly articulated strategic vision communicates management's aspirations to stakeholders and helps steer the energies of company personnel in a common direction. For instance, Henry Ford's vision of a car in every garage had power because it captured the imagination of others, aided internal efforts to mobilize the Ford Motor Company's resources, and served as a reference point for gauging the merits of the company's strategic actions.

CORE CONCEPT

A *strategic vision* describes the route a company intends to take in developing and strengthening its business. It lays out the company's strategic course in preparing for the future.

Well-conceived visions are *distinctive* and *specific* to a particular organization; they avoid generic, feel-good statements like "We will become a global leader and the first choice of customers in every market we choose to serve"—which could apply to any of hundreds of organizations.[1] And they are not the product of a committee charged with coming up with an innocuous one-sentence vision that wins approval from various stakeholders. Nicely worded vision statements with no specifics about the company's product/market/customer/technology focus fall well short of what it takes for a vision to measure up. A strategic vision proclaiming management's quest "to be the market leader" or "to be the first choice of customers" or "to be the most innovative" or "to be recognized as the best company in the industry" offer scant guidance about a company's direction and what changes and challenges lie on the road ahead.

For a strategic vision to function as a valuable managerial tool, it must (1) illuminate the company's directional path and (2) provide managers with a reference point for making strategic decisions and preparing the company for the future. It must say something definitive about the company's future product/market/customer/technology focus. A good vision always needs to be beyond a company's immediate reach so as to help unleash unified actions on the part of company personnel that move the company

Table 2.2 Characteristics of an Effectively Worded Vision Statement

Graphic	Paints a picture of the kind of company that management is trying to create and the market position(s) the company is striving to stake out.
Directional	Is forward-looking; describes the strategic course that management has charted and the kinds of product/market/customer/technology changes that will help the company prepare for the future.
Focused	Is specific enough to provide managers with guidance in making decisions and allocating resources.
Flexible	Is not a once-and-for-all-time statement—the directional course that management has charted may have to be adjusted as product/market/customer/technology circumstances change.
Feasible	Is within the realm of what the company can reasonably expect to achieve in due time.
Desirable	Indicates why the direction makes good business sense and is in the long-term interests of stakeholders (especially shareowners, employees, and customers).
Easy to communicate	Is explainable in 5–10 minutes and, ideally, can be reduced to a simple, memorable slogan (like Henry Ford's famous vision of "a car in every garage").

Source: Based partly on John P. Kotter, *Leading Change* (Boston: Harvard Business School Press, 1996), p. 72.

down the path of realizing the vision. Table 2.2 lists some characteristics of an effective vision statement.

A sampling of vision statements currently in use shows a range from strong/clear to overly general/generic. A surprising number of the vision statements found on company Web sites and in annual reports are vague about the company's future product/market/customer/technology focus. Some are nice-sounding but say little. Others read like something written by a committee hoping to win the support of different stakeholders. And some are so short on specifics as to apply to most any company in any industry. Many read like a public relations statement—high-sounding words that someone came up with because it is fashionable for companies to have an official vision statement.[2] Table 2.3 provides a list of the most common shortcomings in

Table 2.3 Common Shortcomings in Company Vision Statements

Vague or incomplete	Short on specifics about where the company is headed or what the company is doing to prepare for the future.
Not forward-looking	Doesn't indicate whether or how management intends to alter the company's current product/market/customer/technology focus.
Too broad	So inclusive that the company could head in most any direction, pursue most any opportunity, or enter most any business.
Bland or uninspiring	Lacks the power to motivate company personnel or inspire shareholder confidence about the company's direction or future prospects
Not distinctive	Provides no unique company identity; could apply to companies in any of several industries (or at least several rivals operating in the same industry or market arena).
Too reliant on superlatives	Doesn't say anything specific about the company's strategic course beyond the pursuit of such lofty accolades as *best, most successful, recognized leader, global* or *worldwide leader,* or *first choice of customers.*

Sources: Based on information in Hugh Davidson, *The Committed Enterprise: How to Make Vision and Values Work* (Oxford: Butterworth-Heinemann, 2002), Chapter 2; and Michel Robert, *Strategy Pure and Simple II: How Winning Companies Dominate Their Competitors* (New York: McGraw-Hill, 1998), Chapters 2, 3, and 6.

ILLUSTRATION CAPSULE 2.1
Examples of Strategic Visions—How Well Do They Measure Up?

Vision Statement	Effective Elements	Shortcomings
Red Hat To extend our position as the most trusted Linux and open source provider to the enterprise. We intend to grow the market for Linux through a complete range of enterprise Red Hat Linux software, a powerful Internet management platform, and associated support and services.	• Directional • Focused • Feasible • Desirable • Easy to communicate	• Bland or uninspiring
UBS We are determined to be the best global financial services company. We focus on wealth and asset management, and on investment banking and securities businesses. We continually earn recognition and trust from clients, shareholders, and staff through our ability to anticipate, learn and shape our future. We share a common ambition to succeed by delivering quality in what we do. Our purpose is to help our clients make financial decisions with confidence. We use our resources to develop effective solutions and services for our clients. We foster a distinctive, meritocratic culture of ambition, performance and learning as this attracts, retains and develops the best talent for our company. By growing both our client and our talent franchises, we add sustainable value for our shareholders.	• Focused • Feasible • Desirable	• Not forward-looking • Bland or uninspiring
Caterpillar Be the global leader in customer value.	• Directional • Desirable • Easy to communicate	• Vague or incomplete • Could apply to many companies in many industries
eBay Provide a global trading platform where practically anyone can trade practically anything.	• Graphic • Flexible • Easy to communicate	• Too broad

Sources: Company documents and Web sites.

company vision statements. The one- or two-sentence vision statements most companies make available to the public, of course, provide only a glimpse of what company executives are really thinking and the strategic course they have charted—company personnel nearly always have a much better understanding of the ins and outs of where the company is headed and why than is revealed in the official vision statement. But the real purpose of a vision statement is to serve as a management tool for giving the organization a sense of direction. Like any tool, it can be used properly or improperly, either clearly conveying a company's strategic course or not.

Illustration Capsule 2.1 provides a critique of the strategic visions of several prominent companies.

How a Strategic Vision Differs from a Mission Statement

The defining characteristic of a well-conceived strategic vision is what it says about the company's *future strategic course*—"the direction we are headed and what our future product-customer-market-technology focus will be." While a company's strategic vision and its mission statement could be worded to cover much the same ground, the truth is that the mission statements of most companies say much more about the enterprise's *present business scope and purpose*—"who we are, what we do, and why we are here"—than they say about the strategic course that top management has charted. Very few mission statements are forward-looking in content or emphasis.

The distinction between a strategic vision and a mission statement is fairly clear-cut: A strategic vision portrays a company's *future* business scope ("where we are going"), whereas a company's mission typically describes its *present* business and purpose ("who we are, what we do, and why we are here").

The mission statements that one finds in company annual reports or posted on company Web sites typically provide a brief overview of the company's *present* business purpose and reasons for existing, and sometimes its geographic coverage or standing as a market leader. They may or may not single out the company's present products/services, the buyer needs it is seeking to satisfy, the customer groups it serves, or its technological and business capabilities. But rarely do company mission statements say anything about where the company is headed, the anticipated changes in its business, or the kind of company it is trying to become; hence they lack the essential forward-looking quality of a strategic vision in specifying a company's direction and *future* product-market-customer-technology focus. Consider, for example, the mission statement of Trader Joe's, a specialty grocery chain:

> The mission of Trader Joe's is to give our customers the best food and beverage values that they can find anywhere and to provide them with the information required for informed buying decisions. We provide these with a dedication to the highest quality of customer satisfaction delivered with a sense of warmth, friendliness, fun, individual pride, and company spirit.

Trader Joe's mission statement does a good job of conveying "who we are, what we do, and why we are here," but it provides no sense of "where we are headed."

The here-and-now theme that typifies so many company mission statements means that there is value in distinguishing between the forward-looking concept of a strategic vision and the company's current mission. Thus, to mirror actual practice, we will use the term *mission statement* to refer to an enterprise's description of its *present* business and why it exists. (Some companies use the term *business purpose* instead of *mission statement* in characterizing their business activities; in practice, there seems to be no meaningful difference between the terms—which one is used is a matter of preference.)

Ideally, a company mission statement is sufficiently descriptive to *identify the company's products/services and specify the buyer needs it seeks to satisfy, the customer groups or markets it is endeavoring to serve, and its approach to pleasing customers.* Not many company mission statements fully reveal *all* these facets of its business, but most company mission statements do a decent job of indicating "who we are, what we do, and why we are here." A well-conceived mission statement should also distinguish a company's business makeup from that of other enterprises in language specific enough to give the company its own identity. Occasionally, companies couch their mission in terms of making a profit; this is misguided. Profit is more correctly an *objective* and a *result* of what a company does. Moreover, earning a profit is the obvious intent of every commercial enterprise.

An example of a good mission statement with ample specifics about what the organization does is that of the Occupational Safety and Health Administration (OSHA): "to promote the safety and health of America's workers by setting and enforcing standards; providing training, outreach, and education; establishing partnerships; and encouraging continual process improvement in workplace safety and health." Google's mission statement, while short, still captures the essence of the company: "to organize the world's information and make it universally accessible and useful."

Linking the Vision/Mission with Company Values

Many companies have developed a statement of values to guide the company's pursuit of its vision/mission, strategy, and ways of operating. By **values** (or *core values,* as they are often called), we mean the beliefs, traits, and ways of doing things that management has determined should guide the pursuit of its vision and strategy, the conduct of company's operations, and the behavior of company personnel. Values, good and bad, exist in every organization. They relate to such things as fair treatment, integrity, ethical behavior, innovation, teamwork, top-notch quality, superior customer service, social responsibility, and community citizenship. Most companies have built their statements of values around four to eight traits that company personnel are expected to display and that are supposed to be mirrored in how the company conducts its business. At American Express, the core values are customer commitment, quality, integrity, teamwork, and respect for people. Toyota preaches respect for and development of its employees, teamwork, getting quality right the first time, learning, continuous improvement, and embracing change in its pursuit of low-cost, top-notch manufacturing excellence in motor vehicles.[3] DuPont stresses four values—safety, ethics, respect for people, and environmental stewardship; the first three have been in place since the company was founded 200 years ago by E. I. du Pont. Pioneering, achieving, caring, and enduring are the core values that guide decisions and actions at Abbott Laboratories, a pharmaceutical company that appeared on *Fortune*'s "Most Admired Companies" list in 2008. Abbott chose its four core values according to research suggesting these qualities were of utmost importance to the company's key stakeholders—patients, employees, and health care professionals. The company conducted a series of values workshops in 2006 that allowed more than 11,000 employees to identify regularly performed work behaviors that supported the company's values. The company further solidified the values within the organization by asking that each business unit and employee develop annual goals that embodied each of the four values.

CORE CONCEPT

A company's *values* are the beliefs, traits, and behavioral norms that company personnel are expected to display in conducting the company's business and pursuing its strategic vision and strategy.

The extent to which company values statements translate into actually living the values varies widely. At companies such as Abbott, top executives believe in the importance of grounding company operations on sound values and ways of doing business. In their view, holding company personnel accountable for displaying the stated values is a way of infusing the company with the desired character, identity, and behavioral norms—the values become the company's genetic makeup, its DNA.

At the other extreme are companies with values that act as window dressing; the values statement is merely a collection of nice words and phrases that have little discernible impact on either the behavior of company personnel or how the company operates. Such companies have values statements because they are in vogue or because they make the company look good. The now-defunct energy corporation Enron, for example, touted four corporate values—respect, integrity, communication, and excellence—but some top officials engaged in dishonest and fraudulent maneuvers that were concealed by "creative" accounting. The chasm between the company's stated values and the actions of its managers became evident during Enron's dramatic implosion and subsequent bankruptcy, along with criminal indictments, fines, or jail terms for over a dozen Enron executives.

At companies where the stated values are real rather than cosmetic, managers connect values to the pursuit of the strategic vision and mission in one of two ways. In companies with long-standing values that are deeply entrenched in the corporate culture, senior managers are careful to craft a vision, mission, and strategy that match established values; they also reiterate how the value-based behavioral norms contribute to the company's business success. In new companies or companies with weak or incomplete sets of values, top management needs to consider what values, behaviors, and business conduct should characterize the company and help drive the vision and strategy forward. Values and behaviors that complement and support the company's vision are then drafted by these executives and circulated among managers and employees for discussion and possible modification. A final values statement that incorporates the desired behaviors and traits and that connects to the vision/mission is then officially adopted. Some companies combine their vision and values into a single statement or document, circulate it to all organization members, and in many instances post the vision/mission and values statement on the company's Web site. Illustration Capsule 2.2 describes Yahoo's values, and desired behaviors intended to aid it in its mission of "connecting people to their passions, their communities, and the world's knowledge."

Communicating the Strategic Vision

Effectively communicating the strategic vision down the line to lower-level managers and employees is as important as the strategic soundness of the long-term direction top management has chosen. Frontline employees can't be expected to unite behind managerial efforts to get the organization moving in the intended direction until they understand why the strategic course that management has charted is reasonable and beneficial.

CORE CONCEPT

An effectively communicated vision is a valuable management tool for enlisting the commitment of company personnel to actions that get the company moving in the intended direction.

Winning the support of organization members for the vision nearly always means putting "where we are going and why" in writing, distributing the statement organizationwide, and having executives personally explain the vision and its rationale to as many people as feasible. Ideally, executives should present their vision for the company in a manner that reaches out and grabs people. An engaging and convincing strategic vision has enormous motivational value—for the same reason that a stone mason is more inspired by building a great cathedral for the ages than simply laying stones to create floors and walls. When managers articulate a vivid and compelling case for where the company is headed, organization members begin to say, "This is interesting and has a lot of merit. I want to be involved and do my part to make it happen." The more that a vision evokes positive support and excitement, the greater its impact in terms of arousing a committed organizational effort and getting company personnel to move in a common direction.[4] Thus, executive ability to paint a convincing and inspiring picture of a company journey and destination is an important element of effective strategic leadership.

ILLUSTRATION CAPSULE 2.2
Yahoo's Core Values

Our mission is to be the most essential global Internet service for consumers and businesses. How we pursue that mission is influenced by a set of core values—the standards that guide interactions with fellow Yahoos, the principles that direct how we service our customers, the ideals that drive what we do and how we do it. Many of our values were put into practice by two guys in a trailer some time ago; others reflect ambitions as our company grows. All of them are what we strive to achieve every day.

EXCELLENCE

We are committed to winning with integrity. We know leadership is hard won and should never be taken for granted. We aspire to flawless execution and don't take shortcuts on quality. We seek the best talent and promote its development. We are flexible and learn from our mistakes.

INNOVATION

We thrive on creativity and ingenuity. We seek the innovations and ideas that can change the world. We anticipate market trends and move quickly to embrace them. We are not afraid to take informed, responsible risk.

CUSTOMER FIXATION

We respect our customers above all else and never forget that they come to us by choice. We share a personal responsibility to maintain our customers' loyalty and trust. We listen and respond to our customers and seek to exceed their expectations.

TEAMWORK

We treat one another with respect and communicate openly. We foster collaboration while maintaining individual accountability. We encourage the best ideas to surface from anywhere within the organization. We appreciate the value of multiple perspectives and diverse expertise.

COMMUNITY

We share an infectious sense of mission to make an impact on society and empower consumers in ways never before possible. We are committed to serving both the Internet community and our own communities.

FUN

We believe humor is essential to success. We applaud irreverence and don't take ourselves too seriously. We celebrate achievement. We yodel.

WHAT YAHOO *DOESN'T* VALUE

At the end of its values statement, Yahoo makes a point of singling out 54 things that it does not value, including bureaucracy, losing, "good enough," arrogance, the status quo, following, formality, quick fixes, passing the buck, micromanaging, Monday-morning quarterbacks, 20/20 hindsight, missing the boat, playing catch-up, punching the clock, and "shoulda coulda woulda."

Source: www.yahoo.com (accessed March 24, 2008).

Expressing the Essence of the Vision in a Slogan The task of effectively conveying the vision to company personnel is sometimes made easier when management can capture the vision in a catchy, easily remembered slogan. A number of organizations have summed up their vision in a brief phrase:

Strategic visions become real only when the vision statement is imprinted in the minds of organization members and then translated into hard objectives and strategies.

- FedEx: "Satifying worldwide demand for fast, time-definite, reliable distribution."
- Scotland Yard: "To make London the safest major city in the world."
- The Home Depot: "Helping people improve the places where they live and work."
- Charles Schwab: "To provide customers with the most useful and ethical financial services in the world."

Creating a short slogan to illuminate an organization's direction and purpose helps rally organization members to hurdle whatever obstacles lie in the company's path and to focus their attention on "where we are headed and why."

When External Change Calls for a New Strategic Direction Sometimes there's an order-of-magnitude change in a company's environment that dramatically alters its prospects and mandates radical revision of its strategic course. Such changes come about only rarely, but they do affect almost every industry. The technology company Intel has encountered two strategic inflection points during its history:

1. In the mid-1980s, when memory chips were Intel's principal business, Japanese manufacturers intent on dominating the memory chip business began setting their prices 10 percent below the prices charged by Intel and other U.S. memory chip manufacturers. Each time U.S. companies matched the Japanese price cuts, the Japanese manufacturers responded with another 10 percent price cut. In 1985, Gordon Moore, Intel's chairman and cofounder, and Andrew Grove, Intel's CEO, jointly concluded that the best long-term solution was to abandon the memory chip business even though it accounted for 70 percent of Intel's revenue. A new vision was developed that involved committing Intel's full energies to becoming the preeminent supplier of microprocessors to the personal computing industry. Moore and Grove's new vision and strategic course for Intel produced spectacular results. More than 80 percent of the world's PCs have been made with Intel microprocessors since 1996, and Intel has become the world's most profitable chip maker.
2. In 1998, when its chief managers recognized the growing importance of the Internet, Intel refocused on becoming the preeminent building-block supplier to the Internet economy and spurring efforts to make the Internet more useful. Intel's change in vision played a major role in getting more than 1 billion computers connected to the Internet worldwide, installing millions of servers, and building an Internet infrastructure that would support trillions of dollars of e-commerce and serve as a worldwide communication medium.

As the Intel example forcefully demonstrates, when a company reaches a strategic inflection point, management has some tough decisions to make about the company's course. Often it is a question of how to sustain company success, not just how to avoid possible disaster. Responding quickly to unfolding changes in the marketplace lessens a company's chances of becoming trapped in a stagnant or declining business or letting attractive new growth opportunities slip away.

Breaking Down Resistance to a New Strategic Vision It is particularly important for executives to provide a compelling rationale for a bold new strategic vision that takes a company in a dramatically different direction. Company personnel are prone to resist change that requires new priorities and work practices when they don't understand or accept the need for such redirection. Hence, reiterating the importance of the new vision and addressing employees' concerns about the new direction head-on become part of the task in mobilizing support for the vision. A single instance of stating the case for a new direction is not enough. Executives must repeat the reasons for the new direction often and convincingly at company gatherings and in company publications. In addition, senior managers must reinforce their pronouncements with updates about the company's latest performance and how it confirms the validity of the new vision. Unless and until the vision gains wide acceptance, it will have little effect in moving the organization down the newly chosen path.

The Payoffs of a Clear Vision Statement In sum, a well-conceived, forcefully communicated strategic vision pays off in several respects: (1) it crystallizes senior executives' own views about the firm's long-term direction; (2) it reduces the risk of rudderless decision making; (3) it is a tool for winning the support of organizational members for internal changes that will help make the vision a reality; (4) it provides a beacon for lower-level managers in forming departmental missions, setting departmental objectives, and crafting functional and departmental strategies that are in sync with the company's overall strategy; and (5) it helps an organization prepare for the future. When management is able to demonstrate significant progress in achieving these five benefits, the first step in organizational direction setting has been successfully completed.

PHASE 2: SETTING OBJECTIVES

The managerial purpose of setting **objectives** is to convert the strategic vision into specific performance targets—results and outcomes the company's management wants to achieve. Well-stated objectives are *quantifiable,* or *measurable,* and contain a *deadline for achievement.* As Bill Hewlett, cofounder of Hewlett-Packard, shrewdly observed, "You cannot manage what you cannot measure. . . . And what gets measured gets done."[5] Concrete, measurable objectives are managerially valuable because they serve as yardsticks for tracking a company's performance and progress. Indeed, the experiences of countless companies and managers teach that precisely spelling out *how much* of *what kind* of performance *by when* acts as marching orders for the entire organization and communicates to employees what level of performance is expected.[6] Such an approach definitely beats setting vague targets like "increase sales" or "reduce costs," which specify neither how much nor when, or else exhorting company personnel to "do the best they can" and then living with whatever results they deliver.

CORE CONCEPT

Objectives **are an organization's performance targets—the results and outcomes management wants to achieve. They function as yardsticks for measuring how well the organization is doing.**

The Imperative of Setting Stretch Objectives

Ideally, managers ought to use the objective-setting exercise as a tool for *stretching an organization to perform at its full potential and deliver the best possible results.* Challenging company personnel to exert their best efforts to achieve "stretch" gains in performance pushes an enterprise to be more inventive, to exhibit more urgency in improving both its financial performance and its business position, and to be more intentional and focused in its actions. Stretch objectives spur exceptional performance and help build a firewall against contentment with modest gains in organizational performance. As Mitchell Leibovitz, former CEO of the auto parts and service retailer Pep Boys, once said, "If you want to have ho-hum results, have ho-hum objectives." *There's no better way to avoid ho-hum results than by setting stretch objectives and using compensation incentives to motivate organization members to achieve the stretch performance targets.*

Setting stretch objectives is an effective tool for avoiding ho-hum results.

What Kinds of Objectives to Set—The Need for a Balanced Scorecard

Two very distinct types of performance yardsticks are required: those relating to **financial performance** and those relating to **strategic performance**—outcomes that indicate a company is strengthening its marketing standing, competitive vitality, and future business prospects. Examples of commonly used **financial objectives** and **strategic objectives** include the following:

Financial Objectives	Strategic Objectives
• An *x* percent increase in annual revenues • Annual increases in after-tax profits of *x* percent • Annual increases in earnings per share of *x* percent • Annual dividend increases of *x* percent • Profit margins of *x* percent • An *x* percent return on capital employed (ROCE) or return on equity (ROE) • Increased shareholder value—in the form of an upward-trending stock prices and annual dividend increases • Bond and credit ratings of *x* • Internal cash flows of *x* to fund new capital investment	• Winning an *x* percent market share • Achieving lower overall costs than rivals • Overtaking key competitors on product performance or quality or customer service • Deriving *x* percent of revenues from the sale of new products introduced within the past *x* years • Achieving customer satisfaction rates of *x* percent • Consistently getting new or improved products to market ahead of rivals • Having stronger national or global sales and distribution capabilities than rivals

CORE CONCEPT

Financial objectives **relate to the financial performance targets management has established for the organization to achieve.** ***Strategic objectives*** **relate to target outcomes that indicate a company is strengthening its market standing, competitive vitality, and future business prospects.**

Achieving acceptable financial results is a must. Without adequate profitability and financial strength, a company impairs pursuit of its strategic vision and puts its long-term health and ultimate survival in serious jeopardy. Furthermore, subpar earnings and a weak balance sheet not only alarm shareholders and creditors but also put the jobs of senior executives at risk. Even so, good financial performance, by itself, is not enough. Of equal or greater importance is a company's strategic performance—outcomes that indicate whether the company's market position and competitiveness are deteriorating, holding steady, or improving.

The Case for a Balanced Scorecard: Improved Strategic Performance Fosters Better Financial Performance A company's financial performance measures are really *lagging indicators* that reflect the results of *past* decisions and organizational activities.[7] But a company's past or current financial performance is not a reliable indicator of its future prospects—poor financial performers often turn things around and do better, while good financial performers can fall on hard times. The best and most reliable *leading indicators* of a company's future financial performance and business prospects are strategic outcomes that indicate whether the company's competitiveness and market position are stronger or weaker. For instance, if a company has set aggressive strategic objectives and is achieving them—such that its competitive strength and market position are on the rise—then there's reason to expect that its *future* financial performance will be better than its current or past performance. If a company is losing ground to competitors and its market position is slipping—outcomes that reflect weak strategic performance (and, very likely, failure to set or achieve strategic objectives)—then its ability to maintain its present profitability is highly suspect. Hence, whether a company's managers set, pursue, and achieve stretch strategic objectives tend to be a reliable leading indicator of whether its future financial performance will improve or stall.

CORE CONCEPT

A company that pursues and achieves strategic outcomes that boost its competitiveness and strength in the marketplace is in much better position to improve its future financial performance.

ILLUSTRATION CAPSULE 2.3
Examples of Company Objectives

GENERAL MOTORS

Reduce the percentage of automobiles using conventional internal combustion engines (ICE) through the development of hybrid ICEs, plug-in hybrid ICEs, range-extended electric vehicles, and hydrogen fuel cell electric engines; reduce automotive structural costs to benchmark levels of 23 percent of revenue by 2012 from 34 percent in 2005; and reduce annual U.S. labor costs by an additional $5 billion by 2011.

THE HOME DEPOT

Be the number one destination for professional contractors, whose business accounted for roughly 30 percent of 2006 sales; improve in-stock positions so customers can find and buy exactly what they need; deliver differentiated customer service and the know-how that our customers have come to expect from The Home Depot; repurchase $22.5 billion of outstanding shares during 2008; and open 55 new store locations with 5 store relocations in 2008.

YUM! BRANDS (KFC, PIZZA HUT, TACO BELL)

Open 100+ KFC restaurants in Vietnam by 2010; expand Taco Bell restaurant concept to Dubai, India, Spain and Japan during 2008 and 2009; increase number of international restaurant locations from 12,000 in 2007 to 15,000 in 2012; increase operating profit from international operations from $480 million in 2007 to $770 million in 2012; expand Pizza Hut's menu to include pasta and chicken dishes; decrease the number of company owned restaurant units in U.S. from 20% of units in 2007 to less than 10% of units by 2010; and increase the number of Taco Bell units in the U.S. by 2%–3% annually between 2008 and 2010.

AVON

Increase our beauty sales and market share; strengthen our brand image; enhance the representative experience; realize annualized cost savings of $430 million through improvements in marketing processes, sales model and organizational activities; and achieve annualized cost savings of $200 million through a strategic sourcing initiative.

Sources: Information posted on company Web sites (accessed March 27, 2008).

Consequently, a balanced scorecard for measuring company performance—one that tracks the achievement of both financial objectives and strategic objectives—is optimal.[8] Just tracking a company's financial performance overlooks the fact that what ultimately enables a company to deliver better financial results from its operations is the achievement of strategic objectives that improve its competitiveness and market strength. *The surest path to boosting company profitability quarter after quarter and year after year is to relentlessly pursue strategic outcomes that strengthen the company's market position and produce a growing competitive advantage over rivals.*

In 2006, approximately 70 percent of global companies used a balanced scorecard approach to measuring strategic and financial performance.[9] Organizations that have adopted a balanced scorecard approach to setting objectives and measuring performance include United Parcel Service (UPS), Ann Taylor Stores, the UK Ministry of Defense, Caterpillar, Daimler, Hilton Hotels, Duke University Hospital, and Siemens.[10] Illustration Capsule 2.3 provides selected strategic and financial objectives of four prominent companies.

Why Both Short-Term and Long-Term Objectives Are Needed As a rule, a company's set of financial and strategic objectives ought to include both near-term and longer-term performance targets. Having quarterly and annual objectives focuses attention on delivering immediate performance improvements. Targets to be achieved within three to five years prompt considerations of what to do *now* to put the company in position to perform better later. Long-term objectives take on particular importance because it is generally in the best interest of shareholders for companies to be managed for optimal long-term performance. When trade-offs have to be made between achieving long-run objectives and achieving short-run objectives, long-run objectives should take precedence (unless achieving one or more short-run performance targets has overriding importance). Shareholders are seldom well-served by repeated management actions that sacrifice better long-term performance in order to make quarterly or annual targets.

CORE CONCEPT

A company exhibits *strategic intent* when it relentlessly pursues an ambitious strategic objective, concentrating the full force of its resources and competitive actions on achieving that objective.

Strategic Intent: Relentless Pursuit of an Ambitious Long-Term Strategic Objective Very ambitious companies often establish a long-term strategic objective that clearly signals **strategic intent** to be a winner in the marketplace, often against long odds.[11] A company's strategic intent can entail unseating the existing industry leader, becoming the dominant market share leader, delivering the best customer service of any company in the industry (or the world), or turning a new technology into products capable of changing the way people work and live. For some years, Toyota has been charging to overtake General Motors as the world's largest motor vehicle producer—a goal it achieved in 2007 when its global sales totaled 9.37 million cars and trucks compared to General Motors' 2007 sales of 8.8 million cars and trucks.[12] During the mid-1970s, United Parcel Service (UPS) management, recognizing that the world was becoming more interconnected, developed the strategic intent of becoming a leading shipper of small packages in international markets. The company made multiple mistakes as it expanded into foreign locations and failed to realize consistent returns on its heavy investments outside the United States for more than 20 years, but did not abandon its long-term strategic goal. By 2007, however, shipments of small packages had become the company's fastest growing and most profitable business. Honda, too, has engaged in strategic intent with the development of its very light jet. The company's 20-plus-year dream of producing a "Honda Civic of the sky" began in the mid-1980s. The HondaJet was expected to obtain FAA certification in 2009, with production beginning in 2010.[13]

In many cases, ambitious companies that establish exceptionally bold strategic objectives and have an unshakable commitment to achieving them lack the immediate capabilities and market grasp to achieve such lofty targets. But they pursue their strategic objective relentlessly, sometimes even obsessively. They rally the organization around efforts to make the strategic intent a reality. They go all out to marshal the resources and capabilities to close in on their strategic target (which is often global market leadership) as rapidly as they can. They craft potent offensive strategies calculated to throw rivals off balance, put them on the defensive, and force them into an ongoing game of catch-up. As a consequence, capably managed up-and-coming enterprises with strategic intents exceeding their present reach and resources are a force to be reckoned with, often proving to be more formidable competitors over time than larger, cash-rich rivals that have modest strategic objectives and market ambitions.

The Need for Objectives at All Organizational Levels Objective setting should not stop with top management's establishing of companywide performance targets. Company objectives need to be broken down into performance targets for each of the organization's separate businesses, product lines, functional departments, and individual work units. Company performance can't reach full potential unless each organizational unit sets and pursues performance targets that contribute directly to the desired companywide outcomes and results. Objective setting is thus a top-down process that must extend to the lowest organizational levels. And it means that each organizational unit must set performance targets that support—rather than conflict with or negate—the achievement of companywide strategic and financial objectives.

PHASE 3: CRAFTING A STRATEGY

The task of crafting a strategy entails addressing a series of hows: *how* to grow the business, *how* to please customers, *how* to outcompete rivals, *how* to respond to changing market conditions, *how* to manage each functional piece of the business, *how* to develop needed competencies and capabilities, and *how* to achieve strategic and financial objectives. It also means exercising astute entrepreneurship in choosing among the various strategic alternatives—proactively searching for opportunities to do new things or to do existing things in new or better ways.[14]

The faster a company's business environment is changing, the more critical the need for its managers to be good entrepreneurs in diagnosing the direction and force of the changes under way and in responding with timely adjustments in strategy. Strategy makers have to pay attention to early warnings of future change and be willing to experiment with different ways to establish a market position. When obstacles unexpectedly appear in a company's path, it is up to management to adapt rapidly and innovatively. *Masterful strategies come partly (maybe mostly) by doing things differently from competitors where it counts—innovating more creatively, being more efficient, being more imaginative, adapting faster—rather than running with the herd.* Good strategy making is therefore inseparable from good business entrepreneurship. One cannot exist without the other.

Strategy Making Involves Managers at All Organizational Levels

A company's senior executives obviously have important strategy-making roles. The chief executive officer (CEO), as captain of the ship, carries the mantles of chief direction setter, chief objective setter, chief strategy maker, and chief strategy implementer for the total enterprise. Ultimate responsibility for *leading* the strategy-making, strategy-executing process rests with the CEO. In some enterprises the CEO or owner functions as strategic visionary and chief architect of strategy, personally deciding what the key elements of the company's strategy will be, although others may well assist with data gathering and analysis. Also, the CEO may seek the advice of other senior managers and key employees in fashioning an overall strategy and deciding on important strategic moves. A CEO-centered approach to strategy development is characteristic of small owner-managed companies and sometimes large corporations that have been founded by the present CEO or that have CEOs with strong strategic leadership skills. Larry Ellison at Oracle, Andrea Jung at Avon, Steve Jobs at Apple, and Howard Schultz at Starbucks are prominent examples of corporate CEOs who have wielded a heavy hand in shaping their company's strategy.

In most companies, however, strategy is the product of more than just the CEO's handiwork. Typically, other senior executives—business unit heads; the chief financial officer (CFO); and vice presidents for production, marketing, human resources, and other functional departments have influential strategy-making roles. Normally, a company's CFO is in charge of devising and implementing an appropriate financial strategy; the production vice president takes the lead in developing the company's production strategy; the marketing vice president orchestrates sales and marketing strategy; a brand manager is in charge of the strategy for a particular brand in the company's product lineup, and so on.

But even here it is a mistake to view strategy making as a *top* management function, the exclusive province of owner-entrepreneurs, CEOs, and other senior executives. The more that a company's operations cut across different products, industries, and geographical areas, the more that headquarters executives have little option but to delegate considerable strategy-making authority down the line to managers in charge of particular subsidiaries, geographic sales offices, distribution centers, and plants. On-the-scene managers are in the best position to evaluate the local situation and can be expected to have detailed familiarity with local customer requirements and expectations as well as with other aspects surrounding the strategic issues and choices in their arena of authority. This gives them an edge over headquarters executives in keeping the company's strategy responsive to local market and competitive conditions.

Take, for example, a company like General Electric (GE), a $173 billion corporation with operating segments ranging from financial services to aircraft engine manufacturing to television broadcasting. While top-level GE executives may well be personally involved in shaping GE's *overall* strategy and fashioning *important* strategic moves, it doesn't follow that a few senior executives at GE headquarters have either enough expertise or detailed understanding of all the relevant factors to wisely craft all the strategic initiatives for its diverse business lineup and thousands of products. They simply cannot know enough about the situation in every General Electric organizational unit to decide upon every strategy detail and direct every strategic move made in GE's worldwide organization. Rather, it takes involvement on the part of GE's whole management team—top executives; subsidiary heads; division heads; and key managers in such geographic units as sales offices, distribution centers, and plants—to craft the thousands of strategic initiatives that end up comprising the whole of GE's strategy.

CORE CONCEPT
In most companies, crafting and executing strategy is a *collaborative effort* in which every manager has a role for the area he or she heads. It is flawed thinking to view crafting and executing strategy as something only high-level managers do.

While managers farther down in the managerial hierarchy obviously have a narrower, more specific strategy-making role than managers closer to the top, the important understanding here is that in most of today's companies *every manager typically has a strategy-making role—ranging from minor to major—for the area he or she heads.* Hence, any notion that an organization's strategists are at the top of the management hierarchy and that midlevel and frontline personnel merely carry out their strategic directives needs to be cast aside. In companies with wide-ranging operations, it is far more accurate to view strategy making as a *collaborative effort* involving managers (and sometimes key employees) down through the whole organizational hierarchy. A valuable strength of collaborative strategy making is that the team of people charged with crafting the strategy often include the very people who will also be charged with executing it. Giving people an influential stake in crafting the strategy they must later help execute not only builds commitment to new strategies but also enhances accountability at multiple levels of management—the excuse "It wasn't my idea to do this" won't fly.

A Company's Strategy-Making Hierarchy

It thus follows that *a company's overall strategy is a collection of strategic initiatives and actions* devised by managers and key employees up and down the whole organizational hierarchy. As an enterprise's operations become larger, more diverse, and more geographically scattered, progressively more managers and key employees at more levels in the organizational hierarchy tend to become personally engaged in crafting strategic initiatives and exercise a relevant strategy-making role. Figure 2.2 shows who is generally responsible for devising what pieces of a company's overall strategy.

In diversified, multibusiness companies where the strategies of several different businesses have to be managed, the strategy-making task involves four distinct types or levels of strategy, each of which involves different facets of the company's overall strategy:

1. *Corporate strategy* consists of initiatives to diversify into different industries, boost the combined performance of the set of businesses the company has diversified into, and figure out how to capture cross-business synergies and turn them into competitive advantage. Senior corporate executives normally have lead responsibility for devising corporate strategy and for choosing among whatever recommended actions bubble up from the organization below. Major strategic decisions are usually reviewed and approved by the company's board of directors. We will look deeper into the strategy-making process at diversified companies when we get to Chapter 8.
2. *Business strategy* concerns the actions and approaches crafted to produce successful performance in one specific line of business. Orchestrating the development of business-level strategy is the responsibility of the manager in charge of the business. The business head has at least two other strategy-related roles: (*a*) seeing that lower-level strategies are well conceived and well matched to the overall business strategy, and (*b*) getting major business-level strategic moves approved by corporate-level officers (and sometimes the board of directors) and keeping them informed of emerging strategic issues. In diversified companies, business-unit heads may have the additional obligation of making sure business-level objectives and strategy conform to corporate-level objectives and strategy themes.
3. *Functional-area strategies* concern the actions and practices employed in managing particular functions or business processes or activities within a business. A company's marketing strategy, for example, represents the managerial game plan for running the sales and marketing part of the business. A company's product development strategy represents the managerial game plan for keeping the company's product lineup in tune with what buyers are looking for. The primary role of a functional strategy is to add specifics to a company's business-level strategy. Lead responsibility for functional strategies within a business is normally delegated to the heads of the respective functions, with the general manager of the business having final approval and perhaps even exerting a strong influence over the particular pieces of the strategies.
4. *Operating strategies* concern the relatively narrow strategic initiatives and approaches for managing key operating units (plants, distribution centers, geographic units) and specific operating activities with strategic significance (advertising campaigns, supply chain activities, and Internet sales operations). Operating strategies, while of limited scope, add further detail and completeness to functional strategies and to the overall business strategy. Lead responsibility for operating strategies is usually delegated to frontline managers, subject to review and approval by higher-ranking managers.

Even though operating strategy is at the bottom of the strategy-making hierarchy, its importance should not be downplayed. A major plant that fails in its strategy to achieve production volume, unit cost, and quality targets can damage the company's

Figure 2.2 A Company's Strategy-Making Hierarchy

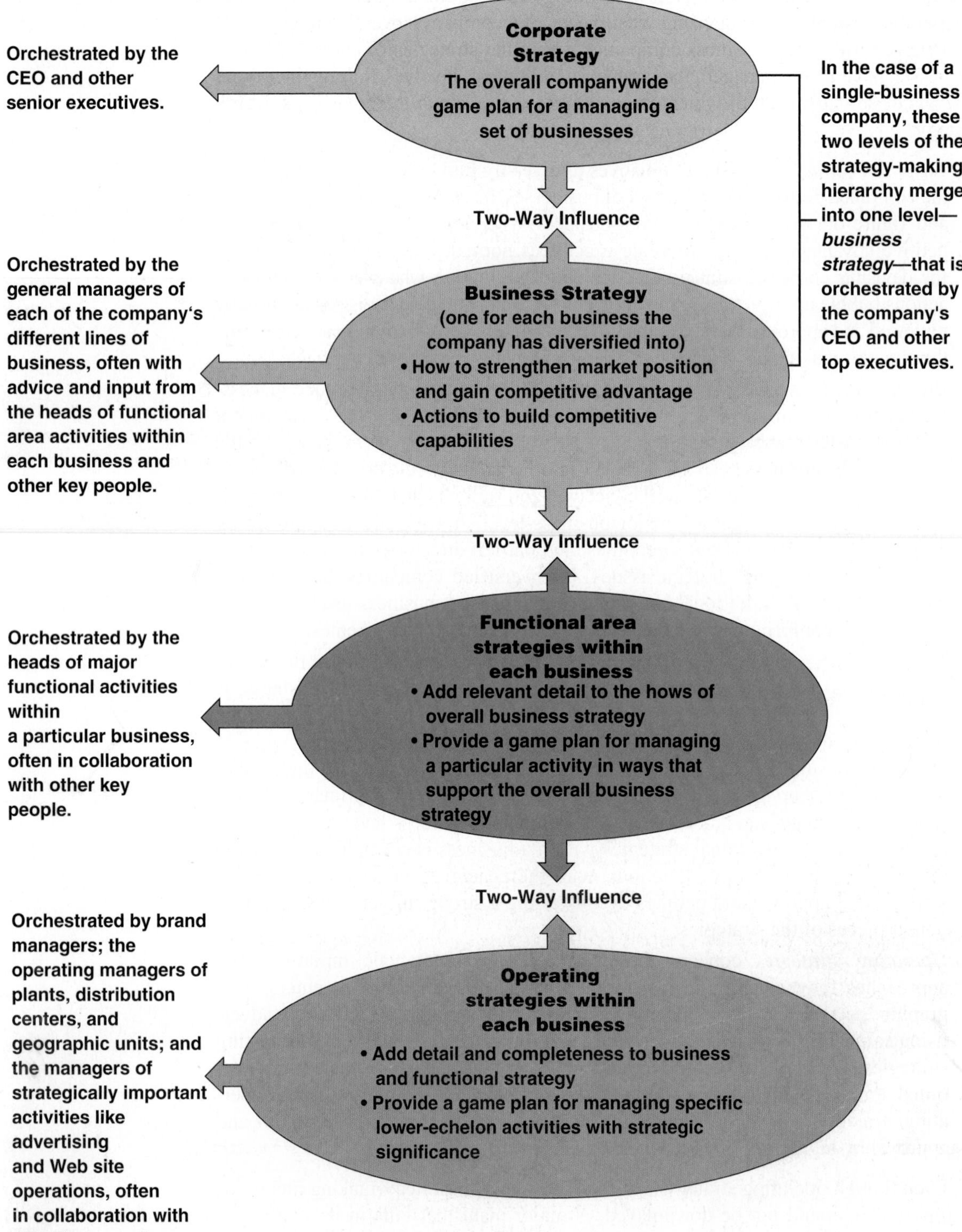
Corporate Strategy
The overall companywide game plan for a managing a set of businesses
Orchestrated by the CEO and other senior executives.
In the case of a single-business company, these two levels of the strategy-making hierarchy merge into one level—*business strategy*—that is orchestrated by the company's CEO and other top executives.
Two-Way Influence
Business Strategy
(one for each business the company has diversified into)
• How to strengthen market position and gain competitive advantage
• Actions to build competitive capabilities
Orchestrated by the general managers of each of the company's different lines of business, often with advice and input from the heads of functional area activities within each business and other key people.
Two-Way Influence
Functional area strategies within each business
• Add relevant detail to the hows of overall business strategy
• Provide a game plan for managing a particular activity in ways that support the overall business strategy
Orchestrated by the heads of major functional activities within a particular business, often in collaboration with other key people.
Two-Way Influence
Operating strategies within each business
• Add detail and completeness to business and functional strategy
• Provide a game plan for managing specific lower-echelon activities with strategic significance
Orchestrated by brand managers; the operating managers of plants, distribution centers, and geographic units; and the managers of strategically important activities like advertising and Web site operations, often in collaboration with other key people

reputation for quality products and undercut the achievement of company sales and profit objectives. Frontline managers are thus an important part of an organization's strategy-making team. One cannot reliably judge the strategic importance of a given action simply by the strategy level or location within the managerial hierarchy where it is initiated.

In single-business enterprises, the corporate and business levels of strategy-making merge into one level—business strategy—because the strategy for the whole company involves only one distinct line of business. Thus, a single-business enterprise has three levels of strategy: business strategy for the company as a whole, functional-area strategies for each main area within the business, and operating strategies undertaken by lower-echelon managers. Proprietorships, partnerships, and owner-managed enterprises may have only one or two strategy-making levels since their strategy-making, strategy-executing process can be handled by just a few key people.

A Strategic Vision + Objectives + Strategy = A Strategic Plan

Developing a strategic vision and mission, setting objectives, and crafting a strategy are basic direction-setting tasks. They map out where a company is headed, the targeted strategic and financial outcomes, and the competitive moves and internal actions to be used in achieving the desired business results. Together, they constitute a **strategic plan** for coping with industry and competitive conditions, combating the expected actions of the industry's key players, and confronting the challenges and issues that stand as obstacles to the company's success.[15]

CORE CONCEPT

A company's *strategic plan* lays out its future direction, performance targets, and strategy.

In companies that do regular strategy reviews and develop explicit strategic plans, the strategic plan usually ends up as a written document that is circulated to most managers and perhaps selected employees. Near-term performance targets are the part of the strategic plan most often spelled out explicitly and communicated to managers and employees. A number of companies summarize key elements of their strategic plans in the company's annual report to shareholders, in postings on their Web site, or in statements provided to the business media, whereas others, perhaps for reasons of competitive sensitivity, make only vague, general statements about their strategic plans. In small, privately owned companies, it is rare for strategic plans to exist in written form. Small companies' strategic plans tend to reside in the thinking and directives of owners/executives, with aspects of the plan being revealed in meetings and conversations with company personnel, and the understandings and commitments among managers and key employees about where to head, what to accomplish, and how to proceed.

PHASE 4: IMPLEMENTING AND EXECUTING THE STRATEGY

Managing the implementation and execution of strategy is an operations-oriented, make-things-happen activity aimed at performing core business activities in a strategy-supportive manner. It is easily the most demanding and time-consuming part of the strategy management process. Converting strategic plans into actions and results tests a manager's ability to direct organizational change, motivate people, build and strengthen company competencies and competitive capabilities, create and nurture a strategy-supportive work climate, and meet or beat performance targets. Initiatives to put the strategy in place and execute it proficiently have to be launched and managed on many organizational fronts.

Management's action agenda for implementing and executing the chosen strategy emerges from assessing what the company will have to do differently or better to achieve the targeted financial and strategic performance. Each company manager has to think through the answer to the following questions: "What has to be done in my area to execute my piece of the strategic plan?" and "What actions should I take to get the process under way?" How much internal change is needed depends on how much of the strategy is new, how far internal practices and competencies deviate from what the strategy requires, and how well the present work climate/culture supports good strategy execution. Depending on the amount of internal change involved, full implementation and proficient execution of company strategy (or important new pieces thereof) can take several months to several years.

In most situations, managing the strategy execution process includes the following principal aspects:

- Staffing the organization with the needed skills and expertise, consciously building and strengthening strategy-supportive competencies and competitive capabilities, and organizing the work effort.
- Allocating ample resources to activities critical to strategic success.
- Ensuring that policies and procedures facilitate rather than impede effective execution.
- Using the best-known practices to perform core business activities and pushing for continuous improvement. Organizational units have to periodically reassess how things are being done and diligently pursue useful changes and improvements.
- Installing information and operating systems that enable company personnel to do their jobs better and quicker.
- Motivating people to pursue the target objectives energetically and, if need be, modifying their duties and job behavior to better fit the requirements of successful strategy execution.
- Tying rewards and incentives directly to the achievement of performance objectives and good strategy execution.
- Creating a company culture and work climate conducive to successful strategy execution.
- Exerting the internal leadership needed to drive implementation forward and keep improving the strategy execution process. When stumbling blocks or weaknesses are encountered, management has to see that they are addressed and rectified in timely and effective fashion.

Good strategy execution requires diligent pursuit of operating excellence. It is a job for a company's whole management team. And success hinges on the skills and cooperation of operating managers who can push needed changes in their organizational units and consistently deliver good results. Implementation of the chosen strategy can be considered successful if the company meets or beats its strategic and financial performance targets and shows good progress in achieving management's strategic vision.

PHASE 5: EVALUATING PERFORMANCE AND INITIATING CORRECTIVE ADJUSTMENTS

The fifth phase of the strategy management process—monitoring external developments, evaluating the company's progress, and making corrective adjustments—is the trigger point for deciding whether to continue or change the company's vision, objectives, strategy, and/or strategy execution methods. So long as the company's direction and strategy seem well matched to industry and competitive conditions and performance targets are being met, company executives may well decide to stay the course. Simply fine-tuning the strategic plan and continuing with efforts to improve strategy execution are sufficient.

But whenever a company encounters disruptive changes in its environment, questions need to be raised about the appropriateness of its direction and strategy. If a company experiences a downturn in its market position or persistent shortfalls in performance, then company managers are obligated to ferret out the causes—do they relate to poor strategy, poor strategy execution, or both?—and take timely corrective action. A company's direction, objectives, and strategy have to be revisited anytime external or internal conditions warrant. It is to be expected that a company will modify its strategic vision, direction, objectives, and strategy over time.

Likewise, it is not unusual for a company to find that one or more aspects of its strategy implementation and execution are not going as well as intended. Proficient strategy execution is always the product of much organizational learning. It is achieved unevenly—coming quickly in some areas and proving nettlesome in others. It is both normal and desirable to periodically assess strategy execution to determine which aspects are working well and which need improving. Successful strategy execution entails vigilantly searching for ways to improve and then making corrective adjustments whenever and wherever it is useful to do so.

CORE CONCEPT
A company's vision, objectives, strategy, and approach to strategy execution are never final; managing strategy is an ongoing process, not an every-now-and-then task.

LEADING THE STRATEGIC MANAGEMENT PROCESS

The litany for leading the process of making and executing strategy is simple enough: Craft a sound strategic plan, implement it, execute it to the fullest, adjust it as needed, and win! But the leadership challenges are significant and diverse. Exerting take-charge leadership, being a spark plug for change and action, ramrodding things through, and achieving results thrusts top executives and senior mangers in charge of business units, product categories, geographic regions, and major production and distribution facilities into a variety of leadership roles: visionary, strategist, resource acquirer, capabilities builder, motivator, and crisis solver, to mention a few. There are times when leading the strategic management process entails being a hard-nosed authoritarian, and times when it is best to be a perceptive listener and a compromising decision maker; there are times when matters are best delegated to people closest to the scene of the action, and times when being a coach is the proper role. Many occasions call for company leaders to assume a highly visible role and put in long hours guiding the process, while others entail only a brief ceremonial performance with the details delegated to subordinates.

In general, leading the strategic management process calls for the following six actions on the part of senior executives:

1. Staying on top of how well things are going.
2. Making sure the company has a good strategic plan.
3. Putting constructive pressure on organizational units to achieve good results and operating excellence.
4. Pushing corrective actions to improve both the company's strategy and how well it is being executed.
5. Leading the development of stronger core competencies and competitive capabilities.
6. Displaying ethical integrity and leading social responsibility initiatives.

Staying on Top of How Well Things Are Going

To stay on top of whether the company's direction and strategy are on track and how well the strategy execution process is going, a manager needs to develop a broad network of contacts and sources of information, both formal and informal. The regular channels include talking with key subordinates, attending presentations and meetings, talking to customers, watching the competitive reactions of rival firms, exchanging e-mail and holding telephone conversations with people in outlying locations, making onsite visits, and listening to rank-and-file employees. However, some sources of information are more trustworthy than the rest, and the views and perspectives offered by different people can vary widely. Presentations and briefings by subordinates may not represent the whole truth. Bad news or problems may be minimized or in some cases not reported at all by subordinates in hopes that they can turn things around before the shortcomings are noticed. Hence, senior managers have to make sure that they have accurate information and a feel for the existing situation. They have to confirm whether things are on track, learn what obstacles lie in the path of good financial and strategic performance, and develop a basis for determining what, if anything, they can personally do to improve the strategy management process.

CORE CONCEPT
Management by walking around (MBWA) **is one of the techniques that effective leaders use to stay on top of how well things are going and to learn what issues they need to address.**

One of the best ways for executives to stay on top of things is by making regular visits to the field and talking with many different people at many different levels—a technique often labeled **managing by walking around (MBWA)**. Wal-Mart executives have had a long-standing practice of spending two to three days every week visiting Wal-Mart's stores and talking with store managers and employees. Sam Walton, Wal-Mart's founder, insisted, "The key is to get out into the store and listen to what the associates have to say." Jack Welch, the highly effective CEO of General Electric (GE) from 1980 to 2001, not only spent several days each month personally visiting GE operations and talking with major customers but also arranged his schedule so that he could spend time exchanging information and ideas with GE managers from all over the world who were attending classes at the company's leadership development center near GE's headquarters. Some companies have weekly get-togethers in each division (often on Friday afternoons), attended by both executives and employees, to create a regular opportunity for tidbits of information to flow freely between down-the-line employees and executives. Many manufacturing executives make a point of strolling the factory floor to talk with workers and meeting regularly with union officials. Some managers operate out of open cubicles in big spaces populated with other personnel in open cubicles so that they can interact easily and frequently with coworkers. Jeff Bezos, Amazon.com's CEO, is noted for his practice of MBWA, firing off a battery of questions when he tours facilities and insisting that Amazon managers spend time in the trenches to prevent overly abstract thinking and disconnections from the reality of what's happening.[16]

Most managers rightly attach great importance to gathering information and opinions firsthand from people at different organizational levels about how well various aspects of the strategy-execution process are going. Such contacts give managers a feel for what progress is being made, what problems are being encountered, and whether additional resources or different approaches may be needed. Just as important, MBWA provides opportunities for managers to give encouragement, lift spirits, shift attention from the old to the new priorities, and create some excitement—all of which generate positive energy and help mobilize organizational efforts behind strategy execution.

Making Sure a Company Has a Good Strategic Plan

It is the responsibility of top executives—most especially the CEO—to ensure that a company has a sound and cohesive strategic plan. There are two things that the CEO and other top-level executives should do in leading the development of a good strategic plan. One is to *effectively communicate the company's vision, objectives, and major strategy components* to down-the-line managers and key personnel. The company's vision, mission, objectives, and overall strategy paint the white lines for strategy makers throughout the organization. *Midlevel and frontline managers cannot craft unified strategic moves without first understanding the company's long-term direction and knowing the major components of the company's strategy that their strategy-making efforts are supposed to support and enhance.* Thus, *leading* the development of a strategic plan is very much a top management *responsibility,* even though the tasks of setting objectives and formulating the details of strategy are most definitely *a team effort,* involving company personnel at the corporate and business levels on down to the associated functional and operating levels—as displayed in Figure 2.2.

When the strategizing process is effectively led by the CEO and other top executives, with lower-level strategy-making efforts taking their cues from the higher-level strategy elements they are supposed to complement and support, there's less potential for conflict between different levels in the strategy hierarchy. An absence of strong strategic leadership from the top sets the stage for some degree of strategic confusion and disunity.

A second responsibility of senior managers is leading the development of a good strategic plan. There are two things that the CEO and other top-level executives should do in leading the development of a good strategic plan. The first is to *effectively communicate the company's vision, objectives, and major strategy components to down-the-line managers and key personnel.* The greater the numbers of company personnel who know, understand, and buy into the company's long-term direction and overall strategy, the smaller the risk that organization units will go off in conflicting strategic directions. The second is to *exercise due diligence in reviewing lower-level strategies for consistency* and support of higher-level strategies. Any strategy conflicts must be addressed and resolved, either by modifying the lower-level strategies with conflicting elements or by adapting the higher-level strategy to accommodate more appealing strategy ideas and initiatives bubbling up from below. *Anything less than a unified collection of strategies weakens the overall strategy and is likely to impair company performance.*

The Importance of Corporate Intrapreneurship in the Strategy-Making Process Keeping the organization bubbling with fresh supplies of ideas and suggestions for improvement is another key demand of strategic leadership. Managers cannot mandate innovative suggestions by simply exhorting people to "be creative." Rather, they have to foster a culture where innovative ideas and experimentation with new ways of doing things can blossom and thrive. In some companies, top management makes a regular practice of encouraging individuals and teams to develop and champion proposals for new product lines and new business ventures. The idea is to unleash the talents and energies of promising "corporate intrapreneurs," letting them try out untested business ideas and giving them the room to pursue new strategic initiatives. Executives judge which proposals merit support, give the chosen intrapreneurs the organizational and budgetary support they need, and let them run with the ball. Thus, important pieces of company strategy can originate with those intrapreneurial individuals and teams who succeed in championing a proposal through the approval stage and then end up being charged with the lead role in launching new products, overseeing the company's entry into new geographic markets, or heading up new business ventures.

At IBM, the company's chief managers found that its reward system—which focused on short-term results, fostered a managerial preoccupation with current markets, and bred an analysis-driven culture—discouraged new business development and slowed the strategy-making process to 12–18 months. To encourage corporate intrapreneurship, IBM developed a new set of policies to foster growth through emerging business opportunities. The new approach encouraged senior managers to push promising entrepreneurial business ventures proposed by subordinates into the market through experiments with existing customers. Those ideas that customers valued and that were deemed capable of generating acceptable revenues and profits went on to be marketed to new customers. Within five years, IBM's corporate intrapreneurship efforts had developed 25 new businesses; 3 of those failed, but the remaining 22 generated more than $15 billion in revenues in 2004.[17]

Organizational leaders can promote innovation and keep the strategy fresh in any of the following ways:

- *Encouraging individuals and groups to brainstorm proposals for new business ventures or improving existing products*—The leadership trick in promoting corporate intrapreneurship is to keep a sense of urgency alive in the business so that people see change and innovation as necessities.
- *Taking special pains to foster, nourish, and support people who are eager to test new business ventures and explore adding new or improved products*—People with maverick ideas or out-of-the-ordinary proposals have to be given room to operate. Above all, would-be champions who advocate radical or different ideas must not be looked on as disruptive or troublesome. The best champions and change agents are persistent, tenacious, and committed to seeing their idea through to success.
- *Ensuring that the rewards for successful champions are large and visible and that people who champion ideas for new products or business ventures that end up being discarded are not punished but rather encouraged to try again*—Encouraging lots of tries is important, since many ideas for new products and business ventures won't pan out.
- *Using all kinds of ad hoc organizational forms to support ideas and experimentation*— Forming venture teams and new business task forces to explore promising ideas, along with top management willingness to give entrepreneurial employees the latitude to work on a promising project without official authorization, are just a few of the possible organizational means a company can use to foster innovation. (*Skunkworks* is a term for a group of people who work on a project outside the usual norms or rules in an organization.)

Putting Constructive Pressure on Organizational Units to Achieve Good Results and Operating Excellence

Managers have to be out front in mobilizing organizational energy behind the drive for good financial and strategic performance and operating excellence. Part of the leadership requirement here entails nurturing a results-oriented work climate, where performance standards are high and a spirit of achievement is pervasive. If management wants to drive the strategic management process by instilling a results-oriented work climate, then senior executives have to take the lead in promoting a culture of innovation and high performance, a strong sense of involvement on the part of company personnel, emphasis on individual initiative and creativity, respect for the contribution of individuals and groups, and pride in doing things right.

Organizational leaders who succeed in creating a results-oriented work climate typically are intensely people-oriented, and they are skilled users of people-management practices that win the emotional commitment of company personnel and inspire them to do their best.[18] They understand that treating employees well generally leads to increased teamwork, higher morale, greater loyalty, and increased employee commitment to making a contribution. All of these foster an esprit de corps that energizes organizational members to contribute to the drive for a top-flight strategic plan, operating excellence and better-than-average financial performance.

While leadership efforts to instill a results-oriented culture usually accentuate the positive, there are negative reinforcers, too. Managers whose units consistently perform poorly have to be replaced. Low-performing workers and people who reject the results-oriented cultural emphasis have to be weeded out or at least moved to out-of-the-way positions. Average performers have to be candidly counseled that they have limited career potential unless they show more progress in the form of more effort, better skills, and ability to deliver better results.

Pushing Corrective Actions to Improve Both the Company's Strategy and How Well It Is Being Executed

The leadership challenge of making corrective adjustments is twofold: deciding when adjustments are needed and deciding what adjustments to make. Both decisions are a normal and necessary part of managing the strategy execution process, since no scheme for implementing and executing strategy can foresee all the events and problems that will arise.[19] There comes a time at every company when managers have to fine-tune or overhaul the approaches to strategy execution and push for better results. Clearly, when a company's strategy execution effort is not delivering good results and making measured progress toward operating excellence, it is the leader's responsibility to step forward and push corrective actions.

The *process* of making corrective adjustments involves sensing needs; gathering information; developing options and exploring their pros and cons; putting forth action proposals and partial solutions; striving for a consensus; and, finally, formally adopting an agreed-on course of action.[20] The time frame for deciding what corrective changes to initiate can vary from a few hours or days to a few months—depending on the complexity of the issue and the urgency of the matter. In a crisis, it is typical for leaders to have key subordinates gather information, identify and evaluate options, and perhaps prepare a preliminary set of recommended actions for consideration. The organizational leader then usually meets with key subordinates and personally presides over extended discussions of the proposed responses, trying to build a quick consensus among members of the executive inner circle. If no consensus emerges and action is required immediately, the burden falls on the manager in charge to choose the response and urge its support.

Leading the Development of Better Competencies and Capabilities

A company that proactively tries to strengthen its competencies and competitive capabilities not only adds power to its strategy and to its potential for winning competitive advantage but also enhances its chances for achieving good strategy execution and operating excellence. Senior management usually has to *lead* the strengthening effort because competencies and competitive capabilities are spawned by the combined efforts of different work groups, departments, and strategic allies. The tasks of developing human skills, knowledge bases, and intellectual assets and then integrating them to forge competitively advantageous competencies and capabilities is an exercise best orchestrated by senior managers who appreciate their significance and who have the clout to enforce the necessary cooperation among individuals, groups, departments, and external allies.

Aside from leading efforts to strengthen *existing* competencies and capabilities, effective strategy leadership also entails trying to anticipate changes in customer/market requirements and proactively build *new* competencies and capabilities that hold promise for building an enduring competitive edge over rivals. Senior managers are in the best position to see the need and potential of such new capabilities and then to play a lead role in the capability-building, resource-strengthening process. *Proactively building new competencies and capabilities ahead of rivals to gain a competitive edge is strategic leadership of the best kind,* but strengthening the company's resource base in reaction to newly developed capabilities of pioneering rivals occurs more frequently.

Displaying Ethical Integrity and Undertaking Social Responsibility Initiatives

For an organization to avoid the pitfalls of scandal and disgrace associated with unethical strategies and operating practices, top executives must be openly and unswervingly committed to conducting the company's business in an ethical manner and to operating according to socially redeeming values and to business principles. Leading the effort to operate the company's business in an ethically principled fashion has three pieces.

- First and foremost, the CEO and other senior executives must set an excellent example in their own ethical behavior, demonstrating character and personal integrity in their actions and decisions. The behavior of senior executives, always watched carefully, sends a clear message to company personnel regarding the real standards of personal conduct.
- Second, top executives must declare unequivocal support for high ethical standards (perhaps even expressing these standards in a company code of ethics) and take an uncompromising stand on expecting all company personnel to adhere to high ethical standards (and comply fully with the company's code of ethics).
- Third, top executives must reprimand those who have been lax in enforcing ethical compliance. Failure to act swiftly and decisively in punishing ethical misconduct is interpreted as a lack of commitment.

Undertaking Social Responsibility Initiatives Like the observance of ethical principles, the exercise of social responsibility requires visible and forthright leadership on the part of top executives. What separates companies that make a sincere effort to be good corporate citizens from companies that are content to do only what is legally required are company leaders who believe strongly that just making a profit is not good enough. Such leaders are committed to a higher standard of performance that includes social and environmental metrics as well as financial and strategic metrics. The strength of the commitment from the top—typically a company's CEO and board of directors—ultimately determines whether a company will implement and execute a full-fledged strategy of social responsibility whereby it pursues initiatives to protect the environment, actively participate in community affairs, support charitable causes, and positively impact workforce diversity and the overall well-being of employees.

Companies with socially conscious strategy leaders and a core value of corporate social responsibility move beyond the rhetorical flourishes of corporate citizenship and enlist the full support of company personnel behind social responsibility initiatives

CORPORATE GOVERNANCE: THE ROLE OF THE BOARD OF DIRECTORS IN THE STRATEGY-MAKING, STRATEGY-EXECUTING PROCESS

Although senior managers have *lead responsibility* for crafting and executing a company's strategy, it is the duty of the board of directors to exercise strong oversight and see that the five tasks of strategic management are done in a manner that benefits shareholders (in the case of investor-owned enterprises) or stakeholders (in the case of not-for-profit organizations). In watching over management's strategy-making, strategy-executing actions, a company's board of directors has four important obligations to fulfill:

1. *Be inquiring critics and oversee the company's direction, strategy, and business approaches.* Board members must ask probing questions and draw on their business acumen to make independent judgments about whether strategy proposals have been adequately analyzed and whether proposed strategic actions appear to have greater promise than alternatives.
2. *Evaluate the caliber of senior executives' strategy-making and strategy-executing skills.* The board is always responsible for determining whether the current CEO is doing a good job of strategic leadership.
3. *Institute a compensation plan for top executives that rewards them for actions and results that serve stakeholder interests, and most especially those of shareholders.* A basic principle of corporate governance is that the owners of a corporation delegate managerial control to top management in return for compensation. In their role as an *agent* of shareholders, top executives have a duty to make decisions and operate the company in accord with shareholder interests. Boards of directors must develop salary and incentive compensation plans that make it in the self-interest of executives to operate the business in a manner that benefits the owners. It is also incumbent on the board of directors to prevent management from gaining executive perks and privileges that simply line the pockets of executives. Numerous media reports have recounted instances in which boards of directors have gone along with opportunistic executive efforts to secure excessive, if not downright obscene, compensation of one kind or another (multimillion-dollar interest-free loans, personal use of corporate aircraft, lucrative severance and retirement packages, outsized stock incentive

awards, and so on). The compensation plan developed by General Electric's board of directors' compensation committee makes a significant portion of the CEO's compensation contingent on GE's financial performance and growth in its stock price. In 2007, the company's strong performance allowed GE chairman and CEO Jeffrey Immelt to receive total compensation of $9.1 million. Immelt's capabilities and track record at leading GE had regularly ranked him as one of the world's best CEOs by *Barron's* and kept GE atop *Fortune*'s "Most Admired Companies" list.

4. *Oversee the company's financial accounting and financial reporting practices.* While top executives, particularly the company's CEO and CFO, are primarily responsible for seeing that the company's financial statements accurately report the results of the company's operations, board members have a fiduciary duty to protect shareholders by exercising oversight of the company's financial practices. In addition, corporate boards must ensure that generally accepted accounting principles (GAAP) are properly used in preparing the company's financial statements and determine whether proper financial controls are in place to prevent fraud and misuse of funds.

Every corporation should have a strong, independent board of directors that (1) is well informed about the company's performance, (2) guides and judges the CEO and other top executives, (3) has the courage to curb management actions they believe are inappropriate or unduly risky, (4) certifies to shareholders that the CEO is doing what the board expects, (5) provides insight and advice to management, and (6) is intensely involved in debating the pros and cons of key decisions and actions.[21] Boards of directors that lack the backbone to challenge a strong-willed or imperial CEO or that rubber-stamp most anything the CEO recommends without probing inquiry and debate abandon their duty to represent and protect shareholder interests. The whole fabric of effective corporate governance is undermined when boards of directors shirk their responsibility to maintain ultimate control over the company's strategic direction, the major elements of its strategy, the business approaches management is using to implement and execute the strategy, executive compensation, and the financial reporting process.

KEY POINTS

The managerial process of crafting and executing a company's strategy consists of five interrelated and integrated phases:

1. *Developing a strategic vision* of where the company needs to head and what its future product/customer/market/technology focus should be. This managerial step provides long-term direction, infuses the organization with a sense of purposeful action, and communicates to stakeholders what management's aspirations for the company are.
2. *Setting objectives* and using the targeted results and outcomes as yardsticks for measuring the company's performance and progress. Objectives need to spell out *how much* of *what kind* of performance *by when,* and they need to require a significant amount of organizational stretch. Measuring company performance entails setting both *financial objectives* and *strategic objectives.* A *balanced scorecard approach* tracks both types of objectives.

3. *Crafting a strategy to achieve the objectives* and move the company along the strategic course that management has charted. Crafting strategy is concerned principally with forming responses to changes under way in the external environment, devising competitive moves and market approaches aimed at producing sustainable competitive advantage, building competitively valuable competencies and capabilities, and uniting the strategic actions initiated in various parts of the company. The more that a company's operations cut across different products, industries, and geographical areas, the more that strategy making becomes a *collaborative effort* involving managers and company personnel at many organizational levels. The total strategy that emerges in such companies is really a collection of strategic actions and business approaches initiated partly by senior company executives, partly by the heads of major business divisions, partly by functional-area managers, and partly by operating managers on the frontlines. The larger and more diverse the operations of an enterprise, the more points of strategic initiative it has and the more managers and employees at more levels of management that have a relevant strategy-making role. A single-business enterprise has three levels of strategy—business strategy for the company as a whole, functional-area strategies for each main area within the business, and operating strategies undertaken by lower-echelon managers to flesh out strategically significant aspects for the company's business and functional area strategies. In diversified, multibusiness companies, the strategy-making task involves four distinct types or levels of strategy: corporate strategy for the company as a whole, business strategy (one for each business the company has diversified into), functional-area strategies within each business, and operating strategies. Typically, the strategy-making task is more top-down than bottom-up, with higher-level strategies serving as the guide for developing lower-level strategies.
4. *Implementing and executing the chosen strategy efficiently and effectively.* Managing the implementation and execution of strategy is an operations-oriented, make-things-happen activity aimed at shaping the performance of core business activities in a strategy-supportive manner. Management's handling of the strategy implementation process can be considered successful if things go smoothly enough that the company meets or beats its strategic and financial performance targets and shows good progress in achieving management's strategic vision.
5. *Evaluating performance and initiating corrective adjustments* in vision, long-term direction, objectives, strategy, or execution in light of actual experience, changing conditions, new ideas, and new opportunities. This phase of the strategy management process is the trigger point for deciding whether to continue or change the company's vision, objectives, strategy, and/or strategy execution methods.

A company's strategic vision plus its objectives plus its strategy equals a *strategic plan* for coping with industry and competitive conditions, outcompeting rivals, and addressing the challenges and issues that stand as obstacles to the company's success.

Successful managers have to do several things in leading the drive for good strategy execution and operating excellence. First, they stay on top of things. They keep a finger on the organization's pulse by spending considerable time outside their offices, listening and talking to organization members, coaching, cheerleading, and picking up important information. Second, they are active and visible in putting constructive pressure on the organization to achieve good results. Generally, this is best accomplished by promoting an esprit de corps that mobilizes and energizes organizational members to execute strategy in a competent fashion and deliver the targeted results. Third, they keep the organization focused on operating excellence by championing innovative ideas for improvement and promoting the use of best practices to ensure value-creating activities are performed in a first-rate fashion. Fourth, they exert their clout in developing competencies and competitive capabilities that enable better execution. Fifth, they serve as a role model in displaying high ethical standards, and they insist that company personnel conduct the company's business ethically and in a socially responsible manner. They demonstrate unequivocal and visible commitment to the ethics enforcement process. Sixth and finally, when a company's strategy execution effort is not delivering good results and the organization is not making measured progress toward operating excellence, it is the leader's responsibility to step forward and push corrective actions.

Boards of directors have a duty to shareholders to play a vigilant role in overseeing management's handling of a company's strategy-making, strategy-executing process. A company's board is obligated to (1) critically appraise and ultimately approve strategic action plans; (2) evaluate the strategic leadership skills of the CEO and others in line to succeed the incumbent CEO; (3) institute a compensation plan for top executives that rewards them for actions and results that serve stakeholder interests, most especially those of shareholders; and (4) ensure that the company issues accurate financial reports and has adequate financial controls.

ASSURANCE OF LEARNING EXERCISES

1. Using the information in Table 2.2 and Table 2.3, critique the adequacy and merit of the following vision statements, listing effective elements and shortcomings. Rank the vision statements from best to worst once you complete your evaluation.

Vision Statement	Effective Elements	Shortcomings
Wells Fargo We want to satisfy all of our customers' financial needs, help them succeed financially, be the premier provider of financial services in every one of our markets, and be known as one of America's great companies.		
Hilton Hotels Corporation Our vision is to be the first choice of the world's travelers. Hilton intends to build on the rich heritage and strength of our brands by: • Consistently delighting our customers • Investing in our team members • Delivering innovative products and services • Continuously improving performance • Increasing shareholder value • Creating a culture of pride • Strengthening the loyalty of our constituents		
The Dental Products Division of 3M Corporation Become THE supplier of choice to the global dental professional markets, providing world-class quality and innovative products. [Note: All employees of the division wear badges bearing these words, and whenever a new product or business procedure is being considered, management asks, "Is this representative of THE leading dental company?"]		

(Continued)

Vision Statement	Effective Elements	Shortcomings
H. J. Heinz Company Be the world's premier food company, offering nutritious, superior tasting foods to people everywhere. Being the premier food company does not mean being the biggest but it does mean being the best in terms of consumer value, customer service, employee talent, and consistent and predictable growth.		
Chevron To be *the* global energy company most admired for its people, partnership and performance. Our vision means we: • provide energy products vital to sustainable economic progress and human development throughout the world; • are people and an organization with superior capabilities and commitment; • are the partner of choice; • deliver world-class performance; • earn the admiration of all our stakeholders—investors, customers, host governments, local communities and our employees—not only for the goals we achieve but how we achieve them.		

Sources: Company Web sites and annual reports.

2. Go to **www.dell.com/speeches** and read Michael Dell's recent speeches. Do Michael Dell's speeches provide evidence that he is an effective leader at Dell? Using evidence from his speeches, discuss whether he is concerned with (*a*) staying on top of what is happening and identifying obstacles to good strategy execution, (*b*) pushing the organization to achieve good results and operating excellence, and (*c*) displaying ethical integrity and spearheading social responsibility initiatives.
3. Go to **www.dell.com/leadership** and read the sections dedicated to its board of directors and corporate governance. Using evidence from these sections, discuss whether there is effective governance at Dell in regard to (*a*) a critical appraisal of strategic action plans, (*b*) evaluation of the strategic leadership skills of the CEO, (*c*) executive compensation, and (*d*) accurate financial reports and controls.

EXERCISES FOR SIMULATION PARTICIPANTS

1. Meet with your co-managers and prepare a strategic vision statement for your company. It should be no shorter than one sentence but no longer than a brief paragraph. When you are finished, check to see if your vision statement meets the conditions for an effectively worded strategic vision set forth in Table 2.2 and avoids the shortcomings set forth in Table 2.3. If not, then revise it accordingly. What would be a good slogan that captures the essence of your strategic vision and that could be used to help communicate the vision to company personnel, shareholders, and other stakeholders?
2. Write a sentence that expresses your company's strategic intent.
3. What are your company's financial objectives? What are your company's strategic objectives?
4. What are the three or four key elements of your company's strategy?

CHAPTER

3 Evaluating a Company's External Environment

LEARNING OBJECTIVES

1. To gain command of the basic concepts and analytical tools widely used to diagnose a company's industry and competitive conditions.
2. To become adept at recognizing the factors that cause competition in an industry to be fierce, more or less normal, or relatively weak.
3. To learn how to determine whether an industry's outlook presents a company with sufficiently attractive opportunities for growth and profitability.
4. To understand why in-depth evaluation of specific industry and competitive conditions is a prerequisite to crafting a strategy well matched to a company's situation.

Analysis is the critical starting point of strategic thinking.

— **Kenichi Ohmae**
Consultant and Author

Things are always different—the art is figuring out which differences matter.

— **Laszlo Birinyi**
Investments Manager

Competitive battles should be seen not as one-shot skirmishes but as a dynamic multiround game of moves and countermoves.

— **Anil K. Gupta**
Professor

In the opening paragraph of Chapter 1, we said that one of the three central questions that managers must address in evaluating their company's business prospects is "What's the company's present situation?" Two facets of a company's situation are especially pertinent: (1) the industry and competitive environment in which the company operates and (2) the company's collection of resources and capabilities, its strengths and weaknesses vis-à-vis rivals, and its windows of opportunity.

Insightful analysis of a company's external and internal environment is a prerequisite for crafting a strategy that is an excellent fit with the company's situation, is capable of building competitive advantage, and holds good prospect for boosting company performance—the three criteria of a winning strategy. As depicted in Figure 3.1, the task of crafting a company's strategy should always begin with appraisals of the company's external environment and internal environment (as a basis for deciding on a long-term strategic direction and developing a strategic vision), then proceed to an evaluation of the most promising alternative strategic options and business models, and culminate in choosing a specific strategy.

This chapter presents the concepts and analytical tools for zeroing in on a single-business company's external environment. Attention centers on the competitive arena in which a company operates, the drivers of market change, and rival companies' actions. In Chapter 4 we explore the methods of evaluating a company's internal circumstances and competitiveness.

Figure 3.1 From Thinking Strategically about the Company's Situation to Choosing a Strategy

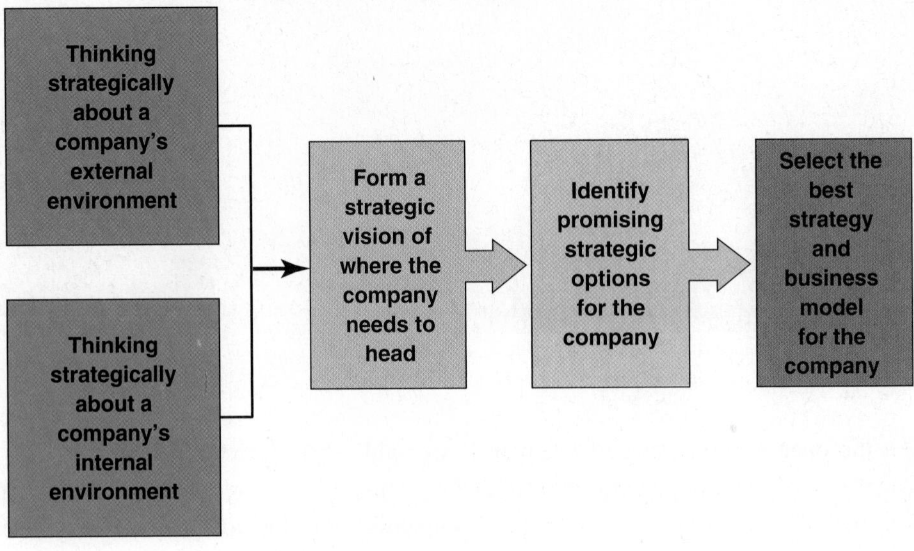

THE STRATEGICALLY RELEVANT COMPONENTS OF A COMPANY'S EXTERNAL ENVIRONMENT

All companies operate in a macroenvironment shaped by influences emanating from general economic conditions; population demographics; societal values and lifestyles; legislation and regulations; technology; and, closer to home, the industry and competitive environment in which the company operates (see Figure 3.2). Strictly speaking, a company's macroenvironment includes *all relevant factors and influences* outside the company's boundaries; by *relevant,* we mean important enough to have a bearing on the decisions the company ultimately makes about its direction, objectives, strategy, and business model. Strategically relevant influences coming from the outer ring of the macroenvironment can sometimes have a high impact on a company's business situation and have a very significant impact on the company's direction and strategy. The strategic opportunities of cigarette producers to grow their business are greatly reduced by antismoking ordinances and the growing cultural stigma attached to smoking. Motor vehicle companies must adapt their strategies (especially as concerns the fuel mileage of their vehicles) to customer concerns about gasoline prices. The demographics of an aging population and longer life expectancies are having a dramatic impact on the business prospects and strategies of health care and prescription drug companies. Companies in most all industries have to craft strategies that are responsive to environmental regulations, growing use of the Internet, and energy prices. Companies in the food processing, restaurant, sports, and fitness industries have to pay special attention to changes in lifestyles, eating habits, leisure-time preferences, and attitudes toward nutrition and fitness in fashioning their strategies.

Figure 3.2 The Components of a Company's Macroenvironment

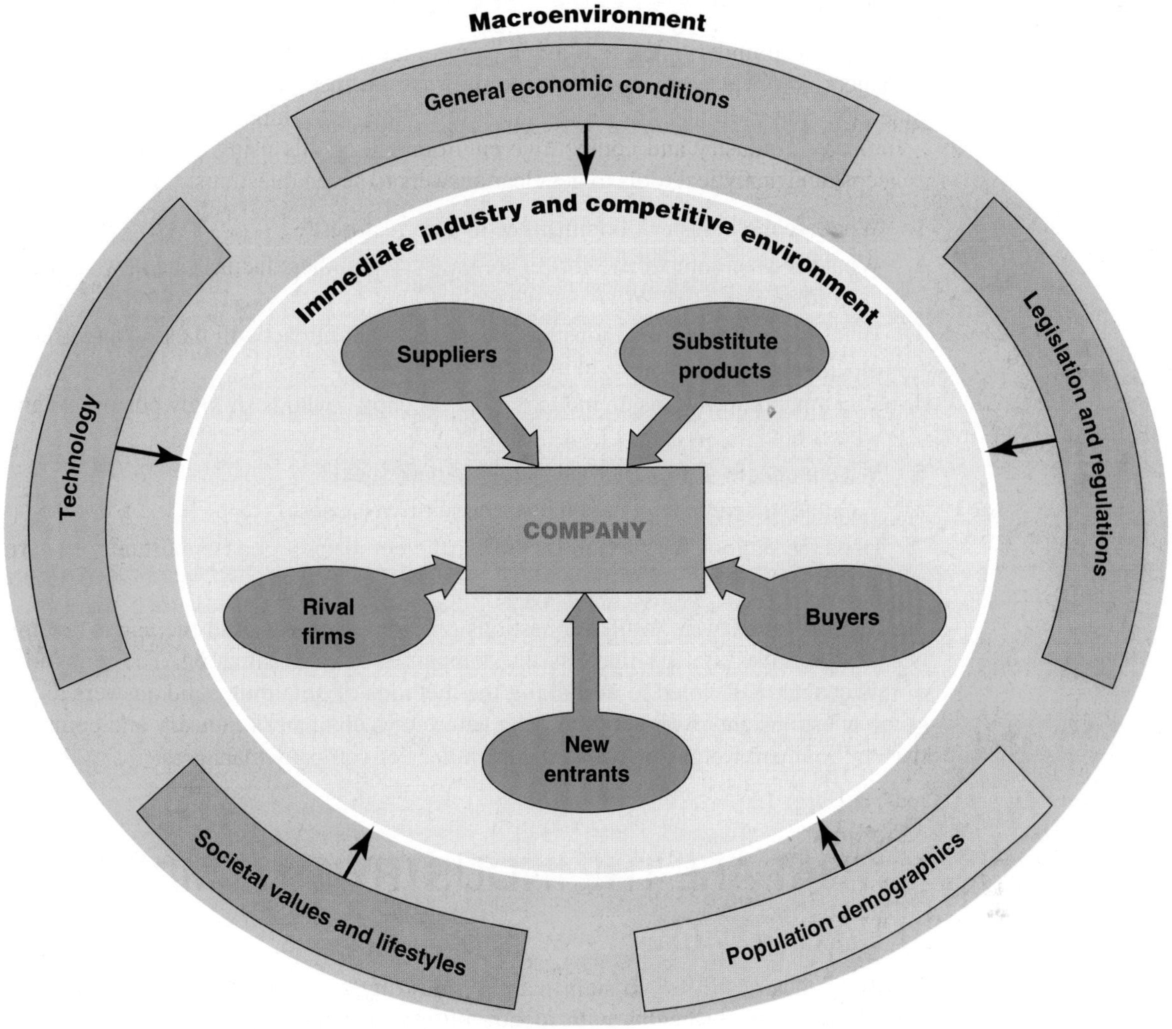

Happenings in the outer ring of the macroenvironment may occur rapidly or slowly, with or without advance warning. The impact of outer-ring factors on a company's choice of strategy can range from big to small. But even if the factors in the macroenvironment change slowly or affect a company's situation only modestly, there are enough strategically relevant outer-ring trends and events to justify a watchful eye. As company managers scan the external environment, they must be alert for potentially important outer-ring developments, assess their impact and influence, and adapt the company's direction and strategy as needed.

However, the factors and forces in a company's macroenvironment having the *biggest* strategy-shaping impact typically pertain to the company's immediate industry and competitive environment—the actions of rivals firms, buyer behavior, supplier-related considerations, and so on. Consequently, it is on a company's industry and competitive environment that we concentrate our attention in this chapter.

THINKING STRATEGICALLY ABOUT A COMPANY'S INDUSTRY AND COMPETITIVE ENVIRONMENT

To gain a deep understanding of a company's industry and competitive environment, managers do not need to gather all the information they can find and spend lots of time digesting it. Rather, the task is much more focused. Thinking strategically about a company's industry and competitive environment entails using some well-defined concepts and analytical tools to get clear answers to seven questions:

1. What are the industry's dominant economic features?
2. What kinds of competitive forces are industry members facing, and how strong is each force?
3. What forces are driving industry change and what impact will these changes have on competitive intensity and industry profitability?
4. What market positions do industry rivals occupy—who is strongly positioned and who is not?
5. What strategic moves are rivals likely to make next?
6. What are the key factors for future competitive success?
7. Does the outlook for the industry offer the company a good opportunity to earn attractive profits?

Analysis-based answers to these questions provide managers with the understanding needed to craft a strategy that fits the company's external situation. The remainder of this chapter is devoted to describing the methods of obtaining solid answers to the seven questions and explaining how the nature of a company's industry and competitive environment weighs on the strategic choices of company managers.

QUESTION1: WHAT ARE THE INDUSTRY'S DOMINANT ECONOMIC FEATURES?

Because industries differ so significantly, analyzing a company's industry and competitive environment begins with identifying an industry's dominant economic features and gaining an an accurate and insightful view of the industry landscape. An industry's dominant economic features are defined by such factors as market size and growth rate, the number and sizes of buyers and sellers, the geographic boundaries of the market (which can extend from local to worldwide), whether sellers' products are virtually identical or highly differentiated, the pace of technological change, and the extent of vertical integration. Table 3.1 provides a convenient summary of what economic features to look at and the corresponding questions to consider in profiling an industry's landscape.

Getting a handle on an industry's distinguishing economic features not only allows managers to prepare for the analysis to come but also helps them understand the kinds of strategic moves that industry members are likely to employ. For example, in industries characterized by one product advance after another—such as the video game, computer, and pharmaceuticals industries—companies must invest in research and development (R&D) and maintain strong product innovation capabilities. An industry that has recently passed through the rapid-growth stage and is looking at single-digit percentage increases

Table 3.1 What to Consider in Identifying an Industry's Dominant Economic Features

Economic Feature	Questions to Answer
Market size and growth rate	• How big is the industry and how fast is it growing? • What does the industry's position in the product life cycle (early development, rapid growth and takeoff, early maturity and slowing growth, saturation and stagnation, decline) reveal about the industry's growth prospects?
Number of rivals	• Is the industry fragmented into many small companies or concentrated and dominated by a few large companies? • Is the industry consolidating to a smaller number of competitors?
Scope of competitive rivalry	• Is the geographic area over which most companies compete local, regional, national, multinational, or global? • Is having a presence in foreign markets becoming more important to a company's long-term competitive success?
Number of buyers	• Is market demand fragmented among many buyers? • Do some buyers have bargaining power because they purchase in large volume?
Degree of product differentiation	• Are the products of rivals becoming more differentiated or less differentiated? • Are the products of rivals becoming increasingly similar and causing heightened price competition?
Product innovation	• Is the industry characterized by rapid product innovation and short product life cycles? • How important is R&D and product innovation? • Are there opportunities to overtake key rivals by being first-to-market with next-generation products?
Demand–supply conditions	• Is a surplus of capacity pushing prices and profit margins down? • Is the industry overcrowded with competitors?
Pace of technological change	• What role does advancing technology play in this industry? • Are ongoing upgrades of facilities/equipment essential because of rapidly advancing production process technologies? • Do most industry members have or need strong technological capabilities? Why?
Vertical integration	• Do most competitors operate in only one stage of the industry (parts and components production, manufacturing and assembly, distribution, retailing), or do some competitors operate in multiple stages? • Is there any cost or competitive advantage or disadvantage associated with being fully or partially integrated?
Economies of scale	• Is the industry characterized by economies of scale in purchasing, manufacturing, advertising, shipping, or other activities? • Do companies with large-scale operations have an important cost advantage over small-scale firms?
Learning/experience curve effects	• Are certain industry activities characterized by strong learning and experience effects ("learning by doing") such that unit costs decline as a company's experience in performing the activity builds? • Do any companies have significant cost advantages because of their learning/experience in performing particular activities?

in buyer demand is likely to be experiencing a competitive shake-out and much stronger strategic emphasis on cost reduction and improved customer service.

In industries like semiconductors, strong *learning/experience effects* in manufacturing cause unit costs to decline about 20 percent each time cumulative production volume doubles. With a 20 percent experience curve effect, if the first 1 million chips cost $100 each, the unit cost would drop to $80 (80 percent of $100) when production volume reaches 2 million and then drop further to $64 (80 percent of $80) when production volume reaches 4 million.[1] The bigger the learning or experience curve effect, the bigger the cost advantage of the company with the largest cumulative production volume. Thus, when an industry is characterized by important learning/experience curve effects (or by economies of scale), industry members are strongly motivated to adopt volume-increasing strategies to capture the resulting cost-saving economies and maintain their competitiveness. Unless small-scale firms succeed in pursuing strategic options that allow them to grow sales sufficiently to remain cost-competitive with larger-volume rivals, they are unlikely to survive. The bigger the learning/experience curve effects and/or scale economies in an industry, the more imperative it becomes for competing sellers to pursue strategies to win additional sales and market share—the company with the biggest sales volume gains sustainable competitive advantage as the low-cost producer.

QUESTION 2: HOW STRONG ARE COMPETITIVE FORCES?

Competitive forces are never the same from one industry to another. Far and away the most powerful and widely used tool for systematically diagnosing the principal competitive pressures in a market and assessing the strength and importance of each is the *five-forces model of competition.*[2] This model, depicted in Figure 3.3, holds that the state of competition in an industry is a composite of competitive pressures operating in five areas of the overall market:

1. Competitive pressures associated with the market maneuvering and jockeying for buyer patronage that goes on among *rival sellers* in the industry.
2. Competitive pressures associated with the threats of new entrants.
3. Competitive pressures coming from the attempts of companies in other industries to win buyers over to their own substitute products.
4. Competitive pressures stemming from supplier bargaining power and supplier–seller collaboration.
5. Competitive pressures stemming from buyer bargaining power and seller–buyer collaboration.

The way one uses the five-forces model to determine the makeup and strength of competitive pressures in a given industry is to build the picture of competitive landscape in three steps:

- *Step 1:* Identify the *specific* competitive pressures associated with each of the five forces.
- *Step 2:* Evaluate how strong the pressures comprising each of the five forces are (fierce, strong, moderate to normal, or weak).
- *Step 3:* Determine whether the collective strength of the five competitive forces is conducive to earning attractive profits.

Figure 3.3 The Five-Forces Model of Competition: A Key Analytical Tool

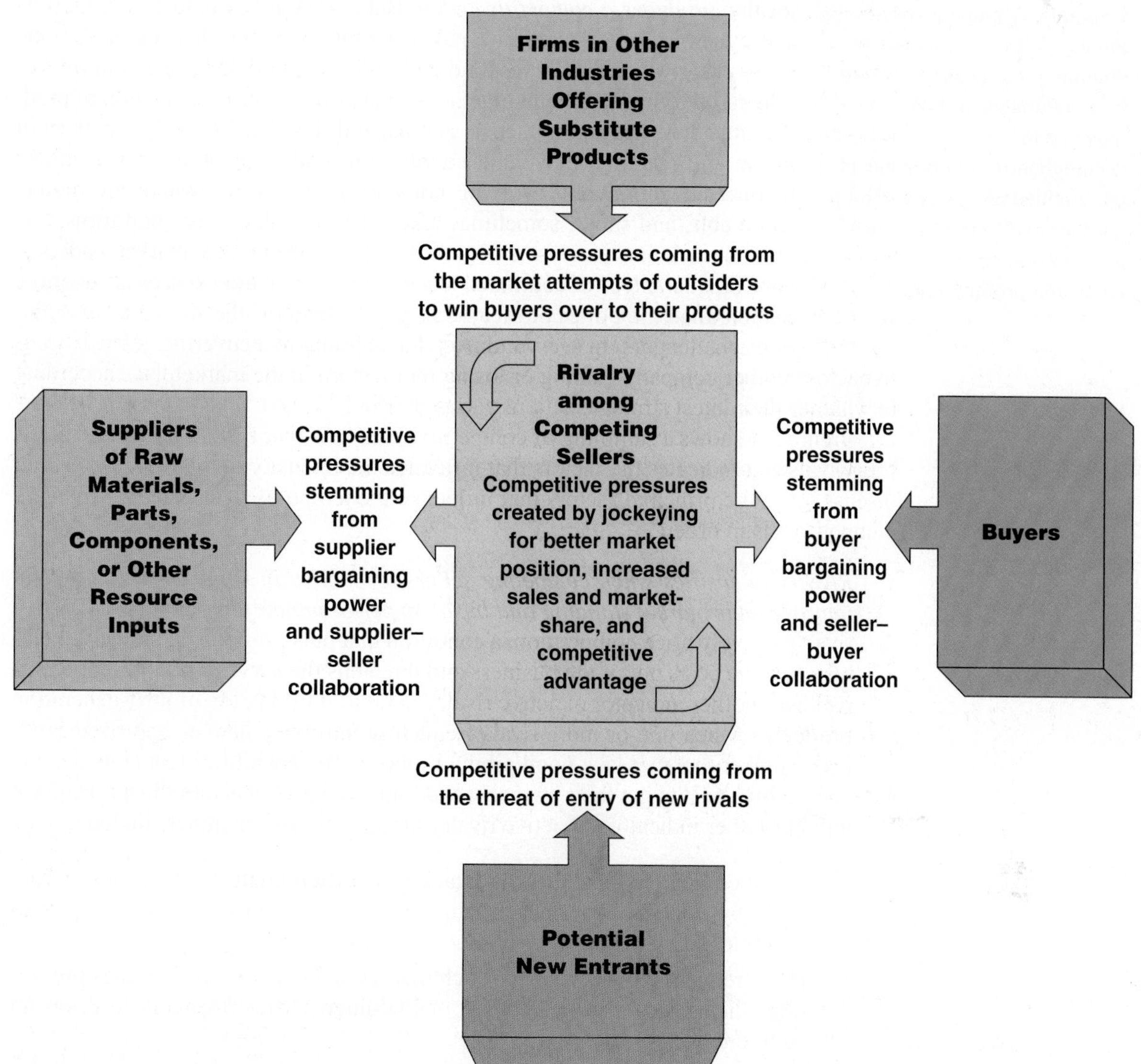

Source: Adapted from Michael E. Porter, "How Competitive Forces Shape Strategy," *Harvard Business Review* 57, no. 2 (March–April 1979), pp. 137–45; and Michael E. Porter, "The Five Competitive Forces That Shape Strategy," *Harvard Business Review* 86, no. 1 (January 2008), pp. 80–86.

The strongest of the five competitive forces is nearly always the market maneuvering for buyer patronage that goes on among rival sellers of a product or service. In effect, *a market is a competitive battlefield* where there's no end to the maneuvering for buyer patronage. Rival sellers employ whatever weapons they have in their business arsenal to strengthen their market positions, attract and retain buyers, and earn good profits.

CORE CONCEPT

Competitive maneuvering among industry rivals is ever changing, as rivals (1) initiate fresh offensive and defensive moves and (2) emphasize first one mix of competitive weapons and then another in efforts to improve their market position and boost sales and profitability.

The challenge for company managers is to craft a competitive strategy that, at the very least, allows the company to hold its own against rivals and that, ideally, *produces a competitive edge.* But competitive contests are ongoing and dynamic. When one firm makes a strategic move that produces good results, its rivals typically respond with offensive or defensive countermoves of their own, shifting their strategic emphasis from one combination of product attributes, marketing tactics, and capabilities to another. This pattern of action and reaction, move and countermove, adjustment and readjustment produces a continually evolving competitive landscape where the market battle ebbs and flows, sometimes takes unpredictable twists and turns, and produces winners and losers. But the winners—the current market leaders—have no guarantees of continued leadership; their market success is no more durable than the power of their strategies to fend off the strategies of ambitious challengers. In every industry, the ongoing maneuvering of rivals leads to one or another company gaining or losing momentum in the marketplace according to whether their latest strategic actions succeed or fail.[3]

Figure 3.4 shows a sampling of competitive weapons that firms can deploy in battling rivals and indicates the factors that influence the intensity of their rivalry. A brief discussion of the principal factors that influence the tempo of rivalry among industry competitors is in order:[4]

- *Rivalry intensifies when competing sellers are active in making fresh moves to improve their market standing and business performance.* One indicator of active rivalry is lively price competition, a condition that puts pressure on industry members to drive costs out of the business and threatens the survival of high-cost companies. Another indicator of active rivalry is rapid introduction of next-generation products—when one or more rivals frequently introduce new or improved products, competitors that lack good product-innovation capabilities feel considerable competitive heat to get their own new and improved products into the marketplace quickly. Other indicators of active rivalry among industry members include:

    - Whether industry members are racing to differentiate their products from rivals by offering better performance features or higher-quality or improved customer service or a wider product selection.
    - How frequently rivals resort to such marketing tactics as special sales promotions, heavy advertising, rebates, or low-interest-rate financing to drum up additional sales.
    - How actively industry members are pursuing efforts to build stronger dealer networks or establish positions in foreign markets or otherwise expand their distribution capabilities and market presence.
    - How hard companies are striving to gain a market edge over rivals by developing valuable expertise and capabilities that rivals are hard-pressed to match.

    Normally, competitive jockeying among rival sellers is active and fairly intense because competing companies are highly motivated to launch whatever fresh actions and creative market maneuvers they can think of to try to strengthen their market positions and business performance.

- *Rivalry is usually stronger when buyer demand is growing slowly and weaker when buyer demand is growing rapidly.* Rapidly expanding buyer demand

Figure 3.4 Weapons for Competing and Factors Affecting the Strength of Rivalry

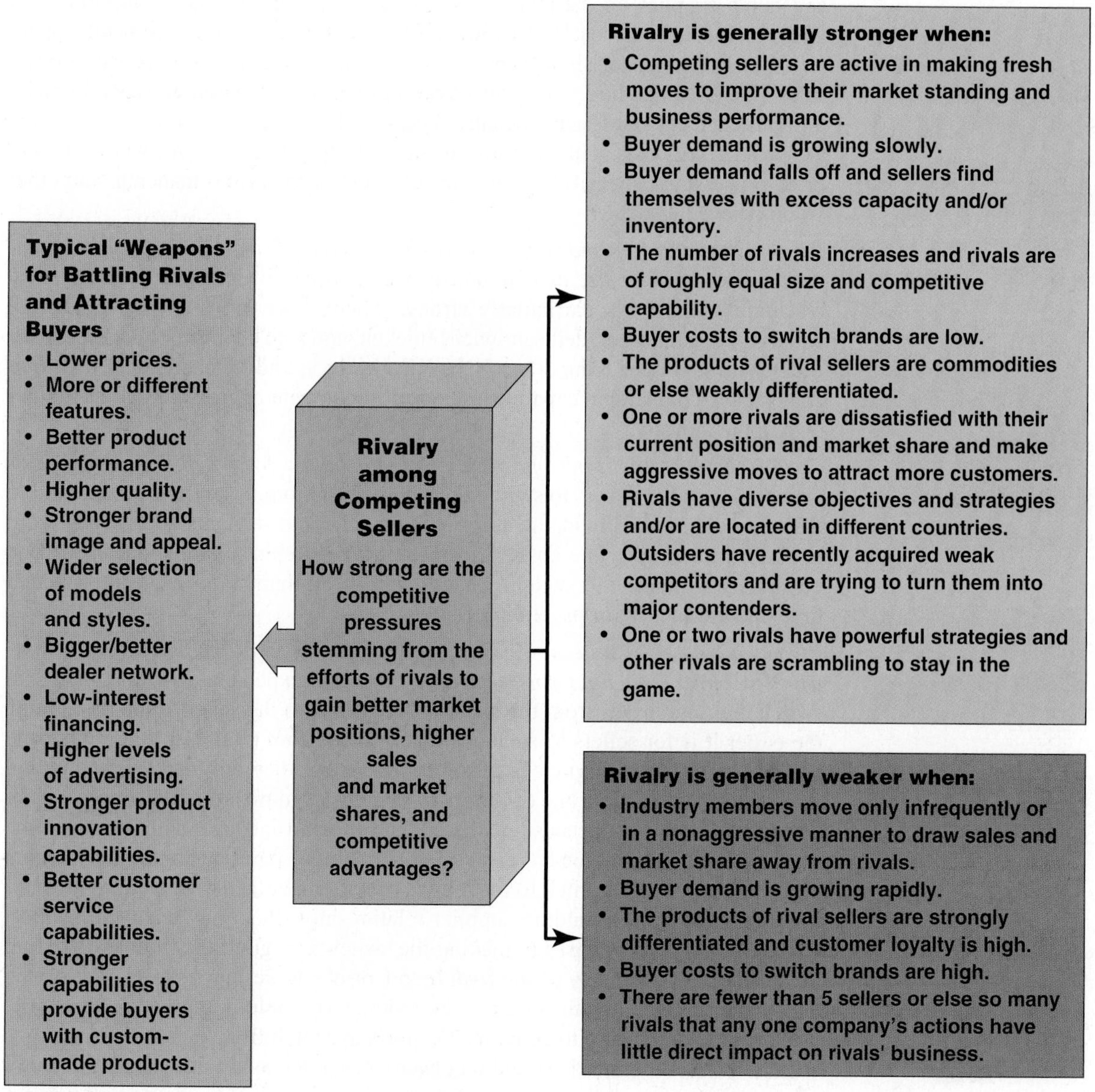

Typical "Weapons" for Battling Rivals and Attracting Buyers
- Lower prices.
- More or different features.
- Better product performance.
- Higher quality.
- Stronger brand image and appeal.
- Wider selection of models and styles.
- Bigger/better dealer network.
- Low-interest financing.
- Higher levels of advertising.
- Stronger product innovation capabilities.
- Better customer service capabilities.
- Stronger capabilities to provide buyers with custom-made products.

Rivalry among Competing Sellers

How strong are the competitive pressures stemming from the efforts of rivals to gain better market positions, higher sales and market shares, and competitive advantages?

Rivalry is generally stronger when:
- Competing sellers are active in making fresh moves to improve their market standing and business performance.
- Buyer demand is growing slowly.
- Buyer demand falls off and sellers find themselves with excess capacity and/or inventory.
- The number of rivals increases and rivals are of roughly equal size and competitive capability.
- Buyer costs to switch brands are low.
- The products of rival sellers are commodities or else weakly differentiated.
- One or more rivals are dissatisfied with their current position and market share and make aggressive moves to attract more customers.
- Rivals have diverse objectives and strategies and/or are located in different countries.
- Outsiders have recently acquired weak competitors and are trying to turn them into major contenders.
- One or two rivals have powerful strategies and other rivals are scrambling to stay in the game.

Rivalry is generally weaker when:
- Industry members move only infrequently or in a nonaggressive manner to draw sales and market share away from rivals.
- Buyer demand is growing rapidly.
- The products of rival sellers are strongly differentiated and customer loyalty is high.
- Buyer costs to switch brands are high.
- There are fewer than 5 sellers or else so many rivals that any one company's actions have little direct impact on rivals' business.

that can threaten the survival of competitively weak firms.

- *Rivalry increases when buyer demand falls off and sellers find themselves with excess capacity and/or inventory.* Excess supply conditions create a "buyer's market," putting added competitive pressure on industry rivals to scramble for profitable sales levels. When a product is perishable, seasonal, or costly to hold in inventory, competitive pressures build quickly anytime one or more firms decide to cut prices and dump supplies on the market. Likewise, whenever fixed costs account for a large fraction of total cost (so that unit costs tend to be lowest at or near full capacity), firms come under significant pressure to cut prices or otherwise try to boost sales whenever they are operating below full capacity. Unused capacity imposes a significant cost-increasing penalty, because there are fewer units over which to spread fixed costs. The pressure of high fixed costs can push rival firms into price concessions, special discounts, rebates, low-interest-rate financing, and other volume-boosting tactics.

- *Rivalry is stronger in industries where the number of rivals increases and competitors are equal in size and capability.* Competitive rivalry in the quick-service restaurant industry is particularly strong, where there are numerous relatively equal-sized hamburger, deli sandwich, chicken, and taco chains. For the most part, McDonald's, Burger King, Taco Bell, KFC, Arby's, and other national fast-food chains have comparable capabilities and must compete aggressively to hold their own in the industry.
- *Rivalry increases as it becomes less costly for buyers to switch brands.* The less expensive it is for buyers to switch their purchases from the seller of one brand to the seller of another brand, the easier it is for sellers to steal customers away from rivals. But the higher the costs associated with switching brands, the less prone buyers are to make the switch. Abandoning a familiar brand may entail added time, inconvenience, or psychological costs.
- *Rivalry increases as it becomes less costly for buyers to switch brands and diminishes as buyer switching costs increase.* The less expensive it is for buyers to switch their purchases from the seller of one brand to the seller of another brand, the easier it is for sellers to steal customers away from rivals. But the higher the costs buyers incur to switch brands, the less prone they are to brand switching. Even if consumers view one or more rival brands as more attractive, they may not be inclined to switch because of the added time and inconvenience that may be involved or the psychological costs of abandoning a familiar brand. Distributors and retailers may not switch to the brands of rival manufacturers because they are hesitant to sever longstanding supplier relationships, incur any technical support costs or retraining expenses in making the switchover, go to the trouble of testing the quality and reliability of the rival brand, or devote resources to marketing the new brand (especially if the brand is lesser-known). Apple Computer, for example, has long had to struggle to convince PC users to switch from Windows-based PCs because of the time burdens and inconvenience associated with learning Apple's operating system and because so many Windows-based applications will not run on a MacIntosh due to operating system incompatibility. In short, unless buyers are dissatisfied with the brand they are presently purchasing, high switching costs can significantly weaken the rivalry among competing sellers.
- *Rivalry increases as the products of rival sellers become more standardized and diminishes as the products of industry rivals become more differentiated.* When the offerings of rivals are identical or weakly differentiated, buyers have less reason to be brand-loyal—a condition that makes it easier for rivals to convince buyers to switch to their offering. And since the brands of different sellers have comparable attributes, buyers can shop the market for the best deal and switch brands at will. On the other hand, strongly differentiated product offerings among rivals breed

high brand loyalty on the part of buyers—because many buyers view the attributes of certain brands as better suited to their needs. Strong brand attachments make it tougher for sellers to draw customers away from rivals. Unless meaningful numbers of buyers are open to considering new or different product attributes being offered by rivals, the high degree of brand loyalty that accompanies strong product differentiation works against fierce rivalry among competing sellers.

- *Rivalry is more intense when industry conditions tempt competitors to use price cuts or other competitive weapons to boost unit volume.* When a product is perishable, seasonal, or costly to hold in inventory, competitive pressures build quickly anytime one or more firms decide to cut prices and dump supplies on the market. Likewise, whenever fixed costs account for a large fraction of total cost so that unit costs tend to be lowest at or near full capacity, firms come under significant pressure to cut prices or otherwise try to boost sales whenever they are operating below full capacity. Unused capacity imposes a significant cost-increasing penalty because there are fewer units over which to spread fixed costs. The pressure of high fixed costs can push rival firms into price concessions, special discounts, rebates, low-interest-rate financing, and other volume-boosting tactics.
- *Rivalry increases when one or more competitors become dissatisfied with their market position.* Firms that are losing ground or in financial trouble often initiate aggressive (perhaps even desperate) turnaround strategies that can involve price discounts, greater advertising, or merger with other rivals—such strategies can turn competitive pressures up a notch.
- *Rivalry becomes more volatile and unpredictable as the diversity of competitors increases in terms of visions, strategic intents, objectives, strategies, resources, and countries of origin.* A diverse group of sellers often contains one or more mavericks willing to try novel or rule-breaking market approaches, thus generating a livelier and less predictable competitive environment. Globally competitive markets usually boost the intensity of rivalry, especially when aggressors having lower costs or products with more attractive features are intent on gaining a strong foothold in new country markets.
- *Rivalry increases when strong companies outside the industry acquire weak firms in the industry and launch aggressive, well-funded moves to transform their newly acquired competitors into major market contenders.* A concerted effort to turn a weak rival into a market leader nearly always entails launching well-financed strategic initiatives to dramatically improve the competitor's product offering, excite buyer interest, and win a much bigger market share—actions that, if successful, put added pressure on rivals to counter with fresh strategic moves of their own.
- *When one or two companies employ powerful, successful competitive strategies, the competitive pressures on other industry members intensify significantly.* Industry members that suddenly start to lose sales and market share to offensive-minded

- *Rivalry is usually weaker in industries made up of vast numbers of small rivals; likewise, it is often weak when there are fewer than five competitors.* When an industry is populated with so many rivals that the impact of successful moves by any one company ripple out to have little discernible impact on the businesses of its many rivals, then head-to-head rivalry turns out to be relatively weak—industry members soon learn that it is not imperative to respond every time one or another rival does something to enhance its market position. Rivalry also tends to be weak if an industry consists of just two to four sellers because each competitor soon learns that aggressive moves to grow its sales and market share have immediate adverse impact on rivals' businesses and will almost certainly provoke vigorous retaliation. Hence, there is a tendency for competition among the few to produce a live-and-let-live approach to competing because rivals see the merits of restrained efforts to wrest sales and market share from competitors as opposed to undertaking hard-hitting offensives that escalate into a profit-eroding arms race or price war. However, some caution must be exercised in concluding that rivalry is weak just because there are only a few competitors. The fierceness of the current battle between Linux and Microsoft in operating system software and between Intel and AMD in microprocessors for PCs and servers and the decades-long war between Coca-Cola and Pepsi are prime examples.

Rivalry can be characterized as *cutthroat* or *brutal* when competitors engage in protracted price wars or habitually employ other aggressive tactics that are mutually destructive to profitability. Rivalry can be considered *fierce* to *strong* when the battle for market share is so vigorous that the profit margins of most industry members are squeezed to bare-bones levels. Rivalry can be characterized as *moderate* or *normal* when the maneuvering among industry members, while lively and healthy, still allows most industry members to earn acceptable profits. Rivalry is *weak* when most companies in the industry are content with their sales growth and market shares, rarely undertake offensives to steal customers away from one another, and have comparatively attractive earnings and returns on investment.

Competitive Pressures Associated with the Threat of New Entrants

Several factors determine whether the threat of new companies entering the marketplace poses significant competitive pressure (see Figure 3.5). One factor relates to the size of the pool of likely entry candidates. As a rule, the bigger the pool of entry candidates, the stronger is the threat of potential entry. Frequently, the strongest competitive pressures associated with potential entry come not from outsiders but from current industry participants looking for growth opportunities. *Existing industry members are often strong candidates to enter market segments or geographic areas where they currently do not have a market presence.* Companies already well established in certain product categories or geographic areas often possess the resources, competencies, and competitive capabilities to hurdle the barriers of entering a different market segment or new geographic area.

A second factor concerns whether the likely entry candidates face high or low entry barriers. High barriers reduce the competitive threat of potential entry, while low barriers make entry more likely, especially if the industry is growing and offers attractive profit opportunities. The most widely encountered barriers that entry candidates must hurdle include:[5]

- *The presence of sizable economies of scale in production or other areas of operation*—When incumbent companies enjoy cost advantages associated with large-scale operations, outsiders must either enter on a large scale (a costly and perhaps risky move) or accept a cost disadvantage and consequently lower profitability.
- *Cost and resource disadvantages not related to scale of operation*—Industry incumbents can have cost advantages that stem from experience/learning curve

Figure 3.5 Factors Affecting the Threat of Entry

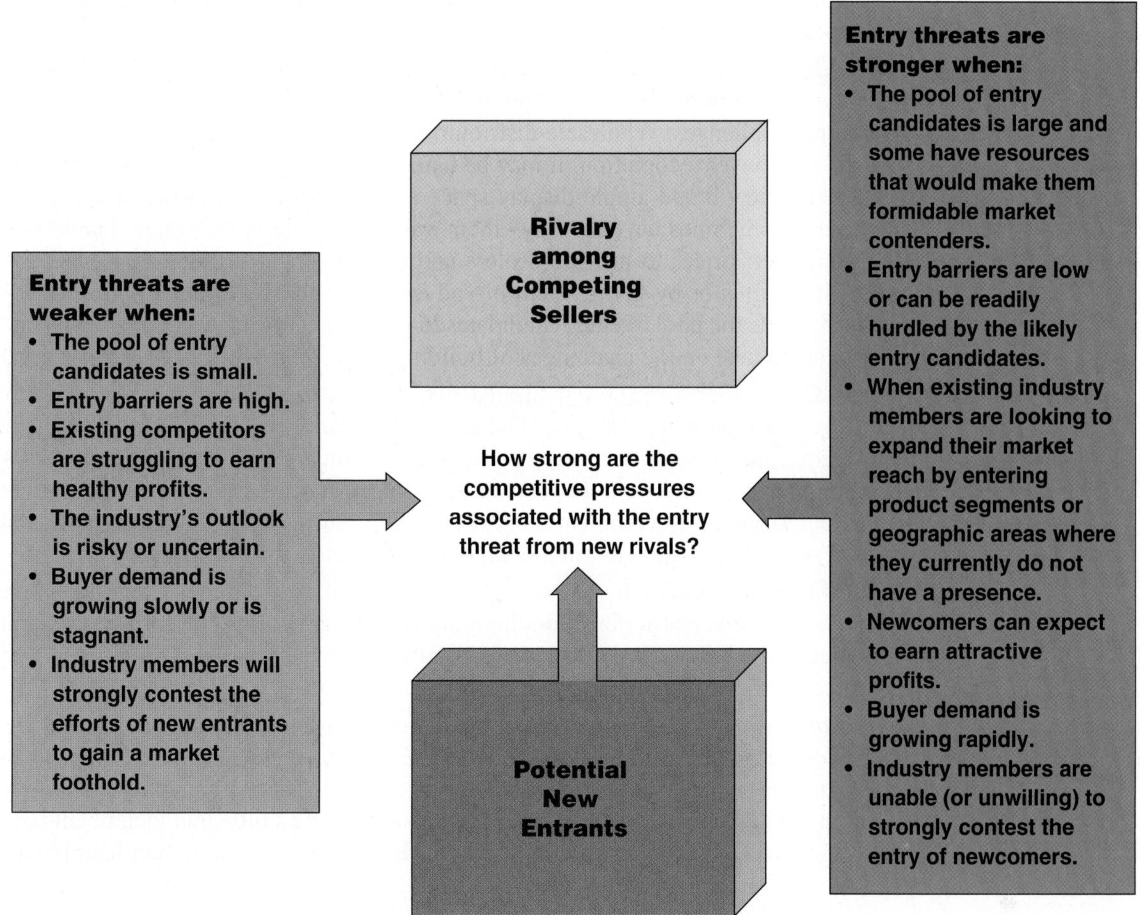
Rivalry among Competing Sellers
Entry threats are weaker when:
• The pool of entry candidates is small.
• Entry barriers are high.
• Existing competitors are struggling to earn healthy profits.
• The industry's outlook is risky or uncertain.
• Buyer demand is growing slowly or is stagnant.
• Industry members will strongly contest the efforts of new entrants to gain a market foothold.
How strong are the competitive pressures associated with the entry threat from new rivals?
Entry threats are stronger when:
• The pool of entry candidates is large and some have resources that would make them formidable market contenders.
• Entry barriers are low or can be readily hurdled by the likely entry candidates.
• When existing industry members are looking to expand their market reach by entering product segments or geographic areas where they currently do not have a presence.
• Newcomers can expect to earn attractive profits.
• Buyer demand is growing rapidly.
• Industry members are unable (or unwilling) to strongly contest the entry of newcomers.
Potential New Entrants

effects, the possession of proprietary technology, partnerships with the best and cheapest suppliers, and low fixed costs (because they have older facilities that have been mostly depreciated).

- *Strong brand preferences and high degrees of customer loyalty*—The stronger the attachment of buyers to established brands, the harder it is for a newcomer to break into the marketplace. In such cases, a new entrant must have the financial resources to spend enough on advertising and sales promotion to overcome customer loyal

for a customer to switch to a new brand, a new entrant must persuade buyers that its brand is worth the switching costs. To overcome switching-cost barriers, new entrants may have to offer buyers a discounted price or an extra margin of quality or service. Such barriers discourage new entry because they act to boost financial requirements and lower expected profit margins for new entrants.

- *High capital requirements*—The larger the total dollar investment needed to enter the market successfully, the more limited the pool of potential entrants. The most obvious capital requirements for new entrants relate to manufacturing facilities and equipment, introductory advertising and sales promotion campaigns, working capital to finance inventories and customer credit, and sufficient cash to cover start-up costs.

- *The difficulties of building a distributor/retailer network and securing adequate space on retailers' shelves*—A potential entrant can face numerous distribution channel challenges. Wholesale distributors may be reluctant to take on a product that lacks buyer recognition. It may be hard to recruit retailers and convince them to give a new brand ample display space and an adequate trial period. Potential entrants sometimes have to "buy" their way into wholesale or retail channels by cutting their prices to provide dealers and distributors with higher markups and profit margins or by giving them big advertising and promotional allowances—this restricts the pool of entry candidates to companies with deep enough financial pockets to take on the challenges of building a viable network of distributors and retailers.
- *Restrictive regulatory policies*—Government agencies can limit or even bar entry by requiring licenses and permits. Regulated industries like cable TV, telecommunications, electric and gas utilities, and radio and television broadcasting are characterized by government-controlled entry. Stringent government-mandated safety regulations and environmental pollution standards raise entry costs.
- *Tariffs and international trade restrictions*—National governments commonly use tariffs and trade restrictions (antidumping rules, local content requirements, local ownership requirements, quotas, etc.) to raise entry barriers for foreign firms and protect domestic producers from outside competition.
- *The ability and willingness of industry incumbents to launch vigorous initiatives to block a newcomer's successful entry*—Even if a potential entrant has or can acquire the needed competencies and resources to attempt entry, it must still worry about the reaction of existing firms.[6] Sometimes, there's little that incumbents can do to throw obstacles in an entrant's path. But there are times when incumbents use price cuts, increase advertising, introduce product improvements, and launch legal attacks to prevent the entrant from building a clientele. Cable TV companies have vigorously fought the entry of satellite TV into the industry by seeking government intervention to delay satellite providers in offering local stations, offering satellite customers discounts to switch back to cable, and charging satellite customer high monthly rates for cable Internet access.

CORE CONCEPT

The threat of entry is stronger when entry barriers are low, when there's a sizable pool of entry candidates, when industry growth is rapid and profit potentials are high, and when incumbent firms are unable or unwilling to vigorously contest a newcomer's entry

Whether an industry's entry barriers ought to be considered high or low depends on the resources and competencies possessed by the pool of potential entrants. Companies with sizable financial resources, proven competitive capabilities, and a respected brand name may be able to hurdle an industry's entry barriers rather easily. Small start-up enterprises may find the same entry barriers insurmountable. When Honda opted to enter the U.S. lawn-mower market in competition against Toro, Snapper, Craftsman, John Deere, and others, it was easily able to hurdle entry barriers that would have been formidable to other newcomers because it had long-standing expertise in gasoline engines and because its well-known reputation for quality and durability gave it instant credibility with homeowners. Honda had to spend relatively little on advertising to attract buyers and gain a market foothold, distributors and dealers were quite willing to handle the Honda lawn-mower line, and Honda had ample capital to build a U.S. assembly plant.

In evaluating whether the threat of additional entry is strong or weak, company managers must also look at how attractive the growth and profit prospects are for new entrants. *Rapidly growing market demand and high potential profits act as magnets, motivating potential entrants to commit the resources needed to hurdle entry barriers.*[7] When growth and profit opportunities are sufficiently attractive, entry barriers are unlikely to be an effective entry deterrent. *The best test of whether potential entry is a strong or weak competitive force in the marketplace is to ask if the industry's growth and profit prospects are strongly attractive to potential entry candidates.* The stronger the threat of entry, the more that incumbent firms must seek ways to fortify their positions against newcomers and make entry more costly or difficult.

One additional point: *The threat of entry changes as the industry's prospects grow brighter or dimmer and as entry barriers rise or fall.* For example, in the pharmaceutical industry the expiration of a key patent on a widely prescribed drug virtually guarantees that one or more drug makers will enter with generic offerings of their own. Use of the Internet for shopping is making it much easier for e-tailers to enter into competition against some of the best-known retail chains. In international markets, entry barriers for foreign-based firms fall as tariffs are lowered, as host governments open up their domestic markets to outsiders, as domestic wholesalers and dealers seek out lower-cost foreign-made goods, and as domestic buyers become more willing to purchase foreign brands.

High entry barriers and weak entry threats today do not always translate into high entry barriers and weak entry threats tomorrow.

Competitive Pressures from the Sellers of Substitute Products

Companies in one industry come under competitive pressure from the actions of companies in a closely adjoining industry whenever buyers view the products of the two industries as good substitutes. For instance, the producers of sugar experience competitive pressures from the sales and marketing efforts of the makers of Equal, Splenda, and Sweet'N Low. Similarly, the producers of eyeglasses and contact lenses face competitive pressures from doctors who do corrective laser surgery. The makers of disc-based music players are facing such stiff competition from Apple's iPod and other brands of MP3 players that devices whose chief purpose is to play of music CDs and DVDs are fast becoming obsolete. Newspapers are struggling to maintain their relevance to subscribers who can readily turn to cable news channels for late-breaking news and use Internet sources to get information about sports results, stock quotes, and job opportunities. First-run movie theater chains are feeling competitive heat as consumers are staying home to watch movies on their big-screen, high-definition TVs, using either DVDs or movies-on-demand services. The producers of metal cans are becoming increasingly engaged in a battle with the makers of retort pouches (multi-layer packages made from polypropylene, aluminum foil, or polyester) for the business of companies producing packaged fruits, vegetables, meats, and pet foods. [illegible]

Just how strong the competitive pressures are from the sellers of substitute products depends on three factors:

1. *Whether substitutes are readily available and attractively priced.* The presence of readily available and attractively priced substitutes creates competitive pressure by placing a ceiling on the prices industry members can charge.[8] When substitutes are cheaper than an industry's product, industry members come under heavy

competitive pressure to reduce their prices and find ways to absorb the price cuts with cost reductions.

2. *Whether buyers view the substitutes as being comparable or better in terms of quality, performance, and other relevant attributes.* Customers are prone to compare performance and other attributes as well as price. For example, consumers have found digital cameras to be a superior substitute for film cameras not only because digital cameras are easy to use but also because they allow people to download images to a home computer and delete bad shots without paying for film developing. Competition from good-performing substitutes unleashes competitive pressures on industry participants to incorporate new performance features and attributes that makes their product offerings more competitive.
3. *Whether the costs that buyers incur in switching to the substitutes are high or low.* High switching costs deter switching to substitutes, while low switching costs make it easier for the sellers of attractive substitutes to lure buyers to their products.[9] Typical switching costs include the inconvenience of switching to a substitute, the costs of additional equipment, the psychological costs of severing old supplier relationships, and employee retraining costs.

Figure 3.6 summarizes the conditions that determine whether the competitive pressures from substitute products are strong, moderate, or weak.

As a rule, the lower the price of substitutes, the higher their quality and performance, and the lower the user's switching costs, the more intense the competitive pressures posed by substitute products. Other market indicators of the competitive strength of substitute products include (1) whether the sales of substitutes are growing faster than the sales of the industry being analyzed (a sign that the sellers of substitutes may be drawing customers away from the industry in question), (2) whether the producers of substitutes are moving to add new capacity, and (3) whether the profits of the producers of substitutes are on the rise.

Competitive Pressures Stemming from Supplier Bargaining Power and Supplier–Seller Collaboration

Whether supplier–seller relationships represent a weak competitive force or a strong one depends on (1) whether the major suppliers can exercise sufficient bargaining power to influence the terms and conditions of supply in their favor, and (2) how closely one or more industry members collaborate with their suppliers to achieve supply chain efficiencies.

How Supplier Bargaining Power Can Create Competitive Pressures

Sometimes the actions of important suppliers bring competitive pressures to bear on the companies they are supplying. For instance, Microsoft and Intel, both of whom supply PC makers with products that most PC users consider essential, are known for using their dominant market status not only to charge PC makers premium prices but also to leverage PC makers in other ways. Microsoft pressures PC makers to position the icons for Microsoft software prominently on the screens of new computers that come with factory-loaded software. Intel tends to give PC makers who use the biggest percentages of Intel chips in their PC models top priority in filling orders for newly introduced Intel chips. Being on Intel's list of preferred customers helps a PC maker get an allocation of the first production runs of Intel's latest and greatest chips and thus get new PC models to market ahead of rivals. The ability of Microsoft and Intel

Figure 3.6 Factors Affecting the Strength of Competitive Pressures from Substitute Products

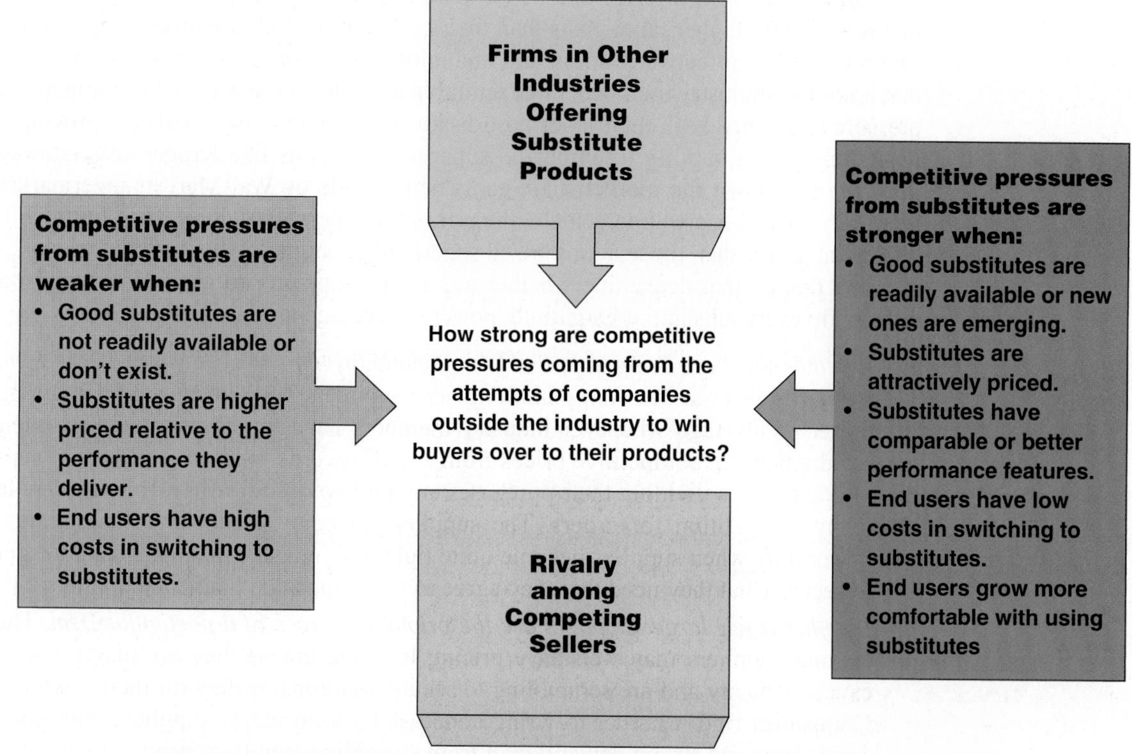

to pressure PC makers for preferential treatment of one kind or another in turn affects competition among rival PC makers.

Firms in Other Industries Offering Substitute Products
Competitive pressures from substitutes are weaker when:
• Good substitutes are not readily available or don't exist.
• Substitutes are higher priced relative to the performance they deliver.
• End users have high costs in switching to substitutes.
How strong are competitive pressures coming from the attempts of companies outside the industry to win buyers over to their products?
Competitive pressures from substitutes are stronger when:
• Good substitutes are readily available or new ones are emerging.
• Substitutes are attractively priced.
• Substitutes have comparable or better performance features.
• End users have low costs in switching to substitutes.
• End users grow more comfortable with using substitutes
Rivalry among Competing Sellers
Signs That Competition from Substitutes Is Strong
• Sales of substitutes are growing faster than sales of the industry being analyzed (an indication that the sellers of substitutes are drawing customers away from the industry in question).
• Producers of substitutes are moving to add new capacity.
• Profits of the producers of substitutes are on the rise.

Small-scale retailers must often contend with the power of manufacturers whose products enjoy prestigious and well-respected brand names; when a manufacturer knows that a retailer needs to stock the manufacturer's product because consumers

power over the terms and conditions with which they supply new vehicles to their independent automobile dealerships. The operators of franchised units of such chains as McDonald's, Dunkin' Donuts, Pizza Hut, Sylvan Learning Centers, and Hampton Inns must frequently agree not only to source some of their supplies from the franchisor at prices and terms favorable to that franchisor but also to operate their facilities in a manner largely dictated by the franchisor.

Strong supplier bargaining power is also a competitive factor in industries where unions have been able to organize the workforces of some industry members but not others; those industry members that must negotiate wages, fringe benefits, and working conditions with powerful unions (which control the supply of labor) often find themselves with higher labor costs than their competitors with nonunion labor forces. The bigger the gap between union and nonunion labor costs in an industry, the more that unionized industry members must scramble to find ways to relieve the competitive pressure associated with their labor cost disadvantage. High labor costs are proving a huge competitive liability to unionized supermarket chains like Kroger and Safeway in trying to combat the market share gains being made by Wal-Mart in supermarket retailing—at Wal-Mart Supercenters, the prices for supermarket items tend to run 5 to 20 percent lower than those at unionized supermarket chains.

The factors that determine whether any of the suppliers to an industry are in a position to exert substantial bargaining power or leverage are fairly clear-cut:[10]

- *Whether the item being supplied is a commodity that is readily available from many suppliers at the going market price.* Suppliers have little or no bargaining power or leverage whenever industry members have the ability to source their requirements at competitive prices from any of several alternative and eager suppliers, perhaps dividing their purchases among two or more suppliers to promote lively competition for orders. The suppliers of commodity items have market power only when supplies become quite tight and industry members are so eager to secure what they need that they agree to terms more favorable to suppliers.
- *Whether a few large suppliers are the primary sources of a particular item.* The leading suppliers may well have pricing leverage unless they are plagued with excess capacity and are scrambling to secure additional orders for their products. Companies find it harder to wring concessions from major suppliers with good reputations and strong demand than from struggling suppliers striving to broaden their customer base or more fully utilize their production capacity.
- *Whether it is difficult or costly for industry members to switch their purchases from one supplier to another or to switch to attractive substitute inputs.* High switching costs signal strong bargaining power on the part of suppliers, whereas low switching costs and ready availability of good substitute inputs signal weak bargaining power. Soft drink bottlers, for example, can counter the bargaining power of aluminum can suppliers by shifting or threatening to shift to greater use of plastic containers and introducing more attractive plastic container designs.
- *Whether certain needed inputs are in short supply.* Suppliers of items in short supply have some degree of pricing power, whereas a surge in the availability of particular items greatly weakens supplier pricing power and bargaining leverage.
- *Whether certain suppliers provide a differentiated input that enhances the performance or quality of the industry's product.* The more valuable that a particular input is in terms of enhancing the performance or quality of the products of industry members or of improving the efficiency of their production processes, the more bargaining leverage its suppliers are likely to possess.
- *Whether certain suppliers provide equipment or services that deliver valuable cost-saving efficiencies to industry members in operating their production processes.* Suppliers who provide cost-saving equipment or other valuable or necessary production-related services are likely to possess bargaining leverage. Industry members that do not source from such suppliers may find themselves at a cost

disadvantage and thus under competitive pressure to do so (on terms that are favorable to the suppliers).

- *Whether suppliers provide an item that accounts for a sizable fraction of the costs of the industry's product.* The bigger the cost of a particular part or component, the more opportunity for the pattern of competition in the marketplace to be affected by the actions of suppliers to raise or lower their prices.
- *Whether industry members are major customers of suppliers.* As a rule, suppliers have less bargaining leverage when their sales to members of this one industry constitute a big percentage of their total sales. In such cases, the well-being of suppliers is closely tied to the well-being of their major customers. Suppliers then have a big incentive to protect and enhance their customers' competitiveness via reasonable prices, exceptional quality, and ongoing advances in the technology of the items supplied.
- *Whether it makes good economic sense for industry members to integrate backward and self-manufacture items they have been buying from suppliers.* The make-or-buy issue generally boils down to how purchased components compare to self-manufactured components in quality and price. For instance, boat manufacturers find it cheaper to source marine engines from outside manufacturers who specialize in engine manufacturing rather than make their own engines because the quantity of engines they need is too small to justify the investment in manufacturing facilities, master the production process, and capture scale economies. Specialists in marine engine manufacturing, by supplying engines to the entire boating industry, can obtain a big enough sales volume to fully realize scale economies, become proficient in all the manufacturing techniques, and keep costs low. As a rule, suppliers are safe from the threat of self-manufacture by their customers *until* the volume of parts a customer needs becomes large enough for the customer to justify backward integration into self-manufacture.

Figure 3.7 summarizes the conditions that tend to make supplier bargaining power strong or weak.

How Collaborative Partnerships Between Industry Members and Their Suppliers Can Create Competitive Pressures In more and more industries, industry members are forging strategic partnerships with select suppliers in efforts to (1) reduce inventory and logistics costs (e.g., through just-in-time deliveries); (2) speed the availability of next-generation components; (3) enhance the quality of the parts and components being supplied and reduce defect rates; and (4) squeeze out important cost savings for both themselves and their suppliers. Numerous Internet technology applications are now available that permit real-time data sharing, eliminate paperwork, and produce cost savings all along the supply chain. The many benefits of effective seller–supplier collaboration can translate into competitive advantage for industry members who do the best job of managing supply chain relationships.

... managed its supply chain relationships in ways that contribute to a low-cost, high-quality competitive edge in components supply, it has put enormous pressure on its PC rivals to try to imitate its supply chain management practices. Effective partnerships with suppliers on the part of one or more industry members can thus become a major source of competitive pressure for rival firms.

The more opportunities that exist for win–win efforts between a company and its suppliers, the less their relationship is characterized by who has the upper hand in

Figure 3.7 Factors Affecting the Bargaining Power of Suppliers

Supplier bargaining power is stronger when:

- Industry members incur high costs in switching their purchases to alternative suppliers.
- Needed inputs are in short supply (which gives suppliers more leverage in setting prices).
- A supplier has a differentiated input that enhances the quality or performance of sellers' products or is a valuable or critical part of sellers' production process.
- There are only a few suppliers of a particular input.
- Some suppliers threaten to integrate forward into the business of industry members and perhaps become a powerful rival.

Supplier bargaining power is weaker when:

- The item being supplied is a commodity, that is, an item readily available from many suppliers at the going market price.
- Seller switching costs to alternative suppliers are low.
- Good substitute inputs exist or new ones emerge.
- There is a surge in the availability of supplies (thus greatly weakening supplier pricing power).
- Industry members account for a big fraction of suppliers' total sales and continued high volume purchases are important to the well-being of suppliers.
- Industry members are a threat to integrate backward into the business of suppliers and to self-manufacture their own requirements.
- Seller collaboration or partnering with selected suppliers provides attractive win–win opportunities.

bargaining with the other. Collaborative partnerships between a company and a supplier tend to last so long as the relationship is producing valuable benefits for both parties. Only if a supply partner is falling behind alternative suppliers is a company likely to switch suppliers and incur the costs and trouble of building close working ties with a different supplier.

Competitive Pressures Stemming from Buyer Bargaining Power and Seller–Buyer Collaboration

Whether seller–buyer relationships represent a weak or strong competitive force depends on (1) whether some or many buyers have sufficient bargaining leverage to obtain price concessions and other favorable terms and conditions of sale, and

(2) whether strategic partnerships between certain industry members and their customers produce competitive pressures that adversely affect other industry members.

How Buyer Bargaining Power Creates Competitive Pressures As with suppliers, the leverage that certain types of buyers have in negotiating favorable terms can range from weak to strong. Individual consumers, for example, rarely have much bargaining power in negotiating price concessions or other favorable terms with sellers. The primary exceptions involve situations in which price haggling is customary, such as the purchase of new and used motor vehicles, homes, and big-ticket items like jewelry and pleasure boats. For most consumer goods and services, individual buyers have no bargaining leverage—their option is to pay the seller's posted price, delay their purchase until prices and terms improve, or take their business elsewhere.

In contrast, large retail chains like Wal-Mart, Best Buy, Staples, and Home Depot typically have considerable negotiating leverage in purchasing products from manufacturers since retailers usually stock just two or three competing brands of a product. In addition, the strong bargaining power of major supermarket chains like Kroger and Safeway allows them to demand promotional allowances and lump-sum payments (called slotting fees) from food products manufacturers in return for stocking certain brands or putting them in the best shelf locations. Motor vehicle manufacturers have strong bargaining power in negotiating to buy original equipment tires from Goodyear, Michelin, Bridgestone/Firestone, Continental, and Pirelli not only because they buy in large quantities but also because tire makers have judged original equipment tires to be important contributors to brand awareness and brand loyalty. "Prestige" buyers have a degree of clout in negotiating with sellers because a seller's reputation is enhanced by having prestige buyers on its customer list.

Even if buyers do not purchase in large quantities or offer a seller important market exposure or prestige, they gain a degree of bargaining leverage in the following circumstances:[11]

- *If buyers' costs of switching to competing brands or substitutes are relatively low*—Buyers who can readily switch between several sellers have more negotiating leverage than buyers who have high switching costs. When the products of rival sellers are virtually identical, it is relatively easy for buyers to switch from seller to seller at little or no cost. For example, the screws, rivets, steel, and capacitors used in the production of large home appliances like washers and dryers are nearly indistinguishable products available from many sellers. The potential for buyers to easily switch from one seller to another encourages sellers to make concessions to win or retain a buyer's business.
- *If the number of buyers is small or if a customer is particularly important to a seller*—The smaller the number of buyers of the part or component being supplied, the less easy it is for suppliers to find alternative sales opportunities when a customer is lost to a competitor. The prospect of losing a customer that

other components have little bargaining power because there are a relatively small number of digital camera makers that need their components.
- *If demand for the item being supplied is weak*—Weak or declining demand for suppliers' products creates a buyer's market; conversely, strong or rapidly growing demand for suppliers' products creates a seller's market and shifts bargaining power to suppliers.

- *If buyers of the item being supplied are well informed about the purchase they are considering*—The more information buyers have about market conditions surrounding the item being supplied and about the products, prices, and costs of alternative suppliers, the better their bargaining position. The mushrooming availability of product information on the Internet is giving added bargaining power to individuals. Buyers can easily use the Internet to compare prices and features of vacation packages, shop for the best interest rates on mortgages and loans, and find the best prices on big-ticket items such as high-definition TVs. Bargain-hunting individuals can shop around for the best deal on the Internet and use that information to negotiate a better deal from local retailers; this method is becoming commonplace in buying new and used motor vehicles. Further, the Internet has created opportunities for manufacturers, wholesalers, retailers, and sometimes individuals to join online buying groups to pool their purchasing power and approach vendors for better terms than could be gotten individually. A multinational manufacturer's geographically scattered purchasing groups can use Internet technology to pool their orders with parts and components suppliers and bargain for volume discounts. Purchasing agents at some companies are banding together at third-party websites to pool corporate purchases to get better deals or special treatment.
- *If buyers pose a credible threat of integrating backward into the business of their suppliers*—Companies like Anheuser-Busch, Coors, and Heinz have integrated backward into metal can manufacturing to gain bargaining power in obtaining the balance of their can requirements from otherwise powerful metal can manufacturers. Retailers gain bargaining power by stocking and promoting their own private-label brands alongside manufacturers' name brands.
- *If buyers have discretion in whether and when they purchase the product*—Consumers who are unhappy with the present deals offered on discretionary items such as furniture, large appliances, and home electronics may choose to delay purchases until prices and financing terms improve. If college students believe that the prices of new textbooks are too high, they can purchase used copies. Business customers who are not happy with the prices or features of such discretionary items as new manufacturing equipment or computer software upgrades can opt to delay purchase until either terms improve or next-generation products become available.

Figure 3.8 highlights the factors causing buyer bargaining power to be strong or weak.

A final point to keep in mind is that *not all buyers of an industry's product have equal degrees of bargaining power,* and some may be less sensitive than others to price, quality, or service differences. For example, apparel manufacturers confront significant bargaining power when selling to big retailers like Macy's, T. J. Maxx, or Target; but those same manufacturers can command much better prices from small owner-managed apparel boutiques.

How Collaborative Partnerships Between Certain Industry Members and Their Key Customers Can Create Competitive Pressures Partnerships between sellers and buyers are an increasingly important element of the competitive picture in *business-to-business relationships* (as opposed to business-to-consumer relationships). Many sellers that provide items to business customers have found it in their mutual interest to collaborate closely with buyers on such matters as just-in-time deliveries, order processing, electronic invoice payments, and data sharing. Wal-Mart,

Figure 3.8 Factors Affecting the Bargaining Power of Buyers

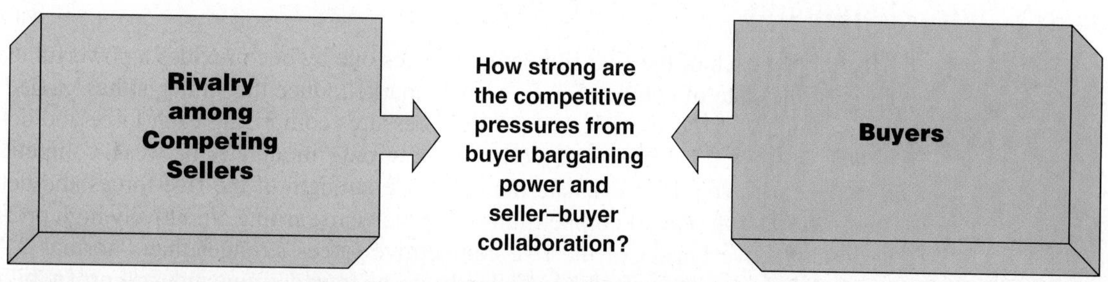
Rivalry among Competing Sellers
How strong are the competitive pressures from buyer bargaining power and seller–buyer collaboration?
Buyers

Buyer bargaining power is stronger when:

- Buyer switching costs to competing brands or substitute products are low.
- Buyers are large and can demand concessions when purchasing large quantities.
- Large volume purchases by buyers are important to sellers.
- Buyer demand is weak or declining.
- There are only a few buyers—so that each one's business is important to sellers.
- Identity of buyer adds prestige to the seller's list of customers.
- Quantity and quality of information available to buyers improves.
- Buyers have the ability to postpone purchases until later if they do not like the present deals being offered by sellers.
- Some buyers are a threat to integrate backward into the business of sellers and become important competitors.

Buyer bargaining power is weaker when:

- Buyers purchase the item infrequently or in small quantities.
- Buyer switching costs to competing brands are high.
- There is a surge in buyer demand that creates a seller's market.
- A seller's brand reputation is important to a buyer.
- A particular seller's product delivers quality or performance that is very important to buyer and that is not matched in other brands.
- Buyer collaboration or partnering with selected sellers provides attractive win–win opportunities.

for example, has entered into partnerships with manufacturers to keep merchandise in stock and to lower its inventory costs. Wal-Mart allows vendors like Procter & Gamble, Sara Lee, or Unilever to monitor store bar-code scanner data to determine when Wal-Mart's distribution centers need shipments and how big those shipments must be. In some instances, sellers ship inventory directly to each Wal-Mart store as merchandi-

an opportunity to boost the sales of their products in Wal-Mart stores. RFID receivers in each Wal-Mart store or distribution center allowed suppliers to track RFID-tagged inventory by number and location. Procter & Gamble and other Wal-Mart suppliers could then connect to Wal-Mart's computer networks to watch the real-time inventory flow of the items they supplied to Wal-Mart and make just-in-time shipments to prevent inventory stockouts.

Is the Collective Strength of the Five Competitive Forces Conducive to Good Profitability?

Scrutinizing each of the five competitive forces one by one provides a powerful diagnosis of the state of competition in a given market. Once the strategist has gained an understanding of the specific competitive pressures comprising each force and determined whether these pressures constitute a strong, moderate, or weak competitive force, the next step is to evaluate the collective strength of the five forces and determine whether the state of competition is conducive to earning attractively high profits. Is the collective impact of the five competitive forces stronger than "normal"? Are some of the competitive forces sufficiently strong to undermine industry profitability? Can companies in this industry reasonably expect to earn decent profits in light of the prevailing competitive forces?

The stronger the forces of competition, the harder it becomes for industry members to earn attractive profits.

Is the Industry Competitively Attractive or Unattractive? *As a rule, the stronger the collective impact of the five competitive forces, the lower the combined profitability of industry participants.* The most extreme case of a "competitively unattractive" industry is when all five forces are producing strong competitive pressures: rivalry among sellers is vigorous, low entry barriers allow new rivals to gain a market foothold, competition from substitutes is intense, and both suppliers and customers are able to exercise considerable bargaining leverage. Fierce to strong competitive pressures coming from all five directions nearly always drive industry profitability to unacceptably low levels, frequently producing losses for many industry members and forcing some out of business. But an industry can be competitively unattractive without all five competitive forces being strong. Intense competitive pressures from just two or three of the five forces may suffice to destroy the conditions for good profitability. Unattractive competitive conditions that include strong substitutes, fierce competitive rivalry, and low buyer switching costs have created a dismal outlook for the movie rental business. In 2007, Blockbuster recorded a net loss of $85 million on revenues of $5.5 billion, while the industry runner-up, Movie Gallery, filed bankruptcy in October 2007 after recording losses for three consecutive years. Movie Gallery lost an additional $70 million by the end of 2007, and its shares were delisted by the NASDAQ in 2008.

In contrast, when the collective impact of the five competitive forces is moderate to weak, an industry is competitively attractive in the sense that industry members can reasonably expect to earn good profits and a nice return on investment. The ideal competitive environment for earning superior profits is one in which both suppliers and customers are in weak bargaining positions, there are no good substitutes, high barriers block further entry, and rivalry among present sellers generates only moderate competitive pressures. Weak competition is the best of all possible worlds for also-ran companies because even they can usually eke out a decent profit—if a company can't earn adequate profits when competition is weak, then its business outlook is indeed grim.

In most industries, the collective strength of the five competitive forces is somewhere near the middle of the two extremes of very intense and very weak, typically ranging from slightly stronger than normal to slightly weaker than normal, and typically allowing well-managed companies with sound strategies to earn attractive profits.

Matching Company Strategy to Competitive Conditions Working through the five-forces model step by step not only aids strategy makers in assessing whether the intensity of competition allows good profitability but also promotes sound strategic thinking about how to better match company strategy to the specific competitive character of the marketplace. Effectively matching a company's strategy to prevailing competitive conditions has two aspects:

1. Pursuing avenues that shield the firm from as many of the different competitive pressures as possible.
2. Initiating actions calculated to shift competition in the company's favor, put added competitive pressure on rivals, and perhaps even define the business model for the industry.

A company's strategy is increasingly effective the more it provides some insulation from competitive pressures and shifts the competitive battle in the company's favor.

But making headway on these two fronts first requires identifying competitive pressures, gauging the relative strength of each of the five competitive forces, and gaining a deep enough understanding of the state of competition in the industry to know which strategy buttons to push.

QUESTION 3: WHAT FORCES ARE DRIVING INDUSTRY CHANGE AND WHAT IMPACTS WILL THEY HAVE?

While it is critical to understand the nature and intensity of competitive forces in an industry, it is just as important to understand that general industry conditions and an industry's overall outlook are fluid and subject to change. All industries are affected by new developments and ongoing trends that gradually or speedily produce new industry conditions important enough to require a strategic response from participating firms. The popular hypothesis that industries go through a life cycle of takeoff, rapid growth, early maturity and slowing growth, market saturation, and eventual stagnation or decline helps explain industry change—but there are more causes of industry change than an industry's normal progression through the life cycle.[12] Just what are the other drivers of industry change? Might they be even stronger drivers of change than progression through the life cycle? And don't strategy makers need to be alert to all the drivers of industry change, as well as to their likely impacts on industry and competitive conditions, in order to craft company strategies that will fit future industry circumstances?

The Concept of Driving Forces

CORE CONCEPT
Industry conditions change because important forces are *driving* industry participants (competitors, customers [illegible] in an industry are the *major underlying causes* of changing industry and competitive conditions—they have the biggest influence on how the industry landscape will be altered.

The important thing to understand about industry change is that it occurs because agents of change are working to entice or pressure certain industry participants (competitors, customers, suppliers) to alter their actions in important ways.[13] The most powerful of the change agents are called **driving forces** [illegible] (see Figure 3.2), but most originate in the company's more immediate industry and competitive environment.

Driving-forces analysis has three steps: (1) identifying what the driving forces are; (2) assessing whether the drivers of change are, on the whole, acting to make the industry more or less attractive; and (3) determining what strategy changes are needed to prepare for the impacts of the driving forces. All three steps merit further discussion.

Identifying an Industry's Driving Forces

Many developments can affect an industry powerfully enough to qualify as driving forces. Some drivers of change are unique, but most fall into one of the following categories (these 14 driving forces are summarized in Table 3.2):[14]

- *Changes in an industry's long-term growth rate*—Shifts in industry growth up or down are a driving force for industry change, affecting the balance between industry supply and buyer demand, entry and exit, and the character and strength of competition. An upsurge in buyer demand triggers a race among established firms and newcomers to capture the new sales opportunities; ambitious companies with trailing market shares may see the upturn in demand as a golden opportunity to launch offensive strategies to broaden their customer base and move up several notches in the industry standings. A slowdown in the rate at which buyer demand is growing nearly always intensifies rivalry because growth-oriented companies may try to launch aggressive initiatives to take sales and market share away from rivals. If industry sales suddenly turn flat or begin to shrink after years of rising at double-digit levels, competition is certain to intensify. Stagnating sales usually prompt both competitively weak and growth-oriented companies to sell their business operations to those industry members who elect to stick it out; as demand for the industry's product continues to shrink, the remaining industry members may be forced to close inefficient plants and retrench to a smaller production base. Thus, either a higher or lower rate of industry growth acts to produce new industry conditions, transform the competitive landscape, and trigger strategy changes on the part of some industry members.
- *Increasing globalization*—Competition begins to shift from primarily a regional or national focus to an international or global focus when industry members begin

Table 3.2 The Most Common Driving Forces

1. Changes in the long-term industry growth rate
2. Increasing globalization
3. Emerging new Internet capabilities and applications
4. Changes in who buys the product and how they use it
5. Product innovation
6. Technological change and manufacturing process innovation
7. Marketing innovation
8. Entry or exit of major firms
9. Diffusion of technical know-how across more companies and more countries
10. Changes in cost and efficiency
11. Growing buyer preferences for differentiated products instead of standardized commodity product (or for a more standardized product instead of strongly differentiated products)
12. Reductions in uncertainty and business risk
13. Regulatory influences and government policy changes
14. Changing societal concerns, attitudes, and lifestyles

seeking out customers in foreign markets or when production activities begin to migrate to countries where costs are lowest. Globalization of competition really starts to take hold when one or more ambitious companies precipitate a race for worldwide market leadership. Globalization can also be precipitated by the blossoming of consumer demand in more and more countries and by the actions of government officials to reduce trade barriers or open up once-closed markets to foreign competitors, as is occurring in many parts of Europe, Latin America, and Asia. Significant differences in labor costs among countries give manufacturers a strong incentive to locate plants for labor-intensive products in low-wage countries and use these plants to supply market demand across the world. Wages in China, India, Vietnam, Mexico, and Brazil, for example, are about one-fourth those in the United States, Germany, and Japan. The forces of globalization are sometimes such a strong driver that companies find it highly advantageous, if not necessary, to spread their operating reach into more and more country markets. Globalization is very much a driver of industry change in such industries as credit cards, cell phones, digital cameras, golf and ski equipment, motor vehicles, steel, petroleum, personal computers, video games, public accounting, and textbook publishing.

- *Emerging new Internet capabilities and applications*—Since the late 1990s, the Internet has woven its way not only into everyday business operations but also into the social fabric of life all across the world. Growing acceptance of Internet shopping and file sharing, the emergence of high-speed connections and Voice over Internet Protocol (VoIP) technology, and an ever-growing series of Internet applications have been major drivers of change in industry after industry. Mounting consumer preferences for buying or sharing music files have profoundly reshaped the music industry and affected traditional brick-and-mortar music retailers. Widespread use of e-mail has forever eroded the revenues of fax services and governmental postal services worldwide. Online course offerings at universities are beginning to revolutionize higher education. Companies are increasingly using online technology to (1) collaborate closely with suppliers and streamline their supply chains and (2) revamp internal operations and squeeze out cost savings. The ability of companies to reach consumers via the Internet increases the number of rivals a company faces and often escalates rivalry by pitting pure online sellers against combination brick-and-click sellers against pure brick-and-mortar sellers. The Internet of the future will feature faster speeds, dazzling applications, and over a billion connected gadgets performing an array of functions, thus driving further industry and competitive changes. But Internet-related impacts vary from industry to industry. The challenges here are to assess precisely how emerging Internet developments are altering a particular industry's landscape and to factor these impacts into the strategy-making equation.
- *Changes in who buys the product and how they use it*—Shifts in buyer demographics and the ways products are used can alter competition by affecting how customers

formed how music is bought and played; album sales in the United States, for example, declined from 785.1 million units in 2000 to 500.5 million units in 2007, whereas there were an estimated 840 million downloads of single digital recordings in 2007. The explosion of features and functions being incorporated into cell phones and their enormous popularity with cell phone users is causing all kinds of waves in telecommunications, video games, and digital photography. Longer life expectancies and growing percentages of relatively well-to-do retirees are driving big changes in buyer demographics in such industries as health care, prescription drugs, recreational living, and vacation travel.

- *Product innovation*—Industry conditions and the competitive landscape are always affected by rivals racing to be first to introduce one new product or product enhancement after another. An ongoing stream of product innovations tends to alter the pattern of competition in an industry by attracting more first-time buyers, rejuvenating industry growth, and/or creating wider or narrower product differentiation. Successful product introductions strengthen the market positions of the innovating companies, usually at the expense of companies that stick with their old products or that are slow to follow with their own versions of the new product. Product innovation has been a key driving force in such industries as cell phones, big-screen televisions, digital cameras, golf clubs, video games, toys, and prescription drugs.
- *Technological change and manufacturing process innovation*—Advances in technology can dramatically alter an industry's landscape, making it possible to produce new and better products at lower cost and opening up whole new industry frontiers. For instance, Voice over Internet Protocol (VoIP) has spawned low-cost, Internet-based phone networks that have begun competing with traditional telephone companies worldwide (whose higher-cost technology depends on hard-wire connections via overhead and underground telephone lines). LCD and plasma screen technology and high-definition technology are transforming the television industry. Satellite radio technology has made it possible for satellite radio companies with their largely commercial-free programming to draw millions of listeners away from traditional radio stations whose revenue streams from commercials are dependent on audience size. Technological developments can also produce competitively significant changes in capital requirements, minimum efficient plant sizes, distribution channels and logistics, and experience/learning curve effects. In the steel industry, ongoing advances in electric arc minimill technology (which involve recycling scrap steel to make new products) have allowed steelmakers with state-of-the-art minimills to gradually expand into the production of more and more steel products and steadily take sales and market share from higher-cost integrated producers (which make steel from scratch using iron ore, coke, and traditional blast furnace technology). Nucor Corporation, the leader of the minimill technology revolution in the United States, began operations in 1970 and has ridden the wave of technological advances in minimill technology to become the biggest U.S. steel producer, with 2007 revenues of nearly $16.6 billion. In a space of 30 years, advances in minimill technology have changed the face of the steel industry worldwide.
- *Marketing innovation*—When firms are successful in introducing *new ways* to market their products, they can spark a burst of buyer interest, widen industry demand, increase product differentiation, and lower unit costs—any or all of which can alter the competitive positions of rival firms and force strategy revisions.
- *Entry or exit of major firms*—The entry of one or more foreign companies into a geographic market once dominated by domestic firms nearly always shakes up competitive conditions. Likewise, when an established domestic firm from another industry attempts entry either by acquiring other companies or by launching its own start-up venture, it usually applies its skills and resources in some innovative fashion that pushes competition in new directions. Entry by a major firm thus often

produces a new ball game, not only with new key players but also with new rules for competing. Similarly, the exit of a major firm changes the competitive structure by reducing the number of market leaders (perhaps increasing the dominance of the leaders who remain) and causing a rush to capture the exiting firm's customers.

- *Diffusion of technical know-how across more companies and more countries*—As knowledge about how to perform a particular activity or execute a particular manufacturing technology spreads, the competitive advantage held by firms originally possessing this know-how erodes. Knowledge diffusion can occur through scientific journals, trade publications, on-site plant tours, word of mouth among suppliers and customers, employee migration, and Internet sources. In recent years, rapid technology transfer across national boundaries has been a prime factor in causing industries to become more globally competitive.
- *Changes in cost and efficiency*—Widening or shrinking differences in the costs among key competitors tend to dramatically alter the state of competition. Advances in fluorescent lightbulb technology and light-emitting diode (LED) technology have enabled manufacturers to produce energy-efficient fluorescent-based spiral lightbulbs and LED lighting products that last several times longer than traditional incandescent bulbs. While the prices of compact fluorescent and LED bulbs are several times greater than incandescent bulbs, they are proving to be far cheaper to use because of their longer lives (as much as eight years between replacements) and the considerable energy savings (as much as $50 over the life of the bulb). As a consequence, sales of incandescent bulbs were on the decline while sales of compact fluorescent and LED bulbs were growing rapidly. When sharply rising prices for crude oil in 2007–2008 caused big jumps in gasoline prices, automakers scrambled to boost the fuel efficiency of their car and truck models—sales of fuel-efficient vehicles like Toyota's popular hybrid Prius rose while sales of gas-guzzling SUVs fell off dramatically. Declining costs to produce PCs have enabled price cuts and spurred PC sales (especially lower-priced models) by making them more affordable to low-income households worldwide.
- *Growing buyer preferences for differentiated products instead of a commodity product (or for a more standardized product instead of strongly differentiated products)*—When buyer tastes and preferences start to diverge, sellers can win a loyal following with product offerings that stand apart from those of rival sellers. In recent years, beer drinkers have grown less loyal to a single brand and have begun to drink a variety of domestic and foreign beers; as a consequence, beer manufacturers have introduced a host of new brands. Buyer preferences for motor vehicles are becoming increasingly diverse, with few models generating sales of more than 250,000 units annually. When a shift from standardized to differentiated products occurs, the driver of change is the contest among rivals to cleverly outdifferentiate one another.

  However, buyers sometimes decide that a standardized, budget-priced product suits their [illegible] competition and force rival sellers to drive down their costs to maintain profitability. The lesson here is that competition is driven partly by whether the market forces in motion are acting to increase or decrease product differentiation.
- *Reductions in uncertainty and business risk*—Emerging industries are typically characterized by uncertainty over such issues as potential market size, how much

time and money will be needed to surmount technological problems, and what distribution channels and buyer segments to emphasize. Emerging industries tend to attract only risk-taking entrepreneurial companies. Over time, however, if the business model of industry pioneers proves profitable and market demand for the product appears durable, more conservative firms are usually enticed to enter the market. Often, these later entrants are large, financially strong firms looking to invest in attractive growth industries.

Lower business risks and less industry uncertainty also affect competition in international markets. In the early stages of a company's entry into foreign markets, conservatism prevails—firms limit their downside exposure by using less risky strategies like exporting, licensing, joint marketing agreements, or joint ventures with local companies to accomplish entry. Then, as experience accumulates and perceived risk levels decline, companies move more boldly and more independently, making acquisitions, constructing their own plants, putting in their own sales and marketing capabilities to build strong competitive positions in each country market, and beginning to link the strategies in each country to create a more globalized strategy.

- *Regulatory influences and government policy changes*—Governments can drive competitive changes by opening their domestic markets to foreign participation or closing them to protect domestic companies. (Note that this driving force is spawned by forces in a company's macroenvironment.) Government incentives to attract companies to locate plants in their communities can impact competitive conditions. Several southern U.S. states created lucrative incentive packages that induced a number of foreign automakers to build new multibillion-dollar plants employing thousands of workers in their states; these plants, which mostly have nonunion workforces, now provide formidable competition for the unionized plants operated by Ford, General Motors, and Chrysler. In contrast, the National Do Not Call Registry, established in 2003, made it difficult for telemarketers to generate new customers. For example, Scholastic Inc., the world's largest publisher and distributor of children's books (including the Harry Potter and Baby-Sitters Club series), had for years relied on telemarketing to sign up new book club members; when its telemarketing campaigns were hampered by the restrictions imposed by the federal Do Not Call legislation, Scholastic turned to Internet-based marketing approaches to generate new customers. But when the Internet campaigns failed to keep Scholastic's book club subscriber base from eroding and resulted in direct-to-home operating losses of nearly $3 million in 2005, $13 million in 2006, and more than $29 million in 2007, Scholastic management concluded in 2008 that the marketplace changes brought about by the Do Not Call legislation had irreparably harmed the book club industry and made it wise to divest its book club business.
- *Changing societal concerns, attitudes, and lifestyles*—Emerging social issues and changing attitudes and lifestyles can be powerful instigators of industry change. (As with the preceding driving force, this driving force springs from factors at work in a company's macroenvironment.) Growing antismoking sentiment has emerged as a major driver of change in the tobacco industry. Concerns about high gasoline prices are causing lifestyle changes in both vehicle purchases and driving habits. Consumer concerns about salt, sugar, chemical additives, saturated fat, cholesterol, carbohydrates, and nutritional value have forced food producers to revamp food-processing techniques, redirect R&D efforts, and compete in developing nutritious, good-tasting products. Safety concerns have driven product

design changes in the automobile, toy, and outdoor power equipment industries, to mention a few. Increased interest in physical fitness has spawned new industries in exercise equipment, biking, outdoor apparel, sports gyms and recreation centers, vitamin and nutrition supplements, and medically supervised diet programs. Social concerns about air and water pollution have forced industries to incorporate expenditures for controlling pollution into their cost structures. Shifting societal concerns, attitudes, and lifestyles alter the pattern of competition, usually favoring those players that respond quickly and creatively with products targeted to the new trends and conditions.

The large number of different *potential driving forces* explains why it is too simplistic to view industry change only in terms of moving through the different stages in an industry's life cycle and why a full understanding of all types of change drivers is a fundamental part of industry analysis. However, while many forces of change may be at work in a given industry, no more than three or four are likely to be true driving forces powerful enough to qualify as the *major determinants* of why and how the industry is changing. Thus, company strategists must resist the temptation to label every change they see as a driving force; the analytical task is to evaluate the forces of industry and competitive change carefully enough to separate major factors from minor ones.

Assessing the Impact of the Driving Forces

Just identifying the driving forces is not sufficient, however. The second, and more important, step in driving-forces analysis is to determine whether the prevailing driving forces are, on the whole, acting to make the industry environment more or less attractive. Answers to three questions are needed here:

1. Are the driving forces collectively acting to cause demand for the industry's product to increase or decrease?
2. Are the driving forces acting to make competition more or less intense?
3. Will the combined impacts of the driving forces lead to higher or lower industry profitability?

An important part of driving forces analysis is to determine whether the collective impact of the driving forces will be to increase or decrease market demand, make competition more or less intense, and lead to higher or lower industry profitability.

Getting a handle on the collective impact of the driving forces usually requires looking at the likely effects of each force separately, since the driving forces may not all be pushing change in the same direction. For example, two driving forces may be acting to spur demand for the industry's product while one driving force may be working to curtail demand. Whether the net effect on industry demand is up or down hinges on which driving forces are the more powerful. The analyst's objective here is to get a good grip on what external factors are shaping industry change and what difference these factors will make.

of the Driving Forces into Account

when done properly, pushes company managers to think about what's around the corner and what the company needs to be doing to get ready for it.

The third step of driving-forces analysis—where the real payoff for strategy-making comes—is for managers to draw some conclusions about what strategy adjustments will be needed to deal with the impacts of the driving

The real payoff of driving forces analysis is to help managers understand what strategy changes are needed to prepare for the impacts of the driving forces.

forces. The real value of doing driving forces analysis is to gain better understanding of what strategy adjustments will be needed to cope with the drivers of industry change and the impacts they are likely to have on market demand, competitive intensity, and industry profitability. In short, the strategy-making challenge that flows from driving-forces analysis is what to do to prepare for the industry and competitive changes being wrought by the driving forces. Indeed, without understanding the forces driving industry change and the impacts these forces will have on the character of the industry environment and on the company's business over the next one to three years, managers are ill-prepared to craft a strategy tightly matched to emerging conditions. So driving-forces analysis is not something to take lightly; it has practical value and is basic to the task of thinking strategically about where the industry is headed and how to prepare for the anticipated changes.

QUESTION 4: WHAT MARKET POSITIONS DO RIVALS OCCUPY—WHO IS STRONGLY POSITIONED AND WHO IS NOT?

Since competing companies commonly sell in different price/quality ranges, emphasize different distribution channels, incorporate product features that appeal to different types of buyers, have different geographic coverage, and so on, it stands to reason that some companies enjoy stronger or more attractive market positions than other companies. Understanding which companies are strongly positioned and which are weakly positioned is an integral part of analyzing an industry's competitive structure. The best technique for revealing the market positions of industry competitors is **strategic group mapping.**[15] This analytical tool is useful for comparing the market positions of each firm separately or for grouping them into like positions when an industry has so many competitors that it is not practical to examine each one in depth.

CORE CONCEPT
Strategic group mapping **is a technique for displaying the different market or competitive positions that rival firms occupy in the industry.**

Using Strategic Group Maps to Assess the Market Positions of Key Competitors

A **strategic group** consists of those industry members with similar competitive approaches and positions in the market.[16] Companies in the same strategic group can resemble one another in any of several ways: they may have comparable product-line breadth, sell in the same price/quality range, emphasize the same distribution channels, use essentially the same product attributes to appeal to similar types of buyers, depend on identical technological approaches, or offer buyers similar services and technical assistance.[17] An industry contains only one strategic group when all sellers pursue essentially identical strategies and have comparable market positions. At the other extreme, an industry may contain as many strategic groups as there are competitors when each rival pursues a distinctively different competitive approach and occupies a substantially different market position.

CORE CONCEPT
A *strategic group* is a cluster of industry rivals that have similar competitive approaches and market positions.

The procedure for constructing a *strategic group map* is straightforward:

- Identify the competitive characteristics that differentiate firms in the industry; typical variables are price/quality range (high, medium, low); geographic coverage (local, regional, national, global); degree of vertical integration (none, partial, full); product-line breadth (wide, narrow); use of distribution channels (one, some, all); and degree of service offered (no-frills, limited, full).
- Plot the firms on a two-variable map using pairs of these differentiating characteristics.
- Assign firms that fall in about the same strategy space to the same strategic group.
- Draw circles around each strategic group, making the circles proportional to the size of the group's share of total industry sales revenues.

This produces a two-dimensional diagram like the one for the world automobile industry in Illustration Capsule 3.1.

Several guidelines need to be observed in mapping the positions of strategic groups in the industry's overall strategy space.[18] First, the two variables selected as axes for the map should *not* be highly correlated; if they are, the circles on the map will fall along a diagonal and strategy makers will learn nothing more about the relative positions of competitors than they would by considering just one of the variables. For instance, if companies with broad product lines use multiple distribution channels while companies with narrow lines use a single distribution channel, then looking at broad versus narrow product lines reveals just as much about who is positioned where as looking at single versus multiple distribution channels; that is, one of the variables is redundant. Second, the variables chosen as axes for the map should expose big differences in how rivals position themselves to compete in the marketplace. This, of course, means analysts must identify the characteristics that differentiate rival firms and use these differences as variables for the axes and as the basis for deciding which firm belongs in which strategic group. Third, the variables used as axes don't have to be either quantitative or continuous; rather, they can be discrete variables or defined in terms of distinct classes and combinations. Fourth, drawing the sizes of the circles on the map proportional to the combined sales of the firms in each strategic group allows the map to reflect the relative sizes of each strategic group. Fifth, if more than two good competitive variables can be used as axes for the map, several maps can be drawn to give different exposures to the competitive positioning relationships present in the industry's structure. Because there is not necessarily one best map for portraying how competing firms are positioned in the market, it is advisable to experiment with different pairs of competitive variables.

What Can Be Learned from Strategic Group Maps?

Strategic group maps are revealing in several respects. The most important has to

rivalry tends to be. Although firms in the same strategic group are the closest rivals, the next closest rivals are in the immediately adjacent groups.[19] Often, firms in strategic groups that are far apart on the map hardly compete at all. For instance, BMW's car lineup, customer base, and pricing points are much too different from those of Mazda, Suzuki, and Ford to justify calling them close competitors of

Strategic group maps reveal which companies are close competitors and which are distant competitors.

ILLUSTRATION CAPSULE 3.1

Comparative Market Positions of Selected Automobile Manufacturers: A Strategic Group Map Application

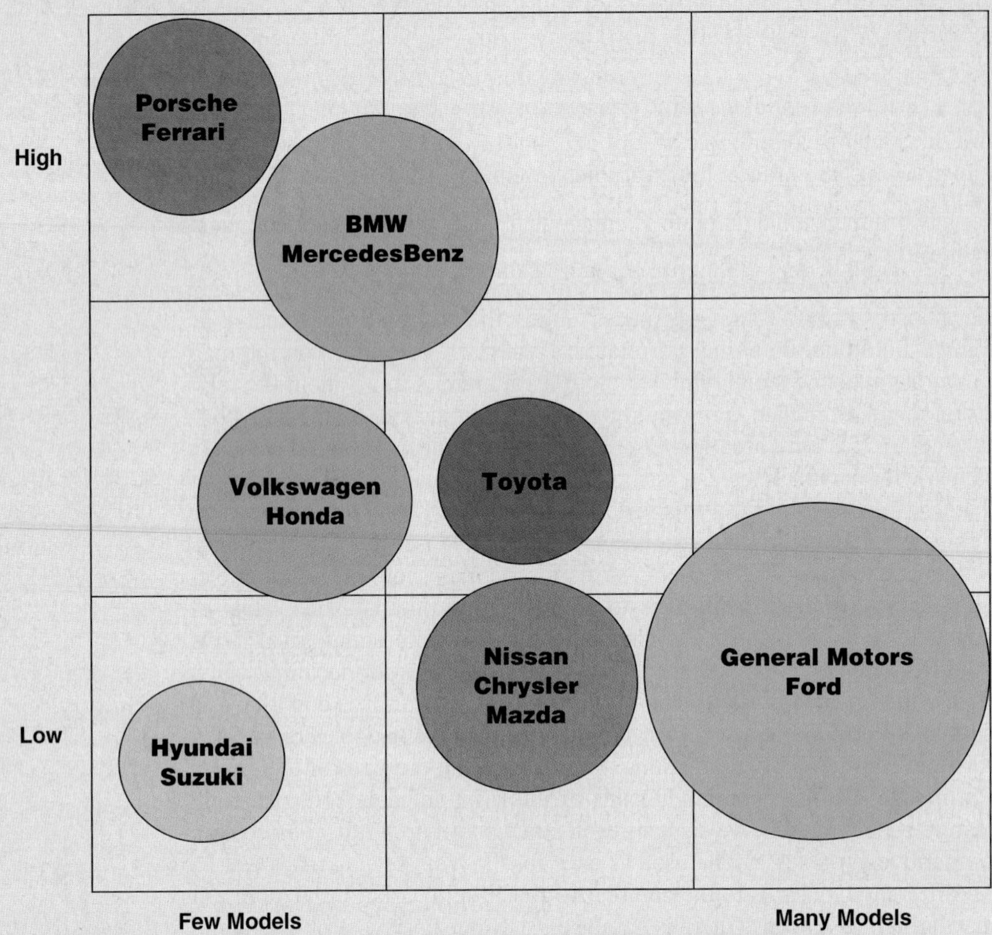

Note: Circles are drawn roughly proportional to the total revenues of manufacturers included in each strategic group.

CORE CONCEPT

Not all positions on a strategic group map are equally attractive.

BMW. For the same reason, Timex is not a meaningful competitive rival of Rolex, and Holiday Inn Express is not a close competitor of such luxury hotel chains as Ritz-Carlton and Four Seasons.

The second thing to be gleaned from strategic group mapping is that *not all positions on the map are equally attractive.* Two reasons account for why some positions can be more attractive than others:

1. *Prevailing competitive pressures and industry driving forces favor some strategic groups and hurt others.*[20] Discerning which strategic groups are advantaged and disadvantaged requires scrutinizing the map in light of what has also been learned

from the prior analysis of competitive forces and driving forces. Quite often the strength of competition varies from group to group—there's little reason to believe that all firms in an industry feel the same types or degrees of competitive pressure, since their strategies and market positions may well differ in important respects. For instance, the battle among Ford, Nissan, Hyundai, Toyota, and Honda for customers looking for low-cost, fuel-efficient vehicles is of a different character than the competition among Mercedes, BMW, and Porsche whose models appeal to upper-income buyers more interested in vehicle styling, performance, and brand image cachet. Likewise, the competitive battle between Wal-Mart and Target is more fierce than the rivalry among the flagship stores of couture brands such as Gucci, Chanel, Fendi, Louis Vuitton, Prada, and Versace. Furthermore, industry driving forces may be acting to grow the demand for the products of firms in some strategic groups and shrink the demand for the products of firms in other strategic groups—as is the case in the news industry, where Internet news services and cable news networks are gaining ground at the expense of newspapers and network television. The industry driving forces of emerging Internet capabilities and applications; changes in who buys the product and how they use it; and changing societal concerns, attitudes, and lifestyles are making it increasingly difficult for traditional media to increase audiences and attract new advertisers.

Firms in strategic groups that are being adversely impacted by intense competitive pressures or driving forces may try to shift to a more favorably situated group. But shifting to a different position on the map can prove difficult when entry barriers for the target strategic group are high. Moreover, attempts to enter a new strategic group nearly always increase competitive pressures in the target strategic group. If certain firms are known to be trying to change their competitive positions on the map, then attaching arrows to the circles showing the targeted direction helps clarify the picture of competitive maneuvering among rivals.

2. *The profit potential of different strategic groups varies due to the strengths and weaknesses in each group's market position.* The profit prospects of firms in different strategic groups can vary from good to ho-hum to poor because of differing growth rates for the principal buyer segments served by each group, differing degrees of competitive rivalry within strategic groups, differing degrees of exposure to competition from substitute products outside the industry, and differing degrees of supplier or customer bargaining power from group to group.

Thus, part of strategic group map analysis always entails drawing conclusions about where on the map is the "best" place to be and why. Which companies/strategic groups are destined to prosper because of their positions? Which companies/strategic groups seem destined to struggle because of their positions? And equally important, how might firms in poorly positioned strategic groups reposition themselves to improve their prospects for good financial performance?

WHAT STRATEGIC MOVES ARE RIVALS LIKELY TO MAKE NEXT?

Unless a company pays attention to what competitors are doing and knows their strengths and weaknesses, it ends up flying blind into competitive battle. As in sports, scouting the opposition is essential. *Competitive intelligence* about rivals' strategies,

Good scouting reports on rivals provide a valuable assist in anticipating what moves rivals are likely to make next and outmaneuvering them in the marketplace.

their latest actions and announcements, their resource strengths and weaknesses, the efforts being made to improve their situation, and the thinking and leadership styles of their executives is valuable for predicting or anticipating the strategic moves competitors are likely to make next. Good information allows a company to prepare defensive countermoves, to craft its own strategic moves with some confidence about what market maneuvers to expect from rivals, and to exploit any openings that arise from competitors' missteps or strategy flaws.

Identifying Competitors' Strategies and Resource Strengths and Weaknesses

Keeping close tabs on a competitor's strategy entails monitoring what the rival is doing in the marketplace and what its management is saying in company press releases, Web postings (especially the presentations management has recently made to securities analysts), and such public documents as annual reports and 10-K filings. (Figure 1.1 in Chapter 1 indicates what to look for in identifying a company's strategy.) Company personnel may be able to pick up useful information from a rival's exhibits at trade shows and from conversations with a rival's customers, suppliers, and former employees.[21] Many companies have a competitive intelligence unit that sifts through the available information to construct up-to-date strategic profiles of rivals—their current strategies, resource strengths and competitive capabilities, and competitive shortcomings. Such profiles are typically updated regularly and made available to managers and other key personnel.

Those who gather competitive intelligence on rivals, however, can sometimes cross the fine line between honest inquiry and unethical or even illegal behavior. For example, calling rivals to get information about prices, the dates of new product introductions, or wage and salary levels is legal, but misrepresenting one's company affiliation during such calls is unethical. Pumping rivals' representatives at trade shows is ethical only if one wears a name tag with accurate company affiliation indicated. Avon Products at one point secured information about its biggest rival, Mary Kay Cosmetics (MKC), by having its personnel search through the garbage bins outside MKC's headquarters.[22] When MKC officials learned of the action and sued, Avon claimed it did nothing illegal, since a 1988 Supreme Court case had ruled that trash left on public property (in this case, a sidewalk) was anyone's for the taking. Avon even produced a videotape of its removal of the trash at the MKC site. Avon won the lawsuit—but Avon's action, while legal, scarcely qualifies as ethical.

In sizing up competitors, it makes sense for company strategists to make three assessments:

1. Which competitor has the best strategy? Which competitors appear to have flawed or weak strategies?
2. Which competitors are poised to gain market share, and which ones seem destined to lose ground?
3. Which competitors are likely to rank among the industry leaders five years from now? Do one or more up-and-coming competitors have powerful strategies and sufficient resource capabilities to overtake the current industry leader?

The industry's *current* major players are generally easy to identify, but today's market leaders don't automatically become tomorrow's. Some of the industry's largest firms may be plagued with weaknesses that are causing them to lose ground, while the superior strategies and capabilities of up-and-coming companies may likely soon place them in the position of industry leader. In evaluating which competitors are favorably or unfavorably positioned to gain market ground, company strategists need to focus on why there is potential for some rivals to do better or worse than other rivals. Usually, a competitor's prospects are a function of whether it is in a strategic group that is being favored or hurt by competitive pressures and driving forces, whether its strategy has resulted in competitive advantage or disadvantage, and whether its resources and capabilities are well suited for competing on the road ahead.

Predicting Rivals' Next Moves

Predicting the next strategic moves of competitors is the hardest yet most useful part of competitor analysis. Good clues about what actions a specific company is likely to undertake can often be gleaned from how well it is faring in the marketplace, the problems or weaknesses it needs to address, and how much pressure it is under to improve its financial performance. Content rivals are likely to continue their present strategy with only minor fine-tuning. Ailing rivals can be performing so poorly that fresh strategic moves are virtually certain. Ambitious rivals looking to move up in the industry ranks are strong candidates for launching new strategic offensives to pursue emerging market opportunities and exploit the vulnerabilities of weaker rivals.

Since the moves a competitor is likely to make are generally predicated on the views their executives have about the industry's future and their beliefs about their firm's situation, it makes sense to closely scrutinize not only company executives' past actions and leadership styles but also their public pronouncements about where the industry is headed, what it will take to be successful, and what their firm's situation is. Information from the grapevine about what rivals are doing can also be analyzed. Other considerations in trying to predict what strategic moves rivals are likely to make next include the following:

Managers who fail to study competitors closely risk being caught napping when rivals make fresh and perhaps bold strategic moves.

- Which rivals badly need to increase their unit sales and market share? What strategic options are they most likely to pursue: lowering prices, adding new models and styles, expanding their dealer networks, entering additional geographic markets, boosting advertising to build better brand-name awareness, acquiring a weaker competitor, or placing more emphasis on direct sales via their Web site?
- Which rivals have a strong incentive, along with the resources, to make major strategic changes, perhaps moving to a different position on the strategic group map? Which rivals are probably locked in to pursuing the same

make an acquisition and are financially able to do so?

- Which rivals are likely to enter new geographic markets?
- Which rivals are strong candidates to expand their product offerings and enter new product segments where they do not currently have a presence?

To succeed in predicting a competitor's next moves, company strategists need to have a good feel for each rival's situation, how its managers think, and what the rival's best strategic options are. Doing the necessary detective work can be tedious and time-consuming, but scouting competitors well enough to anticipate their next moves allows managers to prepare effective countermoves (perhaps even beat a rival to the punch) and to take rivals' probable actions into account in crafting their own best course of action.

QUESTION 6: WHAT ARE THE KEY FACTORS FOR FUTURE COMPETITIVE SUCCESS?

CORE CONCEPT

Key success factors **are the product attributes, competencies, competitive capabilities, and market achievements with the greatest impact on future competitive success in the marketplace.**

An industry's **key success factors (KSFs)** are those competitive factors that most affect industry members' ability to prosper in the marketplace—the particular strategy elements, product attributes, resources, competencies, competitive capabilities, and market achievements that spell the difference between being a strong competitor and a weak competitor—and sometimes between profit and loss. KSFs by their very nature are so important to future competitive success that *all firms* in the industry must pay close attention to them or risk becoming an industry also-ran. To indicate the significance of KSFs another way, how well a company's product offering, resources, and capabilities measure up against an industry's KSFs determines just how financially and competitively successful that company will be. Identifying KSFs, in light of the prevailing and anticipated industry and competitive conditions, is therefore always a top priority analytical and strategy-making consideration. Company strategists need to understand the industry landscape well enough to separate the factors most important to competitive success from those that are less important.

In the bottled water industry, the KSFs are access to distribution (to get the company's brand stocked and favorably displayed in retail outlets where bottled water is sold), image (the product's name and the attractiveness of its packaging are deciding factors in choosing a brand for many consumers), low-cost production capabilities, and sufficient sales volume to achieve scale economies in marketing expenditures. In the ready-to-wear apparel industry, the KSFs are appealing designs and color combinations, low-cost manufacturing, a strong network of retailers or company-owned stores, distribution capabilities that allow stores to keep the best-selling items in stock, and advertisements that effectively convey the brand's image. These attributes and capabilities apply to all brands of apparel ranging from private-label brands sold by discounters to premium-priced ready-to-wear brands sold by upscale department stores. Key success factors thus vary from industry to industry, and even from time to time within the same industry, as driving forces and competitive conditions change. Table 3.3 lists the most common types of industry key success factors.

An industry's key success factors can usually be deduced through identifying the industry's dominant economic characteristics, assessing what competition is like, considering the impacts of the driving forces, comparing the market positions of industry

Table 3.3 Common Types of Industry Key Success Factors (KSFs)

Technology-related KSFs	• Expertise in a particular technology or in scientific research (important in pharmaceuticals, Internet applications, mobile communications, and most other high-tech industries) • Proven ability to improve production processes (important in industries where advancing technology opens the way for higher manufacturing efficiency and lower production costs)
Manufacturing-related KSFs	• Ability to achieve scale economies and/or capture experience curve effects (important to achieving low production costs) • Quality control know-how (important in industries where customers insist on product reliability) • High utilization of fixed assets (important in capital-intensive/high-fixed-cost industries) • Access to attractive supplies of skilled labor • High labor productivity (important for items with high labor content) • Low-cost product design and engineering (reduces manufacturing costs) • Ability to manufacture or assemble products that are customized to buyer specifications
Distribution-related KSFs	• A strong network of wholesale distributors/dealers • Strong direct sales capabilities via the Internet and/or having company-owned retail outlets • Ability to secure favorable display space on retailer shelves
Marketing-related KSFs	• Breadth of product line and product selection • A well-known and well-respected brand name • Fast, accurate technical assistance • Courteous, personalized customer service • Accurate filling of buyer orders (few back orders or mistakes) • Customer guarantees and warranties (important in mail-order and online retailing, big-ticket purchases, new product introductions) • Clever advertising
Skills and capability–related KSFs	• A talented workforce (superior talent is important in professional services like accounting and investment banking) • National or global distribution capabilities • Product innovation capabilities (important in industries where rivals are racing to be first-to-market with new product attributes or performance features) • Design expertise (important in fashion and apparel industries) • Short delivery time capability • Supply chain management capabilities
	• Overall low costs (not just in manufacturing) so as to be able to meet customers' expectations of low prices • Convenient locations (important in many retailing businesses) • Ability to provide fast, convenient after-the-sale repairs and service • A strong balance sheet and access to financial capital (important in newly emerging industries with high degrees of business risk and in capital-intensive industries) • Patent protection

members, and forecasting the likely next moves of key rivals. In addition, the answers to three questions help identify an industry's KSFs:

1. On what basis do buyers of the industry's product choose between the competing brands of sellers? That is, what product attributes are crucial?
2. Given the nature of competitive rivalry and the competitive forces prevailing in the marketplace, what resources and competitive capabilities does a company need to have to be competitively successful?
3. What shortcomings are almost certain to put a company at a significant competitive disadvantage?

CORE CONCEPT

A sound strategy incorporates the intent to stack up well on all of the industry's key success factors and to excel on one or two KSFs.

Only rarely are there more than five or six key factors for future competitive success. And even among these, two or three usually outrank the others in importance. Managers should therefore resist the temptation to label a factor that has only minor importance a KSF. To compile a list of every factor that matters even a little bit defeats the purpose of concentrating management attention on the factors truly critical to long-term competitive success.

Correctly diagnosing an industry's KSFs raises a company's chances of crafting a sound strategy. The goal of company strategists should be to design a strategy aimed at stacking up well on all of the industry's current and future KSFs and trying to be *distinctively better* than rivals on one (or possibly two) of the KSFs. Indeed, companies that stand out or excel on a particular KSF are likely to enjoy a stronger market position—*being distinctively better than rivals on one or two key success factors tends to translate into competitive advantage.* Hence, using the industry's KSFs as *cornerstones* for the company's strategy and trying to gain sustainable competitive advantage by excelling at one particular KSF is a fruitful competitive strategy approach.[23]

QUESTION 7: DOES THE OUTLOOK FOR THE INDUSTRY OFFER THE COMPANY A GOOD OPPORTUNITY TO EARN ATTRACTIVE PROFITS?

The final step in evaluating the industry and competitive environment is to use the preceding analysis to decide whether the outlook for the industry presents the company with a sufficiently attractive business opportunity. The important factors on which to base such a conclusion include:

- The industry's growth potential.
- Whether powerful competitive forces are squeezing industry profitability to subpar levels and whether competition appears destined to grow stronger or weaker.
- Whether industry profitability will be favorably or unfavorably affected by the prevailing driving forces.
- The degrees of risk and uncertainty in the industry's future.
- Whether the industry as a whole confronts severe problems—regulatory or environmental issues, stagnating buyer demand, industry overcapacity, mounting competition, and so on.
- The company's competitive position in the industry vis-à-vis rivals. (Being a well-entrenched leader or strongly positioned contender in a lackluster industry may present adequate opportunity for good profitability; however, having to fight a

steep uphill battle against much stronger rivals may hold little promise of eventual market success or good return on shareholder investment, even though the industry environment is attractive.)

- The company's potential to capitalize on the vulnerabilities of weaker rivals (perhaps converting a relatively unattractive *industry* situation into a potentially rewarding *company* opportunity).
- Whether the company has sufficient competitive strength to defend against or counteract the factors that make the industry unattractive.

As a general proposition, *if an industry's overall profit prospects are above average, the industry environment is basically attractive; if industry profit prospects are below average, conditions are unattractive.* However, it is a mistake to think of a particular industry as being equally attractive or unattractive to all industry participants and all potential entrants. Attractiveness is relative, not absolute, and conclusions one way or the other have to be drawn from the perspective of a particular company. Industries attractive to insiders may be unattractive to outsiders. Industry environments unattractive to weak competitors may be attractive to strong competitors. A favorably positioned company may survey a business environment and see a host of opportunities that weak competitors cannot capture.

CORE CONCEPT

The degree to which an industry is attractive or unattractive is not the same for all industry participants and all potential entrants; the attractiveness of the opportunities an industry presents depends heavily on whether a company has the resource strengths and competitive capabilities to capture them.

When a company decides an industry is fundamentally attractive and presents good opportunities, a strong case can be made that it should invest aggressively to capture the opportunities it sees and to improve its long-term competitive position in the business. When a strong competitor concludes that an industry is relatively unattractive, it may elect to simply protect its present position, invest cautiously if at all, and look for opportunities in other industries. A competitively weak company in an unattractive industry may see its best option as finding a buyer, perhaps a rival, to acquire its business.

KEY POINTS

Thinking strategically about a company's external situation involves probing for answers to the following seven questions:

1. *What are the industry's dominant economic features?* Industries differ significantly on such factors as market size and growth [illegible] conditions, the extent of vertical integration, and the extent of scale economies and experience/learning curve effects. In addition to setting the stage for the analysis to come, identifying an industry's economic features also promotes understanding of the kinds of strategic moves that industry members are likely to employ.
2. *What kinds of competitive forces are industry members facing, and how strong is each force?* The strength of competition is a composite of five forces: (1) competitive pressures stemming from the competitive maneuvering among industry rivals,

(2) competitive pressures associated with the market inroads being made by the sellers of substitutes, (3) competitive pressures associated with the threat of new entrants into the market, (4) competitive pressures stemming from supplier bargaining power and supplier–seller collaboration, and (5) competitive pressures stemming from buyer bargaining power and seller–buyer collaboration. The nature and strength of the competitive pressures associated with these five forces have to be examined force by force to identify the specific competitive pressures they each comprise and to decide whether these pressures constitute a strong or weak competitive force. The next step in competition analysis is to evaluate the collective strength of the five forces and determine whether the state of competition is conducive to good profitability. Working through the five-forces model step by step not only aids strategy makers in assessing whether the intensity of competition allows good profitability but also promotes sound strategic thinking about how to better match company strategy to the specific competitive character of the marketplace. Effectively matching a company's strategy to the particular competitive pressures and competitive conditions that exist has two aspects: (1) pursuing avenues that shield the firm from as many of the prevailing competitive pressures as possible, and (2) initiating actions calculated to produce sustainable competitive advantage, thereby shifting competition in the company's favor, putting added competitive pressure on rivals, and perhaps even defining the business model for the industry.

3. *What forces are driving changes in the industry, and what impact will these changes have on competitive intensity and industry profitability?* Industry and competitive conditions change because forces are in motion that create incentives or pressures for change. The first phase is to identify the forces that are driving change in the industry; the most common driving forces include changes in the long-term industry growth rate, globalization of competition in the industry, emerging Internet capabilities and applications, changes in buyer composition, product innovation, technological change and manufacturing process innovation, marketing innovation, entry or exit of major firms, diffusion of technical know-how, changes in cost and efficiency, growing buyer preferences for differentiated versus standardized products (or vice versa), reductions in uncertainty and business risk, regulatory influences and government policy changes, and changing societal and lifestyle factors. The second phase of driving-forces analysis is to determine whether the driving forces, taken together, are acting to make the industry environment more or less attractive. Are the driving forces causing demand for the industry's product to increase or decrease? Are the driving forces acting to make competition more or less intense? Will the driving forces lead to higher or lower industry profitability?

4. *What market positions do industry rivals occupy—who is strongly positioned and who is not?* Strategic group mapping is a valuable tool for understanding the similarities, differences, strengths, and weaknesses inherent in the market positions of rival companies. Rivals in the same or nearby strategic groups are close competitors, whereas companies in distant strategic groups usually pose little or no immediate threat. The lesson of strategic group mapping is that some positions on the map are more favorable than others. The profit potential of different strategic groups varies due to strengths and weaknesses in each group's market position. Often, industry driving forces and competitive pressures favor some strategic groups and hurt others.

5. *What strategic moves are rivals likely to make next?* This analytical step involves identifying competitors' strategies, deciding which rivals are likely to be strong contenders and which are likely to be weak, evaluating rivals' competitive options, and predicting their next moves. Scouting competitors well enough to anticipate their actions can help a company prepare effective countermoves (perhaps even beating a rival to the punch) and allows managers to take rivals' probable actions into account in designing their own company's best course of action. Managers who fail to study competitors risk being caught unprepared by the strategic moves of rivals.
6. *What are the key factors for future competitive success?* An industry's key success factors (KSFs) are the particular strategy elements, product attributes, competitive capabilities, and business outcomes that spell the difference between being a strong competitor and a weak competitor—and sometimes between profit and loss. KSFs by their very nature are so important to competitive success that *all firms* in the industry must pay close attention to them or risk becoming an industry also-ran. Correctly diagnosing an industry's KSFs raises a company's chances of crafting a sound strategy. The goal of company strategists should be to design a strategy aimed at stacking up well on all of the industry KSFs and trying to be *distinctively better* than rivals on one (or possibly two) of the KSFs. Indeed, using the industry's KSFs as *cornerstones* for the company's strategy and trying to gain sustainable competitive advantage by excelling at one particular KSF is a fruitful competitive strategy approach.
7. *Does the outlook for the industry present the company with sufficiently attractive prospects for profitability?* If an industry's overall profit prospects are above average, the industry environment is basically attractive; if industry profit prospects are below average, conditions are unattractive. Conclusions regarding industry attractive are a major driver of company strategy. When a company decides an industry is fundamentally attractive, a strong case can be made that it should invest aggressively to capture the opportunities it sees and to improve its long-term competitive position in the business. When a strong competitor concludes an industry is relatively unattractive, it may elect to simply protect its present position, investing cautiously if at all and looking for opportunities in other industries. A competitively weak company in an unattractive industry may see its best option as finding a buyer, perhaps a rival, to acquire its business. On occasion, an industry that is unattractive overall is still very attractive to a favorably situated company with the skills and resources to take business away from weaker rivals.

A competently conducted industry and competitive analysis generally tells a clear, easily understood story about the company's external environment. Different analysts can have different judgments about competitive intensity, the impacts of driving forces, how industry conditions will evolve, how good the outlook is for industry profitability, and the degree to which the industry environment offers the [illegible] this doesn't justify shortcutting hard-nosed strategic analysis and relying instead on opinion and casual observation. Managers become better strategists when they know what questions to pose and what tools to use. This is why this chapter has concentrated on suggesting the right questions to ask, explaining concepts and analytical approaches, and indicating the kinds of things to look for. There's no substitute for doing cutting-edge strategic thinking about a company's external situation—anything less weakens managers' ability to craft strategies that are well matched to industry and competitive conditions.

ASSURANCE OF LEARNING EXERCISES

1. Using your favorite Internet search engine, do some research on competitive forces and driving forces that are at work in the snack food industry. Draw a five-forces diagram for the snack food industry and briefly discuss the nature and strength of each of the five competitive forces. Make a list of the driving forces operating in the snack foods industry and draw some conclusions about whether the likely impact of these driving forces on snack foods companies will be favorable or unfavorable.
2. Refer back to the strategic group map in Illustration Capsule 3.1: Who are Toyota's closest competitors? Between which two strategic groups is competition the strongest? Why do you think no automobile manufacturers are positioned in the upper right corner of the map? Which company/strategic group faces the weakest competition from the members of other strategic groups?
3. Using the information provided in Table 3.2 and your knowledge as a casual dining patron, what are the key success factors for restaurants such as Outback Steakhouse or Carrabba's Italian Grill? Your list should contain no more than six industry key success factors. In deciding on your list, it's important to distinguish between factors critical to success in the industry and factors that enhance a company's overall well-being.

EXERCISES FOR SIMULATION PARTICIPANTS

1. Which of the five competitive forces is creating the strongest competitive pressures for your company?
2. What are the "weapons of competition" that rival companies in your industry can use to gain sales and market share? Refer back to Figure 3.4 to help you identify the various competitive factors.
3. What are the factors affecting the intensity of rivalry in the industry in which your company is competing. Use Figure 3.4 and the accompanying discussion to help you pinpoint the specific factors most affecting competitive intensity. Would you characterize the rivalry and jockeying for better market position, increased sales, and market share among the companies in your industry as fierce, very strong, strong, moderate, or relatively weak? Why?
4. Are there any driving forces in the industry in which your company is competing? What impact will these driving forces have? Will they cause competition to be more or less intense? Will they act to boost or squeeze profit margins? List at least two actions your company should consider taking in order to combat any negative impacts of the driving forces.

5. Draw a strategic group map showing the market positions of the companies in your industry. Which companies do you believe are in the most attractive position on the map? Which companies are the most weakly positioned? Which companies do you believe are likely to try to move to a different position on the strategic group map?
6. What do you see as the key factors for being a successful competitor in your industry? List at least three KSFs.

CHAPTER

4

Evaluating a Company's Resources and Competitive Position

LEARNING OBJECTIVES

1. Understand how to evaluate a company's internal situation and capabilities and identify the resource strengths capable of becoming the cornerstone of the company's strategic approach.
2. Grasp how and why activities performed internally by a company and those performed externally by its suppliers and forward channel allies determine a company's cost structure and ability to compete successfully.
3. Learn how to evaluate a company's competitive strength relative to key rivals.
4. Understand the role and importance of industry and competitive analysis and internal situation analysis in identifying strategic issues company managers must address.

Before executives can chart a new strategy, they must reach common understanding of the company's current position.

—**W. Chan Kim and Rene Mauborgne**

The real question isn't how well you're doing today against your own history, but how you're doing against your competitors.

— **Donald Kress**

Organizations succeed in a competitive marketplace over the long run because they can do certain things their customers value better than can their competitors.

— **Robert Hayes, Gary Pisano, and David Upton**

Only firms who are able to continually build new strategic assets faster and cheaper than their competitors will earn superior returns over the long term.

— **C. C. Markides and P. J. Williamson**

In Chapter 3 we described how to use the tools of industry and competitive analysis to assess a company's external environment and lay the groundwork for matching a company's strategy to its external situation. In this chapter we discuss the techniques of evaluating a company's resource capabilities, relative cost position, and competitive strength versus rivals, so as to lay the groundwork for matching the company's strategy to its internal situation. The analytical spotlight for assessing a company's situation will be trained on five questions:

1. How well is the company's present strategy working?
2. What are the company's resource strengths and weaknesses, and its external opportunities and threats?
3. Are the company's prices and costs competitive with those of rivals?
4. Is the company competitively stronger or weaker than key rivals?
5. What strategic issues and problems merit front-burner managerial attention?

In probing for answers to these questions, four analytical tools—SWOT analysis, value chain analysis, benchmarking, and competitive strength assessment—will be used. All four are valuable techniques for revealing a company's competitiveness and for helping company managers match their strategy to the company's own particular circumstances.

QUESTION 1: HOW WELL IS THE COMPANY'S PRESENT STRATEGY WORKING?

In evaluating how well a company's present strategy is working, a manager has to start with what the strategy is. Figure 4.1 shows the key components of a single-business company's strategy. The first thing to pin down is the company's competitive approach. Is the company striving to be a low-cost leader *or* stressing ways to differentiate its product offering from rivals? Is the company's competitive approach tied to resource strengths and capabilities that allow it to deliver value to customers in ways that are unmatched by rivals? Is it concentrating its efforts on serving a broad spectrum of customers *or* a narrow market niche? Another strategy-defining consideration is the firm's competitive scope within the industry—what

Figure 4.1 Identifying the Components of a Single-Business Company's Strategy

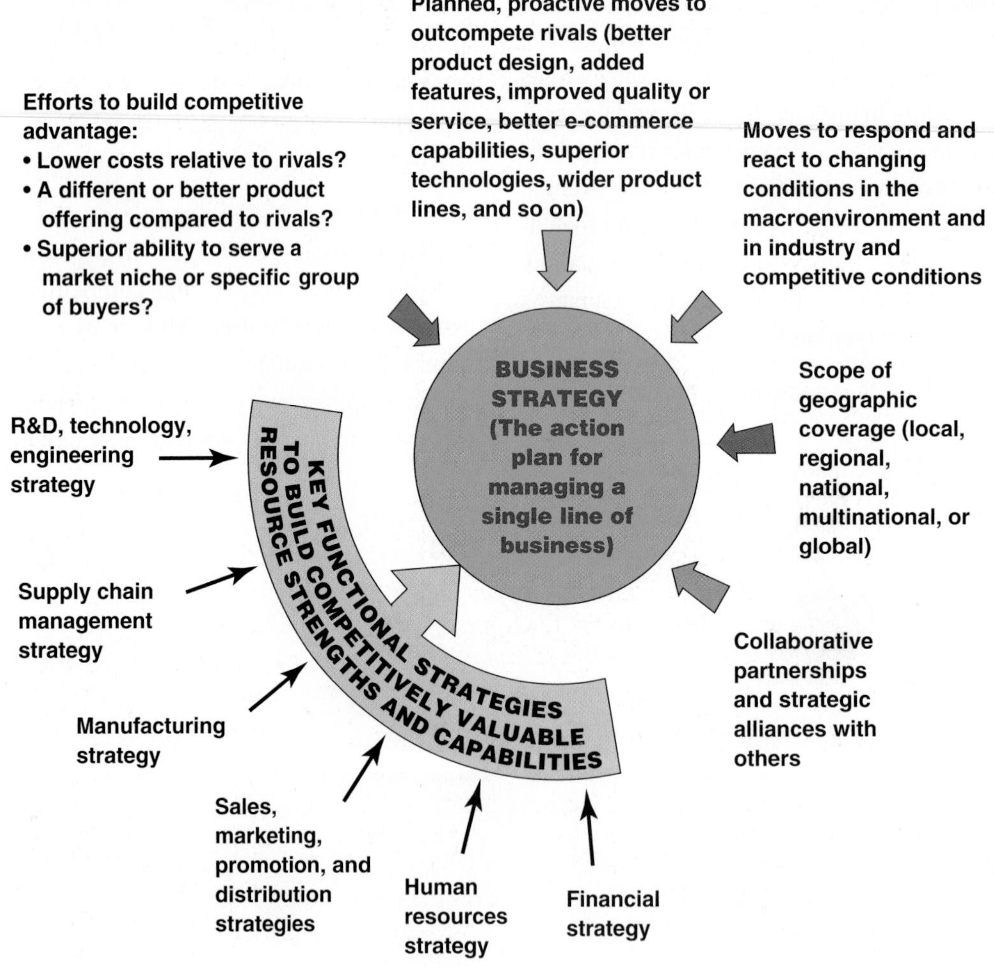

its geographic market coverage is and whether it operates in just a single stage of the industry's production/distribution chain or is vertically integrated across several stages. Another good indication of the company's strategy is whether the company has made moves recently to improve its competitive position and performance—for instance, by cutting prices, improving design, stepping up advertising, entering a new geographic market (domestic or foreign), or merging with a competitor. The company's functional strategies in research and development (R&D), production, marketing, finance, human resources, information technology (IT), and so on further characterize company strategy.

While there's merit in evaluating the strategy from a *qualitative* standpoint (its completeness, internal consistency, rationale, and relevance), the best *quantitative* evidence of how well a company's strategy is working comes from its results. The two best empirical indicators are (1) whether the company is achieving its stated financial and strategic objectives, and (2) whether the company is an above-average industry performer. Persistent shortfalls in meeting company performance targets and weak performance relative to rivals are reliable warning signs that the company suffers from poor strategy making, less-than-competent strategy execution, or both. Other indicators of how well a company's strategy is working include:

- Whether the firm's sales are growing faster, slower, or about the same pace as the market as a whole, thus resulting in a rising, eroding, or stable market share.
- Whether the company is acquiring new customers at an attractive rate as well as retaining existing customers.
- Whether the firm's profit margins are increasing or decreasing and how well its margins compare to rival firms' margins.
- Trends in the firm's net profits and return on investment, and how these compare to the same trends for other companies in the industry.
- Whether the company's overall financial strength and credit rating are improving or on the decline.
- Whether the company can demonstrate continuous improvement in such internal performance measures as days of inventory, employee productivity, unit cost, defect rate, scrap rate, misfilled orders, delivery times, warranty costs, and so on.
- How shareholders view the company based on trends in the company's stock price and shareholder value (relative to the stock price trends at other companies in the industry).
- The firm's image and reputation with its customers.
- How well the company stacks up against rivals on technology, product innovation, customer service, product quality, delivery time, price, getting newly developed products to market quickly, and other relevant factors on which buyers base their choice of brands.

The str[illegible]

[illegible] current strategy must be questioned. Weak performance is almost always a sign of weak strategy, weak execution, or both.

market position, the more likely it has a well-conceived, well-executed strategy.

Table 4.1 provides a compilation of the financial ratios most commonly used to evaluate a company's financial performance and balance sheet strength.

Table 4.1 Key Financial Ratios: How to Calculate Them and What They Mean

Ratio	How Calculated	What It Shows
Profitability ratios		
1. Gross profit margin	$\frac{\text{Revenues} - \text{Cost of goods sold}}{\text{Revenues}}$	Shows the percentage of revenues available to cover operating expenses and yield a profit. Higher is better, and the trend should be upward.
2. Operating profit margin (or return on sales)	$\frac{\text{Revenues} - \text{Operating expenses}}{\text{Revenues}}$ or $\frac{\text{Operating income}}{\text{Revenues}}$	Shows the profitability of current operations without regard to interest charges and income taxes. Higher is better, and the trend should be upward.
3. Net profit margin (or net return on sales)	$\frac{\text{Profits after taxes}}{\text{Revenues}}$	Shows after-tax profits per dollar of sales. Higher is better, and the trend should be upward.
4. Return on total assets	$\frac{\text{Profits after taxes} + \text{Interest}}{\text{Total assets}}$	A measure of the return on total investment in the enterprise. Interest is added to after-tax profits to form the numerator, since total assets are financed by creditors as well as by stockholders. Higher is better, and the trend should be upward.
5. Return on stockholder's equity	$\frac{\text{Profits after taxes}}{\text{Total stockholders' equity}}$	Shows the return stockholders are earning on their investment in the enterprise. A return in the 12–15 percent range is average, and the trend should be upward.
6. Earnings per share	$\frac{\text{Profits after taxes}}{\text{Number of shares of common stock outstanding}}$	Shows the earnings for each share of common stock outstanding. The trend should be upward, and the bigger the annual percentage gains, the better.
Liquidity ratios		
1. Current ratio	$\frac{\text{Current assets}}{\text{Current liabilities}}$	Shows a firm's ability to pay current liabilities using assets that can be converted to cash in the near term. Ratio should definitely be higher than 1.0; ratios of 2 or higher are better still.
2. Quick ratio (or acid-test ratio)	$\frac{\text{Current assets} - \text{Inventory}}{\text{Current liabilities}}$	Shows a firm's ability to pay current liabilities without relying on the sale of its inventories.
3. Working capital	Current assets – Current liabilities	Bigger amounts are better because the company has more internal funds available to (1) pay its current liabilities on a timely basis and (2) finance inventory expansion, additional accounts receivable, and a larger base of operations without resorting to borrowing or raising more equity capital.
Leverage ratios		
1. Debt-to-assets ratio	$\frac{\text{Total debt}}{\text{Total assets}}$	Measures the extent to which borrowed funds have been used to finance the firm's operations. Low fractions or ratios are better—high fractions indicate overuse of debt and greater risk of bankruptcy.

(*Continued*)

Ratio	How Calculated	What It Shows
2. Long-term debt-to-capital ratio	$\frac{\text{Long-term debt}}{\text{Long-term debt} + \text{Total stockholders' equity}}$	An important measure of creditworthiness and balance sheet strength. Indicates the percentage of capital investment which has been financed by creditors and bondholders. Fractions or ratios below .25 or 25% are usually quite satisfactory since monies invested by stockholders account for 75% or more of the company's total capital. The lower the ratio, the greater the capacity to borrow additional funds. Debt-to-capital ratios above 50% and certainly above 75% indicate a heavy and perhaps excessive reliance on debt, lower creditworthiness, and weak balance sheet strength.
3. Debt-to-equity ratio	$\frac{\text{Total debt}}{\text{Total stockholders' equity}}$	Should usually be less than 1.0. High ratios (especially above 1.0) signal excessive debt, lower creditworthiness, and weaker balance sheet strength.
4. Long-term debt-to-equity ratio	$\frac{\text{Long-term debt}}{\text{Total stockholders' equity}}$	Shows the balance between debt and equity in the firm's *long-term* capital structure. Low ratios indicate greater capacity to borrow additional funds if needed.
5. Times-interest-earned (or coverage) ratio	$\frac{\text{Operating income}}{\text{Interest expenses}}$	Measures the ability to pay annual interest charges. Lenders usually insist on a minimum ratio of 2.0, but ratios above 3.0 signal better creditworthiness.
Activity ratios		
1. Days of inventory	$\frac{\text{Inventory}}{\text{Cost of goods sold} \div 365}$	Measures inventory management efficiency. Fewer days of inventory are usually better.
2. Inventory turnover	$\frac{\text{Cost of goods sold}}{\text{Inventory}}$	Measures the number of inventory turns per year. Higher is better.
3. Average collection period	$\frac{\text{Accounts receivable}}{\text{Total sales} \div 365}$ or $\frac{\text{Accounts receivable}}{\text{Average daily sales}}$	Indicates the average length of time the firm must wait after making a sale to receive cash payment. A shorter collection time is better.
Other important financial measures		
1. Dividend yield on common stock	$\frac{\text{Annual dividends per share}}{\text{Current market price per share}}$	A measure of the return to owners received in the form of dividends.
2. Price/earnings (P/E)	[illegible]	[illegible] likely to grow slowly typically have ratios below 12.
3. Dividend payout ratio	$\frac{\text{Annual dividends per share}}{\text{Earnings per share}}$	Indicates the percentage of after-tax profits paid out as dividends.
4. Internal cash flow	After-tax profits + Depreciation	A quick and rough estimate of the cash a company's business is generating after payment of operating expenses, interest, and taxes. Such amounts can be used for dividend payments or funding capital expenditures.

QUESTION 2: WHAT ARE THE COMPANY'S RESOURCE STRENGTHS AND WEAKNESSES AND ITS EXTERNAL OPPORTUNITIES AND THREATS?

SWOT analysis **is a simple but powerful tool for sizing up a company's resource capabilities and deficiencies, its market opportunities, and the external threats to its future well-being.**

Appraising a company's resource **s**trengths and **w**eaknesses and its external **o**pportunities and **t**hreats, commonly known as **SWOT analysis,** provides a good overview of whether the company's overall situation is fundamentally healthy or unhealthy. Just as important, a first-rate SWOT analysis provides the basis for crafting a strategy that capitalizes on the company's resources, aims squarely at capturing the company's best opportunities, and defends against the threats to its well-being.

Identifying Company Resource Strengths, Competencies, and Competitive Capabilities

A *resource strength* is something a company is good at doing or an attribute that enhances its competitiveness in the marketplace. Resource strengths can take any of several forms:

- *A skill, an area of specialized expertise, or a competitively important capability*—skills in keeping operating costs low, proven capabilities in creating and introducing innovative products, skills in creating a cost-efficient supply chain, expertise in getting new products to market quickly, and expertise in providing consistently good customer service.
- *Valuable physical assets*—attractive real estate locations, ownership of valuable natural resource deposits, and state-of-the-art plants, equipment, and distribution facilities.
- *Valuable human assets and intellectual capital*—an experienced and capable workforce, talented employees in key areas, cutting-edge technological knowledge, collective learning embedded in the organization, or proven managerial know-how.[1]
- *Valuable organizational assets*—proven quality control systems, proprietary technology, key patents, state-of-the-art systems for doing business via the Internet, a cadre of highly trained customer service representatives, a strong network of distributors or retail dealers, sizable amounts of cash and marketable securities, and a strong balance sheet and credit rating (thus giving the company access to additional financial capital).
- *Valuable intangible assets*—a powerful or well-known brand name or strong buyer loyalty.
- *An achievement or attribute that puts the company in a position of market advantage*—low overall costs relative to competitors, market share leadership, a superior product, a wider product line than rivals, wide geographic coverage, or award-winning customer service.
- *Competitively valuable alliances or cooperative ventures*—fruitful partnerships with suppliers that reduce costs and/or enhance product quality and performance; alliances or joint ventures that provide access to valuable technologies, specialized know-how, or geographic markets.

A company's resource strengths represent its *competitive assets* and determine whether its competitive power in the marketplace will be impressively strong or disappointingly weak. A company that is well-endowed with potent resource strengths and competitive capabilities normally has considerable competitive power—especially when its management team skillfully utilizes the company's resources in ways that build sustainable competitive advantage. Companies with modest on weak competitive assets nearly always are relegated to a trailing position in the industry.[2]

Assessing a Company's Competencies and Capabilities—What Activities Does It Perform Well? One of the most important aspects of appraising a company's resource strengths has to do with its competence level in performing key pieces of its business—such as supply chain management, R&D, production, distribution, sales and marketing, and customer service. Which activities does it perform especially well? Are there any activities it performs better than rivals? A company's proficiency in conducting different facets of its operations can range from merely a competence in performing an activity to a core competence to a distinctive competence:

1. A **competence** is something an organization is good at doing. It is nearly always the product of experience, representing an accumulation of learning and the buildup of proficiency in performing an internal activity. Usually a company competence originates with deliberate efforts to develop the organizational ability to do something, however imperfectly or inefficiently. Such efforts involve selecting people with the requisite knowledge and skills, upgrading or expanding individual abilities as needed, and then molding the efforts and work products of individuals into a cooperative effort to create organizational ability. Then, as experience builds, such that the company gains proficiency in performing the activity consistently well and at an acceptable cost, the ability evolves into a true competence and company capability. Some competencies relate to specific skills and expertise (like just-in-time inventory control, low-cost manufacturing know-how, picking good locations for new stores, designing an unusually appealing and user-friendly Web site); they spring from proficiency in a single discipline or function and may be performed in a single department or organizational unit. Other competencies, however, are inherently multidisciplinary and cross-functional—they are the result of effective collaboration among people with different expertise working in different organizational units. A competence in continuous product innovation, for example, comes from teaming the efforts of people and groups with expertise in market research, new product R&D, design and engineering, cost-effective manufacturing, and market testing.

CORE CONCEPT
A ***competence*** is an activity that a company has learned to perform well.

2. A **core competence** is a proficiently performed internal activity that is *central* to a company's strategy and competitiveness. A core competence is a more valuable resource strength than a competence because of the well-performed activity's core role in the company's strategy and business. expertise in integrating multiple technologies to create families of new products, know-how in creating and operating systems for cost-efficient supply chain management, the capability to speed new or next-generation products to market, good after-sale service capabilities, skills in manufacturing a high-quality product at a low cost, or the capability to fill customer orders accurately and swiftly. A company may have more than one core competence in its

CORE CONCEPT
A ***core competence*** is a

resource portfolio, but rare is the company that can legitimately claim more than two or three core competencies. Most often, *a core competence is knowledge-based, residing in people and in a company's intellectual capital rather than in its assets on the balance sheet.* Moreover, a core competence is more likely to arise from cross-department combinations of knowledge and expertise than from a single department or work group. 3M Corporation has a core competence in product innovation—3M's record of introducing new products goes back several decades, and new product introduction is central to the company's strategy of growing its business. MySpace, a subsidiary of News Corporation, has a core competence in anticipating features that will appeal to Internet users who join social networking sites. The ability of Internet users to share information, photos, videos, Karaoke-type audio recordings, and interesting news stories with friends and others made MySpace the world's largest social networking site as of 2008, with more than 117 million unique visitors each month. Ben & Jerry's Homemade, which was acquired by Unilever in 2000, has a core competence in creating unusual flavors of ice cream and marketing them with catchy names like Chunky Monkey, Imagine Whirled Peace, Chubby Hubby, Dublin Mudslide, Pfish Food, Karamel Sutra, Turtle Soup, Vermonty Python, and Fossil Fuel.

3. A **distinctive competence** is a competitively valuable activity that a company *performs better than its rivals.* A distinctive competence thus signifies even greater proficiency than a core competence. But what is especially important about a distinctive competence is that the company enjoys *competitive superiority in performing that activity*—a distinctive competence represents a level of proficiency that rivals do not have. Because a distinctive competence represents uniquely strong capability relative to rival companies, it qualifies as a *competitively superior resource strength* with competitive advantage potential. This is particularly true when the distinctive competence enables a company to deliver standout value to customers (in the form of lower costs and prices or better product performance or superior service). Toyota has worked diligently over several decades to establish a distinctive competence in low-cost, high-quality manufacturing of motor vehicles; its "lean production" system is far superior to that of any other automaker, and the company is pushing the boundaries of its production advantage with a new type of assembly line—called the Global Body Line—that costs 50 percent less to install and can be changed to accommodate a new model for 70 percent less than its previous production system.[3] Starbucks' distinctive competence in creating innovative coffee drinks and an inviting store ambience has propelled it to the forefront among coffee retailers.

CORE CONCEPT

A *distinctive competence* is a competitively important activity that a company performs better than its rivals—it thus represents *a competitively superior resource strength*.

The conceptual differences between a competence, a core competence, and a distinctive competence draw attention to the fact that a company's resource strengths and competitive capabilities are not all equal.[4] Some competencies and competitive capabilities merely enable market survival because most rivals have them—indeed, not having a competence or capability that rivals have can result in competitive disadvantage. If an apparel company does not have the competence to produce its apparel items very cost-efficiently, it is unlikely to survive given the intense price competition in the apparel industry. Every Web retailer requires a basic competence in designing an appealing and user-friendly Web site.

Core competencies are *competitively* more important resource strengths than competencies because they add power to the company's strategy and have a bigger positive impact on its market position and profitability. Distinctive competencies are even more competitively important. A distinctive competence is a competitively potent resource strength for three reasons: (1) it gives a company competitively valuable capability that is unmatched by rivals, (2) it has potential for being the cornerstone of the company's strategy, and (3) it can produce a competitive edge in the marketplace since it represents a level of proficiency that is superior to rivals. It is always easier for a company to build competitive advantage when it has a distinctive competence in performing an activity important to market success, when rival companies do not have offsetting competencies, and when it is costly and time-consuming for rivals to imitate the competence. A distinctive competence is thus potentially the mainspring of a company's success—unless it is trumped by more powerful resources of rivals.

CORE CONCEPT

A distinctive competence is a competitively potent resource strength for three reasons: (1) it gives a company competitively valuable capability that is unmatched by rivals, (2) it can underpin and add real punch to a company's strategy, and (3) it is a basis for sustainable competitive advantage.

What Is the Competitive Power of a Resource Strength? Most telling about a company's resource strengths is how powerful they are in the marketplace. The competitive power of a resource strength is measured by how many of the following four tests it can pass:[5]

1. *Is the resource really competitively valuable?* All companies possess a collection of resources and competencies—some have the potential to contribute to a competitive advantage, while others may not. Apple's Mac OS X operating system is by most accounts a world beater (compared to Windows Vista), but Apple has struggled to convert its resource strength in operating system design into competitive success in the global PC market.
2. *Is the resource strength rare—is it something rivals lack?* Companies have to guard against pridefully believing that their core competencies are distinctive competencies or that their brand name is more powerful than the brand names of rivals. Who can really say whether Coca-Cola's consumer marketing prowess is better than PepsiCo's or whether the Mercedes-Benz brand name is more powerful than that of BMW or Lexus? Although many retailers claim to be quite proficient in product selection and in-store merchandising, a number run into trouble in the marketplace because they encounter rivals whose competencies in product selection and in-store merchandising are equal to or better than theirs.
3. *Is the resource strength hard to copy?* The more difficult and more expensive it is to imitate a company's resource strength, the greater its potential competitive value. Resources tend to be difficult to copy when they are unique (a fantastic real estate location, patent protection); when they must be built over time (a brand name, a strategy-supportive organizational culture); and when they carry big capital requirements (a cost-effective plant to manufacture cutting-edge microprocessors). Wal-Mart's competitors have failed miserably in their attempts over the past two decades to match its state-of-the-art distribution capabilities.
4. *Can the resource strength be trumped by substitute resource strengths and competi-*

advantage in production activities may find their technology-based advantage nullified by rivals' use of low-wage offshore manufacturing. Resources can contribute to a competitive advantage only when resource substitutes don't exist.

In-depth understanding of the competitive power of company resource strengths enables managers to consider the merits of boosting existing strengths and/or striving to develop altogether new competencies and capabilities that could prove competitively valuable.

CORE CONCEPT
Companies that lack a standalone resource strength that is competitively powerful may nonetheless be able to bundle several resource strengths into a competitively valuable core competence.

In addition, management may determine that it doesn't possess a resource that independently passes all four tests listed above with high marks, but does have a *bundle of resources* that can be leveraged to develop a core competence. Although Callaway Golf Company's engineering capabilities and market research capabilities are matched relatively well by rivals Cobra Golf and Ping Golf, it has bundled good product development resources, technological know-how, and understanding of golfers and the golfing marketplace to remain the largest seller of golf equipment for more than a decade. Callaway's unique bundle of resource strengths qualifies as a distinctive competence and is the basis of the company's competitive advantage.

CORE CONCEPT
A *resource-based strategy* uses a company's valuable and rare resource strengths and competitive capabilities to deliver value to customers in ways that rivals find it difficult to match.

Competitively Valuable Resource Strengths and Competencies Call for the Use of a Resource-Based Strategy Companies that possess competitively valuable resource strengths and competencies typically deploy these resources and capabilities in a manner that boosts the competitive power of their overall strategy and bolsters their position in the marketplace. **Resource-based strategies** attempt to exploit company resources in a manner that offers value to customers in ways rivals are unable to match. Indeed, the whole point of a resource-based strategy is to deliberately develop and deploy competencies and capabilities that add to a company's competitive power in the marketplace and make its overall strategy more potent in battling rivals. For example, a company pursuing a broad low-cost strategy might invest in superefficient distribution centers that give it the capability to distribute its products at a lower cost than rivals. Wal-Mart's distribution efficiency is one factor in its being able to underprice rivals. Over a period of more than a decade, Dell has put considerable time and money into cultivating relationships with its key suppliers that give it exceptionally low inventory carrying costs (as well as access to low-cost, quality components for its PC models). Many Dell plants operate with only several hours' inventory of certain parts and components because the suppliers have online access to Dell's daily production schedule and make frequent deliveries (sometimes every two hours) of the precise components that particular work stations on the floor of Dell's assembly plants need to build each PC to a customer's specifications. Resource strengths and competitive capabilities can also facilitate differentiation in the marketplace. Because Fox News and CNN can devote more air time to breaking news stories and get reporters on the scene quicker than ABC, NBC, and CBS can, many viewers turn to the cable networks when a major news event occurs.

CORE CONCEPT
Rather than try to play catch-up and match the resource strengths possessed by a rival company, a company's managers may deliberately cultivate the development of entirely different resources and competencies that effectively substitute for the strengths of the rival.

Resource-based strategies can also be directed at eroding or at least neutralizing the competitive potency of a particular rival's resource strengths by identifying and developing substitute resources that accomplish the purpose. For example, Amazon.com lacks a big network of retail stores to compete with those operated by rival Barnes & Noble, but Amazon's much larger book inventory (as compared to any retail store), coupled with its vast selection of other products and short delivery times, is more attractive to many busy consumers than visiting a big-box bookstore. In other words, Amazon has carefully and consciously developed competitively valuable online resource capabilities that have proved to be effective substitutes for competing head-to-head against Barnes & Noble's retail stores and those of other brick-and-mortar retailers without having to invest in hundreds of brick-and-mortar retail stores of its own. Whereas many cosmetics companies sell their products through department stores and specialty retailers, Avon and Mary

Kay Cosmetics have substituted for the lack of a retail dealer network by assembling a direct sales force numbering in the hundreds of thousands—their sales associates can personally demonstrate products to interested buyers in their homes or at parties, take orders on the spot, and deliver the items to buyers' homes.[6]

Identifying Company Resource Weaknesses, Missing Capabilities, and Competitive Deficiencies

A *resource weakness,* or *competitive deficiency,* is something a company lacks or does poorly (in comparison to others) or a condition that puts it at a disadvantage in the marketplace. A company's resource weaknesses can relate to (1) inferior or unproven skills, expertise, or intellectual capital in competitively important areas of the business; (2) deficiencies in competitively important physical, organizational, or intangible assets; or (3) missing or competitively inferior capabilities in key areas. *Internal weaknesses are thus shortcomings in a company's complement of resources and represent competitive liabilities.* Nearly all companies have competitive liabilities of one kind or another. Whether a company's resource weaknesses make it competitively vulnerable depends on how much they matter in the marketplace and whether they are offset by resource strengths that substitute for missing capabilities.

Table 4.2 lists the kinds of factors to consider in compiling a company's resource strengths and weaknesses. Sizing up a company's complement of resource capabilities and deficiencies is akin to constructing a *strategic balance sheet,* where resource strengths represent *competitive assets* and resource weaknesses represent *competitive liabilities.* Obviously, the ideal condition is for the company's competitive assets to outweigh its competitive liabilities by an ample margin—a 50–50 balance is definitely not the desired condition!

CORE CONCEPT

A company's resource strengths represent competitive assets; its resource weaknesses represent competitive liabilities.

Identifying a Company's External Market Opportunities

Market opportunity is a big factor in shaping a company's strategy. Indeed, managers can't properly tailor strategy to the company's situation without first identifying its market opportunities and appraising the growth and profit potential each one holds. (See Table 4.2, under "Potential Market Opportunities.") Depending on the prevailing circumstances, a company's opportunities can be plentiful or scarce, fleeting or lasting, and can range from wildly attractive (an absolute must to pursue) to marginally interesting (because the growth and profit potential are questionable) to unsuitable (because there's not a good match with the company's resource strengths and capabilities).

While stunningly big opportunities sometimes appear fairly frequently in volatile, fast-changing markets (typically due to important technological developments or rapidly shifting consumer preferences), they are nonetheless hard to see in advance. [illegible] ... of the future, identify one or more upcoming opportunities, and get a jump on rivals in pursuing it.[7] In mature markets, unusually attractive market opportunities emerge sporadically, often after long periods of relative calm. But future market conditions here may be less foggy, thus facilitating good market reconnaissance and making emerging opportunities easier for industry members to detect. But in both volatile and stable markets, the rise of a

Table 4.2 What to Look for in Identifying a Company's Strengths, Weaknesses, Opportunities, and Threats

Potential Resource Strengths and Competitive Capabilities	Potential Resource Weaknesses and Competitive Deficiencies
• A powerful strategy • Core competencies in ________ • A distinctive competence in ________ • A product that is strongly differentiated from those of rivals • Competencies and capabilities that are well matched to industry key success factors • A strong financial condition; ample financial resources to grow the business • Strong brand-name image/company reputation • An attractive customer base • Economy of scale or learning/experience curve advantages over rivals • Proprietary technology/superior technological skills/ important patents • Superior intellectual capital relative to key rivals • Cost advantages over rivals • Strong advertising and promotion • Product innovation capabilities • Proven capabilities in improving production processes • Good supply chain management capabilities • Good customer service capabilities • Better product quality relative to rivals • Wide geographic coverage and/or strong global distribution capability • Alliances/joint ventures with other firms that provide access to valuable technology, competencies, and/or attractive geographic markets	• No clear strategic direction • Resources that are not well matched to industry key success factors • No well-developed or proven core competencies • A weak balance sheet, burdened with too much debt • Higher overall unit costs relative to key competitors • Weak or unproven product innovation capabilities • A product/service with ho-hum attributes or features inferior to those of rivals • Too narrow a product line relative to rivals • Weak brand image or reputation • Weak dealer networks; lack of adequate global distribution capability • Behind on product quality, R&D, and/or technological know-how • In the wrong strategic group • Losing market share because . . . • Lack of management depth • Inferior intellectual capital relative to leading rivals • Subpar profitability because . . . • Plagued with internal operating problems or obsolete facilities • Behind rivals in e-commerce capabilities • Short on financial resources to grow the business and pursue promising initiatives • Too much underutilized plant capacity
Potential Market Opportunities	**Potential External Threats to a Company's Prospects**
• Openings to win market share from rivals • Sharply rising buyer demand for the industry's product • Serving additional customer groups or market segments • Expanding into new geographic markets • Expanding the company's product line to meet a broader range of customer needs • Utilizing existing company skills or technological know-how to enter new product lines or new businesses • Online sales • Integrating forward or backward • Falling trade barriers in attractive foreign markets • Acquiring rival firms or companies with attractive technological expertise or capabilities • Entering into alliances or joint ventures to expand the firm's market coverage or boost its competitive capability • Openings to exploit emerging new technologies	• Increasing intensity of competition among industry rivals—may squeeze profit margins • Slowdowns in market growth • Likely entry of potent new competitors • Loss of sales to substitute products • Growing bargaining power of customers or suppliers • A shift in buyer needs and tastes away from the industry's product • Adverse demographic changes that threaten to curtail demand for the industry's product • Vulnerability to unfavorable industry driving forces • Restrictive trade policies on the part of foreign governments • Costly new regulatory requirements

golden opportunity is almost never under the control of a single company or manufactured by company executives—rather, it springs from the simultaneous alignment of several external factors. For instance, in China the recent upsurge in demand for motor vehicles was spawned by a convergence of many factors—increased disposable income, rising middle-class aspirations, a major government road-building program, the demise of employer-provided housing, and easy credit.[8] But golden opportunities are nearly always seized rapidly—and the companies that seize them are usually those that have been staying alert with diligent market reconnaissance and preparing themselves to capitalize on shifting market conditions by patiently assembling an arsenal of competitively valuable resources. New market opportunities are most easily seized by companies possessing talented personnel, technical know-how, valuable strategic partnerships, and a war chest of cash to finance aggressive action when the time comes.[9]

In evaluating a company's market opportunities and ranking their attractiveness, managers have to guard against viewing every *industry* opportunity as a *company* opportunity. Not every company is equipped with the resources to successfully pursue each opportunity that exists in its industry. Some companies are more capable of going after particular opportunities than others, and a few companies may be hopelessly outclassed. *The market opportunities most relevant to a company are those that match up well with the company's financial and organizational resource capabilities, offer the best growth and profitability, and present the most potential for competitive advantage.*

A company is well advised to pass on a particular industry opportunity unless the company has or can acquire the resources to capture it.

Identifying the External Threats to Profitability

Often, certain factors in a company's external environment pose *threats* to its profitability, competitive well-being, and growth prospects. Threats can stem from the emergence of cheaper or better technologies, rivals' introduction of new or improved products, the entry of lower-cost foreign competitors into a company's market stronghold, new regulations that are more burdensome to a company than to its competitors, vulnerability to a rise in interest rates, the potential of a hostile takeover, unfavorable demographic shifts, adverse changes in foreign exchange rates, political upheaval in a foreign country where the company has facilities, and the like. (See Table 4.2, under "Potential External Threats to a Company's Prospects.")

External threats may pose no more than a moderate degree of adversity (all companies confront some threatening elements in the course of doing business), or they may be so imposing as to make a company's situation and outlook quite tenuous. On rare occasions, market shocks can give birth to a *sudden-death* threat that throws a company into a battle to survive. Many of the world's major airlines have been plunged into unprecedented financial crisis because of a combination of factors: rising prices for jet fuel; slower-than-expected growth in passenger traffic (which resulted in having too many empty seats on too many flights); mounting competition from low-fare carriers; shifting traveler preferences for low fares

... their impact.

What Can Be Learned from a SWOT Analysis?

SWOT analysis involves more than making four lists. The two most important parts of SWOT analysis are *drawing conclusions* from the SWOT listings about the company's

Simply making lists of a company's strengths, weaknesses, opportunities, and threats is not enough; the payoff from SWOT analysis comes from the conclusions about a company's situation and the implications for strategy improvement that flow from the four lists.

overall situation, and *translating these conclusions into strategic actions* to better match the company's strategy to its resource strengths and market opportunities, to correct the important weaknesses, and to defend against external threats. Figure 4.2 shows the three steps of SWOT analysis.

Just what story the SWOT listings tell about the company's overall situation is often revealed in the answers to the following sets of questions:

- Does the company have an attractive set of resource strengths? Does it have any strong core competencies or a distinctive competence? Are the company's strengths and capabilities well matched to the industry key success factors? Do they add adequate power to the company's strategy, or are more or different strengths needed? Will the company's current strengths and capabilities matter in the future?
- How serious are the company's weaknesses and competitive deficiencies? Are they mostly inconsequential and readily correctable, or could one or more prove fatal if not remedied soon? Are some of the company's weaknesses in areas that relate to the industry's key success factors? Are there any weaknesses that, if uncorrected,

Figure 4.2 The Three Steps of SWOT Analysis: Identify, Draw Conclusions, Translate into Strategic Action

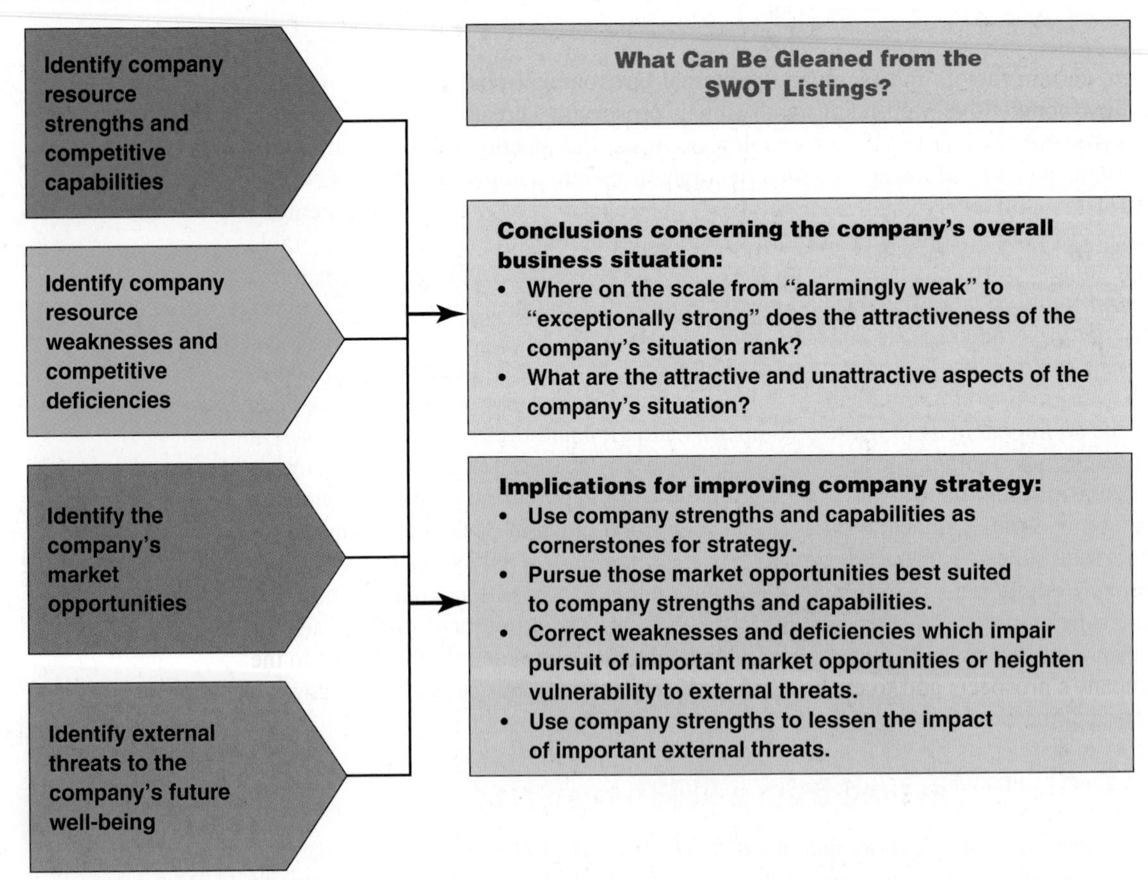

would keep the company from pursuing an otherwise attractive opportunity? Does the company have important resource gaps that need to be filled for it to move up in the industry rankings and/or boost its profitability?

- Do the company's resource strengths and competitive capabilities (its competitive assets) outweigh its resource weaknesses and competitive deficiencies (its competitive liabilities) by an attractive margin?
- Does the company have attractive market opportunities that are well suited to its resource strengths and competitive capabilities? Does the company lack the resources and capabilities to pursue any of the most attractive opportunities?
- Are the threats alarming, or are they something the company appears able to deal with and defend against?
- All things considered, how strong is the company's overall situation? Where on a scale of 1 to 10 (where 1 is alarmingly weak and 10 is exceptionally strong) should the firm's position and overall situation be ranked? What aspects of the company's situation are particularly attractive? What aspects are of the most concern?

The final piece of SWOT analysis is to translate the diagnosis of the company's situation into actions for improving the company's strategy and business prospects. The following questions point to implications the SWOT listings have for strategic action:

- Which competitive capabilities need to be strengthened immediately (so as to add greater power to the company's strategy and boost sales and profitability)? Do new types of competitive capabilities need to be put in place to help the company better respond to emerging industry and competitive conditions? Which resources and capabilities need to be given greater emphasis, and which merit less emphasis? Should the company emphasize leveraging its existing resource strengths and capabilities, or does it need to create new resource strengths and capabilities?
- What actions should be taken to reduce the company's competitive liabilities? Which weaknesses or competitive deficiencies are in urgent need of correction?
- Which market opportunities should be top priority in future strategic initiatives (because they are good fits with the company's resource strengths and competitive capabilities, present attractive growth and profit prospects, and/or offer the best potential for securing competitive advantage)? Which opportunities should be ignored, at least for the time being (because they offer less growth potential or are not suited to the company's resources and capabilities)?
- What should the company be doing to guard against the threats to its well-being?

A company's resource strengths should generally form the cornerstones of strategy because they represent the company's best chance for market success.[10] As a rule, strategies that place heavy demands on areas where the company is weakest or has unproven ability are suspect and should be avoided. If a company doesn't have the resources and competitive capabilities around which to craft an [illegible]

[illegible] with firms possessing the needed expertise. Plainly, managers have to look toward correcting competitive weaknesses that make the company vulnerable, hold down profitability, or disqualify it from pursuing an attractive opportunity.

At the same time, sound strategy making requires sifting through the available market opportunities and aiming strategy at capturing those that are most attractive and suited to the company's circumstances. Rarely does a company have the resource depth to pursue all available market opportunities simultaneously without spreading itself too thin. How much attention to devote to defending against external threats to the company's market position and future performance hinges on how vulnerable the company is, whether there are attractive defensive moves that can be taken to lessen their impact, and whether the costs of undertaking such moves represent the best use of company resources.

QUESTION 3: ARE THE COMPANY'S PRICES AND COSTS COMPETITIVE?

The higher a company's costs are above those of close rivals, the more competitively vulnerable it becomes.

Company managers are often stunned when a competitor cuts its price to "unbelievably low" levels or when a new market entrant comes on strong with a very low price. The competitor may not, however, be *dumping* (an economic term for selling below cost), buying its way into the market with a superlow price, or waging a desperate move to gain sales—it may simply have substantially lower costs. One of the most telling signs of whether a company's business position is strong or precarious is whether its prices and costs are competitive with industry rivals. For a company to compete successfully, its costs must be *in line* with those of close rivals.

Price–cost comparisons are especially critical in a commodity-product industry where the value provided to buyers is the same from seller to seller, price competition is typically the ruling market force, and lower-cost companies have the upper hand. But even in industries where products are differentiated and competition centers on the different attributes of competing brands as much as on price, rival companies have to keep their costs *in line* and make sure that any added costs they incur—and any price premiums they charge—create ample value that buyers are willing to pay extra for. While some cost disparity is justified so long as the products or services of closely competing companies are sufficiently differentiated, a high-cost firm's market position becomes increasingly vulnerable the more its costs exceed those of close rivals.

Two analytical tools are particularly useful in determining whether a company's prices and costs are competitive: value chain analysis and benchmarking.

The Concept of a Company Value Chain

CORE CONCEPT

A company's *value chain* identifies the primary activities that create customer value and the related support activities.

Every company's business consists of a collection of activities undertaken in the course of designing, producing, marketing, delivering, and supporting its product or service. All of the various activities that a company performs internally combine to form a **value chain**—so called because the underlying intent of a company's activities is to do things that ultimately *create value for buyers.* A company's value chain also includes an allowance for profit because a markup over the cost of performing the firm's value-creating activities is customarily part of the price (or total cost) borne by buyers—unless an enterprise succeeds in creating and delivering sufficient value to buyers to produce an attractive profit, it can't survive for long.

As shown in Figure 4.3 (on page 118), a company's value chain consists of two broad categories of activities: (1) the *primary activities* that are foremost in creating value for customers, (2) and the requisite *support activities* that facilitate and enhance the performance of the primary activities.[11] For example, the primary value-creating activities for a maker of bakery goods include supply chain management, recipe development and testing, mixing and baking, packaging, sales and marketing, and distribution; related support activities include quality control, human resource management, and administration. A wholesaler's primary activities and costs deal with merchandise selection and purchasing, inbound shipping and warehousing from suppliers, and outbound distribution to retail customers. The primary activities for a department store retailer include merchandise selection and buying, store layout and product display, advertising, and customer service; its support activities include site selection, hiring and training, and store maintenance, plus the usual assortment of administrative activities. A hotel chain's primary activities and costs are in site selection and construction, reservations, operation of its hotel properties (check-in and check-out, maintenance and housekeeping, dining and room service, and conventions and meetings), and managing its lineup of hotel locations; principal support activities include accounting, hiring and training hotel staff, advertising, building a brand and reputation, and general administration. Supply chain management is a crucial activity for Nissan, L. L. Bean, and PetSmart but is not a value chain component at Google or Bank of America. Sales and marketing are dominant activities at Procter & Gamble and Sony but have minor roles at oil drilling companies and natural gas pipeline companies. Thus, what constitutes primary and secondary activities varies according to the specific nature of a company's business, meaning that you should view the listing of the primary and support activities in Figure 4.3 as illustrative rather than definitive.

A Company's Primary and Secondary Activities Identify the Major Components of Its Cost Structure Segregating a company's operations into different types of primary and secondary activities is the first step in understanding its cost structure. Each activity in the value chain gives rise to costs and ties up assets. Assigning the company's operating costs and assets to each individual activity in the chain provides cost estimates and capital requirements—a process that accountants call *activity-based cost accounting.* Quite often, there are links between activities such that the manner in which one activity is done can affect the costs of performing other activities. For instance, how a product is designed has a huge impact on the number of different parts and components, their respective manufacturing costs, and the expense of assembly.

The combined costs of all the various activities in a company's value chain define the company's internal cost structure. Further, the cost of each activity contributes to whether the company's overall cost position relative to rivals is favorable or unfavorable. The tasks of value chain analysis and benchmarking are to develop the data for comparing a company's costs activity-by-activity against the costs of key rivals and to learn which internal activities are a source of cost advantage or disadvantage. A company's relative cost position is a function of how the overall costs of the activities it performs in conducting business compare to the overall costs of the activities performed by rivals.

chain reflects the evolution of its own particular business and internal operations, the technology and operating practices it employs, its strategy, the approaches it is using to execute its strategy, and the underlying economics of the activities themselves.[12] Because these factors differ from company to company (even among companies in the same industry), the value chains of rival companies sometimes differ substantially—a condition that complicates the task of assessing rivals'

Figure 4.3 A Representative Company Value Chain

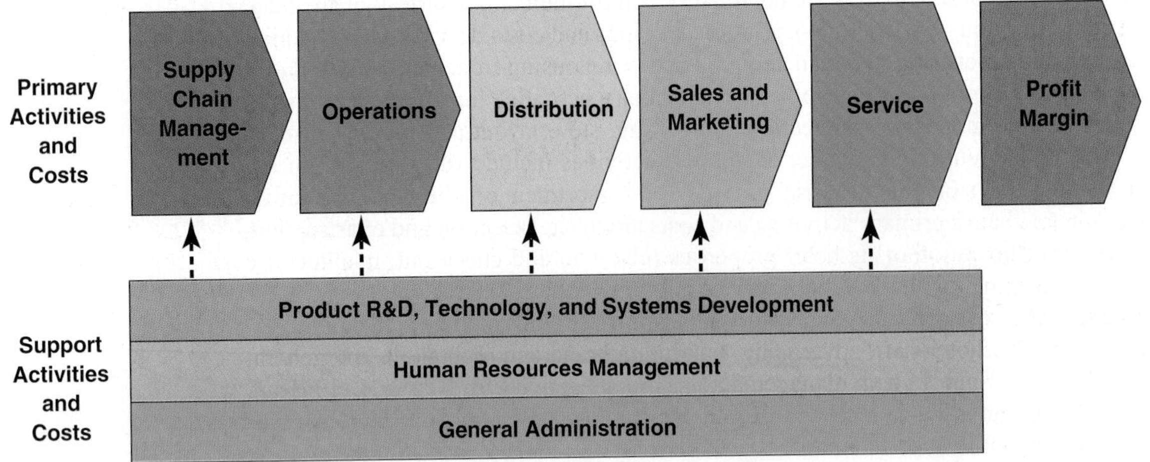

PRIMARY ACTIVITIES

- **Supply Chain Management—Activities, costs, and assets associated with purchasing fuel, energy, raw materials, parts and components, merchandise, and consumable items from vendors; receiving, storing, and disseminating inputs from suppliers; inspection; and inventory management.**
- **Operations—Activities, costs, and assets associated with converting inputs into final product form (production, assembly, packaging, equipment maintenance, facilities, operations, quality assurance, environmental protection).**
- **Distribution—Activities, costs, and assets dealing with physically distributing the product to buyers (finished goods warehousing, order processing, order picking and packing, shipping, delivery vehicle operations, establishing and maintaining a network of dealers and distributors).**
- **Sales and Marketing—Activities, costs, and assets related to sales force efforts, advertising and promotion, market research and planning, and dealer/distributor support.**
- **Service—Activities, costs, and assets associated with providing assistance to buyers, such as installation, spare parts delivery, maintenance and repair, technical assistance, buyer inquiries, and complaints.**

SUPPORT ACTIVITIES

- **Product R&D, Technology, and Systems Development—Activities, costs, and assets relating to product R&D, process R&D, process design improvement, equipment design, computer software development, telecommunications systems, computer-assisted design and engineering, database capabilities, and development of computerized support systems.**
- **Human Resources Management—Activities, costs, and assets associated with the recruitment, hiring, training, development, and compensation of all types of personnel; labor relations activities; and development of knowledge-based skills and core competencies.**
- **General Administration—Activities, costs, and assets relating to general management, accounting and finance, legal and regulatory affairs, safety and security, management information systems, forming strategic alliances and collaborating with strategic partners, and other "overhead" functions.**

Source: Based on the discussion in Michael E. Porter, *Competitive Advantage* (New York: Free Press, 1985), pp. 37–43.

relative cost positions. For instance, music retailers like Blockbuster and F.Y.E., which purchase CDs from recording studios and wholesale distributors and sell them in their own retail store locations, have different value chains and different cost structures than rival online music stores like Apple's iTunes Store and Yahoo! Music, which sell downloadable files directly to music shoppers. Competing companies may differ in their degrees of vertical integration.

The operations component of the value chain for a manufacturer that *makes* all of its own parts and components and assembles them into a finished product differs from the operations of a rival producer that *buys* the needed parts and components from outside suppliers and only performs assembly operations. Likewise, there is legitimate reason to expect value chain and cost differences between a company that is pursuing a low-cost/low-price strategy and a rival that is positioned on the high end of the market. The costs of certain activities along the low-cost company's value chain should indeed be relatively low, whereas the high-end firm may understandably be spending relatively more to perform those activities that create the added quality and extra features of its products.

Moreover, cost and price differences among rival companies can have their origins in activities performed by suppliers or by distribution channel allies involved in getting the product to end users. Suppliers or wholesale/retail dealers may have excessively high cost structures or profit margins that jeopardize a company's cost-competitiveness even though its costs for internally performed activities are competitive. For example, when determining Michelin's cost-competitiveness vis-à-vis Goodyear and Bridgestone in supplying replacement tires to vehicle owners, we have to look at more than whether Michelin's tire manufacturing costs are above or below Goodyear's and Bridgestone's. Let's say that a motor vehicle owner looking for a new set of tires has to pay $400 for a set of Michelin tires and only $350 for a set of Goodyear or Bridgestone tires. The $50 difference can stem not only from Michelin's higher manufacturing costs (reflecting, perhaps, the added costs of Michelin's strategic efforts to build a better-quality tire with more performance features) but also from (1) differences in what the three tire makers pay their suppliers for materials and tire-making components, and (2) differences in the operating efficiencies, costs, and markups of Michelin's wholesale–retail dealer outlets versus those of Goodyear and Bridgestone.

The Value Chain System for an Entire Industry

As the tire industry example makes clear, a company's value chain is embedded in a larger system of activities that includes the value chains of its suppliers and the value chains of whatever distribution channel allies it uses in getting its product or service to end users.[13] Suppliers' value chains are relevant because suppliers perform activities and incur costs in creating and delivering the purchased inputs used in a company's own value-creating activities. The costs, performance features, and quality of these inputs influence a company's own costs and product differentiation capabilities. Anything a company can do to help its suppliers drive down the

in managing supply chain activities.[14]

performed activities (its own value chain) but also on costs in the value chains of its suppliers and forward channel allies.

The value chains of forward channel partners and/or the customers to whom a company sells are relevant because (1) the costs and margins of a company's distributors and retail dealers are part of the price the ultimate consumer pays, and (2) the activities that distribution allies perform affect customer satisfaction. For these reasons, companies normally work closely with their forward channel allies (who are their direct customers) to perform value chain activities in mutually beneficial ways. For instance, motor vehicle manufacturers work closely with their local automobile dealers to keep the retail prices of their vehicles competitive with rivals' models and to ensure that owners are satisfied with dealers' repair and maintenance services. Some aluminum can producers have constructed plants next to beer breweries and deliver cans on overhead conveyors directly to the breweries' can-filling lines; this has resulted in significant savings in production scheduling, shipping, and inventory costs for both container producers and breweries.[15] Many automotive parts suppliers have built plants near the auto assembly plants they supply to facilitate just-in-time deliveries, reduce warehousing and shipping costs, and promote close collaboration on parts design and production scheduling. Irrigation equipment companies; suppliers of grape-harvesting and winemaking equipment; and firms making barrels, wine bottles, caps, corks, and labels all have facilities in the California wine country to be close to the nearly 700 winemakers they supply.[16] The lesson here is that a company's value chain activities are often closely linked to the value chains of their suppliers and the forward allies or customers to whom they sell.

As a consequence, *accurately assessing a company's competitiveness from the perspective of the consumers who ultimately use its products or services thus requires that company managers understand an industry's entire value chain system for delivering a product or service to customers, not just the company's own value chain.* A typical industry value chain that incorporates the value chains of suppliers and forward channel allies (if any) is shown in Figure 4.4. However, industry value chains vary significantly by industry. The primary value chain activities in the pulp and paper industry (timber farming, logging, pulp mills, and papermaking) differ from the primary value chain activities in the home appliance industry (parts and components manufacture, assembly, wholesale distribution, retail sales). The value chain for the soft drink industry (processing of basic ingredients and syrup manufacture, bottling and can filling, wholesale distribution, advertising, and retail merchandising) differs from that for the computer software industry (programming, disk loading, marketing, distribution). Producers of bathroom and kitchen faucets depend heavily on the activities of wholesale distributors and building supply retailers in winning sales to

Figure 4.4 Representative Value Chain for an Entire Industry

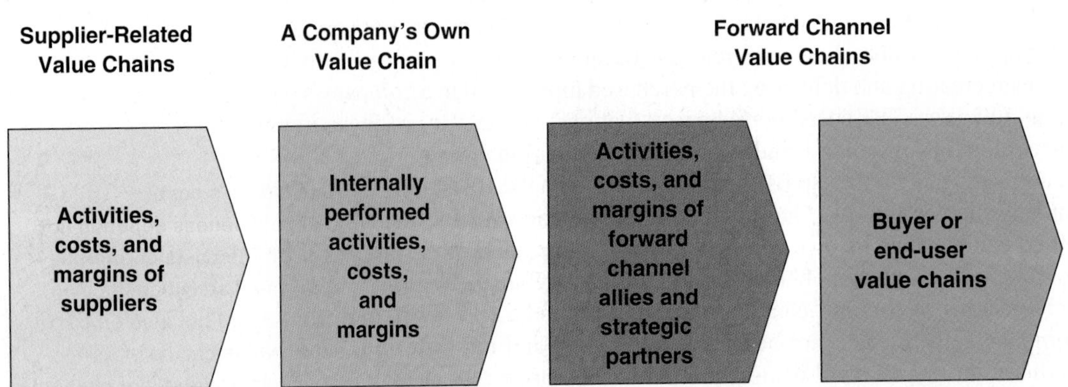

Source: Based in part on the single-industry value chain displayed in Michael E. Porter, *Competitive Advantage* (New York: Free Press, 1985), p. 35.

ILLUSTRATION CAPSULE 4.1
Estimated Value Chain Costs for Recording and Distributing Music CDs through Traditional Music Retailers

The following table presents the representative costs and markups associated with producing and distributing a music CD retailing for $15 in brick-and-mortar music stores.

Value Chain Activities and Costs in Producing and Distributing a CD		
1. Record company direct production costs:		$2.40
Artists and repertoire	$0.75	
Pressing of CD and packaging	1.65	
2. Royalties		.99
3. Record company marketing expenses		1.50
4. Record company overhead		1.50
5. Total record company costs		6.39
6. Record company's operating profit		1.86
7. Record company's selling price to distributor/wholesaler		8.25
8. Average wholesale distributor markup to cover distribution activities and profit margins		1.50
9. Average wholesale price charged to retailer		9.75
10. Average retail markup over wholesale cost		5.25
11. Average price to consumer at retail		$15.00

Source: Developed by the authors from information in "Fight the Power," a case study prepared by Adrian Aleyne, Babson College, 1999 and other sources.

homebuilders and do-it-yourselfers but producers of papermaking machines internalize their distribution activities by selling directly to the operators of paper plants. Illustration Capsule 4.1 shows representative costs for various activities performed by the producers and marketers of music CDs.

Activity-Based Cost Accounting: A Tool for Determining the Costs of Value Chain Activities

Once the major value chain activities are identified, the next step in evaluating a company's cost-competitiveness involves using the company's cost accounting system to determine the costs of performing specific value chain activities using what accountants call [illegible], interest, general administration, and so on. But activity-based cost accounting involves establishing expense categories for specific value chain activities and assigning costs to the activity responsible for creating the cost. An illustrative example is shown in Table 4.3. Perhaps 25 percent of the companies that have explored the feasibility of activity-based costing have adopted this accounting approach.

Table 4.3 **The Difference between Traditional Cost Accounting and Activity-Based Cost Accounting: An Example from Air Conditioner Manufacturing**

Traditional Cost Accounting Categories for Air Conditioner Manufacturing		Cost of Performing Specific Air Conditioner Manufacturing Activities Using Activity-Based Cost Accounting	
Wages and benefits	$2,786,900	Operating production machinery	$ 435,400
Computers and software	731,405	Maintaining product and customer data	132,500
Product transportation	319,800	Moving parts from warehouse to assembly area	1,500,400
Energy	170,600	Production-run setup for seven model types	723,300
Facility and vehicle rent	165,870	Production scheduling for seven model types	24,800
Business and training travel	66,000	Receiving and handling raw materials	877,100
Miscellaneous	65,480	Shipping finished goods to customers	561,000
Depreciation	48,200	Customer service (communications with customers concerning design changes and production status)	144,220
Advertising	40,000	Total costs	$4,398,720
Office and utilities	4,465		
Total costs	$4,398,720		

Source: Developed from information in Heather Nachtmann and Mohammad Hani Al-Rifai, "An Application of Activity Based Costing in the Air Conditioner Manufacturing Industry," *Engineering Economics* 40 (2004), pp. 221–36.

The degree to which a company's costs should be disaggregated into specific activities depends on how valuable it is to develop cross-company cost comparisons for narrowly defined activities as opposed to broadly defined activities. Generally speaking, cost estimates are needed at least for each broad category of primary and secondary activities, but finer classifications may be needed if a company discovers that it has a cost disadvantage vis-à-vis rivals and wants to pin down the exact source or activity causing the cost disadvantage. It can also be necessary to develop cost estimates for activities performed in the competitively relevant portions of suppliers' and customers' value chains—which requires going to outside sources for reliable cost information.

Once a company has developed good cost estimates for each of the major activities in its value chain and perhaps has cost estimates for subactivities within each primary/secondary value chain activity, then it is ready to see how its costs for these activities compare with the costs of rival firms. This is where benchmarking comes in.

Benchmarking: A Tool for Assessing Whether a Company's Value Chain Activities Are Competitive

CORE CONCEPT

Benchmarking **is a potent tool for learning which companies are best at performing particular activities and then using their techniques (or best practices) to improve the cost and effectiveness of a company's own internal activities.**

Many companies today are **benchmarking** their costs of performing a given activity against competitors' costs (and/or against the costs of a noncompetitor that efficiently and effectively performs much the same activity in another industry). *Benchmarking is a tool that allows a company to determine whether the manner in which it performs particular functions and activities represents industry "best practices" when both cost and effectiveness are taken into account.*

Benchmarking entails comparing how different companies perform various value chain activities—how materials are purchased, how suppliers are paid, how inventories are managed, how products are assembled, how fast the company can get new products to market, how the quality control function is performed, how customer orders are filled and shipped, how employees are trained, how payrolls are processed, and how maintenance is performed—and then making cross-company comparisons of the costs of these activities.[18] The objectives of benchmarking are to identify the best practices in performing an activity, to learn how other companies have actually achieved lower costs or better results in performing benchmarked activities, and to take action to improve a company's competitiveness whenever benchmarking reveals that its costs and results of performing an activity are not on a par with what other companies (either competitors or noncompetitors) have achieved.

Xerox became one of the first companies to use benchmarking when, in 1979, Japanese manufacturers began selling midsize copiers in the United States for $9,600 each—less than Xerox's production costs.[19] Xerox management suspected its Japanese competitors were dumping, but it sent a team of line managers to Japan, including the head of manufacturing, to study competitors' business processes and costs. With the aid of Xerox's joint venture partner in Japan, Fuji-Xerox, who knew the competitors well, the team found that Xerox's costs were excessive due to gross inefficiencies in the company's manufacturing processes and business practices. The findings triggered a major internal effort at Xerox to become cost-competitive and prompted Xerox to begin benchmarking 67 of its key work processes against companies identified as employing the best practices. Xerox quickly decided not to restrict its benchmarking efforts to its office equipment rivals but to extend them to any company regarded as "world class" in performing *any activity* relevant to Xerox's business. Other companies quickly picked up on Xerox's approach. Toyota managers got their idea for just-in-time inventory deliveries by studying how U.S. supermarkets replenished their shelves. Southwest Airlines reduced the turnaround time of its aircraft at each scheduled stop by studying pit crews on the auto racing circuit. Over 80 percent of Fortune 500 companies reportedly use benchmarking for comparing themselves against rivals on cost and other competitively important measures.

Benchmarking the costs of company activities against rivals provides hard evidence of whether a company is cost-competitive.

The tough part of benchmarking is not whether to do it, but rather how to gain access to information about other companies' practices and costs. Sometimes benchmarking can be accomplished by collecting information from published reports, trade groups, and industry research firms and by talking to knowledgeable industry analysts, customers, and suppliers. Sometimes field trips to the facilities of competing or noncompeting companies can be arranged to observe how things are done, compare practices and processes, and perhaps exchange data on productivity and other cost components. However, such companies, even if they agree to host facilities tours and answer questions, are unlikely to share competitively sensitive cost information. Furthermore, comparing one company's costs to another's costs may not involve comparing apples to apples if the two companies employ different cost accounting principles to calculate the costs of particular activities.

However, a third and fairly [illegible]

[illegible] Kearney, The Benchmarking Exchange, Towers Perrin, and Best Practices, LLC) and several councils and associations (e.g., APQC, the Qualserve Benchmarking Clearinghouse, and the Strategic Planning Institute's Council on Benchmarking) to gather benchmarking data, distribute information about best practices, and provide comparative cost data without identifying the names of particular companies. Independent reporting that disguises the names of individual companies protects competitively sensitive data

ILLUSTRATION CAPSULE 4.2
Benchmarking and Ethical Conduct

Because discussions between benchmarking partners can involve competitively sensitive data, conceivably raising questions about possible restraint of trade or improper business conduct, many benchmarking organizations urge all individuals and organizations involved in benchmarking to abide by a code of conduct grounded in ethical business behavior. One of the most widely used codes of conduct is the one developed by APQC (formerly the American Productivity and Quality Center) and advocated by the Qualserve Benchmarking Clearinghouse; it is based on the following principles and guidelines:

- Avoid discussions or actions that could lead to or imply an interest in restraint of trade, market and/or customer allocation schemes, price fixing, dealing arrangements, bid rigging, or bribery. Don't discuss costs with competitors if costs are an element of pricing.
- Refrain from the acquisition of trade secrets from another by any means that could be interpreted as improper, including the breach of any duty to maintain secrecy. Do not disclose or use any trade secret that may have been obtained through improper means or that was disclosed by another in violation of duty to maintain its secrecy or limit its use.
- Be willing to provide your benchmarking partner with the same type and level of information that you request from that partner.
- Communicate fully and early in the relationship to clarify expectations, avoid misunderstanding, and establish mutual interest in the benchmarking exchange.
- Be honest and complete.
- The use or communication of a benchmarking partner's name with the data obtained or practices observed requires the prior permission of the benchmarking partner.
- Honor the wishes of benchmarking partners regarding how the information that is provided will be handled and used.
- In benchmarking with competitors, establish specific ground rules up front. For example, "We don't want to talk about things that will give either of us a competitive advantage, but rather we want to see where we both can mutually improve or gain benefit."
- Check with legal counsel if any information gathering procedure is in doubt. If uncomfortable, do not proceed. Alternatively, negotiate and sign a specific nondisclosure agreement that will satisfy the attorneys representing each partner.
- Do not ask competitors for sensitive data or cause benchmarking partners to feel they must provide data to continue the process.
- Use an ethical third party to assemble and "blind" competitive data, with inputs from legal counsel in direct competitor sharing. (Note: When cost is closely linked to price, sharing cost data can be considered to be the same as sharing price data.)
- Any information obtained from a benchmarking partner should be treated as internal, privileged communications. If "confidential" or proprietary material is to be exchanged, then a specific agreement should be executed to specify the content of the material that needs to be protected, the duration of the period of protection, the conditions for permitting access to the material, and the specific handling requirements necessary for that material.

Source: APQC, www.apqc.org, and the Qualserve Benchmarking Clearinghouse, www.awwa.org (accessed April 30, 2008).

and lessens the potential for unethical behavior on the part of company personnel in gathering their own data about competitors. Illustration Capsule 4.2 presents a widely recommended code of conduct for engaging in benchmarking.

Strategic Options for Remedying a Cost Disadvantage

Value chain analysis and benchmarking can reveal a great deal about a firm's cost-competitiveness. Examining the costs of a company's own value chain activities and comparing them to rivals' indicates who has how much of a cost advantage or disadvantage and which cost components are responsible. Such information is vital in strategic actions to eliminate a cost disadvantage or create a cost advantage. One of the fundamental insights of value chain analysis and benchmarking is that *a company's competitiveness on cost depends on how efficiently it manages its value chain activities relative to how well competitors manage theirs.*[20] There are three main areas in a company's overall value chain where important differences in the costs of competing firms can occur: a company's own activity segments, suppliers' part of the industry value chain, and the forward channel portion of the industry chain.

Remedying an Internal Cost Disadvantage When a company's cost disadvantage stems from performing internal value chain activities at a higher cost than key rivals, managers can pursue any of several strategic approaches to restore cost parity:[21]

1. Implement the use of best practices throughout the company, particularly for high-cost activities.
2. Try to eliminate some cost-producing activities altogether by revamping the value chain. Examples include cutting out low-value-added activities or bypassing the value chains and associated costs of distribution allies and marketing directly to end users (the approach used by Dell in PCs and by airlines that encourage passengers to purchase tickets directly from airline Web sites instead of from travel agents).
3. Relocate high-cost activities (e.g., manufacturing) to geographic areas (e.g., Asia, Latin America, Eastern Europe) where they can be performed more cheaply.
4. See if certain internally performed activities can be outsourced from vendors or performed by contractors more cheaply than they can be done in-house.
5. Invest in productivity-enhancing, cost-saving technological improvements (robotics, flexible manufacturing techniques, state-of-the-art electronic networking).
6. Find ways to detour around the activities or items where costs are high—computer chip makers regularly design around the patents held by others to avoid paying royalties; automakers have substituted lower-cost plastic and rubber for metal at many exterior body locations.
7. Redesign the product and/or some of its components to facilitate speedier and more economical manufacture or assembly.
8. Try to make up the internal cost disadvantage by reducing costs in the supplier or forward channel portions of the industry value chain—usually a last resort.

Remedying a Supplier-Related Cost Disadvantage Supplier-related cost disadvantages can be attacked by pressuring suppliers for lower prices, switching to lower-priced substitute inputs, and collaborating closely with suppliers to identify mutual cost-saving opportunities.[22] [illegible] outcome for both. In a few instances, companies may find that it is cheaper to integrate backward into the business of high-cost suppliers and make the item in-house instead of buying it from outsiders. If a company strikes out in wringing savings out of its high-cost supply chain activities, then it must resort to finding cost savings either in-house or in the forward channel portion of the industry value chain to offset its supplier-related cost disadvantage.

Remedying a Cost Disadvantage Associated with Activities Performed by Forward Channel Allies There are three main ways to combat a cost disadvantage in the forward portion of the industry value chain:

1. Pressure dealer-distributors and other forward channel allies to reduce their costs and markups so as to make the final price to buyers more competitive with the prices of rivals.
2. Work closely with forward channel allies to identify win–win opportunities to reduce costs. For example, a chocolate manufacturer learned that by shipping its bulk chocolate in liquid form in tank cars instead of 10-pound molded bars, it could not only save its candy-bar-manufacturing customers the costs associated with unpacking and melting but also eliminate its own costs of molding bars and packing them.
3. Change to a more economical distribution strategy, including switching to cheaper distribution channels (perhaps direct sales via the Internet) or perhaps integrating forward into company-owned retail outlets.

If these efforts fail, the company can either try to live with the cost disadvantage or pursue cost-cutting earlier in the value chain system.

Translating Proficient Performance of Value Chain Activities into Competitive Advantage

Performing value chain activities in ways that give a company the capabilities to either outmatch the competencies and capabilities of rivals or else beat them on costs are two good ways to secure competitive advantage.

A company that does a *first-rate job* of managing its value chain activities *relative to competitors* stands a good chance of achieving sustainable competitive advantage. As shown in Figure 4.5, a company can outmanage rivals in performing value chain activities in either or both of two ways: (1) by astutely developing core competencies and maybe a distinctive competence that rivals don't have or can't quite match and that are instrumental in helping it deliver attractive value to customers, and/or (2) by simply doing an overall better job than rivals of lowering its combined costs of performing all the various value chain activities, such that it ends up with a low-cost advantage over rivals.

The first of these two approaches begins with management efforts to build more organizational expertise in performing certain competitively important value chain activities, deliberately striving to develop competencies and capabilities that add power to its strategy and competitiveness. If management begins to make selected competencies and capabilities cornerstones of its strategy and continues to invest resources in building greater and greater proficiency in performing them, then one (or maybe several) of the targeted competencies/capabilities may rise to the level of a core competence. Later, following additional organizational learning and investments in gaining still greater proficiency, a core competence could evolve into a distinctive competence, giving the company superiority over rivals in performing an important value chain activity. Such superiority, if it gives the company significant competitive clout in the marketplace, can produce an attractive competitive edge over rivals and, more important, prove difficult for rivals to match or offset with competencies and capabilities of their own making. *As a general rule, it is substantially harder for rivals to achieve "best in industry" proficiency in performing a key value chain activity than it is for them to clone the features and attributes of a hot-selling product or service.*[23] This is especially true when a company with a distinctive competence avoids becoming

Figure 4.5 Translating Company Performance of Value Chain Activities into Competitive Advantage

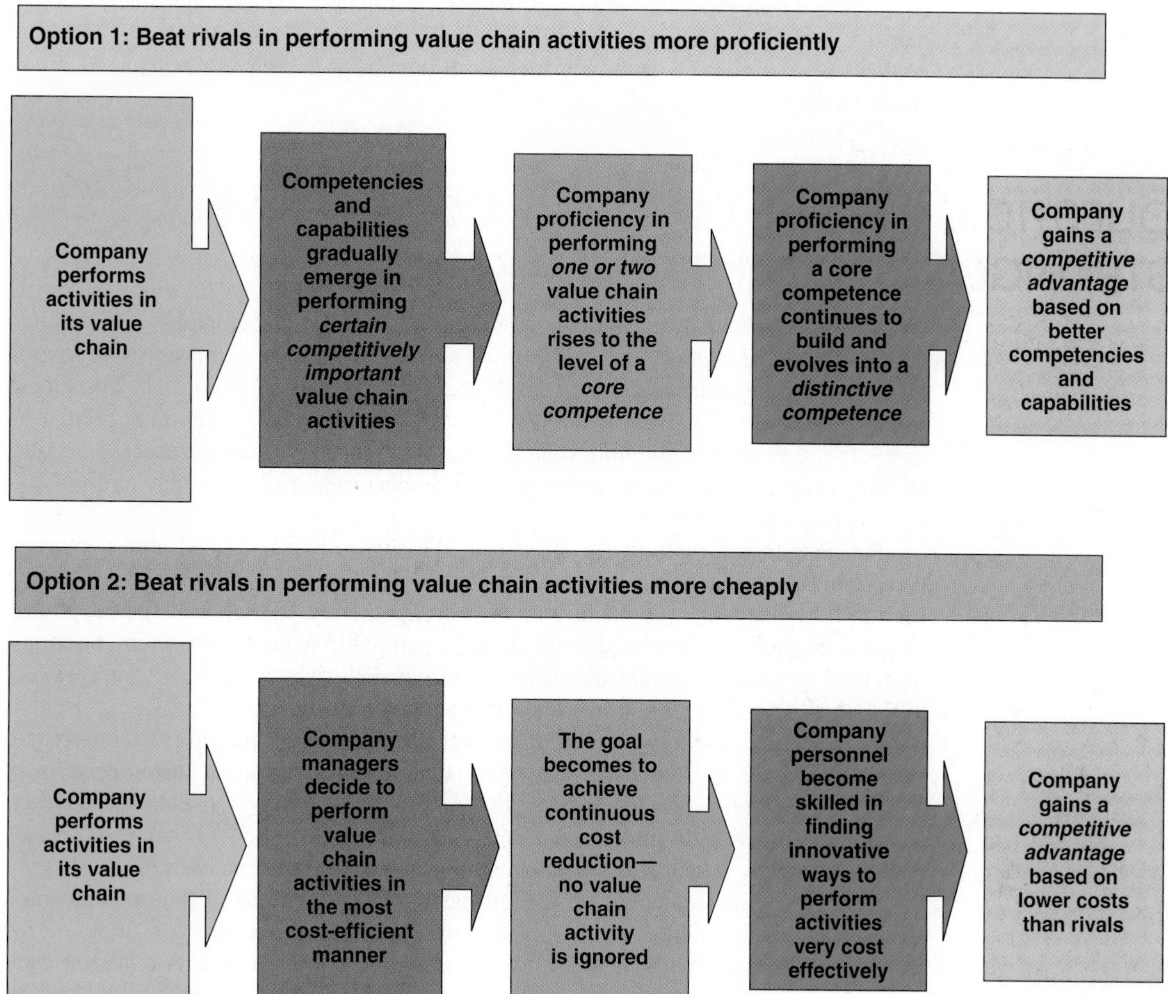
Option 1: Beat rivals in performing value chain activities more proficiently
Company performs activities in its value chain
Competencies and capabilities gradually emerge in performing *certain competitively important* value chain activities
Company proficiency in performing *one or two* value chain activities rises to the level of a *core competence*
Company proficiency in performing a core competence continues to build and evolves into a *distinctive competence*
Company gains a *competitive advantage* based on better competencies and capabilities
Option 2: Beat rivals in performing value chain activities more cheaply
Company performs activities in its value chain
Company managers decide to perform value chain activities in the most cost-efficient manner
The goal becomes to achieve continuous cost reduction—no value chain activity is ignored
Company personnel become skilled in finding innovative ways to perform activities very cost effectively
Company gains a *competitive advantage* based on lower costs than rivals

complacent and works diligently to maintain its industry-leading expertise and capability. GlaxoSmithKline, one of the world's most competitively capable pharmaceutical companies, has built its business position around expert performance of a few competitively crucial activities: [illegible] and sales-force capabilities.[illegible] FedEx's astute management of its value chain has produced unmatched competencies and capabilities in overnight package delivery.

The second approach to building competitive advantage entails determined management efforts to be cost-efficient in performing value chain activities. Such efforts have to be ongoing and persistent, and they have to involve each and every value chain activity. The goal must be continuous cost reduction, not a one-time or on-again/off-again effort.

Companies whose managers are truly committed to low-cost performance of value chain activities and succeed in engaging company personnel to discover innovative ways to drive costs out of the business have a real chance of gaining a durable low-cost edge over rivals. It is not as easy as it seems to imitate a company's low-cost practices. Companies like Wal-Mart, Dell, Nucor Steel, Southwest Airlines, Toyota, and French discount retailer Carrefour have been highly successful in managing their value chains in a low-cost manner.

QUESTION 4: IS THE COMPANY COMPETITIVELY STRONGER OR WEAKER THAN KEY RIVALS?

Using value chain analysis and benchmarking to determine a company's competitiveness on price and cost is necessary but not sufficient. A more comprehensive assessment needs to be made of the company's overall competitive strength. The answers to two questions are of particular interest: First, how does the company rank relative to competitors on each of the important factors that determine market success? Second, all things considered, does the company have a net competitive advantage or disadvantage versus major competitors?

An easy-to-use method for answering the two questions posed above involves developing quantitative strength ratings for the company and its key competitors on each industry key success factor and each competitively pivotal resource capability. Much of the information needed for doing a competitive strength assessment comes from previous analyses. Industry and competitive analysis reveals the key success factors and competitive capabilities that separate industry winners from losers. Benchmarking data and scouting key competitors provide a basis for judging the competitive strength of rivals on such factors as cost, key product attributes, customer service, image and reputation, financial strength, technological skills, distribution capability, and other competitively important resources and capabilities. SWOT analysis reveals how the company in question stacks up on these same strength measures.

Step 1 in doing a competitive strength assessment is to make a list of the industry's key success factors and most telling measures of competitive strength or weakness (6 to 10 measures usually suffice). Step 2 is to rate the firm and its rivals on each factor. Numerical rating scales (e.g., from 1 to 10) are best to use, although ratings of stronger (+), weaker (−), and about equal (=) may be appropriate when information is scanty and assigning numerical scores conveys false precision. Step 3 is to sum the strength ratings on each factor to get an overall measure of competitive strength for each company being rated. Step 4 is to use the overall strength ratings to draw conclusions about the size and extent of the company's net competitive advantage or disadvantage and to take specific note of areas of strength and weakness.

Table 4.4 provides two examples of competitive strength assessment, using the hypothetical ABC Company against four rivals. The first example employs an *unweighted rating system.* With unweighted ratings, each key success factor/competitive strength measure is assumed to be equally important (a rather dubious assumption). Whichever company has the highest strength rating on a given measure has an implied competitive edge on that factor; the size of its edge is mirrored in the margin of difference between its rating and the ratings assigned to rivals—a rating of 9 for one company versus ratings of 5, 4, and 3, respectively, for three other companies indicates a bigger advantage than a rating of 9 versus ratings of 8, 7, and 6. Summing a

Table 4.4 Il[illegible]ions of Unweighted and Weighted Competitive Strength Assessments

A. Sample of a[illegible]ighted Competitive Strength Assessment

Key Success F[illegible]trength Measure	Strength Rating (Scale: 1 = Very weak; 10 = Very strong)				
	ABC Co.	Rival 1	Rival 2	Rival 3	Rival 4
Quality/product [illegible]ance	8	5	10	1	6
Reputation/ima[illegible]	8	7	10	1	6
Manufacturing c[illegible]	2	10	4	5	1
Technological s[illegible]	10	1	7	3	8
Dealer network/[illegible]on capability	9	4	10	5	1
New product inr[illegible] capability	9	4	10	5	1
Financial resour[illegible]	5	10	7	3	1
Relative cost po[illegible]	5	10	3	1	4
Customer servic[illegible]ilities	5	7	10	1	4
Unweighted [illegible]trength rating	**61**	**58**	**71**	**25**	**32**

B. Sample of a [illegible]d Competitive Strength Assessment (Rating scale[illegible]ry weak; 10 = Very strong)

Key Success Fa[illegible] Strength Measu[illegible]	Importance Weight	ABC Co. Strength Rating	ABC Co. Score	Rival 1 Strength Rating	Rival 1 Score	Rival 2 Strength Rating	Rival 2 Score	Rival 3 Strength Rating	Rival 3 Score	Rival 4 Strength Rating	Rival 4 Score
Quality/product p[illegible]nce	0.10	8	0.80	5	0.50	10	1.00	1	0.10	6	0.60
Reputation/image[illegible]	0.10	8	0.80	7	0.70	10	1.00	1	0.10	6	0.60
Manufacturing ca[illegible]	0.10	2	0.20	10	1.00	4	0.40	5	0.50	1	0.10
Technological ski[illegible]	0.05	10	0.50	1	0.05	7	0.35	3	0.15	8	0.40
Dealer network/d[illegible]n capability	0.05	9	0.45	4	0.20	10	0.50	5	0.25	1	0.05
New product inno[illegible] capability	0.05	9	0.45	4	0.20	10	0.50	5	0.25	1	0.05
Financial resourc[illegible]	0.10	5	0.50	10	1.00	7	0.70	3	0.30	1	0.10
Relative cost posi[illegible]	0.30	5	1.50	10	3.00	3	0.90	1	0.30	4	1.20
Customer service[illegible]ies	0.15	5	0.75	7	1.05	10	1.50	1	0.15	4	0.60
Sum of importa[illegible]hts	**1.00**										
Weighted ov[illegible] strength rati[illegible]		61	**5.95**	58	**7.70**	71	**6.85**	25	**2.10**	32	**3.70**

company's ratings on all the measures produces an overall strength rating. The higher a company's overall strength rating, the stronger its overall competitiveness versus rivals. The bigger the difference between a company's overall rating and the scores of *lower-rated* rivals, the greater its implied *net competitive advantage.* Conversely, the bigger the difference between a company's overall rating and the scores of *higher-rated* rivals, the greater its implied *net competitive disadvantage.* Thus, ABC's total score of 61 (see the top half of Table 4.4) signals a much greater net competitive advantage over Rival 4 (with a score of 32) than over Rival 1 (with a score of 58) but indicates a moderate net competitive disadvantage against Rival 2 (with an overall score of 71).

A weighted competitive strength analysis is conceptually stronger than an unweighted analysis because of the inherent weakness in assuming that all the strength measures are equally important.

However, a better method is a *weighted rating system* (shown in the bottom half of Table 4.4) because the different measures of competitive strength are unlikely to be equally important. In an industry where the products/services of rivals are virtually identical, for instance, having low unit costs relative to rivals is nearly always the most important determinant of competitive strength. In an industry with strong product differentiation, the most significant measures of competitive strength may be brand awareness, amount of advertising, product attractiveness, and distribution capability. In a weighted rating system, each measure of competitive strength is assigned a weight based on its perceived importance in shaping competitive success. A weight could be as high as 0.75 (maybe even higher) in situations where one particular competitive variable is overwhelmingly decisive, or a weight could be as low as 0.20 when two or three strength measures are more important than the rest. Lesser competitive strength indicators can carry weights of 0.05 or 0.10. No matter whether the differences between the importance weights are big or little, *the sum of the weights must add up to 1.0.*

Weighted strength ratings are calculated by rating each competitor on each strength measure (using the 1 to 10 rating scale) and multiplying the assigned rating by the assigned weight (a rating of 4 times a weight of 0.20 gives a weighted rating, or score, of 0.80). Again, the company with the highest rating on a given measure has an implied competitive edge on that measure, with the size of its edge reflected in the difference between its rating and rivals' ratings. The weight attached to the measure indicates how important the edge is. Summing a company's weighted strength ratings for all the measures yields an overall strength rating. Comparisons of the weighted overall strength scores indicate which competitors are in the strongest and weakest competitive positions and who has how big a net competitive advantage over whom.

Note in Table 4.4 that the unweighted and weighted rating schemes produce different orderings of the companies. In the weighted system, ABC Company drops from second to third in strength, and Rival 1 jumps from third into first because of its high strength ratings on the two most important factors. Weighting the importance of the strength measures can thus make a significant difference in the outcome of the assessment.

Interpreting the Competitive Strength Assessments

High competitive strength ratings signal a strong competitive position and possession of competitive advantage; low ratings signal a weak position and competitive disadvantage.

Competitive strength assessments provide useful conclusions about a company's competitive situation. The ratings show how a company compares against rivals, factor by factor or capability by capability, thus revealing where it is strongest and weakest, and against whom. Moreover, the overall competitive strength scores indicate how all the different factors add up—whether the company is at a net competitive advantage or disadvantage against each rival. The firm with the largest overall competitive strength rating enjoys the strongest competitive position, with the size of its net competitive advantage reflected by how much its score exceeds the scores of rivals.

In addition, the strength ratings provide guidelines for designing wise offensive and defensive strategies. For example, consider the ratings and weighted scores in the bottom half of Table 4.4. If ABC Co. wants to go on the offensive to win additional sales and market share, such an offensive probably needs to be aimed directly at winning customers away from Rivals 3 and 4 (which have lower overall strength scores) rather than Rivals 1 and 2 (which have higher overall strength scores). Moreover, while ABC has high ratings for technological skills (a 10 rating), dealer network/distribution capability (a 9 rating), new product innovation capability (a 9 rating), quality/product performance (an 8 rating), and reputation/image (an 8 rating), these strength measures have low importance weights—meaning that ABC has strengths in areas that don't translate into much competitive clout in the marketplace. Even so, it outclasses Rival 3 in all five areas, plus it enjoys lower costs than Rival 3 (ABC has a 5 rating on relative cost position versus a 1 rating for Rival 3)—and relative cost position carries the highest importance weight of all the strength measures. ABC also has greater competitive strength than Rival 3 as concerns customer service capabilities (which carries the second-highest importance weight). Hence, because ABC's strengths are in the very areas where Rival 3 is weak, ABC is in good position to attack Rival 3—it may well be able to persuade a number of Rival 3's customers to switch their purchases over to ABC's product.

But in mounting an offensive to win customers away from Rival 3, ABC should note that Rival 1 has an excellent relative cost position—its rating of 10, combined with the importance weight of 0.30 for relative cost, means that Rival 1 has meaningfully lower costs in an industry where low costs are competitively important. Rival 1 is thus strongly positioned to retaliate against ABC with lower prices if ABC's strategy offensive ends up drawing customers away from Rival 1. Moreover, Rival 1's very strong relative cost position vis-à-vis all the other companies arms it with the ability to use its lower-cost advantage to underprice all of its rivals and gain sales and market share at their expense. If ABC wants to defend against its vulnerability to potential price-cutting by Rival 1, then it needs to aim a portion of its strategy at lowering its costs.

A company's competitive strength scores pinpoint its strengths and weaknesses against rivals and point directly to the kinds of offensive/defensive actions it can use to exploit its competitive strengths and reduce its competitive vulnerabilities.

The point here is that a competitively astute company should use the strength scores in deciding what strategic moves to make—what strengths to exploit in winning business away from rivals and which competitive weaknesses to try to correct. When a company has important competitive strengths in areas where one or more rivals are weak, it makes sense to consider offensive moves to exploit rivals' competitive weaknesses. When a company has important competitive weaknesses in areas where one or more rivals are strong, it makes sense to consider defensive moves to curtail its vulnerability.

PROBLEMS MERIT FRONT-BURNER MANAGERIAL ATTENTION?

The final and most important analytical step is to zero in on exactly what strategic issues that company managers need to address—and resolve—for the company to be more financially and competitively successful in the years ahead. This step involves

Zeroing in on the strategic issues a company faces and compiling a "worry list" of problems and roadblocks creates a strategic agenda of problems that merit prompt managerial attention.

Actually deciding upon a strategy and what specific actions to take is what comes *after* developing the list of strategic issues and problems that merit front-burner management attention.

A good strategy must contain ways to deal with all the strategic issues and obstacles that stand in the way of the company's financial and competitive success in the years ahead.

drawing on the results of both industry and competitive analysis and the evaluations of the company's own competitiveness. The task here is to get a clear fix on exactly what strategic and competitive challenges confront the company, which of the company's competitive shortcomings need fixing, what obstacles stand in the way of improving the company's competitive position in the marketplace, and what specific problems merit front-burner attention by company managers. *Pinpointing the precise things that management needs to worry about sets the agenda for deciding what actions to take next to improve the company's performance and business outlook.*

The "worry list" of issues and problems that have to be wrestled with can include such things as *how* to stave off market challenges from new foreign competitors, *how* to combat the price discounting of rivals, *how* to reduce the company's high costs and pave the way for price reductions, *how* to sustain the company's present rate of growth in light of slowing buyer demand, *whether* to expand the company's product line, *whether* to correct the company's competitive deficiencies by acquiring a rival company with the missing strengths, *whether* to expand into foreign markets rapidly or cautiously, *whether* to reposition the company and move to a different strategic group, *what to do* about growing buyer interest in substitute products, and *what to do* to combat the aging demographics of the company's customer base. The worry list thus always centers on such concerns as "how to . . . ," "what to do about . . . ," and "whether to . . ."—the purpose of the worry list is to identify the specific issues/problems that management needs to address, not to figure out what specific actions to take. Deciding what to do—which strategic actions to take and which strategic moves to take—comes later (when it is time to craft the strategy and choose among the various strategic alternatives).

If the items on the worry list are relatively minor—which suggests the company's strategy is mostly on track and reasonably well matched to the company's overall situation, company managers seldom need to go much beyond fine-tuning of the present strategy. If, however, the issues and problems confronting the company are serious and indicate the present strategy is not well suited for the road ahead, the task of crafting a better strategy has got to go to the top of management's action agenda.

KEY POINTS

There are five key questions to consider in analyzing a company's own particular competitive circumstances and its competitive position vis-à-vis key rivals:

1. *How well is the present strategy working?* This involves evaluating the strategy from a qualitative standpoint (completeness, internal consistency, rationale, and suitability to the situation) and also from a quantitative standpoint (the strategic and financial results the strategy is producing). The stronger a company's current overall performance, the less likely the need for radical strategy changes. The weaker a company's performance and/or the faster the changes in its external situation

(which can be gleaned from industry and competitive analysis), the more its current strategy must be questioned.

2. *What are the company's resource strengths and weaknesses, and its external opportunities and threats?* A SWOT analysis provides an overview of a firm's situation and is an essential component of crafting a strategy tightly matched to the company's situation. The two most important parts of SWOT analysis are (1) drawing conclusions about what story the compilation of strengths, weaknesses, opportunities, and threats tells about the company's overall situation, and (2) acting on those conclusions to better match the company's strategy to its resource strengths and market opportunities, to correct the important weaknesses, and to defend against external threats. A company's resource strengths, competencies, and competitive capabilities are strategically relevant because they are the most logical and appealing building blocks for strategy; resource weaknesses are important because they may represent vulnerabilities that need correction. External opportunities and threats come into play because a good strategy necessarily aims at capturing a company's most attractive opportunities and at defending against threats to its well-being.

3. *Are the company's prices and costs competitive?* One telling sign of whether a company's situation is strong or precarious is whether its prices and costs are competitive with those of industry rivals. Value chain analysis and benchmarking are essential tools in determining whether the company is performing particular functions and activities cost-effectively, learning whether its costs are in line with competitors, and deciding which internal activities and business processes need to be scrutinized for improvement. Value chain analysis teaches that how competently a company manages its value chain activities relative to rivals is a key to building a competitive advantage based on either better competencies and competitive capabilities or lower costs than rivals.

4. *Is the company competitively stronger or weaker than key rivals?* The key appraisals here involve how the company matches up against key rivals on industry key success factors and other chief determinants of competitive success and whether and why the company has a competitive advantage or disadvantage. Quantitative competitive strength assessments, using the method presented in Table 4.4, indicate where a company is competitively strong and weak, and provide insight into the company's ability to defend or enhance its market position. As a rule a company's competitive strategy should be built around its competitive strengths and should aim at shoring up areas where it is competitively vulnerable. When a company has important competitive strengths in areas where one or more rivals are weak, it makes sense to consider offensive moves to exploit rivals' competitive weaknesses. When a company has important competitive weaknesses in areas where one or more rivals are strong, it makes sense to consider defensive moves to curtail its vulnerability.

[illegible] problems that stand in the way of the company's success. It involves using the results of both industry and competitive analysis and company situation analysis to identify a "worry list" of issues to be resolved for the company to be financially and competitively successful in the years ahead. The worry list always centers on such concerns as "how to . . . ," "what to do about . . . ," and "whether to . . ."—the purpose of the worry list is to identify the specific issues/problems that management needs to address. Actually deciding on a strategy and what specific actions to take is what comes after the list of strategic issues and problems that merit front-burner management attention is developed.

Good company situation analysis, like good industry and competitive analysis, is a valuable precondition for good strategy making. A competently done evaluation of a company's resource capabilities and competitive strengths exposes strong and weak points in the present strategy and how attractive or unattractive the company's competitive position is and why. Managers need such understanding to craft a strategy that is well suited to the company's competitive circumstances.

ASSURANCE OF LEARNING EXERCISES

1. Review the information in Illustration Capsule 4.1 concerning the costs of the different value chain activities associated with recording and distributing music CDs through traditional brick-and-mortar retail outlets. Then answer the following questions:

    a. Does the growing popularity of downloading music from the Internet give rise to a new music industry value chain that differs considerably from the traditional value chain? Explain why or why not.
    b. What costs would be cut out of the traditional value chain or bypassed in the event recording studios sell downloadable files of artists' recordings direct to online buyers?
    c. What happens to the traditional value chain if more and more consumers use peer-to-peer file-sharing software to download music from the Internet rather than purchase CDs or downloadable files?

2. Using the information in Table 4.1 and the financial statement information for Avon Products below, calculate the following ratios for Avon for both 2006 and 2007:

    a. Gross profit margin
    b. Operating profit margin
    c. Net profit margin
    d. Times-interest-earned (coverage) ratio
    e. Return on shareholders' equity
    f. Return on assets
    g. Debt-to-equity ratio
    h. Long-term debt-to-capital ratio
    i. Days of inventory
    j. Inventory turnover ratio
    k. Average collection period

Based on these ratios, did Avon's financial performance improve, weaken, or remain about the same from 2006 to 2007?

Consolidated Statements of Income for Avon Products, Inc., 2006–2007 (in millions, except per share data)

	Years ended December 31	
	2007	2006
Total revenue	$ 9,938.7	$ 8,763.9
Costs, expenses and other:		
Cost of sales	3,941.2	3,416.5
Selling, general, and administrative expenses	5,124.8	4,586.0
Operating profit	872.7	761.4
Interest expense	112.2	99.6
Interest income	(42.2)	(55.3)
Other expense, net	6.6	13.6
Total other expenses	76.6	57.9
Income before taxes and minority interest	796.1	703.5
Income taxes	**262.8**	223.4
Income before minority interest	**533.3**	480.1
Minority interest	**(2.6)**	(2.5)
Net income	**$ 530.7**	$ 477.6
Earnings per share:		
Basic	**$ 1.22**	$ 1.07
Diluted	**$ 1.21**	$ 1.06
Weighted-average shares outstanding:		
Basic	**433.47**	447.40
Diluted	**436.89**	449.16

Consolidated Balance Sheets for Avon Products, Inc. (in millions, except per share data)

	Years ended December 31	
	2007	2006
Assets		
Current assets		
Cash, including cash equivalents of $492.3 and $825.1	$ 963.4	$ 1,198.9
Accounts receivable (less allowances of $141.1 and $119.1)	840.4	700.4
[illegible]		[illegible]
Total current assets	3,515.4	3,334.4

(Continued)

	Years ended December 31	
	2007	2006
Property, plant and equipment, at cost		
Land	71.8	65.3
Buildings and improvements	972.7	910.0
Equipment	1,317.9	1,137.0
	2,362.4	2,112.3
Less accumulated depreciation	(1,084.2)	(1,012.1)
	1,278.2	1,100.2
Other assets	922.6	803.6
Total assets	$ 5,716.2	$ 5,238.2
Liabilities and Shareholders' Equity		
Current liabilities		
Debt maturing within one year	$ 929.5	$ 615.6
Accounts payable	800.3	655.8
Accrued liabilities	1,221.3	1,044.6
Income taxes	102.3	209.2
Total current liabilities	3,053.4	2,525.2
Long-term debt	1,167.9	1,170.7
Other liabilities (including minority interest of $38.2 and $37.0)	783.3	751.9
Total liabilities	$ 5,004.6	$ 4,447.8
Shareholders' Equity		
Common stock, par value $0.25 — authorized 1,500 shares; issued 736.3 and 732.7 shares	184.7	183.5
Additional paid-in capital	1,724.6	1,549.8
Retained earnings	3,586.5	3,396.8
Accumulated other comprehensive loss	(417.0)	(656.3)
Treasury stock, at cost—308.6 and 291.4 shares	(4,367.2)	(3,683.4)
Total shareholders' equity	$ 711.6	$ 790.4
Total liabilities and shareholders' equity	$ 5,716.2	$ 5,238.2

Source: Avon Products Inc. 2007 10-K.

EXERCISES FOR SIMULATION PARTICIPANTS

1. What hard evidence can you cite that indicates your company's strategy is working fairly well (or perhaps not working so well, if your company's performance is lagging that of rival companies)?
2. What resource strengths and resource weaknesses does your company have? What external market opportunities for growth and increased profitability exist for your company? What external threats to your company's future well-being and profitability do you and your co-managers see? What does the preceding SWOT

analysis indicate about your company's present situation and future prospects—where on the scale from "exceptionally strong" to "alarmingly weak" does the attractiveness of your company's situation rank?

3. Does your company have any core competencies? If so, what are they?
4. What are the key elements of your company's value chain? Refer to Figure 4.3 in developing your answer.
5. Using the methodology presented in Table 4.4, do a weighted competitive strength assessment for your company and two other companies that you and your co-managers consider to be very close competitors.

CHAPTER

5 The Five Generic Competitive Strategies

Which One to Employ?

LEARNING OBJECTIVES

1. Gain command of how each of the five generic competitive strategies lead to competitive advantage and deliver superior value to customers.
2. Learn why some of the five generic strategies work better in certain kinds of industry and competitive conditions than in others.
3. Learn the major avenues for achieving a competitive advantage based on lower costs.
4. Learn the major avenues for developing a competitive advantage based on differentiating a company's product or service offering from the offerings of rivals in ways that better satisfy buyer needs and preferences.

Competitive strategy is about being different. It means deliberately choosing to perform activities differently or to perform different activities than rivals to deliver a unique mix of value.

—**Michael E. Porter**

Strategy . . . is about first analyzing and then experimenting, trying, learning, and experimenting some more.

—**Ian C. McMillan and Rita Gunther McGrath**

Winners in business play rough and don't apologize for it. The nicest part of playing hardball is watching your competitors squirm.

—**George Stalk Jr. and Rob Lachenauer**

Indeed, if your firm's strategy can be applied to any other firm, you don't have a very good one.

—**David J. Collis and Michael G. Rukstad**

The essence of strategy lies in creating tomorrow's competitive advantages faster than competitors mimic the ones you possess today.

—**Gary Hamel and C. K. Prahalad**

This chapter describes the five *basic competitive strategy options*—which of the five to employ is a company's first and foremost choice in crafting an overall strategy and beginning its quest for competitive advantage. A company's **competitive strategy** *deals exclusively with the specifics of management's game plan for competing successfully—its specific efforts to please customers, its offensive and defensive moves to counter the maneuvers of rivals, its responses to whatever market conditions prevail at the moment, its initiatives to strengthen its market position, and its approach to securing a competitive advantage vis-à-vis rivals.* A company achieves competitive advantage whenever it has some type of edge over rivals in attracting buyers and coping with competitive forces. There are many routes to competitive advantage, but they all involve giving buyers what they perceive as superior value compared to the offerings of rival sellers *Superior value* can mean a good product at a lower price; a superior product that is worth paying more for; or a best-value offering that represents an attractive combination of price, features, quality, service, and other appealing attributes. Delivering superior value—whatever form it takes—nearly always requires performing value chain activities differently than rivals and building competencies and resource capabilities that are not readily matched.

CORE CONCEPT

A *competitive strategy* concerns the specifics of management's game plan for competing successfully and securing a competitive advantage over rivals.

CORE CONCEPT

The objective of competitive strategy is to knock the socks off rival companies by doing a better job of satisfying buyer needs and preferences.

THE FIVE GENERIC COMPETITIVE STRATEGIES

There are countless variations in the competitive strategies that companies employ, mainly because each company's strategic approach entails custom-designed actions to fit its own circumstances and industry environment. The chances are remote that any two companies—even companies in the same industry—will employ strategies that are exactly alike in every detail. Managers at different companies always have a slightly different spin on how to best align their company's strategy with market conditions; moreover, they have different notions of how they intend to outmaneuver rivals and what strategic options make the most sense for their particular company. However, when one strips away the details to get at the real substance, the biggest and most important differences among competitive strategies boil down to (1) whether a company's market target is broad or narrow, and (2) whether the company is pursuing a competitive advantage linked to low costs or product differentiation. Five distinct competitive strategy approaches stand out:[1]

1. *A low-cost provider strategy*—striving to achieve lower overall costs than rivals and appealing to a broad spectrum of customers, usually by underpricing rivals.
2. *A broad differentiation strategy*—seeking to differentiate the company's product offering from rivals' in ways that will appeal to a broad spectrum of buyers.
3. *A best-cost provider strategy*—giving customers more value for the money by incorporating good-to-excellent product attributes at a lower cost than rivals; the target is to have the lowest (best) costs and prices compared to rivals offering products with comparable attributes.
4. *A focused (or market niche) strategy based on low costs*—concentrating on a narrow buyer segment and outcompeting rivals by having lower costs than rivals and thus being able to serve niche members at a lower price.
5. *A focused (or market niche) strategy based on differentiation*—concentrating on a narrow buyer segment and outcompeting rivals by offering niche members customized attributes that meet their tastes and requirements better than rivals' products.

Each of these five generic competitive approaches stakes out a different market position, as shown in Figure 5.1. Each involves distinctively different approaches to competing and operating the business. The remainder of this chapter explores the ins and outs of the five generic competitive strategies and how they differ.

LOW-COST PROVIDER STRATEGIES

CORE CONCEPT

A low-cost leader's basis for competitive advantage is lower overall costs than competitors. Successful low-cost leaders are exceptionally good at finding ways to drive costs out of their businesses.

Striving to be the industry's overall low-cost provider is a powerful competitive approach in markets with many price-sensitive buyers. A company achieves low-cost leadership when it becomes the industry's lowest-cost provider rather than just being one of perhaps several competitors with comparatively low costs. A low-cost provider's strategic target is meaningfully lower costs than rivals—but not necessarily the absolutely lowest cost possible. In striving for a cost advantage over rivals, managers must take care to include features and services that buyers consider essential—*even if it is priced lower than competing products, a product offering that is too frills-free sabotages the attractiveness of the company's product and can turn*

Figure 5.1 The Five Generic Competitive Strategies: Each Stakes Out a Different Market Position

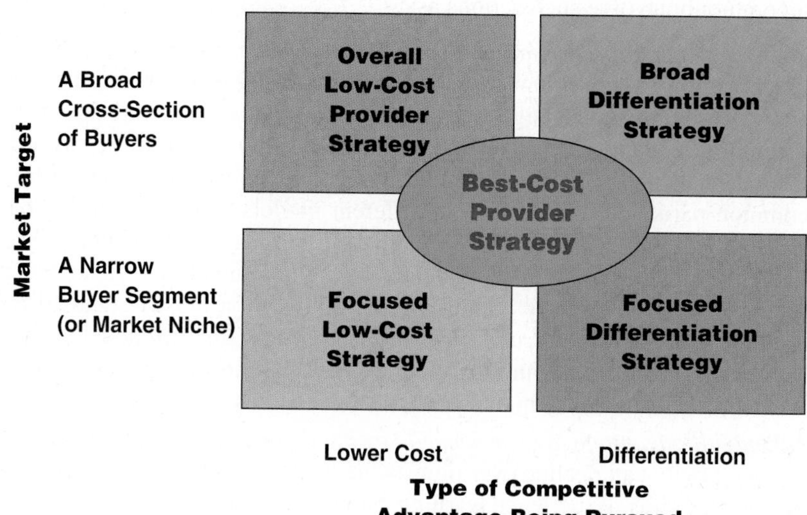

Source: This is an author-expanded version of a three-strategy classification discussed in Michael E. Porter, *Competitive Strategy* (New York: Free Press, 1980), pp. 35–40.

buyers off. For maximum effectiveness, companies employing a low-cost provider strategy need to achieve their cost advantage in ways difficult for rivals to copy or match. If rivals find it relatively easy or inexpensive to imitate the leader's low-cost methods, then the leader's advantage will be too short-lived to yield a valuable edge in the marketplace.

A company has two options for translating a low-cost advantage over rivals into attractive profit performance. Option 1 is to use the lower-cost edge to underprice competitors and attract price-sensitive buyers in great enough numbers to increase total profits. Option 2 is to maintain the present price, be content with the present market share, and use the lower-cost edge to earn a higher profit margin on each unit sold, thereby raising the firm's total profits and overall return on investment.

The Two Major Avenues for Achieving a Cost Advantage

To achieve a low-cost edge over rivals, a firm's cumulative costs across its overall value chain must be lower than competitors' cumulative costs—and the means of achieving the cost advantage must be durable. There are two ways to accomplish this:[2]

1. Perform value chain activities more cost-effectively than rivals

Let's look at each of the two approaches to securing a cost advantage.

Cost-Efficient Management of Value Chain Activities For a company to do a more cost-efficient job of managing its value chain than rivals, managers must launch a concerted, ongoing effort to ferret out cost-saving opportunities in every part of the value chain. No activity can escape cost-saving scrutiny, and all company personnel must be expected to use their talents and ingenuity to come up with innovative and effective ways to keep costs down. All avenues for performing value chain activities at a lower cost than rivals have to be explored. Attempts to outmanage rivals on cost commonly involve such actions as:

1. *Striving to capture all available economies of scale.* Economies of scale stem from an ability to lower unit costs by increasing the scale of operation—there are many occasions when a large plant is more economical to operate than a small or medium-size plant, or when a large distribution warehouse is more cost-efficient than a small one. Often, manufacturing economies can be achieved by using common parts and components in different models and/or by cutting back on the number of models offered (especially slow-selling ones) and then scheduling longer production runs for fewer models. In global industries, making separate products for each country market instead of selling a mostly standard product worldwide tends to boost unit costs because of lost time in model changeover, shorter production runs, and inability to reach the most economic scale of production for each country model.
2. *Taking full advantage of experience/learning curve effects.* The cost of performing an activity can decline over time as the learning and experience of company personnel builds. Experience/learning economies can stem from debugging and mastering newly introduced technologies, using the experiences and suggestions of workers to install more efficient plant layouts and assembly procedures, and the added speed and effectiveness that accrues from repeatedly picking sites for and building new plants, retail outlets, or distribution centers. Aggressively managed low-cost providers pay diligent attention to capturing the benefits of learning and experience and to keeping these benefits proprietary to whatever extent possible.
3. *Trying to operate facilities at full capacity.* Whether a company is able to operate at or near full capacity has a big impact on unit costs when its value chain contains activities associated with substantial fixed costs. Higher rates of capacity utilization allow depreciation and other fixed costs to be spread over a larger unit volume, thereby lowering fixed costs per unit. The more capital-intensive the business, or the higher the percentage of fixed costs as a percentage of total costs, the more important that full-capacity operation becomes, because there's such a stiff unit-cost penalty for underutilizing existing capacity.
4. *Pursuing efforts to boost sales volumes and thus spread such costs as research and development (R&D), advertising, and selling and administrative costs out over more units.* The more units a company sells, the more it lowers its unit costs for R&D, sales and marketing, and administrative overhead. PepsiCo and Anheuser-Busch can afford to spend $2.7 million on a 30-second Super Bowl ad because the cost of such an ad can be spread out over the hundreds of millions of units they sell. In contrast, a small company with a sales volume of only 1 million units would find the $2.7 million cost of a Super Bowl ad prohibitive—just one ad would raise costs over $2.00 per unit even if the ad was unusually effective and caused sales volume to jump 25 percent, to 1.25 million units.
5. *Improving supply chain efficiency.* Partnering with suppliers to streamline the ordering and purchasing process, to reduce inventory carrying costs via just-in-time inventory practices, to economize on shipping and materials handling, and to ferret out other cost-saving opportunities is a much-used approach to cost reduction. A company with a core competence (or better still a distinctive

competence) in cost-efficient supply chain management can sometimes achieve a sizable cost advantage over less adept rivals.

6. *Substituting the use of low-cost for high-cost raw materials or component parts.* If certain raw materials and parts cost too much, a company can either substitute lower-cost items or maybe even design the high-cost components out of the product altogether.
7. *Using online systems and sophisticated software to achieve operating efficiencies.* Sharing data with suppliers—from the latest customer orders to detailed forecasts of components requirements—and using enterprise resource planning (ERP) or manufacturing execution system (MES) software can greatly reduce production times and labor costs. Southwest Airlines developed software enabling it to schedule flights and assign flight crews cost-effectively. MTD—a global manufacturer of lawn mowers, garden tractors, and other outdoor power equipment—implemented ERP and MES systems to track critical supply chain activities. Within the first six months of adopting the software systems, MTD management was able to cut $6 million from annual operating expenses by reducing costly supply chain inefficiencies.
8. *Adopting labor-saving operating methods.* There are numerous ways for a company to economize on labor costs—installing labor-saving technology, shifting production from geographic areas where labor costs are high to those where labor costs are low, avoiding the use of union labor where possible (so as to detour costly union work rules that can stifle productivity and union demands for above-market pay scales and costly fringe benefits), and using incentive compensation systems that promote high labor productivity.
9. *Using the company's bargaining power vis-à-vis suppliers to gain concessions.* Many large enterprises (e.g., Wal-Mart, Home Depot, the world's major motor vehicle producers) have used their bargaining clout in purchasing large volumes to wrangle good prices from suppliers. Having greater buying power than rivals can translate to an important cost advantage.
10. *Being alert to the cost advantages of outsourcing and vertical integration.* Outsourcing the performance of certain value chain activities can be more economical than performing them in-house if outside specialists, by virtue of their expertise and volume, can perform the activities at lower cost. Indeed, outsourcing has in recent years become a widely used cost-reduction approach. However, there can be times when integrating into the activities of either suppliers or distribution channel allies can allow an enterprise to detour suppliers or buyers who have an adverse impact on costs because of their considerable bargaining power.

In addition to the above means of trying to perform value chain activities more efficiently than rivals, a company can also achieve important cost savings by deliberately opting for an [illegible]

[illegible] its product offering that do not have much value to customers.

- Having lower specifications for purchased materials, parts, and components than do rivals. Thus, a maker of personal computers can use the cheapest hard drives, microprocessors, monitors, DVD drives, and other components that it can find so as to end up with lower production costs than rival PC makers.

- Distributing the company's product only through low-cost distribution channels and avoiding high-cost distribution channels.
- Choosing to use the most economical method for delivering customer orders (even if it results in longer delivery times).

Deliberately incorporating strategy elements that keep costs low can greatly assist a company's drive to be the industry's low-cost provider.

Revamping the Value Chain to Curb or Eliminate Unnecessary Activities Dramatic cost advantages can emerge from finding innovative ways to cut back on or entirely bypass certain cost-producing value chain activities. There are two primary ways companies can achieve a cost advantage by reconfiguring their value chains:

- *Bypassing the activities and costs of distributors and dealers by selling direct to customers.* Selling direct can involve (1) having the company's own direct sales force (which adds the costs of maintaining and supporting a sales force but which may be cheaper than accessing customers through distributors and dealers), and/or (2) conducting sales operations at the company's Web site (sales costs at a company's Web site may be a substantially less than those incurred by selling through distributor-dealer channels). Costs in the wholesale/retail portions of the value chain frequently represent 35–50 percent of the price final consumers pay. There are several prominent examples where companies have instituted a sell-direct approach to cutting costs out of the value chain. Software developers are increasingly using the Internet to market and deliver their products directly to buyers; allowing customers to download software directly from the Internet eliminates the costs of producing and packaging CDs and cuts out the host of activities, costs, and markups associated with shipping and distributing software through wholesale and retail channels. By cutting all these costs and activities out of the value chain, software developers have the pricing room to boost their profit margins and still sell their products below levels that retailers would have to charge. The major airlines now sell most of their tickets directly to passengers via their Web sites, ticket counter agents, and telephone reservation systems, allowing them to save hundreds of millions of dollars in commissions once paid to travel agents.
- *Replacing certain value chain activities with faster and cheaper online technology.* Internet technology applications have become powerful and pervasive tools for conducting business and reengineering company and industry value chains. For instance, Internet technology has revolutionized supply chain management, turning many time-consuming and labor-intensive activities into paperless transactions performed instantaneously. Company procurement personnel can—with only a few mouse clicks within one seamless system—check materials inventories against incoming customer orders, check suppliers' stocks, check the latest prices for parts and components at auction and e-sourcing Web sites, and check FedEx or UPS delivery schedules. Various e-procurement software packages streamline the purchasing process by eliminating much of the manual handling of data and by substituting electronic communication for paper documents such as requests for quotations, purchase orders, order acceptances, and shipping notices. There is software that permits the relevant details of incoming customer orders to be instantly shared with the suppliers of needed parts and components. All this facilitates just-in-time deliveries of parts and components and matching the production of parts

and components to assembly plant requirements and production schedules, cutting out unnecessary activities and producing savings for both suppliers and manufacturers. Retailers can install online systems that relay data from cash register sales at the checkout counter back to manufacturers and their suppliers. Manufacturers can use online systems to collaborate closely with parts and components suppliers in designing new products and shortening the time it takes to get them into production. Online systems allow warranty claims and product performance problems involving supplier components to be instantly relayed to the relevant suppliers so that corrections can be expedited. Substituting the use of online systems for activities once performed manually has the further effect of breaking down corporate bureaucracies and reducing overhead costs. The whole back-office data management process (order processing, invoicing, customer accounting, and other kinds of transaction costs) can be handled fast, accurately, and with less paperwork and fewer personnel. New online video conferencing technology is currently allowing companies to slice huge sums from their travel budgets by having company personnel at different geographic locations participate in online meetings rather than traveling to meet face-to-face; online meetings, which can now be conducted very effectively, not only are very cost-effective but they facilitate faster decision-making and boost the productivity of company personnel (by eliminating wasteful travel time).

- *Streamlining operations by eliminating low-value-added or unnecessary work steps and activities.* Examples include using computer-assisted design (CAD) techniques, standardizing parts and components across models and styles, having suppliers collaborate to combine parts and components into modules so that products can be assembled in fewer steps, and shifting to an easy-to-manufacture product design. At Wal-Mart, some items supplied by manufacturers are delivered directly to retail stores rather than being routed through Wal-Mart's distribution centers and delivered by Wal-Mart trucks; in other instances, Wal-Mart unloads incoming shipments from manufacturers' trucks arriving at its cross-docked distribution centers directly onto outgoing Wal-Mart trucks headed to particular stores without ever moving the goods into the distribution center. Many supermarket chains have greatly reduced in-store meat butchering and cutting activities by shifting to meats that are cut and packaged at the meat-packing plant and then delivered in ready-to-sell form.
- *Relocating facilities so as to curb the need for shipping and handling activities.* Having suppliers locate facilities adjacent to the company's plant or locating the company's plants or warehouses near customers can help curb or eliminate shipping and handling costs.
- *Offering a frills-free product.* Deliberately restricting the company's product offering to the essentials can help a company cut costs associated with snazzy attributes and a full lineup of options and extras. Activities and costs can also be [illegible]

reserved seating is a favorite technique of budget airlines like Southwest Airlines, Ryanair (Europe), easyJet (Europe), and Gol (Brazil).
- *Offering a limited product line.* Pruning slow-selling items from the product lineup and being content to meet the needs of most buyers rather than all buyers can eliminate activities and costs associated with numerous product versions and wide selection.

ILLUSTRATION CAPSULE 5.1
How Wal-Mart Managed Its Value Chain to Achieve a Huge Low-Cost Advantage over Rival Supermarket Chains

Wal-Mart has achieved a substantial cost and pricing advantage over rival supermarket chains by both revamping portions of the grocery retailing value chain and by out-managing its rivals in efficiently performing various value chain activities. Its cost advantage stems from a series of initiatives and practices:

- Instituting extensive information-sharing with vendors via online systems that relay sales at its checkout counters directly to suppliers of the items, thereby providing suppliers with real-time information on customer demand and preferences (creating an estimated 6 percent cost advantage). It is standard practice at Wal-Mart to collaborate extensively with vendors on all aspects of the purchasing and store delivery process to squeeze out mutually beneficial cost savings. Procter & Gamble, Wal-Mart's biggest supplier, went so far as to integrate its enterprise resource planning (ERP) system with Wal-Mart's.
- Pursuing global procurement of some items and centralizing most purchasing activities so as to leverage the company's buying power (creating an estimated 2.5 percent cost advantage).
- Investing in state-of-the-art automation at its distribution centers, efficiently operating a truck fleet that makes daily deliveries to Wal-Mart's stores, and putting assorted other cost-saving practices into place at its headquarters, distribution centers, and stores (resulting in an estimated 4 percent cost advantage).
- Striving to optimize the product mix and achieve greater sales turnover (resulting in about a 2 percent cost advantage).
- Installing security systems and store operating procedures that lower shrinkage rates (producing a cost advantage of about 0.5 percent).
- Negotiating preferred real estate rental and leasing rates with real estate developers and owners of its store sites (yielding a cost advantage of 2 percent).
- Managing and compensating its workforce in a manner that produces lower labor costs (yielding an estimated 5 percent cost advantage).

Altogether, these value chain initiatives give Wal-Mart an approximately 22 percent cost advantage over Kroger, Safeway, and other leading supermarket chains. With such a sizable cost advantage, Wal-Mart has been able to underprice its rivals and become the world's leading supermarket retailer in little more than a decade.

Source: Developed by the authors from information at www.wal-mart.com (accessed September 15, 2004) and in Marco Iansiti and Roy Levien, "Strategy as Ecology," *Harvard Business Review* 82, no. 3 (March 2004), p. 70.

Illustration Capsule 5.1 describes how Wal-Mart has managed its value chain in the retail grocery portion of its business to achieve a dramatic cost advantage over rival supermarket chains and become the world's biggest grocery retailer.

Examples of Companies That Revamped Their Value Chains to Reduce Costs Nucor Corporation, the most profitable steel producer in the United States and one of the largest steel producers worldwide, drastically revamped the value chain process for manufacturing steel products by using relatively inexpensive electric arc furnaces where scrap steel and directly reduced iron ore are melted and then sent to a continuous caster and rolling mill to be shaped into steel bars, steel beams, steel plate, and sheet steel. Using electric arc furnaces to make new steel products by recycling scrap steel eliminated many of the expensive steps in making steel products from scratch. For instance, Nucor's value chain approach makes the use of coal, coke, and iron ore unnecessary; cuts investment in facilities and equipment (eliminating coke ovens, blast furnaces, basic oxygen furnaces, and ingot casters); and requires only a modest number of employees. As a consequence, Nucor was able to make steel with a far lower capital investment and far lower operating costs than traditional steel mills using iron ore, coke, and coal to make pig iron and then running the pig iron through a variety of capital- and labor-intensive processes to eventually end up with steel products in a variety of shapes and thicknesses. Nucor's low-cost value chain approach has made it one of the lowest-cost producers of steel in the world, enabled Nucor to outcompete traditional steel companies using make-it-from-scratch technology, and earn attractive profits for its shareholders. Nucor has reported profits for every quarter in every year since 1966—a remarkable accomplishment in a mature and cyclical industry notorious for poor profitability.

Southwest Airlines has reconfigured the traditional value chain of commercial airlines to lower costs and thereby offer dramatically lower fares to passengers. Its mastery of fast turnarounds at the gates (about 25 minutes versus 45 minutes for rivals) allows its planes to fly more hours per day. This translates into being able to schedule more flights per day with fewer aircraft, allowing Southwest to generate more revenue per plane on average than rivals. Southwest does not offer in-flight meals, assigned seating, baggage transfer to connecting airlines, or first-class seating and service, thereby eliminating all the cost-producing activities associated with these features. The company's fast and user-friendly online reservation system facilitates e-ticketing and reduces staffing requirements at telephone reservation centers and airport counters. Its use of automated check-in equipment reduces staffing requirements for terminal check-in.

The Keys to Success in Achieving Low-Cost Leadership

Success in achieving a low-cost edge over rivals comes from outmanaging rivals in performing value chain activities cost-effectively and eliminating or curbing nonessential value chain activities

To succeed with a low-cost provider strategy, company managers have to scrutinize each cost-creating activity and determine what factors cause costs to be high or low. Then they have to use this knowledge to keep the unit costs of each activity low, exhaustively pursuing cost efficiencies throughout the value chain. They have to be proactive in restructuring the value chain to eliminate nonessential work steps and low-value activities. Normally, low-cost producers work diligently to create cost-conscious corporate cultures that feature broad employee participation in continuous cost improvement efforts and limited perks and frills for executives. They strive to operate with exceptionally small corporate staffs to keep administrative costs to a minimum. Many successful low-cost leaders also use benchmarking to keep close tabs on how their costs compare with rivals and firms performing comparable activities in other industries.

But while low-cost providers are champions of frugality, they are usually aggressive in investing in resources and capabilities that promise to drive costs out of the business. Wal-Mart, one of the foremost practitioners of low-cost leadership, employs state-of-the-art technology throughout its operations—its distribution facilities are an automated showcase, it uses online systems to order goods from suppliers and [illegible] systems and capabilities are more sophisticated than those of virtually any other retail chain in the world.

Other companies noted for their successful use of low-cost provider strategies include Lincoln Electric in arc welding equipment, Briggs & Stratton in small gasoline engines, Bic in ballpoint pens, Black & Decker in power tools, and General Electric and Whirlpool in major home appliances.

When a Low-Cost Provider Strategy Works Best

A competitive strategy predicated on low-cost leadership is particularly powerful when:

1. *Price competition among rival sellers is especially vigorous.* Low-cost providers are in the best position to compete offensively on the basis of price, to use the appeal of lower price to grab sales (and market share) from rivals, to remain profitable in the face of strong price competition, and to survive price wars.
2. *The products of rival sellers are essentially identical and supplies are readily available from any of several eager sellers.* Commodity-like products and/or ample supplies set the stage for lively price competition; in such markets, it is less efficient, higher-cost companies whose profits get squeezed the most.
3. *There are few ways to achieve product differentiation that have value to buyers.* When the differences between brands do not matter much to buyers, buyers are nearly always sensitive to price differences and shop the market for the best price.
4. *Most buyers use the product in the same ways.* With common user requirements, a standardized product can satisfy the needs of buyers, in which case low selling price, not features or quality, becomes the dominant factor in causing buyers to choose one seller's product over another's.
5. *Buyers incur low costs in switching their purchases from one seller to another.* Low switching costs give buyers the flexibility to shift purchases to lower-priced sellers having equally good products or to attractively priced substitute products. A low-cost leader is well positioned to use low price to induce its customers not to switch to rival brands or substitutes.
6. *Buyers are large and have significant power to bargain down prices.* Low-cost providers have partial profit-margin protection in bargaining with high-volume buyers, since powerful buyers are rarely able to bargain price down past the survival level of the next most cost-efficient seller.
7. *Industry newcomers use introductory low prices to attract buyers and build a customer base.* The low-cost leader can use price cuts of its own to make it harder for a new rival to win customers; the pricing power of the low-cost provider acts as a barrier for new entrants.

A low-cost provider is in the best position to win the business of price-sensitive buyers, set the floor on market price, and still earn a profit.

As a rule, the more price-sensitive buyers are, the more appealing a low-cost strategy becomes. A low-cost company's ability to set the industry's price floor and still earn a profit erects protective barriers around its market position.

The Pitfalls of a Low-Cost Provider Strategy

Perhaps the biggest pitfall of a low-cost provider strategy is getting carried away with price cutting and ending up with lower, rather than higher, profitability. A low-cost/low-price advantage results in superior profitability only if (1) prices are cut by less than the size of the cost advantage or (2) the added gains in unit sales are large enough to bring in a bigger total profit despite lower margins per unit sold. A company with a 5 percent cost advantage cannot cut prices 20 percent, end up with a volume gain of only 10 percent, and still expect to earn higher profits!

A second big pitfall is not emphasizing avenues of cost advantage that can be kept proprietary or that relegate rivals to playing catch-up. The value of a cost advantage depends on its sustainability. Sustainability, in turn, hinges on whether the company achieves its cost advantage in ways difficult for rivals to copy or match.

A third pitfall is becoming too fixated on cost reduction. Low cost cannot be pursued so zealously that a firm's offering ends up being too features-poor to generate buyer appeal. Furthermore, a company driving hard to push its costs down has to guard against misreading or ignoring increased buyer interest in added features or service, declining buyer sensitivity to price, or new developments that start to alter how buyers use the product. A low-cost zealot risks losing market ground if buyers start opting for more upscale or features-rich products.

A low-cost provider's product offering must always contain enough attributes to be attractive to prospective buyers—low price, by itself, is not always appealing to buyers

Even if these mistakes are avoided, a low-cost competitive approach still carries risk. Cost-saving technological breakthroughs or the emergence of still-lower-cost value chain models can nullify a low-cost leader's hard-won position. The current leader may have difficulty in shifting quickly to the new technologies or value chain approaches because heavy investments lock it in (at least temporarily) to its present value chain approach.

BROAD DIFFERENTIATION STRATEGIES

Differentiation strategies are attractive whenever buyers' needs and preferences are too diverse to be fully satisfied by a standardized product or by sellers with identical capabilities. A company attempting to succeed through differentiation must study buyers' needs and behavior carefully to learn what buyers consider important, what they think has value, and what they are willing to pay for.[3] Then the company has to incorporate buyer-desired attributes into its product or service offering that will clearly set it apart from rivals. Competitive advantage results once a sufficient number of buyers become strongly attached to the differentiated attributes.

CORE CONCEPT
The essence of a broad differentiation strategy is to be unique in ways that are valuable to a wide range of customers.

Successful differentiation allows a firm to do one or more of the following:

- Command a premium price for its product.
- Increase unit sales (because additional buyers are won over by the differentiating features).
- Gain buyer loyalty to its brand (because some buyers are strongly attracted to the differentiating features and bond with the company and its products).

Differentiation enhances profitability whenever the extra price the product commands outweighs the added costs of achieving the differentiation. Company differentiation strategies fail when buyers don't value the brand's uniqueness and/or when a company's approach to differentiation is easily copied or matched by its rivals.

Types of Differentiation Themes

Companies can pursue differentiation from many angles: a unique taste (Dr Pepper, Listerine); multiple features [illegible]

[illegible] parts delivery to any customer anywhere in the world or else the part is furnished free); engineering design and performance (Mercedes, BMW); prestige and distinctiveness (Rolex); product reliability (Johnson & Johnson in baby products); quality manufacture (Karastan in carpets, Michelin in tires, Toyota and Honda in automobiles); technological leadership (3M Corporation in bonding and coating products); a full range of services (Charles Schwab in stock brokerage); a complete line of products (Campbell's soups); and top-of-the-line image and reputation (Ralph Lauren and Starbucks).

Easy-to-copy differentiating features cannot produce sustainable competitive advantage; differentiation based on competencies and capabilities tends to be more sustainable.

The most appealing approaches to differentiation are those that are hard or expensive for rivals to duplicate. Indeed, resourceful competitors can, in time, clone almost any product or feature or attribute. If Coca-Cola introduces a vanilla-flavored soft drink, so can Pepsi; if Ford offers a 50,000-mile bumper-to-bumper warranty on its new vehicles, so can Nissan and General Motors. If Apple introduces a cell phone with a variety of advanced Internet features, so can Nokia, Samsung, and Research in Motion (the maker of the popular BlackBerry models). As a rule, differentiation yields a longer-lasting and more profitable competitive edge when it is based on product innovation, technical superiority, product quality and reliability, comprehensive customer service, and unique competitive capabilities. Such differentiating attributes are generally tougher and take longer for rivals to match, and buyers widely perceive them as having value.

Where along the Value Chain to Create the Differentiating Attributes

Differentiation is not something hatched in marketing and advertising departments, nor is it limited to the catchalls of quality and service. Differentiation opportunities can exist in activities all along an industry's value chain; possibilities include the following:

- *Supply chain activities* that ultimately spill over to affect the performance or quality of the company's end product. Starbucks gets high ratings on its coffees partly because it has strict specifications on the coffee beans purchased from suppliers.
- *Product R&D activities* that aim at improved product designs and performance features, expanded end uses and applications, more frequent first-on-the-market victories, wider product variety and selection, added user safety, greater recycling capability, or enhanced environmental protection.
- *Production R&D and technology-related activities* that permit custom-order manufacture at an efficient cost; make production methods safer for the environment; or improve product quality, reliability, and appearance. Many manufacturers have developed flexible manufacturing systems that allow different models and product versions to be made on the same assembly line. Being able to provide buyers with made-to-order products can be a potent differentiating capability.
- *Manufacturing activities* that reduce product defects, prevent premature product failure, extend product life, allow better warranty coverage, improve economy of use, result in more end-user convenience, or enhance product appearance. The quality edge enjoyed by Japanese automakers stems partly from their distinctive competence in performing assembly-line activities.
- *Distribution and shipping activities* that allow for fewer warehouse and on-the-shelf stockouts, quicker delivery to customers, more accurate order filling, and/or lower shipping costs.
- *Marketing, sales, and customer service activities* that result in superior technical assistance to buyers, faster maintenance and repair services, more and better product information provided to customers, more and better training materials for end users, better credit terms, quicker order processing, or greater customer convenience.

Managers need keen understanding of the sources of differentiation and the activities that drive uniqueness to evaluate various differentiation approaches and design durable ways to set their product offering apart from those of rival brands.

The Four Best Routes to Competitive Advantage via a Broad Differentiation Strategy

While it is easy enough to grasp that a successful differentiation strategy must entail creating buyer value in ways unmatched by rivals, the big issue in crafting a differentiation strategy is which of four basic routes to take in delivering unique buyer value via a broad differentiation strategy. Usually, building a sustainable competitive advantage via differentiation involves pursuing one of four basic routes to delivering superior value to buyers. One route is to *incorporate product attributes and user features that lower the buyer's overall costs of using the company's product.* Making a company's product more economical for a buyer to use can be done by reducing the buyer's raw materials waste (providing cut-to-size components), reducing a buyer's inventory requirements (providing just-in-time deliveries), increasing maintenance intervals and product reliability so as to lower a buyer's repair and maintenance costs, using online systems to reduce a buyer's procurement and order processing costs, and providing free technical support. Rising costs for gasoline have dramatically spurred the efforts of motor vehicle manufacturers worldwide to introduce models with better fuel economy.

A second route is to *incorporate features that raise product performance.*[4] This can be accomplished with attributes that provide buyers greater reliability, durability, convenience, or ease of use. Other performance-enhancing options include making the company's product or service cleaner, safer, quieter, or more maintenance-free than rival brands. Cell phone manufacturers are in a race to introduce next-generation phones with a more appealing, trendsetting set of user features and options.

CORE CONCEPT
A differentiator's basis for competitive advantage is either a product/service offering whose attributes differ significantly from the offerings of rivals or a set of capabilities for delivering customer value that rivals don't have.

A third route to a differentiation-based competitive advantage is to *incorporate features that enhance buyer satisfaction in noneconomic or intangible ways.* Toyota's Prius appeals to environmentally conscious motorists who wish to help reduce global carbon dioxide emissions. Rolls-Royce, Ralph Lauren, Gucci, Tiffany, Cartier, and Rolex have differentiation-based competitive advantages linked to buyer desires for status, image, prestige, upscale fashion, superior craftsmanship, and the finer things in life. L. L. Bean makes its mail-order customers feel secure in their purchases by providing an unconditional guarantee with no time limit: "All of our products are guaranteed to give 100 percent satisfaction in every way. Return anything purchased from us at any time if it proves otherwise. We will replace it, refund your purchase price, or credit your credit card, as you wish."

The fourth route is *to deliver value to customers by differentiating on the basis of competencies and competitive capabilities that rivals don't have or can't afford to match.*[5] The importance of cultivating competencies and capabilities that add power to a company's resource strengths and competitiveness comes into play here. Core and/or distinctive competencies may give a company unique capabilities that deliver important value to customers and help set the company apart from its rivals. Th

preferences for one vehicle style versus another because they have the capabilities to bring new models to market faster than American and European automakers. Apple's competencies in product innovation produced the iPod and the iPhone, both of which have been immensely popular with consumers and put Apple very much in the spotlight. Samsung's competencies and capabilities in liquid crystal display (LCD) technology have made it a global leader in LCD TVs with screen sizes of 27-inches and larger.

The Importance of Perceived Value and Signaling Value

Buyers seldom pay for value they don't perceive, no matter how real the unique extras may be.[6] Thus, the price premium commanded by a differentiation strategy reflects both *the value actually delivered* to the buyer and *the value perceived* by the buyer (even if not actually delivered). Actual and perceived value can differ whenever buyers have trouble assessing what their experience with the product will be. Incomplete knowledge on the part of buyers often causes them to judge value according to such signals as price (where price connotes quality); packaging; the extent of ad campaigns (i.e., how well-known the product is); ad content and image; the quality of brochures and sales presentations; the seller's facilities; the seller's list of customers; the firm's market share; the length of time the firm has been in business; and the professionalism, appearance, and personality of the seller's employees. Such signals of value may be as important as actual value (1) when the nature of differentiation is subjective or hard to quantify, (2) when buyers are making a first-time purchase, (3) when repurchase is infrequent, and (4) when buyers are unsophisticated.

When a Differentiation Strategy Works Best

Differentiation strategies tend to work best in market circumstances where:

- *Buyer needs and uses of the product are diverse.* Diverse buyer preferences present competitors with a bigger window of opportunity to do things differently and set themselves apart with product attributes that appeal to particular buyers. For instance, the diversity of consumer preferences for menu selection, ambience, pricing, and customer service gives restaurants exceptionally wide latitude in creating a differentiated product offering. Other companies having many ways to strongly differentiate themselves from rivals include the publishers of magazines, the makers of motor vehicles, and the manufacturers of cabinetry and countertops.
- *There are many ways to differentiate the product or service and many buyers perceive these differences as having value.* There's plenty of room for retail apparel competitors to stock different styles and quality of apparel merchandise but very little room for the makers of paper clips or copier paper or sugar to set their products apart. Likewise, the sellers of different brands of gasoline or aspirin or plastic cups have little differentiation opportunity compared to the sellers of watches or magazines or patio furniture or breakfast cereal. Unless different buyers have distinguishably different preferences for certain features and product attributes, profitable differentiation opportunities are very restricted.
- *Few rival firms are following a similar differentiation approach.* The best differentiation approaches involve trying to appeal to buyers on the basis of attributes that rivals are not emphasizing. A differentiator encounters less head-to-head rivalry when it goes its own separate way in creating uniqueness and does not try to outdifferentiate rivals on the very same attributes—when many rivals are all claiming "Ours tastes better than theirs" or "Ours gets your clothes cleaner than theirs," the most likely result is weak brand differentiation and *strategy overcrowding*—where competitors end up chasing much the same buyers with much the same product offerings.
- *Technological change is fast-paced and competition revolves around rapidly evolving product features.* Rapid product innovation and frequent introductions of next-version products not only provide space for companies to

pursue separate differentiating paths but also heighten buyer interest. In video game hardware and video games, golf equipment, PCs, cell phones, and MP3 players, competitors are locked into an ongoing battle to set themselves apart by introducing the best next-generation products—companies that fail to come up with new and improved products and distinctive performance features quickly lose out in the marketplace. In network TV broadcasting in the United States, NBC, ABC, CBS, Fox, and several others are always scrambling to develop a lineup of TV shows that will win higher audience ratings and pave the way for charging higher advertising rates and boosting ad revenues.

The Pitfalls of a Differentiation Strategy

Differentiation strategies can fail for any of several reasons. *A differentiation strategy is always doomed when competitors are able to quickly copy most or all of the appealing product attributes a company comes up with.* Rapid imitation means that no rival achieves differentiation, since whenever one firm introduces some aspect of uniqueness that strikes the fancy of buyers, fast-following copycats quickly reestablish similarity. This is why a firm must search out sources of uniqueness that are time-consuming or burdensome for rivals to match if it hopes to use differentiation to win a competitive edge over rivals.

CORE CONCEPT
Any differentiating feature that works well is a magnet for imitators.

A second pitfall is that the company's differentiation strategy produces a ho-hum market reception because buyers see little value in the unique attributes of a company's product. Thus, even if a company sets the attributes of its brand apart from the brands of rivals, its strategy can fail because of trying to differentiate on the basis of something that does not deliver adequate value to buyers (such as lowering a buyer's cost to use the product or enhancing a buyer's well-being). Anytime many potential buyers look at a company's differentiated product offering and conclude "So what," the company's differentiation strategy is in deep trouble—buyers will likely decide the product is not worth the extra price and sales will be disappointingly low.

The third big pitfall of a differentiation strategy is overspending on efforts to differentiate the company's product offering, thus eroding profitability. Company efforts to achieve differentiation nearly always raise costs. The trick to profitable differentiation is either to keep the costs of achieving differentiation below the price premium the differentiating attributes can command in the marketplace (thus increasing the profit margin per unit sold) or to offset thinner profit margins per unit by selling enough additional units to increase total profits. If a company goes overboard in pursuing costly differentiation efforts and then unexpectedly discovers that buyers are unwilling to pay a sufficient price premium to cover the added costs of differentiation, it ends up saddled with unacceptably thin profit margins or even losses. The need to contain differentiation costs is why many companies add little touches of

noon. FedEx, UPS, and many catalog and online retailers allow customers to track packages in transit via the Internet. Some hotels and motels provide free continental breakfasts, exercise facilities, and in-room coffeemaking amenities. Publishers are using their Web sites to deliver supplementary educational materials to the buyers of their textbooks. Laundry detergent and soap manufacturers offer both scented and scent-free products.

Other common pitfalls and mistakes in crafting a differentiation strategy include:[7]

- *Overdifferentiating so that product quality or service levels exceed buyers' needs.* Even if buyers like the differentiating extras, they may not find them sufficiently valuable for their purposes to pay extra to get them. Many shoppers shy away from buying top-of-the-line items because they have no particular interest in all the bells and whistles, and believe that a less deluxe model or style makes better economic sense.
- *Trying to charge too high a price premium.* Even if buyers view certain extras or deluxe features as nice to have, they may still conclude that the added cost is excessive relative to the value they deliver. A differentiator must guard against turning off would-be buyers with what is perceived as price gouging. Normally, the bigger the price premium for the differentiating extras, the harder it is to keep buyers from switching to the lower-priced offerings of competitors.
- *Being timid and not striving to open up meaningful gaps in quality or service or performance features vis-à-vis the products of rivals.* Tiny differences between rivals' product offerings may not be visible or important to buyers. If a company wants to generate the fiercely loyal customer following needed to earn superior profits and open up a differentiation-based competitive advantage over rivals, then its strategy must result in strong rather than weak product differentiation. In markets where differentiators do no better than achieve weak product differentiation (because the attributes of rival brands are fairly similar in the minds of many buyers), customer loyalty to any one brand is weak, the costs of brand switching are fairly low, and no one company has enough of a market edge that it can get by with charging a price premium over rival brands.

A low-cost provider strategy can defeat a differentiation strategy when buyers are satisfied with a basic product and don't think extra attributes are worth a higher price.

BEST-COST PROVIDER STRATEGIES

CORE CONCEPT

***The competitive advantage of a best-cost provider is lower costs than rivals* in incorporating upscale attributes, putting the company in a position to underprice rivals whose products have similar upscale attributes.**

Best-cost provider strategies aim at giving customers *more value for the money.* The objective is to deliver superior value to buyers by satisfying their expectations on key quality/features/performance/service attributes and beating their expectations on price (given what rivals are charging for much the same attributes). *A company achieves best-cost status from an ability to incorporate attractive or upscale attributes at a lower cost than rivals.* The attractive attributes can take the form of appealing features, good-to-excellent product performance or quality, or attractive customer service. If a company has the resource strengths and competitive capabilities to incorporate these upscale attributes into its product offering *at a lower cost than rivals,* then it enjoys best-cost status—it is the low-cost provider *of an upscale product.*

Being a best-cost provider is different from being a low-cost provider because the additional upscale features entail additional costs (that a low-cost provider can avoid by offering buyers a basic product with few frills). As Figure 5.1 indicates, best-cost provider strategies stake out a middle ground between pursuing a low-cost advantage and a differentiation advantage and between appealing to the broad market as a whole and a narrow market niche. From a competitive positioning standpoint, best-cost strategies are thus a *hybrid,* balancing a strategic emphasis on low cost against a strategic emphasis on differentiation (upscale features delivered at a price that constitutes superior value).

The competitive advantage of a best-cost provider is its capability to include upscale attributes at a lower cost than rivals whose products have comparable attributes. A best-cost provider can use its low-cost advantage to underprice rivals whose products have similar upscale attributes—it is usually not difficult to entice customers away from rivals charging a higher price for an item with highly comparable features, quality, performance, and/or customer service attributes. To achieve competitive advantage with a best-cost provider strategy, it is critical that a company have the resources and capabilities to incorporate upscale attributes at a lower cost than rivals. In other words, it must be able to (1) incorporate attractive features at a lower cost than rivals whose products have similar features, (2) manufacture a product of good-to-excellent quality at a lower cost than rivals, (3) develop a product that delivers good-to-excellent performance at a lower cost than rivals, or (4) provide attractive customer service at a lower cost than rivals who provide comparably attractive customer service. What makes a best-cost provider strategy so appealing is being able to incorporate upscale attributes at a lower cost than rivals and then using the company's low-cost advantage to underprice rivals whose products have similar upscale attributes.

The target market for a best-cost provider is value-conscious buyers—buyers who are looking for appealing extras at an appealingly low price. Value-hunting buyers (as distinct from buyers looking only for bargain-basement prices) often constitute a sizable part of the overall market. Normally, value-conscious buyers are willing to pay a fair price for extra features, but they shy away from paying top dollar for items having all the bells and whistles. It is the desire to cater to *value-conscious buyers* as opposed to *budget-conscious buyers* that sets a best-cost provider apart from a low-cost provider—the two strategies aim at distinguishably different market targets.

When a Best-Cost Provider Strategy Is Appealing

A best-cost provider strategy is very well-suited for markets where buyer diversity makes product differentiation the norm and where many buyers are also sensitive to price and value. This is because a best-cost provider can position itself near the middle of the market with either a medium-quality product at a below-average price or a high-quality product at an average or slightly higher price. Often, substantial numbers of buyers prefer midrange products rather than the cheap, basic products of low-cost producers or the expensive products of top-of-the-line differentiators. But unless a company has the resources, know-how, and capabilities to incorporate upscale product or service attributes at a lower cost than rivals, adopting a best-cost strategy is ill-advised—a winning strategy must always be matched to a company's resource strengths and capabilities.

Illustration Capsule 5.2 describes how Toyota has applied the principles of a best-cost provider strategy in producing and marketing its Lexus brand.

The Big Risk of a Best-Cost Provider Strategy

tiation strategies. Low-cost providers may be able to siphon customers away with the appeal of a lower price (despite their less-appealing product attributes). High-end differentiators may be able to steal customers away with the appeal of better product attributes (even though their products carry a higher price tag). Thus, to be successful, a best-cost provider must offer buyers *significantly* better product attributes in order to justify a price above what low-cost leaders are charging. Likewise, it has to achieve significantly lower costs in providing upscale features so that it can outcompete high-end differentiators on the basis of a *significantly* lower price.

ILLUSTRATION CAPSULE 5.2
Toyota's Best-Cost Provider Strategy for Its Lexus Line

Toyota Motor Company is widely regarded as a low-cost provider among the world's motor vehicle manufacturers. Despite its emphasis on product quality, Toyota has achieved low-cost leadership because it has developed considerable skills in efficient supply chain management and low-cost assembly capabilities, and because its models are positioned in the low-to-medium end of the price spectrum, where high production volumes are conducive to low unit costs. But when Toyota decided to introduce its new Lexus models to compete in the luxury-car market, it employed a classic best-cost provider strategy. Toyota took the following four steps in crafting and implementing its Lexus strategy:

- Designing an array of high-performance characteristics and upscale features into the Lexus models so as to make them comparable in performance and luxury to other high-end models and attractive to Mercedes, BMW, Audi, Jaguar, Cadillac, and Lincoln buyers.
- Transferring its capabilities in making high-quality Toyota models at low cost to making premium-quality Lexus models at costs below other luxury-car makers. Toyota's supply chain capabilities and low-cost assembly know-how allowed it to incorporate high-tech performance features and upscale quality into Lexus models at substantially less cost than comparable Mercedes and BMW models.
- Using its relatively lower manufacturing costs to underprice comparable Mercedes and BMW models. Toyota believed that with its cost advantage it could price attractively equipped Lexus cars low enough to draw price-conscious buyers away from Mercedes and BMW. Toyota's pricing policy also allowed it to induce Toyota, Honda, Ford, or GM owners desiring more luxury to switch to a Lexus. Lexus's pricing advantage over Mercedes and BMW was sometimes quite significant. For example, in 2008 the Lexus RX 350, a midsized SUV, carried a sticker price in the \$37,000–\$48,000 range (depending on how it was equipped), whereas variously equipped Mercedes ML 350 SUVs had price tags in the \$42,000–\$85,000 range and a BMW X5 SUV could range anywhere from \$46,000 to \$75,000, depending on the optional equipment chosen.
- Establishing a new network of Lexus dealers, separate from Toyota dealers, dedicated to providing a level of personalized, attentive customer service unmatched in the industry.

Lexus's best-cost provider strategy allowed it to become the number one selling luxury car brand worldwide in 2000—a distinction that it held through 2007 and may well to continue to hold.

FOCUSED (OR MARKET NICHE) STRATEGIES

What sets focused strategies apart from low-cost leadership or broad differentiation strategies is concentrated attention on a narrow piece of the total market. The target segment, or niche, can be defined by geographic uniqueness, by specialized requirements in using the product, or by special product attributes that appeal only to niche members. Community Coffee, the largest family-owned specialty coffee retailer in the United States, has a geographic focus on the state of Louisiana and communities across the Gulf of Mexico. Community Coffee holds only a 1.1 percent share of the national coffee market, but it has recorded sales in excess of \$100 million and has won a 50 percent share of the coffee business in the 11-state region where it is distributed. Other examples of firms that concentrate on a well-defined market niche keyed to a particular product or buyer segment include Animal Planet and the History Channel (in cable TV); Porsche (in sports cars); Bandag (a specialist in truck tire recapping that promotes its recaps aggressively at more than 1,000 truck stops); CGA Inc. (a specialist in providing insurance to cover the cost of lucrative hole-in-one prizes at golf tournaments); and Match.com (the world's largest online dating service). Microbreweries, local bakeries, bed-and-breakfast inns, and local owner-managed retail boutiques are all good examples of enterprises that have scaled their operations to serve narrow or local customer segments.

A Focused Low-Cost Strategy

A focused strategy based on low cost aims at securing a competitive advantage by serving buyers in the target market niche at a lower cost and a lower price than rival competitors. This strategy has considerable attraction when a firm can lower costs significantly by limiting its customer base to a well-defined buyer segment. The avenues to achieving a cost advantage over rivals also serving the target market niche are the same as for low-cost leadership—outmanage rivals in keeping the costs of value chain activities contained to a bare minimum and search for innovate ways to reconfigure the firm's value chain and bypass or reduce certain value chain activities. The only real difference between a low-cost provider strategy and a focused low-cost strategy is the size of the buyer group that a company is trying to appeal to—the former involves a product offering that appeals broadly to most buyer groups and market segments, whereas the latter involves meeting the needs of only those buyers in a narrow market segment.

Focused low-cost strategies are fairly common. Producers of private-label goods are able to achieve low costs in product development, marketing, distribution, and advertising by concentrating on making generic items similar to name-brand merchandise and selling directly to retail chains wanting a low-priced store brand. The Perrigo Company has become a leading manufacturer of over-the-counter health care products, with 2007 sales of more than $1.4 billion, by focusing on producing private-label brands for retailers such as Wal-Mart, CVS, Walgreens, Rite Aid, and Safeway. Motel 6 has used a low-cost strategy in catering to budget-conscious travelers who just want to pay for a clean, no-frills place to spend the night. Illustration Capsule 5.3 describes how Vizio's low costs and focus on big-box retailers allowed it to become a major seller of flat-panel TVs in the United States in less than five years from its start-up.

A Focused Differentiation Strategy

A focused strategy keyed to differentiation aims at securing a competitive advantage with a product offering carefully designed to appeal to the unique preferences and needs of a narrow, well-defined group of buyers (as distinguished from a broad differentiation strategy aimed at many buyer groups and market segments). Successful use of a focused differentiation strategy depends on the existence of a buyer segment that is looking for special product attributes or seller capabilities and on a firm's ability to stand apart from rivals competing in the same target market niche.

Companies like Godiva Chocolates, Chanel, Gucci, Rolls-Royce, Häagen-Dazs, and W. L. Gore (the maker of Gore-Tex) employ successful differentiation-based focused strategies targeted at upscale buyers wanting products and services with world-class attributes. Indeed, most markets contain a buyer segment willing to pay a big price premium for the very finest items available, thus opening the strategic window for some competitors to pursue differentiation-based focused strategies aimed at the very top of the market pyramid. Ferrari markets its 1,500 cars sold in North America each year to a list of just

one of the 20 $1.1 million FXX models planned for sale in North America.

Another successful focused differentiator is Trader Joe's, a 300-store, 11-state chain that is a combination gourmet deli and food warehouse. Customers shop Trader Joe's as much for entertainment as for conventional grocery items—the store stocks out-of-the-ordinary culinary treats like raspberry salsa, salmon burgers, and jasmine fried rice, as well as the standard goods normally found in supermarkets. What sets Trader Joe's apart is not just its unique combination of food novelties and competitively priced grocery items but also its capability to turn an otherwise mundane grocery excursion into a whimsical treasure hunt that is just plain fun.

ILLUSTRATION CAPSULE 5.3
Vizio's Focused Low-Cost Strategy

California-based Vizio Inc. designs flat-panel LCD and plasma TVs that range in size from 20 to 52 inches and are sold only by big-box discount retailers such as Wal-Mart, Sam's Club, Costco Wholesale, Best Buy, and Circuit City. If you've shopped for a flat-panel TV recently, you've probably noticed that Vizio is among the lowest-priced brands and that its picture quality is surprising good considering the price. The company is able to keep its cost low by only designing TVs and then sourcing its production to a limited number of contract manufacturers in Taiwan. In fact, 80 percent of its production is handled by a company called AmTran Technology. Such a dependence on a supplier can place a buyer in a precarious situation, making them vulnerable to price increases or product shortages, but Vizio has countered this possible threat by making AmTran a major stockholder. AmTran Technology owns a 23 percent stake in Vizio and earns about 80 percent of its revenues from its sales of televisions to Vizio. This close relationship with its major supplier and its focus on a single product category sold through limited distribution channels allows it to offer its customers deep price discounts.

Vizio's first major account was landed in 2003 when it approached Costco buyers with a 46-inch plasma TV whose wholesale price was half that of the next-lowest-price competitor. Within two months, Costco was carrying Vizio flat-panel TVs in 320 of its warehouse stores in the United States. In October 2007, Vizio approached buyers for Sam's Club with a 20-inch LCD TV that could be sold at retail for under $350. The price and quality of the 20-inch TV led Sam's Club buyers to place an order for 20,000 TVs for a March 2008 delivery. At year-end 2007, Vizio was the third largest seller of flat-panel TVs in the United States, with a market share of 12.4 percent and within one-tenth of a percentage point of matching number two Sony's 12.5 percent market share. Vizio recorded revenues of $2 billion in 2007 and was the industry's most profitable seller of TVs. Vizio management expected to challenge Samsung for the title of market share leader in 2008, which had a market share of 14.2 percent in 2007.

Source: Christopher Lawton, Yukari Iwatani Kane, and Jason Dean, "Picture Shift: U.S. Upstart Takes On TV Giants in Price War," *Wall Street Journal,* April 15, 2008, p. A1.

Illustration Capsule 5.4 describes Progressive Insurance's focused differentiation strategy.

When a Focused Low-Cost or Focused Differentiation Strategy Is Attractive

A focused strategy aimed at securing a competitive edge based on either low cost or differentiation becomes increasingly attractive as more of the following conditions are met:

- The target market niche is big enough to be profitable and offers good growth potential.
- Industry leaders do not see that having a presence in the niche is crucial to their own success—in which case focusers can often escape battling head-to-head against some of the industry's biggest and strongest competitors.
- It is costly or difficult for multisegment competitors to put capabilities in place to meet the specialized needs of buyers comprising the target market niche and at the same time satisfy the expectations of their mainstream customers.
- The industry has many different niches and segments, thereby allowing a focuser to pick a competitively attractive niche suited to its resource strengths and capabilities. Also, with more niches there is more room for focusers to avoid each other in competing for the same customers.

ILLUSTRATION CAPSULE 5.4
Progressive Insurance's Focused Differentiation Strategy in Auto Insurance

Progressive Insurance has fashioned a strategy in auto insurance focused on people with a record of traffic violations who drive high-performance cars, drivers with accident histories, motorcyclists, teenagers, and other high-risk categories of drivers that most auto insurance companies steer away from. Progressive discovered that some of these high-risk drivers are affluent and pressed for time, making them less sensitive to paying premium rates for their car insurance. Management learned that it could charge such drivers high enough premiums to cover the added risks, plus it differentiated Progressive from other insurers by expediting the process of obtaining insurance. Progressive pioneered the low-cost direct sales model of allowing customers to purchase insurance online and over the phone.

Progressive also studied the market segments for insurance carefully enough to discover that some motorcycle owners were not especially risky (middle-aged suburbanites who sometimes commuted to work or used their motorcycles mainly for recreational trips with their friends). Progressive's strategy allowed it to become a leader in the market for luxury-car insurance for customers who appreciated Progressive's streamlined approach to doing business.

In further differentiating and promoting Progressive's policies, management created teams of roving claims adjusters who would arrive at accident scenes to assess claims and issue checks for repairs on the spot. Progressive introduced 24-hour claims reporting, now an industry standard. In addition, it developed a sophisticated pricing system so that it could quickly and accurately assess each customer's risk and weed out unprofitable customers.

By being creative and excelling at the nuts and bolts of its business, Progressive has won a 7.6 percent share of the $150 billion market for auto insurance and has the highest underwriting margins in the auto-insurance industry.

Sources: www.progressiveinsurance.com; Ian C. McMillan, Alexander van Putten, and Rita Gunther McGrath, "Global Gamesmanship," *Harvard Business Review* 81, no. 5 (May 2003), p. 68; *Fortune,* May 16, 2005, p. 34; and "Motorcyclists Age, Affluence Trending Upward," *BestWire,* July 24, 2007

- Few, if any, other rivals are attempting to specialize in the same target segment—a condition that reduces the risk of segment overcrowding.
- The focuser has a reservoir of customer goodwill and loyalty (accumulated from having catered to the specialized needs and preferences of niche members over many years) that it can draw on to help stave off the ambitious challengers looking to horn in on its business.

The advantages of focusing a company's entire competitive effort on a single market niche are considerable, especially for small and medium-sized companies that may lack the breadth and depth of resources to tackle going after a broad customer base with a something-for-everyone lineup of models, styles, and product selection. By focusing its attention on online auctions—at one time a small niche in the overall auction business—eBay made a huge name for itself and attractive profits for shareholders. Google has capitalized on its specialized expertise in Internet search engines to become one of the most spectacular growth companies of the past 10 years. Two hippie

superpremium segment of the ice cream business.

The Risks of a Focused Low-Cost or Focused Differentiation Strategy

Focusing carries several risks. One is the chance that competitors will find effective ways to match the focused firm's capabilities in serving the target niche—perhaps by coming up with products or brands specifically designed to appeal to buyers in the target niche or by developing expertise and capabilities that offset the focuser's strengths. In the lodging business, large chains like Marriott and Hilton have launched multibrand strategies that allow them to compete effectively in several lodging segments simultaneously. Marriott has flagship hotels with a full complement of services and amenities that allow it to attract travelers and vacationers going to major resorts; it has J. W. Marriot and Ritz-Carlton hotels that provide deluxe comfort and service to business and leisure travelers; it has a Courtyard by Marriott and SpringHill Suites brands for business travelers looking for moderately priced lodging; it has Marriott Residence Inns and TownePlace Suites designed as a "home away from home" for travelers staying five or more nights; and it has 520 Fairfield Inn locations that cater to travelers looking for quality lodging at an affordable price. Similarly, Hilton has a lineup of brands (Conrad Hotels, Doubletree Hotels, Embassy Suite Hotels, Hampton Inns, Hilton Hotels, Hilton Garden Inns, and Homewood Suites) that enable it to compete in multiple segments and compete head-to-head against lodging chains that operate in only a single segment. Multibrand strategies are attractive to large companies like Marriott and Hilton precisely because they enable a company to enter a market niche and siphon business away from companies that employ a focus strategy.

A second risk of employing a focus strategy is the potential for the preferences and needs of niche members to shift over time toward the product attributes desired by the majority of buyers. An erosion of the differences across buyer segments lowers entry barriers into a focuser's market niche and provides an open invitation for rivals in adjacent segments to begin competing for the focuser's customers. A third risk is that the segment may become so attractive it is soon inundated with competitors, intensifying rivalry and splintering segment profits.

THE CONTRASTING FEATURES OF THE FIVE GENERIC COMPETITIVE STRATEGIES: A SUMMARY

Choosing the generic competitive strategy to serve as the framework on which to build the rest of the company's strategy is not a trivial matter. Each of the five generic competitive strategies positions the company differently in its market and competitive environment. Each establishes a central theme for how the company will endeavor to outcompete rivals. Each creates some boundaries or guidelines for maneuvering as market circumstances unfold. Each points to different ways of experimenting and tinkering with the basic strategy—for example, employing a low-cost provider strategy means experimenting with ways that costs can be cut and value chain activities can be streamlined, whereas a broad differentiation strategy means exploring ways to add new differentiating features or to perform value chain activities differently. Each entails differences in terms of product line, production emphasis, marketing emphasis, and means of sustaining the strategy—as shown in Table 5.1.

Thus, a choice of which generic strategy to employ spills over to affect several aspects of how the business will be operated and the manner in which value chain activities must be managed. Deciding which generic strategy to employ is perhaps the most important strategic commitment a company makes—it tends to drive the rest of the company's strategic actions.

One of the big dangers in crafting a competitive strategy is that managers, torn between the pros and cons of the various generic strategies, will opt for *stuck-in-the-middle strategies* that represent compromises between lower costs and greater differentiation and between broad and narrow market appeal. Compromise or

Table 5.1 Dis[illegible]shing Features of the Five Generic Competitive Strategies

	L[illegible] Provider	Broad Differentiation	Best-Cost Provider	Focused Low-Cost Provider	Focused Differentiation
Strategic target	• [illegible] d cross-section of [illegible] rket	• A broad cross-section of the market	• Value-conscious buyers	• A narrow market niche where buyer needs and preferences are distinctively different	• A narrow market niche where buyer needs and preferences are distinctively different
Basis of competitive advantage	• [illegible] overall costs than [illegible] titors	• Ability to offer buyers something attractively different from competitors	• Ability to give customers more value for the money	• Lower overall cost than rivals in serving niche members	• Attributes that appeal specifically to niche members
Product line	• [illegible] basic product [illegible] w frills (acceptable [illegible] and limited [illegible] on)	• Many product variations, wide selection; emphasis on differentiating features	• Items with appealing attributes; assorted upscale features	• Features and attributes tailored to the tastes and requirements of niche members	• Features and attributes tailored to the tastes and requirements of niche members
Production emphasis	• [illegible] uous search for [illegible] luction without [illegible] ng acceptable [illegible] and essential [illegible]	• Build in whatever differentiating features buyers are willing to pay for; strive for product superiority	• Build in upscale features and appealing attributes at lower cost than rivals	• A continuous search for cost reduction while incorporating features and attributes matched to niche member preferences	• Custom-made products that match the tastes and requirements of niche members
Marketing emphasis	• [illegible] ake a virtue out [illegible] ct features that [illegible] low cost	• Tout differentiating features • Charge a premium price to cover the extra costs of differentiating features	• Tout delivery of best value • Either deliver comparable features at a lower price than rivals or else match rivals on prices and provide better features	• Communicate attractive features of a budget-priced product offering that fits niche buyers' expectations	• Communicate how product offering does the best job of meeting niche buyers' expectations
Keys to sustaining the strategy	• [illegible] ical prices/good [illegible] • [illegible] manage costs [illegible] ear after year, [illegible] area of the [illegible] s	• Stress constant innovation to stay ahead of imitative competitors • Concentrate on a few key differentiating features	• Unique expertise in simultaneously managing costs down while incorporating upscale features and attributes	• Stay committed to serving the niche at lowest overall cost; don't blur the firm's image by entering other market segments or adding other products to widen market appeal	• Stay committed to serving the niche better than rivals; don't blur the firm's image by entering other market segments or adding other products to widen market appeal

middle-ground strategies rarely produce sustainable competitive advantage or a distinctive competitive position—well-executed best-cost provider strategies are the only exception. Usually, companies with compromise strategies end up with a middle-of-the-pack industry ranking—they have average costs, some but not a lot of product differentiation relative to rivals, an average image and reputation, and little prospect of industry leadership. Having a competitive edge over rivals is the single most dependable contributor to above-average company profitability. Hence only if a company makes a strong and unwavering commitment to one of the five generic competitive strategies does it stand much chance of achieving the sustainable competitive advantage that such strategies can deliver if properly executed.

KEY POINTS

Early in the process of crafting a strategy, company managers have to decide which of the five basic competitive strategies to employ—overall low-cost, broad differentiation, best-cost, focused low-cost, or focused differentiation.

In employing a low-cost provider strategy, a company must do a better job than rivals of cost-effectively managing value chain activities and/or it must find innovative ways to eliminate or bypass cost-producing activities. Low-cost provider strategies work particularly well when the products of rival sellers are virtually identical or very weakly differentiated and supplies are readily available from eager sellers, when there are not many ways to differentiate that have value to buyers, when many buyers are price sensitive and shop the market for the lowest price, and when buyer switching costs are low.

Broad differentiation strategies seek to produce a competitive edge by incorporating attributes and features that set a company's product/service offering apart from rivals in ways that buyers consider valuable and worth paying for. Successful differentiation allows a firm to (1) command a premium price for its product, (2) increase unit sales (because additional buyers are won over by the differentiating features), and/or (3) gain buyer loyalty to its brand (because some buyers are strongly attracted to the differentiating features and bond with the company and its products). Differentiation strategies work best in markets with diverse buyer preferences where there are big windows of opportunity to strongly differentiate a company's product offering from those of rival brands, in situations where few other rivals are pursuing a similar differentiation approach, and in circumstances where companies are racing to bring out the most appealing next-generation product. A differentiation strategy is doomed when competitors are able to quickly copy most or all of the appealing product attributes a company comes up with, when a company's differentiation efforts meet with a ho-hum or so what market reception, or when a company erodes profitability by overspending on efforts to differentiate its product offering.

Best-cost provider strategies combine a strategic emphasis on low cost with a strategic emphasis on more than minimal quality, service, features, or performance. The aim is to create competitive advantage by giving buyers more value for the money—an approach that entails matching close rivals on key quality/service/features/performance attributes and beating them on the costs of incorporating such attributes into the product or service. A best-cost provider strategy works best in markets where buyer diversity makes product differentiation the norm and where many buyers are also sensitive to price and value.

A focus strategy delivers competitive advantage either by achieving lower costs than rivals in serving buyers comprising the target market niche or by developing specialized ability to offer niche buyers an appealingly differentiated offering than meets their needs better than rival brands. A focused strategy based on either low cost or differentiation becomes increasingly attractive when the target market niche is big enough to be profitable and offers good growth potential, when it is costly or difficult for multisegment competitors to put capabilities in place to meet the specialized needs of the target market niche and at the same time satisfy the expectations of their mainstream customers, when there are one or more niches that present a good match with a focuser's resource strengths and capabilities, and when few other rivals are attempting to specialize in the same target segment.

Deciding which generic strategy to employ is perhaps the most important strategic commitment a company makes—it tends to drive the rest of the strategic actions a company decides to undertake and it sets the whole tone for the pursuit of a competitive advantage over rivals.

ASSURANCE OF LEARNING EXERCISES

1. Best Buy is the largest consumer electronics retailer in the United States; its sales in 2007 reached nearly $36 billion. The company competes aggressively on price with rivals such as Circuit City, Costco Wholesale, Sam's Club, Wal-Mart, and Target, but it is also known by consumers for its first-rate customer service. Best Buy customers have commented that the retailer's sales staff is exceptionally knowledgeable about the products they sell and can direct them to the exact location of difficult-to-find items. Best Buy customers also appreciate that demonstration models of PC monitors, MP3 players, and other electronics are fully powered and ready for in-store use. Best Buy's Geek Squad tech support and installation services are additional customer service features that are valued by many customers. How would you characterize Best Buy's competitive strategy? Should it be classified as a low-cost provider strategy? A differentiation strategy? A best-cost strategy? Explain your answer.
2. Stihl is the world's leading manufacturer and marketer of chain saws, with annual sales exceeding $2 billion. With innovations dating to its 1929 invention of the gasoline-powered chain saw, the company holds over 1,000 patents related to chain saws and outdoor power tools. The company's chain saws, leaf blowers, and hedge trimmers sell at price points well above competing brands and are sold only by its network of 8,000 independent dealers. The company boasts in its advertisements that its products are rated number one by consumer magazines and are *not* sold at Lowe's or The Home Depot. How does Stihl's choice of distribution channels and advertisements contribute to its differentiation strategy?
3. Explore BMW's Web site (www.bmw.com) and see if you can identify at least three ways in which the company seeks to differentiate itself from rival automakers. Is there reason to believe that BMW's differentiation strategy has been successful in producing a competitive [illegible]

[illegible] PARTICIPANTS

1. Which one of the five generic competitive strategies best characterizes your company's strategic approach to competing successfully?
2. Which rival companies appear to be employing a low-cost provider strategy?
3. Which rival companies appear to be employing a broad differentiation strategy?
4. Which rival companies appear to be employing a best-cost provider strategy?
5. Which rival companies appear to be employing some type of focus strategy?

CHAPTER

6 Supplementing the Chosen Competitive Strategy

Other Important Business Strategy Choices

LEARNING OBJECTIVES

1. Gain an understanding of how strategic alliances and collaborative partnerships can bolster a company's competitive capabilities and resource strengths.
2. Become aware of the strategic benefits of mergers and acquisitions.
3. Understand when a company should consider using a vertical integration strategy to extend its operations to more stages of the overall industry value chain.
4. Understand the conditions that favor farming out certain value chain activities to vendors and strategic allies.
5. Recognize how and why different types of market situations shape business strategy choices.
6. Understand when being a first-mover or a fast-follower or a late-mover can lead to competitive advantage.

Strategies for taking the hill won't necessarily hold it.

—**Amar Bhide**

Successful business strategy is about actively shaping the game you play, not just playing the game you find.

—**Adam M. Brandenburger and Barry J. Nalebuff**

The sure path to oblivion is to stay where you are.

— **Bernard Fauber**

Strategy is all about combining choices of what to do and what not to do into a system that creates the requisite fit between what the environment needs and what the company does.

— **Costas Markides**

Once a company has settled on which of the five generic strategies to employ, attention turns to what other *strategic actions* it can take to complement its competitive approach and maximize the power of its overall strategy. As discussed in earlier chapters, a company's overall business strategy includes not only the details of its competitive strategy to deliver value to customers in a unique way (and the related functional-area and operating-level strategies) but also any other strategic initiatives that can embellish its competitive capabilities and resource strengths and promote sustainable competitive advantage. Several measures to enhance a company's strategy have to be considered:

- Whether entering into strategic alliances and/or partnerships can enhance a company's competitive capabilities and resource strengths.
- Whether to bolster the company's market position via merger or acquisitions.
- Whether to integrate backward or forward into more stages of the industry value chain.
- Which value chain activities, if any, should be outsourced.
- How best to tailor the company's strategy to such industry conditions as rapid growth, slow growth, market stagnation, rapid-fire change and market turbulence, and industry fragmentation.
- When to undertake strategic moves—whether it is advantageous to be a first-mover or a fast-follower or a late-mover.

The chapter contains sections discussing the pros and cons of each of these strategy-enhancing measures.

STRATEGIC ALLIANCES AND PARTNERSHIPS

Companies in all types of industries and in all parts of the world have elected to form strategic alliances and partnerships to complement their own strategic initiatives and strengthen their competitiveness in domestic and international markets. This is an about-face from times past, when the vast majority of companies were content to go it alone, confident that they already had or could independently develop whatever resources and know-how were needed to be successful in their markets. But globalization of the world economy; revolutionary advances in technology across a broad front; and untapped opportunities in national markets in Asia, Latin America, and Europe have made strategic partnerships of one kind or another integral to competing on a broad geographic scale.

Many companies now find themselves thrust into two very demanding competitive races: (1) *the global race to build a market presence in many different national markets* and join the ranks of companies recognized as global market leaders, and (2) *the race to seize opportunities on the frontiers of advancing technology* and build the resource strengths and business capabilities to compete successfully in the industries and product markets of the future.[1] Even the largest and most financially sound companies have concluded that simultaneously running the races for global market leadership and for a stake in the industries of the future requires more diverse and expansive skills, resources, technological expertise, and competitive capabilities than they can assemble and manage alone. Such companies, along with others that are missing the resources and competitive capabilities needed to pursue promising opportunities, have determined that the fastest way to fill the gap is often to form alliances with enterprises having the desired strengths. Consequently, these companies form strategic alliances or partnerships in which two or more companies jointly work to achieve mutually beneficial strategic outcomes. Thus, a **strategic alliance** is a formal agreement between two or more separate companies in which there is strategically relevant collaboration of some sort, joint contribution of resources, shared risk, shared control, and mutual dependence. Often, alliances involve joint marketing, joint sales or distribution, joint production, design collaboration, joint research, or projects to jointly develop new technologies or products. The relationship between the partners may be contractual or merely collaborative; the arrangement commonly stops short of formal ownership ties between the partners (although there are a few strategic alliances where one or more allies have minority ownership in certain of the other alliance members). Five factors make an alliance "strategic," as opposed to just a convenient business arrangement:[2]

CORE CONCEPT

Strategic alliances **are collaborative arrangements where two or more companies join forces to achieve mutually beneficial strategic outcomes. The competitive attraction of alliances is in allowing companies to bundle competencies and resources that are more valuable in a joint effort than when kept separate.**

1. It is critical to the company's achievement of an important objective.
2. It helps build, sustain, or enhance a core competence or competitive advantage.
3. It helps block a competitive threat.
4. It helps open up important new market opportunities.
5. It mitigates a significant risk to a company's business.

Strategic cooperation is a much-favored, indeed necessary, approach in industries where new technological developments are occurring at a furious pace along many different paths and where advances in one technology spill over to affect others (often blurring industry boundaries). Whenever industries are experiencing high-velocity technological advances in many areas simultaneously, firms find it virtually essential to have cooperative relationships with other enterprises to stay on the leading edge of technology and product performance even in their own area of specialization.

Companies in many different industries all across the world have made strategic alliances a core part of their overall strategy; U.S. companies alone announced nearly 68,000 alliances from 1996 through 2003.[3] In the personal computer (PC) industry, alliances are pervasive because the different components of PCs and the software to run them are supplied by so many different companies—one set of companies provides the microprocessors, another group makes the circuit boards, another the monitors, another the disk drives, another the memory chips, and so on. Moreover, their facilities are scattered across the United States, Japan, Taiwan, Singapore, Malaysia, and parts of Europe. Strategic alliances among companies in the various parts of the PC industry facilitate the close cross-company collaboration required on next-generation product development, logistics, production, and the timing of new product releases.

Since 2003, Samsung, a global electronics company headquartered in South Korea, has entered into more than 30 major strategic alliances involving such companies as Sony, Nokia, Intel, Microsoft, Dell, Toshiba, Lowe's, IBM, Hewlett-Packard, and Disney Automation; the alliances involved joint investments, technology transfer arrangements, joint R&D projects, and agreements to supply parts and components—all of which facilitated Samsung's strategic efforts to globalize its business and secure it position as a leader in the worldwide electronics industry. Microsoft collaborates very closely with independent software developers to ensure that their programs will run on the next-generation versions of Windows. Genentech, a leader in biotechnology and human genetics, has a partnering strategy to increase its access to novel biotherapeutics products and technologies and has formed R&D alliances with over 30 companies to boost its prospects for developing new cures for various diseases and ailments. United Airlines, American Airlines, Continental, Delta, and Northwest created an alliance to form Orbitz, an Internet travel site that enabled them to compete head-to-head against Expedia and Travelocity and, further, to give them more economical access to travelers and vacationers shopping online for airfares, rental cars, lodging, cruises, and vacation packages.

Intel and wireless telephone provider Clearwire launched a strategic alliance in 2004 to create an advanced Wi-Fi technology that would allow portable PC users to link to the Internet via cellular telephone signals. In 2008, Intel and Clearwire were in negotiations with Google, Time Warner, Comcast, and Sprint to expand Clearwire's WiMAX network in the United States. WiMAX, a fourth-generation Wi-Fi technology, allowed people to browse the Internet at speeds as great as 10 times faster than other cellular Wi-Fi technologies. Intel planned to support the WiMAX alliance with the launch of laptop computers equipped with WiMAX wireless cards by late 2008. The appeal of the partnership for Time Warner and Comcast was the ability to bundle the sale of wireless services to its cable customers, while Clearwire and Sprint hoped

Toyota has forged long-term strategic partnerships with many of its suppliers of automotive parts and components, both to achieve lower costs and to improve the quality and reliability of its vehicles. In 2008, when Chrysler found itself unable to build hybrid SUVs and trucks using its Two Mode technological innovation (because it lacked the economies of scale necessary to produce proprietary components at a reasonable cost), it entered into a strategic alliance with Nissan whereby Nissan would build Chrysler vehicles with the hybrid technology and Chrysler would take over the production of certain Nissan truck models. Chrysler also entered into an alliance with China's Chery Automobile Company to expand Chrysler's line of small cars with a Chery-produced model. Johnson & Johnson and Merck entered into an alliance to market Pepcid AC; Merck developed the stomach distress remedy, and Johnson & Johnson functioned as marketer—the alliance made Pepcid products the best-selling remedies for acid indigestion and heartburn.

Company use of alliances is quite widespread.

Studies indicate that large corporations are commonly involved in 30 to 50 alliances and that a number have hundreds of alliances. One recent study estimated that about 35 percent of corporate revenues in 2003 came from activities involving strategic alliances, up from 15 percent in 1995.[4] Another study reported that the typical large corporation relied on alliances for 15 to 20 percent of its revenues, assets, or income.[5] Companies that have formed a host of alliances have a need to manage their alliances like a portfolio—terminating those that no longer serve a useful purpose or that have produced meager results, forming promising new alliances, and restructuring certain existing alliances to correct performance problems and/or redirect the collaborative effort.[6]

Why and How Strategic Alliances Are Advantageous

The best alliances are highly selective, focusing on particular value chain activities and on obtaining a particular competitive benefit. They tend to enable a firm to build on its strengths and to learn.

The most common reasons why companies enter into strategic alliances are to expedite the development of promising new technologies or products, to overcome deficits in their own technical and manufacturing expertise, to bring together the personnel and expertise needed to create desirable new skill sets and capabilities, to improve supply chain efficiency, to gain economies of scale in production and/or marketing, and to acquire or improve market access through joint marketing agreements.[7] Manufacturers frequently pursue alliances with parts and components suppliers to gain the efficiencies of better supply chain management and to speed new products to market. By joining forces in components production and/or final assembly, companies may be able to realize cost savings not achievable with their own small volumes. Allies can learn much from one another in performing joint research, sharing technological know-how, and collaborating on complementary new technologies and products—sometimes enough to enable them to pursue other new opportunities on their own.[8] In industries where technology is advancing rapidly, alliances are all about fast cycles of learning, staying abreast of the latest developments, and gaining quick access to the latest round of technological know-how. In bringing together firms with different skills and knowledge bases, alliances open up learning opportunities that help partner firms better leverage their own resource strengths.[9]

There are several other instances in which companies find strategic alliances particularly valuable. A company that is racing for *global market leadership* needs alliances to:

- *Get into critical country markets quickly* and accelerate the process of building a potent global market presence.
- *Gain inside knowledge about unfamiliar markets and cultures through alliances with local partners.* For example, U.S., European, and Japanese companies wanting to build market footholds in the fast-growing Chinese market have pursued

partnership arrangements with Chinese companies to help in getting products through the tedious and typically corrupt customs process; to help guide them through the maze of government regulations; to supply knowledge of local markets; to provide guidance on adapting their products to better match the buying preferences of Chinese consumers; to set up local manufacturing capabilities; and to assist in distribution, marketing, and promotional activities. The Chinese government has long required foreign companies operating in China to have a state-owned Chinese company as a minority or maybe even 50 percent partner—only recently has it backed off this requirement for foreign companies operating in selected parts of the Chinese economy.

- *Access valuable skills and competencies* that are concentrated in particular geographic locations (such as software design competencies in the United States, fashion design skills in Italy, and efficient manufacturing skills in Japan and China).

A company that is racing to *stake out a strong position in an industry of the future* needs alliances to:

- *Establish a stronger beachhead* for participating in the target industry.
- *Master new technologies and build new expertise and competencies* faster than would be possible through internal efforts.
- *Open up broader opportunities* in the target industry by melding the firm's own capabilities with the expertise and resources of partners.

Capturing the Benefits of Strategic Alliances

The extent to which companies benefit from entering into alliances and partnerships seems to be a function of six factors:[10]

1. *Picking a good partner*—A good partner not only has the desired expertise and capabilities but also shares the company's vision about the purpose of the alliance. Experience indicates that it is generally wise to avoid a partnership in which there is strong potential of direct competition—agreements to jointly market each other's products hold much potential for conflict unless the products are complements rather than substitutes and unless there is good chemistry among key personnel. Experience also indicates that alliances between strong and weak companies rarely work, because the alliance is unlikely to provide the strong partner with useful resources or skills, plus there's a greater chance of the alliance producing mediocre results.
2. *Being sensitive to cultural differences*—Unless the outsider exhibits respect for the local culture and local business practices, productive working relationships are unlikely to emerge.
3. *Recognizing that the alliance must* [illegible] are learning. Also, if either partner plays games with information or tries to take advantage of the other, the resulting friction can quickly erode the value of further collaboration.
4. *Ensuring that both parties live up to their commitments*—Both parties have to deliver on their commitments for the alliance to produce the intended benefits.

The division of work has to be perceived as fairly apportioned, and the caliber of the benefits received on both sides has to be perceived as adequate.

5. *Structuring the decision-making process so that actions can be taken swiftly when needed*—In many instances, the fast pace of technological and competitive changes dictates an equally fast decision-making process. If the parties get bogged down in discussion or in gaining internal approval from higher-ups, the alliance can turn into an anchor of delay and inaction.
6. *Managing the learning process and then adjusting the alliance agreement over time to fit new circumstances*—One of the keys to long-lasting success is adapting the nature and structure of the alliance to be responsive to shifting market conditions, emerging technologies, and changing customer requirements. Wise allies are quick to recognize the merit of an evolving collaborative arrangement, where adjustments are made to accommodate changing market conditions and to overcome whatever problems arise in establishing an effective working relationship. Most alliances encounter troubles of some kind within a couple of years—those that are flexible enough to evolve are better able to recover.

Most alliances that aim at sharing technology or providing market access turn out to be temporary, fulfilling their purpose after a few years because the benefits of mutual learning have occurred and because the businesses of both partners have developed to the point where they are ready to go their own ways. In such cases, it is important for each partner to learn thoroughly and rapidly about the other partner's technology, business practices, and organizational capabilities and then transfer valuable ideas and practices into its own operations promptly. Although long-term alliances sometimes prove mutually beneficial, most partners don't hesitate to terminate the alliance and go it alone when the payoffs run out.

Alliances are more likely to be long-lasting when (1) they involve collaboration with suppliers or distribution allies and each party's contribution involves activities in different portions of the industry value chain, or (2) both parties conclude that continued collaboration is in their mutual interest, perhaps because new opportunities for learning are emerging or perhaps because further collaboration will allow each partner to extend its market reach beyond what it could accomplish on its own.

Why Many Alliances Are Unstable or Break Apart

The stability of an alliance depends on how well the partners work together, their success in responding and adapting to changing internal and external conditions, and their willingness to renegotiate the bargain if circumstances so warrant. A successful alliance requires real in-the-trenches collaboration, not merely an arm's-length exchange of ideas. Unless partners place a high value on the skills, resources, and contributions each brings to the alliance and the cooperative arrangement results in valuable win–win outcomes, it is doomed. A surprisingly large number of alliances never live up to expectations. In 2007, a *Harvard Business Review* article reported that even though the number of strategic alliances increases by about 25 percent annually, about 60 to 70 percent continue to fail each year.[11]

The high divorce rate among strategic allies has several causes—diverging objectives and priorities, an inability to work well together (the alliance between Disney and Pixar is a classic example of an alliance coming apart because of clashes between high-level executives), changing conditions that render the purpose of the alliance obsolete, the emergence of more attractive technological paths, and marketplace rivalry between one or more allies.[12] Experience indicates that *alliances stand a reasonable chance of helping a company reduce competitive disadvantage, but very rarely have they proved a strategic option for gaining a durable competitive edge over rivals.*

The Strategic Dangers of Relying Heavily on Alliances and Partnerships

The Achilles' heel of alliances and cooperative strategies is a dependence on other companies for *essential* expertise and capabilities. To be a market leader (and perhaps even a serious market contender), a company must ultimately develop its own capabilities in areas where internal strategic control is pivotal to protecting its competitiveness and building competitive advantage. Moreover, some alliances hold only limited potential because the partner guards its most valuable skills and expertise; in such instances, acquiring or merging with a company possessing the desired know-how and resources is a better solution.

MERGER AND ACQUISITION STRATEGIES

Combining the operations of two companies, via merger or acquisition, is an attractive strategic option for achieving operating economies, strengthening the resulting company's competencies and competitiveness, and opening up avenues of new market opportunity.

Mergers and acquisitions are much-used strategic options—for example, the total worldwide value of mergers and acquisitions completed between 2002 and late 2007 approached $16 trillion.[13] Mergers and acquisitions are especially well-suited for situations in which alliances and partnerships do not go far enough in providing a company with access to needed resources and capabilities.[14] Ownership ties are more permanent than partnership ties, allowing the operations of the merger/acquisition participants to be tightly integrated and creating more in-house control and autonomy. A *merger* is a pooling of equals, with the newly created company often taking on a new name. An *acquisition* is a combination in which one company, the acquirer, purchases and absorbs the operations of another, the acquired. The difference between a merger and an acquisition relates more to the details of ownership, management control, and financial arrangements than to strategy and competitive advantage. The resources, competencies, and competitive capabilities of the newly created enterprise end up much the same whether the combination is the result of acquisition or merger.

Many mergers and acquisitions are driven by strategies to achieve any of five strategic objectives:[15]

1. *To create a more cost-efficient operation out of the combined companies*—When a company acquires another company in the same industry, there's usually enough overlap in operations that certain inefficient plants can be closed or distribution activities partly combined and downsized (when nearby centers serve some of the same geographic areas) [illegible] of buying in greater volume from common suppliers and from closer collaboration with supply chain partners. Likewise, it is usually feasible to squeeze out cost savings in administrative activities, again by combining and downsizing such administrative activities as finance and accounting, information technology, human resources, and so on. Delta Air Lines and Northwest Airlines entered into a merger agreement in 2008 that would create the world's largest airline and

hopefully give the new company a reasonable chance of survival in the troubled airline industry. Both companies had emerged from bankruptcy in 2007 and, at the time of the merger announcement, were still struggling to keep costs low and earn profits as fuel costs soared. The merger was expected to allow the new airline to cut $1 billion from its annual operating costs by eliminating redundant activities and improving aircraft utilization. In addition, the merger would allow the new airline to narrow the size of its fleet and retire many older fuel-hungry planes. Quite a number of acquisitions are undertaken with the objective of transforming two or more otherwise high-cost companies into one lean competitor with average or below-average costs.

2. *To expand a company's geographic coverage*—One of the best and quickest ways to expand a company's geographic coverage is to acquire rivals with operations in the desired locations. And if there is some geographic overlap, then a side benefit is being able to reduce costs by eliminating duplicate facilities in those geographic areas where undesirable overlap exists. Banks like Wells Fargo, Bank of America, Wachovia, and SunTrust have pursued geographic expansion by making a series of acquisitions over the years, enabling them to establish a market presence in an ever-growing number of states and localities. Many companies use acquisitions to expand internationally—food-products companies like Nestlé, Kraft, Unilever, and Procter & Gamble—all racing for global market leadership—have made acquisitions an integral part of their strategies to widen their geographic reach.
3. *To extend the company's business into new product categories*—Many times a company has gaps in its product line that need to be filled. Acquisition can be a quicker and more potent way to broaden a company's product line than going through the exercise of introducing a company's own new product to fill the gap. PepsiCo's Frito-Lay division acquired Flat Earth, a maker of fruit and vegetable crisps, to broaden its lineup of snacks that appeal to health-conscious consumers. Coca-Cola added to its lineup of healthy beverages with the $4.1 billion acquisition of Glacéau in 2007. Glacéau is the maker of VitaminWater, which is the leading enhanced-water brand in the United States.
4. *To gain quick access to new technologies or other resources and competitive capabilities*—Making acquisitions to bolster a company's technological know-how or to fill resource holes is a favorite of companies racing to establish a position in an industry or product category about to be born. Making acquisitions aimed at filling meaningful gaps in technological expertise allows a company to bypass a time-consuming and perhaps expensive R&D effort (which might not succeed). Cisco Systems purchased over 75 technology companies between 2000 and 2008 to give it more technological reach and product breadth, thereby buttressing its standing as the world's biggest supplier of systems for building the infrastructure of the Internet. Intel has made over 300 acquisitions in the past five or so years to broaden its technological base, obtain the resource capabilities to produce and market a variety of Internet-related and electronics-related products, and make it less dependent on supplying microprocessors for PCs.
5. *To try to invent a new industry and lead the convergence of industries whose boundaries are being blurred by changing technologies and new market opportunities*—A company's management may conclude that two or more distinct industries are converging into one and decide to establish a strong position in the consolidating markets by bringing together the resources and products of several different companies. Microsoft TV has made a series of acquisitions that have enabled it to

launch Internet Protocol Television (IPTV). Microsoft TV allows broadband users to use their home computers or Xbox game consoles to download live programming, video on demand, pictures, and music. News Corporation has also prepared for the convergence of media services with the purchase of satellite TV companies to complement its media holdings in TV broadcasting (the Fox network, and TV stations in various countries); cable TV (Fox News, Fox Sports, and FX); filmed entertainment (Twentieth Century Fox and Fox Studios); and newspaper, magazine, and book publishing. Most recently, News Corp. acquired Dow Jones, the publisher of *The Wall Street Journal,* to further extend its media business holdings.

Numerous companies have employed an acquisition strategy to catapult themselves from the ranks of the unknown into positions of market leadership. During the 1990s, North Carolina National Bank (NCNB) pursued a series of acquisitions to transform itself into a major regional bank in the Southeast. But NCNB's strategic vision was to become a bank with offices across most of the United States; it therefore changed its name to NationsBank. In 1998, NationsBank acquired Bank of America for $66 billion and also adopted its name. In 2004, Bank of America acquired Fleet Boston Financial for $48 billion. Bank of America spent $35 billion in 2005 to acquire MBNA, a leading credit card company, and acquired U.S. Trust Corporation and LaSalle Bank in 2007. In 2008, Bank of America had a network of 6,150 branch banks in 31 states and the District of Columbia, and held deposits of more than $800 billion. It ranked as the largest U.S. bank in terms of shareholders' equity and market capitalization, the second largest U.S. bank in total assets (more than $1.7 trillion in 2007), and the second most profitable U.S. bank, with 2007 net income of nearly $15 billion. Illustration Capsule 6.1 describes how Clear Channel Communications has used acquisitions to build a leading global position in outdoor advertising and radio broadcasting.

Why Mergers and Acquisitions Sometimes Fail to Produce Anticipated Results

All too frequently, mergers and acquisitions do not produce the hoped-for outcomes.[16] Cost savings may prove smaller than expected. Gains in competitive capabilities may take substantially longer to realize or, worse, may never materialize at all. Efforts to mesh the corporate cultures can stall due to formidable resistance from organization members. Managers and employees at the acquired company may argue forcefully for continuing to do certain things the way they were done prior to the acquisition. Key employees at the acquired company can quickly become disenchanted and leave; the morale of company personnel who remain can drop to disturbingly low levels because they disagree with newly instituted changes. Differences in management styles and operating procedures can prove hard to resolve. The managers appointed to oversee the integration of a newly acquired company can make mistakes in deciding what activities to leave alone and what [illegible] Time Warner, the merger of Daimler-Benz and Chrysler, Ford's acquisition of Jaguar and Land Rover, and Boston Scientific's acquisition of Guidant Corporation are prime examples. The AOL–Time Warner merger proved to be a disaster, partly because AOL's once-rapid growth had evaporated, partly because of a huge clash of corporate cultures, and partly because most of the expected benefits from industry convergence never materialized. Ford paid a handsome price to acquire Jaguar but was

ILLUSTRATION CAPSULE 6.1

Clear Channel Communications: Using Mergers and Acquisitions to Become a Global Market Leader

In 2008, Clear Channel Communications was among the worldwide leaders in radio broadcasting and outdoor advertising. Clear Channel owned and operated more than 1,000 radio stations in the United States and operated an additional 240 radio stations in Australia, New Zealand, and Mexico. Clear Channel's total number of outdoor advertising displays across the world exceeded 850,000 in 2008. The company, which was founded in 1972 by Lowry Mays and Billy Joe McCombs, got its start by acquiring an unprofitable country-music radio station in San Antonio, Texas. Over the next 10 years, Mays learned the radio business and slowly bought other radio stations in a variety of states. Going public in 1984 helped the company raise the equity capital needed to continue acquiring radio stations in additional geographic markets.

When the Federal Communications Commission loosened the rules regarding the ability of one company to own both radio and TV stations in the late 1980s, Clear Channel broadened its strategy and began acquiring small, struggling TV stations. By 1998, Clear Channel had used acquisitions to build a leading position in radio and television stations. Domestically, it owned, programmed, or sold airtime for 69 AM radio stations, 135 FM stations, and 18 TV stations in 48 local markets in 24 states. Clear Channel's big move was to begin expanding internationally, chiefly by acquiring interests in radio station properties in a variety of countries.

In 1997, Clear Channel used acquisitions to establish a major position in outdoor advertising. Its first acquisition was Phoenix-based Eller Media Company, an outdoor advertising company with over 100,000 billboard facings. This was quickly followed by additional acquisitions of outdoor advertising companies, the most important of which were ABC Outdoor in Milwaukee, Wisconsin; Paxton Communications (with operations in Tampa and Orlando, Florida); Universal Outdoor; the More Group, with outdoor operations and 90,000 displays in 24 countries; and the Ackerley Group.

Then in October 1999, Clear Channel made a major move by acquiring AM-FM Inc. and changed its name to Clear Channel Communications; the AM-FM acquisition gave Clear Channel operations in 32 countries, including 830 radio stations, 19 TV stations, and more than 425,000 outdoor displays.

Additional acquisitions were completed during the 2000–2003 period. The emphasis was on buying radio, TV, and outdoor advertising properties with operations in many of the same local markets, which made it feasible to (1) cut costs by sharing facilities and staffs, (2) improve programming, and (3) sell advertising to customers in packages for all three media simultaneously. Packaging ads for two or three media not only helped Clear Channel's advertising clients distribute their messages more effectively but also allowed the company to combine its sales activities and have a common sales force for all three media, achieving significant cost savings and boosting profit margins. But in 2000 Clear Channel broadened its media strategy by acquiring SFX Entertainment, one of the world's largest promoters, producers, and presenters of live entertainment events.

In 2006, Clear Channel management recognized that the company's outdoor advertising and radio businesses were by far the company's most profitable businesses and began a search for buyers of its lesser-performing businesses. The company spun off its live entertainment business in 2006 and entered into an agreement to sell its 56 television stations in 2007. In 2008, it was seeking a buyer for 288 of its 1,005 radio stations that operated in small markets. Its remaining 717 radio stations all operated in the top 100 markets in the United States. In 2008, Clear Channel's outdoor advertising business owned and operated more than 200,000 billboards in the United States and 687,000 outdoor displays in 50 other countries.

Sources: www.clearchannel.com (accessed May 2008), and *BusinessWeek,* October 19, 1999, p. 56.

not able to make the Jaguar brand a major factor in the luxury-car segment in competition against Mercedes, BMW, and Lexus. In 2008, Ford sold Jaguar to India's Tata Motors. In the same deal, Ford also sold its Land Rover division to Tata because of disappointingly low sales volumes—Land Rover was another failed acquisition Ford made to broaden its lineup of models and boost sales volumes. The combination of the engineering expertise of Daimler-Benz and Chrysler's styling and design capabilities was expected to address each of the two merger partners' shortcomings. Daimler-Benz, maker of the Mercedes-Benz brand of vehicles, had long been known for its superior quality and performance, but stodgy styling, while Chrysler had a long tradition of producing beautifully styled vehicles with dismal defect rates and engineering imperfections. The 1998 merger, which formed DaimlerChrysler, did in fact help Daimler-Benz improve its styling, but it also resulted in the esteemed Mercedes brand recording its lowest reliability ratings in the company's history. Chrysler was spun off in 2007, and the now-separate companies are simply called Daimler and Chrysler. Similarly, Boston Scientific's $25 billion acquisition of Guidant Corporation in 2006 has yet to prove successful. At the time of the acquisition, Guidant was a leader in the $10 billion market for pacemakers and other medical devices to treat cardiac disease with 2005 earnings of $355 million. The lofty price paid for Guidant was funded by $6.5 billion in loans and an equity issue that increased outstanding Boston Scientific shares by 80 percent. The addition of $300 million in interest expense to service Boston Scientific's long-term debt contributed to its 2007 net loss of $495 million.

VERTICAL INTEGRATION STRATEGIES: OPERATING ACROSS MORE STAGES OF THE INDUSTRY VALUE CHAIN

Vertical integration extends a firm's competitive and operating scope within the same industry. It involves expanding the firm's range of activities backward into sources of supply and/or forward toward end users. Thus, if a manufacturer invests in facilities to produce certain component parts that it formerly purchased from outside suppliers, it remains in essentially the same industry as before. The only change is that it has operations in two stages of the industry value chain. For example, paint manufacturer Sherwin-Williams remains in the paint business even though it has integrated forward into retailing by operating more than 3,300 retail stores that market its paint products directly to consumers.

Vertical integration strategies can aim at *full integration* (participating in all stages of the industry value chain) or *partial integration* (building positions in selected stages of the industry's total value chain). A firm can pursue vertical integration by starting its own operations in other stages in the industry's activity chain or by acquiring a company already performing the activities it wants to bring in-house.

The Advantages of a Vertical Integration Strategy

The two best reasons for investing company resources in vertical integration are to strengthen the firm's competitive position and to boost its profitability.[17] Vertical integratio [illegible] ... and competitive strengths, and/or helps differentiate the company's product offering.

CORE CONCEPT

[illegible] ... nificantly strengthens a firm's competitive position.

Integrating Backward to Achieve Greater Competitiveness It is harder than one might think to generate cost savings or boost profitability by integrating backward into activities such as parts and components manufacture (which could otherwise be purchased from suppliers with specialized expertise in making these parts and components). For backward integration to be a viable and profitable strategy, a company must be able to (1) achieve the same scale economies as outside suppliers and (2) match or beat suppliers' production efficiency with no drop-off in quality. Neither outcome is a slam dunk. To begin with, a company's in-house requirements are often too small to reach the optimum size for low-cost operation—for instance, if it takes a minimum production volume of 1 million units to achieve mass-production economies and a company's in-house requirements are just 250,000 units, then it falls way short of being able to capture the scale economies of outside suppliers (who may readily find buyers for 1 million or more units). Furthermore, matching the production efficiency of suppliers is fraught with problems when suppliers have considerable production experience of their own, when the technology they employ has elements that are hard to master, and/or when substantial R&D expertise is required to develop next-version parts and components or keep pace with advancing technology in parts/components production.

But that being said, there are still occasions when a company can improve its cost position and competitiveness by performing a broader range of value chain activities in-house rather than having certain of these activities performed by outside suppliers. The best potential for being able to reduce costs via a backward integration strategy exists in situations where suppliers have outsize profit margins, where the item being supplied is a major cost component, and where the requisite technological skills are easily mastered or can be gained by acquiring a supplier with the desired technological know-how. Furthermore, when a company has proprietary know-how that it wants to keep from rivals, then in-house performance of value chain activities related to this know-how is beneficial even if such activities could be performed by outsiders.

Backward vertical integration can produce a differentiation-based competitive advantage when a company ends up with a better-quality product/service offering, improves the caliber of its customer service, or in other ways enhances the performance of its final product. On occasion, integrating into more stages along the industry value chain can add to a company's differentiation capabilities by allowing it to build or strengthen its core competencies, better master key skills or strategy-critical technologies, or add features that deliver greater customer value. Other potential advantages of backward integration include sparing a company the uncertainty of being dependent on suppliers for crucial components or support services and lessening a company's vulnerability to powerful suppliers inclined to raise prices at every opportunity. Panera Bread has been quite successful with a backward vertical integration strategy that involves internally producing fresh dough for company-owned and franchised bakery-cafés to use in making baguettes, pastries, bagels, and other types of bread—the company has earned substantial profits from producing both these items internally rather than having these supplied by outsiders. Furthermore, Panera Bread's vertical integration strategy makes good competitive sense because it helps lower store operating costs and facilitates consistent product quality at the company's 1,185 U.S. locations.

Integrating Forward to Enhance Competitiveness The strategic impetus for forward integration is to gain better access to end users and better market visibility. In many industries, independent sales agents, wholesalers, and retailers handle competing brands of the same product; having no allegiance to any one company's brand, they tend to push whatever sells and earns them the biggest profits. An independent insurance agency, for example, represents a number of different insurance companies—in trying to find the best match between a customer's insurance requirements and the policies of alternative insurance companies, there's plenty of opportunity for independent agents to end up promoting the policies of certain insurance companies ahead of other insurance companies. An insurance company may conclude, therefore, that it is better off integrating forward and setting up its own local sales offices with its own local agents to promote the company's insurance policies exclusively. Likewise, a tire manufacturer may find it better to integrate forward into tire retailing than to use independent distributors and retailers that stock multiple brands. A number of house-ware and apparel manufacturers have integrated forward into retailing so as to move seconds, overstocked items, and slow-selling merchandise through their own branded factory outlet stores. Some producers have opted to integrate forward into retailing by selling directly to customers at the company's Web site. Bypassing regular wholesale/retail channels in favor of direct sales and Internet retailing can have appeal if it lowers distribution costs, produces a relative cost advantage over certain rivals, and results in lower selling prices to end users.

The Disadvantages of a Vertical Integration Strategy

Vertical integration has some substantial drawbacks, however.[18] It boosts a firm's capital investment in the industry, increasing business risk (what if industry growth and profitability go sour?) and boosting a company's vested interests in sticking with its vertically integrated value chain (what if some aspects of its technology and production facilities become obsolete before they are worn out or fully depreciated?). Vertically integrated companies that have invested heavily in a particular technology or in parts/components manufacture are often slow to embrace technological advances or more efficient production methods compared to partially integrated or nonintegrated firms. This is because less integrated firms can pressure suppliers to provide only the latest and best parts and components (even going so far as to shift their purchases from one supplier to another if need be), whereas a vertically integrated firm that is saddled with older technology or facilities that make items it no longer needs is looking at the high costs of premature abandonment. Second, integrating forward or backward locks a firm into relying on its own in-house activities and sources of supply (which later may prove more costly than outsourcing) and potentially results in less flexibility in accommodating shifting buyer preferences or a product design that doesn't include parts and components that it makes in-house. *In today's world of close working relationships with suppliers and efficient supply chain management systems, very few businesses can make a case for integrating backward into the business of suppliers to ensure a reliable supply of materials and components or to reduce production costs.* The best materials and components suppliers stay abreast of advancing technology and are adept in boosting their efficiency and keeping their costs and prices as low as possible. A company that pursues a vertical integration strategy and tries to produce many parts and components in-house is likely to find itself hard-pressed to keep up with technological advances and cutting-edge production practices for each part and component used in making its product.

Third, vertical integration poses all kinds of capacity-matching problems. In [illegible] transmissions. Building the capacity to produce just the right number of axles, radiators, engines, and transmissions in-house—and doing so at the lowest unit costs for each—is much easier said than done. If internal capacity for making transmissions is deficient, the difference has to be bought externally. Where internal capacity for radiators proves excessive, customers need to be found for the surplus. And if by-products are generated—as occurs in the processing of many chemical products—they require arrangements for disposal. Consequently, integrating across several production stages in ways that achieve the lowest feasible costs is not as easy as it might seem.

Fourth, integration forward or backward often calls for radical changes in skills and business capabilities. Parts and components manufacturing, assembly operations, wholesale distribution and retailing, and direct sales via the Internet are different businesses with different key success factors. Managers of a manufacturing company should consider carefully whether it makes good business sense to invest time and money in developing the expertise and merchandising skills to integrate forward into wholesaling and retailing. Many manufacturers learn the hard way that company-owned wholesale/retail networks present many headaches, fit poorly with what they do best, and don't always add the kind of value to their core business they thought they would. Selling to customers via the Internet poses still another set of problems—it is usually easier to use the Internet to sell to business customers than to consumers.

Finally, integrating backward into parts and components manufacture can impair a company's operations when it comes to changing out the use of certain parts and components. It is one thing to design out a component made by a supplier and another to design out a component being made in-house (which can mean laying off employees and writing off the associated investment in equipment and facilities). Companies that alter designs and models frequently in response to shifting buyer preferences often find outsourcing the needed parts and components to be cheaper and less complicated than producing them in-house. Most of the world's automakers, despite their expertise in automotive technology and manufacturing, have concluded that purchasing many of their key parts and components from manufacturing specialists results in higher quality, lower costs, and greater design flexibility than does the vertical integration option.

Weighing the Pros and Cons of Vertical Integration

All in all, a strategy of vertical integration can have both important strengths and weaknesses. The tip of the scales depends on (1) whether vertical integration can enhance the performance of strategy-critical activities in ways that lower cost, build expertise, protect proprietary know-how, or increase differentiation; (2) the impact of vertical integration on investment costs, flexibility and response times, and the administrative costs of coordinating operations across more value chain activities; and (3) whether the integration substantially enhances a company's competitiveness and profitability. *Vertical integration strategies have merit according to which capabilities and value chain activities truly need to be performed in-house and which can be performed better or cheaper by outsiders.* Absent solid benefits, integrating forward or backward is not likely to be an attractive strategy option.

OUTSOURCING STRATEGIES: NARROWING THE BOUNDARIES OF THE BUSINESS

CORE CONCEPT
Outsourcing **involves farming out certain value chain activities to outside vendors.**

Outsourcing involves a conscious decision to abandon or forgo attempts to perform certain value chain activities internally and instead to farm them out to outside specialists and strategic allies. The two big reasons for outsourcing are (1) that outsiders can often perform certain activities better or cheaper and (2) that outsourcing allows a firm to focus its entire energies on those activities at the center of its expertise (its core competencies) and that are the most critical to its competitive and financial success.

The current interest of many companies in making outsourcing a key component of their overall strategy and their approach to supply chain management represents a big departure from the way that companies used to deal with their suppliers and vendors. In years past, it was common for companies to maintain arm's-length relationships with suppliers and outside vendors, insisting on items being made to precise specifications and negotiating long and hard over price.[19] Although a company might place orders with the same supplier repeatedly, there was no expectation that this would be the case; price usually determined which supplier was awarded an order, and companies used the threat of switching suppliers to get the lowest possible prices. To enhance their bargaining power and to make the threat of switching credible, it was standard practice for companies to source key parts and components from several suppliers as opposed to dealing with only a single supplier. But today, most companies are abandoning such approaches in favor of forging alliances and strategic partnerships with a small number of highly capable suppliers. Collaborative relationships are replacing contractual, purely price-oriented relationships because companies have discovered that many of the advantages of performing value chain activities in-house can be captured and many of the disadvantages avoided by forging close, long-term cooperative partnerships with able suppliers and vendors and tapping into the expertise and capabilities that they have painstakingly developed.

When Outsourcing Strategies Are Advantageous

Outsourcing pieces of the value chain to narrow the boundaries of a firm's business makes strategic sense whenever:

> **CORE CONCEPT**
> **A company should generally *not* perform any value chain activity internally that can be performed more efficiently or effectively by outsiders—the chief exception is when a particular activity is strategically crucial and internal control over that activity is deemed essential.**

- *An activity can be performed better or more cheaply by outside specialists.* Many PC makers, for example, have abandoned in-house assembly of their PC models, opting to outsource assembly activities from contract specialists that assemble several brands of PCs—such contract assemblers are able to perform assembly activities at lower cost because their larger-scale operations (1) enable them to purchase PC components in bigger volume and typically at lower costs and (2) provide maximum access to scale economies. Similarly, Nikon—by outsourcing the shipment of digital cameras to UPS—gained the capability to deliver its cameras to retailers in the United States, Latin America, and the Caribbean in as little as two days after an order was placed even though Nikon's camera production was located at facilities in Japan, Korea, and Indonesia.
- *The activity is not crucial to the firm's ability to achieve sustainable competitive advantage and won't hollow out its core competencies, capabilities, or technical know-how.* Outsourcing of maintenance services, data processing and data storage, fringe benefit management, Web site operations, and similar administrative support activities to specialists has become [illegible]

  [illegible] A number of companies have begun outsourcing their call center operations to foreign-based contractors who have access to lower-cost labor supplies and can employ lower-paid call center personnel to respond to customer inquiries or requests for technical support.
- *It reduces the company's risk exposure to changing technology and/or changing buyer preferences.* When a company outsources certain parts, components, and

services, its suppliers must bear the burden of incorporating state-of-the-art technologies and/or undertaking redesigns and upgrades to accommodate a company's plans to introduce next-generation products. If what a supplier provides falls out of favor with buyers or is designed out of next-generation products, it is the supplier's business that suffers rather than a company's own internal operations.

- *It improves a company's ability to innovate.* Collaborative partnerships with world-class suppliers who have cutting-edge intellectual capital and are early adopters of the latest technology give a company access to ever better parts and components—such supplier-driven innovations, when incorporated into a company's own product offering, fuel a company's ability to introduce its own new and improved products.
- *It streamlines company operations in ways that improve organizational flexibility and cuts the time it takes to get new products into the marketplace.* Outsourcing gives a company the flexibility to switch suppliers in the event that its present supplier falls behind competing suppliers. To the extent that its suppliers can speedily get next-generation parts and components into production, then a company can get its own next-generation product offerings into the marketplace quicker. Moreover, seeking out new suppliers with the needed capabilities already in place is frequently quicker, easier, less risky, and cheaper than hurriedly retooling internal operations to replace obsolete capabilities or try to install and master new technologies.
- *It allows a company to assemble diverse kinds of expertise speedily and efficiently.* A company can nearly always gain quicker access to first-rate capabilities and expertise by partnering with suppliers who already have them in place than it can by trying to build them from scratch with its own company personnel.
- *It allows a company to concentrate on its core business, leverage its key resources, and do even better what it already does best.* A company is better able to build and develop its own competitively valuable competencies and capabilities when it concentrates its full resources and energies on performing those activities internally that it can perform better than outsiders and/or that it needs to have under its direct control. Coach, for example, devotes its energy to designing new styles of handbags and leather accessories, opting to outsource handbag production to 40 contract manufacturers in 15 countries. Hewlett-Packard, IBM, and others have sold manufacturing plants to suppliers and then contracted to purchase the output. Starbucks finds purchasing coffee beans from independent growers far more advantageous than trying to integrate backward into the coffee-growing business.

The Big Risk of an Outsourcing Strategy

The biggest danger of outsourcing is that a company will farm out too many or the wrong types of activities and thereby hollow out its own capabilities.[20] In such cases, a company loses touch with the very activities and expertise that over the long run determine its success. But most companies are alert to this danger and take actions to protect against being held hostage by outside suppliers. Cisco Systems guards against loss of control and protects its manufacturing expertise by designing the production methods that its contract manufacturers must use. Cisco keeps the source code for its designs proprietary, thereby controlling the initiation of all improvements and safeguarding its innovations from imitation. Further, Cisco uses the Internet to monitor the factory operations of contract manufacturers around the clock; it can therefore know immediately when problems arise and decide whether to get involved.

BUSINESS STRATEGY CHOICES FOR SPECIFIC MARKET SITUATIONS

As we began emphasizing back in Chapter 3, a good strategy is always well matched to (1) prevailing industry and competitive conditions and (2) a company's own internal resource strengths and weaknesses. We saw in Chapter 3 that a good fit between strategy and the external situation of a company requires an assessment of the industry's driving forces, competitive forces, and key success factors, but there's more to be revealed about matching strategy to specific kinds of industry conditions. This section looks at the various options for matching a company's strategy to six commonly encountered types of market conditions:

- Freshly emerging markets.
- Rapidly growing markets.
- Mature, slow-growth markets.
- Stagnant or declining markets.
- Turbulent markets characterized by rapid-fire change.
- Fragmented markets comprised of a large number of relatively small sellers.

Competing in Emerging Markets

An emerging market is one in the formative stage. Examples include Voice over Internet Protocol (VoIP) telephone communications, online education, e-book publishing, solar energy production, genetic engineering, and nanoelectronics. Many companies striving to establish a strong foothold in a freshly emerging market are start-up enterprises that are busily engaged in perfecting technology, gearing up operations, and trying to broaden distribution and gain buyer acceptance. Important product design issues or technological problems may still have to be worked out. The business models and strategies of companies in an emerging marketplace are unproved—they may look promising but may or may not ever result in attractive profitability.

The Unique Characteristics of an Emerging Market Competing in emerging markets presents managers with some unique strategy-making challenges:[21]

- Because the market is in its infancy, there's usually much speculation about how it will function, how fast it will grow, and how big it will get. The little historical information available is virtually useless in making sales and profit projections. There's lots of guesswork about how rapidly buyers will be attracted and how much they will be willing to pay. For example, there is much uncertainty about how many users of traditional telephone service will be inclined to switch over to VoIP technology and how rapidly any such switchovers will occur.
- In many cases, much of the technological [illegible] use are key factors in securing competitive advantage. In other cases, numerous companies have access to the requisite technology and may be racing to perfect it, often in collaboration with others. In still other instances, there can be competing technological approaches, with much uncertainty over whether multiple technologies will end up competing alongside one another or whether one approach will ultimately win out because of lower costs or better performance—such a battle

is currently under way in the emerging market for hydrogen fuel cell engines for automobiles. General Motors has pioneered one design, while Volkswagen, Honda, Toyota, Ford, Daimler, and BMW have developed their own slightly different fuel cell designs.

- Just as there may be uncertainties surrounding an emerging industry's technology, there may also be no consensus regarding which product attributes will prove decisive in winning buyer favor. Rivalry therefore centers on each firm's efforts to get the market to ratify its own strategic approach to technology, product design, marketing, and distribution. Such rivalry can result in wide differences in product quality and performance from brand to brand.
- Since in an emerging industry all buyers are first-time users, the marketing task is to induce initial purchase and to overcome customer concerns about product features, performance reliability, and conflicting claims of rival firms.
- Many potential buyers expect first-generation products to be rapidly improved, so they delay purchase until technology and product design mature and second- or third-generation products appear on the market.
- Entry barriers tend to be relatively low, even for entrepreneurial start-up companies. Large, well-known, opportunity-seeking companies with ample resources and competitive capabilities are likely to enter if the industry has promise for explosive growth or if its emergence threatens their present business. For instance, many traditional local telephone companies, seeing the potent threat of wireless communications technology and VoIP, have opted to enter the mobile communications business and begin offering landline customers a VoIP option.
- Strong learning/experience curve effects may be present, allowing significant price reductions as volume builds and costs fall.
- Sometimes firms have trouble securing ample supplies of raw materials and components (until suppliers gear up to meet the industry's needs).
- Undercapitalized companies, finding themselves short of funds to support needed R&D and get through several lean years until the product catches on, end up merging with competitors or being acquired by financially strong outsiders looking to invest in a growth market.

CORE CONCEPT

Companies in an emerging industry have wide latitude in experimenting with different strategic approaches.

Strategy Options for Emerging Industries The lack of established rules of the game gives industry participants considerable freedom to experiment with a variety of different strategic approaches. Competitive strategies keyed either to low cost or differentiation are usually viable. Focusing makes good sense when resources and capabilities are limited and the industry has too many technological frontiers or too many buyer segments to pursue at once. Broad or focused differentiation strategies keyed to technological or product superiority typically offer the best chance for early competitive advantage.

In addition to choosing a competitive strategy, companies in an emerging industry usually have to fashion a strategy containing one or more of the following elements:[22]

1. Push to perfect the technology, improve product quality, and develop additional attractive performance features. Out-innovating the competition is often one of the best avenues to industry leadership.
2. Consider merging with or acquiring another firm to gain added expertise and pool resource strengths.

3. As technological uncertainty clears and a dominant technology emerges, try to capture any first-mover advantages by adopting it quickly. However, while there's merit in trying to be the industry standard-bearer on technology and to pioneer the dominant product design, firms have to beware of betting too heavily on their own preferred technological approach or product design—especially when there are many competing technologies, R&D is costly, and technological developments can quickly move in surprising new directions.
4. Acquire or form alliances with companies that have related or complementary technological expertise as a means of helping outcompete rivals on the basis of technological superiority.
5. Pursue new customer groups, new user applications, and entry into new geographical areas (perhaps using strategic partnerships or joint ventures if financial resources are constrained).
6. Make it easy and cheap for first-time buyers to try the industry's first-generation product.
7. As the product becomes familiar to a wide portion of the market, shift the advertising emphasis from creating product awareness to increasing frequency of use and building brand loyalty.
8. Use price cuts to attract the next layer of price-sensitive buyers into the market.
9. Form strategic alliances with key suppliers whenever effective supply chain management provides important access to specialized skills, technological capabilities, and critical materials or components.

Young companies in emerging industries face four strategic hurdles: (1) raising the capital to finance initial operations until sales and revenues take off, profits appear, and cash flows turn positive; (2) developing a strategy to ride the wave of industry growth (what market segments and competitive advantages to go after); (3) managing the rapid expansion of facilities and sales in a manner that positions them to contend for industry leadership; and (4) defending against competitors trying to horn in on their success.[23] Up-and-coming companies can help their cause by selecting knowledgeable members for their boards of directors and by hiring entrepreneurial managers with experience in guiding young businesses through the start-up and takeoff stages. *A firm that develops solid resource capabilities, an appealing business model, and a good strategy has a golden opportunity to shape the rules and establish itself as the recognized industry front-runner.*

But strategic efforts to win the early race for growth and market-share leadership in an emerging industry have to be balanced against the longer-range need to build a durable competitive edge and a defendable market position.[24] The initial front-runners in a fast-growing emerging industry that shows signs of good profitability will almost certainly have to defend their positions against opportunity-seeking competitors trying to horn in on their success. Well-financed outsiders can be counted on to enter [illegible] of new entrants, attracted by the growth and profit potential, overcrowds the market and forces industry consolidation to a smaller number of players. Resource-rich latecomers, aspiring to industry leadership, may become major players by acquiring and merging the operations of weaker competitors and then using their own perhaps considerable brand-name recognition to draw customers and build market share. Hence, the strategies of the early leaders must be aimed at competing for the long haul and making a point of developing the resources, capabilities, and market recognition needed to sustain early successes and stave off competition from capable, ambitious newcomers.

Competing in Rapidly Growing Markets

In a fast-growing market, a company needs a strategy predicated on growing faster than the market average so that it can boost its market share and improve its competitive standing vis-à-vis rivals.

Companies that have the good fortune to be in an industry growing at double-digit rates have a golden opportunity to achieve double-digit revenue and profit growth. If market demand is expanding 20 percent annually, then a company can grow 20 percent annually simply by doing little more than contentedly riding the tide—it simply has to be aggressive enough to secure enough new customers to realize a 20 percent gain in sales, not a particularly impressive strategic feat. What is more interesting, however, is to craft a strategy that enables sales to grow at 25 or 30 percent when the overall market is growing by 20 percent. Should a company's strategy deliver sales growth of only 12 percent in a market growing at 20 percent, then it is actually losing ground in the marketplace—a condition that signals a weak strategy and a less appealing product offering. The point here is that, in a rapidly growing market, a company must aim its strategy at producing gains in revenue that exceed the market average; otherwise, the best it can hope for is to maintain its market standing (if it is able to boost sales at a rate equal to the market average) and its market standing may indeed erode if its sales rise by less than the market average.

To be able to grow at a pace exceeding the market average, a company generally must have a strategy that incorporates one or more of the following elements:

- *Driving down costs per unit so as to enable price reductions that attract droves of new customers.* Charging a lower price always has strong appeal in markets where customers are price-sensitive, and lower prices can help push up buyers' demand by drawing new customers into the marketplace. But since rivals can lower their prices also, a company must really be able to drive its unit costs down *faster than rivals,* such that it can use its low-cost advantage to underprice rivals. The makers of Global Positioning System (GPS) navigation devices are aggressively pursuing cost reductions to make their products more affordable for a wider range of end uses and consumers.
- *Pursuing rapid product innovation, both to set a company's product offering apart from rivals and to incorporate attributes that appeal to growing numbers of customers.* Differentiation strategies, when keyed to product attributes that draw in large numbers of new customers, help bolster a company's reputation for product superiority and lay the foundation for sales gains in excess of the overall rate of market growth. If the market is one where technology is advancing rapidly and product life cycles are short, then it becomes especially important to be first-to-market with next-generation products. But product innovation strategies require competencies in R&D and new product development and design, plus organizational agility in getting new and improved products to market quickly. At the same time they are pursuing cost reductions, the makers of GPS navigation devices are pursuing all sorts of product improvements to enhance performance and functionality and drive sales up at an even faster clip.
- *Gaining access to additional distribution channels and sales outlets.* Pursuing wider distribution access so as to reach more potential buyers is a particularly good strategic approach for realizing above-average sales gains. But usually this

requires a company to be a first-mover in positioning itself in new distribution channels and forcing rivals into playing catch-up.

- *Expanding the company's geographic coverage.* Expanding into areas, either domestic or foreign, where the company does not have a market presence can also be an effective way to reach more potential buyers and pave the way for gains in sales that outpace the overall market average.
- *Expanding the product line to add models/styles that appeal to a wider range of buyers.* Offering buyers a wider selection can be an effective way to draw new customers in numbers sufficient to realize above-average sales gains. Makers of MP3 players and mobile phones are adding new models to stimulate buyer demand; McDonald's has added new coffee drinks and other menu selections to build store traffic. Marketers of VoIP technology are rapidly introducing a wider variety of plans to broaden their appeal to customers with different calling habits and needs.

Competing in Slow-Growth, Mature Markets

A market is said to be *mature* when nearly all potential buyers are already users of the industry's products and growth in market demand closely parallels that of the economy as a whole. In a mature market, demand consists mainly of replacement sales to existing users, with growth hinging on the industry's abilities to attract the few remaining new buyers and to convince existing buyers to up their usage. Consumer goods industries that are mature typically have a growth rate under 5 percent—roughly equal to the growth of the customer base or overall economy.

How Slowing Growth Alters Market Conditions An industry's transition to maturity does not begin on an easily predicted schedule. Industry maturity can be forestalled by technological advances, product innovations, or other driving forces that keep rejuvenating market demand. Nonetheless, when growth rates do slacken, the onset of market maturity usually produces fundamental changes in the industry's competitive environment:[25]

1. *Slowing growth in buyer demand generates more head-to-head competition for market share.* Firms that want to continue on a rapid-growth track start looking for ways to take customers away from competitors. Outbreaks of price cutting, increased advertising, and other aggressive tactics to gain market share are common.
2. *Buyers become more sophisticated, often driving a harder bargain on repeat purchases.* Since buyers have experience with the product and are familiar with competing brands, they are better able to evaluate different brands and can use their knowledge to negotiate a better deal with sellers.
3. *Competition often produces a greater emphasis on cost and service.* As sellers

4. *Firms have a topping-out problem in adding new facilities.* Reduced rates of industry growth mean slowdowns in capacity expansion for manufacturers—adding too much plant capacity at a time when growth is slowing can create oversupply conditions that adversely affect manufacturers' profits well into the future. Likewise, retail chains that specialize in the industry's product have to cut back on the number of new stores being opened to keep from saturating localities with too many stores.

5. *Product innovation and new end-use applications are harder to come by.* Producers find it increasingly difficult to create new product features, find further uses for the product, and sustain buyer excitement.
6. *International competition increases.* Growth-minded domestic firms start to seek out sales opportunities in foreign markets. Some companies, looking for ways to cut costs, relocate plants to countries with lower wage rates. Greater product standardization and diffusion of technological know-how reduce entry barriers and make it possible for enterprising foreign companies to become serious market contenders in more countries. Industry leadership passes to companies that succeed in building strong competitive positions in most of the world's major geographic markets and in winning the biggest global market shares.
7. *Industry profitability falls temporarily or permanently.* Slower growth, increased competition, more sophisticated buyers, and occasional periods of overcapacity put pressure on industry profit margins. Weaker, less-efficient firms are usually the hardest hit.
8. *Stiffening competition induces a number of mergers and acquisitions among former competitors, driving industry consolidation to a smaller number of larger players.* Inefficient firms and firms with weak competitive strategies can achieve respectable results in a fast-growing industry with booming sales. But the intensifying competition that accompanies industry maturity exposes competitive weakness and throws second- and third-tier competitors into a survival-of-the-fittest contest.

Strategies That Fit Conditions in Slow-Growth, Mature Markets As the new competitive character of industry maturity begins to hit full force, any of several strategic moves can strengthen a firm's competitive position: pruning the product line, improving value chain efficiency, trimming costs, increasing sales to present customers, acquiring rival firms, expanding internationally, and strengthening capabilities.[26]

Pruning Marginal Products and Models A wide selection of models, features, and product options sometimes has competitive value during the growth stage, when buyers' needs are still evolving. But such variety can become too costly as price competition stiffens and profit margins are squeezed. Maintaining many product versions works against achieving design, parts inventory, and production economies at the manufacturing levels and can increase inventory stocking costs for distributors and retailers. In addition, the prices of slow-selling versions may not cover their true costs. Pruning marginal products from the line opens the door for cost savings and permits more concentration on items whose margins are highest and/or where a firm has a competitive advantage. General Motors has been cutting slow-selling models and brands from its lineup of offerings—it has eliminated the entire Oldsmobile division. Similarly, Ford is said to be considering the elimination of the Mercury brand from its lineup of vehicle offerings. Textbook publishers are discontinuing publication of those books that sell only a few thousand copies annually (where profits are marginal at best) and are instead focusing their resources on texts that are more widely adopted and generate sales of at least 5,000 copies per edition.

Improving Value Chain Efficiency Efforts to reinvent the industry value chain can have a fourfold payoff: lower costs, better product or service quality, greater capability to turn out multiple or customized product versions, and shorter design-to-market cycles. Manufacturers can mechanize high-cost activities, redesign production lines to improve labor efficiency, build flexibility into the assembly process so that customized product versions can be easily produced, and increase use of advanced technology (robotics, computerized controls, and automated assembly). Suppliers of parts and components, manufacturers, and distributors can collaboratively deploy online systems and product coding techniques to streamline activities and achieve cost savings all along the value chain—from supplier-related activities all the way through distribution, retailing, and customer service.

Trimming Costs Stiffening price competition gives firms extra incentive to drive down unit costs. Company cost-reduction initiatives can cover a broad front. Some of the most frequently pursued options are pushing suppliers for better prices, implementing tighter supply chain management practices, cutting low-value activities out of the value chain, developing more economical product designs, reengineering internal processes using e-commerce technology, and shifting to more economical distribution arrangements.

Increasing Sales to Present Customers In a mature market, growing by taking customers away from rivals may not be as appealing as expanding sales to existing customers. Strategies to increase purchases by existing customers can involve adding more sales promotions, providing complementary items and ancillary services, and finding more ways for customers to use the product. Wal-Mart, for example, has boosted average sales per customer by adding dry-cleaning services, optical centers, in-store restaurants, gasoline sales, and tire and battery service centers.

Acquiring Rival Firms at Bargain Prices Sometimes a firm can acquire the facilities and assets of struggling rivals quite cheaply. Bargain-priced acquisitions can help create a low-cost position if they also present opportunities for greater operating efficiency. In addition, an acquired firm's customer base can provide expanded market coverage and opportunities for greater scale economies. The most desirable acquisitions are those that will significantly enhance the acquiring firm's competitive strength.

Expanding Internationally As its domestic market matures, a firm may seek to enter foreign markets where attractive growth potential still exists and competitive pressures are not so strong. Many multinational companies are expanding into such emerging markets as China, India, Brazil, Argentina, and the Philippines, where the long-term growth prospects are quite attractive. Strategies to expand internationally also make sense when a domestic firm's skills, reputation, and product are readily transferable to foreign markets. For example, even though the U.S. market for beverages is mature, Coca-Cola has remained a growth company by upping its efforts to penetrate emerging markets where sales of bottled water, soft drinks, fruit juices, and energy drinks are expanding rapidly.

[illegible] competencies or capabilities, deepening existing competencies to make them harder to imitate, or striving to make core competencies more adaptable to changing customer requirements and expectations. Microsoft has responded to challenges by such competitors as Google and Linux by expanding its competencies in search engine software and revamping its entire approach to programming next-generation operating systems.

ILLUSTRATION CAPSULE 6.2

PepsiCo's Strategy for Growing Rapidly in Mature, Slow-Growth Markets

PepsiCo's net revenues of approximately $40 billion in 2007 made it the world's largest snack and beverage company. The company's business lineup in 2008 included Frito-Lay salty snacks, Quaker Chewy granola bars, Pepsi soft drink products, Tropicana orange juice, Lipton Brisk tea, Gatorade, Propel, SoBe, Aquafina, Flat Earth, Naked Juice, and many other regularly consumed products. PepsiCo's ability to achieve growth in industries long characterized by low-single-digit growth rates is a result of the impressive strategies crafted by its CEO, Indra Nooyi, and the company's other chief managers.

In 2008, the company's primary strategic priorities were keyed to developing "good-for-you" snacks and beverages, strengthening its position in international markets, and acquiring small, rapidly growing snack food and beverage companies. PepsiCo was able to increase sales in the United States through the introduction of new beverages such as Amp Energy, SoBe Adrenaline Rush, flavored varieties of Aquafina, and new flavors of Gatorade and Propel Fitness Water. The company had also hired the former director of the Mayo Clinic endocrinology department to develop new snacks that would appeal to health-conscious consumers. New snacks like SunChips and acquisitions of brands such as Flat Earth fruit and vegetable crisps and Stacy's Simply Naked pita chips helped healthy snacks and beverages account for 30 percent of PepsiCo's 2007 revenues. The company hoped to make its good-for-you products account for 50 percent of its revenues, with more product innovations and additional acquisitions of grains, nuts, and fruit snack brands.

International markets were also critical to PepsiCo's growth in revenues and earnings. International sales increased by 22 percent in 2007, which was triple the rate of domestic sales growth. The company's fastest growth occurred in markets such as Russia, the Middle East, and Turkey, where both its traditional and its good-for-you snacks and beverages achieved double-digit sales gains. Healthy products such as juices, water, tea, and energy drinks made up more than half of PepsiCo's beverage sales in Russia in 2007. The company planned to increase the percentage of healthy snacks in all country markets where it competed, since most consumers around the world wished to reduce their consumption of saturated fats, cholesterol, trans fats, and simple carbohydrates.

An equally important component of PepsiCo's strategy for competing in mature markets involved divesting marginal products from its lineup of businesses and brands. Shortly after Nooyi joined PepsiCo as head of mergers and acquisitions in 1994, it became clear to PepsiCo's top managers that the company's restaurant brands—Pizza Hut, Taco Bell, and KFC—had to go. The fast-food industry was saturated with too many locations, real estate was becoming more expensive, and a price war was under way, with all of the major chains boasting 99-cent value menus. The spin-off of PepsiCo's restaurant businesses reduced the company's revenues by a third but got the company out of a low-margin, capital-intensive business that was a drag on its overall return on investment.

Source: Betsy Morris, "What Makes Pepsi Great?" *Fortune,* March 3, 2008, pp. 55–66; and PepsiCo's 2007 annual report.

Chevron has developed a best-practices discovery team and a best-practices resource map to enhance the speed and effectiveness with which it is able to transfer efficiency improvements from one oil refinery to another.

Illustration Capsule 6.2 describes how PepsiCo has achieved double-digit growth in revenues and earnings while competing in the mature soft drink and snack food industries.

Mistakes Companies Make in Mature Markets Perhaps the biggest strategic mistake a company can make as an industry matures is steering a middle course between low cost, differentiation, and focusing—blending efforts to achieve low cost with efforts to incorporate differentiating features and efforts to focus on a limited target market. Such strategic compromises typically leave the firm *stuck in the middle* with a fuzzy strategy, too little commitment to winning a competitive advantage, an average image with buyers, and little chance of springing into the ranks of the industry leaders.

Other strategic pitfalls include being slow to mount a defense against stiffening competitive pressures, concentrating more on protecting short-term profitability than on building or maintaining long-term competitive position, waiting too long to respond to price cutting by rivals, overexpanding in the face of slowing growth, overspending on advertising and sales promotion efforts in a losing effort to combat the growth slowdown, failing to invest in product or process innovations that could help the company maintain growth despite slowing industry growth, and failing to pursue cost reductions soon enough or aggressively enough.[27]

Competing in Stagnant or Declining Markets

Many firms operate in industries where demand is growing more slowly than the economywide average or is even declining. The demand for an industry's product can decline for any of several reasons: (1) advancing technology gives rise to better-performing substitute products (slim LCD monitors displace bulky CRT monitors; MP3 players replace portable CD players; wrinkle-free fabrics replace the need for laundry/dry-cleaning services) or lower costs (cheaper synthetics replace expensive leather); (2) the customer group shrinks (mountain biking); (3) lifestyles and buyer tastes change (smoking cigarettes and wearing dress hats go out of vogue); (4) the prices of complementary products rise (higher gasoline prices drive down purchases of gas-guzzling vehicles).[28] The most attractive declining industries are those in which sales are eroding only slowly, there are pockets of stable or even growing demand, and some market niches present good profit opportunities. But in some stagnant or declining industries, decaying buyer demand precipitates a desperate competitive battle among industry members for the available business, replete with price discounting, costly sales promotions, growing amounts of idle plant capacity, and fast-eroding profit margins. It matters greatly whether buyer demand falls gradually or sharply, and whether competition proves to be fierce or moderate.

It is erroneous to assume that companies in a declining industry are doomed to suffer falling revenues and profits.

Businesses competing in stagnant or declining industries have to make a fundamental strategic choice—whether to remain committed to the industry for the long term despite the industry's dim prospects or whether to pursue an end-game strategy to withdraw gradually or quickly from the market. Deciding to stick with the industry despite eroding market demand can have considerable merit. Stagnant demand by itself is not enough to make an industry unattractive. Market demand may be decaying slowly. Some segments of the market may still present good profit opportunities. Cash flows from operations may still remain strongly positive. Strong competitors may well be able to grow and boost profits by taking market share from weaker competitors.[29] Furthermore, the acquisition or exit of [illegible] industry can lead to above-average profitability even though overall market demand is stagnant or eroding. On the other hand, if the market environment of a declining industry is characterized by bitter warfare for customers and lots of overcapacity, such that companies are plagued with heavy operating losses, then an early exit makes much more strategic sense.

If a company decides to stick with a declining industry—because top management is encouraged by the remaining opportunities and/or sees merit in striving for market share leadership (or even just being one of the few remaining companies in the industry), then its three best strategic alternatives are usually the following:[30]

1. *Pursue a focused strategy aimed at the fastest-growing or slowest-decaying market segments within the industry.* Stagnant or declining markets, like other markets, are composed of numerous segments or niches. Frequently, one or more of these segments is growing rapidly (or at least decaying much more slowly), despite stagnation in the industry as a whole. An astute competitor who zeroes in on fast-growing segments and does a first-rate job of meeting the needs of buyers comprising these segments can often escape stagnating sales and profits and even gain decided competitive advantage. For instance, both Abercrombie & Fitch and American Eagle Outfitters have achieved success by focusing on the growing teen segment of the otherwise stagnant market for ready-to-wear apparel; revenue growth and profit margins are substantially higher for trendy apparel than is the case with other segments of the ready-to-wear apparel industry. Companies that focus on the one or two most attractive market segments in a declining business may well decide to ignore the other segments altogether—withdrawing from them entirely or at least gradually or rapidly disinvesting in them. But the key is to *move aggressively* to establish a strong position in the most attractive parts of the stagnant or declining industry.
2. *Stress differentiation based on quality improvement and product innovation.* Either enhanced quality or innovation can rejuvenate demand by creating important new growth segments or inducing buyers to trade up. Successful product innovation opens up an avenue for competing that bypasses meeting or beating rivals' prices. Differentiation based on successful innovation has the additional advantage of being difficult and expensive for rival firms to imitate. The New Covent Garden Food Company has met with success by introducing packaged fresh soups for sale in major supermarkets, where the typical soup offerings are canned or dry mixes. Procter & Gamble rejuvenated sales of its toothbrushes with its new line of Crest battery-powered spin toothbrushes, and it revitalized interest in tooth care products with a series of product innovations related to teeth whitening. Bread makers are countering the decline in sales of their bleached-flour white breads by introducing all kinds of whole-grain breads (which have far more nutritional value).
3. *Strive to drive costs down and become the industry's low-cost leader.* Companies in stagnant industries can improve profit margins and return on investment by pursuing innovative cost reduction year after year. Potential cost-saving actions include (*a*) cutting marginally beneficial activities out of the value chain; (*b*) outsourcing functions and activities that can be performed more cheaply by outsiders; (*c*) redesigning internal business processes to exploit cost-reducing e-commerce technologies; (*d*) consolidating underutilized production facilities; (*e*) adding more distribution channels to ensure the unit volume needed for low-cost production; (*f*) closing low-volume, high-cost retail outlets; and (*g*) pruning marginal products from the firm's offerings. Japan-based Asahi Glass (a low-cost producer of flat glass), PotashCorp and IMC Global (two low-cost leaders in potash production), Safety Components International (a low-cost producer of air bags for motor vehicles), Alcan Aluminum, and Nucor Steel have all been successful in driving costs down in competitively tough and largely stagnant industry environments.

These three strategic themes are not mutually exclusive.[31] Introducing innovative versions of a product can create a fast-growing market segment. Similarly, relentless pursuit of greater operating efficiencies permits price reductions that create price-conscious growth segments. Note that all three themes are spin-offs of the five generic competitive strategies, adjusted to fit the circumstances of a tough industry environment.

End-Game Strategies for Declining Industries An *end-game strategy* can take either of two paths: (1) a *slow-exit strategy* that involves a gradual phasing down of operations coupled with an objective of getting the most cash flow from the business even if it means sacrificing market position or profitability, and (2) a *fast-exit* or *sell-out-quickly strategy* to disengage from the industry during the early stages of the decline and recover as much of the company's investment as possible for deployment elsewhere.[32]

A Slow-Exit Strategy With a slow-exit strategy, *the key objective is to generate the greatest possible harvest of cash from the business for as long as possible.* Management either eliminates or severely curtails new investment in the business. Capital expenditures for new equipment are put on hold or given low financial priority (unless replacement needs are unusually urgent); instead, efforts are made to stretch the life of existing equipment and make do with present facilities as long as possible. Old plants with high costs may be retired from service. The operating budget is chopped to a rock-bottom level. Promotional expenses may be cut gradually, quality reduced in not-so-visible ways, nonessential customer services curtailed, and maintenance of facilities held to a bare minimum. The resulting increases in cash flow (and perhaps even bottom-line profitability and return on investment) compensate for whatever declines in sales might be experienced. Withering buyer demand is tolerable if sizable amounts of cash can be reaped in the interim. If and when cash flows dwindle to meager levels as sales volumes decay, the business can be sold or, if no buyer can be found, closed.

A Fast-Exit Strategy The challenge of a sell-out-quickly strategy is to find a buyer willing to pay an agreeable price for the company's business assets. Buyers may be scarce since there's a tendency for investors to shy away from purchasing a stagnant or dying business. And even if willing buyers appear, they will be in a strong bargaining position once it's clear that the industry's prospects are permanently waning. How much prospective buyers will pay is usually a function of how rapidly they expect the industry to decline, whether they see opportunities to rejuvenate demand (at least temporarily), whether they believe that costs can be cut enough to still produce attractive profit margins or cash flows, whether there are pockets of stable demand where buyers are not especially price-sensitive, and whether they believe that fading market demand will weaken competition (which could enhance profitability) or trigger strong competition for the remaining business (which could put pressure on profit margins). Thus, the expectations of prospective buyers will tend to

Competing in Turbulent, Fast-Changing Markets

Many companies operate in industries characterized by rapid technological change, short product life cycles, the entry of important new rivals, lots of competitive maneuvering by rivals, and fast-evolving customer requirements and expectations—all occurring in a manner that creates swirling market conditions. Since news of this or that important competitive development arrives daily, it is an imposing task just to monitor and assess developing events. High-velocity change is plainly the prevailing condition in computer/server hardware and software, video games, networking, wireless telecommunications, medical equipment, biotechnology, prescription drugs, and online retailing.

Ways to Cope with Rapid Change The central strategy-making challenge in a turbulent market environment is managing change.[33] As illustrated in Figure 6.1, a company can assume any of three strategic postures in dealing with high-velocity change:[34]

- *It can react to change.* The company can respond to a rival's new product with a better product. It can counter an unexpected shift in buyer tastes and buyer demand by redesigning or repackaging its product, or shifting its advertising emphasis to different product attributes. Reacting is a defensive strategy and is therefore unlikely to create fresh opportunity, but it is nonetheless a necessary component in a company's arsenal of options.
- *It can anticipate change.* The company can make plans for dealing with the expected changes and follow its plans as changes occur (fine-tuning them as may be needed). Anticipation entails looking ahead to analyze what is likely to occur and then preparing and positioning for that future. It entails studying buyer behavior, buyer needs, and buyer expectations to get insight into how the market will evolve, then lining up the necessary production and distribution capabilities ahead of time. Like reacting to change, anticipating change is still fundamentally defensive in that forces outside the enterprise are in the driver's seat. Anticipation, however, can open up new opportunities and thus is a better way to manage change than just pure reaction.
- *It can lead change.* Leading change entails initiating the market and competitive forces that others must respond to—it is an offensive strategy aimed at putting a company in the driver's seat. Leading change means being first to market with an important new product or service. It means being the technological leader, rushing next-generation products to market ahead of rivals, and having products whose features and attributes shape customer preferences and expectations. It means proactively seeking to shape the rules of the game.

A sound way to deal with turbulent market conditions is to try to lead change with proactive strategic moves while at the same time trying to anticipate and prepare for upcoming changes and being quick to react to unexpected developments.

As a practical matter, a company's approach to managing change should, ideally, incorporate all three postures (though not in the same proportion). The best-performing companies in high-velocity markets consistently seek to lead change with proactive strategies that often entail the flexibility to pursue any of several strategic options, depending on how the market actually evolves. Even so, an environment of relentless change makes it incumbent on any company to anticipate and prepare for the future and to react quickly to unpredictable or uncontrollable new developments.

Strategy Options for Fast-Changing Markets Competitive success in fast-changing markets tends to hinge on a company's ability to improvise, experiment, adapt, reinvent, and regenerate as market and competitive conditions shift rapidly and sometimes unpredictably.[35] The company has to constantly reshape

Figure 6.1 Meeting the Challenge of High-Velocity Change

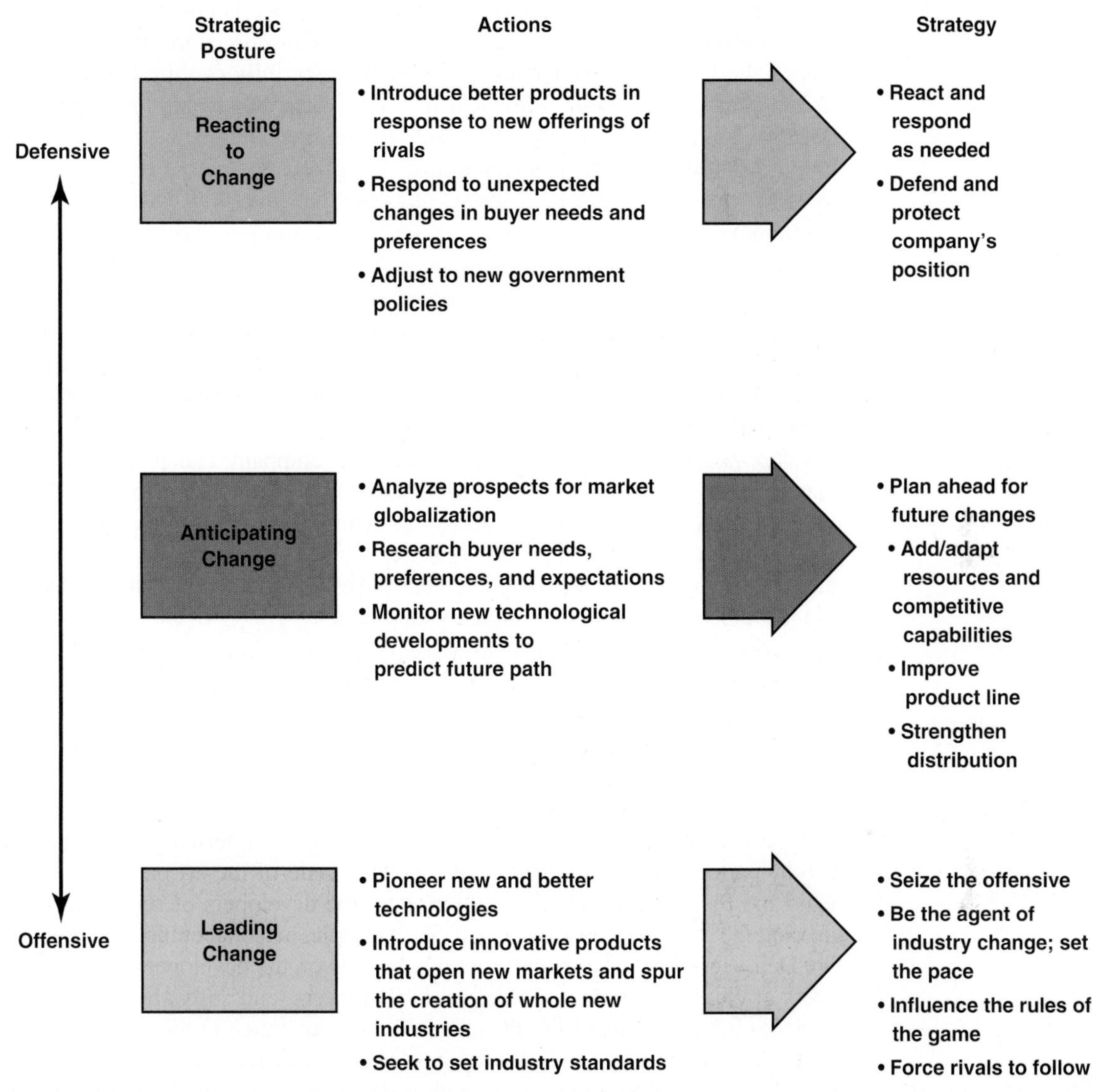

Strategic Posture
Actions
Strategy
Defensive
Reacting to Change
• Introduce better products in response to new offerings of rivals
• Respond to unexpected changes in buyer needs and preferences
• Adjust to new government policies
• React and respond as needed
• Defend and protect company's position
Anticipating Change
• Analyze prospects for market globalization
• Research buyer needs, preferences, and expectations
• Monitor new technological developments to predict future path
• Plan ahead for future changes
• Add/adapt resources and competitive capabilities
• Improve product line
• Strengthen distribution
Offensive
Leading Change
• Pioneer new and better technologies
• Introduce innovative products that open new markets and spur the creation of whole new industries
• Seek to set industry standards
• Seize the offensive
• Be the agent of industry change; set the pace
• Influence the rules of the game
• Force rivals to follow

Source: Adapted from Shona L. Brown and Kathleen M. Eisenhardt, *Competing on the Edge. Strategy as Structured Chaos* (Boston, MA: Harvard Business School Press, 1998) p. 5.

obsolescing strategy—is worse. The following five strategic moves seem to offer the best payoffs:

1. *Invest aggressively in R&D to stay on the leading edge of technological know-how.* Translating technological advances into innovative new products

(and remaining close on the heels of whatever advances and features are pioneered by rivals) is a necessity in industries where technology is the primary driver of change. But it is often desirable to focus the R&D effort on a few critical areas, not only to avoid stretching the company's resources too thin but also to deepen the firm's expertise, master the technology, fully capture learning curve effects, and become the dominant leader in a particular technology or product category.[36] When a fast-evolving market environment entails many technological areas and product categories, competitors have little choice but to employ some type of focus strategy and concentrate on being the leader in a particular product/technology category.

2. *Keep the company's products and services fresh and exciting enough to stand out in the midst of all the change that is taking place.* One of the risks of rapid change is that products and even companies can get lost in the shuffle. The marketing challenge here is to keep the firm's products and services in the limelight and, further, to keep them innovative and well matched to the changes that are occurring in the marketplace.
3. *Develop quick-response capability.* Because no company can predict all of the changes that will occur, it is crucial to have the organizational capability to be able to react quickly, improvising if necessary. This means shifting resources internally, adapting existing competencies and capabilities, creating new competencies and capabilities, and not falling far behind rivals. Companies that are habitual late-movers are destined to be industry also-rans.
4. *Rely on strategic partnerships with outside suppliers and with companies making tie-in products.* In many high-velocity industries, technology is branching off to create so many new technological paths and product categories that no company has the resources and competencies to pursue them all. Specialization (to promote the necessary technical depth) and focus (to preserve organizational agility and leverage the firm's expertise) are desirable strategies. Companies build their competitive position not just by strengthening their own internal resource base but also by partnering with those suppliers making state-of-the-art parts and components and by collaborating closely with both the developers of related technologies and the makers of tie-in products. For example, personal computer companies like Dell, Hewlett-Packard, and Acer rely heavily on the developers and manufacturers of chips, monitors, hard drives, DVD players, and software for innovative advances in PCs. None of the PC makers have done much in the way of integrating backward into parts and components because they have learned that the most effective way to provide PC users with a state-of-the-art product is to outsource the latest, most advanced components from technologically sophisticated suppliers who make it their business to stay on the cutting edge of their specialization and who can achieve economies of scale by mass-producing components for many PC assemblers. An outsourcing strategy also allows a company the flexibility to replace suppliers that fall behind on technology or product features or that cease to be competitive on price. The managerial challenge here is to strike a good balance between building a rich internal resource base that, on the one hand, keeps the firm from being at the mercy of its suppliers and allies and, on the other hand, maintains organizational agility by relying on the resources and expertise of capable (and perhaps best-in-world) outsiders.
5. *Initiate fresh actions every few months, not just when a competitive response is needed.* In some sense, change is partly triggered by the passage of time rather than

solely by the occurrence of events. A company can be proactive by making time-paced moves—introducing a new or improved product every four months, rather than when the market tapers off or a rival introduces a next-generation model.[37] Similarly, a company can expand into a new geographic market every six months rather than waiting for a new market opportunity to present itself; it can also refresh existing brands every two years rather than waiting until their popularity wanes. The keys to successfully using time pacing as a strategic weapon are choosing intervals that make sense internally and externally, establishing an internal organizational rhythm for change, and choreographing the transitions. 3M Corporation has long pursued an objective of having 25 percent of its revenues come from products less than four years old, a force that established the rhythm of change and created a relentless push for new products. Recently, the firm's CEO upped the tempo of change at 3M by increasing the objective from 25 to 30 percent.

Cutting-edge know-how and first-to-market capabilities are valuable competitive assets in fast-evolving markets. Moreover, action-packed competition demands that a company have quick reaction times and flexible, adaptable resources—organizational agility is a huge competitive asset. Even so, companies will make mistakes and some things a company does are going to work better than others. When a company's strategy doesn't seem to be working well, it has to quickly regroup—probing, experimenting, improvising, and trying again and again until it finds something that strikes the right chord with buyers and that puts it in sync with market and competitive realities.

Competing in Fragmented Industries

A number of industries are populated by hundreds, even thousands, of small and medium-sized companies, many privately held and none with a substantial share of total industry sales.[38] The standout competitive feature of a fragmented industry is the absence of market leaders with king-sized market shares or widespread buyer recognition. Examples of fragmented industries include book publishing, landscaping and plant nurseries, real estate development, convenience stores, building materials, health and medical care, computer software development, custom printing, trucking, auto repair, radio broadcasting, restaurants and fast food, public accounting, apparel manufacture and apparel retailing, paperboard boxes, hotels and motels, and furniture.

Reasons for Supply-Side Fragmentation Any of several reasons can account for why the supply side of an industry is comprised of hundreds or even thousands of companies:

- *The product or service is delivered at neighborhood locations so as to be conveniently accessible to local residents.* Retail and service businesses, for example, are inherently local—gas stations and car washes, pharmacies, dry-cleaning facili-

  the market, the way is opened for many enterprises to be engaged in providing products/services to local residents and businesses (and such enterprises can operate at just one location or at multiple locations).
- *Buyer preferences and requirements are so diverse that very large numbers of firms can easily coexist trying to accommodate differing buyer tastes, expectations, and pocketbooks.* This is true in the market for apparel where there are

thousands of apparel manufacturers making garments of various styles and price ranges. There's a host of different hotels and restaurants in places like New York City, London, Buenos Aires, Mexico City, and Tokyo. The software development industry is highly fragmented because there are so many types of software applications and because the needs and expectations of software users are so highly diverse—hence, there's ample market space for a software company to concentrate its attention on serving a particular market niche.

- *Low entry barriers allow small firms to enter quickly and cheaply.* Such tends to be the case in many areas of retailing, residential real estate, insurance sales, beauty shops, and the restaurant business.
- *An absence of scale economies permits small companies to compete on an equal cost footing with larger firms.* The markets for business forms, interior design, kitchen cabinets, and picture framing are fragmented because buyers require relatively small quantities of customized products; since demand for any particular product version is small, sales volumes are not adequate to support producing, distributing, or marketing on a scale that yields cost advantages to a large-scale firm. A locally owned pharmacy can be cost-competitive with the pharmacy operations of large drugstore chains like Walgreens or Rite Aid or CVS. Small trucking companies can be cost-competitive with companies having huge truck fleets. A local pizzeria is not necessarily cost-disadvantaged in competing against such chains as Pizza Hut, Domino's, and Papa John's.
- *The scope of the geographic market for the industry's product or service is transitioning from national to global.* A globalizing marketplace puts companies in more and more countries in the same competitive market arena. In the apparel industry increasing numbers of garment makers are shifting their production operations to low-wage countries and then shipping the finished goods to retailers across the world.
- *The technologies embodied in the industry's value chain are exploding into so many new areas and along so many different paths that specialization is essential just to keep abreast in any one area of expertise.* Technology branching accounts for why the manufacture of electronic parts and components is fragmented and why there's fragmentation in prescription drug research.
- *The industry is young and crowded with aspiring contenders.* In an emerging industry, no firm may yet have developed the resource base, competitive capabilities, and market recognition to command a significant market share (as in solar power and ethanol production).

Competitive Conditions in a Fragmented Market Competitive rivalry in fragmented industries can vary from moderately strong to fierce. Low barriers tend to make entry of new competitors an ongoing threat. Competition from substitutes may or may not be a major factor. The relatively small size of companies in fragmented industries puts them in a relatively weak position to bargain with powerful suppliers and buyers, although sometimes they can become members of a cooperative formed for the purpose of using their combined leverage to negotiate better sales and purchase terms. In such an environment, the best a firm can expect is to cultivate a loyal customer base and grow a bit faster than the industry average.

Some fragmented industries consolidate over time as growth slows and the market matures. The stiffer competition that accompanies slower growth produces a shake-out of weak, inefficient firms and a greater concentration of larger, more visible sellers. Others remain atomistic because it is inherent in the nature of their businesses. And still others remain stuck in a fragmented state because existing firms lack the resources or ingenuity to employ a strategy powerful enough to drive industry consolidation.

Strategy Options for Competing in a Fragmented Market In fragmented industries, firms generally have the strategic freedom to pursue broad or narrow market targets and low-cost or differentiation-based competitive advantages. Many different strategic approaches can exist side by side (unless the industry's product is highly standardized or a commodity—like concrete blocks, sand and gravel, or paperboard boxes). Fragmented industry environments are usually ideal for focusing on a well-defined market niche—a particular geographic area or buyer group or product type. In an industry that is fragmented due to highly diverse buyer tastes or requirements, focusing usually offers more competitive advantage potential than trying to come up with a product offering that has broad market appeal.

Some of the most suitable strategy options for competing in a fragmented industry include:

- *Constructing and operating "formula" facilities*—This strategic approach is frequently employed in restaurant and retailing businesses operating at multiple locations. It involves constructing standardized outlets in favorable locations at minimum cost and then operating them cost-effectively. This is a favorite approach for locally owned fast-food enterprises and convenience stores that have multiple locations serving a geographically limited market area. Major fast-food companies like Yum! Brands—the parent of Pizza Hut, Taco Bell, KFC, Long John Silver's, and A&W restaurants—and big convenience store retailers like 7-Eleven have, of course, perfected the formula facilities strategy.
- *Becoming a low-cost operator*—When price competition is intense and profit margins are under constant pressure, companies can stress no-frills operations featuring low overhead, high-productivity/low-cost labor, lean capital budgets, and dedicated pursuit of total operating efficiency. Successful low-cost producers in a fragmented industry can play the price-discounting game and still earn profits above the industry average. Many e-tailers compete on the basis of bargain prices; so do budget motel chains like Econo Lodge, Super 8, and Days Inn.
- *Specializing by product type*—When a fragmented industry's products include a range of styles or services, a strategy to focus on one product or service category can be effective. Some firms in the furniture industry specialize in only one furniture type such as brass beds, rattan and wicker, lawn and garden, or early American. In auto repair, companies specialize in transmission repair, body work, or speedy oil changes.
- *Specializing by customer type*—A firm can stake out a market niche in a frag-

dining, and still others cater to the sports bar crowd. Bed-and-breakfast inns cater to a particular type of traveler/vacationer (and also focus on a very limited geographic area).

- *Focusing on a limited geographic area*—Even though a firm in a fragmented industry can't win a big share of total industrywide sales, it can still try to dominate a local or regional geographic area. Concentrating company efforts on a limited

ILLUSTRATION CAPSULE 6.3
Just Play Golf's Strategy in the Fragmented Market for Golf Accessories

The golf accessory industry is highly fragmented—there are hundreds of companies that manufacture and market items such as ball markers, divot tools, cleats and spikes, towels, tees, training aids, instructional books and videos, pull carts, range finders, travel bags, and head covers. The window of opportunity for employing a focus strategy is big. The Club Caddy, a simple clip that attaches to a golf club and allows a golfer to place a club on the ground in an upright position, came onto the market in 2007. The Club Caddy is manufactured and marketed by Just Play Golf Inc. and was developed by company founder David Jones after playing golf at a South Carolina resort in 1995. On a day when the ground was exceptionally wet, the pro shop asked Jones to keep his cart on the paved path and not drive on the turf. Jones never seemed to hit a shot near the cart path and found himself frequently walking to his ball, carrying his putter and the one or two clubs he might need to hit the shot to the green. As he kept picking up clubs from the ground and wiping the dampness from the grips, he felt there should be a market for some type of product that would allow a golfer to place clubs down without the grips making contact with the wet ground. Six months later, Jones awoke at 3:00 a.m. with an idea for the Club Caddy clear in his mind. He ran to the dining room table with pencil and paper and began drawing the concept for his new golf accessory. Over the next eleven years, Jones spent about $25,000 to patent the Club Caddy and bring it to market, with its modest sales made mostly to local golfing buddies.

Jones's access to broad distribution for the Club Caddy didn't come until 2007, after he appeared on a reality television program produced by The Golf Channel called *Fore Inventors Only.* By this time, David Jones had invested about all he could in the Club Caddy, but he took the additional risk of asking for a $300 advance on his salary to travel to Orland, Florida, to audition for the program. Jones was among more than 1,000 inventors who were each given three minutes to make their pitch. The Club Caddy was one of 103 inventions selected to compete on the reality television series. The prize included shelf space at all 74 Golfsmith retail stores throughout North America for one year, a fully developed infomercial produced by The Golf Channel, and $50,000 worth of airtime for commercials on The Golf Channel.

The inventors' products were evaluated by a panel of judges made up of former PGA Tour player Fulton Allen, *Golf for Women* magazine editor Stina Sternberg, and golf instructor Billy Harmon. The three judges narrowed the list to five inventions, which were voted on by viewers as the best new golf product. Jones's Club Caddy won the competition with 30 percent of the vote. By 2008, Jones's new company, Just Play Golf Inc., had expanded retail distribution of the Club Caddy to several large retail stores in addition to Golfsmith, had signed a nonexclusive license with a large distributor to make the product available to a broader range of U.S. retailers, and had been contacted by retailers outside the United States for distribution of the Club Caddy in international markets.

Source: Information provided by Just Play Golf Inc. personnel; Chris Gay, "Inventor Hopes to Swing Vote," *Augusta Chronicle,* July 7, 2007, p. C1; Jeremy Friedman, "Champion Crowned on Fore Inventors," www.thegolfchannel.com, September 5, 2007; and Stan Awtrey, "Invention Stands Up to Competition; Winning Device Lets Clubs Be Placed Upright," *Atlanta Journal-Constitution,* September 6, 2007, p. 3D.

territory can produce greater operating efficiency, speed delivery and customer services, promote strong brand awareness, and permit saturation advertising, while avoiding the diseconomies of stretching operations out over a much wider area. Several locally owned banks, drugstores, and sporting goods retailers successfully operate multiple locations within a limited geographic area. Numerous local restaurant operators have pursued operating economies by opening anywhere from 4 to 10 restaurants (each with each its own distinctive theme and menu) scattered across a single metropolitan area like Chicago or Denver or Houston.

Illustration Capsule 6.3 describes how a start-up company in the fragmented golf accessory industry has employed a product-niche type of focus strategy.

TIMING STRATEGIC MOVES—TO BE AN EARLY MOVER OR A LATE MOVER?

When to make a strategic move is often as crucial as *what* move to make. Certain market environments reward first-movers with competitive advantage, while in other markets it is more advantageous to be a late-mover.[39] Consequently, it is important for company strategists to be aware of what conditions favor being a first-mover, a fast-follower, or a late-mover.

CORE CONCEPT

Because of first-mover advantages and disadvantages, competitive advantage can spring from *when* a move is made as well as from *what* move is made.

When Being a First-Mover Leads to Competitive Advantage

Being first to initiate a strategic move can have a high payoff when (1) pioneering helps build a firm's image and reputation with buyers; (2) early commitments to new technologies, new-style components, new or emerging distribution channels, and so on can produce an absolute cost advantage over rivals; (3) first-time customers remain strongly loyal to pioneering firms in making repeat purchases; and (4) moving first constitutes a preemptive strike, making imitation extra hard or unlikely. The bigger the first-mover advantages, the more attractive making the first move becomes.[40] In e-commerce, companies that were first with a new technology, network solution, or business model—like Amazon.com, Yahoo, eBay, and Priceline.com—enjoyed lasting first-mover advantages in gaining the visibility and reputation needed to remain market leaders. However, other first-movers such as Xerox in fax machines, eToys (an online toy retailer), Webvan and Peapod (in online groceries), and scores of other dot-com companies never converted their first-mover status into any sort of competitive advantage (or even a business that was able to survive for that matter). Sometimes markets are slow to accept the innovative product offering of a first-mover; sometimes, a fast-follower with greater resources and marketing muscle can easily overtake the first-mover (as Microsoft was able to do when it introduced Internet Explorer against Netscape, the pioneer of Internet browsers with a lion-sized market share); and sometimes furious technological change or product innovation makes a first-mover vulnerable to quickly appearing next-generation technology or products. Hence, just being a first-mover by itself is seldom enough to win a sustainable competitive advantage.[41]

To sustain any advantage that may initially accrue to a pioneer, a first-mover needs to be a fast learner and continue to move aggressively to capitalize on any initial pioneering advantage. It helps immensely if the first-mover has deep financial pockets, important competencies and competitive capabilities, and astute managers. If a first-mover's skills, know-how, and actions are easily copied or even surpassed, then fast- [illegible] precise combination of features, customer value, and sound revenue/cost/profit economics that gives it an edge over rivals in the battle for market leadership.[42] If the marketplace quickly takes to a first-mover's innovative product offering, a first-mover must have large-scale production, marketing, and distribution capabilities if it is to stave off fast-followers who possess these capabilities. If technology is advancing at a

ILLUSTRATION CAPSULE 6.4
Amazon.com's First-Mover Advantage in Online Retailing

Amazon.com's path to becoming the world's largest online retailer began in 1994 when Jeff Bezos, a Manhattan hedge fund analyst at the time, noticed that the number of Internet users was increasing by 2,300 percent annually. Bezos saw the tremendous growth as an opportunity to sell products that would be demanded by a large number of Internet users and could be easily shipped. Bezos launched the online bookseller Amazon.com in 1995. The start-up's revenues soared to $148 million in 1997, $610 million in 1998, and $1.6 billion in 1999. The business plan Bezos hatched while on a cross-country trip with his wife in 1994 made him *Time*'s Person of the Year in 1999.

Amazon.com's early entry into online retailing had delivered a first-mover advantage, but between 2000 and 2008, Bezos undertook a series of additional strategic initiatives to solidify the company's number one ranking in the industry. Bezos undertook a massive building program in the late 1990s that added five new warehouses and fulfillment centers totaling $300 million. The additional warehouse space was added years before it was needed, but Bezos wanted to ensure that, as demand continued to grow, the company could continue to offer its customers the best selection, the lowest prices, and the cheapest and most convenient delivery. The company also expanded its product line to include sporting goods, tools, toys, grocery items, electronics, and digital music downloads. Amazon.com's 2007 revenues of $14.8 billion accounted for 6 percent of the $136 billion U.S. online retail market and made it number 177 on *Fortune*'s list of America's 500 largest corporations. Also, Jeff Bezos's shares in Amazon.com made him the 110th wealthiest person in the world, with an estimated net worth of $8.2 billion.

Not all of Bezos's efforts to maintain a first-mover advantage in online retailing were a success. Bezos commented in a 2008 *Fortune* article profiling the company, "We were investors in every bankrupt, 1999-vintage e-commerce startup. Pets.com, living.com, kozmo.com. We invested in a lot of high-profile flameouts." He went on to specify that although the ventures were a "waste of money," they didn't take Amazon away from its own mission. Bezos also suggested that gaining advantage as a first-mover is "taking a million tiny steps—and learning quickly from your missteps."

Source: Josh Quittner, "How Jeff Bezos Rules the Retail Space," *Fortune,* May 5, 2008, pp. 126–34.

torrid pace, a first-mover cannot hope to sustain its lead without having strong capabilities in R&D, design, and new product development, along with the financial strength to fund these activities.

Illustration Capsule 6.4 describes how Amazon.com achieved a first-mover advantage in online retailing.

Blue Ocean Strategy: A Powerful First-Mover Approach

A *blue ocean strategy* seeks to gain a dramatic and durable competitive advantage by *abandoning efforts to beat out competitors in existing markets and, instead, inventing a new industry or distinctive market segment that renders existing competitors largely irrelevant and allows a company to create and capture altogether new demand.*[43] This strategy views the business universe as consisting of two distinct types of market space. One is where industry boundaries are defined and accepted, the competitive rules of the game are well understood by all industry members, and companies try to outperform rivals by capturing a bigger share of existing demand; in such markets, lively competition constrains a company's prospects for rapid growth and superior profitability since rivals move quickly to either imitate or counter the successes of competitors. The second type of market space is where the industry does not really exist yet, is untainted by competition, and offers wide open opportunity for profitable and rapid growth if a company can come up with a product offering and strategy that allows it to create new demand rather than fight over existing demand. A terrific example of blue ocean market space is the online auction industry that eBay created and now dominates.

Another company that has employed a blue ocean strategy is Cirque du Soleil, which increased its revenues by 22 times during the 1993–2003 period in the circus business, an industry that had been in long-term decline for 20 years. How did Cirque du Soleil pull this off against legendary industry leader Ringling Bros. and Barnum & Bailey? By reinventing the circus: creating a distinctively different market space for its performances (Las Vegas night clubs and theater-type settings), and pulling in a whole new group of customers—adults and corporate clients—who were noncustomers of traditional circuses and were willing to pay several times more than the price of a conventional circus ticket to have an "entertainment experience" featuring sophisticated clowns and star-quality acrobatic acts in a comfortable tentlike atmosphere. Cirque du Soleil studiously avoided the use of animals not only because of costs but also because of concerns over the treatment of circus animals; Cirque do Soleil's market research led management to conclude that the lasting allure of the traditional circus came down to just three factors: the clowns, classic acrobatic acts, and a tentlike stage. As of 2007, Cirque du Soleil was presenting 15 different shows each with its own theme and story line, was performing before audiences of about 10 million people annually, and had performed 250 engagements in 100 cities since its formation in 1984.

Other examples of companies that have achieved competitive advantages by creating blue ocean market spaces include Starbucks in the coffee shop industry, The Home Depot in big-box retailing of hardware and building supplies, Dollar General in extreme discount retailing, and FedEx in overnight package delivery. Companies that create blue ocean market spaces can usually sustain their initially won competitive advantage without encountering major competitive challenge for 10 to 15 years because of high barriers to imitation and the strong brand-name awareness that a blue ocean strategy can produce.

When Being a Late-Mover Can Be Advantageous

There are instances when there are actually *advantages* to being an adept follower rather than a first-mover. Late-mover advantages (or *first-mover disadvantages*) arise in four instances:

- When pioneering leadership is more costly than imitating followership and only negligible learning/experience curve benefits accrue to the leader—a condition that allows a follower to end up with lower costs than the first-mover.
- When the products of an innovator are somewhat primitive and do not live up to

technology or product being pioneered by a first-mover.

- When rapid market evolution (due to fast-paced changes in either technology or buyer needs and expectations) gives fast-followers and maybe even cautious late-movers the opening to leapfrog a first-mover's products with more attractive next-version products.

Deciding Whether to Be an Early Mover or a Late Mover

In weighing the pros and cons of being a first-mover versus a fast-follower versus a late-mover, it matters whether the race to market leadership in a particular industry is a marathon or a sprint. In marathons, a slow-mover is not unduly penalized—first-mover advantages can be fleeting, and there's ample time for fast-followers and sometimes even late-movers to play catch-up.[44] Thus, the speed at which the pioneering innovation is likely to catch on matters considerably as companies struggle with whether to pursue a particular emerging market opportunity aggressively (as a first-mover or fast-follower) or cautiously (as a late-mover). For instance, it took 18 months for 10 million users to sign up for Hotmail, 5.5 years for worldwide mobile phone use to grow from 10 million to 100 million, and close to 10 years for the number of at-home broadband subscribers to grow to 100 million worldwide. The lesson here is that there is a market-penetration curve for every emerging opportunity; typically, the curve has an inflection point at which all the pieces of the business model fall into place, buyer demand explodes, and the market takes off. The inflection point can come early on a fast-rising curve (like use of e-mail) or farther up on a slow-rising curve (like use of broadband). Any company that seeks competitive advantage by being a first-mover thus needs to ask some hard questions:

- Does market takeoff depend on the development of complementary products or services that currently are not available?
- Is new infrastructure required before buyer demand can surge?
- Will buyers need to learn new skills or adopt new behaviors? Will buyers encounter high switching costs?
- Are there influential competitors in a position to delay or derail the efforts of a first-mover?

When the answer to any of these questions is yes, then a company must be careful not to pour too many resources into getting ahead of the market opportunity—the battle for market leadership is likely going to be more of a 10-year marathon than a short-lived contest.

Being first off the starting block turns out to be competitively important only when pioneering early introduction of a technology or product delivers clear and substantial benefits to early adopters and buyers, thus winning their immediate support, perhaps giving the pioneer a reputational head-start advantage, and forcing competitors to quickly follow the pioneer's lead. In the remaining instances where the race for industry leadership is more of a marathon, the companies that end up capturing and dominating new-to-the-world markets are almost never the pioneers that gave birth to them—there is time for a company to marshal the needed resources and to ponder its best time and method of entry.[45] Plus, being a late-mover into industries of the future has the advantages of being less risky and skirting the costs of pioneering.

But while a company is right to be cautious about quickly entering virgin territory where all kinds of risks abound, rarely does a company have much to gain from consistently being a late-mover whose main concern is avoiding the mistakes of first-movers. Companies that are habitual late-movers regardless of the circumstances, while often able to survive, can find themselves scrambling to keep pace with more progressive and innovative rivals. For a habitual late-mover to catch up, it must count on first-movers to be slow learners and complacent in letting their lead dwindle. It also has to hope that buyers will be slow to gravitate to the products of first-movers, again giving it time to catch up. And it has to have competencies and capabilities that are sufficiently strong to allow it to close the gap fairly quickly once it makes its move. Counting on all first-movers to stumble or otherwise be easily overtaken is usually a bad bet that puts a late-mover's competitive position at risk.

KEY POINTS

Many companies are using strategic alliances and collaborative partnerships to help them in the race to build a global market presence or be a leader in the industries of the future. Strategic alliances are an attractive, flexible, and often cost-effective means by which companies can gain access to missing technology, expertise, and business capabilities.

Mergers and acquisitions are another attractive strategic option for strengthening a firm's competitiveness. When the operations of two companies are combined via merger or acquisition, the new company's competitiveness can be enhanced in any of several ways—lower costs; stronger technological skills; more or better competitive capabilities; a more attractive lineup of products and services; wider geographic coverage; and/or greater financial resources with which to invest in R&D, add capacity, or expand into new areas.

Vertically integrating forward or backward makes strategic sense only if it strengthens a company's position via either cost reduction or creation of a differentiation-based advantage. Otherwise, the drawbacks of vertical integration (increased investment, greater business risk, increased vulnerability to technological changes, and less flexibility in making product changes) are likely to outweigh any advantages.

Outsourcing pieces of the value chain formerly performed in-house can enhance a company's competitiveness whenever an activity (1) can be performed better or more cheaply by outside specialists; (2) is not crucial to the firm's ability to achieve sustainable competitive advantage and won't hollow out its core competencies, capabilities, or technical know-how; (3) reduces the company's risk exposure to changing technology and/or changing buyer preferences; (4) streamlines company operations in ways that improve organizational flexibility, cut cycle time, speed decision making, and reduce coordination costs; and/or (5) allows a company to concentrate on its core business and do what it does best.

Crafting a strategy tightly matched to a company's external situation thus involves

[illegible]

stagnant/declining, high-velocity/turbulent, fragmented) and what strategic options and strategic postures are usually best suited to the specific type of environment.

The timing of strategic moves also has relevance in the quest for competitive advantage. Company managers are obligated to carefully consider the advantages or disadvantages that attach to being a first-mover versus a fast-follower versus a wait-and-see late-mover.

A blue ocean offensive strategy seeks to gain a dramatic and durable competitive advantage by abandoning efforts to beat out competitors in existing markets and, instead, inventing a new industry or distinctive market segment that renders existing competitors largely irrelevant and allows a company to create and capture altogether new demand.

ASSURANCE OF LEARNING EXERCISES

1. Use your favorite search engine to identify at least two companies in different industries that have outsourced certain activities to specialized vendors. Identify what value chain activities the companies have chosen to outsource and evaluate whether any of the outsourcing arrangements seem likely to threaten any of the companies' competitive capabilities.
2. Using your university library's subscription to Lexis-Nexis, EBSCO, or a similar database (or an Internet search engine), perform a search on *acquisition strategy.* Identify at least two companies in different industries that are using acquisitions to strengthen their market positions. How have these acquisitions enhanced the acquiring companies' resource strengths and competitive capabilities?
3. Go to **www.bridgestone.co.jp/english/info** and click on the Data Library link to review information about Bridgestone Corporation's tire and raw materials operations. To what extent is the company vertically integrated? What segments of the industry value chain has the company chosen to perform? What are the benefits and liabilities of Bridgestone's vertical integration strategy?
4. Listed below are ten industries. Classify each one as (*a*) emerging, (*b*) rapid-growth, (*c*) mature/slow-growth, (*d*) stagnant/declining, (*e*) high-velocity/turbulent, and (*f*) fragmented. Do research on the Internet, if needed, to locate information on industry conditions and reach a conclusion on what classification to assign each of the following:

    a. Network television
    b. Dry-cleaning industry
    c. Beef industry
    d. Camera film and film-developing industry
    e. Wine, beer, and liquor retailing
    f. Watch industry
    g. Mobile phone industry
    h. Recorded music industry (DVDs, CDs, MP3s)
    i. Computer software industry
    j. Petroleum industry

EXERCISES FOR SIMULATION PARTICIPANTS

1. Does your company have the option to merge with or acquire other companies? If so, which rival companies would you like to acquire or merge with?
2. Is your company vertically integrated? Explain.

3. Is your company able to engage in outsourcing? If so, what do you see as the pros and cons of outsourcing?
4. What options for being a first-mover does your company have? Do any of these first-mover options hold competitive advantage potential?
5. Is your company facing the prospects of slowing market growth? If so, which, if any, of the strategic options discussed above in the section entitled Strategies for Competing in Slow-Growth, Mature Markets seem most promising for your company?

CHAPTER

7 Strategies for Competing in Foreign Markets

LEARNING OBJECTIVES

1. Develop an understanding of why companies that have achieved competitive advantage in their domestic market may opt to enter foreign markets.
2. Learn how and why differing market conditions in different countries influence a company's strategy for competing in foreign markets.
3. Gain familiarity with the major strategic options for entering and competing in foreign markets.
4. Understand the principal approaches used by multinational companies in building competitive advantage in foreign markets.
5. Gain an understanding of the unique characteristics of competing in emerging markets.

You have no choice but to operate in a world shaped by globalization and the information revolution. There are two options: Adapt or die.

—**Andrew S. Grove**
Co-founder and Senior Advisor, Intel Corporation

You do not choose to become global. The market chooses for you; it forces your hand.

—**Alain Gomez**
Former CEO, Thomson S.A.

Industries actually vary a great deal in the pressures they put on a company to sell internationally.

—**Niraj Dawar and Tony Frost**
Professors, Richard Ivey School of Business

Any company that aspires to industry leadership in the 21st century must think in terms of global, not domestic, market leadership. The world economy is globalizing at an accelerating pace as countries previously closed to foreign companies open up their markets, as the Internet shrinks the importance of geographic distance, and as ambitious growth-minded companies race to build stronger competitive positions in the markets of more and more countries. Companies in industries that are already globally competitive or in the process of becoming so are under the gun to come up with a strategy for competing successfully in foreign markets. This chapter focuses on strategy options for expanding beyond domestic boundaries and competing in the markets of either a few or a great many countries. The spotlight will be on four strategic issues unique to competing multinationally:

1. Whether to customize the company's offerings in each different country market to more precisely match the tastes and preferences of local
2. Whether to employ essentially the same basic competitive strategy in all countries or modify the strategy country by country.
3. Where to locate the company's production facilities, distribution centers, and customer service operations so as to realize the greatest location advantages.
4. How to efficiently transfer the company's resource strengths and capabilities from one country to another in an effort to secure competitive advantage.

In the process of exploring these issues, we will introduce such concepts as multicountry competition; global competition; and cross-country differences in cultural, demographic, and market conditions. The chapter also includes sections on strategy options for entering and competing in foreign markets; the importance of locating operations in the most advantageous countries; and the special circumstances of competing in such emerging markets as China, India, Brazil, Russia, and Eastern Europe.

WHY COMPANIES EXPAND INTO FOREIGN MARKETS

A company may opt to expand outside its domestic market for any of four major reasons:

1. *To gain access to new customers*—Expanding into foreign markets offers potential for increased revenues, profits, and long-term growth and becomes an especially attractive option when a company's home markets are mature. Firms like Cisco Systems, Dell, Sony, Nokia, Avon, and Toyota, which are racing for global leadership in their respective industries, are moving rapidly and aggressively to extend their market reach into all corners of the world.
2. *To achieve lower costs and enhance the firm's competitiveness*—Many companies are driven to sell in more than one country because domestic sales volume is not large enough to fully capture manufacturing economies of scale or learning/experience curve effects and thereby substantially improve the firm's cost-competitiveness. The relatively small size of country markets in Europe explains why companies like Michelin, BMW, and Nestlé long ago began selling their products all across Europe and then moved into markets in North America and Latin America.
3. *To capitalize on its core competencies*—A company may be able to leverage its competencies and capabilities into a position of competitive advantage in foreign markets as well as just domestic markets. Nokia's competencies and capabilities in mobile phones have propelled it to global market leadership in the wireless telecommunications business. Wal-Mart is capitalizing on its considerable expertise in discount retailing to expand into China, Latin America, Japan, South Korea, and the United Kingdom; specifically, Wal-Mart executives believe the company has tremendous growth opportunities in China.
4. *To spread its business risk across a wider market base*—A company spreads business risk by operating in a number of different foreign countries rather than depending entirely on operations in its domestic market. Thus, if the economies of certain Asian countries turn down for a period of time, a company with operations across much of the world may be sustained by buoyant sales in Latin America or Europe.

In a few cases, companies in industries based on natural resources (e.g., oil and gas, minerals, rubber, and lumber) often find it necessary to operate in the international arena because attractive raw material supplies are located in foreign countries.

The Difference between Competing Internationally and Competing Globally

Typically, a company will start to compete internationally by entering just one or maybe a select few foreign markets. Competing on a truly global scale comes later, after the company has established operations on several continents and is racing against rivals for global market leadership. Thus, there is a meaningful distinction between the competitive scope of a company that operates in a few foreign countries (with perhaps modest ambitions to enter several more country markets) and a company that markets its products in 50 to 100 countries and is expanding its operations into additional country markets annually. The former is most accurately termed an *international competitor* while the latter qualifies as a *global competitor*. In the discussion that follows, we'll continue to make a distinction between strategies for competing internationally and strategies for competing globally.

FACTORS THAT SHAPE STRATEGY CHOICES IN FOREIGN MARKETS

There are four important factors that shape a company's strategic approach to competing in foreign markets: (1) the degree to which there are important cross-country differences in cultural, demographic, and market conditions; (2) whether opportunities exist to gain competitive advantage based on whether a company's activities are located in some countries rather than in others; (3) the risks of adverse shifts in currency exchange rates; and (4) the extent to which the policies of foreign governments lead to more favorable business environments in some countries than in other countries.

Cross-Country Differences in Cultural, Demographic, and Market Conditions

Regardless of a company's motivation for expanding outside its domestic markets, the strategies it uses to compete in foreign markets must be situation-driven. Cultural, demographic, and market conditions vary significantly among the countries of the world.[1] Cultures and lifestyles are the most obvious areas in which countries differ; market demographics and income levels are close behind. Consumers in Spain do not have the same tastes, preferences, and buying habits as consumers in Norway; buyers differ yet again in Greece, Chile, New Zealand, and Taiwan. Less than 20 percent of the populations of Brazil, India, and China have annual purchasing power equivalent to \$25,000. Middle-class consumers represent a much smaller portion of the population in these and other emerging countries than in North America, Japan, and much of Western Europe—China's middle class numbers about 125 million out of a population of 1.3 billion.[2] Sometimes product designs suitable in one country are inappropriate in another—for example, in the United States electrical devices run on 110-volt systems, but in some European countries the standard is a 220–240-volt system, necessitating the use of different electrical designs and components. In parts of Asia refrigerators are a status symbol and may be placed in the living room, leading to preferences for stylish designs and colors—in India bright blue and red are popular colors. In other Asian countries household space is constrained and many refrigerators are only four feet high so that the top can be used for storage. In Italy most people use automatic washing machines, but there is a strongly entrenched cultural preference for hanging the clothes out to dry—the widespread belief that sun-dried clothes are fresher virtually shuts down any opportunities for

the more mature economies of Britain, Denmark, Canada, and Japan. In automobiles, for example, the potential for market growth is explosive in China, where 2007 sales of new vehicles amounted to less than 9 million in a country with 1.3 billion people. In India there are efficient, well-developed national channels for distributing trucks, scooters, farm equipment, groceries, personal care items, and other packaged products to the country's 3 million retailers, whereas in China distribution is primarily local and there is no national network for distributing most products. The marketplace is intensely competitive in some countries and only moderately so in others. Industry driving forces may be one thing in Spain, quite another in Canada, and different yet again in Turkey or Argentina or South Korea.

One of the biggest concerns of companies competing in foreign markets is whether to customize their offerings in each different country market to match the tastes and preferences of local buyers or whether to offer a mostly standardized product worldwide. While closely matching products to local tastes makes them more appealing to local buyers, customizing a company's products country by country may have the effect of raising production and distribution costs due to the greater variety of designs and components, shorter production runs, and the complications of added inventory handling and distribution logistics. Greater standardization of a global company's product offering, on the other hand, can lead to scale economies and learning/experience curve effects, thus contributing to the achievement of a low-cost advantage. *The tension between the market pressures to localize a company's product offerings country by country and the competitive pressures to lower costs is one of the big strategic issues that participants in foreign markets have to resolve.*

Aside from the basic cultural and market differences among countries, a company also has to pay special attention to location advantages that stem from country-to-country variations in manufacturing and distribution costs, the risks of adverse shifts in exchange rates, and the economic and political demands of host governments.

Gaining Competitive Advantage Based on Where Activities Are Located

Differences in wage rates, worker productivity, inflation rates, energy costs, tax rates, government regulations, and the like create sizable variations in manufacturing costs from country to country. Plants in some countries have major manufacturing cost advantages because of lower input costs (especially labor), relaxed government regulations, the proximity of suppliers, or unique natural resources. In such cases, the low-cost countries become principal production sites, with most of the output being exported to markets in other parts of the world. Companies that build production facilities in low-cost countries (or that source their products from contract manufacturers in these countries) have a competitive advantage over rivals with plants in countries where costs are higher. The competitive role of low manufacturing costs is most evident in low-wage countries like China, India, Pakistan, Cambodia, Vietnam, Mexico, Brazil, Guatemala, the Philippines, and several countries in Africa that have become production havens for manufactured goods with high labor content (especially textiles and apparel). Labor costs in China were estimated to be about $0.70 an hour in 2006 versus $2.75 in Mexico, $4.91 in Brazil, $6.29 in Hungary, $7.65 in Portugal, $23.82 in the United States, $25.74 in Canada, $34.21 in Germany, and $41.05 in Norway.[3] China is fast becoming the manufacturing capital of the world—virtually all of the world's major manufacturing companies now have facilities in China, and China attracted $69.5 billion in foreign direct investment in 2006, an amount greater than any other country in the world. Likewise, concerns about short delivery times and low shipping costs make some countries better locations than others for establishing distribution centers.

The quality of a country's business environment also offers locational advantages—the governments of some countries are anxious to attract foreign investments and go all out to create a business climate that outsiders will view as favorable. A good example is Ireland, which has one of the world's most pro-business environments. Ireland offers companies very low corporate tax rates, has a government that is responsive to the needs of industry, and aggressively recruits high-tech manufacturing facilities and multinational companies. Ireland's policies were a major factor in Intel's decision to locate a $2.5 billion chip manufacturing plant in Ireland that employs over 4,000 people. Another locational advantage is the clustering of suppliers of components and capital equipment; infrastructure suppliers (universities, vocational training providers, research enterprises); trade associations; and makers of complementary products in a geographic area—such clustering can be an important source of cost savings in addition to facilitating close collaboration with key suppliers.

The Risks of Adverse Exchange Rate Shifts

The volatility of exchange rates greatly complicates the issue of geographic cost advantages. Currency exchange rates often move up or down 20 to 40 percent annually. Changes of this magnitude can either totally wipe out a country's low-cost advantage or transform a former high-cost location into a competitive-cost location. For instance, in the mid-1980s, when the dollar was strong relative to the Japanese yen (meaning that $1 would purchase, say, 125 yen as opposed to only 100 yen), Japanese heavy-equipment maker Komatsu was able to undercut U.S.-based Caterpillar's prices by as much as 25 percent, causing Caterpillar to lose sales and market share. But starting in 1985, when exchange rates began to shift and the dollar grew steadily weaker against the yen (meaning that $1 was worth fewer and fewer yen and that a Komatsu product made in Japan at a cost of 20 million yen translated into costs of many more dollars than before), Komatsu had to raise its prices to U.S. buyers six times over two years. With its competitiveness against Komatsu restored because of the weaker dollar and Komatsu's higher prices, Caterpillar regained sales and market share. *The lesson of fluctuating exchange rates is that companies that export goods to foreign countries always gain in competitiveness when the currency of the country in which the goods are manufactured is weak. Exporters are disadvantaged when the currency of the country where goods are being manufactured grows stronger.* Sizable long-term shifts in exchange rates thus shuffle the global cards of which rivals have the upper hand in the marketplace and which countries represent the low-cost manufacturing location.

> **CORE CONCEPT**
> **Companies with manufacturing facilities in a particular country are more cost-competitive in exporting goods to world markets when the local currency is weak (or declines in value relative to other currencies); their competitiveness erodes when the local currency grows stronger relative to the currencies of the countries to which the locally made goods are being exported.**

As a further illustration of the risks associated with fluctuating exchange rates, consider the case of a U.S. company that has located manufacturing facilities in Brazil (where the currency is reals—pronounced *ray-alls*) and that exports most of the Brazilian-made goods to markets in the European Union (where the currency is euros). To keep the numbers simple, assume that the exchange rate is 2.5 Brazilian reals for 1 euro and that the product being made in Brazil has a manufacturing cost of 2.5

and that the euro is stronger). Making the product in Brazil is now more cost-competitive because a Brazilian good costing 2.5 reals to produce has fallen to only 0.8 euros at the new exchange rate. If, in contrast, the value of the Brazilian real grows stronger in relation to the euro—resulting in an exchange rate of 2 reals to 1 euro—the same good costing 2.5 reals to produce now has a cost of 1.5 euros. Clearly, the attraction of manufacturing a good in Brazil and selling it in Europe is far greater when the euro is strong (an exchange rate of 1 euro for 3 Brazilian reals) than when the euro is weak (an exchange rate of 1 euro for only 2 Brazilian reals).

Insofar as U.S.-based manufacturers are concerned, declines in the value of the U.S. dollar against foreign currencies act to reduce or eliminate whatever cost advantage foreign manufacturers might have over U.S. manufacturers and can even prompt foreign companies to establish production plants in the United States. Likewise, a weak euro enhances the cost-competitiveness of companies manufacturing goods in Europe for export to foreign markets; a strong euro versus other currencies weakens the cost-competitiveness of European plants that manufacture goods for export. The growing strength of the euro relative to the U.S. dollar has encouraged a number of European manufacturers such as Volkswagen, Fiat, and Airbus to shift production from European factories to new facilities in the United States. Also, the weakening dollar caused Chrysler to discontinue its contract manufacturing agreement with a Austrian firm for assembly of minivans and Jeeps sold in Europe. Beginning in 2008, Chrysler's vehicles sold in Europe were exported from its factories in Illinois and Missouri. The weak dollar was also a factor in Ford's and GM's recent decisions to begin exporting U.S.-made vehicles to China and Latin America.

CORE CONCEPT

Fluctuating exchange rates pose significant risks to a company's competitiveness in foreign markets. Exporters win when the currency of the country where goods are being manufactured grows weaker, and they lose when the currency grows stronger. Domestic companies under pressure from lower-cost imports are benefited when their government's currency grows weaker in relation to the countries where the imported goods are being made.

It is important to note that *currency exchange rates are rather unpredictable, swinging first one way and then another way, so the competitiveness of any company's facilities in any country is partly dependent on whether exchange rate changes over time have a favorable or unfavorable cost impact.* Companies producing goods in one country for export abroad always improve their cost-competitiveness when the country's currency grows weaker relative to currencies of the countries to which the goods are being exported, and they find their cost-competitiveness eroded when the local currency grows stronger. On the other hand, domestic companies that are under pressure from lower-cost imported goods become more cost-competitive when their currency grows weaker in relation to the currencies of the countries where the imported goods are made—in other words, a U.S. manufacturer views a weaker U.S. dollar as a *favorable exchange rate shift* because such shifts help make its costs more competitive versus those of foreign rivals.

The Impact of Host Government Policies on the Local Business Climate

National governments enact all kinds of measures affecting business conditions and the operation of foreign companies in their markets. They may set local content requirements on goods made inside their borders by foreign-based companies, have rules and policies that protect local companies from foreign competition, put restrictions on exports to ensure adequate local supplies, regulate the prices of imported and locally produced goods, enact deliberately burdensome procedures and requirements for imported goods to pass customs inspection, and impose tariffs or quotas on the imports of certain goods. Until 2001, when it joined the World Trade Organization, China imposed a 100 percent tariff on motor vehicle imports. The European Union imposes quotas on textile and apparel imports from China, as a measure to protect European producers in southern Europe. India has a long history of utilizing excise taxes of as much as 50 percent on newly purchased products to protect its domestic producers. However, such duties were lowered to 8 to 14 percent in 2008 to help boost consumer demand to further accelerate India's overall economic growth rate.

National governments also vary in the degree to which they impose burdensome tax structures and regulatory requirements upon foreign companies doing business within their borders. In 2008, for example, China raised the tax on purchases of SUVs (most all of which were made outside China) from 20 percent to 40 percent. Sometimes outsiders face a web of regulations regarding technical standards, product certification, prior approval of capital spending projects, withdrawal of funds from the country, and required minority (sometimes majority) ownership of foreign company operations by local companies or investors. Some national governments tend to be hostile to or suspicious of foreign companies operating within their borders. Some governments provide subsidies and low-interest loans to domestic companies to help them compete against foreign-based companies. On the other hand, a number of national governments, anxious to obtain new plants and jobs, offer foreign companies a helping hand in the form of subsidies, privileged market access, and technical assistance. Hence, in deciding which foreign country markets to participate in and which ones to avoid, companies carefully weigh local government politics and policies toward business in general, and foreign companies in particular,.

Companies desirous of expanding their participation in foreign markets tend to put most of their energies and resources into those country markets not only where market opportunities are attractive but also where the business climate is favorable.

THE CONCEPTS OF MULTICOUNTRY COMPETITION AND GLOBAL COMPETITION

There are important differences in the patterns of international competition from industry to industry.[4] At one extreme is **multicountry competition,** in which there's so much cross-country variation in market conditions and in the companies contending for leadership that the market contest among rivals in one country is localized and not closely connected to the market contests in other countries. The standout features of multicountry competition are that (1) buyers in different countries are attracted to different product attributes, (2) sellers vary from country to country, and (3) industry conditions and competitive forces in each national market differ in important respects. Take the banking industry in Italy, Brazil, and Japan as an example—the requirements and expectations of banking customers vary among the three countries, the lead banking competitors in Italy differ from those in Brazil or in Japan, and the competitive battle among the leading banks in Italy is unrelated to the rivalry in Brazil or Japan. Thus, with multicountry competition, rival firms battle for national championships and winning in one country does not necessarily signal the ability to fare well in other countries. In multicountry competition, the power of a company's strategy and resource capabilities in one country may not enhance its competitiveness to the same degree in other countries where it operates. Moreover, any competitive advantage a company secures in one country is largely confined to that

CORE CONCEPT

Multicountry competition **exists when competition in one national market is localized and not closely connected to competition in another national market. When competition in each country differs in important respects, there is no global market but rather a collection of self-contained country markets.**

ing, life insurance, apparel, metals fabrication, many types of food products (coffee, cereals, breads, canned goods, frozen foods), and retailing.

At the other extreme is **global competition,** in which prices and competitive conditions across country markets are strongly linked and the term global or world market has true meaning. In a globally competitive industry, much the same group of rival companies competes in many different countries, but especially so in countries where sales volumes are large and where

across national markets are linked strongly enough to form a true international market and when leading competitors compete head to head in many different countries.

having a competitive presence is strategically important to building a strong global position in the industry. Thus, a company's competitive position in one country both affects and is affected by its position in other countries. In global competition, a firm's overall competitive advantage grows out of its entire worldwide operations; the competitive advantage it creates at its home base is supplemented by advantages growing out of its operations in other countries (having plants in low-wage countries, being able to transfer expertise from country to country, having the capability to serve customers who also have multinational operations, and brand-name recognition in many parts of the world). Rival firms in globally competitive industries vie for worldwide leadership. Global competition exists in motor vehicles, television sets, tires, mobile phones, personal computers, copiers, watches, digital cameras, bicycles, and commercial aircraft.

An industry can have segments that are globally competitive and segments in which competition is country by country.[5] In the hotel/motel industry, for example, the low- and medium-priced segments are characterized by multicountry competition—competitors mainly serve travelers within the same country. In the business and luxury segments, however, competition is more globalized. Companies like Nikki, Marriott, Sheraton, and Hilton have hotels at many international locations, use worldwide reservation systems, and establish common quality and service standards to gain marketing advantages in serving businesspeople and other travelers who make frequent international trips. In lubricants, the marine engine segment is globally competitive—ships move from port to port and require the same oil everywhere they stop. Brand reputations in marine lubricants have a global scope, and successful marine engine lubricant producers (Exxon Mobil, BP, and Shell) operate globally. In automotive motor oil, however, multicountry competition dominates—countries have different weather conditions and driving patterns, production of motor oil is subject to limited scale economies, shipping costs are high, and retail distribution channels differ markedly from country to country. Thus, domestic firms—like Quaker State and Pennzoil in the United States and Castrol in Great Britain—can be leaders in their home markets without competing globally.

It is also important to recognize that an industry can be in transition from multicountry competition to global competition. In a number of today's industries—beer and major home appliances are prime examples—leading domestic competitors have begun expanding into more and more foreign markets, often acquiring local companies or brands and integrating them into their operations. As some industry members start to build global brands and a global presence, other industry members find themselves pressured to follow the same strategic path—especially if establishing multinational operations results in important scale economies and a powerhouse brand name. As the industry consolidates to fewer players, such that many of the same companies find themselves in head-to-head competition in more and more country markets, global competition begins to replace multicountry competition.

At the same time, consumer tastes in a number of important product categories are converging across the world. Less diversity of tastes and preferences opens the way for companies to create global brands and sell essentially the same products in most countries of the world. Even in industries where consumer tastes remain fairly diverse, companies are learning to use "custom mass production" to economically create different versions of a product and thereby satisfy the tastes of people in different countries.

In addition to taking the obvious cultural and political differences between countries into account, a company has to shape its strategic approach to competing in foreign markets according to whether its industry is characterized by multicountry competition, global competition, or a transition from one to the other.

STRATEGY OPTIONS FOR ENTERING AND COMPETING IN FOREIGN MARKETS

There are a host of generic strategic options for a company that decides to expand outside its domestic market and compete internationally or globally:

1. *Maintain a national (one-country) production base and export goods to foreign markets,* using either company-owned or foreign-controlled forward distribution channels.
2. *License foreign firms to use the company's technology or to produce and distribute the company's products.*
3. *Employ a franchising strategy.*
4. *Use strategic alliances or joint ventures with foreign companies as the primary vehicle for entering foreign markets* and perhaps also use alliances as an ongoing strategic arrangement aimed at maintaining or strengthening competitiveness.
5. *Follow a multicountry strategy,* varying the company's strategic approach (perhaps a little, perhaps a lot) from country to country in response to differing local market and competitive conditions and differing buyer tastes and preferences.
6. *Follow a global strategy,* using essentially the same competitive strategy approach in all country markets where the company has a presence.

The following sections discuss these six strategic options in more detail.

Export Strategies

Using domestic plants as a production base for exporting goods to foreign markets is an excellent initial strategy for pursuing international sales. It is a conservative way to test the international waters. The amount of capital needed to begin exporting is often quite minimal; existing production capacity may well be sufficient to make goods for export. With an export strategy, a manufacturer can limit its involvement in foreign markets by contracting with foreign wholesalers experienced in importing to handle the entire distribution and marketing function in their countries or regions of the world. If it is more advantageous to maintain control over these functions, however, a manufacturer can establish its own distribution and sales organizations in some or all of the target foreign markets. Either way, a home-based production and export strategy helps the firm minimize its direct investments in foreign countries. Such strategies are commonly favored by Chinese, Korean, and Italian companies—products are designed and manufactured at home and then distributed through local channels in the importing countries; the primary functions performed abroad relate chiefly to establishing a network of distributors and perhaps conducting sales promotion and brand awareness activities.

centralizing production in one or several giant plants whose output capability exceeds demand in any one country market; obviously, a company must export to capture such economies. However, an export strategy is vulnerable when (1) manufacturing costs in the home country are substantially higher than in foreign countries where rivals have plants, (2) the costs of shipping the product to distant foreign markets are relatively high, or (3) adverse shifts occur in currency exchange rates. Unless an exporter can both keep its production and shipping costs competitive with rivals and successfully hedge against unfavorable changes in currency exchange rates, its success will be limited.

Licensing Strategies

Licensing makes sense when a firm with valuable technical know-how or a unique patented product has neither the internal organizational capability nor the resources to enter foreign markets. Licensing also has the advantage of avoiding the risks of committing resources to country markets that are unfamiliar, politically volatile, economically unstable, or otherwise risky. By licensing the technology or the production rights to foreign-based firms, the firm does not have to bear the costs and risks of entering foreign markets on its own, yet it is able to generate income from royalties. The big disadvantage of licensing is the risk of providing valuable technological know-how to foreign companies and thereby losing some degree of control over its use; monitoring licensees and safeguarding the company's proprietary know-how can prove quite difficult in some circumstances. But if the royalty potential is considerable and the companies to whom the licenses are being granted are both trustworthy and reputable, then licensing can be an attractive option. Many software and pharmaceutical companies use licensing strategies.

Franchising Strategies

While licensing works well for manufacturers and owners of proprietary technology, franchising is often better suited to the global expansion efforts of service and retailing enterprises. McDonald's, Yum! Brands (the parent of A&W, Pizza Hut, KFC, Long John Silver's, and Taco Bell), The UPS Store, 7-Eleven, and Hilton Hotels have all used franchising to build a presence in foreign markets. Franchising has much the same advantages as licensing. The franchisee bears most of the costs and risks of establishing foreign locations; a franchisor has to expend only the resources to recruit, train, support, and monitor franchisees. The big problem a franchisor faces is maintaining quality control; foreign franchisees do not always exhibit strong commitment to consistency and standardization, especially when the local culture does not stress the same kinds of quality concerns. Another problem that can arise is whether to allow foreign franchisees to make modifications in the franchisor's product offering so as to better satisfy the tastes and expectations of local buyers. Should McDonald's allow its franchised units in Japan to modify Big Macs to suit Japanese tastes? Should the franchised Pizza Hut units in China be permitted to substitute spices that appeal to Chinese consumers? Or should the same menu offerings be rigorously and unvaryingly required of all franchisees worldwide?

Strategic Alliances and Joint Ventures with Foreign Partners

Cross-border alliances have proved to be popular and viable vehicles for companies to edge their way into the markets of foreign countries.

Strategic alliances, joint ventures, and other cooperative agreements with foreign companies are a favorite and potentially fruitful means for entering a foreign market or strengthening a firm's competitiveness in world markets.[6] Historically, export-minded firms in industrialized nations sought alliances with firms in less-developed countries to import and market their products locally—such arrangements were often necessary to win approval for entry from the host country's government. Restrictions on investment in China by its government prior to the country's 2001 entry into the World Trade

Organization helped create about 10,000 joint ventures annually in China between 1998 and 2001. However, as those restrictions were lifted, the number of wholly foreign-owned enterprises in China grew from about 10,000 per year prior to 2001 to 30,000 per year between 2003 and 2007. Even with fewer restrictions on foreign investment, many U.S. and European companies have continued to ally with Chinese companies in their efforts to enter the market, with the number of new joint ventures created between 2002 and 2007 ranging from 7,000 to 12,000.[7]

Both Japanese and American companies are actively forming alliances with European companies to strengthen their ability to compete in the 27-nation European Union and to capitalize on the opening up of Eastern European markets. Companies in Europe, Latin America, and Asia are, of course, particularly interested in strategic partnerships that will strengthen their ability to gain a foothold in the U.S. market. In general, companies intent on international expansion commonly look to alliances and joint ventures as a means of strengthening their ability to compete across a wider geographical area.

However, cooperative arrangements between domestic and foreign companies have strategic appeal for reasons besides gaining better access to attractive country markets.[8] A second big appeal of cross-border alliances is to capture economies of scale in production and/or marketing. By joining forces in producing components, assembling models, and marketing their products, companies can realize cost savings not achievable with their own small volumes. A third motivation for entering into a cross-border alliance is to fill gaps in technical expertise and/or knowledge of local markets (buying habits and product preferences of consumers, local customs, and so on). Allies learn much from one another in performing joint research, sharing technological know-how, studying one another's manufacturing methods, and understanding how to tailor sales and marketing approaches to fit local cultures and traditions. Indeed, one of the win-win benefits of an alliance is to learn from the skills, technological know-how, and capabilities of alliance partners and implant the knowledge and know-how of these partners in personnel throughout the company.

A fourth motivation for cross-border alliances is to share distribution facilities and dealer networks, thus mutually strengthening their access to buyers. A fifth benefit is that cross-border allies can direct their competitive energies more toward mutual rivals and less toward one another; teaming up may help them close the gap on leading companies. A sixth driver of cross-border alliances comes into play when companies desiring to enter a new foreign market conclude that alliances with local companies are an effective way to establish working relationships with key officials in the host-country government.[9] And, finally, alliances can be a particularly useful way for companies across the world to gain agreement on important technical standards—they have been used to arrive at standards for assorted PC devices, Internet-related technologies, high-definition televisions, and mobile phones.

What makes cross-border alliances an attractive strategic means of gaining the above types of benefits (as compared to acquiring or merging with

of one kind or another allows a company to preserve its independence (which is not the case with a merger) and avoid using perhaps scarce financial resources to fund acquisitions. Furthermore, an alliance offers the flexibility to readily disengage once its purpose has been served or if the benefits prove elusive, whereas an acquisition is a more permanent sort of arrangement (although the acquired company can, of course, be divested).[10]

Cross-border alliances enable

coverage and strengthen its competitiveness in foreign markets while, at the same time, offering flexibility and allowing a company to retain some degree of autonomy and operating control.

Illustration Capsule 7.1 provides five examples of cross-border strategic alliances.

ILLUSTRATION CAPSULE 7.1
Five Examples of Cross-Border Strategic Alliances

1. Cisco, the worldwide leader in networking components, entered into a strategic alliance with the Finnish telecommunications firm Nokia Siemens Networks to develop communications networks capable of transmitting data either across the Internet or by mobile technologies. Nokia Siemens Networks itself was created through a 2006 international joint venture between German-based Siemens AG and the Finnish communications giant Nokia. The Cisco–Nokia Siemens alliance was created to better position both companies for convergence among Internet technologies and wireless communication devices that was expected to dramatically change how both computer networks and wireless telephones would be used.
2. Verio, a subsidiary of Japan-based NTT Communications and one of the leading global providers of Web hosting services and IP data transport, operates with the philosophy that in today's highly competitive and challenging technology market, companies must gain and share skills, information, and technology with technology leaders across the world. Believing that no company can be all things to all customers in the Web hosting industry, Verio executives have developed an alliance-oriented business model that combines the company's core competencies with the skills and products of best-of-breed technology partners. Verio's strategic partners include Accenture, Cisco Systems, Microsoft, Sun Microsystems, Oracle, Arsenal Digital Solutions (a provider of worry-free tape backup, data restore, and data storage services), Internet Security Systems (a provider of firewall and intrusion detection systems), and Mercantec (which develops storefront and shopping cart software). Verio management believes that its portfolio of strategic alliances allows it to use innovative, best-of-class technologies in providing its customers with fast, efficient, accurate data transport and a complete set of Web hosting services. An independent panel of 12 judges recently selected Verio as the winner of the Best Technology Foresight Award for its efforts in pioneering new technologies.
3. A 2003 strategic alliance between British oil producer BP and Russian oil and gas producer Alfa, Access, Renova (AAR) has produced Russia's third largest crude oil producer. The strategic alliance provided BP with access to AAR's vast oil reserves and allowed AAR access to BP's assets in Russia, including BP's retail refined gasoline network. The addition of BP's oil field production expertise increased the field production by 250 percent between 2003 and 2007. BP's exploration and drilling capabilities also contributed to the development new greenfield projects that were expected to come online in 2009.
4. Toyota and First Automotive Works, China's biggest automaker, entered into an alliance in 2002 to make luxury sedans, sport-utility vehicles, and minivehicles for the Chinese market. The intent was to make as many as 400,000 vehicles annually by 2010, an amount equal to the number that Volkswagen, the company with the largest share of the Chinese market, was making as of 2002. The alliance envisioned a joint investment of about $1.2 billion. At the time of the announced alliance, Toyota was lagging behind Honda, General Motors, and Volkswagen in setting up production facilities in China. Capturing a bigger share of the Chinese market was seen as crucial to Toyota's success in achieving its strategic objective of having a 15 percent share of the world's automotive market by 2010.
5. European Aeronautic Defence and Space (EADS) was formed by an alliance of aerospace companies from Britain, Spain, Germany, and France that included British Aerospace, Daimler-Benz Aerospace, and Aerospatiale. The objective of the alliance was to create a European aircraft company capable of competing with U.S.-based Boeing Corporation. The alliance has proved highly successful, infusing its commercial airline division, Airbus, with the know-how and resources to compete head-to-head with Boeing for world leadership in large commercial aircraft (over 100 passengers). The company also established an alliance with U.S. military aircraft manufacturer Northrop Grumman to develop a highly sophisticated refueling tanker based on the A330 airliner for the U.S. Air Force. As of 2008, the U.S. government was still evaluating competing bids from EADS/Northrop Grumman and Boeing, but the alliance had yielded contracts to produce the tanker for the United Kingdom, Australia, Saudi Arabia, and the United Arab Emirates.

Sources: Company Web sites and press releases; Yves L. Doz and Gary Hamel, *Alliance Advantage: The Art of Creating Value through Partnering* (Boston, MA: Harvard Business School Press, 1998).

The Risks of Strategic Alliances with Foreign Partners Alliances and joint ventures with foreign partners have their pitfalls, however. Cross-border allies typically have to overcome language and cultural barriers and figure out how to deal with diverse (or perhaps conflicting) operating practices. The communication, trust-building, and coordination costs are high in terms of management time.[11] It is not unusual for there to be little personal chemistry among some of the key people on whom success or failure of the alliance depends—the rapport such personnel need to work well together may never emerge. And even if allies are able to develop productive personal relationships, they can still have trouble reaching mutually agreeable ways to deal with key issues or resolve differences. There is a natural tendency for allies to struggle to collaborate effectively in competitively sensitive areas, thus spawning suspicions on both sides about forthright exchanges of information and expertise. Occasionally, the egos of corporate executives can clash—an alliance between Northwest Airlines and KLM Royal Dutch Airlines resulted in a bitter feud among both companies' top officials (who, according to some reports, refused to speak to each other).[12] Plus there is the thorny problem of getting alliance partners to sort through issues and reach decisions fast enough to stay abreast of rapid advances in technology or fast-changing market conditions.

It requires many meetings of many people working in good faith to iron out what is to be shared, what is to remain proprietary, and how the cooperative arrangements will work. Often, once the bloom is off the rose, partners discover they have conflicting objectives and strategies, deep differences of opinion about how to proceed, and/or important differences in corporate values and ethical standards. Tensions build up, working relationships cool, and the hoped-for benefits never materialize.[13]

Even if the alliance becomes a win–win proposition for both parties, there is the danger of becoming overly dependent on foreign partners for essential expertise and competitive capabilities. If a company is aiming for global market leadership and needs to develop capabilities of its own, then at some juncture cross-border merger or acquisition may have to be substituted for cross-border alliances and joint ventures. One of the lessons about cross-border alliances is that they are more effective in helping a company establish a beachhead of new opportunity in world markets than they are in enabling a company to achieve and sustain global market leadership. Global market leaders, while benefiting from alliances, usually must guard against becoming overly dependent on the assistance they get from alliance partners—otherwise they are not masters of their own destiny.

Strategic alliances are more effective in helping establish a beachhead of new opportunity in world markets than in achieving and sustaining global leadership.

When a Cross-Border Alliance May Be Unnecessary Experienced multinational companies that market in 50 to 100 or more countries across the world find less need for entering into cross-border alliances than do companies in the early stages of globalizing their operations.[14] Multinational companies make it a point to develop

in entering the markets of different countries wants to detour the hazards of allying with local businesses, it can simply assemble a capable management team consisting of both senior managers with considerable international experience and local managers. The role of its own in-house managers with international business savvy is to transfer technology, business practices, and the corporate culture into the company's operations in the new country market and to serve as conduits for the flow of information between the corporate office and local operations. The role of local managers is to contribute needed understanding of the local market conditions, local buying habits, and local ways of doing business and, often, to head up local operations.

Hence, one cannot automatically presume that a company needs the wisdom and resources of a local partner to guide it through the process of successfully entering the markets of foreign countries. Indeed, experienced multinationals often discover that local partners do not always have adequate local market knowledge—much of the so-called experience of local partners can predate the emergence of current market trends and conditions, and sometimes their operating practices can be archaic.[15]

Choosing between a Localized Multicountry Strategy and a Global Strategy

The issue of whether to vary the company's competitive approach to fit specific market conditions and buyer preferences in each host country or whether to employ essentially the same strategy in all countries is perhaps the foremost strategic issue that companies must address when they operate in two or more foreign markets. Figure 7.1 shows a company's options for resolving this issue.

Think-Local, Act-Local Approaches to Strategy-Making The bigger the differences in buyer tastes, cultural traditions, and market conditions in different countries, the stronger the case for a "think-local, act-local" approach to strategy making, where a company tailors its product offerings and perhaps its basic competitive strategy to fit buyer tastes and market conditions in each country where it opts to compete. The strength of employing a set of *localized* or *multicountry strategies* is that the company's actions and business approaches are deliberately crafted to accommodate the differing tastes and expectations of buyers in each country and to stake out the most attractive market positions vis-à-vis local competitors. A think-local, act-local approach means giving local managers considerable strategy-making latitude. It means having plants produce different product versions for different local markets, and adapting marketing and distribution to fit local customs and cultures. The bigger the country-to-country variations, the more that a company's overall strategy is a collection of its localized country strategies rather than a common or "global" strategy.[16]

CORE CONCEPT

A *localized or multicountry strategy* is one where a company varies its product offering and competitive approach from country to country in response to important cross-country variations in buyer preferences and market conditions.

A think-local, act-local approach to strategy making is essential when there are significant country-to-country differences in customer preferences and buying habits; when there are significant cross-country differences in distribution channels and marketing methods; when host governments enact regulations requiring that products sold locally meet strict manufacturing specifications or performance standards; and when the trade restrictions of host governments are so diverse and complicated that they preclude a uniform, coordinated worldwide market approach. With localized strategies, a company often has different product versions for different countries and sometimes sells them under different brand names. Castrol, a specialist in oil lubricants, has over 3,000 different formulas of lubricants, many of which have been tailored for different climates, vehicle types and uses, and equipment applications that characterize different country markets. In the food products industry, it is common for companies to vary the ingredients in their products and sell the localized versions under local brand names in order to cater to country-specific tastes and eating preferences. After an unsuccessful launch of the Dasani bottled water brand in Europe, Coca-Cola found that it

Figure 7.1 A Company's Strategic Options for Dealing with Cross-Country Variations in Buyer Preferences and Market Conditions

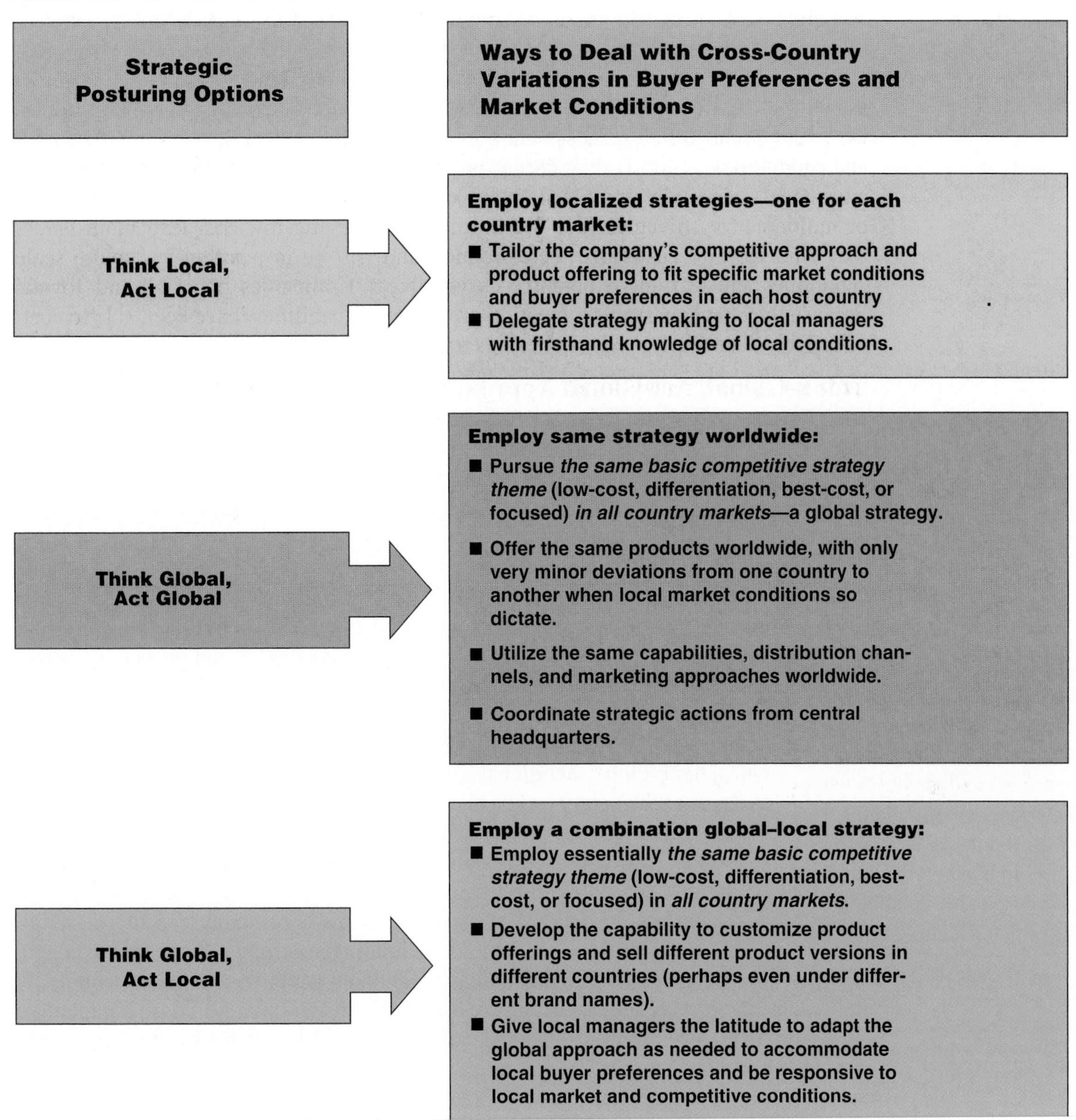

was best to adapt its strategy for competing in the bottled water industry to local market conditions. European consumers' preference for spring water rather than purified water forced Coca-Cola into a strategy of acquiring local brands rather than entering foreign markets with a global brand.[17] Deutsche Telekom markets broadband services, land-based telephone systems, wireless telephone services, and information and communication services to millions of customers in about 50 countries around the world.

Strategic Posturing Options
Ways to Deal with Cross-Country Variations in Buyer Preferences and Market Conditions
Think Local, Act Local
Employ localized strategies—one for each country market:
■ Tailor the company's competitive approach and product offering to fit specific market conditions and buyer preferences in each host country
■ Delegate strategy making to local managers with firsthand knowledge of local conditions.
Think Global, Act Global
Employ same strategy worldwide:
■ Pursue the same basic competitive strategy theme (low-cost, differentiation, best-cost, or focused) in all country markets—a global strategy.
■ Offer the same products worldwide, with only very minor deviations from one country to another when local market conditions so dictate.
■ Utilize the same capabilities, distribution channels, and marketing approaches worldwide.
■ Coordinate strategic actions from central headquarters.
Think Global, Act Local
Employ a combination global-local strategy:
■ Employ essentially the same basic competitive strategy theme (low-cost, differentiation, best-cost, or focused) in all country markets.
■ Develop the capability to customize product offerings and sell different product versions in different countries (perhaps even under different brand names).
■ Give local managers the latitude to adapt the global approach as needed to accommodate local buyer preferences and be responsive to local market and competitive conditions.

The company employs a localized, multicountry strategy, with its broadband and land-based telephone systems marketed only in Germany. Its information and communication services are marketed primarily to government agencies throughout Europe and manufacturers located in about 40 countries. Deutsche Telekom's T-Mobile wireless service is marketed in nine European countries and the United States.

Think-local, act-local strategies do have two big drawbacks: (1) They hinder transfer of a company's competencies and resources across country boundaries (since the strategies in different host countries can be grounded in varying competencies and capabilities), and (2) they do not promote building a single, unified competitive advantage—especially one based on low cost. Companies employing highly localized or multicountry strategies face big hurdles in achieving low-cost leadership *unless* they find ways to customize their products and *still* be in position to capture scale economies and learning/experience curve effects. Companies like Dell and Toyota, because they have mass customization production capabilities, have been able to cost-effectively adapt their product offerings to local buyer tastes.

Think-Global, Act-Global Approaches to Strategy Making While multicountry or localized strategies are best suited for industries where multicountry competition dominates and a fairly high degree of local responsiveness is competitively imperative, global strategies are best suited for globally competitive industries. A *global strategy* is one in which the company's approach is predominantly the same in all countries—it sells the same products under the same brand names everywhere, uses much the same distribution channels in all countries, and competes on the basis of the same capabilities and marketing approaches worldwide. A "think-global, act-global" strategic theme prompts company managers to integrate and coordinate the company's strategic moves worldwide and to expand into most if not all nations where there is significant buyer demand. It puts considerable strategic emphasis on building a *global* brand name and aggressively pursuing opportunities to transfer ideas, new products, and capabilities from one country to another.[18] Indeed, with a think-global, act-global approach to strategy making, a company's operations in each country can be viewed as experiments that result in learning and in capabilities that may merit transfer to other country markets.

CORE CONCEPT

A *global strategy* is one where a company employs the same basic competitive approach in all countries where it operates, sells much the same products everywhere, strives to build global brands, and coordinates its strategic moves worldwide.

Whenever country-to-country differences are small enough to be accommodated within the framework of a global strategy, a global strategy is preferable to localized strategies because a company can more readily unify its operations and focus on building a strong *global* brand image. Moreover, with a global strategy a company is better able to concentrate its full resources on achieving a sustainable low-cost or differentiation-based competitive advantage over rivals, putting itself in better position to contend strongly for world market leadership.[19] Figure 7.2 summarizes the basic differences between a localized or multicountry strategy and a global strategy.

Think-Global, Act-Local Approaches to Strategy Making Often a company can accommodate cross-country variations in buyer tastes, local customs, and market conditions with a "think-global, act-local" approach to developing strategy. This middle-ground approach entails using the same basic competitive theme (low-cost, differentiation, best-cost, or focused) in each country but allowing local mangers the latitude to (1) incorporate whatever country-specific variations in product attributes are needed to best satisfy local buyers and (2) make whatever adjustments in production, distribution, and marketing are needed to be responsive to local

Figure 7.2 How a Localized or Multicountry Strategy Differs from a Global Strategy

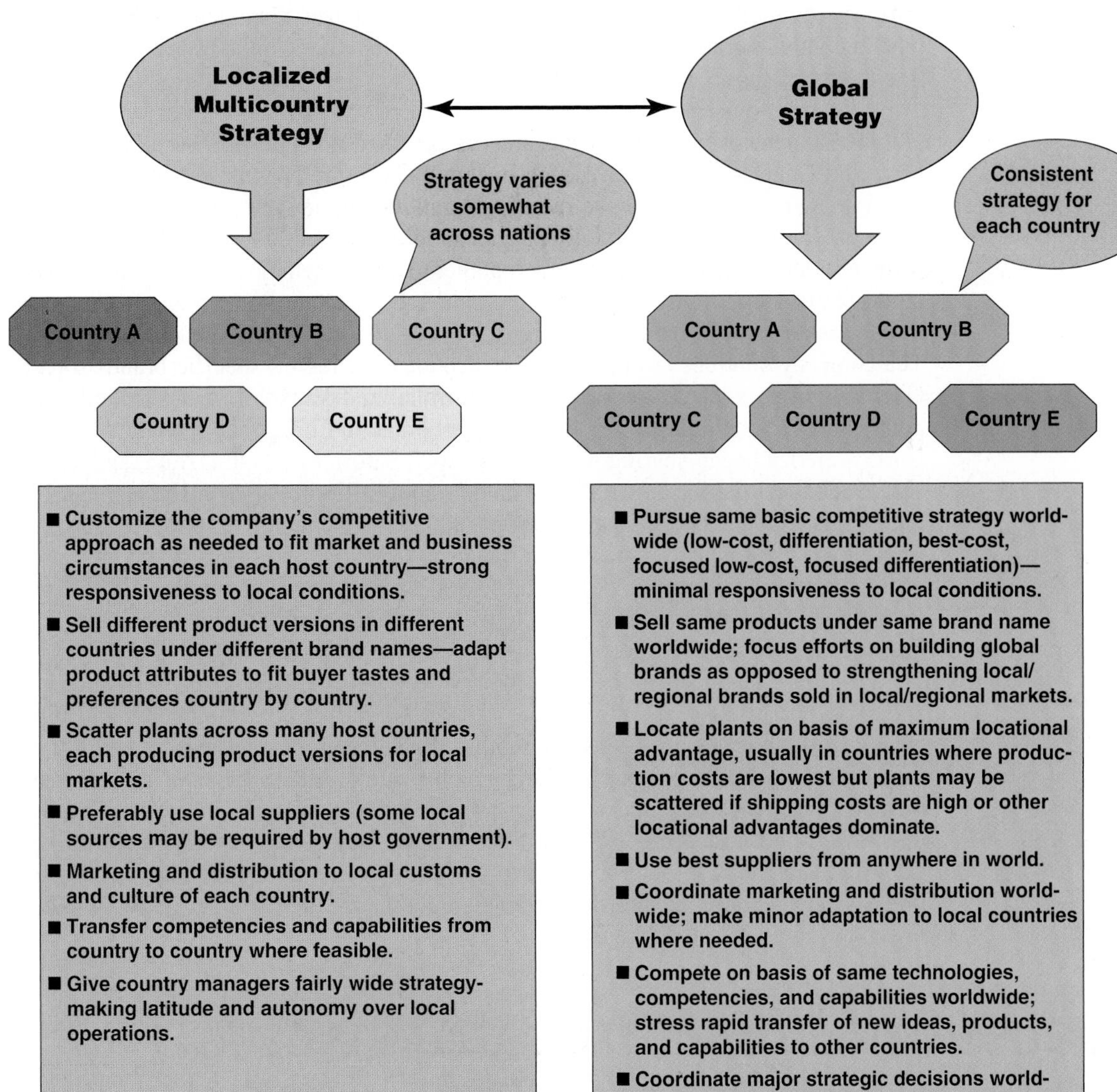
Localized Multicountry Strategy
Global Strategy
Strategy varies somewhat across nations
Consistent strategy for each country
Country A
Country B
Country C
Country D
Country E
Country A
Country B
Country C
Country D
Country E
■ Customize the company's competitive approach as needed to fit market and business circumstances in each host country—strong responsiveness to local conditions.
■ Sell different product versions in different countries under different brand names—adapt product attributes to fit buyer tastes and preferences country by country.
■ Scatter plants across many host countries, each producing product versions for local markets.
■ Preferably use local suppliers (some local sources may be required by host government).
■ Marketing and distribution to local customs and culture of each country.
■ Transfer competencies and capabilities from country to country where feasible.
■ Give country managers fairly wide strategy-making latitude and autonomy over local operations.
■ Pursue same basic competitive strategy worldwide (low-cost, differentiation, best-cost, focused low-cost, focused differentiation)—minimal responsiveness to local conditions.
■ Sell same products under same brand name worldwide; focus efforts on building global brands as opposed to strengthening local/regional brands sold in local/regional markets.
■ Locate plants on basis of maximum locational advantage, usually in countries where production costs are lowest but plants may be scattered if shipping costs are high or other locational advantages dominate.
■ Use best suppliers from anywhere in world.
■ Coordinate marketing and distribution worldwide; make minor adaptation to local countries where needed.
■ Compete on basis of same technologies, competencies, and capabilities worldwide; stress rapid transfer of new ideas, products, and capabilities to other countries.
■ Coordinate major strategic decisions worldwide; expect local managers to stick close to global strategy.

product versions sold under the same brand name may suffice to satisfy local tastes, and it may be feasible to accommodate these versions rather economically in the course of designing and manufacturing the company's product offerings. Philip Morris International markets brands such as Marlboro, Chesterfield, Parliament, and Virginia Slims worldwide. However, the company also makes different versions of Marlboro cigarettes available in different parts of the world to better meet the somewhat different preferences and habits of smokers in each market. The company's Marlboro Mix 9 is a high-nicotine, clove-infused cigarette sold in Indonesia, where smokers prefer powerful, sweet-smelling cigarettes. It's Marlboro Intense was formulated for the Turkish market, while its smooth-tasting Marlboro Filter Plus caters to the tastes of smokers in South Korea, Russia, Kazakhstan, and Ukraine.

As a rule, most companies that operate multinationally endeavor to employ as global a strategy as customer needs and market conditions permit. Ford Motor Company and General Motors have each operated successfully with localized strategies for more than 80 years but have recently begun moving toward more globalized multicountry strategies. General Motors began an initiative in 2004 to insist that its worldwide units share basic parts and work together to design vehicles that can be sold, with modest variations, anywhere around the world; by reducing the types of radios used in its cars and trucks from 270 to 50, it expected to save 40 percent in radio costs. The company continues to produce many country- or region-specific brands such as Opel in Europe and Africa, Holden in Australia, and Vauxhall in the United Kingdom. However, beginning in 2006, GM's Opel brand in Europe and its Saturn brand in North America began sharing models. The 2008 Saturn Sky, Astra, Aura, and Vue all shared identical platforms with Opel models sold in Europe. GM also began executing a think-global, act-local approach in China. GM planned to export 15,000 Buick Enclave SUVs produced in the United States to China and was considering importing its popular four-cylinder Buick Excelle sold in China to the U.S. market. GM planned to equip the U.S. version of the Excelle with an engine slightly larger than that of the Chinese version.

Whirlpool has been globalizing its low-cost leadership strategy in home appliances for nearly 20 years, striving to standardize parts and components and move toward worldwide designs for as many of its appliance products as possible. But it has found it necessary to continue producing significantly different versions of refrigerators, washing machines, and cooking appliances for consumers in different regions of the world because the needs and tastes of local buyers for appliances of different sizes and designs have not converged sufficiently to permit standardization. Illustration Capsule 7.2 describes how three companies localize their strategies for competing in country markets across the world.

THE QUEST FOR COMPETITIVE ADVANTAGE IN FOREIGN MARKETS

There are three important ways in which a firm can gain competitive advantage (or offset domestic disadvantages) by expanding outside its domestic market.[20] First, it can use location to lower costs or achieve greater product differentiation. Second, it can transfer competitively valuable competencies and capabilities from its domestic markets to foreign markets. And, third, it can use cross-border coordination in ways that a domestic-only competitor cannot.

Using Location to Build Competitive Advantage

Location-based advantages range from access to low-cost labor to obtaining low corporate tax rates in pro-business countries to improving innovation by locating activities in countries with unusually large pools of talented and skilled employees.[21]

ILLUSTRATION CAPSULE 7.2
Multicountry Strategies at Electronic Arts, Coca-Cola, and BP

ELECTRONIC ARTS' MULTICOUNTRY STRATEGY IN VIDEO GAMES

Electronic Arts (EA), the world's largest independent developer and marketer of video games, designs games that are suited to the differing tastes of game players in different countries and also designs games in multiple languages. EA has two major design studios—one in Vancouver, British Columbia, and one in Los Angeles—and smaller design studios in San Francisco, Orlando, London, and Tokyo. This dispersion of design studios helps EA design games that are specific to different cultures—for example, the London studio took the lead in designing the popular FIFA Soccer game to suit European tastes and to replicate the stadiums, signage, and team rosters; the U.S. studio took the lead in designing games involving NFL football, NBA basketball, and NASCAR racing. No other game software company had EA's ability to localize games or to launch games on multiple platforms in multiple countries in multiple languages. EA's The Sims was the best-selling PC game series of all time, with more than 100 million copies sold worldwide between 2000 and 2008. The Sims was published in 22 languages and sold in 60 countries.

COCA-COLA'S MULTICOUNTRY STRATEGY IN BEVERAGES

Coca-Cola strives to meet the demands of local tastes and cultures, offering 300 brands in some 200 countries. Its network of bottlers and distributors is distinctly local, and the company's products and brands are formulated to cater to local tastes. The ways in which Coca-Cola's local operating units bring products to market, the packaging that is used, and the advertising messages that are employed are all intended to match the local culture and fit in with local business practices. Many of the ingredients and supplies for Coca-Cola's products are sourced locally.

BP'S MULTICOUNTRY STRATEGY IN THE GASOLINE AND SERVICE STATION BUSINESS

Country differences in requirements for gasoline formulations mean that most oil producers employ think-local, act-local strategies to some extent. Government requirements for gasoline additives that help reduce carbon monoxide, smog, and other emissions are almost never the same from country to country. BP uses localized strategies in its gasoline and service station business segment because of these cross-country formulation differences and because of customer familiarity with local brand names. For example, the company markets gasoline in the United States under its BP and Arco brands, but it markets gasoline in Germany, Belgium, Poland, Hungary, and the Czech Republic under the Aral brand. Aral has been among Germany's most well-known gasoline brands and service station chains for more than 70 years. In 1937, Aral ran 8,000 gas stations in Germany and held a 25 percent share of the German market for gasoline sales. Over the next 30 years, the company continued to expand its chain of service stations to 11,000 locations. BP acquired Aral in 2002 and, as part of its think-local, act-local strategy, converted its 630 BP gas stations in Germany to Aral stations.

Sources: www.ea.com, www.cocacola.com, and www.bp.com (accessed September 2004 and July 2008).

To use location to build competitive advantage, a company must consider two issues: (1) whether to concentrate each activity it performs in a few select countries or to

When to Concentrate Activities in a Few Locations Companies tend to concentrate their activities in a limited number of locations in the following circumstances:

- *When the costs of manufacturing or other activities are significantly lower in some geographic locations than in others*—For example, much of the world's athletic footwear is manufactured in Asia (China and Malaysia) because of low labor costs; much of the production of motherboards for PCs is located in Taiwan because of both low costs and the high-caliber technical skills of the Taiwanese labor force.

- *When there are significant scale economies*—The presence of significant economies of scale in components production or final assembly means that a company can gain major cost savings from operating a few super-efficient plants as opposed to a host of small plants scattered across the world. Achieving low-cost provider status often requires a company to have the largest worldwide manufacturing share (as distinct from brand share or market share), with production centralized in one or a few world-scale plants. Some companies even use such plants to manufacture units sold under the brand names of rivals to further boost production-related scale economies. Chinese makers of apparel, footwear, housewares, toys, sporting goods, and parts for computers and peripherals have used their large manufacturing share and low labor costs to establish a low-cost advantage. Marketing and distribution economies associated with multinational operations can also yield scale economies necessary for low-cost leadership.

Companies that compete multinationally can pursue competitive advantage in world markets by locating their value chain activities in whatever nations prove most advantageous.

- *When there is a steep learning curve associated with performing an activity in a single location*—In some industries learning/experience curve effects in parts manufacture or assembly are so great that a company establishes one or two large plants from which it serves the world market. The key to riding down the learning curve is to concentrate production in a few locations to increase the accumulated volume at a plant (and thus the experience of the plant's workforce) as rapidly as possible.
- *When certain locations have superior resources, allow better coordination of related activities, or offer other valuable advantages*—A research unit or a sophisticated production facility may be situated in a particular nation because of its pool of technically trained personnel. Samsung became a leader in memory chip technology by establishing a major R&D facility in Silicon Valley and transferring the know-how it gained back to headquarters and its plants in South Korea. Also, parts manufacturing plants may be geographically concentrated and clustered around final assembly plants where just-in-time inventory practices yield big cost savings and/or where an assembly firm has long-term partnering arrangements with its key suppliers.

When to Disperse Activities Across Many Locations There are several instances when dispersing activities is more advantageous than concentrating them. Buyer-related activities—such as distribution to dealers, sales and advertising, and after-sale service—usually must take place close to buyers. This means physically locating the capability to perform such activities in every country market where a global firm has major customers (unless buyers in several adjoining countries can be served quickly from a nearby central location). For example, firms that make mining and oil-drilling equipment maintain operations in many international locations to support customers' needs for speedy equipment repair and technical assistance. The four biggest public accounting firms have numerous international offices to service the foreign operations of their multinational corporate clients. A global competitor that effectively disperses its buyer-related activities can gain a service-based competitive edge in world markets over rivals whose buyer-related activities are more concentrated—this is one reason the Big Four public accounting firms

(PricewaterhouseCoopers, KPMG, Deloitte & Touche, and Ernst & Young) have been so successful relative to regional and national firms. Dispersing activities to many locations is also competitively advantageous when high transportation costs, diseconomies of large size, and trade barriers make it too expensive to operate from a central location. Many companies distribute their products from multiple locations to shorten delivery times to customers. In addition, it is strategically advantageous to disperse activities to hedge against the risks of fluctuating exchange rates; supply interruptions (due to strikes, mechanical failures, and transportation delays); and adverse political developments. Such risks are greater when activities are concentrated in a single location.

Using Cross-Border Transfers of Competencies and Capabilities to Build Competitive Advantage

One of the best ways for a company with valuable competencies and resource strengths to grow sales and profits is to use its considerable resource strengths to enter additional country markets. Transferring competencies, capabilities, and resource strengths from country to country may also contribute to the development of broader or deeper competencies and capabilities—ideally helping a company achieve dominating depth in some competitively valuable area. Dominating depth in a competitively valuable capability, resource, or value chain activity is a strong basis for sustainable competitive advantage over other international or global competitors, and especially so over domestic-only competitors. A one-country customer base is often too small to support the resource buildup needed to achieve such depth; this is particularly true when the market is just emerging and sophisticated resources have not been required.

Whirlpool, the leading global manufacturer of home appliances, with 72 plants and technology centers in 17 countries and sales in 170 countries, has used the Internet to create a global information technology platform that allows the company to transfer key product innovations and production processes across regions and brands quickly and effectively. Wal-Mart is slowly but forcefully expanding its operations with a strategy that involves transferring its considerable domestic expertise in distribution and discount retailing to store operations recently established in China, Japan, Latin America, and the United Kingdom. Its status as the largest, most resource-deep, and most sophisticated user of distribution-retailing know-how has served it well in building its foreign sales and profitability. But Wal-Mart is not racing madly to position itself in many foreign markets; rather, it is establishing a strong presence in select country markets and learning how to be successful in these before tackling entry into other countries well suited to its business model.

However, cross-border resource transfers are not a guaranteed recipe for success.

27 billion euros, but as of 2007 Philips had lost money for 19 consecutive years in its U.S. consumer electronics business. In the United States, the company's televisions and DVD recorders (sold under the Magnavox and Philips brands) are slow sellers. Philips has been notoriously slow in introducing new products into the U.S. market, struggling to change its image as a low-end brand and convince U.S. electronics retailers to stock the Philips brand.

Using Cross-Border Coordination to Build Competitive Advantage

International and global competitors are able to coordinate activities across different countries to build competitive advantage.[23] If a firm learns how to assemble its product more efficiently at, say, its Brazilian plant, the accumulated expertise can be quickly communicated via the Internet to assembly plants in other world locations. Knowledge gained in marketing a company's product in Great Britain can readily be exchanged with company personnel in New Zealand or Australia. A global or international manufacturer can shift production from a plant in one country to a plant in another to take advantage of exchange rate fluctuations, to enhance its leverage with host-country governments, and to respond to changing wage rates, components shortages, energy costs, or changes in tariffs and quotas. Production schedules can be coordinated worldwide; shipments can be diverted from one distribution center to another if sales rise unexpectedly in one place and fall in another.

Multinational companies can use online systems to involve their best design and engineering personnel (wherever they are located) in collectively coming up with next-generation products. Efficiencies can also be achieved by shifting workloads from where they are unusually heavy to locations where personnel are underutilized. Whirlpool's efforts to link its product R&D and manufacturing operations in North America, Latin America, Europe, and Asia allowed it to accelerate the discovery of innovative appliance features, coordinate the introduction of these features in the appliance products marketed in different countries, and create a cost-efficient worldwide supply chain. Whirlpool's conscious efforts to integrate and coordinate its various operations around the world have helped it become a low-cost producer and also speed product innovations to market, thereby giving Whirlpool an edge over rivals in designing and rapidly introducing innovative and attractively priced appliances worldwide.

Furthermore, a multinational company that consistently incorporates the same differentiating attributes in its products worldwide has enhanced potential to build a global brand name with significant power in the marketplace. The reputation for quality that Honda established worldwide first in motorcycles and then in automobiles gave it competitive advantage in positioning Honda lawn mowers at the upper end of the U.S. outdoor power equipment market—the Honda name gave the company immediate credibility with U.S. buyers of power equipment and enabled it to become an instant market contender without all the fanfare and cost of a multimillion-dollar ad campaign to build brand awareness.

STRATEGIES TO COMPETE IN THE MARKETS OF EMERGING COUNTRIES

Companies racing for global leadership have to consider competing in emerging markets like China, India, Brazil, Indonesia, Thailand, Poland, Russia, and Mexico—countries where the business risks are considerable but where the opportunities for growth are huge, especially as their economies develop and living standards climb toward levels in the industrialized world.[24] With the world now comprising more than 6 billion people—fully one-third of whom are in India and China, and hundreds of millions more in other less-developed countries in Asia and Latin America—a

ILLUSTRATION CAPSULE 7.3
Yum! Brands' Strategy for Becoming the Leading Food Service Brand in China

In 2007, Yum! Brands operated more than 35,000 restaurants in more than 110 countries. Its best-known brands were KFC, Taco Bell, Pizza Hut, A&W, and Long John Silver's. Its fastest revenue growth in 2007 came from its 3,100 restaurants in China, which recorded revenues of $2.1 billion and operating profits of $375 million during the year. KFC was the largest quick-service chain in China, with 2,140 units in 2007, while Pizza Hut was the largest casual dining chain, with nearly 1,000 units. Yum! Brands planned to open at least 425 new restaurant locations annually in China, including new Pizza Hut Home delivery units and East Dawning units, which had a menu offering traditional Chinese food. All of Yum! Brands' menu items for China were developed in its R&D facility in Shanghai.

In addition to adapting its menu to local tastes and adding new units at a rapid pace, Yum! Brands also adapted the restaurant ambiance and decor to appeal to local consumer preferences and behavior. The company changed its KFC store formats to provide educational displays that supported parents' priorities for their children and to make KFC a fun place for children to visit. The typical KFC outlet in China averaged two birthday parties per day.

In 2008, Yum! Brands operated 60 KFC, Taco Bell, Pizza Hut, A&W, and Long John Silver's restaurants for every 1 million Americans. The company's 3,100 units in China represented only 2 restaurants per 1 million people in China. Yum! Brands' management believed that its strategy keyed to continued expansion in the number of units in China and additional menu refinements would allow its operating profits from restaurants located in China to account for 40 percent of systemwide operating profits by 2017.

Sources: Yum! Brands 2007 10-K report; information posted at www.yum.com.

company that aspires to world market leadership (or to sustained rapid growth) cannot ignore the market opportunities or the base of technical and managerial talent such countries offer. For example, in 2008 China was the world's second largest economy (behind the United States), measured by purchasing power. In 2003, its population of 1.3 billion people consumed nearly 33 percent of the world's annual cotton production, 51 percent of the world's pork, 35 percent of all cigarettes, 23 percent of televisions, 20 percent of cell phones, and 18 percent of all washing machines. China is also the world's largest consumer of many commodities—accounting for 50 percent of the world's demand for cement, 33 percent of all steel produced, 31 percent of worldwide coal production, and over 25 percent of the world's aluminum purchases. China's growth in demand for consumer goods had put it on track to become the second largest market for motor vehicles by 2010 and the world's largest market for luxury goods by 2014.[25] Thus, no company that aspires to global market leadership can afford to ignore the strategic importance of establishing competitive market positions in China, India, other parts of the Asia-Pacific region, Latin America, and Eastern Europe. Illustration Capsule 7.3 describes Yum! Brands' strategy to boost its sales and market share in China.

familiar with local cultures.[26] Ford's attempt to sell a Ford Escort in India at a price of $21,000—a luxury-car price, given that India's best-selling Maruti-Suzuki model sold at the time for $10,000 or less, and that fewer than 10 percent of Indian households have annual purchasing power greater than $20,000—met with a less-than-enthusiastic market response. McDonald's has had to offer vegetable burgers in parts of Asia and to rethink its prices, which are often high by local standards and affordable only by the well-to-do. Kellogg has struggled to introduce its cereals successfully because consumers in many less-developed countries do not eat cereal for breakfast—changing habits is difficult and expensive. In several emerging countries, Coca-Cola has found that advertising its world image does not strike a chord with the local populace in a number of emerging-country markets. Single-serving packages of detergents, shampoos, pickles, cough syrup, and cooking oils are very popular in India because they allow buyers to conserve cash by purchasing only what they need immediately. Thus, many companies find that trying to employ a strategy akin to that used in the markets of developed countries is hazardous.[27] Experimenting with some, perhaps many, local twists is usually necessary to find a strategy combination that works.

Strategy Options for Emerging-Country Markets

The following are options for tailoring a company's strategy to fit the sometimes unusual or challenging circumstances presented in emerging-country markets:

- *Prepare to compete on the basis of low price.* Consumers in emerging markets are often highly focused on price, which can give low-cost local competitors the edge unless a company can find ways to attract buyers with bargain prices as well as better products.[28] For example, when Unilever entered the market for laundry detergents in India, it realized that 80 percent of the population could not afford the brands it was selling to affluent consumers there (or the brands it was selling in wealthier countries). To compete against a very low-priced detergent made by a local company, Unilever came up with a low-cost formula that was not harsh to the skin, constructed new low-cost production facilities, packaged the detergent (named Wheel) in single-use amounts so that it could be sold very cheaply, distributed the product to local merchants by hand carts, and crafted an economical marketing campaign that included painted signs on buildings and demonstrations near stores. The new brand quickly captured $100 million in sales and was the number one detergent brand in India in 2008, measured by dollar sales. Unilever later replicated the strategy with low-priced packets of shampoos and deodorants in India and in South America with a detergent brand named Ala.
- *Be prepared to modify aspects of the company's business model or strategy to accommodate local circumstances (but not so much that the company loses the advantage of global scale and global branding).*[29] For instance, when Dell entered China, it discovered that individuals and businesses were not accustomed to placing orders through the Internet. (In contrast, in North America, over 50 percent of Dell's sales in 2002–2007 were online.) To adapt, Dell modified its direct sales model to rely more heavily on phone and fax orders and decided to be patient in getting Chinese customers to place Internet orders. Further, because numerous Chinese government departments and state-owned enterprises insisted that hardware vendors make their bids through distributors and systems integrators (as opposed to dealing directly with Dell salespeople, as did large enterprises in other countries), Dell opted to use third parties in marketing its products to this buyer segment (although it did sell through its own sales force where it could). But Dell was careful not to abandon those parts of its business model that gave it a competitive edge over rivals. When McDonald's moved into Russia in the 1990s, it was forced to alter its practice of obtaining needed supplies from outside vendors because capable local suppliers were not available; to supply its Russian outlets and stay true to its core principle of serving consistent-quality fast food, McDonald's set up its own vertically integrated supply chain—cattle were imported from Holland, and russet potatoes were imported from the United States.

McDonald's management also worked with a select number of Russian bakers for its bread; brought in agricultural specialists from Canada and Europe to improve the management practices of Russian farmers; built its own 100,000-square-foot McComplex to produce hamburger, French fries, ketchup, mustard, and Big Mac sauce; and set up a trucking fleet to move supplies to restaurants.

- *Try to change the local market to better match the way the company does business elsewhere.*[30] A multinational company often has enough market clout to drive major changes in the way a local market operates. When Hong Kong–based STAR launched its first satellite TV channel in 1991, it generated profound impacts on the TV marketplace in India. The Indian government lost its monopoly on TV broadcasts. Several other satellite TV channels aimed at Indian audiences quickly emerged. The excitement of additional TV channels in India triggered a boom in TV manufacturing in India. When Japan's Suzuki entered India in 1981, it triggered a quality revolution among Indian auto parts manufacturers. Local parts and components suppliers teamed up with Suzuki's vendors in Japan and worked with Japanese experts to produce higher-quality products. Over the next two decades, Indian companies became proficient in making top-notch parts and components for vehicles, won more prizes for quality than companies in any country other than Japan, and broke into the global market as suppliers to many automakers in Asia and other parts of the world. Mahindra and Mahindra, one of India's premier automobile manufacturers, has been recognized by a number of organizations for its product quality. Among its most noteworthy awards was its number one ranking by J. D. Power Asia Pacific in 2007 for new vehicle overall quality.
- *Stay away from those emerging markets where it is impractical or uneconomic to modify the company's business model to accommodate local circumstances.*[31] The Home Depot expanded into Mexico in 2001 and China in 2006, but it has avoided entry into other emerging countries because its value proposition of good quality, low prices, and attentive customer service relies on (1) good highways and logistical systems to minimize store inventory costs, (2) employee stock ownership to help motivate store personnel to provide good customer service, and (3) high labor costs for housing construction and home repairs to encourage homeowners to engage in do-it-yourself projects. Relying on these factors in the U.S. and Canadian markets has worked spectacularly for Home Depot, but Home Depot has found that it cannot count on these factors in nearby Latin America.

Profitability in emerging markets rarely comes quickly or easily—new entrants have to adapt their business models and strategies to local conditions and be patient in earning a profit.

Company experiences in entering developing markets like China, India, Russia, and Brazil indicate that profitability seldom comes quickly or easily. Building a market for the company's products can often turn into a long-term process that involves reeducation of consumers, sizable investments in advertising and promotion to alter tastes and buying habits, and upgrades of the local infrastructure (the supplier base, transportation systems, distribution

... revenues and profits once conditions are ripe for market takeoff.

Defending against Global Giants: Strategies for Local Companies in Emerging Markets

If opportunity-seeking, resource-rich multinational companies are looking to enter emerging markets, what strategy options can local companies use to survive? As it turns out, the prospects for local companies facing global giants are by no means grim.

Studies of local companies in developing markets have disclosed five strategies that have proved themselves in defending against globally competitive multinationals:[32]

1. *Develop business models that exploit shortcomings in local distribution networks or infrastructure.* In many instances, the extensive collection of resources possessed by multinationals is of little help in building a presence in emerging markets. The lack of well-established wholesaler and distributor networks, telecommunication systems, consumer banking, or media necessary for advertising make it difficult for multinationals to migrate business models proved in developed markets to emerging countries. Such markets sometimes favor local companies whose managers are familiar with the local language and culture and are skilled in selecting large numbers of conscientious employees to carry out labor-intensive tasks. Grupo Elektra is an electronics, furniture, and household goods retailer in Mexico that has overcome a void in Mexico's credit-reporting system that maintains few records on middle- and low-income consumers. To make financing available to its customers, Elektra has launched its own bank and placed a branch inside each store. Since credit reports are not available for most of its customers, its loan officers make their lending decisions after visiting the homes of applicants and determining if the applicant's standard of living appears consistent with the amount of household income stated on their loan application. The system has helped Elektra grow at a compound annual rate of 133 percent between 2002 and 2007. In addition, Grupo Elektra's Banco Azteca had a loan repayment rate of 90 percent in 2006.

   Shanda, a Chinese producer of massively multiplayer online role-playing games (MMORPGs), has overcome China's lack of an established credit card network by selling prepaid access cards through local merchants. The company's focus on online games also addresses shortcomings in China's software piracy laws. Emerge Logistics has used its understanding of China's extensive government bureaucracy and fragmented network of delivery services to deliver goods for multinationals doing business in China. Many foreign firms have found it difficult to get their goods to market, since the average Chinese trucking company owns only one or two trucks. An India-based electronics company has been able to carve out a market niche for itself by developing an all-in-one business machine designed especially for India's 1.2 million small shopkeepers that tolerates the frequent power outages in that country.[33]

2. *Utilize keen understanding of local customer needs and preferences to create customized products or services.* In many emerging markets, multinationals find it difficult to attract the business of customers unable to pay global prices. When emerging markets are largely made up of customers who are satisfied with local standard or near-global standard products, a good strategy option is to concentrate on customers who prefer a local touch and to accept the loss of customers attracted to global brands.[34] In many cases, a local company enjoys a significant cost advantage over global rivals (perhaps because of simpler product design or lower operating and overhead costs), allowing it to compete on the basis of price. Also, a local company may be able to astutely exploit its local orientation—its familiarity with local preferences, its expertise in traditional products, its long-standing customer relationships.

   A small Middle Eastern cell phone manufacturer competes successfully against industry giants Nokia, Samsung, and Motorola by selling a model designed especially for Muslims—it is loaded with the Koran, alerts people at prayer times, and is equipped with a compass that points them toward Mecca. Shenzhen-based Tencent has become the leader in instant messaging in China, with a 70 to 80 percent share of the market in 2006, through its unique understanding of Chinese behavior and culture. Chinese consumers are among the most frequent users of instant messaging and use cybercommunities to express their individuality. The company generated more than $375 million in revenues in 2006 by allowing its 220 million QQ instant messengers to customize their digital avatars used during messaging and chat sessions with an extensive array of outfits and accessories (including digital cars). Users were allowed to download QQ for free but were required to pay 1–2 yuan (about 15–30 cents) for each accessory.

3. *Take advantage of low-cost labor and other competitively important local work-force qualities.* Local companies that lack the technological capabilities possessed by multinational entrants to emerging markets may be able to rely on low-cost labor or knowledge of the capabilities of the local labor force to offset any cost disadvantage. Focus Media is China's largest outdoor advertising firm and has relied on access to China's low-cost labor to update its 130,000 liquid crystal displays (LCDs) and billboards in 90 cities. While multinationals operating in China use electronically networked screens that allow messages to be changed remotely, Focus uses an army of employees who ride to each display by bicycle to change advertisements with programming contained on a USB flash drive or DVD. Indian information technology firms such as Infosys Technologies and Satyam Computer Services have been able to keep personnel costs lower than multinational competitors EDS and Accenture because of their familiarity with local labor markets. While multinationals have focused recruiting efforts in urban centers like Bangalore and Delhi and have subsequently helped to drive up engineering and computer science salaries in such cities, local companies have shifted recruiting efforts to second-tier cities that are unfamiliar to foreign firms.

4. *Use acquisition and rapid growth strategies to better defend against expansion-minded multinationals.* With the growth potential of emerging markets such as China, India, and Brazil obvious to the world, local companies must attempt to develop scale as quickly as possible to defend against the stronger multinationals' arsenal of resources. Most successful regional companies in emerging markets have pursued mergers and acquisitions at a rapid-fire pace to build a nationwide presence. Acquisitions allow small firms to broaden product offerings and achieve the economies of scale necessary to compete against global rivals. For example, Focus Media built its network of 130,000 LCDs in China through multiple acquisitions and, by 2006, held a 2-to-1 advantage over Clear Channel Communications in terms of total number of displays in China. Chinese baby-related products manufacturer and marketer Goodbaby had defended itself against foreign entrants by setting up company offices in 35 cities to establish broad distribution across China. In 2008, Goodbaby's 1,500 products that included strollers, baby monitors, bicycles, and toys were sold in more than 4,000 retail locations in throughout China.

5. *Transfer company expertise to cross-border markets and initiate actions to contend on a global level.* When a company has

Mexico's largest media company, used its expertise in Spanish culture and linguistics to become the world's most prolific producer of Spanish-language soap operas. Jollibee Foods, a family-owned company with 56 percent of the fast-food business in the Philippines, combated McDonald's entry first by upgrading service and delivery standards and then by using its expertise in seasoning hamburgers with garlic and soy sauce and making noodle and rice meals with fish to open outlets catering to Asian residents in Hong Kong, the Middle East, and California.

ILLUSTRATION CAPSULE 7.4

How Ctrip Successfully Defended against Multinationals to Become China's Largest Online Travel Agency

Ctrip has used a business model tailored to the Chinese travel market, its access to low-cost labor, and its unique understanding of customer preferences and buying habits to build scale rapidly and defeat foreign rivals such as Expedia and Travelocity in becoming the largest travel agency in China. The company was founded in 1999 with a focus on business travelers, since corporate travel accounts for the majority of China's travel bookings. The company also placed little emphasis on online transactions since, at the time, there was no national ticketing system in China, most hotels did not belong to a national or global chain, and most consumers preferred paper tickets to electronic tickets. To overcome this infrastructure shortcoming, the company established its own central database of 5,600 hotels located throughout China and flight information for all major airlines operating in China. Ctrip set up a call center of 3,000 representatives that could use its proprietary database to provide travel information for up to 100,000 customers per day. Because most of its transactions were not done over the Internet, the company hired couriers in all major cities in China to ride by bicycle or scooter to collect payments and deliver tickets to Ctrip's corporate customers. Ctrip also initiated a loyalty program that provided gifts and incentives to the administrative personnel who arranged travel for business executives. In 2006, more than 70 percent of Ctrip's bookings came from off-line reservations made by business customers.

Sources: Based on information in Arindam K. Bhattacharya and David C. Michael, "How Local Companies Keep Multinationals at Bay," *Harvard Business Review* 86, no. 3 (March 2008), pp. 85–95.

If a local company in an emerging market has transferable resources and capabilities, it can sometimes launch successful initiatives to meet the pressures for globalization head-on and start to compete on a global level itself.[36] When General Motors (GM) decided to outsource the production of radiator caps for all of its North American vehicles, Sundaram Fasteners of India pursued the opportunity; it purchased one of GM's radiator cap production lines, moved it to India, and became GM's sole supplier of radiator caps in North America—at 5 million units a year. As a participant in GM's supplier network, Sundaram learned about emerging technical standards, built its capabilities, and became one of the first Indian companies to achieve QS 9000 certification, a quality standard that GM now requires for all suppliers. Sundaram's acquired expertise in quality standards enabled it then to pursue opportunities to supply automotive parts in Japan and Europe. Haier became the leader in the appliance industry in China through its low-cost manufacturing capabilities and its intimate understanding of consumer needs. Rather than producing only traditional washing machines and dryers, Haier produced small appliances that met just about any type of consumer need. For example, the company produces a tiny washer that cleans a single set of clothes that has become very popular in regions of China where humidity is very high and people tend to change clothes often. Haier has transferred its expertise in producing low-cost specialty appliances to meet the unique needs of consumers in Europe and North America. Haier's air conditioners, wine cellars, mini refrigerators, beer keg cooler/dispensers, and other compact appliances—which can be found in the United States at The Home Depot, Best Buy, and Wal-Mart—are best-sellers in their categories.

Illustration Capsule 7.4 discusses how a travel agency in China used a combination of these five strategies to become that country's largest travel consolidator and online travel agent.

KEY POINTS

Most issues in competitive strategy that apply to domestic companies apply also to companies that compete internationally. But there are four strategic issues unique to competing across national boundaries:

1. Whether to customize the company's offerings in each different country market to match the tastes and preferences of local buyers or offer a mostly standardized product worldwide.
2. Whether to employ essentially the same basic competitive strategy in all countries or modify the strategy country by country to fit the specific market conditions and competitive circumstances it encounters.
3. Where to locate the company's production facilities, distribution centers, and customer service operations so as to realize the greatest locational advantages.
4. How to efficiently transfer the company's resource strengths and capabilities from one country to another in an effort to secure competitive advantage.

Strategy options for competing in world markets include maintaining a national (one-country) production base and exporting goods to foreign markets, licensing foreign firms to use the company's technology or produce and distribute the company's products, employing a franchising strategy, using strategic alliances or other collaborative partnerships to enter a foreign market or strengthen a firm's competitiveness in world markets, following a multicountry strategy, or following a global strategy.

Strategic alliances with foreign partners have appeal from several angles: gaining wider access to attractive country markets, allowing capture of economies of scale in production and/or marketing, filling gaps in technical expertise and/or knowledge of local markets, saving on costs by sharing distribution facilities and dealer networks, helping gain agreement on important technical standards, and helping combat the impact of alliances that rivals have formed.

Multicountry competition refers to situations where competition in one national market is largely independent of competition in another national market—there is no "international market," just a collection of self-contained country (or maybe regional) markets. Global competition exists when competitive conditions across national markets are linked strongly enough to form a true world market and when leading competitors compete head-to-head in many different countries.

Once a company has chosen to establish international operations, it has three basic options: (1) a think-local, act-local approach to crafting a strategy; (2) a think-global, act-global approach to crafting a strategy; and (3) a combination think-global, act-local approach. A *think-local, act-local* strategy is appropriate for industries where multicountry competition dominates; a localized approach to strategy making calls for a company to vary its product offering and competitive approach from country to country in order to accommodate differing buyer preferences and market conditions. A *think-global, act-global* approach [illegible] country markets and marketing essentially the same products under the same brand names in all countries where the company operates. A *think-global, act-local* approach can be used when it is feasible for a company to employ essentially the same basic competitive strategy in all markets but still customize its product offering and some aspect of its operations to fit local market circumstances.

There are three ways in which a firm can gain competitive advantage (or offset domestic disadvantages) in global markets. One way involves locating various value chain activities among nations in a manner that lowers costs or achieves greater product differentiation. A second way involves efficient and effective transfer of competitively valuable competencies and capabilities from its domestic markets to foreign markets. A third way draws on a multinational or global competitor's ability to deepen or broaden its resource strengths and capabilities and to coordinate its dispersed activities in ways that a domestic-only competitor cannot.

Companies racing for global leadership have to consider competing in emerging markets like China, India, Brazil, Indonesia, and Mexico—countries where the business risks are considerable but the opportunities for growth are huge. To succeed in these markets, companies often have to (1) compete on the basis of low price, (2) be prepared to modify aspects of the company's business model or strategy to accommodate local circumstances (but not so much that the company loses the advantage of global scale and global branding), and/or (3) try to change the local market to better match the way the company does business elsewhere. Profitability is unlikely to come quickly or easily in emerging markets, typically because of the investments needed to alter buying habits and tastes and/or the need for infrastructure upgrades. And there may be times when a company should simply stay away from certain emerging markets until conditions for entry are better suited to its business model and strategy.

Local companies in emerging country markets can seek to compete against multinational companies by (1) developing business models that exploit shortcomings in local distribution networks or infrastructure, (2) utilizing understanding of local customer needs and preferences to create customized products or services, (3) taking advantage of low-cost labor and other competitively important qualities of the local workforce, (4) using economies of scope and scale to better defend against expansion-minded multinationals, or (5) transferring company expertise to cross-border markets and taking initiatives to compete on a global level themselves.

ASSURANCE OF LEARNING EXERCISES

1. Harley-Davidson has chosen to compete in various country markets in Europe and Asia using an export strategy. Read the sections of its latest annual report at www.harley-davidson.com related to its international operations. Why has the company avoided developing production facilities outside the United States?
2. Log on to www.ford.co.uk and review the information provided under the Vehicles and Company pull-down menus. Given this information and what you know about Ford's operations in North America, does it appear that Ford is pursuing a global strategy or a localized multicountry strategy? Support your answer.
3. The Hero Group is among the 10 largest corporations in India, with 19 business segments and annual revenues of $3.19 billion in fiscal 2005–2006. Many of the corporation's business units have used strategic alliances with foreign partners to compete in new product and geographic markets. Review the company's statements concerning its alliances and international business operations at www.herogroup.com/alliance.htm and prepare a two-page report that outlines the Hero Group's successful use of international strategic alliances.
4. Assume you are in charge of developing the strategy for a multinational company selling products in some 50 different countries around the world. One of the issues you face is whether to employ a multicountry strategy or a global strategy.

a. If your company's product is personal computers, do you think it would make better strategic sense to employ a multicountry strategy or a global strategy? Why?

b. If your company's product is dry soup mixes and canned soups, would a multicountry strategy seem to be more advisable than a global strategy? Why?

c. If your company's product is washing machines, would it seem to make more sense to pursue a multicountry strategy or a global strategy? Why?

d. If your company's product is basic work tools (hammers, screwdrivers, pliers, wrenches, saws), would a multicountry strategy or a global strategy seem to have more appeal? Why?

EXERCISES FOR SIMULATION PARTICIPANTS

The questions below are for simulation participants whose companies operate in an international or global market arena. If your company competes only in a single country, then skip the questions in this section.

1. Is the international market arena in which your company competes characterized by multicountry competition or global competition? Explain.
2. Which of the strategies for competing in foreign markets is your company employing?
3. Which one of the following best describes the strategic approach your company is taking in trying to compete successfully?
   - Think local, act local
   - Think global, act local
   - Think global, act global

   Explain your answer.
4. To what extent, if any, have you and your co-managers adapted your company's strategy to take shifting exchange rates into account? In other words, have you undertaken any actions to try to minimize the impact of adverse shifts in exchange rates?
5. To what extent, if any, have you and your co-managers adapted your company's strategy to take geographic differences in import tariffs or import duties into account?

CHAPTER

8 Diversification

Strategies for Managing a Group of Businesses

LEARNING OBJECTIVES

1. Understand when and how business diversification can enhance shareholder value.
2. Gain an understanding of how related diversification strategies can produce cross-business strategic fits capable of delivering competitive advantage.
3. Become aware of the merits and risks of corporate strategies keyed to unrelated diversification.
4. Gain command of the analytical tools for evaluating a company's diversification strategy.
5. Become familiar with a company's five main corporate strategy options after it has diversified.

To acquire or not to acquire: that is the question.

—**Robert J. Terry**

Fit between a parent and its businesses is a two-edged sword: a good fit can create value; a bad one can destroy it.

—**Andrew Campbell, Michael Goold, and Marcus Alexander**

Make winners out of every business in your company. Don't carry losers.

—**Jack Welch**
Former CEO, General Electric

We measure each of our businesses against strict criteria: growth, margin, and return-on-capital hurdle rate, and does it have the ability to become number one or two in its industry? We are quite pragmatic. If a business does not contribute to our overall vision, it has to go.

—**Richard Wambold**
CEO, Pactiv

In this chapter, we move up one level in the strategy-making hierarchy, from strategy making in a single-business enterprise to strategy making in a diversified enterprise. Because a diversified company is a collection of individual businesses, the strategy-making task is more complicated. In a one-business company, managers have to come up with a plan for competing successfully in only a single industry environment—the result is what we labeled in Chapter 2 as *business strategy* (or *business-level strategy*). But in a diversified company, the strategy-making challenge involves assessing multiple industry environments and developing a *set* of business strategies, one for each industry arena in which the diversified company operates. And top executives at a diversified company must still go one step further and devise a companywide or *corporate strategy* for improving the attractiveness and performance of the company's overall business lineup and for making a rational whole out of its diversified collection of individual businesses.

authority to the heads of each business, usually giving them the latitude to craft a business strategy suited to their particular industry and competitive circumstances and holding them accountable for producing good results. But the task of crafting a diversified company's overall or corporate strategy falls squarely in the lap of top-level executives and involves four distinct facets:

1. *Picking new industries to enter and deciding on the means of entry*—The first concerns in diversifying are what new industries to get into and whether to enter by starting a new business from the ground up, acquiring a company already in the target industry, or forming a joint venture or strategic alliance with another company. A company can diversify narrowly into a few industries or broadly into many industries. The choice of whether to enter an industry via (*a*) a start-up operation; (*b*) a joint venture; or (*c*) an acquisition of an established leader, an up-and-coming company, or a troubled company with turnaround potential shapes what position the company will initially stake out for itself.
2. *Initiating actions to boost the combined performance of the businesses the firm has entered*

strengthen the long-term competitive positions and profits of the businesses the firm has invested in. Corporate parents can help their business subsidiaries by providing financial resources, by supplying missing skills, or technological know-how or managerial expertise to better perform key value chain activities, and by providing new avenues for cost reduction. They can also acquire another company in the same industry and merge the two operations into a stronger business, or acquire new businesses that strongly complement existing businesses. Typically, a diversified company will pursue rapid-growth strategies in its most promising businesses, initiate turnaround efforts in weak-performing businesses with potential, and divest businesses that are no longer attractive or that don't fit into management's long-range plans.

3. *Pursuing opportunities to leverage cross-business value chain relationships and strategic fits into competitive advantage*—A company that diversifies into businesses with competitively important value chain matchups (pertaining to technology, supply chain logistics, production, overlapping distribution channels, or common customers) gains competitive advantage potential not open to a company that diversifies into businesses whose value chains are totally unrelated. Capturing this competitive advantage potential requires that corporate strategists spend considerable time trying to capitalize on such cross-business opportunities as transferring skills or technology from one business to another, reducing costs via sharing use of common facilities and resources, and utilizing the company's well-known brand names and distribution muscle to grow the sales of newly acquired products.
4. *Establishing investment priorities and steering corporate resources into the most attractive business units*—A diversified company's different businesses are usually not equally attractive from the standpoint of investing additional funds. It is incumbent on corporate management to (*a*) decide on the priorities for investing capital in the company's different businesses, (*b*) channel resources into areas where earnings potentials are higher and away from areas where they are lower, and (*c*) divest business units that are chronically poor performers or are in an increasingly unattractive industry. Divesting poor performers and businesses in unattractive industries frees up unproductive investments either for redeployment to promising business units or for financing attractive new acquisitions.

The demanding and time-consuming nature of these four tasks explains why corporate executives generally refrain from becoming immersed in the details of crafting and implementing business-level strategies, preferring instead to delegate lead responsibility for business strategy to the heads of each business unit.

In the first portion of this chapter we describe the various means a company can use to become diversified and explore the pros and cons of related versus unrelated diversification strategies. The second part of the chapter looks at how to evaluate the attractiveness of a diversified company's business lineup, decide whether it has a good diversification strategy, and identify ways to improve its performance. In the chapter's concluding section, we survey the strategic options open to already-diversified companies.

WHEN TO DIVERSIFY

So long as a company has its hands full trying to capitalize on profitable growth opportunities in its present industry, there is no urgency to pursue diversification. The big risk of a single-business company, of course, is having all of the firm's eggs in one industry basket. If demand for the industry's product is eroded by the appearance of alternative technologies, substitute products, or fast-shifting buyer preferences, or if the industry becomes competitively unattractive and unprofitable, then a company's prospects can quickly dim. Consider, for example, what growing use of debit cards and online bill payment have done to the check printing business; what iPods, other brands of digital music players, and online music stores have done to the business outlook for the retailers of music CDs; and what cell phone companies and marketers of Voice over Internet Protocol (VoIP) have done to the revenues of such once-dominant long-distance providers as AT&T, British Telecommunications, and Japan's NTT.

Thus, diversifying into new industries always merits strong consideration whenever a single-business company encounters diminishing market opportunities and stagnating sales in its principal business—most landline-based telecommunications companies across the world are quickly diversifying their product offerings to include wireless and VoIP services. In addition, there are four other instances in which a company becomes a prime candidate for diversifying:[1]

1. When it spots opportunities for expanding into industries whose technologies and products complement its present business.
2. When it can leverage existing competencies and capabilities by expanding into businesses where these same resource strengths are key success factors and valuable competitive assets.
3. When diversifying into closely related businesses opens new avenues for reducing costs.
4. When it has a powerful and well-known brand name that can be transferred to the products of other businesses and thereby used as a lever for driving up the sales and profits of such businesses.

The decision to diversify presents wide-open possibilities. A company can diversify into closely related businesses or into totally unrelated businesses. It can diversify its present revenue and earning base to a small extent (such that new businesses account for less than 15 percent of companywide revenues and profits) or to a major extent (such that new businesses produce 30 or more percent of revenues and profits). It can move into one or two large new businesses or a greater number of small ones. It can achieve multibusiness/multi-industry status by acquiring an existing company already in a business/industry it wants to enter, starting up a new business subsidiary from scratch, or forming a joint venture with one or more companies to enter new businesses.

BUILDING SHAREHOLDER VALUE: THE ULTIMATE JUSTIFICATION FOR DIVERSIFYING

Diversification must do more for a company than simply spread its business risk across various industries. In principle, diversification cannot be considered a success unless it results in *added shareholder value*—value that shareholders cannot capture on their own by purchasing stock in companies in different industries or investing in mutual funds so as to spread their investments across several industries.

For there to be reasonable expectations that a company's diversification efforts can produce added value, a move to diversify into a new business must pass three tests:[2]

1. *The industry attractiveness test*—The industry to be entered must be attractive enough to yield consistently good returns on investment. Whether an industry is attractive depends chiefly on the presence of industry and competitive conditions that are conducive to earning as good or better profits and return on investment as the company is earning in its present business(es). It is hard to justify diversifying into an industry where profit expectations are *lower* than in the company's present businesses.
2. *The cost-of-entry test*—The cost to enter the target industry must not be so high as to erode the potential for good profitability. A catch-22 can prevail here, however. The more attractive an industry's prospects are for growth and good long-term profitability, the more expensive it can be to get into. Entry barriers for start-up companies are likely to be high in attractive industries; were barriers low, a rush of new entrants would soon erode the potential for high profitability. And buying a well-positioned company in an appealing industry often entails a high acquisition cost that makes passing the cost-of-entry test less likely. For instance, suppose that the price to purchase a company is $3 million and that the company is earning after-tax profits of $200,000 on an equity investment of $1 million (a 20 percent annual return). Simple arithmetic requires that the profits be tripled if the purchaser (paying $3 million) is to earn the same 20 percent return. Building the acquired firm's earnings from $200,000 to $600,000 annually could take several years—and require additional investment on which the purchaser would also have to earn a 20 percent return. Since the owners of a successful and growing company usually demand a price that reflects their business's profit prospects, it's easy for such an acquisition to fail the cost-of-entry test.
3. *The better-off test*—Diversifying into a new business must offer potential for the company's existing businesses and the new business to perform better together under a single corporate umbrella than they would perform operating as independent, stand-alone businesses. For example, let's say that company A diversifies by purchasing company B in another industry. If A and B's consolidated profits in the years to come prove no greater than what each could have earned on its own, then A's diversification won't provide its shareholders with added value. Company A's shareholders could have achieved the same 1 + 1 = 2 result by merely purchasing stock in company B. Shareholder value is not created by diversification unless it produces a 1 + 1 = 3 effect where sister businesses *perform better together* as part of the same firm than they could have performed as independent companies.

CORE CONCEPT
Creating added value for shareholders via diversification requires building a multibusiness company where the whole is greater than the sum of its parts.

Diversification moves that satisfy all three tests have the greatest potential to grow shareholder value over the long term. Diversification moves that can pass only one or two tests are suspect.

STRATEGIES FOR ENTERING NEW BUSINESSES

The means of entering new businesses can take any of three forms: acquisition, internal start-up, or joint ventures with other companies.

Acquisition of an Existing Business

Acquisition is the most popular means of diversifying into another industry. Not only is it quicker than trying to launch a brand-new operation, but it also offers an effective way to hurdle such entry barriers as acquiring technological know-how, establishing supplier relationships, becoming big enough to match rivals' efficiency and unit costs, having to spend large sums on introductory advertising and promotions, and securing adequate distribution. Buying an ongoing operation allows the acquirer to move directly to the task of building a strong market position in the target industry rather than getting bogged down in going the internal start-up route and trying to develop the knowledge, resources, scale of operation, and market reputation necessary to become an effective competitor within a few years.

The big dilemma an acquisition-minded firm faces is whether to pay a premium price for a successful company or to buy a struggling company at a bargain price.[3] If the buying firm has little knowledge of the industry but ample capital, it is often better off purchasing a capable, strongly positioned firm—unless the price of such an acquisition is prohibitive and flunks the cost-of-entry test. However, when the acquirer sees promising ways to transform a weak firm into a strong one and has the resources, the know-how, and the patience to do it, a struggling company can be the better long-term investment.

Internal Start-Up

Achieving diversification through *internal start-up* involves building a new business subsidiary from scratch. This entry option takes longer than the acquisition option and poses some hurdles. A newly formed business unit not only has to overcome entry barriers but also has to invest in new production capacity, develop sources of supply, hire and train employees, build channels of distribution, grow a customer base, and so on. Generally, forming a start-up subsidiary to enter a new business has appeal only when (1) the parent company already has in-house most or all of the skills and resources it needs to piece together a new business and compete effectively; (2) there is ample time to launch the business; (3) internal entry has lower costs than entry via acquisition; (4) the targeted industry is populated with many relatively small firms such that the new start-up does not have to compete head-to-head against larger, more powerful rivals; (5) adding new production capacity will not adversely impact the supply–demand balance in the industry; and (6) incumbent firms are likely to be slow or ineffective in responding to a new entrant's efforts to crack the market.[4]

The biggest drawbacks to entering an industry by forming an internal start-up are the costs of over-coming entry barriers and the extra time it takes to build a strong and profitable competitive position.

Joint Ventures

Joint ventures entail forming a new corporate entity owned by two or more companies, where the purpose of the joint venture is to pursue a mutually attractive opportunity. The terms and [illegible]

[illegible] the arrangement between the partners is one of limited collaboration for a limited purpose and a partner can choose to simply walk away or reduce its commitment to collaborating at any time.

A joint venture to enter a new business can be useful in at least three types of situations.[5] First, a joint venture is a good vehicle for pursuing an opportunity that is too complex, uneconomical, or risky for one company to pursue alone. Second, joint ventures make sense when the opportunities in a new industry require a broader range of competencies and know-how than a company can marshal. Many of the opportunities in satellite-based telecommunications, biotechnology, and network-based systems that blend hardware, software, and services call for the coordinated development of complementary innovations and tackling an intricate web of financial, technical, political, and regulatory factors simultaneously. In such cases, pooling the resources and competencies of two or more companies is a wiser and less risky way to proceed.

Third, companies sometimes use joint ventures to diversify into a new industry when the diversification move entails having operations in a foreign country—several governments require foreign companies operating within their borders to have a local partner that has minority, if not majority, ownership in the local operations. Aside from fulfilling host government ownership requirements, companies usually seek out a local partner with expertise and other resources that will aid the success of the newly established local operation.

However, as discussed in Chapters 6 and 7, partnering with another company—in the form of either a joint venture or a collaborative alliance—has significant drawbacks due to the potential for conflicting objectives, disagreements over how to best operate the venture, culture clashes, and so on. Joint ventures are generally the least durable of the entry options, usually lasting only until the partners decide to go their own ways.

CHOOSING THE DIVERSIFICATION PATH: RELATED VERSUS UNRELATED BUSINESSES

CORE CONCEPT

Related businesses **possess competitively valuable cross-business value chain match-ups;** ***unrelated businesses*** **have dissimilar value chains, containing no competitively useful cross-business relationships.**

Once a company decides to diversify, its first big strategy decision is whether to diversify into related businesses, unrelated businesses, or some mix of both (see Figure 8.1). **Related businesses** are those whose value chains possess competitively valuable cross-business relationships that present opportunities for the businesses to perform better under the same corporate umbrella than they could by operating as stand-alone entities. The big appeal of related diversification is to build shareholder value by leveraging these cross-business relationships into competitive advantage, thus allowing the company as a whole to perform better than just the sum of its individual businesses. **Unrelated businesses** are those whose value chain activities are so dissimilar that no competitively valuable cross-business relationships are present.

The next two sections explore the ins and outs of related and unrelated diversification.

THE CASE FOR DIVERSIFYING INTO RELATED BUSINESSES

A related diversification strategy involves building the company around businesses whose value chains possess competitively valuable strategic fits, as shown in Figure 8.2. **Strategic fit** exists whenever one or more activities comprising the value chains of different businesses are sufficiently similar as to present opportunities for:[6]

- Transferring competitively valuable expertise, technological know-how, or other capabilities from one business to another.

Figure 8.1 Strategy Alternatives for a Company Looking to Diversify

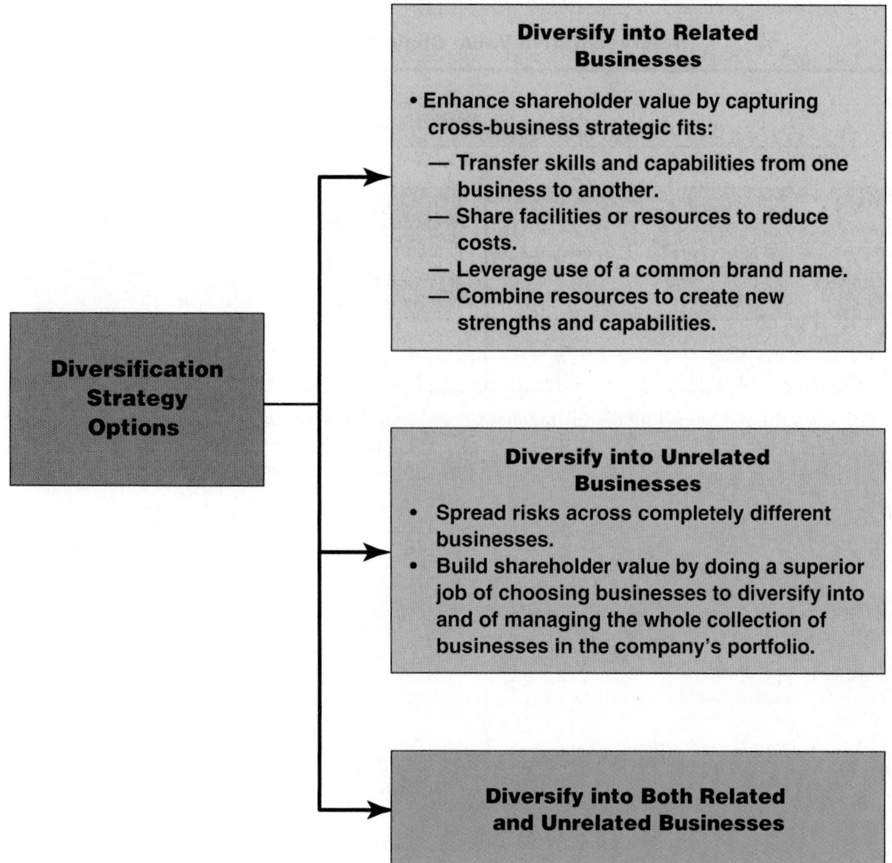

- Combining the related value chain activities of separate businesses into a single operation to achieve lower costs. For instance, it is often feasible to manufacture the products of different businesses in a single plant or use the same warehouses for shipping and distribution or have a single sales force for the products of different businesses (because they are marketed to the same types of customers).
- Exploiting common use of a well-known and potent brand name. For example, Yamaha's name in motorcycles gave it instant credibility and recognition in entering the personal watercraft business, allowing it

asset that facilitated the company's diversification into digital music players. Sony's name in consumer electronics made it easier for it to enter the market for video games with its PlayStation console and lineup of PlayStation video games.
- Cross-business collaboration to create competitively valuable resource strengths and capabilities.

CORE CONCEPT

Strategic fit exists when the value chains of different businesses present opportunities for cross-business resource transfer, lower costs through combining the performance of related value chain activities,

new or stronger competitive capabilities.

Figure 8.2 Related Businesses Possess Related Value Chain Activities and Competitively Valuable Strategic Fits

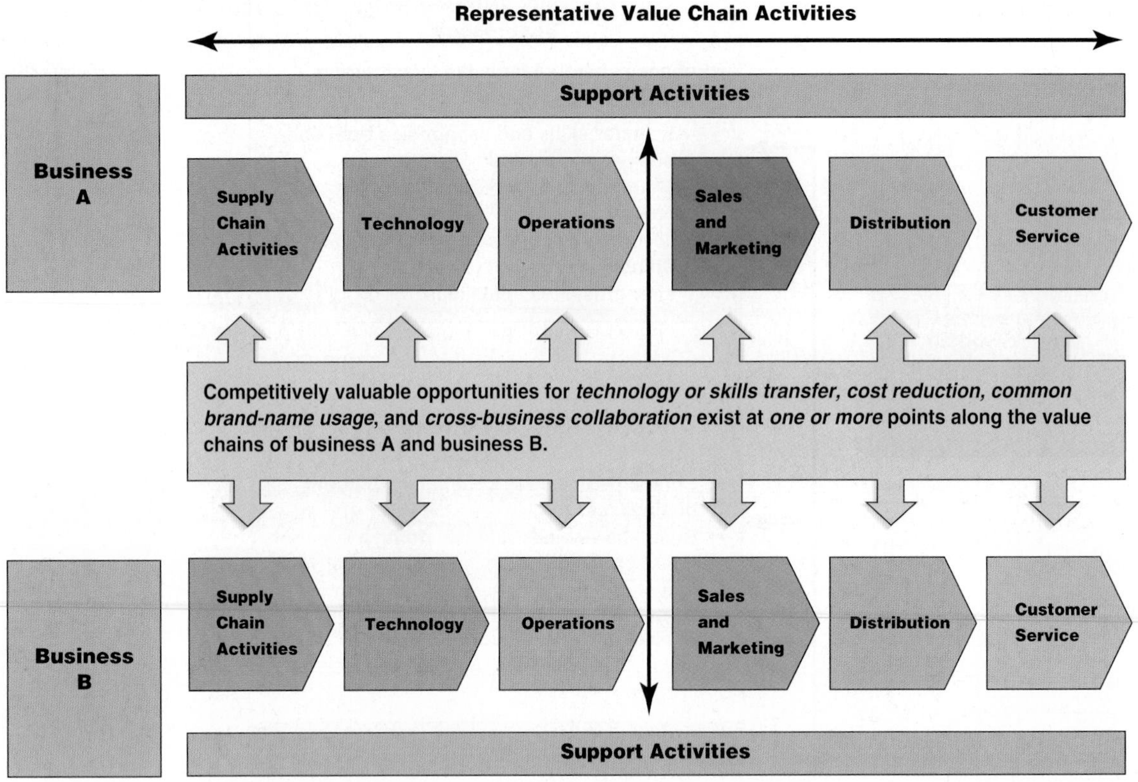

Related diversification thus has strategic appeal from several angles. It allows a firm to reap the competitive advantage benefits of skills transfer, lower costs, a powerful brand name, and/or stronger competitive capabilities and still spread investor risks over a broad business base. Furthermore, the relatedness among the different businesses provides sharper focus for managing diversification and a useful degree of strategic unity across the company's various business activities.

Identifying Cross-Business Strategic Fits along the Value Chain

Cross-business strategic fits can exist anywhere along the value chain: in R&D and technology activities, in supply chain activities and relationships with suppliers, in manufacturing, in sales and marketing, in distribution activities, or in administrative support activities.[7]

Strategic Fits in R&D and Technology Activities Diversifying into businesses where there is potential for sharing common technology, exploiting the full range of business opportunities associated with a particular technology and its derivatives, or transferring technological know-how from one business to another has considerable appeal. Businesses with technology-sharing benefits can perform better together than apart because of potential cost savings in R&D and potentially shorter times in getting new products to market; also, technological advances in one business can lead to increased sales for both. Technological innovations have been the driver behind the efforts of cable TV companies to diversify into high-speed Internet access (via the use of cable modems) and, further, to explore providing local and long-distance telephone service to residential and commercial customers via either a single wire or VoIP technology.

Strategic Fits in Supply Chain Activities Businesses that have supply chain strategic fits can perform better together because of the potential for skills transfer in procuring materials, greater bargaining power in negotiating with common suppliers, the benefits of added collaboration with common supply chain partners, and/or added leverage with shippers in securing volume discounts on incoming parts and components. Dell's strategic partnerships with leading suppliers of microprocessors, circuit boards, disk drives, memory chips, flat-panel displays, wireless capabilities, long-life batteries, and other PC-related components have been an important element of the company's strategy to diversify into servers, data storage devices, networking components, and LCD TVs—products that include many components common to PCs and that can be sourced from the same strategic partners that provide Dell with PC components.

Manufacturing-Related Strategic Fits Cross-business strategic fits in manufacturing-related activities can represent an important source of competitive advantage in situations where a diversifier's expertise in quality manufacture and cost-efficient production methods can be transferred to another business. When Emerson Electric diversified into the chain-saw business, it transferred its expertise in low-cost manufacturing to its newly acquired Beaird-Poulan business division; the transfer drove Beaird-Poulan's new strategy—to be the low-cost provider of chain-saw products—and fundamentally changed the way Beaird-Poulan chain saws were designed and manufactured. Another benefit of production-related value chain matchups is the ability to consolidate production into a smaller number of plants and significantly reduce overall production costs. When snowmobile maker Bombardier diversified into motorcycles, it was able to set up motorcycle assembly lines in the same manufacturing facility where it was assembling snowmobiles. When Smucker's acquired Procter & Gamble's Jif peanut butter business, it was able to combine the manufacture of its own Smucker's peanut butter products with those of Jif—plus, it gained greater leverage with vendors in purchasing its peanut supplies.

Distribution-Related Strategic Fits Businesses with closely related distribution activities can perform better together than apart because of potential cost savings in sharing the same distribution facilities [illegible] business in 2007, it was able to consolidate its own distribution centers for hair dryers and curling irons with those of Allegro, thereby generating cost savings for both businesses. Likewise, since Conair products and Allegro's neck rests, ear plugs, luggage tags, and toiletry kits were sold by the same types of retailers (discount stores, supermarket chains, and drugstore chains), Conair was able to convince many of the retailers not carrying Allegro products to take on the line.

Strategic Fits in Sales and Marketing Activities Various cost-saving opportunities spring from diversifying into businesses with closely related sales and marketing activities. The same distribution centers can be utilized for warehousing and shipping the products of different businesses. When the products are sold directly to the same customers, sales costs can often be reduced by using a single sales force and avoiding having two different salespeople call on the same customer. The products of related businesses can be promoted at the same Web site, and included in the same media ads and sales brochures. After-sale service and repair organizations for the products of closely related businesses can often be consolidated into a single operation. There may be opportunities to reduce costs by consolidating order processing and billing and using common promotional tie-ins (cents-off couponing, free samples and trial offers, seasonal specials, and the like). When global power-tool maker Black & Decker acquired Vector Products, it was able to use its own global sales force and distribution facilities to sell and distribute the newly acquired Vector power inverters, vehicle battery chargers, and rechargeable spotlights because the types of customers that carried its power tools (discounters like Wal-Mart and Target, home centers, and hardware stores) also stocked the types of products produced by Vector.

A second category of benefits arises when different businesses use similar sales and marketing approaches; in such cases, there may be competitively valuable opportunities to transfer selling, merchandising, advertising, and product differentiation skills from one business to another. Procter & Gamble's product lineup includes Folgers coffee, Tide laundry detergent, Crest toothpaste, Ivory soap, Charmin toilet tissue, Gillette razors and blades, Duracell batteries, Oral-B toothbrushes, and Head & Shoulders shampoo. All of these have different competitors and different supply chain and production requirements, but they all move through the same wholesale distribution systems, are sold in common retail settings to the same shoppers, are advertised and promoted in much the same ways, and require the same marketing and merchandising skills.

Strategic Fits in Managerial and Administrative Support Activities Often, different businesses require comparable types managerial know-how, thereby allowing know-how in one line of business to be transferred to another. At General Electric (GE), managers who were involved in GE's expansion into Russia were able to expedite entry because of information gained from GE managers involved in expansions into other emerging markets. The lessons GE managers learned in China were passed along to GE managers in Russia, allowing them to anticipate that the Russian government would demand that GE build production capacity in the country rather than enter the market through exporting or licensing. In addition, GE's managers in Russia were better able to develop realistic performance expectations and make tough upfront decisions since experience in China and elsewhere warned them (1) that there would likely be increased short-term costs during the early years of start-up and (2) that if GE committed to the Russian market for the long term and aided the country's economic development it could eventually expect to be given the freedom to pursue profitable penetration of the Russian market.[8]

Likewise, different businesses can often use the same administrative and customer service infrastructure. For instance, an electric utility that diversifies into natural gas, water, appliance sales and repair services, and home security services can use the same customer data network, the same customer call centers and local offices, the same billing and customer accounting systems, and the same customer service infrastructure to support all of its products and services.

ILLUSTRATION CAPSULE 8.1
Related Diversification at Darden Restaurants, L'Oréal, and Johnson & Johnson

See if you can identify the value chain relationships that make the businesses of the following companies related in competitively relevant ways. In particular, you should consider whether there are cross-business opportunities for (1) skills/technology transfer (2) combining related value chain activities to achieve lower costs, (3) leveraging use of a well-respected brand name, and/or (4) cross-business collaboration to create new resource strengths and capabilities.

DARDEN RESTAURANTS

- Olive Garden restaurant chain (Italian-themed).
- Red Lobster restaurant chain (seafood-themed).
- Longhorn Steakhouse chain (steak-themed).
- Seasons 52 chain (a sophisticated wine bar and grill featuring fresh, flavorful natural foods).
- Bahama Breeze restaurant chain (Caribbean-themed).

L'ORÉAL

- Maybelline, Lancôme, Helena Rubenstein, Kiehl's, Garnier, and Shu Uemura cosmetics.
- L'Oréal and Soft Sheen/Carson hair care products.
- Redken, Matrix, L'Oréal Professional, and Kérastase Paris professional hair care and skin care products.
- Ralph Lauren and Giorgio Armani fragrances.
- Biotherm skin care products.
- La Roche–Posay and Vichy Laboratories dermo-cosmetics.

JOHNSON & JOHNSON

- Baby products (powder, shampoo, oil, lotion).
- Band-Aids and other first-aid products.
- Women's health and personal care products (Stayfree, Carefree, Sure & Natural).
- Neutrogena and Aveeno skin care products.
- Nonprescription drugs (Tylenol, Motrin, Pepcid AC, Mylanta, Monistat).
- Prescription drugs.
- Prosthetic and other medical devices.
- Surgical and hospital products.
- Accuvue contact lenses.

Sources: Company Web sites, annual reports, and 10-K reports.

Illustration Capsule 8.1 lists the businesses of three companies that have pursued a strategy of related diversification.

Strategic Fit, Economies of Scope, and Competitive Advantage

What makes related diversification an attractive strategy is the opportunity to convert cross-business strategic fits into a competitive advantage over business rivals whose operations do not offer comparable strategic-fit benefits. The greater the relatedness among a diversified company's sister businesses, the bigger a company's

cross-business collaboration to create new resource strengths and capabilities.

Economies of Scope: A Path to Competitive Advantage One of the most important competitive advantages that a related diversification strategy can produce is lower costs than competitors. Related businesses often present opportunities to eliminate or reduce the costs of performing certain value chain activities; such cost

CORE CONCEPT

Economies of scope **are cost reductions that flow from operating in multiple businesses; such economies stem directly from strategic fit efficiencies along the value chains of related businesses.**

savings are termed **economies of scope**—a concept distinct from *economies of scale.* Economies of *scale* are cost savings that accrue directly from a larger-sized operation; for example, unit costs may be lower in a large plant than in a small plant, lower in a large distribution center than in a small one, lower for large-volume purchases of components than for small-volume purchases. Economies of *scope,* however, stem directly from cost-saving strategic fits along the value chains of related businesses. Such economies are open only to a multibusiness enterprise and are the result of a related diversification strategy that allows sister businesses to share technology, perform R&D together, use common manufacturing or distribution facilities, share a common sales force or distributor/dealer network, use the same established brand name, and/or share the same administrative infrastructure. *The greater the cross-business economies associated with cost-saving strategic fits, the greater the potential for a related diversification strategy to yield a competitive advantage based on lower costs than rivals.*

From Competitive Advantage to Added Profitability and Gains in Shareholder Value The competitive advantage potential that flows from economies of scope and the capture of other strategic-fit benefits is what enables a company pursuing related diversification to achieve 1 + 1 = 3 financial performance and the hoped-for gains in shareholder value. The strategic and business logic is compelling: Capturing strategic fits along the value chains of its related businesses gives a diversified company a clear path to achieving competitive advantage over undiversified competitors and competitors whose own diversification efforts don't offer equivalent strategic-fit benefits.[9] Such competitive advantage potential provides a company with a dependable basis for earning profits and a return on investment that exceed what the company's businesses could earn as stand-alone enterprises. Converting the competitive advantage potential into greater profitability is what fuels 1 + 1 = 3 gains in shareholder value—the necessary outcome for satisfying the better-off test and proving the business merit of a company's diversification effort.

CORE CONCEPT

Diversifying into related businesses where competitively valuable strategic fit benefits can be captured puts sister businesses in position to perform better financially as part of the same company than they could have performed as independent enterprises, thus providing a clear avenue for boosting shareholder value.

There are three things to bear in mind here. One, capturing cross-business strategic fits via a strategy of related diversification builds shareholder value in ways that shareholders cannot undertake by simply owning a portfolio of stocks of companies in different industries. Two, the capture of cross-business strategic-fit benefits is possible only via a strategy of related diversification. Three, the benefits of cross-business strategic fits are not automatically realized when a company diversifies into related businesses; *the benefits materialize only after management has successfully pursued internal actions to capture them.*

THE CASE FOR DIVERSIFYING INTO UNRELATED BUSINESSES

An unrelated diversification strategy discounts the merits of pursuing cross-business strategic fits and, instead, focuses squarely on entering and operating businesses in industries that allow the company as a whole to grow its revenues and earnings. Companies that pursue a strategy of unrelated diversification generally exhibit a willingness to diversify into *any industry* where senior managers see *opportunity* to realize

Figure 8.3 Unrelated Businesses Have Unrelated Value Chains and No Strategic Fits

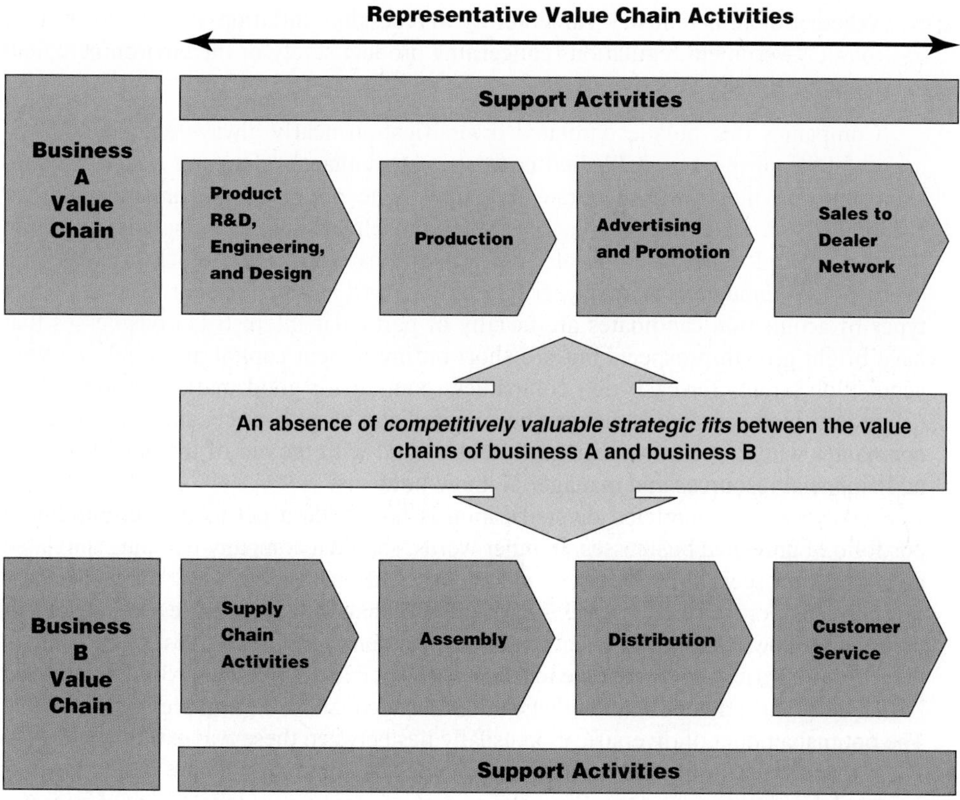

consistently good financial results—*the basic premise of unrelated diversification is that any company or business that can be acquired on good financial terms and that has satisfactory growth and earnings potential represents a good acquisition and a good business opportunity.* Such companies are frequently labeled *conglomerates* because their business interests range broadly across diverse industries.

With a strategy of unrelated diversification, the emphasis is on satisfying the attractiveness and cost-of-entry tests and each business's prospects for good financial performance. As indicated in Figure 8.3, there's no deliberate effort to satisfy the better-off test in the sense of diversifying only into businesses having strategic fits with the firm's other businesses. Thus, with an unrelated diversification strategy, company managers spend much time and effort screening acquisition candidates and evaluating the pros and cons of keeping or divesting existing businesses, using such criteria as:

- Whether the business is in an industry with attractive growth potential.
- Whether the business is big enough to contribute *significantly* to the parent firm's bottom line.
- Whether the business has burdensome capital requirements (associated with replacing out-of-date plants and equipment, growing the business, and/or providing working capital).

- Whether the business is plagued with chronic union difficulties and labor problems.
- Whether there is industry vulnerability to recession, inflation, high interest rates, tough government regulations concerning product safety or the environment, and other potentially negative factors.

Companies that pursue unrelated diversification nearly always enter new businesses by acquiring an established company rather than by forming a start-up subsidiary within their own corporate structures. The premise of acquisition-minded corporations is that growth by acquisition can deliver enhanced shareholder value through upward-trending corporate revenues and earnings and a stock price that *on average* rises enough year after year to amply reward and please shareholders. Three types of acquisition candidates are usually of particular interest: (1) businesses that have bright growth prospects but are short on investment capital are highly coveted acquisition targets for cash-rich companies scouting for good market opportunities, (2) undervalued companies that can be acquired at a bargain price, and (3) struggling companies whose operations can be turned around with the aid of the parent company's financial resources and managerial know-how.

A key issue in unrelated diversification is how wide a net to cast in building a portfolio of unrelated businesses. In other words, should a company pursuing unrelated diversification seek to have few or many unrelated businesses? How much business diversity can corporate executives successfully manage? A reasonable way to resolve the issue of how much diversification comes from answering two questions: "What is the least diversification it will take to achieve acceptable growth and profitability?" and "What is the most diversification that can be managed, given the complexity it adds?"[10] The optimal amount of diversification usually lies between these two extremes.

Illustration Capsule 8.2 lists the businesses of three companies that have pursued unrelated diversification. Such companies are frequently labeled *conglomerates* because their business interests range broadly across diverse industries.

The Merits of an Unrelated Diversification Strategy

A strategy of unrelated diversification has appeal from several angles:

1. Business risk is scattered over a set of truly *diverse* industries. In comparison to related diversification, unrelated diversification more closely approximates *pure* diversification of financial and business risk because the company's investments are spread over businesses whose technologies and value chain activities bear no close relationship and whose markets are largely disconnected.[11]
2. The company's financial resources can be employed to maximum advantage by (*a*) investing in *whatever industries* offer the best profit prospects (as opposed to considering only opportunities in industries with related value chain activities) and (*b*) diverting cash flows from company businesses with lower growth and profit prospects to acquiring and expanding businesses with higher growth and profit potentials.
3. To the extent that corporate managers are exceptionally astute at spotting bargain-priced companies with big upside profit potential, shareholder wealth can be enhanced by buying distressed businesses at a low price, turning their operations around fairly quickly with infusions of cash and managerial know-how supplied by the parent company, and then riding the crest of the profit increases generated by the newly acquired businesses.

ILLUSTRATION CAPSULE 8.2
Unrelated Diversification at General Electric, Fortune Brands, and United Technologies

The defining characteristic of unrelated diversification is few competitively valuable cross-business relationships. Peruse the business group listings for General Electric, Fortune Brands, and United Technologies and see if you can confirm why these three companies have unrelated diversification strategies.

GENERAL ELECTRIC

- Major household appliances (refrigerators, dishwashers, ranges, cooking tops, ovens, microwaves, clothes washers and dryers).
- Jet engines and aviation services.
- Lighting products and lighting controls.
- Oil and gas equipment.
- Locomotive engines, rail traffic control and dispatch systems, and signaling products.
- Monitoring and video surveillance systems, building access and control systems, and fire detection and security systems for businesses and homes.
- Water treatment systems and water treatment chemicals.
- Rechargeable lithium-ion batteries.
- Advanced materials (engineering thermoplastics, silicon-based products and technology platforms, and fused quartz and ceramics).
- Capital management services and financial products for businesses and consumers, including all types of business loans, operating leases, real estate and equipment financing programs, inventory financing, health care financial services, asset management services, business and consumer credit cards, personal loans and debt consolidation services, home equity loans, commercial insurance, and identity theft protection services.
- Trailer rentals, along with online fleet management and maintenance software.
- Electric power [...] plant equipment, and equipment for fossil-fuel-generating plants.
- Electrical distribution equipment, including power transformers, high-voltage breakers, distribution transformers and breakers, capacitors, relays, regulators, substation equipment, and metering products.
- X-ray and advanced imaging products, medical diagnostic technologies and equipment, patient monitoring systems, disease research, drug discovery, and biopharmaceuticals.
- Media and entertainment—GE's NBC Universal business unit owned and operated the NBC television network, a Spanish-language network (Telemundo), several news and entertainment networks (CNBC, MSNBC, Bravo, Sci-Fi Channel, USA Network), Universal Studios, various television production operations, a group of television stations, and several theme parks.

FORTUNE BRANDS

- Premium spirits—Jim Beam, Maker's Mark, Knob Creek, Canadian Club, and 10 other brands.
- Titleist, Footjoy, Cobra, and Pinnacle golf products.
- Home and hardware businesses, including Moen faucets, Therma Tru doors, Simonton windows, Master Lock security hardware, Master Brand kitchen and bath cabinetry, Waterloo tool storage products, and 10 other home and hardware businesses.

UNITED TECHNOLOGIES

- Pratt & Whitney aircraft engines.
- Carrier heating and air-conditioning equipment.
- Otis elevators and escalators.
- Sikorsky military and commercial helicopters.

Sources: Company web sites and 2007 10-K reports.

4. Company profitability may prove somewhat more stable over the course of economic upswings and downswings because market conditions in all industries don't move upward or downward simultaneously—in a broadly diversified company, there's a chance that market downtrends in some of the company's businesses will be partially offset by cyclical upswings in its other businesses, thus producing somewhat less earnings volatility. (In practice, however, there is no convincing evidence that the consolidated profits of firms with unrelated diversification strategies are more stable or less subject to reversal in periods of recession and economic stress than the profits of firms with related diversification strategies.)

Unrelated diversification certainly merits consideration when a firm is trapped in or overly dependent on an endangered or unattractive industry, especially when it has no competitively valuable resources or capabilities it can transfer to an adjacent industry. A case can also be made for unrelated diversification when a company has a strong preference for spreading business risks widely and not restricting itself to investing in a family of closely related businesses.

Building Shareholder Value via Unrelated Diversification Given the absence of cross-business strategic fits with which to capture added competitive advantage, the task of building shareholder value via unrelated diversification ultimately hinges on the business acumen of corporate executives. To succeed in using a strategy of unrelated diversification to produce companywide financial results above and beyond what the businesses could generate operating as stand-alone entities, corporate executives must:

- Do a superior job of diversifying into new businesses that can produce consistently good earnings and returns on investment (thereby satisfying the attractiveness test).
- Do an excellent job of negotiating favorable acquisition prices (thereby satisfying the cost-of-entry test).
- Do such a good job overseeing the firm's business subsidiaries and contributing to how they are managed—by providing expert problem-solving skills, creative strategy suggestions, and high-caliber decision-making guidance to the heads of the various business subsidiaries—that the subsidiaries perform at a higher level than they would otherwise be able to do through the efforts of the business-unit heads alone (a possible way to satisfy the better-off test).
- Be shrewd in identifying when to shift resources out of businesses with dim profit prospects and into businesses with above-average prospects for growth and profitability.
- Be good at discerning when a business needs to be sold (because it is on the verge of confronting adverse industry and competitive conditions and probable declines in long-term profitability) and also finding buyers who will pay a price higher than the company's net investment in the business (so that the sale of divested businesses will result in capital gains for shareholders rather than capital losses).

To the extent that corporate executives are able to craft and execute a strategy of unrelated diversification that produces enough of the above outcomes to result in a stream of dividends and capital gains for stockholders greater than a 1 + 1 = 2 outcome, a case can be made that shareholder value has truly been enhanced.

The Drawbacks of Unrelated Diversification

Unrelated diversification strategies have two important negatives that undercut the pluses: very demanding managerial requirements and limited competitive advantage potential.

Demanding Managerial Requirements Successfully managing a set of fundamentally different businesses operating in fundamentally different industry and competitive environments is an exceptionally challenging proposition for corporate-level managers. It is difficult because key executives at the corporate level, while perhaps having personally worked in one or two of the company's businesses, rarely have the time and expertise to be sufficiently familiar with all the circumstances surrounding each of the company's businesses to be in a position to give high-caliber guidance to business-level managers. Indeed, the greater the number of businesses a company is in and the more diverse they are, the harder it is for corporate managers to (1) stay abreast of what's happening in each industry and each subsidiary and thus judge whether a particular business has bright prospects or is headed for trouble, (2) know enough about the issues and problems facing each subsidiary to pick business-unit heads having the requisite combination of managerial skills and know-how, (3) be able to tell the difference between those strategic proposals of business-unit managers that are prudent and those that are risky or unlikely to succeed, and (4) know what to do if a business unit stumbles and its results suddenly head downhill.[12]

CORE CONCEPT

The two biggest drawbacks to unrelated diversification are the difficulties of competently managing many different businesses and being without the added source of competitive advantage that cross-business strategic fit provides.

In a company like General Electric or United Technologies (see Illustration Capsule 8.2) or Tyco International (which acquired over 1,000 companies between 1994 and 2001), corporate executives are constantly scrambling to stay on top of fresh industry developments and the strategic progress and plans of each subsidiary, often depending on briefings by business-level managers for many of the details. As a rule, the more unrelated businesses that a company has diversified into, the more corporate executives depend on briefings from business-unit heads and "managing by the numbers"—that is, keeping a close track on the financial and operating results of each subsidiary and assuming that the heads of the various subsidiaries have most everything under control so long as the latest key financial and operating measures look good. Managing by the numbers works if the heads of the various business units are capable and consistently meet their numbers. The problem comes when things start to go awry in a business despite the best effort of business-unit managers; in that case corporate management has to get deeply involved in turning around a business it does not know all that much about—as the former chairman of a Fortune 500 company advised, "Never acquire a business you don't know how to run." Because every business tends to encounter rough sledding, a good way to gauge the merits of acquiring a company in an unrelated industry is to ask, "If the business got into trouble, is corporate management likely to know how to bail it out?" When the answer is no (or even a qualified yes or maybe), growth via acquisition into unrelated businesses is a chancy strategy.[13] Just one or two unforeseen problems or big strategic mistakes (like misjudging the importance of certain competitive forces or the impact of driving forces or key success factors, not recognizing that a newly acquired business has some serious

Hence, competently overseeing a set of widely diverse businesses can turn out to be much harder than it sounds. In practice, comparatively few companies have proved that they have top management capabilities that are up to the task. There are far more companies whose corporate executives have failed at delivering consistently good financial results with an unrelated diversification strategy than there are companies with corporate executives who have been successful.[14] It is simply very difficult for

Relying solely on the expertise of corporate executives to wisely manage a set of unrelated businesses is *a much weaker foundation for enhancing shareholder value* than is a strategy of related diversification where corporate performance can be boosted by competitively valuable cross-business strategic fits.

corporate executives to achieve 1 + 1 = 3 gains in shareholder value based on their expertise in (*a*) picking which industries to diversify into and which companies in these industries to acquire, (*b*) shifting resources from low-performing businesses into high-performing businesses, and (*c*) giving high-caliber decision-making guidance to the general managers of their business subsidiaries. The odds are that the result of unrelated diversification will be 1 + 1 = 2 or less.

Limited Competitive Advantage Potential The second big negative is that *unrelated diversification offers no potential for competitive advantage beyond what each individual business can generate on its own.* Unlike a related diversification strategy, there are no cross-business strategic fits to draw on for reducing costs, beneficially transferring skills and technology, leveraging use of a powerful brand name, or collaborating to build mutually beneficial competitive capabilities and thereby *adding to any competitive advantage possessed by individual businesses.* Yes, a cash-rich corporate parent pursuing unrelated diversification can provide its subsidiaries with the capital and maybe even the managerial know-how to help resolve problems in particular business units, but otherwise it has little to offer in the way of enhancing the competitive strength of its individual business units. *Without the competitive advantage potential of strategic fits, consolidated performance of an unrelated group of businesses stands to be little or no better than the sum of what the individual business units could achieve if they were independent.*

COMBINATION RELATED–UNRELATED DIVERSIFICATION STRATEGIES

There's nothing to preclude a company from diversifying into both related and unrelated businesses. Indeed, in actual practice the business makeup of diversified companies varies considerably. Some diversified companies are really *dominant-business enterprises*—one major "core" business accounts for 50 to 80 percent of total revenues and a collection of small related or unrelated businesses accounts for the remainder. Some diversified companies are *narrowly diversified* around a few (two to five) related or unrelated businesses. Others are *broadly diversified* around a wide-ranging collection of related businesses, unrelated businesses, or a mixture of both. And a number of multibusiness enterprises have diversified into unrelated areas but have a collection of related businesses within each area—thus giving them a business portfolio consisting of *several unrelated groups of related businesses.* There's ample room for companies to customize their diversification strategies to incorporate elements of both related and unrelated diversification, as may suit their own risk preferences and strategic vision.

The various corporate strategy initiatives that help identify management's approach to building shareholder value through diversification are shown in Figure 8.4. Having a clear fix on the company's current corporate strategy sets the stage for evaluating how good the strategy is and proposing strategic moves to boost the company's performance.

Figure 8.4 Identifying a Diversified Company's Strategy

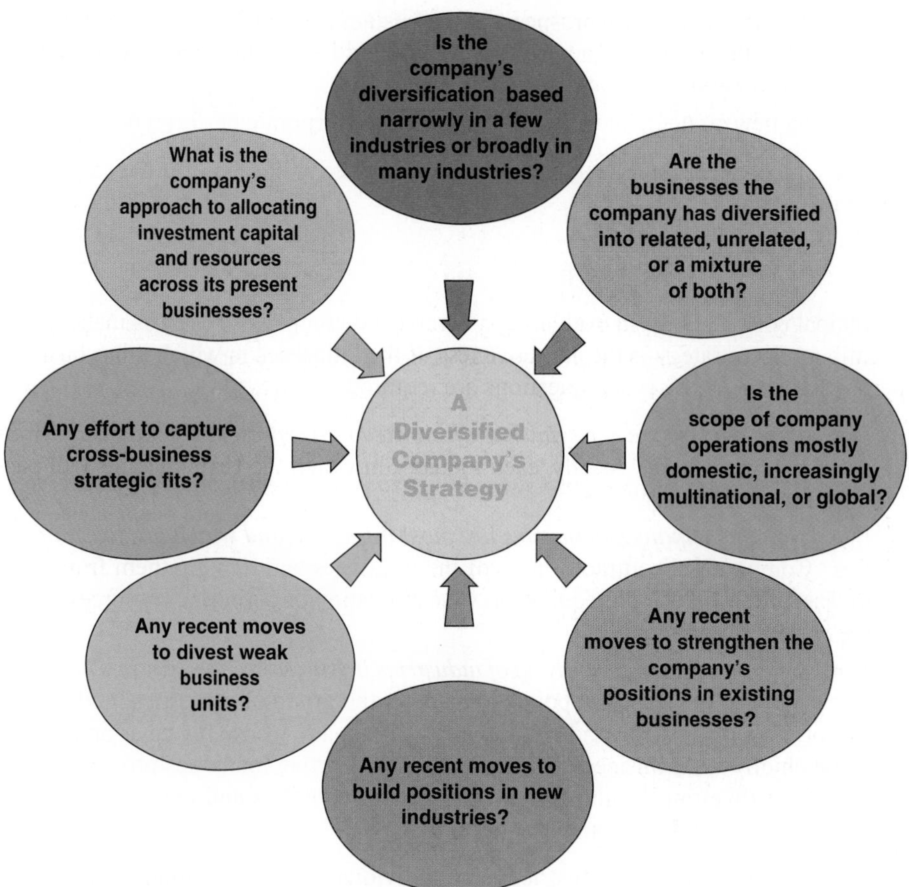

EVALUATING THE STRATEGY OF A DIVERSIFIED COMPANY

Strategic analysis of diversified companies builds on the concepts and methods used for single-business companies. But there are some additional aspects to consider and a couple of new analytical tools to master. The procedure for evaluating the pluses and minuses of a diversified company's strategy and deciding what actions to take to improve the company's performance involves six steps:

both individually and as a group.

2. Assessing the competitive strength of the company's business units and determining how many are strong contenders in their respective industries.
3. Checking the competitive advantage potential of cross-business strategic fits among the company's various business units.

4. Checking whether the firm's resources fit the requirements of its present business lineup.
5. Ranking the performance prospects of the businesses from best to worst and determine what the corporate parent's priority should be in allocating resources to its various businesses.
6. Crafting new strategic moves to improve overall corporate performance.

The core concepts and analytical techniques underlying each of these steps merit further discussion.

Step 1: Evaluating Industry Attractiveness

A principal consideration in evaluating a diversified company's business makeup and the caliber of its strategy is the attractiveness of the industries in which it has business operations. Answers to several questions are required:

1. *Does each industry the company has diversified into represent a good business for the company to be in?* Ideally, each industry in which the firm operates will pass the attractiveness test.
2. *Which of the company's industries are most attractive and which are least attractive?* Comparing the attractiveness of the industries and ranking them from most to least attractive is a prerequisite to wise allocation of corporate resources across the various businesses.
3. *How appealing is the whole group of industries in which the company has invested?* The answer to this question points to whether the group of industries holds promise for attractive growth and profitability. A company whose revenues and profits come chiefly from businesses in relatively unattractive industries probably needs to look at divesting businesses in unattractive industries and entering industries that qualify as highly attractive.

The more attractive the industries (both individually and as a group) a diversified company is in, the better its prospects for good long-term performance.

Calculating Industry Attractiveness Scores for Each Industry into Which the Company Has Diversified A simple and reliable analytical tool involves calculating quantitative industry attractiveness scores, which can then be used to gauge each industry's attractiveness, rank the industries from most to least attractive, and make judgments about the attractiveness of all the industries as a group.

The following measures are typically used to gauge an industry's attractiveness:

- *Market size and projected growth rate*—Big industries are more attractive than small industries, and fast-growing industries tend to be more attractive than slow-growing industries, other things being equal.
- *The intensity of competition*—Industries where competitive pressures are relatively weak are more attractive than industries where competitive pressures are strong.
- *Emerging opportunities and threats*—Industries with promising opportunities and minimal threats on the near horizon are more attractive than industries with modest opportunities and imposing threats.
- *The presence of cross-industry strategic fits*—The more the industry's value chain and resource requirements match up well with the value chain activities of other

industries in which the company has operations, the more attractive the industry is to a firm pursuing related diversification. However, cross-industry strategic fits may be of no consequence to a company committed to a strategy of unrelated diversification.

- *Resource requirements*—Industries having resource requirements within the company's reach are more attractive than industries where capital and other resource requirements could strain corporate financial resources and organizational capabilities.
- *Seasonal and cyclical factors*—Industries where buyer demand is relatively steady year-round and not unduly vulnerable to economic ups and downs tend to be more attractive than industries where there are wide swings in buyer demand within or across years. However, seasonality may be a plus for a company that is in several seasonal industries, if the seasonal highs in one industry correspond to the lows in another industry, thus helping even out monthly sales levels.
- *Social, political, regulatory, and environmental factors*—Industries with significant problems in such areas as consumer health, safety, or environmental pollution or that are subject to intense regulation are less attractive than industries where such problems are not burning issues.
- *Industry profitability*—Industries with healthy profit margins and high rates of return on investment are generally more attractive than industries where profits have historically been low or unstable.
- *Industry uncertainty and business risk*—Industries with less uncertainty on the horizon and lower overall business risk are more attractive than industries whose prospects for one reason or another are quite uncertain, especially when the industry has formidable resource requirements.

After settling on a set of attractiveness measures that suit a diversified company's circumstances, each attractiveness measure is assigned a weight reflecting its relative importance in determining an industry's attractiveness—it is weak methodology to assume that the various attractiveness measures are equally important. The intensity of competition in an industry should nearly always carry a high weight (say, 0.20 to 0.30). Strategic-fit considerations should be assigned a high weight in the case of companies with related diversification strategies; but, for companies with an unrelated diversification strategy, strategic fits with other industries may be given a low weight or even dropped from the list of attractiveness measures altogether. Seasonal and cyclical factors generally are assigned a low weight (or maybe even eliminated from the analysis) unless a company has diversified into industries strongly characterized by seasonal demand and/or heavy vulnerability to cyclical upswings and downswings. The importance weights must add up to 1.0.

Next, each industry is rated on each of the chosen industry attractiveness measures, using a rating scale of 1 to 10 (where a *high* rating signifies *high* attractiveness and a

higher the capital and resource requirements associated with being in a particular industry, the lower the attractiveness rating. And an industry subject to stringent pollution control regulations or that causes societal problems (like cigarettes or alcoholic beverages) should usually be given a low attractiveness rating. Weighted attractiveness scores are then calculated by multiplying the industry's rating on each measure by the corresponding weight. For example, a rating of 8 times a weight of 0.25 gives a

Table 8.1 Calculating Weighted Industry Attractiveness Scores

Industry Attractiveness Measure	Importance Weight	Industry A Rating/Score	Industry B Rating/Score	Industry C Rating/Score	Industry D Rating/Score
Market size and projected growth rate	0.10	8/0.80	5/0.50	2/0.20	3/0.30
Intensity of competition	0.25	8/2.00	7/1.75	3/0.75	2/0.50
Emerging opportunities and threats	0.10	2/0.20	9/0.90	4/0.40	5/0.50
Cross-industry strategic fits	0.20	8/1.60	4/0.80	8/1.60	2/0.40
Resource requirements	0.10	9/0.90	7/0.70	5/0.50	5/0.50
Seasonal and cyclical influences	0.05	9/0.45	8/0.40	10/0.50	5/0.25
Societal, political, regulatory, and environmental factors	0.05	10/0.50	7/0.35	7/0.35	3/0.15
Industry profitability	0.10	5/0.50	10/1.00	3/0.30	3/0.30
Industry uncertainty and business risk	0.05	5/0.25	7/0.35	10/0.50	1/0.05
Sum of the assigned weights	1.00				
Overall weighted industry attractiveness scores		**7.20**	**6.75**	**5.10**	**2.95**

[Rating scale: 1 = Very unattractive to company; 10 = Very attractive to company]

weighted attractiveness score of 2.00. The sum of the weighted scores for all the attractiveness measures provides an overall industry attractiveness score. This procedure is illustrated in Table 8.1.

Interpreting the Industry Attractiveness Scores Industries with a score much below 5.0 probably do not pass the attractiveness test. If a company's industry attractiveness scores are all above 5.0, it is probably fair to conclude that the group of industries the company operates in is attractive as a whole. But the group of industries takes on a decidedly lower degree of attractiveness as the number of industries with scores below 5.0 increases, especially if industries with low scores account for a sizable fraction of the company's revenues.

For a diversified company to be a strong performer, a substantial portion of its revenues and profits must come from business units with relatively high attractiveness scores. It is particularly important that a diversified company's principal businesses be in industries with a good outlook for growth and above-average profitability. Having a big fraction of the company's revenues and profits come from industries with slow growth, low profitability, or intense competition tends to drag overall company performance down. Business units in the least attractive industries are potential candidates for divestiture, unless they are positioned strongly enough to overcome the unattractive aspects of their industry environments or they are a strategically important component of the company's business makeup.

The Difficulties of Calculating Industry Attractiveness Scores There are two hurdles to using this method of evaluating industry attractiveness. One is deciding on appropriate weights for the industry attractiveness measures. Not only may different analysts have different views about which weights are appropriate for the different attractiveness measures, but different weightings may also be appropriate for different companies—based on their strategies, performance targets, and financial circumstances. For instance, placing a low weight on industry resource requirements may be justifiable for a cash-rich company, whereas a high weight may be more appropriate for a financially strapped company. The second hurdle is gaining sufficient command of the industry to assign accurate and objective ratings. Generally, a company can come up with the statistical data needed to compare its industries on such factors as market size, growth rate, seasonal and cyclical influences, and industry profitability. Cross-industry fits and resource requirements are also fairly easy to judge. But the attractiveness measure where judgment weighs most heavily is that of intensity of competition. It is not always easy to conclude whether competition in one industry is stronger or weaker than in another industry because of the different types of competitive influences that prevail and the differences in their relative importance. In the event that the available information is too skimpy to confidently assign a rating value to an industry on a particular attractiveness measure, then it is usually best to use a score of 5, which avoids biasing the overall attractiveness score either up or down.

But despite the hurdles, calculating industry attractiveness scores is a systematic and reasonably reliable method for ranking a diversified company's industries from most to least attractive—numbers like those shown for the four industries in Table 8.1 help pin down the basis for judging which industries are more attractive and to what degree.

Step 2: Evaluating Business-Unit Competitive Strength

The second step in evaluating a diversified company is to appraise how strongly positioned its business units are in their respective industries. Doing an appraisal of each business unit's strength and competitive position in its industry not only reveals its chances for industry success but also provides a basis for ranking the units from competitively strongest to competitively weakest and sizing up the competitive strength of all the business units as a group.

Calculating Competitive Strength Scores for Each Business Unit Quantitative measures of each business unit's competitive strength can be calculated using a procedure similar to that for measuring industry attractiveness. The following factors are useful in quantifying the competitive strengths of a diversified company's business subsidiaries:

- *Relative market share*—A business unit's *relative market share* is defined as the ratio of its market share to the market share held by the largest rival firm in the industry, with market share measured in unit volume, not dollars. For instance, if business A has a market-leading share of 40 percent and its largest rival has 30 percent, A's relative market share is 1.33. (Note that only business units that are market share leaders in their respective industries can have relative market shares greater than 1.0.) If business B has a 15 percent market share and B's largest rival has 30 percent, B's relative market share is 0.5. *The further below 1.0 a business unit's relative market share is, the weaker its competitive strength and market position* [illegible] quite strong if the leader's share is only 12 percent (a 0.83 relative market share)—this why a company's relative market share is a better measure of competitive strength than a company's market share based on either dollars or unit volume.

Using relative market share to measure competitive strength is analytically superior to using straight-percentage market share.

- *Costs relative to competitors' costs*—Business units that have low costs relative to key competitors' costs tend to be more strongly positioned in their industries than business units struggling to maintain cost parity with major rivals. Assuming that the prices charged by industry rivals are about the same, there's reason to expect that business units with higher relative market shares have lower unit costs than competitors with lower relative market shares because their greater unit sales volumes offer the possibility of economies from larger-scale operations and the benefits of any learning/experience curve effects. Another indicator of low cost can be a business unit's supply chain management capabilities. The only time when a business unit's competitive strength may not be undermined by having higher costs than rivals is when it has incurred the higher costs to strongly differentiate its product offering and its customers are willing to pay premium prices for the differentiating features.

- *Ability to match or beat rivals on key product attributes*—A company's competitiveness depends in part on being able to satisfy buyer expectations with regard to features, product performance, reliability, service, and other important attributes.
- *Ability to benefit from strategic fits with sister businesses*—Strategic fits with other businesses within the company enhance a business unit's competitive strength and may provide a competitive edge.
- *Ability to exercise bargaining leverage with key suppliers or customers*—Having bargaining leverage signals competitive strength and can be a source of competitive advantage.
- *Caliber of alliances and collaborative partnerships with suppliers and/or buyers*—Well-functioning alliances and partnerships may signal a potential competitive advantage vis-à-vis rivals and thus add to a business's competitive strength. Alliances with key suppliers are often the basis for competitive strength in supply chain management.
- *Brand image and reputation*—A strong brand name is a valuable competitive asset in most industries.
- *Competitively valuable capabilities*—Business units recognized for their technological leadership, product innovation, or marketing prowess are usually strong competitors in their industry. Skills in supply chain management can generate valuable cost or product differentiation advantages. So can unique production capabilities. Sometimes a company's business units gain competitive strength because of their knowledge of customers and markets and/or their proven managerial capabilities. *An important thing to look for here is how well a business unit's competitive assets match industry key success factors.* The more a business unit's resource strengths and competitive capabilities match the industry's key success factors, the stronger its competitive position tends to be.
- *Profitability relative to competitors*—Business units that consistently earn above-average returns on investment and have bigger profit margins than their rivals usually have stronger competitive positions. Moreover, above-average profitability signals competitive advantage, while below-average profitability usually denotes competitive disadvantage.

After settling on a set of competitive-strength measures that are well matched to the circumstances of the various business units, weights indicating each measure's importance need to be assigned. A case can be made for using different weights for different business units whenever the importance of the strength measures differs significantly from business to business, but otherwise it is simpler just to go with a single set of weights and avoid the added complication of multiple weights. As before, the

Table 8.2 Calculating Weighted Competitive Strength Scores for a Diversified Company's Business Units

Competitive Strength Measure	Importance Weight	Business A in Industry A Rating/ Score	Business B in Industry B Rating/ Score	Business C in Industry C Rating/ Score	Business D in Industry D Rating/ Score
Relative market share	0.15	10/1.50	1/0.15	6/0.90	2/0.30
Costs relative to competitors' costs	0.20	7/1.40	2/0.40	5/1.00	3/0.60
Ability to match or beat rivals on key product attributes	0.05	9/0.45	4/0.20	8/0.40	4/0.20
Ability to benefit from strategic fits with sister businesses	0.20	8/1.60	4/0.80	4/0.80	2/0.60
Bargaining leverage with suppliers/ buyers; caliber of alliances	0.05	9/0.45	3/0.15	6/0.30	2/0.10
Brand image and reputation	0.10	9/0.90	2/0.20	7/0.70	5/0.50
Competitively valuable capabilities	0.15	7/1.05	2/0.30	5/0.75	3/0.45
Profitability relative to competitors	0.10	5/0.50	1/0.10	4/0.40	4/0.40
Sum of the assigned weights	1.00				
Overall weighted competitive strength scores		**7.85**	**2.30**	**5.25**	**3.15**

[Rating scale: 1 = Very weak; 10 = Very strong]

importance weights must add up to 1.0. Each business unit is then rated on each of the chosen strength measures, using a rating scale of 1 to 10 (where a *high* rating signifies competitive *strength* and a *low* rating signifies competitive *weakness*). In the event that the available information is too skimpy to confidently assign a rating value to a business unit on a particular strength measure, then it is usually best to use a score of 5, which avoids biasing the overall score either up or down. Weighted strength ratings are calculated by multiplying the business unit's rating on each strength measure by the assigned weight. For example, a strength score of 6 times a weight of 0.15 gives a weighted strength rating of 0.90. The sum of weighted ratings across all the strength measures provides a quantitative measure of a business unit's overall market strength and competitive standing. Table 8.2 provides sample calculations of competitive strength ratings for four businesses.

Interpreting the Competitive Strength Scores Business units with competitive strength ratings above 6.7 (on a scale of 1 to 10) are strong market contenders in their industries. Businesses with ratings in the 3.3–6.7 range have moderate competitive strength vis-à-vis rivals. Businesses with ratings below 3.3 are in competitively [illegible] in their respective industries. But as the number of business units with scores below 5.0 increases, there's reason to question whether the company can perform well with so many businesses in relatively weak competitive positions. This concern takes on even more importance when business units with low scores account for a sizable fraction of the company's revenues.

Figure 8.5 A Nine-Cell Industry Attractiveness–Competitive Strength Matrix

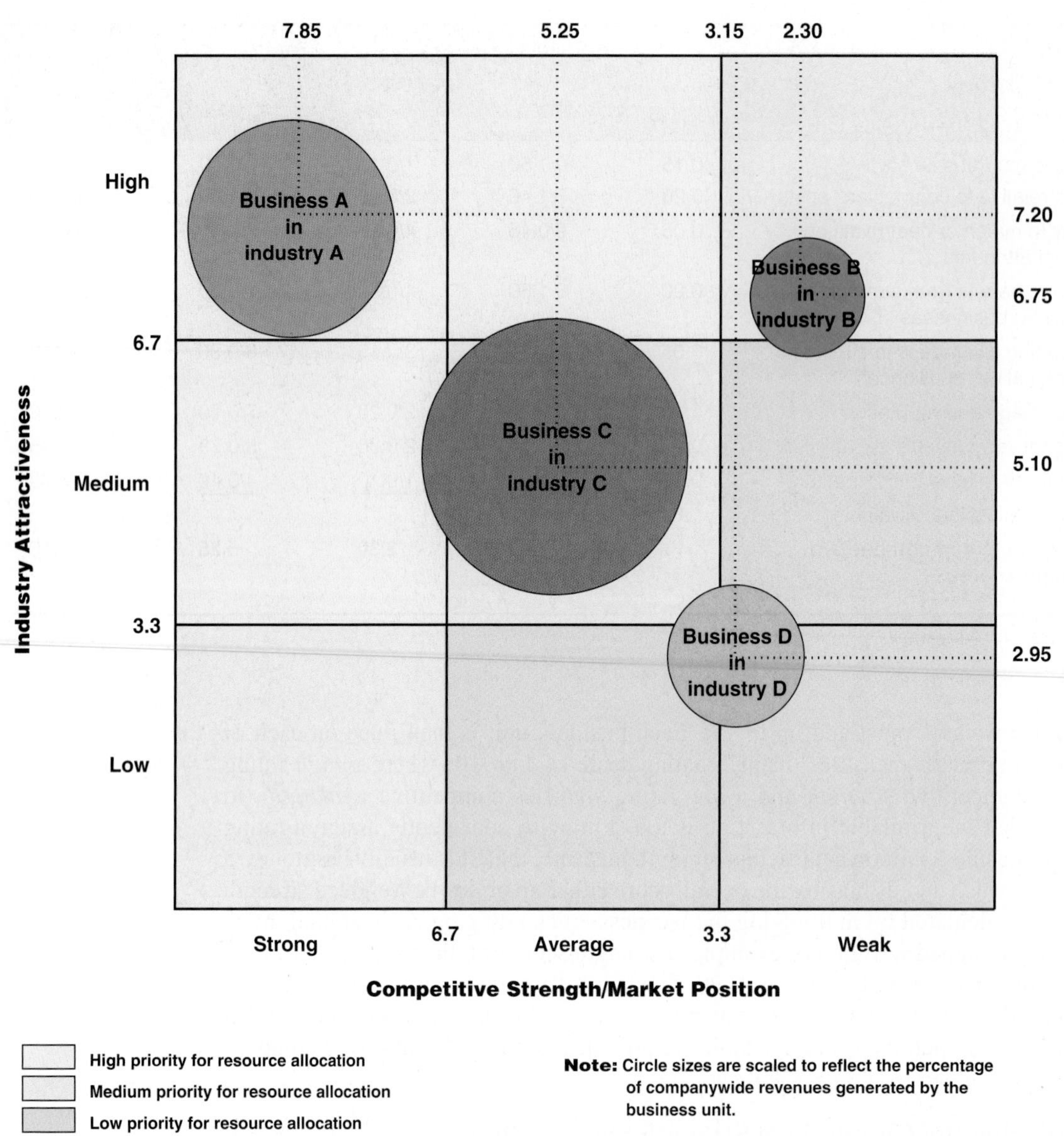

Using a Nine-Cell Matrix to Simultaneously Portray Industry Attractiveness and Competitive Strength The industry attractiveness and business strength scores can be used to portray the strategic positions of each business in a diversified company. Industry attractiveness is plotted on the vertical axis, and competitive strength on the horizontal axis. A nine-cell grid emerges from dividing the vertical axis into three regions (high, medium, and low attractiveness) and the horizontal axis into three regions (strong, average, and weak competitive strength). As shown in Figure 8.5, high attractiveness is associated with scores of 6.7 or greater on a rating scale of 1 to 10, medium attractiveness to scores of 3.3 to 6.7, and low attractiveness to scores below 3.3.

Likewise, high competitive strength is defined as a score greater than 6.7, average strength as scores of 3.3 to 6.7, and low strength as scores below 3.3. *Each business unit is plotted on the nine-cell matrix according to its overall attractiveness score and strength score, and then shown as a "bubble."* The size of each bubble is scaled to what percentage of revenues the business generates relative to total corporate revenues. The bubbles in Figure 8.5 were located on the grid using the four industry attractiveness scores from Table 8.1 and the strength scores for the four business units in Table 8.2.

The locations of the business units on the attractiveness–strength matrix provide valuable guidance in deploying corporate resources to the various business units. In general, *a diversified company's prospects for good overall performance are enhanced by concentrating corporate resources and strategic attention on those business units having the greatest competitive strength and positioned in highly attractive industries*—specifically, businesses in the three cells in the upper left portion of the attractiveness-strength matrix, where industry attractiveness and competitive strength/market position are both favorable. The general strategic prescription for businesses falling in these three cells (for instance, business A in Figure 8.5) is "grow and build," with businesses in the high–strong cell standing first in line for resource allocations by the corporate parent.

Next in priority come businesses positioned in the three diagonal cells stretching from the lower left to the upper right (businesses B and C in Figure 8.5). Such businesses usually merit medium or intermediate priority in the parent's resource allocation ranking. However, some businesses in the medium-priority diagonal cells may have brighter or dimmer prospects than others. For example, a small business in the upper right cell of the matrix (like business B), despite being in a highly attractive industry, may occupy too weak a competitive position in its industry to justify the investment and resources needed to turn it into a strong market contender and shift its position leftward in the matrix over time. If, however, a business in the upper right cell has attractive opportunities for rapid growth and a good potential for winning a much stronger market position over time, it may merit a high claim on the corporate parent's resource allocation ranking and be given the capital it needs to pursue a grow-and-build strategy—the strategic objective here would be to move the business leftward in the attractiveness–strength matrix over time.

Businesses in the three cells in the lower right corner of the matrix (like business D in Figure 8.5) typically are weak performers and have the lowest claim on corporate resources. Most such businesses are good candidates for being divested (sold to other companies) or else managed in a manner calculated to squeeze out the maximum cash flows from operations—the cash flows from low-performing/low-potential businesses can then be diverted to financing expansion of business units with greater market opportunities. In exceptional cases where a business located in the three lower right cells is nonetheless fairly profitable (which it might be if it is in the low–average cell) or has the potential for good earnings and return on investment, the business merits retention and the allocation of sufficient resources to achieve better performance.

The nine-cell attractiveness–strength [illegible] good case can be made for concentrating resources in those businesses that enjoy higher degrees of attractiveness and competitive strength, being very selective in making investments in businesses with intermediate positions on the grid, and withdrawing resources from businesses that are lower in attractiveness and strength unless they offer exceptional profit or cash flow potential.

Step 3: Checking the Competitive Advantage Potential of Cross-Business Strategic Fits

CORE CONCEPT
A company's related diversification strategy derives its power in large part from the presence of competitively valuable strategic fits among its businesses.

While this step can be bypassed for diversified companies whose business are all unrelated (since, by design, no strategic fits are present), a high potential for converting strategic fits into competitive advantage is central to concluding just how good a company's related diversification strategy is. Checking the competitive advantage potential of cross-business strategic fits involves searching for and evaluating how much benefit a diversified company can gain from value chain matchups that present (1) opportunities to combine the performance of certain activities, thereby reducing costs and capturing economies of scope; (2) opportunities to transfer skills, technology, or intellectual capital from one business to another, thereby leveraging use of existing resources; (3) opportunities to share use of a well-respected brand name; and (4) opportunities for sister businesses to collaborate in creating valuable new competitive capabilities (such as enhanced supply chain management capabilities, quicker first-to-market capabilities, or greater product innovation capabilities).

CORE CONCEPT
The greater the value of cross-business strategic fits in enhancing a company's performance in the marketplace or on the bottom line, the more competitively powerful is its strategy of related diversification.

Figure 8.6 illustrates the process of comparing the value chains of sister businesses and identifying competitively valuable cross-business strategic fits. *But more than just strategic fit identification is needed. The real test is what competitive value can be generated from these fits.* To what extent can cost savings be realized? How much competitive value will come from cross-business transfer of skills, technology, or intellectual capital? Will transferring a potent brand name to the products of sister businesses grow sales significantly? Will cross-business collaboration to create or strengthen competitive capabilities lead to significant gains in the marketplace or in financial performance? Absent significant strategic fits and dedicated company efforts to capture the benefits, one has to be skeptical about the potential for a diversified company's businesses to perform better together than apart.

CORE CONCEPT
Sister businesses possess *resource fit* when they add to a company's overall resource strengths and when a company has adequate resources to support their requirements.

Step 4: Checking for Resource Fit

The businesses in a diversified company's lineup need to exhibit good **resource fit.** Resource fit exists when (1) businesses add to a company's overall resource strengths and (2) a company has adequate resources to support its entire group of businesses without spreading itself too thin. One important dimension of resource fit concerns whether a diversified company can generate the internal cash flows sufficient to fund the capital requirements of its businesses, pay its dividends, meet its debt obligations, and otherwise remain financially healthy.

CORE CONCEPT
A *cash hog* business generates cash flows that are too small to fully fund its operations and growth; a cash hog business requires cash infusions to provide additional working capital and finance new capital investment.

Financial Resource Fits: Cash Cows versus Cash Hogs Different businesses have different cash flow and investment characteristics. For example, business units in rapidly growing industries are often **cash hogs**—so labeled because the cash flows they are able to generate from internal operations aren't big enough to fund their expansion. To keep pace with rising buyer demand, rapid-growth businesses frequently need sizable annual capital investments—for new facilities and equipment, for new product development or technology improvements, and for additional working

Figure 8.6 Identifying the Competitive Advantage Potential of Cross-Business Strategic Fits

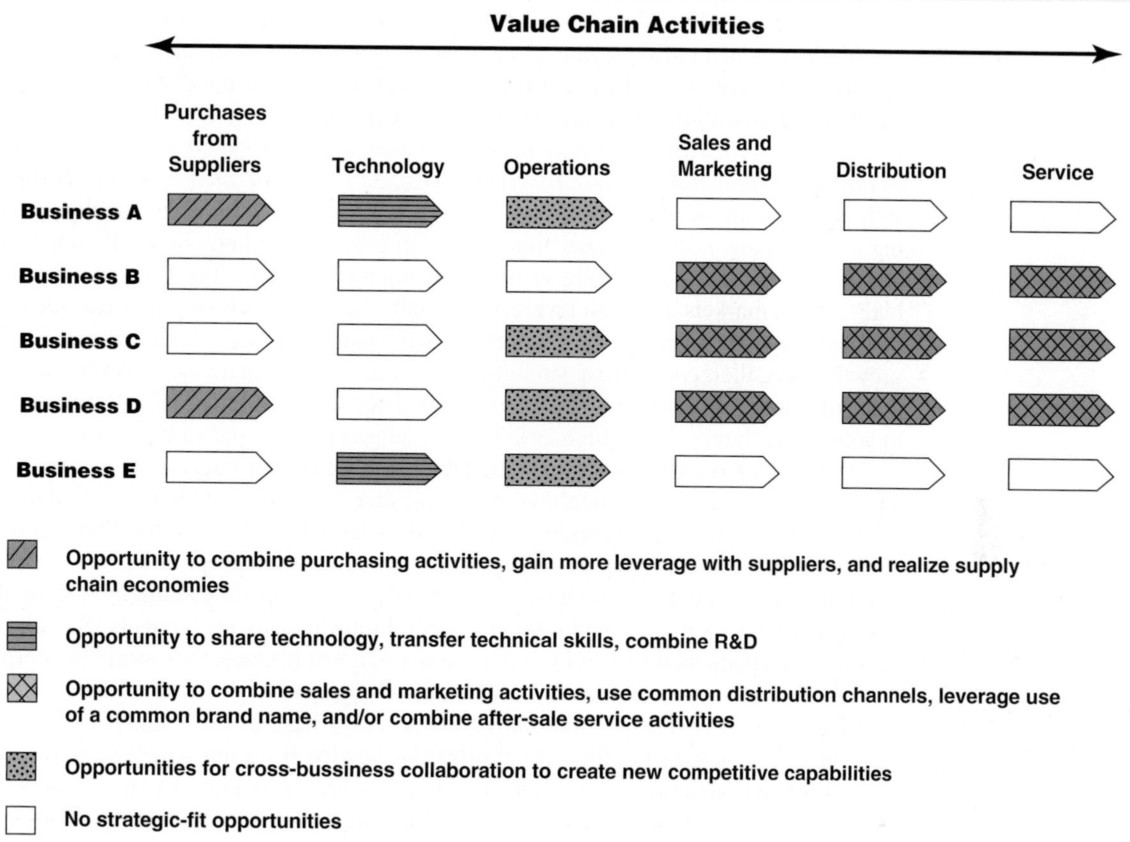
Value Chain Activities
Purchases from Suppliers
Technology
Operations
Sales and Marketing
Distribution
Service
Business A
Business B
Business C
Business D
Business E
Opportunity to combine purchasing activities, gain more leverage with suppliers, and realize supply chain economies
Opportunity to share technology, transfer technical skills, combine R&D
Opportunity to combine sales and marketing activities, use common distribution channels, leverage use of a common brand name, and/or combine after-sale service activities
Opportunities for cross-bussiness collaboration to create new competitive capabilities
No strategic-fit opportunities

capital to support inventory expansion and a larger base of operations. A business in a fast-growing industry becomes an even bigger cash hog when it has a relatively low market share and is pursuing a strategy to become an industry leader. Because a cash hog's financial resources must be provided by the corporate parent, corporate managers have to decide whether it makes good financial and strategic sense to keep pouring new money into a business that continually needs cash infusions.

In contrast, business units with leading market positions in mature industries may, however, be **cash cows**—businesses that generate substantial cash surpluses over what is needed to adequately fund their operations. Market leaders in slow-growth industries of

to earn attractive profits and because the slow-growth nature of their industry often entails relatively modest annual investment requirements. Cash cows, though not always attractive from a growth standpoint, are valuable businesses from a financial resource perspective. The surplus cash flows they generate can be used to pay corporate dividends, finance acquisitions, and provide funds for investing in the company's promising cash hogs. It makes good

CORE CONCEPT

its internal requirements, thus providing a corporate parent with funds for investing in cash hog businesses, financing new acquisitions, or paying dividends.

financial and strategic sense for diversified companies to keep cash cows healthy, fortifying and defending their market position so as to preserve their cash-generating capability over the long term and thereby have an ongoing source of financial resources to deploy elsewhere. The cigarette business is one of the world's biggest cash cows.

Viewing a diversified group of businesses as a collection of cash flows and cash requirements (present and future) is a major step forward in understanding what the financial ramifications of diversification are and why having businesses with good financial resource fit is so important. For instance, *a diversified company's businesses exhibit good financial resource fit when the excess cash generated by its cash cows is sufficient to fund the investment requirements of promising cash hogs.* Ideally, investing in promising cash hogs over time results in growing the hogs into self-supporting *star businesses* that have strong or market-leading competitive positions in attractive, high-growth markets and high levels of profitability. Star businesses are often the cash cows of the future—when the markets of star businesses begin to mature and their growth slows, their competitive strength should produce self-generated cash flows more than sufficient to cover their investment needs. The "success sequence" is thus cash hog to young star (but perhaps still a cash hog) to self-supporting star to cash cow.

If, however, a cash hog has questionable promise (either because of low industry attractiveness or a weak competitive position), then it becomes a logical candidate for divestiture. Pursuing an aggressive invest-and-expand strategy for a cash hog with an uncertain future seldom makes sense because it requires the corporate parent to keep pumping more capital into the business with only a dim hope of eventually turning the cash hog into a future star and realizing a good return on its investments. Such businesses are a financial drain and fail the resource-fit test because they strain the corporate parent's ability to adequately fund its other businesses. Divesting a less-attractive cash hog is usually the best alternative unless (1) it has valuable strategic fits with other business units or (2) the capital infusions needed from the corporate parent are modest relative to the funds available and there's a decent chance of growing the business into a solid bottom-line contributor yielding a good return on invested capital.

Other Tests of Resource Fit Aside from cash flow considerations, there are two other factors to consider in determining whether the businesses comprising a diversified company's portfolio exhibit good resource fit from a financial perspective:

- *Does the business adequately contribute to achieving companywide performance targets?* A business has good financial fit when it contributes to the achievement of corporate performance objectives (growth in earnings per share, above-average return on investment, recognition as an industry leader, etc.) and when it materially enhances shareholder value via helping drive increases in the company's stock price. A business exhibits poor financial fit if it soaks up a disproportionate share of the company's financial resources, makes subpar or inconsistent bottom-line contributions, is unduly risky and failure would jeopardize the entire enterprise, or remains too small to make a material earnings contribution even though it performs well.
- *Does the company have adequate financial strength to fund its different businesses and maintain a healthy credit rating?* A diversified company's strategy fails the resource-fit test when its financial resources are stretched across so many businesses that its credit rating is impaired. Severe financial strain sometimes occurs when a company borrows so heavily to finance new acquisitions that it has to trim way back on capital expenditures for existing businesses and use the big majority of its financial resources to meet interest obligations and to pay down debt. Time

Warner, Royal Ahold, and AT&T, for example, have found themselves so financially overextended that they have had to sell off some of their business units to raise the money to pay down burdensome debt obligations and continue to fund essential capital expenditures for the remaining businesses.

- *Does the company have (or can it develop) the specific resource strengths and competitive capabilities needed to be successful in each of its businesses?*[15] Sometimes the resource strengths a company has accumulated in its core or mainstay business prove to be a poor match with the key success factors and competitive capabilities needed to succeed in one or more businesses it has diversified into. For instance, LVMH, a multibusiness company in France, discovered that the company's resources and managerial skills were quite well suited for parenting luxury goods businesses including Louis Vuitton, Christian Dior, Givenchy, Fendi, Dom Perignon, Moët & Chandon, and Hennessy but not for parenting art auctions and radio stations; as a consequence, LVMH decided to divest its art auctioning and radio broadcasting businesses after those businesses had run up significant operating losses and proved to be a drain on the corporate treasury. Another company with businesses in restaurants and retailing decided that its resource capabilities in site selection, controlling operating costs, management selection and training, and supply chain logistics would enable it to succeed in the hotel business and in property management; but what management missed was that these businesses had some significantly different key success factors—namely, skills in controlling property development costs, maintaining low overheads, product branding (hotels), and ability to recruit a sufficient volume of business to maintain high levels of facility utilization.[16] Thus, a mismatch between the company's resource strengths and the key success factors in a particular business can be serious enough to warrant divesting an existing business or not acquiring a new business. In contrast, when a company's resources and capabilities are a good match with the key success factors of industries it is not presently in, it makes sense to take a hard look at acquiring companies in these industries and expanding the company's business lineup.
- *Are recently acquired businesses acting to strengthen a company's resource base and competitive capabilities or are they causing its competitive and managerial resources to be stretched too thin?* A diversified company has to guard against overtaxing its resource strengths and managerial capabilities, a condition that can arise (1) when it goes on an acquisition spree and management is called on to assimilate and oversee many new businesses very quickly or (2) when it lacks sufficient resource and managerial depth to do a creditable job of transferring skills and competences from one of its businesses to another. The broader the diversification, the greater the concern about whether the company has sufficient managerial depth to cope with the diverse range of operating problems its wide business lineup presents. And the more a company's diversification strategy is tied to transferring its existing know-how or technologies to new businesses, the more [illegible] spread too thin across many businesses and the opportunity for competitive advantage slips through the cracks.

A Cautionary Note about Transferring Resources from One Business to Another Hitting a home run in one business doesn't mean that a company can easily enter a new business with similar resource requirements and hit a second home run.[18] Noted British retailer Marks & Spencer—despite possessing a range of impressive resource capabilities (ability to choose excellent store locations, a supply chain that gives it both low costs and high merchandise quality, loyal employees, an excellent reputation with consumers, and strong management expertise) that have made it one of Britain's premier retailers for 100 years—has failed repeatedly in its efforts to diversify into department store retailing in the United States. Even though Philip Morris (now named Altria) had built powerful consumer marketing capabilities in its cigarette and beer businesses, it floundered in soft drinks and ended up divesting its acquisition of 7UP after several frustrating years of competing against strongly entrenched and resource-capable rivals like Coca-Cola and PepsiCo. Then in 2002 it decided to divest its Miller Brewing business—despite its long-standing marketing successes in cigarettes and in its Kraft Foods subsidiary—because it was unable to grow Miller's market share in head-to-head competition against the considerable marketing prowess of Anheuser-Busch.

Step 5: Ranking the Performance Prospects of Business Units and Assigning a Priority for Resource Allocation

Once a diversified company's strategy has been evaluated from the perspective of industry attractiveness, competitive strength, strategic fit, and resource fit, the next step is to rank the performance prospects of the businesses from best to worst and determine which businesses merit top priority for resource support and new capital investments by the corporate parent.

The most important considerations in judging business-unit performance are sales growth, profit growth, contribution to company earnings, and return on capital invested in the business. Sometimes, cash flow is a big consideration. Information on each business's past performance can be gleaned from a company's financial records. While past performance is not necessarily a good predictor of future performance, it does signal whether a business already has good to excellent performance or has problems to overcome.

Furthermore, the industry attractiveness/business strength evaluations provide a solid basis for judging a business's prospects. Normally, strong business units in attractive industries have significantly better prospects than weak businesses in unattractive industries. And, normally, the revenue and earnings outlook for businesses in fast-growing industries is better than for businesses in slow-growing industries—one important exception is when a business in a slow-growing industry has the competitive strength to draw sales and market share away from its rivals and thus achieve much faster growth than the industry as whole. As a rule, the prior analyses, taken together, signal which business units are likely to be strong performers on the road ahead and which are likely to be laggards. And it is a short step from ranking the prospects of business units to drawing conclusions about whether the company as a whole is capable of strong, mediocre, or weak performance in upcoming years.

The rankings of future performance generally determine what priority the corporate parent should give to each business in terms of resource allocation. *Business subsidiaries with the brightest profit and growth prospects and solid strategic and resource fits generally should head the list for corporate resource support.* More specifically, corporate executives must be diligent in steering resources out of low-opportunity areas into high-opportunity areas. Divesting marginal businesses is one of the best ways of freeing unproductive assets for redeployment. Surplus funds from cash cows also can be used to finance the range of chief strategic and financial options

Figure 8.7 The Chief Strategic and Financial Options for Allocating a Diversified Company's Financial Resources

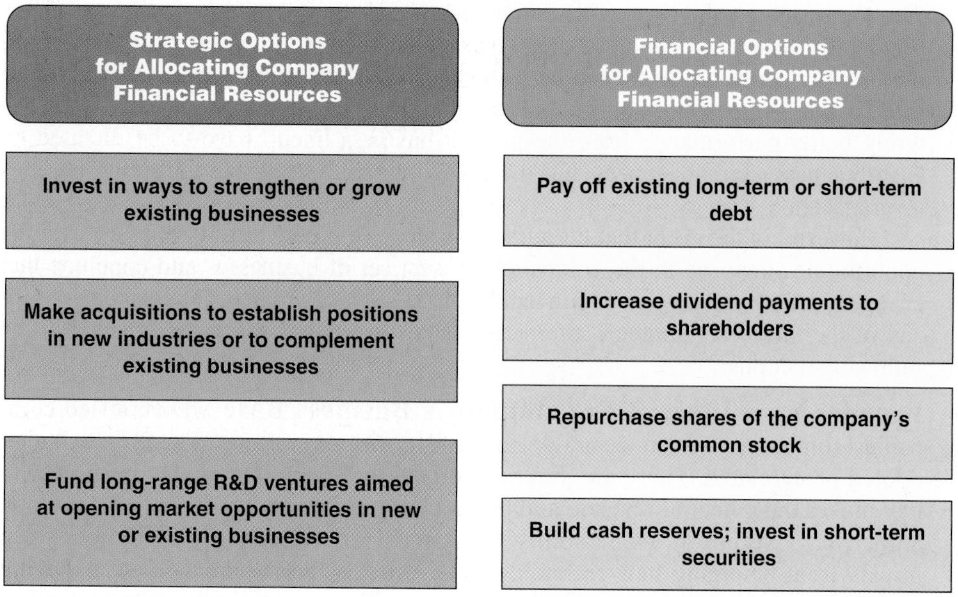

Strategic Options for Allocating Company Financial Resources

- Invest in ways to strengthen or grow existing businesses
- Make acquisitions to establish positions in new industries or to complement existing businesses
- Fund long-range R&D ventures aimed at opening market opportunities in new or existing businesses

Financial Options for Allocating Company Financial Resources

- Pay off existing long-term or short-term debt
- Increase dividend payments to shareholders
- Repurchase shares of the company's common stock
- Build cash reserves; invest in short-term securities

shown in Figure 8.7. Ideally, a company will have enough funds to do what is needed, both strategically and financially. If not, strategic uses of corporate resources should usually take precedence unless there is a compelling reason to strengthen the firm's balance sheet or divert financial resources to pacify shareholders.

Step 6: Crafting New Strategic Moves to Improve Overall Corporate Performance

The diagnosis and conclusions flowing from the five preceding analytical steps set the agenda for crafting strategic moves to improve a diversified company's overall performance. Corporate strategy options once a company has diversified boil down to five broad categories of actions (see Figure 8.7):

1. Sticking closely with the existing business lineup and pursuing the opportunities these businesses present.
2. Broadening the company's business scope by making new acquisitions in new industries.
3. Divesting some businesses and retrenching to a narrower base of busi

and new acquisitions to put a whole new face on the company's business makeup.

5. Pursuing multinational diversification and striving to globalize the operations of several of the company's business units.

Sticking Closely with the Existing Business Lineup The option of sticking with the current business lineup makes sense when the company's present businesses offer attractive growth opportunities and can be counted on to generate good earnings and cash flows. As long as the company's set of existing businesses puts it in good position for the future and these businesses have good strategic and/or resource fits, then rocking the boat with major changes in the company's business mix is usually unnecessary. Corporate executives can concentrate their attention on getting the best performance from each of its businesses, steering corporate resources into those areas of greatest potential and profitability. The specifics of "what to do" to wring better performance from the present business lineup have to be dictated by each business's circumstances and the preceding analysis of the corporate parent's diversification strategy.

However, in the event that corporate executives are not entirely satisfied with the opportunities they see in the company's present set of businesses and conclude that changes in the company's direction and business makeup are in order, they can opt for any of the four other strategic alternatives shown in Figure 8.8 and described in the following sections.

Broadening a Diversified Company's Business Base Diversified companies sometimes find it desirable to build positions in new industries, whether related or unrelated. There are several motivating factors. One is sluggish growth that makes the potential revenue and profit boost of a newly acquired business look attractive. A second is vulnerability to seasonal or recessionary influences or to threats from emerging new technologies. A third is the potential for transferring resources and capabilities to other related or complementary businesses. A fourth is rapidly changing conditions in one or more of a company's core businesses brought on by technological, legislative, or new product innovations that alter buyer requirements and preferences. For instance, the passage of legislation in the United States allowing banks, insurance companies, and stock brokerages to enter one another's businesses spurred a raft of acquisitions and mergers to create full-service financial enterprises capable of meeting the multiple financial needs of customers. Citigroup, already the largest U.S. bank with a global banking franchise, acquired Salomon Smith Barney to position itself in the investment banking and brokerage business and acquired insurance giant Travelers Group to enable it to offer customers insurance products.

A fifth, and often very important, motivating factor for adding new businesses is to complement and strengthen the market position and competitive capabilities of one or more of its present businesses. Procter & Gamble's 2005 acquisition of Gillette strengthened and extended P&G's reach into personal care and household products—Gillette's businesses included Oral-B toothbrushes, Gillette razors and razor blades, Duracell batteries, Braun shavers and small appliances (coffeemakers, mixers, hair dryers, and electric toothbrushes), and toiletries (Right Guard, Foamy, Soft & Dry, White Rain, and Dry Idea). Unilever, a leading maker of food and personal care products, expanded its business lineup by acquiring SlimFast, Ben & Jerry's Homemade Ice Cream, and Bestfoods (whose brands included Knorr's soups, Hellman's mayonnaise, Skippy peanut butter, and Mazola cooking oils). Unilever saw these businesses as giving it more clout in competing against such other diversified food and household products companies as Nestlé, Kraft, Procter & Gamble, Campbell Soup, and General Mills. Cisco Systems built itself into a worldwide leader in networking systems for the Internet by making 130 technology-based acquisitions from 1993 to 2008 that extended its market reach from routing and switching into IP telephony, home networking, wireless LAN, storage networking, network security, broadband, and optical and broadband systems.

Figure 8.8 A Company's Five Main Strategic Alternatives after It Diversifies

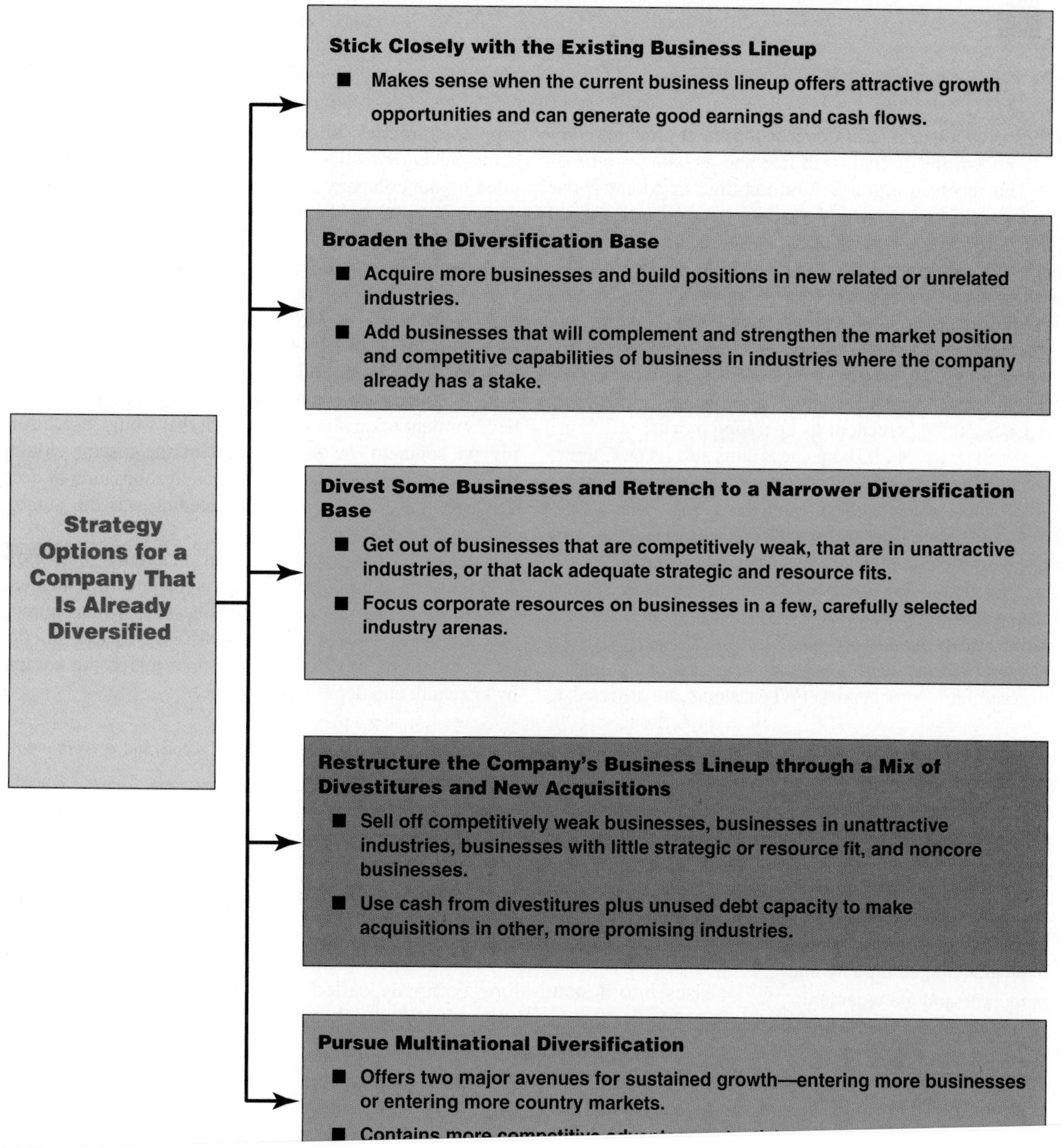

Strategy Options for a Company That Is Already Diversified
Stick Closely with the Existing Business Lineup
Makes sense when the current business lineup offers attractive growth opportunities and can generate good earnings and cash flows.
Broaden the Diversification Base
Acquire more businesses and build positions in new related or unrelated industries.
Add businesses that will complement and strengthen the market position and competitive capabilities of business in industries where the company already has a stake.
Divest Some Businesses and Retrench to a Narrower Diversification Base
Get out of businesses that are competitively weak, that are in unattractive industries, or that lack adequate strategic and resource fits.
Focus corporate resources on businesses in a few, carefully selected industry arenas.
Restructure the Company's Business Lineup through a Mix of Divestitures and New Acquisitions
Sell off competitively weak businesses, businesses in unattractive industries, businesses with little strategic or resource fit, and noncore businesses.
Use cash from divestitures plus unused debt capacity to make acquisitions in other, more promising industries.
Pursue Multinational Diversification
Offers two major avenues for sustained growth—entering more businesses or entering more country markets.

Illustration Capsule 8.3 describes how Johnson & Johnson has used acquisitions to diversify far beyond its well-known Band-Aid and baby care businesses and become a major player in pharmaceuticals, medical devices, and medical diagnostics.

Divesting Some Businesses and Retrenching to a Narrower Diversification Base A number of diversified firms have had difficulty managing a diverse group of businesses and have elected to get out of some of them. Retrenching

ILLUSTRATION CAPSULE 8.3

Managing Diversification at Johnson & Johnson: The Benefits of Cross-Business Strategic Fits

Johnson & Johnson (J&J), once a consumer products company known for its Band-Aid line and its baby care products, has evolved into a $61 billion diversified enterprise consisting of some 250-plus operating companies organized into three divisions: pharmaceuticals, medical devices and diagnostics, and consumer health care products. Over the past decade J&J has made acquisitions totaling more than $50 billion; about 10 to 15 percent of J&J's annual growth in revenues has come from acquisitions. Much of the company's recent growth has been in the pharmaceutical division, which in 2007 accounted for 41 percent of J&J's revenues and 48 percent of its operating profits.

While each of J&J's business units sets its own strategies and operates with its own finance and human resource departments, corporate management strongly encourages cross-business cooperation and collaboration, believing that many of the advances in 21st-century medicine will come from applying advances in one discipline to another. J&J's drug-coated stent grew out of a discussion between a drug researcher and a researcher in the company's stent business. The innovative product helps prevent infection after cardiatric procedures. (When stents are inserted to prop open arteries following angioplasty, the drug coating helps prevent infection.) A gene technology database compiled by the company's gene research lab was shared with personnel from the diagnostics division, who developed a test that the drug researchers used to predict which patients would most benefit from an experimental cancer therapy. J&J's liquid Band-Aid product (a liquid coating applied to hard-to-cover places like fingers and knuckles) is based on a material used in a wound-closing product sold by the company's hospital products company. In 2007, scientists from three separate business units were working toward the development of an absorbable patch that would stop bleeding on contact. The development of the instant clotting patch was expected to save the lives of thousands of accident victims since uncontrolled bleeding was the number one cause of death due to injury.

J&J's corporate management maintains that close collaboration among people in its diagnostics, medical devices, and pharmaceuticals businesses—where numerous cross-business strategic fits exist—gives J&J an edge on competitors, most of whom cannot match the company's breadth and depth of expertise.

Sources: Amy Barrett, "Staying on Top," *BusinessWeek,* May 5, 2003, pp. 60–68; Johnson & Johnson 2007 annual report; and www.jnj.com (accessed July 25, 2008).

Focusing corporate resources on a few core and mostly related businesses avoids the mistake of diversifying so broadly that resources and management attention are stretched too thin.

to a narrower diversification base is usually undertaken when top management concludes that its diversification strategy has ranged too far afield and that the company can improve long-term performance by concentrating on building stronger positions in a smaller number of core businesses and industries. Hewlett-Packard spun off its testing and measurement businesses into a stand-alone company called Agilent Technologies so that it could better concentrate on its PC, workstation, server, printer and peripherals, and electronics businesses.

But there are other important reasons for divesting one or more of a company's present businesses. Sometimes divesting a business has to be considered because market conditions in a once-attractive industry have badly deteriorated. A business can become a prime candidate for divestiture because it lacks adequate strategic or resource fit, because it is a cash hog with questionable long-term potential, or because it is weakly positioned in its industry with little prospect that the corporate parent can realize a decent return on its investment in the business. Sometimes a company acquires businesses that, down the road, just do not work out as expected even though management has tried all it can think of to make them profitable. Subpar performance by some business units is bound to occur, thereby raising questions of whether to divest them or keep them and attempt a turnaround. Other business units, despite adequate financial performance, may not mesh as well with the rest of the firm as was originally thought.

On occasion, a diversification move that seems sensible from a strategic-fit standpoint turns out to be a poor *cultural fit.*[19] Several pharmaceutical companies had just this experience. When they diversified into cosmetics and perfume, they discovered their personnel had little respect for the "frivolous" nature of such products compared to the far nobler task of developing miracle drugs to cure the ill. The absence of shared values and cultural compatibility between the medical research and chemical-compounding expertise of the pharmaceutical companies and the fashion/marketing orientation of the cosmetics business was the undoing of what otherwise was diversification into businesses with technology-sharing potential, product-development fit, and some overlap in distribution channels.

Time Warner's 2000 merger with America Online (AOL) proved to be a dismal failure—its planned convergence of Time Warner Entertainment's movies, music, magazine content, and cable network programming with AOL's Internet platform and Time Warner Cable's broadband capabilities never materialized; the cultures of the three divisions prevented the capture of strategic-fit benefits; and shareholder value eroded by nearly 80 percent. After struggling for more than seven years to make a success of its diversification, Time Warner management spun off its Time Warner Cable operations into an independent business and began evaluating offers from buyers interested in purchasing AOL.

Tyco International began a restructuring program in 2004 to narrow its diversification base from more than 2,000 separate businesses with operations in over 100 countries. Much of Tyco's diversification came during the 1994–2001 tenure of CEO Dennis Kozlowski, who made over 1,000 acquisitions, totaling approximately $63 billion. The company's far-flung diversification included businesses in electronics, electrical components, fire and security systems, health care products, valves, undersea telecommunications systems, plastics, and adhesives. Tyco's corporate restructuring was capped with the 2007 spin-off of its electronics and health care businesses; once completed, the restructuring reduced the size of the company from approximately $40 billion in revenues and $70 billion in assets in 2001 to $18 billion in revenues and $33 billion in assets in 2007.

There's evidence indicating that pruning businesses and narrowing a firm's diversification base improves corporate performance.[20] But corporate parents often end up selling off unwanted or under-performing businesses too late and at too low a price, sacrificing shareholder value.[21] A useful guide to determine whether or when to divest a business subsidiary is to ask, "If we were not in this business today, would we want to get into it now?"[22] When the answer is no or probably not, divestiture should be considered. Another signal that a business should become a divestiture candidate is whether it is worth more to another company than to the present parent; in such cases, shareholders would be well served if the company sells the business and collects a premium price from the buyer for whom the business is a valuable fit.[23]

Diversified companies need to divest low-performing businesses or businesses that don't fit in order to concentrate on expanding existing businesses and entering new ones where opportunities are more promising.

the most frequently used option for divesting a business. But sometimes a business selected for divestiture has ample resource strengths to compete successfully on its own. In such cases, a corporate parent may elect to spin the unwanted business off as a financially and managerially independent company, either by selling shares to the investing public via an initial public offering or by distributing shares in the new company to existing shareholders of the corporate parent. When a corporate parent decides to spin off one of its businesses as a separate company, there's the issue of whether or not to retain partial ownership. Retaining partial ownership makes sense when the business to be divested has a hot product or technological capabilities that give it good profit prospects. When Bank of America elected to divest its CTC Consulting business unit, which made independent investment recommendations to clients with extreme wealth, it elected to retain an ownership interest in the business so as to provide Bank of America shareholders a way of participating in whatever future market success that CTC might have on its own. Investors expected CTC Consulting to perform better as an independent company since it would no longer be burdened by the conflict of interest that resulted from its corporate affiliation with a financial institution that offered its own investment products. In 2005, Cendant announced it would split its diversified businesses into four separate publicly traded companies—one for vehicle rental services (which consisted of Avis and Budget car rental companies); one for real estate and mortgage services (which included Century 21, Coldwell Banker, ERA, Sotheby's International Realty, and NRT—a residential real estate brokerage company); one for hospitality and lodging (consisting of such hotels and motel chains as Wyndam, Ramada, Days Inn, Howard Johnson, Travelodge, AmeriHost Inn, and Knights Inn, plus an assortment of timeshare resort properties); and one for travel (consisting of various travel agencies, online ticket and vacation travel sites like Orbitz and Cheap Tickets, and vacation rental operations handling some 55,000 villas and condos). Cendant said the reason for the split-up was that shareholders would realize more value from operating the businesses independently—a clear sign that Cendant's diversification strategy had failed to deliver added shareholder value and that the parts were worth more than the whole. Similarly, IAC/InterActive, which operated a host of Internet properties such as Ask.com and Match.com, spun off several businesses in 2008 because of lackluster performance and challenging industry conditions. The company's spin-off of its Lending Tree mortgage loan service unit, a timeshare-exchange business, Ticketmaster, and the Home Shopping Network yielded $1.3 billion that management planned to use to support investments in remaining businesses and fund a share buyback plan intended to help boost the company's dramatically declining stock price.

Selling a business outright requires finding a buyer. This can prove hard or easy, depending on the business. As a rule, a company selling a troubled business should not ask, "How can we pawn this business off on someone, and what is the most we can get for it?"[24] Instead, it is wiser to ask, "For what sort of company would this business be a good fit, and under what conditions would it be viewed as a good deal?" Enterprises for which the business is a good fit are likely to pay the highest price. Of course, if a buyer willing to pay an acceptable price cannot be found, then a company must decide whether to keep the business until a buyer appears; spin it off as a separate company; or, in the case of a crisis-ridden business that is losing substantial sums, simply close it down and liquidate the remaining assets. Liquidation is obviously a last resort.

CORE CONCEPT
Restructuring **involves divesting some businesses and acquiring others so as to put a whole new face on the company's business lineup.**

Restructuring a Company's Business Lineup through a Mix of Divestitures and New Acquisitions **Restructuring** strategies involve divesting some businesses and acquiring others so as to put a whole new face on the company's business lineup. Performing radical surgery on a company's group of businesses is an appealing strategy alternative when its financial performance is being squeezed or eroded by:

- Too many businesses in slow-growth, declining, low-margin, or otherwise unattractive industries (a condition indicated by the number and size of businesses with industry attractiveness ratings below 5 and located on the bottom half of the attractiveness–strength matrix—see Figure 8.5).

- Too many competitively weak businesses (a condition indicated by the number and size of businesses with competitive strength ratings below 5 and located on the right half of the attractiveness–strength matrix).
- Ongoing declines in the market shares of one or more major business units that are falling prey to more market-savvy competitors.
- An excessive debt burden with interest costs that eat deeply into profitability.
- Ill-chosen acquisitions that haven't lived up to expectations.

Restructuring can also be mandated by the emergence of new technologies that threaten the survival of one or more of a diversified company's important businesses or by the appointment of a new CEO who decides to redirect the company. On occasion, restructuring can be prompted by special circumstances—like when a firm has a unique opportunity to make an acquisition so big and important that it has to sell several existing business units to finance the new acquisition or when a company needs to sell off some businesses in order to raise the cash for entering a potentially big industry with wave-of-the-future technologies or products.

Candidates for divestiture in a corporate restructuring effort typically include not only weak or up-and-down performers or those in unattractive industries but also business units that lack strategic fit with the businesses to be retained, businesses that are cash hogs or that lack other types of resource fit, and businesses incompatible with the company's revised diversification strategy (even though they may be profitable or in an attractive industry). As businesses are divested, corporate restructuring generally involves aligning the remaining business units into groups with the best strategic fits and then redeploying the cash flows from the divested business to either pay down debt or make new acquisitions to strengthen the parent company's business position in the industries it has chosen to emphasize.[25]

Over the past decade, corporate restructuring has become a popular strategy at many diversified companies, especially those that had diversified broadly into many different industries and lines of business. For instance, between 1994 and 2005 Ingersoll Rand radically restructured its business lineup by divesting its automotive components and mining components business units that accounted for 56 percent of its total revenues. During the same period, Ingersoll Rand made acquisitions of new businesses that went on to account for 52 percent of its 2005 total revenues. In 2007, the company executed the $6.2 billion sale of its road development, Bobcat, and utility equipment businesses and completed a variety of small acquisitions. Its corporate restructuring continued into 2008, with its $9.5 billion acquisition of Trane, a maker of heating and air-conditioning products. Trane had just undergone its own restructuring one year earlier when American Standard divested its legacy plumbing fixture business, spun off an automotive braking unit, and changed its name to Trane to reflect its new focus on heating and air-conditioning.

PerkinElmer used a series of divestitures and new acquisitions to transform itself [illegible] ics, medical instruments, and fluid control and containment services (for customers in aerospace, power generation, and semiconductors). In 2005, PerkinElmer took a second restructuring step by divesting its entire fluid control and containment business group so that it could concentrate on its higher growth health sciences and optoelectronics businesses; the company's CEO said, "While fluid services is an excellent business, it does not fit with our long-term strategy."[26]

During Jack Welch's first four years as CEO of General Electric (GE), the company divested 117 business units, accounting for about 20 percent of GE's assets; these divestitures, coupled with several important acquisitions, resulted in GE having 14 major business divisions and led to Welch's challenge to the managers of GE's divisions to become number one or number two in their industry. Ten years after Welch became CEO, GE was a different company, having divested operations worth $9 billion, made new acquisitions totaling $24 billion, and cut its workforce by 100,000 people. Then, during the 1990–2001 period, GE continued to reshuffle its business lineup, acquiring over 600 new companies, including 108 in 1998 and 64 during a 90-day period in 1999. Most of the new acquisitions were in Europe, Asia, and Latin America and were aimed at transforming GE into a truly global enterprise. In 2003, GE's new CEO, Jeffrey Immelt, began a further restructuring of GE's business lineup with three initiatives: (1) spending $10 billion to acquire British-based Amersham and extend GE's Medical Systems business unit into diagnostic pharmaceuticals and biosciences, thereby creating a $15 billion business designated as GE Healthcare; (2) acquire the entertainment assets of debt-ridden French media conglomerate Vivendi Universal Entertainment (Universal Studios, five Universal theme parks, USA Network, Sci-Fi Channel, the Trio cable channel, and Spanish-language broadcaster Telemundo) and integrate its operations into GE's NBC division (the owner of NBC, 29 television stations, and cable networks CNBC, MSNBC, and Bravo), thereby creating a broad-based $13 billion media business positioned to compete against Walt Disney, Time Warner, Fox, and Viacom; and (3) beginning a withdrawal from the insurance business by divesting several companies in its insurance division and preparing to spin off its remaining life and mortgage insurance businesses through an initial public offering (IPO) for a new company called Genworth Financial. In 2008, Jeffrey Immelt announced that GE would spin off its Industrial division, which included GE appliances, lighting, and various industrial businesses.

In a study of the performance of the 200 largest U.S. corporations from 1990 to 2000, McKinsey & Company found that those companies that actively managed their business portfolios through acquisitions and divestitures created substantially more shareholder value than those that kept a fixed lineup of businesses.[27] Illustration Capsule 8.4 discusses how VF Corporation shareholders have benefited through the company's large-scale restructuring program.

Pursuing Multinational Diversification The distinguishing characteristics of a multinational diversification strategy are a *diversity of businesses* and a *diversity of national markets.*[28] Such diversity makes multinational diversification a particularly challenging and complex strategy to conceive and execute. Managers have to develop business strategies for each industry (with as many multinational variations as conditions in each country market dictate). Then they have to pursue and manage opportunities for cross-business and cross-country collaboration and strategic coordination in ways calculated to result in competitive advantage and enhanced profitability.

Moreover, the geographic operating scope of individual businesses within a diversified multinational company (DMNC) can range from one country only to several countries to many countries to global. Thus, each business unit within a DMNC often competes in a somewhat different combination of geographic markets than the other businesses do—adding another element of strategic complexity, and perhaps an element of opportunity.

ILLUSTRATION CAPSULE 8.4
The Corporate Restructuring Strategy That Made VF the Star of the Apparel Industry

VF Corporation's corporate restructuring—which included a mix of divestitures and acquisitions—has provided its shareholders with returns that are more than five times greater than shareholder returns provided by competing apparel manufacturers. In fact, VF delivered a total shareholder return of 110 percent between 1998 and 2007, and its 2007 revenues of $7 billion and annual revenue growth and earnings growth of 16 percent and 14 percent, respectively, made it number 335 on *Fortune*'s list of 500 largest U.S. companies. The company's corporate restructuring began in 2000 when it divested its slow-growing businesses, including its namesake Vanity Fair brand of lingerie and sleepwear. The company's $136 million acquisition of North Face in 2000 was the first in the series of many acquisitions of "lifestyle brands" that connected with the way people lived, worked, and played. Since the acquisition and turnaround of North Face, VF has spent $2.8 billion to acquire 18 additional businesses. New apparel brands acquired by VF Corporation include Vans skateboard shoes, Nautica, John Varvatos, 7 For All Mankind sportswear, Reef surf wear, and Lucy athletic wear. The company also acquired a variety of apparel companies specializing in apparel segments such as uniforms for professional baseball and football teams and law enforcement.

VF Corporation's acquisitions came after years of researching each company and developing a relationship with an acquisition candidate's chief managers before closing the deal. The company made a practice of leaving management of acquired companies in place, while bringing in new managers only when necessary talent and skills were lacking. In addition, companies acquired by VF were allowed to keep long-standing traditions that shaped culture and spurred creativity. For example, the Vans headquarters in Cypress, California, retained its halfpipe and concrete floor so that its employees could skateboard to and from meetings.

In 2007, VF Corporation was the most profitable apparel firm in the industry, with net earnings of $591 million. The company expected new acquisitions that would push the company's revenues to $11 billion by 2012.

Sources: Suzanne Kapner, "How a 100-Year Old Apparel Firm Changed Course," *Fortune,* April 9, 2008, online edition; and www.vf.com (accessed July 24, 2008).

Illustration Capsule 8.5 on the next page shows the scope of four prominent DMNCs.

The Appeal of Multinational Diversification: More Opportunities for Sustained Growth and Maximum Competitive Advantage Potential Despite their complexity, multinational diversification strategies have great appeal. They contain *two major avenues* for growing revenues and profits: One is to grow by entering additional businesses, and the other is to grow by extending the operations of existing businesses into additional country markets. Moreover, a strategy of multinational diversification also contains five attractive paths to competitive advantage, *all of which can be pursued simultaneously:*

1. *Full capture of* [illegible] exceeding the volume that can be achieved operating within the boundaries of a single country market, especially a small one. *The ability to drive down unit costs by expanding sales to additional country markets is one reason why a diversified multinational may seek to acquire a business and then rapidly expand its operations into more and more foreign markets.*

ILLUSTRATION CAPSULE 8.5
The Global Scope of Four Prominent Diversified Multinational Corporations

Company	Global Scope	Businesses into Which the Company Has Diversified
Sony	Operations in more than 100 countries and sales offices in more than 200 countries	• Televisions, VCRs, DVD players, Walkman radios and digital music players, clock radios, digital cameras and camcorders, car audio and GPS systems, mobile phones, Vaio PCs, Blu-ray technology products; PlayStation game consoles, portable video game players, video game software; Columbia, Epic, and Sony Classical prerecorded music; Columbia TriStar motion pictures; syndicated television programs; entertainment complexes, semiconductors, and financial services (insurance and banking)
Nestlé	Factories in 80 countries and sales offices in more than 200 countries	• Beverages (Nescafé and Taster's Choice coffees, Nestea, 72 brands of bottled waters including Perrier, San Pellegrino, Acqua Panna, Arrowhead, Deer Park, and Poland Springs); milk and dairy products (including Carnation, Coffee Mate, Milkmaid, Nestlé ice cream and yogurt, Dreyer's/Edy's ice creams and frozen yogurt); infant foods (including Gerber and 16 other brands); nutritional foods (PowerBar, Jenny Craig, and 8 other brands); pet foods (Friskies, Alpo, Fancy Feast, Purina, Beneful, ProPlan, and 7 other brands); Stouffer's, Lean Cuisine, Hot Pockets, and Buitoni food products and prepared dishes; Nestlé, Toll House, and Buitoni refrigerated products; Maggi soups; chocolate and confectionery products (Nestlé Crunch, Smarties, Polo, Butterfinger, KitKat); and pharmaceuticals (Alcon ophthalmic products, Galderma dermatological products)
Siemens	Operations in 160 countries and sales offices in more than 190 countries	• Electrical power generation, transmission, and distribution equipment and products; manufacturing automation systems; industrial motors, machinery, and tools; plant construction and maintenance services; telephones, VoIP and WiMax devices; PCs, mainframes, computer network products, consulting services; mass transit and light rail systems, rail cars, locomotives, lighting products (bulbs, lamps, automotive lighting, theater and television lighting systems); semiconductors; fire safety systems; industrial water treatment products; heating and ventilation systems; and financial, procurement, and logistics services.
Samsung	Operations in more than 60 countries and sales in more than 200 countries	• Personal computers, hard disk drives, CD/DVD drives for PCs, monitors, printers, fax machines, memory chips, televisions; DVD players; digital music players; cell phones and various other telecommunications products, home appliances (washing machines, dryers, refrigerators, air conditioners, cooking appliances), optical fibers, fiber-optic cables, and fiber-optic connectors.

Sources: Company annual reports and Web sites.

2. *Opportunities to capitalize on cross-business economies of scope.* Diversifying into related businesses offering economies of scope can drive the development of a low-cost advantage over less diversified rivals. For example, a DMNC that uses mostly the same distributors and retail dealers worldwide can diversify into new businesses using these same worldwide distribution channels at relatively little incremental expense. The cost savings of piggybacking distribution activities can be substantial. Moreover, with more business selling more products in more countries, a DMNC acquires more bargaining leverage in its purchases from suppliers and more bargaining leverage with retailers in securing attractive display

space for its products. Consider, for example, the competitive power that Sony derived from these very sorts of economies of scope when it decided to diversify into the video game business with its PlayStation product line. Sony had in-place capability to go after video game sales in all country markets where it presently did business in other electronics product categories (TVs, computers, DVD players, VCRs, radios, and CD players, and camcorders). And it had the marketing clout and brand-name credibility to persuade retailers to give Sony's PlayStation products prime shelf space and visibility. These strategic-fit benefits helped Sony quickly overtake longtime industry leaders Nintendo and Sega and defend its market leadership against Microsoft's new Xbox.

3. *Opportunities to transfer competitively valuable resources both from one business to another and from one country to another.* A company pursuing related diversification can gain a competitive edge over less diversified rivals by transferring competitively valuable resources from one business to another; a multinational company can gain competitive advantage over rivals with narrower geographic coverage by transferring competitively valuable resources from one country to another. But a strategy of multinational diversification enables simultaneous pursuit of both sources of competitive advantage.
4. *Ability to leverage use of a well-known and competitively powerful brand name.* Diversified multinational companies whose businesses have brand names that are well known and respected across the world possess a valuable strategic asset with competitive advantage potential. For example, Sony's well-established global brand-name recognition gives it an important marketing and advertising advantage over rivals with lesser-known brands. When Sony goes into a new marketplace with the stamp of the Sony brand on its product families, it can command prominent display space with retailers. It can expect to win sales and market share simply on the confidence that buyers place in products carrying the Sony name. While Sony may spend money to make consumers aware of the availability of its new products, it does not have to spend nearly as much on achieving brand recognition and market acceptance as would a lesser-known competitor looking at the marketing and advertising costs of entering the same new product/business/country markets and trying to go head-to-head against Sony. Further, if Sony moves into a new country market for the first time and does well selling Sony PlayStations and video games, it is easier to sell consumers in that country Sony TVs, digital cameras, PCs, MP3 players, and so on—plus, the related advertising costs are likely to be less than they would be without having already established the Sony brand strongly in the minds of buyers.
5. *Ability to capitalize on opportunities for cross-business and cross-country collaboration and strategic coordination.*[29] A multinational diversification strategy allows competitively valuable cross-business and cross-country coordination of certain value chain activities. For instance, by channeling [illegible]

[illegible] it, a DMNC can merge its expertise and efforts *worldwide* to advance core technologies, expedite cross-business and cross-country product improvements, speed the development of new products that complement existing products, and pursue promising technological avenues to create altogether new businesses—all significant contributors to competitive advantage and better corporate performance.[30] Honda has been very successful in building R&D expertise in gasoline engines and transferring the resulting technological advances to its businesses in automobiles, motorcycles, outboard engines, snow blowers, lawn mowers, garden tillers, and portable power generators. Further, a DMNC can reduce costs through cross-business and cross-country coordination of purchasing and procurement from suppliers, from collaborative introduction and shared use of e-commerce technologies and online sales efforts, and from coordinated product introductions and promotional campaigns. Firms that are less diversified and less global in scope have less such cross-business and cross-country collaborative opportunities.

The Combined Effects of These Advantages Is Potent A strategy of diversifying into *related* industries and then competing *globally* in each of these industries thus has great potential for being a winner in the marketplace because of the long-term growth opportunities it offers and the multiple corporate-level competitive advantage opportunities it contains. *Indeed, a strategy of multinational diversification contains more competitive advantage potential (above and beyond what is achievable through a particular business's own competitive strategy) than any other diversification strategy.* The strategic key to maximum competitive advantage is for a DMNC to concentrate its diversification efforts in those industries where there are resource-sharing and resource-transfer opportunities and where there are important economies of scope and brand name benefits. The more a company's diversification strategy yields these kinds of strategic-fit benefits, the more powerful a competitor it becomes and the better its profit and growth performance is likely to be.

CORE CONCEPT
A strategy of multinational diversification has more built-in potential for competitive advantage than any other diversification strategy.

KEY POINTS

The purpose of diversification is to build shareholder value. Diversification builds shareholder value when a diversified group of businesses can perform better under the auspices of a single corporate parent than they would as independent, stand-alone businesses—the goal is to achieve not just a $1 + 1 = 2$ result but rather to realize important $1 + 1 = 3$ performance benefits. Whether getting into a new business has potential to enhance shareholder value hinges on whether a company's entry into that business can pass the attractiveness test, the cost-of-entry test, and the better-off test.

Entry into new businesses can take any of three forms: acquisition, internal start-up, or joint venture/strategic partnership. Each has its pros and cons, but acquisition is the most frequently used; internal start-up takes the longest to produce home-run results, and joint venture/strategic partnership, though used second most frequently, is the least durable.

There are two fundamental approaches to diversification—into related businesses and into unrelated businesses. The rationale for *related* diversification is *strategic:* Diversify into businesses with strategic fits along their respective value chains, capitalize on strategic-fit relationships to gain competitive advantage, and then use competitive advantage to achieve the desired $1 + 1 = 3$ impact on shareholder value.

The basic premise of unrelated diversification is that any business that has good profit prospects and can be acquired on good financial terms is a good business to diversify into. Unrelated diversification strategies surrender the competitive advantage potential of strategic fit in return for such advantages as (1) spreading business risk over a variety of industries and (2) providing opportunities for financial gain (if candidate acquisitions have undervalued assets, are bargain-priced and have good upside potential given the right management, or need the backing of a financially strong parent to capitalize on attractive opportunities). However, the greater the number of businesses a company has diversified into and the more diverse these businesses are, the harder it is for corporate executives to select capable managers to run each business, know when the major strategic proposals of business units are sound, or decide on a wise course of recovery when a business unit stumbles.

Analyzing how good a company's diversification strategy is a six-step process:

Step 1: *Evaluate the long-term attractiveness of the industries into which the firm has diversified.* Industry attractiveness needs to be evaluated from three angles: the attractiveness of each industry on its own, the attractiveness of each industry relative to the others, and the attractiveness of all the industries as a group.

Step 2: *Evaluate the relative competitive strength of each of the company's business units.* Again, quantitative ratings of competitive strength are preferable to subjective judgments. The purpose of rating the competitive strength of each business is to gain clear understanding of which businesses are strong contenders in their industries, which are weak contenders, and the underlying reasons for their strength or weakness. The conclusions about industry attractiveness can be joined with the conclusions about competitive strength by drawing an industry attractiveness–competitive strength matrix that helps identify the prospects of each business and what priority each business should be given in allocating corporate resources and investment capital.

Step 3: *Check for cross-business strategic fits.* A business is more attractive strategically when it has value chain relationships with sister business units that offer potential to (1) realize economies of scope or cost-saving efficiencies; (2) transfer technology, skills, know-how, or other resource capabilities from one business to another; (3) leverage use of a well-known and trusted brand name; and (4) build new or stronger resource strengths and competitive capabilities via cross-business collaboration. Cross-business strategic fits represent a significant avenue for producing competitive advantage beyond what any one business can achieve on its own.

Step 4: *Check whether the firm's resource strengths fit the resource requirements of its present business lineup.* Resource fit exists when (1) businesses add to a company's resource strengths, either financially or strategically, (2) a company has the resources to adequately support the resource requirements of its businesses as a group without spreading itself too thin, and (3) there are close matches between a company's resources and industry key success factors. One important

Step 5: *Rank the performance prospects of the businesses from best to worst and determine what the corporate parent's priority should be in allocating resources to its various businesses.* The most important considerations in judging business-unit performance are sales growth, profit growth, contribution to company earnings, and the return on capital invested in the business. Sometimes, cash flow generation is a big consideration. Normally, strong business units in attractive industries have significantly better performance prospects than weak businesses or businesses in unattractive industries. Business subsidiaries with the brightest profit and growth prospects and solid strategic and resource fits generally should head the list for corporate resource support.

Step 6: *Crafting new strategic moves to improve overall corporate performance.* This step entails using the results of the preceding analysis as the basis for devising actions to strengthen existing businesses, make new acquisitions, divest weak-performing and unattractive businesses, restructure the company's business lineup, expand the scope of the company's geographic reach multinationally or globally, and otherwise steer corporate resources into the areas of greatest opportunity. Once a company has diversified, corporate management's task is to manage the collection of businesses for maximum long-term performance. There are five different strategic paths for improving a diversified company's performance: (1) sticking with the existing business lineup, (2) broadening the firm's business base by diversifying into additional businesses, (3) retrenching to a narrower diversification base by divesting some of its present businesses, (4) restructuring the company's business lineup with a combination of divestitures and new acquisitions to put a whole new face on the company's business makeup, and (5) pursuing multinational diversification and striving to globalize the operations of several of the company's business units.

ASSURANCE OF LEARNING EXERCISES

1. See if you can identify the value chain relationships that make Outback Steakhouse's different restaurant businesses (listed below) related in competitively relevant ways. In particular, you should consider whether there are cross-business opportunities for (*a*) skills/technology transfer, (*b*) combining related value chain activities to achieve lower costs, and/or (*c*) leveraging use of a well-respected brand name.
    - Outback Steakhouse
    - Carrabba's Italian Grill
    - Roy's Restaurant (Hawaiian fusion cuisine)
    - Bonefish Grill (market-fresh fine seafood)
    - Fleming's Prime Steakhouse & Wine Bar
    - Lee Roy Selmon's (Southern comfort food)
    - Cheeseburger in Paradise
    - Blue Coral Seafood & Spirits (fine seafood)
2. Go to Unilever's Web site (www.unilever.com) and peruse the company's lineup of brands and businesses. Is Unilever's strategy best characterized as one of related diversification, unrelated diversification, or a combination of related and unrelated diversification? Be prepared to justify and explain your answer in terms of the extent to which the value chains of Unilever's different businesses seem to have competitively valuable cross-business relationships.
3. Go to the Web site of the diversified luxury goods company LVMH (www.lvmh.com) and peruse the company's lineup of luxury brands and businesses. Is LVMH's strategy best characterized as one of related diversification, unrelated diversification, or a combination of related and unrelated diversification? Do you see any

competitively valuable cross-business relationships at LVMH? Might the expertise of LVMH's corporate executives in managing a portfolio of luxury brands be valuable to each of the business/brands and also act to help build added value for LVMH shareholders? Why or why not?

4. The defining characteristic of unrelated diversification is few competitively valuable cross-business relationships. Peruse the business group listings for Lancaster Colony below and see if you can confirm why it is pursuing an unrelated diversification strategy.

- Specialty food products: Cardini, Marzetti, Girard's, and Pheiffer salad dressings; Chatham Village croutons; Jack Daniels mustards; Inn Maid noodles; and Romanoff caviar
- Candle-lite brand candles marketed to retailers and private-label customer chains
- Glassware, plasticware, coffee urns, and matting products marketed to the food service and lodging industries

If you need additional information about Lancaster Colony's business lineup to determine its strategy to answer the question, visit the company's Web site (www.lancastercolony.com).

5. The Walt Disney Company is in the following businesses:

- Theme parks
- Disney Cruise Line
- Resort properties
- Movie, video, and theatrical productions (for both children and adults)
- Television broadcasting (ABC, Disney Channel, Toon Disney, Classic Sports Network, ESPN and ESPN2, E!, Lifetime, and A&E networks)
- Radio broadcasting (Disney Radio)
- Musical recordings and sales of animation art
- Anaheim Mighty Ducks NHL franchise
- Anaheim Angels Major League Baseball franchise (25 percent ownership)
- Books and magazine publishing
- Interactive software and Internet sites
- The Disney Store retail shops

Based on the above list, would you say that Walt Disney's business lineup reflects a strategy of related diversification, unrelated diversification, or a combination of related and unrelated diversification? Be prepared to justify and explain your answer in terms of the extent to which the value chains of Disney's different businesses seem to have competitively valuable cross-business relationships.

6. The Jarden Corporation has recently acquired a number of businesses that

- Völkl and K2 ski equipment
- Mr. Coffee coffemakers
- Rival, VillaWare, and Crock-Pot cookware
- Shakespeare and Penn fishing rods and reels
- Marmot and ExOfficio outdoor apparel
- Coleman camping equipment

- Rawlins sporting goods
- Hoyle playing cards
- Ball jars (used for home canning)
- Bionaire and Holmes humidifiers, fans, and other home comfort products
- Healthometer scales
- Jarden zinc and electroplated products
- First Alert alarm systems

Based on the above list, would you say that Jarden's acquisition strategy involves the pursuit of related diversification, unrelated diversification, or a combination of both? Explain.

7. General Electric recently organized its broadly diversified lineup of products and services into the following six business groups:

    - GE Commercial Finance: commercial and consumer finance (loans, operating leases, financing programs and financial services provided to corporations, retailers, and consumers in 35 countries)—revenues of $34.3 billion in 2007.
    - GE Healthcare: medical imaging and information technologies, medical diagnostics, patient monitoring systems, disease research, drug discovery and biopharmaceuticals—revenues of $17 billion in 2007.
    - GE Industrial: consumer appliances, lighting, and electrical equipment; industrial automation hardware and software, controls, sensors, and security systems—revenues of $17.7 billion in 2007.
    - GE Infrastructure: jet engines for military and civil aircraft, freight and passenger locomotives, motorized systems for mining trucks and drills, and gas turbines for marine and industrial applications, electric power generation equipment, power transformers, high-voltage breakers, distribution transformers and breakers, capacitors, relays, regulators, substation equipment, metering products, water treatment and purification—revenues of $57.9 billion in 2007.
    - GE Money: credit cards, consumer personal loans, automobile loans, mortgage loans—revenues of $25 billion in 2007.
    - NBC Universal: owns and operates the NBC television network, a Spanish-language network (Telemundo), several news and entertainment networks (CNBC, MSNBC, Bravo, Sci-Fi Channel, Sleuth, USA Network), Universal Pictures, Universal Studios Home Entertainment, various television production operations, several special interest Internet sites; a group of television stations, and theme parks—revenues of $15.4 billion in 2007.

    a. Is GE's diversified business lineup best characterized as unrelated diversification or a combination of related and unrelated diversification?

    b. Is GE more accurately categorized as a dominant business-enterprise or a broadly diversified conglomerate or something else?

    c. Do you see any strategic-fit opportunities in GE's business lineup? Are these strategic-fit opportunities, if any, more within each of the six business groupings or do they cut across the six business groupings? Explain.

EXERCISES FOR SIMULATION PARTICIPANTS

1. If your company can diversify into multiple products/businesses, are the diversification opportunities best characterized as related or unrelated? Explain. If the diversification opportunities are related, what precisely are the strategic-fit relationships that are available for capture?
2. Irrespective of whether your company has the option to diversify into other products/businesses, what specific resources does your company have that would make it attractive to diversify into related businesses? List as many resource strengths as you think are transferable to other businesses and also indicate what kinds of strategic-fit benefits could be captured with these resource strengths.
3. Assuming your company has the option to diversify into other products or businesses of your choosing, would you prefer to pursue a strategy of related or unrelated diversification? Why?

CHAPTER

9

Ethical Business Strategies, Social Responsibility, and Environmental Sustainability

LEARNING OBJECTIVES

1. Understand why business conduct is judged according to the ethical standards of society at large rather than a special set of ethical standards for businesses only.
2. Understand the principal drivers of unethical strategies and business behavior.
3. Learn why unethical business conduct can be very costly for a company's shareholders.
4. Become familiar with the various approaches to managing a company's ethical conduct.
5. Gain an understanding of the concepts of corporate social responsibility, corporate citizenship, and environmental sustainability.
6. Become familiar with both the moral case and the business case for ethical business conduct and socially responsible business behavior.

When morality comes up against profit, it is seldom profit that loses.

—Shirley Chisholm
Former Congresswoman

But I'd shut my eyes in the sentry box so I didn't see nothing wrong.

—Rudyard Kipling
"The Shut-Eye Sentry"

Corporations are economic entities, to be sure, but they are also social institutions that must justify their existence by their overall contribution to society.

—Henry Mintzberg, Robert Simons, and Kunal Basu
Professors

Integrity violations are no-brainers. In such cases, you don't need to hesitate for a moment before firing someone or fret about it either. Just do it, and make sure the organization knows why, so that the consequences of breaking the rules are not lost on anyone.

—Jack Welch
Former CEO, General Electric

There is one and only one social responsibility of business—to use its resources and engage in activities designed to increase its profits so long as it stays within the rules of the game, which is to say engages in free and open competition, without deception or fraud.

—Milton Friedman
Nobel Prize–winning Economist

Clearly, a company has a responsibility to make a profit and grow the business—in capitalistic or market economies, management's fiduciary duty to create value for shareholders is not a matter for serious debate. Just as clearly, a company and its personnel also have a duty to obey the law and play by the rules of fair competition. But does a company have a duty to operate according to the ethical norms of the societies in which it operates—should it be held to some standard of ethical conduct? And does it have a duty or obligation to contribute to the betterment of society independent of the needs and preferences of the customers it serves? Should a company display a social conscience and devote a portion of its resources to bettering society? Should a company alter its business practices to help protect the environment and sustain the world's natural resources?

The focus of this chapter is to examine what link, if any, there should be between a company's efforts to craft and execute a winning strategy and its duties to (1) conduct its activities in an ethical manner; (2) demonstrate socially responsible behavior by being a committed corporate citizen and directing corporate resources to the betterment of employees, the communities in which it operates, and society as a whole; and (3) limit its strategic initiatives to those that meet the needs of consumers without depleting resources needed by future generations.

WHAT DO WE MEAN BY *BUSINESS ETHICS?*

CORE CONCEPT
Business ethics **concerns the application of general ethical principles and standards to the actions and decisions of companies and the conduct of company personnel.**

Business ethics is the application of ethical principles and standards to business behavior.[1] Ethical principles in business are not materially different from ethical principles in general because business actions have to be judged in the context of society's standards of right and wrong. There is not a special set of ethical standards or guidelines that businesspeople can decide to apply to their own conduct. If dishonesty is considered to be unethical and immoral, then dishonest behavior in business—whether it relates to customers, suppliers, employees, or shareholders—qualifies as equally unethical and immoral. If being ethical entails not deliberately harming others, then recalling a defective or unsafe product is ethically necessary and failing to undertake such a recall or correct the problem in future shipments of the product is likewise unethical. If society deems bribery to be unethical, then it is unethical for company personnel to make payoffs to government officials to facilitate business transactions or bestow gifts and other favors on prospective customers to win or retain their business. In short, ethical behavior in business situations requires adhering to generally accepted norms about conduct that determine whether an action is right or wrong. As a consequence, company managers have an obligation—indeed, a duty—to observe ethical norms when crafting and executing strategy.

How and Why Ethical Standards Impact the Tasks of Crafting and Executing Strategy

Many companies have acknowledged their ethical obligations in official codes and values statements. In the United States, for example, the Sarbanes-Oxley Act, passed in 2002, requires that companies whose stock is publicly traded have a code of ethics or else explain in writing to the Securities and Exchange Commission (SEC) why they do not. But there's a big difference between having a code of ethics that serves merely as public window dressing and having ethical standards that truly paint the white lines for a company's actual strategy and business conduct.[2] *The litmus test of a company's code of ethics is the extent to which it is embraced in crafting strategy and in operating the business day to day.*

It is up to senior executives to walk the talk and make a point of considering two sets of questions whenever a new strategic initiative is under review:

- Is what we are proposing to do fully compliant with our code of ethical conduct? Is there anything here that could be considered ethically objectionable?
- Is it apparent that this proposed action is in harmony with our core values? Are any conflicts or concerns evident?

Unless questions of this nature are posed—either in open discussion or by force of habit in the minds of strategy makers—then there's room for strategic initiatives to become disconnected from the company's code of ethics and stated core values. If a company's executives believe strongly in living up to the company's stated core values, there's a good chance they will unhesitatingly reject strategic initiatives and operating approaches that don't measure up. However, in companies with window-dressing ethics and core values, any strategy-ethics-values linkage stems mainly from a desire to avoid the risks of embarrassment and of possible disciplinary action should strategy makers be held accountable for approving a strategic initiative that is deemed by society to be unethical or perhaps illegal.

While most company managers are usually careful to ensure that a company's strategy is legal, the available evidence indicates they are not always so careful to ensure that all elements of their strategies and operating activities are within the bounds of what is generally deemed ethical. In recent years, there have been revelations of ethical misconduct on the part of managers at such companies as Enron, Tyco International, HealthSouth, Rite Aid, Citicorp, Bristol-Myers Squibb, Adelphia, Royal Dutch/Shell, the Italy-based food products company Parmalat, the Mexican oil giant Pemex, Marsh & McLennan and other insurance brokers, several leading brokerage houses and investment banking firms, and a host of mutual fund companies. In 2005, four global companies—Samsung and Hynix Semiconductor in South Korea, Infineon Technologies in Germany, and Micron Technology in the United States—pleaded guilty to conspiring to fix the prices of dynamic random access memory (DRAM) chips sold to such companies as Dell, Apple, and Hewlett-Packard. Alstom SA, a giant France-based engineering firm and maker of power plant turbines and high-speed trains and subway cars, has been accused by French and Swiss prosecutors of using a Swiss slush fund to pay $500 million in bribes to foreign officials to win contracts abroad during 2001–2008; executives at Siemens AG of Germany, one of Alstom's competitors, have been charged by German authorities with paying bribes of about $2 billion to win large contracts in 12 foreign countries during 2000–2006. Much of the crisis in residential real estate that emerged in the United States in 2007–2008 stemmed from consciously unethical strategies at certain banks and mortgage companies to boost the fees they earned on processing home mortgage applications by deliberately lowering lending standards and finding ways to secure mortgage approvals for home buyers who lacked sufficient income to make their monthly mortgage payments. Once these lenders earned their fees on the so-called subprime loans (a term used for high-risk mortgage loans made to home buyers with dubious qualifications to repay the loans), they secured the assistance of investment banking firms to bundle those and other mortgages into collateralized debt obligations (CDOs), found means of having the CDOs assigned triple-A bond ratings, and auctioned them to unsuspecting investors, who later suffered huge losses when the high-risk borrowers began to default on their loan payments and foreclosure procedures had to be initiated (government authorities later forced some of the firms that auctioned off these CDOs to repurchase them at the auction price and bear the losses themselves).

The consequences of crafting strategies that cannot pass the test of moral scrutiny are manifested in sharp drops in stock prices that cost shareholders billions of dollars, devastating public relations hits, sizable fines, and criminal indictments and convictions of company executives. The fallout from recent business scandals has resulted in heightened management attention to legal and ethical considerations in crafting strategy.

WHERE DO ETHICAL STANDARDS COME FROM—ARE

AND SITUATIONAL CIRCUMSTANCES?

Notions of right and wrong, fair and unfair, moral and immoral, ethical and unethical are present in all societies, organizations, and individuals. But there are three schools of thought about the extent to which the ethical standards travel across cultures and whether multinational companies can apply the same set of ethical standards in any and all of the locations where they operate.

The School of Ethical Universalism

CORE CONCEPT
According to the school of ***ethical universalism,*** the same standards of what's ethical and what's unethical resonate with peoples of most societies regardless of local traditions and cultural norms; hence, common ethical standards can be used to judge the conduct of personnel at companies operating in a variety of country markets and cultural circumstances.

According to the school of **ethical universalism,** some concepts of what is right and what is wrong are *universal* and transcend most cultures, societies, and religions.[3] For instance, being truthful (or not lying or not being deliberately deceitful) strikes a chord of what's right in the peoples of all nations. Likewise, demonstrating integrity of character, not cheating, and treating people with dignity and respect are concepts that resonate with people of most cultures and religions. In most societies, people believe that companies should not pillage or degrade the environment in the course of conducting their operations. In most societies, people would concur that it is unethical to knowingly expose workers to toxic chemicals and hazardous materials or to sell products known to be unsafe or harmful to the users. *To the extent there is common moral agreement about right and wrong actions and behaviors across multiple cultures and countries, there exists a set of universal ethical standards to which all societies, all companies, and all individuals can be held accountable.*

Ethical norms considered universal by many ethicists include honesty, trustworthiness, respecting the rights of others, practicing the Golden Rule (i.e., treat others as you would like to be treated), exercising due diligence in product safety, and not acting in a manner that harms others or pillages the environment. These universal ethical principles or norms put limits on what actions and behaviors fall inside the boundaries of what is right and which ones fall outside; they set forth the traits and behaviors that a virtuous person is supposed to believe in and to display.[4] Adherents of the school of ethical universalism maintain that the conduct of personnel at companies operating in a variety of country markets and cultural circumstances can be judged against this set of universal ethical standards.

The strength of ethical universalism is that it draws on the collective views of multiple societies and cultures to put some clear boundaries on business behavior no matter what country market or culture a company or its personnel are operating in. This means that in those instances where basic moral standards really do not vary significantly according to local cultural beliefs, traditions, religious convictions, or time and circumstance, a multinational company can develop a code of ethics that it applies more or less evenly across its worldwide operations.[5] It can avoid the slippery slope that comes from having different ethical standards for different company personnel depending on where in the world they are working.

The School of Ethical Relativism

CORE CONCEPT
According to the school of ***ethical relativism*** different societal cultures and customs have divergent values and standards of right and wrong—thus what is ethical or unethical must be judged in the light of local customs and social mores and can vary from one culture or nation to another.

But apart from select universal basics—honesty, trustworthiness, fairness, a regard for worker safety, and respect for the environment—there are meaningful variations in what societies generally agree to be right and wrong in the conduct of business activities. Divergent religious beliefs, historic traditions, social customs, and prevailing political and economic doctrines (whether a country leans more toward a capitalistic market economy or one heavily dominated by socialistic or communistic principles) frequently produce ethical norms that vary from one country to another. The school of **ethical relativism** holds that when there are cross-country or cross-cultural differences in what is deemed ethical or unethical in business situations, it is appropriate for local moral standards to take precedence over what the ethical standards may be elsewhere—for instance, in a company's home market.

The thesis is that whatever a culture thinks is right or wrong really is right or wrong for that culture.[6] Consider the following examples.

The Use of Underage Labor In industrialized nations, the use of child workers is considered taboo; social activists are adamant that child labor is unethical and that companies should neither employ children under the age of 18 as full-time nor source any products from foreign suppliers that employ underage workers. Many countries have passed legislation forbidding the use of underage labor or, at a minimum, regulating the employment of people under 18. However, in India, Bangladesh, Botswana, Sri Lanka, Ghana, Somalia, Turkey, and 100-plus other countries, it is customary to view children as potential, even necessary, workers. Many poverty-stricken families cannot subsist without the income earned by young family members; sending their children to school instead of having them work is not a realistic option. In 2006, the International Labor Organization estimated that 191 million children ages 5 to 14 were working around the world.[7] If such children are not permitted to work—due to pressures imposed by activist groups in industrialized nations—they may be forced to take lower-wage jobs in "hidden" parts of the economy, to go out on the street begging, or even to traffic in drugs or engage in prostitution.[8] So if all businesses succumb to the protests of activist groups and government organizations that, based on their values and beliefs, loudly proclaim that underage labor is unethical, then have either businesses or the protesting groups really done something good on behalf of society in general?

The Payment of Bribes and Kickbacks A particularly thorny issue facing multinational companies is the degree of cross-country variability in paying bribes.[9] In many countries in Eastern Europe, Africa, Latin America, and Asia, it is customary to pay bribes to government officials in order to win a government contract, obtain a license or permit, or facilitate an administrative ruling.[10] Senior managers in China often use their power to obtain kickbacks and offer bribes when they purchase materials or other products for their companies.[11] In some developing nations, it is difficult for any company, foreign or domestic, to move goods through customs without paying off low-level officials.[12] Some people stretch to justify the payment of bribes and kickbacks on grounds that bribing government officials to get goods through customs or giving kickbacks to customers to retail their business or win an order is simply a payment for services rendered, in the same way that people tip for service at restaurants.[13] But even though it is a clever and pragmatic rationalization, this argument rests on moral quicksand.

Companies that forbid the payment of bribes and kickbacks in their codes of ethical conduct and that are serious about enforcing this prohibition face a particularly vexing problem in those countries where bribery and kickback payments have been entrenched as a local custom for decades and are not considered unethical by the local population.[14] Refusing to pay bribes or kickbacks (so as to comply with the company's

ethical companies and ethical individuals are penalized. On the other hand, the payment of bribes or kickbacks not only undercuts enforcement of and adherence to the company's code of ethics but can also risk breaking the law. U.S. companies are prohibited by the Foreign Corrupt Practices Act (FCPA) from paying bribes to government officials, political parties, political candidates, or others in all countries where they do business; the FCPA requires U.S. companies with foreign operations to adopt accounting practices that ensure full disclosure of a company's transactions so that illegal payments can be detected. The 35 member countries of the Organization for Economic Cooperation and Development (OECD) in 1997 adopted a convention to combat bribery in international business transactions; the Anti-Bribery Convention obligated the countries to criminalize the bribery of foreign public officials, including payments made to political parties and party officials. However, so far there has been only token enforcement of the OECD convention and the payment of bribes in global business transactions remains a common practice in many countries.

Ethical Relativism Equates to Multiple Sets of Ethical Standards The existence of varying ethical norms such as those cited above explains why the adherents of ethical relativism maintain that there are few absolutes when it comes to business ethics and thus few ethical absolutes for consistently judging a company's conduct in various countries and markets. Indeed, the thesis of ethical relativists is that while there are sometimes general moral prescriptions that apply in most every society and business circumstance, there are plenty of situations where ethical norms must be contoured to fit the local customs, traditions, and the notions of fairness shared by the parties involved. They argue that a "one-size-fits-all" template for judging the ethical appropriateness of business actions and the behaviors of company personnel simply does not exist—in other words, ethical problems in business cannot be fully resolved without appealing to the shared convictions of the parties in question.[15] European and American managers may want to impose standards of business conduct that give heavy weight to such core human rights as personal freedom, individual security, political participation, the ownership of property, and the right to subsistence as well as the obligation to respect the dignity of each human person, provide a safe workplace, and respect the environment; managers in China have a much weaker commitment to these kinds of human rights. Japanese managers may prefer ethical standards that show respect for the collective good of society. Muslim managers may wish to apply ethical standards compatible with the teachings of Mohammed. Individual companies may want to give explicit recognition to the importance of company personnel living up to the company's own espoused values and business principles. Clearly, there is merit in the school of ethical relativism's view that what is deemed right or wrong, fair or unfair, moral or immoral, ethical or unethical in business situations depends partly on the context of each country's local customs, religious traditions, and societal norms. Hence, there is a kernel of truth in the argument that businesses need some room to tailor their ethical standards to fit local situations. A company has to be cautious about exporting its home-country values and ethics to foreign countries where it operates—"photocopying" ethics is disrespectful of other cultures and neglects the important role of moral free space.

Under ethical relativism, there can be no one-size-fits-all set of authentic ethical norms against which to gauge the conduct of company personnel.

Pushed to Extremes, Ethical Relativism Breaks Down While the ethically relativist rule of "When in Rome, do as the Romans do" appears reasonable, it nonetheless presents a big problem—when the envelope starts to be pushed, as will inevitably be the case, *it is tantamount to rudderless ethical standards.* Consider, for instance, the following example: In 1992, the owners of the SS *United States,* an aging luxury ocean liner constructed with asbestos in the 1940s, had the liner towed to Turkey, where a contractor had agreed to remove the asbestos for $2 million (versus a far higher cost in the United States, where asbestos removal safety standards were much more stringent).[16] When Turkish officials blocked the asbestos removal because of the dangers to workers of contracting cancer, the owners had the liner towed to the Black Sea port of Sevastopol, in the Crimean Republic, where the asbestos removal standards were quite lax and where a contractor had agreed to remove more than 500,000 square feet of carcinogenic asbestos for less than $2 million. There are no moral grounds for arguing that exposing workers to carcinogenic asbestos is ethically correct, irrespective of what a country's law allows or the value the country places on worker safety.

A company that adopts the principle of ethical relativism and holds company personnel to local ethical standards necessarily assumes that what prevails as local morality is an adequate guide to ethical behavior. This can be ethically dangerous—it leads to the conclusion that if a country's culture is accepting of bribery or environmental degradation or exposing workers to dangerous conditions (toxic chemicals or bodily harm), then so much the worse for honest people and protection of the environment and safe working conditions. Such a position is morally unacceptable. Even though bribery of government officials in China is a common practice, when Lucent Technologies found that managers in its Chinese operations had bribed government officials, it fired the entire senior management team.[17]

Managers in multinational enterprises have to figure out how to navigate the gray zone that arises when operating in two cultures with two sets of ethics.

Moreover, from a global markets perspective, ethical relativism results in a maze of conflicting ethical standards for multinational companies wanting to address the very real issue of what ethical standards to enforce companywide. It is a slippery slope indeed to resolve such ethical diversity without any kind of higher-order moral compass. Imagine, for example, that a multinational company says it is okay for company personnel to pay bribes and kickbacks in countries where such payments are customary but not okay in countries where they are considered unethical or illegal. Or that the company says it is fine to use child labor in its plants in those countries where underage labor is acceptable but not fine to employ child labor at the remainder of its plants. Having thus adopted conflicting ethical standards for operating in different countries, company managers have little moral basis for enforcing ethical standards companywide—rather, the clear message to employees would be that the company has no ethical standards or principles of its own. This is scarcely strong moral ground to stand on.

Ethics and Integrative Social Contracts Theory

Social contract theory provides a middle position between the opposing views of universalism (that the same set of ethical standards should apply everywhere) and relativism (that ethical standards vary according to local custom).[18] According to **integrative social contracts theory,** the ethical standards a company should try to uphold are governed both by (1) a limited number of universal ethical principles that are widely recognized as putting legitimate ethical boundaries on actions and behavior in *all* situations and (2) the circumstances of local cultures, traditions, and shared values that further prescribe what constitutes ethically permissible behavior and what does not. *The uniform agreements about what is morally right and* [illegible] *behaviors.* But these universal ethical principles or norms nonetheless still leave some "moral free space" for the people in a particular country (or local culture or even a company) to make specific interpretations of what other actions may or may not be permissible within the bounds defined by universal ethical principles. Hence, while firms, industries, professional associations, and other business-relevant groups are "contractually obligated"

CORE CONCEPT
According to ***integrative social contracts theory,*** universal ethical principles or norms based on the collective views of multiple cultures and societies combine to form a "social contract" that all individuals in all situations have [illegible] tract, local cultures or groups can specify other impermissible actions; however, universal ethical norms always take precedence over local ethical norms.

to society to observe universal ethical norms, they have the discretion to go beyond these universal norms and specify other behaviors that are out of bounds and place further limitations on what is considered ethical. Both the legal and medical professions have standards regarding what kinds of advertising are ethically permissible and what kinds are not. Food producers are beginning to establish ethical guidelines for judging what is and is not appropriate advertising for food products that are inherently unhealthy and may cause dietary or obesity problems for people who eat them regularly or consume them in large quantities. Likewise, fast-food chains and restaurants are beginning to exhibit ethical concerns about the calorie content and nutritional value of their menu offerings.

The strength of integrative social contracts theory is that it accommodates the best parts of ethical universalism and ethical relativism. It is indisputable that cultural differences impact how business is conducted in various parts of the world and that these cultural differences sometimes give rise to different ethical norms. But it is just as indisputable that some ethical norms are more authentic or universally applicable than others, meaning that in many instances of cross-country differences one side may be more "ethically correct" than another. In circumstances where local ethical norms are more permissive, resolving the conflict between universal, or "first-order," ethical norms and local, or "second-order," ethical norms *requires* adhering to universal ethical norms and overriding local ethical norms. A good example is the payment of bribes and kickbacks. Yes, bribes and kickbacks seem to be common in some countries, but does this justify paying them? Just because bribery flourishes in a country does not mean that it is an authentic or legitimate ethical norm. Virtually all of the world's major religions (Buddhism, Christianity, Confucianism, Hinduism, Islam, Judaism, Sikhism, and Taoism) and all moral schools of thought condemn bribery and corruption.[19] Bribery is commonplace in India, but, in one set of interviews, Indian CEOs whose companies constantly engaged in payoffs indicated their disgust for the practice and expressed no illusions about its impropriety.[20] Therefore, a multinational company might reasonably conclude that the right ethical standard is one of refusing to condone bribery and kickbacks on the part of company personnel no matter what the local custom is and no matter what the sales consequences are.

Granting an automatic preference to local ethical norms presents vexing problems to multinational company managers when the ethical standards followed in a foreign country are lower than those in its home country or are in conflict with the company's code of ethics. Sometimes—as with bribery and kickbacks—there can be no compromise on what is ethically permissible and what is not. *This is precisely what integrative social contracts theory maintains: Adherence to universal or first-order ethical norms should always take precedence over local or second-order norms.* Consequently, integrative social contracts theory offers managers in multinational companies some valuable guidance in dealing with different ethical standards in different countries: those parts of the company's code of ethics that involve universal ethical norms must be enforced worldwide, but *within these boundaries* ethical diversity is acceptable and there is room for company personnel to observe the moral and ethical standards of host country cultures. Such an accommodation of the second-order ethical norms in various countries detours the somewhat scary case of a self-righteous multinational company trying to operate as the standard-bearer of moral truth and imposing its interpretation of its code of ethics worldwide no matter what. And it avoids the equally scary case for a company's ethical conduct to be no higher than local ethical norms in situations where local ethical norms permit practices that are generally considered immoral or when local norms clearly conflict with a company's code of ethical conduct. But even with the guidance provided by integrative social contracts theory, there are many instances where cross-country differences in ethical norms create "gray areas" where it is tough to draw a line in the sand between right and wrong decisions, actions, and business practices.

THE THREE CATEGORIES OF MANAGEMENT MORALITY

Three categories of managers stand out with regard to ethical and moral principles in business affairs:[21]

- *The moral manager*—Moral managers are dedicated to high standards of ethical behavior, both in their own actions and in their expectations of how the company's business is to be conducted. They see themselves as stewards of ethical behavior and believe it is important to exercise ethical leadership. Moral managers may well be ambitious and have a powerful urge to succeed, but they pursue success in business within the confines of both the letter and the spirit of what is ethical and legal—they typically regard the law as an ethical minimum and have a habit of operating well above what the law requires.
- *The immoral manager*—Immoral managers have no regard for so-called ethical standards in business and pay no attention to ethical principles in making decisions and conducting the company's business. Their philosophy is that good business-people cannot spend time watching out for the interests of others and agonizing over "the ethically correct thing to do." In the minds of immoral managers, nice guys come in second and the competitive nature of business requires that you either trample on others or get trampled yourself. They believe what really matters is single-minded pursuit of their own best interests—they are living examples of self-serving greed, caring only about their own or their organization's gains and successes. Immoral managers may even be willing to short-circuit legal and regulatory requirements if they think they can escape detection. And they are always on the lookout for legal loopholes and creative ways to get around rules and regulations that block or constrain actions they deem in their own or their company's self-interest. Immoral managers are thus the bad guys—they have few scruples, little or no integrity, and are willing to do most anything they believe they can get away with. It doesn't bother them much to be seen by others as wearing the black hats.
- *The amoral manager*—Amoral managers appear in two forms: the intentionally amoral manager and the unintentionally amoral manager. Intentionally amoral managers are of the strong opinion that business and ethics are not to be mixed. They are not troubled by failing to factor ethical considerations into their decisions and actions because it is perfectly legitimate for businesses to do anything they wish so long as they stay within legal and regulatory bounds—in other words, if particular actions and behaviors are legal and comply with existing regulations, then they qualify as permissible and should not be seen as unethical. Intentionally amoral managers [illegible] considerations may be appropriate in life outside of business. Their concept of right and wrong tends to be lawyer-driven—"How much can we get by with?" and "Can we go ahead even if it is borderline?" Like immoral managers, intentionally amoral managers hold firmly to the view that anything goes, but differ from immoral managers in that they acknowledge that business actions and behaviors must comply with prevailing legal and regulatory requirements.

Unintentionally amoral managers do not pay much attention to the concept of business ethics either, but for different reasons. They are simply casual about, careless about, or inattentive to the fact that certain kinds of business decisions or company activities are unsavory or may have deleterious effects on others—in short, they go about their jobs as best they can without giving serious thought to the ethical dimension of decisions and business actions. They are ethically unconscious when it comes to business matters, partly or mainly because they have just never stopped to consider whether and to what extent business decisions or company actions sometimes spill over to create adverse impacts on others. Unintentionally amoral managers may even see themselves as people of integrity and as personally ethical. But their behaviors and actions send the message to subordinates that businesses ought to be able to do whatever the current legal and regulatory framework allows them to do without being shackled by ethical considerations.

CORE CONCEPT

Amoral managers believe that businesses ought to be able to do whatever current laws and regulations allow them to do without being shackled by ethical considerations—they think that what is permissible and what is not is governed entirely by prevailing laws and regulations, not by societal concepts of right and wrong.

By some accounts, the population of managers is distributed among all three types in a bell-shaped curve, with immoral managers and moral managers occupying the two tails of the curve, and the amoral managers (especially the intentionally amoral managers) occupying the broad middle ground.[22] Furthermore, within the population of managers, there is experiential evidence that while the average manager may be amoral most of the time, he or she may slip into a moral or immoral mode on occasion, given impinging factors and circumstances.

Evidence of Managerial Immorality in the Global Business Community

There is considerable evidence that a sizable majority of managers are either amoral or immoral. Recent issues of the *Global Corruption Report* sponsored by Berlin-based Transparency International present credible evidence that corruption among public officials and in business transactions is widespread across the world. Table 9.1 shows some of the countries where corruption is believed to be lowest and highest. This same report also presents data showing the perceived likelihood that companies in large exporting countries are paying bribes to win business in the markets of such countries as Argentina, Brazil, Colombia, Hungary, India, Indonesia, Mexico, Morocco, Nigeria, the Philippines, Poland, Russia, South Africa, South Korea, and Thailand. Bribery seems to occur most often in (1) public works contracts and construction, (2) the arms and defense industry, and (3) the oil and gas industry. Corruption, of course, extends beyond just bribes and kickbacks; price-fixing, securities fraud, and efforts to skirt regulations relating to the payment of minimum wages, use of child labor, and environmental protection are three other areas where unethical behavior is common.

A global business community that is apparently so populated with unethical business practices and managerial immorality leaves scant basis for concluding that most companies ground their strategies on exemplary ethical principles or that company managers diligently try to ingrain ethical behavior into company personnel. And as many business school professors have noted, there are considerable numbers of amoral business students in our classrooms. So efforts to root out shady and corrupt business practices and implant high ethical principles into the managerial

TABLE 9.1 Corruption Perceptions Index (CPI), Selected Countries, 2007

Country	2007 CPI Score*	High–Low Range	Number of Surveys Used
Finland	9.4	9.2–9.6	6
New Zealand	9.4	9.2–9.6	6
Denmark	9.4	9.2–9.6	6
Singapore	9.3	9.0–9.5	9
Sweden	9.3	9.1–9.4	6
Iceland	9.2	8.3–9.6	6
Netherlands	9.0	8.8–9.2	6
Switzerland	9.0	8.8–9.4	6
Canada	8.7	8.3–9.1	6
Norway	8.7	8.0–9.2	6
Australia	8.6	8.1–9.0	8
United Kingdom	8.4	7.9–8.9	6
Hong Kong	8.3	7.6–8.8	8
Germany	7.8	7.3–8.4	6
Japan	7.5	7.1–8.0	8
France	7.3	6.9–7.8	6
United States	7.2	6.5–7.6	8
Chile	7.0	6.5–7.4	7
Spain	6.7	6.2–7.0	6
Israel	6.1	5.6–6.7	6
United Arab Emirates	5.7	4.8–6.5	5
Taiwan	5.7	5.4–6.1	9
Italy	5.2	4.7–5.7	6
Malaysia	5.1	4.5–5.7	9
South Africa	5.1	4.9–5.5	9
South Korea	5.1	4.7–5.5	9
Turkey	4.1	3.8–4.5	7
Romania	3.7	3.4–4.1	8
Brazil	3.5	3.2–4.0	7
China	3.5	3.0–4.2	9
India	3.5	3.3–3.7	10
Mexico	3.5	3.3–3.8	7
Saudi Arabia	3.4	2.7–3.9	4
Thailand	3.3	2.9–3.7	9
Argentina	2.9	2.6–3.2	7
Vietnam	2.6	2.4–2.9	9
Pakistan	2.4	2.0–2.8	7
Russia	2.3	2.1–2.6	8
Nigeria	2.2	2.0–2.4	8
Venezuela	2.0	1.9–2.1	7
Somalia	1.4	1.1–1.7	4
Myanmar	1.4	1.1–1.7	4

**Note:* The CPI scores range between 10 (highly clean) and 0 (highly corrupt); the data were collected between 2006 and 2007 and represent a composite of 14 polls and surveys from 12 independent institutions. The CPI score represents the perceptions of the degree of corruption as seen by businesspeople, academics, and risk analysts. CPI scores were reported for 180 countries.

Source: Transparency International, *2008 Global Corruption Report,* www.globalcorruptionreport.org (accessed July 30, 2008), pp. 296–302.

process of crafting and executing strategy is unlikely to produce an ethically strong global business climate anytime soon, barring perhaps further scandals resulting in a major effort to address and correct the ethical laxness of company managers.

DRIVERS OF UNETHICAL STRATEGIES AND BUSINESS BEHAVIOR

The apparent pervasiveness of immoral and amoral businesspeople is one obvious reason why ethical principles are an ineffective moral compass in business dealings and

[illegible] stand out:

- Faulty oversight by top management and the board of directors that implicitly allows the overzealous pursuit of personal gain, wealth, and other self-interests.
- Heavy pressures on company managers to meet or beat performance targets.
- A company culture that puts profitability and "good" business performance ahead of ethical behavior.

Overzealous Pursuit of Personal Gain, Wealth, and Self-Interest

People who are obsessed with wealth accumulation, greed, power, status, and other self-interests often push ethical principles aside in their quest for personal gain. Driven by their ambitions, they exhibit few qualms in skirting the rules or doing whatever is necessary to achieve their goals. A general disregard for business ethics can prompt all kinds of unethical strategic maneuvers and behaviors at companies. Top executives, directors, and majority shareholders at cable-TV company Adelphia Communications ripped off the company for amounts totaling well over $1 billion, diverting hundreds of millions of dollars to fund their Buffalo Sabres hockey team, build a private golf course, and buy timber rights—among other things—and driving the company into bankruptcy. Their actions, which represent one of the biggest instances of corporate looting and self-dealing in American business, took place despite the company's public pontifications about the principles it would observe in trying to care for customers, employees, stockholders, and the local communities where it operated. Andrew Fastow, Enron's chief financial officer (CFO), set himself up as the manager of one of Enron's off-the-books partnerships and as the part-owner of another, allegedly earning extra compensation of $30 million for his owner-manager roles in the two partnerships; Enron's board of directors agreed to suspend the company's conflict-of-interest rules designed to protect the company from this very kind of executive self-dealing.

According to a civil complaint filed by the Securities and Exchange Commission (SEC), the chief executive officer (CEO) of Tyco International, a well-known $35.6 billion manufacturing and services company, conspired with the company's CFO to steal more than $170 million, including a company-paid $2 million birthday party for the CEO's wife held on Sardinia, an island off the coast of Italy; a $7 million Park Avenue apartment for his wife; and secret low-interest and interest-free loans to fund private businesses and investments and purchase lavish artwork, yachts, estate jewelry, and vacation homes in New Hampshire, Connecticut, Massachusetts, and Utah. The CEO allegedly lived rent-free in a $31 million Fifth Avenue apartment that Tyco purchased in his name, directed millions of dollars of charitable contributions in his own name using Tyco funds, diverted company funds to finance his personal businesses and investments, and sold millions of dollars of Tyco stock back to Tyco itself through Tyco subsidiaries located in offshore bank-secrecy jurisdictions. Tyco's CEO and CFO were further charged with conspiring to reap more than $430 million from sales of stock, using questionable accounting to hide their actions, and engaging in deceptive accounting practices to distort the company's financial condition from 1995 to 2002. At the trial on the charges filed by the SEC, the prosecutor told the jury in his opening statement, "This case is about lying, cheating and stealing. These people didn't win the jackpot—they stole it." Defense lawyers countered that "every single transaction . . . was set down in detail in Tyco's books and records" and that the authorized and disclosed multimillion-dollar compensation packages were merited by the company's financial performance and stock price gains. The two Tyco executives were convicted and sentenced to jail.

Ten prominent Wall Street securities firms in 2003 paid $1.4 billion to settle charges that they knowingly issued misleading stock research to investors in an effort to prop up the stock prices of client corporations. A host of mutual-fund firms made under-the-table arrangements to regularly buy and sell stock for their accounts at special after-hours trading prices that disadvantaged long-term investors and had to pay nearly $2.0 billion in fines and restitution when their unethical practices were discovered by authorities during 2002–2003. Salomon Smith Barney, Goldman Sachs, Credit Suisse First Boston, and several other financial firms were assessed close to $2 billion in fines and restitution for the unethical manner in which they contributed to the scandals at Enron and WorldCom (now MCI) and for the shady practice of allocating shares of hot stocks to a select list of corporate executives who either steered or were in a position to steer investment banking business their way.

Heavy Pressures on Company Managers to Meet or Beat Earnings Targets

Performance expectations of Wall Street analysts and investors may create enormous pressure on management to do whatever it takes to sustain the company's reputation for delivering good financial performance. Executives at high-performing companies know that investors will see the slightest sign of a slowdown in earnings growth as a red flag and drive down the company's stock price. In addition, slowing growth or declining profits could lead to a downgrade of the company's credit rating if it has used lots of debt to finance its growth. The pressure to watch the scoreboard and "never miss a quarter"—so as not to upset the expectations of Wall Street analysts and fickle stock market investors—prompts managers to cut costs wherever savings show up immediately, squeeze extra sales out of early deliveries, and engage in other short-term maneuvers to make the numbers. As the pressure builds to "meet or beat the numbers," company personnel start stretching the rules further and further, until the limits of ethical conduct are overlooked.[24]

Several top executives at WorldCom (now MCI), a company built with scores of acquisitions in exchange for WorldCom stock, allegedly concocted a fraudulent $11 billion accounting scheme to hide costs and inflate revenues and profit over several years; the scheme was said to have helped the company keep its stock price propped up high enough to make additional acquisitions, support its nearly $30 billion debt load, and allow executives to cash in on their lucrative stock options. At Qwest Communications, a company created by the merger of a go-go telecom start-up and U.S. West (one of the regional Bell companies), management was charged with scheming to improperly book $2.4 billion in revenues from a variety of sources and deals, thereby inflating the company's profits and making it appear that the company's strategy to create a telecommunications company of the future was on track when, in fact, it was faltering badly behind the scenes. Top-level Qwest executives were dismissed and in 2004 new management agreed to $250 million in fines for all the misdeeds.

At Bristol-Myers Squibb, the world's fifth largest drug maker, management apparently engaged in a series of numbers-game maneuvers to meet earnings targets, including such actions as:

- Offering special [illegible] to spur purchases and beef up operating profits.
- Setting up excessive reserves for restructuring charges and then reversing some of the charges as needed to bolster operating profits.
- Making repeated asset sales small enough that the gains could be reported as additions to operating profit rather than being flagged as one-time gains.

Such numbers games were said to be a common "earnings management" practice at Bristol-Myers and, according to one former executive, "sent a huge message across the organization that you make your numbers at all costs."[25]

Company executives often feel pressured to hit financial performance targets because their compensation depends heavily on the company's performance. During the late 1990s, it became fashionable for boards of directors to grant lavish bonuses, stock option awards, and other compensation benefits to executives for meeting specified performance targets. So outlandishly large were these rewards that executives had strong personal incentives to bend the rules and engage in behaviors that allowed the targets to be met. Much of the accounting hocus-pocus at the root of recent corporate scandals has entailed situations in which executives benefited enormously from misleading accounting or other shady activities that allowed them to hit the numbers and receive incentive awards ranging from $10 million to $100 million. At Bristol-Myers Squibb, for example, the pay-for-performance link spawned strong rules-bending incentives. About 94 percent of one top executive's $18.5 million in total compensation in 2001 came from stock-option grants, a bonus, and long-term incentive payments linked to corporate performance; about 92 percent of a second executive's $12.9 million of compensation was incentive-based.[26]

The fundamental problem with a "make the numbers and move on" syndrome is that a company doesn't really create additional value for customers or improve its competitiveness in the marketplace—these outcomes are the most reliable drivers of higher profits and added shareholder value. Cutting ethical corners or stooping to downright illegal actions in the name of profits first carries exceptionally high risk for shareholders—the steep stock price decline and tarnished brand image that accompany the discovery of scurrilous behavior leaves shareholders with a company worth much less than before—and the rebuilding task can be arduous, taking both considerable time and resources.

Company Cultures That Put the Bottom Line Ahead of Ethical Behavior

When a company's culture spawns an ethically corrupt or amoral work climate, people have a company-approved license to ignore "what's right" and engage in most any behavior or employ most any strategy they think they can get away with.[27] At such companies, ethically immoral or amoral people are given free rein and otherwise honorable people may succumb to the many opportunities around them to engage in unethical practices. A perfect example of a company culture gone awry on ethics is Enron.[28]

Enron's leaders encouraged company personnel to focus on the current bottom line and to be innovative and aggressive in figuring out what could be done to grow current revenues and earnings. Employees were expected to pursue opportunities to the utmost in the electric utility industry, which was undergoing a loosening of regulation. Enron executives viewed the company as a laboratory for innovation; the company hired the best and brightest people and pushed them to be creative, look at problems and opportunities in new ways, and exhibit a sense of urgency in making things happen. Employees were encouraged to make a difference and do their part in creating an entrepreneurial environment where creativity flourished, people could achieve their full potential, and everyone had a stake in the outcome. Enron employees got the message—pushing the limits and meeting one's numbers were viewed as survival skills. Enron's annual "rank and yank" formal evaluation process—in which the 15 to 20 percent lowest-ranking employees were let go or encouraged to seek other employment—made it abundantly clear that what counted were bottom-line results and being the "mover-and-shaker" in the marketplace. The name of the game at Enron became devising clever ways to boost revenues and earnings, even if it sometimes meant operating outside established policies and without the knowledge of superiors. In fact, outside-the-lines behavior was celebrated if it generated profitable new business. Enron's energy contracts and its trading and hedging activities grew increasingly more complex and diverse as employees pursued first one avenue and then another to help keep Enron's financial performance looking good.

As a consequence of Enron's well-publicized successes in creating new products and businesses and leveraging the company's trading and hedging expertise into new market arenas, Enron came to be regarded as an exceptionally innovative company. It was ranked by its corporate peers as the most innovative U.S. company for three consecutive years in *Fortune* magazine's annual surveys of the most admired companies. A high-performance/high-rewards climate came to pervade the Enron culture, as the best workers (determined by who produced the best bottom-line results) received impressively large incentives and bonuses (amounting to as much as $1 million for traders and even more for senior executives). On Car Day at Enron, an array of luxury sports cars arrived for presentation to the most successful employees. Understandably, employees wanted to be seen as part of Enron's star team and partake in the benefits that being one of Enron's best and smartest employees entailed. The high monetary rewards, the ambitious and hard-driving people whom the company hired and promoted, and the competitive, results-oriented culture combined to give Enron a reputation not only for trampling competitors at every opportunity but also for internal ruthlessness. The company's super-aggressiveness and win-at-all-costs mind-set nurtured a culture that gradually and then more rapidly fostered the erosion of ethical standards, eventually making a mockery of the company's stated values of integrity and respect. When it became evident in the fall of 2001 that Enron was a house of cards propped up by deceitful accounting and a myriad of unsavory practices, the company imploded in a matter of weeks—the biggest bankruptcy of all time cost investors $64 billion in losses (between August 2000, when the stock price was at its five-year high, and November 2001), and Enron employees lost their retirement assets, which were almost totally invested in Enron stock.

More recently, a team investigating an ethical scandal at oil giant Royal Dutch/Shell Group that resulted in the payment of $150 million in fines found that an ethically flawed culture was a major contributor to why managers made rosy forecasts that they couldn't meet and why top executives engaged in maneuvers to mislead investors by overstating Shell's oil and gas reserves by 25 percent (equal to 4.5 billion barrels of oil). The investigation revealed that [illegible] Shell [illegible] and production group, were being used to overstate reserves. An e-mail written by Shell's top executive for exploration and production (who was caught up in the ethical misdeeds and later forced to resign) said, "I am becoming sick and tired of lying about the extent of our reserves issues and the downward revisions that need to be done because of our far too aggressive/optimistic bookings."[29]

WHY ETHICAL STRATEGIES MATTER

Company managers may formulate strategies that are ethical in all respects, or they may decide to employ strategies that, for one reason or another, have unethical or at least gray-area components. Senior executives with strong ethical convictions are normally proactive in insisting that all aspects of company strategy fall within ethical boundaries. But at companies whose senior executives are either immoral or amoral, shady strategies and unethical or borderline business practices may well be used, especially if their managers are clever at devising schemes to keep ethically questionable actions hidden from view.

There are two reasons why a company's strategy should be ethical: (1) a strategy that is unethical in whole or in part is morally wrong and reflects badly on the character of the company personnel involved, and (2) an ethical strategy is good business and in the best interest of shareholders.

The Moral Case for an Ethical Strategy

Managers do not dispassionately assess what strategic course to steer. Ethical strategy making generally begins with managers who themselves have strong character (i.e., who are honest, have integrity, and truly care about how they conduct the company's business). Managers with high ethical principles and standards are usually advocates of a corporate code of ethics and strong ethics compliance, and they are typically genuinely committed to certain corporate values and business principles. They walk the talk in displaying the company's stated values. They understand there's a big difference between adopting values statements and codes of ethics that serve merely as window dressing and those that truly paint the white lines for a company's actual strategy and business conduct. As a consequence, ethically strong managers consciously opt for strategic actions that can pass moral scrutiny—they display no tolerance for strategies with ethically controversial components.

The Business Case for an Ethical Strategy

There are solid business reasons to adopt ethical strategies even if most company managers are not of strong moral character and personally committed to high ethical standards. Pursuing unethical strategies not only damages a company's reputation but can also have costly consequences that are wide ranging. Some of the costs are readily visible; others are hidden and difficult to track down—as shown in Figure 9.1. The costs of fines and penalties and any declines in the stock price are easy enough to calculate. The administrative cleanup (or Level 2) costs are usually buried in the general costs of doing business and can be difficult to ascribe to any one ethical misdeed. Level 3 costs can be quite difficult to quantify but can sometimes be the most devastating—the Enron debacle left Arthur Andersen's reputation in shreds and led to the once-revered accounting firm's almost immediate demise. It remains to be seen whether Merck, once one of the world's most respected pharmaceutical firms, can survive the revelation that senior management deliberately concealed that its Vioxx painkiller, which the company pulled off the market in September 2004, was tied to much greater risk of heart attack and strokes—some 20 million people in the United States had taken Vioxx over the years, and Merck executives had reason to suspect as early as 2000 (and perhaps earlier) that Vioxx had dangerous side effects.[30]

Figure 9.1 The Business Costs of Ethical Failures

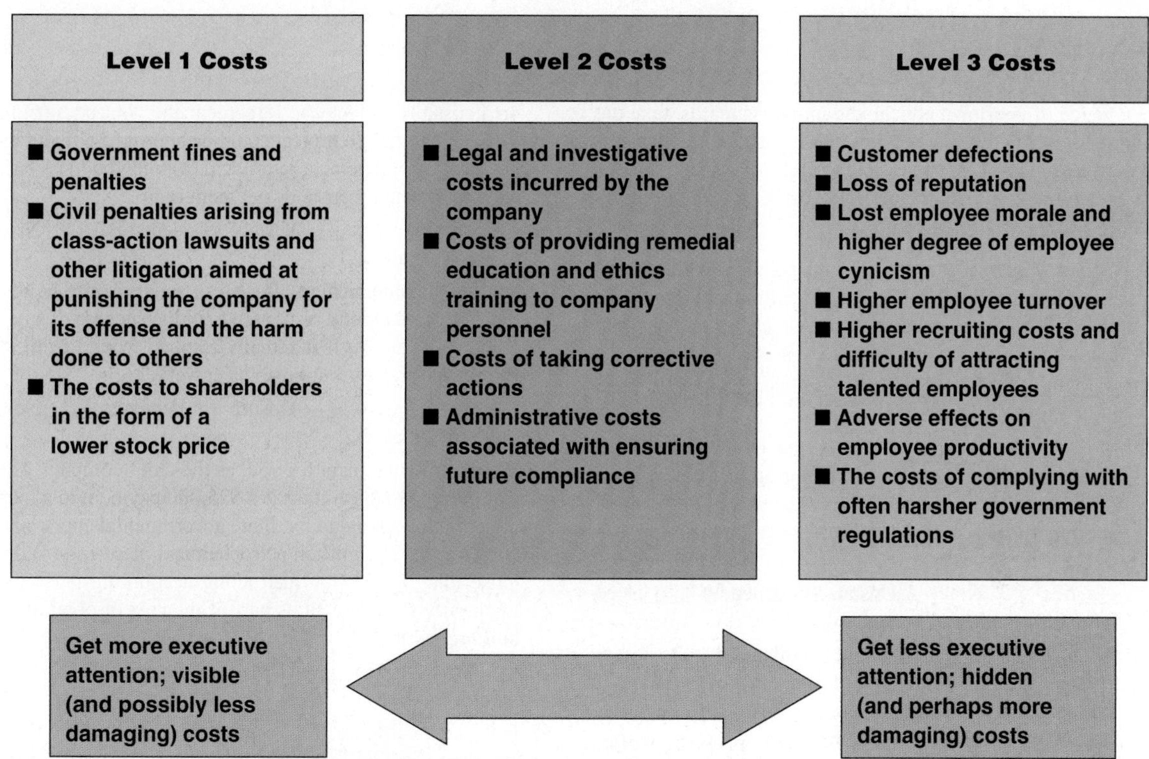

Level 1 Costs
Level 2 Costs
Level 3 Costs
Government fines and penalties
Civil penalties arising from class-action lawsuits and other litigation aimed at punishing the company for its offense and the harm done to others
The costs to shareholders in the form of a lower stock price
Legal and investigative costs incurred by the company
Costs of providing remedial education and ethics training to company personnel
Costs of taking corrective actions
Administrative costs associated with ensuring future compliance
Customer defections
Loss of reputation
Lost employee morale and higher degree of employee cynicism
Higher employee turnover
Higher recruiting costs and difficulty of attracting talented employees
Adverse effects on employee productivity
The costs of complying with often harsher government regulations
Get more executive attention; visible (and possibly less damaging) costs
Get less executive attention; hidden (and perhaps more damaging) costs

Source: Adapted from Terry Thomas, John R. Schermerhorn, and John W. Dienhart, "Strategic Leadership of Ethical Behavior," *Academy of Management Executive* 18, no. 2 (May 2004), p. 58.

Rehabilitating a company's shattered reputation is time-consuming and costly. Customers shun companies known for their shady behavior. Companies with reputations for unethical conduct have considerable difficulty in recruiting and retaining talented employees. Most hardworking, ethically upstanding people are repulsed by a work environment where unethical behavior is condoned; they don't want to get entrapped in a compromising situation, nor do they want their personal reputations tarnished by the actions of an unsavory employer. A 1997 survey revealed that 42 percent of the respondents took into account a company's ethics when deciding whether to accept a job.[31] Creditors are usually unnerved by the unethical actions of a borrower because of the potential business fallout and subsequent risk of

both their reputations and their long-term well-being are tied to conducting their business in a manner that wins the approval of suppliers, employees, investors, and society at large.

As a test of your own business ethics and where you stand on the importance of companies having an ethical strategy, take the test in Illustration Capsule 9.1.

ILLUSTRATION CAPSULE 9.1

A Test of Your Business Ethics

As a gauge of your own ethical and moral standards, take the following quiz and see how you stack up against other members of your class. For the test to be valid, you need to answer the questions candidly and not on the basis of what you think the "ethically correct" answer is.

1. Do you think that it would be unethical for you to give two Super Bowl tickets to an important customer? Would your answer be different if the customer is likely to place an order that would qualify you for a large year-end sales bonus?

   ____Yes ____No ____Unsure (it depends) ____Need more information

2. Would it be wrong to accept a case of fine wine from an important customer? Would your answer be different if you have just convinced your superiors to authorize a special price discount on a big order that the customer has just placed?

   ____Yes ____No ____Unsure (it depends) ____Need more information

3. Is it unethical for a high school or college coach to accept a "talent fee" or similar type of payment from a maker of sports apparel or sports equipment when the coach has authority to determine which brand of apparel or equipment to use for his or her team and subsequently chooses the brand of the company making the payment? Is it unethical for the maker of the sports apparel or equipment to make such payments in expectation that the coach will reciprocate by selecting the company's brand? Would you answer be different if "everybody else" is doing it?

   ____Yes ____No ____Unsure (it depends) ____Need more information

4. Is it unethical to accept an invitation from a supplier to spend a holiday weekend skiing at the supplier company's resort home in Colorado? Would your answer be different if you were presently considering a proposal from that supplier to purchase $1 million worth of components?

   ____Yes ____No ____Unsure (it depends) ____Need more information

5. Is it unethical for a food products company to use ingredients that have trans fats, given that trans fats are known to be very unhealthy for consumers and that alternative ingredients (which might be somewhat more expensive) can be used?

   ____Yes ____No ____Unsure (it depends) ____Need more information

6. Would it be wrong to keep quiet if you, as a junior financial analyst, had just calculated that the projected return on a possible project was 18 percent and your boss (*a*) informed you that no project could be approved without the prospect of a 25 percent return and (*b*) told you to go back and redo the numbers and "get them right"?

   ____Yes ____No ____Unsure (it depends) ____Need more information

7. Would it be unethical to allow your supervisor to believe that you were chiefly responsible for the success of a new company initiative if it actually resulted from a team effort or major contributions by a coworker?

   ____Yes ____No ____Unsure (it depends) ____Need more information

8. Would it be unethical for you, as the chief company official in India to (*a*) authorize a $25,000 payment to a local government official to facilitate governmental approval to construct a $200 million petrochemical plant and (*b*) disguise this payment by instructing accounting personnel to classify the payment as part of the cost of obtaining a building permit?

   ____Yes ____No ____Unsure (it depends) ____Need more information

9. Is it unethical for a motor vehicle manufacturer to resist recalling some of its vehicles when governmental authorities present it with credible evidence that the vehicles have safety defects?

   ____Yes ____No ____Unsure (it depends) ____Need more information

10. Is it unethical for a credit card company to aggressively try to sign up new accounts when, after an introductory period of interest-free or low-interest charges on unpaid monthly balances, the interest rate on unpaid balances jumps to 18 percent or more annually (even though the rate is disclosed in fine print)?

    ____Yes ____No ____Unsure (it depends) ____Need more information

11. Is it unethical to bolster your résumé with exaggerated claims of your credentials and prior job accomplishments in hopes of improving your chances of gaining employment?

    ____Yes ____No ____Unsure (it depends) ____Need more information

12. Is it unethical for a company to spend as little as possible on pollution control when, with some extra effort and expenditures, it could substantially reduce the amount of pollution caused by its operations?

    ____Yes ____No ____Unsure (it depends) ____Need more information

Answers: The answers to questions 1, 2, and 4 probably shift from no/unsure to a definite yes when the second part of the circumstance comes into play. We think a strong case can be made that the answers to the remaining 9 questions are yes, although it can be argued that more information about the circumstances might be needed in responding to questions 5, 7, 9, and 12.

APPROACHES TO MANAGING A COMPANY'S ETHICAL CONDUCT

A company can take can take any of four basic approaches with regard to ethical conduct:[32]

- The unconcerned or nonissue approach.
- The damage control approach.
- The compliance approach.
- The ethical culture approach.

The differences in these four approaches are discussed briefly below and summarized in Table 9.2.

The Unconcerned or Nonissue Approach

The unconcerned approach is prevalent at companies whose executives are immoral and unintentionally amoral. Senior executives at companies using this approach subscribe to the view that notions of right and wrong in matters of business are defined entirely by the prevailing laws and government regulations. They maintain that trying to enforce ethical standards above and beyond what is legally required is a nonissue because businesses are entitled to conduct their affairs in whatever manner they wish so long as they comply with the letter of what is legally required. Hence, there is no need to spend valuable management time trying to prescribe and enforce standards of conduct that go above and beyond legal and regulatory requirements. In companies where senior managers are immoral, the prevailing view may well be that under-the-table dealing can be good business if it can be kept hidden or if it can be justified on grounds that others are doing it too. Companies in this mode usually engage in most any business practices they believe they can get away with, and the strategies they employ may include elements that are either borderline from a legal perspective or ethically shady.

The Damage Control Approach

Damage control is favored at companies whose managers are intentionally amoral but who are wary of scandal and adverse public relations fallout that could cost them their jobs or tarnish their careers. Companies using this approach, not wanting to raise doubts about their commitment to ethical business conduct, will often adopt a code of ethics for window-dressing purposes. But it quickly becomes understood that the code exists mainly as nice [illegible] practice the damage control approach are prone to look the other way when shady or borderline behavior occurs. They may even condone questionable actions that help the company reach earnings targets or bolster its market standing—such as pressuring customers to stock up on the company's product (channel stuffing), making under-the-table payments to win new business, or stonewalling the recall of products claimed to be unsafe. But they are usually careful to do such things in a manner that lessens the risks of exposure or damaging consequences. This generally includes making token gestures

The main objective of the damage control approach is to protect against adverse publicity and any damaging litigation, punitive government action, or angry or vocal stakeholders.

Table 9.2 Four Approaches to Managing Business Ethics

	Unconcerned or Nonissue Approach	Damage Control Approach	Compliance Approach	Ethical Culture Approach
Underlying beliefs	• The business of business is business, not ethics • Ethics has no place in the conduct of business • Companies should not be morally accountable for their actions	• Need to make a token gesture in the direction of ethical standards (a code of ethics)	• Company must be committed to ethical standards and monitoring ethics performance • Unethical behavior must be prevented and punished if discovered • Important to have a reputation for high ethical standards	• Ethics is basic to the culture • Behaving ethically must be a deeply held corporate value and become a "way of life" • Everyone is expected to walk the talk
Ethics management approaches	• There's no need to make decisions concerning business ethics—if its legal, it is okay • No intervention regarding the ethical component of decisions is needed	• Act to protect against the dangers of unethical strategies and behavior • Ignore unethical behavior or allow it to go unpunished unless the situation is extreme and requires action	• Establish a clear, comprehensive code of ethics • Prevent unethical behavior • Provide ethics training for all personnel • Have formal ethics compliance procedures, an ethics compliance office, and a chief ethics officer	• Ethical behavior is ingrained and reinforced as part of the culture • Much reliance on co-worker peer pressure—"that's not how we do things here" • Everyone is an ethics watchdog—whistle-blowing is required • Ethics heroes are celebrated; ethics stories are told
Challenges	• Financial consequences can become unaffordable • Some stakeholders are alienated	• Credibility problems with stakeholders can arise • The company is susceptible to ethical scandal • The company has a sub-par ethical reputation—executives and company personnel don't walk the talk	• Organizational members come to rely on the existing rules for moral guidance—fosters a mentality of what is not forbidden is allowed • Rules and guidelines proliferate • The locus of moral control resides in the code and in the ethics compliance system rather than in an individual's own moral responsibility for ethical behavior	• New employees must go through strong ethics induction program • Formal ethics management systems can be underutilized • Relying on peer pressures and cultural norms to enforce ethical standards can result in eliminating some or many of the compliance trappings and, over time, induce moral laxness

Source: Adapted from Gedeon J. Rossouw and Leon J. van Vuuren, "Modes of Managing Morality: A Descriptive Model of Strategies for Managing Ethics," *Journal of Business Ethics* 46, no. 4 (September 2003), pp. 392–93.

to police compliance with codes of ethics and relying heavily on all sorts of spin to help extricate the company or themselves from claims that the company's strategy has unethical components or that company personnel have engaged in unethical practices.

The Compliance Approach

Anywhere from light to forceful compliance is favored at companies whose managers (1) lean toward being somewhat amoral but are highly concerned about having ethically upstanding reputations or (2) are moral and see strong compliance methods as the best way to impose and enforce ethical rules and high ethical standards. Companies that adopt a compliance mode usually do some or all of the following to display their commitment to ethical conduct: make the code of ethics a visible and regular part of communications with employees, implement ethics training programs, appoint a chief ethics officer, have ethics committees to give guidance on ethics matters, institute formal procedures for investigating alleged ethics violations, conduct ethics audits to measure and document compliance, and/or try to deter violations by setting up ethics hotlines for anonymous callers to use in reporting possible violations. Ethics code violators at these companies are disciplined and sometimes subjected to public reprimand and punishment (including dismissal), thereby sending a clear signal to company personnel that complying with ethical standards needs to be taken seriously.

The driving force behind the company's commitment to eradicate unethical behavior normally stems from a desire to avoid the cost and damage associated with unethical conduct or else a quest to gain favor from stakeholders (especially ethically conscious customers, employees, and investors) for having a highly regarded reputation for ethical behavior. One of the weaknesses of the compliance approach is that moral control resides in the company's code of ethics and in the ethics compliance system rather than in (1) the strong peer pressures for ethical behavior that come from ingraining a highly ethical corporate culture and (2) an individual's own moral responsibility for ethical behavior.[33]

The Ethical Culture Approach

At some companies, top executives believe that high ethical principles must be deeply ingrained in the corporate culture and function as guides for "how we do things around here." A company using the ethical culture approach seeks to gain employee buy-in to the company's ethical standards, business principles, and corporate values. The ethical principles embraced in the company's code of ethics and/or in its statement of corporate values are seen as integral to the company's identity, self-image, and ways of operating. The strength of the ethical culture approach depends heavily on the ethical

decisions and behavior. Further, it is essential that the strategy be ethical in all respects and that company personnel execute the strategy in an ethical manner. Such strong commitment to ethical business conduct is what creates an ethical work climate and a workplace where displaying integrity is the norm.

Many of the ethical enforcement mechanisms used in the compliance approach are also employed in the ethical culture mode, but one other is added—strong peer pressure from coworkers to observe ethical norms. Thus, responsibility for ethics compliance is widely dispersed throughout all levels of management and the rank and file. Stories of former and current moral heroes are kept in circulation, and the deeds of company personnel who display ethical values and are dedicated to walking the talk are celebrated at internal company events. The message that ethics matters—and matters a lot—resounds loudly and clearly throughout the organization and in its strategy and decisions.

However, one of the challenges to overcome in the ethical culture approach is relying too heavily on peer pressure and cultural norms to enforce ethics compliance rather than on an individual's own moral responsibility for ethical behavior—absent unrelenting peer pressure or strong internal compliance systems, there is a danger that over time company personnel may become lax about ethical standards. Compliance procedures need to be an integral part of the ethical culture approach to help send the message that management takes the observance of ethical norms seriously and that behavior that falls outside ethical boundaries will have negative consequences. Illustration Capsule 9.2 discusses General Electric's approach to building a culture that combines demands for high performance with expectations for ethical conduct.

Why Companies Change Their Ethics Management Approach

Regardless of the approach they have used to managing ethical conduct, a company's executives may sense they have exhausted a particular mode's potential for managing ethics and that they need to become more forceful in their approach to ethics management. Such changes typically occur when the company's ethical failures have made the headlines and created an embarrassing situation for company officials or when the business climate changes. For example, the number of recent highly publicized corporate scandals, coupled with aggressive enforcement of anticorruption legislation (such as the Sarbanes-Oxley Act of 2002 which penalizes lax corporate governance and illicit accounting practices), has prompted numerous executives and boards of directors to clean up their acts in accounting and financial reporting, review their ethical standards, and tighten up ethics compliance procedures. Intentionally amoral managers using the unconcerned or nonissue approach to ethics management may see less risk in shifting to the damage control approach (or, for appearance's sake, maybe a "light" compliance mode). Senior managers who have employed the damage control mode may be motivated by bad experiences to mend their ways and shift to a compliance mode. In the wake of so many embarrassing corporate scandals, companies in the compliance mode may move closer to the ethical culture approach.

SOCIAL RESPONSIBILITY AND CORPORATE CITIZENSHIP STRATEGIES

That businesses have an obligation to be good citizens and foster the betterment of society, a much-debated topic in the past 40 years, took root in the 19th century when progressive companies began, in the aftermath of the industrial revolution, to provide workers with housing and other amenities. The notion that corporate executives should

ILLUSTRATION CAPSULE 9.2
How General Electric's Top Management Built a Culture That Fuses High Performance with High Integrity

Jack Welch and his successor as General Electric's CEO, Jeffrey Immelt, have fostered a culture built on high ethical standards. The company's heavy reliance on financial controls and performance-based reward systems—which are necessary because of GE's broad multinational diversification—could easily tempt managers at all levels to cut corners, engage in unethical sales tactics, inaccurately record revenues or expenses, or participate in corrupt practices prevalent in the many emerging markets where GE competes. Welch, Immelt, and GE's other top managers clearly recognize that, absent a strong ethical culture, there would be little to deter the company's thousands of managers across the globe to pursue all types of unethical behavior that would, on the surface, boost performance.

GE's top management was not so naive as to believe that it had successfully hired only moral managers with the highest personal expectations for ethical behavior, but was well aware that many among its managerial ranks were either intentionally or unintentionally amoral. The first step in establishing an ethical culture at GE was for its top management to forcefully communicate the company's principles that should guide decision making. Jeffrey Immelt begins and ends each annual meeting of the company's 220 officers and 600 senior managers with a recitation of the company's fundamental ethical principles. Immelt and GE's other managers are careful to not violate these principles themselves or give implied consent for others to skirt these principles, since human nature makes subordinates at all levels ever vigilant for the signs of hypocrisy in the actions of higher-ups. The importance of walking the talk justifies GE's "one strike and you're out" standard for its top management. For example, a high-level manager in an emerging market was terminated for failing to conduct required diligence on a third-party vendor known for its shady business practices, including the payment of bribes to local officials. Another executive was fired from GE for agreeing to a large and important Asian customer's request to falsify supplier documents that were used by regulatory agencies.

With so many ethical standards prevailing in the more than 100 countries where GE operates, the company has turned to global ethical standards rather than allow local cultures to shape business behavior. The company's global standards cover such topics as how to best evaluate suppliers' environmental records and working conditions in its manufacturing businesses and how to avoid money-laundering schemes or aiding and abetting financial services customers engaged in tax evasion or accounting fraud. Operating-level managers were formally responsible for ensuring ethical compliance in their divisions and were required to submit quarterly tracking reports to GE's corporate offices on key indicators such as spills, accident rates, and violation notices. Managers of operating units falling in the bottom quartile on such quarterly assessments were required to submit plans for improving the ethical shortcomings. GE also evaluated the ethical performance of its 4,000 managers who were responsible for profit centers or were key contributors on business teams.

GE's approach to culture building also included instilling such principles into the behavior of the company's 300,000-plus employees with no managerial responsibility. Employees are provided training to help them understand the company's ethical principles and how those principles can help them make decisions in the ethical gray areas that arise while making everyday decisions. GE also allows employees to lodge complaints about ethics compliance anonymously; those complaints are evaluated by more than 500 employees around the world with either full-time or part-time ombudsperson capacity. About 20 percent of the 1,500 concerns lodged annually lead to serious discipline. Hourly employees are also included in annual assessments of ethical performance and are rewarded through bonuses, promotions, or recognition for identifying or resolving ethical issues at the operating level.

balance the interests of all stakeholders—shareholders, employees, customers, suppliers, the communities in which they operated, and society at large—began to blossom in the 1960s. Some years later, a group of chief executives of America's 200 largest corporations, calling themselves the Business Roundtable, took a strong stance and forcefully advocated that corporations conduct their business in a manner that benefited all

CORE CONCEPT

The notion of social responsibility as it applies to businesses concerns a company's *duty* to operate in an honorable manner, provide good working conditions for employees, be a good steward of the environment, and actively work to better the quality of life in the local communities where it operates and in society at large.

stakeholders; the Roundtable's "Statement on Corporate Responsibility," written in 1981, said:

> Balancing the shareholder's expectations of maximum return against other priorities is one of the fundamental problems confronting corporate management. The shareholder must receive a good return but the legitimate concerns of other constituencies (customers, employees, communities, suppliers and society at large) also must have the appropriate attention. . . . [Leading managers] believe that by giving enlightened consideration to balancing the legitimate claims of all its constituents, a corporation will best serve the interest of its shareholders.[34]

Today, corporate social responsibility is a concept that resonates in Western Europe, the United States, Canada, and such developing nations as Brazil and India.

What Do We Mean by *Social Responsibility* and *Corporate Citizenship?*

The essence of socially responsible business behavior is that a company should balance strategic actions to benefit shareholders against the *duty* to be a good corporate citizen. Company managers must display a *social conscience* in operating the business and specifically take into account how management decisions and company actions affect the well-being of employees, local communities, the environment, and society at large. Acting in a socially responsible manner thus encompasses more than just complying with the laws and regulations of the countries in which it operates, participating in community service projects, and donating monies to charities and other worthy social causes. Demonstrating social responsibility also entails undertaking actions that earn trust and respect from all stakeholders—operating in an honorable and ethical manner, striving to make the company a great place to work, demonstrating genuine respect for the environment, and trying to make a difference in bettering society. As depicted in Figure 9.2, the menu for demonstrating a social conscience and choosing specific ways to exercise social responsibility includes:

- *Efforts to employ an ethical strategy and observe ethical principles in operating the business*—A sincere commitment to observing ethical principles is necessary here simply because unethical strategies and conduct are incompatible with the concept of good corporate citizenship and socially responsible business behavior.
- *Making charitable contributions, donating money and the time of company personnel to community service endeavors, supporting various worthy organizational causes, and reaching out to make a difference in the lives of the disadvantaged*—Some companies fulfill their corporate citizenship and community outreach obligations by spreading their efforts over a multitude of charitable and community activities; for instance, Microsoft and Johnson & Johnson support a broad variety of community, art, social welfare, and environmental programs. Others prefer to focus their energies more narrowly. McDonald's, for example, concentrates on sponsoring the Ronald McDonald House program (which provides a home away from home for the families of seriously ill children receiving treatment at nearby hospitals), preventing child abuse and neglect, and participating in local community service activities. British Telecom gives 1 percent of its profits directly to communities, largely for education—teacher training, in-school workshops, and digital technology. Leading prescription drug maker GlaxoSmithKline and

Figure 9.2 **Demonstrating a Social Conscience: The Five Components of Socially Responsible Business Behavior**

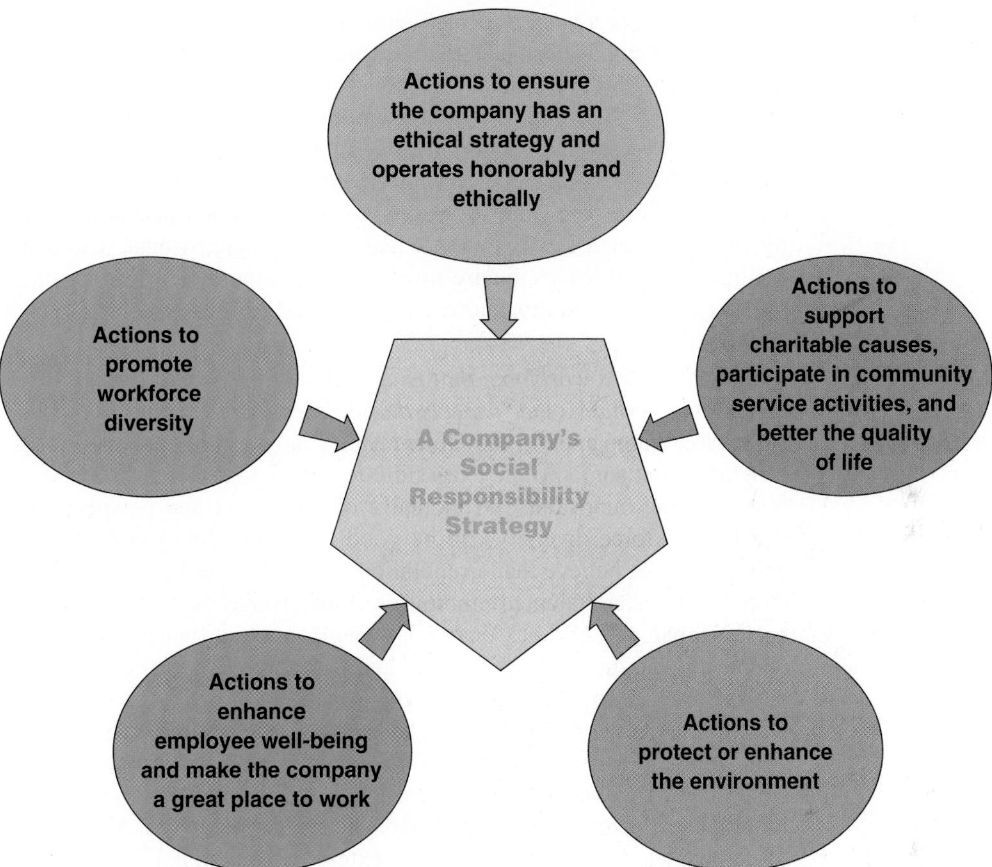

Source: Adapted from material in Ronald Paul Hill, Debra Stephens, and Iain Smith, "Corporate Social Responsibility: An Examination of Individual Firm Behavior," *Business and Society Review* 108, no. 3 (September 2003), p. 348.

other pharmaceutical companies either donate or heavily discount medicines for distribution in the least-developed nations. Companies frequently reinforce their philanthropic efforts by encouraging employees to support charitable causes and participate in community affairs, often through programs to match employee contributions.

- *Actions to protect or enhance the environment and, in particular, to minimize or*

tection means doing more than what is legally required. From a social responsibility perspective, companies have an obligation to be stewards of the environment. This means using the best available science and technology to achieve higher-than-required environmental standards. Even more ideally, it means putting time and money into improving the environment in ways that extend past a company's own industry boundaries—such as participating in recycling projects, adopting energy conservation practices, and supporting efforts to clean up local water supplies. Retailers such as Home Depot and Wal-Mart in the United States and B&Q in the United Kingdom have begun pressuring their suppliers to adopt stronger environmental protection practices.[35]

- *Actions to create a work environment that enhances the quality of life for employees and makes the company a great place to work*—Numerous companies go beyond providing the ordinary kinds of compensation and exert extra efforts to enhance the quality of life for their employees, both at work and at home. This can include varied and engaging job assignments, career development programs and mentoring, rapid career advancement, appealing compensation incentives, ongoing training to ensure future employability, added decision-making authority, onsite day care, flexible work schedules for single parents, workplace exercise facilities, special leaves to care for sick family members, work-at-home opportunities, gender pay equity, showcase plants and offices, special safety programs, and the like.
- *Actions to build a workforce that is diverse with respect to gender, race, national origin, and perhaps other aspects that different people bring to the workplace*—Most large companies in the United States have established workforce diversity programs, and some go the extra mile to ensure that their workplaces are attractive to ethnic minorities and inclusive of all groups and perspectives. The pursuit of workforce diversity can be good business—Johnson & Johnson, Pfizer, and Coca-Cola believe that a reputation for workforce diversity makes recruiting employees easier (talented employees from diverse backgrounds often seek out such companies). And at Coca-Cola, where strategic success depends on getting people all over the world to become loyal consumers of the company's beverages, efforts to build a public persona of inclusiveness for people of all races, religions, nationalities, interests, and talents has considerable strategic value. Multinational companies are particularly inclined to make workforce diversity a visible strategic component; they recognize that respecting individual differences and promoting inclusiveness resonate well with people all around the world. At growing numbers of companies the diversity initiative extends to suppliers—sourcing items from small businesses owned by women or ethnic minorities.

CORE CONCEPT

A company's *social responsibility strategy* is defined by the specific combination of socially beneficial and community citizenship activities it opts to support with its contributions of time, money, and other resources.

The particular combination of socially responsible endeavors a company elects to pursue defines its **social responsibility strategy.**

Some companies use the terms *corporate social responsibility* and *corporate citizenship* interchangeably, but there's a body of thought that only companies pursuing discretionary activities in the pursuit of bettering society can be described as good corporate citizens. Adherents of corporate citizenship theories suggest that corporations, as citizens of the communities in which they operate, have an obligation to contribute to society, particularly in areas where governments have chosen not to focus or where government efforts have fallen short.[36]

Environmental Sustainability Strategies: A New and Growing Priority

A rapidly growing number of companies are expanding their exercise of social responsibility and corporate citizenship to include the impact of their strategies and operations on future generations and the well-being of the planet. Corporate strategies aimed at operating in an environmentally sustainable fashion entail deliberate and concerted actions to operate the company's business in a manner that protects and maybe even enhances natural resources and ecological support systems, guards against outcomes that will ultimately endanger the planet, and is therefore sustainable for centuries.

CORE CONCEPT

A company's environmental sustainability strategy consists of its deliberate actions to meet the current needs of customers, suppliers, shareholders, employees, and other stakeholders in a manner that protects the environment, provides for the longevity of natural resources, maintains ecological support systems for future generations, and guards against ultimate endangerment of the planet.

Sustainability initiatives undertaken by companies are frequently directed at improving the company's "Triple-P" performance—people, planet, and profit.[37] Unilever, a diversified producer of processed foods, personal care, and home cleaning products, is among the many committed corporations pursuing sustainable business practices. The company tracks 11 sustainable agricultural indicators in its processed foods business and has launched a variety of programs to improve the environmental performance of its suppliers. Examples of such programs include special low-rate financing for tomato suppliers choosing to switch to water-conserving irrigation systems and training programs in India that have allowed contract cucumber growers to reduce pesticide use by 90 percent, while improving yields by 78 percent. Unilever has also reengineered many internal processes to improve the company's overall performance on sustainability measures. For example, the company's factories have reduced water usage by 50 percent and manufacturing waste by 14 percent through the implementation of sustainability initiatives. Unilever has also redesigned packaging for many of its products to conserve natural resources and reduce the volume of consumer waste. The company's Suave shampoo bottles in the United States were reshaped to save almost 150 tons of plastic resin per year, which is the equivalent of 15 million fewer empty bottles making it to landfills annually. Also, the width of Unilever's Lipton soup cartons was reduced to save 154 tons of cardboard per year. Since 40 percent of Unilever's sales are made to consumers in developing countries, the company also is committed to addressing societal needs of consumers in those countries. Examples of the company's social performance include free laundries in poor neighborhoods in developing countries, start-up assistance for women-owned microbusinesses in India, and free drinking water provided to villages in Ghana.

Sometimes cost savings and improved profitability are drivers of environmental sustainability strategies. DuPont's sustainability initiatives regarding energy usage have resulted in energy conservation savings of more than $2 billion between 1990 and 2005. Procter & Gamble's Swiffer cleaning system, one of the company's best-selling new products, was developed as a sustainable product; not only does the Swiffer system have an earth-friendly design, but it also outperforms less-ecological alternatives. Although most consumers probably aren't aware that the Swiffer mop reduces demands on municipal water sources, saves electricity that would be needed to heat mopwater, and doesn't add to the amount of detergent making its way into waterways and waste-treatment facilities, they are attracted to purchasing Swiffer mops because they prefer Swiffer's disposable cleaning sheets to filling and refilling a mop bucket

sustainability reports for consumers and investors to review. Just as investment firms some years ago created mutual funds made up of companies passing some threshold of social responsibility, they are now creating mutual funds comprised of companies that are pursuing potent sustainability strategies in order to attract funds from environmentally and socially aware investors. The Dow Jones Sustainability World Index consists of the top 10 percent of the 2,500 companies listed in the Dow Jones World

Table 9.3 Companies with Exceptional Commitments to Sustainability

Name	Market Sector	Country
BMW	Automobiles & Parts	Germany
Australia & New Zealand Banking Group	Banks	Australia
Norsk Hydro	Basic Resources	Norway
Akzo Nobel	Chemicals	Netherlands
Holcim	Construction & Materials	Switzerland
Sodexho	Travel & Leisure	France
Statoil	Oil & Gas	Norway
Land Securities Group	Financial Services	United Kingdom
Unilever	Food & Beverage	Netherlands
Novo Nordisk	Health Care	Denmark
TNT	Industrial Goods & Services	Netherlands
Allianz	Insurance	Germany
Pearson	Media	United Kingdom
Philips Electronics	Personal & Household Goods	Netherlands
Marks & Spencer	Retail	United Kingdom
Intel Corp.	Technology	United States
BT Group Plc	Telecommunications	United Kingdom
CEMIG	Utilities	Brazil

Sources: Dow Jones Indexes, STOXX Limited, and SAM Group; http://www.sustainability-indexes.com/07_htmle/indexes/djsiworld_supersectorleaders_07.html (accessed August 1, 2008).

Index in terms of economic performance, environmental performance, and social performance. Table 9.3 shows companies with exceptional commitments to sustainability (judged according to their being designated as worldwide supersector leaders in the Dow Jones Sustainability World Index for 2007/2008). However, achieving a prominent ranking in sustainability indexes is no guarantee that a company will outperform industry rivals when it comes to social responsibility. For example, BP's $8 billion investment in alternative energy sources and its strong involvement in community and environmental groups had allowed it to be consistently ranked near the top among sustainability indexes, but between 2005 and 2007, the company was fined for safety violations at an Ohio refinery, was investigated by the U.S. Department of Justice for suspected manipulation of oil prices, had a major oil pipeline leak in Alaska, and was hit with a refinery explosion in Texas that claimed the lives of 15 employees.[38]

Crafting Social Responsibility and Sustainability Strategies

While striving to be socially responsible and to engage in environmentally sustainable business practices entails choosing from the menu outlined in the preceding sections and Figure 9.2, there's plenty of room for every company to make its own statement about what charitable contributions to make, what kinds of community service projects to emphasize, what environmental actions to support, how to make the company a good place to work, where and how workforce diversity fits into the picture, and what else it will do to support worthy causes and projects that benefit society.

A company may choose to focus its social responsibility strategy on generic social issues, but social responsibility strategies keyed to points of intersection between a company and society may also contribute to a company's competitive advantage.[39] Almost all activities performed by a company (such as hiring practices, emissions, and waste disposal) have either a positive effect on society or a negative one. In addition, society affects the competitive environment in which companies operate—society provides a company with labor and transportation infrastructure, sets the rules that govern competition, determines the demand for a company's products or services, and shapes the availability of supporting industries. Social responsibility strategies that focus on these points of intersection between society and the company's ability to execute various value chain activities or better serve customer needs provide social benefits as well as build competitive advantage. For example, while carbon emissions may be a generic social issue for a financial institution such as Wells Fargo, Toyota's social responsibility strategy aimed at reducing carbon emissions has produced both competitive advantage and environmental benefits. Toyota's Prius hybrid electric/gasoline automobile is not only among the least polluting automobiles but also the best-selling hybrid vehicle in the United States. The Prius has earned the company the loyalty of fuel-conscious buyers and given Toyota a green image.

Business leaders who want their companies to be regarded as exemplary corporate citizens not only must see that their companies operate ethically but also must personally display a social conscience in making decisions that affect employees, the environment, the communities in which they operate, and society at large.

However, unless a company's social responsibility initiatives become part of the way it operates its business every day, the initiatives are unlikely to be fully effective. As an executive at Royal Dutch/Shell put it, corporate social responsibility "is not a cosmetic; it must be rooted in our values. It must make a difference to the way we do business."[40] A few companies have integrated social responsibility and/or environmental sustainability objectives into their missions and overall performance targets—they see social performance and environmental metrics as an essential component of judging the company's overall future performance. Some 2,500 companies around the world are issuing annual social responsibility reports (much like an annual report) that set forth their commitments and the progress they are making for all the world to see and evaluate.[41]

Green Mountain Coffee Roasters' commitment to protect the welfare of coffee growers and their families (in particular, making sure they receive a fair price) also intersects with the company's competitively important value chain activities. In its dealings with suppliers at small farmer cooperatives in Peru, Mexico, and Sumatra, Green Mountain pays "fair-trade" prices for coffee beans (in 2002, the fair-trade prices per pound of coffee were a minimum of $1.26 for conventional coffee and $1.41 for organically grown, versus market prices of 24 to 50 cents). Green Mountain also purchases about 25 percent of its coffee direct from farmers so as to cut out intermediaries and see that farmers realize a higher price for their efforts—coffee is the world's second most heavily traded commodity after oil

Social responsibility strategies that have the effect of both providing valuable social benefits and fulfilling customer needs in a superior fashion can lead to competitive advantage.

job training to the chronically unemployed. Ninety percent of the graduates from the job training program take jobs with Marriott and about two-thirds of those remain with Marriott for more than a year. Patagonia encourages customers to return worn-out cotton, fleece, and nylon clothing items so that the fibers can be recycled into fabrics for new clothing items.

reputation but are unlikely to improve its competitive strength in the marketplace.

Whole Foods Market's social responsibility strategy is evident in almost every segment of its company value chain and is a big part of its differentiation strategy. The company's procurement policies encourage stores to purchase fresh fruits and vegetables from local farmers and screen processed food items for more than 100 common ingredients that the company considers unhealthy or environmentally unsound. Spoiled food items are sent to regional composting centers rather than landfills, and all cleaning products used in Whole Foods stores are biodegradable. The company also has created the Animal Compassion Foundation to develop natural and humane ways of raising farm animals and has converted all of its vehicles to run on biofuels.

However, not all companies choose to link their corporate social agendas to their own business or industry. Chick-Fil-A, an Atlanta-based fast-food chain with over 1,200 outlets in 38 states, has a charitable foundation that supports 14 foster homes and a summer camp for some 1,800 campers from 22 states and several foreign countries.[43] Toys "R" Us supports initiatives addressing the issues of child labor and fair labor practices around the world. Levi Strauss & Company has made AIDS prevention and awareness a major component of its social agenda for a number of years. The company and the Levi Strauss Foundation have supported the Syringe Access Fund (which makes sterile syringes available to intravenous drug users in the United States) and Preventoons (cartoons directed at children between the ages 8 and 10 that discuss how to best prevent the transmission of the AIDS virus). The Preventoons were distributed to more than 20,000 teachers in Argentina and Uruguay to use in their classrooms.

It is common for companies engaged in natural resource extraction, electric power production, forestry and paper products, motor vehicles, and chemicals production to place more emphasis on addressing environmental concerns than, say, software and electronics firms or apparel manufacturers. Companies whose business success is heavily dependent on high employee morale or attracting and retaining the best and brightest employees are somewhat more prone to stress the well-being of their employees and foster a positive, high-energy workplace environment that elicits the dedication and enthusiastic commitment of employees, thus putting real meaning behind the claim "Our people are our greatest asset." Ernst & Young, one of the four largest global accounting firms, stresses its "People First" workforce diversity strategy, which is all about respecting differences, fostering individuality, and promoting inclusiveness so that its 105,000 employees in 140 countries can feel valued, engaged, and empowered in developing creative ways to serve the firm's clients.

Thus, while the strategies and actions of all socially responsible companies have a sameness in the sense of drawing on the five categories of socially responsible behavior shown in Figure 9.2, each company's version of being socially responsible is unique.

The Moral Case for Corporate Social Responsibility and Environmentally Sustainable Business Practices

The moral case for why businesses should actively promote the betterment of society and act in a manner that benefits all of the company's stakeholders—not just the interests of shareholders—boils down to "It's the right thing to do." In today's social and political climate, most business leaders can be expected to acknowledge that socially responsible actions and environmental sustainability are important and that businesses have a duty to be good corporate citizens. But there is a complementary school of thought that business operates on the basis of an implied social contract with the members of society. According to this contract, society grants a business the right to conduct its business affairs and agrees not to unreasonably restrain its pursuit of a fair profit for the goods or services it sells. In return for this "license to operate," a business is obligated to act as a responsible citizen and do its fair share to promote the general welfare. Such a view clearly puts a moral burden on a company to take corporate citizenship into consideration and to do what's best for shareholders within the confines of discharging its duties to operate honorably, provide good working conditions to employees, be a good environmental steward, and display good corporate citizenship.

The Business Case for Socially Responsible Behavior and Environmentally Sustainable Business Practices

Whatever the merits of the moral case for socially responsible business behavior and environmentally sustainable business practices, it has long been recognized that it is in the enlightened self-interest of companies to be good citizens and devote some of their energies and resources to the betterment of employees, the communities in which they operate, and society in general. In short, there are several reasons why the exercise of social responsibility is good business:

- *It generates internal benefits (particularly as concerns employee recruiting, workforce retention, employee morale, and training costs)*—Companies with deservedly good reputations for contributing time and money to the betterment of society are better able to attract and retain employees compared to companies with tarnished reputations. Some employees just feel better about working for a company committed to improving society.[44] This can contribute to lower turnover and better worker productivity. Other direct and indirect economic benefits include lower costs for staff recruitment and training. For example, Starbucks is said to enjoy much lower rates of employee turnover because of its full benefits package for both full-time and part-time employees, management efforts to make Starbucks a great place to work, and the company's socially responsible practices. When a U.S. manufacturer of recycled paper, taking eco-efficiency to heart, discovered how to increase its fiber recovery rate, it saved the equivalent of 20,000 tons of waste paper—a factor that helped the company become the industry's lowest-cost producer.[45] Various benchmarking and measurement mechanisms have shown that workforce diversity initiatives promote the success of companies that stay behind them. Making a company a great place to work pays dividends in recruiting talented workers, more creativity and energy on the part of workers, higher worker productivity, and greater employee commitment to the company's business mission/vision and success in the marketplace.
- *It reduces the risk of reputation-damaging incidents and can lead to increased buyer patronage*—Firms may well be penalized by employees, consumers, and shareholders for actions that are not considered socially responsible. When a major oil company suffered damage to its reputation on environmental and social grounds, the CEO repeatedly said that the most negative impact the company suffered—and the one that made him fear for the future of the company—was that bright young graduates were no longer attracted to work for the company.[46] Consumer, environmental, and human rights activist groups are quick to criticize businesses whose behavior they consider to be out of line, and they are adept at getting their message into the media and onto the Internet. Pressure groups can generate widespread adverse publicity, promote boycotts, and influence like-minded or sympathetic buyers to avoid an offender's

products. Research has shown that product boycott announcements are associated with a decline in a company's stock price.[47] For many years, Nike received stinging criticism for not policing sweatshop conditions in the Asian factories of its contractors, causing Nike CEO Phil Knight to observe that "Nike has become synonymous with slave wages, forced overtime, and arbitrary abuse." In 1997, Nike began an extensive effort to monitor conditions in the 800 overseas factories from which it outsourced its shoes; Knight said, "Good shoes come from good factories and good factories have good labor relations."[48] Nonetheless, Nike has continually been plagued by complaints from human rights activists that its monitoring procedures are flawed and that it is not doing enough to correct the plight of factory workers. In contrast, to the extent that a company's socially responsible behavior wins applause from consumers and fortifies its reputation, the company may win additional patronage; Whole Foods Market, Patagonia, Chick-Fil-A, Starbucks, and Green Mountain Coffee Roasters have definitely expanded their customer bases because of their visible and well-publicized activities as socially conscious companies. More and more companies are recognizing the strategic value of social responsibility strategies that reach out to people of all cultures and demographics—in the United States, women are said to having buying power of $3.7 trillion, retired and disabled people close to $4.1 trillion, Hispanics nearly $600 billion, African Americans some $500 billion, and Asian Americans about $255 billion.[49] In sum, reaching out in ways that appeal to such groups can pay off at the cash register. Some observers and executives are convinced that a strong, visible social responsibility strategy gives a company an edge in differentiating itself from rivals and in appealing to those consumers who prefer to do business with companies that are solid corporate citizens. Yet there is only limited evidence that consumers go out of their way to patronize socially responsible companies if it means paying a higher price or purchasing an inferior product.[50]

The higher the public profile of a company or brand, the greater the scrutiny of its activities and the higher the potential for it to become a target for pressure group action.

- *It is in the best interest of shareholders*—Well-conceived social responsibility strategies and strategies to promote environmental sustainability work to the advantage of shareholders in several ways. Socially responsible business behavior and environmentally sustainable business practices help avoid or preempt legal and regulatory actions that could prove costly and otherwise burdensome. Increasing numbers of mutual funds and pension benefit managers are restricting their stock purchases to companies that meet social responsibility criteria. According to one survey, one out of every eight dollars under professional management in the United States involved socially responsible investing.[51] Moreover, the growth in socially responsible investing and identifying socially responsible companies has led to a substantial increase in the number of companies that publish formal reports on their social and environmental activities.[52] The stock prices of companies that rate high on social and environmental performance criteria have been found to perform 35 to 45 percent better than the average of the 2,500 companies comprising the Dow Jones Global Index.[53] A two-year study of leading companies found that improving environmental compliance and developing environmentally friendly products can enhance earnings per share, profitability, and the likelihood of winning contracts.[54] Nearly 100 studies have examined the relationship between corporate citizenship and corporate financial performance over the past 30 years; the majority point to a positive relationship. Of the 80 studies that examined whether a company's social performance is a good predictor of its financial performance, 42 concluded yes, 4 concluded no, and the remainder reported mixed or inconclusive

There's little hard evidence indicating shareholders are disadvantaged in any meaningful way by a company's actions to be socially responsible and to engage in environmentally sustainable business practices.

findings.[55] To the extent that socially responsible behavior is good business, then, a social responsibility strategy that packs some punch and is more than rhetorical flourish turns out to be in the best interest of shareholders.

In sum, companies that take social responsibility and environmental sustainability seriously can improve their business reputations and operational efficiency while also reducing their risk exposure and encouraging loyalty and innovation. Overall, companies that take special pains to protect the environment (beyond what is required by law), are active in community affairs, and are generous supporters of charitable causes and projects that benefit society are more likely to be seen as good investments and as good companies to work for or do business with. Shareholders are likely to view the business case for social responsibility as a strong one, even though they certainly have a right to be concerned whether the time and money their company spends to carry out its social responsibility strategy outweighs the benefits and reduces the bottom line by an unjustified amount.

Companies are, of course, sometimes rewarded for bad behavior—a company that is able to shift environmental and other social costs associated with its activities onto society as a whole can reap large short-term profits. The major cigarette producers for many years were able to earn greatly inflated profits by shifting the health-related costs of smoking onto others and escaping any responsibility for the harm their products caused to consumers and the general public. Numerous companies will, of course, try to evade paying for the social harms of their operations for as long as they can. Calling a halt to such actions usually hinges on (1) the effectiveness of activist social groups in publicizing the adverse consequences of a company's social irresponsibility and marshaling public opinion for something to be done, (2) the enactment of legislation or regulations to correct the inequity, and (3) widespread actions on the part of socially conscious buyers to take their business elsewhere.

KEY POINTS

Ethics involves concepts of right and wrong, fair and unfair, moral and immoral. Beliefs about what is ethical serve as a moral compass in guiding the actions and behaviors of individuals and organizations. Ethical principles in business are not materially different from ethical principles in general.

There are three schools of thought about ensuring a commitment to ethical standards for companies with international operations:

- According to the *school of ethical universalism,* the same standards of what's ethical and what's unethical resonate with peoples of most societies regardless of local traditions and cultural norms; hence, common ethical standards can be used to judge the conduct of personnel at companies operating in a variety of country markets and cultural circumstances.
- According to the *school of ethical relativism* different societal cultures and customs have divergent values and standards of right and wrong—thus, what is ethical or unethical must be judged in the light of local customs and social mores and can vary from one culture or nation to another.

- According to *integrative social contracts theory,* universal ethical principles or norms based on the collective views of multiple cultures and societies combine to form a "social contract" that all individuals in all situations have a duty to observe. Within the boundaries of this social contract, local cultures can specify other impermissible actions; however, universal ethical norms always take precedence over local ethical norms.

Three categories of managers stand out with regard to their prevailing beliefs in and commitments to ethical and moral principles in business affairs: the moral manager; the immoral manager, and the amoral manager. By some accounts, the population of managers is said to be distributed among all three types in a bell-shaped curve, with immoral managers and moral managers occupying the two tails of the curve, and the amoral managers, especially the intentionally amoral managers, occupying the broad middle ground.

The moral case for social responsibility boils down to a simple concept: It's the right thing to do. The business case for social responsibility holds that it is in the enlightened self-interest of companies to be good citizens and devote some of their energies and resources to the betterment of such stakeholders as employees, the communities in which they operate, and society in general.

The apparently large numbers of immoral and amoral businesspeople are one obvious reason why some companies resort to unethical strategic behavior. Three other main drivers of unethical business behavior also stand out:

- Overzealous or obsessive pursuit of personal gain, wealth, and other selfish interests.
- Heavy pressures on company managers to meet or beat earnings targets.
- A company culture that puts profitability and good business performance ahead of ethical behavior.

The stance a company takes in dealing with or managing ethical conduct at any given time can take any of four basic forms:

- The unconcerned or nonissue approach.
- The damage control approach.
- The compliance approach.
- The ethical culture approach.

The idea of *corporate social responsibility* calls for companies to find balance between (1) their *economic responsibilities* to reward shareholders with profits, (2) *legal responsibilities* to comply with the laws of countries where they operate, (3) *ethical responsibilities* to abide by society's norms of what is moral and just, and (4) *philanthropic responsibilities* to contribute to the noneconomic needs of society. The menu of actions and behavior for demonstrating social responsibility includes:

- Employing an ethical strategy and observing ethical principles in operating the business.
- Making charitable contributions, donating money and the time of company personnel to community service endeavors, supporting various worthy organizational causes, and making a difference in the lives of the disadvantaged. Corporate commitments are further reinforced by encouraging employees to support charitable and community activities.

- Protecting or enhancing the environment and, in particular, striving to minimize or eliminate any adverse impact on the environment stemming from the company's own business activities.
- Creating a work environment that makes the company a great place to work.
- Employing a workforce that is diverse with respect to gender, race, national origin, and perhaps other aspects that different people bring to the workplace.

There's ample room for every company to tailor its social responsibility strategy to fit its core values and business mission, thereby making its own statement about "how we do business and how we intend to fulfill our duties to all stakeholders and society at large."

Some companies use the terms *corporate social responsibility* and *corporate citizenship* interchangeably, but typically, corporate citizenship places expectations on companies to go beyond consistently demonstrating ethical strategies and business behavior by addressing unmet noneconomic needs of society. Corporate sustainability involves strategic efforts to meet the needs of current customers, suppliers, shareholders, employees, and other stakeholders, while protecting, and perhaps enhancing, the resources needed by future generations.

ASSURANCE OF LEARNING EXERCISES

1. Consider the following portrayal of strategies employed by the major recording studios:

> Some recording artists and the Recording Artists' Coalition claim that the world's five major music recording studios—Universal, Sony, Time Warner, EMI/Virgin, and Bertelsmann—deliberately employ strategies calculated to take advantage of musicians who record for them. One practice to which they strenuously object is that the major-label record companies frequently require artists to sign contracts committing them to do six to eight albums, an obligation that some artists say can entail an indefinite term of indentured servitude. Further, it is claimed that audits routinely detect unpaid royalties to musicians under contract; according to one music industry attorney, record companies misreport and underpay artist royalties by 10 to 40 percent and are "intentionally fraudulent." One music writer was recently quoted as saying the process was "an entrenched system whose prowess and conniving makes Enron look like amateur hour." Royalty calculations are based on complex formulas that are paid only after artists pay for recording costs and other expenses and after any advances are covered by royalty earnings.
>
> A *Baffler* magazine article outlined a hypothetical but typical record deal in which a promising young band is given a $250,000 royalty advance on a new album. The album subsequently sells 250,000 copies, earning $710,000 for the record company; but the band, after repaying the record company for $264,000 in expenses ranging from recording fees and video budgets to catering, wardrobe, and bus tour costs for promotional events related to the album, ends up $14,000 in the hole, owes the record company money, and is thus paid no royalties on any of the $710,000 in revenues the recording company receives from the sale of the band's music. It is also standard practice in the music industry for recording studios to sidestep payola laws by hiring independent promoters to lobby and compensate radio stations for playing certain records. Record companies are often entitled to damages for undelivered albums if an artist

leaves a recording studio for another label after seven years. Record companies also retain the copyrights in perpetuity on all music recorded under contract, a practice that artists claim is unfair. The Dixie Chicks, after a year-long feud with Sony over contract terms, ended up refusing to do another album; Sony sued for breach of contract, prompting a countersuit by the Dixie Chicks charging "systematic thievery" to cheat them out of royalties. The suits were settled out of court. One artist said, "The record companies are like cartels." Recording studios defend their strategic practices by pointing out that fewer than 5 percent of the signed artists ever deliver a hit and that they lose money on albums that sell poorly.[56]

a. If you were a recording artist, would you be happy with some of the strategic practices of the recording studios? Would you feel comfortable signing a recording contract with studios engaging in any of the practices?

b. Which, if any, of the practices of the recording studios do you view as unethical?

2. Suppose you found yourself in the following situation: In preparing a bid for a multimillion-dollar contract in a foreign country, you are introduced to a "consultant" who offers to help you in submitting the bid and negotiating with the customer company. You learn in conversing with the consultant that she is well connected in local government and business circles and knows key personnel in the customer company extremely well. The consultant quotes you a six-figure fee. Later, your local coworkers tell you that the use of such consultants is normal in this country—and that a large fraction of the fee will go directly to people working for the customer company. They further inform you that bidders who reject the help of such consultants have lost contracts to competitors who employed them. What would you do, assuming your company's code of ethics expressly forbids the payments of bribes or kickbacks in any form?

3. Assume that you are the sales manager at a European company that makes sleepwear products for children. Company personnel discover that the chemicals used to flameproof the company's line of children's pajamas might cause cancer if absorbed through the skin. Following this discovery, the pajamas are then banned from sale in the European Union and the United States, but senior executives of your company learn that the children's pajamas in inventory and the remaining flameproof material can be sold to sleepwear distributors in certain countries where there are no restrictions against the material's use. Your superiors instruct you to make the necessary arrangements to sell the inventories of banned pajamas and flameproof materials to distributors in those countries. Would you comply if you felt that your job would be in jeopardy if you didn't?

4. Review Microsoft's statements about its corporate citizenship programs at www.microsoft.com/about/corporatecitizenship. How does the company's commitment to global citizenship provide positive benefits for its stakeholders? How does Microsoft plan to improve social and economic empowerment in developing countries through its Unlimited Potential program? Why is this important to Microsoft shareholders?

5. Go to www.nestle.com and read the company's latest sustainability report. What are Nestlé's key sustainable environmental policies? How is the company addressing sustainable social development? How do these initiatives relate to the company's principles, values, and culture and its approach to competing in the food industry?

EXERCISES FOR SIMULATION PARTICIPANTS

1. Is your company's strategy ethical? Why or why not? Is there anything that your company is doing that could be considered shady by your competitors?
2. In what ways, if any, is your company exercising social responsibility and good corporate citizenship? Could (should) the list of things your company is doing be longer? If so, indicate what additional actions you think your company could take (assuming it had the option to do so).
3. Is your company conducting its business in an environmentally sustainable manner? What specific actions could your company take that would make an even greater contribution to environmental sustainability?

CHAPTER

10

Building an Organization Capable of Good Strategy Execution

LEARNING OBJECTIVES

1. Gain command of what managers must do to promote successful strategy execution.
2. Understand why good strategy execution requires astute managerial actions to build core competencies and competitive capabilities.
3. Learn what issues to consider in organizing the work effort and why strategy-critical activities should be the main building blocks of the organizational structure.
4. Become aware of the pros and cons of centralized and decentralized decision making in implementing and executing the chosen strategy.

The best game plan in the world never blocked or tackled anybody.

—Vince Lombardi

Strategies most often fail because they aren't executed well.

—Larry Bossidy and Ram Charan
CEO, Honeywell International; Author and Consultant

A second-rate strategy perfectly executed will beat a first-rate strategy poorly executed every time.

—Richard M. Kovacevich
Chairman and CEO, Wells Fargo

People are *not* your most important asset. The right people are.

—Jim Collins

Organizing is what you do before you do something, so that when you do it, it is not all mixed up.

—A. A. Milne

Once managers have decided on a strategy, the emphasis turns to converting it into actions and good results. Putting the strategy into place and getting the organization to execute it well call for different sets of managerial skills. Whereas crafting strategy is largely a market-driven activity, implementing and executing strategy is primarily an operations-driven activity revolving around the management of people and business processes. Whereas successful strategy making depends on business vision, solid industry and competitive analysis, and shrewd market positioning, successful strategy execution depends on doing a good job of working with and through others, building and strengthening competitive capabilities, motivating and rewarding people in a strategy-supportive manner, and instilling a discipline of getting things done. Executing strategy is an action-oriented, make-things-happen task that tests a manager's ability to direct organizational change, achieve continuous improvement in operations and business processes, create and nurture a strategy-supportive culture, and consistently meet or beat performance targets.

Experienced managers are emphatic in declaring that it is a whole lot easier to develop a sound strategic plan than it is to execute the plan and achieve the desired outcomes. According to one executive, "It's been rather easy for us to decide where we wanted to go. The hard part is to get the organization to act on the new priorities."[1] In a recent study of 1,000 companies, government agencies, and not-for-profit organizations in over 50 countries, 60 percent of employees rated their organizations poor in terms of strategy implementation.[2] *Just because senior managers announce a new strategy doesn't mean that organizational members will agree with it or enthusiastically move forward in implementing it.* Senior executives cannot simply direct immediate subordinates to abandon old ways and take up new ways, and they certainly cannot expect the needed actions and changes to occur in rapid-fire fashion and lead to the desired outcomes. Some managers and employees may be skeptical about the merits of the strategy, seeing it as contrary to the organization's best interests, unlikely to succeed, or threatening to their departments or careers. Moreover, different employees may have misconceptions about the new strategy or have different ideas about what internal changes are needed to execute it. Long-standing attitudes, vested interests, inertia, and ingrained organizational practices don't melt away when managers decide on a new strategy and begin efforts to implement it—especially when only a few people have been involved in crafting the strategy and when the rationale for strategic change requires quite a bit of salesmanship. It takes adept managerial leadership to convincingly communicate the new strategy and the reasons for it, overcome pockets of doubt and disagreement, secure the commitment and enthusiasm of key personnel, build consensus on all the hows of implementation and execution, and move forward to get all the pieces into place. Company personnel have to understand—in their heads and in their hearts—why a new strategic direction is necessary and where the new strategy is taking them.[3] Instituting change is, of course, easier when the problems with the old strategy have become obvious and/or the company has spiraled into a financial crisis.

But the challenge of successfully implementing new strategic initiatives goes well beyond managerial adeptness in overcoming resistance to change. What really makes executing strategy a tougher, more time-consuming management challenge than crafting strategy are the wide array of managerial activities that have to be attended to and the number of bedeviling issues that must be worked out. It takes first-rate "managerial smarts" to zero in on what exactly needs to be done to put new strategic initiatives in place and, further, how best to get these things done in a timely manner that yields good results. Highly demanding people-management skills are required. Plus, it takes follow-through and perseverance to get a variety of initiatives launched and moving, and to integrate the efforts of many different work groups into a smoothly functioning whole. Depending on how much consensus building and organizational change is involved, the process of implementing strategy changes can take several months to several years. And it takes still longer to achieve *real proficiency* in executing the strategy.

Like crafting strategy, *executing strategy is a job for the whole management team, not just a few senior managers.* While an organization's chief executive officer and the heads of major units (business divisions, functional departments, and key operating units) are ultimately responsible for seeing that strategy is executed successfully, the process typically affects every part of the firm, from the biggest operating unit to the smallest frontline work group. Top-level managers have to rely on the active support and cooperation of middle and lower managers in launching new strategic initiatives, in putting all of the pieces of the strategy into place, and in getting rank-and-file employees to execute the strategy with real proficiency and dedication. It is middle and lower-level managers who ultimately must ensure that work groups and frontline employees do a good job of performing strategy-critical value chain activities and produce the operating results that allow companywide performance targets to be met. Hence, the role of middle and lower-level managers on the company's strategy execution team is by no means minimal.

CORE CONCEPT
Good strategy execution requires a *team effort*. All managers have strategy-executing responsibility in their areas of authority, and all employees are participants in the strategy execution process.

Strategy execution thus requires every manager to think through the answer to "What does my area have to do to implement its part of the strategic plan, and what should I do to get these things accomplished effectively and efficiently?" The bigger the organization or the more geographically scattered its operating units, the more that successful strategy execution depends on the cooperation and implementing skills of operating managers who can push the needed changes at the lowest organizational levels and, in the process, deliver good results. Only in small organizations can top-level managers get around the need for a team effort on the part of management and personally orchestrate the action steps required for good strategy execution and operating excellence.

A FRAMEWORK FOR EXECUTING STRATEGY

Executing strategy entails figuring out all the hows—the specific techniques, actions, and behaviors that are needed for a smooth strategy-supportive operation—and then following through to get things done and deliver results. The idea is to make things happen and make them happen right. The first step in implementing strategic changes is for management to communicate the case for organizational change so clearly and persuasively to organizational members that a determined commitment takes hold throughout the ranks to find ways to put the strategy into place, make it work, and meet performance targets. The ideal condition is for managers to arouse enough enthusiasm for the strategy to turn the implementation process into a companywide crusade. *Management's handling of the strategy implementation process can be considered successful if and when the company achieves the targeted strategic and financial performance and shows good progress in making its strategic vision a reality.*

The specific hows of executing a strategy—the exact items that need to be placed on management's action agenda—always have to be customized to fit the particulars of a company's situation. Making minor changes in an existing strategy differs from implementing radical strategy changes. The hot buttons for successfully executing a low-cost provider strategy are different from those in executing a high-end differentiation strategy. Implementing and executing a new strategy for a struggling company in the midst of a financial crisis is a different job from that of improving strategy execution in a company where the execution is already pretty good. Moreover, some managers are more adept than others at using this or that approach to achieving the desired kinds of organizational changes. Hence, there's no definitive managerial recipe for successful strategy execution that cuts across all company situations and all types of strategies or that works for all types of managers. Rather, the specific hows of implementing and executing a strategy—the "to-do list" that constitutes management's agenda for action—always represents management's judgment about how best to proceed in light of the prevailing circumstances.

The Principal Managerial Components of the Strategy Execution Process

Despite the need to tailor a company's strategy-executing approaches to the particulars of its situation, certain managerial bases have to be covered no matter what the circumstances. Eight managerial tasks crop up repeatedly in company efforts to execute strategy (see Figure 10.1):

1. Building an organization with the competencies, capabilities, and resource strengths to execute strategy successfully.
2. Marshaling sufficient money and people behind the drive for strategy execution.
3. Instituting policies and procedures that facilitate rather than impede strategy execution.

Figure 10.1 The Eight Components of Strategy Execution

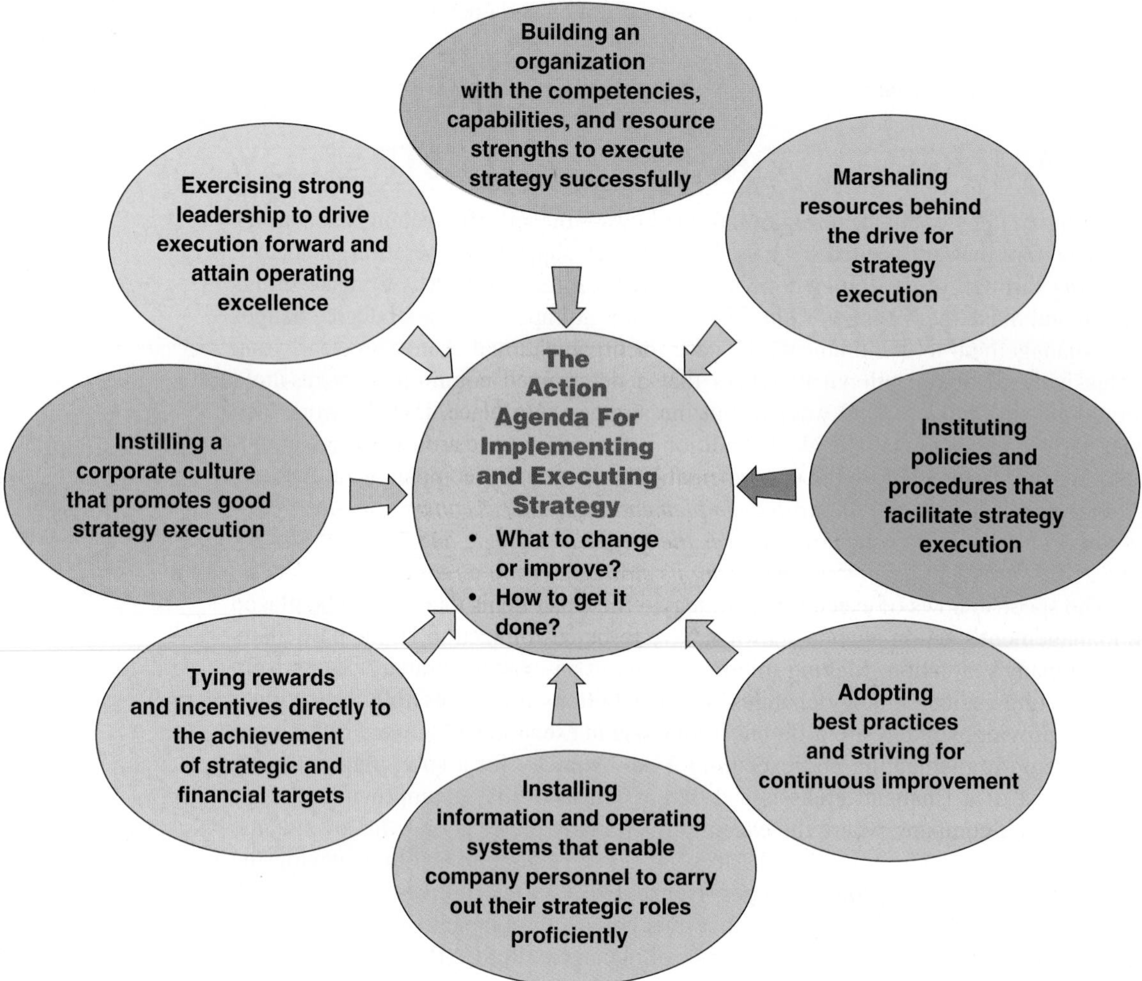

4. Adopting best practices and pushing for continuous improvement in how value chain activities are performed.
5. Installing information and operating systems that enable company personnel to carry out their strategic roles proficiently.
6. Tying rewards directly to the achievement of strategic and financial targets and to good strategy execution.
7. Instilling a corporate culture that promotes good strategy execution.
8. Exercising strong leadership to drive execution forward, keep improving on the details of execution, and achieve operating excellence as rapidly as feasible.

How well managers perform these eight tasks has a decisive impact on whether the outcome is a spectacular success, a colossal failure, or something in between.

In devising an action agenda for implementing and executing strategy, the place for managers to start is with *a probing assessment of what the organization must do differently and better to carry out the strategy successfully.* They should then consider *precisely how to make the necessary internal changes* as rapidly as possible. Successful strategy implementers have a knack for diagnosing what their organizations need to do to execute the chosen strategy well and figuring out how to get things done—they are masters in promoting results-oriented behaviors on the part of company personnel and following through on making the right things happen in a timely fashion.[4]

When strategies fail, it is often because of poor execution—things that were supposed to get done slip through the cracks.

In big organizations with geographically scattered operating units, the action agenda of senior executives mostly involves communicating the case for change to others, building consensus for how to proceed, installing strong allies to push implementation along in key organizational units, urging and empowering subordinates to keep the process moving, establishing deadlines and measures of progress, recognizing and rewarding those who achieve implementation milestones, directing resources to the right places, and personally leading the strategic change process. Thus, the bigger the organization, the more successful strategy execution depends on the cooperation and implementing skills of operating managers who can push needed changes at the lowest organizational levels and deliver results. In small organizations, top managers can deal directly with frontline managers and employees, personally orchestrating the action steps and implementation sequence, observing firsthand how implementation is progressing, and deciding how hard and how fast to push the process along. Regardless of the organization's size and whether implementation involves sweeping or minor changes, the most important leadership traits are a strong, confident sense of what to do and how to do it. Having a strong grip on these two things comes from understanding the circumstances of the organization and the requirements for effective strategy execution. Then it remains for those managers and company personnel in strategy-critical areas to step up to the plate and produce the desired results.

What's Covered in Chapters 10, 11, and 12 In the remainder of this chapter and the next two chapters, we will discuss what is involved in performing the eight key managerial tasks (shown in Figure 10.1) that shape the process of implementing and executing strategy. This chapter explores building resource strengths and organizational capabilities. Chapter 11 looks at marshaling resources, instituting strategy-facilitating policies and procedures, adopting best practices, installing operating systems, and tying rewards to the achievement of good results. Chapter 12 deals with creating a strategy-supportive corporate culture and exercising appropriate strategic leadership.

BUILDING AN ORGANIZATION CAPABLE OF GOOD STRATEGY EXECUTION

Proficient strategy execution depends heavily on competent personnel, better-than-adequate competitive capabilities, and effective internal organization. Building a capable organization is thus always a top priority in strategy execution. As shown in Figure 10.2, three types of organization-building actions are paramount:

1. *Staffing the organization*—putting together a strong management team, and recruiting and retaining employees with the needed experience, technical skills, and intellectual capital.

Figure 10.2 The Three Components of Building an Organization Capable of Proficient Strategy Execution

Staffing the Organization
■ Putting together a strong management team
■ Recruiting and retaining talented employees
Building Core Competencies and Competitive Capabilities
■ Developing a set of competencies and capabilities suited to the current strategy
■ Updating and revising this set as external conditions and strategy change
■ Training and retraining Company personnel as needed to maintain skills-based competencies
Structuring the Organization and Work Effort
■ Instituting organizational arrangements that facilitate good strategy execution
■ Deciding how much decision-making authority to push down to lower-level managers and frontline employees
A Company with the Competencies and Capabilities Needed for Proficient Strategy Execution

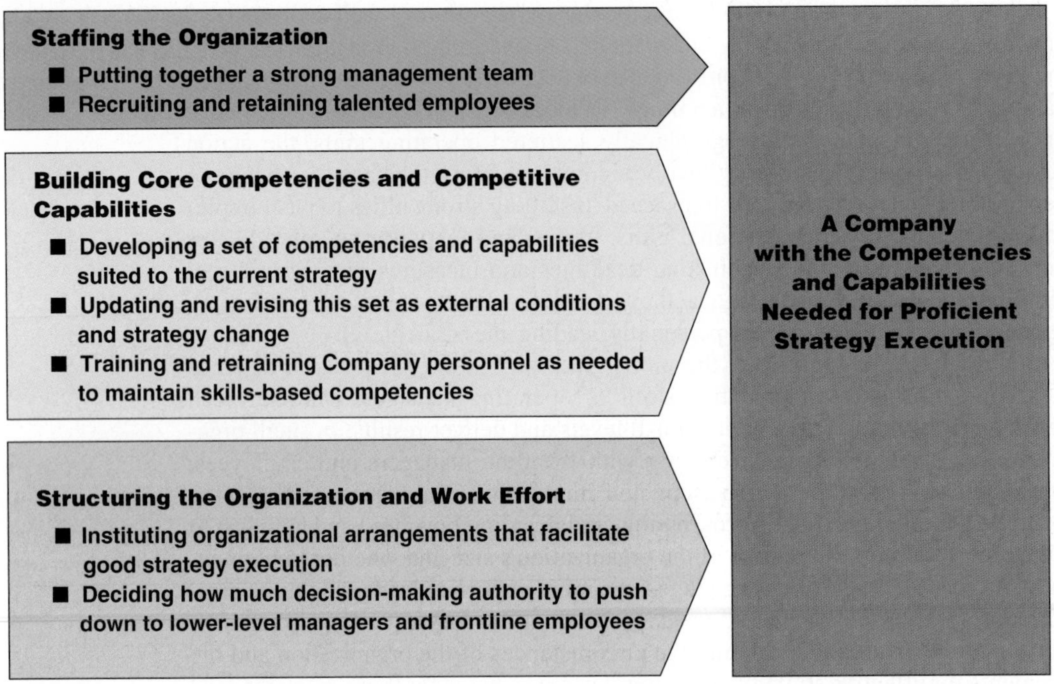

2. *Building core competencies and competitive capabilities*—developing proficiencies in performing strategy-critical value chain activities and updating them to match changing market conditions and customer expectations.
3. *Structuring the organization and work effort*—organizing value chain activities and business processes and deciding how much decision-making authority to push down to lower-level managers and frontline employees.

STAFFING THE ORGANIZATION

No company can hope to perform the activities required for successful strategy execution without attracting and retaining talented managers and employees with suitable skills and *intellectual capital.*

Putting Together a Strong Management Team

Assembling a capable management team is a cornerstone of the organization-building task.[5] While different strategies and company circumstances sometimes call for different mixes of backgrounds, experiences, management styles, and know-how, *the most important consideration is to fill key managerial slots with smart people who are clear thinkers, good at figuring out what needs to be done, skilled in "making it happen" and delivering good results.*[6] The task of implementing and executing challenging strategic initiatives must be assigned to executives who can be counted on to turn their decisions and actions into results that meet or beat the established performance targets. It helps enormously when a company's top management team has several people who are particularly good change agents—true believers who champion change, know how to make it happen, and love every second of the process.[7] Without a smart, capable, results-oriented management team, the implementation-execution process ends up being hampered by missed deadlines, misdirected or wasteful efforts, and/or managerial ineptness.[8] Weak executives are serious impediments to getting optimal results because they are unable to differentiate between ideas and approaches that have merit and those that are misguided—the caliber of work done under their supervision suffers.[9] In contrast, managers with strong strategy-implementing capabilities have a talent for asking tough, incisive questions. They know enough about the details of the business to ensure the soundness of the approaches and decisions of the people around them, and they can discern whether the resources people are asking for to put the strategy in place make sense. They are good at getting things done through others, typically by making sure they have the right people under them and that these people are put in the right jobs.[10] They consistently follow through on issues, monitor progress carefully, make adjustments when needed, and keep important details from slipping through the cracks. In short, they know how to drive organizational change, and they have the managerial skills to promote first-rate strategy execution.

CORE CONCEPT

Putting together a talented management team with the right mix of experiences, skills, and abilities to get things done is one of the first strategy-implementing steps.

Sometimes a company's existing management team is up to the task; at other times it may need to be strengthened or expanded by promoting qualified people from within or by bringing in outsiders whose experiences, talents, and leadership styles better suit the situation. In turnaround and rapid-growth situations, and in instances when a company doesn't have insiders with the requisite know-how, filling key management slots from the outside is a fairly standard organization-building approach. In addition, it is important to ferret out and replace managers who, for whatever reasons, either do not buy into the case for making organizational changes or do not see ways to make things better.[11] For a top management team to be truly effective, it has got to consist of true believers who recognize that organizational changes are needed and are ready to get on with the process. Weak executives and diehard resisters have to be replaced or sidelined, perhaps by shifting them to positions of lesser influence where they cannot hamper new strategy execution initiatives.

The overriding aim in building a management team should be to assemble a *critical mass* of talented managers who can function as agents of change and further the cause of first-rate strategy execution—every manager's success is enhanced (or limited) by the quality of his or her managerial colleagues and the degree to which they freely exchange ideas, debate how to improve approaches that have merit, and join forces to tackle issues and solve problems.[12] When a first-rate manager enjoys the help and support of other first-rate managers, it's possible to create a managerial whole that is greater than the sum of individual efforts—talented managers who work well together as a team can produce organizational results that are dramatically better than what one or two star managers acting individually can achieve. The chief lesson here is that *a company needs to get the right executives on the bus—and the wrong executives off the bus—before trying to drive the bus in the desired direction.*[13]

Illustration Capsule 10.1 describes General Electric's widely acclaimed approach to developing a top-caliber management team.

Recruiting and Retaining Capable Employees

Assembling a capable management team is not enough. Staffing the organization with the right kinds of people must go much deeper than managerial jobs in order for value chain activities to be performed competently. *The quality of an organization's*

ILLUSTRATION CAPSULE 10.1
How General Electric Develops a Talented and Deep Management Team

General Electric (GE) is widely considered to be one of the best-managed companies in the world, partly because of its concerted effort to develop outstanding managers. For starters, GE strives to hire talented people with high potential for executive leadership; it then goes to great lengths to expand the leadership, business, and decision-making capabilities of all its managers. The company spends about $1 billion annually on training and education programs. In 2008, all of its 189 most-senior executives had spent at least 12 months in training and professional development.

Four key elements undergird GE's efforts to build a talent-rich stable of managers:

1. GE makes a practice of transferring managers across divisional, business, or functional lines for sustained periods. Such transfers allow managers to develop relationships with colleagues in other parts of the company, help break down insular thinking in business "silos," and promote the sharing of cross-business ideas and best practices. There is an enormous emphasis at GE on transferring ideas and best practices from business to business and making GE a "boundaryless" company.
2. In selecting executives for key positions, GE is strongly disposed to candidates who exhibit what are called the four Es—enormous personal *energy*, the ability to *energize* others, *edge* (a GE code word for instinctive competitiveness and the ability to make tough decisions in a timely fashion, saying yes or no, and not maybe), and *execution* (the ability to carry things through to fruition). Considerable attention is also paid to problem-solving ability, experience in multiple functions or businesses, and experience in driving business growth (as indicated by good market instincts, in-depth knowledge of particular markets, customer touch, and technical understanding).
3. All managers are expected to be proficient at what GE calls *workout*—a process in which managers and employees come together to confront issues as soon as they come up, pinpoint the root cause of the issues, and bring about quick resolutions so the business can move forward. Workout is GE's way of training its managers to diagnose what to do and how to do it.
4. Each year GE sends about 10,000 newly hired and longtime managers to its John F. Welch Leadership Development Center (generally regarded as one of the best corporate training centers in the world) for a three-week course on the company's Six Sigma quality initiative. Close to 10,000 "Master Black Belt" and "Black Belt" Six Sigma experts have graduated from the program to drive forward thousands of quality initiatives throughout GE. Six Sigma training is an ironclad requirement for promotion to any professional or managerial position and any stock option award. GE's Leadership Development Center also offers advanced courses for senior managers that may focus on a single management topic for a month. All classes involve managers from different GE businesses and different parts of the world. Some of the most valuable learning comes in between formal class sessions when GE managers from different businesses trade ideas about how to improve processes and better serve the customer. This knowledge sharing not only spreads best practices throughout the organization but also improves each GE manager's knowledge.

Each of GE's 85,000 managers and professionals is graded in an annual process that divides them into five tiers: the top 10 percent, the next 15 percent, the middle 50 percent, the next 15 percent, and the bottom 10 percent. Everyone in the top tier gets stock awards, nobody in the fourth tier gets shares of stock, and most of those in the fifth tier become candidates for being weeded out. Business heads are pressured to wean out "C" players. GE's CEO personally reviews the performance of the top 3,000 managers. Senior executive compensation is heavily weighted toward Six Sigma commitment and producing successful business results. In 2007, over 70 percent of total compensation for GE's five most-senior executives was contingent on the company's performance.

According to Jack Welch, GE's CEO from 1980 to 2001, "The reality is, we simply cannot afford to field anything but teams of 'A' players."

Sources: GE's 1998, 2003, and 2007 annual reports; www.ge.com; John A. Byrne, "How Jack Welch Runs GE," *BusinessWeek,* June 8, 1998, p. 90; Miriam Leuchter, "Management Farm Teams," *Journal of Business Strategy,* May 1998, pp. 29–32; and "The House That Jack Built, *The Economist,* September 18, 1999.

people is always an essential ingredient of successful strategy execution—knowledgeable, engaged employees are a company's best source of creative ideas for the nuts-and-bolts operating improvements that lead to operating excellence. Companies like Google, Microsoft, McKinsey & Company, Southwest Airlines, Cisco Systems, Amazon.com, Procter & Gamble, PepsiCo, Nike, Electronic Data Systems (EDS), Goldman Sachs,and Intel make a concerted effort to recruit the best and brightest people they can find and then retain them with excellent compensation packages, opportunities for rapid advancement and professional growth, and challenging and interesting assignments. Having a pool of "A" players with strong skill sets and lots of brainpower is essential to their business. Microsoft makes a point of hiring the very brightest and most talented programmers it can find and motivating them with both good monetary incentives and the challenge of working on cutting-edge software design projects. McKinsey & Company, one of the world's premier management consulting companies, recruits only cream-of-the-crop MBAs at the nation's top 10 business schools; such talent is essential to McKinsey's strategy of performing high-level consulting for the world's top corporations. The leading global accounting firms screen candidates not only on the basis of their accounting expertise but also on whether they possess the people skills needed to relate well with clients and colleagues. Southwest Airlines goes to considerable lengths to hire people who can have fun and be fun on the job; it uses special interviewing and screening methods to gauge whether applicants for customer-contact jobs have outgoing personality traits that match its strategy of creating a high-spirited, fun-loving, in-flight atmosphere for passengers; it is so selective that only about 3 percent of the people who apply are offered jobs.

CORE CONCEPT

In many industries, adding to a company's talent base and building intellectual capital is more important to good strategy execution than additional investments in plants, equipment, and capital projects.

In high-tech companies, the challenge is to staff work groups with gifted, imaginative, and energetic people who can bring life to new ideas quickly and inject into the organization what one Dell executive calls "hum."[14] The saying "People are our most important asset" may seem hollow, but it fits high-technology companies dead-on. Besides checking closely for functional and technical skills, Dell tests applicants for their tolerance of ambiguity and change, their capacity to work in teams, and their ability to learn on the fly. Companies like Amazon.com, Google, and Cisco Systems have broken new ground in recruiting, hiring, cultivating, developing, and retaining talented employees—most of whom are in their 20s and 30s. Cisco goes after the top 10 percent, raiding other companies and endeavoring to retain key people at the companies it acquires. Cisco executives believe that a cadre of star engineers, programmers, managers, salespeople, and support personnel is the backbone of the company's efforts to execute its strategy and remain the world's leading provider of Internet infrastructure products and technology.

In instances where intellectual capital greatly aids good strategy execution, companies have instituted a number of practices aimed at staffing jobs with the best people they can find:

1. Spending considerable effort in screening and evaluating job applicants, selecting only those with suitable skill sets, energy, initiative, judgment, aptitudes for learning, and personality traits that mesh well with the company's work environment and culture.
2. Putting employees through training programs that continue throughout their careers.

3. Providing promising employees with challenging, interesting, and skill-stretching assignments.
4. Rotating people through jobs that not only have great content but also span functional and geographic boundaries. Providing people with opportunities to gain experience in a variety of international settings is increasingly considered an essential part of career development in multinational or global companies.
5. Encouraging employees to challenge existing ways of doing things, to be creative and innovative in proposing better ways of operating, and to push their ideas for new products or businesses. Progressive companies work hard at creating an environment in which ideas and suggestions bubble up from below and employees are made to feel that their views and suggestions count.
6. Making the work environment stimulating and engaging such that employees will consider the company a great place to work.
7. Striving to retain talented, high-performing employees via promotions, salary increases, performance bonuses, stock options and equity ownership, fringe benefit packages, and other perks.
8. Coaching average performers to improve their skills and capabilities, while weeding out underperformers and benchwarmers.

The best companies make a point of recruiting and retaining talented employees—the objective is to make the company's entire workforce (managers and rank-and-file employees) a genuine resource strength.

It is very difficult for a company to competently execute its strategy and achieve operating excellence without a large band of capable employees who are actively engaged in the process of making ongoing operating improvements.

BUILDING CORE COMPETENCIES AND COMPETITIVE CAPABILITIES

High among the organization-building priorities in the strategy implementing/executing process is the need to build and strengthen competitively valuable core competencies and organizational capabilities. Whereas managers identify the desired competencies and capabilities in the course of crafting strategy, good strategy execution requires putting the desired competencies and capabilities in place, upgrading them as needed, and then modifying them as market conditions evolve. Sometimes a company already has some semblance of the needed competencies and capabilities, in which case managers can concentrate on strengthening and nurturing them to promote better strategy execution. More often, however, company managers have to significantly broaden or deepen certain capabilities or even add entirely new competencies in order to put strategic initiatives in place and execute them proficiently.

A number of prominent companies have succeeded in establishing core competencies and capabilities that have been instrumental in making them winners in the marketplace. Intel's core competence is in the design and mass production of complex chips for personal computers, servers, and other electronic products. Procter & Gamble's core competencies reside in its superb marketing/distribution skills and its R&D capabilities in five core technologies—fats, oils, skin chemistry, surfactants, and emulsifiers. Ciba Specialty Chemicals has technology-based competencies that allow it to quickly manufacture products for customers wanting customized products relating to coloration, brightening and whitening, water treatment and paper processing, freshness, and cleaning. Disney has core competencies in theme park operation and family entertainment.

The Three-Stage Process of Developing and Strengthening Competencies and Capabilities

Building core competencies and competitive capabilities is a time-consuming, managerially challenging exercise. While some organization-building assist can be gotten from discovering how best-in-industry or best-in-world companies perform a particular activity, trying to replicate and then improve on the competencies and capabilities of others is much easier said than done, for the same reasons that one is unlikely to ever become a good golfer just by studying what Tiger Woods does. Putting a new capability in place is more complicated than charging a group of people to become highly competent in performing the desired activity, using whatever information can be gleaned from other companies having similar competencies or capabilities. Rather, it takes a series of deliberate and well-orchestrated organizational steps to achieve mounting proficiency in performing an activity. The capability-building process has three stages:

> ***Stage 1***—First, the organization must develop the *ability* to do something, however imperfectly or inefficiently. This entails selecting people with the requisite skills and experience, upgrading or expanding individual abilities as needed, and then molding the efforts and work products of individuals into a collaborative effort to create organizational ability.
>
> ***Stage 2***—As experience grows and company personnel learn how to perform the activity *consistently well and at an acceptable cost,* the ability evolves into a tried-and-true *competence* or *capability.*
>
> ***Stage 3***—Should company personnel continue to polish and refine their know-how and otherwise sharpen their performance of an activity such that the company eventually becomes *better than rivals* at performing the activity, the core competence rises to the rank of a *distinctive competence* (or the capability becomes a competitively superior capability), thus providing a path to competitive advantage.

Many companies are able to get through stages 1 and 2 in performing a strategy-critical activity, but comparatively few achieve sufficient proficiency in performing strategy-critical activities to qualify for the third stage.

Managing the Process Four traits concerning core competencies and competitive capabilities are important in successfully managing the organization-building process:[15]

1. *Core competencies and competitive capabilities are bundles of skills and know-how that most often grow out of the combined efforts of cross-functional work groups and departments performing complementary activities at different locations in the firm's value chain.* Rarely does a core competence or capability consist of narrow skills attached to the work efforts of a single department. For instance, a core competence in speeding new products to market involves the collaborative efforts of personnel in R&D, engineering and design, purchasing, production, marketing, and distribution. Similarly, the capability to provide superior customer service is a team effort among people in customer call centers (where orders are taken and inquiries are answered), shipping and delivery, billing and accounts receivable, and after-sale support. Complex activities (like designing and manufacturing an ultra-fuel-efficient SUV using innovative engine technology or creating software security systems that can foil the efforts of hackers) usually involve a number

of component skills, technological disciplines, competencies, and capabilities—some performed in-house and some provided by suppliers/allies. An important part of the organization-building function is to think about which activities of which groups need to be linked and made mutually reinforcing and then to forge the necessary collaboration both internally and with outside resource providers.

CORE CONCEPT

Building competencies and capabilities is a multistage process that occurs over months and years, not something that is accomplished overnight.

2. *Normally, a core competence or capability emerges incrementally* out of company efforts either to bolster skills that contributed to earlier successes or to respond to customer problems, new technological and market opportunities, and the competitive maneuverings of rivals. Migrating from the one-time ability to do something up the ladder to a core competence or competitively valuable capability is usually an organization-building process that takes months and often years to accomplish—it is definitely not an overnight event.
3. The key to leveraging a core competence into a distinctive competence (or a capability into a competitively superior capability) is *concentrating more effort and more talent than rivals on deepening and strengthening the competence or capability, so as to achieve the dominance needed for competitive advantage.* This does not necessarily mean spending more money on such activities than competitors, but it does mean consciously focusing more talent on them and striving for best-in-industry, if not best-in-world, status. To achieve dominance on lean financial resources, companies like Cray in large computers and Honda in gasoline engines have leveraged the expertise of their talent pool by frequently re-forming high-intensity teams and reusing key people on special projects. The experiences of these and other companies indicate that the usual keys to successfully building core competencies and valuable capabilities are superior employee selection, thorough training and retraining, powerful cultural influences, effective cross-functional collaboration, empowerment, motivating incentives, short deadlines, and good databases—not big operating budgets.
4. Evolving changes in customers' needs and competitive conditions often require *tweaking and adjusting a company's portfolio of competencies and intellectual capital to keep its capabilities freshly honed and on the cutting edge.* This is particularly important in high-tech industries and fast-paced markets where important developments occur weekly. As a consequence, wise company managers work at anticipating changes in customer-market requirements and staying ahead of the curve in proactively building a package of competencies and capabilities that can win out over rivals.

Managerial actions to develop core competencies and competitive capabilities generally take one of two forms: either strengthening the company's base of skills, knowledge, and intellect, or coordinating and networking the efforts of the various work groups and departments. Actions of the first sort can be undertaken at all managerial levels, but actions of the second sort are best orchestrated by senior managers who not only appreciate the strategy-executing significance of strong competencies/capabilities but also have the clout to enforce the necessary networking and cooperation among individuals, groups, departments, and external allies.

One organization-building question is whether to develop the desired competencies and capabilities internally or to outsource them by partnering with key suppliers or forming strategic alliances. The answer depends on what can be safely delegated to outside suppliers or allies versus what internal capabilities are key to the company's long-term success. Either way, though, calls for action. Outsourcing means launching initiatives to identify the most attractive providers and to establish collaborative relationships. Developing the capabilities in-house means marshaling personnel with relevant skills and experience, collaboratively networking the individual skills and related cross-functional activities to form organizational capability, and building the desired levels of proficiency through repetition (practice makes perfect).[16]

Sometimes the tediousness of internal organization building can be shortcut by buying a company that has the requisite capability and integrating its competencies into the firm's value chain. Indeed, a pressing need to acquire certain capabilities quickly is one reason to acquire another company—an acquisition aimed at building greater capability can be every bit as competitively valuable as an acquisition aimed at adding new products or services to the company's business lineup. Capabilities-motivated acquisitions are essential (1) when a market opportunity can slip by faster than a needed capability can be created internally, and (2) when industry conditions, technology, or competitors are moving at such a rapid clip that time is of the essence. But usually there's no good substitute for ongoing internal efforts to build and strengthen the company's competencies and capabilities in performing strategy-critical value chain activities.

Updating and Remodeling Competencies and Capabilities as External Conditions and Company Strategy Change Even after core competencies and competitive capabilities are in place and functioning, company managers can't relax. Competencies and capabilities that grow stale can impair competitiveness unless they are refreshed, modified, or even phased out in response to ongoing market changes and shifts in company strategy. Indeed, the buildup of knowledge and experience over time, coupled with the imperatives of keeping capabilities in step with ongoing strategy and market changes, makes it appropriate to view a company as *a bundle of evolving competencies and capabilities.* Management's organization-building challenge is one of deciding when and how to recalibrate existing competencies and capabilities, and when and how to develop new ones. Although the task is formidable, ideally it produces a dynamic organization with "hum" and momentum as well as a distinctive competence.

Toyota, en route to overtaking General Motors as the global leader in motor vehicles, has aggressively upgraded its capabilities in fuel-efficient hybrid engine technology and constantly fine-tuned its famed Toyota Production System to enhance its already proficient capabilities in manufacturing top-quality vehicles at relatively low costs—see Illustration Capsule 10.2. Likewise, Honda, which has long had a core competence in gasoline engine technology and small engine design, has recently accelerated its efforts to broaden its expertise and capabilities in hybrid engines so as to stay close behind Toyota. Microsoft totally retooled the manner in which its programmers attacked the task of writing code for its Vista operating systems for PCs and servers. TV broadcasters have upgraded their capabilities in digital broadcasting technology in readiness for the 2009 switchover from analog to digital signal transmission.

The Strategic Role of Employee Training

Training and retraining are important when a company shifts to a strategy requiring different skills, competitive capabilities, managerial approaches, and operating methods. Training is also strategically important in organizational efforts to build skills-based competencies. And it is a key activity in businesses where technical know-how

ILLUSTRATION CAPSULE 10.2

Toyota's Legendary Production System: A Capability That Translates into Competitive Advantage

The heart of Toyota's strategy in motor vehicles is to outcompete rivals by manufacturing world-class, quality vehicles at low costs and selling them at competitive price levels. Executing this strategy requires top-notch manufacturing capability and superefficient management of people, equipment, and materials. Toyota began conscious efforts to improve its manufacturing competence over 50 years ago. Through tireless trial and error, the company gradually took what started as a loose collection of techniques and practices and integrated them into a full-fledged process that has come to be known as the Toyota Production System (TPS). The TPS drives all plant operations and the company's supply chain management practices. TPS is grounded in the following principles, practices, and techniques:

- *Use just-in-time delivery of parts and components to the point of vehicle assembly.* The idea here is to cut out all the bits and pieces of transferring materials from place to place and to discontinue all activities on the part of workers that don't add value (particularly activities where nothing ends up being made or assembled).
- *Develop people who can come up with unique ideas for production improvements.* Toyota encourages employees at all levels to question existing ways of doing things—even if it means challenging a boss on the soundness of a directive. Toyota president Katsuaki Watanabe encourages the company's employees to "pick a friendly fight." Also, Toyota doesn't fire its employees who, at first, have little judgment for improving work flows; instead, the company gives them extensive training to become better problem solvers.
- *Emphasize continuous improvement.* Workers are expected to use their heads and develop better ways of doing things, rather than mechanically follow instructions. Toyota managers tout messages such as "Never be satisfied" and "There's got to be a better way." Another mantra at Toyota is that the *T* in TPS also stands for "Thinking." The thesis is that a work environment where people have to think generates the wisdom to spot opportunities for making tasks simpler and easier to perform, increasing the speed and efficiency with which activities are performed, and constantly improving product quality.
- *Empower workers to stop the assembly line when there's a problem or a defect is spotted.* Toyota views worker efforts to purge defects and sort out the problem immediately as critical to the whole concept of building quality into the production process. According to TPS, "If the line doesn't stop, useless defective items will move on to the next stage. If you don't know where the problem occurred, you can't do anything to fix it."
- *Deal with defects only when they occur.* TPS philosophy holds that when things are running smoothly, they should not be subject to control; if attention is directed to fixing problems that are found, quality control along the assembly line can be handled with fewer personnel.
- *Ask yourself "Why?" five times.* While errors need to be fixed whenever they occur, the value of asking "Why?" five times enables identifying the root cause of the error and correcting it so that the error won't recur.
- *Organize all jobs around human motion to create a production/assembly system with no wasted effort.* Work organized in this fashion is called "standardized work," and people are trained to observe standardized work procedures (which include supplying parts to each process on the assembly line at the proper time, sequencing the work in an optimal manner, and allowing workers to do their jobs continuously in a set sequence of subprocesses).
- *Find where a part is made cheaply and use that price as a benchmark.*

The TPS utilizes a unique vocabulary of terms (such as *kanban, takt-time, jikoda, kaizen, heijunka, monozukuri, poka yoke,* and *muda*) that facilitates precise discussion of specific TPS elements. In 2003, Toyota established a Global Production Center to efficiently train large numbers of shop-floor experts in the latest TPS methods and better operate an increasing number of production sites worldwide.

There's widespread agreement that Toyota's ongoing effort to refine and improve on its renowned TPS gives it important manufacturing capabilities that are the envy of other motor vehicle manufacturers. Not only have such auto manufacturers as Ford, Daimler, Volkswagen, and General Motors attempted to emulate key elements of TPS, but elements of Toyota's production philosophy has been adopted by hospitals and postal services.

Sources: Information posted at www.toyotageorgetown.com; Hirotaka Takeuchi, Emi Osono, and Norihiko Shimizu, "The Contradictions That Drive Toyota's Success," *Harvard Business Review* 86, no. 6 (June 2008), pp. 96–104; and Taiichi Ohno, *Toyota Production System: Beyond Large-Scale Production* (New York: Sheridan, 1988).

is changing so rapidly that a company loses its ability to compete unless its skilled people have cutting-edge knowledge and expertise. Successful strategy implementers see to it that the training function is both adequately funded and effective. If the chosen strategy calls for new skills, deeper technological capability, or building and using new capabilities, training should be placed near the top of the action agenda.

The strategic importance of training has not gone unnoticed. Over 600 companies have established internal "universities" to lead the training effort, facilitate continuous organizational learning, and help upgrade company competencies and capabilities. Many companies conduct orientation sessions for new employees, fund an assortment of competence-building training programs, and reimburse employees for tuition and other expenses associated with obtaining additional college education, attending professional development courses, and earning professional certification of one kind or another. A number of companies offer online, just-in-time training courses to employees around the clock. Increasingly, employees at all levels are expected to take an active role in their own professional development, assuming responsibility for keeping their skills and expertise up-to-date and in sync with the company's needs.

From Competencies and Capabilities to Competitive Advantage

While strong core competencies and competitive capabilities are a major assist in executing strategy, they are an equally important avenue for securing a competitive edge over rivals in situations where it is relatively easy for rivals to copy smart strategies. Anytime rivals can readily duplicate successful strategy features, making it difficult or impossible to outstrategize rivals and beat them in the marketplace with a superior strategy, the chief way to achieve lasting competitive advantage is to outexecute them (beat them by performing certain value chain activities in superior fashion). *Building core competencies and competitive capabilities that are difficult or costly for rivals to emulate and that push a company closer to true operating excellence promotes proficient strategy execution.* Moreover, because cutting-edge core competencies and competitive capabilities represent resource strengths that are often time-consuming and expensive for rivals to match or trump, any competitive edge they produce tends to be sustainable and pave the way for above-average company performance.

CORE CONCEPT
Building competencies and capabilities that are very difficult or costly for rivals to emulate has a huge payoff—improved strategy execution and a potential for competitive advantage.

It is easy to cite instances where companies have gained a competitive edge based on superior competencies and capabilities. Dell's competitors have spent years and millions of dollars in what so far is a futile effort to match Dell's cost-efficient supply chain management capabilities. FedEx has unmatched capabilities in reliable overnight delivery of documents and small parcels. Various business news media have been unable to match the competence of *The Wall Street Journal* to report business news with such breadth and depth.

EXECUTION-RELATED ASPECTS OF ORGANIZING THE WORK EFFORT

There are few hard-and-fast rules for organizing the work effort to support good strategy execution. Every firm's organization chart is partly a product of its particular situation, reflecting prior organizational patterns, varying internal circumstances, executive judgments about reporting relationships, and the politics of who gets which assignments.

Moreover, every strategy is grounded in its own set of key success factors and value chain activities. But some organizational considerations are common to all companies. These are summarized in Figure 10.3 and discussed in turn in the following sections.

Deciding Which Value Chain Activities to Perform Internally and Which to Outsource

The advantages of a company having an outsourcing component in its strategy were discussed in Chapter 6 (pp. 164–205), but there is also a need to consider the role of outsourcing in executing the strategy. Aside from the fact than an outsider, because of its expertise and specialized know-how, may be able to perform certain value chain activities better or cheaper than a company can perform them internally, outsourcing can also have several organization-related benefits. Managers too often spend inordinate amounts of time, mental energy, and resources haggling with functional support groups and other internal bureaucracies over needed services, leaving less time for them to devote to performing strategy-critical activities in the most proficient manner. One way to reduce such distractions is to outsource the performance of assorted administrative support functions and perhaps even selected core or primary value chain activities to outside vendors, thereby enabling the company to *concentrate its full energies and resources on even more competently performing those value chain activities that are at the core of its strategy and for which it can create unique value.*

Figure 10.3 Structuring the Work Effort to Promote Successful Strategy Execution

Decide which value chain activities to perform internally and which ones to outsource
Make internally performed strategy-critical activities the main building blocks in the organization structure
Decide how much authority to centralize at the top and how much to delegate to down-the-line managers and employees
Provide for cross-unit coordination
Provide for the necessary collaboration with suppliers and strategic allies
An Organization Structure Matched to the Requirements of Successful Strategy Execution

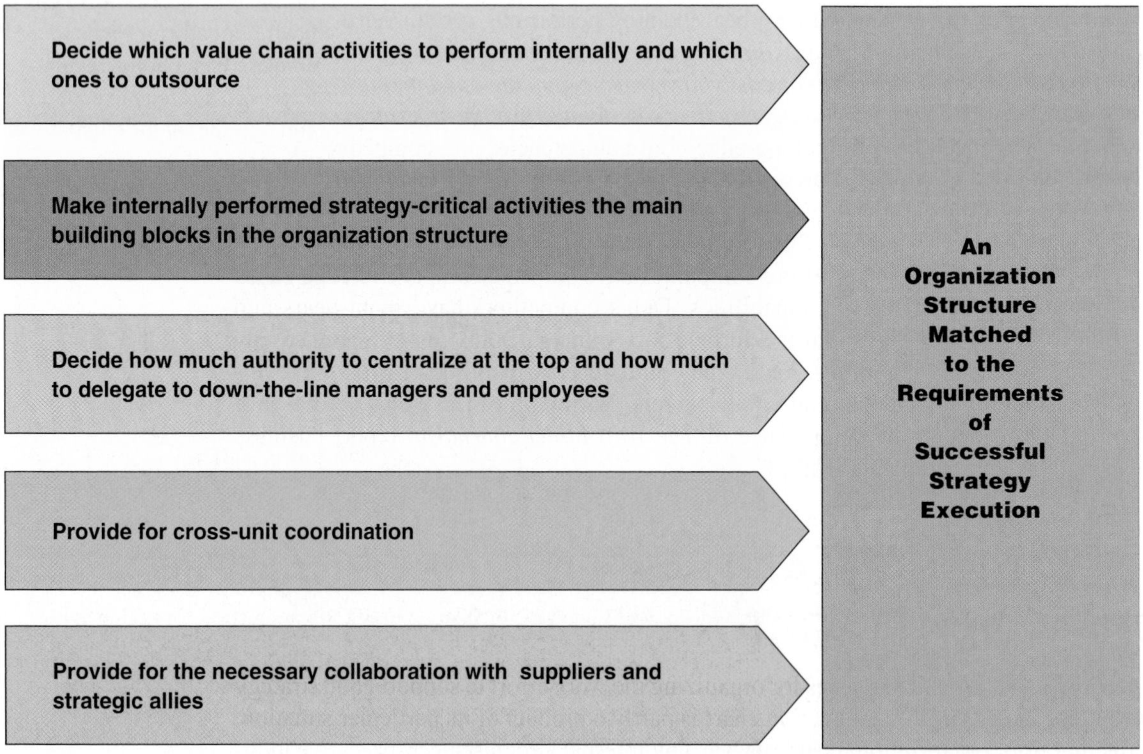

For example, E. & J. Gallo Winery outsources 95 percent of its grape production, letting farmers take on the weather and other grape-growing risks while it concentrates its full energies on wine production and sales.[17] A number of PC makers outsource the mundane and highly specialized task of PC assembly, concentrating their energies instead on product design, sales and marketing, and distribution.

When a company uses outsourcing to zero in on ever better performance of those truly strategy-critical activities where its expertise is most needed, then it may be able to realize three very positive benefits:

1. *The company improves its chances for outclassing rivals in the performance of these activities and turning a core competence into a distinctive competence.* At the very least, the heightened focus on a performing a select few value chain activities should meaningfully strengthen the company's existing core competencies and promote more innovative performance of those activities—either of which could lower costs or materially improve competitive capabilities. ING Insurance, Circuit City, Hugo Boss, Japan Airlines, Whirlpool, and Chevron have outsourced their data processing activities to computer service firms, believing that outside specialists can perform the needed services at lower costs and equal or better quality. A relatively large number of companies outsource the operation of their Web sites to Web design and hosting enterprises. Many business that get a lot of inquiries from customers or that have to provide 24/7 technical support to users of their products across the world have found that it is considerably less expensive to outsource these functions to specialists (often located in foreign countries where skilled personnel are readily available and worker compensation costs are much lower) than to operate their own call centers.
2. *The streamlining of internal operations that flows from outsourcing often acts to decrease internal bureaucracies, flatten the organization structure, speed internal decision making and shorten the time it takes to respond to changing market conditions.*[18] In consumer electronics, where advancing technology drives new product innovation, organizing the work effort in a manner that expedites getting next-generation products to market ahead of rivals is a critical competitive capability. The world's motor vehicle manufacturers have found that they can shorten the cycle time for new models, improve the quality and performance of those models, and lower overall production costs by outsourcing the big majority of their parts and components from independent suppliers and then working closely with their vendors to advance the design and functioning of the items being supplied, to swiftly incorporate new technology, and to better integrate individual parts and components to form engine cooling systems, transmission systems, and electrical systems.
3. *Partnerships can add to a company's arsenal of capabilities and contribute to better strategy execution.* By building, continually improving, and then leveraging partnerships, a company enhances its overall organizational capabilities and builds resource strengths—strengths that deliver value to customers and consequently pave the way for competitive success. Soft-drink and beer manufacturers all cultivate their relationships with their bottlers and distributors to strengthen access to local markets and build the loyalty, support, and commitment for corporate marketing programs, without which their own sales and growth are weakened. Similarly, fast-food enterprises like McDonald's and Taco Bell find it essential to work hand-in-hand with franchisees on outlet cleanliness, consistency

CORE CONCEPT

Wisely choosing which activities to perform internally and which to outsource can lead to several strategy-executing advantages—lower costs, heightened strategic focus, less internal bureaucracy, speedier decision making, and a better arsenal of competencies and capabilities.

of product quality, in-store ambience, courtesy and friendliness of store personnel, and other aspects of store operations. Unless franchisees continuously deliver sufficient customer satisfaction to attract repeat business, a fast-food chain's sales and competitive standing will suffer quickly. Companies like Boeing, Aerospatiale, Verizon Communications, and Dell have learned that their central R&D groups cannot begin to match the innovative capabilities of a well-managed network of supply chain partners having the ability to advance the technology, lead the development of next-generation parts and components, and supply them at a relatively low price.[19]

As a general rule, companies refrain from outsourcing those value chain activities over which they need direct strategic and operating control in order to build core competencies, achieve competitive advantage, and effectively manage key customer–supplier–distributor relationships. It is the strategically less important activities—like handling customer inquiries and providing technical support, doing the payroll, administering employee benefit programs, providing corporate security, managing stockholder relations, maintaining fleet vehicles, operating the company's Web site, conducting employee training, and managing an assortment of information and data processing functions—where outsourcing is most used.

Even so, a number of companies have found ways to successfully rely on outside vendors to perform strategically significant value chain activities.[20] Broadcom, a global leader in chips for broadband communications systems, outsources the manufacture of its chips to Taiwan Semiconductor, thus freeing company personnel to focus their full energies on R&D, new chip design, and marketing. Nike concentrates on design, marketing, and distribution to retailers, while outsourcing virtually all production of its shoes and sporting apparel. Cisco Systems outsources virtually all of its manufacturing of its routers, switches, and other Internet gear; yet, it protects its market position by retaining tight internal control over product design and it closely monitors the daily operations of its manufacturing vendors. Large numbers of electronics companies outsource the design, engineering, manufacturing, and shipping of their products to such companies as Flextronics and Solectron, both of which have built huge businesses as providers of such services to companies worldwide. So while performing *core* value chain activities in-house normally makes good sense, there can be times when outsourcing some of them works to good advantage.

The Dangers of Excessive Outsourcing Critics contend that a company can go overboard on outsourcing and so hollow out its knowledge base and capabilities as to leave itself at the mercy of outside suppliers and short of the resource strengths to be a master of its own destiny.[21] The point is well taken, but most companies appear alert to the danger of taking outsourcing to an extreme or failing to maintain control of the work performed by specialist vendors or offshore suppliers. Many companies refuse to source key components from a single supplier, opting to use two or three suppliers as a way of avoiding single supplier dependence or giving one supplier too much bargaining power. Moreover, they regularly evaluate their suppliers, looking not only at the supplier's overall performance but also at whether they should switch to another supplier or even bring the activity back in-house. To avoid loss of control, companies typically work closely with key suppliers, meeting often and setting up online systems to share data and information, collaborate on work in progress, monitor performance, and otherwise document that suppliers' activities are closely integrated with their own requirements and expectations. Indeed, the advent of sophisticated online systems makes it feasible for companies to work in "real time" with suppliers 10,000 miles away, making rapid response possible whenever concerns or problems arise. Hence, *the real debate surrounding outsourcing is not about whether too much outsourcing risks loss of control but about how to use outsourcing in a manner that produces greater competitiveness.*

Making Strategy-Critical Activities the Main Building Blocks of the Organization Structure

In any business, some activities in the value chain are always more critical to strategic success and competitive advantage than others. For instance, hotel/motel enterprises have to be good at fast check-in/check-out, housekeeping and facilities maintenance, food service, and creating a pleasant ambience. In discount stock brokerage, the strategy-critical activities are fast access to information, accurate order execution, efficient record keeping and transactions processing, and good customer service. In specialty chemicals, the critical activities are R&D, product innovation, getting new products onto the market quickly, effective marketing, and expertise in assisting customers. Where such is the case, it is important for management to build its organization structure around proficient performance of these activities, making them the centerpieces or main building blocks on the organization chart.

The rationale for making strategy-critical activities the main building blocks in structuring a business is compelling: If activities crucial to strategic success are to have the resources, decision-making influence, and organizational impact they need, they have to be centerpieces in the organizational scheme. Plainly, implementing a new or changed strategy is likely to entail new or different key activities, competencies, or capabilities and therefore to require new or different organizational arrangements. If workable organizational adjustments are not forthcoming, the resulting mismatch between strategy and structure can open the door to execution and performance problems.[22] Attempting to carry out a new strategy with an old organizational structure is usually unwise.

What Types of Organization Structures Fit Which Strategies? It is generally agreed that some type of *functional or specialized-activity structure* is the best organizational arrangement when a company is in just one particular business (irrespective of which of the five competitive strategies it opts to pursue). The primary organizational building blocks within a business are usually traditional *functional departments* (R&D, engineering and design, production and operations, sales and marketing, information technology, finance and accounting, and human resources) and *process departments* (where people in a single work unit have responsibility for all the aspects of a certain process like supply chain management, new product development, customer service, quality control, or Web sales). For instance, a technical instruments manufacturer may be organized around research and development, engineering, supply chain management, assembly, quality control, marketing, technical services, and corporate administration. A hotel may have a functional organization based on front-desk operations, housekeeping, building maintenance, food service, convention services and special events, guest services, personnel and training, and accounting. A discount retailer may organize around such functional units as purchasing, warehousing and distribution, store operations, advertising, merchandising and promotion, customer service, and corporate administrative services.

In enterprises with operations in various countries around the world (or with geographically scattered organizational units within a country), the basic building blocks may also include *geographic organizational units,* each of which has profit/loss responsibility for its assigned geographic area. In vertically integrated firms, the major building blocks are *divisional units performing one or more of the major processing steps along the value chain* (raw materials production, components manufacture, assembly, wholesale distribution, retail store operations); each division in the value chain may operate as a profit center for performance measurement purposes.

The typical building blocks of a diversified company are its *individual businesses,* with each business unit usually operating as an independent profit center and with corporate headquarters performing assorted support functions for all of its business units. But a divisional business-unit structure can present problems to a company pursuing related diversification because independent business units—each running its own business in its own ways—inhibit cross-business collaboration and the capture of cross-business strategic fits.

Determining the Degree of Authority and Independence to Give Each Unit and Each Employee

In executing the strategy and conducting daily operations, companies must decide how much authority to delegate to the managers of each organization unit—especially the heads of business subsidiaries, functional and process departments, and plants, sales offices, distribution centers and other operating units—and how much decision-making latitude to give individual employees in performing their jobs. The two extremes are to *centralize decision making* at the top (the CEO and a few close lieutenants) or to *decentralize decision making* by giving managers and employees considerable decision-making latitude in their areas of responsibility. As shown in Table 10.1, the two approaches are based on sharply different underlying principles and beliefs, with each having its pros and cons.

There are disadvantages to having a small number of top-level managers micromanage the business either by personally making decisions or by requiring lower-level subordinates to gain approval before taking action.

Centralized Decision Making: Pros and Cons *In a highly centralized organization structure, top executives retain authority for most strategic and operating decisions and keep a tight rein on business-unit heads, department heads, and the managers of key operating units; comparatively little discretionary authority is granted to frontline supervisors and rank-and-file employees.* The command-and-control paradigm of centralized structures is based on the underlying assumption that frontline personnel have neither the time nor the inclination to direct and properly control the work they are performing, and that they lack the knowledge and judgment to make wise decisions about how best to do it—hence the need for managerially prescribed policies and procedures, close supervision, and tight control. The thesis underlying authoritarian structures is that strict enforcement of detailed procedures backed by rigorous managerial oversight is the most reliable way to keep the daily execution of strategy on track.

The big advantage of an authoritarian structure is tight control by the manager in charge—it is easy to know who is accountable when things do not go well. But there are some serious disadvantages. Hierarchical command-and-control structures make an organization sluggish in responding to changing conditions because of the time it takes for the review/approval process to run up all the layers of the management bureaucracy. Furthermore, to work well, centralized decision making requires top-level managers to gather and process whatever information is relevant to the decision. When the relevant knowledge resides at lower organizational levels (or is technical, detailed, or hard to express in words), it is difficult and time-consuming to get all of

TABLE 10.1 Advantages and Disadvantages of Centralized versus Decentralized Decision Making

Centralized Organizational Structures	Decentralized Organizational Structures
Basic Tenets • Decisions on most matters of importance should be pushed to managers up the line who have the experience, expertise, and judgment to decide what is the wisest or best course of action. • Front-line supervisors and rank-and-file employees can't be relied upon to make the right decisions—because they seldom know what is best for the organization and because they do not have the time or the inclination to properly manage the tasks they are performing (letting them decide what to do is thus risky). **Chief Advantage** • Tight control from the top fixes accountability. **Primary Disadvantages** • Lengthens response times because management bureaucracy must decide on a course of action. • Does not encourage responsibility among lower level managers and rank-and-file employees. • Discourages lower level managers and rank-and-file employees from exercising any initiative—they are expected to wait to be told what to do.	**Basic Tenets** • Decision-making authority should be put in the hands of the people closest to and most familiar with the situation and these people should be trained to exercise good judgment. • A company that draws on the combined intellectual capital of all its employees can outperform a command-and-control company. **Chief Advantages** • Encourages lower level managers and rank-and-file employees to exercise initiative and act responsibly. • Promotes greater motivation and involvement in the business on the part of more company personnel. • Spurs new ideas and creative thinking. • Allows fast response times. • Entails fewer layers of management. **Primary Disadvantages** • Puts the organization at risk if many bad decisions are made at lower levels—top management lacks full control. • Impedes cross-business coordination and capture of strategic fits in diversified companies.

the facts and nuances in front of a high-level executive located far from the scene of the action—full understanding of the situation cannot be readily copied from one mind to another.[23] Hence, centralized decision making is often impractical—the larger the company and the more scattered its operations, the more that decision-making authority has to be delegated to managers closer to the scene of the action.

Decentralized Decision-Making: Pros and Cons *In a highly decentralized organization, decision-making authority is pushed down to the lowest organizational level capable of making timely, informed, competent decisions.* The objective is to put adequate decision-making authority in the hands of the people closest to and most familiar with the situation and train them to weigh all the factors and exercise good judgment. Decentralized decision making means that the managers of each organizational unit are delegated lead responsibility for deciding how best to execute strategy (as well as some role in shaping the strategy for the units they head). Decentralization thus requires selecting strong managers to head each organizational unit and holding them accountable for crafting and executing appropriate strategies for their units. Managers who consistently produce unsatisfactory results have to be weeded out.

The ultimate goal of decentralized decision making is to put decision-making authority in the hands of those persons or teams closest to and most knowledgeable about the situation.

The case for empowering down-the-line managers and employees to make decisions related to daily operations and executing the strategy is based on the belief that a company that draws on the combined intellectual capital of all its employees can outperform a command-and-control company.[24] Decentralized decision making means, for example, that in a diversified company the various business-unit heads have broad authority to execute the agreed-on business strategy with comparatively little interference from corporate headquarters; moreover, the business-unit heads delegate considerable decision-making latitude to functional and process department heads and the heads of the various operating units (plants, distribution centers, sales offices) in implementing and executing their pieces of the strategy. In turn, work teams may be empowered to manage and improve their assigned value chain activity, and employees with customer contact may be empowered to do what it takes to please customers. At Starbucks, for example, employees are encouraged to exercise initiative in promoting customer satisfaction—there's the story of a store employee who, when the computerized cash register system went offline, enthusiastically offered free coffee to waiting customers.[25] *With decentralized decision making, top management maintains control by limiting empowered managers' and employees' discretionary authority and holding people accountable for the decisions they make.*

The benefits of decentralized organization structures are considerable. Delegating greater authority to subordinate managers and employees creates a more horizontal organization structure with fewer management layers. Whereas in a centralized vertical structure managers and workers have to go up the ladder of authority for an answer, in a decentralized horizontal structure they develop their own answers and action plans—making decisions in their areas of responsibility and being accountable for results is an integral part of their job. Pushing decision-making authority down to middle and lower-level managers and then further on to work teams and individual employees shortens organizational response times and spurs new ideas, creative thinking, innovation, and greater involvement on the part of subordinate managers and employees. In worker-empowered structures, jobs can be defined more broadly, several tasks can be integrated into a single job, and people can direct their own work. Fewer managers are needed because deciding how to do things becomes part of each person's or team's job. Further, today's online communication systems make it easy and relatively inexpensive for people at all organizational levels to have direct access to data, other employees, managers, suppliers, and customers. They can access information quickly (via the Internet or company intranet), readily check with superiors or whomever else as needed, and take responsible action. Typically, there are genuine gains in morale and productivity when people are provided with the tools and information they need to operate in a self-directed way. Decentralized decision making can not only shorten organizational response times but also spur new ideas, creative thinking, innovation, and greater involvement on the part of subordinate managers and employees.

In the past 15 years, there has been a pronounced shift from authoritarian, multilayered hierarchical structures to flatter, more decentralized structures that stress employee empowerment. There's strong and growing consensus that authoritarian, hierarchical organization structures are not well suited to implementing and executing strategies in an era when extensive information and instant communication are the norm and when a big fraction of the organization's most valuable assets consists of intellectual capital and resides in the knowledge and capabilities of its employees. Many companies have therefore begun empowering lower-level managers and employees throughout their organizations, giving them greater discretionary authority to make strategic adjustments in their areas of responsibility and to decide what needs to be done to put new strategic initiatives into place and execute them proficiently.

Maintaining Control in a Decentralized Organization Structure Pushing decision-making authority deep down into the organization structure and empowering employees presents its own organizing challenge: *how to exercise adequate control* *over the actions of empowered employees so that the business is not put at risk at the same time that the benefits of empowerment are realized.*[26] Maintaining adequate organizational control over empowered employees is generally accomplished by placing limits on the authority that empowered personnel can exercise, holding people accountable for their decisions, instituting compensation incentives that reward people for doing their jobs in a manner to contributes to good company performance, and creating a corporate culture where there's strong peer pressure on individuals to act responsibly.

Capturing Strategic Fits in a Decentralized Structure Diversified companies striving to capture cross-business strategic fits have to beware of allowing business heads to operate independently when cross-business collaboration is essential in order to gain strategic fit benefits. Cross-business strategic fits typically have to be captured either by enforcing close cross-business collaboration or by centralizing performance of functions having strategic fits at the corporate level.[27] For example, if businesses with overlapping process and product technologies have their own independent R&D departments—each pursuing their own priorities, projects, and strategic agendas—it's hard for the corporate parent to prevent duplication of effort, capture either economies of scale or economies of scope, or broaden the company's R&D efforts to embrace new technological paths, product families, end-use applications, and customer groups. Where cross-business R&D fits exist, the best solution is usually to centralize the R&D function and have a coordinated corporate R&D effort that serves both the interests of individual business and the company as a whole. Likewise, centralizing the related activities of separate businesses makes sense when there are opportunities to share a common sales force, use common distribution channels, rely on a common field service organization to handle customer requests or provide maintenance and repair services, use common e-commerce systems and approaches, and so on.

The point here is that efforts to decentralize decision making and give organizational units leeway in conducting operations have to be tempered with the need to maintain adequate control and cross-unit coordination—decentralization doesn't mean delegating authority in ways that allow organization units and individuals to do their own thing. There are numerous instances when decision-making authority must be retained at high levels in the organization and ample cross-unit coordination strictly enforced.

Providing for Internal Cross-Unit Coordination

The classic way to coordinate the activities of organizational units is to position them in the hierarchy so that the most closely related ones report to a single person (a functional department head, a process manager, a geographic area head, a senior executive). Managers higher up in the ranks generally have the clout to coordinate, integrate, and arrange for the cooperation of units under their supervision. In such structures, the chief executive officer, chief operating officer, and business-level managers end up as central points of coordination because of their positions of authority over the whole unit. When a firm is pursuing a related diversification strategy, coordinating the related activities of independent business units often requires the centralizing authority of a single corporate-level officer. Also, diversified companies commonly centralize such staff support functions as public relations, finance and accounting, employee benefits, and information technology at the corporate level both to contain the costs of support activities and to facilitate uniform and coordinated performance of such functions within each business unit.

However, close cross-unit collaboration is usually needed to build core competencies and competitive capabilities in such strategically important activities as speeding new products to market and providing superior customer service which involve employees scattered across several internal organization units (and perhaps the employees of outside strategic partners or specialty vendors). A big weakness of traditional functionally organized structures is that pieces of strategically relevant activities and capabilities often end up scattered across many departments, with the result that no one group or manager is accountable. Consider, for example, how the following strategy-critical activities cut across different functions:

- *Filling customer orders accurately and promptly*—a process that involves personnel from sales (which wins the order); finance (which may have to check credit terms or approve special financing); production (which must produce the goods and replenish warehouse inventories as needed); warehousing (which has to verify whether the items are in stock, pick the order from the warehouse, and package it for shipping); and shipping (which has to choose a carrier to deliver the goods and release the goods to the carrier).[28]
- *Fast, ongoing introduction of new products*—a cross-functional process involving personnel in R&D, design and engineering, purchasing, manufacturing, and sales and marketing.
- *Improving product quality*—a process that entails the collaboration of personnel in R&D, design and engineering, purchasing, in-house components production, manufacturing, and assembly.
- *Supply chain management*—a collaborative process that cuts across such functional areas as purchasing, inventory management, manufacturing and assembly, and warehousing and shipping.
- *Building the capability to conduct business via the Internet*—a process that involves personnel in information technology, supply chain management, production, sales and marketing, warehousing and shipping, customer service, finance, and accounting.
- *Obtaining feedback from customers and making product modifications to meet their needs*—a process that involves personnel in customer service and after-sale support, R&D, design and engineering, purchasing, manufacturing and assembly, and marketing research.

Handoffs from one department to another lengthen completion time and frequently drive up administrative costs, since coordinating the fragmented pieces can soak up hours of effort on the parts of many people.[29] This is not a fatal flaw of functional organization—organizing around specific functions normally works to good advantage in support activities like finance and accounting, human resource management, and engineering, and in such primary activities as R&D, manufacturing, and marketing. But the tendency for pieces of a strategy-critical activity to be scattered across several functional departments is an important weakness of functional organization and accounts for why a company's competencies and capabilities are typically cross-functional and don't reside in the activities of a single functional department.

Many companies have found that rather than continuing to scatter related pieces of a strategy-critical business process across several functional departments and scrambling to integrate their efforts, it is better to reengineer the work effort and pull the people who performed the pieces in functional departments into a group that works together to perform the whole process, thus creating *process departments* (like customer service or new product development or supply chain management). And sometimes the coordinating mechanisms involve the use of cross-functional task forces, dual reporting relationships, informal organizational networking, voluntary cooperation, incentive compensation tied to measures of group performance, and strong executive-level insistence on teamwork and cross-department cooperation (including removal of recalcitrant managers who stonewall collaborative efforts). At one European-based company, a top executive promptly replaced the managers of several plants who were not fully committed to collaborating closely on eliminating duplication in product development and production efforts among plants in several different countries. Earlier, the executive, noting that negotiations among the managers had stalled on which labs and plants to close, had met with all the managers, asked them to cooperate to find a solution, discussed with them which options were unacceptable, and given them a deadline to find a solution. When the asked-for teamwork wasn't forthcoming, several managers were replaced.

Providing for Collaboration with Outside Suppliers and Strategic Allies

Someone or some group must be authorized to collaborate as needed with each major outside constituency involved in strategy execution. Forming alliances and cooperative relationships presents immediate opportunities and opens the door to future possibilities, but nothing valuable is realized until the relationship grows, develops, and blossoms. Unless top management sees that constructive organizational bridge-building with strategic partners occurs and that productive working relationships emerge, the value of alliances is lost and the company's power to execute its strategy is weakened. If close working relationships with suppliers are crucial, then supply chain management must be given formal status on the company's organization chart and a significant position in the pecking order. If distributor/dealer/franchisee relationships are important, someone must be assigned the task of nurturing the relationships with forward channel allies. If working in parallel with providers of complementary products and services contributes to enhanced organizational capability, then cooperative organizational arrangements have to be put in place and managed to good effect.

Building organizational bridges with external allies can be accomplished by appointing "relationship managers" with responsibility for making particular strategic partnerships or alliances generate the intended benefits. Relationship managers have many roles and functions: getting the right people together, promoting good rapport, seeing that plans for specific activities are developed and carried out, helping adjust internal organizational procedures and communication systems, ironing out operating dissimilarities, and nurturing interpersonal cooperation. Multiple cross-organization ties have to be established and kept open to ensure proper communication and coordination.[30] There has to be enough information sharing to make the relationship work and periodic frank discussions of conflicts, trouble spots, and changing situations.[31]

Current Organizational Trends

Many of today's companies are winding up the task of remodeling their traditional hierarchical structures once built around functional specialization and centralized authority. Much of the corporate downsizing movement in the late 1980s and early 1990s was aimed at recasting authoritarian, pyramidal organizational structures into flatter, decentralized structures. The change was driven by growing realization that command-and-control hierarchies were proving a liability in businesses where customer preferences were shifting from standardized products to custom orders and special features, product life cycles were growing shorter, custom mass production methods were replacing standardized mass production techniques, customers wanted to be treated as individuals, technological change was ongoing, and market conditions were fluid. Layered management hierarchies with lots of checks and controls that required people to look upward in the organizational structure for answers and approval were failing to deliver responsive customer service and timely adaptations to changing conditions.

The organizational adjustments and downsizing of companies in 2001–2003 brought further refinements and changes to streamline organizational activities and shake out inefficiencies. The goals have been to make companies leaner, flatter, and more responsive to change. Many companies are drawing on five tools of organizational design: (1) managers and workers empowered to act on their own judgments, (2) work process redesign (to achieve greater streamlining and tighter cohesion), (3) self-directed work teams, (4) rapid incorporation of Internet technology applications, and (5) networking with outsiders to improve existing organization capabilities and create new ones. Considerable management attention is being devoted to building a company capable of outcompeting rivals on the basis of superior resource strengths and competitive capabilities—capabilities that are increasingly based on intellectual capital and cross-unit collaboration.

Several other organizational characteristics are emerging:

- Extensive use of Internet technology and e-commerce business practices—real-time data and information systems, greater reliance on online systems for transacting business with suppliers and customers, and Internet-based communication and collaboration with suppliers, customers, and strategic partners.
- Fewer barriers between different vertical ranks, between functions and disciplines, between units in different geographic locations, and between the company and its suppliers, distributors/dealers, strategic allies, and customers—an outcome partly due to pervasive use of online systems.
- Rapid dissemination of information, rapid learning, and rapid response times—also an outcome partly due to pervasive use of online systems.
- Collaborative efforts among people in different functional specialties and geographic locations—essential to create organization competencies and capabilities.
- Assembling work teams that include more members and have a greater geographic dispersion of team members. During the 1990s, most formal team arrangements contained 20 or fewer members. Today, teams at many multinational corporations include 100 or more members that might be scattered across 10 or more countries.

KEY POINTS

Implementing and executing strategy is an operation-driven activity revolving around the management of people and business processes. The managerial emphasis is on converting strategic plans into actions and good results. *Management's handling of the process of implementing and executing the chosen strategy can be considered successful if and when the company achieves the targeted strategic and financial performance and shows good progress in making its strategic vision a reality.* Shortfalls in performance signal weak strategy, weak execution, or both.

The place for managers to start in implementing and executing a new or different strategy is with *a probing assessment of what the organization must do differently and better to carry out the strategy successfully.* They should then consider *precisely how to make the necessary internal changes* as rapidly as possible.

Like crafting strategy, executing strategy is a job for a company's whole management team, not just a few senior managers. Top-level managers have to rely on the active support and cooperation of middle and lower managers to push strategy changes into functional areas and operating units and to see that the organization actually operates in accordance with the strategy on a daily basis.

Eight managerial tasks crop up repeatedly in company efforts to execute strategy:

1. Building an organization with the competencies, capabilities, and resource strengths to execute strategy successfully.
2. Marshaling sufficient money and people behind the drive for strategy execution.
3. Instituting policies and procedures that facilitate rather than impede strategy execution.
4. Adopting best practices and pushing for continuous improvement in how value chain activities are performed.
5. Installing information and operating systems that enable company personnel to carry out their strategic roles proficiently.
6. Tying rewards directly to the achievement of strategic and financial targets and to good strategy execution.
7. Shaping the work environment and corporate culture to fit the strategy.
8. Exercising strong leadership to drive execution forward, keep improving on the details of execution, and achieve operating excellence as rapidly as feasible.

Building an organization capable of good strategy execution entails three types of organization-building actions: (1) *staffing the organization*—assembling a talented, can-do management team, and recruiting and retaining employees with the needed experience, technical skills, and intellectual capital, (2) *building core competencies and competitive capabilities* that will enable good strategy execution and updating them as strategy and external conditions change, and (3) *structuring the organization and work effort*—organizing value chain activities and business processes and deciding how much decision-making authority to push down to lower-level managers and frontline employees.

Building core competencies and competitive capabilities is a time-consuming, managerially challenging exercise that involves three stages: (1) developing the *ability* to do something, however imperfectly or inefficiently, by selecting people with the requisite skills and experience, upgrading or expanding individual abilities as needed, and then molding the efforts and work products of individuals into a collaborative group effort; (2) coordinating group efforts to learn how to perform the activity *consistently well and at an acceptable cost,* thereby transforming the ability into a tried-and-true *competence* or *capability;* and (3) continuing to polish and refine the organization's know-how and otherwise sharpen performance such that it becomes *better than rivals* at performing the activity, thus raising the core competence (or capability) to the rank of a *distinctive competence* (or competitively superior capability) and opening an avenue to competitive advantage. Many companies manage to get through stages 1 and 2 in performing a strategy-critical activity but comparatively few achieve sufficient proficiency in performing strategy-critical activities to qualify for the third stage.

Strong core competencies and competitive capabilities are an important avenue for securing a competitive edge over rivals in situations where it is relatively easy for rivals to copy smart strategies. Anytime rivals can readily duplicate successful strategy features, making it difficult or impossible to *outstrategize* rivals and beat them in the marketplace with a superior strategy, the chief way to achieve lasting competitive advantage is to *outexecute* them (beat them by performing certain value chain activities in superior fashion). *Building core competencies and competitive capabilities that are difficult or costly for rivals to emulate and that push a company closer to true operating excellence is one of the best and most reliable ways to achieve a durable competitive edge.*

Structuring the organization and organizing the work effort in a strategy-supportive fashion has five aspects: (1) deciding which value chain activities to perform internally and which ones to outsource; (2) making internally performed strategy-critical activities the main building blocks in the organization structure; (3) deciding how much authority to centralize at the top and how much to delegate to down-the-line managers and employees; (4) providing for internal cross-unit coordination and collaboration to build and strengthen internal competencies/capabilities; and (5) providing for the necessary collaboration and coordination with suppliers and strategic allies.

ASSURANCE OF LEARNING EXERCISES

1. Review the Careers link on L'Oréal's worldwide corporate Web site (go to **www.loreal.com** and click on the company's worldwide corporate Web site option). The section provides extensive information about personal development, international learning opportunities, integration of new hires into existing teams, and other areas of management development. How do the programs discussed help build core competencies and competitive capabilities at L'Oréal? Please use the chapter's discussion of building core competencies and competitive capabilities as a guide for preparing your answer.
2. Examine the overall corporate organizational structure chart for Exelon Corporation. The chart can be found by going to **www.exeloncorp.com** and using the Web site search feature to locate "organizational charts." Does it appear that strategy-critical activities are the building blocks of Exelon's organizational arrangement? Is its organizational structure best characterized as a departmental structure tied to functional, process, or geographic departments? Is the company's organizational structure better categorized as a divisional structure? Would you categorize Exelon's organizational structure as a matrix arrangement? Explain your answer.

3. Using Google Scholar or your university library's access to EBSCO, InfoTrac, or other online databases, do a search for recent writings on decentralized decision making and employee empowerment. According to the articles you found in the various management journals, what are the conditions for effectively pushing decision making down to lower levels of management?

EXERCISES FOR SIMULATION PARTICIPANTS

1. How would you describe the organization of your company's top management team? Is some decision making decentralized and delegated to individual managers? If so, explain how the decentralization works. Or are decisions made more by consensus, with all co-managers having input? What do you see as the advantages and disadvantages of the decision-making approach your company is employing?
2. Have you and your co-managers made a special effort to develop any core competencies or competitive capabilities that can contribute to achieving a competitive advantage? Why or why not? Explain.
3. Does your company have the ability to outsource any value chain activities? If so, have you and your co-managers opted to engage in outsourcing? Why or why not?

CHAPTER

11 Managing Internal Operations: Actions That Promote Good Strategy Execution

LEARNING OBJECTIVES

1. Learn why resource allocation should always be based on strategic priorities.
2. Understand why policies and procedures should be designed to facilitate good strategy execution.
3. Understand why and how benchmarking, best-practices adoption, and tools for continuously improving the performance of value chain activities help an organization achieve operating excellence and superior strategy execution.
4. Understand the role of information and operating systems in enabling company personnel to carry out their strategic roles proficiently.
5. Learn how and why the use of well-designed incentives and rewards can be management's single most powerful tool for promoting proficient strategy execution and operating excellence.

Winning companies know how to do their work better.

—Michael Hammer and James Champy

If you want people motivated to do a good job, give them a good job to do.

—Frederick Herzberg

Companies that make best practices a priority are thriving, thirsty, learning organizations. They believe that everyone should always be searching for a better way. Those kinds of companies are filled with energy and curiosity and a spirit of can-do.

—Jack Welch
Former CEO, General Electric

You ought to pay big bonuses for premier performance . . . Be a top payer, not in the middle or low end of the pack.

—Lawrence Bossidy
Former CEO, Honeywell International

In Chapter 10 we emphasized the importance of building organization capabilities and structuring the work effort so as to perform strategy-critical activities in a coordinated and highly competent manner. In this chapter we discuss five additional managerial actions that promote successful strategy execution:

1. Marshaling resources behind the drive for good strategy execution.
2. Instituting policies and procedures that facilitate strategy execution.
3. Adopting best practices and striving for continuous improvement in how value chain activities are performed.
4. Installing information and operating systems that enable company personnel to carry out their strategic roles proficiently.
5. Tying rewards and incentives directly to the achievement of strategic and financial targets and to good strategy execution.

MARSHALLING RESOURCES BEHIND THE DRIVE FOR GOOD STRATEGY EXECUTION

Early in the process of implementing and executing a new or different strategy, managers need to determine what resources will be needed and then consider whether the current budgets of organizational units are suitable. Plainly, organizational units must have the budgets and resources for executing their parts of the strategic plan effectively and efficiently. Developing a strategy-driven budget requires top management to determine what funding is needed to execute new strategic initiatives and to strengthen or modify the company's competencies and capabilities. This includes careful screening of requests for more people and new facilities and equipment, approving those that hold promise for making a contribution to strategy execution, and turning down those that don't. Should internal cash flows prove insufficient to fund the planned strategic initiatives, then management must raise additional funds through borrowing or selling additional shares of stock to willing investors.

A company's ability to marshal the resources needed to support new strategic initiatives and steer them to the appropriate organizational units has a major impact on the strategy execution process. Too little funding (stemming either from constrained financial resources or from sluggish management action to adequately increase the budgets of strategy-critical organizational units) slows progress and impedes the efforts of organizational units to execute their pieces of the strategic plan proficiently. Too much funding wastes organizational resources and reduces financial performance. Both outcomes argue for managers to be deeply involved in reviewing budget proposals and directing the proper kinds and amounts of resources to strategy-critical organization units.

A change in strategy nearly always calls for budget reallocations and resource shifting. Previously important organizational units having a lesser role in the new strategy may need downsizing. Units that now have a bigger and more critical strategic role may need more people, new equipment, additional facilities, and above-average increases in their operating budgets. More resources may have to be devoted to quality control or to adding new product features or to building a better brand image or to cutting costs or to employee retraining. Strategy implementers need to be active and forceful in downsizing some functions and upsizing others, not only to amply fund activities with a critical role in the new strategy but also to avoid inefficiency and achieve profit projections. They have to put enough resources behind new strategic initiatives to make things happen, and they have to make the tough decisions to kill projects and activities that are no longer justified. Honda's strong support of R&D activities allowed it to develop the first motorcycle airbag, the first low-polluting four-stroke outboard marine engine, a wide range of ultralow-emission cars, the first hybrid car (Honda Insight) in the U.S. market, and the first hydrogen fuel cell car (Honda Clarity). However, Honda managers had no trouble stopping production of the Insight in 2006 when its sales failed to take off and then shifting resources to the development and manufacture of other promising new models.

CORE CONCEPT

The funding requirements of a new strategy must drive how capital allocations are made and the size of each unit's operating budgets. Underfunding organizational units and activities pivotal to strategic success impedes execution and the drive for operating excellence.

Visible actions to reallocate operating funds and move people into new organizational units signal a determined commitment to strategic change and frequently are needed to catalyze the implementation process and give it credibility. Microsoft has made a practice of regularly shifting hundreds of programmers to new high-priority programming initiatives within a matter of weeks or even days. At Harris Corporation, where the strategy was to diffuse research ideas into areas that were commercially viable, top management regularly moved groups of engineers out of low-opportunity activities into its most promising new commercial venture divisions. Fast-moving developments in many markets are prompting companies to abandon traditional annual or semiannual budgeting and resource allocation cycles in favor of speedily adapting the strategy to newly developing events.

Merely fine-tuning the execution of a company's existing strategy seldom requires big movements of people and money from one area to another. But the bigger the change in strategy (or the more obstacles that lie in the path of good strategy execution), the bigger the resource shifts that tend to be required. The desired improvements can usually be accomplished through above-average budget increases to organizational units launching new initiatives and below-average increases (or even small budget cuts) for the remaining organizational units. However, there are times when strategy changes or new execution initiatives need to be made without boosting budget requirements. In such circumstances, managers have to work their way through the existing budget line by line and activity by activity, looking for ways to shift resources from low-value-adding activities to high-priority activities where new execution initiatives are needed.

INSTITUTING POLICIES AND PROCEDURES THAT FACILITATE STRATEGY EXECUTION

A company's policies and procedures can either assist or block good strategy execution. Anytime a company moves to put new strategy elements in place or improve its strategy-execution capabilities, managers are well advised to undertake a careful review of existing policies and procedures, proactively revising or discarding those that are out of sync. A change in strategy or a push for better strategy execution generally requires some changes in work practices and the behavior of company personnel. One way of promoting such changes is to institute a select set of new policies and procedures deliberately aimed at steering the actions and behavior of company personnel in a direction more conducive to good strategy execution and operating excellence.

CORE CONCEPT
Well-conceived policies and procedures aid strategy execution; out-of-sync ones are barriers.

As shown in Figure 11.1, prescribing new policies and operating procedures acts to facilitate strategy execution in three ways:

1. *Instituting new policies and procedures provides top-down guidance regarding how certain things now need to be done.* Asking people to alter established habits and procedures, of course, always upsets the internal order of things. It is normal for pockets of resistance to develop and for people to exhibit some degree of stress and anxiety about how the changes will affect them, especially when the changes may eliminate jobs. But when existing ways of doing things pose a barrier to improving strategy execution, actions and behaviors have to be changed. The managerial role of establishing and enforcing new policies and operating practices is to paint a different set of white lines, place limits on independent behavior, and channel individual and group efforts along a path more conducive to executing the strategy. Instituting new policies and procedures to steer the actions and behavior of company personnel in strategy-supportive directions becomes especially important when there are doubts among rank-and-file employees about the soundness of a new strategy or the necessity of change. Most employees will refrain from violating company policy or going against recommended practices and procedures without first gaining clearance or having strong justification.[1]

Figure 11.1 How Prescribed Policies and Procedures Facilitate Strategy Execution

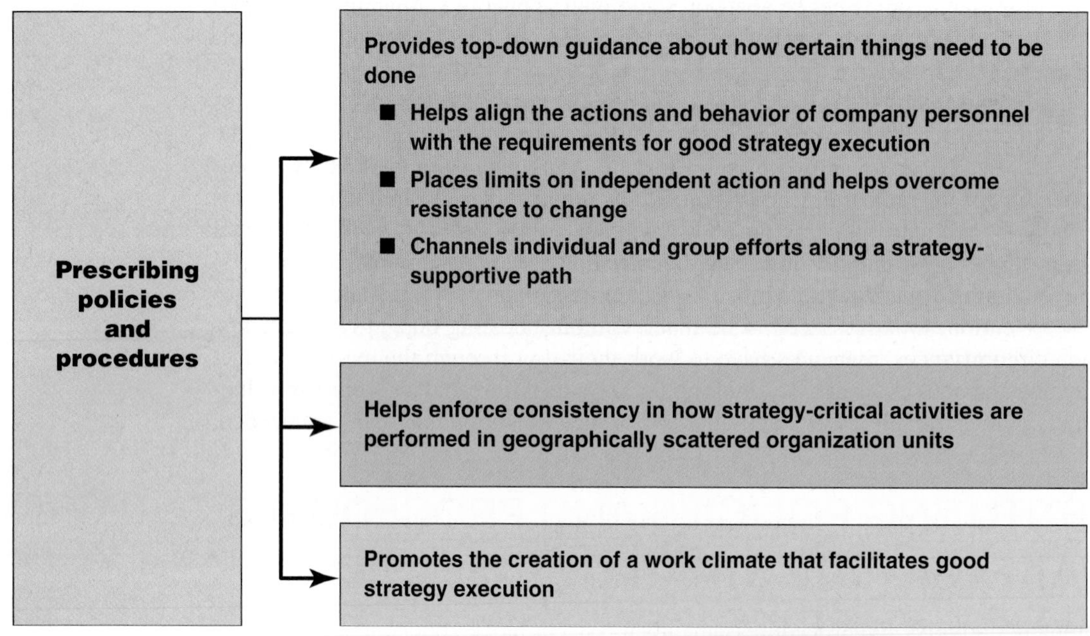

2. *Policies and procedures help enforce needed consistency in how particular strategy-critical activities are performed in geographically scattered operating units.* Standardization and strict conformity are sometimes desirable components of good strategy execution. Eliminating significant differences in the operating practices of different plants, sales regions, customer service centers, or the individual outlets in a chain operation helps a company deliver consistent product quality and service to customers. Good strategy execution nearly always entails an ability to replicate product quality and the caliber of customer service at every location where the company does business—anything less blurs the company's image and fails to meet customer expectations.
3. *Well-conceived policies and procedures promote the creation of a work climate that facilitates good strategy execution.* Because discarding old policies and procedures in favor of new ones invariably alters the internal work climate, managers can use the policy-changing process as a powerful lever for changing the corporate culture in ways that produce a stronger fit with the new strategy. The trick here, obviously, is to hit on a new policy that will catch the immediate attention of the whole organization, quickly shift actions and behavior, and then become embedded in how things are done.

In an attempt to steer "crew members" into stronger quality and service behavior patterns, McDonald's policy manual spells out detailed procedures that personnel in each McDonald's unit are expected to observe; for example, "Cooks must turn, never flip, hamburgers. If they haven't been purchased, Big Macs must be discarded in 10 minutes after being cooked and French fries in 7 minutes. Cashiers must make eye contact with and smile at every customer."

Nordstrom's strategic objective is to make sure that each customer has a pleasing shopping experience in its department stores and returns time and again; to get store personnel to dedicate themselves to outstanding customer service, Nordstrom has a policy of promoting only those people whose personnel records contain evidence of "heroic acts" to please customers—especially customers who may have made "unreasonable requests" that require special efforts. To keep its R&D activities responsive to customer needs and expectations, Hewlett-Packard requires R&D people to make regular visits to customers to learn about their problems and learn their reactions to HP's latest new products.

One of the big policymaking issues concerns what activities need to be rigidly prescribed and what activities ought to allow room for independent action on the part of empowered personnel. Few companies need thick policy manuals to direct the strategy-execution process or prescribe exactly how daily operations are to be conducted. Too much policy promotes excessive and stifling bureaucracy, erecting as many obstacles as wrong policy and being as confusing as no policy. There is wisdom in a middle approach: *Prescribe enough policies to give organization members clear direction in implementing strategy and to place desirable boundaries on employees' actions; then empower them to act within these boundaries however they think makes sense.* Allowing company personnel to act anywhere between the "white lines" is especially appropriate when individual creativity and initiative are more essential to good strategy execution than standardization and strict conformity. Instituting strategy-facilitating policies can therefore mean more policies, fewer policies, or different policies. It can mean policies that require things to be done a certain way or policies that give employees leeway to do activities the way they think best.

ADOPTING BEST PRACTICES AND STRIVING FOR CONTINUOUS IMPROVEMENT

Company managers can significantly advance the cause of competent strategy execution by pushing organization units and company personnel to identify and adopt the best practices for performing value chain activities and, further, insisting on continuous improvement in how internal operations are conducted. One of the most widely used and effective tools for gauging how well a company is executing pieces of its strategy entails benchmarking the company's performance of particular activities and business processes against "best-in-industry" and "best-in-world" performers.[2] It can also be useful to look at "best-in-company" performers of an activity if a company has a number of different organizational units performing much the same function at different locations. Identifying, analyzing, and understanding how top companies or individuals perform particular value chain activities and business processes provides useful yardsticks for judging the effectiveness and efficiency of internal operations and setting performance standards for organization units to meet or beat.

CORE CONCEPT

Managerial efforts to identify and adopt best practices are a powerful tool for promoting operating excellence and better strategy execution.

Identifying and Incorporating Best Practices to Improve Operating Effectiveness and Efficiency

A **best practice** is a technique for performing an activity or business process that at least one company has demonstrated works particularly well. To qualify as a legitimate best practice, the technique must have a proven record in significantly lowering costs, improving quality or performance,

CORE CONCEPT

A *best practice* is any practice that at least one company has proved works particularly well.

shortening time requirements, enhancing safety, or delivering some other highly positive operating outcome. Best practices thus identify a path to operating excellence. For a best practice to be valuable and transferable, it must demonstrate success over time, deliver quantifiable and highly positive results, and be repeatable.

Benchmarking is the backbone of the process of identifying, studying, and implementing outstanding practices. A company's benchmarking effort looks outward to find best practices and then proceeds to develop the data for measuring how well a company's own performance of an activity stacks up against the best-practice standard. A strong commitment to and belief in benchmarking involves being humble enough to admit that others have come up with world-class ways to perform particular activities yet wise enough to try to learn how to match, and even surpass, them. But, as shown in Figure 11.2, the payoff of benchmarking comes from adapting the top-notch approaches pioneered by other companies in the company's own operation and thereby boosting, perhaps dramatically, the proficiency with which value chain tasks are performed.

However, benchmarking is more complicated than simply identifying which companies are the best performers of an activity and then trying to imitate their approaches—especially if these companies are in other industries. Normally, the outstanding practices of other organizations have to be *adapted* to fit the specific circumstances of a company's own business and operating requirements. Since most companies believe "our work is different" or "we are unique," the telling part of any best-practice initiative is how well the company puts its own version of the best practice into place and makes it work.

Indeed, a best practice remains little more than another company's interesting success story unless company personnel buy into the task of translating what can be learned from other companies into real action and results. The agents of change must be frontline employees who are convinced of the need to abandon the old ways of doing things and switch to a best-practice mind-set. *The more that organizational units use best practices in performing their work, the closer a company moves toward performing its value chain activities as effectively and efficiently as possible.* This is what operational excellence is all about.

Legions of companies across the world now engage in benchmarking to improve their strategy execution efforts and, ideally, gain a strategic, operational, and financial advantage over rivals. Scores of trade associations and special interest organizations have undertaken efforts to collect best-practice data relevant to a particular industry or business function and make their databases available online to members—good examples include The Benchmarking Exchange (www.benchnet.com); Best Practices, LLC

Figure 11.2 From Benchmarking and Best-Practice Implementation to Operating Excellence

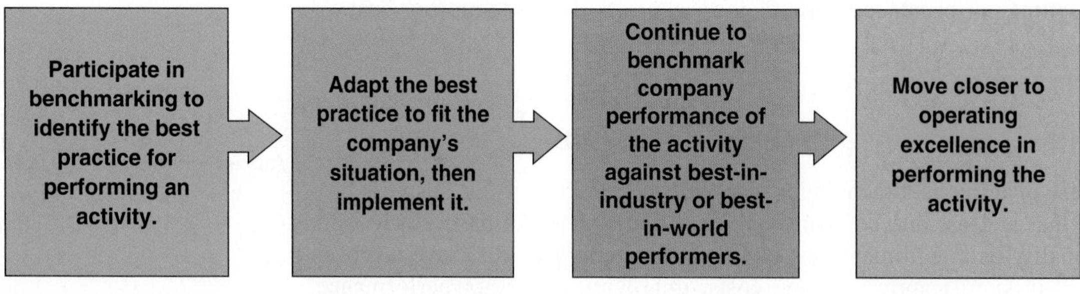

(www.best-in-class.com); and the American Productivity and Quality Center (www.apqc.org). Benchmarking and best-practice implementation have clearly emerged as legitimate and valuable managerial tools for promoting operational excellence.

Business Process Reengineering, Six Sigma Quality Programs, and TQM: Tools for Promoting Operating Excellence

In striving for operating excellence, many companies have also come to rely on three other potent management tools: business process reengineering, Six Sigma quality control techniques, and total quality management (TQM) programs. Indeed, these three tools have become globally pervasive techniques for implementing strategies keyed to cost reduction, defect-free manufacture, superior product quality, superior customer service, and total customer satisfaction. The following sections describe how business process reengineering, Six Sigma, and TQM can contribute to operating excellence and better strategy execution.

Business Process Reengineering Companies scouring for ways to improve their operations have sometimes discovered that the execution of strategy-critical activities is hindered by an organizational arrangement where pieces of the activity are performed in several different functional departments, with no one manager or group being accountable for optimum performance of the entire activity. This can easily occur in such inherently cross-functional activities as customer service (which can involve personnel in order filling, warehousing and shipping, invoicing, accounts receivable, after-sale repair, and technical support); new product development (which can typically involve personnel in R&D, design and engineering, purchasing, manufacturing, and sales and marketing); and supply chain management (which cuts across such areas as purchasing, inventory management, manufacturing and assembly, warehousing, and shipping). Even if personnel in all the different departments and functional areas are inclined to collaborate closely, the activity may not end up being performed optimally or cost-efficiently.

To address such shortcomings in strategy execution, many companies during the past decade have opted to *reengineer the work effort* by pulling the pieces of strategy-critical activities out of different departments and unifying their performance in a single department or cross-functional work group. Reorganizing the people who performed the pieces in functional departments into a close-knit group that has charge over the whole process and that can be held accountable for performing the activity in a cheaper, better, and/or more strategy-supportive fashion is called business process reengineering.[3]

When done properly, business process reengineering can produce dramatic operating benefits. In the order-processing section of General Electric's circuit breaker division, elapsed time from order receipt to delivery was cut from three weeks to three days by consolidating six production units into one, reducing a variety of former inventory and handling steps, automating the design system to replace a human custom-design process, and cutting the organizational layers between managers and workers from three to one. Productivity rose by 20 percent in one year, and unit manufacturing costs dropped by 30 percent. Northwest Water, a British utility, used business process reengineering to eliminate 45 work depots that served as home bases to crews who installed and repaired water and sewage lines and equipment. Now crews work directly from their vehicles, receiving assignments and reporting work completion from computer terminals in their trucks. Crew members are no longer employees but contractors to Northwest Water. These reengineering efforts not only eliminated the need for the work depots but also allowed Northwest Water to eliminate a big percentage of the bureaucratic personnel and supervisory organization that managed the crews.[4]

Since the early 1990s, reengineering of value chain activities has been undertaken at many companies in many industries all over the world, with some companies achieving excellent results.[5] While reengineering has produced only modest results in some instances, usually because of ineptness and/or lack of wholehearted commitment, it has nonetheless proved itself as a useful tool for streamlining a company's work effort and moving closer to operational excellence.

Total Quality Management Programs *Total quality management (TQM) is a philosophy of managing a set of business practices that emphasizes continuous improvement in all phases of operations, 100 percent accuracy in performing tasks, involvement and empowerment of employees at all levels, team-based work design, benchmarking, and total customer satisfaction.*[6] While TQM concentrates on the production of quality goods and fully satisfying customer expectations, it achieves its biggest successes when it is also extended to employee efforts in *all departments*—human resources, billing, R&D, engineering, accounting and records, and information systems—that may lack pressing, customer-driven incentives to improve. It involves reforming the corporate culture and shifting to a total quality/continuous improvement business philosophy that permeates every facet of the organization.[7] TQM aims at instilling enthusiasm and commitment to doing things right from the top to the bottom of the organization. Management's job is to kindle an organizationwide search for ways to improve, a search that involves all company personnel exercising initiative and using their ingenuity. TQM doctrine preaches that there's no such thing as "good enough" and that everyone has a responsibility to participate in continuous improvement. TQM is thus a race without a finish. Success comes from making little steps forward each day, a process that the Japanese call *kaizen.*

CORE CONCEPT

TQM entails creating a total quality culture bent on continuously improving the performance of every task and value chain activity.

TQM takes a fairly long time to show significant results—very little benefit emerges within the first six months. The long-term payoff of TQM, if it comes, depends heavily on management's success in implanting a culture within which TQM philosophies and practices can thrive. TQM is a managerial tool that has attracted numerous users and advocates over several decades, and it can deliver good results when used properly.

Six Sigma Quality Control *Six Sigma quality control consists of a disciplined, statistics-based system aimed at producing not more than 3.4 defects per million iterations for any business process—from manufacturing to customer transactions.*[8] The Six Sigma process of define, measure, analyze, improve, and control (DMAIC, pronounced *Dee-may-ic*) is an improvement system for existing processes falling below specification and needing incremental improvement. The Six Sigma process of define, measure, analyze, design, and verify (DMADV) is used to develop *new* processes or products at Six Sigma quality levels. DMADV is sometimes referred to as a Design for Six Sigma (DFSS). Six Sigma programs for both improving existing processes or developing new processes are executed by personnel who have earned Six Sigma "green belts" and Six Sigma "black belts," and are overseen by personnel who have completed Six Sigma "master black belt" training. According to the Six Sigma Academy, personnel with black belts can save companies approximately $230,000 per project and can complete four to six projects a year.[9]

The statistical thinking underlying Six Sigma is based on the following three principles: All work is a process, all processes have variability, and all processes create data that explains variability.[10] To illustrate how these three principles drive the metrics of DMAIC, consider the case of a janitorial company that wants to improve the caliber of work done by its cleaning crews and thereby boost customer satisfaction. The janitorial company's Six Sigma team can pursue quality enhancement and continuous improvement via the DMAIC process as follows:

- *Define.* Because Six Sigma is aimed at reducing defects, the first step is to define what constitutes a defect. Six Sigma team members might decide that leaving streaks on windows is a defect because it is a source of customer dissatisfaction.
- *Measure.* The next step is to collect data to find out why, how, and how often this defect occurs. This might include a process flow map of the specific ways that cleaning crews go about the task of cleaning a commercial customer's windows. Other metrics may include recording what tools and cleaning products the crews use to clean windows.
- *Analyze.* After the data are gathered and the statistics analyzed, the company's Six Sigma team discovers that the tools and window cleaning techniques of certain employees are better than those of other employees because their tools and procedures leave no streaked windows—a "best practice" for avoiding window streaking is thus identified and documented.
- *Improve.* The Six Sigma team implements the documented best practice as a standard way of cleaning windows.
- *Control.* The company teaches new and existing employees the best practice technique for window cleaning. Over time, there's significant improvement in customer satisfaction and increased business.

Six Sigma's DMAIC process is a particularly good vehicle for improving performance when there are *wide variations* in how well an activity is performed.[11] For instance, airlines striving to improve the on-time performance of their flights have more to gain from actions to curtail the number of flights that are late by more than 30 minutes than from actions to reduce the number of flights that are late by less than 5 minutes. Likewise, FedEx might have a 16-hour average delivery time for its overnight package service operation, but if the actual delivery time varies around the 16-hour average from a low of 12 hours to a high of 26 hours, such that 10 percent of its packages are delivered over 6 hours late, then it has a huge *reliability* problem.

Since the mid-1990s, thousands of companies and nonprofit organizations around the world have begun using Six Sigma programs to promote operating excellence. Such manufacturers as Motorola, Allied Signal, Caterpillar, DuPont, Xerox, Alcan Aluminum, BMW, Volkswagen, Nokia, Owens Corning, and Emerson Electric have employed Six Sigma techniques to good advantage in improving production quality. General Electric (GE), one of the most successful companies implementing Six Sigma training and pursuing Six Sigma perfection, estimated benefits on the order of $10 billion during the first five years of implementation. GE first began Six Sigma in 1995 after Motorola and Allied Signal blazed the Six Sigma trail. One of GE's successes was in its Lighting division where Six Sigma was used to cut invoice defects and disputes by 98 percent, a particular benefit to Wal-Mart, the division's largest customer. GE Capital Mortgage improved the chances of a caller reaching a "live" GE person from 76 to 99 percent.[12] Illustration Capsule 11.1 describes Whirlpool's use of Six Sigma in its appliance business.

ILLUSTRATION CAPSULE 11.1
Whirlpool's Use of Six Sigma to Promote Operating Excellence

Top management at Whirlpool Corporation, the leading global manufacturer and marketer of home appliances in 2007, with 72 manufacturing and technology centers around the globe and sales in some 170 countries, has a vision of Whirlpool appliances in "Every Home . . . Everywhere with Pride, Passion, and Performance." One of management's chief objectives in pursuing this vision is to build unmatched customer loyalty to the Whirlpool brand. Whirlpool's strategy to win the hearts and minds of appliance buyers the world over has been to produce and market appliances with top-notch quality and innovative features that users will find appealing. In addition, Whirlpool's strategy has been to offer a wide selection of models (recognizing that buyer tastes and needs differ) and to strive for low-cost production efficiency, thereby enabling Whirlpool to price its products very competitively. Executing this strategy at Whirlpool's operations in North America (where it is the market leader), Latin America (where it is also the market leader), Europe (where it is ranks third), and Asia (where it is number one in India and has a foothold with huge growth opportunities elsewhere) has involved a strong focus on continuous improvement, lean manufacturing capabilities, and a drive for operating excellence. To marshal the efforts of its 73,000 employees in executing the strategy successfully, management developed a comprehensive Operational Excellence program with Six Sigma as one of the centerpieces.

The Operational Excellence initiative, which began in the 1990s, incorporated Six Sigma techniques to improve the quality of Whirlpool products, while at the same time lowering costs and trimming the time it took to get product innovations into the marketplace. The Six Sigma program helped Whirlpool save $175 million in manufacturing costs in its first three years.

To sustain the productivity gains and cost savings, Whirlpool embedded Six Sigma practices within each of its manufacturing facilities worldwide and instilled a culture based on Six Sigma and lean manufacturing skills and capabilities. Beginning in 2002, each of Whirlpool's operating units began taking the Six Sigma initiative to a higher level by first placing the needs of the customer at the center of every function—R&D, technology, manufacturing, marketing, and administrative support—and then striving to consistently improve quality levels while eliminating all unnecessary costs. The company systematically went through every aspect of its business with the view that company personnel should perform every activity at every level in a manner that delivers value to the customer and that leads to continuous improvement on how things are done.

Whirlpool management believes that the company's Operational Excellence process has been a major contributor in sustaining the company's global leadership in appliances.

Source: www.whirlpool.com (accessed September 25, 2003; November 15, 2005; and August 16, 2008).

Six Sigma is, however, not just a quality-enhancing tool for manufacturers. At one company, product sales personnel typically wined and dined customers to close their deals.[13] But the costs of such entertaining were viewed as excessively high in many instances. A Six Sigma project that examined sales data found that although face time with customers was important, wining, dining, and other types of entertainment were not. The data showed that regular face time helped close sales, but that time could be spent over a cup of coffee instead of golfing at a resort or taking clients to expensive restaurants. In addition, analysis showed that too much face time with customers was counterproductive. A regularly scheduled customer picnic was found to be detrimental to closing sales because it was held at a busy time of year, when customers preferred not to be away from their offices. Changing the manner in which prospective customers were wooed resulted in a 10 percent increase in sales. Six Sigma has also been used to improve processes in health care. A Milwaukee hospital used Six Sigma to map the process of filling prescriptions—the prescriptions originated with a doctor's writeup, were filled by the hospital pharmacy, and then administered by nurses. DMAIC analysis revealed that most mistakes came from misreading the doctor's handwriting.[14] The hospital implemented a program requiring doctors to type the prescription into a computer, which slashed the number of errors dramatically.

A problem tailor-made for Six Sigma occurs in the insurance industry, where it is common for top agents to outsell poor agents by a factor of 10 to 1 or more. If insurance executives offer a trip to Hawaii in a monthly contest to motivate low-performing agents, the typical result is to motivate top agents to be even more productive and make the performance gap even wider. A DMAIC Six Sigma project to reduce the variation in the performance of agents and correct the problem of so many low-performing agents would begin by measuring the performance of all agents, perhaps discovering that the top 20 percent sell seven times more policies than the bottom 40 percent. Six Sigma analysis would then consider such steps as mapping how top agents spend their day, investigating the factors that distinguish top performers from low performers, learning what techniques training specialists have employed in converting low-performing agents into high performers, and examining how the hiring process could be improved to avoid hiring underperformers in the first place. The next step would be to *test* proposed solutions—better training methods or psychological profiling to identify and weed out candidates likely to be poor performers—to identify and measure which alternative solutions really work, which don't, and why. Only those actions that prove statistically beneficial are then introduced on a wide scale. The DMAIC method thus entails empirical analysis to diagnose the problem (*design, measure, analyze*), test alternative solutions (*improve*) and then *control* the variability in how well the activity is performed by implementing actions shown to truly fix the problem.

However, while Six Sigma programs often improve the efficiency of many operating activities and processes, there is evidence that innovation can be stifled by Six Sigma programs. The essence of Six Sigma is to reduce variability in processes, but creative processes include quite a bit of variability. In many instances, breakthrough innovations occur only after thousands of ideas have been abandoned and promising ideas have gone through multiple iterations and extensive prototyping. James McNerney, a GE executive schooled in constructive use of Six Sigma, became CEO at 3M Corporation and proceeded to institute a series of Six Sigma-based principles. McNerney's dedication to Six Sigma and his elimination of 8 percent of the company's workforce did cause 3M's profits to jump shortly after his December 2000 arrival, but the application of Six Sigma in 3M's R&D and new product development activities soon proved to stifle innovation and new product introductions, undermining 3M's long-standing reputation for innovation. 3M's researchers complained that the innovation process did not lend itself well to the extensive data collection and analysis required under Six Sigma and that too much time was spent completing reports that outlined the market potential and possible manufacturing concerns for projects in all stages of the R&D pipeline. Six Sigma rigidity and a freeze on 3M's R&D budget from McNerney's first year as CEO through 2005 was blamed for the company's drop from first to seventh place on the Boston Consulting Group's Most Innovative Companies list.[15]

Moreover, there are several other prominent instances when Six Sigma proponents who used Six Sigma to great advantage at one company fell flat when trying to utilize Six Sigma principles in managing another company. Robert Nardelli, another executive whose management skills were honed at GE and based on the Six Sigma philosophy, struggled during short tenure as CEO at The Home Depot because a number of the changes he introduced ended up damaging worker morale and customer satisfaction. Under Nardelli, The Home Depot's ranking on the American Customer Satisfaction Index for major U.S. retailers dropped from first to last among major U.S.

retailers. Ann Fudge, a GE board member who was also well versed in GE's management approaches, failed as CEO of Young & Rubicam after attempting to implement Six Sigma processes at the advertising agency. So while Six Sigma principles have certainly been used to good advantage in numerous companies and have a track record of promoting operating excellence, Six Sigma is not a panacea for improving operations at all organizations—there are occasions where it has been used unwisely and inadvertently produced counterproductive outcomes.

A blended approach to Six Sigma implementation that is gaining in popularity pursues incremental improvements in operating efficiency, while R&D and other processes that allow the company to develop new ways of offering value to customers are given freer rein. Managers of these *ambidextrous organizations* are adept at employing continuous improvement in operating processes but allowing R&D to operate under a set of rules that allows for the development of breakthrough innovations. However, the two distinctly different approaches to managing employees must be carried out by tightly integrated senior managers to ensure that the separate and diversely oriented units operate with a common purpose. Ciba Vision, a global leader in contact lenses, has dramatically reduced operating expenses through the use of continuous improvement programs, while simultaneously and harmoniously developing new series of contact lens products that have allowed its revenues to grow by 300 percent over a 10-year period.[16]

In summary, a company that systematically and wisely applies Six Sigma methods to its value chain, activity by activity, can make major strides in improving the proficiency with which its strategy is executed. As is the case with TQM, obtaining managerial commitment, establishing a quality culture, and fully involving employees are the three most intractable challenges encountered in the implementation of Six Sigma quality programs.[17]

The Difference between Business Process Reengineering and Continuous Improvement Programs like Six Sigma and TQM Business process reengineering and continuous improvement efforts like TQM and Six Sigma both aim at improved efficiency and reduced costs, better product quality, and greater customer satisfaction. The essential difference between business process reengineering and continuous improvement programs is that reengineering aims at *quantum gains* on the order of 30 to 50 percent or more, whereas total quality programs stress *incremental progress,* striving for inch-by-inch gains again and again in a never-ending stream. The two approaches to improved performance of value chain activities and operating excellence are not mutually exclusive; it makes sense to use them in tandem. Reengineering can be used first to produce a good basic design that yields quick, dramatic improvements in performing a business process. Total quality programs can then be used as a follow-on to reengineering and/or best-practice implementation, delivering gradual improvements. Such a two-pronged approach to implementing operational excellence is like a marathon in which you run the first four miles as fast as you can, then gradually pick up speed the remainder of the way.

Business process reengineering aims at one-time quantum improvement; continuous improvement programs like TQM and Six Sigma aim at ongoing incremental improvements.

Capturing the Benefits of Initiatives to Improve Operations

Usually, the biggest beneficiaries of benchmarking and best-practice initiatives, reengineering, TQM, and Six Sigma are companies that view such programs not as ends in themselves but as tools for implementing and executing company strategy more effectively. The skimpiest payoffs occur when company managers seize them as something worth trying—novel ideas that could improve things. In most such instances, they result in strategy-blind efforts to simply manage better. There's an important lesson here. Best practices, TQM, Six Sigma quality, and business process reengineering all need to be seen and used as part of a bigger-picture effort to execute strategy proficiently. Only strategy can point to which value chain activities matter and what performance targets make the most sense. Absent a strategic framework, managers lack the context in which to fix things that really matter to business-unit performance and competitive success.

To get the most from initiatives to better execute strategy, managers must have a clear idea of what specific outcomes really matter. Is it a Six Sigma defect rate, high on-time delivery percentages, low overall costs relative to rivals, fewer customer complaints, shorter cycle times, a higher percentage of revenues coming from recently introduced products, or what? Benchmarking best-in-industry and best-in-world performance of most or all value chain activities provides a realistic basis for setting internal performance milestones and longer-range targets.

Once initiatives to improve operations are linked to the company's strategic priorities, then comes the managerial task of building a total quality culture that is genuinely committed to achieving the performance outcomes that strategic success requires.[18] Managers can take the following action steps to realize full value from TQM or Six Sigma initiatives and promote a culture of operating excellence:[19]

CORE CONCEPT

The purpose of using benchmarking, best practices, business process reengineering, TQM, Six Sigma, or other operational improvement programs is to improve the performance of strategy-critical

1. Visible, unequivocal, and unyielding commitment to total quality and continuous improvement, including a quality vision and specific, measurable objectives for boosting quality and making continuous improvement.
2. Nudging people toward quality-supportive behaviors by:
   a. Screening job applicants rigorously and hiring only those with attitudes and aptitudes right for quality-based performance.
   b. Providing quality training for most employees.
   c. Using teams and team-building exercises to reinforce and nurture individual effort. (The creation of a quality culture is facilitated when teams become more cross-functional, multitask-oriented, and increasingly self-managed.)
   d. Recognizing and rewarding individual and team efforts regularly and systematically.
   e. Stressing prevention (doing it right the first time), not inspection (instituting ways to correct mistakes).
3. Empowering employees so that authority for delivering great service or improving products is in the hands of the doers rather than the overseers—*improving quality has to be seen as part of everyone's job.*
4. Using online systems to provide all relevant parties with the latest best practices and actual experiences with them, thereby speeding the diffusion and adoption of best practices throughout the organization and also allowing them to exchange data and opinions about how to upgrade the prevailing best practices.
5. Preaching that performance can, and must, be improved because competitors are not resting on their laurels and customers are always looking for something better.

If the targeted performance measures are appropriate to the strategy and if all organizational members (top executives, middle managers, professional staff, and line employees) buy into a culture of operating excellence, then a company's work climate becomes decidedly more conducive to proficient strategy execution. Benchmarking, best practices implementation, reengineering, TQM, and Six Sigma initiatives can greatly enhance a company's product design, cycle time, production costs, product quality, service, customer satisfaction, and other operating capabilities—and they can even deliver competitive advantage.[20] Not only do improvements from such initiatives add up over time and strengthen organizational capabilities, but the benefits they produce have hard-to-imitate aspects. While it is relatively easy for rivals to undertake benchmarking, process improvement, and quality training, it is much more difficult and time-consuming for them to instill a deeply ingrained culture of operating excellence (as occurs when such techniques are religiously employed) and top management exhibits lasting commitment to operational excellence throughout the organization.

INSTALLING INFORMATION AND OPERATING SYSTEMS

Company strategies can't be executed well without a number of internal systems for business operations. Southwest Airlines, Singapore Airlines, Lufthansa, British Airways, and other successful airlines cannot hope to provide passenger-pleasing service without a user-friendly online reservation system, an accurate and speedy baggage handling system, and a strict aircraft maintenance program that minimizes equipment failures requiring at-the-gate service and delaying plane departures. FedEx has internal communication systems that allow it to coordinate its 70,000-plus vehicles in handling an average of 5.5 million packages a day. Its leading-edge flight operations systems allow a single controller to direct as many as 200 of FedEx's 650 aircraft simultaneously, overriding their flight plans should weather or other special emergencies arise. In addition, FedEx has created a series of e-business tools for customers that allow them to ship and track packages online (either at FedEx's Web site or on their own company intranets or Web sites), create address books, review shipping history, generate custom reports, simplify customer billing, reduce internal warehousing and inventory management costs, purchase goods and services from suppliers, and respond quickly to changing customer demands. All of FedEx's systems support the company's strategy of providing businesses and individuals with a broad array of package delivery services (from premium next-day to economical five-day deliveries) and boosting its competitiveness against United Parcel Service, Airborne Express, and the U.S. Postal Service.

Otis Elevator, the world's largest manufacturer of elevators, has a 24-hour communications service center called OtisLine to coordinate its maintenance efforts for the 1.5 million-plus elevators and escalators it has installed worldwide.[21] Electronic monitors installed on each user's site can detect when an elevator or escalator has any of 325 problems and will automatically place a service call to the nearest service center. Trained operators take all trouble calls, input critical information into a computer, and dispatch trained mechanics from one of 325 locations across the world to the local trouble spot. All customers have online access to performance data on each of their Otis elevators. More than 80 percent of mechanics in North America carry Web-enabled phones connected to Otis's e*Service that transport needed information quickly and allow mechanics to update data in Otis computers for future reference. The OtisLine system helps keep outage times to less than two and a half hours. All the trouble-call data is relayed to design and manufacturing personnel, allowing them to quickly alter design specifications or manufacturing procedures when needed to correct recurring problems.

Amazon.com ships customer orders from fully computerized, 1,300-by-600-foot warehouses containing about 3 million books, CDs, toys, and houseware items.[22] The warehouses are so technologically sophisticated that they require about as many lines of code to run as Amazon's Web site does. Using complex picking algorithms, computers initiate the order-picking process by sending signals to workers' wireless receivers, telling them which items to pick off the shelves in which order. Computers also generate data on misboxed items, chute backup times, line speed, worker productivity, and shipping weights on orders. Systems are upgraded regularly, and productivity improvements are aggressively pursued. In 2003, Amazon's six warehouses were able to handle three times the volume handled in 1999 at costs averaging 10 percent of revenues (versus 20 percent in 1999); in addition, they turned their inventory over 20 times annually in an industry whose average was 15 turns. Amazon's warehouse efficiency and cost per order filled was so low that one of the fastest-growing and most profitable parts of Amazon's business was using its warehouses to run the e-commerce operations of Toys "R" Us and Target.

Most telephone companies, electric utilities, and TV broadcasting systems have online monitoring systems to spot transmission problems within seconds and increase the reliability of their services. At eBay, there are systems for real-time monitoring of new listings, bidding activity, Web site traffic, and page views. Kaiser Permanente spent $3 billion to digitize the medical records of its 8.2 million members so that it could manage patient care more efficiently.[23] IBM has created a database of 36,000 employee profiles that enable it to better assign the most qualified IBM consultant to the projects it is doing for clients. In businesses such as public accounting and management consulting, where large numbers of professional staff need cutting-edge technical know-how, companies have developed systems that identify when it is time for certain employees to attend training programs to update their skills and know-how. Many companies have cataloged best-practice information on their intranets to promote faster transfer and implementation organizationwide.[24]

Well-conceived state-of-the-art operating systems not only enable better strategy execution but also strengthen organizational capabilities—perhaps enough to provide a competitive edge over rivals. For example, a company with a differentiation strategy based on superior quality has added capability if it has systems for training personnel in quality techniques, tracking product quality at each production step, and ensuring that all goods shipped meet quality standards. A company striving to be a low-cost provider is competitively stronger if it has a benchmarking system that identifies opportunities to implement best practices and drive costs out of the business. Fast-growing companies get an important assist from having capabilities in place to recruit and train new employees in large numbers and from investing in infrastructure that gives them the capability to handle rapid growth as it occurs. It is nearly always better to put infrastructure and support systems in place before they are actually needed than to have to scramble to catch up to customer demand.

CORE CONCEPT

State-of-the-art support systems can be a basis for competitive advantage if they give a firm capabilities that rivals can't match.

Instituting Adequate Information Systems, Performance Tracking, and Controls

Accurate and timely information about daily operations is essential if managers are to gauge how well the strategy execution process is proceeding. Information systems need to cover five broad areas: (1) customer data, (2) operations data, (3) employee data, (4) supplier/partner/collaborative ally data, and (5) financial performance data. All key strategic performance indicators have to be tracked and reported as often as practical. Monthly profit-and-loss statements and monthly statistical summaries, long the norm, are fast being replaced by daily statistical updates and even up-to-the-minute performance monitoring that online technology makes possible. Many retail companies have automated online systems that generate daily sales reports for each store and maintain up-to-the-minute inventory and sales records on each item. Manufacturing plants typically generate daily production reports and track labor productivity on every shift. Many retailers and manufacturers have online data systems connecting them with their suppliers that monitor the status of inventories, track shipments and deliveries, and measure defect rates.

Real-time information systems permit company managers to stay on top of implementation initiatives and daily operations, and to intervene if things seem to be drifting off course. Tracking key performance indicators, gathering information from operating personnel, quickly identifying and diagnosing problems, and taking corrective actions are all integral pieces of the process of managing strategy implementation and execution and exercising adequate organization control. A number of companies have recently begun creating "electronic scorecards" for senior managers that gather daily or weekly statistics from different databases about inventory, sales, costs, and sales trends; such information enables these managers to easily stay abreast of what's happening and make better decisions in real time.[25] Telephone companies have elaborate information systems to measure signal quality, connection times, interrupts, wrong connections, billing errors, and other measures of reliability that affect customer service and satisfaction. British Petroleum (BP) has outfitted rail cars carrying hazardous materials with sensors and global-positioning systems (GPS) so that it can track the status, location, and other information about these shipments via satellite and relay the data to its corporate intranet. Companies that rely on empowered customer-contact personnel to act promptly and creatively in pleasing customers have installed online information systems that put essential customer data on their computer monitors with a few keystrokes so that they can respond effectively to customer inquiries and deliver personalized customer service.

CORE CONCEPT
Having good information systems and operating data is integral to competent strategy execution and operating excellence.

Statistical information gives managers a feel for the numbers, briefings and meetings provide a feel for the latest developments and emerging issues, and personal contacts add a feel for the people dimension. All are good barometers. Managers have to identify problem areas and deviations from plan before they can take actions to get the organization back on course, by either improving the approaches to strategy execution or fine-tuning the strategy. Jeff Bezos, Amazon's CEO, an ardent proponent of managing by the numbers, says, "Math-based decisions always trump opinion and judgment. The trouble with most corporations is that they make judgment-based decisions when data-based decisions could be made."[26]

Exercising Adequate Controls over Empowered Employees

Another important aspect of effectively managing and controlling the strategy execution process is monitoring the performance of empowered workers to see that they are acting within the specified limits.[27] Leaving empowered employees to their own devices in meeting performance standards without appropriate checks and balances can expose an organization to excessive risk.[28] Instances abound of employees' decisions or behavior having gone awry, sometimes costing a company huge sums or producing lawsuits, aside from just generating embarrassing publicity.

Managers shouldn't have to devote big chunks of their time to making sure that the decisions and behavior of empowered employees stay between the white lines—this would defeat the major purpose of empowerment and, in effect, lead to the reinstatement of a managerial bureaucracy engaged in constant over-the-shoulder supervision. Yet managers have a clear responsibility to exercise sufficient control over empowered employees to protect the company against out-of-bounds behavior and unwelcome surprises. Scrutinizing daily and weekly operating statistics is one of the important ways in which managers can monitor the results that flow from the actions of empowered subordinates—if the operating results flowing from the actions of empowered employees look good, then it is reasonable to assume that empowerment is working.

But close monitoring of real-time or daily operating performance is only one of the control tools at management's disposal. Another valuable lever of control in companies that rely on empowered employees, especially in those that use self-managed work groups or other such teams, is peer-based control. Most team members feel responsible for the success of the whole team and tend to be relatively intolerant of any team member's behavior that weakens team performance or puts team accomplishments at risk (especially when team performance has a big impact on each team member's compensation). Because peer evaluation is such a powerful control device, companies organized into teams can remove some layers of the management hierarchy and rely on strong peer pressure to keep team members operating between the white lines. This is especially true when a company has the information systems capability to monitor team performance daily or in real time.

TYING REWARDS AND INCENTIVES TO STRATEGY EXECUTION

It is important for both organization units and individuals to be enthusiastically committed to executing strategy and achieving performance targets. Company managers typically use an assortment of motivational techniques and rewards to enlist organizationwide commitment to executing the strategic plan. A manager has to do more than just talk to everyone about how important new strategic practices and performance targets are to the organization's well-being. No matter how inspiring, talk seldom commands people's best efforts for long. *To get employees' sustained, energetic commitment, management has to be resourceful in designing and using motivational incentives—both monetary and nonmonetary.* The more a manager understands what motivates subordinates and the more he or she relies on motivational incentives as a tool for achieving the targeted strategic and financial results, the greater will be employees' commitment to good day-in, day-out strategy execution and achievement of performance targets.[29]

CORE CONCEPT
A properly designed reward structure is management's most powerful tool for mobilizing organizational commitment to successful strategy execution.

Strategy-Facilitating Motivational Practices

Financial incentives generally head the list of motivating tools for trying to gain wholehearted employee commitment to good strategy execution and operating excellence. Monetary rewards generally include some combination of base pay increases,

CORE CONCEPT

One of management's biggest strategy-executing challenges is to employ motivational techniques that build wholehearted commitment to operating excellence and winning attitudes among employees.

performance bonuses, profit-sharing plans, stock awards, company contributions to employee 401(k) or retirement plans, and piecework incentives (in the case of production workers). But successful companies and managers normally make extensive use of such nonmonetary carrot-and-stick incentives as frequent words of praise (or constructive criticism), special recognition at company gatherings or in the company newsletter, more (or less) job security, stimulating assignments, opportunities to transfer to attractive locations, increased (or decreased) autonomy, and rapid promotion (or the risk of being sidelined in a routine or dead-end job). In addition, companies use a host of other motivational approaches to make their workplaces more appealing and spur stronger employee commitment to the strategy execution process; the following are some of the most important:[30]

- *Providing attractive perks and fringe benefits*—The various options here include full coverage of health insurance premiums; full tuition reimbursement for work on college degrees; paid vacation time of three or four weeks; on-site child care at major facilities; on-site gym facilities and massage therapists; getaway opportunities at company-owned recreational facilities (beach houses, ranches, resort condos); personal concierge services; subsidized cafeterias and free lunches; casual dress every day; personal travel services; paid sabbaticals; maternity leaves; paid leaves to care for ill family members; telecommuting; compressed workweeks (four 10-hour days instead of five 8-hour days); reduced summer hours; college scholarships for children; on-the-spot bonuses for exceptional performance; and relocation services.
- *Relying on promotion from within whenever possible*—This practice helps bind workers to their employer and employers to their workers; plus, it is an incentive for good performance. Promotion from within also helps ensure that people in positions of responsibility actually know something about the business, technology, and operations they are managing.
- *Making sure that the ideas and suggestions of employees are valued and that those with merit are promptly acted on*—Many companies find that their best ideas for nuts-and-bolts operating improvements come from the suggestions of employees. Moreover, research indicates that the moves of many companies to push decision making down the line and empower employees increases employee motivation and satisfaction, as well as boosting their productivity. The use of self-managed teams has much the same effect.
- *Creating a work atmosphere in which there is genuine sincerity, caring, and mutual respect among workers and between management and employees*—A "family" work environment where people are on a first-name basis and there is strong camaraderie promotes teamwork and cross-unit collaboration.
- *Stating the strategic vision in inspirational terms that make employees feel they are a part of doing something very worthwhile in a larger social sense*—There's strong motivating power associated with giving people a chance to be part of something exciting and personally satisfying. Jobs with noble purpose tend to turn employees on. At Pfizer, Merck, and most other pharmaceutical companies, it is the notion of helping sick people get well and restoring patients to full life. At Whole Foods Market (a natural foods grocery chain), it is helping customers discover good eating habits and thus improving human health and nutrition.
- *Sharing information with employees about financial performance, strategy, operational measures, market conditions, and competitors' actions*—Broad disclosure

and prompt communication send the message that managers trust their workers. Keeping employees in the dark denies them information useful to performing their job, prevents them from being "students of the business," and usually turns them off.

- *Having knockout facilities*—An appealing work environment with appealing features and amenities usually has decidedly positive effects on employee morale and productivity.
- *Being flexible in how the company approaches people management (motivation, compensation, recognition, recruitment) in multinational, multicultural environments*—There is usually some merit in giving local managers in foreign operations leeway to adapt their motivation, compensation, recognition, and recruitment practices to fit local customs, habits, values, and business practices rather than insisting on consistent people-management practices worldwide. But the one area where consistency is essential is conveying the message that the organization values people of all races and cultural backgrounds and that discrimination of any sort will not be tolerated.

For specific examples of the motivational tactics employed by several prominent companies (many of which appear on *Fortune*'s annual list of the 100 best companies to work for in America), see Illustration Capsule 11.2.

Striking the Right Balance between Rewards and Punishment

While most approaches to motivation, compensation, and people management accentuate the positive, companies also embellish positive rewards with the risk of punishment. At General Electric, McKinsey & Company, several global public accounting firms, and other companies that look for and expect top-notch individual performance, there's an "up-or-out" policy—managers and professionals whose performance is not good enough to warrant promotion are first denied bonuses and stock awards and eventually weeded out. A number of companies deliberately give employees heavy workloads and tight deadlines—personnel are pushed hard to achieve "stretch" objectives and expected to put in long hours (nights and weekends if need be). At most companies, senior executives and key personnel in underperforming units are pressured to boost performance to acceptable levels and keep it there or risk being replaced.

As a general rule, it is unwise to take off the pressure for good individual and group performance or play down the stress, anxiety, and adverse consequences of shortfalls in performance. There is no evidence that a no-pressure/no-adverse-consequences work environment leads to superior strategy execution or operating excellence. As the CEO of a major bank put it, "There's a deliberate policy here to create a level of anxiety. Winners usually play like they're one touchdown behind."[31] *High-performing organizations nearly always have a cadre of ambitious people who relish the opportunity to climb the ladder of success, love a challenge, thrive in a performance-oriented environment, and find some competition and pressure useful to satisfy their own drives for personal recognition, accomplishment, and self-satisfaction.*

However, if an organization's motivational approaches and reward structure induce too much stress, internal competitiveness, job insecurity, and unpleasant consequences, the impact on workforce morale and strategy execution can be counterproductive. Evidence shows that managerial initiatives to improve strategy execution should incorporate more positive than negative motivational elements because when cooperation

ILLUSTRATION CAPSULE 11.2
What Companies Do to Motivate and Reward Employees

Companies have come up with an impressive variety of motivational and reward practices to help create a work environment that energizes employees and promotes better strategy execution. Here's a sampling of what companies are doing:

- Google has a sprawling four-building complex known as the Googleplex where the roughly 1,000 employees are provided with free food, unlimited ice cream, pool and Ping-Pong tables, and complimentary massages—management built the Googleplex to be "a dream environment." Moreover, the company gives its employees the ability to spend 20 percent of their work time on any outside activity. Google has helped extend its social mission to employees' lives away from work by giving employees $1,000 toward the purchase of a hybrid car and covering a portion of the cost of having solar panels installed at their homes.
- Lincoln Electric, widely known for its piecework pay scheme and incentive bonus plan, rewards individual productivity by paying workers for each nondefective piece produced. Workers have to correct quality problems on their own time—defects in products used by customers can be traced back to the worker who caused them. Lincoln's piecework plan motivates workers to pay attention to both quality and volume produced. In addition, the company sets aside a substantial portion of its profits above a specified base for worker bonuses. To determine bonus size, Lincoln Electric rates each worker on four equally important performance measures: dependability, quality, output, and ideas and cooperation. The higher a worker's merit rating, the higher the incentive bonus earned; the highest rated workers in good profit years receive bonuses of as much as 110 percent of their piecework compensation.
- At JM Family Enterprises, a Toyota distributor in Florida, employees get a great lease on new Toyotas and are flown to the Bahamas for cruises on the 172-foot company yacht, plus the company's office facility has such amenities as a heated lap pool, a fitness center, on-site child care, and a free nail salon. Employees get free prescriptions delivered by a "pharmacy concierge" and professionally made take-home dinners.
- Wegmans, a family owned grocer with 71 stores on the East Coast of the United States, provides employees with flexible schedules and benefits that include on-site fitness centers. The company's approach to managing people allows it to provide a very high level of customer service not found in other grocery chains. Employees ranging from cashiers to butchers to store managers are all treated equally and viewed as experts in their jobs. Employees receive 50 hours of formal training per year and are allowed to make decisions that they believe are appropriate for their jobs. The company's annual turnover rate is only 6 percent, which is less than one-half the 14 percent average turnover rate in the U.S. supermarket industry.
- Nordstrom, widely regarded for its superior in-house customer service experience, typically pays its retail salespeople an hourly wage higher than the prevailing rates paid by other department store chains plus a commission on each sale. Spurred by a culture that encourages salespeople to go all out to satisfy customers and to seek for and promote new fashion ideas, Nordstrom salespeople often earn twice the average incomes of sales employees at competing stores. The typical Nordstrom salesperson earns nearly $38,000 a year, and sales department managers earn, on average, $48,500 a year. Nordstrom's rules for employees are simple: "Rule #1: Use your good judgment in all situations. There will be no additional rules."
- Employees at W. L. Gore (the maker of Gore-Tex) get to choose what project/team they work on, and each team member's compensation is based on other team members' rankings of his or her contribution to the enterprise.
- At Ukrop's Super Markets, a family-owned chain, stores stay closed on Sunday; the company pays out 20 percent of pretax profits to employees in the form of quarterly bonuses; and the company picks up the membership tab for employees if they visit their health club 30 times a quarter.
- At biotech leader Amgen, employees get 16 paid holidays, generous vacation time, tuition reimbursements up to $10,000, on-site massages, a discounted car wash, and the convenience of shopping at on-site farmers' markets.

Sources: Fortune's lists of the 100 best companies to work for in America, 2002, 2004, 2005, and 2008; Jefferson Graham, "The Search Engine That Could," *USA Today,* August 26, 2003, p. B3; and Fred Vogelstein, "Winning the Amazon Way," *Fortune,* May 26, 2003, p. 73.

is positively enlisted and rewarded, rather than strong-armed by orders and threats (implicit or explicit), people tend to respond with more enthusiasm, dedication, creativity, and initiative.[32] Something of a middle ground is generally optimal—not only handing out decidedly positive rewards for meeting or beating performance targets but also imposing sufficiently negative consequences (if only withholding rewards) when actual performance falls short of the target. But the negative consequences of underachievement should never be so severe or demoralizing as to impede a renewed and determined effort to overcome existing obstacles and hit the targets in upcoming periods.

Linking the Reward System to Strategically Relevant Performance Outcomes

The most dependable way to keep people focused on strategy execution and the achievement of performance targets is to *generously* reward and recognize individuals and groups who meet or beat performance targets and deny rewards and recognition to those who don't. *The use of incentives and rewards is the single most powerful tool management has to win strong employee commitment to diligent, competent strategy execution and operating excellence.* Decisions on salary increases, incentive compensation, promotions, key assignments, and the ways and means of awarding praise and recognition are potent attention-getting, commitment-generating devices.[33] Such decisions seldom escape the closest employee scrutiny, saying more about what is expected and who is considered to be doing a good job than about any other factor. Hence, when meeting or beating strategic and financial targets becomes *the dominating basis* for designing incentives, evaluating individual and group efforts, and handing out rewards, company personnel quickly grasp that it is in their own self-interest to do their best in executing the strategy competently and achieving key performance targets.[34] Indeed, it is usually through the company's system of incentives and rewards that workforce members emotionally ratify their commitment to the company's strategy execution effort.

Ideally, performance targets should be set for every organization unit, every manager, every team or work group, and perhaps every employee—targets that measure whether strategy execution is progressing satisfactorily. If the company's strategy is to be a low-cost provider, the incentive system must reward actions and achievements that result in lower costs. If the company has a differentiation strategy predicated on superior quality and service, the incentive system must reward such outcomes as Six Sigma defect rates, infrequent need for product repair, low numbers of customer complaints, speedy order processing and delivery, and high levels of customer satisfaction. If a company's growth is predicated on a strategy of new product innovation, incentives should be tied to factors such as the percentages of revenues and profits coming from newly introduced products.

CORE CONCEPT

A properly designed reward system aligns the well-being of organization members with their contributions to competent strategy execution and the achievement of performance targets.

Illustration Capsule 11.3 provides two vivid examples of how companies have designed incentives linked directly to outcomes reflecting good strategy execution.

The Importance of Basing Incentives on Achieving Results, Not on Performing Assigned Duties

To create a strategy-supportive system of rewards and incentives, a company must emphasize rewarding people for accomplishing results,

ILLUSTRATION 11.3

Nucor and Bank One: Two Companies That Tie Incentives Directly to Strategy Execution

The strategy at Nucor Corporation, one of the two largest steel producers in the United States, is to be *the* low-cost producer of steel products. Because labor costs are a significant fraction of total cost in the steel business, successful implementation of Nucor's low-cost leadership strategy entails achieving lower labor costs per ton of steel than competitors' costs. Nucor management uses an incentive system to promote high worker productivity and drive labor costs per ton below rivals'. Each plant's workforce is organized into production teams (each assigned to perform particular functions), and weekly production targets are established for each team. Base pay scales are set at levels comparable to wages for similar manufacturing jobs in the local areas where Nucor has plants, but workers can earn a 1 percent bonus for each 1 percent that their output exceeds target levels. If a production team exceeds its weekly production target by 10 percent, team members receive a 10 percent bonus in their next paycheck; if a team exceeds its quota by 20 percent, team members earn a 20 percent bonus. Bonuses, paid every two weeks, are based on the prior two weeks' actual production levels measured against the targets.

Nucor's piece-rate incentive plan has produced impressive results. The production teams put forth exceptional effort; it is not uncommon for most teams to beat their weekly production targets anywhere from 20 to 50 percent. When added to their base pay, the bonuses earned by Nucor workers make Nucor's work force among the highest-paid in the U.S. steel industry. From a management perspective, the incentive system has resulted in Nucor having labor productivity levels 10 to 20 percent above the average of the unionized workforces at several of its largest rivals, which in turn has given Nucor a significant labor cost advantage over most rivals.

At Bank One (recently acquired by JPMorgan Chase), management believed it was strategically important to boost its customer satisfaction ratings in order to enhance its competitiveness vis-à-vis rivals. Targets were set for customer satisfaction and monitoring systems for measuring customer satisfaction at each branch office were put in place. Then, to motivate branch office personnel to be more attentive in trying to please customers and also to signal that top management was truly committed to achieving higher levels of overall customer satisfaction, top management opted to tie pay scales in each branch office to that branch's customer satisfaction rating—the higher the branch's ratings, the higher that branch's pay scales. Management believed its shift from a theme of equal pay for equal work to one of equal pay for equal performance contributed significantly to its customer satisfaction priority.

It is folly to reward one outcome in hopes of getting another outcome.

not for just dutifully performing assigned tasks. Focusing jobholders' attention and energy on what to *achieve* as opposed to what to *do* makes the work environment results-oriented. It is flawed management to tie incentives and rewards to satisfactory performance of duties and activities in hopes that the by-products will be the desired business outcomes and company achievements.[35] In any job, performing assigned tasks is not equivalent to achieving intended outcomes. Diligently showing up for work and attending to job assignments does not, by itself, guarantee results. As any student knows, the fact that an instructor teaches and students go to class doesn't necessarily mean that the students are learning. The enterprise of education would no doubt take on a different character if teacher compensation dropped when student learning was unacceptably low and rose when student learning increased. Employee productivity among employees at Best Buy's corporate headquarters rose by 35 percent after the company began to focus on the results of each employee's work rather than on whether employees came to work early and stayed late.

Incentive compensation for top executives is typically tied to such financial measures as revenue and earnings growth, stock price performance, return on investment, and creditworthiness and perhaps such strategic measures as market share, product quality, or customer satisfaction. However, incentives for department heads, teams, and individual workers may be tied to performance outcomes more closely related to their strategic area of responsibility. In manufacturing, incentive compensation may be tied to unit manufacturing costs, on-time production and shipping, defect rates, the number and extent of work stoppages due to labor disagreements and equipment breakdowns, and so on. In sales and marketing, there may be incentives for achieving dollar sales or unit volume targets, market share, sales penetration of each target customer group, the fate of newly introduced products, the frequency of customer complaints, the number of new accounts acquired, and customer satisfaction. Which performance measures to base incentive compensation on depends on the situation—the priority placed on various financial and strategic objectives, the requirements for strategic and competitive success, and what specific results are needed in different facets of the business to keep strategy execution on track.

Guidelines for Designing Incentive Compensation Systems The concepts and company experiences discussed above yield the following prescriptive guidelines for creating an incentive compensation system to help drive successful strategy execution:

1. *Make the performance payoff a major, not minor, piece of the total compensation package.* Payoffs must be at least 10 to 12 percent of base salary to have much impact. Incentives that amount to 20 percent or more of total compensation are big attention-getters, likely to really drive individual or team effort; incentives amounting to less than 5 percent of total compensation have comparatively weak motivational impact. Moreover, the payoff for high-performing individuals and teams must be meaningfully greater than the payoff for average performers, and the payoff for average performers meaningfully bigger than for below-average performers.
2. *Have incentives that extend to all managers and all workers, not just top management.* It is a gross miscalculation to expect that lower-level managers and employees will work their hardest to hit performance targets just so a few senior executives can get lucrative rewards.
3. *Administer the reward system with scrupulous objectivity and fairness.* If performance standards are set unrealistically high or if individual/group performance evaluations are not accurate and well documented, dissatisfaction with the system will overcome any positive benefits.
4. *Tie incentives to performance outcomes directly linked to good strategy execution and financial performance.* Incentives should never be paid just because people are thought to be "doing a good job" or because they "work hard." Performance evaluation based on factors not tightly related to good strategy execution signal that either the strategic plan is incomplete (because important performance targets were left out) or management's real agenda is something other than the stated strategic and financial objectives.
5. *Make sure that the performance targets each individual or team is expected to achieve involve outcomes that the individual or team can personally affect.* The role of incentives is to enhance individual commitment and channel behavior in beneficial directions. This role is not well served when the performance measures by which company personnel are judged are outside their arena of influence.
6. *Keep the time between achieving the target performance outcome and the payment of the reward as short as possible.* Companies like Nucor and Continental

CORE CONCEPT
The role of the reward system is to align the well-being of organization members with realizing the company's vision, so that organization members benefit by helping the company execute its strategy competently and fully satisfy customers.

Airlines have discovered that weekly or monthly payments for good performance work much better than annual payments. Nucor pays weekly bonuses based on prior-week production levels; Continental awards employees a monthly bonus for each month that on-time flight performance meets or beats a specified percentage companywide. Annual bonus payouts work best for higher-level managers and for situations where target outcome relates to overall company profitability or stock price performance.

7. *Make liberal use of nonmonetary rewards; don't rely solely on monetary rewards.* When used properly, money is a great motivator, but there are also potent advantages to be gained from praise, special recognition, handing out plum assignments, and so on.
8. *Absolutely avoid skirting the system to find ways to reward effort rather than results.* Whenever actual performance falls short of targeted performance, there's merit in determining whether the causes are attributable to subpar individual/group performance or to circumstances beyond the control of those responsible. An argument can be made that exceptions should be made in giving rewards to people who've tried hard, gone the extra mile, yet still come up short because of circumstances beyond their control. The problem with making exceptions for unknowable, uncontrollable, or unforeseeable circumstances is that once good excuses start to creep into justifying rewards for subpar results, the door is open for all kinds of reasons why actual performance failed to match targeted performance. A "no excuses" standard is more evenhanded and certainly easier to administer.

CORE CONCEPT

The unwavering standard for judging whether individuals, teams, and organizational units have done a good job must be whether they meet or beat performance targets that reflect good strategy execution.

Once the incentives are designed, they have to be communicated and explained. Everybody needs to understand how their incentive compensation is calculated and how individual/group performance targets contribute to organizational performance targets. The pressure to achieve the targeted strategic and financial performance and continuously improve on strategy execution should be unrelenting, with few (if any) loopholes for rewarding shortfalls in performance. People at all levels have to be held accountable for carrying out their assigned parts of the strategic plan, and they have to understand their rewards are based on the caliber of results that are achieved. But with the pressure to perform should come meaningful rewards. Without an ample payoff, the system breaks down, and managers are left with the less workable options of barking orders, trying to enforce compliance, and depending on the goodwill of employees.

Performance-Based Incentives and Rewards in Multinational Enterprises In some foreign countries, incentive pay runs counter to local customs and cultural norms. Professor Steven Kerr cites the time he lectured an executive education class on the need for more performance-based pay and a Japanese manager protested, "You shouldn't bribe your children to do their homework, you shouldn't bribe your wife to prepare dinner, and you shouldn't bribe your employees to work for the company."[36] Singling out individuals and commending them for unusually good effort can also be a problem; Japanese culture considers public praise of an individual an affront to the harmony of the group. In some countries, employees have a preference for nonmonetary rewards—more leisure time, important titles, access to vacation villages, and nontaxable perks. Thus, multinational companies have to build some degree of flexibility into the design of incentives and rewards in order to accommodate cross-cultural traditions and preferences.

KEY POINTS

Managers implementing and executing a new or different strategy must identify the resource requirements of each new strategic initiative and then consider whether the current pattern of resource allocation and the budgets of the various subunits are suitable.

Anytime a company alters its strategy, managers should review existing policies and operating procedures, proactively revise or discard those that are out of sync, and formulate new ones to facilitate execution of new strategic initiatives. Prescribing new or freshly revised policies and operating procedures aids the task of strategy execution (1) by providing top-down guidance to operating managers, supervisory personnel, and employees regarding how certain things need to be done and what the boundaries are on independent actions and decisions; (2) by enforcing consistency in how particular strategy-critical activities are performed in geographically scattered operating units; and (3) by promoting the creation of a work climate and corporate culture that promotes good strategy execution.

Competent strategy execution entails visible, unyielding managerial commitment to best practices and continuous improvement. Benchmarking, the discovery and adoption of best practices, business process reengineering, and continuous improvement initiatives like total quality management (TQM) or Six Sigma programs all aim at improved efficiency, lower costs, better product quality, and greater customer satisfaction. *These initiatives are important tools for learning how to execute a strategy more proficiently.*

Company strategies can't be implemented or executed well without a number of support systems to carry on business operations. Well-conceived state-of-the-art support systems not only facilitate better strategy execution but also strengthen organizational capabilities enough to provide a competitive edge over rivals. Real-time information and control systems further aid the cause of good strategy execution.

Strategy-supportive motivational practices and reward systems are powerful management tools for gaining employee commitment. The key to creating a reward system that promotes good strategy execution is to make strategically relevant measures of performance *the dominating basis* for designing incentives, evaluating individual and group efforts, and handing out rewards. Positive motivational practices generally work better than negative ones, but there is a place for both. There's also a place for both monetary and nonmonetary incentives.

For an incentive compensation system to work well (1) the monetary payoff should be a major percentage of the compensation package, (2) the use of incentives should extend to all managers and workers, (3) the system should be administered with care and fairness, (4) the incentives should be linked to performance targets spelled out in the strategic plan, (5) each individual's performance targets should involve outcomes the person can personally affect, (6) rewards should promptly follow the determination of good performance, (7) monetary rewards should be supplemented with liberal use of nonmonetary rewards, and (8) skirting the system to reward nonperformers or subpar results should be scrupulously avoided. Companies with operations in multiple countries often have to build some degree of flexibility into the design of incentives and rewards in order to accommodate cross-cultural traditions and preferences.

ASSURANCE OF LEARNING EXERCISES

1. Using your favorite search engine, do a search on the term *best practices*. Browse through the search results to identify at least five organizations that have gathered a set of best practices and are making the best-practices library they have assembled available to members.

2. Do an Internet search on Six Sigma quality programs. Browse through the search results and (*a*) identify at least three companies that offer Six Sigma training and (*b*) find lists of companies that have implemented Six Sigma programs in their pursuit of operational excellence—be prepared to cite at least 10 companies that are Six Sigma users.
3. Read some of the recent Six Sigma articles posted at **www.isixsigma.com**. Prepare a one-page report to your instructor detailing how Six Sigma is being used in various companies and what benefits these companies are reaping from Six Sigma implementation.
4. Review the profiles and applications of the latest Malcolm Baldrige National Quality Award recipients at **www.quality.nist.gov**. What are the standout features of the companies' approaches to managing operations? What do you find impressive about the companies' policies and procedures, use of best practices, emphasis on continuous improvement, and use of rewards and incentives?
5. Go to **www.dell.com/casestudies** and read how Dell's clients have used information and operating systems to facilitate good strategy execution. Choosing one of the case studies provided in PDF format, describe how the information systems solution improved the effectiveness of the client's value creating business processes.
6. Consult the latest issue of *Fortune* containing the annual "100 Best Companies to Work For" (usually a late-January or early-February issue), or go to **www.fortune.com** to access the list, and identify at least five compensation incentives and work practices that these companies use to enhance employee motivation and reward them for good strategic and financial performance. You should identify compensation methods and work practices that are different from those cited in Illustration Capsule 11.2.
7. Using Google Scholar or your university library's access to online business periodicals, search for the term *incentive compensation* and prepare a one- to two-page report to your instructor discussing the successful (or unsuccessful) use of incentive compensation plans by various instructors. Given the results of your research, what factors seem to determine whether incentive compensation plans succeed or fail?

EXERCISES FOR SIMULATION PARTICIPANTS

1. Do you and your co-managers deliberately shift resources from one area to another to better support strategy execution efforts? If so, cite at least three such instances.
2. Is benchmarking data available in the simulation exercise in which you are participating? If so, do you and your co-managers regularly study the benchmarking data to see how well your company is doing? Do you consider the benchmarking information provided to be valuable? Why or why not? Cite three recent instances in which your examination of the benchmarking statistics has caused you and your co-managers to take corrective actions to boost company performance.
3. Do you and your co-managers have an opportunity to (*a*) adopt best practices or (*b*) use TQM or Six Sigma tools? If so, explain how your company has used these tools to try to improve strategy execution and boost company performance.

4. Does your company have opportunities to use incentive compensation techniques? If so, explain your company's approach to incentive compensation. Is there any hard evidence you can cite that indicates your company's use of incentive compensation techniques has worked? For example, have your company's compensation incentives actually boosted productivity? Can you cite evidence indicating that the productivity gains have resulted in lower labor costs? If the productivity gains have *not* translated into lower labor costs, then is it fair to say that your company's use of incentive compensation is a failure?
5. Are you and your co-managers consciously trying to achieve operating excellence? What are the indicators of operating excellence at your company? Given these indicators, how well does your company measure up? Is there any evidence indicating that your company's management team is doing a better job of achieving operating excellence than are the management teams at rival companies?

CHAPTER 12

Corporate Culture and Leadership

Keys to Good Strategy Execution

LEARNING OBJECTIVES

1. Be able to identify the key features of a company's corporate culture.
2. Understand how and why a company's culture can aid the drive for proficient strategy execution and operating excellence.
3. Learn the kinds of actions management can take to change a problem corporate culture.
4. Learn why corporate cultures tend to be grounded in core values and ethical principles and help establish a corporate conscience.
5. Understand what constitutes effective managerial leadership in achieving superior strategy execution and operating excellence.

The biggest levers you've got to change a company are strategy, structure, and culture. If I could pick two, I'd pick strategy and culture.

—Wayne Leonard
CEO, Entergy

An organization's capacity to execute its strategy depends on its "hard" infrastructure—its organizational structure and systems—and on its "soft" infrastructure—its culture and norms.

—Amar Bhide

You have to transform the culture, not just the strategy. Culture is what people do when no one is watching.

—Lou Gerstner
Former CEO, IBM

Weak leadership can wreck the soundest strategy; forceful execution of even a poor plan can often bring victory.

—Sun Zi

In the previous two chapters we examined six of the managerial tasks that are important to good strategy execution and operating excellence—building a capable organization, marshaling the needed resources and steering them to strategy-critical operating units, establishing policies and procedures that facilitate good strategy execution, adopting best practices and pushing for continuous improvement in how value chain activities are performed, creating internal operating systems that enable better execution, and employing motivational practices and compensation incentives that gain wholehearted employee commitment to the strategy execution process. In this chapter we explore the two remaining managerial tasks that shape the outcome of efforts to execute a company's strategy: creating a strategy-supportive corporate culture and exerting the internal leadership needed to drive the implementation of strategic initiatives forward and achieve higher plateaus of operating excellence.

INSTILLING A CORPORATE CULTURE THAT PROMOTES GOOD STRATEGY EXECUTION

Every company has its own unique culture. The character of a company's culture or work climate is a product of the core values and business principles that executives espouse, the standards of what is ethically acceptable and what is not, the work practices and behaviors that define "how we do things around here," its approach to people management and style of operating, the "chemistry" and the "personality" that permeates its work environment, and the stories that get told over and over to illustrate and reinforce the company's values, business practices, and traditions. The meshing together of stated beliefs, business principles, style of operating, ingrained behaviors and attitudes, and work climate define a company's **corporate culture.** A company's culture is important because it influences the organization's actions and approaches to conducting business—in a very real sense, the culture is the company's "operating system" or organizational DNA.[1]

CORE CONCEPT

Corporate culture **refers to the character of a company's internal work climate and personality—as shaped by its core values, beliefs, business principles, traditions, ingrained behaviors, work practices, and style of operating.**

Corporate cultures vary widely. For instance, the bedrock of Wal-Mart's culture is dedication to customer satisfaction, zealous pursuit of low costs and frugal operating practices, a strong work ethic, ritualistic Saturday-morning headquarters meetings to exchange ideas and review problems, and company executives' commitment to visiting stores, listening to customers, and soliciting suggestions from employees. General Electric's culture is founded on a hard-driving, results-oriented atmosphere (where all of the company's business divisions are held to a standard of being number one or two in their industries as well as achieving good business results); extensive cross-business sharing of ideas, best practices, and learning; the reliance on "workout sessions" to identify, debate, and resolve burning issues; a commitment to Six Sigma quality; and globalization of the company. At Nordstrom, the corporate culture is centered on delivering exceptional service to customers; the company's motto is "Respond to unreasonable customer requests"—each out-of-the-ordinary request is seen as an opportunity for a "heroic" act by an employee that can further the company's reputation for a customer-pleasing shopping environment. Illustration Capsule 12.1 relates how Google and Alberto-Culver describe their corporate cultures.

Identifying the Key Features of a Company's Corporate Culture

A company's corporate culture is mirrored in the character or "personality" of its work environment—the factors that underlie how the company tries to conduct its business and the behaviors that are held in high esteem. The chief things to look for include the following:

- The values, business principles, and ethical standards that management preaches and *practices*—actions speak much louder than words here.
- The company's approach to people management and the official policies, procedures, and operating practices that paint the white lines for the behavior of company personnel.
- The spirit and character that pervades the work climate. Is the workplace vibrant and fun? Methodical and all-business? Tense and harried? Highly competitive and

ILLUSTRATION CAPSULE 12.1
The Corporate Cultures at Google and Alberto-Culver

Founded in 1998 by Larry Page and Sergey Brin, two Ph.D. students in computer science at Stanford University, Google has become world renowned for its search engine technology. Google.com was the most frequently visited Internet site in 2008, attracting over 530 million unique visitors monthly from around the world. Google has some unique ways of operating, and its culture is also rather quirky. The company describes its culture as follows:

> Though growing rapidly, Google still maintains a small company feel. At the Googleplex headquarters almost everyone eats in the Google café (known as "Charlie's Place"), sitting at whatever table has an opening and enjoying conversations with Googlers from all different departments. Topics range from the trivial to the technical, and whether the discussion is about computer games or encryption or ad serving software, it's not surprising to hear someone say, "That's a product I helped develop before I came to Google."
>
> Google's emphasis on innovation and commitment to cost containment means each employee is a hands-on contributor. There's little in the way of corporate hierarchy and everyone wears several hats. The international webmaster who creates Google's holiday logos spent a week translating the entire site into Korean. The chief operations engineer is also a licensed neurosurgeon. Because everyone realizes they are an equally important part of Google's success, no one hesitates to skate over a corporate officer during roller hockey.
>
> Google's hiring policy is aggressively nondiscriminatory and favors ability over experience. The result is a staff that reflects the global audience the search engine serves. Google has offices around the globe and Google engineering centers are recruiting local talent in locations from Zurich to Bangalore. Dozens of languages are spoken by Google staffers, from Turkish to Telugu. When not at work, Googlers pursue interests from cross-country cycling to wine tasting, from flying to Frisbee. As Google expands its development team, it continues to look for those who share an obsessive commitment to creating search perfection and having a great time doing it.

The Alberto-Culver Company, with fiscal 2007 revenues of about $1.5 billion, is the producer and marketer of Alberto VO5, TRESemmé, Motions, Soft & Beautiful, Just for Me, and Nexxus hair care products; St. Ives skin care products; and such brands as Molly McButter, Mrs. Dash, Sugar Twin, and Static Guard. Alberto-Culver brands are sold in more than 100 countries.

At the careers section of its Web site, the company described its culture in the following words:

> Building careers is as important to us as building brands. We believe that passionate people create powerful growth. We believe in a workplace built on values and believe our best people display those same values in their families and their communities. We believe in recognizing and rewarding accomplishment and celebrating our victories.
>
> We believe the best ideas work their way—quickly—up an organization, not down. We believe that we should take advantage of every ounce of your talent on teams and cross-functional activities, not just assign you to a box.
>
> We believe in open communication. We believe that you can improve what you measure, so we survey and spot check all the time. For that same reason, everyone has specific goals so that their expectations are in line with their managers' and the company's.
>
> We believe that victory is a team accomplishment. We believe in personal development. We believe if you talk with us you will catch our enthusiasm and want to be a part of the Alberto-Culver team.

Sources: Information posted at www.google.com and www.alberto.com (accessed August 18, 2008).

politicized? Are people excited about their work and emotionally connected to the company's business, or are they just there to draw a paycheck? Is there an emphasis on empowered worker creativity, or do people have little discretion in how jobs are done?

- How managers and employees interact and relate to each other—the reliance on teamwork and open communication, the extent to which there is good camaraderie, whether people are called by their first names, whether coworkers spend little or lots of time together outside the workplace, and what the dress codes are (the accepted styles of attire and whether there are casual days).

- The strength of peer pressures to do things in particular ways and conform to expected norms—what actions and behaviors are approved (and rewarded by management in the form of compensation and promotion) and which ones are frowned on.
- The company's revered traditions and oft-repeated stories about "heroic acts" and "how we do things around here."
- The manner in which the company deals with external stakeholders (particularly vendors and local communities where it has operations)—whether it treats suppliers as business partners or prefers hardnosed, arm's-length business arrangements and the strength and genuineness of the commitment to corporate citizenship and environmental sustainability.

Some of these sociological forces are readily apparent, and others operate quite subtly.

The values, beliefs, and practices that undergird a company's culture can come from anywhere in the organization hierarchy, most often representing the business philosophy and managerial style of influential executives but also resulting from exemplary actions on the part of company personnel and consensus agreement about "how we ought to do things around here."[2] Typically, key elements of the culture originate with a founder or certain strong leaders who articulated them as a set of business principles; company policies; operating approaches; and ways of dealing with employees, customers, vendors, shareholders, and local communities where the company has operations. Over time, these cultural underpinnings take root, become embedded in how the company conducts its business, come to be accepted by company managers and employees alike, and then persist as new employees are encouraged to adopt and follow the professed values, behaviors, and work practices.

The Role of Stories Frequently, a significant part of a company's culture is captured in the stories that get told over and over again to illustrate to newcomers the importance of certain values and the depth of commitment that various company personnel have displayed. One of the folktales at FedEx, world renowned for the reliability of its next-day package delivery guarantee, is about a deliveryman who had been given the wrong key to a FedEx drop box. Rather than leave the packages in the drop box until the next day when the right key was available, the deliveryman unbolted the drop box from its base, loaded it into the truck, and took it back to the station. There, the box was pried open and the contents removed and sped on their way to their destination the next day. Nordstrom keeps a scrapbook commemorating the heroic acts of its employees and uses it as a regular reminder of the above-and-beyond-the-call-of-duty behaviors that employees are encouraged to display. At Frito-Lay, there are dozens of stories about truck drivers who went to extraordinary lengths in overcoming adverse weather conditions in order to make scheduled deliveries to retail customers and keep store shelves stocked with Frito-Lay products. At Microsoft, there are stories of the long hours programmers put in, the emotional peaks and valleys in encountering and overcoming coding problems, the exhilaration of completing a complex program on schedule, the satisfaction of working on cutting-edge projects, the rewards of being part of a team responsible for a popular new software program, and the tradition of competing aggressively. Such stories serve the valuable purpose of illustrating the kinds of behavior the company encourages and reveres. Moreover, each retelling of a legendary story puts a bit more peer pressure on company personnel to display core values and do their part in keeping the company's traditions alive.

Perpetuating the Culture Once established, company cultures are perpetuated in six important ways: (1) by screening and selecting new employees that will mesh well with the culture, (2) by systematic indoctrination of new members in the culture's fundamentals, (3) by the efforts of senior group members to reiterate core values in daily conversations and pronouncements, (4) by the telling and retelling of company legends, (5) by regular ceremonies honoring members who display desired cultural behaviors, and (6) by visibly rewarding those who display cultural norms and penalizing those who don't.[3] *The more new employees a company is hiring, the more important it becomes to screen job applicants every bit as much for how well their values, beliefs, and personalities match up with the culture as for their technical skills and experience.* For example, a company that stresses operating with integrity and fairness has to hire people who themselves have integrity and place a high value on fair play. A company whose culture revolves around creativity, product innovation, and leading change has to screen new hires for their ability to think outside the box, generate new ideas, and thrive in a climate of rapid change and ambiguity. Southwest Airlines—whose two core values, "LUV" and fun, permeate the work environment and whose objective is to ensure that passengers have a positive and enjoyable flying experience—goes to considerable lengths to hire flight attendants and gate personnel who are witty, cheery, and outgoing and who display "whistle while you work" attitudes. Fast-growing companies risk creating a culture by chance rather than by design if they rush to hire employees mainly for their talents and credentials and neglect to screen out candidates whose values, philosophies, and personalities aren't a good fit with the organizational character, vision, and strategy being articulated by the company's senior executives.

As a rule, companies are careful to hire people who they believe will fit in and embrace the prevailing culture. And, usually, job seekers lean toward accepting jobs at companies where they feel comfortable with the atmosphere and the people they will be working with. Employees who don't hit it off at a company tend to leave quickly, while employees who thrive and are pleased with the work environment stay on, eventually moving up the ranks to positions of greater responsibility. The longer people stay at an organization, the more that they come to embrace and mirror the corporate culture—their values and beliefs tend to be molded by mentors, fellow workers, company training programs, and the reward structure. Normally, employees who have worked at a company for a long time play a major role in indoctrinating new employees into the culture.

Forces That Cause a Company's Culture to Evolve However, even stable cultures aren't static—just like strategy and organization structure, they evolve. New challenges in the marketplace, revolutionary technologies, and shifting internal conditions—especially eroding business prospects, an internal crisis, or top executive turnover—tend to breed new ways of doing things and, in turn, cultural evolution. An incoming CEO who decides to shake up the existing business and take it in new directions often triggers a cultural shift, perhaps one of major proportions. Likewise, diversification into new businesses, expansion into foreign countries, rapid growth, an influx of new employees, and merger with or acquisition of another company can all precipitate cultural changes of one kind or another.

Company Subcultures: The Problems Posed by New Acquisitions and Multinational Operations Although it is common to speak about corporate culture in the singular, it is not uncommon for companies to have multiple cultures (or subcultures).[4] Values, beliefs, and practices within a company sometimes vary significantly by department, geographic location, division, or business unit. A company's subcultures can clash, or at least not mesh well, if they embrace conflicting business philosophies or operating approaches, if key executives employ different approaches to people management, or if important differences between a company's culture and those of recently acquired companies have not yet been ironed out. *Global and multinational companies tend to be at least partly multicultural* because cross-country organization units have different operating histories and work climates, as well as members who have grown up under different social customs and traditions and who have different sets of values and beliefs. The human resources manager of a global pharmaceutical company who took on an assignment in the Far East discovered, to his surprise, that one of his biggest challenges was to persuade his company's managers in China, Korea, Malaysia, and Taiwan to accept promotions—their cultural values were such that they did not believe in competing with their peers for career rewards or personal gain, nor did they relish breaking ties to their local communities to assume cross-national responsibilities.[5] Many companies that have merged with or acquired foreign companies have to deal with language- and custom-based cultural differences.

Nonetheless, the existence of subcultures does not preclude important areas of commonality and compatibility. For example, General Electric's cultural traits of boundarylessness, workout, and Six Sigma quality have been implanted and practiced successfully in many different countries. AES, a global power company with operations in 29 countries, has found that the core values of integrity, fun, sharing knowledge, and social responsibility underlying its culture are readily embraced by people in different countries. Moreover, AES tries to define and practice its cultural values the same way in all of its locations while still being sensitive to differences in languages, geography, lifestyles, and local customs.

In today's globalizing world, multinational companies are learning how to make strategy-critical cultural traits travel across country boundaries and create a workably uniform culture worldwide. Likewise, company managements are quite alert to the importance of cultural compatibility in making acquisitions and the need to address how to merge and integrate the cultures of newly acquired companies—cultural due diligence is often as important as financial due diligence in deciding whether to go forward on an acquisition or merger.[6] On a number of occasions, companies have decided to pass on acquiring particular companies because of culture conflicts that they believed would be hard to resolve.

Strong versus Weak Cultures

Company cultures vary widely in strength and influence. Some are strongly embedded and have a big impact on a company's practices and behavioral norms. Others are weak and have comparatively little influence on company operations.

Strong-Culture Companies The hallmark of a strong-culture company is the dominating presence of certain deeply rooted values and operating approaches that "regulate" the conduct of a company's business and the climate of its workplace.[7] Strong cultures take years (sometimes decades) to emerge and are never an overnight phenomenon. In strong-culture companies, senior managers make a point of reiterating these principles and values to organization members and explaining how they relate to its business environment. But, more important, they make a conscious effort to display these principles in their own actions and behavior—they walk the talk, and they *insist* that *company values and business principles be reflected in the decisions and actions taken by all company personnel.* An unequivocal expectation that company personnel will act and behave in accordance with the adopted values and ways of doing business leads to two important outcomes: (1) over time the values come to be widely shared by rank-and-file employees—people who dislike the culture tend to leave; and (2) individuals encounter strong peer pressure from coworkers to observe the culturally approved norms and behaviors. Hence, a strongly implanted corporate culture ends up having a powerful influence on "how we do things around here" because so many company personnel are accepting of cultural traditions and because this acceptance is reinforced by both management expectations and coworker peer pressure. Since cultural traditions and norms have such a dominating influence in strong-culture companies, the character of the culture becomes the company's soul or psyche.

CORE CONCEPT

In a strong-culture company, culturally approved behaviors and ways of doing things are nurtured while culturally disapproved behaviors and work practices get squashed.

Three factors contribute to the development of strong cultures: (1) a founder or strong leader who establishes values, principles, and practices that are consistent and sensible in light of customer needs, competitive conditions, and strategic requirements; (2) a sincere, long-standing company commitment to operating the business according to these established traditions, thereby creating an internal environment that supports decision making and strategies based on cultural norms; and (3) a genuine concern for the well-being of the organization's three biggest constituencies—customers, employees, and shareholders. Continuity of leadership, small group size, stable group membership, geographic concentration, and considerable organizational success all contribute to the emergence and sustainability of a strong culture.[8]

In strong-culture companies, values and behavioral norms are so ingrained that they can endure leadership changes at the top—although their strength can erode over time if new CEOs cease to nurture them or move aggressively to institute cultural adjustments. And the cultural norms in a strong-culture company may not change much as strategy evolves and the organization acts to make strategy adjustments, either because the new strategies are compatible with the present culture or because the dominant traits of the culture are somewhat strategy-neutral and compatible with evolving versions of the company's strategy.

In a strong-culture company, values and behavioral norms are like crabgrass: deeply rooted and hard to weed out.

Weak-Culture Companies In direct contrast to strong-culture companies, weak-culture companies lack values and principles that are consistently preached or widely shared (usually because the company has had a series of CEOs with differing values and differing views about how the company's business ought to be conducted). As a consequence, the company has few widely revered traditions and few culture-induced norms are evident in operating practices. Because top executives at a weak-culture company don't repeatedly espouse any particular business philosophy or exhibit long-standing commitment to particular values or extol particular operating practices and behavioral norms, individuals encounter little coworker peer pressure to do things in particular ways. Moreover, a weak company culture breeds no strong employee allegiance to what the company stands for or to operating the business in well-defined ways. While individual employees may well have some bonds of identification with and loyalty toward their department, their colleagues, their union, or their boss, there's neither passion about the company nor emotional commitment to what it is trying to accomplish—a condition that often results in many employees viewing their company as just a place to work and their job as just a way to make a living. Very often, cultural weakness stems from moderately entrenched subcultures that block the emergence of a well-defined companywide work climate.

As a consequence, *weak cultures provide little or no assistance in executing strategy* because there are no traditions, beliefs, values, common bonds, or behavioral norms that management can use as levers to mobilize commitment to executing the chosen strategy. The only plus of a weak culture is that it does not usually pose a strong barrier to strategy execution, but the negative of not providing any support means that culture-building has to be high on management's action agenda. Absent a work climate that channels organizational energy in the direction of good strategy execution, managers are left with the options of either using compensation incentives and other motivational devices to mobilize employee commitment or trying to establish cultural roots that will in time start to nurture the strategy execution process.

Unhealthy Cultures

The distinctive characteristic of an unhealthy corporate culture is the presence of counterproductive cultural traits that adversely impact the work climate and company performance.[9] The following four traits are particularly unhealthy:

1. A highly politicized internal environment in which many issues get resolved and decisions made on the basis of which individuals or groups have the most political clout to carry the day.
2. Hostility to change and a general wariness of people who champion new ways of doing things.
3. An insular "not-invented-here" mind-set that makes company personnel averse to looking outside the company for best practices, new managerial approaches, and innovative ideas.
4. A disregard for high ethical standards and overzealous pursuit of wealth and status on the part of key executives.

Politicized Cultures What makes a politicized internal environment so unhealthy is that political infighting consumes a great deal of organizational energy, often with the result that what's best for the company takes a backseat to political maneuvering. In companies where internal politics pervades the work climate, empire-building managers jealously guard their decision-making prerogatives. They have their own agendas and operate the work units under their supervision as autonomous "fiefdoms," and the positions they take on issues are usually aimed at protecting or expanding their turf. Collaboration with other organizational units is viewed with suspicion (What are "they" up to? How can "we" protect "our" flanks?), and cross-unit cooperation occurs grudgingly. When an important proposal moves to the front burner, advocates try to ram it through and opponents try to alter it in significant ways or even kill it. The support or opposition of politically influential executives and/or coalitions among departments with vested interests in a particular outcome typically weigh heavily in deciding what actions the company takes. All this maneuvering takes away from efforts to execute strategy with real proficiency and frustrates company personnel who are less political and more inclined to do what is in the company's best interests.

Change-Resistant Cultures In less-adaptive cultures where skepticism about the importance of new developments and resistance to change are the norm, managers prefer waiting until the fog of uncertainty clears before steering a new course, making fundamental adjustments to their product line, or embracing a major new technology. They believe in moving cautiously and conservatively, preferring to follow others rather than take decisive action to be in the forefront of change. Change-resistant cultures place a premium on not making mistakes, prompting managers to lean toward safe, don't-rock-the-boat options that will have only a ripple effect on the status quo, protect or advance their own careers, and guard the interests of their immediate work groups.

Change-resistant cultures encourage a number of undesirable or unhealthy behaviors—avoiding risks, not making bold proposals to pursue emerging opportunities, a lax approach to both product innovation and continuous improvement in performing value chain activities, and following rather than leading market change. In change-resistant cultures, word quickly gets around that proposals to do things differently face an uphill battle and that people who champion them may be seen as something of a nuisance. Executives who don't value managers or employees with initiative and new ideas quickly put a damper on product innovation, experimentation, and efforts to improve. At the same time, change-resistant companies have little appetite for being first-movers or fast-followers, believing that being in the forefront of change is too risky and that acting too quickly increases vulnerability to costly mistakes. They are more inclined to adopt a wait-and-see posture, carefully analyze several alternative responses, learn from the missteps of early movers, and then move forward cautiously and conservatively with initiatives that are deemed safe. Hostility to change is most often found in companies with multilayered management bureaucracies that have enjoyed considerable market success in years past and that are wedded to the "We have done it this way for years" syndrome.

When such companies encounter business environments with accelerating change, going slow on altering traditional ways of doing things can be become a liability rather than an asset. General Motors, IBM, Sears, and Eastman Kodak are classic examples of companies whose change-resistant bureaucracies were slow to respond to fundamental changes in their markets; clinging to the cultures and traditions that made them successful, they were reluctant to alter operating practices and modify their business approaches. As strategies of gradual change won out over bold innovation and being an early mover, all four lost market share to rivals that quickly moved to institute changes more in tune with evolving market conditions and buyer preferences. These companies are now struggling to recoup lost ground with cultures and behaviors more suited to market success—the kinds of fit that caused them to succeed in the first place.

Insular, Inwardly Focused Cultures Sometimes a company reigns as an industry leader or enjoys great market success for so long that its personnel start to believe they have all the answers or can develop them on their own. There is a strong tendency to neglect what customers are saying and how their needs and expectations are changing. Such confidence in the correctness of how it does things and in the company's skills and capabilities breeds arrogance—company personnel discount the merits of what outsiders are doing and what can be learned by studying best-in-class performers. Benchmarking and a search for the best practices of outsiders are seen as offering little payoff. Any market share gains on the part of up-and-coming rivals are regarded as temporary setbacks, soon to be reversed by the company's own forthcoming initiatives (which, it is confidently predicted, will be an instant market hit with customers).

Insular thinking, internally driven solutions, and a must-be-invented-here mindset come to permeate the corporate culture. An inwardly focused corporate culture gives rise to managerial inbreeding and a failure to recruit people who can offer fresh thinking and outside perspectives. The big risk of insular cultural thinking is that the company can underestimate the competencies and accomplishments of rival companies and overestimate its own progress—with a resulting loss of competitive advantage over time.

Unethical and Greed-Driven Cultures Companies that have little regard for ethical standards or that are run by executives driven by greed and ego gratification are scandals waiting to happen. Enron's collapse in 2001 was largely the product of an ethically dysfunctional corporate culture—while the culture embraced the positives of product innovation, aggressive risk-taking, and a driving ambition to lead global change in the energy business, its executives exuded the negatives of arrogance, ego, greed, and an "ends-justify-the-means" mentality in pursuing stretch revenue and profitability targets.[10] A number of Enron's senior managers were all too willing to wink at unethical behavior, to cross over the line to unethical (and sometimes criminal) behavior themselves, and to deliberately stretch generally accepted accounting principles to make Enron's financial performance look far better than it really was. In the end, Enron came unglued because a few top executives chose unethical and illegal paths to pursue corporate revenue and profitability targets—in a company that publicly preached integrity and other notable corporate values but was lax in making sure that key executives walked the talk. Unethical cultures and executive greed have produced scandals at WorldCom, Quest, HealthSouth, Adelphia, Tyco, McWane, Parmalat, Rite Aid, Hollinger International, Refco, and Marsh & McLennan, with executives being indicted and/or convicted of criminal behavior. The U.S. Attorney's office elected not to prosecute KPMG with "systematic" criminal acts to market illegal tax shelters to wealthy clients (which KPMG tried mightily to cover up) because a criminal indictment would have resulted in the immediate collapse of KPMG and cut the number of global public accounting firms from four to just three; instead, criminal charges were filed against the company officials deemed most responsible. In 2005, U.S. prosecutors elected not to press criminal charges against Royal Dutch Petroleum (Shell Oil) for repeatedly and knowingly reporting inflated oil reserves to the Securities and Exchange Commission and not to indict Tommy Hilfiger USA for multiple tax law violations—but both companies agreed to sign nonprosecution agreements, the terms of which were not made public but almost certainly involved fines and a long-term company commitment to cease and desist.

High-Performance Cultures

Some companies have so-called high-performance cultures where the standout cultural traits are a can-do spirit, pride in doing things right, no-excuses accountability, and a pervasive results-oriented work climate where people go the extra mile to meet or beat stretch objectives. In high-performance cultures, there's a strong sense of involvement on the part of company personnel and emphasis on individual initiative and creativity. Performance expectations are clearly delineated for the company as a whole, for each organizational unit, and for each individual. Issues and problems are promptly addressed—a strong bias for being proactive instead of reactive exists. There's a razor-sharp focus on what needs to be done. Results-oriented cultures are permeated with a spirit of achievement and have a good track record in meeting or beating performance targets.

The challenge in creating a high-performance culture is to inspire high loyalty and dedication of the part of employees, such that they are both energized and preoccupied with putting forth their very best efforts to do things right and be unusually productive. Managers have to take pains to reinforce constructive behavior, reward top performers, and purge habits and behaviors that stand in the way of high productivity and good results. They must work at knowing the strengths and weaknesses of their subordinates, so as to better match talent with task and enable people to make meaningful contributions by doing what they do best.[11] They have to stress learning from mistakes and building on strengths, and put an unrelenting emphasis on moving forward and making good progress—in effect, there has to be a disciplined, performance-focused approach to managing the organization.

Adaptive Cultures

The hallmark of adaptive corporate cultures is willingness on the part of organizational members to accept change and take on the challenge of introducing and executing new strategies.[12] Company personnel share a feeling of confidence that the organization can deal with whatever threats and opportunities come down the pike; they are receptive to risk taking, experimentation, innovation, and changing strategies and practices. In direct contrast to change-resistant cultures, adaptive cultures are very supportive of managers and employees at all ranks who propose or help initiate useful change. Internal entrepreneurship on the part of individuals and groups is encouraged and rewarded. Senior executives seek out, support, and promote individuals who exercise initiative, spot opportunities for improvement, and display the skills to implement them. Managers openly evaluate ideas and suggestions, fund initiatives to develop new or better products, and take prudent risks to pursue emerging market opportunities. As in high-performance cultures, the company exhibits a proactive approach to identifying issues, evaluating the implications and options, and quickly moving ahead with workable solutions. Strategies and traditional operating practices are modified as needed to adjust to or take advantage of changes in the business environment.

CORE CONCEPT

In adaptive cultures, there's a spirit of doing what's necessary to ensure long-term organizational success provided the new behaviors and operating practices that management is calling for are seen as legitimate and consistent with the core values and business principles underpinning the culture.

But why is change so willingly embraced in an adaptive culture? Why are organization members not fearful of how change will affect them? Why does an adaptive culture not become unglued with ongoing changes in strategy, operating practices, and behavioral norms? The answers lie in two distinctive and dominant traits of an adaptive culture: (1) Any changes in operating practices and behaviors must *not* compromise core values and long-standing business principles, and (2) the changes that are instituted must satisfy the legitimate interests of stakeholders—customers, employees, shareowners, suppliers, and the communities where the company operates.[13] In other words, what sustains an adaptive culture is that organization members perceive the changes that management is trying to institute as legitimate and in keeping with the core values and business principles that form the heart and soul of the culture.

Thus, for an adaptive culture to remain intact over time, top management must orchestrate organizational changes in a manner that (1) demonstrates genuine care for the well-being of all key constituencies and (2) tries to satisfy all their legitimate interests simultaneously. Unless fairness to all constituencies is a decision-making principle and a commitment to doing the right thing is evident to organization members, the changes are not likely to be seen as legitimate and thus be readily accepted and implemented wholeheartedly.[14] Making changes that will please customers and/or that protect, if not enhance, the company's long-term well-being are generally seen as legitimate and are often seen as the best way of looking out for the interests of employees, stockholders, suppliers, and communities where the company operates.

At companies with adaptive cultures, management concern for the well-being of employees is nearly always a big factor in gaining employee support for change—company personnel are usually receptive to change as long as employees understand that changes in their job assignments are part of the process of adapting to new conditions and that their employment security will not be threatened unless the company's business unexpectedly reverses direction. In cases where workforce downsizing becomes necessary, management concern for employees dictates that separation be handled humanely, making employee departure as painless as possible. Management efforts to make the process of adapting to change fair and equitable for customers, employees, stockholders, suppliers, and communities where the company operates breeds acceptance of and support for change among all organization stakeholders.

Adaptive cultures are exceptionally well suited to companies with fast-changing strategies and market environments.

Technology companies, software companies, and Internet-based companies are good illustrations of organizations with adaptive cultures. Such companies thrive on change—driving it, leading it, and capitalizing on it (but sometimes also succumbing to change when they make the wrong move or are swamped by better technologies or the superior business models of rivals). Companies like Google, Intel, Cisco Systems, eBay, Nokia, Amazon.com, and Dell cultivate the capability to act and react rapidly. They are avid practitioners of entrepreneurship and innovation, with a demonstrated willingness to take bold risks to create altogether new products, new businesses, and new industries. To create and nurture a culture that can adapt rapidly to changing to shifting business conditions, they make a point of staffing their organizations with people who are proactive, rise to the challenge of change, and have an aptitude for adapting.

In fast-changing business environments, a corporate culture that is receptive to altering organizational practices and behaviors is a virtual necessity. However, adaptive cultures work to the advantage of all companies, not just those in rapid-change environments. Every company operates in a market and business climate that is changing to one degree or another and that, in turn, requires internal operating responses and new behaviors on the part of organization members. *As a company's strategy evolves, an adaptive culture is a definite ally in the strategy-implementing, strategy-executing process as compared to cultures that have to be coaxed and cajoled to change.*

Culture: Ally or Obstacle to Strategy Execution?

A company's present culture and work climate may or may not be compatible with what is needed for effective implementation and execution of the chosen strategy. *When a company's present work climate promotes attitudes and behaviors that are well suited to first-rate strategy execution, its culture functions as a valuable ally in the strategy execution process.* When the culture is in conflict with some aspect of the company's direction, performance targets, or strategy, the culture becomes a stumbling block.[15]

How a Company's Culture Can Promote Better Strategy Execution A culture grounded in strategy-supportive values, practices, and behavioral norms adds significantly to the power and effectiveness of a company's strategy execution effort. For example, a culture characterized by frugality and thrift nurtures employee actions to identify cost-saving opportunities—the very behavior needed for successful execution of a low-cost leadership strategy. A culture built around such business principles as pleasing customers, operating excellence, and employee empowerment promotes employee behaviors that facilitate execution of strategies keyed to high product quality and superior customer service. A culture that includes taking initiative, challenging the status quo, exhibiting creativity, embracing change, and working collaboratively is conducive to successful execution of product innovation and technological leadership strategies.[16] Good alignment between ingrained cultural norms and the behaviors needed for good strategy execution makes the culture a valuable ally in the strategy execution process. In a company where strategy and culture are misaligned, some of the very behaviors needed to execute strategy successfully run contrary to the behaviors and values imbedded in the prevailing culture. Such a clash nearly always poses a formidable hurdle that has to be cleared for strategy execution to get very far.

CORE CONCEPT

The tighter the culture–strategy fit, the more that the culture steers company personnel into displaying behaviors and adopting operating practices that promote good strategy execution.

A tight culture–strategy matchup furthers a company's strategy execution effort in three ways:[17]

1. *A culture that encourages actions, behaviors, and work practices supportive of good strategy execution not only provides company personnel with clear guidance regarding "how we do things around here" but also produces significant peer pressure from coworkers to conform to culturally acceptable norms.* The stronger the admonishments from top executives about "how we need to do things around here" and the stronger the peer pressures from coworkers, the more the culture influences people to display behaviors and observe operating practices that support good strategy execution.
2. *A deeply embedded culture tightly matched to the strategy aids the cause of competent strategy execution by steering company personnel to culturally approved behaviors and work practices, thus making it far simpler for management to root out operating practices that are a misfit.* This is why it is very much in management's best interests to build and nurture a deeply rooted culture where ingrained behaviors and operating practices marshal organizational energy behind the drive for good strategy execution.
3. *A culture imbedded with values and behaviors that facilitate strategy execution promotes strong employee identification with and commitment to the company's vision, performance targets, and strategy.* When a company's culture is grounded in many of the needed strategy-executing behaviors, employees feel genuinely better about their jobs, the company they work for, and the merits of what the company is trying to accomplish. As a consequence, greater numbers of company personnel exhibit some passion about their work and exert their best efforts to execute the strategy and achieve performance targets. All this helps move the company closer to realizing its strategic vision and, from employees' standpoint, makes the company a more engaging place to work.

CORE CONCEPT

It is in management's best interest to dedicate considerable effort to building a corporate culture that encourages behaviors and work practices conducive to good strategy execution—a tight strategy–culture fit automatically nurtures culturally approved behaviors and squashes culturally disapproved behaviors.

These benefits of close culture–strategy alignment say something important about the task of managing the strategy executing process: *Closely aligning corporate culture with the requirements for proficient strategy execution merits the full attention of senior executives.* The culture-building objective is to create a work climate and style of operating that mobilize the energy and behavior of company personnel squarely behind efforts to execute strategy competently. The more deeply that management can embed strategy-supportive ways of doing things, the more that management can rely on the culture to automatically steer company personnel toward behaviors and work practices that aid good strategy execution.[18]

Furthermore, culturally astute managers understand that nourishing the right cultural environment not only adds power to their push for proficient strategy execution but also promotes strong employee identification with and commitment to the company's vision, performance targets, and strategy. A culture–strategy fit prompts employees with emotional allegiance to the culture to feel genuinely better about their jobs, the company they work for, and the merits of what the company is trying to accomplish. As a consequence, their morale is higher and their productivity is higher. In addition, greater numbers of company personnel exhibit passion for their work and exert their best efforts to make the strategy succeed and achieve performance targets. All this helps move the company closer to realizing its strategic vision and, from employees' standpoint, makes the company a more engaging place to work.

The Perils of Strategy–Culture Conflict Conflicts between behaviors approved by the culture and behaviors needed for good strategy execution pose a real dilemma for company personnel. Should they be loyal to the culture and company traditions (to which they are likely to be emotionally attached) and thus resist or be indifferent to actions and behaviors that will promote better strategy execution? Or should they go along with the strategy execution effort and engage in actions and behaviors that run counter to the culture—a choice that will likely impair morale and lead to less-than-wholehearted commitment to management's strategy execution efforts? Neither choice leads to desirable outcomes, and the solution is obvious: Eliminate the conflict.

When a company's culture is out of sync with the actions and behaviors needed to execute the strategy successfully, the culture has to be changed as rapidly as can be managed—this, of course, presumes that it is one or more aspects of the culture that are out of whack rather than the strategy execution approaches management wishes to institute. While correcting a strategy–culture conflict can occasionally mean revamping a company's approach to executing the strategy to produce good cultural fit, more usually it means altering aspects of the mismatched culture to ingrain new behaviors and work practices that will enable first-rate strategy execution. The more entrenched the mismatched aspects of the culture, the greater the difficulty of implementing and executing new or different strategies until better strategy–culture alignment emerges. A sizable and prolonged strategy–culture conflict weakens and may even defeat managerial efforts to make the strategy work.

Changing a Problem Culture

Changing a problem culture is among the toughest management tasks because of the heavy anchor of ingrained behaviors and ways of doing things. It is natural for company personnel to cling to familiar practices and to be wary, if not hostile, to new approaches of how things are to be done. Consequently, it takes concerted management action over a period of time to root out certain unwanted behaviors and replace an out-of-sync culture with behaviors and ways of doing things that are more conducive to executing the strategy. *The single most visible factor that distinguishes successful culture-change efforts from failed attempts is competent leadership at the top.* Great power is needed to force major cultural change and overcome the springback resistance of entrenched cultures—and great power is possessed only by the most senior executives, especially the CEO. However, while top management must be out front leading the effort, instilling new cultural behaviors is a job for the whole management team. Middle managers and frontline supervisors play a key role in implementing the new work practices and operating approaches, helping win rank-and-file acceptance of and support for the desired behavioral norms.

As shown in Figure 12.1, the first step in fixing a problem culture is for top management to identify those facets of the present culture that are dysfunctional and pose obstacles to executing new strategic initiatives and meeting or beating company performance targets. Second, managers have to clearly define the desired new behaviors and features of the culture they want to create. Third, managers have to convince company personnel why the present culture poses problems and why and how new behaviors and operating approaches will improve company performance—the case for cultural reform has to be persuasive. Finally, and most important, all the talk about remodeling the present culture has to be followed swiftly by visible, forceful actions to promote the desired new behaviors and work practices—actions that company personnel will interpret as a determined top management commitment to bring about a different work climate and new ways of operating.

Making a Compelling Case for Culture Change The place for management to begin a major remodeling of the corporate culture is by selling company personnel on the need for new-style behaviors and work practices. This means making a compelling

Figure 12.1 Changing a Problem Culture

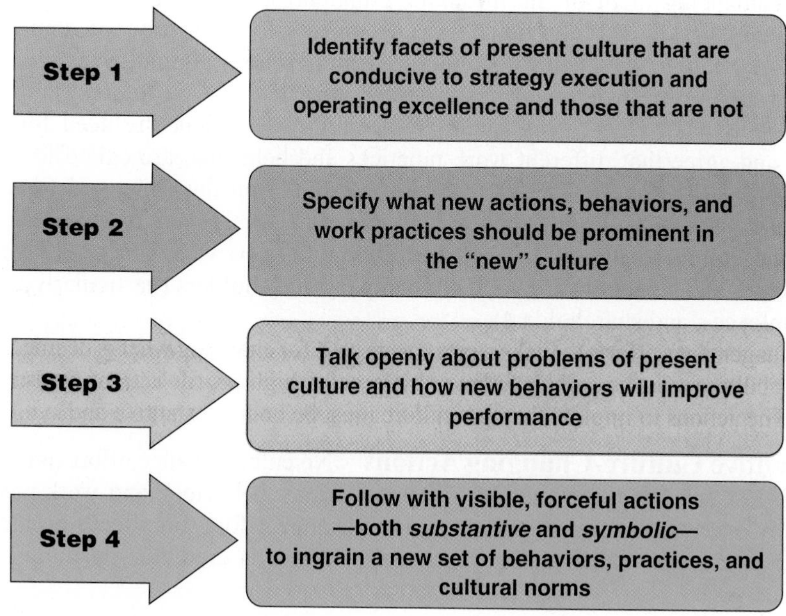
Step 1
Identify facets of present culture that are conducive to strategy execution and operating excellence and those that are not
Step 2
Specify what new actions, behaviors, and work practices should be prominent in the "new" culture
Step 3
Talk openly about problems of present culture and how new behaviors will improve performance
Step 4
Follow with visible, forceful actions —both *substantive* and *symbolic*— to ingrain a new set of behaviors, practices, and cultural norms

case for why the company's new strategic direction and culture-remodeling efforts are in the organization's best interests and why company personnel should wholeheartedly join the effort to doing things somewhat differently. Skeptics and opinion leaders have to be convinced that all is not well with the status quo. This can be done by:

- Citing reasons why the current strategy has to be modified and why new strategic initiatives that are being undertaken will bolster the company's competitiveness and performance. The case for altering the old strategy usually needs to be predicated on its shortcomings—why sales are growing slowly, why rivals are doing so much better, why too many customers are opting to go with the products of rivals, why costs are too high, why the company's price has to be lowered, and so on. In some instances, management must sell the case for culture change when signs of problems are just emerging. It is far easier to change elements of a problem culture before they become deeply ingrained work behaviors.[19] Building the case for culture change is easier if managers and other key personnel are forced to listen to dissatisfied customers, the complaints of strategic allies, alienated employees, or disenchanted stockholders.
- Explaining why and how certain behavioral norms and work practices in the current culture pose obstacles to good execution of new strategic initiatives.
- Explaining how new behaviors and work practices that are to have important roles in the new culture will be more advantageous and produce better results. Effective culture-change leaders are good at telling stories to describe the new values and desired behaviors and connect them to everyday practices.

It is essential for the CEO and other top executives to personally talk to company personnel all across the company about the reasons for modifying work practices and culture-related behaviors. Senior officers and department heads have to play the lead role in explaining the behaviors, practices, and operating approaches that are to be introduced and why they are beneficial—and the explanations will likely have to be repeated many times. For the culture-change effort to be successful, frontline supervisors and employee opinion leaders must be won over to the cause, which means convincing them of the merits of *practicing* and *enforcing* cultural norms at the lowest levels in the organization. Arguments for new ways of doing things and new work practices tend to be embraced more readily if employees understand how they will benefit company stakeholders (particularly customers, employees, and shareholders). Until a big majority of employees accept the need for a new culture and agree that different work practices and behaviors are called for, there's more work to be done in selling company personnel on the whys and wherefores of culture change. Building widespread organizational support requires taking every opportunity to repeat the messages of why the new work practices, operating approaches, and behaviors are good for company stakeholders (particularly customers, employees, and shareholders).

Management's efforts to make a persuasive case for changing what is deemed to be a problem culture must be *quickly followed* by forceful, high-profile actions across several fronts. The actions to implant the new culture must be both substantive and symbolic.

Substantive Culture-Changing Actions No culture change effort can get very far with just talk about the need for different actions, behaviors, and work practices. Company executives have to give the culture-change effort some teeth by initiating *a series of actions* that company personnel will see as credible and unmistakably indicative of the seriousness of management's commitment to new strategic initiatives and the associated cultural changes. The strongest signs that management is truly committed to instilling a new culture include:

1. Replacing key executives who are strongly associated with the old culture and are stonewalling needed organizational and cultural changes.
2. Promoting individuals who are known to possess the desired cultural traits, who have stepped forward to advocate the shift to a different culture, and who can serve as role models for the desired cultural behavior.
3. Appointing outsiders with the desired cultural attributes to high-profile positions—bringing in new-breed managers to serve as role models and help drive the culture-change movement sends an unmistakable message that a new era is dawning and acts to reinforce company personnel who have already gotten on board the culture-change effort.
4. Screening all candidates for new positions carefully, hiring only those who appear to fit in with the new culture—this helps build a critical mass of people to help turn the tide in favor of the new culture.
5. Mandating that all company personnel attend culture-training programs to learn more about the new work practices and operating approaches and to better understand the cultured-related actions and behaviors that are expected.
6. Pushing hard to implement new-style work practices and operating procedures.
7. Designing compensation incentives that boost the pay of teams and individuals who display the desired cultural behaviors and hit change-resisters in the pocketbook—company personnel are much more inclined to exhibit the desired kinds of actions and behaviors when it is in their financial best interest to do so.
8. Granting generous pay raises to individuals who step out front, lead the adoption of the desired work practices, display the new-style behaviors, and achieve pace-setting results.
9. Revising policies and procedures in ways that will help drive cultural change.

Executives must take care to launch enough companywide culture-change actions at the outset to leave no room for doubt that management is dead serious about changing the present culture and that a cultural transformation is inevitable. To convince doubters and skeptics that they cannot just wait things out in hopes the culture-change initiative will soon die out, the series of actions initiated by top management must create lots of hallway talk across the whole company, get the change process off to a fast start, and be followed by unrelenting efforts to firmly establish the new work practices and style of operating as standard.

Symbolic Culture-Changing Actions There's also an important place for symbolic managerial actions to alter a problem culture and tighten the strategy–culture fit. The most important symbolic actions are those that top executives take to *lead by example*. For instance, if the organization's strategy involves a drive to become the industry's low-cost producer, senior managers must display frugality in their own actions and decisions: inexpensive decorations in the executive suite, conservative expense accounts and entertainment allowances, a lean staff in the corporate office, scrutiny of budget requests, few executive perks, and so on. At Wal-Mart, all the executive offices are simply decorated; executives are habitually frugal in their own actions, and they are zealous in their own efforts to control costs and promote greater efficiency. At Nucor, one of the world's low-cost producers of steel products, executives fly coach class and use taxis at airports rather than limousines. If the culture change imperative is to be more responsive to customers' needs and to pleasing customers, the CEO can instill greater customer awareness by requiring all officers and executives to spend a significant portion of each week talking with customers about their needs. Top executives must be alert to the fact that company personnel will be watching their actions and decisions to see if they are walking the talk. Hence they need to make sure that their current decisions will be construed as consistent with new-culture values and behaviors.[20]

Another category of symbolic actions includes holding ceremonial events to single out and honor people whose actions and performance exemplify what is called for in the new culture. A point is made of holding events to celebrate each culture-change success (and any other outcome that management would like to see happen again). Executives sensitive to their role in promoting strategy–culture fits make a habit of appearing at ceremonial functions to praise individuals and groups that get with the program. They show up at employee training programs to stress strategic priorities, values, ethical principles, and cultural norms. Every group gathering is seen as an opportunity to repeat and ingrain values, praise good deeds, expound on the merits of the new culture, and cite instances of how the new work practices and operating approaches have worked to good advantage.

The use of symbols in culture-building is widespread. Many universities give outstanding teacher awards each year to symbolize their commitment to good teaching and their esteem for instructors who display exceptional classroom talents. Numerous businesses have employee-of-the-month awards. The military has a long-standing custom of awarding ribbons and medals for exemplary actions. Mary Kay Cosmetics awards an array of prizes—from ribbons to pink automobiles—to its beauty consultants for reaching various sales plateaus.

How Long Does It Take to Change a Problem Culture? Planting and growing the seeds of a new culture require a determined effort by the chief executive and other senior managers. Neither charisma nor personal magnetism is essential. But a sustained and persistent effort to reinforce the culture at every opportunity through both word and deed is very definitely required. Changing a problem culture is never a short-term exercise. It takes time for a new culture to emerge and prevail. Overnight transformations simply don't occur. And it takes even longer for a new culture to become deeply embedded. The bigger the organization and the greater the cultural shift needed to produce a strategy–culture fit, the longer it takes. In large companies, fixing a problem culture and instilling a new set of attitudes and behaviors can take two to five years. In fact, it is usually tougher to reform an entrenched problematic culture than it is to instill a strategy-supportive culture from scratch in a brand-new organization. Sometimes executives succeed in changing the values and behaviors of small groups of managers and even whole departments or divisions, only to find the changes eroded over time by the actions of the rest of the organization—what is communicated, praised, supported, and penalized by an entrenched majority undermines the new emergent culture and halts its progress. Executives, despite a series of well-intended actions to reform a problem culture, are likely to fail at weeding out embedded cultural traits when widespread employee skepticism about the company's new directions and culture-change effort spawns covert resistance to the cultural behaviors and operating practices advocated by top management. This is why management must take every opportunity to convince employees of the need for culture change and communicate to them how new attitudes, behaviors, and operating practices will benefit the interests of organizational stakeholders.

ILLUSTRATION CAPSULE 12.2
Changing the "Old Detroit" Culture at Chrysler

Shortly after Robert Nardelli became CEO of Chrysler in August 2007, he announced that the company, which had just been spun off from DaimlerChrysler AG in May, would record an annual loss of $1.6 billion. Nardelli believed that Chrysler's problems in the marketplace and its inability to control costs were rooted in a corporate culture formed during an era when U.S. automobile manufacturers had no serious competition from abroad, gasoline was inexpensive, and high profit margins from the sale of trucks, SUVs, and minivans helped disguise weaknesses in the company's passenger car lineup. In early 2008, Nardelli placed himself in charge of a wide-ranging culture change program that included the following elements:

- Chrysler's top 300 executives were required to participate in multiday in-house management seminars aimed at creating the mind-set that decisions should be based on what is best for the customer. Chrysler executives participating in the seminars are not allowed to accept phone calls or e-mails via PDAs and wireless phones during the sessions.
- Nardelli has replaced Chrysler managers unwilling to break from past work behaviors and attitudes. A well-regarded engineer who was put in charge of a key vehicle project was ousted after resisting key principles of the new culture Nardelli hoped to install at Chrysler.
- Chrysler's compensation plan and promotion policies were changed to reward performance rather than seniority.
- Chrysler's purchasing managers were required to abandon the procurement policies that gave preference to the cheapest parts even if the parts were of inferior quality. Purchasing managers were retrained to consider the ownership experience of the customers who purchase Chrysler vehicles when making decisions about the quality and price of parts used in the company's vehicles.
- Nardelli selected a former Toyota executive to become vice chairman of the company to help with the culture change effort and push the drive for improved product quality forward. When given an opportunity to test-drive the new Dodge Challenger as it was headed to production, the former Toyota executive sent the new vehicle back to engineering because its push-button starter needed be held down too long before the engine turned over. Chrysler's vice chairman sent other new vehicles back to engineering after his test drives—including the Chrysler Sebring, which received new bushings and more sound-deadening materials.

Chrysler's culture-change program was expected to take years of effort on the part of management at all levels to break the ingrained behaviors that damaged the company's reputation for quality and had been in place for decades. In mid-2008, Chrysler, Dodge, and Jeep all ranked below the industry average on J. D. Power and Associates' initial quality survey, with Jeep placing last among all automobile manufacturers.

Source: Based on information in Neal E. Boudette, "Nardelli Tries to Shift Chrysler's Culture," *The Wall Street Journal,* June 18, 2008, p. B1.

Illustration Capsule 12.2 discusses the approaches being used at Chrysler in 2007–2008 to change a culture that was grounded in a 1970s view of the automobile industry.

Grounding the Culture in Core Values and Ethics

CORE CONCEPT
A company's culture is grounded in and shaped by its core values and the bar it sets for ethical behavior.

The foundation of a company's corporate culture nearly always resides in its dedication to certain core values and the bar it sets for ethical behavior. The culture-shaping significance of core values and ethical behaviors accounts for why so many companies have developed a formal values statement and a code of ethics—see Table 12.1 for representative core values and the ground usually covered in codes of ethics. Many companies today convey their values and codes of ethics to stakeholders and interested parties in their annual reports and on their Web sites The trend of making stakeholders aware of a company's commitment

Table 12.1 Representative Content of Company Values Statements and Codes of Ethics

Typical Core Values	Areas Covered by Codes of Ethics
• Satisfying and delighting customers • Dedication to superior customer service, top-notch quality, product innovation, and/or technological leadership • A commitment to excellence and results • Exhibiting such qualities as integrity, fairness, trustworthiness, pride of workmanship, Golden Rule behavior, respect for coworkers, and ethical behavior • Creativity, exercising initiative, and accepting responsibility • Teamwork and cooperative attitudes • Fair treatment of suppliers • Making the company a great place to work • A commitment to having fun and creating a fun work environment • Being stewards of shareholders' investments and remaining committed to profits and growth • Exercising social responsibility and being a good community citizen • Caring about protecting the environment • Having a diverse workforce	• Expecting all company personnel to display honesty and integrity in their actions and avoid conflicts of interest • Mandating full compliance with all laws and regulations, specifically: —Antitrust laws prohibiting anticompetitive practices, conspiracies to fix prices, or attempts to monopolize —Foreign Corrupt Practices Act —Securities laws and prohibitions against insider trading —Environmental and workplace safety regulations —Discrimination and sexual harassment regulations —Political contributions and lobbying activities • Prohibiting giving or accepting bribes, kickbacks, or gifts • Engaging in fair selling and marketing practices • Not dealing with suppliers that employ child labor or engage in other unsavory practices • Being above-board in acquiring and using competitively sensitive information about rivals and others • Avoiding use of company assets, resources, and property for personal or other inappropriate purposes • Responsibility to protect proprietary information and not divulge trade secrets

to core values and ethical business conduct is attributable to three factors: (1) greater management understanding of the role these statements play in culture-building, (2) a renewed focus on ethical standards stemming from the numerous corporate scandals that hit the headlines during 2001–2005, and (3) the sizable fraction of consumers and suppliers who prefer doing business with ethical companies.

At Darden Restaurants—the world's largest casual dining company that employs more than 180,000 people and serves 350 million meals annually at 1,700 Red Lobster, Olive Garden, LongHorn Steakhouse, Capital Grille, Bahama Breeze, and Seasons 52 restaurants in North America—the core values are operating with integrity and fairness, caring and respect, being of service, teamwork, excellence, always learning and teaching, and welcoming and celebrating workforce diversity. Top executives at Darden believe the company's practice of these values has been instrumental in creating a culture characterized by trust, exciting jobs and career opportunities for employees, and a passion to provide "a terrific dining experience to every guest, every time, in every one of our restaurants."[21]

Of course, sometimes a company's stated core values and codes of ethics are cosmetic, existing mainly to impress outsiders and help create a positive company image. But more usually they have been developed to shape the culture. Many executives want the work climate at their companies to mirror certain values and ethical standards, partly because they are personally committed to these values and ethical standards but mainly because they are convinced that adherence to such values and ethical principles will make the company a much better performer and improve its image with both insiders and external constituents alike. As discussed earlier, values-related cultural norms promote better strategy execution and mobilize company personnel behind the drive to achieve stretch objectives and the company's strategic vision. Hence, a corporate culture grounded in well-chosen core values and high ethical standards contributes mightily to a company's long-term strategic success.[22] And, not incidentally, strongly ingrained values and ethical standards reduce the likelihood of lapses in ethical and socially approved behavior that mar a company's reputation and put its financial performance and market standing at risk.

A company's values statement and code of ethics communicate expectations of how employees should conduct themselves in the workplace.

The Culture-Building Role of Values and Codes of Ethics At companies where executives believe in the merits of practicing the values and ethical standards that have been espoused, *the stated core values and ethical principles are the cornerstones of the corporate culture.* As depicted in Figure 12.2, a company's stated core values and ethical principles have two roles in the culture-building process. One, a company that works hard at putting its stated core values and ethical principles into practice fosters a work climate where company personnel share strongly held convictions about how the company's business is to be conducted. Second, the stated values and ethical principles provide company personnel with guidance about the manner in which they are to do their jobs—which behaviors and ways of doing things are approved (and expected) and which are out of bounds.

Transforming Core Values and Ethical Standards into Cultural Norms Once values and ethical standards have been formally adopted, they must be institutionalized in the company's policies and practices and embedded in the conduct of company personnel. This can be done in a number of different ways.[23] Tradition-steeped companies with a rich folklore rely heavily on word-of-mouth indoctrination

Figure 12.2 The Two Culture-Building Roles of a Company's Core Values and Ethical Standards

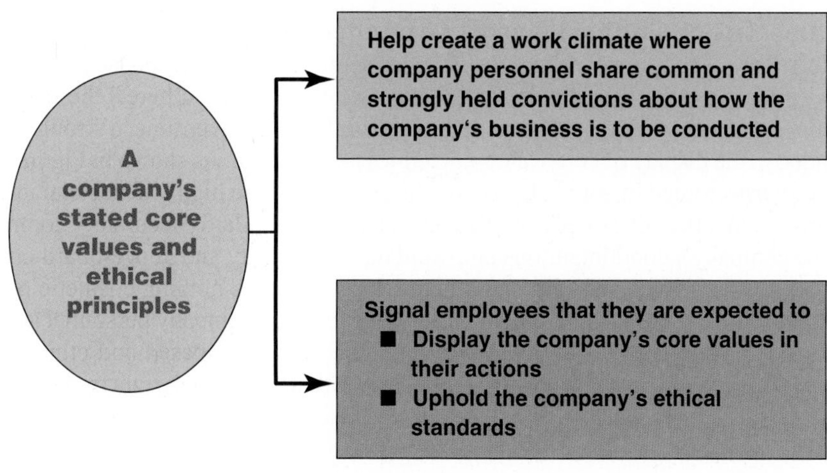

and the power of tradition to instill values and enforce ethical conduct. But most companies employ a variety of techniques to hammer in core values and ethical standards, using some or all of the following:

1. Giving explicit attention to values and ethics in recruiting and hiring to screen out applicants who do not exhibit compatible character traits.
2. Incorporating the statement of values and the code of ethics into orientation programs for new employees and training courses for managers and employees.
3. Having senior executives frequently reiterate the importance and role of company values and ethical principles at company events and internal communications to employees.
4. Using values statements and codes of ethical conduct as benchmarks for judging the appropriateness of company policies and operating practices.
5. Making the display of core values and ethical principles a big factor in evaluating each person's job performance—there's no better way to win the attention and commitment of company personnel than by using the degree to which individuals observe core values and ethical standards as a basis for compensation increases and promotion.
6. Making sure that managers, from the CEO down to frontline supervisors, are diligent in stressing the importance of ethical conduct and observance of core values. Line managers at all levels must give serious and continuous attention to the task of explaining how the values and ethical code apply in their areas.
7. Encouraging everyone to use their influence in helping enforce observance of core values and ethical standards—strong peer pressures to exhibit core values and ethical standards are a deterrent to outside-the-lines behavior.
8. Periodically having ceremonial occasions to recognize individuals and groups who display the values and ethical principles.
9. Instituting ethics enforcement procedures.

To deeply ingrain the stated core values and high ethical standards, companies must turn them into *strictly enforced cultural norms.* They must put a stake in the ground, making it unequivocally clear that living up to the company's values and ethical standards has to be a way of life at the company and that there will be little toleration of outside-the-lines behavior

The Benefits of Cultural Norms Grounded in Core Values and Ethical Principles The more that managers succeed in making the espoused values and ethical principles the main drivers of "how we do things around here," the more that the values and ethical principles function as cultural norms. Over time, a strong culture grounded in the display of core values and ethics may emerge. As shown in Figure 12.3, *cultural norms* rooted in core values and ethical behavior are highly beneficial in three respects.[24] One, the advocated core values and ethical standards accurately communicate the company's good intentions and validate the integrity and above-board character of its business principles and operating methods. There's nothing cosmetic or fake about the company's values statement and code of ethics—company personnel actually strive to practice what is being preached. Second, the values-based and ethics-based cultural norms steer company personnel toward both doing things right and doing the right thing. Third, they establish a "corporate conscience" and provide yardsticks for gauging the appropriateness of particular actions, decisions, and policies.

Figure 12.3 The Benefits of Cultural Norms Strongly Grounded in Core Values and Ethical Principles

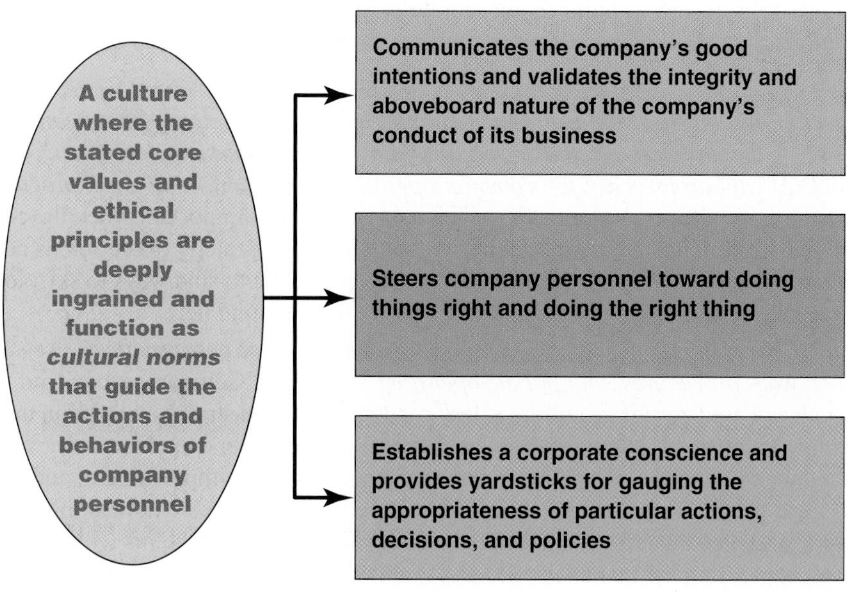
A culture where the stated core values and ethical principles are deeply ingrained and function as *cultural norms* that guide the actions and behaviors of company personnel
Communicates the company's good intentions and validates the integrity and aboveboard nature of the company's conduct of its business
Steers company personnel toward doing things right and doing the right thing
Establishes a corporate conscience and provides yardsticks for gauging the appropriateness of particular actions, decisions, and policies

Establishing a Strategy–Culture Fit in Multinational and Global Companies

In multinational and global companies, establishing a tight strategy–culture fit is complicated by the diverse societal circumstances surrounding the company's operations in different countries. The nature of the local economies, living conditions, per capita incomes, and lifestyles can give rise to considerable cross-border diversity in a company's workforce and to subcultures within the corporate culture. Leading cross-border culture-change initiatives requires sensitivity to prevailing differences in local circumstances; company managers must discern when local subcultures have to be accommodated and when cross-border differences in the company's corporate culture can and should be narrowed.[25] Cross-country diversity in a multinational enterprise's corporate culture are more tolerable if the company is pursuing a multicountry strategy and if the company's culture in each country is well aligned with its strategy in that country. But significant cross-country differences in a company's culture are likely to impede execution of a global strategy and have to be addressed.

As discussed earlier in this chapter, *the trick to establishing a workable strategy–culture fit in multinational companies is to ground the culture in strategy-supportive values and operating practices that travel well across country borders* and strike a chord with managers and workers in many different areas of the world, despite varying local customs and traditions. A multinational enterprise with a misfit between its strategy and culture in certain countries where it operates can attack the problem by rewording its values statement so as to express core values in ways that have universal appeal. The alternative is to allow *some leeway* for certain core values to be reinterpreted

CORE CONCEPT

A multinational company needs to build its corporate culture around values and operating practices that travel well across borders.

or de-emphasized or applied somewhat differently from country to country whenever local customs and traditions in a country really need to be accommodated. But such accommodation needs to be done in ways that do not impede good strategy execution.

Aside from trying to build the corporate culture around a set of core values that have universal appeal, management can seek to minimize the existence of subcultures and promote greater cross-country cultural uniformity by:

- *Instituting culture training in each country to (1) communicate the meaning of core values in language that resonates with company personnel in that country and (2) explain the case for common operating approaches and work practices.* The use of uniform work practices becomes particularly important when the company's work practices are more efficient and aid good strategy execution as compared to others—in such instances, local managers have to find ways to skirt local preferences and win support for "how we do things around here."
- *Creating a cultural climate where it is the norm to adopt best practices, use common work procedures, and pursue operating excellence.* Companies may find that a values-based corporate culture is less conducive to good strategy execution than a cultural climate of operating excellence where company personnel are energized to do things in the best possible manner, achieve continuous improvement, and meet or beat performance targets. A results-oriented culture keyed to operating excellence and meeting stretch objectives sidesteps many of the problems with trying to get people from different societies and traditions to embrace common values.
- *Giving local managers the flexibility to modify people management approaches or operating styles in those situations where adherence to companywide cultural traditions simply doesn't work well.* But local modifications have to be infrequent and done in a manner that doesn't undermine the establishment of a mostly uniform corporate culture.
- *Giving local managers discretionary authority to use somewhat different motivational and compensation incentives to induce local personnel to adopt and practice the desired cultural behaviors.* Personnel in different countries may respond better to some compensation structures and reward systems than others.

Generally, a high degree of cross-country homogeneity in a multinational company's corporate culture is desirable and has to be pursued, particularly when it comes to ingraining universal core values and companywide enforcement of such ethical standards as the payment of bribes and kickbacks, the use of underage labor, and environmental stewardship. Having too much variation in the culture from country to country not only makes it difficult to use the culture to drive the strategy execution process but also works against the establishment of a one-company mind-set and a consistent corporate identity.

LEADING THE STRATEGY-EXECUTION PROCESS

For an enterprise to execute its strategy in truly proficient fashion and approach operating excellence, top executives have to be out front personally leading the implementation/execution process and driving the pace of progress. Top executives—and, to some degree, the enterprise's entire management team—must seek to engage the full organization. A fully engaged workforce, one where individuals bring their best every day, is a necessary element to producing great results.[26] So is having a group of high-impact people looking to make a big difference at work. Top-level executives can usually best create a fully engaged organization by delegating authority to middle and lower-level managers to get the implementation/execution process moving and by creating a sense of empowerment among employees as well. It is unwise for company personnel to feel powerless to change anything significant and just wait to follow orders from top executives.

But delegating and empowering does not mean that senior managers can stay in their offices, content to receive reports from subordinates and monitor the latest metrics. Rather, they have to be out in the field, seeing for themselves how well operations are going, gathering information firsthand, and gauging the progress being made. Proficient strategy execution requires company managers to be diligent and adept in spotting gridlock, ferreting out problems and issues, learning what obstacles lie in the path of good execution, and then clearing the way for progress—the goal must be to produce better results speedily and productively. And there has to be constructive, but unrelenting, pressure on organizational units to (1) demonstrate growing consistency in strategy execution and (2) achieve performance targets—ultimately, it's all about producing excellent strategy execution and financial results.

Making Corrective Adjustments in Timely Fashion

The leadership challenge in achieving consistently good strategy execution ultimately boils down to two things: deciding when corrective adjustments are needed and deciding what adjustments to make. Both decisions are a normal and necessary part of managing the strategy execution process, since no scheme for implementing and executing strategy can foresee all the events and problems that will arise. There comes a time at every company when managers have to fine-tune or overhaul the approaches to strategy execution and push for better results. Clearly, when a company's strategy execution effort is not delivering good results and making measurable progress toward operating excellence, it is the leader's responsibility to step forward and push corrective actions—*there is no substitute for decisive and effective action to resolve problems and improve outcomes.*

The *process* of making corrective adjustments varies according to the situation. In a crisis, taking remedial action fairly quickly is of the essence. But it still takes time to review the situation, examine the available data, identify and evaluate options (crunching whatever numbers may be appropriate to determine which options may generate the best outcomes), and decide what to do. The organizational leader then usually meets with key subordinates and personally presides over extended discussions of the proposed responses, trying to build a quick consensus among members of the executive inner circle. If no consensus emerges and/or if action is required so swiftly that consultation with others is infeasible, the burden falls on the manager in charge to make the decision and get the chosen actions under way.

When the situation allows managers to proceed more deliberately in deciding when to make changes and what changes to make, most managers seem to prefer a process of incrementally solidifying commitment to a particular course of action.[27] The process that managers go through in deciding on corrective adjustments is essentially the same for both proactive and reactive changes: They sense needs, gather information, broaden and deepen their understanding of the situation, develop options and explore their pros and cons, put forth action proposals, generate partial (comfort-level) solutions, strive for a consensus, and finally formally adopt an agreed-on course of action.[28] The time frame for deciding what corrective changes to initiate can take a few hours, a few days, a few weeks, or even a few months if the situation is particularly complicated.

Success in initiating corrective actions usually hinges on thorough analysis of the situation, the exercise of good business judgment in deciding what actions to take, and good implementation of the corrective actions that are initiated. Successful managers are skilled in getting an organization back on track rather quickly; they (and their staffs) are good at discerning what actions to take and in ramrodding them through to a successful conclusion. Managers that struggle to show measurable progress in generating good results and improving the performance of strategy-critical value chain activities are candidates for being replaced.

The challenges of leading a successful strategy execution effort are, without question, substantial.[29] But the job is definitely doable. Because each instance of executing strategy occurs under different organizational circumstances, the managerial agenda for executing strategy always needs to be situation-specific—there's no neat generic procedure to follow. And, as we said at the beginning of Chapter 10, executing strategy is an action-oriented, make-the-right-things-happen task that challenges a manager's ability to lead and direct organizational change, create or reinvent business processes, manage and motivate people, and achieve performance targets. If you now better understand what the challenges are, what approaches are available, which issues need to be considered, and why the action agenda for implementing and executing strategy sweeps across so many aspects of administrative and managerial work, then we will look on our discussion in Chapters 10, 11, and 12 as a success.

A FINAL WORD ON MANAGING THE PROCESS OF CRAFTING AND EXECUTING STRATEGY

In practice, it is hard to separate the leadership requirements of executing strategy from the other pieces of the strategy process. As we emphasized in Chapter 2, the job of crafting, implementing, and executing strategy is a five-task process with much looping and recycling to fine-tune and adjust strategic visions, objectives, strategies, capabilities, implementation approaches, and cultures to fit one another and to fit changing circumstances. The process is continuous, and the conceptually separate acts of crafting and executing strategy blur together in real-world situations. The best tests of good strategic leadership are whether the company has a good strategy and whether the strategy execution effort is delivering the hoped-for results. If these two conditions exist, the chances are excellent that the company has good strategic leadership.

KEY POINTS

The character of a company's culture is a product of the core values and business principles that executives espouse, the standards of what is ethically acceptable and what is not, the work practices and behaviors that define "how we do things around here," the company's approach to people management and style of operating, the chemistry and the personality that permeates its work environment, and the stories that get told over and over to illustrate and reinforce the company's values, business practices, and traditions. A company's culture is important because it influences the organization's actions and approaches to conducting business—in a very real sense, the culture is the company's "operating system" or organizational DNA.[30]

The psyche of corporate cultures varies widely. Moreover, company cultures vary widely in strength and influence. Some are strongly embedded and have a big impact on a company's practices and behavioral norms. Others are weak and have comparatively little influence on company operations. There are four types of unhealthy cultures: (1) those that are highly political and characterized by empire building, (2) those that are change resistant, (3) those that are insular and inwardly focused, and (4) those that are ethically unprincipled and are driven by greed. High-performance cultures and adaptive cultures both have positive features that are conducive to good strategy execution.

A culture grounded in values, practices, and behavioral norms that match what is needed for good strategy execution helps energize people throughout the company to do their jobs in a strategy-supportive manner, adding significantly to the power of a company's strategy execution effort and the chances of achieving the targeted results. But when the culture is in conflict with some aspect of the company's direction, performance targets, or strategy, the culture becomes a stumbling block. Thus, an important part of managing the strategy execution process is establishing and nurturing a good fit between culture and strategy.

A company's present culture and work climate may or may not be compatible with what is needed for effective implementation and execution of the chosen strategy. *When a company's present work climate promotes attitudes and behaviors that are well suited to first-rate strategy execution, its culture functions as a valuable ally in the strategy execution process.* When the culture is in conflict with some aspect of the company's direction, performance targets, or strategy, the culture becomes a stumbling block.

Changing a company's culture, especially a strong one with traits that don't fit a new strategy's requirements, is a tough and often time-consuming challenge. Changing a culture requires competent leadership at the top. It requires symbolic actions and substantive actions that unmistakably indicate serious commitment on the part of top management. The more that culture-driven actions and behaviors fit what's needed for good strategy execution, the less managers have to depend on policies, rules, procedures, and supervision to enforce what people should and should not do.

The taproot of a company's corporate culture nearly always is its dedication to certain core values and the bar it sets for ethical behavior. Of course, sometimes a company's stated core values and codes of ethics are cosmetic, existing mainly to impress outsiders and help create a positive company image. But more usually they have been developed to shape the culture. If management practices what it preaches, a company's core values and ethical standards nurture the corporate culture in three highly positive ways: (1) they communicate the company's good intentions and validate the integrity and above-board character of its business principles and operating methods; (2) they steer company personnel toward both doing the right thing and doing things right; and (3) they establish a corporate conscience that gauges the appropriateness of particular actions, decisions, and policies. Companies that really care about how they conduct their business put a stake in the ground, making it unequivocally clear that company personnel are expected to live up to the company's values and ethical standards—how well individuals display core values and adhere to ethical standards is often part of the job performance evaluations. Peer pressure to conform to cultural norms is quite strong, acting as an important deterrent to outside-the-lines behavior.

Leading the drive for good strategy execution and operating excellence calls for five actions on the part of the manager in charge:

1. Staying on top of what is happening, closely monitoring progress, ferreting out issues, and learning what obstacles lie in the path of good execution.
2. Putting constructive pressure on the organization to achieve good results and operating excellence.
3. Leading the development of stronger core competencies and competitive capabilities.
4. Displaying ethical integrity and leading social responsibility initiatives.
5. Pushing corrective actions to improve strategy execution and achieve the targeted results.

ASSURANCE OF LEARNING EXERCISES

1. Go to www.google.com. Click on the "About Google" link and then on the "Corporate Info" link. Read what Google has to say about its culture under the "Culture" link. Also, read the "Ten Things Google Has Found to Be True" in the "Our Philosophy" section. How do the "Ten Things" and Google's culture aid in management's attempts to execute the company's strategy?
2. Go to the Jobs section at www.intel.com and see what Intel has to say about its culture under the links for Careers, Diversity, and The Workplace. Does what's on this Web site appear to be just recruiting propaganda, or does it convey the type of work climate that management is actually trying to create? Explain your answer.
3. Using Google Scholar or your university library's access to EBSCO, Lexis-Nexis, or other databases, search for recent articles in business publications on culture change. Give examples of three companies that have recently undergone culture-change initiatives. What are the key features of each company's culture-change program? What results did management achieve at each company?
4. Go to www.jnj.com, the Web site of Johnson & Johnson, and read the "J&J Credo," which sets forth the company's responsibilities to customers, employees, the community, and shareholders. Then read the "Our Company" section. Why do you think the credo has resulted in numerous awards and accolades that recognize the company as a good corporate citizen?
5. Go to www.avoncompany.com/investor and read the "Management Discussion and Analysis of Financial Condition and Results of Operations" section of Avon's 2007 annual report. The company provides a great deal of information about its turnaround plan launched in 2005 and its ongoing corrective actions to achieve operating excellence. Describe in one to two pages how management at Avon demonstrates the internal leadership needed for superior strategy execution.

EXERCISES FOR SIMULATION PARTICIPANTS

1. If you were making a speech to company personnel, what would you tell them about the kind of corporate culture you would like to have at your company? What specific cultural traits would you like your company to exhibit? Explain.

2. What core values would you want to ingrain in your company's culture? Why?
3. Following each decision round, how important is it for you and your co-managers to make corrective adjustments in either your company's strategy or how well the strategy is being executed? Explain. What will happen to your company's performance if you and your co-managers stick with the status quo and fail to make corrective adjustments?

part two 2

Cases in Crafting and Executing Strategy

CASE 1 Whole Foods Market in 2008: Vision, Core Values, and Strategy

Arthur A. Thompson
The University of Alabama

Founded in 1980, Whole Foods Market evolved from a local supermarket for natural and health foods in Austin, Texas, into the world's largest retail chain of natural and organic foods supermarkets. The company had 2007 sales of $6.6 billion and in early 2008 had 276 stores in the United States, Canada, and Great Britain. Revenues had grown at a compound annual rate of 30 percent since 1991 and 20 percent since 2000. Management's near-term growth objectives for Whole Foods were to have 400 stores and sales of $12 billion in fiscal year 2010.

During its 27-year history, Whole Foods Market had been a leader in the natural and organic foods movement across the United States, helping the industry gain acceptance among growing numbers of consumers concerned about the food they ate. The company sought to offer the highest quality, least processed, most flavorful and naturally preserved foods available. John Mackey, the company's cofounder and CEO, believed that Whole Foods' rapid growth and market success had much to do with its having "remained a uniquely mission-driven company—highly selective about what we sell, dedicated to our core values and stringent quality standards and committed to sustainable agriculture."

Mackey's vision was for Whole Foods to become an international brand synonymous not just with natural and organic foods but also with being the best food retailer in every community in which Whole Foods stores were located. He wanted Whole Foods Market to set the standard for excellence in food retailing. Mackey's philosophy was that marketing high-quality natural and organic foods to more and more customers in more and more communities would over time gradually transform the diets of individuals in a manner that would help them live longer, healthier, more pleasurable lives. But as the company's motto, "Whole Foods, Whole People, Whole Planet," implied, its core mission extended well beyond food retailing—see Exhibit 1. At its Web site, the company proclaimed that its deepest purpose as an organization was helping support the health, well-being, and healing of both people—customers, team members, and business organizations in general —and the planet.[1]

THE NATURAL AND ORGANIC FOODS INDUSTRY

The combined sales of foods and beverages labeled as "natural" or organic—about $62 billion in 2007—represented about 7.3 percent of the roughly $850 billion in total U.S. grocery store sales. *Natural foods* are defined as foods that are minimally processed; largely or completely free of artificial ingredients, preservatives, and other non–naturally occurring chemicals; and as near to their whole, natural state as possible. The U.S. Department of Agriculture's Food and Safety Inspection Service defines *natural food* as "a product containing no artificial ingredient or added color and that is minimally processed." While sales of natural foods products had increased at double-digit rates in the 1990s, growth had slowed to the 7–9 percent range since 2000.

Exhibit 1 Whole Foods Market's Motto: Whole Foods, Whole People, Whole Planet

Whole Foods

We obtain our products locally and from all over the world, often from small, uniquely dedicated food artisans. We strive to offer the highest quality, least processed, most flavorful and naturally preserved foods. We believe that food in its purest state—unadulterated by artificial additives, sweeteners, colorings and preservatives—is the best tasting and most nutritious food available.

Whole People

We recruit the best people we can to become part of our team. We empower them to make many operational decisions, creating a respectful workplace where team members are treated fairly and are highly motivated to succeed. We look for team members who are passionate about food, but also well-rounded human beings who can play a critical role in helping build our Company into a profitable and beneficial part of every community in which we operate.

Whole Planet

We believe companies, like individuals, must assume their share of responsibility for our planet. We actively support organic farming on a global basis because we believe it is the best method for promoting sustainable agriculture and protecting the environment and farm workers. On a local basis, we are actively involved in our communities by supporting food banks, sponsoring neighborhood events, and contributing at least 5 percent of our after-tax profits in the form of cash or products to not-for-profit organizations.

Source: Company overview, posted at www.wholefoodsmarket.com (accessed March 21, 2008), and 2007 10-K report, p. 5.

Organic foods were a special subset of the natural foods category; to be labeled as organic, foods had to be grown and processed without the use of pesticides, antibiotics, hormones, synthetic chemicals, artificial fertilizers, preservatives, dyes or additives, or genetic engineering. Organic foods included fresh fruits and vegetables, meats, and processed foods that had been produced using any or all of the following:

- Agricultural management practices that promoted a healthy and renewable ecosystem. These practices could include no genetically engineered seeds or crops, petroleum-based fertilizers, fertilizers made from sewage sludge, synthetic pesticides, herbicides, or fungicides.
- Livestock management practices that involved organically grown feed, fresh air and outdoor access for the animals, and no use of antibiotics or growth hormones.
- Food processing practices that protected the integrity of the organic product and did not involve the use of radiation, genetically modified organisms, or synthetic preservatives.

In 1990, passage of the Organic Food Production Act started the process of establishing national standards for organically grown products in the United States, a movement that included farmers, food activists, conventional food producers, and consumer groups. In October 2002, the U.S. Department of Agriculture (USDA) officially established labeling standards for organic products, overriding both the patchwork of inconsistent state regulations for what could be labeled as organic and the different rules of some 43 agencies for certifying organic products. The new USDA regulations established four categories of food with organic ingredients, with varying levels of organic purity:

1. *100 percent organic products:* Such products were usually whole foods, such as fresh fruits and vegetables, grown by organic methods—which meant that the product had been grown without the use of synthetic pesticides or sewage-based fertilizers; had not been subjected to irradiation; and had not been genetically modified or injected with bioengineered organisms, growth hormones, or antibiotics. Products that were 100 percent organic could carry the green USDA organic certification seal, provided the merchant could document that the food product had been organically grown (usually by a certified organic producer).
2. *Organic products:* Such products, often processed, had to have at least 95 percent organically certified ingredients. These could also carry the green USDA organic certification seal.
3. *Made with organic ingredients:* Such products had to have at least 70 percent organic ingredients; they could be labeled "made with organic ingredients" but could not display the USDA seal.

4. *All other products with organic ingredients:* Products with less than 70 percent organic ingredients could not use the word *organic* on the front of a package, but organic ingredients could be listed among other ingredients in a less prominent part of the package.

An official with the National Organic Program, commenting on the appropriateness and need for the new USDA regulations, said, "For the first time, when consumers see the word *organic* on a package, it will have consistent meaning."[2] The new labeling program was not intended as a health or safety program (organic products have not been shown to be more nutritious than conventionally grown products, according to the American Dietetic Association), but rather as a marketing solution. An organic label had long been a selling point for shoppers wanting to avoid pesticides or to support environmentally friendly agricultural practices. However, the new regulations required documentation on the part of growers, processors, exporters, importers, shippers, and merchants to verify that they were certified to grow, process, or handle organic products carrying the USDA's organic seal. In 2003, Whole Foods was designated as the first national "Certified Organic" grocer by Quality Assurance International, a federally recognized independent third-party certification organization.

According to the Organic Consumers Association, sales of organic foods in the United States hit $17 billion in 2006, up 22 percent from $13.8 billion in 2005. When natural foods and beverages (defined narrowly as those with no artificial ingredients) were lumped in with organic foods and beverages, the U.S. retail sales total came to $28.2 billion in 2006, up from $23.0 billion in 2005. Natural and organic foods and beverages were projected to reach nearly $33 billion in 2008. Organic food sales were said to represent about 3 percent of total U.S. retail sales of food and beverages. About 31 percent of overall organic sales in 2006 were through mainstream supermarkets/grocery stores, and 24 percent were through the leading natural food supermarket chains such as Whole Foods, Wild Oats, and Trader Joe's. Another 22 percent of all organic sales were through independent, small natural grocery store chains. Organic foods and beverages were available in nearly every food category in 2008 and were available in over 75 percent of U.S. retail food stores. Most observers believed that organic products had staying power in the marketplace as opposed to being a passing fad.

Major food processing companies like Kraft, General Mills, Groupe Danone (the parent of Dannon Yogurt), Dean Foods, and Kellogg had all purchased organic food producers in an effort to capitalize on growing consumer interest in purchasing organic foods. Heinz had introduced an organic ketchup and bought a 19 percent stake in Hain Celestial Group, one of the largest organic and natural foods producers. Campbell Soup had introduced organic tomato juice. Starbucks, Green Mountain Coffee, and several other premium coffee marketers were marketing organically grown coffees; Coca-Cola's Odwalla juices were organic; Del Monte and Hunt's were marketing organic canned tomatoes; and Tyson Foods and several other chicken producers had introduced organic chicken products. Producers of organically grown beef were selling all they could produce, and sales were expected to grow 30 percent annually through 2008.

Organic farmland in the United States totaled 4.1 million acres (about 1.7 million acres of cropland and 2.4 million acres of rangeland and pasture) in 2005, up from 2.1 million acres in 2001.[3] There were 8,400 certified organic farms in 2005, and perhaps another 9,000 small farmers growing organic products. All 50 states had some certified organic farmland, with California, North Dakota, Montana, Minnesota, Wisconsin, Texas, and Idaho having the largest amount of certified organic cropland. While only about 1 percent of U.S. farmland was certified organic in 2005, farmers were becoming increasingly interested in and attracted to organic farming, chiefly because of the substantially higher prices they could get for organically grown fruits, vegetables, and meats.

RETAILING OF ORGANIC FOODS

According to the USDA, 2000 was the first year in which more organic food was sold in conventional U.S. supermarkets than in the nation's 14,500 natural foods stores. Since 2002, most mainstream supermarkets had been expanding their selections of natural and organic products, which ranged from fresh produce to wines, cereals, pastas, cheeses, yogurts, vinegars, potato chips, beef, chicken, and canned and frozen fruits and vegetables. Fresh produce was the most popular organic product—lettuce, broccoli, cauliflower, celery, carrots, and apples were the biggest sellers. Meat, dairy, bread, and snack foods were among the fastest-growing organic product categories. Most supermarket chains stocked a selection of natural and organic food items, and the number and variety of items they carried was growing. Leading supermarket chains like Wal-Mart, Kroger, Publix, Safeway, and Supervalu/Save-a-Lot had created special "organic and health food" sections for nonperishable items in most of their stores. Kroger, Publix, and several other chains also had special sections for fresh organic fruits and vegetables in their produce cases in most of their stores in 2007. Safeway, Publix, and Kroger were stocking organic beef and chicken in a number of their stores, while Whole Foods was struggling to find organic beef and chicken suppliers big enough to supply all its stores. Two chains—upscale Harris Teeter in the southeastern United States and Whole Foods Market—had launched their own private-label brands of organics. Exhibit 2 shows the leading supermarket retailers in North America in 2006. Whole Foods Market was ranked 24th in 2006, up from 26th in 2004.

Most industry observers expected that, as demand for organic foods increased, conventional supermarkets would continue to expand their offerings and selection. Supermarkets were attracted to merchandising organic foods for several reasons: Consumer demand for organic foods was growing at close to 20 percent annually, and mounting consumer enthusiasm for organic products allowed retailers to command attractively high profit margins on organic products. In contrast, retail sales of general food products were growing slowly (in part because more and more consumers were eating out rather than cooking at home) and price competition among rival supermarket chains was intense (which dampened profit margins on many grocery items).

Several factors had combined to transform organic foods retailing, once a niche market, into the fastest-growing segment of U.S. food sales:

- Healthier eating patterns on the part of a populace that was becoming better educated about foods, nutrition, and good eating habits. Among those most interested in organic products were aging, affluent people concerned about health and better-for-you foods.
- Increasing consumer concerns over the purity and safety of food due to the presence of pesticide residues, growth hormones, artificial ingredients, chemicals, and genetically engineered ingredients.
- A "wellness," or health-consciousness, trend among people of many ages and ethnic groups.
- Growing belief that organic farming had positive environmental effects, particularly in contributing to healthier soil and water conditions and to sustainable agricultural practices (which was confirmed by a series of studies done at the University of Michigan and the University of Illinois).[4]

A 2005 survey commissioned by Whole Foods found that 65 percent of U.S. consumers had tried organic foods and beverages, up from 54 percent in both 2003 and 2004; 27 percent of respondents indicated they consumed more organic foods and beverages than they did one year before.[5] Ten percent consumed organic foods several times per week, up from just 7 percent in 2004. The top three reasons why consumers were buying organic foods and beverages were avoidance of pesticides (70.3 percent), freshness (68.3 percent), and health and nutrition (67.1 percent); 55 percent reported buying organic to avoid genetically modified foods. Also, many respondents agreed that organic foods and beverages were better for their health (52.8 percent) and better for the environment (52.4 percent). The categories of organic foods and beverages purchased most frequently by those participating in Whole Foods' survey were fresh fruits and vegetables (73 percent), nondairy beverages (32 percent), bread or baked goods (32 percent), dairy items (24.6 percent), packaged goods such as soup or pasta (22.2 percent), meat (22.2 percent), snack foods (22.1 percent), frozen foods (16.6 percent), prepared and ready-to-eat meals (12.2 percent), and baby food (3.2 percent).

The higher prices of organic products were the primary barrier for most consumers in trying or using organic products—75 percent of those participating in the 2005 Whole Foods survey believed organics were too expensive. Other reasons for not consuming more organics were availability (46.1 percent) and loyalty to non-organic brands (36.7 percent).

WHOLE FOODS MARKET

Whole Foods Market was founded in Austin, Texas, when John Mackey, the current CEO, and two other local natural foods grocers in Austin decided the natural foods industry was ready for a supermarket format. The original Whole Foods Market opened in 1980 with a staff of only 19. It was an immediate success. At the time, there were fewer than half a dozen natural foods supermarkets in the United States. By 1991, the company had 10 stores, revenues of $92.5 million, and net income of $1.6 million. Whole Foods became a public company in 1992, with its stock trading on the NASDAQ; Whole Foods stock was added to the Standard & Poor's Mid-Cap 400 Index in May 2002 and to the NASDAQ-100 Index in December 2002.

Core Values

In 1997, when Whole Foods developed the "Whole Foods, Whole People, Whole Planet" slogan, John Mackey, known as a go-getter with a "cowboy way of doing things," said:

> This slogan taps into perhaps the deepest purpose of Whole Foods Market. It's a purpose we seldom talk about because it seems pretentious, but a purpose nevertheless felt by many of our team members

Exhibit 2 Leading North American Supermarket Chains, 2006

Rank/Company	Number of Stores	2006 Sales Revenues (in billions)	Share of Total U.S. Grocery Sales ($850 billion)
1. Wal-Mart	2,297	$209.9 [a]	9.4%
2. Kroger	2,477	66.1 [b]	7.8
3. Costco	458	59.0 [c]	4.3
4. Sam's Club	580	42.2 [d]	3.0
5. Safeway	1,767	40.5	4.8
6. Supervalu	434	37.4 [e]	4.4
7. Loblaw [f]	1,072	26.5	3.1
8. Ahold USA [g]	827	24.0	2.8
9. Publix Supermarkets	885	21.7	2.6
10. Delhaize [h]	1,544	17.3	2.0
11. Meijer	176	13.2	1.6
		. . .	
24. Whole Foods Market	188	5.6	0.7

[a] Sales revenue numbers include all store items in Wal-Mart Discount Stores and Supercenters, not just those related to food and groceries. Sales of grocery, candy, tobacco, and health and beauty aids represented about 38 percent of total sales at Wal-Mart Discount Stores and Supercenters. Wal-Mart's market share percentage is based on grocery- and supermarket-item sales of $79.8 billion (38 percent of $209.9 billion).

[b] Sales data for Kroger (whose supermarket brands also include City Market, King Sooper, Ralph's, and 11 smaller chains) include revenues from all company-owned retail outlets (fuel centers, drugstores, apparel, and jewelry) that are not supermarket-related.

[c] The sales revenue figure for Costco includes all items sold at Costco stores; sales of only grocery items (food, sundries, fresh produce, gasoline, and pharmacy) were $36.6 billion; the market share percentage is based on that $36.6 billion.

[d] Sales revenue numbers include all store items sold at Sam's Club, not just those related to food and groceries; food and sundries accounted for 61 percent of sales (about $25.7 billion). The market share percentage is based on estimated food and grocery-related sales of $25.7 billion.

[e] Sales data for Supervalu includes 1,368 supermarkets (including 1,124 of which were recently acquired from Albertson's), 301 corporate-owned Save-A-Lots, 867 licensed Save-A-Lots, and 31 licensed Cub Foods stores.

[f] Loblaw is a Canadian chain; sales and market shares are based only on Loblaw store sales in the United States.

[g] Ahold USA , the U.S. division of Netherlands-based Ahold, includes 386 Stop & Shops, 192 Giant Foods (Landover, Maryland), 126 Giant Foods (Carlisle, Pennsylvania), and 123 Tops Markets.

[h] Delhaize includes 1,171 Food Lion stores, 158 Hannaford Bros. stores, 108 Sweetbay and Kash 'n Karry stores, 68 Harvey's stores, 22 Bloom units, and 17 Bottom Dollar stores.

Sources: Wal-Mart's 2007 10-K report and "Top 75 North American Food Retailers," www.supermarketnews.com (accessed March 20, 2008).

> and by many of our customers (and hopefully many of our shareholders too). Our deepest purpose as an organization is helping support the health, well-being, and healing of both people (customers and Team Members) and of the planet (sustainable agriculture, organic production and environmental sensitivity). When I peel away the onion of my personal consciousness down to its core in trying to understand what has driven me to create and grow this company, I come to my desire to promote the general well-being of everyone on earth as well as the earth itself. This is my personal greater purpose with the company and the slogan perfectly reflects it.

Complementing the slogan were five core values shared by both top management and company personnel (see Exhibit 3). In the company's 2003 annual report, John Mackey said:

> Our core values reflect the sense of collective fate among our stakeholders and are the soul of our company. Our Team Members, shareholders, vendors, community and environment must flourish together through their affiliation with us or we are not succeeding as a business. It is leadership's role to balance the needs and desires of all our stakeholders and increase the productivity of Whole Foods Market. By growing the collective pie, we create larger slices for all of our shareholders.

Growth Strategy

Since going public in 1991, Whole Foods' growth strategy had been to expand via a combination of opening its own new stores and acquiring small, owner-managed chains that had capable personnel and were located in desirable markets—the company's most significant acquisitions are shown in Exhibit 4. But since the retailers of natural and organic foods were mostly one-store operations and small, regional chains having stores in the 5,000- to 20,000-square-foot range, attractive acquisition candidates were hard to find. From 2002 to 2006, Whole Foods' management decided to drive growth by opening 10 to 15 decidedly bigger stores in metropolitan areas each year—stores that ranged from 40,000 square feet to as much as 70,000 square feet and were on the same scale or even larger than the standard supermarkets operated by Kroger, Safeway, Publix, and other chains.

The Wild Oats Market Acquisition In 2007, Whole Foods moved to purchase struggling Wild Oats Markets—Whole Foods' biggest competitor in natural and organic foods—for $700 million. Wild Oats operated 109 stores in 23 states under the Wild Oats Market, Henry's Farmer's Market, and Sun Harvest

Exhibit 3 Whole Foods Market's Core Values

Our Core Values

The following list of core values reflects what is truly important to us as an organization. These are not values that change from time to time, situation to situation or person to person, but rather they are the underpinning of our company culture. Many people feel Whole Foods is an exciting company of which to be a part and a very special place to work. These core values are the primary reasons for this feeling, and they transcend our size and our growth rate. By maintaining these core values, regardless of how large a company Whole Foods becomes, we can preserve what has always been special about our company. These core values are the soul of our company.

Selling the Highest Quality Natural and Organic Products Available

- **Passion for Food**—We appreciate and celebrate the difference natural and organic products can make in the quality of one's life.
- **Quality Standards**—We have high standards and our goal is to sell the highest quality products we possibly can. We define quality by evaluating the ingredients, freshness, safety, taste, nutritive value and appearance of all of the products we carry. We are buying agents for our customers and not the selling agents for the manufacturers.

Satisfying and Delighting Our Customers

- **Our Customers**—They are our most important stakeholders in our business and the lifeblood of our business. Only by satisfying our customers first do we have the opportunity to satisfy the needs of our other stakeholders.
- **Extraordinary Customer Service**—We go to extraordinary lengths to satisfy and delight our customers. We want to meet or exceed their expectations on every shopping trip. We know that by doing so we turn customers into advocates for our business. Advocates do more than shop with us, they talk about Whole Foods to their friends and others. We want to serve our customers competently, efficiently, knowledgeably and with flair.

(*continued*)

Exhibit 3 (Continued)

- **Education**—We can generate greater appreciation and loyalty from all of our stakeholders by educating them about natural and organic foods, health, nutrition and the environment.
- **Meaningful Value**—We offer value to our customers by providing them with high quality products, extraordinary service and a competitive price. We are constantly challenged to improve the value proposition to our customers.
- **Retail Innovation**—We value retail experiments. Friendly competition within the company helps us to continually improve our stores. We constantly innovate and raise our retail standards and are not afraid to try new ideas and concepts.
- **Inviting Store Environments**—We create store environments that are inviting and fun, and reflect the communities they serve. We want our stores to become community meeting places where our customers meet their friends and make new ones.

Team Member Happiness and Excellence

- **Empowering Work Environments**—Our success is dependent upon the collective energy and intelligence of all of our Team Members. We strive to create a work environment where motivated Team Members can flourish and succeed to their highest potential. We appreciate effort and reward results.
- **Self-Responsibility**—We take responsibility for our own success and failures. We celebrate success and see failures as opportunities for growth. We recognize that we are responsible for our own happiness and success.
- **Self-Directed Teams**—The fundamental work unit of the company is the self-directed Team. Teams meet regularly to discuss issues, solve problems and appreciate each others' contributions. Every Team Member belongs to a Team.
- **Open & Timely Information**—We believe knowledge is power and we support our Team Members' right to access information that impacts their jobs. Our books are open to our Team Members, including our annual individual compensation report. We also recognize everyone's right to be listened to and heard regardless of their point of view.
- **Incremental Progress**—Our company continually improves through unleashing the collective creativity and intelligence of all of our Team Members. We recognize that everyone has a contribution to make. We keep getting better at what we do.
- **Shared Fate**—We recognize there is a community of interest among all of our stakeholders. There are no entitlements; we share together in our collective fate. To that end we have a salary cap that limits the compensation (wages plus profit incentive bonuses) of any Team Member to fourteen times the average total compensation of all full-time Team Members in the company.

Creating Wealth Through Profits & Growth

- **Stewardship**—We are stewards of our shareholders' investments and we take that responsibility very seriously. We are committed to increasing long-term shareholder value.
- **Profits**—We earn our profits every day through voluntary exchange with our customers. We recognize that profits are essential to creating capital for growth, prosperity, opportunity, job satisfaction and job security.

Caring About Our Communities & Our Environment

- **Sustainable Agriculture**—We support organic farmers, growers and the environment through our commitment to sustainable agriculture and by expanding the market for organic products.
- **Wise Environmental Practices**—We respect our environment and recycle, reuse, and reduce our waste wherever and whenever we can.
- **Community Citizenship**—We recognize our responsibility to be active participants in our local communities. We give a minimum of 5% of our profits every year to a wide variety of community and non-profit organizations. In addition, we pay our Team Members to give of their time to community and service organizations.
- **Integrity in All Business Dealings**—Our trade partners are our allies in serving our stakeholders. We treat them with respect, fairness and integrity at all times and expect the same in return.

Source: www.wholefoodsmarket.com (accessed March 21, 2008).

Exhibit 4 Major Acquisitions by Whole Foods Market, 1992–2007

Year	Company Acquired	Location	Number of Stores	Acquisition Costs
1992	Bread & Circus	Northeastern United States	6	$20 million plus $6.2 million in common stock
1993	Mrs. Gooch's	Southern California	7	2,970,596 shares of common stock
1996	Fresh Fields Markets	East Coast and Chicago area	22	4.8 million shares of stock plus options for 549,000 additional shares
1997	Merchant of Vino	Detroit area	6	Approximately 1 million shares of common stock
1997	Bread of Life	South Florida	2	200,000 shares of common stock
1999	Nature's Heartland	Boston area	4	$24.5 million in cash
2000	Food 4 Thought (Natural Abilities, Inc.)	Sonoma County, CA	3	$25.7 million in cash, plus assumption of certain liabilities
2001	Harry's Farmer's Market	Atlanta	3	Approximately $35 million in cash
2004	Fresh & Wild	Great Britain	7	$20 million in cash plus 239,000 shares of common stock
2007	Wild Oats Natural Marketplace	United States and Canada	74 (after sale of 35 stores)	$565 million plus the assumption of $137 million in debt; however, Whole Foods received approximately $166 million for the 35 stores that were subsequently sold (out of the total of 109 stores that were acquired)

Source: Investor relations section of www.wholefoodsmarket.com (accessed November 18, 2004, and March 21, 2008).

brands and had total annual sales of about $1.2 billion. The Federal Trade Commission (FTC) opposed the acquisition on grounds that the competition in the organic foods retailing segment would be weakened; however, a U.S. district court found that the FTC's position lacked merit. When the district court's ruling was upheld on appeal, Whole Foods was legally cleared to complete its acquisition of Wild Oats in late August 2007. Acquiring Wild Oats gave Whole Foods entry into 15 new metropolitan markets and 5 new states. Whole Foods then quickly sold 35 Henry's and Sun Harvest stores in California and Texas previously acquired by Wild Oats, along with a California distribution center, to Los Angeles food retailer Smart & Final, realizing almost $166 million from the sale and reducing its net purchase price for Wild Oats Market to about $534 million (which included the assumption of $137 million in Wild Oats' debt). In addition, Whole Foods immediately closed nine Wild Oats stores that did not fit with its brand strategy or real estate strategy and began planning to relocate seven smaller Wild Oats stores to existing or soon-to-be-opened Whole Foods locations.

Whole Foods' CEO, John Mackey, believed that the addition of the Wild Oats stores would give Whole Foods additional bargaining power with suppliers, boost the overall utilization of the company's facilities, and allow general and administrative expenses for the combined companies to be reduced significantly. Moreover, while Wild Oats stores were older and smaller than Whole Foods stores (the average Wild Oats store was 24,100 square feet versus a Whole Foods average of 34,000 square feet), management believed that over time it would be able to boost customer traffic and sales per square foot at the former Wild Oats stores to levels in line with those at Whole Foods stores. Three months after the close of the acquisition, sales at Wild Oats stores were said to be "rapidly improving" due to expanded product offerings and price cuts on more than 1,000 items.[6] During 2008, Whole Foods planned to spend close to $45 million renovating Wild Oats stores and rebranding them as Whole Foods stores.

Store Sizes and Locations

Whole Foods' stores had an open format and generated average annual sales of about $32 million. The company's "sweet spot" for most markets it had entered since 2000 was a store footprint between

45,000 and 60,000 square feet. All told, in early 2008, it had 82 stores that were 40,000 square feet or larger—the biggest was a 99,800-square-foot store in London. The 100-plus stores that company had opened since 2000 averaged 48,000 square feet, and 18 Whole Foods stores were over 60,000 square feet. Whole Foods had the two largest supermarket stores in New York City, a 58,000-square-foot store on Columbus Circle in Manhattan and a 71,000-square-foot store in the Bowery. Whole Foods had a 74,500-square-foot store in Columbus, Ohio; a flagship 78,000-square-foot store in Austin, Texas; a 77,000-square-foot store in Pasadena, California; and two 75,000-square-foot stores in the suburbs of Atlanta, Georgia. It was the company's practice each year not only to open new stores but also to relocate some of its smaller stores to larger sites with improved visibility and parking. In early 2008, the company had 89 stores averaging 51,500 square feet in varying stages of development; 13 of these were over 65,000 square feet (the new stores of supermarket chains like Safeway and Kroger averaged around 55,000 square feet), and 15 were in new geographic markets. Exhibit 5 provides store-related statistics.

In 2008, Whole Foods had stores in 36 states. Whole Foods favored store locations in the upscale areas of urban metropolitan centers, frequently on premier real estate sites. Most stores were in high-traffic shopping locations; some were freestanding, some were in strip centers, and some were in high-density mixed-use projects. Whole Foods had its own internally developed model to analyze potential markets according to education levels, population density, and income within certain drive times. After picking a target metropolitan area, the company's site consultant did a comprehensive site study and developed sales projections; potential sites had to pass certain financial hurdles. New stores opened 12 to 24 months after a lease was signed.

The cash investment needed to get a new Whole Foods Market site ready for opening varied with the metropolitan area, store size, amount of work performed by the landlord, and the complexity of site development issues—the average capital cost was $15.1 million in 2007.[7] In addition to the capital cost of a new store, it took about $850,000 to stock a store with inventory, a portion of which was financed by vendors. Pre-opening expenses (including rent) averaged $2.6 million for the 21 new stores opened and relocated in fiscal 2007.

Product Line

While product and brand selections varied from store to store (because stores were different sizes and had different clientele), Whole Foods' product line included some 30,000 natural, organic, and gourmet food products and nonfood items:

- Fresh produce—fruits and vegetables, including seasonal, exotic, and specialty products like cactus pears, cippolini onions, and Japanese eggplant.
- Meat and poultry—natural and organic meats, house-made sausages, turkey, and chicken products from animals raised on wholesome grains, pastureland, and well water (and grown without the use of by-products, hormones, or steroids).
- Fresh seafood—a selection of fresh fish; shrimp; oysters; clams; mussels; homemade marinades; and exotic items like octopus, sushi, and black tip shark. A portion of the fresh fish selections at the seafood station came from the company's

Exhibit 5 Number of Stores in the Whole Foods Markets Chain, 1991–2007, and Selected Store Operating Statistics, 2000–2007

Year	Number of Stores at End of Fiscal Year
1991	10
1992	25
1993	42
1994	49
1995	61
1996	68
1997	75
1998	87
1999	100
2000	117
2001	126
2002	135
2003	145
2004	163
2005	175
2006	186
2007	276

(continued)

Exhibit 5 (Continued)

	Fiscal Year					
	2000	2002	2004	2005	2006	2007
Store sales (000s)	$1,838,630	$2,690,475	$3,864,950	$4,701,289	$5,607,376	$6,591,773
Average weekly sales	$324,710	$392,837	$482,061	$536,986	$593,439	$616,706
Comparable store sales growth*	8.6%	10.0%	14.9%	12.8%	11.0%	7.1%
Total square footage of all stores, end of year	3,180,207	4,098,492	5,145,261	5,819,843	6,376,817	9,312,107
Average store size, end of year, in square feet	27,181	30,359	31,566	33,200	34,284	33,740
Gross margin, all-store average	34.5%	34.6%	34.2%	35.1%	34.9%	34.8%
Store contribution, all-store average†	9.4%	9.6%	9.3%	9.6%	9.6%	8.9%

*Defined as average annual sales increases at stores open a full year or more; represents the rate at which sales at existing stores are increasing annually on average.

†Defined as gross profit minus direct store expenses, where gross profit equals store revenues less cost of goods sold.

Sources: Information posted at www.wholefoodsmarket.com (accessed March 14, 2008), and the company's 2007 10-K report.

Pigeon Cove and Select Fish seafood processing subsidiaries. Seafood items coming from distant supply sources were flown in to stores to ensure maximum freshness.

- A selection of daily baked goods—breads, cakes, pies, cookies, bagels, muffins, and scones.
- Prepared foods—soups, canned and packaged goods, oven-ready meals, rotisserie meats, hearth-fired pizza, pastas, patés, salad bars, a sandwich station, and a selection of entrées and side foods prepared daily.
- Fine-quality cheeses, olives (up to 40 varieties in some stores), chocolates, and confections.
- Frozen foods, juices, yogurt and dairy products, smoothies, and bottled waters.
- A wide selection of dried fruits, nuts, and spices (either prepackaged or dispensed from bins).
- Beer and wines—the selection of domestic and imported wines varied from store to store. Organic wines were among those available.
- Coffees and teas—the company's Allegro coffee subsidiary supplied all stores with specialty and organic coffees, and several of the newer stores had in-store coffee-roasting equipment that allowed customers to order any of 20 varieties to be roasted while they shopped. The tea selections included environmentally correct, premium exotic teas from remote forests. Most stores had a coffee and tea bar where shoppers could enjoy freshly brewed drinks.
- A body care and nutrition department containing a wide selection of natural and organic body care products and cosmetics, along with assorted vitamin supplements, homeopathic remedies, yoga supplies, and aromatherapy products—all items entailed the use of non-animal testing methods and contained no artificial ingredients.
- Natural and organic pet foods (including the company's own private-label line), treats, toys, and pest control remedies.
- Grocery and household products—canned and packaged goods, pastas, soaps, cleaning products, and other conventional household items that helped make Whole Foods' larger stores a one-stop grocery shopping destination where people could get everything on their shopping list.
- A floral department with sophisticated flower bouquets and a selection of plants for inside and outside the home.
- A "365 Everyday Value" line and a "365 Organic Everyday Value" line of private-label products that were less expensive than comparable name brands, as well as a family of private-label products with consistent logos and packaging for

specific departments—examples included "Whole Kitchen" for prepackaged fresh and frozen grocery items; "Whole Treat" for cookies, candies, and frozen desserts; "Whole Pantry" for herbs, spices, and condiments; and "Whole Catch" for prepackaged fresh and frozen seafood items.

- Educational products (information on alternative health care) and books relating to healing, cookery, diet, and lifestyle. In some stores, there were cooking classes and nutrition sessions.

Whole Foods was the world's biggest seller of organic produce. Perishables accounted for about 67 percent of Whole Foods' sales in 2007, considerably higher than the 40–50 percent that perishables represented at conventional supermarkets. The acquisition of the three 75,000-plus-square-foot Harry's Market superstores in Atlanta, where 75 percent of sales were perishables, had provided the company with personnel having valuable intellectual capital in creatively merchandising all major perishables categories. Management believed that the company's emphasis on fresh fruits and vegetables, bakery goods, meats, seafood, and other perishables differentiated Whole Foods stores from other supermarkets and attracted a broader customer base. According to John Mackey:

> First-time visitors to Whole Foods Market are often awed by our perishables. We devote more space to fresh fruits and vegetables, including an extensive selection of organics, than most of our competitors. Our meat and poultry products are natural—no artificial ingredients, minimal processing, and raised without the use of artificial growth hormones, antibiotics or animal by-products in their feed. Our seafood is either wild-caught or sourced from aquaculture farms where environmental concerns are a priority. Also, our seafood is never treated with chlorine or other chemicals, as is common practice in the food retailing industry. With each new store or renovation, we challenge ourselves to create more entertaining, theatrical, and scintillatingly appetizing prepared foods areas. We bake daily, using whole grains and unbleached, unbromated flour and feature European-style loaves, pastries, cookies and cakes as well as gluten-free baked goods for those allergic to wheat. We also offer many vegetarian and vegan products for our customers seeking to avoid all animal products. Our cheeses are free of artificial flavors, colors, and synthetic preservatives, and we offer an outstanding variety of both organic cheeses and cheeses made using traditional methods.[8]

Whole Foods' three-story showcase Union Square store in Manhattan carried locally made New York offerings, seasonal items from the nearby Greenmarket farmer's market, and numerous exotic and gourmet items. A 28-foot international section featured such items as Lebanese fig jam, preserved lemons from Morocco, Indian curries, Thai rice, stuffed grape leaves from Greece, and goulash from Hungary. The prepared foods section had a Grilling Station where shoppers could get grilled-to-order dishes such as swordfish in red pepper Romesco sauce and steak with a mushroom demi-glace.

One of Whole Foods Market's foremost commitments to its customers was to sell foods that met strict standards and that were of high quality in terms of nutrition, freshness, appearance, and taste. Whole Foods guaranteed 100 percent satisfaction on all items purchased and went to great lengths to live up to its core value of satisfying and delighting customers. Buyers personally visited the facilities of many of the company's suppliers and were very picky about the items they chose and the ingredients they contained. For the benefit of prospective food suppliers, the company maintained a list of ingredients it considered unacceptable in food products. Exhibit 6 shows the company's quality standards.

Pricing Because the costs of growing and marketing organic foods ran 25 to 75 percent more than conventionally grown items, prices at Whole Foods were higher than at conventional supermarkets. For the most part, Whole Foods sold premium products at premium prices. Price-sensitive consumers and some media critics had dubbed Whole Foods as "Whole Paycheck." Some of the exotic items sold at Whole Foods had eye-popping price tags—for example, Graffiti eggplants grown in Holland were $4 per pound, lobster mushrooms from Oregon were $25 per pound, and a three-ounce can of organic pearl jasmine tea was $14.[9] The earth-friendly detergents, toilet papers, and other household items that Whole Foods merchandised frequently were priced higher than the name brands of comparable products found in traditional supermarkets. However, as one analyst noted, "If people believe that the food is healthier and they are doing something good for themselves, they are willing to invest a bit more, particularly as they get older. It's not a fad."[10] Another grocery industry analyst noted that while Whole Foods served a growing niche, it had managed to attract a new kind of customer, one who was willing to pay a premium

Exhibit 6 Whole Foods Market's Product Quality Standards and Customer Commitments

Our business is to sell the highest quality foods we can find at the most competitive prices possible. We evaluate quality in terms of nutrition, freshness, appearance, and taste. Our search for quality is a never-ending process involving the careful judgment of buyers throughout the company.

- We carefully evaluate each and every product we sell.
- We feature foods that are free of artificial preservatives, colors, flavors, sweeteners, and hydrogenated fats.
- We are passionate about great tasting food and the pleasure of sharing it with others.
- We are committed to foods that are fresh, wholesome and safe to eat.
- We seek out and promote organically grown foods.
- We provide food and nutritional products that support health and well-being.

Whole Foods Market's Quality Standards team maintains an extensive list of unacceptable ingredients. . . . However, creating a product with no unacceptable ingredients does not guarantee that Whole Foods Market will sell it. Our buyers are passionate about seeking out the freshest, most healthful, minimally processed products available. [As of 2008, there were 81 chemicals on Whole Foods' list of unacceptable ingredients, including artificial colors, artificial flavors, aspartame, bleached flour, cyclamates, foie gras, hydrogenated fats, irradiated foods, nitrates and nitrites, saccharin, sorbic acid, sucralose, and sulfites (sulfur dioxide).]

Source: The quality standards section of www.wholefoodsmarket.com (accessed March 24, 2008).

to dabble in health food without being totally committed to vegetarianism or an organic lifestyle.[11]

Store Description and Merchandising

Whole Foods Market did not have a standard store design. Instead, each store's layout was customized to fit the particular site and building configuration and to best show off the particular product mix for the store's target clientele. The driving concept of Whole Foods' merchandising strategy was to create an inviting and interactive store atmosphere that turned shopping for food into a fun, pleasurable experience. Management at Whole Foods wanted customers to view company stores as a "third place" (besides home and office) where people could gather, learn, and interact while at the same time enjoying an intriguing food-shopping and eating experience. Stores had a colorful décor, and products were attractively merchandised (see Exhibit 7). According to one industry analyst, Whole Foods had "put together the ideal model for the foodie who's a premium gourmet and the natural foods buyer. When you walk into a Whole Foods store, you're overwhelmed by a desire to look at everything you see."[12]

Most stores featured hand-stacked produce, instore chefs working in open kitchens, scratch bakeries, prepared-foods stations, European-style charcuterie departments, "Whole Body" departments with a wide selection of personal care items and natural cosmetics (as well as a makeup station), salad bars, sit-down dining areas, gourmet food sections with items from around the world, and ever-changing selections and merchandise displays. Many stores had recipe cards at the end of key aisles. A few stores offered valet parking, home delivery, and massages. Management believed that the extensive and attractive displays of fresh produce, seafood, meats and house-made sausages (up to 40 varieties), baked goods, and prepared foods in its larger stores appealed to a broader customer base and were responsible for the fact that Whole Foods stores larger than 30,000 square feet were generally better performers than smaller stores.

Whole Foods' 78,000-square-foot flagship Austin store was a top central Texas tourist destination and a downtown Austin landmark; it had an intimate village-style layout; six mini restaurants within the store; a raw food and juice bar; more than 600 varieties of cheese and 40 varieties of olives; a selection of 1,800 wines; a Candy Island with handmade lollipops and popcorn balls; a hot nut bar with an in-house nut roaster; a world foods section; a walk-in beer cooler with 800 selections; 14 pastry chefs making a variety of items; a natural home section with organic cotton apparel and household linens; an extensive meat department with an in-house smoker and 50 oven-ready items prepared by in-house chefs; and a theater-like seafood department with more than 150 fresh seafood items and on-the-spot shucking, cooking, smoking, slicing and frying to order.

Exhibit 7 Scenes from Whole Foods Stores

The Columbus Circle store in Manhattan had a 248-seat café where shoppers could enjoy restaurant-quality prepared foods while relaxing in a comfortable community setting; a Jamba Juice smoothie station that served freshly blended-to-order fruit smoothies and juices; a full-service sushi bar by Genji Express where customers sat on bar stools enjoying fresh-cut sushi wrapped in organic seaweed; a walk-in greenhouse showcasing fresh-cut and exotic flowers; a wine shop with more than 700 varieties of wine from both large and small vineyards and family estates; and a chocolate enrobing station in the bakery where customers could request just about anything covered in chocolate. The two-story store in Pasadena, California (Whole Foods' largest store west of the Rocky Mountains), had a wine and tapas lounge; a seafood bar; an Italian trattoria; 1,200 selections of wine; fresh doughnuts made hourly; a 6,000-square-foot produce department that featured more than 500 items daily; and free wireless Internet access. The three-story, 99,800-square-foot store in London had 55 in-store chefs; 13 dining venues (including a tapas bar, a champagne and oyster bar, a pub, and a sushi and dim sum eatery) that accommodated 350 diners; a self-service bulk foods center with 100 selections; and a 12-meter display of fresh seafood (many of the seafood selections were hook-and-line caught off the shores of the United Kingdom).

Whole Foods got very high marks from merchandising experts and customers for its presentation—from the bright colors of the produce displays, to the quality of the foods and customer service, to the wide aisles and cleanliness. Management was continually experimenting with new merchandising concepts to keep stores fresh and exciting for customers. According to a Whole Foods regional manager, "We take the best ideas from each of our stores and try to incorporate them in all our other stores. We're constantly making our stores better."[13] Whole Foods' merchandising skills were said to be a prime factor in its success in luring shoppers back time and again—Whole Foods stores had annual sales averaging more than $800 per square foot of space (about double the sales per square foot of Kroger and Safeway).

To further a sense of community and interaction with customers, stores typically included customer comment boards and "Take Action" centers for customers who wanted information on such topics as sustainable agriculture, organics, overfishing problems and the sustainability of seafood supplies, the environment, and similar issues. The Toronto store had biographies of farmers suspended from the ceiling on placards and a board calling attention to Whole Foods' "Sustainable Seafood Policy" hung above the seafood station. In 2008, Whole Foods began introducing signage and brochures in all its stores informing shoppers of the company's Five-Step Animal Welfare Rating Program, which laid out a set of "animal compassionate" standards expected of Whole Foods' meat and poultry suppliers; these standards focused on humane living conditions for the animals and specified permissible and prohibited production and handling techniques from parent stock through slaughter.

Marketing and Customer Service

Whole Foods spent about 0.5 percent of its revenues on advertising, a much smaller percentage than conventional supermarkets, preferring instead to rely primarily on word-of-mouth recommendations and testimonials from customers. The corporate marketing budget was allocated to regionwide programs, marketing efforts for individual stores, and a national brand-awareness initiative focused primarily on national in-store marketing programs. Stores spent most of their marketing budgets on in-store signage and store events such as taste fairs, classes, and product samplings. Store personnel were encouraged to extend company efforts to encourage the adoption of a natural and organic lifestyle by going out into the community and conducting a proactive public relations campaign. Each store also had a separate budget for making contributions to philanthropic activities and community outreach programs.

Since one of its core values was to satisfy and delight customers (see Exhibit 3), Whole Foods Market empowered team members to do whatever it took to meet or exceed customer expectations on every shopping trip. Competent, knowledgeable, and friendly service was a hallmark of shopping at a Whole Foods Market. The aim was to turn highly satisfied customers into advocates for Whole Foods who talked to close friends and acquaintances about their positive experiences shopping at Whole Foods. Store personnel were personable and chatty with shoppers. Customers could get personal attention in every department of the store. When customers asked where an item was located, team members often took them to the spot, making conversation along the way and offering to answer any questions. Team members were quite knowledgeable and enthusiastic about the products in their particular department and tried to take advantage of opportunities to inform and educate customers about natural foods, organics, healthy eating, and food-related environmental issues. They took pride in helping customers navigate the extensive variety to make the best choices. Meat department personnel provided customers with custom cuts, cooking instructions, and personal recommendations.

Store Operations

Whole Foods employed a team approach to store operations. Depending on store size and traffic volume, Whole Foods stores employed between 85 and 600 team members, who were organized into as many as 13 teams, each led by a team leader. Each team within a store was responsible for a different product category or aspect of store operations, such as customer service, prepared foods, produce, and customer checkout stations. Teams were empowered to make many decisions at the store level pertaining to merchandising, departmental operations, and efforts to please customers.

Whole Foods' commitment to team-based management of store operations stemmed from the conviction that the company's long-term success was advanced by having happy employees actively helping to create happy customers. The team approach, complemented by a strong emphasis on empowering employees, was seen as promoting a strong corporate culture and contributing to a work environment where motivated team members could flourish, build a career, and reach their highest potential. Whole Foods' top management believed that empowered teams helped harness the collective energy and intelligence of team members to operate their departments effectively and efficiently—thereby enabling Whole Foods to manage its stores better than rival supermarket chains managed their stores. Management also believed that team members were further motivated and inspired by the company's strategic vision—many team members felt good about their jobs and had a greater sense of purpose because the work they did contributed to better diets and eating habits on the part of Whole Foods shoppers and to the overall well-being of society at large. Indeed, many job candidates were drawn to interview at Whole Foods because they identified with the company's mission of selling natural and organic foods, advancing the cause of long-term sustainable agricultural practices, and promoting a cleaner environment—a mission that was captured and reflected in the company's motto of "Whole Foods, Whole People, Whole Planet."

A team member at Whole Foods' store in Austin, Texas, said, "I really feel like we're a part of making the world a better place. When I joined the company 17 years ago, we only had four stores. I have always loved—as a customer and now as a Team Member—the camaraderie, support for others, and progressive atmosphere at Whole Foods Market."[14] According to the company's vice president of human resources, "Team members who love to take initiative, while enjoying working as part of a team and being rewarded through shared fate, thrive here."

Top executives at Whole Foods were acutely aware that the company's decentralized team approach to store operations—where many personnel, merchandising, and operating decisions were made by teams at the individual store level—made it critical to have an effective store team leader. The store team leader worked with one or more associate store team leaders, as well as with all the department team leaders, to operate the store as efficiently and profitably as possible. Team leaders screened candidates for job openings on their team, but a two-thirds majority of the team had to approve a new hire—and that approval came only after a 30-day trial for the candidate. Store team leaders were paid a salary plus a bonus based on the store's economic value added (EVA) contribution; they were also eligible to receive stock options.[15] Twice yearly, team members were asked to complete a confidential, third-party administered team leader survey that provided them with an opportunity to give team leaders constructive feedback. Store team leaders reported directly to one of 11 regional presidents.

Starting in 2002, team members across the company were encouraged to actively contribute ideas about the benefits they would like the company to offer. The suggestions were compiled, put into a choice of packages, and the choices submitted to team members for a vote. The benefits plan that was adopted for 2003 through 2006 was approved by 83 percent of the 79 percent of the team members participating in the benefits vote. Under the adopted plan, team members could select their own benefits package. The resulting health insurance plan that the company put in place in January 2003 involved the company paying 100 percent of the premium for full-time employees and the establishment of company-funded "personal wellness accounts," which team members could use to pay the higher deductibles; any unused balances in a team member's account could roll over and accumulate for future expenses. A second companywide benefits vote was held in fiscal 2006 to determine the benefits program that would be in place from 2007 through 2009. One outcome of the second vote, in which approximately 77 percent of eligible team members participated, was that the company again provided health care at no cost to eligible full-time employees (defined as those who worked 30 or more hours per week and had worked a minimum of 800 hours); the cost of dependent health care premiums was shared between the company and the team member, with the percentage paid by the team member declining as years of service with the company increased. Other key benefits included paid time off, a 20 percent discount on all purchases at Whole Foods, dental and eye care plans, life insurance and disability insurance plans, and an emergency assistance plan.

Every year, management gave team members an opportunity to complete a morale survey covering job satisfaction, opportunity and empowerment, pay, training, and benefits. In 2004, the overall participation rate was 63 percent (versus 71 percent in 2003). Of the team members responding in 2004, 86 percent said they almost always or frequently enjoyed their job (the same percentage as in 2003), and 82 percent said they almost always or frequently felt empowered to do their best work at Whole Foods Market (up slightly from 81 percent in 2003). Common responses to the question "What is the best thing about working at Whole Foods Market?" included coworkers, customers, flexibility, work environment, growth and learning opportunities, the products Whole Foods sold, benefits, the team concept, and the culture of empowerment.

Whole Foods Market had 54,000 employees in 2008, of whom approximately 85 percent were full-time. None were represented by unions, although there had been a couple of unionization attempts. John Mackey was viewed as fiercely anti-union and had once said: "The union is like having herpes. It doesn't kill you, but it's unpleasant and inconvenient and it stops a lot of people from becoming your lover."[16] When workers at a Whole Foods Market in Madison, Wisconsin, voted to unionize in 2002, John Mackey spent over nine months going to all of the company's stores to speak with store employees personally, listen to what was on their minds, and gather suggestions for improving working conditions. Unionization efforts had never made any headway at Whole Foods, and the company was widely regarded as very progressive and genuinely committed to creating a positive, satisfying work environment.

Whole Foods had made *Fortune*'s "100 Best Companies to Work For" list for 11 consecutive years (1998–2008); it was one of only 14 companies to make the list every year since its inception and was the only national supermarket chain to ever make the list (although Wegmans, a regional supermarket chain, was the top-ranked company on *Fortune*'s 2005 list and was the third-ranked company in both 2007 and 2008). In scoring companies, *Fortune* placed two-thirds weight on responses to a 57-question survey of 400 randomly selected employees and one-third on *Fortune*'s own evaluation of a company's demographic makeup, pay and benefits, and culture.

Compensation and Incentives

Whole Foods strived to create a "shared-fate consciousness" on the part of team members by uniting the self-interests of team members with those of shareholders. One way management reinforced this concept was through a gain-sharing program that rewarded a store's team members according to their store's contribution to operating profit (store sales less cost of goods sold less store operating expenses)—gain-sharing distributions added 5 to 7 percent to team member wages. The company also encouraged stock ownership on the part of team members through three other programs:

1. *A team member stock option plan.* All full-time and part-time team members were eligible for a grant of stock options each year based on team member performance and length of service to the company. In 2007, options to purchase 1.7 million shares were granted to 13,400 team members .
2. *A team member stock purchase plan.* Through payroll deductions, team members could purchase

a restricted number of shares at 95 percent of the market price on the purchase date. Approximately 2,000 team members participated in this plan in fiscal 2007.

3. *A team member 401(k) plan.* Whole Foods Market stock was one of the investment options in the 401(k) plan.

All the teams at each store were continuously evaluated on measures relating to sales, operations, and morale; the results were made available to team members and to headquarters personnel.[17] Teams competed not only against the goals they had set for themselves but also against other teams at their stores or in their region—competition among teams was encouraged. In addition, stores went through two review processes—a store tour and a "customer snapshot." Each store was toured periodically and subjected to a rigorous evaluation by a group of 40 personnel from another region; the group included region heads, store team leaders, associate team leaders, and leaders from two operating teams. Customer snapshots involved a surprise inspection by a headquarters official or regional president who rated the store on 300 items; each store had 10 surprise inspections annually, with the results distributed to every store and included in the reward system. Rewards were team-based and tied to performance metrics.

Whole Foods had a salary cap that limited the compensation (wages plus profit incentive bonuses) of any team member to 19 times the average total compensation of all full-time team members in the company—a policy mandated in the company's core values (see Exhibit 3). The salary cap was raised from 14 to 19 times the average total compensation in 2007—it had been 8 times in 2003; the increases stemmed from the need to attract and retain key executives. For example, if the average total compensation was $50,000, then a cap of 19 times the average meant that an executive could not be paid more than $950,000. All team members had access to the company's financial books, including an annual compensation report listing the gross pay of each team member and company executive. Cofounder and CEO John Mackey had recently reduced his annual salary to $1, with future compensation from his personal stock options going to Whole Foods' two not-for-profit foundations.

The company promoted from within as much as possible, with team members often moving up to assume positions at stores soon to be opened or at stores in other regions.

The Use of Economic Value Added to Measure Performance In 1999, Whole Foods adopted an economic value added (EVA) management and incentive system. EVA is defined as net operating profits after taxes minus a charge for the cost of capital necessary to generate that profit. At Whole Foods, EVA at the store level was based on store contribution (store revenues minus cost of goods sold minus store operating expenses) relative to store investment over and above a weighted average cost of capital of 9 percent—average store contribution percentages for 2000–2007 are shown in Exhibit 5. Senior executives managed the company with the goal of *improving* EVA at the store level and companywide; they believed that an EVA-based bonus system was the best financial framework for team members to use in helping make decisions that created sustainable shareholder value. The teams in all stores were challenged to find ways to boost store contribution and EVA—the team member bonuses paid on EVA improvement averaged 6 percent in 2003.

In 2007, more than 750 senior executives, regional managers, store team leaders, and assistant store team leaders throughout the company were on EVA-based incentive compensation plans. The primary measure for payout was EVA *improvement.* The company's overall EVA climbed from a negative $30.4 million in fiscal 2001 to $2.6 million in fiscal 2003, $15.6 million in fiscal 2004, $25.8 million in 2005, and $64.4 million in 2006, but then dropped sharply to $35.4 million in 2007.

In addition, management used EVA calculations to determine whether the sales and profit projections for new stores would yield a positive and large enough EVA to justify the investment. EVA calculations were also used to guide decisions on store closings and to evaluate new acquisitions.

Purchasing and Distribution

Whole Foods' buyers purchased most of the items retailed in the company's stores from local, regional, and national wholesale suppliers and vendors. Much of the buying responsibility was located at the regional and national levels in order to put the company in a better position to negotiate volume discounts with major vendors and distributors. Whole Foods Market was the largest account for many suppliers of natural and organic foods. United Natural Foods was the company's biggest supplier, accounting for about 24 percent of Whole Foods' total purchases in fiscal 2007; United was the company's primary supplier of dry grocery and frozen food products. However, regional and store managers had discretionary authority to source from local organic farmers and suppliers that meet the company's quality standards. In 2007–2008, the company's buyers began to place stronger emphasis on buying directly from producers and manufacturers.

Whole Foods owned two produce procurement centers that facilitated the procurement and distribution of the majority of the produce Whole Foods sold. However, where feasible, local store personnel sourced produce items from local organic farmers as part of the company's commitment to promote and support organic farming methods. Two subsidiaries, the Pigeon Cove seafood processing facility in Massachusetts and the Select Fish seafood processing facility on the West Coast, supplied a portion of the company's seafood requirements. A regional seafood distribution facility had recently been established in Atlanta.

The company operated nine regional distribution centers to supply its stores. Nine regional bake houses and five commissary kitchens supplied area stores with various prepared foods. A central coffee-roasting operation supplied stores with the company's Allegro brand of coffees.

Community Citizenship and Social Activism

Whole Foods demonstrated its social conscience and community citizenship in a variety of ways:

- By donating at least 5 percent of its after-tax profits in cash or products to nonprofit or educational organizations. In fiscal 2007, Whole Foods made charitable donations of just under $15 million, equal to about 8 percent of after-tax profits in fiscal 2007.
- Whole Foods' Green Mission Task Force promoted environmentally sound practices for every aspect of store and facility operations. In early 2008, Whole Foods began using all-natural-fiber packaging at its salad and food bars. As of Earth Day 2008 (April 22), Whole Foods ended the use of disposable plastic bags at the checkout lanes of all its stores, chiefly because such bags did not break down in landfills. Company officials said the move would eliminate use of 100 million plastic bags annually—in their place, customers were offered reusable paper bags made of 100 percent recycled paper (at a cost of 10 cents each) and an opportunity to purchase stylish long-life canvas bags for 99 cents (80 percent of the content of the canvas bags came from recycled plastic bottles).
- The company was in the process of converting its distribution fleet vehicles to biodiesel fuel.
- The company purchased renewable energy credits to offset 100 percent of the electricity used in all of its locations (retail and nonretail) in North America. In both 2006 and 2007, Whole Foods won a Green Power Partnership award from the U.S. Environmental Protection Agency for supporting the development of renewable energy.
- Whole Foods created the not-for-profit Animal Compassion Foundation in January 2005, which strived to help producers adopt and improve their practices for raising farm animals naturally and humanely.
- In October 2005, Whole Foods had established a not-for-profit Whole Planet Foundation that was charged with combating poverty and promoting self-sufficiency in third-world countries that supplied Whole Foods with some of the products it sold.
- Whole Foods participated in a Whole Trade program that committed the company to paying small-scale producers (chiefly in impoverished, low-wage countries where living standards were low) a price for their products that more than covered the producer's costs; the goal was to make sure that the producers of products meeting Whole Foods' quality standards could always afford to create, harvest or grow their product so that they did not have to abandon their work or jeopardize the well-being of their family to make ends meet. The commitment to paying such producers a premium price was viewed as an investment in such producers and their communities, a way for producers to be able to put money back into their operations, enable them to invest in training and education for their workers, and have sufficient take-home pay to help support a better life. Whole Foods' goal

was to have more than 50 percent of its products imported from developing nations meet its Whole Trade qualifications within 10 years. In 2007, the Whole Trade Guarantee label was featured on more than 400 items at Whole Foods' stores. Whole Foods donated 1 percent of the retail sale of each Whole Trade product sold to the Whole Planet Foundation.

- In 2007, Whole Foods established a Local Producer Loan Program that awarded low-interest loans to small-scale food producers and growers. So far, Whole Foods had committed $10 million to its microlending program to help aspiring local producers of organic and natural agricultural crops, body care products, and artisan foods (such as nut butters, ice cream, granolas, and cheeses) to grow and flourish. Loan recipients had to meet Whole Foods Market's quality standards, use the funds for expansion, and have a viable business plan. Loan amounts were between $1,000 and $100,000 with fixed interest rates that ranged between 5 and 9 percent in 2007.
- Team members at every Whole Foods store were heavily involved in such community citizenship activities as sponsoring blood donation drives, preparing meals for seniors and the homeless, holding fund-raisers to help the disadvantaged, growing vegetables for a domestic violence shelter, participating in housing renovation projects, and working as deliverypeople for Meals on Wheels.
- Individual Whole Foods stores held "5% Days" (or "Community Giving Days"), donating 5 percent of that day's net store sales to a local or regional nonprofit or educational organization.

In an effort to "walk the talk" about its commitment to its core values and "Whole Foods, Whole People, Whole Planet" motto, Whole Foods had gathered information about key issues that could affect people's health and well-being—the genetic engineering of food supplies, food irradiation practices, and the organic standards process—and disseminated that information via in-store brochures, presentations to groups, and postings on the company's Web site. Further, the company had developed position statements on sustainable seafood practices (see Exhibit 8), the merits of organic farming, and wise environmental practices. Whole Foods regularly publicized its position statements in its stores and on its Web site, along with the company's commitment to selling only those meats that had been raised without the use of growth hormones, antibiotics, and animal by-products.

Mackey's Ethics Are Called into Question

Business Ethics named Whole Foods Market to its list of the "100 Best Corporate Citizens" in 2004, 2006, and 2007. However, during 2007, CEO John Mackey was the center of attention in two ethics-related incidents. The first involved a discovery that, over a seven-year period, Mackey had typed out more than 1,100 entries on Yahoo Finance's

Exhibit 8 Whole Foods' Position on Seafood Sustainability

The simple fact is our oceans are soon to be in trouble. Our world's fish stocks are disappearing from our seas because they have been overfished or harvested using damaging fishing practices. To keep our favorite seafood plentiful for us to enjoy and to keep it around for future generations, we must act now.

As a shopper, you have the power to turn the tide. When you purchase seafood from fisheries using ocean-friendly methods, you reward their actions and encourage other fisheries to operate responsibly.

At Whole Foods Market, we demonstrate our long-term commitment to seafood preservation by:

- Supporting fishing practices that ensure the ecological health of the ocean and the abundance of marine life.
- Partnering with groups who encourage responsible practices and provide the public with accurate information about the issue.
- Operating our own well-managed seafood facility and processing plant, Pigeon Cove Seafood, located in Gloucester, Massachusetts.
- Helping educate our customers on the importance of practices that can make a difference now and well into the future.
- Promoting and selling the products of well-managed fisheries.

Source: www.wholefoodsmarket.com (accessed November 26, 2004).

message board touting his company's stock and occasionally making uncomplimentary remarks about rival Wild Oats Markets. Mackey's postings stopped several months prior to Whole Foods' offer to buy Wild Oats Market. In making his postings, Mackey used the alias Rahodeb—a variation of his wife's name, Deborah. The *Wall Street Journal* reported that in January 2005 Rahodeb posted that no one would buy Wild Oats at its current price of $8 per share and that Whole Foods had nothing to gain by buying Wild Oats because Wild Oats' stores were too small.[18] A *New York Times* article reported that, on March 28, 2006, Rahodeb wrote, "OATS has lost their way and no longer has a sense of mission or even a well-thought-out theory of the business. They lack a viable business model that they can replicate. They are floundering around hoping to find a viable strategy that may stop their erosion. Problem is they lack the time and the capital now."[19] The *New York Times* article quoted Mackey as saying, "I posted on Yahoo! under a pseudonym because I had fun doing it. I never intended any of those postings to be identified with me." Mackey's postings, which came to light in June–July 2007 and spurred calls for his resignation on grounds that he breached his fiduciary responsibility, were first discovered by the Federal Trade Commission (FTC) in Whole Foods' documents that the FTC obtained in the course of challenging the Wild Oats acquisition. According to Mackey, the views he expressed in his Rahodeb postings sometimes represented his personal beliefs and sometimes were different because he would occasionally play the role of devil's advocate. He said no proprietary information about Whole Foods was disclosed.[20] In the days following the media reports of the postings, Mackey expressed remorse for his postings, apologized for his behavior, and asked stakeholders to forgive him for exercising bad judgment. Nonetheless, certain Mackey postings were cited in court documents filed by the FTC as reasons why Whole Foods' acquisition of Wild Oats should be blocked. On July 17, 2007, the Securities and Exchange Commission (SEC) announced that it had begun an investigation of the postings. That same day, Whole Foods announced that the company's board of directors had formed a special committee to investigate the postings and retained legal counsel to advise it during the investigation. Whole Foods said it would cooperate fully with the SEC inquiry.

In October 2007, Whole Foods announced that the special committee had completed its investigation of Mackey's message board postings and that the board of directors affirmed its support of CEO John Mackey; the company indicated that the special committee's findings would be turned over to the SEC and that the company would have no further comment pending the SEC investigation.[21] As of April 2008, there had been no public announcement regarding the SEC's investigation of Mackey's postings.

A second controversy-stirring incident involved a Mackey-authored blog entitled "Whole Foods, Wild Oats and the FTC" that was posted on the company's Web site on June 19, 2007. Mackey, who objected strenuously to the grounds on which the FTC was trying to block Whole Foods' acquisition of Wild Oats, authored the blog, which was dedicated to posting updates and information regarding the FTC proceedings and to making the case for why the company's acquisition of Wild Oats Market should be allowed to go forward. Mackey explained the basis for the blog:

> My blog posting provides a detailed look into Whole Foods Market's decision-making process regarding the merger, as well as our company's experience interacting with the FTC staff assigned to this merger. I provide explanations of how I think the FTC, to date, has neglected to do its homework appropriately, especially given the statements made regarding prices, quality, and service levels in its complaint. I also provide a glimpse into the bullying tactics used against Whole Foods Market by this taxpayer-funded agency. Finally, I provide answers in my FAQ section to many of the questions that various Team Members have fielded from both the media and company stakeholders. As previously announced, we set an intention as a company to be as transparent as possible throughout this legal process, and this blog entry is my first detailed effort at transparency.

The blog posting by Mackey included the following headings:

- Why Whole Foods Market Wants to Buy Wild Oats.
- Whole Foods Market's Objections to the FTC's Investigation.
- What the FTC Is Claiming in Its Objections to the Merger.
- FAQs.

Critics of the Mackey blog posting said it was inappropriate for a CEO to publicly air the company's position, to take issue with the FTC, and to make the company's case for why the acquisition should be allowed to proceed. At the least, some critics opined, the blog should be toned down. When the SEC announced on July 17, 2007, that it would investigate John Mackey's financial message board postings, Mackey put a hold on further blog postings regarding the FTC's actions to try to block the Wild Oats acquisition.

Whole Foods Market's Financial Performance

Since becoming a public company in 1991, Whole Foods Market had been profitable every year except one—2000, which involved a net loss of $8.5 million. That loss stemmed from a decision to divest a nutritional supplement business and losses in two affiliated dot-com enterprises (Gaiam.com and WholePeople.com) in which Whole Foods owned a minority interest. The company's net income rose at a compound average rate of 17.6 percent from fiscal 2003 through fiscal 2007 despite a falloff in 2007 net income to $182.7 million from $203.8 million in 2006. Whole Foods paid its first quarterly dividend in January 2004; since then, dividends had been increased several times. The company began paying a quarterly dividend of $0.20 as of the first quarter of fiscal 2008; this dividend level resulted in cash outlays of about $28 million quarterly.

Whole Foods' business generated cash flows from operations of $410.8 million in fiscal 2005, $452.7 million in fiscal 2006, and $398.6 million in fiscal 2007. For the most part, the company's capital expenditures went into funding the development or acquisition of new stores and the acquisition of property and equipment for existing stores. Capital expenditures totaled $324.1 million in fiscal 2005, $340.2 million in fiscal 2006, and $529.7 million in fiscal 2007, of which $207.8 million, $208.6 million, and $389.3 million, respectively, was for new store development and $116.3 million, $131.6 million, and $140.3 million, respectively, was for remodeling and other additions. During fiscal 2008, Whole Foods expected capital expenditures to be in the range of $575 to $625 million, of which 65 to 70 percent was related to new store openings in 2008 and beyond and approximately 7 to 8 percent related to remodeling the acquired Wild Oats stores. To aid in financing the Wild Oats acquisition and continue fast-paced opening of new stores, Whole Foods had taken on long-term debt of more than $700 million and negotiated a $250 million line of credit with its banks. Exhibits 9, 10, and 11 present the company's recent statements of operations and consolidated balance sheets.

Late-Breaking Developments at Whole Foods

In 2008, the souring U.S. economy hit Whole Foods rather hard. Sales increases at Whole Foods stores open at least a year rose a meager and unexpectedly low 0.8 percent in 2008 versus a robust 8.2 percent in 2007; however, much of the sluggish sales growth was at the former Wild Oats stores rather than at stores that Whole Foods had opened—comparable store sales growth was 5 percent at Whole Foods stores (but this was still well below the 10.9 percent average annual sales growth increases that Whole Foods had realized in the 2003–2007 period). During the July–September 2008 period, sales at the 55 Wild Oats stores that remained open (45 had been rebranded as Whole Foods stores) were $159.3 million and sales at these stores had grown at 4.6 percent during September 2008.

On July 29, 2008, the United States Court of Appeals for the District of Columbia reversed the lower court order allowing Whole Foods' acquisition of Wild Oats to go forward and directed the U.S. District Court to reopen the proceedings for further evidentiary hearings. Separately, the Federal Trade Commission had reopened its administrative action challenging Whole Foods acquisition of Wild Oats. The administrative case was scheduled to go to trial in February 2009. Whole Foods was vigorously contesting the FTC's administrative case.

In August 2008, Whole Foods announced that planned new store openings for 2009 would be reduced. While it was unclear how much flexibility Whole Foods had to back out of signed leases or revise the lease terms for the 70 new stores that had been scheduled to open in 2009 and 2010, it had so far been able to terminate the leases for 13 of its planned new store openings at a cost of $5.5 million. In addition, Whole Foods announced that quarterly dividend payments would be suspended indefinitely. The company had cash of about $30 million

Exhibit 9 Whole Foods Market, Statement of Operations, Fiscal Years 2003–2007 ($ in thousands, except per share data)

	Fiscal Year				
	2007	2006	2005	2004	2003
Sales	$6,591,773	$5,607,376	$4,701,289	$3,864,950	$3,148,593
Cost of goods sold and occupancy costs	4,295,170	3,647,734	3,052,184	2,523,816	2,070,334
Gross profit	2,296,603	1,959,642	1,649,105	1,341,134	1,078,259
Direct store expenses	1,711,229	1,421,968	1,223,473	986,040	794,422
Store contribution	585,374	537,674	425,632	355,094	283,837
General and administrative expenses	217,743	181,244	158,864	119,800	100,693
Pre-opening and relocation costs	70,180	37,421	37,035	18,648	15,765
Operating income	297,451	319,009	229,733	216,646	167,379
Interest expense, net	(4,208)	(32)	(2,223)	(7,249)	(8,114)
Investment and other income	11,324	20,736	9,623	6,456	5,593
Income before income taxes	304,567	339,713	237,133	215,853	164,858
Provision for income taxes	121,827	135,885	100,782	86,341	65,943
Net income	$182,740	$203,828	$136,351	$129,512	$98,915
Basic earnings per share	$1.30	$1.46	$1.05	$1.06	$0.84
Weighted average shares outstanding	140,088	139,328	130,090	122,648	118,070
Diluted earnings per share	$1.29	$1.41	$0.99	$0.99	$0.79
Weighted average shares outstanding, diluted basis	141,836	145,082	139,950	135,454	130,660
Dividends declared per share	$0.87	$2.45	$0.47	$0.30	—

Source: Whole Foods Market, 2007 10-K report, p. 25.

and about $100 million available on existing lines of credit as of November 2008; in recent quarters, Whole Foods' capital expenditures for store expansion had exceeded its cash flows from operations, pushing total debt to $929 million. To bolster its financial position and provided needed funding for opening additional stores and revamping former Wild Oats stores, Whole Foods had recently arranged to sell $425 million of preferred stock to private equity investors, which equated to an ownership interest of 17 percent in the event the private equity investors exercised rights to convert their preferred stock into common stock.

COMPETITORS

The food retailing business was intensely competitive. The degree of competition Whole Foods faced varied from locality to locality, and to some extent from store location to store location within a given locale. Competitors included local, regional, and national supermarkets, along with specialty grocery stores and health and natural foods stores. Most supermarkets offered at least a limited selection of natural and organic foods, and some had chosen to expand their offerings aggressively. Whole Foods' executives had said it was to the company's benefit for conventional supermarkets to offer natural and organic foods for two reasons: first, it helped fulfill the company's mission of improving the health and well-being of people and the planet and, second, it helped create new customers for Whole Foods by providing a gateway experience. They contended that as more people were exposed to natural and organic products, they were more likely to become Whole Foods customers because Whole Foods was the category leader for natural and organic products, offered the largest selection at competitive prices, and provided the most informed customer service.

Whole Foods Market's two biggest competitors in the natural foods and organics segment of the food

Exhibit 10 Whole Foods Market, Consolidated Balance Sheet, Fiscal Years 2006–2007 ($ in thousands)

	Year Ending	
	September 30, 2007	September 24, 2006
Assets		
Current assets:		
Cash and cash equivalents	—	$ 2,252
Short-term investments	—	193,847
Restricted cash	2,310	60,065
Proceeds receivable from store divestitures	165,054	—
Accounts receivable	105,209	82,137
Merchandise inventories	288,112	203,727
Deferred income taxes	40,402	48,149
Prepaid expenses and other current assets	66,899	33,804
Total current assets	667,986	623,981
Property and equipment, net of accumulated depreciation and amortization	1,666,559	1,236,133
Goodwill	668,850	113,494
Intangible assets, net of accumulated amortization	97,683	34,767
Deferred income taxes	104,877	29,412
Other assets	7,173	5,209
Total assets	$3,213,128	$2,042,996
Liabilities and Shareholders' Equity		
Current liabilities:		
Current installments of long-term debt and capital lease obligations	$ 24,781	$ 49
Accounts payable	225,728	121,857
Accrued payroll, bonus, and other benefits due team members	181,290	153,014
Dividends payable	25,060	—
Other current liabilities	327,657	234,850
Total current liabilities	784,516	509,770
Long-term debt and capital lease obligations, less current installments	736,087	8,606
Deferred rent liability	152,552	120,421
Other long-term liabilities	81,169	56
Total liabilities	1,754,324	638,853
Shareholders' equity: Common stock, no par value, 300,000 shares authorized; 143,787 and 142,198 shares issued; 139,240 and 139,607 shares outstanding in 2007 and 2006, respectively	1,232,845	1,147,872
Common stock in treasury, at cost	(199,961)	(99,964)
Accumulated other comprehensive income	15,772	6,975
Retained earnings	410,198	349,260
Total shareholders' equity	1,458,804	1,404,143
Commitments and contingencies		
Total liabilities and shareholders' equity	$3,213,128	$2,042,996

Source: Whole Foods Market, 2007 10-K report, p. 41.

Exhibit 11 Whole Foods Market, Selected Cash Flow Data, Fiscal Years 2005–2007 ($ in thousands)

	2007	2006	2005
Net cash provided by operating activities	$ 398,603	$ 452,664	$ 410,819
Cash flows from investing activities			
Development costs of new store locations	(389,349)	(208,588)	(207,792)
Other property, plant and equipment expenditures	(140,333)	(131,614)	(116,318)
Purchase of available-for-sale securities	(277,283)	(555,095)	—
Sale of available-for-sale securities	475,625	362,209	—
Payment for purchase of acquired entities, net of cash acquired	(596,236)	—	—
Other items	32,595	(36,167)	1,868
Net cash used in investing activities	$(894,981)	$(569,255)	$(322,242)
Cash flows from financing activities			
Dividends paid	$ (96,742)	$(358,075)*	$ (54,683)
Issuance of common stock	54,383	222,030	85,816
Purchase of treasury stock	(99,997)	(99,964)	—
Excess tax benefit related to exercise of team member stock options	12,839	52,008	—
Proceeds form long-term borrowing	717,000	—	—
Payments on long-term debt and capital lease obligations	(93,357)	(5,680)	(5,933)
Net cash provided by (used in) financing activities	$494,126	$(189,681)	$ 25,200
Other cash flow data			
Cash and cash equivalents at beginning of year	$ 2,252	$ 308,524	$ 194,747
Cash and cash equivalents at end of year	—	2,252	308,524
Net change in cash and cash equivalents	(2,252)	(306,272)	113,777
Interest paid	4,561	607	1,063
Federal and state income taxes paid	152,626	70,220	74,706

*Includes cash outlays for a special one-time dividend of $4.00 per share that was paid just prior to a 2-for-1 stock split in early 2006.

Source: Whole Foods Market, 2007 10-K report, p. 44.

retailing industry were Wild Oats Markets (until its 2007 acquisition by Whole Foods) and Fresh Market. Another competitor with some overlap in products and shopping ambience was Trader Joe's. Supervalu/ Save-a-Lot, the sixth largest supermarket chain in North America (see Exhibit 2), had begun an initiative to launch a chain of small natural and organic foods stores called Sunflower Markets.

Wild Oats Market

Prior to being acquired by Whole Foods in August 2007, Wild Oats Market ranked second behind Whole Foods in the natural foods and organics segment and was Whole Foods' biggest and closest competitor in terms of merchandise mix, product offerings, store ambience, and target clientele. The company's 109 stores in 23 states and British Columbia, Canada, operated under four names (Wild Oats Natural Marketplace, Henry's Farmer's Market, Sun Harvest, and Capers Community Markets) and generated combined sales of about $1.2 billion. Mike Gilliland, a cofounder of Wild Oats and its original CEO, had gone on an aggressive acquisition streak during the late 1990s to expand Wild Oats' geographic coverage. But Gilliland's acquisition binge piled up extensive debt and dropped the company into a money-losing position with too many stores, a dozen different store names, a dozen different ways of operating, and inconsistent product selection and customer service from one location to another.

When Perry Odak, formerly the CEO of Ben & Jerry's Homemade until it was acquired by Unilever in 2000, joined the company in 2001, he streamlined operations, closed 28 unprofitable stores, cut prices, trimmed store staffing by 100 employees, and launched a new, smaller prototype store with a heavier emphasis on fresh food. Merchandising and marketing were revamped. The strategy was to draw in more "crossover" shoppers with lower-priced produce, meat, and seafood and raise the average customer purchase at checkout above the current $19 level. When this strategy produced only mixed results, Odak over the next several years tried a series of different strategic initiatives—accelerating new store openings, remodeling a number of existing stores, changing store layouts, expanding fresh produce selections, offering more private-label products, making efficiency improvements in distribution and store operations, and tinkering with the product mix and product selection. But none of Odak's initiatives delivered the hoped-for improvements in profit margins and company profitability, although sales did grow from $969 million in 2003 to $1.2 billion in 2006–2007. Wild Oats recorded a net loss of $43.9 million in 2001, net income of $5.1 million in 2002, net income of $1.6 million in 2003, a net loss of $40.0 million in 2004, net income of $3.2 million in 2005, and a net loss of $16.6 million in 2006.

While both Whole Foods and Wild Oats had stores in some of the same urban areas, for the most part their stores were not in the same neighborhoods. Wild Oats' latest stores were 22,000 to 24,000 square feet and featured a grocery-store layout (in which produce, dairy, meat, seafood, and baked goods were around the perimeters of the store), an expanded produce section at the front of the store, a deli, a sushi bar, a juice and java bar, a reduced selection of canned and packaged items, and store-within-a-store sections for supplements and specialty personal care products.

Fresh Market

Fresh Market, headquartered in Greensboro, North Carolina, was a family-owned 77-store chain operating in 17 states in the Southeast and the Midwest. Founded by Ray Berry, a former vice president with Southland Corporation who had responsibility over some 3,600 7-Eleven stores, the first Fresh Market store opened in 1982 in Greensboro. Berry's concept was to develop a small neighborhood store with the feel and atmosphere of an open European-style market that was service-oriented and focused on perishable goods (particularly fresh produce and meats and seafood displayed in glass-front refrigerated cases). All fixtures and display pieces were purchased used, as the store was financed entirely with the family's savings. After the Greensboro store, which had low-level lighting and classical music playing in the background, proved to be a hit with customers, Berry began to open similar stores in other locales. During the 1982–2000 period, Fresh Market's sales revenues grew at a 25.2 percent compound rate, reaching $193 million in 2000; revenues were an estimated $350 million in 2007. The company had almost 7,000 employees in early 2008. Management planned to open 15–20 new stores annually. Expansion was funded by internal cash flows and bank debt. Financial data were not available because the company was privately owned, but Fresh Market's profitability was believed to be above the industry average.

Fresh Market's product line included meats; seafood; 300 fresh produce items (including a growing organic selection); fresh-baked goods; prepared foods; 40 varieties of coffees; a selection of grocery and dairy items; bulk products; cheeses; deli items (including rotisserie meats, sandwiches, wraps, and signature soups); wine and beer; and floral and gift items. Fresh Market stores were typically in the 18,000- to 22,000-square-feet range and were located in neighborhood shopping areas near educated, high-income residents. Newer stores had an open-air design that evoked "old-world European charm, artful sophistication, old-fashioned retail sentiment, and a warm and friendly atmosphere." Warm lights, classical background music, and terracotta-colored tiles made Fresh Market stores a cozier place to shop than a typical supermarket.

Aside from store ambience, Fresh Market differentiated itself from natural foods stores and traditional supermarkets with what management considered as superlative service; attractive fresh produce displays; appealing fresh meat and seafood selections; and "upscale grocery boutique" items such as pick-and-pack spices, gourmet coffees, chocolates, hard-to-get H&H bagels from New York City, Ferrara's New York cheesecake, fresh Orsini parmesan cheese, and Acqua della Madonna bottled water; and an extended selection of olive oils, mustards, bulk products (granolas, nuts, beans, dried fruits, spices, and snack mixes), wine, and beer. Stores also stocked a small assortment of floral items and gifts (cookbooks, gift cards, baskets, cutting boards, and gift baskets) and a bare lineup of general grocery products. The product line emphasized variety, freshness, and quality. Each department had at least one employee in the area constantly to help shoppers—the idea was to force interaction between store employees and shoppers. From time to time, stores had cooking classes, wine tastings, and food sampling events. Fresh Market sponsored an annual fund-raiser for the Juvenile Diabetes Research Foundation called the Root Beer Float.

Stores had 75–100 employees, resulting in labor costs about double those of supermarket chains. All full-time employees were eligible immediately upon hire to enroll in a medical, dental, and life insurance plan. After 90 days, eligible full-time employees were offered additional benefits that included domestic partner medical and dental coverage, short- and long-term disability insurance, holiday bonuses, employee discounts, and a 401(K) plan with 50 percent company matching of employee contributions. Immediately upon hire, all part-time employees were eligible to enroll for medical, dental, and life insurance.

Trader Joe's

Based in Pasadena, California, Trader Joe's was a specialty supermarket chain with more than 315 stores in 22 states (Arizona, California, Connecticut, Delaware, Georgia, Illinois, Indiana, Maryland, Massachusetts, Michigan, Missouri, Nevada, New Jersey, North Carolina, New Mexico, New York, Ohio, Oregon, Pennsylvania, Virginia, Washington, and Wisconsin). Management described the company's mission and business as follows:

> At Trader Joe's, our mission is to bring our customers the best food and beverage values and the information to make informed buying decisions. There are more than 2,000 unique grocery items in our label, all at honest everyday low prices. We work hard at buying things right: Our buyers travel the world searching for new items and we work with a variety of suppliers who make interesting products for us, many of them exclusive to Trader Joe's. All our private label products have their own "angle," i.e., vegetarian, Kosher, organic or just plain decadent, and all have minimally processed ingredients.
>
> Customers tell us, "I never knew food shopping could be so much fun!" Some even call us "The home of cheap thrills!" We like to be part of our neighborhoods and get to know our customers. And where else do you shop that even the CEO, Dan Bane, wears a loud Hawaiian shirt?
>
> Our tasting panel tastes every product before we buy it. If we don't like it, we don't buy it. If customers don't like it, they can bring it back for a no-hassle refund.
>
> We stick to the business we know: good food at the best prices! Whenever possible we buy direct from our suppliers, in large volume. We bargain hard and manage our costs carefully. We pay in cash, and on time, so our suppliers like to do business with us.
>
> Trader Joe's Crew Members are friendly, knowledgeable and happy to see their customers. They taste our items too, so they can discuss them with their customers. All our stores regularly cook up new and interesting products for our customers to sample.[22]

Plans called for ongoing development and introduction of new, one-of-a-kind food items at value prices, and continued expansion of store locations across the country.

Prices and product offerings varied somewhat by region and state. Customers could choose from a variety of baked goods, organic foods, fresh fruits and vegetables, imported and domestic cheeses, gourmet chocolates and candies, coffees, fresh salads, meatless entrées and other vegan products, low-fat and low-carbohydrate foods, frozen fish and seafood, heat-and-serve entrées, packaged meats, juices, wine and beer, snack foods, energy bars, vitamins, nuts and trail mixes, and whatever other exotic items the company's buyers had come upon. About 10–15 new, seasonal, or one-time-buy items were introduced each week. Products that weren't selling well were dropped. Trader Joe's had recently worked with its vendors to remove genetically modified ingredients from all of its private-label products. It had also discontinued sale of duck meat because of the cruel conditions under which ducks were grown.

Stores were open, with wide aisles, appealing displays, cedar plank walls, a nautical decor, and crew members wearing colorful Hawaiian shirts. Because of its combination of low prices, an emporium-like atmosphere, intriguing selections, and friendly service, customers viewed shopping at Trader Joe's as an enjoyable experience. The company was able to keep the prices of its unique products attractively low (relative to those at Whole Foods, Fresh Market, and Wild Oats) partly because its buyers were always on the lookout for exotic items they could buy at a discount (all products had to pass a taste test and a cost test) and partly because most items were sold under the Trader Joe's label.

Sunflower Farmers Markets

Sunflower Markets, out to establish a discount niche in organic and natural foods, entered the market in 2003 with four stores—two in Phoenix, one in Albuquerque, and one in Denver.[23] As of 2008, the company, based in Boulder, Colorado, had 14 stores in Arizona, Colorado, Nevada, and New Mexico and a distribution center in Phoenix. Sunflower's strategy borrowed from concepts employed by Trader Joe's and small farmer's-market-type stores. The company's mission statement described its four-pronged strategic approach:

- **We Will Always Offer the Best Quality Food at the Lowest Prices in Town.** "Better-than-supermarket quality at better-than-supermarket prices" is our motto.
- **We Keep Our Overhead Low.** No fancy fixtures or high rent. No corporate headquarters . . . just regular people, like you, looking for the best deals we can find.
- **We Buy Big.** We source directly, we pay our vendors quickly, and we buy almost everything by the pallet or truckload. That buying power means big savings for you!
- **We Keep It Simple.** We don't charge our vendors "slotting allowances" or shelf space fees. Just honest-to-goodness negotiating for the lowest possible price and we pass the savings on to you.

The company's tagline was "Serious Food . . . Silly Prices." According to founding partner Mark Gilliland, "The last thing we want to be is another wanna-be Whole Foods." Gilliland was formerly the founder and president of Wild Oats but was forced out when his aggressive expansion strategy put Wild Oats in a financial bind. Gilliland's ambitions for Sunflower were to have 50 locations in 2013 and become a company with annual sales of $500 million. In late 2007, Sunflower raised $30 million in equity financing from PCG Capital Partners to fund its store expansion initiative; plans called for opening about eight new locations annually.

Sunflower Farmers Market stores ranged from 25,000 to 27,000 square feet and had a warehouse-like atmosphere, with no customer service except for checkout personnel. Stores stocked about 5,000 different items, a number of which were one-of-a-kind products purchased in large lots from brokers. The product focus was on organic, natural, and minimally processed food items. Pallets of goods were placed wherever there was floor space available. Each store stocked fresh produce, meats and seafood, cereals, nutrition bars, health drinks, pastas, frozen meals, trail mixes, coffee, nuts, candy, salads, cheeses, breads, vitamins, supplements, natural remedies, medications, soaps, shampoos, and books. Some stores had food bars with live chefs. Each store had a weekly sales flyer, and Wednesdays were promoted as "Double Ad Day" because the previous week's ad prices also overlapped with the current weekly ad prices (which began on Wednesday); shoppers could thus find virtually twice the amount of items on sale throughout the store on Wednesdays. Stores also served the community by organizing activities, lectures, and events that emphasized the value of good nutrition and a healthy lifestyle.

Fresh & Easy Neighborhood Markets

In 2007, a new chain, Fresh & Easy Neighborhood Market, emerged as a competitor in the natural and organic segment of the retail grocery industry. Fresh & Easy was a newly established subsidiary of British supermarket giant Tesco, the world's third largest retailer (sales of £51.86 billion for fiscal year ending February 23, 2008, equivalent to about $95 billion). Tesco did extensive research on 60 American families and had numerous focus groups in California provide comments on store prototypes before opening its first 21 stores in Phoenix, followed quickly by an additional 38 stores in Las Vegas, San Diego, and Los Angeles. Some of the stores were located in low-income central-city neighborhoods, while others were adjacent to medium- and upper-income residential areas. Tesco's ambitious growth strategy called for opening Fresh & Easy locations at the rate of 3 per week, with 200 stores open by February 2009 and as many as 500 stores by 2011. The company opened an 820,000-square-foot distribution center (big enough to supply about 400 stores) in a Los Angeles suburb that was used both to create and package prepared foods and to supply area stores; a warehouse for northern California was being planned for when store expansion moved northward.

The Fresh & Easy concept called for stores to be in readily accessible neighborhood locations; have about 10,000 square feet of shopping space (about the size of an average Walgreen's); stock around 3,500 items (versus about 60,000 at a typical supermarket); and convey a theme of fresh, wholesome, and easy-to-prepare foods in a convenient and pleasant setting. Product offerings ranged from gourmet items to everyday staples and included natural and organic foods; fruits and vegetables; meats, fish, and poultry; and a selection of prepared foods and grab-and-go products—all intended to convey a theme of fresh, wholesome, and easy to prepare. About 45 percent of the products on the shelves were house-branded Fresh & Easy items—one of the biggest-selling private-label items was a $1.99 bottle of Fresh & Easy "Big Kahuna" Australian wine (an idea said to be an imitation of Trader Joe's "Two-Buck Chuck" wine offering).[24] Other key features of Fresh & Easy stores included:

- Low prices (around 20–25 percent below traditional supermarkets and on a par with the prices at Wal-Mart Supercenters).
- Locally sourced and mostly packaged fresh produce with expiration dates.
- Wide aisles and simple store layouts.
- Low shelves that allowed shoppers to see all across the store.
- All self-checkout.
- Energy-efficient store designs, lighting, and equipment (and the 820,000-square-foot distribution center had the largest solar panel roof in California).
- Most Fresh & Easy brand products, particularly prepared foods, were packaged so shoppers could see what was inside.
- A taste-before-you-buy policy where shoppers were encouraged to take almost any product to the "Kitchen Table" area of the store, where a staff person would open it or cook it and dole out samples.

However, in April 2008, top executives at Fresh & Easy announced that the company would put a three-month hold on further new store openings "to kick the tires, smooth out any wrinkles and make some improvements customers have asked for."[25] Management had already corrected a problem of stores frequently running out of certain items and responded to unexpectedly high demand for prepared foods by adding more than 100 new selections. A flyer campaign backed by the United Food and Commercial Workers Union (which represented workers at competing supermarket chains) had cast doubts about the freshness and safety of the meat and produce sold at Fresh & Easy stores (where the workforce was nonunion)—the flyers directed readers to a union-produced Web site with links to news articles detailing instances in Europe where Tesco supermarkets were found to be selling old or expired food products.

But there was also thought to be a more fundamental strategic issue about whether the Fresh & Easy concept of offering a limited selection of organic and natural foods at relatively cheap prices was really working. One analyst estimated that weekly sales at Fresh & Easy stores had only been about $170,000 instead of the projected $200,000.[26] A research report by another analyst was considerably more downbeat, suggesting that weekly sales could be averaging as little as $60,000.[27] Skeptics of the Fresh & Easy format believed that health-conscious food shoppers could find a far wider and more appealing selection at Whole Foods stores (and to a lesser extent at Trader Joe's), and the shopping ambience was far superior at both Whole Foods and Trader Joe's. Inexpensive packaged foods were commonplace at supermarkets and full-range superstores.

However, bullish observers saw the Fresh & Easy concept of trying to meld quality, low price, and convenience as a promising opportunity that could fill a big hole in the U.S. market. One very bullish retail analyst had gone out on a limb and projected that Fresh & Easy could have 5,000 U.S. stores and annual sales of $60 billion by 2020, making it one of the top 10 U.S. grocers.[28] And Tesco was widely viewed as a formidable retailer with ample resources to fine-tune Fresh & Easy's business concept and strategy and to eventually generate a return on its $700-million-plus investment in Fresh & Easy.

In commenting on the Fresh & Easy venture in the United States, Tesco CEO Sir Terry Leahy said, "Clearly, it is high risk. If it fails it's embarrassing. . . . If it succeeds then it's transformational."[29] In April 2008, Leahy announced that while Tesco expected to report losses of about $200 million in 2008 on its launch of Fresh & Easy stores in Arizona, California, and Nevada because of start-up expenses, sales were "ahead of budget" and the best-performing stores were exceeding $20 in sales per square foot per week—a typical new grocery store in the United States was said to average $9 to $10 in sales per square foot during the first year of operations.[30] He indicated that the company planned to have 200 Fresh & Easy stores open in the United States by mid-2009 and would begin releasing sales numbers for Fresh & Easy stores in September 2008.

Independent Natural and Health Food Grocers

In 2005, there were approximately 14,000 small, independent retailers of natural and organic foods, vitamins/supplements, and beauty and personal care products. Most were single-store, owner-managed enterprises serving small to medium-sized communities and particular neighborhoods in metropolitan areas. Combined sales of the 14,000 independents were in the $18 billion range in 2007. Two other vitamin/supplement chains, General Nutrition and Vitamin World, dominated the vitamin/supplement segment with about 7,500 store locations; vitamin/supplement chains were an alternative source for many of the products that Whole Foods stocked in the vitamin/supplement section of its stores. Most of the independent stores had less than 2,500 square feet of retail sales space and generated revenues of less than $1 million annually, but there were roughly 850 natural foods and organic retailers with store sizes exceeding 6,000 square feet and sales of between $1 million and $5 million annually.

Product lines and range of selection at the stores of independent natural and health foods retailers varied from narrow to moderately broad, depending on a store's market focus and the shopper traffic it was able to generate. Inventories at stores under 1,000 square feet could run as little as $10,000, while those at stores of 6,000 square feet or more often ranged from $400,000 to $1,200,000. Many of the independents had some sort of deli or beverage bar, and some even had a small dine-in area with a limited health food menu. Revenues and customer traffic at most independent stores were trending upward, reflecting growing buyer interest in natural and organic products. Most independent retailers had average annual sales per square foot of store space of $200 (for stores under 2,000 square feet) to as much as $470 (for stores greater than 6,000 square feet)—Whole Foods' average was over $850 per square foot in 2007 (excluding the newly acquired Wild Oats stores).[31]

Endnotes

[1] The careers section of www.wholefoodsmarket.com (accessed March 26, 2008).

[2] As quoted in Elizabeth Lee, "National Standards Now Define Organic Food," *Atlanta Journal and Constitution,* October 21, 2002.

[3] Economic Research Service, U.S. Department of Agriculture, data at www.ers.usda.gov (accessed March 25, 2008).

[4] Information posted at www.rodaleinstitute.org (accessed March 25, 2008).

[5] Company press release, November 18, 2005.

[6] John Mackey's letter to the shareholders in the company's 2007 annual report, November 2007.

[7] Company press release, February 19, 2008, p. 4.

[8] Letter to Shareholders, 2003 annual report.

[9] Prices cited in "Eating Too Fast at Whole Foods," *BusinessWeek,* October 24, 2005, p. 84.

[10] Hollie Shaw, "Retail-Savvy Whole Foods Opens in Canada," *National Post,* May 1, 2002, p. FP9.

[11] See Karin Schill Rives, "Texas-Based Whole Foods Market Makes Changes to Cary, N.C., Grocery Store," *News and Observer,* March 7, 2002.

[12] As quoted in Marilyn Much, "Whole Foods Markets: Austin, Texas Green Grocer Relishes Atypical Sales," *Investors Business Daily,* September 10, 2002.

[13] As quoted in "Whole Foods Market to Open in Albuquerque, N.M.," *Santa Fe New Mexican,* September 10, 2002.

[14] Company press release, January 21, 2003.

[15] EVA at the store level was based on store contribution (store revenues minus cost of goods sold minus store operating expenses) relative to store investment over and above the cost of capital.

[16] As quoted in John K. Wilson, "Going Whole Hog with Whole Foods," Bankrate.com, posted December 23, 1999. Mackey made the statement in 1991 when efforts were being made to unionize the company's store in Berkeley, California.

[17] Information contained in John R. Wells and Travis Haglock, "Whole Foods Market, Inc.," Harvard Business School case study 9-705-476.

[18] David Kesmodel and John. R. Wilke, "Whole Foods Is Hot, Wild Oats a Dud—So Said Rahodeb," *Wall Street Journal,* July 12, 2007, http://online.wsj.com/article/SB118418782959963745.html (accessed April 7,2008).

[19] Andrew Martin, "Whole Foods Executive Used Alias," *New York Times,* July 12, 2007, www.nytimes.com/2007/07/12/business/12foods.html (accessed April 7, 2008).

[20] Ibid.

[21] Company press release, October 5, 2007. According to a July 13, 2007, posting on a *BusinessWeek* message board, www.businessweek.com/careers/managementiq/archives/2007/07/who_advises_joh.html (accessed April 7, 2008).

[22] Information posted at www.traderjoes.com (accessed December 1, 2005).

[23] This section is based on information posted at www.sunflowermarkets.com and in Joe Lewandowski, "Naturals Stores Freshen Their Strategies," *Natural Foods Merchandiser,* January 1, 2004, www.naturalfoodsmerchandiser.com (accessed November 19, 2004).

[24] Matthew Boyle, "Tesco Needs a Fresh Start in the U.S.," *Fortune,* December 4, 2007, www.cnnmoney.com (accessed April 7, 2008).

[25] As quoted in Bruce Horovitz, "British Invasion Hits Grocery Stores," *USA Today,* April 7, 2008, p. B2.

[26] Ibid.

[27] Ibid.

[28] Ibid.

[29] As quoted in "Fresh, But Far from Easy," *Economist,* June 21, 2007, www.economist.com (accessed April 7, 2008).

[30] Company press release, April 15, 2008.

[31] *Natural Foods Merchandiser,* June 2004, p. 27.

CASE 2 Costco Wholesale in 2008: Mission, Business Model, and Strategy

Arthur A. Thompson
The University of Alabama

Jim Sinegal, cofounder and CEO of Costco Wholesale, was the driving force behind Costco's 25-year march to become the fourth largest retailer in the United States and the eighth largest in the world. He was far from the stereotypical CEO. A grandfatherly 71-year-old, Sinegal dressed casually and unpretentiously, often going to the office or touring Costco stores wearing an open-collared cotton shirt that came from a Costco bargain rack and sporting a standard employee name tag that only said "Jim." His informal dress, mustache, gray hair, and unimposing appearance made it easy for Costco shoppers to mistake him for a store clerk. He answered his own phone, once telling ABC News reporters, "If a customer's calling and they have a gripe, don't you think they kind of enjoy the fact that I picked up the phone and talked to them?"[1]

Sinegal spent much of his time touring Costco stores, using the company plane to fly from location to location and sometimes visiting as many as 8 to 10 stores daily (the record for a single day was 12). Treated like a celebrity when he appeared at a store (news that "Jim's in the store" spread quickly), Sinegal made a point of greeting store employees, observing, "The employees know that I want to say hello to them, because I like them. We have said from the very beginning: 'We're going to be a company that's on a first-name basis with everyone.'"[2] Employees genuinely seemed to like Sinegal. He talked quietly, in a commonsensical manner that suggested what he was saying was no big deal.[3] He came across as kind yet stern, but he was prone to display irritation when he disagreed sharply with what people were saying to him.

In touring a Costco store with the local store manager, Sinegal was very much the person in charge. He functioned as producer, director, and knowledgeable critic. He cut to the chase quickly, exhibiting intense attention to detail and pricing, wandering through store aisles firing a barrage of questions at store managers about sales volumes and stock levels of particular items, critiquing merchandising displays or the position of certain products in the stores, commenting on any aspect of store operations that caught his eye, and asking managers to do further research and get back to him with more information whenever he found their answers to his questions less than satisfying. It was readily apparent that Sinegal had tremendous merchandising savvy, that he demanded much of store managers and employees, and that his views about discount retailing set the tone for how the company operated. Knowledgeable observers regarded Jim Sinegal's merchandising know-how and expertise as being on a par with those of the legendary Sam Walton.

In 2008, Costco's sales totaled almost $71 billion at 544 warehouses in 40 states, Puerto Rico, Canada, the United Kingdom, Taiwan, Japan, Korea, and Mexico. More than 50 of Costco's warehouses generated sales exceeding $200 million annually, and 2 stores had sales exceeding $300 million. Sales per store averaged $130 million annually, about

75 percent more than the $75 million per store average at Sam's Club, Costco's chief competitor in the membership warehouse retail segment. In 2008, about 53.5 million individuals, 29.2 million households, and 5.6 million businesses had membership cards entitling them to shop at Costco, generating $1.5 billion in membership fees for Costco.

COMPANY BACKGROUND

The membership warehouse concept was pioneered by discount merchandising sage Sol Price, who opened the first Price Club in a converted airplane hangar on Morena Boulevard in San Diego, California, in 1976. While Price Club lost $750,000 in its first year of operation, in 1979 it earned a profit of $1 million and had 200,000 members, two stores, and 900 employees. Years earlier, Sol Price had experimented with discount retailing at a San Diego store called Fed-Mart; Jim Sinegal got his start in retailing there at the age of 18 loading mattresses for $1.25 an hour while attending San Diego Community College. When Sol Price sold Fed-Mart, Sinegal left with Price to help him start the San Diego Price Club store; within a few years, Sol Price's Price Club stores emerged as the unchallenged leader in member warehouse retailing, operating primarily on the West Coast.

Having originally conceived Price Club as a place where local small-business members could obtain needed merchandise at economical prices, Sol Price soon concluded that his fledgling operation could achieve far greater sales volumes and gain buying clout with suppliers by also granting membership to individuals—Price's decision to add individual memberships was the trigger that made deep-discount warehouse clubs a fast-growing business. When Sinegal was 26, Sol Price made him the manager of the original San Diego store, which had become unprofitable. Price saw that Sinegal had a special knack for discount retailing and for spotting what a store was doing wrong (usually either not being in the right merchandise categories or not selling items at the right price points)—the very things that Sol Price was good at and that were at the roots of Price Club's growing success in the marketplace. Sinegal soon got the San Diego store back into the black. Over the next several years, Sinegal continued to hone his talent for discount merchandising. He mirrored Sol Price's attention to detail and absorbed all the nuances and subtleties of his mentor's style of operating—constantly improving store operations, keeping operating costs and overhead low, stocking items that moved quickly, and charging ultra-low prices that kept customers coming back to shop. Deciding that he had mastered the tricks of running a successful membership warehouse business from Sol Price, Sinegal decided to leave Price Club and form his own warehouse club operation.

Sinegal joined with Seattle entrepreneur Jeff Brotman (now chairman of the board of directors) to found Costco. The first Costco store began operations in Seattle in 1983, the same year that Wal-Mart launched its warehouse membership format called Sam's Club. By the end of 1984, there were nine Costco stores in five states serving more than 200,000 members. In December 1985, Costco became a public company, selling shares to the public and raising additional capital for expansion. Costco became the first U.S. company ever to reach $1 billion in sales in less than six years. In October 1993, Costco merged with Price Club. Following the merger, Jim Sinegal became CEO, presiding over 206 PriceCostco locations, which in total generated $16 billion in annual sales. Jeff Brotman, who had functioned as Costco's chairman since the company's founding, became vice chairman of PriceCostco in 1993 and was elevated to chairman in December 1994. Brotman kept abreast of company operations but stayed in the background and concentrated on managing the company's $9 billion investment in real estate operations—in 2008, Costco owned the land and buildings for about 80 percent of its stores.

In January 1997, after the spin-off of most of its non-warehouse assets to Price Enterprises, Inc., PriceCostco changed its name to Costco Companies, Inc. When the company reincorporated from Delaware to Washington in August 1999, the name was changed to Costco Wholesale Corporation. The company's headquarters was in Issaquah, Washington, not far from Seattle.

Exhibit 1 contains a financial and operating summary for Costco for fiscal years 2000–2008.

Exhibit 1 Financial and Operating Summary, Costco Wholesale Corp., Fiscal Years 2000–2008 ($ in millions, except for per share data)

	Fiscal Years Ending on Sunday Closest to August 31				
Income Statement Data	2008	2007	2006	2005	2000
Net sales	$70,977	$63,088	$58,963	$51,862	$31,621
Membership fees	1,506	1,313	1,188	1,073	544
Total revenue	72,483	64,400	60,151	52,935	32,164
Operating expenses					
Merchandise costs	63,503	56,450	52,745	46,347	28,322
Selling, general, and administrative	6,954	6,273	5,732	5,044	2,755
Preopening expenses	57	55	43	53	42
Provision for impaired assets and store closing costs	0	14	5	16	7
Operating income	1,969	1,609	1,626	1,474	1,037
Other income (expense)					
Interest expense	(103)	(64)	(13)	(34)	(39)
Interest income and other	133	165	138	109	54
Income before income taxes	1,999	1,710	1,751	1,549	1,052
Provision for income taxes	716	627	648	486	421
Net income	$1,283	$1,083	$1,103	$1,063	$631
Diluted net income per share	$2.89	$2.37	$2.30	$2.18	$1.35
Dividends per share	$0.61	0.55	$0.49	0.43	0.00
Millions of shares used in per share calculations	444.2	457.6	480.3	492.0	475.7
Balance Sheet Data					
Cash and cash equivalents	$2,619	$2,780	$1,511	$2,063	$525
Merchandise inventories	5,039	4,879	4,561	4,015	2,490
Current assets	9,462	9,324	8,232	8,238	3,470
Current liabilities	8,874	8,582	7,819	6,761	3,404
Working capital	588	742	413	1,477	66
Net property and equipment	10,355	9,520	8,564	7,790	4,834
Total assets	20,692	19,607	17,495	16,514	8,634
Short-term borrowings	134	54	41	54	10
Long-term debt	2,206	2,108	215	711	790
Stockholders' equity	9,192	8,623	9,143	8,881	4,240
Cash Flow Data					
Net cash provided by operating activities	$1,827	$2,076	$1,831	$1,773	$1,070
Warehouses in Operation*					
Beginning of year	488	458	433	417	292
Opened	34	30	28	21	25
Closed	(10)	—	(3)	(5)	(4)
End of year	512	488	458	433	313
Primary Members at Year-End					
Businesses (000s)	5,600	5,400	5,214	5,050	4,358
Gold Star members (000s)	20,200	18,600	17,338	16,233	12,737

Note: Some totals may not add due to rounding.
*Data for warehouses in operation does not include the warehouses in Mexico operated in a joint venture.
Sources: Costco, company 10-K reports 2007, 2005, and 2000; and company press release, October 8, 2008.

COSTCO'S MISSION AND BUSINESS MODEL

Costco's mission in the membership warehouse business was "To continually provide our members with quality goods and services at the lowest possible prices." The company's business model was to generate high sales volumes and rapid inventory turnover by offering members very low prices on a limited selection of nationally branded and select private-label products in a wide range of merchandise categories. Management believed that rapid inventory turnover—when combined with the operating efficiencies achieved by volume purchasing, efficient distribution, and reduced handling of merchandise in no-frills, self-service warehouse facilities—enabled Costco to operate profitably at significantly lower gross margins than traditional wholesalers, mass merchandisers, supermarkets, and supercenters. Examples of the incredible volume that Costco generated included selling 110,000 carats of diamonds (2007), 40 million rotisserie chickens (2008), 40 percent of the Tuscan olive oil bought in the United States, 29 million prescriptions (2007), 150 million croissants (2007), 100 million pounds of ground beef (2007), 1 million pumpkin pies during Thanksgiving week (2007), annual gasoline sales of $4.6 billion (2007), and 1.5 million $1.50 hot dog/soda pop combinations per week; Costco was also the largest seller of fine wines in the world ($499 million out of total 2007 wine sales of $1.01 billion).[4] At one of Costco's largest-volume stores, which had annual sales of $285 million and 232,000 members, annual volume ran 283,000 rotisserie chickens, 375,000 gallons of milk, and 8.4 million rolls of toilet paper—this store had an average customer bill per trip of $150.[5]

Furthermore, Costco's high sales volume and rapid inventory turnover generally allowed it to sell and receive cash for inventory before it had to pay many of its merchandise vendors, even when vendor payments were made in time to take advantage of early-payment discounts. Thus, Costco was able to finance a big percentage of its merchandise inventory through the payment terms provided by vendors rather than by having to maintain sizable working capital (defined as current assets minus current liabilities) to facilitate timely payment of suppliers.

COSTCO'S STRATEGY

The cornerstones of Costco's strategy were low prices, a limited product line and limited selection, and a "treasure hunt" shopping environment.

Pricing

Costco was known for selling top-quality national and regional brands at prices consistently below traditional wholesale or retail outlets. The company stocked only those items that could be priced at bargain levels and provide members with significant cost savings; this was true even for items often requested by customers. A key element of Costco's strategy to keep prices low to members was to cap the margins on brand-name merchandise at 14 percent (compared to 20 to 50 percent margins at other discounters and many supermarkets). The margins on Costco's private-label Kirkland Signature items—which included juice, cookies, coffee, spices, tires, housewares, luggage, appliances, clothing, and detergent—were a maximum of 15 percent, but the fractionally higher markups on Costco's private-label items still resulted in the company's private-label prices being about 20 percent below comparable name-brand items. The specifications for Kirkland Signature products resulted in Costco's private-label offerings being of equal or better quality than national brands.

Costco's philosophy was to keep members coming in to shop by wowing them with low prices. Jim Sinegal explained the company's approach to pricing as follows:

> We always look to see how much of a gulf we can create between ourselves and the competition. So that the competitors eventually say, "These guys are crazy. We'll compete somewhere else." Some years ago, we were selling a hot brand of jeans for $29.99. They were $50 in a department store. We got a great deal on them and could have sold them for a higher price but we went down to $29.99. Why? We knew it would create a riot.[6]

At another time, he explained:

> We're very good merchants, and we offer value. The traditional retailer will say: "I'm selling this for $10. I wonder whether we can get $10.50 or $11." We say: "We are selling this for $9. How do we get it down to

> $8?" We understand that our members don't come and shop with us because of the window displays or the Santa Claus or the piano player. They come and shop with us because we offer great values.[7]

Indeed, Costco's markups and prices were so low that Wall Street analysts had criticized Costco management for going all out to please customers at the expense of the company's shareholders. One retailing analyst said, "They could probably get more money for a lot of the items they sell."[8] Sinegal was unimpressed with Wall Street's calls for Costco to abandon its ultra-low markups and pricing strategy, commenting, "Those people are in the business of making money between now and next Tuesday. We're trying to build an organization that's going to be here 50 years from now."[9] He went on to explain why Costco's approach to pricing would remain unaltered during his tenure:

> When I started, Sears, Roebuck was the Costco of the country, but they allowed someone else to come in under them. We don't want to be one of the casualties. We don't want to turn around and say, "We got so fancy we've raised our prices, and all of a sudden a new competitor comes in and beats our prices."[10]

Product Selection

Whereas typical supermarkets stocked about 40,000 items and a Wal-Mart Supercenter or SuperTarget might have as many as 150,000 items for shoppers to choose from, Costco's merchandising strategy was to provide members with a selection of only about 4,000 items.

Costco's product range did cover a broad spectrum—rotisserie chicken, prime steaks, caviar, flat-screen TVs, digital cameras, fresh flowers, fine wines, caskets, baby strollers, toys and games, musical instruments, ceiling fans, vacuum cleaners, books, DVDs, chandeliers, stainless-steel cookware, seat-cover kits for autos, prescription drugs, gasoline, and one-hour photo finishing—but it deliberately limited the selection in each product category to fast-selling models, sizes, and colors. Many consumable products like detergents, canned goods, office supplies, and soft drinks were sold only in big-container, case, carton, or multiple-pack quantities. For example, Costco stocked only a 325-count bottle of Advil—a size many shoppers might find too large for their needs; Sinegal explained the reason for the deliberately limited selection:

> If you had ten customers come in to buy Advil, how many are not going to buy any because you just have one size? Maybe one or two. We refer to that as the intelligent loss of sales. We are prepared to give up that one customer. But if we had four or five sizes of Advil, as most grocery stores do, it would make our business more difficult to manage. Our business can only succeed if we are efficient. You can't go on selling at these margins if you are not.[11]

The selections of appliances, equipment, and tools often included commercial and professional models because so many of Costco's members were small businesses. The approximate percentage of net sales accounted for by each major category of items stocked by Costco is shown in the following table:

	2007	2006	2005	2004	2003
Food (fresh produce, meats and fish, bakery and deli products, and dry and institutionally packaged foods)	31%	30%	30%	31%	30%
Sundries (candy, snack foods, tobacco, alcoholic and nonalcoholic beverages, and cleaning and institutional supplies)	23	24	25	25	26
Hard lines (major appliances, electronics, health and beauty aids, hardware, office supplies, garden and patio, sporting goods, furniture, cameras, and automotive supplies)	21	20	20	20	20
Soft lines (including apparel, domestics, jewelry, housewares, books, movie DVDs, video games and music, home furnishings, and small appliances)	11	12	12	13	14
Ancillary and other (gasoline, pharmacy, food court, optical, one-hour photo, hearing aids, and travel)	14	14	13	11	10

To encourage members to shop at Costco more frequently, the company operated ancillary businesses within or next to most Costco warehouses; the number of ancillary businesses at Costco warehouses is shown in the following table:

	2007	2006	2005	2004
Total number of warehouses	488	458	433	417
Warehouses having stores with:				
Food court and hot dog stands	482	452	427	412
One-hour photo centers	480	450	423	408
Optical dispensing centers	472	442	414	397
Pharmacies	429	401	374	359
Gas stations	279	250	225	211
Hearing aid centers	237	196	168	143
Print shops and copy centers	8	9	10	10

Treasure-Hunt Merchandising

About one-fourth of Costco's line of 4,000 products was constantly changing. Costco's merchandise buyers remained on the lookout to make one-time purchases of items that would appeal to the company's clientele and that would sell out quickly. A sizable number of these items were high-end or name-brand products that carried big price tags—like big-screen HDTVs selling for $1,000 to $2,500 or $800 leather sofas. The idea was to entice shoppers by offering irresistible deals on luxury items. According to Jim Sinegal, "Of that 4,000, about 3,000 can be found on the floor all the time. The other 1,000 are the treasure-hunt stuff that's always changing. It's the type of item a customer knows they better buy because it will not be there next time, like Waterford crystal. We try to get that sense of urgency in our customers."[12] In many cases, Costco did not obtain its luxury offerings directly from high-end manufacturers like Calvin Klein or Waterford (who were unlikely to want their merchandise marketed at deep discounts at places like Costco); rather, Costco buyers searched for opportunities to source such items legally on the gray market from other wholesalers or distressed retailers looking to get rid of excess or slow-selling inventory. Examples of treasure-hunt specials included $800 espresso machines, expensive jewelry and diamond rings (with price tags of $50,000 to as high as $250,000), Italian-made Hathaway shirts priced at $29.99, Movado watches, exotic cheeses, Coach bags, $5,000 necklaces, cashmere sport coats, $1,500 digital pianos, and Dom Perignon champagne.

Marketing and Advertising

Costco's low prices and its reputation for making shopping at Costco something of a treasure hunt made it unnecessary to engage in extensive advertising or sales campaigns. Marketing and promotional activities were generally limited to special campaigns for new warehouse openings, occasional direct mail marketing to prospective new members, and regular direct mail programs promoting selected merchandise to existing members. The company's primary direct mail program for members was "The Costco Connection," a multipage mailout that contained a host of savings coupons for featured specials. For new warehouse openings, marketing teams personally contacted businesses in the area that were potential wholesale members; these contacts were supplemented with direct mailings during the period immediately prior to opening. Potential Gold Star (individual) members were contacted by direct mail or by promoting membership offerings at local employee associations and businesses with large numbers of employees. After a membership base was established in an area, most new memberships came from word of mouth (existing members telling friends and acquaintances about their shopping experiences at Costco), follow-up messages distributed through regular payroll or other organizational communications to employee groups, and ongoing direct solicitations to prospective Business and Gold Star members. Management believed that its emphasis on direct mail advertising kept its marketing expenses low relative to those at typical retailers, discounters, and supermarkets.

Growth Strategy

Costco's strategy to grow sales and profits had three main elements: open more new warehouses, build an ever larger and fiercely loyal membership base, and employ well-executed merchandising techniques to induce members to shop at Costco more often and purchase more per shopping trip. Costco opened 127 new warehouses in fiscal years 2005–2008; management planned to open another 20–24 by the end of fiscal 2009. Most were in the United States, where efforts were focused on entering cities and states where Costco did not yet have a warehouse (as of 2008 there were no Costco stores in 10 states) and opening additional warehouses in metropolitan areas big enough to support two or more Costco locations. Expansion was under way internationally as well. As of October 2008, Costco had a total of 102 wholly owned warehouses outside the United States, including 76 in Canada, 20 in the United Kingdom, 8 in Japan, 6 in Korea, and 5 in Taiwan. Costco was a 50-50 partner in a venture to operate 31 Costco warehouses in Mexico. Exhibit 2 shows a breakdown of Costco's geographic operations for fiscal years 2005–2008—the data in the Exhibit 2 presentation do not include the 31 warehouses in Mexico because the 50-50 venture in Mexico was accounted for using the equity method.

Costco had opened two freestanding high-end furniture warehouse businesses called Costco Home in 2004. Sales in 2005 at these two locations increased 132 percent over 2004 levels, and profits were up significantly. Since 2004, rather than open additional Costco Home stores, management had opted to experiment with adding about 45,000 square feet to the size of selected new Costco stores and using the extra space to stock a much bigger selection of furniture—furniture was one of the top three best-selling categories at Costco's Web site.

Costco's strategy to attract more members and entice members to do a bigger percentage of their shopping at Costco had three components:

- Give members a place to buy supplies of practical, frequently used business and household items at money-saving prices. A recent initiative that management believed would spur sales was to expand the offerings of Kirkland Signature private-label items from some 400 items in 2005 to as many as 600 items by 2009.
- Make shopping at Costco interesting and rewarding because of opportunities to purchase an ever-changing array of big-ticket items and indulgences at rock-bottom prices—in this regard, it was important that members be able to spot appealing new items on the sales floor each time they shopped at Costco. Costco buyers constantly scanned the manufacturing landscape, looking for one-time opportunities to buy items that would appeal to bargain-hunting members. And warehouse personnel diligently tried to do an effective job of displaying and merchandising the special buys on the sales floor.
- Acclimate members to the merits of visiting Costco weekly or bimonthly so as to not miss out on the special one-time-only merchandise selections that typically sold out in a matter of days.

Web Site Sales

Costco operated two Web sites—www.costco.com in the United States and www.costco.ca in Canada—both to provide another shopping alternative for members and to provide members with a way to purchase products and services that might not be available at the warehouse where they customarily shopped, especially such services as digital photo processing, prescription drugs and pharmacy products, and travel and other membership services. At Costco's online photo center, customers could upload images and pick up the prints at their local warehouse in little over an hour. Costco's e-commerce sales totaled $1.2 billion in fiscal 2007, up from $534 million in fiscal 2005 and $376 million in fiscal 2004.

WAREHOUSE OPERATIONS

In Costco's 2005 annual report, Jim Sinegal summed up the company's approach to operations as follows:

> Costco is able to offer lower prices and better values by eliminating virtually all the frills and costs historically associated with conventional wholesalers and retailers, including salespeople, fancy buildings, delivery, billing, and accounts receivable. We run a tight operation with extremely low overhead which enables us to pass on dramatic savings to our members.

Costco warehouses ranged in size from 70,000 to 205,000 square feet; the average size was 141,000

Exhibit 2 Geographic Operating Data, Costco Wholesale Corporation, Fiscal Years 2005–2008 ($ in millions)

	United	Canadian	Other	Total
Year Ended August 31, 2008				
Total revenue (including membership fees)	$56,903	$10,528	$5,052	$72,483
Operating income	1,393	420	156	1,969
Depreciation and amortization	511	92	50	653
Capital expenditures	1,190	246	163	1,599
Property and equipment	8,016	1,371	968	10,355
Total assets	16,345	2,477	1,860	20,682
Net assets	6,882	1,292	1,018	9,192
Number of warehouses	398	75	39*	512
Year Ended September 2, 2007				
Total revenue (including membership fees)	$51,532	$8,724	$4,144	$64,400
Operating income	1,217	287	105	1,609
Depreciation and amortization	449	73	44	566
Capital expenditures	1,104	207	74	1,386
Property and equipment	7,357	1,237	926	8,564
Total assets	15,543	2,279	1,784	19,607
Net assets	6,417	1,158	1,048	8,623
Number of warehouses	383	71	34*	488
Year Ended September 3, 2006				
Total revenue (including membership fees)	$48,466	$8,122	$3,564	$60,151
Operating income	1,246	293	87	1,626
Depreciation and amortization	413	61	41	515
Capital expenditures	934	188	90	1,213
Property and equipment	6,676	1,032	855	8,564
Total assets	14,009	1,914	1,572	17,495
Net assets	7,190	1,043	910	9,143
Number of warehouses	358	68	32*	458
Year Ended August 28, 2005				
Total revenue (including membership fees)	$43,064	$6,732	$3,155	$52,952
Operating income	1,168	242	65	1,474
Depreciation and amortization	389	51	42	482
Capital expenditures	734	140	122	995
Property and equipment	6,171	834	786	7,790
Total assets	13,203	2,034	1,428	16,665
Net assets	6,769	1,285	827	8,881
Number of warehouses	338	65	30*	433

*Does not include warehouses in Mexico operated under a joint venture.

Source: Costco, company 10-K reports, 2008 and 2007.

square feet. Newer units were usually in the range of 150,000 to 205,000 square feet. Because shoppers were attracted principally by Costco's low prices, its warehouses were rarely located on prime commercial real estate sites. Most warehouses were of a metal preengineered design, with concrete floors and minimal interior decor. Floor plans were designed for economy and efficiency in use of selling space, the handling of merchandise, and the control of inventory. Merchandise was generally stored on racks above the sales floor and displayed on pallets containing large quantities of each item, thereby reducing labor required for handling and stocking. In-store signage was done mostly on laser printers; there were no shopping bags at the checkout counter—merchandise was put directly into the shopping cart or sometimes loaded into empty boxes. Scenes of Costco's warehouses are shown in Exhibit 3.

Warehouses generally operated on a seven-day, 69-hour week, typically being open between 10:00 a.m. and 8:30 p.m. weekdays, with earlier closing hours on the weekend; the gasoline operations outside many stores usually had extended hours. The shorter hours of operation as compared to those of traditional retailers, discount retailers, and supermarkets resulted in lower labor costs relative to the volume of sales.

Warehouse managers were delegated considerable authority over store operations. In effect, warehouse managers functioned as entrepreneurs running their own retail operation. They were responsible for coming up with new ideas about what items would sell in their stores, effectively merchandising the ever-changing lineup of treasure-hunt products, and orchestrating in-store product locations and displays to maximize sales and quick turnover. In experimenting with what items to stock and what in-store merchandising techniques to employ, warehouse managers had to know the clientele that patronized their locations—for instance, big-ticket diamonds sold well at some warehouses but not others. Costco's best managers kept their finger on the pulse of the members who shopped their warehouse location to stay in sync with what would sell well, and they had a flair for creating a certain element of excitement, hum, and buzz in their warehouses that spurred above-average sales volumes (sales at Costco's top-volume warehouses often exceeded $5 million a week, with sales topping $1 million on many days). Successful managers also thrived on the rat race of running a high-traffic store and solving the inevitable crises of the moment.

Costco bought the majority of its merchandise directly from manufacturers, routing it either directly to its warehouse stores or to one of nine cross-docking depots that served as distribution points for nearby stores. Depots received container-based shipments from manufacturers and reallocated these goods for combined shipment to individual warehouses, generally in less than 24 hours. This maximized freight volume and handling efficiencies. When merchandise arrived at a warehouse, it was moved directly onto the sales floor; very little was stored in locations off the sales floor, thereby lowering receiving costs by eliminating many of the costs associated with multiple-step handling of merchandise, such as purchasing from distributors as opposed to manufacturers, use of central receiving, operating regional distribution centers for inventory storage and distribution of merchandise to nearby stores, and having storage areas at retail sites where merchandise could be held in reserve off the sales floor.

Costco had direct buying relationships with many producers of national brand-name merchandise (including Canon, Casio, Coca-Cola, Colgate-Palmolive, Dell, Fuji, Hewlett-Packard, Kimberly-Clark, Kodak, Levi's, Michelin, Nestlé, Panasonic, Procter & Gamble, Samsung, Sony, Kitchen Aid, and Jones of New York) and with manufacturers that supplied its Kirkland Signature private-label products. No one manufacturer supplied a significant percentage of the merchandise that Costco stocked. Costco had not experienced any difficulty in obtaining sufficient quantities of merchandise, and management believed that if one or more of its current sources of supply became unavailable, the company could switch its purchases to alternative manufacturers without experiencing a substantial disruption of its business.

Costco warehouses accepted cash, checks, most debit cards, American Express, and a private-label Costco credit card. Costco accepted merchandise returns when members were dissatisfied with their purchases. Losses associated with dishonored checks were minimal because any member who wrote a bad check was thereafter prevented from paying by check or cashing checks at the point of sale until he or she made restitution. The membership format facilitated strict control over warehouse entrances and exits, resulting in inventory losses of less than two-tenths of 1 percent of net sales—well below those of other retail discounters.

Exhibit 3 Scenes from Costco's Warehouses

Source: Costco management presentation, May 29, 2008.

COSTCO'S MEMBERSHIP BASE AND MEMBER DEMOGRAPHICS

Costco attracted the most affluent customers in discount retailing—the average income of individual members was about $75,000, with over 30 percent having incomes of $100,000 or more annually. Many members were affluent urbanites, living in nice neighborhoods not far from Costco warehouses. One loyal Executive member, a criminal defense lawyer, said, "I think I spend over $20,000–$25,000 a year buying all my products here from food to clothing—except my suits. I have to buy them at the Armani stores."[13] Another Costco loyalist said, "This is the best place in the world. It's like going to church on Sunday. You can't get anything better than this. This is a religious experience."[14]

Costco had two primary types of memberships: Business and Gold Star. Gold Star memberships were for individuals who did not qualify for a Business membership. Small-business owners—including individuals with a business license, retail sales license, or other evidence of business existence—qualified as Business members. Business members generally paid an annual membership fee of $50 for the primary and spouse membership card and could purchase add-on membership cards for an annual fee of $40 each for partners or business employees (these add-ons also included a spouse card). A significant number of Business members also shopped at Costco for their personal needs.

Gold Star members generally paid an annual fee of $50, which included a spouse card. In addition, all members in the United States and Canada could upgrade to an Executive membership for an annual fee of $100; Executive members qualified for 2 percent additional savings on qualified purchases at Costco (redeemable at Costco warehouses), up to a maximum rebate of $500 per year. The Executive membership program also offered members savings and benefits on various business and consumer services offered by Costco, including merchant credit card processing, small-business loans, auto and home insurance, long-distance telephone service, check printing, and real estate and mortgage services; these services were mostly offered by third-party providers and varied by state. In 2008, Executive members represented 23 percent of Costco's primary membership base and generated over 40 percent of consolidated net sales.

As of September 2008, Costco had 53.5 million cardholders:

Gold Star members (including Executive members)	20,200,000
Business members	5,600,000
Total primary cardholders	25,800,000
Add-on cardholders	27,700,000
Total cardholders	53,500,000

Recent trends in membership are shown at bottom of Exhibit 1. Members could shop at any Costco warehouse; member renewal rates were about 87 percent.

COMPENSATION AND WORKFORCE PRACTICES

In September 2008, Costco had 70,000 full-time employees and 57,000 part-time employees worldwide, including approximately 9,000 people employed by Costco Mexico, whose operations were not consolidated in Costco's financial and operating results. Approximately 13,900 hourly employees at locations in California, Maryland, New Jersey, New York and one warehouse in Virginia were represented by the International Brotherhood of Teamsters. All remaining employees were non-union.

Starting wages for new Costco employees were in the range of $10.50 to $11.00 per hour in 2008. Depending on the job classification, the median pay scales for Costco employees with five or more years of experience were in the range of $17 to $21 per hour.[15] Warehouse employees received time-and-a-half pay for working on Sundays and were paid double time in the event they were called on to work more than 12 hours in a given shift. Median salaries for managerial positions at Costco warehouses were in the range of $55,000 to $75,000.[16]

Employees received biannual bonuses and a full spectrum of benefits. Salaried employees were eligible for benefits on the first of the month after the date of hire. Full-time hourly employees were eligible for benefits on the first of the month after working a probationary 90 days; part-time hourly employees became benefit-eligible on the first of the month after working 180 days. The benefit package included the following:

- Health and dental care plans. Full-time employees could choose from among a freedom-of-choice health care plan, a managed-choice health care plan, and two dental plans. A managed-choice health care plan and a core dental plan were available for part-time employees. The company paid about 90 percent of an employee's premiums for health care (far above the more normal 50 percent contributions at many other retailers), but employees did have to pick up the premiums for coverage for family members.
- Convenient prescription pickup at Costco's pharmacies, with co-payments as low as $5 for generic drugs and generally no more than $15 for the most expensive branded drugs.
- A vision program that paid $45 for an optical exam (the amount charged at Costco's optical centers) and generous allowances for the purchase of glasses and contact lenses.
- A 401(k) plan in which Costco matched hourly employee contributions 50 cents on the dollar for the first $1,000 annually (giving a maximum company match of $500 per year). Eligible employees qualified for additional company contributions based on the employee's years of service and eligible earnings. The company's union employees on the West Coast qualified for matching contributions of 50 cents on the dollar to a maximum company match of $250 a year; eligible union employees qualified for additional company contributions based on straight-time hours worked. Company contributions for salaried workers ran about 3 percent of salary during the second tear of employment and could be as high as 9 percent of salary after 25 years. Company contributions to employee 410(k) plans were $238.8 million in fiscal 2007, $233.6 million in fiscal 2006, $191.6 million in fiscal 2005, and $169.7 million in fiscal 2004.
- A dependent care reimbursement plan in which Costco employees whose families qualified could pay for day care for children under 13 or adult day care with pretax dollars and realize savings from $750 to $2,000 per year.
- Confidential professional counseling services.
- Company-paid long-term disability coverage equal to 60 percent of earnings out for more than 180 days on a non–worker's compensation leave of absence.
- All employees who passed their 90-day probation period and were working at least 10 hours per week were automatically enrolled in a short-term disability plan covering non-work-related injuries or illnesses for up to 26 weeks. Weekly short-term disability payments equaled 60 percent of average weekly wages up to a maximum of $1,000 and were tax free.
- Generous life insurance and accidental death and dismemberment coverage, with benefits based on years of service and whether the employee worked full-time or part-time. Employees could elect to purchase supplemental coverage for themselves, their spouses, or their children.
- An employee stock purchase plan allowing all employees to buy Costco stock via payroll deduction and avoid commissions and fees.
- A health care reimbursement plan in which benefit eligible employees could arrange to have pretax money automatically deducted from their paychecks and deposited in a health care reimbursement account that could be used to pay medical and dental bills.
- A long-term care insurance plan for employees with 10 or more years of service; eligible employees could purchase a basic or supplemental policy for nursing home care for themselves, their spouses, or their parents (including in-laws) or grandparents (including in-laws).

Although admitting that paying good wages and good benefits was contrary to conventional wisdom in discount retailing, Jim Sinegal was convinced that having a well-compensated workforce was very important to executing Costco's strategy successfully. He said, "Imagine that you have 120,000 loyal ambassadors out there who are constantly saying good things about Costco. It has to be a significant advantage for you. . . . Paying good wages and keeping your people working with you is very good business."[17] When a reporter asked him about why Costco treated its workers so well compared to other retailers (particularly Wal-Mart, which paid lower wages and had a skimpier benefits package), Sinegal replied: "Why shouldn't employees have the right to good wages and good careers? . . . It absolutely makes good business sense. Most people agree that we're the lowest-cost producer. Yet we pay the highest wages. So it must mean we get better productivity. It's axiomatic in our business—you get what you pay for."[18] In 2007, Sinegal announced his support for raising the minimum wage from $5.15 an hour to $7.25, saying, "The more people make, the better lives they are going to have and the better consumers they're going to be."[19]

About 85 percent of Costco's employees had signed up for health insurance, versus about 50 percent at Wal-Mart and Target. The Teamster's Union's chief negotiator with Costco said, "They gave us the best agreement of any retailer in the country."[20] Good wages and benefits were said to be why employee turnover at Costco ran under 6 percent after the first year of employment. Some Costco employees had been with the company since its founding in 1983. Many others had started working part-time at Costco while in high school or college and opted to make a career at the company. One Costco employee told an ABC *20/20* reporter, "It's a good place to work; they take good care of us."[21] A Costco vice president and head baker said that working for Costco was a family affair: "My whole family works for Costco, my husband does, my daughter does, my new son-in-law does."[22] Another employee, a receiving clerk who made about $40,000 a year, said, "I want to retire here. I love it here."[23] An employee with more than two years of service could not be fired without the approval of a senior company officer.

Selecting People for Open Positions

Top management wanted employees to feel that they could have a long-term career at Costco. It was company policy to fill at least 86 percent of its higher-level openings by promotions from within; in actuality, the percentage ran close to 98 percent, which meant that the majority of Costco's management team members (including warehouse, merchandise, administrative, membership, front-end, and receiving managers) were "home grown." Many of the company's vice presidents had started in entry-level jobs; according to Jim Sinegal, "We have guys who started pushing shopping carts out on the parking lot for us who are now vice presidents of our company."[24] Costco made a point of recruiting at local universities; Sinegal explained why: "These people are smarter than the average person, hardworking, and they haven't made a career choice."[25] On another occasion, he said, "If someone came to us and said he just got a master's in business at Harvard, we would say fine, would you like to start pushing carts?"[26] Those employees who demonstrated smarts and strong people management skills moved up through the ranks.

But without an aptitude for the details of discount retailing, even up-and-coming employees stood no chance of being promoted to a position of warehouse manager. Sinegal and other top Costco executives who oversaw warehouse operations insisted that candidates for warehouse managers be top-notch merchandisers with a gift for the details of making items fly off the shelves; Sinegal said, "People who have a feel for it just start to get it. Others, you look at them and it's like staring at a blank canvas. I'm not trying to be unduly harsh, but that's the way it works."[27] Most newly appointed warehouse managers at Costco came from the ranks of assistant warehouse managers who had a track record of being shrewd merchandisers and tuned into what new or different products might sell well given the clientele that patronized their particular warehouse—just having the requisite skills in people management, crisis management, and cost-effective warehouse operations was not enough.

Executive Compensation

Executives at Costco did not earn the outlandish salaries that had become customary over the past decade at most large corporations. In fiscal 2007, both Jeff Brotman and Jim Sinegal were paid identical salaries of $350,000 and earned bonuses of $80,000 each (versus identical salaries of $350,000 and bonuses of $200,000 in fiscal 2004). As of late 2007, Brotman owned about 1.6 million shares of Costco stock (worth about $112 million as of December 2007) and had been awarded options to purchase an additional 1.12 million shares; Sinegal owned 2.4 million shares of Costco stock (worth about $168 million as of December 2007) and had also been awarded options for an additional 1.12 million shares. The best-paid senior executives at Costco were paid 2007 salaries in the range of $500,000 to $550,000 and bonuses of $30,000 to $50,000. Sinegal explained why executive compensation at Costco was only a fraction of the millions paid to top-level executives at other corporations with sales of $50 billion or more: "I figured that if I was making something like 12 times more than the typical person working on the floor, that that was a fair salary."[28] To another reporter, he said: "Listen, I'm one of the founders of this business. I've been very well rewarded. I don't require a salary that's 100 times more than the people who work on the sales floor."[29] Sinegal's employment contract was only one page long and provided that he could be terminated for cause.

COSTCO'S BUSINESS PHILOSOPHY, VALUES, AND CODE OF ETHICS

Jim Sinegal, who was the son of a steelworker, had ingrained five simple and down-to-earth business principles into Costco's corporate culture and the manner in which the company operated. The following are excerpts of these principles and operating approaches:

1. **Obey the law**—The law is irrefutable! Absent a moral imperative to challenge a law, we must conduct our business in total compliance with the laws of every community where we do business. We pledge to:

- Comply with all laws and other legal requirements.
- Respect all public officials and their positions.
- Comply with safety and security standards for all products sold.
- Exceed ecological standards required in every community where we do business.
- Comply with all applicable wage and hour laws.
- Comply with all applicable anti-trust laws.
- Conduct business in and with foreign countries in a manner that is legal and proper under United States and foreign laws.
- Not offer, give, ask for, or receive any form of bribe or kickback to or from any person or pay to expedite government action or otherwise act in violation of the Foreign Corrupt Practices Act.
- Promote fair, accurate, timely, and understandable disclosure in reports filed with the Securities and Exchange Commission and in other public communications by the Company.

2. **Take care of our members**—Costco membership is open to business owners, as well as individuals. Our members are our reason for being—the key to our success. If we don't keep our members happy, little else that we do will make a difference. There are plenty of shopping alternatives for our members and if they fail to show up, we cannot survive. Our members have extended a trust to Costco by virtue of paying a fee to shop with us. We will succeed only if we do not violate the trust they have extended to us, and that trust extends to every area of our business. We pledge to:

- Provide top-quality products at the best prices in the market.
- Provide high quality, safe and wholesome food products by requiring that both vendors and employees be in compliance with the highest food safety standards in the industry.
- Provide our members with a 100% satisfaction guaranteed warranty on every product and service we sell, including their membership fee.
- Assure our members that every product we sell is authentic in make and in representation of performance.
- Make our shopping environment a pleasant experience by making our members feel welcome as our guests.
- Provide products to our members that will be ecologically sensitive.
- Provide our members with the best customer service in the retail industry.
- Give back to our communities through employee volunteerism and employee and corporate contributions to United Way and Children's Hospitals.

3. **Take care of our employees**—Our employees are our most important asset. We believe we have the very best employees in the warehouse club industry, and we are committed to providing them with rewarding challenges and ample opportunities for personal and career growth. We pledge to provide our employees with:

- Competitive wages.
- Great benefits.
- A safe and healthy work environment.
- Challenging and fun work.
- Career opportunities.
- An atmosphere free from harassment or discrimination.

- An Open Door Policy that allows access to ascending levels of management to resolve issues.
- Opportunities to give back to their communities through volunteerism and fundraising.

4. **Respect our suppliers**—Our suppliers are our partners in business and for us to prosper as a company, they must prosper with us. To that end, we strive to:

- Treat all suppliers and their representatives as you would expect to be treated if visiting their places of business.
- Honor all commitments.
- Protect all suppliers' property assigned to Costco as though it were our own.
- Not accept gratuities of any kind from a supplier.
- Avoid actual or apparent conflicts of interest, including creating a business in competition with the Company or working for or on behalf of another employer in competition with the Company.

If we do these four things throughout our organization, then we will achieve our ultimate goal, which is to:

5. **Reward our shareholders**—As a company with stock that is traded publicly on the NASDAQ stock exchange, our shareholders are our business partners. We can only be successful so long as we are providing them with a good return on the money they invest in our company. . . . We pledge to operate our company in such a way that our present and future stockholders, as well as our employees, will be rewarded for our efforts.

COMPETITION

The wholesale club and warehouse segment of retailing in 2008 was estimated to be a $120 billion business in the United States, and it was growing about 20 percent faster than retailing as a whole. There were 1,200-plus warehouse locations across the United States and Canada; most every major metropolitan area had one, if not several, warehouse club operations. The three main competitors were Costco Wholesale, Sam's Club (713 warehouses in six countries—the United States, Canada, Brazil, Mexico, China, and Puerto Rico), and BJ's Wholesale (177 locations in 16 states). Costco had close to a 53 percent share of warehouse club sales across the United States and Canada, with Sam's Club (a division of Wal-Mart) having roughly a 37 percent share and BJ's Wholesale and several small warehouse club competitors about a 10 percent share. Exhibit 4 shows selected financial and operating data for Sam's Club and BJ's Wholesale.

Competition among the warehouse clubs was based on such factors as price, merchandise quality and selection, warehouse location, and member service. However, warehouse clubs also competed with other types of retailers, including discounters like Wal-Mart and Dollar General, supermarkets, general merchandise chains like Target and Kohl's, gasoline stations, Internet retailers, and low-cost operators selling a single category or narrow range of merchandise, such as The Home Depot, Lowe's, Office Depot, Staples, Best Buy, Trader Joe's, PetSmart, and Barnes & Noble.

Sam's Club

In 2008, Sam's Club had 713 warehouse locations and more than 47 million members. Wal-Mart Stores opened the first Sam's Club in 1984, and management had pursued rapid expansion of the membership club format over the next 24 years, creating a chain of 591 U.S. locations in 48 states and 122 international locations in Brazil, Canada, China, Mexico, and Puerto Rico as of 2007. Many Sam's Club locations were adjacent to Wal-Mart Supercenters. The concept of the Sam's Club format was to sell merchandise at very low profit margins, resulting in low prices to members.

The sizes of Sam's Clubs ranged between 70,000 and 190,000 square feet, with the average being about 132,000 square feet. All warehouses had concrete floors; sparse decor; and goods displayed on pallets, simple wooden shelving, or racks in the case of apparel. Sam's Club stocked brand-name merchandise, including hard goods, some soft goods, institutional-size grocery items, and select private-label items sold under the Member's Mark, Bakers & Chefs, and Sam's Club brands. Generally, each Sam's Club also carried software, electronics, jewelry, sporting goods, toys, tires and batteries, stationery and books—and most clubs had fresh foods departments that included bakery, meat, produce, floral products, and a Sam's Cafe. A significant number of clubs had a one-hour photo-processing department, a pharmacy that filled prescriptions, an optical department, and self-service gasoline pumps.

Exhibit 4 Selected Financial and Operating Data for Sam's Club and BJ's Wholesale Club, 2000–2007

	2007	2006	2005	2000
Sam's Club [a]				
U.S. sales [c] (millions of $)	$44,357	$41,582	$39,798	$26,798
Operating income (millions of $)	1,618	1,480	1,407	942
Assets (millions of $)	11,722	11,448	10,588	3,843
Number of locations at year-end	713	693	670	564
U.S.	591	579	567	475
International	122	114	103	64
Average sales per U.S. location (millions of $)	$75.1	$71.8	$70.2	$56.8
Average warehouse size (square feet)	132,000	132,000	129,400	122,100
BJ's Wholesale [b]				
Net sales (millions of $)	$8,815	$8,303	$7,784	$4,767
Membership fees and other (millions of $)	190	177	166	102
Total revenues (millions of $)	9,905	8,480	7,950	4,869
Selling, general, and administrative expenses (millions of $)	694	705	611	335
Operating income (millions of $)	195	144	215	209
Net income (millions of $)	123	72	129	132
Total assets (millions of $)	2,047	1,993	1,990	1,234
Number of clubs at year-end	177	172	165	118
Number of members (000s)	8,800	8,700	8,619	6,596
Average sales per location (millions of $)	$49.8	$48.3	$47.2	$40.4

[a]Fiscal years end in January 31; data for 2007 are for the year ending January 31, 2008; data for 2006 are for the year ending January 31, 2007; data for 2005 are for year ending January 31, 2006; and so on.
[b]Fiscal years ending on last Saturday of January; data for 2007 are for year ending February 2, 2008; data for 2006 are for year ending February 3, 2007; data for 2005 are for year ending January 28, 2006; and so on.
[c]For financial reporting purposes, Wal-Mart consolidates the operations of all foreign-based stores into a single "international" segment figure; thus, financial information for foreign-based Sam's Club locations is not separately available.

Members could shop for a broad assortment of merchandise and services online at www.samsclub.com.

Like Costco Wholesale, Sam's Club stocked about 4,000 items, a big fraction of which were standard and a small fraction of which represented special buys and one-time offerings. The treasure-hunt items at Sam's tended to be less upscale than those at Costco. The reported percentage composition of sales at Sam's Club was as follows:

	2007	2006	2005	2004
Food	28%	32%	30%	31%
Sundries	37	36	31	31
Hard goods	18	19	23	23
Soft goods	5	5	5	6
Service businesses	12%	11%	11%	9%

In 2006–2008, Sam's Club launched a series of initiatives to grow its sales and market share:

- *Adding new lines of merchandise, with more emphasis on products for the home as opposed to small businesses.* In particular, Sam's had put more emphasis on furniture, flat-screen TVs and other electronics products, jewelry, and select other big-ticket items. The 2007 spring catalog included a 36-foot Windsor Craft yacht for $495,000, a trip for four persons to the Kentucky Derby for $89,000, and an Italian Getaway to a private villa for $54,000. A larger jewelry collection was added for the 2008 holiday season; offerings included an Asscher cut diamond ring for $347,000 and square emerald drop earrings for $210,000.
- *Instituting new payment methods.* Starting November 10, 2006, Sam's began accepting payment via MasterCard credit cards; prior to

then, payment was limited to cash, check, Discover credit cards, and debit cards. Early results with MasterCard were favorable; company officials reported that in the week following the MasterCard acceptance, the average ticket checkout at Sam's was up 35 percent.

- *Running ads on national TV.* Sam's spent about $50 million annually on advertising and direct mail promotions. Although the bulk of advertising expenditures at Sam's Club was for direct mail, during the 2006 holiday season, Sam's ran national TV ads on high-profile TV programs like *Deal or No Deal,* NBC's coverage of the Macy's Thanksgiving Day Parade, and an NFL game on Thanksgiving Day. In 2008, to celebrate its 25th anniversary, Sam's Club ran ads on TV and in newspapers announcing a weekend open-house in April that allowed nonmembers to shop at Sam's without paying the usual 10 percent surcharge on purchases and members to buy in bulk at special discount prices.
- *Adding a collegiate membership.* In 2008, Sam's announced that college students with a valid college ID and collegiate e-mail address could obtain a year-long, Sam's Club Collegiate Membership for $40 and receive a $15 gift card to help offset the cost of their first purchase. Each Collegiate Membership came with a complimentary add-on card so roommates or housemates could share with shopping duties and enjoy the savings.
- *Launching a holiday catering program.* In 2008, Sam's expanded its offering for caterers to include menu planning and additional selections of catering supplies and seasonal decorating items.

The annual fee for Sam's Club business members was $35 for the primary membership card, with a spouse card available at no additional cost. Business members could add up to eight business associates for $35 each and could purchase memberships for employees at $30 per membership for 50 to 999 employees and $25 for 1,000 or more employees. The annual membership fee for an individual Advantage member was $40, which included a spouse card. There was a Sam's Club Plus premium membership costing $100 that included an assortment of additional benefits and services such as health care insurance, merchant credit card processing, Web site operation, personal and financial services, and an auto, boat, and recreational vehicle program. Regular hours of operations were Monday through Friday, 10:00 a.m. to 8:30 p.m.; Saturday, 9:30 a.m. to 8:30 p.m.; and Sunday, 10:00 a.m. to 6:00 p.m.

Approximately 65 percent of the nonfuel merchandise at Sam's Club was shipped from the division's own distribution facilities and, in the case of perishable items, from some of Wal-Mart's grocery distribution centers; the balance was shipped by suppliers directly to Sam's Club locations. Like Costco, Sam's Club distribution centers employed cross-docking techniques whereby incoming shipments were transferred immediately to outgoing trailers destined for Sam's Club locations; shipments typically spent less than 24 hours at a cross-docking facility and in some instances were there only an hour. The Sam's Club distribution center network consisted of 7 company-owned-and-operated distribution facilities and 17 third-party-owned-and-operated facilities. A combination of company-owned trucks and independent trucking companies was used to transport merchandise from distribution centers to club locations.

BJ's Wholesale

BJ's Wholesale introduced the member warehouse concept to the northeastern United States in the mid-1980s. Since then it had expanded to 177 stores operating in 16 states from Maine to Florida; it also had three cross-dock distribution centers. BJ's had 158 "full-sized" warehouses averaging 113,000 square feet and 19 smaller-format warehouses averaging 71,000 square feet that were located in markets too small to support a full-sized warehouse. About 100 clubs had a self-service gasoline station operation. In early 2007, BJ's abandoned prescription filling and closed all of its 46 in-club pharmacies.

BJ's clubs were located in both freestanding and shopping center locations. Construction and site development costs for a full-sized owned BJ's club were in the range of $5 to $8 million; land acquisition costs could run $6 to $10 million (significantly higher in some locations). Each warehouse generally had an investment of $3 to $4 million for fixtures and equipment. Preopening expenses at a new club were close to $1 million. Full-sized clubs had approximately $2 million in inventory. Merchandise was generally displayed on pallets containing large quantities of each item, thereby reducing labor required for handling, stocking, and restocking.

Backup merchandise was generally stored in steel racks above the sales floor. Most merchandise was premarked by the manufacturer so that it did not require ticketing at the club.

Like Costco and Sam's, BJ's Wholesale sold high-quality, brand-name merchandise at prices that were significantly lower than the prices found at supermarkets, discount retail chains, department stores, drugstores, and specialty retail stores like Best Buy. Its merchandise lineup of about 7,300 items included consumer electronics, prerecorded media, small appliances, tires, jewelry, health and beauty aids, household products, computer software, books, greeting cards, apparel, furniture, toys, seasonal items, frozen foods, fresh meat and dairy products, beverages, dry grocery items, fresh produce, flowers, canned goods, and household products. About 70 percent of BJ's product line could be found in supermarkets. Food categories accounted for approximately 61 percent of BJ's total food and general merchandise sales in 2007; about 13 percent of sales consisted of BJ's private-label products that were primarily premium quality and typically priced well below name-brand products. In some product assortments, BJ's had three price categories for members to choose from—good, deluxe, and luxury.

To encourage more frequent trips to its clubs and also to provide members with more of a one-stop shopping opportunity, most BJ's locations offered a variety of specialty products and services, provided mostly by outside operators that leased warehouse space from BJ's; these included photo developing, full-service optical centers, brand-name fast-food service, garden and storage sheds, patios and sunrooms, vacation packages, propane-tank-filling services, discounted home heating oil, an automobile buying service, installation of home security services, printing of business forms and checks, and muffler and brake services.

BJ's Wholesale had about 8.8 million members at year-end 2007 (see Exhibit 4). It charged $45 per year for a primary Inner Circle membership, which included one free supplemental membership; members in the same household could purchase additional supplemental memberships for $20. A business membership also cost $45 per year, which included one free supplemental membership and the ability to purchase additional supplemental memberships for $20. BJ's launched a membership rewards program in 2003 that offered members a 2 percent rebate, capped at $500 per year, on most in-club purchases; members who paid the $80 annual fee to enroll in the rewards program accounted for 5 percent of all members and 13 percent of total merchandise and food sales in 2007.

BJ's was the only warehouse club that accepted MasterCard, Visa, Discover, and American Express cards at all locations; members could also pay for purchases by cash, check, and debit cards. BJ's accepted returns of most merchandise within 30 days after purchase.

BJ's Wholesale increased customer awareness of its clubs primarily through direct mail, public relations efforts, marketing programs for newly opened clubs, and a publication called *BJ's Journal,* which was mailed to members throughout the year; during the holiday season, BJ's engaged in radio and TV advertising, a portion of which was funded by vendors.

Merchandise purchased from manufacturers was shipped either to a BJ's cross-docking facility or directly to clubs. Personnel at the cross-docking facilities broke down truckload quantity shipments from manufacturers and reallocated goods for shipment to individual clubs, generally within 24 hours.

Strategy Features That Differentiated BJ's

Top management believed that several factors set BJ's Wholesale operations apart from those of Costco and Sam's Club:

- Offering a wide range of choice—7,300 items versus 4,000 items at Costco and Sam's Club. Focusing on the individual consumer via merchandising strategies that emphasized a customer-friendly shopping experience.
- Clustering club locations to achieve the benefit of name recognition and maximize the efficiencies of management support, distribution, and marketing activities.
- Trying to establish and maintain the first or second industry leading position in each major market where it operated.
- Creating an exciting shopping experience for members with a constantly changing mix of food and general merchandise items and carrying a broader product assortment than competitors.
- Supplementing the warehouse format with aisle markers, express checkout lanes, self-checkout lanes, and low-cost video-based sales aids to make shopping more efficient for members.

- Being open longer hours than competitors.
- Offering smaller package sizes of many items.
- Accepting manufacturers' coupons.
- Accepting more credit card payment options.

Endnotes

[1] As quoted in Alan B. Goldberg and Bill Ritter, "Costco CEO Finds Pro-Worker Means Profitability," *20/20,* August 2, 2006, http://abcnews.go.com/2020/Business/story?id=1362779 (accessed November 15, 2006).
[2] Ibid.
[3] As described in Nina Shapiro, "Company for the People," *Seattle Weekly,* December 15, 2004, www.seattleweekly.com (accessed November 14, 2006).
[4] 2005 and 2006 annual reports.
[5] Matthew Boyle, "Why Costco Is So Damn Addictive," *Fortune,* October 30, 2006, p. 130.
[6] As quoted in ibid., pp. 128–29.
[7] Steven Greenhouse, "How Costco Became the Anti-Wal-Mart," *New York Times,* July 17, 2005, www.wakeupwalmart.com/news (accessed November 28, 2006).
[8] As quoted in ibid.
[9] As quoted in Shapiro, "Company for the People."
[10] As quoted in Greenhouse, "How Costco Became the Anti-Wal-Mart."
[11] Boyle, "Why Costco Is So Damn Addictive," p.132.
[12] Ibid., p.130.
[13] Goldberg and Ritter, "Costco CEO Finds Pro-Worker Means Profitability."
[14] Ibid.
[15] Based on data for Costco posted at www.payscale.com (accessed October 9, 2008).
[16] Ibid.
[17] As quoted in Goldberg and Ritter, "Costco CEO Finds Pro-Worker Means Profitability."
[18] Shapiro, "Company for the People."
[19] As quoted in Lori Montgomery, "Maverick Costco CEO Joins Push to Raise Minimum Wage," *Washington Post,* January 30, 2007, p. D4.
[20] Greenhouse, "How Costco Became the Anti-Wal-Mart."
[21] As quoted in Goldberg and Ritter, "Costco CEO Finds Pro-Worker Means Profitability."
[22] Ibid.
[23] As quoted in Greenhouse, "How Costco Became the Anti-Wal-Mart."
[24] As quoted in Goldberg and Ritter, "Costco CEO Finds Pro-Worker Means Profitability."
[25] Boyle, "Why Costco Is So Damn Addictive," p. 132.
[26] As quoted in Shapiro, "Company for the People."
[27] Ibid.
[28] As quoted in Goldberg and Ritter, "Costco CEO Finds Pro-Worker Means Profitability."
[29] As quoted in Shapiro, "Company for the People."

JetBlue Airways: A Cadre of New Managers Takes Control

CASE 3

Janet Rovenpor
Manhattan College

Mary Michel
Manhattan College

On February 14, 2007, Valentine's Day, Genevieve McCaw and her boyfriend arrived at JFK International Airport and boarded JetBlue flight number 351 bound for Burbank, California. The plane, however, never took off. An ice storm grounded the Airbus A320 on the tarmac for almost an entire day. When the ordeal was over, McCaw created a blog and posted the following message: "Nothing says 'I love you' like being held hostage on a frozen plane with the man you love, 99 strangers, 4 other people you happen to know, 4 screaming babies and 3 rambunctious kids running about, nothing but chips and soda for sustenance, faulty power, unreliable direct TV and an overfilled sewage system for 11 hours" (see **www.jetbluehostage.com**). McCaw was not the only traveler who was angry. The ice storm affected 130,000 passengers, caused the cancellation of 1,100 flights over a six-day period, and cost JetBlue an estimated \$30 million.[1]

Industry observers and loyal customers were left to wonder how this could happen. After all, JetBlue was founded by David Neeleman, a Salt Lake City entrepreneur, to "bring humanity back to air travel."[2] As the eighth largest passenger carrier in the United States, JetBlue had won many awards, including "Best Domestic Airline," "Best Domestic Airline for Value," and "Best Overall Airline" for onboard service. Company officials explained that JetBlue's philosophy was to delay flights rather than cancel them. The airline was committed to getting its passengers to their destinations despite bad weather. When the ice storm lasted longer than forecasted, flight delays at JFK caused cancellations at other airports. Outbound passengers in New York could not deplane because there were only 21 gates for 52 airplanes and some airplanes had become frozen to the ground at the gates.

Neeleman issued several apologies on news programs, talk shows, and even on YouTube. In an e-mail to passengers dated February 21, 2007, he wrote: "We are sorry and embarrassed. But most of all, we are deeply sorry. Last week was the worst operational week in JetBlue's seven year history. Following the severe winter ice storm in the Northeast, we subjected our customers to unacceptable delays, flight cancellations, lost baggage. . . . Words cannot express how truly sorry we are for the anxiety, frustration and inconvenience that we caused." Neeleman also announced JetBlue's "Passenger's Bill of Rights," the first of its kind among U.S. airline carriers, in which the company disclosed its policies regarding vouchers and refunds in the event of delays, cancellations, and other inconveniences (see Exhibit 1).

Nonetheless, JetBlue's reputation was tarnished and a new senior management team was assembled. Russell Chew, who had served for four years as the chief operating officer (COO) at the Federal Aviation Administration, was hired as JetBlue's COO in March 2007. He brought with him 17 years of experience as a pilot and manager for American Airlines. Chew assumed the additional post of president on September 13, 2007. John Harvey, JetBlue's chief financial officer (CFO), resigned on November 9, 2007,

 This case was developed for the sole purpose of providing material for class discussion. It is not intended to illustrate either effective or ineffective handling of a managerial situation. We wish to thank Dr. John E. Gamble, Associate Dean and Director of Graduate Studies, Mitchell College of Business, University of South Alabama, for obtaining the data presented in Exhibits 3, 4 and 11; his assistance is greatly appreciated.

Exhibit 1 JetBlue Airways' Customer Bill of Rights

INFORMATION

JetBlue will notify customers of the following:

- Delays prior to scheduled departure
- Cancellations and their cause
- Diversions and their cause

CANCELLATIONS

All customers whose flight is cancelled by JetBlue will, at the customer's option, receive a full refund or reaccommodation on the next available JetBlue flight at no additional charge or fare. If JetBlue cancels a flight within 4 hours of scheduled departure and the cancellation is due to a Controllable Irregularity, JetBlue will also issue the customer a $100 Voucher good for future travel on JetBlue.

DELAYS (Departure Delays or Onboard Ground Delays on Departure)

For customers whose flight is delayed 3 hours or more after scheduled departure, JetBlue will provide free movies on flights that are 2 hours or longer.

DEPARTURE DELAYS

1. Customers whose flight is delayed for 1–1:59 hours after scheduled departure time due to a Controllable Irregularity are entitled to a $25 Voucher good for future travel on JetBlue.
2. Customers whose flight is delayed for 2–3:59 hours after scheduled departure time due to a Controllable Irregularity are entitled to a $50 Voucher good for future travel on JetBlue.
3. Customers whose flight is delayed for 4–5:59 hours after scheduled departure time due to a Controllable Irregularity are entitled to a Voucher good for future travel on JetBlue in the amount paid by the customer for the one-way trip.
4. Customers whose flight is delayed for 6 or more hours after scheduled departure time due to a Controllable Irregularity are entitled to a Voucher good for future travel on JetBlue in the amount paid by the customer for the roundtrip (or the one-way trip, doubled).

ONBOARD GROUND DELAYS

JetBlue will provide customers experiencing an Onboard Ground Delay with 36 channels of DIRECTV®,* food and drink, access to clean restrooms and, as necessary, medical treatment. For customers who experience an Onboard Ground Delay for more than 5 hours, JetBlue will also take necessary action so that customers may deplane.

Arrivals:

1. Customers who experience an Onboard Ground Delay on Arrival for 1–1:59 hours after scheduled arrival time are entitled to a $50 Voucher good for future travel on JetBlue.
2. Customers who experience an Onboard Ground Delay on Arrival for 2 hours or more after scheduled arrival time are entitled to a Voucher good for future travel on JetBlue in the amount paid by the customer for the roundtrip (or the one-way trip, doubled).

Departures:

1. Customers who experience an Onboard Ground Delay on Departure after scheduled departure time for 3–3:59 hours are entitled to a $50 Voucher good for future travel on JetBlue.
2. Customers who experience an Onboard Ground Delay on Departure after scheduled departure time for 4 or more hours are entitled to a Voucher good for future travel on JetBlue in the amount paid by the customer for the roundtrip (or the one-way trip, doubled).

In-flight entertainment:

JetBlue offers 36 channels of DIRECTV® service on its flights in the Continental U.S. If our LiveTV™ system is inoperable on flights in the Continental U.S., customers are entitled to a $15 Voucher good for future travel on JetBlue.

OVERBOOKINGS (As Defined in JetBlue's Contract of Carriage)

Customers who are involuntarily denied boarding shall receive $1,000.

*Available only on flights in the Continental United States.

Source: www.jetblue.com.

after 18 months on the job. Harvey wanted to pursue "other, unspecified professional interests."[3] Ed Barnes, a senior vice president in finance and principal accounting officer, became the interim CFO; he was permanently assigned to that position on February 13, 2008.

Neeleman's tenure as CEO was over. On May 10, 2007, JetBlue's board of directors said that he would resign as CEO and become its nonexecutive board chairman. On April 10, 2008, Neeleman announced that he was leaving the company and starting an airline company in Brazil. David Barger, who had been president, became the new CEO. When asked what his initial goals were, Barger said, "Let's calm things down. What I mean is, we had an awful lot of growth. That's easy to say in hindsight, but the fact is we took on too much."[4]

JetBlue's managers faced many challenges ahead. JetBlue's stock prices were in a downward spiral, dropping from $12.99 per share on February 13, 2007, to $3.97 per share on May 30, 2008. The new management team needed to put in place new operating procedures, communication systems, and information technology solutions to prevent another weather-related debacle. It needed to deal with rising jet fuel prices and the emergence of new competitors just as it was making the transition from a start-up airline to a major domestic carrier. Would Barger, Chew, and Barnes be up to the task?

THE FOUNDING OF JETBLUE AIRWAYS

David Neeleman's idea was to start a company that would combine the low fares of a discount airline carrier with the comforts of a small cozy den in people's homes. Passengers would be able to save money while they munched on gourmet snacks, sat in leather seats, and watched television. Many of JetBlue's original design principles came from Neeleman's own personal experiences. He added leather seats because he once got assigned to a fabric seat on an airplane that was soaked with urine. He realized that leather seats were not only more durable but also easier to clean. To make air travel entertaining, he decided to offer 24-channel live television via satellite—for free. Individual monitors were installed in all seats.

Neeleman was well versed in customer service and had worked in the travel and airline industry before starting JetBlue. He was born in São Paulo, Brazil, in 1959, but his family moved to Sandy, Utah, when he was five years old. One of Neeleman's first jobs was in his grandfather's grocery store in downtown Salt Lake City.[5] As a teenager, he would order items, cut the meat, and stack the beer. He learned from his grandfather never to disappoint customers; satisfied customers would return. Neeleman even pushed the shopping carts of elderly customers to their homes. Later, when Neeleman became CEO of JetBlue, he performed similar good deeds. He once drove an elderly couple from JFK to their home in Connecticut (the state where he had relocated) to save them $200 for a taxi.

As a young man, Neeleman studied accounting at the University of Utah. After his freshman year, he took time off to live in Brazil as a Mormon missionary. There, he learned to be frugal, saving $1,300 out of the $3,000 his parents had given him.[6] Neeleman left college in his junior year. He opened up his own travel agency near Salt Lake City. He sold vacation packages to Hawaii that included airfare and a stay in a time-share. His company grew to 20 employees and brought in $8 million in business.[7] Unfortunately, Pineapple Express, the air charter company with which he had an agreement to transport his customers, ran out of cash. Neeleman was forced to close his own business in 1983.[8]

In 1984, Neeleman joined Morris Air, a small local carrier based in Salt Lake City. He stayed for about eight years, first as executive vice president and later president, during which time he experimented with several strategies that were later implemented at JetBlue. Working for Morris Air, Neeleman sold vacation packages to shoppers in malls and to couples at weddings he attended. When JetBlue started service out of Long Beach, California, Neeleman hired paid college interns to ride local streets in nine Volkswagen Beetles painted in the airline's logo and colors. For a month, they handed out bumper stickers, buttons, and tote bags to potential passengers in hotels, movie studios, and restaurants.[9]

Neeleman introduced electronic ticketing and allowed reservation agents to work from home at Morris Air and then at JetBlue. JetBlue travelers printed boarding passes at check-in kiosks at the airport. This was convenient for people like Neeleman who often forgot their paper tickets at home.

Reservation agents worked six-hour shifts with two 15-minute breaks from home. This was a way to save money on paper tickets, on postage needed to mail out paper tickets, and on rent for office space. Neeleman raised capital for JetBlue from some of the same investors in Morris Air.

In 1993, Southwest Airlines purchased Morris Air for $129 million. The deal made Neeleman $20 million wealthier. Southwest hired Neeleman as a member of the executive planning committee, but Neeleman could not get used to the company's policies and procedures. In short, he was fired. Because he had signed a five-year noncompete agreement with Southwest Airlines, Neeleman could not establish another airline company until 1998. When he was ready to start JetBlue, Neeleman raised $130 million from such investors as George Soros, Weston Presidio, and Chase Manhattan Bank's venture capital group. He contributed $5 million of his own money.

Neeleman staffed his first senior management team carefully. He hired David Barger as president and COO. With 10 years' experience in the airline industry, Barger had been the vice president at Continental Airlines and was responsible for running its Newark, New Jersey, hub. John Owen was hired as executive vice president and CFO. He had prior experience as a financial analyst at American Airlines and as vice president of operations/planning and analysis, and then as treasurer, at Southwest Airlines. Owen served as JetBlue's CFO until 2006. Neeleman's longtime business partner Thomas Kelly became JetBlue's executive vice president and general counsel. Kelly's title changed to executive vice president and secretary in 2003. Ann Rhoades was hired as executive vice president to handle human resources; she held that position for three years. Rhoades had been the head of the People Department at Southwest Airlines and was the one who had fired Neeleman from the carrier back in 1993.

JETBLUE STARTS SERVICE OUT OF NEW YORK CITY

On February 11, 2000, JetBlue launched its first ceremonial flight between Buffalo and New York City, making John F. Kennedy (JFK) International Airport its hub. The one-way fare for the first month was set at $25, which then went up to $98 round-trip. Fares for that route available from other carriers at the time were as high as $600 round-trip.[10] Mayor Rudolph Giuliani and Senator Charles Schumer, the latter of whom had been instrumental in helping the airline obtain its takeoff and landing slots at JFK, were among the celebrity passengers. Schumer wanted to make good on a campaign promise to help stimulate the stagnant economy in upper New York State. By providing low-fare accessibility to such cities as Buffalo and Syracuse, JetBlue might encourage outside employers to open up new businesses.

Later that day, JetBlue introduced its first commercial flight from JFK to Fort Lauderdale, Florida, with 152 passengers aboard. The one-way fare was $159, which was 70 percent lower than the fares of other carriers. JetBlue would soon fly to Tampa, Orlando, West Palm Beach, and Fort Myers. JetBlue's COO, Barger, viewed Florida as "the sixth borough of New York."[11] It became JetBlue's most popular destination.

The decision to start up service at JFK was a risky one. The airport was called the "black sheep of New York airports" because of its crowded skies, high costs, and inevitable hassles.[12] Even Southwest Airlines had entered the region by choosing to fly in and out of a secondary airport, MacArthur Airport in Islip, Long Island, instead of JFK. Yet Neeleman saw an opportunity at JFK that no one else saw. While airlines faced heavy delays during the 3:00–8:00 p.m. time period (when most international flights arrived and departed), the morning hours were relatively free. Neeleman noted that only 15 flights left JFK between the hours of 8:00 and 9:00 a.m.[13] JFK had an average gate utilization of 2.7 flights a day, much lower than LaGuardia's 5.5 flights a day.[14]

Neeleman originally thought that JetBlue's target market consisted of the 8 million people in a five-mile radius around JFK. He later found that his service also appealed to young, affluent professionals with Manhattan zip codes. "You have this large population that makes a lot of money per capita, and everyone in New York would like to get out. At the same time, everyone outside New York would like to get in. It's truly the nirvana of all markets," said Neeleman.[15] New York City travelers had not had access to a low-fare carrier since People Express folded in 1986.

Congestion at JFK got worse. Between March 2006 and August 2007, airline carriers increased their scheduled operations by 41 percent; in the first 10 months of fiscal year 2007, the number of arrival delays that exceeded one hour increased by 114 percent.[16] JFK had the third worst overall delay record among the nation's 32 largest airports in 2007.[17] President George W. Bush and Transportation Secretary Mary Peters suggested that the U.S. government might auction landing/takeoff rights to the highest bidder and/or charge "peak" fees at JFK. When U.S. carriers lobbied against congestion pricing at JFK, a compromise was reached: U.S. airlines operating out of JFK agreed to voluntarily adjust their schedules so that no more than 83 takeoffs and landings would occur per hour.[18] Previously, up to 100 flights could land or take off during a peak hour.

JetBlue managers estimated that congestion at JFK cost $50 million in labor, fuel, and vouchers in 2007.[19] They looked forward to the opening of JetBlue's new Terminal 5 at JFK in late 2008. With 26 gates and 72 acres of space, the terminal could handle up to 250 flights a day. Customers would experience greater convenience and efficiency. There would be a security checkpoint that could accommodate 20 lanes and a baggage sorting system that could process up to 40 bags per hour. Passengers would get from airport entrance to airplane door in less time. To further address constrained air space in the New York City area, JetBlue began service from Stewart Field in Newburgh, New York, and Westchester County Airport in White Plains, New York. Suburbanites would not have to travel to JFK, LaGuardia, or Newark to catch a flight for select destinations.

JETBLUE'S RAPID EXPANSION

Exhibit 2 shows JetBlue's growth. By the end of 2000, JetBlue boarded its millionth passenger. In addition to its Florida destinations, JetBlue provided service from JFK to Buffalo and Rochester, New York; to Burlington, Vermont; to Salt Lake City, Utah; and to Oakland and Ontario, California. Its fare structure was simple. All passengers flew coach and purchased one-way, nonrefundable tickets. The average one-way fare was $88.84. No Saturday stay was required. A $25 fee was charged to passengers who wanted to change their departure times.

In April 2001, JetBlue boarded its 2 millionth passenger. It added service from JFK to Syracuse, New York; Seattle, Washington; Denver, Colorado; Long Beach, California; and New Orleans, Louisiana. More important, it started direct service between Washington, D.C. (Dulles International Airport), and Fort Lauderdale, Florida. This marked the beginning of the company's plans to operate as a point-to-point carrier.

On March 7, 2002, JetBlue flew its 5 millionth passenger. On April 12, JetBlue raised $182 million from its first public offering of stock. It sold 5.87 million shares at a starting price of $27 a share. In September, JetBlue acquired LiveTV, LLC, its provider of in-flight satellite entertainment systems. JetBlue added service from Washington, D.C., to Oakland and Long Beach, California. It significantly expanded its operations out of Long Beach by offering nine flights to Oakland, California; five daily flights to Las Vegas, Nevada; and one daily flight to Salt Lake City, Utah.

Exhibit 2 JetBlue Airways Expansion from 2000 to 2007

	2000	2001	2002	2003	2004	2005	2006	2007
Number of cities served	12	18	20	21	30	33	49	53
Number of departures	10,265	26,334	44,144	66,920	90,532	112,009	159,152	196,594
Number of aircraft (owned and leased)	10	21	37	53	69	92	119	134
Number of tull-time equivalent employees	1,028	1,983	3,572	4,892	6,413	8,326	9,265	9,909
Percentage of sales through JetBlue.com	28.7%	44.1%	63%	73%	75.4%	77.5%	79.1%	75.7%

Sources: JetBlue 10K reports, www.jetblue.com.

On January 1, 2003, JetBlue flew its 10 millionth passenger. It launched service between JFK and San Diego, Long Beach, and Fort Lauderdale. This was also the year in which JetBlue ordered a new type of plane, the Embraer 190. With 100 seats, the Embraer was a smaller plane compared to the Airbus A320. JetBlue pulled out of Atlanta, Georgia, because of competition from Delta and AirTran on its transcontinental routes to Oakland and Long Beach.

In 2004, JetBlue added satellite radio and movie channels to its in-flight entertainment systems. It was a big year for route expansion. JetBlue started service out of Boston (with flights to Long Beach, Denver, Fort Lauderdale, Orlando, and Tampa) and out of New York's LaGuardia airport (with flights to Fort Lauderdale). It launched service out of JFK to seven new cities including Aguadillo, Puerto Rico; Santiago, Dominican Republic; and Nassau, Bahamas.

In 2005, JetBlue added flights from Boston to San Jose, California; Las Vegas, Nevada; and Seattle, Washington. It started a new service between Washington D.C.'s Dulles Airport and San Diego, California. In the New York area, it added flights out of JFK to Burbank, California; Portland, Oregon; and Ponce, Puerto Rico; and out of La Guardia to West Palm Beach, Florida, and to San Juan, Puerto Rico. In November, JetBlue started service between New York's JFK International Airport and Boston's Logan Airport with its Embraer 190 airplanes. JetBlue lost $20.2 million, largely due to sharp rises in fuel costs.

On February 1, 2006, JetBlue began to serve Dunkin' Donuts coffee on its flights. It continued to add new destinations; for example, it began to fly from Austin, Texas, to New York's JFK and Boston's Logan airports. It offered nonstop flights between Washington, D.C., and Boston; between Oakland and Fort Lauderdale; and between New York and Bermuda. JetBlue lost $1 million. It began to scale back its expansion plans. It put five Airbus A320 airplanes up for sale, deferred delivery of six A320s, and modified the timing of its Embraer 190 aircraft purchases.

JetBlue started 2007 by providing service to Chicago's O'Hare International Airport and to San Francisco International Airport. It piloted a new on-board service: e-mail and instant messaging. The German airline company Lufthansa bought a 19 percent equity stake in JetBlue when it purchased shares priced at $7.27 per share (for a total investment of $300 million). By December 2007, JetBlue operated more than 550 flights a day and served 53 destinations in 21 states, Puerto Rico, Mexico, and the Caribbean.

JETBLUE'S OPERATING COSTS AND SERVICE QUALITY

JetBlue was a discount airline carrier. It offered passengers low fares; operated point-to-point systems; used two types of aircraft; served only snacks; and maintained quick turnaround times at airports. Its operating costs were low, especially compared to those of other major U.S. airline companies. In the first quarter of 2008, for example, JetBlue's total operating expenses amounted to 12.77 cents per revenue passenger mile, compared to 20.95 cents per revenue passenger mile for Delta and 13.85 cents per revenue passenger mile for Southwest (see Exhibit 3).

JetBlue chose for its fleet the new Airbus A320, which had 30 additional seats and was more fuel efficient and less costly to operate than a Boeing 737.[20] Since the airplanes were new, repairs and maintenance costs were low for the first couple of years of operations. JetBlue was spared the problems experienced by American Airlines and Southwest Airlines, whose aircraft were older. In March 2008, the Federal Aviation Administration (FAA) fined Southwest for flying airplanes that should have been grounded for required fuselage inspections. Cracks in the fuselage of five airplanes were discovered. In April 2008, American Airlines grounded its entire fleet of 300 MD080 airplanes to recheck wiring that it had failed to repair.

JetBlue added Embraer 190 airplanes to its fleet in 2005. It ran into unexpected technical glitches. Pilots, for example, needed to get used to the new jet. An A-320 pilot could set the parking brake when waiting in line to take off. If an E-190 pilot were to do this, the airplane's electronic systems would act as if the airplane had landed and arrived at the gate.[21] Also, after the February 2007 ice storm, software problems were detected in the Embraers that were later fixed by the manufacturer.

JetBlue managers wanted to realize some of the advantages of using two types of airplanes. Instead of flying an Airbus A320 whose 150 seats were

Exhibit 3 Comparative Operating Cost Statistics, Selected U.S. Airlines, 1995, 2000, 2005–First Quarter 2008 (in cents per revenue passenger mile)

		Pilots and Copilots	Total Salaries and Fringe Benefits	Fuel and Oil	Maintenance	Rentals	Landing Fees	Advertising	General and Administrative	Other Operating Expenses	Total Operating Expenses
America West	**1995**	0.64¢	3.01¢	1.40¢	0.94¢	1.30¢	0.23¢	0.23¢	0.84¢	2.62¢	10.57¢
	2000	0.81	3.14	2.18	1.82	1.73	0.18	0.14	0.55	2.41	12.15
	2005	0.77	3.06	3.32	1.46	0.44	0.23	0.04	0.82	5.13	14.50
	2006	0.76	3.32	3.85	1.41	0.47	0.23	0.05	1.27	5.57	16.15
	2007	0.76	3.28	3.87	1.55	0.55	0.23	0.03	0.43	5.65	15.58
Q1	**2008**	n.a.	n.a.	n.a.	n.a.	n.a.	n.a.	n.a.	n.a.	n.a.	n.a.
American Airlines	**1995**	0.94¢	5.59¢	1.53¢	1.34¢	0.59¢	0.22¢	0.19¢	1.14¢	3.65¢	14.25¢
	2000	1.16	5.77	2.04	1.90	0.48	0.23	0.18	0.58	3.30	14.48
	2005	0.90	4.65	3.67	1.42	0.41	0.32	0.10	0.95	3.66	15.18
	2006	0.85	4.64	4.15	1.46	0.42	0.31	0.11	0.80	3.64	15.55
	2007	0.84	4.63	4.34	1.48	0.42	0.30	0.12	0.91	3.78	15.98
Q1	**2008**	0.90	4.79	5.72	1.75	0.38	0.32	0.13	0.85	4.24	18.18
Continental Air Lines	**1995**	0.95¢	3.69¢	1.67¢	1.50¢	1.25¢	0.27¢	0.25¢	0.56¢	3.68¢	12.87¢
	2000	1.25	4.43	2.18	1.42	1.17	0.24	0.09	0.59	3.57	13.70
	2005	0.79	3.85	3.42	1.18	0.91	0.34	0.13	0.82	5.74	16.38
	2006	0.71	3.76	3.82	1.20	0.87	0.33	0.12	1.03	5.38	16.51
	2007	0.75	3.85	3.97	1.24	0.81	0.30	0.13	1.09	5.17	16.56
Q1	**2008**	0.79	3.82	5.26	1.34	0.85	0.33	0.14	0.92	6.15	18.81
Delta Air Air Lines	**1995**	1.27¢	4.97¢	1.70¢	1.16¢	0.71¢	0.30¢	0.18¢	0.43¢	4.07¢	13.53¢
	2000	1.27	5.08	1.73	1.41	0.54	0.22	0.12	0.74	3.03	12.85
	2005	0.93	4.31	3.68	1.10	0.38	0.22	0.16	0.84	6.01	16.68
	2006	0.73	3.81	4.18	1.15	0.21	0.20	0.15	0.94	6.87	17.50
	2007	0.73	3.64	4.32	1.21	0.15	0.20	0.17	1.18	6.75	17.63
Q1	**2008**	0.83	3.95	5.67	1.27	0.21	0.21	0.12	1.07	8.45	20.95
JetBlue Airways	**1995**	n.a.	n.a.	n.a.	n.a.	n.a.	n.a.	n.a.	n.a.	n.a.	n.a.
	2000	n.a.	n.a.	n.a.	n.a.	n.a.	n.a.	n.a.	n.a.	n.a.	n.a.
	2005	0.51¢	2.31¢	2.42¢	0.68¢	0.38¢	0.25¢	0.16¢	0.51¢	1.44¢	8.13¢
	2006	0.62	2.60	3.37	0.74	0.44	0.30	0.16	0.39	1.63	9.64

(Continued)

Exhibit 3 (Continued)

		Pilots and Copilots	Total Salaries and Fringe Benefits	Fuel and Oil	Maintenance	Rentals	Landing Fees	Advertising	General and Administrative	Other Operating Expenses	Total Operating Expenses
	2007	0.70	2.73	3.76	0.77	0.48	0.31	0.15	0.46	1.76	10.41
Q1	2008	0.73	2.91	4.87	0.90	0.49	0.33	0.20	0.53	1.94	12.17
Northwest Airlines	1995	1.21¢	4.84¢	1.73¢	1.39¢	0.58¢	0.37¢	0.20¢	0.52¢	3.14¢	12.77¢
	2000	1.01	4.76	2.35	1.55	0.53	0.31	0.17	0.55	2.77	12.99
	2005	0.94	5.07	4.01	1.54	0.57	0.38	0.12	0.58	5.13	17.40
	2006	0.73	3.83	4.56	1.38	0.31	0.48	0.10	0.51	5.02	16.20
	2007	0.78	3.60	4.47	1.32	0.28	0.33	0.09	0.71	5.09	15.90
Q1	2008	0.74	3.79	5.94	1.48	0.26	0.31	0.08	0.85	6.54	19.25
Southwest Airlines	1995	0.92¢	3.94¢	1.56¢	1.21¢	0.79¢	0.35¢	0.41¢	1.09¢	1.56¢	10.91¢
	2000	0.86	4.22	1.95	1.22	0.48	0.31	0.35	1.42	0.96	10.91
	2005	1.18	4.70	2.44	1.17	0.31	0.34	0.29	0.73	1.23	11.21
	2006	1.19	4.72	3.37	1.13	0.27	0.33	0.27	0.70	1.24	12.03
	2007	1.22	4.67	3.71	1.27	0.26	0.34	0.26	0.80	1.20	12.53
Q1	2008	1.28	4.80	4.54	1.26	0.27	0.43	0.31	0.90	1.35	13.85
United Air Lines	1995	0.86¢	4.73¢	1.51¢	1.51¢	0.90¢	0.29¢	0.17¢	0.53¢	2.92¢	12.58¢
	2000	1.15	5.75	1.98	1.84	0.73	0.28	0.21	0.76	3.09	14.65
	2005	0.62	3.72	3.53	1.60	0.35	0.30	0.16	0.60	5.09	15.35
	2006	0.61	3.84	4.11	1.71	0.35	0.30	0.09	0.92	4.76	16.07
	2007	0.62	3.86	4.26	1.87	0.35	0.29	0.07	0.91	4.65	16.27
Q1	2008	0.69	4.16	5.85	2.13	0.34	0.32	0.07	1.00	5.26	19.13
US Airways	1995	1.55¢	7.53¢	1.59¢	2.09¢	1.05¢	0.29¢	0.13¢	0.73¢	4.32¢	17.73¢
	2000	1.36	7.59	2.44	2.30	0.97	0.28	0.19	1.10	4.81	19.68
	2005	0.78	3.74	3.89	1.50	1.06	0.31	0.06	0.66	7.27	18.49
	2006	0.73	3.85	4.30	1.62	1.08	0.28	0.05	1.04	7.82	20.03
	2007	0.71	4.25	4.45	1.71	1.12	0.26	0.04	0.86	7.46	20.14
Q1	2008	0.83	4.13	5.63	2.11	1.26	0.24	0.03	0.25	7.81	21.45

n.a. = not available.

Note: US Airways and America West started merging operations in September 2005. US Airways started to report combined data in October 2007. US Airways' and America West's data prior to October 2007 were reported separately.

Source: U.S. Department of Transportation, Bureau of Transportation Statistics, Air Carrier Statistics Form 298C Summary Data and Form 41, Schedules P-6, P-12, P-51, and P-52.

not filled to capacity during an off-peak time, the company could deploy an Embraer with 100 seats. However, JetBlue's passenger load factor actually declined from 80.4 percent in 2007 to 78.2 percent in the first quarter of 2008 (see Exhibit 4).

The Embraer was also used in smaller, regional markets to transport passengers to major hubs for connecting flights. A mix-and-match strategy could provide a better pattern of service for business travelers interested in flying in and out of New York the same day.[22] Instead of operating two Airbus A320s (with 150 seats each) to fly, for example, between JFK and New Orleans, three Embraers (with 100 seats each) could be deployed morning, noon, and evening.

JetBlue's turnaround time ranged from 20 to 30 minutes. Because no meals were served, JetBlue did not have to wait for catering services to replenish the aircraft. To save time, flight attendants themselves stowed carry-on bags and coats in the overhead bins. Everyone—pilots, flight attendants, and passengers—helped throw away the trash after each flight.

JetBlue was one of the first companies to use information technology to keep costs down. It operated Open Skies software to handle electronic ticketing, Internet bookings, and revenue management. It cost $1 to process an e-ticket, compared to $10 for a paper ticket.[23] By June 1, 2008, the International Air Transport Association (representing 240 airline companies) stated that it would no longer support paper tickets. The effort was aimed at saving the industry $3 billion annually.[24] In 2007, JetBlue booked more than 75 percent of its sales on its own Web site, leading the industry and reducing travel agent commissions.

JetBlue hired full-time reservation agents to sell tickets over the telephone. They worked at home with company-supplied computers and second telephone lines. JetBlue needed to operate only a small office in Salt Lake City for training. Starting pay for the agents was $8.50 per hour with a fixed 5 percent annual increase, medical coverage, profit sharing, and flight benefits.[25] Traditional call centers cost about $10 more per employee hour (including overhead and training) to operate than a network of home-based operators.[26]

JetBlue paid attention to the little details that customers found special. It worked with a unit of Bally Total Fitness to offer in-flight yoga cards in seat pockets. Passengers received instruction on how they could hold four yoga poses without removing their seatbelts. In 2005, JetBlue partnered with Oasis Day Spa to offer private massages, manicures, and hair styling to travelers at JetBlue's JFK Terminal 6. A children's play area and big-screen television could be found near its gates. In June 2007, JetBlue entered a partnership with Google Maps so that flights could be tracked live on the airline's Web site and via the

Exhibit 4 Load Factors for Selected U.S. Airlines, 1995, 2000, 2005–First Quarter 2008*

Carrier	1995	2000	2005	2006	2007	First Quarter 2008
America West	69.1%	70.6%	79.8%	79.9%	83.2%	n.a.
American Airlines	65.2%	72.0%	80.3%	82.1%	83.1%	80.3%
Continental Air Lines	65.1%	74.1%	81.5%	83.8%	84.0%	82.3%
Delta Air Lines	63.5%	72.1%	77.1%	79.2%	82.0%	80.0%
JetBlue Airways	n.a.	72.7%	84.9%	81.7%	80.4%	78.2%
Northwest Airlines	68.9%	73.1%	80.0%	83.0%	83.8%	82.8%
Southwest Airlines	64.5%	70.5%	70.7%	73.1%	72.6%	78.2%
United Air Lines	69.2%	71.5%	81.6%	81.9%	83.4%	78.7%
US Airways	64.5%	69.4%	74.2%	79.0%	81.0%	80.0%

*Load factor is a measure of how much of an airline's passenger-carrying capacity is actually utilized; it is calculated by dividing the number of revenue-generating passenger miles flown by the total number of seat miles available. In other words, it is roughly equal to the percentage of total available seats occupied by ticketed passengers.

Notes: America West merged with US Airways in September 2005; stopped reporting in 2007.

US Airways merged with America West in September 2005; combined reporting began in 2007.

Source: U.S. Department of Transportation, Bureau of Transportation Statistics, Air Carrier Statistics Form T-100.

in-seat satellite television system on its aircraft. In April 2008, passengers could pay for their flights using PayPal. In May 2008, JetBlue partnered with Carbonfund.org so that passengers could offset the carbon dioxide emissions generated by their flight.

Exhibit 5 compares JetBlue's on-time performance, mishandling of baggage, and number of passenger complaints to other major U.S. airlines. For the years 2005, 2006, and 2007, between 70.1 and 72.9 percent of JetBlue's flights arrived within 15 minutes

Exhibit 5 On-Time Flights, Mishandled Baggage, and Passenger Complaints of Selected U.S. Airlines, 2005–2007

Percentage of Flights Arriving on Time* and Carrier Rank

	12 Months Ending December 2007		12 Months Ending December 2006		12 Months Ending December 2005	
Airline	**%**	**Rank**	**%**	**Rank**	**%**	**Rank**
Air Tran	76.8	4	74.6	7	71.3	10
Alaska	72.4	6	73.3	10	69.7	11
America West					81.2	1
American	68.7	10	75.5	6	76.9	5
Continental	74.3	5	73.4	9	76.9	4
Delta	76.9	3	76.3	4	76.3	6
Frontier	77.6	2	80.7	1		
JetBlue	70.1	8	72.9	11	71.4	9
Northwest	69.6	9	75.8	5	75.0	8
Southwest	80.1	1	80.2	2	80.7	2
United	70.3	7	73.9	8	77.6	3
US Airways	68.7	11	76.9	3	76.2	7
All-airline average	73.4		75.4		78.7	

*"On time" means an arrival less than 15 minutes after scheduled arrival time.

Mishandled Baggage Reports Filed by Passengers

	January–December 2007		January–December 2006		January–December 2005	
Airline	**Reports Per 1,000 Passengers**	**Rank**	**Reports Per 1,000 Passengers**	**Rank**	**Reports Per 1,000 Passengers**	**Rank**
Air Tran	4.06	1	4.72	3	3.45	1
Alaska	6.39	8	5.71	8	5.03	8
America West					4.33	6
American	7.25	9	6.33	9	5.92	9
Continental	5.33	4	4.76	4	4.12	3
Delta	7.60	10	6.88	10	7.09	10
Frontier	6.16	7	5.18	5		
JetBlue	5.23	3	4.09	1	4.06	2
Northwest	5.01	2	4.60	2	4.86	7
Southwest	5.87	6	5.34	6	4.25	4
United	5.76	5	5.68	7	4.28	5
US Airways	8.47	11	7.82	11	9.62	11
All-airline average	7.03		6.73		6.04	

(Continued)

Exhibit 5 (Continued)

Passenger Complaints

Airline	January–December 2007 Complaints Per 100,000 Passengers Boarded	Rank	January–December 2006 Complaints Per 100,000 Passengers Boarded	Rank	January–December 2005 Complaints Per 100,000 Passengers Boarded	Rank
Air Tran	n.a.	n.a.	0.62	5	1.00	7
Alaska	0.76	3	0.52	4	0.77	3
American	1.65	7	1.09	9	1.02	9
America West					0.96	6
Continental	1.09	5	0.88	6	0.92	4
Delta	1.81	8	1.03	8	1.09	10
Frontier	0.66	2	0.49	3		
JetBlue	0.78	4	0.40	2	0.29	2
Northwest	1.43	6	0.88	7	0.94	5
Southwest	0.26	1	0.18	1	0.18	1
United	2.25	9	1.36	11	1.02	8
US Airways	3.16	10	1.36	10	1.86	11
All-airline average	1.37		0.87		0.89	

n.a. = not available.

Notes: Statistics are displayed to one or two decimal places. Actual ranking order is based on calculations carrying out the number of decimal places to nine. US Airways and America West merged in September 2005 with the US Airways name being retained. Frontier filed for Chapter 11 bankruptcy protection in April 2008 but continued its normal business operations as it reorganized.

Source: U.S. Department of Transportation; *Air Travel Consumer Report,* February 2006, 2007, 2008, www.airconsumer.ost.dot.gov/reports.

of their scheduled times. This was down from its peak performance in 2003, when 84.3 percent of JetBlue's flights arrived within 15 minutes of their scheduled times. In 2005, 2006, and 2007, JetBlue received, respectively, 4.06, 4.09, and 5.23 reports of mishandled baggage (baggage that was lost or damaged) per 1,000 passengers. This compared with 2.88 reports of mishandled baggage per 1,000 passengers in 2003. In 2005, 2006, and 2007, JetBlue had, respectively, 0.29, 0.40, and 0.78 complaints per 100,000 passengers (for such things as canceled flights, poor customer service, and discrimination); in 2003, it had 0.12.

JETBLUE'S ORGANIZATIONAL CULTURE

Ann Rhoades, JetBlue's first executive vice president of human resources, helped JetBlue put in place a strong organizational culture. She believed that "people can accomplish the extraordinary when they are give the authority and responsibility to succeed."[27] She helped the company achieve extraordinary results from its employees by implementing five steps.

The first step was to determine the company's values. At JetBlue, these values were *safety, caring, integrity, fun,* and *passion.* Safety was the company's number one priority, with the other four values being approximately equal in importance.[28] The values guided employees in the decision-making process.

- The carrier's concern over *safety* was exhibited early on when it signed an agreement with Medaire Inc., enabling crew members to immediately consult with land-based emergency physicians anytime a passenger fell ill during a flight. JetBlue's Web site featured a section called "Inflight Health," which offered tips on what to do if flying caused ear pain and how to prevent deep-vein thrombosis, a rare condition that occurred when blood clots formed in the leg and pelvic veins. After September 11, 2001,

JetBlue was the first company to install Kevlar cockpit doors and cabin surveillance cameras in all of its airplanes.

- *Caring,* in the form or respect and understanding, was exhibited after the September 11 terrorist attacks when the company did not lay off anyone and continued paying salaries and benefits.[29] When Neeleman was CEO, he donated part of his salary to a crisis fund, designed, for example, to pay the medical bills of an employee's wife who was sick with cancer or replace the personal belongings of an employee whose home was destroyed by a fire.[30]
- *Integrity* meant "doing the right thing." When JetBlue's security department violated company policy and released passenger data to a U.S. Defense Department contractor, Neeleman took personal responsibility for the incident. He either e-mailed, called, or wrote letters to some passengers whose information had been released and sent out free airline tickets. Neeleman hired the financial advising firm Deloitte & Touche to analyze and further develop the carrier's privacy policies.
- *Fun* was the key to a friendly work environment where people liked to be. At JetBlue's JFK terminal, employees had access to George Foreman grills, which they used for barbecues. In 2002, passengers could hit yellow punching bags to relieve stress. The bags were tagged with such humorous sayings as "Forget where you parked?" and "Left the iron on?"[31]
- Employees demonstrated a *passion* for work and the company's products. They cared about customers. Once, a passenger who had landed at JFK could not board a connecting flight to Italy because she had left her passport at home in Buffalo. A JetBlue customer service agent telephoned a colleague in Buffalo who went to the woman's home, collected her passport, and put it on a flight to JFK. The passenger was able to depart for Italy.[32] Managers cared about employees. When employees in Burlington, Vermont, complained that there were not enough health care providers in their area, the company added a second health insurance plan.

The second step Rhoades implemented was to make sure that managers hired employees who mirrored company values. An example of an outstanding flight attendant who embodied the values of safety and caring was a 63-year-old former firefighter who had rescued people during the 1993 World Trade Center bombing. An example of someone who was not hired was a pilot who promoted himself by saying that he had 15,000 hours of experience in the cockpit. He could fly a plane anywhere, anytime. Yet, when asked by the recruiter what else he had done, he could not provide an answer. JetBlue wanted to hear that a candidate had done something special for someone else.

Rhoades encouraged managers to be creative during the hiring process. Instead of asking, "How should we do a better job of screening flight attendants?" one might ask, "Why don't people want to be flight attendants?" College graduates did not want to commit themselves to a long-term contract, so Rhoades agreed to hire them for a year. That way, they could meet people and visit places. Parents with children did not want to be away from home for long periods, so Rhoades created the Friends Crew Program, which allowed two people to share a job. This was perfect for a mother and daughter. When the daughter worked, the mother cared for her grandchild. Rhoades developed three different paths: one for traditional flight attendants, one for college students, and one for participants in the Friends Crew Program.

The third and fourth steps were to ensure that the company continually exceeded employee expectations and to ensure that it listened to its customers. JetBlue pilots received immediate benefits and profit-sharing opportunities in their first year of service. Passengers told JetBlue that they wanted television shows free of charge and low-carb snacks like almonds. They indicated that there was no need for separate restrooms for men and women. The fifth step was to create a "disciplined culture of excellence." The company had to continually improve its services and differentiate itself from its competitors.

JETBLUE'S HUMAN RESOURCE MANAGEMENT PRACTICES

Rhoades laid the foundations for JetBlue's focus on people. Employees were called "crew members," passengers were referred to as "customers," and vendors were addressed as "business partners." Vincent Stabile, who replaced Rhoades, made sure the company values became an integral part of the company's human resource management practices. His first day at JetBlue was September 11, 2001. He witnessed firsthand how JetBlue employees put their values into action. Soon after the attacks on the World Trade Center, crew members realized that the airports would be closing. At the company's expense, they booked blocks of hotel rooms and reserved buses to transport passengers to their accommodations. They extended the same courtesy to stranded passengers who were booked on the flights of their competitors.[33]

Hiring

Each year, JetBlue received 130,000 résumés, from which 3,000 qualified candidates were hired.[34] According to Stephen Howell, director of the College of Inflight at JetBlue University, a Blue Review recruitment team sifted through online applications, prescreened candidates via phone interviews, and invited qualified applicants to an eight-hour, one-day event in Forest Hills, Queens. The team, which included the director and manager of in-flight recruitment as well as several additional representatives from the company's human resources and from its in-flight crew leadership ranks, interviewed the candidates. At the day's conclusion, team members got together and made their selections. They were looking for individuals who performed especially well during group activities.[35]

In February 2008, JetBlue implemented a program called the Aviation University Gateway to anticipate a shortage of airplane pilots. It partnered with Embry-Riddle Aeronautical University and the University of North Dakota to identify candidates with exceptional potential as professional pilots, to clearly define a career path for them, and to provide them with rigorous academic training and regional airline experience.[36] Candidates would intern at Cape Air, serve as an instructor at a flight school, fly with Cape Air for at least two years, and then be eligible for a final interview at JetBlue.[37]

Faced with rising costs associated with high jet fuel prices, JetBlue implemented a hiring freeze for all management and support staff starting in April 2008. It also stopped accepting applications for first officer (i.e., copilot) positions.

Training

Mike Barger (CEO David Barger's brother) was JetBlue's chief learning officer. A former navy pilot who still flew JetBlue aircraft, Barger helped create JetBlue University. The university was separated into five colleges, one for each discipline: pilots, flight attendants, maintenance crew, gate staff, and reservations agents. Classroom-based training was held in one of five campuses—in New York, Orlando, Salt Lake City, Boston, and Long Beach.[38]

In 2005, results of an employee survey showed a lack of confidence in JetBlue's leadership. The company had promoted qualified frontline employees to leadership positions without providing them with appropriate tools and training. "We identified great 'doers,' but didn't give them a lot of tools, and they found themselves struggling within 18 to 24 months," said Barger.[39] As a result, 800 employees attended more than 14,000 hours of leadership development training.

In 2005, JetBlue completed construction on a 107,000-square-foot building at Orlando International Airport. It became the new home for the airline's training center. It had the capacity for eight flight simulators, two cabin simulators, classrooms, a training pool, a firefighting training station, and a cafeteria. Pilots, in-flight crew members, and customer service representatives received initial and continuous education there. JetBlue's Forest Hills location was used primarily for recurrent training; there, trainees could work with mock-ups, such as simulations of cabin doors.[40]

Paying

JetBlue was known for paying employees lower base salaries than its competitors. In 2004, for example, it was reported that flight attendants started at $25 an hour, mechanics at $26 an hour, and pilots at $108 an hour. US Airways, after implementing cuts, paid its flight attendants $39.95 an hour, its mechanics $28 an hour and its pilots $134 an hour.[41] JetBlue made up for these differences by offering health coverage, profit-sharing, and 401(k) retirement plans. JetBlue had a no-layoff policy and relied on downsizing through voluntary packages and attrition during difficult economic times.[42] CEO David Barger voluntarily reduced his base salary by 50 percent, from $500,000 per year to $250,000 per year, for the period of July 1 to December 31, 2008.[43]

JETBLUE'S FINANCIAL AND OPERATING PERFORMANCE

Despite its early promise and strong organizational culture, JetBlue did not deliver value to its stockholders over the five-year period ending December 31, 2007. None of the major airlines did. Shareholders of another low-fare airline, Southwest, lost less than JetBlue's shareholders over the same period. Exhibit 6 shows that a $100 investment in JetBlue common stock on December 31, 2002, was worth only $49 five years later. A $100 investment in Southwest common stock on December 31, 2002, was worth $89 five years later. Airline stockholders would have achieved similar returns by investing in the AMEX Airline Index. A $100 investment in the AMEX Airline Index on December 31, 2002, was worth $89 after five years. In contrast, a $100 investment in the S&P 500 Index was worth $182 at the end of the same five-year period. Industry observers quipped that it was better to place money under a mattress than invest in an airline stock.[44] According to Michael Boyd, a Colorado-based industry expert, "Airlines are a crummy business, and will always be a crummy business"[45]

The financial and operating data in Exhibits 7 and 8 were consistent with JetBlue's stock performance during the period. JetBlue revenues grew 185 percent, from $998 million in 2003 to $2,842 million in 2007. The growth in operating revenues reflected both the increase in revenue passenger miles flown and a modest increase in the average fare. However, operating expenses grew by 222 percent during the same period. Of the operating expenses, jet fuel expenses grew by 532 percent from 2003 to 2007. Operating expenses excluding jet fuel actually grew slower than revenues (155 percent). JetBlue's largest nonoperating item was interest expense, which grew 658 percent over the period to finance the company's expanded operations.

Exhibit 6 Comparison of Five-Year Cumulative Total Return among JetBlue, Southwest Airlines, the AMEX Airline Index, and the S&P 500 Index*

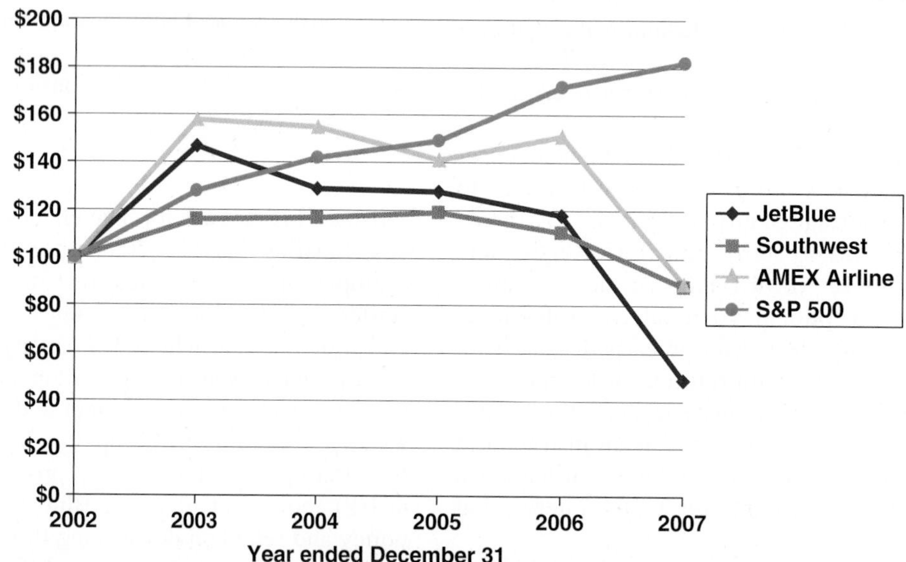

*The graph assumes the investment of $100 in each stock and each of the indexes as of the market close on December 31, 2002, with reinvestment of all dividends on a quarterly basis.

Source: JetBlue and Southwest, 2007 10-K reports.

Exhibit 7 Summary of JetBlue Airways' Financial Performance, 2003–2007 ($ in millions, except per share data)

	2007	2006	2005	2004	2003
Income Statement Data					
Operating revenues	$2,842	$2,363	$1,701	$1,265	$998
Operating expenses					
Aircraft fuel	929	752	488	255	147
Other operating expenses	1,744	1,484	1,165	899	684
Operating income (loss)	169	127	48	111	167
Govt. compensation	—	—	—	—	23
Non-operating income (expense)					
Interest (expense)*	(182)	(146)	(91)	(45)	(24)
Other nonoperating	54	28	19	9	8
Income before income taxes	41	9	(24)	75	174
Income tax expense (benefit)	23	10	(4)	29	71
Net income	18	(1)	(20)	46	103
Earnings (loss) per share, basic	0.10	—	(0.13)	0.30	0.71
Earnings (loss) per share, diluted	0.10	—	(0.13)	0.28	0.64
Other Financial Data					
Cash, cash equivalents and investment securities	$ 834	$ 699	$ 484	$ 450	$ 607
Total assets	5,598	4,843	3,892	2,797	2,185
Total debt	3,048	2,840	2,326	1,545	1,109
Common stockholders' equity	1,036	952	911	754	670
Net cash provided by operating activities	358	274	170	199	287

*Interest expense after deducting interest capitalized for self-constructed assets.

Source: JetBlue, 2007 and 2004 10-K reports.

Exhibit 8 Summary of JetBlue Airways' Operating Performance, 2003–2007

	2007	2006	2005	2004	2003
Revenue passengers (thousands)	21,387	18,565	14,729	11,783	9,012
Revenue passenger miles (millions)	25,737	23,320	20,200	15,730	11,527
Available seat miles (ASMs) (millions)	31,904	28,594	23,703	18,911	13,639
Load factor	80.7%	81.6%	85.2%	83.2%	84.5%
Aircraft utilization (hours per day)	12.8	12.7	13.4	13.4	13.0
Average fare	$123.23	$119.73	$110.03	$103.49	$107.09
Passenger revenue per ASM	8.26¢	7.77¢	6.84¢	6.45¢	7.08¢
Operating revenue per ASM	8.91¢	8.26¢	7.18¢	6.69¢	7.32¢
Operating expense per ASM	8.38¢	7.82¢	6.98¢	6.10¢	6.09¢
Average fuel cost per gallon	$2.09	$1.99	$1.61	$1.06	$0.85
Fuel gallons consumed (millions)	444	377	303	241	173

Source: JetBlue, 2007 10-K report.

Was JetBlue doomed to poor financial performance when fuel costs soared? Why had its stock performed poorly compared to the airline industry as a whole? JetBlue had a different cost and capital structure from Southwest Airlines, its low-fare competitor. Exhibit 9 compares the common size income statements and balance sheets of JetBlue and Southwest for the year ending December 31, 2007. The common size income statements show that JetBlue's fuel cost consumed 33 percent of its operating revenues versus just 26 percent for Southwest. Southwest hedged more of its jet fuel costs. JetBlue's net interest expense was 6 percent of operating revenues versus 1 percent for Southwest. In the 2007 common size balance sheets, JetBlue had a strikingly lower percentage of cash to total assets than Southwest (3.4 percent versus 13.2 percent). JetBlue's long-term debt comprised 46.2 percent of total assets versus 12.2 percent for Southwest.

Southwest hedged jet fuel prices more aggressively than JetBlue in 2007, according to the two companies' 2007 10-K reports. In 2007, Southwest hedged over 90 percent of its fuel consumption at an average crude oil equivalent price of $51 per barrel. For 2008, Southwest had hedges to protect over 70 percent of expected fuel consumption at an average crude oil equivalent price of $51. Southwest even had hedges in place to protect 15 percent of 2012

Exhibit 9 Comparative Income Statement Data, JetBlue versus Southwest Airlines, 2007

	JetBlue		Southwest Airlines	
2007 Income Statement Data*	$ Millions	As a Percent of Operating Revenues	$ Millions	As a Percent of Operating Revenues
Operating revenues	$2,842	100.0%	$ 9,861	100.0%
Operating expenses				
Jet fuel	929	32.7%	2,536	25.7%
Other operating expenses	1,744	61.4%	6,534	66.3%
Operating income	169	5.9%	791	8.0%
Non-operating income (expense)				
Interest (expense)*	(182)	−6.4%	(69)	−0.7%
Other non-operating income	54	1.9%	336	3.4%
Income before income taxes	41	1.4%	1,058	10.7%
Income tax expense	23	0.8%	413	4.2%
Net income	$ 18	0.6%	$ 645	6.5%
2007 Balance Sheet Data*		As a Percent of Total Assets		As a Percent of Total Assets
Cash and cash equivalents	$ 190	3.4%	$ 2,213	13.2%
Other current assets	926	16.5%	2,230	13.3%
Property, plant & equipment	3,794	67.8%	10,874	64.8%
Other assets	688	12.3%	1,455	8.7%
Total assets	5,598	100.0%	16,772	100.0%
Current liabilities	1,256	22.4%	4,838	28.8%
Long-term debt and capital leases	2,588	46.2%	2,050	12.2%
Other liabilities	718	12.8%	2,943	17.5%
Total liabilities	4,562	81.5%	9,831	58.6%
Stockholders' equity	1,036	18.5%	6,941	41.4%
Total liabilities & equity	$5,598	100.0%	$16,772	100.0%

*Interest expense after deducting interest capitalized for self-constructed assets.

Source: JetBlue, 2007 10-K reports.

fuel needs at $63 per barrel. JetBlue hedged 59 percent of its actual fuel consumption in 2007, although it stated no crude oil equivalent price per barrel. At December 31, 2007, JetBlue hedged approximately 13 percent of its projected 2008 fuel requirement. All of its outstanding hedges were scheduled to settle by the end of 2008.

Given the rapid increase in jet fuel prices, why did JetBlue hedge so little? David Neeleman gave some insight in an interview in the *Financial Times* on December 14, 2007: "If oil goes up to $120 and no one is hedged, then you don't look like a fool. But if you do it at $100 and it goes to $80 or $70, then you really look like a fool. You have to be careful at these historically high demand levels."[46]

JetBlue used two types of derivative instruments—option contracts and swap agreements—to hedge its exposure to aircraft fuel prices. It used derivatives for crude oil or heating oil, which were highly correlated with airline fuel prices. There was no derivative market for aircraft fuel. If a cash flow hedge was to be effective, hedge gains (losses) would offset (increase) aircraft fuel expense when the derivative settled and fuel was consumed. If JetBlue used an option contract to hedge increasing fuel prices when prices actually fell, the option would expire worthless and JetBlue would lose only the option premium paid. If JetBlue used a swap agreement to hedge increasing fuel prices and prices fell, it would have to pay the counterparty to the swap the full extent of its losses.

In addition to soaring fuel prices, the airline industry faced an increasing "crack spread" between the cost of a barrel of jet fuel and crude oil. The spread was $3.61 at the beginning of 2002 and $18.59 at the end of 2007.[47] It averaged $23.98 a barrel in the period from January 1 to April 1, 2008.[48] Refiners had increased their profit margins on jet fuel due to a lack of refining capacity. During the question-and-answer portion of JetBlue's presentation to the Merrill Lynch Transportation Conference on June 18, 2008, Dave Barger said that he assumed the crack spread would stay at the "mid-thirties."[49] If crude oil prices were to drop, however, airlines would not necessarily see immediate decreases in the cost of jet fuel.

Because of a conservative financial strategy, JetBlue maintained strong liquidity through the first quarter of 2008. It listed cash and cash equivalents of $713 million on March 31, 2008, in its 10-Q report. The position was within its target range of 20–25 percent of trailing 12-month revenues, according to CFO Ed Barnes during the first-quarter earnings conference call.[50] JetBlue had one of the highest liquidity coverage ratios of the major airlines.

The cash balance excluded $313 million of investments in auction-rate securities collateralized by student loans. Because markets for auction-rate securities began to fail in February 2008, investments in them were reclassified from current assets to long-term investments. Barnes predicted that liquidity would return to this market or that secondary markets would develop for most of JetBlue's auction-rate securities.[51] During its second-quarter 2008 earnings conference call, Barnes announced that JetBlue used its auction-rate securities to obtain a $110 million line of credit from Citigroup Global Markets on July 22, 2008.[52]

JetBlue obtained new equity capital in 2008 according to its March 31, 2008, 10-Q report. In January 2008, JetBlue issued 42.6 million new common shares to Deutsche Lufthansa AG for $301 million, net of transaction costs. This investment represented 19 percent of JetBlue's common shares outstanding. A Lufthansa nominee was appointed to JetBlue's board of directors.

JetBlue was also able to obtain credit. During its first-quarter earnings conference call, Barnes stated that financing was secured for all of its 2008 aircraft deliveries. Minimal cash was due because of favorable financing and pricing terms negotiated by JetBlue.

JetBlue completed its offering of two series of 5.5 percent convertible debentures, according to its 8-K report to the Securities and Exchange Commission on June 4, 2008. The debentures had a combined principal of $201.25 million due in 2038. Owners of the Series A debentures might require JetBlue to repurchase them for cash on October 15 of the years 2013, 2018, 2023, 2028, and 2033. Holders of the Series B debentures might require JetBlue to repurchase them for cash on October 15 of the years 2015, 2020, 2025, 2030, and 2035. JetBlue expected to use the funds to retire $175 million of 3.5 percent convertible notes due in 2033 that it expected to repurchase on July 15, 2008. On March 15, 2010, JetBlue might be required to repurchase $250 million of 3.75 percent convertible debentures due in 2035.

LESSONS IN CRISIS MANAGEMENT

The Valentine's Day 2007 ice storm at JFK that resulted in flight cancellations and delays taught JetBlue's managers several important lessons and set in motion needed changes. JetBlue's Navitaire Open Skies reservation system, which was configured to accommodate up to 650 reservation agents at a time, worked well during normal operations but was inadequate during an emergency. It could not handle the huge volume of telephone calls from stranded passengers who wanted to rebook flights and request compensation. Many passengers waited on the phone for more than an hour, and others could not get through at all. Navitaire managed to expand the system to 950 agents, but JetBlue had difficulty staffing the new lines. Off-duty crews and airport personnel volunteered to help but were not trained in how to use the computerized system.[53]

Because the telephone lines were busy, JetBlue pilots and crew members stuck in different cities across the country could not call in to headquarters with their availability and location. It was difficult, therefore, for crew schedulers to locate and assign crews to new flights once conditions improved and the airplanes could be redeployed. Crew members waiting out a storm along with passengers could not always fly out when a new schedule was made because the FAA set limits on a crew's number of hours of duty. Baggage was piling up at airports but there was no computerized system to record and track lost bags.[54]

JetBlue took several steps to fix these problems. It worked with Navitaire to double the number of agents who could simultaneously use the reservation system. It trained additional staff members at JFK to help out during an emergency. It decided to provide cross-training so that employees could learn the skills necessary to use the reservation, flight, and crew scheduling systems. JetBlue upgraded its Web site to allow passengers on canceled flights to rebook online and at airport kiosks. It set up a system to quickly alert passengers about flight delays and cancellations by e-mail and telephone to prevent long waits at airports. It provided crew members with the ability to inform crew schedulers of their availability and location via the Internet or via handheld devices. In addition, it put in place a computerized baggage tracking system.[55]

In April 2007, JetBlue hired Alex Battaglia to be the troubleshooter at JFK airport. The position of director of JFK operations had been vacant since September 2007. Battaglia (who had previously managed Delta's operations at JFK) was in charge of service and the upcoming move to JetBlue's new $850 million terminal.

In December 2007, JetBlue started a search for a crisis communications agency. It needed access to experts to teach its managers how to better communicate with the media, respond appropriately to lawsuits, and monitor the effectiveness of its advertising.[56] In June 2008, JetBlue hired MWW Group to oversee its communications for "any type of catastrophic event" and to train executives and airport managers in media relations.[57]

JETBLUE'S POSITION IN THE AIRLINE INDUSTRY

In the first six months of 2008, the U.S. economy slowed and crude oil prices rose to a record of $140 per barrel. Businesses began to cut back on employee travel, and consumers started to save money and contemplate "staycations" instead of vacations during the summer. Jet fuel prices skyrocketed as crude oil prices rose. The Airport Transport Association determined that each 1-cent increase in the price of a gallon of jet fuel cost the industry an additional $190 million to $200 million a year.[58] Airline companies struggled to offset higher fuel costs by increasing revenues (adding $25 fuel surcharges; charging $15 for the first checked bag; charging for headphones, pillows, and blankets) or cutting costs (lowering wages, grounding aircraft).

Some airline companies did not survive. Frontier Airlines Holding, a major airline company, filed for protection under Chapter 11 of the U.S. Bankruptcy Code. Three smaller airlines—Aloha Airgroup, ATA Airlines, and SkyBus Airlines—went bankrupt and ceased all operations. Delta Airlines and Northwest Airlines Corporation (both of which had just emerged from bankruptcy) announced plans to merge. Additional industry consolidation could occur. It was rumored, for example, that Continental Airlines and UAL Corporation, the parent of United, held merger talks in February 2008.[59] Exhibit 10 ranks U.S. airline carriers by domestic market share,

Exhibit 10 Comparative Domestic Revenue Passenger Miles for the Major U.S. Airlines, March 2007–February 2008 (in billions of miles)

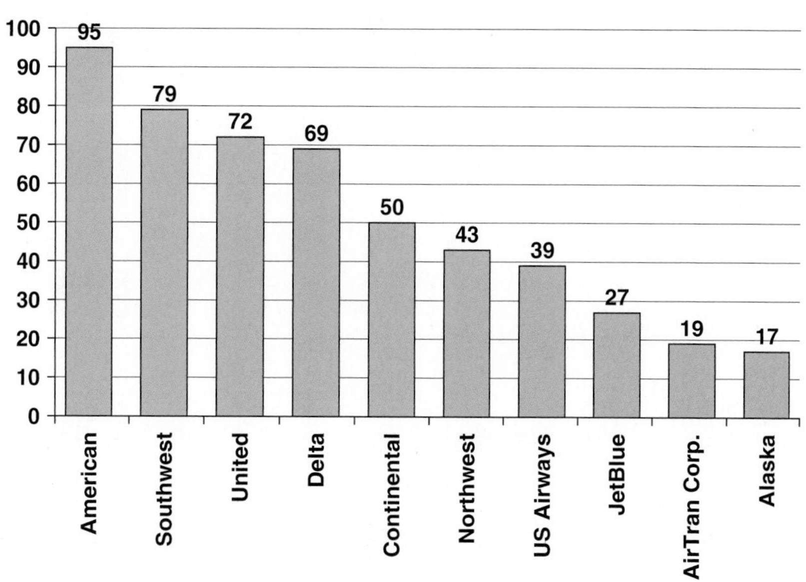

Domestic Market Shares of Major U.S. Airlines, March 2007–February 2008 (based on revenue passenger miles)

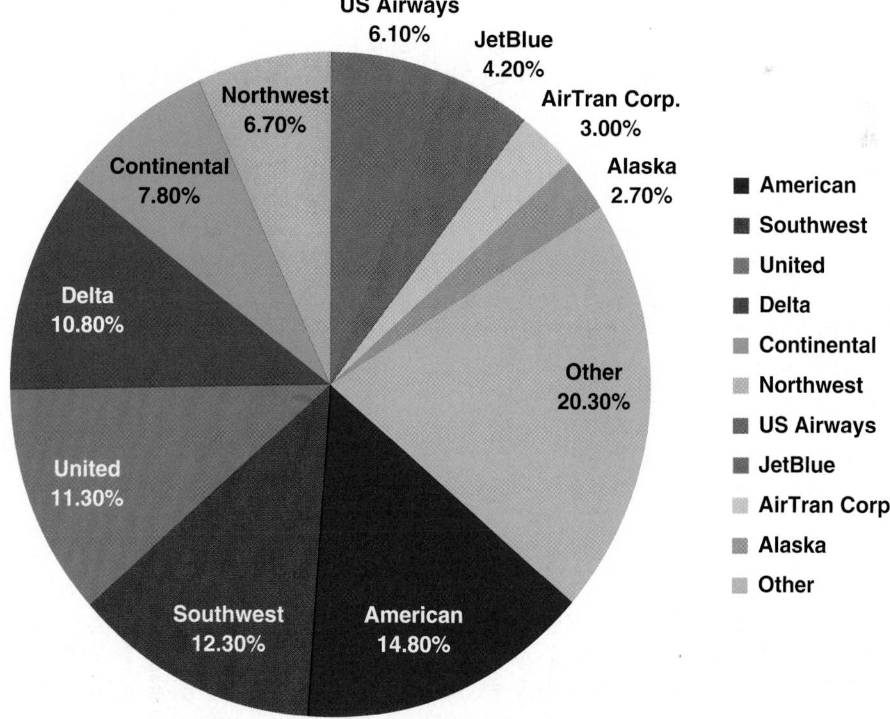

Source: Bureau of Transportation Statistics, www.transtats.bts.gov.

Exhibit 11 Domestic and International Passenger Enplanements by Air Carrier, 1998–First Quarter 2008 (in thousands)

Carrier	1998	1999	2000	2001	2002	2003	2004	2005	2006	2007	First Quarter 2008
America West											
Domestic	17,305	18,265	19,467	19,013	18,799	19,187	20,151	20,868	19,956	14,674	n.a.
International	475	427	478	565	640	861	982	1,262	1,234	991	n.a.
Total	17,780	18,692	19,945	19,578	19,439	20,048	21,133	22,130	21,190	15,665	n.a.
American Airlines											
Domestic	63,987	63,893	68,319	61,704	77,489	72,202	72,648	77,297	76,813	76,581	17,724
International	17,372	17,516	17,951	16,370	16,580	16,560	18,858	20,710	21,313	21,562	n.a.
Total	81,359	81,409	86,270	78,074	94,069	88,762	91,506	98,007	98,126	98,143	n.a.
Continental Air Lines											
Domestic	34,985	36,130	36,591	34,635	31,653	30,853	31,529	32,971	35,795	37,117	8,713
International	6,611	7,814	8,747	8,058	8,247	7,926	9,146	9,795	10,994	11,859	n.a.
Total	41,596	43,944	45,338	42,693	39,900	38,779	40,675	42,766	46,789	48,976	n.a.
Delta Air Lines											
Domestic	97,879	98,212	97,965	86,888	83,747	77,793	79,374	77,581	63,496	61,599	14,307
International	7,259	7,158	7,596	7,150	7,036	6,335	7,416	8,359	10,020	11,435	n.a.
Total	105,138	105,370	105,561	94,038	90,783	84,128	86,790	85,940	73,516	73,034	n.a.
JetBlue Airways	n.a.	n.a.	1,128	3,056	5,672	8,950	11,616	14,463	18,098	20,528	7,024
International	n.a.	n.a.	n.a.	n.a.	n.a.	n.a.	116	218	408	777	n.a.
Total	n.a.	n.a.	1,128	3,056	5,672	8,950	11,732	14,681	18,506	21,305	n.a.
Northwest Airlines											
Domestic	41,931	46,666	48,462	44,786	43,314	43,310	45,959	46,690	45,141	43,812	9,685
International	6,914	7,575	8,228	7,418	7,454	6,871	7,576	7,912	7,831	8,042	n.a.
Total	48,845	54,241	56,690	52,204	50,768	50,181	53,535	54,602	52,972	51,854	n.a.
Southwest Airlines (Domestic Only)	59,053	65,288	72,568	73,629	72,459	74,768	81,121	88,436	96,330	101,948	24,724
United Air Lines											
Domestic	75,058	75,436	72,450	63,947	57,830	56,308	60,081	55,173	57,229	56,402	12,369
International	9,912	9,969	10,625	9,996	9,532	8,541	9,490	10,355	10,770	11,011	n.a.
Total	84,970	85,405	83,075	73,943	67,362	64,849	69,571	65,528	67,999	67,413	n.a.
US Airways											
Domestic	55,603	53,272	56,667	52,658	43,480	37,302	37,810	37,040	31,886	51,895	12,000
International	2,384	2,539	3,105	3,455	3,679	3,954	4,598	4,829	4,609	4,978	n.a.
Total	57,987	55,811	59,772	56,113	47,159	41,256	42,408	41,869	36,495	56,873	n.a.

n.a.= Not available or not applicable.

Notes: US Airways and America West started merging operations in September 2005. US Airways started to report combined traffic data in October 2007. US Airways' and America West's numbers prior to October 2007 were reported separately.

Source: U.S. Department of Transportation, Bureau of Transportation Statistics, Air Carrier Statistics Form T-100.

and Exhibit 11 shows domestic and international passenger enplanements.

Energy conservation became crucial. To save fuel, airlines used one engine instead of two to taxi on runways, installed wing fins to minimize drag, flew at slower speeds to reduce the burn rate, and carried less fuel on long flights to decrease weight. Other strategies included flying at higher altitudes where the air was thinner (meaning less resistance and thus less fuel use), "tankering" (filling up with more fuel than needed at locations where fuel was less expensive), and making planes lighter to conserve fuel (eliminating seats and storing less water).

Besides the volatility of jet fuel prices, airline companies faced the prospects of increased competition from new entrants. With the help of U.S. investors, the British entrepreneur Richard Branson launched a low-fare carrier, Virgin America, with a hub in San Francisco and administrative offices in New York City. It began operating two daily flights between San Francisco and New York and five daily flights between San Francisco and Los Angeles on August 8, 2007. A number of former WestJet executives planned to launch a low-cost airline carrier operating out of Canada. Temporarily named Newair & Tours, the airline planned to sign a deal for a used narrow-body jet and start service in the third quarter of 2008. It would add six more airplanes by the end of 2008. It would fly to destinations in Canada during peak seasons and perhaps target U.S. destinations in the shoulder seasons (i.e., before and after a tourist area's peak season).

The International Air Transport Association estimated that the global airline industry needed 3,000 more pilots each year than training schools were providing.[60] The shortage was caused by the thousands of pilots from the baby-boom generation who were retiring every year and by the thousands of flying hours first officers needed to acquire before they could become captains. Flying schools did not have the instructors to train enough new pilots. The increase in the age limit for a commercial-pilot license from 60 to 65, passed by the International Civil Aviation Organization in 2006, was considered only a stopgap measure.[61] So, along with soaring jet fuel costs, the industry could also face increased labor costs. Large airlines resorted to stealing pilots from small carriers by offering better pay and benefits.

JETBLUE'S STRATEGIES FOR 2008 AND BEYOND

Despite the difficulties facing the airline industry as a whole, JetBlue's new managers spoke confidently of the future. CEO David Barger said, "JetBlue is well positioned with a strong route network, a flexible fleet order book, solid liquidity, the best crew members in the industry, and a management team that understands and has and will continue to respond to the challenges that lie ahead. We will continue to make decisions for the long-term success of JetBlue. We are just being smart about it at the same time."[62] COO Russell Chew felt that proving that a start-up low-cost carrier could mature without giving up its unique attributes was a "once-in-a-generation opportunity to re-invent air travel."[63]

JetBlue began to follow several new strategies. Its managers decided to (1) reevaluate the ways the company was using its assets, (2) reduce capacity and cut costs, (3) raise fares and grow in select markets, (4) offer improved services for corporations and business travelers, (5) form strategic partnerships, and (6) increase ancillary revenues.

JetBlue's managers found new ways of deploying two of the airline's key assets: its JFK terminal and its LiveTV subsidiary. Lufthansa, which held a 19 percent equity stake in JetBlue and a 30 percent equity stake in BMI British Midland (with the option to buy more shares), would be able to use JFK as a "quasi-hub."[64] For several years, Lufthansa had wanted to compete with British Airways on the lucrative London–New York routes. Its partnership with JetBlue would give BMI British Midland access to gates at JFK (once construction of JetBlue's Terminal 5 was completed). In January 2008, JetBlue signed a contract with Continental to provide it with LiveTV. Among LiveTV's other customers were WestJet, Virgin Blue, and AirTran. JetBlue also hired a financial adviser to explore strategic alternatives for the subsidiary (including a divestiture of LiveTV in order to raise cash).

JetBlue planned to reduce capacity and cut costs by:[65]

- Agreeing to sell nine used Airbus A320s in 2008, which would result in a net cash gain of $100 million. It might sell more aircraft in 2009 and 2010.

- Delaying the delivery of 21 new Airbus A320s scheduled for 2009 through 2011 to 2014 and 2015. This would enable JetBlue to postpone payment for the airplanes and save on operating expenses it would incur.
- Reducing its aircraft utilization rate from 13 hours per day to 12.5 hours per day in the fourth quarter of 2008.
- Suspending service in and out of Columbus, Ohio; Nashville, Tennessee; and Tucson, Arizona.
- Canceling planned service between Los Angeles International Airport and Boston and New York. The cost to fill an Airbus 320 with fuel for a transcontinental flight had risen from $9,600 in 2007 to more than $15,000 in 2008.[66]

JetBlue began to grow selectively in certain markets and to slowly raise its fares. In March 2008, JetBlue announced that Orlando would become its seventh "focus city."[67] It opened service between Orlando and Cancún, Mexico, and between Orlando and Santo Domingo, Dominican Republic. It received tentative approval from the U.S. Department of Transportation to start Orlando's only service to South America (with daily nonstop service to Bogotá, Colombia). Two JetBlue partners—Aer Lingus and Lufthansa—also started flying to Orlando. This would offer JetBlue passengers other conveniently scheduled flights to international destinations.

In March 2008, JetBlue's average one-way fare reached an all-time high of $138.[68] This was still very competitive with other airline carriers. The U.S. Department of Transportation noted that the average domestic fare in the fourth quarter of 2007 was $331 (data for the first quarter of 2008 were not yet available).[69] Transcontinental fares rose from $279 to $599. Fares to the Caribbean went from $299 to $599. Barger said that the new fares were being accepted by the traveling public during peak travel periods.[70]

JetBlue tried to appeal to business travelers. It introduced refundable fares and enabled corporate meeting planners to receive meeting-specific discounts and a complimentary travel certificate for every 40 customers booked to the same event destination. It entered into a five-year agreement with Expedia Inc. to reach leisure travelers, managed business travelers, and unmanaged business travelers (unmanaged business travelers were those who booked their business travel on their own as opposed to going through a corporate travel department or a full-service corporate travel management company). JetBlue flights were also available to Travelocity business customers.

At the same time, JetBlue was interested in pursuing partnerships with other airline companies. It developed, for example, an agreement with Aer Lingus that enabled passengers to make a single reservation between Ireland and 40 destinations in the United States through JetBlue's hub at JFK. It had entered into a marketing partnership with Massachusetts-based Cape Air so that passengers could transfer between the two carriers to get to such places as Hyannis, Nantucket, and Martha's Vineyard.

Barger was exploring "ancillary revenue opportunities."[71] He realized this focus would not be a panacea but would enable the airline to offset some of the costs associated with high fuel prices.[72] JetBlue:

- Imposed a call-center charge of $10 on passengers who booked a flight on the phone or at the airport.
- Intended to create a cashless cabin in which passengers could pay for extra food items via handheld devices carried by flight attendants.
- Stopped handing out free headphones and sold only upgraded versions for $1 at the gate.
- Charged passengers additional fees to reserve seats with extra legroom. These seats were popular on long-haul flights. The program generated more than $40 million in incremental revenue in nine months in 2008.
- Charged passengers a $20 service fee for checking a second bag beginning June 1, 2008. The new policy was expected to generate more than $20 million in new revenues in the last six months in 2008.

These were the strategies that JetBlue's management team had developed to deal with what Barger called "the new normal environment" of rising fuel prices and increased competition.[73] The issue was whether they would be enough to ensure JetBlue's survival; the company's performance in the first six months of 2008, as shown in Exhibits 12 and 13, cast doubt on the adequacy of the actions taken so far.

Exhibit 12 JetBlue Airways' Financial Performance, First Six Months of 2008 ($ in millions, except per share data and percentages)

Income Statement Data (unaudited)	Six Months Ending June 30, 2008	Six Months Ending June 30, 2007	Percent Change
OPERATING REVENUES			
Passenger	$1,527	$1,247	22.5%
Other	148	91	62.0%
Total operating revenues	1,675	1,338	25.2%
OPERATING EXPENSES			
Aircraft fuel	678	416	62.8%
Salaries, wages and benefits	346	322	7.3%
Landing fees and rents	100	92	9.3%
Depreciation/amortization	91	85	7.1%
Aircraft rent	64	60	6.5%
Sales and marketing	80	60	35.0%
Maintenance and repairs	65	53	22.5%
Other operating expenses	213	190	11.6%
Total operating expenses	1,637	1,278	28.0%
OPERATING INCOME	38	60	(35.6)%
Operating margin (%)	2.3%	4.5%	(2.2) points
Non-operating income (expense)			
Interest (expense)	(109)	(108)	1.5%
Capitalized interest	28	19	50.3%
Other non-operating	20	27	26.4%
Total other income (expense)	(61)	(62)	(0.7)%
Income (loss) before income taxes	(23)	(2)	
Pre-tax margin (%)	(1.4)%	(0.1)%	(1.3) points
Income tax expense (benefit)	(8)	(1)	
NET INCOME	(15)	(1)	
Earnings (loss) per share, basic	(0.07)	(0.00)	
Earnings (loss) per share, diluted	(0.07)	(0.00)	

Selected Balance Sheet and Cash Flow Data	As of June 30, 2008 (unaudited)	As of December 31, 2007	Percent Change
Cash and cash equivalents	$ 846	$ 190	345.3%
Total investment securities	397	644	−38.4%
Total assets	6,468	5,598	15.5%
Total debt	3,335	3,048	9.4%
Common stockholders' equity	1,378	1,036	33.0%
Net cash provided by operating activities	105	219	−52.1%

Source: JetBlue, 2008 Form 10-Q for the period ended June 30, 2008, and press release on Form 8-K for July 22, 2008.

Exhibit 13 JetBlue Airways' Operating Performance, Six Months Ending June 30, 2008 versus 2007

	Six Months Ending June 30, 2008	Six Months Ending June 30, 2007	Percent Change
Revenue passengers (thousands)	11,155	10,678	4.5%
Revenue passenger miles (millions)	13,319	12,678	5.1%
Available seat miles (ASMs) (millions)	16,778	15,436	8.7%
Load factor	79.4%	82.1%	(2.7) points
Breakeven load factor*	83.1%	83.5%	(0.4) points
Aircraft utilization (hours per day)	12.8	12.9	(1.0)%
Average fare	$136.90	$116.74	17.3%
Yield per passenger mile (cents)	11.47	9.83	16.6%
Passenger revenue per ASM (cents)	9.10	8.08	12.7%
Operating revenue per ASM (cents)	9.98	8.67	15.2%
Operating expense per ASM (cents)	9.75	8.28	17.8%
Operating expense per ASM, excluding fuel (cents)	5.71	5.58	2.3%
Airline operating expense per ASM (cents)	9.53	8.21	16.1%
Departures	104,501	96,087	8.8%
Average stage length (miles)	1,135	1,111	2.1%
Average number of operating aircraft during period	138.0	124.1	11.2%
Average fuel cost per gallon	2.91	1.95	49.5%
Fuel gallons consumed (millions)	233	214	8.9%
Percent of sales through JetBlue.com	77.0%	75.2%	1.8 points
Full-time equivalent employees at period end*	9,856	9,421	4.6%

*Excludes operating expenses and employees of LiveTV, LLC, which are unrelated to airline operations.
Source: JetBlue, 2008 Form 10-Q for the period ended June 30, 2008, and press release on Form 8-K for July 22, 2008.

Meanwhile, there were indications that JetBlue might become a takeover target. Its shares had hit an all-time low of $3.14 on July 11, 2008. JetBlue had put in place a severance plan to protect executives and employees in case a competitor attempted a hostile takeover.[74] Perhaps Lufthansa might have a long-term interest in increasing its minority stake in the airline. The German company could easily increase its stake from 19 to 25 percent; anything above that would require a change in U.S. laws. Foreign airlines were allowed to own only up to 25 percent of a U.S. carrier's stock. Some industry observers suggested that if turmoil in the domestic airline carrier industry continued, policymakers might ease the restriction. "The U.S. airlines badly need more capital to survive, and the only players with the resources to buy in are the [cash-rich] European carriers," noted Robert Mann Jr., an industry consultant.[75] Would JetBlue remain an independent carrier in the future?

Endnotes

[1] N. Weil, "What JetBlue's CIO Learned about Customer Satisfaction," *CIO* 20 (April 15, 2007), p. 1. Retrieved September 3, 2007, from ABI/INFORM (Proquest) database.

[2] R. Newman, "Loyal Clients Key, JetBlue CEO Says," Knight Ridder Tribune Business News, November, 2003, p. 1. Retrieved May 5, 2005, from ABI/INFORM (Proquest) database.

[3] "JetBlue Finance Chief Harvey Resigns," *Wall Street Journal,* November 9, 2007, p. B5. Retrieved April 30, 2008, from ABI/INFORM (Proquest) database.

[4] L. Barack, "Betting on Clear Skies Once More: With Flying in His Blood, JetBlue's Dave Barger Keeps His Head Above the Clouds," *Wall Street Journal,* November 1, 2007, p. 1. Retrieved April 30, 2008, from ABI/INFORM (Proquest) database.

[5] D. Neeleman, "From Milk Crates to High Altitudes," *New York Times,* November 5, 2000, p. 3. Retrieved March 12, 2005, from ABI/INFORM (Proquest) database.

[6] S. B. Donnelly, "Blue Skies," *Time* 158 (July 30, 2001), pp. 24–26. Retrieved March 13, 2005, from ABI/INFORM (Proquest) database.

[7] "On the Record: David Neeleman," *San Francisco Chronicle,* September 12, 2004, p. J1. Retrieved March 6,2005, from ABI/INFORM (Proquest) database.
[8] R. Newman, "Preaching JetBlue," *Chief Executive* 202 (October 2004), pp. 26–29. Retrieved March 5, 2005, from ABI/INFORM (Proquest) database.
[9] C. Woodyard, "JetBlue Turns to Beetles, Beaches, Bars," *USA Today,* August 22, 2001, p. B3. Retrieved March 6, 2005, from ABI/INFORM (Proquest) database.
[10] R. Smothers, "New Airline to Emphasize More Flights for Upstate," *New York Times,* February 11, 2000, p. B8. Retrieved March 2, 2005, from ABI/INFORM (Proquest) database.
[11] J. M. Feldman, "JetBlue Loves New York," *Air Transport World* 38 (June 2001), pp. 78–80. Retrieved March 3, 2005, from ABI/INFORM (Proquest) database.
[12] E. Brown, "A Smokeless Herb," *Fortune* 143 (May 28, 2001), pp. 78–79. Retrieved May 5, 2005, from ABI/INFORM (Proquest) database.
[13] A. Williams, "SuperFly," *New York Magazine,* January 31, 2000, www.newyorkmetro.com/nymetro/news/bizfinance/biz/features/1879 (accessed March 2, 2005).
[14] R. Dwyer, "Blue Skies," *AirFinance Journal* 227 (April 2000), p. 26. Retrieved March 15, 2005, from ABI/INFORM (Proquest) database.
[15] Williams, "SuperFly."
[16] "Bush Administration Moves to Reduce Delays at Kennedy International Airport," *Air Safety Week* 21 (October 22, 2007). Retrieved July 7, 2008, from ABI/INFORM (Proquest) database.
[17] S. Linstedt, "Flight Delays Here Are Below U.S.Average: Top Destination JFK Remains a Problem," McClatchy-Tribune Business News, February 6, 2008. Retrieved July 7, 2008, from ABI/INFORM (Proquest) database.
[18] S. Amoult and A. Karp, "New York Delayed," *Air Transport World* 45 (February 2008), pp. 56–59. Retrieved July 7, 2008, from ABI/INFORM (Proquest) database.
[19] "Q4 2007 JetBlue Airways Earnings Conference Call-Final," Fair Disclosure Wire, January 29, 2008. Retrieved July 9, 2008, from Lexis-Nexis Academic.
[20] D. Armstrong, "David Neeleman, Founder and CEO of JetBlue Airways, Has a Successful Flight Plan," *San Francisco Chronicle,* December 28, 2002, p. B1. Retrieved January 20, 2003, from ABI/INFORM (Proquest) database.
[21] D. Reed, "Loss Shifts JetBlue's Focus to Climbing Back into Black," *USA Today,* February 22, 2006, p. B1. Retrieved June 17, 2008 from ABI/INFORM (Proquest) database.
[22] "JetBlue Airways at Merrill Lynch Transportation Conference—Final," Fair Disclosure Wire, June 18, 2008. Retrieved July 9, 2008 from Lexis Nexis Academic.
[23] "Paper Tickets May Be a Costlier Air Travel Option," *Businessline,* May 7, 2008. Retrieved June 17, 2008 from ABI/INFORM (Proquest) database.
[24] Ibid.
[25] M. Frase-Blunt, "Call Centers Come Home," *HRMagazine* 52 (January 2007), pp. 84–89. Retrieved June 17, 2008 from ABI/INFORM (Proquest) database.
[26] J. Artunian, "Customer Service Finds Spot in Homes; More Companies Use Home-Based Workers to Handle Calls," *Chicago Tribune,* April 11, 2005, p. 1. Retrieved June 17, 2008 from ABI/INFORM (Proquest) database.
[27] J. Ginovsky, "Corporate Excellence," *ABA Bankers News* 12 (March 16, 2004), pp 1–2. Retrieved March 17, 2005, from ABI/INFORM (Proquest) database.
[28] "Corporate Culture," *Air Safety Week* 15 (November 12, 2001), p. 1. Retrieved March 17, 2005, from ABI/INFORM (Proquest) database; www.jetblue.com/about/work/culture.
[29] "Find a Way to Yes! SLA Keynoter's Tips," *Information Outlook* 8 (March 2004). Retrieved March 17, 2005, from ABI/INFORM (Proquest) database.
[30] B. Finn and D. Neeleman, "How to Turn Managers into Leaders," *Business 2.0* 5 (September 2004), p. 70. Retrieved March 17, 2005, from ABI/INFORM (Proquest) database.
[31] F. Fiorino, "Airline Outlook," *Aviation Week and Space Technology* 156 (June 3, 2002). Retrieved June 17, 2008 from ABI/INFORM (Proquest) database.
[32] E. Sanger, "JetBlue Flying High with Service," *New York Newsday,* June 14, 2004, www.nynewsday.com (accessed March 18, 2005).
[33] E. Tahmincioglu, "True Blue," *Workforce Management* 84 (February 2005), pp. 47–50. Retrieved March 17, 2005, from ABI/INFORM (Proquest) database.
[34] G. Ruiz, "Special Report: Talent acquisition," *Workforce Management* 86 (July, 23, 2007), pp. 39–43. Retrieved July 7, 2008, from ABI/INFORM (Proquest) database.
[35] M. Weinstein, "JetBlue: Training in the Air," *Training* 43 (April 2006), pp. 26–27. Retrieved June 13, 2008, from ABI/INFORM (Proquest) database.
[36] "JetBlue Woos Pilot Candidates," *Air Safety Week* 22 (February 4, 2008). Retrieved July 7, 2008, from ABI/INFORM (Proquest) database.
[37] Ibid.
[38] "Striving for Safety Excellence," *T + D* 60 (October 2006), pp. 44–46. Retrieved July 14, 2008, from ABI/INFORM (Proquest) database.
[39] Ibid.
[40] Weinstein, "JetBlue: Training in the Air."
[41] M. Maynard, "Coffee, Tea or Job?" *New York Times,* September 3, 2004, p. C1.
[42] "Q2 2008 JetBlue Airways Earnings Conference Call-Final," Fair Disclosure Wire, July 22, 2008. Retrieved July 31, 2008 from LexisNexis Academic.
[43] JetBlue Airways, 8-K report, July 28, 2008.
[44] L. Steffy, "Airline Investors Find They're Always Losing Altitude," *Houston Chronicle,* April 11, 2008, p. 1. Retrieved June 30, 2008, from ABI/INFORM (Proquest) database.
[45] A. Sloan and T. Ehrenfeld, "Skies Were Cloudy Before Jet Blew It," *Newsweek* 149 (March 5, 2007), p. 26. Retrieved June 12, 2008, from ABI/INFORM (Proquest) database.
[46] "View from the Top, David Neeleman, Founder of JetBlue Airways," *Financial Times,* December 14, 2007, p. 12. Retrieved April 30, 2008, from ABI/INFORM (Proquest) database.
[47] S. Carey and M. Trottman, "Costly Fuel, Economic Woes Weight Down U.S.Airlines," *Wall Street Journal,* March 20, 2008, p. A1. Retrieved June 17, 2008, from ABI/INFORM (Proquest) database.
[48] J. Corridore, "Current Environment," Airlines, *Standard & Poor's Industry Surveys,* May 15, 2008, pp. 1–13.
[49] "JetBlue Airways at Merrill Lynch."
[50] "Q1 2008 JetBlue Airways Earnings Conference Call-Final," Fair Disclosure Wire, April 22, 2008. Retrieved July 9, 2008, from LexisNexis Academic.
[51] Ibid.
[52] "Q2 2008 JetBlue Airways Earnings Conference Call-Final."
[53] M. Duvall and D. Bartholomew, "What Really Happened at JetBlue," *Baseline,* April 2007, pp. 53–58. Retrieved June 17, 2008, from EBSCOHost database.
[54] Ibid.
[55] Ibid.
[56] M. Bush, "JetBlue Seeks PR Shop to Help It Out of the Toilet," *Advertising Age* 79 (May 19, 2008), pp. 3–4. Retrieved July 7, 2008, from ABI/INFORM (Proquest) database.
[57] N. Zerillo, "JetBlue Hires MWW for Crisis Communication," *PR Week,* June 30, 2008, www.prweekus.com/JetBlue-hires-MWW-for-crisis-communications/article/111961/ (accessed July 7, 2008).
[58] D. R. Stewart, "Fuel-Cost Coping," McClatchy-Tribune Business News, March 21, 2008. Retrieved June 17, 2008, from ABI/INFORM (Proquest) database.
[59] Corridore, "Current Environment."
[60] D. Pearson, "Airlines Face Shortage of Pilots," *Wall Street Journal,* April 23, 2008. Retrieved July 14, 2008, from ABI/INFORM (Proquest) database.
[61] Ibid.
[62] "Q1 2008 JetBlue Airways Earnings Conference Call-Final."
[63] D. Reed, "JetBlue's New COO Didn't Follow Traditional Aviation Career Trail," *USA Today,* June 7, 2007, p. B2. Retrieved June 10, 2008, from ABI/INFORM (Proquest) database.

[64] G. Wiesmann, "Lufthansa Poised to Deepen Link with JetBlue to Create JFK Hub," *Financial Times,* March 13, 2008, p. 39. Retrieved July 7, 2008 from Gale Cengage Learning database.
[65] "Q1 2008 JetBlue Airways Earnings Conference Call-Final."
[66] P. Pae, "JetBlue Expected to Delay Service from LAX," *Los Angeles Times,* May 6, 2008, p. C3. Retrieved July 7, 2008, from Lexis Nexis Academic.
[67] "New Focus City at Orlando International Airport Announced by JetBlue," *Airline Industry Information,* March 20, 2008. Retrieved July 7, 2008, from ABI/INFORM (Proquest) database.
[68] "Q1 2008 JetBlue Airways Earnings Conference Call-Final."
[69] "Average Fourth-Quarter Air Fares Rose 4.0 Percent from 2006," U.S.Department of Transportation, Bureau of Transportation Statistics, April 23, 2008, www.bts.gov/press_releases/2008/bts019_08/html/bts019_08.html (accessed July 12, 2008).
[70] "JetBlue Airways at Merrill Lynch."
[71] Barack, "Betting on Clear Skies."
[72] "Q1 2008 JetBlue Airways Earnings Conference Call-Final."
[73] "JetBlue Airways at Merrill Lynch."
[74] J. Bernstein, "Talk of JetBlue Merger in the Air," Knight Ridder Tribune Business News, June 30, 2007, p. 1. Retrieved September 3, 2007, from ABI/INFORM (Proquest) database.
[75] D. Foust, J. Bachman, and A. Aston, "Fly the Shrinking Skies," *BusinessWeek,* June 9, 2008, p. 29. Retrieved June 17, 2008, from ABI/INFORM (Proquest) database.

Competition in the Golf Equipment Industry in 2008

CASE 4

John E. Gamble
University of South Alabama

It is not known with certainty when the game of golf originated, but historians believe it evolved from ball-and-stick games played throughout Europe in the Middle Ages. The first known reference to golf in historical documents was a 1452 decree by King James II of Scotland banning the game. The ban was instituted because King James believed his archers were spending too much time playing golf and not enough time practicing archery. King James III and King James IV reaffirmed the ban in 1471 and 1491, respectively, but King James IV ultimately repealed the ban in 1502 after he himself became hooked on the game. The game became very popular with royalty and commoners alike, with the Archbishop of St. Andrews decreeing in 1553 that the local citizenry had the right to play on the links of St. Andrews and King James VI declaring in 1603 that his subjects had the right to play golf on Sundays.

The first known international golf tournament was played in Leith, Scotland, in 1682; Scotsmen George Patterson and James VII prevailed over two Englishmen. By the 1700s, golf had become an established sport in the British Isles, complete with golfing societies, published official rules, regularly held tournaments, full-time equipment manufacturers, and equipment exports from Scotland to the American colonies. The links of St. Andrews became a private golf society in 1754 and was given the title of Royal & Ancient Golf Club of St. Andrews by King William IV in 1834. The first golf society in the United States was founded in Charleston, South Carolina, in 1786.

In the United States, golf was a game that interested primarily the wealthy until the arrival of televised tournaments in the 1950s and 1960s featuring the charismatic PGA Tour players Arnold Palmer, Gary Player, and Jack Nicklaus. The popularity of golf grew in the United States throughout the 1970s and 1980s and peaked in 1998 with 27.5 million Americans playing golf at least once a year. At the beginning of the 21st century, the U.S. golf economy accounted for approximately \$62 billion worth of goods and services. The golf economy involved core industries such as golf equipment manufacturers, course designers, turf maintenance, and club management services. The golf economy also included such enabled industries as residential golf communities and hospitality and tourism. In 2000, the golf equipment segment of the industry, which included golf clubs, bags, balls, gloves, and footwear, accounted for approximately \$4 billion in retail sales.

Even though golf had grown to be a sizable part of the U.S. economy, the golf equipment industry was faced with serious troubles in 2008. The convergence of a variety of serious hazards to the industry had caused the retail value of the golf equipment industry to decline from approximately \$4 billion in 2000 to about \$3 billion in 2003. Golf equipment sales had rebounded to an estimated \$3.8 billion in 2007, but many threats to the industry continued to exist. The number of golfers in the United States had declined from 1998's all-time high of 27.5 million to 22.7 million in 2007. Also, the number of rounds of golf played in the United States had not grown appreciably since 2000 and had declined by 2.2 percent during the first six months of 2008. In addition, golf equipment manufacturers had become stifled in their abilities to pursue innovation-based strategies directed at making golf easier to play for those of modest talent. Revenues and profits of golf equipment manufacturers soared during the mid-to-late 1990s as such companies as Callaway Golf,

TaylorMade Golf, Titleist, and Ping Golf developed innovation after innovation that helped minimize the negative effects of recreational golfers' swing flaws. But beginning in 1998, golf's governing organizations, the United States Golf Association (USGA) and the Royal & Ancient Golf Club (R&A), put a series of new rules in place that limited manufacturers' abilities to develop more forgiving golf equipment. The major concern of the USGA and the R&A was that the rapid advances in golf club and golf ball technology had given golfers too much of an advantage and that continued technological innovation might pose a threat to the game.

The combined effect of technological limitations imposed by golf's governing organizations, a decline in the number of golfers, and blurred differentiation between brands had all begun to affect profit margins in the industry. Industry leader Callaway Golf Company, which had earned a record \$132 million when it enjoyed a large technology-based competitive advantage over rivals in 1997, had seen its profits drop abruptly and sharply after limitations to innovation were enacted by the USGA and the R&A. The company's share price declined from a peak of \$35 in 1997 to about \$13.50 in mid-2008 as the company turned more and more to price discounting and costly endorsement deals with professional golfers to boost sales. TaylorMade Golf, which was an adidas business unit and another technological leader in the industry, suffered consistent declines in operating profits between 2003 and 2007. Titleist, a division of Fortune Brands and a leader in golf technology, had also struggled to maintain its operating profit margins as it was forced to rely more on discounting and endorsement contracts to capture sales gains.

Some industry rivals with less developed technological capabilities had actually benefited from the USGA and R&A performance regulations, since it provided those companies with an opportunity to catch up to TaylorMade, Titleist, and Callaway Golf from a technology standpoint. Revenues for Adams Golf, which had been a niche seller with limited technological capabilities, increased from \$41.7 million in 2000 to nearly \$95 million in 2007 after the performance of its products grew closer to those offered by industry leaders. The sizable increase in revenues allowed Adams Golf to swing from a \$37 million loss in 2000 to a \$9.4 million profit in 2007.

Even though the equalization of technological capabilities had resulted in increased profits for some golf equipment manufacturers, the overall slim operating profit margins in the industry and a growing reliance on price competition presented a variety of strategy-making challenges for golf's premier equipment manufacturers. Golf equipment retail sales, units sold, and average selling price by product category for 1997–2007 are presented in Exhibit 1.

Exhibit 1 **Retail Value, Units Sold, and Average Selling Price of Golf Equipment in the United States, 1997–2007**

Drivers and Woods			
Year	Retail Value (in millions)	Units Sold (in millions)	Average Selling Price
1997	\$676.8	2.93	\$231
1998	601.1	2.81	214
1999	583.8	2.91	201
2000	599.1	2.94	204
2001	626.6	2.99	210
2002	608.7	3.09	197
2003	660.4	3.28	201
2004	654.1	3.56	184
2005	792.2	4.76	166
2006	883.3	5.12	172
2007	877.7	5.03	174
Irons			
Year	Retail Value (in millions)	Units Sold (in millions)	Average Selling Price Per Club
1997	\$533.4	7.12	\$75
1998	485.4	6.87	71
1999	447.9	6.97	64
2000	475.3	7.14	67
2001	459.3	7.17	64
2002	456.4	7.42	62
2003	461.4	7.66	60
2004	482.6	8.06	60
2005	534.3	8.26	65
2006	570.7	8.35	68
2007	579.5	8.22	71

(Continued)

Exhibit 1 (Continued)

Putters

Year	Retail Value (in millions)	Units Sold (in millions)	Average Selling Price
1997	$142.1	1.70	$83
1998	150.3	1.68	89
1999	160.1	1.68	95
2000	161.5	1.67	97
2001	167.2	1.65	101
2002	184.3	1.65	111
2003	195.2	1.60	122
2004	188.6	1.58	120
2005	188.4	1.56	121
2006	193.8	1.53	127
2007	190.0	1.46	130

Wedges

Year	Retail Value (in millions)	Units Sold (in millions)	Average Selling Price
1997	$67.6	0.78	$86
1998	64.3	0.79	82
1999	65.0	0.81	80
2000	68.3	0.82	83
2001	69.4	0.82	85
2002	71.2	0.83	85
2003	77.0	0.88	87
2004	79.3	0.93	86
2005	87.5	0.99	89
2006	93.9	1.03	91
2007	95.6	1.07	90

Golf Balls

Year	Retail Value (in millions)	Units Sold (in dozens)	Average Selling Price Per Dozen
1997	$458.7	19.97	$22.97
1998	487.4	20.06	24.30
1999	518.1	20.46	25.32
2000	530.8	20.80	25.52
2001	555.6	21.32	26.06
2002	529.9	20.81	25.46
2003	496.4	19.85	25.01
2004	506.3	19.98	25.34
2005	536.0	20.39	26.29
2006	539.0	20.45	26.35
2007	552.3	20.99	26.31

Footwear

Year	Retail Value (in millions)	Units Sold (in millions)	Average Selling Price
1997	$214.3	2.48	$86
1998	204.3	2.43	84
1999	206.9	2.47	84
2000	220.8	2.52	88
2001	217.8	2.57	85
2002	211.7	2.68	79
2003	217.1	2.82	77
2004	234.4	3.00	78
2005	245.2	3.15	78
2006	257.7	3.24	80
2007	275.5	3.42	81

Gloves

Year	Retail Value (in millions)	Units Sold (in dozens)	Average Selling Price (per unit)
1997	$156.7	1.28	$12.23
1998	160.6	1.28	12.56
1999	161.6	1.30	12.46
2000	165.4	1.32	12.53
2001	169.2	1.34	12.61
2002	163.7	1.34	12.26
2003	157.1	1.29	12.16
2004	159.3	1.32	12.11
2005	164.0	1.12	12.22
2006	168.4	1.13	12.45
2007	174.9	1.17	12.46

Golf Bags

Year	Retail Value (in millions)	Units Sold (in millions)	Average Selling Price
1997	$171.8	1.37	$126
1998	165.6	1.32	125
1999	165.4	1.32	125
2000	165.1	1.31	126
2001	163.2	1.32	124
2002	153.4	1.32	116
2003	145.5	1.32	111
2004	146.8	1.34	110
2005	150.7	1.39	109
2006	158.5	1.41	112
2007	165.8	1.43	116

Source: Golf Datatech.

Exhibit 2 Participation Rates for Selected Sports and Recreational Activities, 1996–2007, Various Years (in millions)

	1996	1998	2000	2002	2004	2006	2007
Bicycle riding	53.3	43.5	43.1	39.7	40.3	35.6	37.4
Fishing	45.6	43.6	49.3	44.2	41.2	40.6	35.3
Golf	23.1	27.5	26.4	27.1	24.5	24.4	22.7
Hunting	18.3	17.3	19.1	19.5	17.7	17.8	19.5
Running	22.2	22.5	22.8	24.7	26.7	28.8	30.4
Swimming	60.2	58.2	60.7	53.1	53.4	56.5	52.3
Tennis	11.5	11.2	10.0	11.0	9.6	10.4	12.3
Workout at fitness club	22.5	26.5	24.1	28.9	31.8	37.0	33.8

Source: National Sporting Goods Association.

INDUSTRY CONDITIONS IN 2008

In 2007, approximately 22.7 million Americans played golf at least once a year—which was about 5 million less than the number of Americans playing golf in 1998. The decline in the number of golfers was distributed among men, women, and junior golfers, with the number of men playing golf falling from about 20 million in 2000 to 16.2 million in 2007, the number of women golfers declining from 5.8 million in 2002 to 5.1 million in 2007, and the number of junior golfers declining from 2.4 million in 1998 to 1.4 million in 2007. Minority participation was relatively low in the United States, with only 1.3 million African American golfers, 1.1 million Asian American golfers, and 1.0 million Hispanic American golfers participating in 2003. A 2003 National Golf Foundation study on minority golf participation in the United States found that income tended to reduce differences in participation rates among races. For golfers with household incomes lower than $100,000, white non-Hispanics and Asians were nearly twice as likely to play golf as African Americans or Hispanic Americans. About 28 percent of adults with household incomes exceeding $100,000 played golf, regardless of race.

The availability of municipal and public golf courses in the United States made golf accessible to Americans across a wide range of income levels, but in Europe and Asia golf remained a sport pursued primarily by the affluent. About 2 million Europeans and about 17 million Asians played golf in 2007. Exhibit 2 provides the number of Americans playing golf during various years between 1996 and 2007. The exhibit also provides participation rates for other sports and recreational activities popular with adults.

About one-third of golfers were considered core golfers—those playing at least eight times a year and averaging 37 rounds a year. Industry sales were keyed to the number of core golfers, since these frequent golfers accounted for 91 percent of rounds played each year and 87 percent of industry equipment sales, membership fees, and green fees. Even though core golfers might play once a week or more, only a small fraction of golfers might be confused for PGA touring professionals while on the course. The average score for adult male golfers on an 18-hole course was 96, with only 5 percent of adult male golfers regularly breaking a score of 80. The average score for adult female golfers was 108. The number of golf rounds played for each year between 2001 and 2007 is presented in Exhibit 3.

Exhibit 3 Total Rounds of Golf Played in the United States, 2001–2007 (in millions)

Year	Rounds Played (in millions)	Percent Change
2001	518.1	—
2002	502.4	−3.0%
2003	494.9	−1.5
2004	528.6	6.8
2005	528.1	−0.1
2006	532.3	0.8
2007	529.6	−0.5

Source: National Golf Foundation.

RECENT TRENDS IN THE GOLF EQUIPMENT INDUSTRY

Limited Opportunities for Innovation in Clubface Design

The arrival of Tiger Woods to the PGA Tour in 1996 inspired many people to take up the game of golf, but most soon found that becoming a somewhat accomplished golfer was a highly demanding task. Developing a sound golf swing required regular instruction from a teaching professional, many hours of practice, and the patience to master all aspects of the game—driving the ball from the tee, long iron shots, short approach shots, hitting from the rough, chipping to the green, sand shots, and putting. Few adults had the leisure time to master all elements of the game simultaneously—for example, they might find they were hitting iron shots really well at a particular point but were having trouble off the tee or botching chips and sand shots. Later they might be very pleased with their drives but furious with their poor putting.

Golf equipment manufacturers had developed innovations at a rapid clip during the late 1990s and early 2000s to help make the game easier to play for recreational golfers. The size of the driver was increased to reduce the adverse effect of off-center hits, wedges were given more defined grooves to help improve accuracy on approach shots, and balls were redesigned to provide greater distance off the tee and better control on the green. The technological innovations proved to give golfers of modest skills an assist such that their bad shots were not quite so bad. The primary benefit of technologically advanced golf clubs and balls related to distance. Under no conditions would a poorly struck ball fly as far as a well-struck ball, but the loss of distance using modern equipment was not as great as what would be the case with older 1980s or early-1990s equipment.

The advent of game improvement equipment was also a benefit to the world's elite professional golfers on the PGA Tour, the PGA European Tour, and the Ladies Professional Golf Association Tour (LPGA). The average driving distance on the PGA Tour had increased from 257 yards in 1980 to 290 yards in 2005. Also, it was not uncommon for touring professionals to hit the ball more than 320 yards off the tee and for women on the LPGA Tour to hit the ball as far as 290 yards. Tournament committees responded to the increased driving distance by lengthening the overall distance of the courses hosting professional tournaments. USGA officials believed that it was the organization's responsibility to limit golf club performance to protect historic golf courses that could not be lengthened because of space limitations. The USGA developed a measurement and limitation in 1998 that would defend against any springlike effect that a high-tech driver clubface might deliver. The test involved firing a golf ball at a driver out of a cannon-like machine at 109 miles per hour. The speed that the ball returned to the cannon could not exceed 83 percent of its initial speed (90.47 miles per hour). The USGA called the ratio of incoming to outgoing velocity the coefficient of restitution (COR). Drivers that did not conform to the USGA 0.83 COR threshold were barred from use by recreational or professional golfers in the United States, Canada, and Mexico who intended to play by the USGA's Rules of Golf. The USGA refused to calculate handicaps for golfers who had used a nonconforming club, but it did not attempt to restrict the club's use among players who did not choose to establish or maintain handicaps.

Golf club manufacturers disagreed that a springlike effect could be produced by a metal golf club and believed that the USGA's ruling—which affected recreational as well as professional tournament golfers—would discourage new golfers from taking up the game. During the 2000 Masters Tournament in Augusta, Georgia, Callaway Golf chief engineer Richard Helmstetter challenged the suggestion that clubs with a high COR could produce a springlike effect:

> We do a great deal of research at Callaway Golf and I think we are the most technologically advanced golf company in the world. We have been unable to find any evidence at all that a clubface, no matter how thin, plays a role like a trampoline in striking the ball. We do think that certain kinds of construction and materials will reduce the loss of energy in the golf ball at impact and give the golfer longer drives, but this is quite different from a trampoline. The clubface vibrates during impact at a speed so high that it cannot be timed, we believe, to the compression and release of a golf ball. Consequently, we think that trampoline effect is a misnomer, if not a myth entirely.[1]

Callaway Golf challenged the USGA's COR limitation in 2000 when it introduced for sale in the United States the ERC II driver with a COR of 0.86. The company's management believed that the 6–10 additional yards of carry achieved by recreational golfers using the ERC II posed no threat to the game of golf. Callaway Golf executives did concede that equipment limitations might be set for professional golfers, but they saw no need to limit the performance of equipment used by recreational golfers who might gain more pleasure from hitting longer drives. Callaway Golf founder Ely Callaway suggested that there were "two games of golf—tournament golf and recreational golf, and the two games differ in many respects. . . . We believe that recreational golfers should not be denied the benefits of modern technology that can bring them added enjoyment that comes from occasionally hitting the ball a little bit further."[2]

Upon the announcement that Callaway Golf would make the club available to golfers in the United States, Arnold Palmer supported the company's decision by saying, "I think what Callaway is doing is just right. I have given a lot of thought to conforming and non-conforming clubs. If my daughter, who is a 100s shooter, can shoot 90 with a non-conforming driver, I can't imagine that there would be anything wrong with that."[3]

The ERC II was a failure in the United States since most core golfers did not want to purchase equipment that violated the USGA's Rules of Golf. The USGA clarified its purpose for barring products like the ERC II in 2002 by stating that "the purpose of the Rules is to prevent an over-reliance on technological advances rather than skill and to ensure that skill is the dominant element in determining success throughout the game."[4] Initially, the R&A chose to place limitations only on equipment used in elite competitive events, but it came to an agreement with the USGA in 2006 to regulate driver performance for both professional and recreational golfers. In order to arrive at a worldwide standard, the USGA scrapped the COR test for the R&A's characteristic time (CT) test. The CT test required that the golf ball remain in contact with the face of a driver for 239 microseconds, plus a test tolerance of 18 microseconds. Contact longer than 257 microseconds was considered evidence of a springlike effect and would place a driver on the R&A's nonconforming list.

Once the USGA had successfully eliminated the possibility of a springlike effect produced by a driver clubface, it created additional rules regulating driver dimensions and other elements of driver performance. In 2004, the USGA ruled that driving clubs were not allowed to be larger than 5 inches by 5 inches and could not have a volume of more than 460 cubic centimeters (cc). With clubhead size and clubface CT off limits, golf club manufacturers began to pursue innovations that would increase the clubface area capable of producing the maximum CT. Specifically, drivers offered by all golf club manufacturers produced the maximum CT rating allowed by the USGA and R&A, but the percentage of the surface area of the clubface producing the maximum CT might vary quite a bit between driver models and brands. Therefore, all club manufacturers were in a race to push the allowable CT area out to the perimeter of the clubface. This clubface performance characteristic was referred to as the moment of inertia (MOI). Higher MOI drivers allowed golfers to hit the ball near the inside heel of the club or toward the outer toe of the club and still achieve a near-maximum driving distance. The USGA notified golf equipment manufacturers in 2005 that driver MOI had tripled over the past 15 years and that, beginning in 2006, MOI would be limited to 5,900 g-cm^2 with a tolerance of 100 g-cm^2.

The USGA was also concerned about the performance of technologically advanced golf balls such as the Titleist Pro V1, which was introduced in 2000. The Pro V1, Callaway Golf HX Tour, Nike One, and a few other high-tech golf balls were designed to reduce spin when hit by a driver and increase spin when hit by a wedge during an approach shot. Low spin off the tee made the ball fly much farther than high spin, while high spin on shorter shots allowed golfers to stop the ball quickly once it hit the green. Before the development of the Pro V1, golfers were required to make a choice—low spin off the tee (increased driving distance) and low spin into the green (poor distance control on the green) or high spin off the tee (shorter driving distance) and high spin into the green (good shot-stopping ability). In June 2005, the USGA asked all golf ball manufacturers to develop prototypes of golf balls that would fly 15–25 yards shorter than current models. USGA officials asked that these prototypes be submitted for evaluation by golf's governing body.

The USGA also believed that the tremendous spin that PGA Tour golfers achieved when hitting shots into the green was partly attributable to wedge technology. The combination of soft-cover golf balls like the Pro V1, Callaway Golf HX Tour, or Nike One and the precision-milled grooves of the latest-technology wedges produced ample spin to stop shots near the hole, even when hit from deep rough. The USGA ruled in August 2008 that, beginning January 2010, golf equipment manufacturers must discontinue producing wedges with sharply squared groove edges on irons and wedges. The grooves of irons and wedges produced after January 2010 were required to have rounded edges to minimize spin. Under the new rule concerning groove shape, any remaining inventory of Callaway Golf Mack Daddy, Titleist Spin Milled, or Cleveland Zip Groove wedges would have to be removed from the market after 2009.

Even with all of the technological advances in golf club and golf ball design, there was little evidence that golfers were achieving lower scores. The average score on the PGA Tour had declined only slightly—from 71.18 in 1990 to 71.07 in 2005—and with the exception of Tiger Woods, almost none of the longest drivers on the PGA Tour were at the top of the Tour's Money List. Technology also had a minimal effect on the scores of recreational golfers. The average men's handicap maintained with the USGA had declined from 16.3 in 1993 to just 15.0 in 2005, while the average women's handicap had declined from 29.9 in 1993 to 28.0 in 2005.

In a March 2006 *PGA Magazine* article focusing on the future of golf equipment, Nike Golf's president expressed frustration with USGA and R&A limitations on innovation and pointed out that the capabilities of typical recreational golfers were quite different from those of touring professionals:

> A lot of the heat of the debate has to do with the effects of technology on what you see on TV on the weekend. It skews the debate in a way that is not relevant to the average golfer. It's all emotional, anecdotal hoo-ha.[5]

Golf equipment manufacturers were not alone in their disagreement with recent USGA and R&A rulings. A teaching professional and PGA member argued:

> Technology has had a wonderful impact on golf, and although we see longer drives and some lower scores on the PGA Tour, what's the harm? . . . If the average golfer enjoys the game more by playing a little better through technology, that's a plus.[6]

A 16-year PGA veteran disagreed with the entire premise behind the USGA's technology limitations by commenting:

> Today's high-tech equipment isn't making any courses obsolete for the average player. Maybe technology has made some courses too short for Tiger [Woods] and players on the PGA Tour, but technology has only helped most players gain more gratification from playing the game.[7]

When asked about what impact USGA rulings might have on the health of the game of golf, the USGA's senior communications director commented:

> In a nutshell, we are pleased overall with the state of our game. Growth, however, is not the yardstick by which we judge success or failure. . . . I would contend that we look at our role as one of governing the game responsibly and effectively so that all constituencies—tours, manufacturers, amateurs—enjoy a healthy climate in which to pursue a favorite and rewarding pastime that can be passed down from one generation to the next.[8]

Decline in the Number of Golfers and Rounds Played

The rapid decline in the number of golfers and the recent downturn in the number of rounds played were thought by industry analysts to result from a variety of factors. The overall difficulty of the game and the disappointment of many golfers that low scores didn't come quickly after taking up the sport were certainly factors in people leaving the game. A survey of golfers conducted in June 2003 by the National Golf Foundation found that limited time to practice and play golf was another closely related factor contributing to golf's decline. Golfers who were married with children were most likely to comment that job responsibilities, lack of free time, and family responsibilities prohibited them from playing golf on a more regular basis. Job responsibilities and lack of free time were also barriers to playing golf more frequently for married or single golfers who had no children. Older golfers who were either retired or who were working less than 40 hours per week were more likely to list health concerns or injuries as a major reason for not playing golf more often. About 30 percent of survey respondents cited high golf fees as a barrier to playing more golf.

The Rise of Counterfeiting in the Golf Equipment Industry

In 2007, more than $600 billion worth of counterfeit goods were sold in countries throughout the world. Fake Rolex watches or Ralph Lauren Polo shirts had long been a problem, but by the mid-2000s counterfeiters were even making knockoffs of branded auto parts, shampoo, canned vegetables, and prescription drugs. It was estimated that 90 percent of the world's counterfeit merchandise originated in China and that counterfeit goods accounted for 15–20 percent of all products made in China. The Chinese government did little to prevent counterfeiting and, in fact, allowed China's largest automobile producer to manufacture and market a nearly exact knockoff of the Chevrolet Spark, which was one of GM's top-selling cars in the Chinese market. The Chinese government gave most counterfeiters a green light to produce knockoffs for sale both within China and for export. Interpol testified before the U.S. Congress in 2005 that counterfeits were illegally imported into Western countries by organized crime and terrorist groups such as al Qaeda and Hezbollah. Counterfeiting was an effective approach to funding the activities of organized crime and terrorist groups, since fake brands were as profitable as drugs and there was very little risk of being prosecuted if caught.

Counterfeit clubs were a considerable threat to the industry because good counterfeits were nearly exact copies of legitimate products. The extraordinarily low prices at which counterfeit golf clubs were offered were too great a temptation for many bargain-hunter golfers. In 2008, it was not unusual to see complete sets of new Callaway, TaylorMade, Ping, Titleist, Nike, or Cobra clubs that would retail for more than $2,000 sell on eBay or similar auction Web sites for $150 to $400. The sellers and others who dealt in counterfeit merchandise could purchase counterfeit sets complete with eight irons, a driver, two or three fairway woods, a putter, a golf bag, and a travel bag for as little as $100 in China. Callaway Golf Company posted warnings on its Web site about counterfeiters, noting that "a full set of authentic Callaway Golf clubs, depending on the models, will retail for $2,500–$3,000 or more. If the deal looks too good to be true, it probably is."[9]

The rise of counterfeiting in the golf equipment industry was attributable to the decisions by golf executives to source clubheads and sometimes contract out assembly of golf clubs to manufacturers in China. In 2005, about 60 percent of all golf equipment was produced in China. Counterfeiters were able to make accurate copies of branded golf clubs through reverse engineering or by enticing employees of contract manufacturers to steal clubhead molds that could be used to produce counterfeit clubheads. In some cases, contract manufacturers scheduled production runs after hours to produce black-market clubs. Counterfeiters even copied the details of the packaging in which golf clubs were shipped to better disguise the fakes. It was estimated that counterfeiters in China could produce golf clubs for less than $3 per club.

The golf equipment industry's six leading manufacturers created an alliance in December 2003 to identify and pursue both those who made and those who sold counterfeit clubs. TaylorMade Golf, Fortune Brands (parent of Titleist and Cobra Golf), Callaway Golf, Ping Golf, Cleveland Golf, and Nike Golf had successfully shut down many Internet auction sellers in the United States and Canada that listed counterfeit clubs and had gained cooperation from the Chinese government to confiscate counterfeit goods produced in that country. The Chinese government conducted two raids in 2004 that netted approximately $3 million worth of counterfeit golf equipment, and the Chinese seized more than $1 million worth of counterfeit clubs in 2005. In 2008, a Chinese man was sentenced to three years and six months in jail and ordered to pay a $58,000 fine after being convicted of running an illegal operation selling counterfeit golf equipment during 2007.

Even though the golf industry's alliance against counterfeiting had recorded some successes, it remained quite easy to purchase counterfeit clubs produced in China. In 2008, an Internet search using the words "golf club supplier China" produced results for dozens of Chinese companies offering counterfeit clubs. One such company, Sail Full Golf, located in Shenzhen, China, offered delivery worldwide for orders in any quantity of "100% original" Callaway, TaylorMade, Cleveland, Ping, and other branded golf equipment "taken from the original factory." Sail Full accepted payment by Western Union or Pay Pal and offered a 5 percent discount for orders of three or more sets of golf clubs.[10] A Nike executive commented in 2005 on the difficulty of shutting down counterfeiters of golf equipment: "Often these aren't legitimate businesses, so you can't take the case to a court of law, you have to hunt them down. Many times it isn't even worth the effort. They simply create a new company and move. It's really frustrating."[11]

Key Competitive Capabilities in the Golf Equipment Industry

Competitive rivalry in the golf equipment industry centered on technological innovations as allowed by the USGA and R&A, product performance, brand image, tour exposure, and price. Product innovation, performance, image, tour exposure, and price were also the primary competitive variables at play in the golf ball segment of the industry. During the mid-1990s and until the USGA's 2005 ruling on driver dimensions, most innovation in driver design focused on increasing clubhead size and creating a larger clubface. The larger clubhead size and clubface created a larger "sweet spot," which reduced the negative effects of mis-hit shots by boosting the COR or CT capabilities. With the size of the driver limited to 5 inches by 5 inches and clubhead volume limited to 460 cc, club designers focused on repositioning weight within the clubhead to produce higher launch angles, to create a draw bias, and to increase MOI. The higher launch angles tended to help golfers achieve greater distance, while a draw bias helped many golfers hit straighter shots and a high MOI tended to reduce distance loss related to off-center hits.

In 2008, most golf club manufacturers had met dimension, volume, CT, and MOI limits and were attempting to achieve differentiation in drivers by either lowering the center of gravity to increase launch angle or by offering clubs with adjustable features. For example, the TaylorMade r7 line of drivers allowed golfers to move tungsten weight plugs among a series of slots located in the rear of the driver to adjust launch angle and left/right dispersion. Nike Golf, Callaway Golf, Nickent Golf, and Nicklaus Golf had introduced drivers using square or other geometric shapes to position weight farther behind the clubface to boost MOI and produce a higher launch angle. Some equipment manufacturers had looked to adjustability to differentiate their product lines from competing brands. TaylorMade, Callaway Golf, Ping Golf, and Nickent Golf all launched series of drivers in 2008 that allowed golfers to install different shafts into the driver head to produce different launch characteristics. Interchangeable shafts were allowed under USGA rules that went into effect in January 2008; those rules permitted adjustable features to clubs provided that the adjustable feature was approved by the USGA during the design process.

As product differentiation became more difficult to achieve in the golf equipment industry, golf club manufacturers were relying more on endorsements from touring professionals to enhance their image with consumers. Most recreational golfers who watched televised golf tournaments or read golf magazines were very aware of what brands of clubs and golf balls their favorite touring professionals used. It was not at all unusual for recreational golfers to base purchase decisions on the equipment choices of successful golfers on the PGA Tour. Leading golf equipment companies had always struck endorsement deals with the game's best-known players, but the value of endorsement contracts had escalated since 2000. During the late 1990s, the PGA Tour's top 10 golfers could expect to earn between \$250,000 and \$400,000 annually through endorsement contracts. By 2007, the top 10 golfers on the PGA Tour all earned at least \$4 million annually through endorsements, and PGA Tour professionals who were ranked 40 to 70 on the Money List could expect anywhere from \$450,000 to \$800,000 in annual endorsement fees. Tiger Woods had led the PGA Tour in endorsement fees since his professional debut in 1996, when he earned more than \$12 million from product endorsements. Tiger Woods earned nearly \$100 million from endorsement contracts in 2007, which brought his career earnings from winnings and endorsements to an estimated \$770 million. *Golf Digest* expected Tiger Woods's career earnings to surpass \$1 billion by 2010.

Suppliers to the Industry

Many club makers' manufacturing activities were restricted to club assembly since clubhead production was contracted out to investment casting houses located in Asia and shafts and grips were usually purchased from third-party suppliers. Casting houses like Advanced International Multitech

Company in Taiwan produced clubheads to manufacturers' specifications and shipped the clubheads to the United States for assembly. In some cases, clubheads and shafts were sourced from suppliers in China and shipped to the United States as fully assembled products ready for shipment to retailers.

Manufacturers were quite selective in establishing contracts with offshore casting houses since the quality of clubhead greatly affected consumers' perception of overall golf club quality and performance. Poor casting could result in clubheads that could easily break or fail to perform to the developers' expectations. In addition, it was important that golf equipment manufacturers perform background checks on suppliers and initiate security procedures to prevent finished clubheads and completed golf clubs from leaving the production facility and making it to the black market.

Differentiation based on shaft performance became more important to golf club manufacturers as technological differences between brands of golf clubs decreased after the USGA limitation on clubhead size and performance was enacted. Most golf club manufacturers co-developed modestly sized lines of proprietary shafts with companies specializing in shaft design and manufacturing. The relatively narrow line of shafts bearing the club manufacturer's name was supplemented with branded shafts produced and marketed by companies such as Aldila, UST, Fujikura, or Graphite Designs. Even though third-party-branded shafts were equally available to all manufacturers, they were important in attracting sales to skilled core golfers, since these golfers might have as strong a preference for a particular shaft as for a clubhead design. For example, the purchase decision made by a low-handicap golfer considering two drivers might come down to which club could be ordered with a specific shaft.

The USGA limitation on clubhead size and clubface performance had helped shaft manufacturers record higher revenues and profits. Like many shaft manufacturers, Aldila had struggled during years when consumers' greatest interest was in clubhead innovations, but a shifting consumer focus on shafts had allowed the company to swing from a $1.7 million loss in 2003 to an $11.2 million profit in 2006. Grips had yet to prove to be a point of differentiation, and few golfers showed a strong preference for one brand of grip over another.

Golf Equipment Retailers and the Distribution and Sale of Golf Equipment

Leading golf equipment manufacturers distributed their products through on-course pro shops, off-course pro shops such as Edwin Watts and Nevada Bob's, and online golf retailers such as Golfsmith.com and TGW.com. Most on-course pro shops sold only to members and carried few clubs since their members purchased golf clubs infrequently. Off-course pro shops accounted for the largest portion of retail golf club sales because they carried a wider variety of brands and marketed more aggressively than on-course shops. Off-course pro shops held an advantage over online retailers as well since golf equipment consumers could inspect clubs and try out demo models before committing to a purchase. Also, both on-course and off-course pro shops were able to offer consumers custom fitting and advice from a PGA professional or other individual with the training necessary to properly match equipment to the customer. Most consumers making online purchases had already decided on a brand and model and bought online to get a lower price or to avoid sales taxes. However, most of the top brands required online retailers to sell their equipment at the suggested retail price. Both online retailers and brick-and-mortar retailers were free to sell discontinued models at deep discounts, which was very appealing to golfers who did not mind purchasing models from the previous year.

Custom fitting was offered by most manufacturers and large off-course pro shops with the use of specialized computer equipment. Common swing variables recorded and evaluated in determining the proper clubs for golfers included clubhead speed, launch angle of the ball, back spin on the ball, side spin on the ball, ball flight pattern, ball flight carry distance, and roll distance. Custom fitting had become very important as golf equipment companies expanded shaft flex options during the early 2000s. In 2008, fairway woods, hybrid clubs, and iron sets could be equipped with shafts in senior, regular, stiff, or extra-stiff flex. Most leading equipment manufacturers offered drivers with dozens of different shaft configurations. For example, the Callaway Golf I-Mix FT-5 and FT-i drivers could be ordered with any number of 70 different shafts produced by Aldila, Fujikura, Graffaloy, UST, Mitsubishi Rayon, Matrix, or Graphite Design shafts. Pro shops generally chose to stock only equipment produced by leading manufacturers and did not carry less expensive, less technologically advanced equipment. Low-end manufacturers sold their products mainly through discounters, mass merchandisers, and large sporting goods stores. These retailers had no custom-fitting capabilities and rarely had sales personnel knowledgeable about the performance features of the different brands and models of golf equipment carried in the store. Such retail outlets appealed to customers on low price; they mainly attracted beginning golfers and occasional golfers who were unwilling to invest in more expensive equipment.

PROFILES OF THE LEADING MANUFACTURERS AND MARKETERS OF GOLF EQUIPMENT

Callaway Golf Company

Callaway Golf Company began to take form in 1983 when Ely Reeves Callaway Jr. purchased a 50 percent interest in a Temecula, California, manufacturer and marketer of hickory-shafted wedges and putters for $400,000. Ely Callaway knew from the outset that the company's prospects for outstanding profits were limited as long as its product line was restricted to reproductions of antique golf clubs. Callaway purchased the remaining 50 percent interest in the company and, in 1985, hired a team of aerospace and metallurgical engineers to design and produce the industry's most technologically advanced golf clubs. The company launched noteworthy product lines within a few years, but its revenues skyrocketed from less than $10 million to more than $500 million after its 1991 introduction of the Big Bertha stainless-steel driver. The Big Bertha was revolutionary in that it was much larger than conventional wooden drivers and performed far better than wooden drivers when players made poor contact with the ball. The success of the Big Bertha driver set off a technology race in the industry; Callaway Golf and its chief rivals launched innovations every 12–18 months that further improved the performance of metal drivers. To help his company retain its lead in technological innovation, Ely Callaway provided his product development staff with a budget larger than the R&D budgets of all other golf companies combined. The company's commitment to innovation led to the development of the Great Big Bertha Titanium driver in 1995, the ERC Forged Titanium Driver in 1999, variable-face-thickness X-14 irons in 2000, and the ERC II Forged Titanium Driver in 2000. Also during Ely Callaway's tenure as CEO, the company acquired Odyssey, a leading brand of putters, in 1996 and began manufacturing and marketing golf balls in 2000.

In February 2000, a survey of golf equipment company executives voted Callaway's Big Bertha driver the best golf product of the century by a 2–1 margin. The same group of executives called Ely Callaway the most influential golf trade person of the 1990s. Ely Callaway stepped down as president and CEO of the company on May 15, 2001, after being diagnosed with pancreatic cancer. The company's performance began to decline soon after Ely Callaway's death later that year, with its core driver line suffering the greatest. USGA limitations on driver innovation were partly to blame for Callaway Golf's declining sales of drivers, but some of its misfortune was self-inflicted. When the USGA limited the size of drivers to 460 cc, the typical driver size ranged from 360 cc to 380 cc. Callaway Golf's key rivals saw the USGA ruling as a signal to immediately increase the size of their drivers to the 460 cc maximum allowable size. Callaway managers and engineers chose to take an incremental approach to reaching the size threshold and, as a result, saw its share of driver sales fall from nearly 35 percent in 2002 to about 15 percent in 2004.

Callaway Golf's sales of drivers and fairway woods rebounded to some extent after 2004, but in 2008, Callaway Golf remained the second-largest seller of drivers and fairway woods. Its square FT-i and traditional-shaped FT-5 driver lines featured titanium clubfaces, carbon composite shells, and prepositioned weights that produced a draw, fade, or neutral ball path. Both the FT-i and the FT-5 were available with fixed shafts or any of Callaway's 70 I-Mix interchangeable shafts. The FT-i or FT-5 drivers were priced at $399 with a fixed shaft or $550–$700 with a single I-Mix shaft. Each additional shaft ranged from $149 to $349. Callaway Golf also produced a Hyper X driver line, which sold for $299, and the Big Bertha driver line, which sold at $199. The company's Big Bertha fairway woods sold for $179 in retail stores, its X line of fairway woods were offered at $179–$229, and its FT fairway woods carried a retail price of $249–$299.

In the years following Ely Callaway's death, the company struggled with a series of issues beyond loss of market share in its flagship driver business. The company misread the market potential for hybrid clubs, which were substitutes for low-lofted, long irons. TaylorMade's Rescue was the first hybrid to gain a widespread appeal, but almost all manufacturers raced to get hybrid clubs to the market. Callaway Golf's failure to get its hybrid club to market before 2005 caused it to lose significant sales, as many golfers purchased TaylorMade, Adams Golf, and Cobra hybrid clubs to replace the 2-, 3-, and 4-irons in their bags. It was estimated that 31 percent of all golfers had purchased at least one hybrid club by 2007. In 2008, Callaway Golf's X line of hybrid clubs retailed from $139 to $159, while its FT line of hybrids sold for $199.

As Callaway Golf struggled with its golf club business, its golf ball start-up also failed to perform to management's expectations. The company's golf ball business had lost $90 million between 2000 and 2002 and showed little hope of providing a return on its $170 million investment in a state-of-the-art golf ball plant. In 2003, Callaway Golf Company acquired bankrupt golf ball producer Top-Flite Golf for $125 million. The Top-Flite acquisition was executed to give Callaway Golf Company the volume necessary to achieve economies of scale in golf ball production, since Top-Flite was the second largest seller of golf balls in the United States, with a market share of 16.3 percent. About $175 million of Top-Flite's 2002 revenues were generated from the sale of golf balls. Top-Flite's sales of Top-Flite- and Hogan-branded golf clubs accounted for about $75 million of the company's $250 million total revenues in 2002.

Callaway Golf's acquisition of Top-Flite proved to be more troublesome than management had expected. Top-Flite had invested little in R&D over the years, and the performance of its products had fallen substantially behind that of key industry rivals. Top-Flite golf balls sold at the lowest price points in the industry and had become known among golfers as "Rock-Flite" because of their hard covers and overall poor quality. The perception of poor quality and performance caused Top-Flite's market share to fall to 6.3 percent by 2006. Callaway-branded golf balls, however, had grown to account for nearly 10 percent of industry sales by 2006. Callaway Golf's HX Tour golf ball was a technological equal to Titleist's Pro V1 and was used by such touring professionals as Phil Mickelson, Annika Sorenstam, Lorena Ochoa, and Ernie Els. Even though some of the biggest names in golf endorsed Callaway Golf products, the company had chosen to limit its endorsement contracts to 12 staff professionals and 7 contract professionals in 2008.

In 2007, Callaway Golf launched a broad plan to resurrect the Top-Flite brand. A new line of D2 golf balls was to include some of the innovations found in the HX Tour line of golf balls. The company supported the launch of the D2 line with an advertising campaign called "Rock-Flite Is Dead," which acknowledged the company's reputation for poor quality and performance. The better-performing D2 line allowed Top-Flite to add 900 retailers who had previously not considered Top-Flite to be a legitimate brand. The strong sales for the Callaway Golf's technologically advanced HX Tour golf balls and the sales gains from the D2 line helped its golf ball division record its first profitable year in 2007. Profitability in the golf ball business was also achieved by moving production from Callaway Golf's production facilities in the United States to suppliers in China. Callaway Golf had closed its Carlsbad, California, golf ball plant in 2005 and, in 2008, closed one of its two remaining golf ball plants in the United States in order to outsource a larger percentage of its golf ball production requirements.

Callaway Golf's Odyssey putter line had remained a bright spot for the company since its 1996 acquisition. From quarter to quarter during the late 1990s, Odyssey and Ping shifted spots as the industry's top-selling brand of putter. However, Callaway Golf's 2001 development of the innovative Odyssey 2-Ball putter gave it a decisive lead in the putter category of the golf equipment industry. The popularity of the 2-Ball putter boosted Odyssey's market-leading share in putters from 30.7 percent in 1999 to nearly 50 percent in 2002. In fact, the 2003 sales of 2-Ball putters were greater than the total revenues of any golf company except Titleist/Cobra, TaylorMade, and Ping. Odyssey had a 35 percent market share in the putter category of the industry in 2007. It had retained its market-leading position through the development of new models of 2-Ball putters and a variety of conventional-looking models. Most Odyssey putters sold at price points between $100 and $170, but the company had developed a Black Series of Odyssey putters in 2007 that carried an average sales price of $228. The Black Series was intended to compete against Titleist's Scotty Cameron premium line of putters and had a 1.2 percent market share in 2007.

Callaway Golf became the industry leader in the iron segment with its 2000 introduction of the X-14 series of perimeter-weighted irons. The X-14 series' perimeter-weighted design helped minimize the loss of distance that resulted from off-center shots and became so popular that it catapulted Callaway's market share in irons from 14 percent in 1999 to about 28 percent in 2002. Callaway remained the leader in the iron segment of the industry between 2002 and 2008 through continued innovation in perimeter-weighted irons. Its X-16, X-18, and X-20 model lines incrementally improved the performance of the popular X-14 line. The company also produced a composite construction FT line of irons that featured a titanium face welded to a proprietary metal frame and finished with a thermoplastic urethane cavity-back insert. Callaway's X-Forged irons were designed to compete against Titleist's blade-style irons, which were popular with touring pros and the most skilled recreational golfers. Callaway Golf also produced a Big Bertha line of irons that featured a low center of gravity and produced a high launch angle. The low center of gravity and high launch angle benefited many female and senior male golfers with slower-than-average swing speeds. The company's Ben Hogan line of traditional blade irons, acquired along with Top-Flite in 2003, had changed little since its development in the 1970s and 1980s and accounted for a very small percentage of the company's sales of irons in 2008. There was some belief by industry analysts that Callaway Golf might divest the brand since Hogan irons competed directly with the Callaway Golf X-Forged line of irons. Callaway Golf irons covered all price points between $600 and $1,300 per eight-club set. Callaway Golf also marketed a Top-Flite set of irons that retailed for $250 and were sold primarily by discount sporting goods retailers. The sales of Top-Flite irons accounted for a negligible percentage of Callaway Golf's total iron sales.

Callaway Golf Company also designed and sold a Callaway Golf footwear line and received royalties from the sale of Callaway-branded golf apparel, watches and clocks, travel gear, eyewear, and golf rangefinders. The company recorded footwear and licensing revenues of $8.6 million, $8.2 million, and $7.1 million in 2005, 2006, and 2007, respectively. Discontinued apparel, footwear, accessories, and golf club models could be purchased online at Callaway Golf's Web site (www.callawaygolfpreowned.com). New models of Callaway golf clubs could also be purchased online (at www.shop.callawaygolf.com). Order fulfillment for new clubs purchased online was made by a network of retailers who participated in Callaway Golf's Internet sales program. A financial summary for Callaway Golf Company for the years 1995 to 2007 is presented in Exhibit 4. Exhibit 5 provides the company's revenues by product group for the period 1999 to 2007.

TaylorMade-adidas Golf

TaylorMade was founded in 1979 when Gary Adams mortgaged his house and began production of his "metalwoods" in an abandoned car dealership building in McHenry, Illinois. Both touring pros and golf retailers alike were skeptical of the new club design until they found that the metalwoods actually hit the ball higher and farther than persimmon woods. By 1984, TaylorMade metalwoods were the number one wood on the PGA Tour and the company had grown to be the third largest golf equipment company in the United States. The company was acquired by France-based Salomon SA in 1984, which provided the capital necessary for the company to continue to develop innovative new lines of metalwoods. The company also produced irons and putters, but the majority of TaylorMade's sales were derived from high-margin drivers and fairway woods.

TaylorMade's metalwood drivers were the most technologically advanced in the industry until Callaway Golf's 1991 introduction of the oversized Big Bertha metalwood. During the entire decade of the 1990s, TaylorMade fell further behind Callaway Golf in the technology race but remained runner-up in the driver segment.

Exhibit 4 Callaway Golf Company, Financial Summary, 1995–2007 ($ in thousands, except per share amounts)

	2007	2006	2005	2004	2003	2002	2001	2000	1999	1998	1997	1996	1995
Net sales	$1,124,591	$1,017,907	$998,093	$934,564	$814,032	$792,064	$816,163	$837,627	$719,038	$703,060	$848,941	$683,536	$557,048
Operating income	90,183	37,055	17,206	(24,702)	65,855	111,060	114,317	124,727	79,909	(40,139)	209,189	189,828	154,384
Operating income as a percent of sales	8%	4%	2%	−3%	8%	14%	14%	15%	11%	−6%	25%	28%	28%
Pretax income	88,275	34,998	14,537	(23,713)	67,883	111,671	98,192	128,365	85,497	(38,899)	213,765	195,595	158,401
Pretax income as a percent of sales	8%	3%	1%	−3%	8%	14%	12%	15%	12%	−6%	25%	29%	29%
Net income	$ 54,587	$ 23,290	$ 13,284	($10,103)	$ 45,523	$ 69,446	$ 58,375	$ 80,999	$ 55,322	($25,564)	$132,704	$122,337	$ 97,736
Net income as a percent of sales	5%	2%	1%	−1%	9%	9%	7%	10%	8%	−4%	16%	18%	18%
Fully diluted earnings per share	$0.81	$0.34	$0.19	($0.15)	$0.68	$1.03	$0.82	$1.13	$0.78	($0.38)	$1.85	$1.73	$1.40
Shareholders' equity	$568,230	$577,117	$596,048	$586,317	$589,383	$543,387	$514,349	$511,744	$499,934	$453,096	$481,425	$362,267	$224,934

Source: Callaway Golf Company annual reports.

Exhibit 5 Callaway Golf Company's Net Sales by Product Group, 1999–2007 ($ in thousands)

Product Group	2007	2006	2005	2004	2003	2002	2001	2000	1999
Woods	$ 305.9	$ 266.5	$241.3	$238.6	$252.4	$310.0	$392.9	$403.0	$429.0
Irons	309.6	288	316.5	259.1	280.7	243.5	248.9	299.9	221.3
Putters	109.1	102.7	109.3	—[1]	—[1]	—[1]	—[1]	—[1]	—[1]
Golf balls	213.1	214.8	214.7	231.3	78.4	66	54.9	34	—[2]
Accessories and other	186.9	145.9	116.3	205.6	202.5	172.6	119.5	100.8	68.7
Net sales	$1,124.6	$1,017.9	$998.1	$934.6	$814.0	$792.1	$816.20	$837.60	$719.00

[1]Net sales for putters included in "Accessories and other" for 1999–2004.

[2]Golf ball operations began in 2000.

Source: Callaway Golf Company annual reports.

TaylorMade and its parent were acquired by the athletic footwear and apparel company adidas in 1997 and gained the lead in the market for drivers with its 2003 introduction of its 400 cc R580 driver. The company's R580 driver was 40 cc larger than Callaway's competing Great Big Bertha II driver and matched consumers' preference for the largest possible driver. TaylorMade expanded its lead over Callaway Golf in drivers with its 2004 introduction of its r5 series and r7 Quad drivers. The r5, a 450 cc driver, came in three varieties that used prepositioned weights to produce a draw, slight fade, or straight shot. The r5 was one of the best-selling drivers in the marketplace but was less technologically advanced (and lower-priced) than TaylorMade's r7 Quad driver. The r7's movable weight technology allowed users to use a special tool to move four tungsten weights with a total weight of 48 grams to ports in various positions in the clubhead to produce whatever bias the golfer found necessary on a given day. For example, a golfer who was struggling with a low fade could move the heaviest of the four weights to the toe of the clubhead to favor a high draw. The golfer could later move the weights to a different position if he or she experienced a different ball flight on a different day. The movable weight system allowed golfers to have a single driver that could produce six ball-flight paths.

TaylorMade maintained its lead in the driver category of the golf equipment industry with updated models of the r7 that were launched at 18-month intervals between 2004 and 2008. In 2008, the r7 was sold in four basic configurations that ranged in price from $400 to $600. The price of each model depended on the shaft option selected and the number of extra weights included with the driver. The r7 CGB Max Limited carried a retail price of $1,000 and came with an r7 clubhead, three interchangeable shafts, and nine weight plugs. The three shaft options and nine weights allow golfers to create more than 1,000 different ball-flight paths by choosing different shaft and weight combinations. TaylorMade replaced its popular r5 driver models in 2007 with the relaunch of the Burner driver, which had been a popular TaylorMade sub-brand in the mid-1990s. Burner drivers were equipped with a fixed shaft and did not use movable weights that allowed golfers to adjust launch angles. The TaylorMade Burner carried a retail price of $299. TaylorMade's combined sales of r7 drivers and Burner drivers gave it a 28 percent market share in 2007. As of 2008, TaylorMade's management had not chosen to develop a square driver—managers had commented in 2007 that square drivers did not offer any technological advantage over traditional-shaped drivers.

TaylorMade was also the leading seller of hybrid clubs. TaylorMade introduced its Rescue line of hybrid clubs in 1999, but the clubs did not become a huge success in the marketplace until 2002. In 2005, TaylorMade extended its Rescue line by adding r7 models that featured the movable weight technology used in r7 drivers. TaylorMade Burner Rescue hybrids sold at a retail price of $130, while the r7 Rescue hybrids carried a $200 price tag. TaylorMade's r7 line of fairway woods also featured movable weights and sold for $300 in retail stores. TaylorMade's Burner series of fairway woods sold for $200 at retail and did not have movable weights.

TaylorMade's success in drivers and hybrid clubs had not translated to iron sales, a category in which the company never challenged Callaway Golf for market share leadership. In late 2005, the company introduced its r7 irons in hopes of repeating the success of the r7 driver in irons. The r7 irons were designed much like Callaway Golf's Fusion irons, with a titanium face mounted to a steel perimeter-weighted frame. The r7 irons also featured prepositioned tungsten cartridges imbedded into the stainless-steel clubhead to improve launch angles. The company also produced a Burner line of perimeter-weighted irons, which competed with Callaway Golf X-20 irons, Ping G10 irons, and other perimeter-weighted irons. TaylorMade's forged irons, which were targeted to low-handicap golfers, competed against Titleist irons and Callaway Golf X-Forged irons. In 2008, TaylorMade irons covered all price points between $600 and $1,300 for an eight-club set. TaylorMade's combined sales of all three lines of irons gave it a 15.2 percent market share in the iron category of the industry in 2007.

TaylorMade was a weak competitor in the putter category of the golf equipment industry, with an 11-model product line that had long been ignored by most golfers. The company's putters carried retail prices between $120 and $220 in 2008. As was the case with putters, TaylorMade wedges were not particularly well regarded by core golfers. The company introduced a new line of forged Z groove wedges to better compete against Cleveland, Titleist, and Callaway Golf in the wedge category but, as of 2008, had made no real headway in capturing a larger share of the market for wedges. The retail price of TaylorMade's wedges was $120 in 2008.

The division's Maxfli golf ball business had produced consistently dismal results each year since its acquisition in 2002. Maxfli's Noodle sub-brand had become popular with price-sensitive consumers and had sold more than 2 million dozen per year, but the Maxfli brand in total accounted for less than 5 percent of golf ball sales worldwide. TaylorMade sold the chronic moneyloser in 2008 to Dick's Sporting Goods, which also manufactured and marketed Slazenger- and Walter Hagen–branded golf equipment. At the time of the sale, Maxfli produced only one Maxfli-branded golf ball model and the Noodle sub-brand. The terms of the sale allowed TaylorMade to retain the Noodle brand along with its newly introduced TaylorMade TP Red and TP Black premium-priced golf balls and lower-priced TaylorMade Burner brand of golf balls. TaylorMade had not achieved any significant market success with its TP Red, TP Black, or Burner golf balls, but the company expected to eventually challenge Callaway Golf and Nike for the title of runner-up to golf ball leader Titleist.

The sales of TaylorMade's adidas-branded golf apparel and golf shoes had grown at compounded annual rates of 28 percent and 18 percent, respectively, between 2004 and 2007 through the continued introduction of new styles and exposure on the professional tours by such well-known golfers as Sergio Garcia, Natalie Gulbis, Paula Creamer, and Retief Goosen. In all, TaylorMade-adidas Golf had signed endorsement contracts with 70 golfers on the men's and women's professional tours. The company's endorsement contracts called for golfers to use a TaylorMade driver and 11 other TaylorMade clubs and wear the company's clothing or shoes during tournaments. The heavy reliance on endorsements by touring professionals made adidas the most widely worn apparel brand on the professional tours. Some of its touring staff was also compensated to use TaylorMade's TP Red or TP Black golf balls during tournaments. TaylorMade also had limited contracts with an additional 40 golfers to use TaylorMade drivers during professional tournaments. The table below presents net sales and operating profit between 2004 and 2007 for TaylorMade-adidas Golf. The table on the next page also presents the TaylorMade-adidas Golf division's sales by product category for 2004–2007. The company outsourced 92 percent of its production of golf clubs and 96 percent of accessories such as golf balls and golf bags from suppliers in Asia to improve its operating margins. As of 2008, TaylorMade-adidas Golf did not offer consumers the option of purchasing clubs or apparel while visiting its Web site.

TaylorMade-adidas Golf Financial Performance (€ in millions)

	2007	2006	2005	2004
Net sales	€804	€856	€709	€633
Operating profit	65	73	50	60

Sales Contribution by Product Line (€ in millions)

	2007	2006	2005	2004
Metalwoods	€338	€325	€319	€304
Apparel	145	197	99	70
Footwear	72	60	50	44
Other hardware*	249	274	255	215

*Other hardware includes irons, putters, golf balls, golf bags, gloves, and other accessories.

Source: adidas Group annual reports, various years.

Titleist/Cobra Golf

Titleist golf balls were developed in 1932 after the founder of an Acushnet, Massachusetts, rubber deresinating company concluded that a bad putt during his round of golf was a result of a faulty ball rather than poor putting. Philip Young took the ball to a dentist's office to have it X-rayed and found that the core of the ball was indeed off-center. Young believed that the Acushnet Processing Company could develop and manufacture high-quality golf balls and teamed with a fellow MIT graduate, Fred Bommer, to create the Titleist line of balls. Young and Bommer introduced their first Titleist golf ball in 1935, and by 1949 Titleist had become the most played ball on the PGA Tour.

Acushnet's acquisition of John Reuter Jr. Inc. in 1958 and Golfcraft Inc. in 1969 put Titleist into the golf club business. Titleist's Reuter Bull's Eye putter became a favorite on the PGA Tour during the 1960s, and its AC-108 heel-toe-weighted irons were among the most popular brands of irons during the early 1970s. The company's Pinnacle line of golf balls was developed in 1980 as a lower-priced alternative to Titleist-branded golf balls. In 1996, the Acushnet Company was acquired by tobacco and spirits producer and marketer American Brands. American Brands increased its presence in the golf equipment industry in 1985 when it acquired Foot-Joy, the number one seller of golf gloves and shoes. In 1996, American Brands acquired Cobra Golf for $715 million. The company changed its name to Fortune Brands in 1997 when it completed the divestiture of its tobacco businesses that began in 1994.

In 2007, Fortune Brands' golf division had become the world's largest seller of golf equipment, with sales of $1.4 billion. Titleist was the number one brand of golf balls, with a 40 percent market share and annual sales approximating $600 million in 2007. Fortune Brands' FootJoy brand led the industry in the sale of golf shoes, golf gloves, and golf outerwear, with a 60 percent market share and 2007 revenues of about $400 million. The remainder of the golf division's 2007 revenues was nearly equally divided between Cobra- and Titleist-branded golf clubs and accessories, at about $200 million each.

Most golfers considered Titleist golf balls to be technologically superior to other brands, although Callaway Golf's HX Tour and Nike One golf balls were considered equally impressive by industry analysts and golf retailers. Titleist's Pro V1 golf ball was the company's most advanced and expensive golf ball and was able to offer maximum distance along with spin rates that allowed low-handicap golfers to stop approach shots near the pin. Pro V1 was the best-selling golf ball in the industry and accounted for about 22 percent of industry sales. A box of one dozen Titleist Pro V1 golf balls carried a suggested retail price of $58. The remainder of Titleist's 40 percent market share in golf balls was made up of its lower-priced NXT and DT models and its value-priced Pinnacle sub-brand.

The company had remained the largest seller of golf balls since 1949 through a heavy reliance on endorsements by touring professionals and a long-running advertising campaign boasting Titleist's status as the "most played ball on the Tour."[12] More than 100 PGA Tour professionals had endorsement contracts with Titleist to play the Pro V1, which ensured that the Pro V1 would be played by at least 75 percent of the field in any PGA Tour event. Fifty of its tour staff members also endorsed Titleist golf clubs and FootJoy shoes and apparel. The company also compensated about 50 golfers on other professional tours to use Titleist golf balls during competitive events and gave free boxes of sample golf balls to top amateurs and club champions. The company also gave 15,000 two-ball packs to club professionals in 2007 to distribute to club members.

Titleist's line of golf clubs was targeted toward professional golfers and elite recreational players. The company's forged iron design was not that different from its AC-108 irons produced in the early 1970s and offered no element of forgiveness for poorly struck shots. Titleist's market share in the iron category was less than 2.5 percent in 2007. Even some very good golfers felt that they were "not good enough" to use Titleist irons; such perceptions had allowed the brand's market share to slowly erode from about 10 percent in 2002.[13] Fortune Brand's Cobra line of irons was designed to appeal to lesser-skilled golfers and included many of the technological features found in Callaway Golf and TaylorMade irons. Cobra produced three game-improvement lines, including two multimaterial iron lines and a perimeter-weighted line. Cobra also produced a forged line for better players but, overall, held a modest 5 percent market share in 2007. Even though Cobra had signed endorsement contracts with rising PGA Tour stars like Camillo Villegas, J. B. Holmes, and Ian Poulter, core recreational golfers remained hesitant to abandon more widely used brands for Cobra's $500–$700 iron sets.

Cobra's chief manager was given control over Titleist's line of irons in 2007 to develop products for golfers who aspired to Titleist-branded products, but were realistic about their abilities. Titleist's AP1 and AP2 line of irons, introduced in 2008, retained the look of a forged iron but offered some forgiveness for mis-hit shots. The company's ZM forged irons were used by many of Titleist's staff gofers playing on professional tours, while its ZB line of iron sets included a mix of more-difficult-to-hit forged irons and easier-to-hit perimeter-weighted irons. The new product lines carried retail prices between $700 and $1,000 and had not produced any discernable growth in sales by mid-2008.

Titleist offered one driver model—the 909, which came in a 440 cc version and a 460 cc version. Titleist also produced two versions of its 909 fairway wood and a single line of hybrid clubs. Titleist drivers, fairway woods, and hybrids were popular choices with professionals and better recreational golfers. The 909 driver line carried a retail price of $400, while 909 fairway woods and hybrid clubs sold at price points near those of other premium brands. Fortune Brands' Cobra lines of drivers, fairway woods, and hybrids were targeted to golfers of an average skill level. All three King Cobra driver models met the USGA maximum for size and CT, while its L4V line's name (for "limit four variables") was chosen to reflect that the driver met all four specification limits set by the USGA—MOI, CT, 5 inches by 5 inches, and 460 cc volume. The L4V driver line featured a carbon composite top plate, tungsten weights near the rear of the clubhead, and a titanium clubface. King Cobra L4V drivers were sold at retail for $300, while other Cobra driver lines sold at $200. Cobra fairway woods retailed for $180–$230, while Cobra Baffler hybrid clubs sold in the $150–$180 price range.

Titleist's Vokey forged wedges were frequently used on the PGA Tour and were favorites of many low-handicap golfers. The Vokey wedge line was named for golf club craftsman Bob Vokey and held a 22.5 percent share of the wedge category of the golf equipment industry in 2007. Vokey wedges were second in sales only to Cleveland Golf, which held a 24.8 percent market share in the category. Vokey spin-milled wedge models accounted for half of Titleist's sales of wedges. All Vokey wedges carried a retail price of $110. Vokey spin-milled wedges sold in 2008 did not conform to USGA groove dimension specifications that would go into effect in January 2010. As with its wedge line, Titleist's putter line was named after a famed club designer: the Titleist Scotty Cameron putter line held an approximate 10 percent share of the putter segment and was the most widely purchased premium putter brand. Titleist offered four Scotty Cameron putter models, which were all priced at $300. Cobra's wedges and putters were not widely used on the PGA Tour or among recreational golfers.

Titleist management's biggest concern in 2008 centered on the USGA's interest in lesser-performing golf balls. In a special equipment issue of *Inside the USGA* published in October 2005, the editors worried openly that technology might endanger some of golf's most historic courses. The editors recalled how the wound, rubber-cored Haskell ball—developed in 1898 and popularized during the early 1900s—was eventually "removed for consideration at the Myopia Hunt Club, which hosted four U.S. Opens between 1898 and 1908."[14] The USGA editorial staff continued to speculate that the "confluence of golf science and commercial investment . . . accelerated by the injection of large amounts of capital" might possibly have the same effect on such championship courses as Merion or Oakland Hills.[15] Arguing against the concern, Titleist CEO Wally Uihlein attributed the overall scoring improvement among recreational and tournament golfers to "six contributing factors: (1) the introduction of low-spinning high performance golf balls; (2) the introduction of oversize, thin-faced drivers; (3) improved golf course conditioning and agronomy; (4) player physiology—they're bigger and stronger; (5) improved techniques and instruction; and

(6) launch monitors and the customization of equipment."[16] The following table presents net sales and operating profit between 2004 and 2007 for Fortune Brands' golf division.

Financial Performance for Fortune Brands' Golf Division ($ in millions)

	2007	2006	2005	2004
Net sales	$1,400	$1,313	$1,266	$1,212
Operating profit	168	166	172	154

Source: Fortune Brands' annual reports, various years.

Ping Golf

Perimeter weighting came about due to the poor putting of Karsten Solheim, a General Electric (GE) mechanical engineer who took up golf at the age of 47 in 1954. Solheim designed a putter for himself that he found provided more "feel" when he struck the ball. Solheim moved much of the clubhead weight to the perimeter of the clubface, which created a higher MOI and larger "sweet spot." In addition to perimeter weighting, Karsten Solheim also developed the investment-casting manufacturing process. This process allowed clubheads to be formed from molds rather than forged from steel (the traditional manufacturing process).

Solheim made his putters by hand from 1959 until 1967, when he left GE and founded Karsten Manufacturing. By the 1970s, Karsten manufactured a full line of perimeter-weighted putters and irons that carried the Ping brand. Solheim named the brand Ping because of the sound the perimeter-weighted clubhead made when it struck the ball. Karsten Manufacturing's Ping line of putters and irons were thought to be among the most technologically advanced throughout the 1980s and reigned as the market leaders. Karsten Manufacturing was renamed Ping Inc. in 1999.

Karsten Solheim was also the pioneer of custom fitting, with his fitting activities predating the official founding of the company. During the 1960s touring professionals would meet with Solheim to have him custom-fit putters to their body measurements, and by the 1970s Solheim had developed a fitting system for irons. His system used the golfer's physical measurements, stance and swing, and ball flight to select irons with the optimal lie. The company's irons were sold in 12 color-coded lie configurations to best match recreational golfers' unique fit conditions. Ping invited retailers to three-day training programs in its Phoenix, Arizona, plant to become better skilled at custom fitting and, in 2008, had provided retailers with 2,000 iron-fitting systems, 1,900 driver-fitting systems, and 2,000 putter-fitting systems.

Ping was an industry leader in the iron segment in 2008—frequently trading the number one ranking with Callaway Golf. The company offered four lines of irons: the traditional blade S57 irons featured minimal perimeter weighting, the i10 line offered a medium degree of perimeter weighting, and both the G10 and Rapture lines had expanded perimeter weighting. The S57 line was suitable for professionals and low-handicap recreational golfers, while the i10 was designed for average players looking for a moderate ball flight. The G10 and Rapture iron lines produced a higher ball flight than other models and was intended for average golfers who were able to produce only modest amounts of clubhead speed. Ping irons ranged in price from $615 for an eight-club set of G10 irons to $1,050 for an eight-club set of Rapture irons. The company produced a broad line of putters and was a strong runner-up to Odyssey in the putter category of the industry. The majority of Ping's putter line sold in the $90–$160 range, but its Redwood premium line of putters carried a retail price of $250 to $270. The Redwood putter line held a 1.2 percent market share in 2007.

Even though Ping had been known at one time for only its irons and putters, the privately owned company was the fourth largest seller of drivers behind TaylorMade, Callaway Golf, and Titleist/Cobra Golf. The company's 460 cc G10 titanium driver had become a popular choice for golfers who did not want to tinker with the TaylorMade r7 movable weight system or did not like the carbon composite design of Callaway Golf's FT drivers. The suggested retail price of the Ping G10 driver was $300. Ping's $450 Rapture driver included the use of tungsten weights to produce a higher launch angle than the G10 but was not a popular seller in 2008. Like Callaway Golf, the company had failed to develop a hybrid until 2005 and was struggling to gain market share in the category in 2008. Its $130 G10 hybrid and $200 Rapture hybrid were most frequently purchased by golfers who had purchased either a Ping driver or Ping irons. Ping fairway woods were also frequently purchased by those owning a Ping driver. Ping G10 fairway woods were sold for $220 in retail stores, while Rapture fairway woods typically sold for $250. The company's wedges were not big sellers in the market. Ping Golf had endorsement contracts with 20 golfers on the PGA Tour and 12 LPGA Tour members, including LPGA Money List leader Lorena Ochoa. Ping Golf did not produce a golf ball in 2008.

Nike Golf

Nike seized on the instant popularity of Tiger Woods in 1996 by signing the young star to a five-year, $40 million contract to endorse Nike shoes and apparel. In 1999, Woods extended the contract for an additional five years for $90 million to endorse Nike's golf ball and golf clubs, which would be launched in 2000 and 2002, respectively. Woods extended his contract with Nike a number of times after 1999 for undisclosed amounts, but industry analysts suspected the value of Tiger Woods's endorsement contract with Nike exceeded $25 million per year in 2008.

Nike management's 1996 assessment of Tiger Woods's enduring worldwide popularity was on the mark, with PGA tournament viewership doubling when Tiger Woods was in contention for a Sunday win. However, Woods's appeal with television viewers did not always translate into equipment sales. Nike's entry into the golf equipment industry had proved successful in terms of apparel and footwear sales, where it was the second leading seller of golf shoes behind FootJoy. Similarly, Nike Golf had achieved notable success in golf balls, with its Nike One, Ignite, Juice, and Power Distance balls controlling about 10 percent of the market in 2007. However, Nike's sales of golf clubs had never grown to be more than about 2 to 3 percent of the market.

Much of Nike Golf's troubles in the marketplace had to do with the image it created when it entered the golf equipment industry in 2002. The company had produced a line of clubs that were endorsed by Tiger Woods, but any serious golfer watching a televised tournament could tell that the Nike clubs in Tiger's hands bore no resemblance to the poor-performing Nike clubs on store shelves. To combat the perception that it was not a serious golf equipment manufacturer, Nike introduced a dramatically improved line of drivers in 2006. In fact, its SasQuatch Sumo drivers, offered in 2008, were produced to the USGA limitations for MOI, volume, CT, and dimensions. To further change opinions among core golfers that Nike Golf was primarily a marketer of sporting goods and apparel, the company signed an additional 17 PGA Tour members to endorse its clubs and golf balls. However, the poor performance of its hybrids, irons, wedges, and putters—all of which were far inferior to those produced by other leading manufacturers—may have overshadowed the improvement in its drivers. Many golfers also found the bright yellow paint scheme used for the SasQuatch Sumo distracting. It was also common for golfers to comment that Nike drivers, when hitting a golf ball, made a sound too different from that of other brands of drivers. Many golfers said the SasQuatch Sumo sound was too similar to that of an aluminum bat striking a baseball.

While Callaway Golf, TaylorMade, Ping, Titleist, and Cobra Golf tightly controlled retail prices and allowed markdowns only when a new product line was introduced, Nike Golf equipment almost never sold at the suggested retail price. In 2008, the Nike SasQuatch Sumo 5900, which had a suggested retail price of $479, was sold by most retailers for $300. Its SasQuatch Sumo 5000 had a suggested retail price of $359 but was usually listed at $200 in retail stores. Nike fairway woods carried retail prices of $140 to $230, while its hybrid clubs sold for $100 to $150, depending on model. Nike irons sets carried list prices of $400 to $600, while Nike wedge models sold for $50 to $100. Nike putters ranged from $100 to $140. Nike One golf balls sold for $43 per dozen, while its other models carried retail prices between $16 and $20 per dozen.

Endnotes

[1] As quoted in *The Callaway Connection,* Spring 2000, p. 7.

[2] As quoted in "Callaway Golf Introduced ERC II Forged Titanium Driver—Its Hottest and Most Forgiving Driver Ever," PR Newswire, October 24, 2000.

[3] Ibid.

[4] Joint Statements of Principles, USGA, www.usga.org/equipment/mission/joint_statement.html (accessed September 8, 2008).

[5] As quoted in Mark S. Murphy, "Special Report: Equipment, PGA Professionals Offer Continuing Discussion," *PGA Magazine,* March 2006, p. 40.
[6] Ibid., p. 39.
[7] Ibid., p. 37.
[8] Ibid., pp. 43–44.
[9] www.callawaygolf.com/EN/customerservice.aspx?pid59ways.
[10] www.isailfull.com.
[11] As quoted in "Teed Off: Counterfeiters Are Cashing In on Big-Name Clubs by Hawking Bogus Merchandise on the Internet," *St. Louis Post-Dispatch,* May 18, 2005, p. C1.
[12] Adam Schupak, "Pro V Is Still the 1," *GolfWeek,* February 19, 2007, www.golfweek.com/business/equipment/story/prov1_feature_021907 (accessed August 29, 2008).
[13] Adam Schupak, "Iron Supplement," *GolfWeek,* February 18, 2008, www.golfweek.com/business/equipment/story/titleistap_news_021808 (accessed August 28, 2008).
[14] As quoted in "Keeping Our Eye on the Ball," *Inside the USGA, Special Issue: Equipment,* October 2005, p. 1.
[15] Ibid., p. 9.
[16] As quoted in a reprint of "Mr. Titleist Talks," *Travel & Leisure Golf,* 2005, www.titleist.com.

CASE 5 Competition in the Movie Rental Industry in 2008: Netflix and Blockbuster Battle for Market Leadership

Arthur A. Thompson
The University of Alabama

Since 2000, the introduction of new technologies and electronics products had rapidly multiplied consumer opportunities to view movies. It was commonplace in 2008 for movies to be viewed at theaters, on airline flights, in hotels, from the rear seats of motor vehicles equipped with video consoles, in homes, or most anywhere on a laptop or a handheld device like a video iPod. Home viewing was possible on PCs, televisions, and video game consoles. The digital video disc (DVD) player was one of the most successful consumer electronic products of all time; as of 2008, more than 85 percent of U.S. households had DVD players (many had more than one) and increasing numbers of households had combination DVD player/recorders. Sales of combination DVD player/recorders surpassed sales of play-only DVD players in 2007–2008. Many households were attracted to purchasing a digital video recorder (DVR) so that they could easily record TV programs and movies and then replay them at their convenience. Moreover, consumers were increasingly interested in watching movies on their big-screen high-definition TVs and were upgrading to Blu-ray DVD players or player/recorders; both Blu-ray and high-definition technologies enabled more spectacular pictures and a significantly higher caliber in-home movie-viewing experience. Also, making recordings of movies and TV programs and sometimes burning one's own DVDs from downloaded or recorded files were becoming common means of building a personal media-viewing library.

Consumers could obtain movie DVDs through a wide variety of channels. They could purchase them from such retailers as Wal-Mart, Target, Best Buy, Circuit City, and Amazon.com or rent them from a host of local video outlets that frequently included Blockbuster and/or Movie Gallery. They could join Netflix, Blockbuster, or any of several other subscription services and have movie DVDs mailed directly to their own homes. They could subscribe to any of several cable movie channels (such as HBO, Showtime, and Starz), download movies from Apple iTunes and other Web sites, watch movies streamed to their PCs or TVs from a host of Web sites (including those of Netflix and Blockbuster), use their cable or satellite TV remotes to order movies instantly streamed directly to their TVs on a pay-per-view basis, or use the services of several other video-on-demand providers (including local phone companies like Verizon and AT&T and Web-based sources such as iTunes, Amazon.com, VOD.com, and Hulu.com). There were even vending machines containing movies for purchase or rental. Some consumers obtained movies illicitly on the Internet via file-sharing programs. New services for Internet delivery of movies, as well as better movie-watching devices, were expected to proliferate over the coming years. The biggest problem downloadable movie sites had in attracting customers was that most

 This case is a vastly revised and updated version of a 2004 case that was prepared by Braxton Maddox, under the supervision of Professor A. J. Strickland, The University of Alabama.

people wanted to watch the movies they rented on their biggest TV screen, not their computer monitor. The easiest way to move downloads from a PC to a TV was to burn them onto a DVD, but movie studios so far had been adamantly opposed to using downloaded movie formats that would enable a rented title to play on home DVD players.

Traditionally, movie studios released filmed entertainment content for distribution to companies renting movie DVDs and retailers of movie DVDs three to six months after films were released for showing in theaters. Seven to eight months after theatrical release, movie studios usually released their films to pay-per-view and video-on-demand (VOD) providers. Satellite and cable companies were next in the distribution window, getting access to filmed content one year after theatrical release. Movie studios released films for viewing to basic cable and syndicated networks three years after theatrical release. Recently, however, studios and various movie content aggregators and retailers had experimented with allowing consumers to download certain movies to their computers on the same day that the movie's DVD was released by the studios nationwide for rental or sale in retail stores. In some cases, consumers were permitted to burn the downloaded movie to a blank DVD for playback in a DVD player, allowing them to watch the movies on their TVs or portable devices. It was expected that movie studios would continue to experiment with the timing of the releases to various distribution channels, in an ongoing effort to maximize studio revenues.

MARKET SIZE

According to Adams Media Research (AMR), movie DVD sales and rentals amounted to a $24.9 billion market in the United States in 2007, up from $22.0 million in 2004.[1] Movie DVD purchases totaled $15.4 billion, and consumer expenditures for rental movies amounted to $9.5 billion. Movie rental was the most popular means of obtaining movies for in-home viewing, chiefly because of the much lower cost per movie; an estimated 2.5 billion movies were rented in 2006. The movie rental industry consisted of four segments:

1. In-store rentals (2007 revenues of $5.8 billion).
2. Rentals via mail (2007 revenues of $2.0 billion).
3. Video-on-demand (2007 revenues of $1.3 billion). VOD providers delivered rented movies via (*a*) a file downloaded to a PC (the downloaded movie file could be watched an unlimited number of times during the rental period) or (*b*) streaming the rented movie directly to a TV via a high-speed Internet connection, a cable TV connection, satellite, or a fiber-optic network.
4. Vending machines (2007 revenues of $400 million).

AMR projected that online subscription spending for rented DVDs would increase 68 percent between 2007 and 2011, rising to $3.2 billion, or about 37.5 percent of the total video rental market. Exhibit 1 contains details of the estimated sizes of various segments of the media entertainment industry in the United States.

MARKET TRENDS IN HOME VIEWING OF MOVIES

The wave of the future in viewing movies at home was widely thought to be in streaming rented movies directly to big-screen high-definition TVs. Household members could order the movies they wanted to rent and instantly watch either online (from Netflix, Blockbuster, or other online subscription services with instant video-streaming capability via the Internet) or by using their TV remotes to place orders from their cable or satellite provider. Providing VOD had been technically possible and available for a number of years, but it had not garnered substantial usage because movie studios were leery of the potential for movie-pirating and doubtful of whether they could profit from a VOD business model. But streaming video was less subject to pirating, and recent advances in video-streaming technology were rapidly improving the prospects that VOD would emerge as the dominant movie rental channel within the next 5–10 years.

In addition, there were a number of other important trends and developments in the movie rental marketplace:[2]

- Sales of movie DVDs had slowed from double-digit to single-digit levels in 2006–2007. Online

Exhibit 1 Estimated Sizes of Various Market Segments of the Media Entertainment Industry in the United States, 2006–2008 ($ in millions)

	2008	2007	2006
In-store rentals	$5,826	$6,215	$7,030
Vending machine rentals	388	198	79
By-mail rentals	2,023	1,797	1,291
Total physical film rental market	$8,237	8,210	8,400
Cable video-on-demand (VOD)	1,164	1,038	977
Digital VOD	84	28	12
Subscription VOD	35	11	4
Total digital film rental market	1,283	1,077	993
Total film rental market	9,520	9,287	9,393
Physical DVD movie sales at retail	15,419	15,932	16,460
Digital movie sales at retail	170	90	20
Total movie sales at retail	15,589	16,022	16,480
Video game software (rental and retail)	6,047	6,016	4,864
Video game hardware and accessories	5,161	6,353	4,218
Total video game market	11,208	12,369	9,082
Total U.S. media entertainment market	$36,317	$37,678	$34,955

Source: As reported in Blockbuster's 2008 10-K report, p. 5.

rentals of movie DVDs, computer downloads of music and movie files, growing consumer interest in video-on-demand (VOD) services, and growing popularity of high-definition TV programs were cited as factors.

- Prices for wide-screen, high-definition TVs had been dropping rapidly, and picture quality was exceptionally good, if not stunning, on increasing numbers of models.
- Starting in 2009, all TV stations in the United States were required by law to use digital technology and equipment to broadcast all their programs, a requirement that would result in far more programs being transmitted in high-definition format.
- The flood of new and old TV shows on DVDs that had recently hit retailers' shelves had cut into the sales of movie DVDs—however, the multidisc sets of many of these TV shows were more expensive than most new releases of movie DVDs.
- Hollywood movie producers were hoping that next-generation, high-definition (HD) optical-disc-format DVDs that incorporated Blu-ray technology would rejuvenate sales of movie DVDs. The Blu-ray format offered more than five times the storage capacity of traditional DVDs and used advanced video and audio capabilities that provided users with an unprecedented HD experience. But it remained to be seen whether Blu-ray movie DVDs would spur movie DVD sales, given the growing popularity of digital video recorders (DVRs), VOD, and online rentals.
- Cable companies like Comcast were offering VOD options for many of their premium movie channels. The Starz Entertainment Group claimed its research showed that Comcast customers who were using the Starz on Demand VOD service tended to reduce their purchases and rentals of movie DVDs due to the ease of using the VOD service.
- Cable and satellite TV companies were promoting their VOD services and making more movie titles available to their customers.
- Cable and satellite TV customers with DVRs could readily substitute VOD movie offerings from their cable/satellite TV provider for

purchasing or renting movie DVDs (although selection was generally more limited).

- Online rentals and VOD services were not only cutting into sales of movie DVDs but also taking business away from local video rental stores. Just as Netflix posed a competitive threat to customers patronizing local Blockbuster and Movie Gallery stores in the United States, market research in Great Britain indicated that one out of every five DVDs rented was rented online.

NETFLIX AND ITS SUBSCRIPTION-BASED BUSINESS MODEL FOR RENTING MOVIES

By 2008, having revolutionized the way that many people rented movies, Netflix had become the world's largest online entertainment subscription service. It had attracted 8.4 million subscribers, who paid monthly fees ranging from \$4.99 to \$47.99; subscribers went to Netflix's Web site, selected one or more movies from its library of 100,000 titles, and received the movie DVDs by first-class mail generally within one business day—more than 95 percent of Netflix's subscribers lived within one-day delivery of the company's 50 distribution centers (plus 50 other shipping points) located throughout the United States. Subscribers could keep a DVD for as long as they wished, with no due dates or late fees, although they were limited to having a certain number of DVDs in their possession at any one time (depending on which fee plan they had chosen). Subscribers returned DVDs via the U.S. Postal Service in a prepaid return envelope that came with each movie order. The company also had a growing library of more than 12,000 full-length movies and television episodes that subscribers could watch instantly on their televisions or PCs for no additional cost. Netflix had been rated number one in online retail customer satisfaction by Nielsen Online and for seven consecutive periods by Foresee/FGI Research.

A unique aspect of Netflix's pioneering business model was that it provided subscribers with all the benefits of a local movie rental store but without the hassle of having to drive to the store, pick out movie DVDs from a selection of primarily recent releases, and return the rentals by a specified time. Netflix's positive and rapidly growing profits over the past five years had convinced skeptics that its wholly online business model for renting DVDs and streaming video was indeed viable, despite the fact that movie rental leader Blockbuster (which at one time had 9,000 company-operated and franchised stores worldwide) had entered the online movie rental segment and tried to horn in on the market opportunity that Netflix was so rapidly exploiting. Wal-Mart had pursued online movie rentals for a short time, but in May 2005 had decided to enter into an arrangement with Netflix whereby Wal-Mart would refer customers interested in online DVD rentals to Netflix, while Netflix would steer customers wanting to purchase a movie DVD to Wal-Mart's Web site. Amazon.com had considered entering the online movie rental market but in the end opted not to take on Netflix. Entry barriers into online DVD rentals were relatively low, but the barriers to profitability were considered rather high because of the need to attract 2 to 4 million subscribers in order to operate profitably.

Nonetheless, Reed Hastings, founder and CEO of Netflix, remained concerned about how to make the company's service offerings even better (identifying additional strategic moves to outcompete Blockbuster) and most particularly how to stay ahead of other competitors that were either already offering movies on a pay-per-view basis to Internet customers with high-speed broadband connections or else were gearing up to do so. Hastings's goals for Netflix were simple: to build the world's best Internet movie service and to deliver a growing subscriber base and earnings per share every year.

Company Background

After successfully founding his first company, Pure Software, in 1991, Reed Hastings engineered several acquisitions and grew Pure Software into one of the 50 largest software companies in the world—the company's principal product was a debugging tool for engineers. When Pure Software was acquired by Rational Software in 1997 for \$750 million, Hastings used the money from selling his shares of Pure Software to help fund his pursuit of another, entirely different business venture. Sensing the opportunity for online movie rentals in a climate where the popularity of the Internet was mushrooming, he founded

Netflix in 1997, launched the online subscription service in 1999, and attracted a base of more than 2 million subscribers in just four years. (In contrast, America Online took six years to acquire the same number of subscribers.) Netflix quickly discovered that new subscribers were drawn to try its online movie rental service because of the wide selection; the extensive information Netflix provided about each movie in its rental library (including critic reviews, member reviews, online trailers, ratings); the ease with which they could find and order movies; the elimination of late fees and due dates; and the convenience of being provided a postage-paid return envelope for mailing the DVDs back to Netflix.

The company's extensive marketing campaigns from 2001 into 2008 had produced widespread consumer awareness of the Netflix name, its distinctive red logo, and its movie rental service. By July 2008, Netflix had 8.4 million subscribers. Exhibit 2 shows trends in Netflix's subscriber growth.

Netflix had 2007 revenues of $1.2 billion (up from $501 million in 2004), and its 100,000 movie titles (up from 55,000 in 2005) far outdistanced the selection available in local brick-and-mortar movie rental stores. Netflix's DVD lineup included everything from the latest big Hollywood releases to hard-to-locate documentaries to independent films to TV shows and how-to videos. Subscriber growth had been fueled by the rapid adoption of DVDs as a medium for home entertainment as well as by increased awareness of online DVD rentals.

Netflix's Strategy

Netflix's success in building a bigger subscriber base was due to its six-pronged strategy of providing comprehensive selection of movie DVDs, an easy way to choose movies, fast delivery of selections, no due dates for return, and a convenient drop-it-in-the-mail return procedure, coupled with aggressive marketing to attract subscribers and build widespread awareness of the Netflix brand and service. The sought-for competitive advantage over other movie rental competitors was to deliver compelling customer value and customer satisfaction by eliminating the hassle involved in choosing, renting, and returning movies.

Going forward, Netflix had two primary strategic objectives: (1) to continue to grow a large DVD subscription business and (2) to expand rapidly into Internet-based delivery of content as that market segment developed. Management's long-term growth strategy for Netflix was predicated on two beliefs: (1) that the DVD format, along with high-definition successor formats such as Blu-ray, would be the main vehicle for watching content in the home for the foreseeable future and (2) that by growing a large DVD subscription business based on mail delivery, Netflix would be well positioned to transition its subscribers to Internet-based delivery of content. In January 2007, Netflix introduced an instant-watching feature for PCs that allowed subscribers to view selections from Netflix's library of 12,000 full-length movies and television episodes streamed over the Internet directly to their PC monitors. Shortly thereafter, the company began efforts to broaden the distribution of instant-watching capability to other platforms and partners over time. In 2008, LG Electronics introduced a set-top box device that enabled Netflix's instant-watching selections of movies and TV episodes to be viewed directly on subscribers' television screens. Netflix anticipated that other consumer electronics manufacturers would soon introduce similar devices, thus paving the way for more subscribers to begin the expected switchover from postal delivery to Internet-based delivery.

In October 2008, Netflix and Starz Entertainment, a premium movie service provider operating in the United States, announced an agreement to make movies from Starz, through its Starz Play broadband subscription movie service, available to be streamed instantly at Netflix. Access to the Starz Play service at Netflix was included with Netflix members' current monthly subscription fee. The agreement with Starz Play gave Netflix members access to an additional 2,500 movies that could be streamed directly to their TVs and boosted Netflix's library of instantly watchable movies from 12,000 to 14,500.

Management expected that at some point Internet delivery of media content would surpass postal delivery and that eventually postal delivery would account for a relatively small fraction of Netflix's business. Internet delivery of media content was segmented into the rental of Internet-delivered content, the download-to-own segment, and the advertising-supported online delivery segment. Netflix's objective was to be the clear leader in the rental segment via its instant-watching feature.

Exhibit 2 Subscriber Data for Netflix, 2000–2007

	2000	2001	2002	2003	2004	2005	2006	2007
Total subscribers at beginning of period	107,000	292,000	456,000	857,000	1,487,000	2,610,000	4,179,000	6,316,000
Gross subscriber additions during period	515,000	566,000	1,140,000	1,571,000	2,716,000	3,729,000	5,250,000	5,340,000
Subscriber cancellations during the period	330,000	402,000	739,000	941,000	1,593,000	2,160,000	3,113,000	4,177,000
Total subscribers at end of period	292,000	456,000	857,000	1,487,000	2,610,000	4,179,000	6,316,000	7,479,000
Net subscriber additions during the period	185,000	164,000	401,000	630,000	1,123,000	1,569,000	2,137,000	1,163,000
Free trial subscribers*	n.a.	n.a.	56,000	61,000	71,000	153,000	162,000	153,000
Subscriber acquisition cost	$110.79	$49.96	$37.16	$32.80	$37.02	$38.77	$42.96	$40.88

n.a. = Not available.

*First-time subscribers automatically were eligible for a free two-week trial; membership fees began after the two-week trial expired (unless the membership was canceled).

A Wide Choice of Subscription Plans In 2008, Netflix members had the choice of eight "unlimited" subscription plans:

- $8.99 Unlimited DVDs each month, one title out at a time, plus unlimited streaming.
- $13.99 Unlimited DVDs each month, two titles out at a time, plus unlimited streaming.
- $16.99 Unlimited DVDs each month, three titles out at a time, plus unlimited streaming.
- $23.99 Unlimited DVDs each month, four titles out at a time, plus unlimited streaming .
- $29.99 Unlimited DVDs each month, five titles out at a time, plus unlimited streaming.
- $35.99 Unlimited DVDs each month, six titles out at a time, plus unlimited streaming.
- $41.99 Unlimited DVDs each month, seven titles out at a time, plus unlimited streaming.
- $47.99 Unlimited DVDs each month, eight titles out at a time, plus unlimited streaming.

The company also offered one "limited" plan for $4.99, which entailed a maximum of two DVDs per month with two hours of video streaming to a PC. This plan did not allow members to stream movies to their TV via a Netflix-ready device—as was the case with the eight unlimited plans.

The most popular subscription plan was the $16.99 plan (three DVDs at a time, with unlimited streaming). Subscribers could cancel anytime. New subscribers were automatically eligible for a free two-week trial that provided full access to the whole library of 100,000 movie titles and unlimited streaming to PCs.

Management believed that Netflix's subscriber base consisted of three types of customers: those who liked the convenience of home delivery, bargain hunters who were enthused about being able to watch 10 or more movies a month at an economical price (on the $16.99 plan, 12 movies equated to a rental fee of $1.42 per movie), and movie buffs who wanted access to a very wide selection of films.

Netflix's Proprietary Movie Recommendation Software Netflix had developed proprietary software that enabled it to provide subscribers with detailed information about each title in the Netflix library as well as personalized movie recommendations every time they visited the Netflix Web site. The information provided for each title included length, rating, cast and crew, screen formats, movie trailers, plot synopses, and reviews written by Netflix editors, third parties, and subscribers. The personalized recommendations were based on a subscriber's individual likes and dislikes (determined by their rental history, their personal ratings of movies viewed, movies in the subscriber's queue for future delivery, and titles posted to a wish list), movie ratings, and the average rating by all subscribers. Subscribers often began their search for movie titles by starting from a familiar title and then using the recommendations tool to find other titles they might enjoy.

The recommendation software was designed around an Oracle database and proprietary algorithms that organized Netflix's library of movies into clusters of similar movies and analyzed how customers rated them after they rented them. Those customers who rated similar movies in similar clusters were then matched as like-minded viewers. When a customer was online, the software was programmed to check the clusters the subscriber had rented from in the past, determine which movies the customer had yet to rent in that cluster, and recommend only those movies in the cluster that had been highly rated by viewers. Viewer ratings determined which available titles were displayed to a subscriber and in what order. The recommendations helped subscribers quickly create a list, or queue, of movies they wanted to see. Subscribers used this queue to specify the order in which movies would be delivered; they could alter their queue at any time. Netflix management saw the movie recommendation tool as a powerful means of enticing customers to spend time browsing through its expansive content library and locating movies they would like to see.

In 2008, Netflix had more than 2 billion movie ratings from customers in its database, and the average subscriber had rated more than 200 movies. These ratings were used to determine which titles to feature most prominently on the company's Web site, to generate lists of similar titles, and to select the promotional trailers that a subscriber would see when using the Previews feature. Netflix management believed that more than 50 percent of its rentals came from the recommendations generated by its recommendation software. The software algorithms were thought to be particularly effective in promoting selections of smaller, high-quality films to subscribers who otherwise might have missed spotting them in the company's massive 100,000-film library (to which new titles were continuously being added). On average, more than 85 percent of the movie titles in the Netflix library of offerings were rented each quarter, an indication of the effectiveness of the company's recommendation software in steering subscribers to movies of interest and achieving broader utilization of the company's entire library of titles.

Quick Delivery Capability Netflix had 50 regional shipping centers and another 50 shipping points scattered across the United States, giving it one-business-day delivery capability for 95 percent of its subscribers. In 2008, Netflix was shipping more than 2 million DVDs a day (outside of holidays and weekends) from its inventory of around 70 million DVDs, which was growing as the subscriber base increased.

Netflix had developed sophisticated software to track its inventory and minimize delivery times. Netflix's system allowed the distribution centers to communicate to determine the fastest way of getting the DVDs to the customers. When a customer placed an order for a specific DVD, the system first looked for that DVD at the shipping center closest to the customer. If that center didn't have the DVD in stock, the system then moved the next closest center and checked there. The search continued until the DVD was found, at which point the shipping center was provided with the information needed to initiate the order fulfillment and shipping process. If the DVD was unavailable anywhere in the system, it was waitlisted. The system then moved to the customer's next choice, and the process started all over. And no matter where the DVD was sent from, the system knew to print the return label on the prepaid envelope to send the DVDs to the shipping center closest to the customer to reduce return times and permit more efficient use of the company's DVD inventory.

New Content Acquisition In the first six months of 2008, Netflix spent $120.3 million on the acquisition of new movie DVDs and movie/TV content for online streaming; new content was acquired from movie studios and distributors through direct purchases (usually on a fee-per-DVD basis), revenue-sharing agreements, and licensing. Netflix acquired many of its new-release movie DVDs from studios for a low up-front fee plus a percentage of revenue earned from rentals for a defined period. After a revenue-sharing period expired for a title, Netflix generally had the option of returning the title to the studio, purchasing the title, or destroying its copies of the title. In the case of movie titles and TV episodes that were delivered to subscribers via the Internet for instant viewing, Netflix generally paid a fee to license the content for a defined period of time; in most instances, these license agreements could be extended or renewed.

The company's June 30, 2008, balance sheet indicated that its content had a net value of $126.9 million (after depreciation). New-release DVDs were amortized over one year; the useful life of back-library titles (some of which qualified as classics) were amortized over three years (since the personalized movie recommendations generated significant rentals of older titles). DVDs that the company expected to sell at the end of their useful lives carried a salvage value of $3 per DVD; DVDs that the company did not expect to sell were assigned a salvage value of zero.

Marketing and Advertising Netflix used multiple marketing channels to attract subscribers, including online advertising (paid search listings, banner ads, text on popular sites such as AOL and Yahoo!, and permission-based e-mails), radio stations, regional and national television, direct mail, and print ads. It also participated in a variety of cooperative advertising programs with studios through which Netflix received cash consideration in return for featuring a studio's movies in its advertising.

Advertising campaigns of one type or another were under way more or less continuously, with the lure of two-week free trials usually being a prominent feature of most ads. Management had boosted marketing expenditures from $25.7 million in 2002 (16.8 percent of revenues) to $98 million in 2004 (19.6 percent of revenues) to $142.0 million in 2005 (20.8 percent of revenues) to $223.4 million in 2006 (22.4 percent of revenues) before cutting back slightly to $216.1 million in 2007 (17.9 percent of revenues) and then $95 million in the first six months of 2008 (14.3 percent of revenues). Netflix management believed that its paid advertising efforts were significantly enhanced by the benefits of word-of-mouth advertising, the referrals of satisfied subscribers, and its active public relations programs.

Netflix's Performance and Prospects

Recent financial statement data for Netflix are shown in Exhibits 3 and 4. Management's latest forecast called for having between 9.1 and 9.7 million subscribers by year-end 2008, full-year revenues of about $1.37 billion, net income in the range of $75–$83 million, and diluted earnings per share of $1.19 to $1.31. In January 2008, the company announced that it would spend $100 million to repurchase shares of its common stock; the buyback resulted in the repurchase of 3.8 million shares at an average price of $25.96. In March 2008, Netflix's board of directors authorized a second repurchase program whereby the company would spend an additional $150 million to buy back shares during the remainder of 2008. In September 2008, Netflix's stock was trading in $30–$33 range.

BLOCKBUSTER: THE WORLD LEADER IN MOVIE RENTALS

Blockbuster was the global leader in the movie rental industry. In 2008, it had an estimated 40 percent share of the roughly $9.5 billion U.S. market for renting movies for in-home viewing and a globally recognized brand in movie rentals. Founded in Dallas, Texas, in 1985, Blockbuster had pursued an aggressive growth strategy, reaching a peak of 9,094 company-operated and franchised movie rental stores worldwide by year-end 2004, with 7,265 company-operated stores (including 2,557 outside the United States) and 1,829 franchised Blockbuster stores (some 734 of which were outside the United States). Blockbuster's 3,291 international store locations at year-end 2004 were scattered across 24 countries, but 87 percent were in the following countries: Great Britain (897), Canada (426), Australia (408), Mexico (317), Italy (241), Ireland (199), Brazil (131), Taiwan (128), and Spain (106).

However, during 2005–2007, amid adverse market and competitive conditions and hemorrhaging losses, Blockbuster closed more than 700 of its company-operated stores in the United States and nearly 500 of its company-operated stores outside the United States. The total number of franchised stores had fallen modestly from 1,829 to 1,757 as of year-end 2007. An additional 137 company-owned stores and 96 franchised stores were closed or sold worldwide in the first six months of 2008. As of July 2008, Blockbuster had a total of 7,619 stores in the United States and 20 other countries, including 3,939 company-operated stores in the United States,

Exhibit 3 Netflix's Consolidated Statements of Operations, 2000–2007 ($ in millions, except per share data)

	2000	2002	2004	2005	2006	2007
Revenues	$35.9	$152.8	$500.6	$682.2	$996.7	$1,205.3
Cost of Revenues:						
Subscription costs	24.9	78.1*	273.4	393.7	532.6	664.4
Fulfillment expenses	10.2	19.4	56.6	70.8	93.4	121.3
Total cost of revenues	35.1	97.5	330.0	464.6	626.0	785.7
Gross profit	0.8	55.3	170.6	217.7	370.7	419.6
Operating expenses						
Technology and development	16.8	14.6	22.9	30.9	44.8	67.7
Marketing	25.7	35.8	98.0	142.0	223.4	216.1
General and administrative	7.0	6.7	16.3	29.4	30.1	46.8
Stock-based compensation	9.7	8.8	16.6	14.3	12.7	12.0
Gain (loss) on disposal of DVDs	—	—	(2.6)	(2.0)	(4.8)	(7.2)
Gain on legal settlement	—	—	—	—	—	(7.0)
Total operating expenses	59.2	65.9	151.2	214.7	306.2	328.4
Operating income	(58.4)	(10.7)	19.4	3.0	64.4	91.2
Interest and other income (expense)	(0.2)	(10.3)	2.4	5.3	15.9	20.3
Income before income taxes	—	(20.9)	21.8	8.3	80.3	111.5
Provision for (benefit from) income taxes	—	—	0.2	(33.7)	31.2	44.5
Net income	$(58.5)	$(20.9)	$21.6	$42.0	$49.1	$67.0
Net income per share:						
Basic	$(20.61)	$(0.74)	$0.42	$0.79	$0.78	$1.00
Diluted	(20.61)	(0.74)	0.33	0.64	0.71	0.97
Weighted average common shares outstanding:						
Basic	2.8	28.2	52.0	53.5	62.6	67.1
Diluted	2.8	28.2	64.7	65.5	69.1	68.9

*Includes sales costs of $1.1 million.

Note: Totals may not add due to rounding.

Source: Company 10-K reports for 2003, 2005, and 2007.

2,013 company-owned stores outside the United States, and 1,630 franchised stores domestically and internationally.

Blockbuster recorded net losses of $2.8 billion during the 2003–2005 period, earned a modest $39.2 million after-tax profit in 2006, and lost $85.1 million in 2007—see Exhibit 5 on pages C-110–111. The company had announced that it expected to report full-year 2008 net income in the range of $21 to $36 million, despite reporting a net loss of $2.1 million for the first six months of 2008. To improve the company's 2008 financial performance and avoid another year of losses, senior management had launched efforts to cut general and administrative expenses at the corporate level by $100 million, and during the first half of 2008 alone, advertising expenses had been trimmed by $65 million (about 60 percent).

Exhibit 4 Selected Balance Sheet and Cash Flow Data for Netflix, 2000–2007 ($ in millions)

	2000	2002	2004	2005	2006	2007
Selected Balance Sheet Data						
Cash and cash equivalents	$14.9	$ 59.8	$174.5	$212.3	$400.4	$177.4
Short-term investments	—	43.8	—	—	—	207.7
Current assets	n.a.	107.1	187.3	243.7	428.4	416.5
Net investment in DVD library	n.a.	10.0	42.2	42.2	104.9	132.5
Total assets	52.5	130.5	251.8	251.8	608.8	647.0
Current liabilities	n.a.	40.4	94.9	94.9	193.4	212.6
Working capital*	(1.7)	66.6	92.4	148.8	235.0	203.9
Notes payable, less current portion	1.8	—	—	—	—	—
Stockholders' equity	(73.3)	89.4	156.3	226.3	430.7	414.2
Cash Flow Data						
Net cash provided by operating activities	$(22.7)	$ 40.1	$147.6	$157.5	$247.9	$291.8
Net cash used in investing activities	(25.0)	(67.3)	(68.4)	(133.2)	(185.9)	(450.8)
Net cash provided by financing activities	48.4	70.9	5.6	13.3	126.2	(64.0)

*Defined as current assets minus current liabilities.

Sources: Company 10-K reports for 2003, 2005, and 2007.

Blockbuster's financial troubles stemmed in part from its split-off from media conglomerate Viacom in October 2004 (Viacom had acquired Blockbuster in 1994 for $8.4 billion); part of the split-off arrangement involved paying a special one-time $5 dividend (totaling $905 million) to all shareholders, including Viacom (which owned 81.5 percent of Blockbuster's shares prior to the divestiture deal). A cash payment of this size proved to be a considerable financial burden, thrusting Blockbuster into a weak financial condition and limiting the financial resources available for overcoming sluggish sales at its stores and eroding movie rentals. The company's revenues in 2007 were $500 million below the 2004 level. Since becoming an independent company in 2004 (when it split off from Viacom), Blockbuster had seen its stock price trend steadily downward, falling from a high of $10 in 2004 to $1.90 per share as of October 2, 2008. In July 2007, James F. Keyes, former president and CEO of 7-Eleven, was appointed to replace John F. Antioco, who had served as Blockbuster's CEO since 1997. Keyes quickly initiated a series of efforts to recast Blockbuster's strategy and put the company in better position to improve its dismal bottom-line performance.

Blockbuster's Strategy, 2002–2006

In 2002, Blockbuster announced a strategic vision of becoming the complete source for movies and video games—rental and retail. Already the leader in the movie and game rental market, the company set its sights on increasing sales and market share by launching a variety of promotional campaigns and expanding its in-store selection of movies and gaming equipment, including hardware, software, and accessories.

New Video Game Strategic Initiatives To expand its presence in the gaming marketplace, in 2002 Blockbuster purchased the United Kingdom–based video game retailer Gamestation and proceeded to expand the chain from 64 to more than 150 stores. Meanwhile, Blockbuster started a Game Freedom Pass rental subscription program in all of its U.S. company-operated stores. Customers could purchase a single-month pass for just $19.99 and get unlimited video game rentals for 30 consecutive days with a maximum of one game rented at any given time, and no extended viewing fees during the 30 days; a gamer could keep one game for the entire 30 consecutive days or change out the game daily—or even multiple times a day.

Several other initiatives in video games were launched in 2004–2005. Blockbuster began carrying PlayStation Portable handheld games for rent in all stores. And it had boosted its games offering by creating a special section called Game Rush within certain high-traffic Blockbuster stores; Game Rush customers could rent, sell, or buy new and used game software and hardware. During peak hours, Game Rush sections were staffed by specially trained game specialists. Blockbuster believed that about half of its U.S. stores were suited to having a special Game Rush section.

In-Store Movie Rental Subscription Programs In 2003, Blockbuster initiated an in-store movie rental subscription program in approximately 25 percent of its stores. The program was rolled out to all U.S. company-operated stores in 2004 under the banner Blockbuster Movie Pass. For $24.99 per month, members could take up to two movies out at a time; for $29.99 per month, they could have three movies out on rental at a time. Both plans entitled customers to watch all the movies they wanted, with no specified return dates and no extended viewing fees. Once customers joined the Movie Pass program, their credit card or debit card was automatically charged the monthly fee; subscriptions could be canceled at any time.

Expansion into Online Rentals In August 2004, Blockbuster launched an online subscription service in the United States and a smaller online service in Great Britain (where it also had almost 900 Blockbuster stores). In the United States, customers were offered a choice of three monthly plans (all with unlimited rentals and no due dates or late fees): (1) a $19.99 plan with three DVDs out at a time, (2) a $29.99 plan with five DVDs out at a time, and (3) a $39.99 plan with eight DVDs out at a time. At the time, customers could choose from 25,000 titles, ranging from classics to new releases. In addition, subscribers were e-mailed two e-coupons each month for free in-store rentals; all Blockbuster Online members were eligible for exclusive deals and discounts at participating Blockbuster stores. Rentals were shipped from 11 distribution centers to subscribers via first-class mail and usually arrived in one to three business days. Subscribers were provided with a postage-paid envelope for returning the DVDs. Subscribers could create and maintain a personal queue of movies they wished to rent at Blockbuster's Web site. When Blockbuster received return DVDs from subscribers, it automatically shipped the next available titles in the subscriber's rental queue.

Management said entry into online rentals represented an ongoing effort to transform Blockbuster from a chain of neighborhood movie rental stores into an "anywhere, anytime" entertainment destination that eventually would enable customers to rent, buy, or trade both new and used movies and games, in-store and online. The initial response was promising; according to Blockbuster's CEO, John Antioco, "After six weeks, we had more subscribers than Netflix had in a year and a half of existence."

On December 22, 2004, Blockbuster cut the price on its most popular online subscription plan (unlimited rentals, three titles out at a time) from $19.99 per month to $14.99 and announced it was expanding the copy-depth of new-release movies, boosting the number of titles available for online rental to 30,000, and adding more variety to its library of both TV shows and movies. It also announced that it was increasing the number of shipping centers to 23 and implementing new technology with the U.S. Postal Service that would shorten delivery times.

In August 2005, Blockbuster Online's pricing was raised. Customers could choose from among three plans:

- $9.99, one title out at a time, no monthly rental limits.
- $14.99, two titles out at a time, no monthly rental limits.
- $17.99, three titles out at a time, no monthly rental limits.

The $17.99 plan was the most popular. All new subscribers received a free two-week trial. The company had 1 million online subscribers and, during 2005, reportedly added about as many net new subscribers as Netflix. Also in 2005, Blockbuster integrated its in-store and online subscription program—members paid the same fees and had the same privileges.

As of mid-2005, online subscribers could choose from over 40,000 titles. Blockbuster had 30 distribution centers, and more than 200 local Blockbuster stores were fulfilling online orders for nearby customers (to help shorten delivery times). More local stores were being added daily to fulfill online orders. By year-end 2006, Blockbuster had 65,000 titles in its online rental library; its 35 distribution centers and 90 points for mail entry enabled it to deliver orders to 90 percent of online subscribers within one business day.

Blockbuster's 2005 Decision to Discontinue Late Fees for In-Store Rentals To revitalize stagnant store sales and combat the attractiveness of the no due dates/no late fees policies of Netflix, in January 2005 Blockbuster discontinued its practice of charging late fees on DVD rental returns at its retail stores. However, it held on to the practice of specified due dates—one week for games and two days or one week for movies. If customers kept the rental beyond the due date, they were automatically granted an extra one-week goodwill period at no additional charge. If customers chose to keep their rentals past the end of the seventh day after the due date per the posted rental terms, Blockbuster converted the rental to a sale and charged customers for the movie or game, minus the original rental fee. If customers later decided they did not want to own the movie or game and returned the product within 30 days, Blockbuster reversed the sale and charged a minimal restocking fee of $1.25 (some franchised Blockbuster stores charged a higher restocking fee).

Blockbuster ran extensive ads in December 2004/January 2005 touting its new no-late-fee policy. To help compensate for the estimated $250 to $300 million that late fees were expected to contribute to Blockbuster's revenues in 2005, Blockbuster management reduced 2005 capital spending by more than $100 million, took actions to cut corporate overhead by $70 million on an annualized basis, and put planned strategic initiatives in video games and movie trading on hold until 2006. John Antioco, CEO of Blockbuster at the time, saw the new end-of-late-fees program as the company's best option for addressing one of the biggest complaints that customers had with their in-store rental experience at Blockbuster. Nonetheless, Antioco was under fire from shareholders and some members of the company's board of directors for instituting the no-late-fee policy, given the big revenue erosion impact, Blockbuster's string of huge losses, and the need to increase store inventories of DVDs to compensate for the extra time that customers were keeping the DVDs. Investors and board members were also skeptical about Blockbuster's entry into the online rental market segment because of the heavy costs (estimated at $100 to $200 million) and what some considered as dim prospects for profitability. Later in 2005, about 160 Blockbuster franchisees decided to reinstate late fees because of the loss in revenues and the extra expenses involved in stocking additional copies of popular titles.

Blockbuster's Strategy Overhaul, 2007–2008

To fulfill its mission of "providing convenient access to media entertainment," in 2008 Blockbuster was moving beyond just renting movies to pursue what management saw as bigger growth opportunities in the broader entertainment market. The company was focusing on three strategic priorities:

- Growing its core movie rental business.
- Broadening the product offerings at local Blockbuster stores.
- Developing new channels for delivery of digital content.

Growing Movie Rental Revenues One of new CEO Jim Keyes's first actions had been to significantly improve the in-stock availability of hot new releases at Blockbuster stores. Customers going to a local Blockbuster to rent a popular movie or placing an order online for by-mail delivery were often frustrated upon learning that all copies of the movie were out on rental. To attack the out-of-stock problems, Blockbuster boosted its purchases of new movie DVDs for inventory by about 20 percent and improved its inventory management procedures—moves that boosted in-stock availability from 20 percent in June 2007 to nearly 60 percent in May 2008. All stores had signage alerting customers to Blockbuster's new practice of stocking more copies of hit titles. These actions helped reverse the declines in movie rental revenues and same-store sales that had plagued the company since January 2003 (see Exhibit 5).

Exhibit 5 Selected Financial and Operating Statistics for Blockbuster Inc., 2002–2007 ($ in millions, except for per share data)

	2007	2006	2005	2004	2003	2002
Selected Statement of Operations Data						
Revenues						
Rentals	$4,082.5	$4,029.1	$4,160.7	$4,428.6	$4,533.5	$4,460.4
Merchandise sales	1,400.1	1,431.9	1,488.9	1,532.6	1,281.6	1,019.7
Other	59.8	61.2	72.2	92.0	96.6	85.8
Total	5,542.4	5,522.2	5,721.8	6,053.2	5,911.7	5,565.9
Cost of rental revenues	1,604.0	1,403.9	1,396.6	1,250.7	1,362.1	1,513.8
Gross margin on rentals	60.7%	65.2%	66.4%	71.8%	70.0%	66.1%
Cost of merchandise sold	1,073.8	1,075.8	1,164.4	1,190.7	1,027.7	844.9
Gross margin on merchandise sales	23.3%	24.9%	21.8%	22.3%	19.8%	17.1%
Gross profit	2,864.6	3,042.5	3,160.8	3,611.8	3,521.9	3,207.2
Gross profit margin	51.7%	55.1%	55.2%	59.7%	59.6%	57.6%
Operating expenses						
General and administrative	2,525.1	2,598.6	2,724.8	2,835.2	2,605.9	2,369.5
Share-based compensation	—	—	—	18.3	—	—
Advertising	194.0	154.3	252.7	257.4	181.8	250.9
Depreciation and intangible amortization	185.7	210.9	224.3	249.7	266.0	239.1
Impairment of goodwill and other long-lived assets	2.2	5.1	341.9	1,504.4	1,304.9	—
Gain on sale of Gamestation	(81.5)	—	—	—	—	—
Total operating expenses	2,825.5	2,968.9	3,543.7	4,865.0	4,358.6	2,859.5
Operating income (loss)	39.1	73.6	(382.9)	(1,253.2)	(836.7)	347.7
Interest expense	(88.7)	(101.6)	(98.7)	(38.1)	(33.1)	(49.5)
Interest income	6.5	9.9	4.1	3.6	3.1	4.1
Other items, net	(1.5)	5.4	(4.2)	—	—	—
Income (loss) before income taxes	(44.6)	(12.7)	(481.7)	(1,286.1)	(867.1)	305.2
Net profit (loss)	$ (85.1)	$ 39.2	$ (583.9)	$(1,248.8)	$ (978.7)	$ 195.9
Earnings per share (diluted)	$(0.45)	$0.21	$(3.18)	$(6.89)	$(5.41)	$1.08
Dividends per share	—	—	$0.04	$5.08	$0.08	$0.08
Selected Balance Sheet Data						
Cash and cash equivalents	$184.6	$394.9	$276.2	$330.3	$233.4	$152.5
Merchandise inventories	343.9	343.9	310.3	516.6	415.1	452.1

(Continued)

Exhibit 5 (Continued)

	2007	2006	2005	2004	2003	2002
Current assets	1,319.2	1,562.4	1,423.8	1,217.7	960.3	958.9
Total assets	2,733.6	3,134.6	3,179.6	3,863.4	4,822.0	6,243.8
Current liabilities	1,288.5	1,405.4	1,317.9	1,449.4	1,323.4	1,477.6
Long-term debt, less current portion	665.6	851.0	1,059.4	1,044.9	0.7	328.9
Stockholders' equity	655.7	723.3	631.6	1,062.9	3,188.4	4,100.9
Selected Cash Flow Data						
Net cash flow provided by (used for) operations	$ (56.2)	$ 329.4	$ (70.5)	$1,215.4	$ 1,430.3	$1,462.3
Net cash flow provided by (used for) investing activities	76.7	(41.0)	(114.2)	(1,112.3)	(1,024.6)	(1,314.6)
Net cash flow provided by (used for) financing activities	(241.0)	(183.2)	138.3	(18.8)	(335.5)	(199.2)
Worldwide Store Data						
Same-store revenue increase (decrease)	3.4%	(2.1)%	(4.8)%	(3.2)%	(2.2)%	5.1%
Company-owned stores, end-of-year	6,073	6,551	7,158	7,265	7,105	6,907
Franchised stores, end-of-year	1,757	1,809	1,884	1,829	1,762	1,638
Total stores, end-of-year	7,830	8,360	9,042	9,094	8,867	8,545

Source: Blockbuster's 2003 10-K report, 2006 10-K report, and 2007 10-K report.

Other moves to profitably grow revenues from movie rentals at Blockbuster included the following:

- Expanding the selection of independent films—Blockbuster signed an agreement with IFC, a leading provider of independent films, whereby Blockbuster would have exclusive rights to rent IFC titles for a limited period. As of fall 2008, customers could choose from a library of 85,000 titles.
- Refurbishing stores with brighter paint, lower shelves, and new merchandising displays. Some stores had a Rock the Block café area with seating, snacks, and beverages.
- Placing Blockbuster-branded DVD vending machines and high-speed downloading kiosks at high-traffic retail locations to give Blockbuster more points at which it could access customers interested in renting a movie. In August 2008, Blockbuster and NCR Corporation announced a strategic alliance to deploy Blockbuster-branded state-of-the-art DVD vending kiosks for renting movie DVDs; if the initial pilot program for 50 machines proved successful, plans called for a national rollout of as many as 10,000 vending kiosks where consumers could either rent or purchase movie DVDs and video games. Earlier in 2008, Blockbuster and NCR had partnered to test digital movie downloading kiosks in select Blockbuster stores.
- Creating a program called Total Access, through which customers could choose from among any of 11 subscription plans, ranging from as little as $3.99 (one DVD out at a time, limit of two per month) to as much as $34.99 (three DVDs out at a time, no monthly limits); browse Blockbuster's library of 85,000 titles; place orders; and obtain movies from Blockbuster via mail delivery. Blockbuster's Total Access Premium plans allowed subscribers to go to a local

Blockbuster store and exchange DVDs received by mail for unlimited free in-store movie rentals; Blockbuster Total Access plans entailed two, three, or five free in-store exchanges per month; Blockbuster's by-mail-only plans (with fees from $3.99 to $15.99 per month) called for in-store exchange fees of $1.99 per movie. To induce subscription upgrades, some mail-only subscribers received free in-store rental coupons each month, which could be used toward movie or video game rentals. As of January 2008, Blockbuster had 2.2 million online subscribers, of whom 2.0 million were paying subscribers and 200,000 were free-trial subscribers—all new subscribers were eligible for a free three-week trial.

- Purchasing the membership interests of Movielink, an online movie downloading service owned and operated by a group of movie studios. Movielink had one of the largest libraries of digital content for both rental and sale. Movielink's offerings were integrated into Blockbuster's Web site, giving Blockbuster expanded capability to sell or rent movies and deliver them in digital files (which was a considerably cheaper delivery method for Blockbuster than paying the postage for outgoing DVD orders and incoming DVD returns). Downloaded movies that were rented could be stored for up to 30 days and watched as many times as desired during a 24-hour viewing period that commenced when "Play Movie" was clicked. No subscription, membership, or late fees were charged on downloadable movie rentals from the Movielink library.

Recent sales data indicated that these actions were having a positive effect. Sales at Blockbuster stores had, on average, risen for four consecutive quarters, starting in the second quarter of 2007 and continuing through the second quarter of 2008. Most of the sales gains were in merchandise rather than rentals, however. In the first six months of 2008, rental revenues were $1.575 billion (versus $1.564 billion for the first six months of 2007), while merchandise sales climbed from $201 million in the first half of 2007 to $266 million in the first half of 2008. Moreover, the sales improvement at the company's stores was due in part to recent closures and sales of underperforming stores.

Broadening the Product Offerings at Blockbuster Stores Believing that the company's store network represented a huge competitive advantage, in 2008 Blockbuster executives initiated actions to transform Blockbuster stores into media entertainment destinations. One initiative was to expand the selection of movie DVDs offered for sale. Another initiative was to add a variety of entertainment-related services and products, including video game consoles (PlayStation 3, Xbox 360, Wii, and various handheld devices); a bigger selection of video games for both sale and rental; video game accessories; Discovery Channel products; and products related to hit movies (like Indiana Jones and Batman movies). To help consumers better appreciate the dramatic visual and audio improvements of Blu-ray technology and its high-definition format, during 2008 Blockbuster installed Blu-ray demonstration and sales kiosks in almost all of its U.S. and Canadian stores—the goal was to make Blockbuster the preferred destination for Blu-ray players/recorders and Blu-ray DVDs.

Early in 2008, Blockbuster entered into an agreement to acquire electronics retailer Circuit City—a move seen by top Blockbuster executives as a way to offer consumers a complete set of entertainment solutions; however, in July 2008, Blockbuster had to cancel the planned acquisition due to inability to secure adequate financing.

Expanding Digital Content Delivery Although digital delivery of movies was still a small market, Blockbuster was actively exploring a variety of ways to give customers a convenient way to access digitally delivered content from Blockbuster. The acquisition of Movielink and subsequent integration of Movielink's movie library into Blockbuster's online offerings gave customers the option to download movies to rent or own. But Blockbuster management saw this as only a significant first step toward giving customers a single interface—www.blockbuster.com—to reserve an in-store movie, rent movies for mail delivery, download content to a PC or portable device, and eventually access Blockbuster digital content directly through television sets. Ultimately, what was needed was an electronic device that enabled customers to view high-definition digital content from Blockbuster on their big-screen TVs. Management was actively working to achieve this capability, but as of fall 2008 Blockbuster had not announced when such a device would be available.

The ultimate goal was to provide "whenever, wherever" viewing solutions to customers.

Providing Convenient Access to Media Content Senior Blockbuster executives believed that the company's capability to deliver entertainment content to consumers through its stores, by mail, DVD vending machines, digital downloading kiosks, and online downloads put it in an advantageous competitive position in 2008 compared to other media content providers. No other media provider could provide entertainment content to consumers through as many channels as Blockbuster. According to Jim Keyes, "We believe our distinct competitive advantage and our platform for future profitable growth will be our ability to provide convenient access to physical and electronic media entertainment all under the Blockbuster brand."

Blockbuster's Advertising and Marketing Strategy

Blockbuster relied on in-store conversations with store personnel, in-store signage, direct mail, e-mail, and online advertising to get its messages across to people coming to its stores, help increase store traffic, and acquire new subscribers. Management saw e-mail marketing as a cost-effective and efficient communications channel for building customer awareness and loyalty and boosting shopper traffic in its stores. New and reactivated customers were sent in-store offers. In-store signage and brochures were used to support relevant talking points by store customer service representatives. Store personnel were provided scripts designed to help them up-sell, cross-sell, engage store shoppers, increase transactions, and promote return visits.

A series of e-mail communications to Blockbuster Total Access subscribers was created to encourage in-store purchases during subscribers' in-store DVD exchange visits; these messages were customized according to in-store spend history, last store visit date, and other behaviors. Online subscribers received e-mails intended to educate new members, reinforce membership benefits, inform members of new features and offerings, and offer recommendations for movies to add to their queues.

During 2007, Blockbuster's advertising focus was on attracting more online rental subscribers. In 2008, advertising efforts were aimed at promoting greater hit title availability in stores, growing revenues in the video game category, informing customers of new product introductions, announcing special traffic-driving promotions, and acquiring and retaining Total Access members. Blockbuster used cooperative advertising funds from the studios to promote new DVD releases via direct mail and in-store signage.

Blockbuster's advertising expenditures were \$252.7 million in 2005, \$154.3 million in 2006, \$194.0 million in 2007, and \$43.9 million in the first six months of 2008 (versus \$108.3 million in the first six months of 2007).

Blockbuster's Purchasing and Inventory Strategy

In purchasing movie and video game DVDs for rental, Blockbuster sought to craft an arrangement with each individual studio or game publisher aimed at acquiring sufficient copies to satisfy customer demand for the studio's titles while still holding down the overall costs of purchasing those titles for inventory. In some instances, Blockbuster's strategy for a given studio or game publisher entailed purchasing rental inventory on a title-by-title basis. In other instances, Blockbuster negotiated a revenue-sharing arrangement whereby in return for a lower price per copy, Blockbuster paid the studio/game publisher a percentage of rental revenues earned from its titles. The revenue-sharing payments became due and payable as the rental revenues were earned. In addition to the revenue-sharing component, most arrangements also provided for the method of disposition of the product at the conclusion of the rental cycle and/or additional payments for the early sale of unreturned product that was automatically purchased by the customer.

While the terms of revenue-sharing arrangements were generally similar for rental movie and game software inventory, revenue-sharing arrangements for domestic rental movies were generally negotiated for all titles released during the term of the contract, while revenue-sharing arrangements for rental game software were generally negotiated on a title-by-title basis. Approximately 82 percent of Blockbuster's domestic movie rental units were purchased under revenue-sharing arrangements in

2006 and 2007. The number of domestic game software rental inventory units purchased under revenue-sharing arrangements increased from 53 percent in 2006 to 58 percent in 2007.

Distribution and Inventory Management

All movies and games for Blockbuster's U.S. company-operated stores were delivered to the company's highly automated 850,000-square-foot distribution center in McKinney, Texas, which employed 785 people. At the McKinney facility, incoming copies of new movies and games were mechanically repackaged to make them suitable for rental at Blockbuster stores. The repackaged products were shipped to delivery agents scattered across the United States for distribution to nearby Blockbuster stores. In 2008, Blockbuster was exploring ways to improve the efficiency of its distribution system, including the potential of outsourcing all distribution activities.

In addition to the McKinney distribution center, in 2008 Blockbuster had 39 distribution centers spread strategically throughout the United States to support its by-mail subscription service. To expedite the delivery of rental DVDs to by-mail customers by the U.S. Postal Service, Blockbuster transported packaged DVDs from the distribution centers to 85 mail entry points, enabling one-business-day delivery to more than 90 percent of its online subscribers. Each distribution center operated 16 hours a day, five days a week, and employed approximately 35 people, including one distribution center manager.

Endnotes

[1] Cited by Blockbuster CEO James F. Keyes at Blockbuster's annual shareholders' meeting on May 28, 2008; AMR's market size estimate for 2004 was cited in Sarah McBride, Peter Grant, and Merissa Marr, "Movies May Hit DVD Cable Simultaneously," *Wall Street Journal*, January 4, 2006, p. B1.

[2] Based on information in Shane C. Buettner, "DVD Sales Peaking," posted at Ultimate AV, www.guidetohometheater.com (accessed December 29, 2005).

Dell Inc. in 2008: Can It Overtake Hewlett-Packard as the Worldwide Leader in Personal Computers?

CASE 6

Arthur A. Thompson
The University of Alabama

John E. Gamble
University of South Alabama

In 1984, at the age of 19, Michael Dell invested $1,000 of his own money and founded Dell Computer with a simple vision and business concept—that personal computers (PCs) could be built to order and sold directly to customers. Michael Dell believed his approach to the PC business had two advantages: (1) bypassing distributors and retail dealers eliminated the markups of resellers, and (2) building to order greatly reduced the costs and risks associated with carrying large stocks of parts, components, and finished goods. Between 1986 and 1993, the company worked to refine its strategy, build an adequate infrastructure, and establish market credibility against better-known rivals. In the mid-to-late 1990s, Dell's strategy started to click into full gear. By 2003, Dell's sell-direct and build-to-order business model and strategy had provided the company with the most efficient procurement, manufacturing, and distribution capabilities in the global PC industry and given Dell a substantial cost and profit margin advantage over rival PC vendors.

During 2004–2005, Dell overtook Hewlett-Packard (HP) to become the global market leader in PCs. But Dell's global leadership proved short-lived; HP, energized by a new CEO who engineered a revitalized strategy, dramatically closed the gap on Dell in 2006 and regained the global market share lead by a fairly wide margin in 2007—winning an 18.8 percent global share versus Dell's 14.9 percent. In the United States, Dell also struggled to fend off a resurgent HP during 2006–2007. Whereas Dell had a commanding 33.6 percent share of PC sales in the United States in 2005, comfortably ahead of HP (19.5 percent) and far outdistancing Apple, Acer, Toshiba, Gateway, and Lenovo/IBM, Dell's U.S. share had slipped to 28.0 percent by the end of 2007, while HP's share was up to 23.9 percent. Exhibit 1 shows the shifting domestic and global sales and market share rankings in PCs during 1998–2007.

Since the late 1990s, Dell had also been driving for industry leadership in servers. In the mid-to-late 1990s, a big fraction of the servers sold were proprietary machines running on customized Unix operating systems and carrying price tags ranging from $30,000 to $1 million or more. But a seismic shift in server technology, coupled with growing cost-consciousness on the part of server users, produced a radical shift away from more costly, proprietary, Unix-based servers during 1999–2004 to low-cost x86 machines that were based on standardized components and technology, ran on either Windows or Linux operating systems, and carried price tags below $10,000. Servers with these characteristics fit Dell's strategy and capabilities perfectly, and the company seized on the opportunity to use its considerable resources and capabilities in making low-cost, standard-technology PCs to go after the market for low- and mid-range x86 servers in a big way. During 2004–2007, Dell reigned as the number one domestic seller of x86 servers for Windows and Linux (based on unit volume), with just over a 30 percent market share (up from about 3–4 percent in the mid-1990s). Dell ranked number two in the world in x86 server shipments during this

Exhibit 1 U.S. and Global Market Shares of Leading PC Vendors, 1998–2007

A. U.S. Market Shares of the Leading PC Vendors, 1998–2005

		2007		2006		2005		2004		2002		2000		1998	
2003 Rank	Vendor	Shipments (in 000s)	Market Share	Shipments (in 000s)	Market Share	Shipments (in 000s)	Market Share	Shipments (in 000s)	Market Share	Shipments (in 000s)	Market Share	Shipments (in 000s)	Market Share	Shipments (in 000s)	Market Share
1	Dell	19,645	28.0%	20,472	31.2%	21,466	33.6%	19,296	33.7%	13,324	27.9%	9,645	19.7%	4,799	13.2%
2	Hewlett-Packard[1]	16,759	23.9	11,600	21.5	12,456	19.5	11,600	20.3	8,052	16.8	5,630	11.5	2,832	7.8
	Compaq[1]	—	—			—	—			—	—	7,761	15.9	6,052	16.7
3	Apple	4,081	5.8	3,109	4.7	2,555	4.0	1,935	3.3	1,693	3.5	n.a.	n.a.	n.a.	n.a.
4	Acer[2]	3,860	5.5	1,421	2.2	n.a.	n.a.	n.a.	n.a.	n.a.	n.a.	n.a.	n.a.	n.a.	n.a.
5	Toshiba	3,509	5.0	2,843	4.3	2,327	3.6	n.a.	n.a.	n.a.	n.a.	n.a.	n.a.	n.a.	n.a.
	Gateway	—	—	n.a.	n.a.	n.a.	n.a.	2,945	5.1	2,725	5.7	4,237	8.7	3,039	8.4
	Lenovo/IBM[3]	n.a.	n.a.	n.a.	n.a.	n.a.	n.a.	2,932	5.0	2,531	5.3	2,668	5.5	2,983	8.2
	Others	22,235	31.7	23,350	35.7	25.070	39.2	24,425	33.6	19,514	40.8	18,959	38.8	16,549	45.6
	All vendors	70,088	100.0%	65,481	100.0%	63,874	100.0%	57,256	100.0%	47,839	100.0%	48,900	100.0%	36,254	100.0%

B. Worldwide Market Shares of the Leading PC Vendors, 1998–2007[4]

		2007		2006		2005		2004		2002		2000		1998	
2003 Rank	Vendor	Shipments (in 000s)	Market Share	Shipments (in 000s)	Market Share	Shipments (in 000s)	Market Share	Shipments (in 000s)	Market Share	Shipments (in 000s)	Market Share	Shipments (in 000s)	Market Share	Shipments (in 000s)	Market Share
1	Hewlett Packard[1]	50,526	18.8%	38,838	16.5%	32,575	15.7%	28,063	15.8%	18,432	13.6	10,327	7.4	5,743	6.3
2	Dell	39,993	14.9%	39,094	16.6	37,755	18.2	31,771	17.9	20,672	15.2%	14,801	10.6%	7,770	8.5%
—	Compaq[1]	—	—	—	—	—	—	—	—	—	—	17,399	12.5	13,266	14.5
3	Acer[2]	21,206	7.9	13,594	5.8	9,845	4.7	6,461	3.6	n.a.	n.a.	n.a.	n.a.	n.a.	n.a.
4	Lenovo/IBM[3]	20,224	7.5	16,609	7.1	12,979	6.2	10,492	5.9	8,292	6.2	9,308	6.7	7,946	8.7
5	Toshiba	10,936	4.1	9,292	3.9	7,234	3.5	n.a.	n.a.	n.a.	n.a.	n.a.	n.a.	n.a.	n.a.
	Others	126,075	46.9	117,971	50.1	107,450	51.7	100,693	52.7	73,237	54.9	80,640	58	50,741	55.5
	All Vendors	268,960	100.0%	235,397	100.0%	207,837	100.0%	177,480	100.0%	133,466	100.0%	139,057	100.0%	91,442	100.0%

n.a. = not available; sales and market shares for these companies in the years where n.a. appears are included in the "Others" category because the company was not in the top five in shipments or market share.

[1] Compaq was acquired by Hewlett-Packard in May 2002. The 2002 data for Hewlett-Packard include both Compaq-branded and Hewlett-Packard-branded PCs for the last three quarters of 2002 plus only Hewlett-Packard-branded PCs for Q1 2002. Compaq's worldwide PC shipments during Q1 2002 were 3,367,000; its U.S. PC shipments during Q1 2002 were 1,280,000 units. Compaq's line of PCs were later rebranded and absorbed into Hewlett-Packard PC offerings.

[2] Acer acquired Gateway in 2007. Data for Acer include shipments for Gateway starting in Q4 2007, and only Acer data for prior periods.

[3] Lenovo, a Chinese computer company, completed the acquisition of IBM's PC business in the second quarter of 2005 (the deal was made in December 2004). The numbers for Lenovo/IBM for 1998–2004 reflect sales of IBM branded PCs only; the numbers for 2005–2007 reflect their combined sales beginning in the second quarter of 2005. In 2007, Lenovo rebranded all IBM PCs as Lenovo.

[4] The worldwide market share data includes branded shipments only and excludes sales of units carrying the brands of other PC producers and marketers; shipments of Compaq PCs for last three quarters of 2002 are included in 2002 figures for Hewlett-Packard due to HP's acquisition of Compaq.

Source: International Data Corporation.

same period, with market shares in the 24–26 percent range, which put it in position to contend with HP for global market leadership.

In addition, Dell was making market inroads in other product categories. Its sales of data storage devices had grown to nearly $2.5 billion annually, aided by a strategic alliance with EMC, a leader in data storage. In 2001–2002, Dell began selling low-cost, data-routing switches—a product category where Cisco Systems was the dominant global leader. Starting in 2003, Dell began marketing Dell-branded printers and printer cartridges, product categories that provided global leader HP with the lion's share of its profits; as of 2008, Dell's sales of printers and printer supplies was believed to exceed $3 billion. Also in 2003, Dell began selling flat-screen LCD TVs and retail-store systems, including electronic cash registers, specialized software, services, and peripherals required to link retail-store checkout lanes to corporate information systems. Dell's MP3 player, the Dell DJ, was number two behind the Apple iPod. Dell added plasma screen TVs to its TV product line in 2004. Since the late 1990s, Dell had been marketing CD and DVD drives, printers, scanners, modems, monitors, digital cameras, memory cards, data storage devices, and speakers made by a variety of manufacturers.

So far, Dell's foray into new products and businesses had, in most cases, proved to be profitable—for a time, Dell sold handheld PC devices, an MP3 player (called the Dell DJ) that competed against the Apple iPod, and big-screen TVs, but these products were abandoned when profits proved elusive. According to Michael Dell, "We believe that all our businesses should make money. If a business doesn't make money, if you can't figure out how to make money in that business, you shouldn't be in that business."[1] Dell products were sold in more than 170 countries, but sales in 60 countries accounted for about 95 percent of total revenues.

COMPANY BACKGROUND

At age 12, Michael Dell was running a mail order stamp-trading business, complete with a national catalog, and grossing $2,000 a month. At 16 he was selling subscriptions to the *Houston Post,* and at 17 he bought his first BMW with money he had earned. He enrolled at the University of Texas in 1983 as a premed student (his parents wanted him to become a doctor), but he soon became immersed in computers and started selling PC components out of his college dormitory room. He bought random-access memory (RAM) chips and disk drives for IBM PCs at cost from IBM dealers, who at the time often had excess supplies on hand because they were required to order large monthly quotas from IBM. Dell resold the components through newspaper ads (and later through ads in national computer magazines) at 10–15 percent below the regular retail price.

By April 1984, sales were running about $80,000 per month. Dell decided to drop out of college and form a company, PCs Ltd., to sell both PC components and PCs under the brand name PCs Limited. He obtained his PCs by buying retailers' surplus stocks at cost, then powering them up with graphics cards, hard disks, and memory before reselling them. His strategy was to sell directly to end users; by eliminating the retail markup, Dell's new company was able to sell IBM clones (machines that copied the functioning of IBM PCs using the same or similar components) about 40 percent below the price of IBM's best-selling PCs. The discounting strategy was successful, attracting price-conscious buyers and generating rapid revenue growth. By 1985, the company was assembling its own PC designs with a few people working on six-foot tables. The company had 40 employees, and Michael Dell worked 18-hour days, often sleeping on a cot in his office. By the end of fiscal 1986, sales had reached $33 million.

During the next several years, however, PCs Limited was hampered by growing pains—specifically, a lack of money, people, and resources. Michael Dell sought to refine the company's business model; add needed production capacity; and build a bigger, deeper management staff and corporate infrastructure while at the same time keeping costs low. The company was renamed Dell Computer in 1987, and the first international offices were opened that same year. In 1988, Dell added a sales force to serve large customers, began selling to government agencies, and became a public company—raising $34.2 million in its first offering of common stock. Sales to large customers quickly became the dominant part of Dell's business. By 1990, Dell Computer had sales of $388 million, a market share of 2–3 percent, and an R&D staff of more than 150 people. Michael Dell's vision was for Dell Computer to become one of the top three PC companies.

Thinking its direct sales business would not grow fast enough, in 1990–93, the company began distributing its computer products through Soft Warehouse Superstores (now CompUSA), Staples (a leading office products chain), Wal-Mart, Sam's Club, and Price Club (which merged with Costco in 1993). Dell also sold PCs through Best Buy stores in 16 states and through Xerox in 19 Latin American countries. But when the company learned how thin its margins were in selling through such distribution channels, it realized it had made a mistake and withdrew from selling to retailers and other intermediaries in 1994 to refocus on direct sales. At the time, sales through retailers accounted for only about 2 percent of Dell's revenues.

In 1993, further problems emerged: Dell reportedly lost $38 million in risky foreign-currency hedging, quality difficulties arose with certain PC lines made by the company's contract manufacturers, profit margins declined, and buyers were turned off by the company's laptop PC models. To get laptop sales back on track, the company took a charge of $40 million to write off its laptop line and suspended sales of laptops until it could get redesigned models into the marketplace.

Because of higher costs and unacceptably low profit margins in selling to individuals and households, Dell did not pursue the consumer market aggressively until sales to individuals at the company's Internet site took off in 1996 and 1997. It became clear that PC-savvy individuals, who were buying their second and third computers, wanted powerful computers with multiple features; did not need much technical support; and liked the convenience of buying direct from Dell, ordering a PC configured exactly to their liking, and having it delivered to their door within a matter of days. In early 1997, Dell created an internal sales and marketing group dedicated to serving the individual consumer segment and introduced a product line designed especially for home and personal use.

By late 1997, Dell had become a low-cost leader among PC vendors by wringing greater and greater efficiency out of its direct sales and build-to-order business model. Since then, the company had continued driving hard to reduce its costs by closely partnering with key suppliers to drive costs out of its supply chain and by incorporating e-commerce technology and use of the Internet into its everyday business practices. Throughout 2002–2007, Dell was widely regarded as the lowest-cost producer among all the leading vendors of PCs and servers worldwide. Moreover, its products were highly regarded; in 2007, Dell products received more than 400 awards relating to design, quality, and innovation—this was the largest number of product awards for a single year in the company's history.

In its 2008 fiscal year, Dell posted revenues of $61.1 billion and profits of nearly $3.0 billion. It ranked number 34 on *Fortune*'s list of the 500 largest U.S. corporations for 2007. In 2008, Dell had approximately 88,200 employees worldwide, up from 16,000 at year-end 1997; more than 66 percent of Dell's employees were located in countries outside the United States, and this percentage was growing. The company's headquarters and main office complex was in Round Rock, Texas (an Austin suburb). Its name had been changed from Dell Computer to Dell Inc. in 2003 to reflect the company's growing business base outside of PCs. Exhibits 2 and 3 provide information about Dell's financial performance and geographic operations.

Michael Dell

In the company's early days Michael Dell hung around mostly with the company's engineers. He was so shy that some employees thought he was stuck up because he never talked to them. But people who worked with him closely described him as a likable young man who was slow to warm up to strangers.[2] He was a terrible public speaker and wasn't good at running meetings. But Lee Walker, a 51-year-old venture capitalist brought in by Michael Dell to provide much-needed managerial and financial experience during the company's organization-building years, became Michael Dell's mentor, built up his confidence, and was instrumental in turning him into a polished executive.[3] Walker served as the company's president and chief operating officer from 1986 to 1990; he had a fatherly image, knew everyone by name, and played a key role in implementing Michael Dell's marketing ideas. Under Walker's tutelage, Michael Dell became intimately familiar with all parts of the business, overcame his shyness, learned to control his ego, and turned into a charismatic leader with an instinct for motivating people and winning their loyalty and respect.

When Walker had to leave the company in 1990 for health reasons, Dell turned to Morton Meyerson,

Exhibit 2 Selected Financial Statement Data for Dell Inc., Fiscal Years 2000–2008 ($ in millions, except per share data)

	Fiscal Year Ended						
	February 1, 2008	February 2, 2007	February 3, 2006	January 28, 2005	January 30, 2004	February 1, 2002	January 28, 2000
Results of Operations							
Net revenue	$61,133	$57,420	$55,788	$49,121	$41,327	$31,168	$25,265
Cost of revenue	49,462	47,904	45,897	40,103	33,764	25,661	20,047
Gross margin	11,671	9,516	9,891	9,018	7,563	5,507	5,218
Gross profit margin	19.1%	16.6%	17.7%	18.4%	18.3%	17.7%	20.7%
Operating expenses:							
Selling, general and administrative[a]	7,538	5,948	5,051	4,352	3,604	2,784	2,387
Research, development and engineering[b]	693	498	458	460	434	452	374
Special charges	—	—	—	—	—	482	194
Total operating expenses	8,231	6,446	5,509	4,812	4,038	3,718	2,955
Total operating expenses as a % of net revenues	13.5%	11.2%	9.9%	9.8%	9.8%	10.4%[c]	10.9%[c]
Operating income	3,440	3,070	4,382	4,206	3,525	1,789	2,263
Operating profit margin	5.6%	5.3%	7.9%	8.6%	8.5%	5.7%	9.0%
Investment and other income (loss), net	387	275	26	197	186	(58)	188
Income before income taxes, extraordinary loss, and cumulative effect of change in accounting principle	3,827	3,345	4,608	4,403	3,711	1,731	2,451
Provision for income taxes	880	762	1,006	1,385	1,086	485	785
Net income	$ 2,947	$ 2,583	$ 3,602	$ 3,018	$ 2,625	$ 1,246	$ 1,666
Net profit margin	4.8%	5.8%	6.5%	6.1%	6.4%	4.0%	6.6%
Earnings per common share: Basic	$1.33	$1.15	$1.50	$1.20	$1.02	$0.48	$0.66
Diluted	$1.31	$1.14	$1.47	$1.18	$1.01	$0.46	$0.61
Weighted average shares outstanding: Basic	2,223	2,255	2,403	2,509	2,565	2,602	2,536
Diluted	2,247	2,271	2,449	2,568	2,619	2,726	2,728
Cash Flow and Balance Sheet Data							
Net cash provided by operating activities	$ 3,949	$ 3,969	$ 4,751	$ 5,821	$ 3,670	$ 3,797	$ 3,926
Cash, cash equivalents, and short-term investments	7,972	10,298	9,070	9,807	11,922	8,287	6,853
Total assets	27,561	25,635	23,252	23,215	19,311	13,535	11,560
Long-term debt	362	569	625	505	505	520	508
Total stockholders' equity	3,735	4,328	4,047	6,485	6,280	4,694	5,308

[a] Includes stock-based compensation expenses for fiscal years 2007 and 2008, pursuant to Statement of Financial Accounting Standards No. 123.
[b] Includes one-time in-process research and development charges of $83 million related to companies acquired by Dell during fiscal 2008.
[c] Excluding special charges.

Sources: Dell Inc., 10-K reports, 2002, 2005–2008.

Exhibit 3 Dell's Geographic Area Performance, Fiscal Years 2000–2008 ($ in millions)

	February 1, 2008	February 2, 2007	February 3, 2006	January 28, 2005	January 30, 2004	February 1, 2002	January 28, 2000
Net revenues							
Americas							
Business	$31,144	$29,311	$28,365	$25,289	$21,824	$17,275	$15,160
U.S. consumer	6,244	7,069	7,960	7,614	6,696	4,485	2,719
Total Americas	37,368	36,380	36,325	32,903	28,520	21,760	17,879
Europe/Middle East/Africa	15,267	13,682	12,887	10,753	8,472	6,429	5,590
Asia-Pacific/ Japan	8,498	7,358	6,576	5,465	4,335	2,979	1,796
Total net revenues	$61,133	$57,420	$55,788	$49,121	$41,444	$31,168	$25,265
Operating income							
Americas							
Business	$2,549	$2,388	$2,956	$2,534	$2,229	$1,482	$1,800
U.S. consumer	(59)	135	452	414	373	260	204
Total Americas	2,490	2,523	3,408	2,948	2,602	1,742	2,004
Europe/Middle East/Africa	1,009	583	871	815	614	377	359
Asia-Pacific/ Japan	471	332	524	443	309	152	94
Special charges	(530)	(368)	(421)	—	—	(482)	(194)
Total operating income	$3,440	$3,070	$4,382	$4,206	$3,525	$1,789	$2,263

Sources: Dell Inc., 10-K reports, 2002, 2005 and 2008; financial data posted at www.dell.com (accessed May 6, 2008).

former CEO and president of Electronic Data Systems, for advice and guidance on how to transform Dell Computer from a fast-growing medium-sized company into a billion-dollar enterprise. Though sometimes given to displays of impatience, Michael Dell usually spoke in a quiet, reflective manner and came across as a person with maturity and seasoned judgment far beyond his age. His prowess was based more on an astute combination of technical knowledge and marketing know-how than on being a technological wizard. In 1992, at the age of 27, Michael Dell became the youngest CEO ever to head a Fortune 500 company; he was a billionaire at the age of 31.

By the late 1990s, Michael Dell had become one of the most respected executives in the PC industry. Journalists had described him as "the quintessential American entrepreneur" and "the most innovative guy for marketing computers." He was a much-sought-after speaker at industry and company conferences. His views and opinions about the future of PCs, the Internet, and e-commerce practices carried considerable weight both in the PC industry and among executives worldwide. Once pudgy and bespectacled, in early 2008, 43-year-old Michael Dell was physically fit, considered good-looking, wore contact lenses, ate only health foods, and lived in a three-story 33,000-square-foot home on a 60-acre estate in Austin, Texas, with his wife and four children. In 2008, he owned about 10 percent of Dell's common stock, worth about $4.3 billion.

Michael Dell was considered a very accessible CEO and a role model for young executives because he had done what many of them were trying to do. He delegated authority to subordinates, believing that the best results came from "turning loose talented people who can be relied upon to do what they're supposed to do." Business associates viewed Michael Dell as an aggressive personality, an extremely competitive risk taker who had always played close to the edge. He spent about 30 percent of his time traveling to company operations and meeting with customers. In a typical year, he would make two or three trips to Europe and two trips to Asia.

In mid-2004, Michael Dell, who had been the company's first and only CEO, transferred his title of CEO to Kevin Rollins, the company's president and chief operating officer. Dell remained as chairman of the board. Dell and Rollins had run the company for the past seven years under a shared leadership structure. The changes were primarily ones of title, not of roles or responsibilities. But when the company's performance stalled in 2006, Kevin Rollins was relieved of his responsibilities and Michael Dell reassumed the title of CEO (and continued in the role of chairman of the company's board of directors).

DELL'S STRATEGY AND BUSINESS MODEL

In orchestrating Dell Inc.'s rise to global prominence, company executives had come to believe strongly that four tenets were the key to delivering superior customer value:[4]

1. Selling direct to customers is the most efficient way to market the company's products because it eliminates wholesale and retail dealers that impede Dell's understanding of customer needs and expectations and that add unnecessary time and cost.
2. Allowing customers to purchase custom-built products and custom-tailored services is the most effective way to meet customer needs.
3. A highly efficient supply chain and manufacturing organization, grounded in the use of standardized technologies and selling direct, paves the way for a low-cost structure where cost savings can be passed along to customers in the form of lower prices.
4. Dell can deliver added value to customers by (1) researching all the technological options, (2) trying to determine which ones are "optimal" in the sense of delivering the best combination of performance and efficiency, and (3) being accountable to customers for helping them obtain the highest return on their investment in IT products and services. In almost all cases, non-proprietary, standardized technologies deliver the best value to customers.

With top management holding firmly to these tenets, Dell's strategy during the 2002–2007 period had seven core elements: (1) making build-to-order manufacturing progressively more cost-efficient, (2) partnering closely with suppliers to squeeze cost savings out of the supply chain, (3) using direct sales techniques to gain customers, (4) expanding into additional products and services to capture a bigger share of customers' IT spending, (5) providing good customer service and technical support, (6) keeping R&D and engineering activities focused squarely on better meeting the needs of customers, and (7) using standardized technologies in all product offerings.

The business model on which the strategy was predicated was straightforward: Continuously search for ways to reduce costs—the company's latest initiative was to reduce costs by $3 billion in 2008. Use the company's strong capabilities in supply chain management, low-cost manufacturing, and direct sales to grow sales and market share in both the PC and server segments and expand into product categories where Dell could provide added value to its customers in the form of lower prices. The standard pattern for entering new product categories was to identify an IT product with good margins; figure out how to build it (or else have it built by others) cheaply enough to be able to significantly underprice competitive products; market the new product to Dell's steadily growing customer base; and watch the market share points, incremental revenues, and incremental profits pile up.

Cost-Efficient Build-to-Order Manufacturing

Dell built the vast majority of its computers, workstations, and servers to order; only a small fraction was produced for inventory and shipped to wholesale or retail partners. Dell customers could order custom-equipped servers and workstations according to the needs of their applications. Desktop and laptop customers ordered whatever configuration of microprocessor speed, random-access memory, hard disk capacity, CD or DVD drives, fax/modem/wireless capabilities, graphics cards, monitor size, speakers, and other accessories they preferred. The orders were directed to the nearest factory. In 2008, Dell had assembly plants in Austin, Texas; Nashville, Tennessee; Winston-Salem, North Carolina; Limerick, Ireland; Xiamen, China; Penang, Malaysia; Hortolândia, Brazil; Chennai, India; and Lodz, Poland. In March 2008, the company announced that its desktop assembly plant in Austin, Texas, would be closed. The Winston-Salem plant was Dell's largest when it opened in 2005 and had the capacity to assemble 15,000 to 20,000 desktops per day—it could turn out a new PC every five seconds. Dell shipped about 140,000 products daily—about 1 every second. PCs, workstations, and servers were assembled at all locations; assembly of lower-volume products was concentrated in a more limited number of locations. All plants used much the same production systems and procedures. Typically, a plant had the capability to build and deliver a customer's order in three to five business days; however, the Winston-Salem plant could in most cases deliver orders to customers on the eastern coast of the United States in one to three business days. Dell believed in building its assembly plants close to customers because the labor costs to assemble a PC were about $10 whereas the logistics costs to move parts and ship a finished PC were about $40.[5]

Ongoing Improvements in Assembly Efficiency Until 1997, Dell operated its assembly lines in traditional fashion, with each worker performing a single operation. An order form accompanied each metal chassis across the production floor; drives, chips, and ancillary items were installed to match customer specifications. As a partly assembled PC arrived at a new workstation, the operator, standing beside a tall steel rack with drawers full of components, was instructed what to do by little red and green lights flashing beside the drawers. When the operator was finished, the component drawers were automatically replenished from the other side and the PC chassis glided down the line to the next workstation. However, Dell had reorganized its plants in 1997, shifting to "cell manufacturing" techniques whereby a team of workers operating at a group workstation (or cell) assembled an entire PC according to customer specifications. The shift to cell manufacturing reduced Dell's assembly times by 75 percent and doubled productivity per square foot of assembly space. Assembled computers were first tested and then loaded with the desired software, shipped, and typically delivered five to six business days after the order was placed.

Later, the cell manufacturing approach was gradually abandoned in favor of an even more efficient assembly-line approach that allowed workers to turn out close to 800 desktop PCs per hour on three assembly lines that took half the floor space of the cell manufacturing process, where production had run about 120 units per hour. Here the gains in assembly efficiency were achieved partly by redesigning the PCs to permit easier and faster assembly, partly by making innovations in the assembly process, and partly by reducing (by 50 percent) the number of times a computer was touched by workers during assembly and shipping. In 2005, it took about 66 minutes to assemble and test a PC. Moreover, just-in-time inventory practices that left pallets of parts sitting around everywhere had been tweaked to just-in-the-nick-of-time delivery by suppliers of the exact parts needed every couple of hours; double-decker conveyor belts moved parts and components to designated assembly points. Newly assembled PCs were routed on conveyors to shipping, where they were boxed and shipped to customers the same day.

Dell's new 750,000-square-foot plant in Winston-Salem featured a production layout that allowed computers to be tested as its components and software were installed. This "instantaneous build and test" operation permitted team members to identify and correct any problems on the spot rather than waiting until the PC was fully assembled. Workers at all Dell plants competed with one another to come up with more efficient assembly methods. Cost-saving assembly innovations pioneered in one Dell plant were quickly implemented worldwide.

Dell's latest cost-saving initiative was to move away from 100 percent configure-to-customer-order assembly to a mixture of fixed configurations (for components that rarely varied from order to order) and flexible configurations (for components that were subject to strong and varying customer preferences—like hard drive size, screen displays, amount of memory, graphics cards, type of microprocessor, and version of Windows operating system).

Dell was regarded as a world-class manufacturing innovator and a pioneer in how to mass-produce a customized product—its methods were routinely studied in business schools worldwide. Several of Dell's PC rivals—most notably Hewlett-Packard—had given up on trying to produce their own PCs as cheaply as Dell and shifted to outsourcing their PCs from contract manufacturers who specialized in PC assembly and often assembled a variety of PC brands. Dell management believed that its in-house manufacturing delivered about a 6 percent cost advantage versus outsourcing. Dell's build-to-order strategy meant that the company had only a tiny stock of finished goods inventories in-house and that, unlike competitors using the traditional value chain model, it did not have to wait for resellers to clear out their own inventories before it could push new models into the marketplace—resellers typically operated with 30 to 60 days inventory of prebuilt models (see Exhibit 4). Equally important was the fact that customers who bought from Dell got the satisfaction of having their computers customized to their particular liking and pocketbook.

Quality Control All assembly plants had the capability to run testing and quality control processes on components, parts, and subassemblies obtained from suppliers, as well as on the finished products Dell assembled. Suppliers were urged to participate in a quality certification program that committed them to achieving defined quality specifications. Quality control activities were undertaken at various stages in the assembly process. In addition, Dell's quality control program included testing of completed units after assembly, ongoing production reliability audits, failure tracking for early identification of production and component problems associated with new models shipped to customers, and information obtained from customers through service and technical support programs. All of the company's plants had been certified as meeting

Exhibit 4 Comparative Value Chain Models of PC Vendors

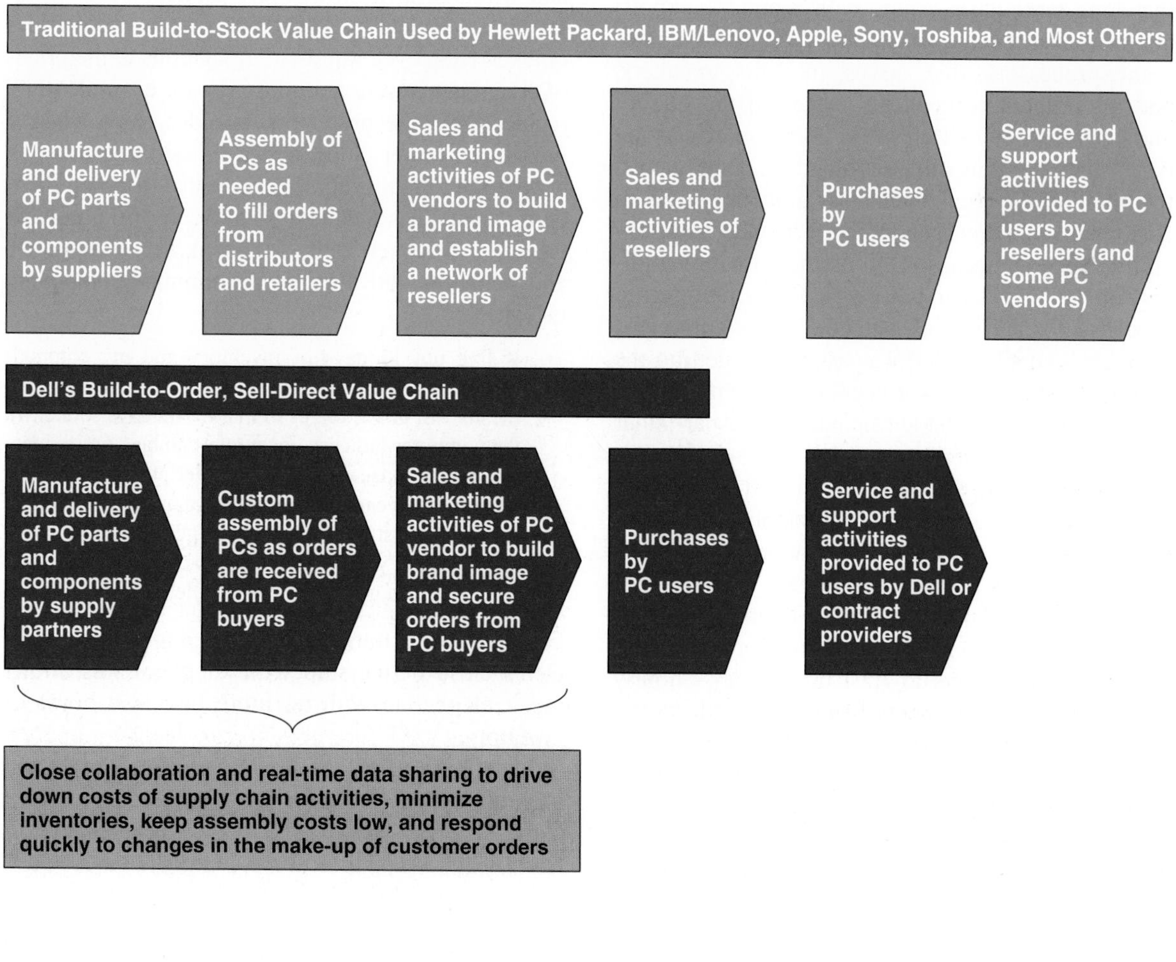

Traditional Build-to-Stock Value Chain Used by Hewlett Packard, IBM/Lenovo, Apple, Sony, Toshiba, and Most Others

Manufacture and delivery of PC parts and components by suppliers → Assembly of PCs as needed to fill orders from distributors and retailers → Sales and marketing activities of PC vendors to build a brand image and establish a network of resellers → Sales and marketing activities of resellers → Purchases by PC users → Service and support activities provided to PC users by resellers (and some PC vendors)

Dell's Build-to-Order, Sell-Direct Value Chain

Manufacture and delivery of PC parts and components by supply partners → Custom assembly of PCs as orders are received from PC buyers → Sales and marketing activities of PC vendor to build brand image and secure orders from PC buyers → Purchases by PC users → Service and support activities provided to PC users by Dell or contract providers

Close collaboration and real-time data sharing to drive down costs of supply chain activities, minimize inventories, keep assembly costs low, and respond quickly to changes in the make-up of customer orders

ISO 9001:2000 standards. But while Dell's quality control program was first-rate, it was not perfect; in fiscal year 2008, Dell incurred special warranty cost charges of $307 million to service or replace certain desktop models that included a vendor part that failed to perform to specifications.

Partnerships with Suppliers Michael Dell believed that it made much better sense for the company to partner with reputable suppliers of PC parts and components than to integrate backward and get into parts and components manufacturing on its own. He explained why:

> If you've got a race with 20 players all vying to make the fastest graphics chip in the world, do you want to be the twenty-first horse, or do you want to evaluate the field of 20 and pick the best one?[6]

Dell management evaluated the various makers of each component; picked the best one or two as suppliers; and then stuck with them as long as they maintained their leadership in technology, performance, quality, and cost. Management believed that long-term partnerships with reputable suppliers had at least five advantages. First, using name-brand processors, disk drives, modems, speakers, and multimedia components enhanced the quality and performance of Dell's PCs. Because of varying performance among different brands of components, the brand of the components was quite important to customers concerned about performance and reliability. Second, because Dell partnered with suppliers for the long term and because it committed to purchase a specified percentage of its requirements from each supplier, Dell was assured of getting the volume of components it needed on a timely basis even when overall market demand for a particular component temporarily exceeded the overall market supply. Third, Dell's long-run commitment to its suppliers made it feasible for suppliers to locate their plants or distribution centers within a few miles of Dell assembly plants, putting them in position to make deliveries daily or every few hours, as needed. Dell supplied data on inventories and replenishment needs to its suppliers at least once a day—hourly in the case of components being delivered several times daily from nearby sources.

Fourth, long-term supply partnerships facilitated having some of the supplier's engineers assigned to Dell's product design teams and being treated as part of Dell. When new products were launched, suppliers' engineers were stationed in Dell's plants; if early buyers called with a problem related to design, further assembly and shipments were halted while the supplier's engineers and Dell personnel corrected the flaw on the spot.[7] Fifth, long-term partnerships enlisted greater cooperation on the part of suppliers to seek new ways to drive costs out of the supply chain. Dell openly shared its daily production schedules, sales forecasts, and new model introduction plans with vendors. Dell also did a three-year plan with each of its key suppliers and worked with suppliers to minimize the number of different stock-keeping units of parts and components in its products and to identify ways to drive costs down.

Commitment to Just-in-Time Inventory Practices Dell's just-in-time inventory emphasis yielded major cost advantages and shortened the time it took for Dell to get new generations of its computer models into the marketplace. New advances were coming so fast in certain computer parts and components (particularly microprocessors, disk drives, and wireless devices) that any given item in inventory was obsolete in a matter of months, sometimes quicker. Moreover, rapid-fire reductions in the prices of components were not unusual—for example, Intel regularly cut the prices on its older chips when it introduced newer chips, and it introduced new chip generations about every three months. In 2003–2004, component costs declined an average of 0.5 percent weekly.[8] Michael Dell explained the competitive and economic advantages of minimal component inventories:

> If I've got 11 days of inventory and my competitor has 80 and Intel comes out with a new chip, that means I'm going to get to market 69 days sooner. In the computer industry, inventory can be a pretty massive risk because if the cost of materials is going down 50 percent a year and you have two or three months of inventory versus 11 days, you've got a big cost disadvantage. And you're vulnerable to product transitions, when you can get stuck with obsolete inventory.[9]

For a growing number of parts and components, Dell's close partnership with suppliers was allowing it to operate with no more than two hours of inventory.

In fiscal year 1995, Dell averaged an inventory turn cycle of 32 days. By the end of fiscal 1997 (January 1997), the average was down to 13 days. In fiscal 1998, Dell's inventory averaged 7 days, which compared very favorably with a 14-day average at Gateway, a 23-day average at then industry leader Compaq, and the estimated industrywide average of over 50 days. In fiscal years 1999 and 2000, Dell operated with an average of 6 days' supply of production materials in inventory; the average dropped to 5 days' supply in fiscal year 2001, 4 days' supply in 2002, and 2.7 to 4 days' supply in fiscal years 2003–2007.

Dell's Direct Sales Strategy and Marketing Efforts

With thousands of phone, fax, and Internet orders daily and ongoing field sales force contact with customers, the company kept its finger on the market pulse, quickly detecting shifts in sales trends, design problems, and quality glitches. If the company got more than a few of the same complaints, the information was relayed immediately to design engineers who checked out the problem. When design flaws or components defects were found, the factory was notified and the problem corrected within a few days. Management believed Dell's ability to respond quickly gave it a significant advantage over PC makers that operated on the basis of large production runs of variously configured and equipped PCs and sold them through retail channels. Dell saw its direct sales approach as a totally customer-driven system, with the flexibility to transition quickly to new generations of components and PC models.

Web Site Strategy Dell's Web site was one of the world's highest volume Internet commerce sites, with nearly 500 million unique visitors, well over 1 billion visits, and close to 10 billion page requests annually. Dell began Internet sales at its Web site in 1995, almost overnight achieving sales of $1 million a day. Sales at its Web site reached $5 million daily in 1998, $35 million daily in 2000, and $60 million a day in 2004. By early 2003, over 50 percent of Dell's sales were Web-enabled—and the percentage trended upward through 2007. The revenues generated at the Web site were greater than those generated at Yahoo, Google, eBay, and Amazon combined.[10]

At the company's Web site, prospective buyers could review Dell's entire product line in detail, configure and price customized PCs, place orders, and track orders from manufacturing through shipping. The closing rate on sales at Dell's Web site was 20 percent higher than that on sales inquiries received via telephone. Management believed that enhancing www.dell.com to shrink transaction and order fulfillment times, increase accuracy, and provide more personalized content resulted in a higher degree of "e-loyalty" than traditional attributes like price and product selection.

Dell's Customer-Based Sales and Marketing Focus Whereas many technology companies organized their sales and marketing efforts around product lines, Dell was organized around customer groups. Dell had placed managers in charge of developing sales and service programs appropriate to the needs and expectations of each customer group. Until the early 1990s, Dell operated with sales and service programs aimed at just two market segments—high-volume corporate and governmental buyers and low-volume business and individual buyers. But as sales took off in 1995–1997, these segments were subdivided into finer, more homogeneous categories that by 2000 included global enterprise accounts, large and midsize companies (over 400 employees), small companies (under 400 employees), health care businesses (over 400 employees), federal government agencies, state and local government agencies, educational institutions, and individual consumers. Many of these customer segments were further subdivided—for instance, in education, there were separate sales and marketing programs for K–12 schools; higher education institutions; and personal-use purchases by faculty, staff, and students.

Dell had a field sales force that called on large business and institutional customers throughout the world. Dell's largest global enterprise accounts were assigned their own dedicated sales force—for example, Dell had a sales force of 150 people dedicated to meeting the needs of General Electric's facilities and personnel scattered across the world. Individuals and small businesses could place orders by telephone or at Dell's Web site. Dell had call centers in the United States, Canada, Europe, and Asia with toll-free lines; customers could talk with a sales representative about specific models, get information faxed or mailed to them, place an order, and pay by credit card. The Asian and European call centers were equipped with technology that routed calls from a particular country to a particular call center. Thus, for example, a customer calling from Lisbon, Portugal, was automatically directed to a Portuguese-speaking sales rep at the call center in Montpelier, France.

However, in some countries Dell's sell-direct-to-customers strategy put it at a disadvantage in appealing to small business customers and individual consumers, since most of these customers were reluctant to place orders by phone or over the Internet. Rivals in Japan and China who marketed PCs through retailers and other resellers were outselling Dell in the small business and household segments. According to an executive at Lenovo, one of Dell's biggest rivals in China, "It takes two years of a person's savings to buy a PC in China. And when two years of savings is at stake, the whole family wants to come out to a store to touch and try the machine."[11] To address the reluctance of households to buy direct from Dell, the head of Dell's consumer PC sales group in Japan installed 34 kiosks in leading electronics stores around Japan, allowing shoppers to test Dell computers, ask questions of staff, and place orders—close to half the sales were to people who did not know about Dell prior to visiting the kiosk. The kiosks proved quite popular and were instrumental in boosting Dell's share of PC sales to consumers in Japan.

Inspired by the success of kiosks in Japan, in 2002 Dell began installing Dell Direct Store kiosks in a variety of U.S. retail settings as a hands-on complement to Internet and phone sales. The kiosk stores showcased Dell's newest notebook and desktop computers, plasma and LCD TVs, printers, and music players. The kiosks did not carry inventory, but customers could talk face-to-face with a knowledgeable Dell sales representative, inspect Dell's products, and order them on the Internet while at the kiosk. The kiosks were considered a success in getting consumers to try Dell products. More kiosks were added and, by December 2005, Dell had 145 Dell Direct Store kiosks in 20 states, within reach of more than 50 percent of the U.S. population.

Supplementing the Direct Sales Strategy with Sales at the Retail Stores of Select Partners In fiscal 2006, Dell's share of PC sales to U.S. households dropped to 25.6 percent from 29.3 percent the prior year. In 2007, its share of the home or consumer market in the United States dropped even more precipitously, to 18.9 percent (see Exhibit 5). Sales to households weakened in other parts of the world market as well. The declines were partly due (1) to Hewlett-Packard's aggressive and successful efforts (mainly, lower pricing and better feature sets) to gain market share at Dell's expense and (2) to surging U.S. sales of Apple's PC models (see Exhibit 1), buoyed chiefly by consumer infatuation with Apple's iPod models and its new iPhone. Dell management responded to the unexpected and unprecedented falloff in sales to households by backing off on its almost 100 percent commitment to selling direct and forging partnerships with such retailers as Wal-Mart, Staples, and Best Buy to begin offering select Dell PCs in retail stores. Similar initiatives to begin selling through retailers were taken in other parts of the world market. In Latin America, Dell forged retailing partnerships with Wal-Mart and Pontofrio. Dell's retailing partners in Europe, the Middle East, and Africa included Carphone Warehouse, Carrefour, Tesco, and DSGi. In China, Japan, and other parts of the Asia-Pacific region, Dell began selling its PCs at the stores of Gome (the leading consumer electronics retailer in China), Suning, Hontu, HiMart, Courts, Croma, Officeworks (104 stores in Australia), and Bic Camera. By mid-2008, Dell had its products available in 12,000 retail stores worldwide and planned to grow this number considerably.

So far, Dell management was pleased with the initial results of its shift to using retail stores as a way to supplement online and telephone sales to consumers and small businesses.

Expansion into New Products

In recent years, Dell had expanded its product offerings to include data storage hardware, switches, handheld PCs, printers, and printer cartridges, and software products in an effort to diversify its revenue stream and use its competitive capabilities in PCs and servers to pursue growth opportunities. Michael Dell explained why Dell had decided to expand into products and services that complemented its sales of PCs and servers:

> We tend to look at what is the next big opportunity all the time. We can't take on too many of these at once, because it kind of overloads the system. But we believe fundamentally that if you think about the whole market, it's about an $800 billion market, all areas of technology over time go through a process of standardization or commoditization. And we try to look at those, anticipate what's happening, and develop strategies that will allow us to get into those

Exhibit 5 Trends in Dell's Market Shares in PCs and x86 Servers, 1994–2007

	Dell's Market Share								
Market Segment	2007	2006	2005	2004	2002	2000	1998	1996	1994
Worldwide share by geographic area	14.9%	17.2%	18.2%	17.7%	14.9%	10.5%	8.0%	4.1%	2.7%
United States	29.3	31.3	33.6	33.1	28.0	18.4	12.0	6.4	4.2
Europe/Middle East/Africa	11.0	12.2	12.5	11.5	9.6	7.8	7.0	3.8	2.4
Asia-Pacific	8.9	8.8	8.2	7.0	4.8	3.4	2.4	1.3	0.3
Japan	14.0	14.2	12.3	11.3	7.7	4.0	3.0	1.6	1.1
Worldwide share by product									
Desktop PCs	15.0%	17.2%	18.2%	18.0%	14.8%	10.1%	7.8%	4.3%	3.0%
Notebook PCs	14.2	16.4	17.3	16.2	14.4	11.3	8.5	3.4	1.1
x86 Servers	25.0	25.6	26.3	24.8	21.7	15.4	9.7	3.4	3.1
U.S. segment share	29.3%	31.3%	33.1%	33.1%	28.0%	18.4%	12.0%	6.4%	4.2%
Education	40.7	43.8	44.6	44.3	34.9	26.2	11.0	3.9	1.1
Government	37.7	33.2	36.0	32.9	33.7	22.9	14.6	6.5	7.1
Home	18.9	25.6	29.3	29.7	22.7	6.5	3.5	2.1	1.2
Large business	43.3	43.7	43.3	44.2	39.9	31.3	21.6	11.2	6.9
Small/medium business	29.1	27.0	29.2	28.5	24.2	22.6	14.3	7.9	5.4

Source: Information posted at www.dell.com (accessed May 6, 2008).

markets. In the server market in 1995 we had a 2 percent market share, today we have over a 30 percent share, we're number 1 in the U.S. How did that happen? Well, first of all it happened because we started to have a high market share for desktops and notebooks. Then customers said, oh yes, we know Dell, those are the guys who have really good desktops and notebooks. So they have servers, yes, we'll test those, we'll test them around the periphery, maybe not in the most critical applications at first, but we'll test them here. [Then they discover] these are really good and Dell provides great support . . . and I think to some extent we've benefited from the fact that our competitors have underestimated the importance of value, and the power of the relationship and the service that we can create with the customer.

And, also, as a product tends to standardize there's not an elimination of the requirement for custom services, there's a reduction of it. So by offering some services, but not the services of the traditional proprietary computer company, we've been able to increase our share. And, in fact, what tends to happen is customers embrace the standards, because they know that's going to save them costs. Let me give you an example . . . about a year ago we entered into the data networking market. So we have Ethernet switches, layer 2 switches. So if you have PCs and servers, you need switches; every PC attaches to a switch, every server attaches to a switch. It's a pretty easy sale, switches go along with computer systems. We looked at this market and were able to come up with products that are priced about 2½ times less than the market leader today, Cisco, and as a result the business has grown very, very quickly. We shipped 1.8 million switch ports in a period of about a year, when most people would have said that's not going to work and come up with all kinds of reasons why we can't succeed.[12]

As Dell's sales of data-routing switches accelerated in 2001–2002 and Dell management mulled over whether to expand into other networking products and Internet gear, Cisco elected to discontinue supplying its switches to Dell for resale as of October 2002. Dell's family of PowerConnect switches—simple commodity-like products generally referred to as layer 2 switches in the industry—were about 75 percent cheaper than those made by Cisco as of 2005.

Senior Dell executives saw external storage devices as a growth opportunity because the company's corporate and institutional customers were making increasing use of high-speed data storage and retrieval devices. Dell's PowerVault line of storage products had data protection and recovery features that made it easy for customers to add and manage storage and simplify consolidation. The PowerVault products used standardized technology and components (which were considerably cheaper than customized ones), allowing Dell to underprice rivals and drive down storage costs for its customers by about 50 percent. Dell's competitors in storage devices included Hewlett-Packard and IBM.

Some observers saw Dell's 2003 entry into the printer market as a calculated effort to go after Hewlett-Packard's biggest and most profitable business segment and believed the Dell offensive was deliberately timed to throw a wrench into HP's efforts to resolve the many challenges of successfully merging its operations with those of Compaq. One of the reasons Dell had entered the market for servers back in 1995 was that Compaq Computer, then its biggest rival in PCs, had been using its lucrative profits on server sales to subsidize charging lower prices on Compaq computers and thus be more price-competitive against Dell's PCs—at the time Compaq was losing money on its desktop and notebook PC business. According to Michael Dell:

> Compaq had this enormous profit pool that they were using to fight against us in the desktop and notebook business. That was not an acceptable situation. Our product teams knew that the servers weren't that complicated or expensive to produce, and customers were being charged unfair prices.[13]

Dell management believed that in 2000–2002 HP was doing much the same thing in printers and printer products, where it had a dominant market share worldwide and generated about 75 percent of its operating profits. Dell believed that HP was using its big margins on printer products to subsidize selling its PCs at prices comparable to Dell's, even though Dell had costs that were about 8 percent lower than HP's. HP's PC operations were either in the red or barely in the black during most of 2000–2003, while Dell consistently had profit margins of 8 percent or more on PCs. Dell management believed the company's entry into the printer market would add value for its customers. Michael Dell explained:

> We think we can drive down the entire cost of owning and using printing products. If you look at any other market Dell has gone into, we have been able to significantly save money for customers. We know we can do that in printers; we have looked at the supply chain all the way through its various cycles and we know there are inefficiencies there. I think the price of the total offering when we include the printer and the supplies . . . can come down quite considerably.[14]

When Dell announced it had contracted with Lexmark to make printers and printer and toner cartridges for sale under the Dell label beginning in 2003, HP immediately discontinued supplying HP printers to Dell for resale at Dell's Web site. Dell had been selling Lexmark printers for two years and, since 2000, had resold about 4 million printers made by such vendors as HP, Lexmark, and other vendors to its customers. Lexmark designed and made critical parts for its printers but used offshore contract manufacturers for assembly. Gross profit margins on printers (sales minus cost of goods sold) were said to be in single digits in 2002–2004, but the gross margins on printer supplies were in the 50–60 percent range—brand-name ink cartridges for printers typically ran \$25 to \$35. As of fall 2005, Dell had sold more than 10 million printers and had an estimated 20 percent of the market for color network lasers and color inkjet printers in the United States.[15]

Dell executives believed the company's entry and market success in printer products had put added competitive pressure on Hewlett-Packard in the printer market and was partly responsible for HP's share of the printer market worldwide slipping from just under 50 percent to around 46 percent in 2004. To further keep the pricing pressure on HP in 2003, Dell had priced its storage and networking products below comparable HP products.

Exhibit 6 shows a breakdown of Dell's sales by product category. Exhibit 7 shows Dell's average revenues per unit sold for fiscal years 1998–2008. The declines were driven by steadily falling costs for components, Dell's ability to improve productivity and take costs out of its value chain, and Dell's strategy of passing along cost savings to its customers and trying to deliver more value to customers than its rivals did. However, the tiny increases in average revenues

Exhibit 6 Dell's Revenues by Product Category, 2006–2008

Product Category	2008		2007		2006	
	Revenues (in billions)	% of Total Revenues	Revenues (in billions)	% of Total Revenues	Revenues (in billions)	% of Total Revenues
Desktop PCs	$19.6	32.1%	$19.8	34.5%	$21.6	38.7%
Mobility products (laptop PCs and workstations)	17.4	28.5	15.5	27.0	14.4	25.8
Software and peripherals (printers, monitors, TVs, projectors, ink and toner cartridges)	9.9	16.2	9.0	15.7	8.3	14.9
Servers and networking hardware	6.5	10.6	5.8	10.1	5.4	9.8
Consulting and enhanced services	5.3	8.8	5.1	8.9	4.2	7.5
Storage products	2.4	3.9	2.3	4.0	1.9	3.4
Totals	$61.1	100.1%	$57.4	100.2%	$55.8	100.1%

Source: Dell's 10-K report, fiscal 2008, p. 90.

Exhibit 7 Trend in Dell's Approximate Average Revenue per Unit Sold, Fiscal Years 1998–2008

Fiscal Year	Dell's Approximate Average Revenue per Unit Sold
1998	$2,600
2000	2,250
2001	2,050
2002	1,700
2003	1,640
2004	1,590
2005	1,560
2006	1,500
2007	1,510
2008	1,540

Source: Company financial records and company postings at www.dell.com (accessed May 3, 2008).

per unit in the past two fiscal years reflected slowing declines in components prices, a shift in the PC sales mix away from desktops to laptops (which carried higher price tags and thus yielded greater average revenues per unit sold), and Dell's more restrained pricing (to protect its operating and net profit margins from further erosion). In fiscal 2007–2008, unlike prior years, Dell had difficulty in lowering unit costs; out-of-proportion increases in operating expenses (see Exhibit 2) made it infeasible for Dell to cut prices and still preserve its operating profit margins. Top executives opted to maintain prices to keep the company's already lower operating profit margins from going down any further (see Exhibit 2); this left Dell vulnerable to HP's strategic offensive to regain sales and market share—an offensive that featured prices for HP products that were more in line with what Dell was charging.

Customer Service and Technical Support

Service became a feature of Dell's strategy in 1986 when the company began providing a year's free on-site service with most of its PCs after users complained about having to ship their PCs back to Austin for repairs. Dell began offering PC buyers the option of buying contracts for on-site repair services for a defined period (usually one to four years). Dell contracted with local service providers to handle customer requests for repairs; on-site service was provided on a four-hour basis to large customers and on a next-day basis to small customers. Dell generally contracted with third-party providers to make the necessary on-site service calls. Customers notified Dell when they had problems; such notices triggered two electronic dispatches—one to ship replacement parts from Dell's factory to the customer, and one to notify the contract service provider to prepare to make the needed repairs as soon as the parts arrived.[16] Bad parts were returned so that Dell could determine what went wrong and how to prevent such problems from happening again (problems relating to faulty components or flawed components design were promptly passed along to the relevant supplier for correction). If business or institutional customers preferred to work with their own service provider, Dell supplied the provider of choice with training and spare parts needed to service the customers' equipment.

Later, Dell began offering contracts for CompleteCare accidental damage service. In 2006, Dell began using an online diagnostics tool called DellConnect to troubleshoot and resolve problems with a customer's computer while the customer was connected to Dell's Web site. In 2007, Dell launched a corporate blog called Direct2Dell, a customer idea engine called IdeaStorm, and several online community forums for the purpose of better listening to and engaging with customers. Dell's online training programs featured more than 1,200 courses for consumer, business, and IT professionals. Over 50 percent of Dell's technical support and customer service activities were conducted via the Internet. Customers could also request technical support via a toll-free phone number and e-mail; Dell received more than 8 million phone calls and 500,000 to 600,000 e-mail messages annually requesting service and support.

Dell had 25 customer service centers worldwide in 2008 that were primarily engaged in handling technical support, requests for repairs, and other issues and inquiries. In a move to trim rising technical support and customer service costs in 2004–2005, Dell opted to move a large portion of its support services to countries where labor costs were low. But according to Dell's president of global services and chief information officer, "We did it way too quickly—we didn't move process management disciplines with it as effectively as we should have, and we wound up making some mistakes with the services experience."[17] The outcome was a sharp rise in customer complaints, especially among small business and individual customers who were most affected—a number of irritated Dell customers went so far as to post their horror stories at Web sites like IhateDell.net, and the resulting media publicity tarnished Dell's reputation for customer service among these buyers. To correct the service problems, Dell had moved many of its service centers back to countries where big numbers of its customers were located. Service processes were standardized worldwide, and best practices from all over the world were built into the standards. Dell's goal was to reach 90 percent customer satisfaction—where customers rated their service experience with Dell as "top notch" or "very satisfied"—as quickly as possible. In early 2008, Dell's customer satisfaction ratings were at 92 percent for Asia, at 90 percent in the Europe/Middle East/Africa region, and in the 80 percent range for the Americas (these ratings included all services for small, medium, and large customers).[18]

Premier Pages Dell had developed customized, password-protected Web sites called Premier Pages for more than 50,000 corporate, governmental, and institutional customers worldwide. These Premier Pages gave customers' personnel online access to information about all Dell products and configurations the company had purchased or that were currently authorized for purchase. Employees could use Premier Pages to (1) obtain customer-specific pricing for whatever machines and options the employee wanted to consider, (2) place an order online that would be routed electronically to higher-level managers for approval and then on to Dell for assembly and delivery, and (3) seek advanced help desk support. Customers could also search and sort all invoices and obtain purchase histories. These features eliminated paper invoices, cut ordering time, and reduced the internal labor customers needed to staff corporate purchasing and accounting functions. Customer use of Premier Pages had boosted the productivity of Dell salespeople assigned to these accounts by 50 percent. Dell was providing Premier Page service to additional customers annually and adding more features to further improve functionality.

Product Design Services One of Dell's latest services for large customers was making special-purpose products for such customers as Internet search providers, social networking sites, and big video content sites that might need 10,000 or more units to accommodate its requirements. Such customers did not want to pay for a general-purpose product with components or performance features it did not need. So Dell created a group that had the capability to provide a big user with thousands of units of a product stripped of unnecessary features and equipped with whatever processor, memory, and disk drive suited the customer's needs. Dell personnel would visit with the customer, ascertain the customer's needs and preferences, provide a prototype within three weeks for evaluation and testing, make any additional changes within another two weeks for further testing and evaluation, and then be in volume production by the thousands of units within another three or four weeks—altogether about a nine-week design-to-production/delivery cycle.

Value-Added Services for Customers with Large IT Operations Dell kept close track of the purchases of its large global customers, country by country and department by department—and customers themselves found this purchase information valuable. Dell's sales and support personnel used their knowledge about a particular customer's needs to help that customer plan PC purchases, to configure the customer's PC networks, and to provide value-added services. For example, for its large customers Dell loaded software and placed ID tags on newly ordered PCs at the factory, thereby eliminating the need for the customer's IT personnel to unpack the PC, deliver it to an employee's desk, hook it up, place asset tags on the PC, and load the needed software—a process that could take several hours and cost \$200–\$300.[19] While Dell charged an extra \$15 or \$20 for the software-loading and asset-tagging services, the savings to customers were still considerable—one large customer reported savings of \$500,000 annually from this service.[20]

In 2007 and early 2008, Dell spent about \$2 billion to make a series of software-related acquisitions that gave it an altogether new value-added capability:

1. Everdream Corporation—Everdream was a leading provider of Software as a Service (SaaS) solutions, with operations in California and North Carolina. This acquisition enabled Dell to extend its capabilities to use the Internet to remotely manage global delivery of software solutions from servers, storage devices, and printers to desktop PCs, laptops, and other end-user devices. Dell management believed that remote-service management of software products would help business customers of all sizes simplify their IT infrastructure—a value-added outcome that Dell was aggressively pursuing. Terms of the acquisition were not disclosed.
2. SilverBack Technologies Inc.—Silverback was a privately owned, Massachusetts-based company that had a delivery platform to remotely manage and monitor SaaS products. Such a platform was essential to Dell's strategy of simplifying customers' IT infrastructures by providing their personnel with desirable software applications on an as-needed basis via the Internet. Terms of the acquisition were not disclosed.
3. MessageOne Inc.—Acquired for \$155 million, MessageOne was an industry leader in SaaS-enabled continuous e-mail service, e-mail archiving, and disaster recovery of e-mail messages. The MessageOne acquisition further enhanced Dell's strategy to use SaaS applications and remote software management tools to deliver configure-to-order IT services to commercial customers over the Internet.
4. EqualLogic—This company, acquired for \$1.4 billion, was a leading provider of high-performance storage area network (SAN) solutions that made storing and processing data easier and cheaper. EqualLogic's technological capabilities allowed Dell to offer its customers a secure data storage solution that used the customer's existing IT infrastructure, could be installed in minutes, managed itself, and was easily expanded as needs increased.
5. ASAP Software—ASAP, acquired at a cost of \$340 million, was a leading software solutions and licensing services provider, with expertise in software licensing and the management of IT assets. The ASAP acquisition expanded Dell's lineup of software offerings from 200 to 2,000.
6. The Networked Storage Company—Networked Storage was a leading IT consulting group that specialized in transitioning customers to proven, simplified, cost-efficient data storage solutions. Dell management saw this acquisition as an important element in its strategy to build the capability to offer Dell customers simple, cost-effective ways to manage their IT infrastructures. Terms of the acquisition were not disclosed.

Dell management saw all six acquisitions as greatly strengthening the company's capabilities to provide an altogether new value-added service to customers with sizable IT operations, all of whom were finding the tasks of managing and maintaining an IT infrastructure to be increasingly complex and costly.

Executives at Dell believed that having greater capability than rivals to offer commercial customers simple, cost-effective ways to manage their IT operations would give Dell added competitiveness in marketing its lineup of product offerings to commercial enterprises worldwide. While Dell already was the sales leader in PCs sold to corporations and businesses in North America and Europe, extending its lead in these regions and growing sales and market share in the remaining parts of the world could make a material contribution not only to growing Dell's overall business but also to overtaking Hewlett-Packard as the global leader in PCs.

Enhanced Services and Support for Large Enterprises Corporate customers paid Dell fees to provide on-site service and help with migrating to new information technologies. Service revenues had climbed from $1.7 billion in 2002 to about $5.3 billion in fiscal 2008. This portion of Dell's business was split between what Michael Dell called close-to-the-box services and management/professional services. Dell estimated that close-to-the-box support services for Dell products represented about a $50 billion market as of 2005, whereas the market for management/professional services (IT life-cycle services, deployment of new technology, and solutions for greater IT productivity) in 2005 was about $90 billion. The market for IT consulting and services was forecast to be in the $850–$900 billion range in 2011. For the most part, IT consulting services were becoming more standardized, driven primarily by growing hardware and software standardization, reduction in on-site service requirements (partly because of online diagnostic and support tools, growing ease of repair and maintenance, increased customer knowledge, and increased remote management capabilities), and declines in the skills and know-how that were required to perform service tasks on standardized equipment and install new, more standardized systems.

Dell's strategy in enhanced services, like its strategy in hardware products, was to bring down the cost of IT-related services for its large enterprise customers and free customers from "overpriced relationships" with such vendors as IBM, Sun Microsystems, and Hewlett-Packard that typically charged premium prices ($250 per hour) and realized hefty profits for their efforts.[21] According to Michael Dell, customers who bought the services being provided by Dell saved 40 to 50 percent over what they would have paid other providers of IT services.

The caliber of technical support and customer service that Dell provided to its large enterprise customers was highly regarded (despite the problems sometimes experienced by small businesses and individuals). In a 2005 survey of IT executives by *CIO* magazine, Dell was rated number one among leading vendors for providing "impeccable customer service" to large enterprises.

Providing Online Shoppers with Customer Reviews of Dell Products Users of Dell products were encouraged to provide Dell with a review of their experiences with the products they had purchased. As part of the review process, customers were asked to provide a rating of the product using a 5-point scale that ran from 1 (poor) to 5 (excellent). Shoppers browsing through Dell's product offerings could view the average customer rating score for each product directly on the screen where the product details were displayed and could click on an adjacent link to read the accompanying reviews. In 2008, about 50,000 customer reviews of Dell products were posted and available for inspection.

Listening to Customers In addition to using its sales and support mechanisms to stay close to customers, Dell periodically held regional forums that gave senior Dell personnel opportunities to listen to the company's biggest and most influential customers and discuss their emerging needs and expectations. The meeting agenda frequently included a presentation by Michael Dell, plus presentations by Dell's senior technologists on the direction of the latest technological developments and what the flow of technology really meant for customers, presentations on what new and upgraded products Dell was planning to introduce, and breakout sessions on topics of current interest.

In February 2007, Dell began inviting customers to post their ideas for improving its products and services at a section of its Web site called IdeaStorm. As of April 2008, customers had posted more than 8,900 ideas, 45 of which had been implemented. Michael Dell believed that the Internet and the speed with which people worldwide were able to connect to the Internet via a growing number of devices had forever redefined what it means to listen to customers:

> Listening used to mean commissioning a customer survey. Now it means engaging directly with customers and critics and using those relationships to create a smarter business. Tapping into the ideas of our customers is like having an open source R&D lab.[22]

Customer-Driven Research and Development and Standardized Technology

Dell's R&D focus was to track and test new developments in components and software, ascertain which ones would prove most useful and cost-effective for customers, and then design them into Dell products. Management's philosophy was that it was Dell's job on behalf of its customers to sort out all the new technology coming into the marketplace and design products having the features, options, and solutions that were the most relevant for customers. Studies conducted by Dell's R&D personnel indicated that, over time, products incorporating standardized technology delivered about twice the performance per dollar of cost as products based on proprietary technology.

At the University of Buffalo, for example, Dell had installed a 5.6 teraflop cluster of about 2,000 Dell servers containing 4,000 microprocessors that constituted one of the most powerful supercomputers in the world and gave researchers the computing power needed to help decode the human genome. The cluster of servers, which were the same as those Dell sold to many other customers, had been installed in about 60 days at a cost of a few million dollars—far less than the cost of another vendor's supercomputer that used proprietary technology. Energy giant Amerada Hess Corporation (now known as Hess Corporation), attracted by Dell's use of standardized and upgradable parts and components, installed a cluster of several hundred Dell workstations and allocated about $300,000 a year to upgrade and maintain it; the cluster replaced an IBM supercomputer that cost $1.5 million a year to lease and operate.

Dell's R&D unit also studied and implemented ways to control quality and to streamline the assembly process. In 2008, Dell had a portfolio of 1,954 U.S. patents and another 2,196 patent applications were pending. Dell's R&D group included about 4,000 engineers, and its annual budget for research, development, and engineering was in the $430–$500 million range before jumping to more than $600 million in fiscal 2008 (see Exhibit 2).

Other Elements of Dell's Business Strategy

Dell's strategy had three other elements that complemented its core strategy: entry into the white-box segment of the PC industry, advertising, and continuous pursuit of cost reduction initiatives.

Dell's Entry into the White-Box PC Segment In 2002, Dell announced it would begin making so-called white-box (i.e., unbranded) PCs for resale under the private labels of retailers. PC dealers that supplied white-box PCs to small businesses and price-conscious individuals under the dealer's own brand name accounted for about one-third of total PC sales and about 50 percent of sales to small businesses. According to one industry analyst, "Increasingly, Dell's biggest competitor these days isn't big brand-name companies like IBM or HP; it's white-box vendors." Dell's thinking in entering the white-box PC segment was that it was cheaper to reach many small businesses through the white-box dealers that already served them than by using its own sales force and support groups to sell and service businesses with fewer than 100 employees. Dell believed that its low-cost supply chain and assembly capabilities would allow it to build generic machines cheaper than white-box resellers could buy components and assemble a customized machine. Management forecast that Dell would achieve $380 million in sales of white-box PCs in 2003 and would generate profit margins equal to those on Dell-branded PCs. Some industry analysts were skeptical of Dell's move into white-box PCs because they expected white-box dealers to be reluctant to buy their PCs from a company that had a history of taking their clients. Others believed this was a test effort by Dell to develop the capabilities to take on white-box dealers in Asia and especially in China, where the sellers of generic PCs were particularly strong.

Advertising Michael Dell was a firm believer in the power of advertising and frequently espoused its importance in the company's strategy. He insisted that the company's ads be communicative and forceful, not soft and fuzzy. The company regularly had prominent ads describing its products and prices in such leading computer publications as *PC Magazine* and *PC World*, as well as in *USA Today*, the *Wall Street Journal*, and other business publications. From time to time, the company ran ads on TV to promote its products to consumers and small businesses. Catalogs of about 25–30 pages describing Dell's latest desktop and laptop PCs, along with its printers and other offerings, were periodically mailed to consumers who had bought Dell products. Other marketing initiatives included printing newspaper inserts and sending newsletters and promotional pieces to customers via the Internet.

Continuous Pursuit of Cost-Reduction Initiatives Michael Dell had long been an ardent advocate of relentless efforts to improve efficiency and keeps costs as low as feasible. But during Kevin Rollins's tenure as CEO, Dell's cost edge over rivals had narrowed, and the company's profit margins had slipped as well (partly because fierce price competition was driving down the prices of many products that Dell sold faster than Dell was able to lower its costs per unit)—Exhibit 7 shows the downward trend in the average revenue Dell received from each unit sold. When he reassumed his role as CEO in 2007, Michael Dell announced that tighter controls over operating expenses would be implemented immediately and that management would begin an in-depth exploration of ways for improving Dell's cost-competitiveness, organizing operations more efficiently, and boosting profitability and cash flows. In May 2007, Dell announced an initiative to reduce the global workforce headcount by 10 percent, or 8,800 people. By March 2008, a net of 3,200 jobs had been eliminated. However, the company had actually hired 2,100 more people to staff frontline operations and customer-facing activities; the net reduction of 3,200 people was achieved by cutting 5,300 personnel engaged in performing what Dell called non-frontline activities. The result was to increase the number of Dell employees engaged in frontline and customer-facing activities from 54 percent to 57 percent.

In March 2008, Dell executives announced that over the next three years the company would seek to achieve annualized savings of $3 billion via productivity improvements and cost-reduction efforts across all the company's value chain—design, supply chain logistics, materials, manufacturing, and other operating activities. Management reaffirmed its commitment to reducing the global employee headcount by 8,800 and achieving the related labor-cost savings. At the same time, Dell also put programs in place to reignite the company's revenue growth in five focus areas: global consumer products, sales to large enterprise customers, laptop computers, sales to small and medium enterprises, and sales in emerging countries.

THE INFORMATION TECHNOLOGY MARKETPLACE IN 2008

Analysts expected the worldwide IT industry to grow from $1.2 trillion in 2007 to $1.5 trillion in 2010, a compound growth rate of about 7.7 percent. Of that projected 2010 total, about $560 billion was expected to be for hardware (PCs, servers, storage devices, networking equipment, and printers and peripherals); $327 billion for software; and $613 billion for services. From 1980 to 2000, IT spending had grown at an average annual rate of 12 percent; thereafter, it had flattened—to a 1 percent decline in 2001, a 2.3 percent decline in 2002, a single-digit increase in 2003—then rose more briskly at rates in the 5–10 percent range in 2004, 2005, 2006 and 2007. The slowdown in IT spending in 2001–2007 compared to earlier years reflected a combination of factors: sluggish economic growth in many countries in 2001–2003; overinvestment in IT in the 1995–1999 period; declining unit prices for many IT products (especially PCs and servers); and a growing preference for lower-priced, standard-component hardware that was good enough to perform a variety of functions using off-the-shelf Windows or Linux operating systems (as opposed to relying on proprietary hardware and customized Unix software). The selling points that appealed most to IT customers were standardization, flexibility, modularity, simplicity, economy of use, and value.

There were several driving forces contributing to increased global spending for information technology products and services starting in 2004.[23] One was the explosion of digital information and content. According to Forrester Research, the world's data doubled approximately every three years, a phenomenon that was expected to produce more than a sixfold increase in data between 2003 and 2010. A second force was the rapid expansion of search engine activity, e-mail, text messages, social networking Web sites like My Space and Facebook, blogs, and online video and images; these fed the worldwide demand for digital devices to create, store, share, and print the mushrooming volume of digital information and content. The third force was the rapidly growing demand for information technology products and services in emerging markets around the world—like Brazil, Russia, China, India, and several other countries in Southeast Asia and Eastern Europe—where over half of the world's population resided. At the same time, several other complicating factors were at work. Much of the growing volume of content lacked authentication and proper security, plus the content was increasingly global and mobile. And consumer expectations were changing—people wanted instantaneous access to content regardless of what kind of device they were using or where they happened to be, and their tolerance for complexity was low. All of these aspects of the global IT marketplace created huge opportunities for IT providers and huge challenges for IT users.

Exhibit 8 shows actual and projected PC sales for 1980–2012 as compiled by industry researcher International Data Corporation (IDC). According to Gartner Research, the billionth PC was shipped sometime in July 2002; of the billion PCs sold, an estimated 550 million were still in use. Forrester Research estimated that the numbers of PCs in use worldwide would exceed 1 billion by the end of 2008 (up from 575 million in 2004) and would approach 1.3 billion by 2011 and 2.0 billion by 2016. With a world population of more than 6 billion, most industry participants believed there was ample opportunity for further growth in the PC market. Growth potential for PCs was particularly strong in Russia, China, India, several other Asian countries, and portions of Latin America (especially Brazil and Mexico). At the same time, forecasters expected full global buildout of the Internet to continue, which would require the installation of millions of servers.

Exhibit 8 **Worldwide Shipments of PCs, Actual and Forecast, 1980–2012 (in millions)**

Year	PCs Shipped
1980	1
1985	11
1990	24
1995	58
2000	139
2001	133
2002	136
2003	153
2004	177
2005	208
2006	235
2007	269
2008*	302
2009*	335
2010*	368
2011*	398
2012*	426

*Forecast.

Source: International Data Corporation.

HOW DELL'S STRATEGY PUT COMPETITIVE PRESSURE ON RIVALS

When the personal computer industry first began to take shape in the early 1980s, the founding companies manufactured many of the components themselves—disk drives, memory chips, graphics chips, microprocessors, motherboards, and software. Subscribing to a philosophy that mandated in-house development of key components, they built expertise in a variety of PC-related technologies and created organizational units to produce components as well as handle final assembly. While certain noncritical items were typically outsourced, if a computer maker was not at least partially vertically integrated and did not produce some components for its PCs, then it was not taken seriously as a manufacturer. But as the industry grew, technology advanced quickly in so many directions on so many parts and components that the early personal computer manufacturers could not keep pace as experts on all fronts. There were too many technologies and manufacturing intricacies to master for a vertically integrated manufacturer to keep its products on the cutting edge.

As a consequence, companies emerged that specialized in making particular components. Specialists could marshal enough R&D capability and resources to either lead the technological developments in their area of specialization or else quickly match the advances made by their competitors. Moreover, specialist firms could mass-produce the component and supply it to several computer manufacturers far cheaper than any one manufacturer could fund the needed component R&D and then make only whatever smaller volume of components it needed for assembling its own brand of PCs. Thus, in the early 1990s, such computer makers as Compaq Computer, IBM, Hewlett-Packard, Sony, Toshiba, and Fujitsu-Siemens began to abandon vertical integration in favor of a strategy of outsourcing most components from specialists and concentrating on efficient assembly and marketing their brand of computers. They adopted the build-to-stock value chain model shown in the top section of Exhibit 4. It featured arm's-length transactions between specialist suppliers, manufacturer/assemblers, distributors and retailers, and end users. However, a few others, most notably Dell and Gateway, employed a shorter value chain model, selling directly to customers and eliminating the time and costs associated with distributing through independent resellers. Building to order avoided (1) having to keep many differently equipped models on retailers' shelves to fill buyer requests for one or another configuration of options and components, and (2) having to clear out slow-selling models at a discount before introducing new generations of PCs—for instance, Hewlett-Packard's retail dealers had an average of 43 days of HP products in stock as of October 2004. Direct sales eliminated retailer costs and markups; retail dealer margins were typically in the range of 4–10 percent.

Because of Dell's success in using its business model and strategy to become the low-cost leader, most other PC makers had tried to emulate various aspects of Dell's strategy, but with only limited success. Nearly all vendors were trying to cut days of inventory out of their supply chains and reduce their costs of goods sold and operating expenses to levels that would make them more cost-competitive with Dell. In an effort to cut their assembly costs, several others (including HP) had begun outsourcing assembly to contract manufacturers and refocusing their internal efforts on product design and marketing. Virtually all PC vendors were trying to minimize the amount of finished goods in dealer/distributor inventories and shorten the time it took to replenish dealer stocks. Collaboration with contract manufacturers was increasing to develop the capabilities to build and deliver PCs equipped to customer specifications within 7 to 14 days, but these efforts were hampered by the use of Asia-based contract manufacturers—delivering built-to-order PCs to North American and European customers within a two-week time frame required the use of costly air freight from assembly plants in Asia.

While most PC vendors would have liked to adopt Dell's sell-direct strategy for at least some of their sales, they confronted big channel conflict problems: if they started to push direct sales hard, they would almost certainly alienate the independent dealers on whom they depended for the bulk of their sales and service to customers. Dealers saw sell-direct efforts on the part of a manufacturer whose brand they represented as a move to cannibalize their business and to compete against them. However, Dell's success in gaining large enterprise customers with its direct sales force had forced growing numbers of PC vendors to supplement the efforts of their independent dealers with direct sales and service efforts of their own. During 2003–2007, several of Dell's rivals were selling 15 to 25 percent of their products direct.

HEWLETT-PACKARD: DELL'S CHIEF RIVAL IN PCS AND x86 SERVERS

In one of the most contentious and controversial acquisitions in U.S. history, Hewlett-Packard shareholders in early 2002 voted by a narrow margin to approve the company's acquisition of Compaq Computer, the world's second largest full-service global computing company (behind IBM), with 2001 revenues of $33.6 billion and a net loss of $785 million. Compaq had passed IBM to become the world leader in PCs in 1995 and remained in first place until it was overtaken by Dell in late 1999. Compaq had acquired Tandem Computer in 1997 and Digital Equipment Corporation in 1998 to give it capabilities, products, and service offerings that allowed it to compete in every sector of the computer industry—PCs, servers, workstations, mainframes, peripherals, and such services as business and e-commerce solutions, hardware and software support, systems integration, and technology consulting.[24] In 2000, Compaq spent $370 million to acquire certain assets of Inacom Corporation that management believed would help Compaq reduce inventories, speed cycle time, and enhance its capabilities to do business with customers via the Internet. Nonetheless, at the time of its acquisition by HP, Compaq was struggling to compete successfully in all of the many product and service arenas where it operated.

Carly Fiorina, who became HP's CEO in 1999, explained why the acquisition of Compaq was strategically sound:[25]

> With Compaq, we become No. 1 in Windows, No. 1 in Linux and No. 1 in Unix . . . With Compaq, we become the No. 1 player in storage, and the leader in the fastest growing segment of the storage market—storage area networks. With Compaq, we double our service and support capacity in the area of mission-critical infrastructure design, outsourcing and support. . . . Let's talk about PCs. . . . Compaq has been able to improve their turns in that business from 23 turns of inventory per year to 62—100 percent improvement year over year—and they are coming close to doing as well as Dell does. They've reduced operating expenses by $130 million, improved gross margins by three points, reduced channel inventory by more than $800 million. They ship about 70 percent of their commercial volume through their direct channel, comparable to Dell. We will combine our successful retail PC business model with their commercial business model and achieve much more together than we could alone. With Compaq, we will double the size of our sales force to 15,000 strong. We will build our R&D budget to more than $4 billion a year, and add important capabilities to HP Labs. We will become the No. 1 player in a whole host of countries around the world—HP operates in more than 160 countries, with well over 60 percent of our revenues coming from outside the U.S. The new HP will be the No. 1 player in the consumer and small- and medium-business segments. . . . We have estimated cost synergies of $2.5 billion by 2004. . . . It is a rare opportunity when a technology company can advance its market position substantially and reduce its cost structure substantially at the same time. And this is possible because Compaq and HP are in the same businesses, pursuing the same strategies, in the same markets, with complementary capabilities.

However, going into 2005 the jury was still out on whether HP's acquisition of Compaq was the success that Carly Fiorina had claimed it would be. The company's only real bright spot was its $24 billion crown jewel printer business, which still reigned as the unchallenged world leader. But the rest of HP's businesses (PCs, servers, storage devices, digital cameras, calculators, and IT services) were underachievers. Its PC and server businesses were struggling, losing money in most quarters and barely breaking even in others—and HP was definitely losing ground to Dell in PCs and low-priced servers. In servers, HP was being squeezed on the low end by Dell's low prices and on the high end by strong competition from IBM. According to most observers, IBM overshadowed HP in corporate computing—high-end servers and IT services. HP had been able to grow revenues in data storage and technical support services, but profit margins and total operating profits were declining. While HP had successfully cut annual operating costs by $3.5 billion—beating the $2.5 billion target set at the time of the Compaq acquisition, the company had missed its earnings forecasts in 7 of the past 20 quarters.

With HP's stock price stuck in the $18–$23 price range, impatient investors in 2004 began clamoring for the company to break itself up and create two separate companies, one for its printer business and one for all the rest of the businesses. While HP's board of directors had looked at breaking the company into smaller pieces, Carly Fiorina was steadfastly opposed, arguing that HP's broad product/business lineup paid off in the form of added sales and lower costs. But in February 2005, shortly after HP released disappointing financials for 2004 (the company's earnings per share total of $1.16 in 2004 was substantially below the earnings per share total of $1.80 reported in 2000), Carly Fiorina resigned her post as HP's CEO amid mounting differences between herself and members of HP's board of directors about what actions were needed to revive HP's earnings.

Mark Hurd, president and CEO of NCR (formerly National Cash Resister Systems), was brought in to replace Fiorina, effective April 1, 2005; Hurd had been at NCR for 25 years in a variety of management positions and was regarded as a no-nonsense executive who underpromised and overdelivered on results.[26] Hurd immediately sought to bolster HP's competitiveness and financial performance by bringing in new managers and attacking bloated costs. In his first seven months as CEO, the results were encouraging. HP posted revenues of $86.7 billion and net profits of $2.4 billion for the fiscal year ending October 31, 2005. HP had the number one ranking worldwide for server shipments (a position it had held for 14 consecutive quarters) and disk storage systems, plus it was the world leader in server revenues for Unix, Windows, and Linux systems. During the first seven months that Hurd was HP's CEO, the company's stock price rose about 25 percent.

With Hurd at the helm, Hewlett-Packard continued to gain traction in the marketplace in the next two fiscal years. For example, HP's sales of laptop computers increased 47 percent in fiscal 2007 and its PC business in China nearly doubled, making China HP's third biggest market for PCs. The company posted revenues of $91.7 billion in fiscal 2006 and $104.3 billion in fiscal 2007. Earnings climbed from $2.4 billion in 2005 to $6.2 billion in 2006 (equal to a diluted earnings per share of $2.18) and to $7.3 billion in 2007 (equal to a diluted earning per share of $2.68). By late fall 2007, HP's stock price was more than double what it had been during Carly Fiorina's last days as CEO. The company's 2007 share of the estimated $1.2 trillion global IT market was almost 9 percent. It was the global leader in both PCs and x86 servers running on Windows and Linux operating systems. About 67 percent of HP's sales were outside the United States. In May 2008, HP announced that it was expecting fiscal 2008 revenues of about $114 billion and a diluted earnings per share in the range of $3.30 to $3.34. Exhibit 9 shows the performance of Hewlett-Packard's four major business groups for fiscal years 2001–2007.

HP's strategy in PCs and servers differed from Dell's in two important respects:

1. Although HP had a direct sales force that sold direct to large enterprises and select other customers, a very sizable share of HP's sales of PCs were made through distributors, retailers, and other channels. These included:

    - Retailers that sold HP products to the public through their own physical or Internet stores.
    - Resellers that sold HP products and services, frequently with their own value-added products or services, to targeted customer groups.
    - Distribution partners that supplied HP products to smaller resellers with which HP had no direct relationships.
    - Independent distributors that sold HP products into geographic areas or customer segments in which HP had little or no presence.
    - Independent software vendors that often assisted HP in selling HP computers, servers, and other products/services to their software clients.
    - Systems integrators that helped large enterprises design and implement custom IT solutions and often recommended that these enterprises purchase HP products when such products were needed to put a customized IT solution in place.

    Much of HP's global market clout in PCs and servers came from having the world's biggest and most diverse network of distribution partners. The percentage of PCs and servers sold by its direct sales force and by its various channel partners varied substantially by geographic region and country, partly because customer buying patterns and different regional market conditions made it useful for HP to tailor its sales, marketing, and distribution accordingly.

2. While in-house personnel designed the company's PCs and x86 servers, the vast majority were assembled by contract manufacturers located in various parts of the world. Big-volume orders from large enterprise customers were assembled to each customer's particular specifications. The remaining units were assembled and shipped to HP's retail and distribution partners; these were configured in a variety of ways (different microprocessor speeds, hard drive sizes, display sizes, memory size, and so on) that HP and its resellers thought would be attractive to customers and then assembled in large productions runs to maximize manufacturing efficiencies.

During 2005–2007, after replacing a number of HP's senior executives, Mark Hurd engineered several strategic moves to strengthen HP's competitiveness

Exhibit 9 Performance of Hewlett-Packard's Four Major Business Groups, Fiscal Years 2001–2007 ($ in billions)

Fiscal Years Ending October 31	Printing and Imaging	Personal Computing Systems	Enterprise Systems and Software	HP Services
2007				
Net revenue	$28,465	$36,409	$21,094	$16,646
Operating income	4,315	1,939	2,327	1,829
2006				
Net revenue	$26,786	$29,169	$18,609	$15,617
Operating income	3,978	1,152	1,531	1,507
2005				
Net revenue	$25,155	$26,741	$17,878	$15,536
Operating income	3,413	657	751	1,151
2004				
Net revenue	$24,199	$24,622	$16,074	$13,778
Operating income	3,847	210	28	1,263
2003				
Net revenue	$22,569	$21,210	$15,367	$12,357
Operating income (loss)	3,596	22	(48)	1,362
2002*				
Net revenue	$20,358	$21,895	$11,105	$12,326
Operating income (loss)	3,365	(372)	(656)	1,369
2001*				
Net revenue	$19,602	$26,710	$20,205	$12,802
Operating income (loss)	2,103	(728)	(579)	1,617

*Results for 2001 and 2002 represent the combined results of both HP and Compaq Computer.
Source: Company 10-K reports 2003, 2004, and 2007.

and ability to deliver better financial performance to shareholders:

- Top executives charged each HP business with identifying and implementing opportunities to boost efficiency and lower costs per unit. Every aspect of the company's supply chain and internal cost structure was scrutinized for ways to become more efficient and reduce costs. The costs of each value chain component—from real estate to procurement to IT to marketing—were examined so that managers could know costs by business group, region, country, site, product, and employee; these levels of cost analysis were then used to scrutinize how each expense supported HP's strategy and whether there were opportunities for cost savings. Corporate overheads were trimmed, negotiations with suppliers were conducted to be sure that HP was getting the best terms and best prices on its purchases, steps were taken to trim HP's workforce by about 15,000 people worldwide, the organizational structure was streamlined resulting in three layers of management being removed, and the company's very complicated IT operations were simplified and the expenses reduced—the objective was to engineer HP's IT architecture and operations to be the world's best showcase for the company's technology. In 2008, HP began trimming the number of sites worldwide at which it conducted activities by 25 percent. The resulting improvements in operating expenses paved the way for HP to price its products more competitively against those of Dell and other rivals.

- Company personnel began working more closely with large enterprise customers to find ways to simplify their experience with information technology.
- A number of new products and services were introduced.
- HP spent close to $7 billion to acquire more than a dozen software, technology, and service companies that management believed would add significant capabilities and technology to HP's portfolio and help fuel revenue growth.
- The company prepared to capitalize on three big growth opportunities that top management saw emerging over the next four or five years: (1) next-generation data center architecture; (2) growing consumer interest in always-ready, always-on mobile computing; and (3) digital printing. Mark Hurd believed that HP had important strengths in all three of these high-growth market arenas but needed to be more adept in getting new products into the marketplace. He directed company personnel to develop a better "go-to-market" model and to arm the sales force with the tools needed to "get quotes and proposals in front of customers as fast as anybody on the planet." HP added 1,000 people to its sales force in 2007 to expand its coverage of key accounts and geographic markets; an additional 1,000 salespeople were added through acquisitions.

Soon after becoming CEO in 2005, Mark Hurd concluded that HP needed to beef up its IT services business in order to go head-to-head against IBM, the unquestioned worldwide leader in IT services; IBM had 2007 revenues of about $54 billion and an estimated 7.2 percent global share of a $748 billion market. Hurd took a major step in that direction in May 2008, making his first really big strategic move as HP's CEO by cutting a deal to acquire Electronic Data Systems (EDS) for a cash price of $13.25 billion. According to Gartner (one of the world's leading technology research firms), EDS had IT service revenues of $22.1 billion in 2007, equal to a global share of 3.0 percent—ahead of HP with revenues of $17.3 billion and a 2.3 percent share (see Exhibit 10 for the sales and market shares of the world's top six IT service providers). While a combined HP/EDS would have IT service revenues of more than $49 billion and market share of 5.3 percent—sufficient for a strong second place in the global market—industry observers were not enamored with the ability of HP/EDS to compete with IBM for high-end, high-profit buyers of IT services. IBM's profit margin in IT services was almost double EDS's 6 percent profit margin, partly because IBM catered to the needs of high-end customers and partly because IBM had about 74,000 employees in India, where wages for IT professionals were considerably lower—only 27,000 of EDS's 140,000 employees were in India.

Exhibit 10 Estimated Sales and Market Shares of the World's Six Leading Providers of Information Technology Services, 2007

Company	2007 Revenues (in billions)	Market Share
IBM	$ 54.1	7.2%
Electronic Data Systems (EDS)	22.1	3.0
Accenture	20.6	2.8
Fujitsu	18.6	2.5
Hewlett-Packard	17.3*	2.3
Computer Sciences Corp. (CSC)	16.3	2.2
All others	599.0	80.0
Totals	$748.0	100.0%

*Gartner's $17.3 billion number for HP's 2007 revenues in IT services exceeds the $16.6 billion reported by HP in its 2007 10-K report and shown in Exhibit 9.

Source: Gartner, as reported in Justin Scheck and Ben Worthen, "Hewlett-Packard Takes Aim at IBM," *Wall Street Journal,* May 14, 2008, p. B1.

EDS, founded in 1962, was best known for its capabilities in running clients' mainframe systems, operating help desks to support personal computer users, developing and running business software for its clients, and handling such automated IT processes as billing and payments for clients.[27] In contrast, HP's IT service business revolved around managing infrastructure—such as back-office server systems—for its large enterprises. There was relatively little overlap between the customer bases of the two companies. HP executives believed there was plenty of opportunity to cut costs at EDS and that there were clear revenue-boosting opportunities, such as expanding sales of managed printing services. Even so, HP's shareholders were unenthusiastic about the EDS acquisition—HP's stock price fell more than $10 per share in the two days following news of the acquisition but recovered $2.50 of the drop within a week.

DELL'S FUTURE PROSPECTS

In a February 2003 article in *Business 2.0,* Michael Dell said, "The best way to describe us now is as a broad computer systems and services company. We have a pretty simple system. The most important thing is to satisfy our customers. The second most important thing is to be profitable. If we don't do the first one well, the second one won't happen."[28] For the most part, Michael Dell was not particularly concerned about the efforts of competitors to copy many aspects of Dell's build-to-order, sell-direct strategy. He explained why on at least two occasions:

> The competition started copying us seven years ago. That's when we were a $1 billion business. . . . And they haven't made much progress to be honest with you. The learning curve for them is difficult. It's like going from baseball to soccer.[29]

> I think a lot of people have analyzed our business model, a lot of people have written about it and tried to understand it. This is an 18½-year process. . . . It comes from many, many cycles of learning. . . . It's very, very different than designing products to be built to stock. . . . Our whole company is oriented around a very different way of operating. . . . I don't, for any second, believe that they are not trying to catch up. But it is also safe to assume that Dell is not staying in the same place.[30]

On other occasions, Michael Dell spoke about the size of the company's future opportunities:

> When technologies begin to standardize or commoditize, the game starts to change. Markets open up to be volume markets and this is very much where Dell has made its mark—first in the PC market in desktops and notebooks and then in the server market and the storage market and services and data networking. We continue to expand the array of products that we sell, the array of services and, of course, expand on a geographic basis. The way we think about it is that there are all of these various technologies out there. . . . What we have been able to do is build a business system that takes those technological ingredients, translates them into products and services and gets them to the customer more efficiently than any company around.[31]

> There are enormous opportunities for us to grow across multiple dimensions in terms of products, with servers, storage, printing and services representing a huge realm of expansion for us. There's geographic expansion and market share expansion back in the core business. The primary focus for us is picking those opportunities, seizing on them, and making sure we have the talent and the leadership growing inside the company to support all that growth. And there's also a network effect here. As we grow our product lines and enter new markets, we see a faster ability to gain share in new markets versus ones we've previously entered.[32]

> A great portion of our growth will come from key markets outside the U.S. We have about 10 percent market share outside the United States, so there's definitely room to grow. We'll grow in the enterprise with servers, storage, and services. Our growth will come from new areas like printing. And, quite frankly, those are really enough. There are other things that I could mention, other things we do, but those opportunities I mentioned can drive us to $80 billion and beyond.[33]

That Dell had ample growth opportunities was indisputable—in 2007, it only had a minuscule 2 percent share of the $1.2 trillion global market for IT products and services. Exhibit 11 shows Dell's principal competitors in each of the industry's major product categories and its estimated 2007 market shares in each category.

In 2008, despite near-term prospects of sluggish economic growth in the United States and perhaps elsewhere, Michael Dell remained enthusiastic about the unrivaled opportunity for the company's business given that the number of people online globally (via PCs, cell phones, and other devices with Internet connectivity) was expected to increase from just over 1 billion in 2008 to over 2 billion by 2011:

> The world is witnessing the most exciting and promising period for technology ever seen. We call it the "Connected Era." The second billion people coming online, many from the world's fast growing and emerging economies, expect a different technology experience to the first. The Internet has unleashed billions of new conversations and made it possible for people to connect in new ways. The emergence of this connected era is arguably the most influential single trend remodeling the world today.[34]

In May 2008, the latest sales and market share data indicated that Dell might be closing the gap on Hewlett-Packard and on the verge of mounting

Exhibit 11 Dell's Principal Competitors and Dell's Estimated Market Shares by Product Category, 2007

Product Category	Dell's Principal Competitors	Estimated Size of Worldwide Market, 2007	Dell's Estimated Worldwide Share, 2007
PCs	Hewlett-Packard (maker of both Compaq and HP brands); Lenovo, Apple, Acer, Toshiba, Sony, Fujitsu-Siemens (in Europe and Japan)	$375 billion	~15%
Servers	Hewlett-Packard, IBM, Sun Microsystems, Fujitsu	$60 billion	~11%
Data storage devices	Hewlett-Packard, IBM, EMC, Hitachi	$48 billion	~5%
Networking switches and related equipment	Cisco Systems, Broadcom, Enterasys, Nortel, 3Com, Airespace, Proxim	~$65 billion	~2%
Printers and printer cartridges	Hewlett-Packard, Lexmark, Canon, Epson	~$50 billion	~5%
Services	Accenture, IBM, Hewlett-Packard, Fujitsu, EDS, many others	$748 billion	<1%

Source: Compiled by the case authors from a variety of sources, including International Data Corporation, www.dell.com, and *The Wall Street Journal,* May 14, 2008, p. B1.

Exhibit 12 Worldwide Unit Sales and Market Shares of Top Five PC Manufacturers, First Quarter 2008 versus Fourth Quarter 2007

Rank	Company	Q1, 2008 Shipments	Market Share	Q4, 2007 Shipments	Market Share	Percentage Growth in Shipments
1	Hewlett-Packard	13,251,000	19.1%	11,291,000	18.6%	17.4%
2	Dell	10,913,000	15.7%	8,971,000	14.8%	21.6%
3	Acer*	6,914,000	9.9%	4,164,000	6.9%	66.0%
4	Lenovo	4,814,000	6.9%	3,980,000	6.6%	21.0%
5	Toshiba	3,069,000	4.4%	2,544,000	4.2%	20.6%
	All Others	30,537,000	43.9%	29,674,000	48.9%	2.9%
	Total	69,498,000	100.0%	60,624,000	100.0%	14.6%

*Figures for Acer include shipments of Gateway, which was acquired by Acer in 2007.

Source: International Data Corporation, as per posting at www.dell.com (accessed May 12, 2008).

another run at being the global leader in PC sales. Exhibit 12 shows the sales and market shares of the world's top five PC vendors in the first quarter of 2008 as compared to the fourth quarter of 2007. Moreover, Dell's senior executives believed that their aggressive moves to reduce costs would help restore profit margins, given that there seemed to be some modest relief from having to contend with eroding average revenues per unit sold (see Exhibit 7).

However, by late Fall 2008, Dell's prospects for overtaking HP were looking more bleak. Global recessionary forces had caused a significant slowdown in global IT spending during 2008 and even larger cutbacks were being forecast for at least the first half of 2009 in light of the global financial crisis that emerged in Fall 2008. Still, HP reported a 5 percent increase in revenues for its 2008 fourth quarter ending October 31 (excluding the effect of its recent acquisition of EDS) versus the year earlier 2007 fourth quarter and a 2008 fourth quarter earnings increase of 4 percent; moreover HP was forecasting that fiscal 2009 revenues would be in the \$127.5 to \$130 billion range, up from \$118.4 billion in 2008. Dell's sales revenues in the third quarter of 2008 were 3 percent below those in the 2007 third quarter on unit-shipment growth of 3 percent; Dell's third quarter 2008 net profits were down 5 percent.

The Wall Street Journal reported in September 2008 that Dell was trying to sell its worldwide network of computer factories in an effort to reduce production costs; the apparent plan was to enter into agreements with contract manufacturers to produce its PCs. While Dell had for many years been the industry leader in lean manufacturing approaches and cost-efficient build-to-order production methods and was still the low-cost leader in producing desktop PCs, it had fallen behind contract manufacturers in producing notebook PCs cost efficiently—and there was a pronounced shift among individual consumers to purchase laptop PCs instead of desktops. Laptop PCs were more complex and labor-intensive to assemble than were desktops. To help contain the assembly costs of laptops, Dell had already begun having Asian contract manufacturers partially assemble its laptops; these partly assembled laptop units were then shipped to Dell's own plants where assembly was completed. Because each laptop was produced at two factories, Dell referred to its assembly of laptops as a "two-two" system. But the two-touch system was more costly than simply having a contract manufacturer in Asia perform the entire assembly. Hence, Dell's interest in abandoning in-house production altogether and shifting to 100 percent outsourcing.

As of late November 2008, Dell had found no buyers for its plants. But the company had nonetheless begun outsourcing the full assembly of some laptop models to contract manufacturers (such as Taiwan's Foxconn Group) to eliminate the extra costs of the two-touch system, and it had made significant progress in cutting operating expenses elsewhere—operating expenses were 12.1 percent of revenues in the 2008 third quarter versus 12.8 percent in the 2007 third quarter. There were some other positives. In the 2008 third quarter, Dell's Global Consumer business posted a 10 percent revenue gain on a 32 percent increase in unit shipments—Dell's revenue growth was double the industry average and the profitability of this business was the highest in 13 quarters. Dell consumer products won 41 awards in the 2008 third quarter—the Inspiron Mini 9 notebook was selected as one of *Time Magazine*'s "Best Inventions of 2008" and as one of CNET's "10 Most Cutting Edge Products of 2008."

Endnotes

[1] As quoted in "Dell Puts Happy Customers First," *Nikkei Weekly,* December 16, 2002.
[2] "Michael Dell: On Managing Growth," *MIS Week,* September 5, 1988, p. 1.
[3] "The Education of Michael Dell," *BusinessWeek,* March 22, 1993, p. 86.
[4] Dell's 2005 10-K report, pp. 1–2.
[5] Remarks by Kevin Rollins in a speech at Peking University, November 2, 2005, and posted at www.dell.com.
[6] As quoted in Joan Magretta, "The Power of Virtual Integration: An Interview with Dell Computer's Michael Dell," *Harvard Business Review,* March–April 1998, p. 74.
[7] Ibid., p. 75.
[8] Speech by Michael Dell at University of Toronto, September 21, 2004, www.dell.com (accessed December 15, 2004).
[9] Ibid., p. 76.
[10] Remarks by Michael Dell, Gartner Symposium, Orlando, FL, October 20, 2005, www.dell.com.
[11] Quoted in Neel Chowdhury, "Dell Cracks China," *Fortune,* June 21, 1999, p. 121.
[12] Remarks by Michael Dell, Gartner Fall Symposium, Orlando, FL, October 9, 2002, www.dell.com.
[13] Remarks by Michael Dell at the University of Toronto, September 21, 2004, www.dell.com.
[14] Quoted in the *Financial Times* Global News Wire, October 10, 2002.
[15] Remarks by Michael Dell, Gartner Symposium, Orlando, FL, October 20, 2005, www.dell.com.
[16] Kevin Rollins, "Using Information to Speed Execution," *Harvard Business Review,* March–April 1998, p. 81.
[17] As quoted in Don Tennant, "Dell Exec Addresses Service Woes in Run-up to IT-as-a-Service Launch," *Computerworld,* March 17, 2008, www.computerworld.com (accessed May 12, 2008).
[18] Ibid.
[19] Magretta, "The Power of Virtual Integration," p. 79.
[20] "Michael Dell Rocks," *Fortune,* May 11, 1998, p. 61
[21] Quoted in Kathryn Jones, "The Dell Way," *Business 2.0,* February 2003.
[22] Company press release, April 6, 2008.
[23] Much of this paragraph was developed by the case authors from information in Hewlett-Packard's 2007 annual report.
[24] "Can Compaq Catch Up?" *BusinessWeek,* May 3, 1999, p. 163.
[25] Company press release and speech posted at www.hp.com, accessed December 11, 2004.

[26] Louise Lee and Peter Burrows, "What's Dogging Dell's Stock," *BusinessWeek,* September 5, 2005, p. 90.
[27] Justin Scheck and Ben Worthen, "Hewlett-Packard Takes Aim at IBM," *Wall Street Journal,* May 14, 2008, p. B1.
[28] *Business 2.0,* February 2003, www.business2.com.
[29] Comments made to students at the University of North Carolina and reported in the *Raleigh News & Observer,* November 16, 1999.
[30] Remarks by Michael Dell, Gartner Fall Symposium, Orlando, FL, October 9, 2002, www.dell.com.
[31] Remarks by Michael Dell, MIT Sloan School of Management, September 26, 2002, www.dell.com.
[32] Remarks by Michael Dell, University of Toronto, September 21, 2004, www.dell.com.
[33] Remarks by Michael Dell, Gartner Symposium, Orlando FL, October 20, 2005, www.dell.com.
[34] Remarks by Michael Dell to reporters in Dubai, company press release, April 6, 2008.

CASE 7

Apple Inc. in 2008

Lou Marino
The University of Alabama

John Hattaway
The University of Alabama

Katy Beth Jackson
The University of Alabama

When the first version of the Apple iPhone was released on June 29, 2007, it took 74 days to sell 1 million units. When Apple released the next generation of the phone, the iPhone 3G, on July 11, 2008, sales reached 1 million units in 3 days—this sales figure easily surpassed analysts' estimates and netted an estimated $330 million. Despite multiple problems associated with the launch, including Apple's servers being overloaded and key applications being unavailable on launch day, the iPhone 3G quickly sold out in 21 states in the United States, with some customers agreeing to wait up to four weeks for delivery. Mirroring the success of the company's iPod/iTunes partnership, Apple's newly launched App Store, which allowed users to download programs for the iPhone, reported more than 10 million downloads in its first week of operations.

Within the same week, Apple's strength in its PC and iPod divisions was also recognized. Regarding the PC division, Gartner, a leading analyst in the PC industry, announced that in the second quarter of 2008 Apple had overtaken Acer to become the third largest PC maker in the United States, capturing 8.5 percent of the market behind Dell (31.9 percent) and Hewlett-Packard (25.3 percent). Regarding the iPod division, Gene Munster, a senior research analyst at the leading investment firm Piper Jaffray, noted that there was no evidence that the iPhone would cannibalize iPod sales, and he raised his estimates of the number of iPods sold in the first half of 2008.

Despite the encouraging news across all of Apple's divisions, a growing number of analysts were becoming increasingly concerned. Specific issues noted by analysts included gross margins that were not increasing despite falling component prices; cutbacks in education budgets in the United States that could impact Apple's revenues; the continued problems with the iPhone 3G launch, including a worldwide crash of the iPhone activation system; and a U.S. economy that did not appear to be gaining traction heading into the second half of 2008. These challenges, combined with speculation about potential health problems for Apple's CEO, Steve Jobs, had some investors and analysts concerned as to whether the company could continue its impressive performance and leadership in innovation into the future.

HISTORY OF APPLE

Steven Wozniak and Steven Jobs founded Apple Computer in 1976 by introducing the initial version of what was to become the first highly successful mass-produced personal computer, the Apple I. Although the original Apple I needed some refinement (it lacked a monitor, a keyboard, and even a case), this idea would influence the computer industry immeasurably. Wozniak and Jobs had attended high school together and maintained contact after graduation despite taking jobs with different Silicon Valley companies (Hewlett-Packard and Atari, respectively). Wozniak was the true designer of the Apple I, but Jobs recognized its commercial potential and insisted that they sell the computer. Although the Apple I launch was not especially successful, Wozniak was already designing the Apple II, which was introduced at a local trade show in 1977 and launched in April 1978. This second machine included a plastic case and color graphics and was instantly much more popular than its predecessor. Apple's president, Michael Scott, and chairman of the board, Mike Markkula, were happy with the computer's sales; by the end of 1980, Apple had sold more than 10,000 Apple IIs.

While the Apple II was relatively successful, the next revision of the product line, code-named Macintosh (Mac), was already in the works by 1979 under the direction of Jeff Raskin, a former professor at the University of California at San Diego and a researcher at Xerox's Palo Alto Research Center (PARC) who had proposed the project to Markkula. Raskin's ambitious goal was to design a user-friendly computer that had a graphical user interface (GUI) and would cost less than $500. At Raskin's urging that year, Jobs visited PARC, where he saw researchers using a GUI to simplify their computing. Jobs immediately recognized the importance of the interface and decided to use it in the project he was spearheading with project manager Ken Rothmuller: the Apple Lisa, named after Jobs's daughter. However, Jobs's constant drive for innovation and demands for refinements drove up costs for the Lisa, delayed the shipping date, and eventually caused Scott to remove Jobs from the project. Due to excessive cost, the Lisa never performed up to Apple's expectations and was retired from the market soon after it was introduced.

Undeterred, Jobs took his passion for the GUI to Raskin's Macintosh project. Jobs's 11 percent share of Apple's equity helped convince Scott to allow him to take over the project, and eventually personality conflicts between Jobs and Raskin forced Raskin to leave Apple in 1981. In the same year, Scott resigned as president of Apple and became the vice chairman of the board. Scott was replaced by Markkula, who became president and CEO. Jobs became chairman of the board upon Markkula's assumption of the presidency, and under Jobs's leadership the Macintosh team was challenged to make something "insanely great"; by many accounts they succeeded.

The Macintosh, introduced in 1984, was hailed as a breakthrough in user-friendly computing. It was also the first computer to use a 3.5-inch disk drive. Unfortunately, the Macintosh did not have the speed, power, or software availability to compete with the PC that IBM had introduced in 1981. One of the reasons the Macintosh lacked the necessary software was that Apple put very strict restrictions on the Apple Certified Developer Program, which made it difficult for software developers to obtain Macs at a discount and receive informational materials about the operating system.

When Scott stepped down in 1981, Jobs began actively working to replace Markkula with John Sculley, then president of Pepsi-Cola. Sculley became president and CEO of Apple in April 1983, and Markkula became the associate chairman. When Apple introduced the Macintosh the following year and it was not as well received as initially expected, Jobs (a volatile individual) and Sculley began to have difficulty working with each other. Finally, in 1985, as Sculley was preparing to visit China, Jobs devised a "boardroom coup" to replace him. Sculley found out about the plan and canceled his trip. After Apple's board voted unanimously to keep Sculley in his position, Jobs, who was retained as chairman of the company but stripped of all decision-making authority, soon resigned. During the remainder of 1985, Apple continued to encounter problems and laid off one-fifth of its employees while posting its first ever quarterly loss. In addition, Sculley entered into a legal battle with Microsoft's Bill Gates over the introduction of Windows 1.0, which used similar technology to the Mac's GUI. Gates eventually signed a document that in effect ensured that Microsoft would not use Mac technology in Windows 1.0 but claimed no such promises for any later versions of Windows. Essentially, Apple had lost the exclusive right to use its own GUI.

Despite these setbacks, Apple kept bringing innovative products to the market, realizing that innovation would have to be the company's strategy against big companies like IBM and Microsoft, especially since Microsoft had made its technology available to any PC company that wanted to incorporate it into their own hardware components. In contrast, Apple was well-known for closely guarding the secrets behind its own technology. In 1987, Apple released a revamped Macintosh computer; like the Apple II, this second version was a phenomenal success. This computer was easy to use, making it a favorite at schools and in homes. In addition, the second Macintosh had excellent graphics capabilities. However, by 1990, PCs with Microsoft software had flooded the market and Windows technology was far more prevalent than Mac technology because Microsoft had licensed its software for use on computers built by many different companies.

In 1991, Apple released its first-generation notebook computer, the PowerBook, which was successful. In the meantime, Sculley began to push for the completion of a project under way to develop a new device called a personal digital assistant (PDA). With Sculley's persistence, Apple's version of the PDA, the Newton, was released to the market in August 1993. However, the Newton did not sell well, partly because it failed to recognize handwriting. Also in 1993, Sculley began to lose interest in Apple's daily operations; in June, the board of directors opted to remove Sculley from the position of CEO. The board chose to place the chief operating officer, Michael Spindler, in the vacated spot. Sculley was given the chance to keep his position as chairman of the board, but he chose to resign from the company altogether a few months later.

Although Spindler was not a personable, accessible leader, he did oversee Apple's development of several important products. First, in 1994, Apple released the PowerMac family of PCs, the first Macs to incorporate the PowerPC chip, a very fast processor co-developed with Motorola and IBM. For the first time since Intel technology had become prevalent, Apple could compete with, and sometimes even surpass, Intel in the area of processor speed. Spindler also made a somewhat halfhearted attempt to license the Macintosh operating system (Mac OS) to other companies. However, very few companies ever chose to license the Mac OS because many felt the licensing agreements were far too restrictive. By 1995, Apple had bigger problems, including $1 billion in back orders and insufficient parts to build those machines. And worse, in the late summer of 1995, Microsoft released its infamous Windows '95 version, which was well suited to compete with the strengths of the Mac OS. During the winter of 1995–96, Apple made some misguided judgments concerning its product line and as a result posted a loss for that quarter. In January 1996, Apple asked Spindler to resign and chose Gil Amelio, former president of National Semiconductor, to take his place.

During his first 100 days in office, Amelio announced many sweeping changes for the company. He split Apple into seven distinct divisions, each responsible for its own profit or loss, and he tried to better inform the developers and consumers of Apple's products and projects. Although Apple announced a staggering first-quarter loss of $740 million in 1996, the company brought down its losses to $33 million quarter two, an achievement that financial experts had not imagined Apple could accomplish. And in the third quarter, Apple again beat the best estimates, reporting a $30 million profit. At the end of 1996, the company astonished the industry when it announced that it planned to acquire NeXT, the company Steve Jobs had founded upon his resignation from Apple in 1985; Jobs was to be rehired by Apple as part of the acquisition. The acquisition was chosen in order to control NeXTstep, the basis Apple planned to use for its next-generation operating system, Rhapsody. During the summer of 1997, after announcing another multimillion-dollar quarterly loss, Apple determined that Gil Amelio had made many significant improvements in Apple's operations but had done all he could. No permanent replacement was announced, but Fred Anderson, chief financial officer, was placed in charge of daily operations; Jobs was also given an expanded role in the company.

Jobs's "expanded role" soon became more clear in terms of his responsibilities—Apple had no CEO, stock prices were at a five-year low, and important decisions needed to be made. Jobs soon began to be referred to as "interim CEO," and 1997 proved to be a landmark year for his company. MacWorld Boston was held in August, and Jobs was the keynote speaker. He used that event to make several significant announcements that would turn Apple around: there would be an almost entirely new board of directors, an aggressive advertising campaign, and an alliance with Microsoft. Microsoft received $150 million in Apple stock, Apple would have a five-year patent cross-license, and the old legal battle between the two companies would finally be resolved. As part of the resolution to the legal dispute, Microsoft paid an undisclosed amount to Apple to quiet the allegations that it had stolen Apple's intellectual property (the Mac GUI) and agreed to make Windows '98 available to Mac users by year's end. Jobs also effectively ended Apple's licensing agreements with other companies, buying out all but one, with the understanding that that company would serve only the low-end market for computers (under $1,000). At a late-1997 press conference, Jobs announced that Apple would begin selling direct to consumers over the Web and by phone. Within a week, the Apple store was the third largest e-commerce site on the Web.

Jobs continued to make several changes during 1998, a year in which Apple reported a profit in all four quarters. Apple's stock price was on the rise, and the company had released the iMac, an all-new design for the Macintosh that was meant to serve the lower-end consumer market. The computer had more than enough processing capabilities than most consumers would ever need and was priced affordably. In the fall of that year, the iMac was the best-selling computer in the United States. Apple followed up that success by introducing the iBook in 1999, the portable counterpart to the iMac, a laptop meant to be stylish, affordable, and powerful. Throughout 1999, Apple's stock continued to soar; in the fall it reached a high in the upper $70s.

In early 2000, Jobs announced that he was now permanent CEO of Apple. The remainder of that year was a slow one for Apple and for the rest of the computer industry. As a result, Apple reported its first quarterly loss in three years. In late 2000, the company cut prices across the board; then, in early 2001, it released a new set of PowerMacs with optical drives that let consumers both listen to and burn CDs as well as both read and write to DVDs as well. In May 2001, Jobs announced that Apple would open several retail stores that would sell Apple products as well as third-party products, including MP3 players, digital cameras, and digital video cameras.

In October 2001, Apple released its first noncomputer product in years, the iPod. This small machine was a portable MP3 player that stored songs on a hard drive and could be taken anywhere. Apple took quite a risk in pricing the small machine at a premium, but the company felt that consumers would be willing to pay more for the unique style, design, and technology.

Over the next few years, Apple made adjustments and additions to its product line, on both the software and hardware sides. Although the latter half of 2002 was a poor time for the entire economy as a whole, Apple did well, with net earnings of $65 million. The company's other products sold well and also enjoyed success, but it was the iPod that would revolutionize the company and the industry. In 2003, when the company released iTunes, the online retail store where consumers could purchase individual songs legally, the success of the venture skyrocketed. The technology was available only for Macs at first but had since become available for PC users as well. By July 2004, 100 million songs had been sold and iTunes had a 70 percent market share among all legal online music download services. Apple's success continued to grow, largely thanks to the iPod and iTunes.

By 2005, Jobs's leadership had placed Apple at the forefront of the MP3 player industry and had established the company as a player once again in the computer industry. From the moment Jobs returned to Apple, he had idea after idea for how to improve the company and turn its performance around. He not only consistently pushed for innovative new ideas and products but also enforced several structural changes, including ridding the company of unprofitable segments and divisions. This blended his leadership style, which epitomized the spirit and standards on which Apple was founded, with the business discipline the younger Jobs had lacked. Jobs also credited Apple's success to its skilled management team, which included Peter Oppenheimer and Timothy Cook.

Having started with Apple in 1996 as controller for the Americas, Peter Oppenheimer had become senior vice president and chief financial officer. He was promoted to these positions after less than two years, due to his extensive experience in business and finance. Oppenheimer supervised the controller, treasury, investor relations, tax, information systems, internal audit, corporate development, and human resources departments. He reported to the CEO and helped return a healthy fiscal discipline to the company. Timothy D. Cook was Apple's executive vice president of worldwide sales and operations. Cook, who also reported to the CEO, managed Apple's supply chain, sales activities, and service and support in all markets and countries. His position was accountable for maintaining Apple's flexibility in serving more demanding consumers. Cook had worked first for IBM and then for Compaq, gaining extensive experience in technological industries. While Jobs provided the vision for the organization, Oppenheimer, Cook, and the other members of the executive staff and the board of directors were responsible for ensuring that all operations of Apple ran efficiently and smoothly. Together they worked to ensure that Apple could continue to be a vital, innovative company in the face of a very competitive environment.

APPLE'S SITUATION IN 2008

In its fiscal 2008 third quarter ending June 28, Apple reported the best third quarter in the company's history, with revenues of $7.646 billion, up from $5.41 billion for the same quarter the previous year, and a net quarterly profit of $1.07 billion, up from $818 million. Apple shipped a record 2,496,000 Macintosh units (up 41 percent from the same quarter the previous year) and 11,011,000 iPods (up 12 percent from the same quarter the previous year). But the company's gross margin for the 2008 third-quarter was only 34.8 percent, down from 36.9 percent the previous year, and the company's stock price dropped by more than 10 percent, to below $155, in response to Apple's statement that it expected the company's gross margin to fall to 31 percent in the 2008 fourth quarter due to a future product transition. Apple's financial performance for fiscal years 2005–2007 is shown in Exhibit 1.

Exhibit 1 Financial Performance for Apple, Fiscal Years 2005–2007 (in millions, except share amounts, employees, and contractors)

	FY 2007	FY 2006	FY 2005
Income statement data			
Net sales			
Domestic	$14,128	$11,486	$ 8,334
International	9,878	7,829	5,597
Total net sales	24,006	19,315	13,931
Cost of sales	15,852	13,717	9,889
Research and development	782	712	535
Selling, general, and administrative	2,963	2,433	1,864
Total operating expenses	3,745	3,145	2,399
Operating income	4,409	2,453	1,643
Other income and expense	599	365	165
Income before provision for income taxes	5,008	2,818	1,808
Provision for income taxes	1,512	829	480
Net income	$3,496	$1,989	$1,328
Earnings per common share—diluted	$3.93	$2.27	$1.55
Shares used in computing earnings per share—diluted (in thousands)	889,292	877,526	856,878
Balance sheet data as of September of year			
Cash, cash equivalents, and short-term investments	$15,386	$10,110	$ 8,261
Accounts receivable, net	1,637	1,252	895
Inventories	346	270	165
Property, plant, and equipment, net	1,832	1,281	817
Total assets	25,347	17,205	11,516
Current liabilities	9,299	6,443	3,487
Noncurrent liabilities	1,516	778	601
Shareholders' equity	$14,532	$ 9,984	$ 7,428
Other data			
Regular employees	21,550	17,787	14,806
Temporary employees and contractors	2,116	2,399	2,020
International net sales as a percentage of total net sales	41%	41%	40%
Gross margin as a percentage of net sales	34%	29%	29%
R&D as a percentage of net sales	3%	4%	4%

Source: From Apple Investor Relations, http://media.corporate-ir.net/media_files/irol/10/107357/AAPL_3YR_Q407.pdf (accessed July 13, 2008).

According to Apple, the company's "business strategy leverages its ability, through the design and development of its own operating system, hardware, and many software applications and technologies, to bring to its customers around the world compelling new products and solutions with superior ease-of-use, seamless integration, and innovative industrial design."[1] Most of the actions Apple had taken over its history were consistent with its underlying philosophy on innovation. Since 2002, Apple had determined that the digital electronics market was converging with the computer market and that consumers would begin to demand more synchronization and harmony between the two. That belief had led Apple to release the iPod and iTunes, and more recently the iPhone and the App Store, as well as to improve the software and available options on its computers.

Apple managed its businesses largely on a geographic basis. Its primary geographic segments included the Americas (North America and South America); Europe, Africa, and the Middle East; and Japan. It also had a Retail division that operated the Apple-owned stores in the United States, Italy, Japan, Canada, and the United Kingdom. The company's primary product lines were Macintosh products (including desktops and portables), iPods, iPhones, iTunes (including other music-related products and services), peripherals (including other hardware), and software, service, and other sales.

In fiscal year 2007, Apple had more than $24 billion in sales, with about $10.3 billion of that from sales of Macintosh computers and approximately $8 billion from iPod sales—see Exhibit 2. Apple's unit sales for the same fiscal year, broken down by product, revealed that approximately 7 million Mac units were sold in 2007, while approximately 51.6 million iPods (all types) and approximately 1.3 million iPhones were sold over the same period.

One other impressive feature of Apple's financial statements was that although the company had some minimal long-term debt in recent years, in February 2004 it retired the $300 million of outstanding debt (unsecured notes) it held, resulting in reporting long-term liabilities of $0. In retiring this debt, Apple did not deprive key operating areas of the necessary levels of funding and much of Apple's operating budget was poured into research and development. These investments were consistent with the company's philosophy that its continued achievement would depend heavily on research and development, innovative products and services, and competitive prices. Perhaps even more important, Apple's investments were intended to convince investors and consumers that the company offered a real advantage over the abundant competition in personal computers, MP3 players, and mobile communications.

Heading into the fourth quarter of 2008, Apple had much to be excited about. Besides the company just having reported record revenues and Mac sales, Apple's new iPhone 3G was receiving rave reviews from many analysts. The company had quickly recovered from the worldwide crash of the computer servers used to activate the phones, allowing Apple to sell more than 1 million phones over the launch weekend. In recognition of the company's competence in design, the Industrial Designers Society of America, sponsor of the 2008 Industrial Design Excellence Awards, presented gold awards to the iPhone, MacBook Air, and Apple Wireless Keyboard, while it gave the iMac a silver award.

However, Apple also faced some significant challenges in its core personal computer and digital music player businesses. In July 2008, the struggling U.S. economy was on the verge of slipping into a recession. While Apple's international sales continued to grow, the United States remained the company's single largest revenue source. Further, analysts were concerned that the slumping U.S. economy would significantly reduce back-to-school spending (traditionally a key revenue source for Apple's computer business) in the fall of 2008. Additionally, several large, well-funded competitors had made significant investments to enter the online digital media distribution channel, which was becoming increasingly crowded. For example, Amazon.com had begun to offer digital music downloads as well as movie and television show downloads through its Amazon Unbox service and had developed a service to provide live video downloads. Finally, while iPods had been a significant portion of Apple's revenue, they were coming under increasing pressure from competitors and from mobile phones that included MP3 players.

Exhibit 2 Apple's Net Sales by Operating Segment, Net Sales by Product, and Unit Sales by Product, Fiscal Years 2003–2007 ($ in millions)

	2007	2006	2005	2004	2003
Net Sales by Operating Segment					
Americas	$11,596	$9,415	$6,950	$4,019	$3,181
Europe	5,460	4,096	3,073	1,799	1,309
Japan	1,082	1,211	920	677	698
Retail	4,115	3,246	2,350	1,185	621
Other segments [a]	1,753	1,347	998	599	398
Total	$24,006	$19,315	$13,931	$8,279	$6,207
Net Sales by Product					
Desktops [b]	$4,020	$3,319	$3,436	$2,373	$2,475
Portables [c]	6,294	4,056	2,839	2,550	2,016
Total Macintosh	10,314	7,375	6,275	4,923	4,491
iPod	8,305	7,375	4,540	1,306	345
Other music-related products and services [d]	2,496	1,885	899	278	36
Peripherals and other hardware [e]	1,260	1,100	1,126	951	691
Software, service, and other sales [f]	1,508	1,279	1,091	821	644
Total	$24,006	$19,315	$13,931	$8,279	$6,207
Unit Sales by Product					
Desktops [b]	2,714	2,434	2,520	1,625	1,761
Portables [c]	4,337	2,869	2,014	1,665	1,251
Total Macintosh	7,051	5,303	4,534	3,290	3,012
Net sales per Macintosh unit sold [g]	$1,463	$1,391	$1,384	$1,496	$1,491
iPod	51,630	39,409	22,497	4,416	939
Net sales per iPod unit sold [h]	$161	$195	$202	$296	$367
iPhone	1,389				

[a] Other segments include Asia Pacific and FileMaker.

[b] Includes iMac, eMac, Mac mini, Power Mac, and Xserve product lines.

[c] Includes MacBook, MacBook Pro, iBook. and PowerBook product lines.

[d] Consists of iTunes Music Store sales, iPod services, and Apple-branded and third-party iPod accessories.

[e] Includes sales of Apple-branded and third-party displays, wireless connectivity and networking solutions, and other hardware accessories.

[f] Includes sales of Apple-branded operating system, application software, third-party software, AppleCare, and Internet services.

[g] Derived by dividing total Macintosh net sales by total Macintosh unit sales.

[h] Derived by dividing total iPod net sales by total iPod unit sales.

Source: Apple Inc., 10K report filed with the SEC on November 15, 2007.

PERSONAL COMPUTER INDUSTRY

In the second quarter of 2008, the worldwide PC market grew by 16 percent over the second quarter of 2007, to 71.9 million units, with growth led by mobile PCs. In the U.S. market, total shipments grew by only 4.2 percent, with Apple having the highest growth rate, 38.1 percent, from the second quarter of 2007. The PC industry was relatively consolidated. As shown in Exhibit 3, the U.S. market was dominated by five main players, who controlled 79 percent of the market. Internationally, the top five

Exhibit 3 U.S. PC Market Shares Second Quarter 2007 and 2008

Company	Q2 2008	Q2 2007
Dell Inc.	31.9%	27.9%
Hewlett-Packard	25.3	25.8
Apple	8.5	6.4
Acer	8.1	10.6
Toshiba	5.5	5.6
Others	20.7	23.7

Source: www.gartner.com, October 2008.

controlled more than 55.2 percent of the market, and Apple accounted for only 2 percent of international volume. While the PC market had experienced substantial growth over the last decade, IDC, a leading expert, predicted that the market in the United States, as well as the market throughout the world, with the exception of Asia, would experience double-digit growth in terms of unit shipments through 2010 but would then slow down to high-single-digit growth through 2012. However, the dollar value of PC shipments was expected to grow at a rate of only 5–6 percent to reach $354 billion by 2012.[2]

Apple's Computer Operations

Even though Apple's revenues were increasingly coming from noncomputer products, primarily the iPod, the company still saw computers as its core business. Apple's approach of handling every facet of the computer in-house differentiated it from its primary competitors in the PC market but left out many of the synergies that Wintel PC makers benefited from. Many analysts still projected that Apple's greatest opportunity for growth would come from the projected halo effect of iPods and iPhones. That is, consumers were expected to switch to Apple computers after being exposed to the Apple brand through the iPod/iTunes combination or through the iPhone.

Apple's computer product line consisted of several models in various configurations. Its desktop lines included the Mac Pro (aimed at professional and business users); the iMac (targeted toward consumer, educational, and business use); and Mac mini (made specifically for consumer use). Apple had three notebook product lines as well: MacBook Pro (for professional and advanced consumer users), the MacBook (designed for education users and consumers), and the MacBook Air (designed for professional and consumer users). In both the desktop and notebook lines, the "Power" products were higher-end and offered more computing power at a premium price. The other models were lower on the price scale but still priced high relative to Wintel sellers.

The MacBook Air was Apple's most recent notebook introduction. The MacBook Air was designed to target users who valued both portability and power. The notebook featured a 13.3-inch screen, a full-size keyboard, a built-in video camera, and cutting-edge wireless connectivity. This sleek notebook was only 0.76 inches at its maximum height when closed and weighed only three pounds. The MacBook Air had won critical acclaim for both its design and its ease of use, and was one of the products helping Apple gain ground in the competitive computer industry.

Competitors in the PC Market

Dell Dell posted revenues of $61.1 billion for the fiscal year ending February 1, 2008. Dell's revenues had been consistently growing, and this trend was expected to continue. Roughly 32 percent of Dell's revenues came from sales of desktop PCs (see Exhibit 4). These PCs ranged from low-end bargain desktops to high-end gaming setups with the latest hardware and software. However, competition in the desktop market was lowering the profitability of desktop sales. Dell, a company that attempted to be a low-cost provider through supply chain and distribution logistics, was beginning to see a shift in consumer demand toward mobility products: laptops/notebooks, MP3 players, and PDAs. Dell's notebook computers, like its desktops, ranged from low-end, low-priced models to state-of-the-art, high-priced models. This segment showed promising revenue growth for Dell. The company also marketed peripherals such as printers, TVs, GPS devices, and cameras in an effort to supply a broader array of customers' needs for electronic products.

Hewlett-Packard Hewlett-Packard's Personal Systems Group (PSG) accounted for about 35 percent of the company's revenues in fiscal year 2007. Imaging and various services accounted for the second largest percentage of the company's revenues, at 27 percent. From fiscal year 2006 to fiscal year 2007, the PSG experienced double-digit revenue growth and a 28 percent increase in unit volume sales. HP attributed the growth to increased sales of notebooks and

Exhibit 4 Dell's Revenues by Product Category (% of total revenues)

Product Category	Fiscal Year Ended February 1, 2008	Fiscal Year Ended February 2, 2007
Desktop PCs	32%	34%
Mobility products (notebooks etc.)	28	27
Software and peripherals	16	16
Servers and networking hardware	11	10
Professional consulting and support services	9	9
Storage products	4	4
Totals	100%	100%

Source: Based on information in Dell's 10-K report filed on March 31, 2008, http://ccbn.10kwizard.com/csv.php/5571911.xls?action=showtablexlsall&ipage=5571911&cik=826083 (accessed July 13, 2008).

sales in emerging markets. The group provided half of the company's net revenue growth from 2003 to 2004; however, earnings from the division were only 0.9 percent of net revenues ($210 million earnings on $24.6 billion in net revenues). Overall revenue growth in the PSG broke down as shown in Exhibit 5.

The desktop and notebook lines were the key growth areas for Hewlett-Packard. At one point, HP offered a branded version of Apple's iPod, but that relationship ended because the partnership wasn't helping HP as much as had been hoped. HP then moved to Microsoft-compatible devices but did not develop its own product for this market. Like Dell, HP offered desktops and notebooks in various configurations, with prices determined by the features offered and hardware contained in the systems. HP also offered peripherals such as televisions and related media devices, and was well-known in the imaging and printer markets.

Exhibit 5 Hewlett-Packard Personal Systems Group, Net Revenue ($ in millions)

Product	2007	2006	2005
Notebooks	$17,642	$12,000	$9,763
Desktop PCs	15,850	14,613	14,406
Workstations	1,721	1,368	1,195
Handhelds	490	620	836
Other	706	565	541
Total	$36,409	$29,166	$26,741

Source: Based on information in Hewlett-Packard's fiscal year 2007 10-K report, http://media.corporate-ir.net/media_files/irol/71/71087/AR2007/pdfs/hp_annual_report_2007.pdf (accessed July 13, 2008).

Acer Acer, a multinational manufacturer based in Taiwan, was founded in 1976 as Multitech, with 11 employees. In 1979, Acer designed the first mass-produced computer for export from Taiwan; in 1985, it founded Taiwan's first and largest franchised retail computer chain. The company was renamed Acer in 1987, and a decade later it purchased the mobile PC division of Texas Instruments. By 2008, Acer was one of the leading computer manufacturers in the world. In fiscal year 2007, which ended December 31, Acer's consolidated revenues rose by 25 percent from the previous year, to $14.07 billion, while operating income increased by 30 percent, to $310.63 million, and global shipments were up over 50 percent. The company's largest and one of its fastest-growing geographic segments was the Europe/Middle East/Africa segment, which accounted for 54.3 percent of the company's PC, desktop, and notebook sales. Acer was one of the fastest-growing vendors in the United States, due in part to its acquisitions of Packard Bell and Gateway. The company based its competitive strategy on its four pillars of success: a winning business model, competitive products, an innovative marketing strategy, and an efficient operation model. The company's PC-centric offering included desktop and mobile PCs, LCD monitors, servers and storage, and high-definition TVs and projectors. The company's distribution of sales is provided in Exhibit 6. Heading into

Exhibit 6 Acer's Segment Sales as a Percentage of Total Revenue

Products	2006	2007
Mobile PCs	60.5%	63.8%
Desktop PCs	15.2	16.1
Displays	18.5	16.0
Others*	5.8	4.1
Total	100%	100%

*Others include servers, projectors, and peripheral products.

Source: Information from Acer's 2007 annual report.

2008, the company expected to be able to continue to grow unit total notebook shipments by 40 percent and total PC unit shipments by more than 30 percent.

PERSONAL MEDIA PLAYER INDUSTRY

The personal electronics industry existed long before the iPod was popular. However, much of the history of the industry was related to the iPod's ancestors: portable music devices. Sony, with its Walkman product line, was one of the early giants in this sector. The first Walkman appeared in 1979 in Japan. The tape player, which notably did not have a record function, was an innovative gamble by Sony's management. After a slow start, sales skyrocketed and music history was made. By 1995, more than 150 million Walkman products had been sold worldwide. The Walkman line eventually included tape- and CD-playing devices.

The history of personal digital assistants (PDAs) reaches back almost as far as the history of portable music players. While Apple is often credited with making and distributing the first true PDA, there were many forerunners to Apple's Newton. Sharp, Toshiba, and Casio, among others, had products whose functions mimicked those included in PDAs. However, Apple's Newton was the first product to successfully bring such functionality into a package for mass marketing.[3]

In more recent years, PDAs had become more and more functional, blurring the line between PDAs and portable computers. Microsoft's specialized edition of Windows for PDAs further blurred this line. PDAs could sync with PC software and hold calendar events, task lists, and even documents. However, despite this increase in functionality, pure PDA sales had been declining since their peak in the early 2000s. According to IDC, sales of PDAs in the fourth quarter of 2007 fell 53.2 percent from the same quarter in 2006. This decline was due not to a lack of demand for portable devices but to a convergence between PDAs and other devices—particularly the cell phone.

The other major consumer electronics product of the past 25 years was the cellular telephone. The first public testing of cell phones was in Chicago in 1977. However, a successful demonstration of cell phone technology had occurred as early as 1973. In 1982, the Federal Communications Commission (FCC) authorized commercial cellular service in the United States. By 1987, demand was so high (more than 1 million users) that the original allocations for bandwidth were no longer sufficient. Changes and improvements were made to the technology, and the FCC allowed broader innovation in the industry. According to the CTIA (which describes itself as an association representing all sectors of wireless communications), there were more than 250 million cell phone users in the United States in 2008, and the Central Intelligence Agency's *2008 World Factbook* reported that there were more than 2.4 billion worldwide.

The past 30 years of consumer electronics history were filled with companies expanding functionality and portability in products. At the same time, personal computers were getting smaller and creeping toward the market that these portable electronics products had historically filled. Apple's foray into the consumer electronics market with its iPod was a perfect example of this movement. While a number of the major computer manufacturers had entered the MP3 player industry, there were more than 100 manufacturers offering digital music players and personal media players (PMP), devices that played video and music. In the United States in 2008, Apple was the undisputed leader of the market. In fact, it was the introduction of the user-friendly iPod in 2001 that spurred growth in the digital music industry. By 2004, sales of digital music players had reached 27.8 million units and the research firm Gartner predicted that more than 150 million units would be shipped in 2010. However, market growth was expected to slow, especially in developed countries, given the number of people who had already purchased the devices and the increasing number of cell phones that had the ability to play digital music and videos.

Apple iPod

In fiscal year 2003, Apple Computer, Inc. reported net revenues of $6.2 billion (up 8.1 percent from 2002) and net income of $69 million. For much of the company's history, Apple had excelled at being the first company to introduce a concept or a new product, but then struggled to maintain control of its market share in that product line. Although Apple didn't introduce the first portable MP3 player

(EigerLabs did in 1998), the iPod, introduced in October 2001, was the first to gain widespread attention and popularity.

When Apple launched its iPod, many critics did not give the product much of a chance for success, as its launch came about one month after the September 11 terrorist attacks and it carried a fairly hefty price tag of $399. However, the success of the iPod had reached such phenomenal proportions that one observer said, "It is now a fashion statement, and any other MP3 player is considered 'Brand X' for many consumers."[4] Industry experts agreed that the iPod's success had revolutionized the portable music industry in a manner similar to the Sony Walkman in 1980.

By June 2005, Apple controlled well over 70 percent of the hard drive MP3 player market and more than 40 percent of the flash memory player market. In July 2008, Apple offered four basic styles in the iPod product line and controlled an estimated 70 percent of the MP3 player market. The four iPod styles were as follows:

- The *iPod Shuffle,* a basic flash-based player with no screen, FM radio, or voice recorder. It came in 1GB and 2GB, and provided up to 12 hours of battery life.
- The *iPod Nano* multimedia player, offered in 4GB (4 hours of video or 1,000 songs) and 8GB (8 hours of video or 2,000 songs) sizes, that used a click wheel interface to navigate the player's controls. It allowed users to view photos and videos as well as to listen to music (in Apple's AAC format). It provided up to 24 hours of music playback and 5 hours of video playback on a single charge.
- The *iPod Classic,* a hard-drive-based click-wheel-controlled multimedia player offered in 80GB and 160GB sizes that, similar to the smaller Nano, played music in Apple's AAC format and showed videos and photos. The 80GB player held up to 20,000 songs or 100 hours of video and provided up to 30 hours of audio playback or 5 hours of video playback on a single charge. The 160GB player held 40,000 songs or 200 hours of video and provided up to 40 hours of audio playback or 7 hours of video playback on a single charge.
- The *iPod Touch,* a multimedia flash-based player controlled though an innovative touch screen interface. It was offered in 8GB (1,750 songs, 10 hours of video), 16GB (3,500 songs, 20 hours of video) and 32GB (7,000 songs, 40 hours of video) sizes, and provided up to 22 hours of music playback and 5 hours of video playback on a single charge. This multimedia player featured a wide 3.5 inch-screen and built-in Wi-Fi, which allowed users to connect to the Internet and access e-mail, buy music from the iTunes store, and surf the Web from wireless hotspots. Touch users also had access to maps, the weather, and stocks, and the ability to write notes to themselves. The Touch featured an accelerometer that detected when the Touch rotated and automatically changed the display from portrait to landscape.

While each new version of the iPod offered innovative technology, the new product introductions were not without their challenges. The original iPods were criticized for short battery life and eventually led to a class action lawsuit against Apple, with users claiming that Apple had misrepresented the life of the rechargeable battery used in the iPod. While Apple denied this claim, the company offered a battery replacement service for $99.00 and offered to settle the class action suit in June 2005, offering purchasers of first-, second-, and third-generation iPods an extended warranty and a $50 voucher. Apple also experienced problems with the launch of the Nano in 2005, with customers complaining about the device freezing, and the ease with which the device (especially the screen) could be scratched or would stop functioning. Apple offered a repair and replacement service for these devices, but it was expected to face a class action suit as a result of these problems, similar to the one filed over the battery life problem.

Regardless of these challenges, a 2007 customer survey by *PC Magazine* showed that Apple iPods ranked significantly higher than other brands in terms of overall quality, sound quality, ease of use, and overall reliability (see Exhibit 7). By the end of 2005, many iPod fans were eagerly awaiting the next version of the iPod, and rivals were striving to take a bite out of Apple's market share.

iTunes

Aside from the iPod's ease of use, one of the primary factors that contributed to the popularity of the iPod was Apple's iPod/iTunes combination. In fact,

Exhibit 7 Comparative Customer Satisfaction Scores for MP3 Players—2007 *PC Magazine* Reader Survey

MP3 Players	Overall	Sound Quality	Ease of Use	Reliability
Apple	8.3	8.7	8.6	8.3
Microsoft	8.1	8.7	8.3	8.2
Creative	7.8	8.4	7.5	8.1
Archos	7.6	8.1	7.6	8.0
iRiver	7.6	8.4	7.2	8.1
Toshiba	7.6	8.5	8.1	8.0
SanDisk	7.5	8.0	7.5	7.9
Samsung	7.4	8.0	7.5	7.9
Sony	7.3	8.0	7.4	7.8
Industry average*	7.4	8.1	7.6	7.8

*Includes scores from Dell, Rio, Panasonic, Philips and RCA as well. The maximum possible score was 10.0.

Source: Based on a *PC Magazine* customer survey, October 31, 2007, www.pcmag.com.

despite the acclaim that had been heaped on it, many industry observers believed that the iPod would not have achieved its dominant position without iTunes

Apple first released the iTunes digital music management software for Macintosh computers in 2001. It was innovative but not alone. Originally, the software was intended to allow users to store their digital (CD) music to their computer hard drives and make the content easily accessible. As features such as the ability to burn custom CDs were added to the software, iTunes became more and more useful to consumers.

When the iPod was released in 2001, iTunes was quickly adjusted to allow for syncing between the music management software and the new music player. This interface made it easy for consumers to move content from their computer to their iPod, an essential part of the product value of the iPod. While the iTunes software was a key component in Apple's strategy, it would not have a significant impact on iPod sales until the iTunes fourth edition was released in April 2003.

With the release of the fourth edition, Steve Jobs announced that he had reached a deal with the five major music labels to sell their content in a copy-protected form from the iTunes Music Store on the Internet, and the world took notice. It marked the first time that such a large library of popular music was available in one place via a simple method. Jobs was able to negotiate the agreement with the labels for two main reasons. First, the labels were eager to offer a legitimate online source for their music that would reduce the flow of pirated music. Second, the music Apple provided from the iTunes Music Store was compressed using Apple's proprietary Advanced Audio Coding (AAC) and the music was protected with Apple's Fairplay Digital Rights Management system, one of the strongest in the country.

In October 2003, a version of iTunes, including the iTunes Music Store, was released for Windows users. This immediately opened up Apple's music store to millions of users who had previously been shut out. By October 2005 Apple had introduced a new version of iTunes that sold not only music but video as well. This version of iTunes was released in conjunction with Apple's video iPod. As in the original launch of iTunes, Apple formed partnerships with major networks such as ABC, NBC, ESPN, and Disney to make content such as television shows, sports programming, news, and children's shows available in a secure, encoded format.

In 2008, iTunes allowed customers not only to purchase music, videos, movies, and television shows that could be played on any of the iPods (with the exception of the Shuffle and the iPhone) but also to rent movies that could be played on the Apple devices. Apple advertised that with a catalog of more than 8 million songs, and with more than 5 billion songs downloaded from the iTunes store since its introduction in 2001, iTunes was the number one music retailer in the United States. Additionally, Apple advertised iTunes as the world's most popular online movie store, with customers purchasing and renting more than 50,000 movies a day.

COMPETITION IN THE MP3 PLAYER INDUSTRY

More than 100 companies manufactured MP3 players in 2008, but only 4 of them legitimately claimed real importance in this market: Apple, Creative, SanDisk, and Microsoft.

A looming recession in North America and a maturing market (analysts estimated that as many as 84 percent of the U.S. market currently owned a cell phone) were taking a toll on U.S. sales. The NPD Group estimated that shipments in the first quarter of 2008 were down 22 percent from the first quarter of 2007. However, worldwide shipments of cell phones grew 14 percent year-over-year in the first quarter of 2008. The growth rate was higher than at any time in 2007, with nearly 282 million cell phones shipping in the first quarter of 2008, compared to 247.2 million in the same quarter of 2007.

The MP3 market was clearly dominated by Apple, with it closest rival, SanDisk, capturing only 10 percent of the market (see Exhibit 8). The leading companies in the industry realized that their continued success depended not only on how well they could satisfy their current customers but also on their ability to attract new customers. Research indicated that most buyers based their choice of player on song capacity, multimedia capabilities, unit battery life, physical size and weight, and ease of use. Apple's success had proved that many consumers were willing to pay a premium for some perceived benefit, whether it was higher quality, more technological sophistication, or greater ease of use. Flash-based players were becoming increasingly popular with consumers, as were touch screens and Bluetooth connectivity. However, as the market matured, price was becoming an increasingly important factor in consumer decisions.

Exhibit 8 MP3 Player Market Shares in Units, Q1 2007 vs. Q1 2008

	Q1 2007	Q1 2008
Apple	72	71
SanDisk	10	11
Creative	4	2
Microsoft	3	4

Source: NPD Group, May 12, 2008.

Creative

Creative Labs (Creative) first became famous for its Sound Blaster sound cards, which set the standard in PC audio in 1989. Since that time, Creative had been an industry leader in PC audio technology and had built a large user base and strong brand name in this area. Leveraging this position, Creative offered the MP3 industry's broadest and most diverse product line:

- The Zen, a credit-card-sized multimedia flash-based player offered in sizes from 2GB to 32GB that featured a 2.5-inch screen and allowed users to listen to music in Apple's AAC format as well as MP3 and WMA formats; to view video, including movies rented from online services; and to view photos. This innovative product was rated as one of the 100 best products of 2008 by *PC World.*
- The Zen Stone line, which included the Zen Stone, the Zen Stone with Speaker, the Zen Stone Plus, and the Zen Stone Plus with Speaker. The Zen Stone line included flash-based players, from 1GB to 4GB, that were positioned to compete against Apple's iPod Shuffle. The most basic player, the Zen Stone, was a 1GB player that did not have a screen but was offered in six colors and provided 10 hours of playback on one charge. The Zen Stone with Speaker was offered in 1GB and 2GB sizes and offered a battery life superior to that of the Zen Stone while also offering an external speaker so the device could be used without earphones. The Zen Stone Plus, offered in 2GB and 4GB sizes, had significantly more features, including a small screen, an FM radio, a voice recorder, a clock, and a stopwatch. The 2GB version provided 9.5 hours of playback per charge, while the 4GB offered 12 hours. The Zen Stone Plus with Speaker was essentially identical to the Zen Stone Plus, with the addition of an external speaker and a longer battery life (of up to 20 hours).

Creative was acknowledged as one of the leaders in innovation in the industry, having won the prestigious Consumer Electronics Show's Best of CES Award three years in a row with its Zen Portable Media Center in 2004, the Zen Microphoto in 2005, and the Zen Vision: M in 2006. In 2008, Creative introduced the Zen X-Fi (8GB), which used Creative's proprietary X-Fi Xtreme Fidelity Audio technology to enhance sound quality. This multimedia player featured a built-in speaker, a memory expansion slot, an FM radio, and voice recorder; also, it allowed users to watch movies, view photos, and play music in Apple's AAC format as well as in MP3 and the Windows WMA format. A significant edition to the X-Fi line was the Zen X-Fi with wireless, available in both 16GB and 32GB, which allowed users to stream music and photos as part of a home network and include Yahoo Messenger and Windows Live Messenger to allow users to stay in touch with their friends on the go.

In Creative's fiscal year ending June 30, 2008, the company reported an operating loss of $61 million but a net income of $28 million due to a $100 million payment from Apple for use of the Zen patent. This compared to an operating loss of $145 million in fiscal year 2006 and loss in net income of $126 million. The struggling company was voluntarily delisted from the NASDAQ stock exchange in 2007, and in March 2008 agreed to sell and lease-back its headquarters building for $250 million in an effort to increase cash flows.

iRiver

iRiver Inc. was owned by Reigncom Ltd., based in South Korea. The company entered the digital music player market relatively early and offered a wide variety of MP3 players worldwide. The brand was especially strong in Korea, where it controlled more than 50 percent of the Korean MP3 player market at one time. However, in 2008 iRiver only offered four styles of players in the U.S. market: the E100, the iRiver Clix, the T60, and the L Series.

Leading the company's product line was the popular and critically acclaimed iRiver Clix, which had won multiple awards, such as an Editor's Choice Award and a World Class Award from *PC World,* and was featured as one of *PC World*'s Top 100 Products of the Year for 2006. *Consumer Reports* (a leading consumer advocate magazine that regularly rated and ranked products) rated the Clix as its top flash player as of April 1, 2007, placing it above players from Apple and SanDisk, among other manufacturers. In 2008, iRiver offered the second-generation Clix in 2GB, 4GB, and 8GB models. The Clix GEN2 offered 24 hours of battery life; played music, videos, and photos; supported subscription music services; and featured a built-in digital FM tuner.

The iRiver T60 was a relatively basic flash-based player that was offered in 1GB, 2GB, and 4GB sizes. The T60 series played music files (including MP3, WMA, and OMG) and featured a small screen, an FM tuner and recorder, and a voice recorder. The e100 flash-based player was launched in April 2008 and was offered in 4GB and 8GB sizes. This multimedia player featured a sleek, sophisticated design, high-quality playback, an FM radio, and a voice recorder, and offered up to 5 hours of video playback and up to 18 hours of audio. T-10 was a flash-based, ultraportable digital music player that, depending on its size, held up to 64 hours of music. The player was offered in 2GB ($149.99), 1GB ($119.99), and 512MB ($99.99) sizes and featured an FM tuner and recorder, a color display, and up to 45 hours of battery life. While the player did not support video or photos, it did support subscription music services and audio content from Audible.com. The iRiver offerings were rounded out by the iRiver Lplayer. The Lplayer was offered in both 4GB and 8GB sizes and resembled a smaller version of the Clix. The Lplayer played audio and video files, and featured high-quality graphics, touch screen navigation, FM radio and recording, and voice recording.

Microsoft

Microsoft Corporation, one of the best known companies in the world, was a late entrant into the MP3 player market, not releasing its Zune brand until November 2006. In 2008, the Zune flash-based players were offered in 4GB and 8GB sizes, and the Zune hard-disk players came in 30GB and 80GB sizes. The Zune flash-based players played both audio and video files and featured a 1.8-inch glass screen, the ability to wirelessly sync music with the user's home network, a built-in FM radio, and access to the Zune Marketplace, an online store that was Microsoft's answer to the iTunes store. The Zune could also be plugged into an Xbox 360 to customize the sound track of games played on the system. The 80GB player offered all of the features of the flash-based players but also offered a 3.2-inch screen. The larger player held up to 20,000 songs, 25,000 pictures, or 250 hours of video. One of the primary distinguishing characteristics of the Zune was its wireless connectivity, which allowed users to share music and photos with other users within 30 feet. A user who received "beamed" songs could listen to the song three times before the Zune's built-in digital rights management (DRM) software prohibited access to the song. Photos had no such limitation. To highlight the song-sharing capability of the Zune, Microsoft marketed the product with the tag line "Welcome to the Social."

Microsoft viewed the Zune's networking feature as a critical element of its strategy for the Zune brand. According to J. Allard, who was charged with overseeing the development of the Zune, Microsoft intended to place this player, and future Zune products, at the center of an "ecosystem" that "helps bring artists closer to their audience and helps people find new music and develop social connections."[5] To further support the ecosystem, Microsoft enlisted more than 100 partners to aid in product development, to offer accessories for the Zune, and to provide content on the Zune Marketplace. Users could access the Zune Marketplace through the software included with the Zune. At the Zune Marketplace, they could purchase accessories for their Zune or select from more than 2 million songs, which they could buy outright or access through an "all you can eat" subscription service known as Zune Pass. For $14.95 a month, the Zune Pass allowed users to download as many songs as they wanted from the Zune Marketplace, but once the subscription expired, users could no longer access the downloaded songs.

SanDisk

Like Microsoft, SanDisk was a relatively new entrant in the MP3 player industry. SanDisk was founded in 1988 and headquartered in Milpitas, California. The company was the leading worldwide supplier of innovative flash memory storage products and leveraged this market position when it integrated forward and shipped its first flash-based players in May 2005. By June 2005, the company had captured 8.9 percent of the flash memory digital music player market.

By July 2008, the company's digital music player portfolio featured more than 8 players. Four of the more notable offerings were the following:

- The *Sansa View,* available in 8GB, 16GB, and 32GB sizes, was introduced in January 2007 and was considered to be the flagship product from SanDisk. The Sansa View players featured a 2.4-inch screen, a built-in FM radio, an expandable memory slot, and a built-in microphone for recording. The 32GB player offered up to 35 hours of audio playback on a single battery charge and could hold up to 48 two-hour movies, 8,000 MP3 songs, or 16,000 photos.
- The *Sansa Connect* MP3 player was a 4GB ($249.99) flash-based player that won two CNET Best of CES Awards in 2007 and was introduced to the U.S. market in March 2007. The player held 1,000 songs and played music, photos, and Internet radio. The highlight of the Sansa Connect was that it was a Wi-Fi-enabled MP3 player that allowed users to connect to their content through any open wireless hot spot. Through a partnership with Yahoo, Sansa Connect users could listen to LAUNCHcast Internet radio and browse Flickr albums and photos. Those users with a Yahoo Music Unlimited subscription could share song recommendations with friends and download tracks and albums.
- The *Sansa Fuze* was a multimedia player that played videos, music, and audiobooks. The Sansa Fuze was available in 2GB, 4GB, and 8GB sizes and featured a digital FM radio, voice recording with a built-in microphone, an expandable memory slot, and up to 24 hours of audio playback on a single battery charge.
- The *Sansa Clip* was a compact, wearable flash-based MP3 player that included a small screen and was offered in 1GB, 2GB, and 4GB capacities. This relatively basic player featured an FM tuner, a voice recorder with a built-in microphone, and up to 15 hours of play time on a single charge.
- The *Sansa Express* MP3 player was a flash-based player introduced in January 2007. The Sansa Express was offered in only a 1GB ($59.99) size. The player held up to 250 songs in MP3 format or 500 in WMA format. The Sansa Express was billed as the first cableless player that connected directly to a user's PC and included a microSD expansion slot as well as an FM tuner with an FM recorder and a microphone for voice recording.

SanDisk was considered by many analysts to be the second strongest competitor in the MP3 player industry and the strongest in the Windows-based segment. SanDisk had made significant strides in the market by offering more features at a lower price than its rivals. For example, the Connect was positioned to compete directly with the iPod Nano, given the Connect's WiFi capabilities, larger screen, expansion slot, and lower price point. The company also attributed its success to aggressive marketing campaigns and retailers who were looking to improve on the razor-thin profit margins Apple allowed its retailers. However, the company was significantly affected by the fierce competition in the MP3 player industry and the volatile flash memory market. In response to falling profits, the company took measures to reduce production costs and operating expenses. Even with this temporary setback, many analysts viewed SanDisk as the leading challenger to Apple and the main rival for Microsoft to overtake in the fiercely competitive Windows-based MP3 player market.

APPLE iPHONE

The iPhone, Apple's Internet-enabled multimedia cellular phone, was considered to be a key product in the future of the company's product portfolio. The first version of the iPhone was released on June 29, 2007. It had a multitouch screen with a virtual keyboard and buttons but a minimal amount of hardware input. The iPhone's functions included those of a camera phone and portable media player (equivalent to the iPod) in addition to text messaging and visual voice mail. It also offered Internet services including e-mail, Web browsing (using access to Apple's Safari Web browser), and local Wi-Fi connectivity. Apple first announced the iPhone on January 9, 2007. The announcement was preceded by rumors and speculations that circulated for several months and was followed by additional rumors of its features until its anticipated release. After its worldwide release, the iPhone was named *Time* magazine's Invention of the Year in 2007.

The iPhone began with Apple CEO Steve Jobs's direction that Apple engineers investigate touch screens. Apple created the device during a secretive and unprecedented collaboration with AT&T Mobility (which was Cingular Wireless at the time of the phone's inception), at a development cost of $150 million by one estimate. During development, the iPhone was code-named Purple 2. The company rejected an early "design by committee" built with Motorola in favor of engineering a custom operating system and interface and building custom hardware. The iPhone went on sale in the United States on June 29, 2007. Apple closed its stores at 2:00 p.m. local time to prepare for the 6:00 p.m. iPhone launch, while hundreds of customers lined up at stores nationwide. Apple sold 270,000 iPhones in the first 30 hours on launch weekend.

On September 5, 2007, the 4GB model was discontinued and the 8GB model price reduced to $399. Those who had purchased an iPhone in the 14-day period before the September 5, 2007, announcement were eligible for a $200 "price protection" rebate from Apple or AT&T. However, it was widely reported that some who bought between the June 29, 2007, launch and the August 22, 2007, price protection kick-in date complained that this was a larger-than-normal price drop for such a relatively short period and accused Apple of unfair pricing. In response to the controversy, on September 6, 2007, Apple CEO Steve Jobs wrote in an open letter to iPhone customers that everyone who purchased an iPhone at the higher price "and who is not receiving a rebate or other consideration," would receive a $100 credit toward the purchase of any product sold in Apple's retail or online stores.

While the cell phone handset industry in the United States was experiencing slowing growth overall, two segments—the smartphone segment and the low-cost handset market—were expected to expand. In the first quarter of 2008, the iPhone controlled 19.2 percent of the smartphone segment, down from 26.7 percent in the fourth quarter of 2007. However, analysts attributed this drop in demand, at least partially, to the impending launch of the iPhone 3G.

The iPhone 3G was released in 70 countries on July 11, 2008, and was available in the United States exclusively on AT&T Mobility with a two-year contract. The new Apple iPhone 3G combined the functionality of a wireless phone and an iPod and allowed users to access the Internet wirelessly at twice the speed of the previous version of the iPhone. Apple's new phone also featured a built-in GPS and, in an effort to increase adoption by corporate users, was compatible with Microsoft Exchange.

Similar to the iTunes/iPod partnership, Apple launched the App Store for the iPhone. The App Store allowed developers to build applications for the iPhone and to offer them either for free or for a fee. On launch day, there were more than 800 applications available. Two hundred of these were available for free, while 90 percent of the applications cost less than $10. By the end of the launch weekend, the App Store reported more than 10 million downloads. To further expand the interconnectivity between its product offerings, including the iPhone, Apple launched its MobileMe service on June 9, 2008. Like Microsoft Exchange, this service delivered push e-mail, contacts, and calendars to applications on the iPhone, iPod touch, Macs, and PCs. However, the launch of MobileMe had not gone smoothly for Apple, leading Apple to post an apology to customers who had lost e-mail access and service as a result of some problems with the new MobileMe Web applications. Despite the June 9, 2008, launch, the problems with MobileMe were still not completely resolved as of July 23, 2008.

The 8GB iPhone 3G was priced at $199, and the 16GB iPhone 3G cost $299. These prices represented a drop of $200 each over the previous generation. However, the consumer data plan for the iPhone 3G cost $30 per month, a price increase of $10. In an interview with technology writer Om Malik, AT&T Mobility president and CEO Ralph de la Vega stated, "The SMS messages are not bundled anymore, and you pay for what you want." The voice plan for the first-generation iPhone included 200 text messages; AT&T currently charged $5 per month for 200 text messages. Several sources, including CNET, Engadget, Gizmodo, *MacWorld, Time,* and Yahoo!, pointed out that this would be an increase of $240 to $360 over the span of the two-year contract, which was greater than the $200 price discount.

Regardless of these price increases, and despite some systemic problems with activations of the iPhone, demand for the iPhone 3G exceeded expectations, with many stores still sold out two weeks after the phone's launch.

THE FUTURE

In assessing Apple's future, most analysts agreed that Apple would undoubtedly continue its well-established track record of introducing innovative, high-quality consumer electronics to the masses. However, many believed that it would be very difficult for Apple to maintain its substantial operating profit margins given increasing competition in its core markets. In a conference call discussing its third-quarter operating results, Apple acknowledged that it expected its operating profit margin to fall from 34.1 percent to 31.5 percent over the next quarter. While Apple offered no details, it attributed this fall in margin at least partially to a product transition that would result in "state-of-the-art products at price points our competitors can't match."[6]

Analysts were also concerned with Steve Jobs's health (he had previously been treated for cancer), Apple's succession plan, falling demand in the personal media player market, and an increasing number of iPhone killers being offered by powerful competitors such as Nokia and Samsung in the mobile phone industry. Most analysts believed that with Jobs at the helm, Apple could overcome the competition and continue to offer innovative market leading products. However, with Apple maintaining strict secrecy regarding its succession plan, it was not clear that the company could continue its success without Jobs, especially if it experienced challenges expanding into new markets as it did in launching its MobileMe service.

Endnotes

[1] Apple Inc., Form 10-K, filed November 15, 2007, p. 36.

[2] Dan Nystedt, "IDC Raises Global PC Shipment Forecast," IDG News Service, June 12, 2008.

[3] See www.snarc.net/pda/pda-treatise.htm (accessed May 27, 2008).

[4] Steve Smith, "iPod's Lessons," *Twice New York* 19, no. 15 (July 26, 2004), p. 12.

[5] Steven Levy, "Trying Apple's Tune," *Newsweek* online, September 17, 2006, www.msnbc.msn.com/id/14866932/site/newsweek (accessed April 10, 2007).

[6] Apple earnings conference call, July 21, 2008, www.apple.com/investor.

CASE

8 Panera Bread Company

Arthur A. Thompson
The University of Alabama

As Panera Bread Company headed into 2007, it was continuing to expand its market presence swiftly. The company's strategic intent was to make great bread broadly available to consumers across the United States. It had opened 155 new company-owned and franchised bakery-cafés in 2006, bringing its total to 1,027 units in 36 states. Plans were in place to open another 170 to 180 café locations in 2007 and to have nearly 2,000 Panera Bread bakery-cafés open by the end of 2010. Management was confident that Panera Bread's attractive menu and the dining ambience of its bakery-cafés provided significant growth opportunity, despite the fiercely competitive nature of the restaurant industry.

Already Panera Bread was widely recognized as the nationwide leader in the specialty bread segment. In 2003, Panera Bread scored the highest level of customer loyalty among quick-casual restaurants, according to a study conducted by TNS Intersearch.[1] J. D. Power and Associates' 2004 restaurant satisfaction study of 55,000 customers ranked Panera Bread highest among quick-service restaurants in the Midwest and Northeast regions of the United States in all categories, which included environment, meal, service, and cost. In 2005, for the fourth consecutive year, Panera Bread was rated among the best of 121 competitors in the Sandleman & Associates national customer satisfaction survey of more than 62,000 consumers. Panera Bread had also won "best of" awards in nearly every market across 36 states.

COMPANY BACKGROUND

In 1981, Louis Kane and Ron Shaich founded a bakery-café enterprise named Au Bon Pain Company Inc. Units were opened in malls, shopping centers, and airports along the East Coast of the United States and internationally throughout the 1980s and 1990s; the company prospered and became the dominant operator within the bakery-café category. In 1993, Au Bon Pain Company purchased Saint Louis Bread Company, a chain of 20 bakery-cafés located in the St. Louis, Missouri, area. Ron Shaich and a team of Au Bon Pain managers then spent considerable time in 1994 and 1995 traveling the country and studying the market for fast-food and quick-service meals. They concluded that many patrons of fast-food chains like McDonald's, Wendy's, Burger King, Subway, Taco Bell, Pizza Hut, and KFC could be attracted to a higher-quality, quick-dining experience. Top management at Au Bon Pain then instituted a comprehensive overhaul of the newly acquired Saint Louis Bread locations, altering the menu and the dining atmosphere. The vision was to create a specialty café anchored by an authentic, fresh-dough artisan bakery and upscale quick-service menu selections. Between 1993 and 1997, average unit volumes at the revamped Saint Louis Bread units increased by 75 percent, and over 100 additional Saint Louis Bread units were opened. In 1997, the Saint Louis Bread bakery-cafés were renamed Panera Bread in all markets outside St. Louis.

By 1998, it was clear that the reconceived Panera Bread units had connected with consumers.

Au Bon Pain management concluded the Panera Bread format had broad market appeal and could be rolled out nationwide. Ron Shaich believed that Panera Bread had the potential to become one of the leading fast-casual restaurant chains in the nation. Shaich also believed that growing Panera Bread into a national chain required significantly more management attention and financial resources than the company could marshal if it continued to pursue expansion of both the Au Bon Pain and Panera Bread chains. He convinced Au Bon Pain's board of directors that the best course of action was for the company to go exclusively with the Panera Bread concept and divest the Au Bon Pain cafés. In August 1998, the company announced the sale of its Au Bon Pain bakery-café division for $73 million in cash to ABP Corporation; the transaction was completed in May 1999. With the sale of the Au Bon Pain division, the company changed its name to Panera Bread Company. The restructured company had 180 Saint Louis Bread and Panera Bread bakery-cafés and a debt-free balance sheet.

Between January 1999 and December 2006, close to 850 additional Panera Bread bakery-cafés were opened, some company-owned and some franchised. Panera Bread reported sales of $829.0 million and net income of $58.8 million in 2006. Sales at franchise-operated Panera Bread bakery-cafés totaled $1.2 billion in 2006. A summary of Panera Bread's recent financial performance is shown in Exhibit 1, and selected operating statistics are given in Exhibit 2.

Exhibit 1 Selected Consolidated Financial Data for Panera Bread, 2002–2006 ($ in millions, except for per share amounts)

	2006	2005	2004	2003	2002
Income Statement Data					
Revenues:					
Bakery-café sales	$666,141	$499,422	$362,121	$265,933	$212,645
Franchise royalties and fees	61,531	54,309	44,449	36,245	27,892
Fresh dough sales to franchisees	101,299	86,544	72,569	61,524	41,688
Total revenues	828,971	640,275	479,139	363,702	282,225
Bakery café expenses:					
Food and paper products	197,182	142,675	101,832	73,885	63,370
Labor	204,956	151,524	110,790	81,152	63,172
Occupancy	48,602	37,389	26,730	18,981	15,408
Other operating expenses	92,176	70,003	51,044	36,804	27,971
Total bakery-café expenses	542,916	401,591	290,396	210,822	169,921
Fresh dough costs of sales to franchisees	85,618	75,036	65,627	54,967	38,432
Depreciation and amortization	44,166	33,011	25,298	18,304	13,794
General and administrative expenses	59,306	46,301	33,338	28,140	24,986
Pre-opening expenses	6,173	3,241	2,642	1,531	1,051
Total costs and expenses	738,179	559,180	417,301	313,764	248,184
Operating profit	90,792	81,095	61,838	49,938	34,041
Interest expense	92	50	18	48	32
Other (income) expense, net	(1,976)	(1,133)	1,065	1,592	467
Provision for income taxes	33,827	29,995	22,175	17,629	12,242
Net income	$ 58,849	$ 52,183	$ 38,430*	$ 30,669	$ 21,300
Earnings per share					
Basic	$1.88	$1.69	$1.28	$1.02	$0.74
Diluted	1.84	1.65	1.25	1.00*	0.71

(Continued)

Exhibit 1 (Continued)

	2006	2005	2004	2003	2002
Weighted average shares outstanding					
Basic	31,313	30,871	30,154	29,733	28,923
Diluted	32,044	31,651	30,768	30,423	29,891
Balance Sheet Data					
Cash and cash equivalents	$ 52,097	$ 24,451	$ 29,639	$ 42,402	$ 29,924
Investments in government securities	20,025	46,308	28,415	9,019	9,149
Current assets	127,618	102,774	58,220	70,871	59,262
Total assets	542,609	437,667	324,672	256,835	195,431
Current liabilities	109,610	86,865	55,705	44,792	32,325
Total liabilities	144,943	120,689	83,309	46,235	32,587
Stockholders' equity	397,666	316,978	241,363	193,805	151,503
Cash Flow Data					
Net cash provided by operating activities	$104,895	$110,628	$ 84,284	$ 73,102	$ 46,323
Net cash used in investing activities	(90,917)	(129,640)	(102,291)	(66,856)	(40,115)
Net cash provided by financing activities	13,668	13,824	5,244	6,232	5,664
Net (decrease) increase in cash and cash equivalents	27,646	(5,188)	(12,763)	12,478	11,872

*After adjustment of $239,000 for cumulative effect of accounting change.

Sources: 2006 10-K report, pp. 36–38; 2005 10-K report, pp. 16–17; 2003 10-K report, pp. 29–31; and company press release, February 8, 2007.

THE PANERA BREAD CONCEPT AND STRATEGY

The driving concept behind Panera Bread was to provide a premium specialty bakery and café experience to urban workers and suburban dwellers. Its artisan sourdough breads made with a craftsman's attention to quality and detail and its award-winning bakery expertise formed the core of the menu offerings. Panera Bread specialized in fresh baked goods, made-to-order sandwiches on freshly baked breads, soups, salads, custom roasted coffees, and other café beverages. Panera's target market was urban workers and suburban dwellers looking for a quick-service meal and a more aesthetically pleasing dining experience than that offered by traditional fast-food restaurants.

In his letter to shareholders in the company's 2005 annual report, Panera chairman and CEO Ron Shaich said:

> We think our continued commitment to providing crave-able food that people trust, served in a warm, community gathering place by associates who make our guests feel comfortable, really matters. When this is rooted in our commitment to the traditions of handcrafted, artisan bread, something special is created. As we say here at Panera, it's our Product, Environment, and Great Service (PEGS) that we count on to deliver our success—year in and year out.

Panera Bread's distinctive menu, signature café design, inviting ambience, operating systems, and unit location strategy allowed it to compete successfully in five submarkets of the food-away-from-home industry: breakfast, lunch, daytime "chill out" (the time between breakfast and lunch and between lunch and dinner when customers visited its bakery-cafés to take a break from their daily activities), light evening fare for eat-in or take-out, and take-home bread. In 2006, Panera began enhancing its menu in ways that would attract more diners during the evening meal hours. Management's long-term objective and strategic intent was to make Panera Bread a nationally recognized brand name and to be the dominant restaurant operator in the specialty bakery-café segment. According to Scott Davis, Panera's senior vice president and chief concept officer, the company was trying to succeed by "being better than the guys across the street" and making the experience of

Exhibit 2 Selected Operating Statistics, Panera Bread Company, 2000–2006

	2006	2005	2004	2003	2002	2001	2000
Revenues at company-operated stores (in millions)	$666.1	$499.4	$362.1	$265.9	$212.6	$157.7	$125.5
Revenues at franchised stores (in millions)	$1,245.5	$1,097.2	$879.1	$711.0	$542.6	$371.7	$199.4
Systemwide store revenues (in millions)	$1,911.6	$1,596.6	$1,241.2	$976.9	$755.2	$529.4	$324.9
Average annualized revenues per company-operated bakery-café (in millions)	$1.967	$1.942	$1.852	$1.830	$1.764	$1.636	$1.473
Average annualized revenues per franchised bakery-café (in millions)	$2.074	$2.016	$1.881	$1.860	$1.872	$1.800	$1.707
Average weekly sales, company-owned cafés	$37,833	$37,348	$35,620	$35,198	$33,924	$31,460	$28,325
Average weekly sales, franchised cafés	$39,894	$38,777	$36,171	$35,777	$35,997	$34,607	$32,832
Comparable bakery-café sales percentage increases*							
Company-owned	3.9%	7.4%	2.9%	1.7%	4.1%	5.8%	8.1%
Franchised	4.1%	8.0%	2.6%	(0.4)%	6.1%	5.8%	10.3%
Systemwide	4.1%	7.8%	2.7%	0.2%	5.5%	5.8%	9.1%
Company-owned bakery-cafés open at year-end	391	311	226	173	132	110	90
Franchised bakery-cafés open at year-end	636	566	515	429	346	259	172
Total bakery-cafés open	1,027	877	741	602	478	369	262

*The percentages for comparable store sales are based on annual changes at stores open at least 18 months.

Sources: Company 10-K reports 2000, 2001, 2003, 2005, and 2006; company press releases, January 4, 2007, and February 8, 2007.

dining at Panera so attractive that customers would be willing to pass by the outlets of other fast-casual restaurant competitors to dine at a nearby Panera Bread bakery-café.[2] Davis maintained that the question about Panera Bread's future was not *if* it would be successful but *by how much.*

Management believed that its concept afforded growth potential in suburban markets sufficient to expand the number of Panera bread locations by 17 percent annually through 2010 (see Exhibits 3 and 4) and to achieve earnings per share growth of 25 percent annually. Panera Bread's growth strategy was to capitalize on Panera's market potential by opening both company-owned and franchised Panera Bread locations as fast as was prudent. So far, franchising had been a key component of the company's efforts to broaden its market penetration. Panera Bread had organized its business around company-owned bakery-café operations, the franchise operations, and fresh dough operations; the fresh bread unit supplied dough to all Panera Bread stores, both company-owned and franchised.

PANERA BREAD'S PRODUCT OFFERINGS AND MENU

Panera Bread's signature product was artisan bread made from four ingredients—water, natural yeast, flour, and salt; no preservatives or chemicals were used. Carefully trained bakers shaped every step of the process, from mixing the ingredients, to kneading the dough, to placing the loaves on hot stone slabs to

Exhibit 3 Areas of High and Low Market Penetration of Panera Bread Bakery-Cafés, 2006

High Penetration Markets			Low Penetration Markets		
Area	Number of Panera Bread Units	Population per Bakery-Café	Area	Number of Panera Bread Units	Population per Bakery-Café
St. Louis	40	67,000	Los Angeles	17	1,183,000
Columbus, OH	19	83,000	Miami	2	1,126,000
Jacksonville	12	98,000	Northern California	10	1,110,000
Omaha	12	101,000	Seattle	5	860,000
Cincinnati	26	108,000	Dallas/Fort Worth	10	590,000
Pittsburgh	25	142,000	Houston	12	335,000
Washington D.C./ Northern Virginia	26	152,000	Philadelphia	25	278,000

Untapped Markets

New York City	Phoenix	Austin
Salt Lake City	Tucson	San Antonio
Memphis	District of Columbia	Green Bay/Appleton
New Orleans	Spokane	Shreveport
Atlantic City	Baton Rouge	Toronto
Albuquerque	Little Rock	Vancouver

Source: Panera Bread management presentation to securities analysts, May 5, 2006.

Exhibit 4 Comparative U.S. Market Penetration of Selected Restaurant Chains, 2006

Restaurant Chain	Number of Locations	Population per Location
Subway	19,965	15,000
McDonald's	13,727	22,000
Starbucks Coffee	7,700	39,000
Applebee's	1,800	166,000
Panera Bread	910	330,000

Note: Management believed that a 17 percent annual rate of expansion of Panera Bread locations through 2010 would result in 1 café per 160,000 people.

Source: Panera Bread management presentation to securities analysts, May 5, 2006.

bake in a traditional European-style stone deck bakery oven. Exhibit 5 shows Panera's lineup of breads.

The Panera Bread menu was designed to provide target customers with products built on the company's bakery expertise, particularly its 20-plus varieties of bread baked fresh throughout the day at each café location. The key menu groups were fresh baked goods, made-to-order sandwiches and salads, soups, light entrées, and café beverages. Exhibit 6 shows a sampling of the items on a typical Panera Bread menu.

The menu offerings were regularly reviewed and revised to sustain the interest of regular customers, satisfy changing consumer preferences, and be responsive to various seasons of the year. The soup lineup, for example, changed seasonally. Product development was focused on providing food that customers would crave and trust to be tasty. New menu items were developed in test kitchens and then introduced in a limited number of the bakery-cafés to determine customer response and verify that preparation and operating procedures resulted in product consistency and high quality standards. If successful, they were then rolled out systemwide. New product rollouts were integrated into periodic or seasonal menu rotations, which Panera referred to as "Celebrations."

Panera recognized in late 2004 that significantly more customers were conscious about eating "good" carbohydrates, prompting the introduction of whole

Exhibit 5 Panera's Lineup of Bread Varieties, 2006

Sourdough
Panera's signature sourdough bread that featured a golden, crackled crust and firm, moderately structured crumb with a satisfying, tangy flavor. *Available in Baguette, Loaf, XL Loaf, Roll and Bread Bowl.*

Asiago Cheese
Chunks of Asiago cheese were added to the standard sourdough recipe and baked right in, with more Asiago cheese sprinkled on top. *Available in Demi and Loaf.*

Focaccia
A traditional Italian flatbread made with Panera's artisan starter dough, olive oil, and chunks of Asiago cheese. *Available in three varieties—Asiago Cheese, Rosemary & Onion and Basil Pesto.*

Nine Grain
Made with cracked whole wheat, rye, corn meal, oats, rice flour, soy grits, barley flakes, millet and flaxseed plus molasses for a semisweet taste. *Available in Loaf.*

Tomato Basil
A sourdough-based bread made with tomatoes and basil, topped with sweet walnut streusel. *Available in XL Loaf.*

Cinnamon Raisin
A light raisin bread with a swirl of cinnamon, sugar and molasses. *Available in Loaf.*

Artisan Sesame Semolina
Made with enriched durum and semolina flours to create a golden yellow crumb, topped with sesame seeds. *Available in Loaf and Miche.*

Artisan Multigrain
Nine grains and sesame, poppy and fennel seeds blended with molasses, topped with rolled oats. *Available in Loaf.*

Artisan French
Made with Panera's artisan starter to create a nutty flavor with a wine-like aroma. *Available in Baguette and Miche.*

Whole Grain
A moist, hearty mixture of whole spelt flour, millet, flaxseed and other wheat flours and grains, sweetened with honey and topped with rolled oats. *Available in loaf, miche and baguette.*

White Whole Grain
A new bread created especially for Panera Kids sandwiches; a sweeter alternative to the Whole Grain bread with a thin, caramelized crust sweetened with honey and molasses. *Available in Loaf.*

French
A classic French bread characterized by a thin, crackly crust, slightly sweet taste and a lighter crumb than our sourdough. *Available in Baguette, Loaf, XL Loaf and Roll.*

Ciabatta
A flat, oval-shaped loaf with a delicate flavor and soft texture; made with Panera's artisan starter and a touch of olive oil. *Available in Loaf.*

Honey Wheat
A mild wheat bread with tastes of honey and molasses; the soft crust and crumb made it great for sandwiches. *Available in Loaf.*

Rye
Special natural leavening, unbleached flour and chopped rye kernels were used to create a delicate rye flavor. *Available in Loaf.*

Sunflower
Made with honey, lemon peel and raw sunflower seeds and topped with sesame and honey-roasted sunflower seeds. *Available in Loaf.*

Artisan Three Seed
The addition of sesame, poppy and fennel seeds created a sweet, nutty, anise-flavored bread. *Available in Demi.*

Artisan Three Cheese
Made with Parmesan, Romano, and Asiago cheeses and durum and semolina flours. *Available in Demi, Loaf and Miche.*

Artisan Stone-Milled Rye
Made with Panera's artisan starter, chopped rye kernels and caraway seeds, topped with more caraway seeds. *Available in Loaf and Miche.*

Artisan Country
Made from artisan starter with a crisp crust and nutty flavor. *Available in loaf, miche and demi.*

Lower-Carb Pumpkin Seed
Made from Panera's artisan starter dough, pumpkin seeds and flax meal to create a subtle, nutty flavor. *Available in Loaf.*

Lower-Carb Italian Herb
Made from Panera's artisan starter dough, roasted garlic, dried herbs and sesame seed topping. *Available in Loaf.*

Source: www.panerabread.com (accessed July 28, 2006).

Exhibit 6 Sample Menu Selections, Panera Bread Company, 2006

Bakery
Loaves of Bread (22 varieties)
Bagels (11 varieties)
Cookies (5 varieties)
Scones (5 varieties)
Cinnamon Rolls Pecan Rolls
Croissants
Coffee Cakes
Muffins (5 varieties)
Artisan and Specialty Pastries (8 varieties)
Brownies (3 varieties)
Mini-Bundt Cakes (3 varieties)

Signature Sandwiches
Pepperblue Steak
Garden Veggie
Tuscan Chicken
Asiago Roast Beef
Italian Combo
Bacon Turkey Bravo
Sierra Turkey
Turkey Romesco
Mediterranean Veggie

Café Sandwiches
Smoked Turkey Breast
Chicken Salad
Tuna Salad
Smoked Ham and Cheese

Hot Panini Sandwiches
Turkey Artichoke
Frontega Chicken
Smokehouse Turkey
Portobello and Mozzarella

Baked Egg Soufflés
Four Cheese
Spinach and Artichoke
Spinach and Bacon

Soups
Broccoli Cheddar
French Onion
Baked Potato
Low Fat Chicken Noodle
Cream of Chicken and Wild Rice
Boston Clam Chowder
Low Fat Vegetarian Garden Vegetable
Low Fat Vegetarian Black Bean
Vegetarian Roasted Red Pepper and Lentil
Tuscan Chicken and Ditalini
Tuscan Vegetable Ditalini

Hand Tossed Salads
Asian Sesame Chicken
Fandango
Greek
Caesar
Grilled Chicken Caesar
Bistro Steak
Classic Café
California Mission Chicken
Fuji Apple Chicken
Strawberry Poppyseed and Chicken
Grilled Salmon Salad

Side Choices
Portion of French Baguette
Portion of Whole Grain Baguette
Kettle-cooked or Baked Chips
Apple

Panera Kids
Grilled Cheese
Peanut Butter and Jelly
Kids Deli

Beverages
Coffee
Hot and Iced Teas
Sodas
Bottled Water
Juice
Organic Milk
Organic Chocolate Milk
Hot Chocolate
Orange Juice
Organic Apple Juice
Espresso
Cappuccino
Lattes
Mango Raspberry Smoothie

Source: Sample menu posted at www.panerabread.com (accessed July 29, 2006).

grain breads. In 2005, several important menu changes were made. Panera introduced a new line of artisan sweet goods made with gourmet European butter, fresh fruit toppings, and appealing fillings; these new artisan pastries represented a significantly higher level of taste and upgraded quality. To expand its breakfast offerings and help boost morning-hour sales, Panera introduced egg soufflés baked in a flaked pastry shell. And, in another health-related move, Panera switched to the use of natural, antibiotic-free chicken in all of its chicken-related sandwiches and salads. During 2006, the chief menu changes involved the addition of light entrées to jump-start dinner appeal; one such menu addition was crispani (a pizzalike topping on a thin crust). In 2006, evening-hour sales represented 20 percent of Panera's business.

PANERA FRESH CATERING

In 2004–2005, Panera Bread introduced a catering program to extend its market reach into the workplace, schools, parties, and gatherings held in homes. Panera saw catering as an opportunity to grow lunch and dinner sales with making capital investments in additional physical facilities. By the end of 2005, catering was generating an additional $80 million in sales for Panera Bread. Management foresaw considerable opportunity for future growth of Panera's catering operation.

MARKETING

Panera's marketing strategy was to compete on the basis of providing an entire dining experience rather than by attracting customers on the basis of price only. The objective was for customers to view dining at Panera as being a good value—meaning high-quality food at reasonable prices—so as to encourage frequent visits. Panera Bread performed extensive market research, including the use of focus groups, to determine customer food and drink preferences and price points. The company tried to grow sales at existing Panera locations through menu development, product merchandising, promotions at everyday prices, and sponsorship of local community charitable events.

Historically, marketing had played only a small role in Panera's success. Brand awareness had been built on customers' satisfaction with their dining experience at Panera and their tendency to share their positive experiences with friends and neighbors. About 85 percent of consumers who were aware that there was a Panera Bread bakery-café in their community or neighborhood had dined at Panera on at least one occasion.[3] The company's marketing research indicated that 57 percent of consumers who had "ever tried" dining at Panera Bread had been customers in the past 30 days. This high proportion of trial customers to repeat customers had convinced management that getting more first-time diners into Panera Bread cafés was a potent way to boost store traffic and average weekly sales per store.

Panera's research also showed that people who dined at Panera Bread very frequently or moderately frequently typically did so for only one part of the day. Yet 81 percent indicated "considerable willingness" to try dining at Panera Bread at other parts of the day.[4]

Franchise-operated bakery-cafés were required to contribute 0.7 percent of their sales to a national advertising fund and 0.4 percent of their sales as a marketing administration fee and were also required to spend 2.0 percent of their sales in their local markets on advertising. Panera contributed similar amounts from company-owned bakery-cafés toward the national advertising fund and marketing administration. The national advertising fund contribution of 0.7 percent had been increased from 0.4 percent starting in 2006. Beginning in fiscal 2006, national advertising fund contributions were raised to 0.7 percent of sales, and Panera could opt to raise the national advertising fund contributions as high as 2.6 percent of sales.

In 2006, Panera Bread's marketing strategy had several elements. One element aimed at raising the quality of awareness about Panera by continuing to feature the caliber and appeal of its breads and baked goods, by hammering the theme "food you crave, food you can trust," and by enhancing the appeal of its bakery-cafés as a neighborhood gathering place. A second marketing initiative was to raise awareness and boost trial of dining at Panera Bread at multiple meal times (breakfast, lunch, "chill out" times, and dinner). Panera avoided hard-sell or in-your-face marketing approaches, preferring instead to employ a range of ways to softly drop the Panera Bread name into the midst of consumers as they moved through their lives and let them "gently collide" with the brand; the idea was to let consumers "discover" Panera Bread and then convert them into loyal customers by providing a very satisfying dining experience. The third marketing initiative was to increase perception of Panera Bread as a viable evening meal option and to drive early trials of Panera for dinner (particularly among existing Panera lunch customers).

Franchise Operations

Opening additional franchised bakery-cafés was a core element of Panera Bread's strategy and management's initiatives to achieve the company's growth targets. Panera Bread did not grant single-unit franchises, so a prospective franchisee could not open just one bakery-café. Rather, Panera Bread's franchising strategy was to enter into franchise agreements that required the franchise developer to open a number of units, typically 15 bakery-cafés in six years. Franchisee candidates had to be well capitalized, have a proven track record as excellent multi-unit restaurant operators, and agree to meet an aggressive development schedule. Applicants had to meet eight stringent criteria to gain consideration for a Panera Bread franchise:

- Experience as a multi-unit restaurant operator.
- Recognition as a top restaurant operator.
- Net worth of $7.5 million.
- Liquid assets of $3 million.
- Infrastructure and resources to meet Panera's development schedule for the market area the franchisee was applying to develop.
- Real estate experience in the market to be developed.
- Total commitment to the development of the Panera Bread brand.
- Cultural fit and a passion for fresh bread.

The franchise agreement typically required the payment of a franchise fee of $35,000 per bakery-café (broken down into $5,000 at the signing of the area development agreement and $30,000 at or before a bakery-café opened) and continuing royalties of 4–5 percent on sales from each bakery-café. Franchise-operated bakery-cafés followed the same standards for in store operating standards, product quality, menu, site selection, and bakery-café construction as did company-owned bakery-cafés. Franchisees were required to purchase all of their dough products from sources approved by Panera Bread. Panera's fresh dough facility system supplied fresh dough products to substantially all franchise-operated bakery-cafés. Panera did not finance franchisee construction or area development agreement payments or hold an equity interest in any of the franchise-operated bakery-cafés. All area development agreements executed after March 2003 included a clause allowing Panera Bread the right to purchase all bakery-cafés opened by the franchisee at a defined purchase price, at any time five years after the execution of the franchise agreement.

Exhibit 7 shows estimated costs of opening a new franchised Panera Bread bakery-café. As of 2006, the typical franchise-operated bakery-café averaged somewhat higher average weekly and annual sales volumes than company-operated cafés (see Exhibit 2), was equal to or slightly more profitable, and produced a slightly higher return on equity investment than company-operated cafés (partly because many franchisees made greater use of debt in financing their operations than did Panera, which had no long-term debt at all).[5] During the 2003–2006 period, in four unrelated transactions, Panera purchased 38 bakery-cafés from franchisees.

Panera provided its franchisees with market analysis and site selection assistance, lease review, design services and new store opening assistance, a comprehensive 10-week initial training program, a training program for hourly employees, manager and baker certification, bakery-café certification, continuing education classes, benchmarking data regarding costs and profit margins, access to company developed marketing and advertising programs, neighborhood marketing assistance, and calendar planning assistance. Panera's surveys of its franchisees indicated high satisfaction with the Panera Bread concept, the overall support received from Panera Bread, and the company's leadership. The biggest franchisee issue was the desire for more territory. In turn, Panera management expressed satisfaction with the quality of franchisee operations, the pace and quality of new bakery-café openings, and franchisees' adoption of Panera Bread initiatives.[6]

As of April 2006, Panera had entered into area development agreements with 42 franchisee groups covering 54 markets in 34 states; these franchisees had commitments to open 423 additional franchise-operated bakery-cafés. If a franchisee failed to

Exhibit 7 Estimated Initial Investment for a Panera Bread Bakery-Café, 2007

Investment Category	Actual or Estimated Amount	To Whom Paid
Franchise fee	$35,000	Panera
Real property	Varies according to site and local real estate market conditions	
Leasehold improvements	$350,000 to $1,250,000	Contractors
Equipment	$250,000 to $300,000	Equipment vendors, Panera
Fixtures	$60,000 to $90,000	Vendors
Furniture	$50,000 to $70,000	Vendors
Consultant fees and municipal impact fees (if any)	$20,000 to $120,000	Architect, engineer, expeditor, others
Supplies and inventory	$19,000 to $24,175	Panera, other suppliers
Smallwares	$24,000 to $29,000	Suppliers
Signage	$20,000 to $72,000	Suppliers
Additional funds (for working capital and general operating expenses for 3 months)	$175,000 to $245,000	Vendors, suppliers, employees, utilities, landlord, others
Total	$1,003,000 to $2,235,175, plus real estate and related costs	

Source: www.panerabread.com (accessed February 9, 2007).

develop bakery-cafés on schedule, Panera had the right to terminate the franchise agreement and develop its own company-operated locations or develop locations through new area developers in that market. As of mid-2006, Panera Bread did not have any international franchise development agreements but was considering entering into franchise agreements for several Canadian locations (Toronto and Vancouver).

SITE SELECTION AND CAFÉ ENVIRONMENT

Bakery-cafés were typically located in suburban, strip mall, and regional mall locations. In evaluating a potential location, Panera studied the surrounding trade area, demographic information within that area, and information on competitors. Based on analysis of this information, including the use of predictive modeling using proprietary software, Panera developed projections of sales and return on investment for candidate sites. Cafés had proved successful as freestanding units, as both in-line and end-cap locations in strip malls, and in large regional malls.

The average Panera bakery-café was approximately 4,600 square feet. The great majority of the locations were leased. Lease terms were typically for 10 years with one, two, or three 5-year renewal option periods thereafter. Leases typically entailed charges for minimum base occupancy, a proportionate share of building and common-area operating expenses and real estate taxes, and a contingent percentage rent based on sales above a stipulated sales level. The average construction, equipment, furniture and fixture, and signage cost for the 66 company-owned bakery-cafés opened in 2005 was $920,000 per bakery-café after landlord allowances.

Each bakery-café sought to provide a distinctive and engaging environment (what management referred to as "Panera Warmth"), in many cases using fixtures and materials complementary to the neighborhood location of the bakery-café. In 2005–2006, the company had introduced a new G2 café design aimed at further refining and enhancing the appeal of Panera bakery-cafés as a warm and appealing neighborhood gathering place (a strategy that Starbucks had used with great success). The G2 design incorporated higher-quality furniture, cozier seating areas and groupings, and a brighter, more open display case. Many locations had fireplaces to further create an alluring and hospitable atmosphere that patrons would flock to on a regular basis, sometimes for a meal, sometimes to meet friends and acquaintances for a meal, sometimes to take a break for a light snack or beverage, and sometimes to just hang out with friends and acquaintances. Many of Panera's bakery-cafés had outdoor seating, and virtually all cafés featured free wireless high-speed (Wi-Fi) Internet access—Panera considered free Wi-Fi part of its commitment to making its bakery-cafés open community gathering places where people could catch up on some work, hang out with friends, read the paper, or just relax. All Panera cafés used real china and stainless silverware instead of paper plates and plastic utensils.

BAKERY-CAFÉ SUPPLY CHAIN

Panera had invested about $52 million in a network of 17 regional fresh dough facilities (16 company-owned and one franchise-operated) to supply fresh dough daily to both company-owned and franchised bakery-cafés. These facilities, totaling some 313,000 square feet, employed about 830 people who were largely engaged in preparing the fresh doughs, a process that took about 48 hours. The dough-making process began with the preparation and mixing of Panera's all-natural starter dough, which then was given time to rise; other all-natural ingredients were then added to create the different bread and bagel varieties (no chemicals or preservatives were used). Another period of rising then took place. Next the dough was cut into pieces, shaped into loaves or bagels, and readied for shipment in fresh dough form. There was no freezing of the dough, and no partial baking was done at the fresh dough facilities. Each bakery-café did all of the baking itself, using the fresh doughs delivered daily. The fresh dough facilities manufactured about 50 different products, with 11 more rotated throughout the year.

Distribution of the fresh bread and bagel doughs was accomplished through a leased fleet of about 140 temperature-controlled trucks operated by Panera personnel. Trucks on average delivered dough to six bakery-cafés, with trips averaging about 300 miles (but in some cases extending to as much as 500 miles—management believed the optimal trip length was about 300 miles). The fresh dough was sold to both company-owned and franchised bakery-cafés at a delivered cost not to exceed 27 percent of the retail value of the product. Exhibit 8 provides financial data relating to each of Panera's three business segments: company-operated bakery-cafés, franchise operations, and fresh dough facilities. The sales and operating profits associated with the fresh doughs supplied to company-operated bakery-cafés are included in the revenues and operating profits of the company-owned bakery-café segment. The sales and operating profits of the fresh dough facilities segment shown in Exhibit 8 all represent transactions with franchised bakery-cafés.

Management claimed that the company's fresh-dough-making capability provided a competitive advantage by ensuring consistent quality and dough-making efficiency. It was more economical to concentrate the dough-making operations in a few facilities dedicated to that function than it was to have each bakery-café equipped and staffed to do all of its baking from scratch.

Panera obtained ingredients for its doughs and other products manufactured at the fresh dough facilities from a variety of suppliers. While some ingredients used at the fresh dough facilities were sourced from a single supplier, there were numerous suppliers of each ingredient and Panera could obtain ingredients from another supplier when necessary. Panera contracted externally for the supply of sweet goods to its bakery-cafés. In November 2002, it entered into a cost-plus agreement with Dawn Food Products Inc. to provide sweet goods for the period 2003–2007. Sweet goods were completed at each bakery-café by professionally trained bakers—completion entailed finishing with fresh toppings and other ingredients and baking to established artisan standards.

Panera had arrangements with independent distributors to handle the delivery of sweet goods and other materials to bakery-cafés. Virtually all other food products and supplies for retail operations, including paper goods, coffee, and smallwares, were contracted for by Panera and delivered by the vendors to the designated distributors for delivery to the bakery-cafés. Individual bakery-cafés placed orders for the needed supplies directly from a distributor two to three times per week. Franchise-operated bakery-cafés operate under individual contracts with one of Panera's three primary independent distributors or other regional distributors.

Exhibit 8 Business Segment Information, Panera Bread Company, 2003–2006 ($ in thousands)

	2006	2005	2004	2003
Segment revenues:				
Company bakery-café operations	$666,141	$499,422	$362,121	$265,933
Franchise operations	61,531	54,309	44,449	36,245
Fresh dough operations	159,050	128,422	103,786	93,874
Intercompany sales eliminations	(57,751)	(41,878)	(31,217)	(32,350)
Total revenues	$828,971	$640,275	$479,139	$363,702
Segment operating profit:				
Company bakery-café operations	$123,225	$97,831	$71,725	$55,111
Franchise operations	54,160	47,652	39,149	32,132
Fresh dough operations	15,681	11,508	6,942	6,557
Total segment operating profit	$193,066	$156,991	$117,816	$93,800
Depreciation and amortization:				
Company bakery-café operations	$32,741	$23,345	$17,786	$12,256
Fresh dough operations	7,097	6,016	4,356	3,298
Corporate administration	4,328	3,650	3,156	2,750
Total	$44,166	$33,011	$25,298	$18,304
Capital expenditures:				
Company bakery-café operations	$86,743	$67,554	$67,374	$33,670
Fresh dough operations	15,120	9,082	9,445	8,370
Corporate administration	7,433	5,420	3,610	3,721
Total capital expenditures	$109,296	$82,056	$80,429	$45,761
Segment assets:				
Company bakery-café operations	$374,795	$301,517	$204,295	$147,920
Franchise operations	3,740	2,969	1,778	1,117
Fresh dough operations	59,919	37,567	39,968	33,442
Other assets	104,155	95,614	78,631	74,356
Total assets	$542,609	$437,667	$324,672	$256,835

Sources: Company 10-K reports, 2004, 2005, and 2006.

COMPETITION

According to the National Restaurant Association, sales at the 925,000 food service locations in the United States were forecast to be about $511 billion in 2006 (up from $308 billion in 1996), and account for 47.5 percent of consumers' food dollars (up from 25 percent in 1955). Commercial eating places accounted for about $345 billion of the projected $511 billion in total food service sales, with the remainder divided among drinking places, lodging establishments with restaurants, managed food service locations, and other types of retail, vending, recreational, and mobile operations with food service capability. The U.S. restaurant industry had about 12.5 million employees in 2006, served about 70 billion meals and snack occasions, and was growing about 5 percent annually.[7] Just over 7 out of 10 eating and drinking places in the United States were independent single-unit establishments with fewer than 20 employees.

Even though the average U.S. consumer ate 76 percent of meals at home, on a typical day, about 130 million U.S. consumers were food service patrons at an eating establishment—sales at commercial eating places averaged close to $1 billion daily. Average household expenditures for food away from home in 2004 were $2,434, or $974 per person. In 2003, unit sales averaged $755,000 at full-service restaurants and $606,000 at limited-service restaurants; however, very popular restaurant locations achieved annual sales volumes in the $2.5 million to $5 million range. The profitability of a restaurant location ranged from exceptional to good to average to marginal to money-losing.

The restaurant business was labor-intensive, extremely competitive, and risky. Industry members pursued differentiation strategies of one variety of another, seeking to set themselves apart from rivals via pricing, food quality, menu theme, signature menu selections, dining ambience and atmosphere, service, convenience, and location. To further enhance their appeal, some restaurants tried to promote greater customer traffic via happy hours, lunch and dinner specials, children's menus, innovative or trendy dishes, diet-conscious menu selections, and beverage/appetizer specials during televised sporting events (important at restaurants/bars with big-screen TVs). Most restaurants were quick to adapt their menu offerings to changing consumer tastes and eating preferences, frequently featuring heart-healthy, vegetarian, organic, low-calorie, and/or low-carb items on their menus. It was the norm at many restaurants to rotate some menu selections seasonally and to periodically introduce creative dishes in an effort to keep regular patrons coming back, attract more patrons, and remain competitive.

Consumers (especially those who ate out often) were prone to give newly opened eating establishments a trial, and if they were pleased with their experience to return, sometimes frequently—loyalty to existing restaurants was low when consumers perceived there were better dining alternatives. It was also common for a once-hot restaurant to lose favor and confront the stark realities of a dwindling clientele, forcing it to either reconceive its menu and dining environment or go out of business. Many restaurants had fairly short lives; there were multiple causes for a restaurant's failure—a lack of enthusiasm for the menu or dining experience, inconsistent food quality, poor service, a bad location, meal prices that patrons deemed too high, and superior competition by rivals with comparable menu offerings.

While Panera Bread competed with specialty food, casual dining, and quick-service restaurant retailers—including national, regional, and locally owned restaurants—its closest competitors were restaurants in the so-called fast-casual restaurant category. Fast-casual restaurants filled the gap between fast-food and casual, full-table-service dining. Fast-casual restaurants provided quick-service dining (much like fast-food enterprises) but were distinguished by enticing menus, higher food quality, and more inviting dining environments; typical meal costs per guest were in the $7–$12 range. Some fast-casual restaurants had limited table service and some were self-service (like fast-food establishments). Exhibit 9 provides information on prominent national and regional chains that were competitors of Panera Bread.

Exhibit 9 Representative Fast-Casual Restaurant Chains and Selected Full-Service Restaurant Chains in the United States, 2006

Company	Number of Locations, 2005–2006	Select 2005 Financial Data	Key Menu Categories
Atlanta Bread Company	160 bakery-cafés in 27 states	Not available (privately held company)	Fresh-baked breads, waffles, salads, sandwiches, soups, wood-fired pizza and pasta (select locations only), baked goods, desserts
Applebee's Neighborhood Grill and Bar*	1,730+ locations in 49 states, plus some 70 locations in 16 other countries	2005 revenues of $1.2 billion; average annual sales of $2.5 million per location; alcoholic beverages accounted for about 12 percent of sales	Beef, chicken, pork, seafood, and pasta entrées plus appetizers, salads, sandwiches, a selection of Weight Watchers branded menu alternatives, desserts, and alcoholic beverages

(*Continued*)

Exhibit 9 (Continued)

Company	Number of Locations, 2005–2006	Select 2005 Financial Data	Key Menu Categories
Au Bon Pain	190 company-owned and franchised bakery-cafés in 23 states; 222 locations internationally	Systemwide sales of about $245 million in 2005	Baked goods (with a focus on croissants and bagels), soups, salads, sandwiches and wraps, and coffee drinks
Baja Fresh	300+ locations across the United States	A subsidiary of Wendy's International	Tacos, burritos, quesadilla, fajitas, salads, soups, sides, and catering services
Bruegger's	260 bakery-cafés in 17 states	2005 revenues of $155.2 million; 3,500 full-time employees	Several varieties of bagels and muffins, sandwiches, salads, and soups
California Pizza Kitchen*	190+ locations in 27 states and 5 other countries	2005 revenues of $480 million; average annual sales of $3.2 million per location	Signature California-style hearth-baked pizzas; creative salads, pastas, soups and sandwiches; appetizers; desserts, beer, wine, coffees, teas, and assorted beverages
Chili's Grill and Bar* (a subsidiary of Brinker International**)	1,074 locations in 49 states and 23 countries	Average revenue per meal of ≈$12.00; average capital investment of $2.4 million per location	Chicken, beef, and seafood entrées, steaks, appetizers, salads, sandwiches, desserts, and alcoholic beverages (13.6 percent of sales)
Chipotle Mexican Grill	500+ locations (all company-owned)	2005 sales of $628 million; 13,000 employees	A selection of gourmet burritos and tacos
Corner Bakery Café (a subsidiary of Brinker International**)	90 locations in 8 states and District of Columbia	Average revenue per meal of ≈$7.44; average capital investment of $1.7 million per location	Breakfast selections (egg scramblers, pastries, mixed berry parfaits); lunch/diner selections (hot and cold sandwiches, salads, soups, and desserts); catering (≈21 percent of sales)
Cracker Barrel	527 combination retail stores and restaurants in 42 states	Restaurant sales of $2.1 billion in 2005; average restaurant sales of $3.3 million	Two menus (breakfast and lunch/dinner); named "Best Family Dining Chain" for 15 consecutive years
Culver's	330 locations in 16 states	Not available (a privately held company)	Signature hamburgers served on buttered buns, fried battered cheese curds, value dinners (chicken, shrimp, cod with potato and slaw), salads, frozen custard, milkshakes, sundaes, and fountain drinks
Fazoli's	380 locations in 32 states	Not available (a privately held company)	Spaghetti and meatballs, fettuccine Alfredo, lasagna, ravioli, submarinos and panini sandwiches, salads, and breadsticks
Fuddruckers	200+ locations in the United States and 6 Middle Eastern countries	Not available (a privately held company)	Exotic hamburgers (the feature menu item), chicken and fish sandwiches, French fries and other sides, soups, salads, desserts
Jason's Deli	150 locations in 20 states	Not available (a privately held company)	Sandwiches, extensive salad bar, soups, loaded potatoes, desserts; catering services, party trays, and box lunches

(*Continued*)

Exhibit 9 (Continued)

Company	Number of Locations, 2005–2006	Select 2005 Financial Data	Key Menu Categories
McAlister's Deli	200+ locations in 18 states	Not available (a privately held company)	Deli sandwiches, loaded baked potatoes, soups, salads, and desserts, plus sandwich trays and lunch boxes
Moe's Southwest Grill	200+ locations in 35 states	Not available (a privately held company)	Tex-Mex foods prepared fresh—tacos, burritos, fajitas, quesadillas, nachos, salads, chips and salsa
Noodles & Company	120+ urban and suburban locations in 16 states	Not available (a privately held company)	Asian, Mediterranean and American noodle/pasta entrées, soups and salads
Nothing But Noodles	39 locations in 20 states	Not available (a privately held company)	Starters, a wide selection of American and Italian pastas, Asian dishes with noodles, pasta-less entrées, soups, salads, and desserts
Qdoba Mexican Grill	280+ locations in 40 states	A subsidiary of Jack in the Box, Inc.; Jack in the Box had 2005 revenues of $2.5 billion, 2,300 + Jack in the Box and Qdoba locations, and 44,600 employees	Signature burritos, a "Naked Burrito" (a burrito served in a bowl without the tortilla), nontraditional taco salads, three-cheese nachos, five signature salsas, and a Q-to-Go Hot Taco Bar catering alternative
Rubio's Fresh Mexican Grill	150 locations in 5 western states	2005 revenues of $141 million; average sales of $960,000 per location	Signature fish tacos; chicken beef, and pork tacos; burritos and quesadillas; salads; proprietary salsas; sides; and domestic and imported beers
Starbucks	7,500+ company-operated and licensed locations in the United States, plus ≈3,000 international locations	2005 revenues of $6.4 billion; estimated retail sales of $1.1 million per company-operated location	Italian-style espresso beverages, teas, sodas, juices, assorted pastries and confections; some locations offer sandwiches and salads

*Denotes a full-service restaurant.

**Brinker International was a multi-concept restaurant operator with over 1,500 restaurants including Chili's Grill & Bar, Chili's Too, Corner Bakery Café, Romano's Macaroni Grill, On the Border Mexican Grill & Cantina, and Maggiano's Little Italy. Brinker had 2005 sales of $3.9 billion.

Sources: Company Web sites and en.wikipedia.org/wiki/Fast_casual_restaurant (accessed August 2, 2006).

Endnotes

[1] According to information in Panera Bread's press kit; the results of the study were reported in a 2003 *Wall Street Journal* article.
[2] As stated in a presentation to securities analysts, May 5, 2006.
[3] As cited in Panera Bread's presentation to securities analysts on May 5, 2006.
[4] Ibid.
[5] Ibid.
[6] Ibid.
[7] Information posted at www.restaurant.org (accessed August 1, 2006).

CASE 9

Rogers' Chocolates

Charlene Zietsma
University of Western Ontario

Steve Parkhill was thinking about his options for growing Rogers' Chocolates (Rogers'). It was March 2007, and he had just started his new job as president of the company, after training with the former president for two months. The board of directors had asked him to double or triple the size of the company within 10 years. Each board member of the privately held company, and each member of the management team (most of whom also held shares), had a different idea about what Rogers' needed to do to achieve that growth. Parkhill needed to devise a strategy that would fit the company's culture, and then gain the support of the board, the management team, and the employees.

THE PREMIUM CHOCOLATE MARKET

The Canadian market size for chocolates was US$167 million in 2006 and it was projected to grow at 2 percent annually.[1] The growth rate in the chocolate industry as a whole had been falling, however, so traditional manufacturers such as Hershey's and Cadburys were moving into the premium chocolate market through acquisitions or upmarket launches. The premium chocolate market was growing at 20 percent annually,[2] as aging baby boomers purchased more chocolate and emphasized quality and brand in their purchases.

About one-quarter of chocolate sales typically occur in the eight weeks prior to Christmas. Twenty percent of "heavy users" accounted for 54 percent of these pre-Christmas sales in 2006. These heavy users tended to be established families, middle-aged childless couples, and empty nesters with high incomes, and they tended to purchase more high-quality boxed chocolate than bars or lower quality chocolate.[3] The margins in premium chocolate were much better than those in lower quality segments.

Purchasers were also demanding more from chocolate than taste. In line with a broad social trend for healthier diets, the demand for organic products, including organic chocolates, was growing. Consumers looked for products with no trans fats.[4] Demand for dark chocolate, traditionally less popular than milk chocolate in North America, was growing in part because of its heart-healthy anti-oxidant properties. At the same time, however, larger chocolate manufacturers were seeking a redefinition of the term "chocolate" under USFDA guidelines, so that they could produce cheaper versions of the product and still call it chocolate.

Consumers and employees were also demanding that chocolate companies (like other companies) follow good corporate social responsibility practices. Environmental concerns, which were very strong in Victoria, influenced packaging, procurement, and operational decisions. Human rights concerns were

also high on the list for consumer expectations of chocolate companies, as forced labor and child labor were still used in some of the production of cocoa beans in West Africa. One customer e-mail received by Rogers' read as follows:

> I am drawing the conclusion that Rogers' buys their raw product from West Africa. Rogers' is uninterested in making a real effort to eradicate this crisis. Furthermore, Rogers' is making contributions to the unethical side of the conflict and in so doing is endorsing the vile acts that continue to occur in West Africa. If any of my conclusions are incorrect, please let me know. I would appreciate it if you kept my e-mail address on file and notified me if Rogers' begins to value the lives of people even though they are not potential consumers.

COMPETITORS

Chocolate competitors in the premium chocolate segment in Canada featured strong regional brands plus a few larger players. Godiva, backed by Nestlé, had taken the business by storm with glitzy packaging, high price points, and widespread distribution among retailers of gift items. Godiva's quality was not as high as Rogers' but it was able to obtain about 15 percent higher price points for standard products on the strength of its packaging, advertising, and distribution. For truffle-only collections and seasonal collections, the price points were often two to three times the price of Rogers' chocolates, though these featured exceptionally sleek and modern packaging, significant variations in chocolate molding, and chocolates of various colors.

Bernard Callebaut[5] was a premium chocolate producer out of Calgary that had begun to grow in similar locations to Rogers' (tourist and downtown retail), though it also had mall locations. There were 32 stores, mostly across the West, but with four in the United States and two in Ontario. The company's quality was good and it excelled in new flavor introductions, with an often seasonal influence. Callebaut's packaging was also superior with copper and gold boxes that could be customized for the consumer at the store, and great seasonal displays. Bernard Callebaut attracted similar price points to Godiva, but emphasized a retail strategy instead of a wholesale strategy, though bars for immediate consumption could be found in grocery outlets and other retailers.

Lindt was a large and well-established Swiss chocolate producer that offered a large variety of chocolates and distributed them broadly in mass merchandisers, drug, and grocery retailers. The product quality and packaging was mid-range and their pricing was about 90 percent of Rogers' pricing. They emphasized bars and small bags of truffles for immediate consumption, though they also produced gift boxes. They also produced the Ghirardelli brand, which was of higher quality but focused on pure chocolate squares.

Purdy's was a Vancouver-based company that was 120 years old and had been very successful with a variety of products, particularly its hedgehogs. Purdy's had over 50 locations, nearly all of which were based in malls. While they had stores nationally, their biggest and most successful presence was in British Columbia. Purdy's had tried to launch its products in Seattle, but had not done well there. Purdy's price point was significantly lower than Rogers' (about 35 percent lower), and product quality level was also lower than Rogers', though still high. Their packaging and store displays were very good. Purdy's did a strong business in corporate gifts and group purchases, offering 20 percent to 25 percent discounts for high-volume orders.

Other premium chocolate companies ranged from the extremely high-end custom chocolatiers that carried a very small line of chocolates in exclusive packaging and often produced custom orders, to Belgian producers that sold in Canada through established retailers or online, to niche players in single varietal bean chocolates or organic chocolates carried only at high-end grocery or retail stores.

There were also companies that commanded price premiums over their quality level because of their distribution and/or store concept. For example, Laura Secord, which emphasized mall stores, and Rocky Mountain Chocolate Company, which sold more candy than chocolate and used a franchise model, had higher price points than Purdy's but lesser quality. Laura Secord had had several ownership changes over the last decade.

ROGERS' COMPANY HISTORY

Founded by Charles "Candy" Rogers in 1885, Rogers' Chocolates, based in Victoria, British Columbia (BC), was Canada's oldest chocolate company and British

Columbia's second oldest company. After Charles's death, his wife ran the company until the late 1920s, when she sold the firm to a customer. Since then the company has changed hands three times. For the last two decades (during which time the company had grown sales by more than 900 percent), the company had been owned by a private group comprised principally of two financial executives and partners with Connor, Clark & Lunn, a Vancouver-based investment firm; an art dealer and private investor; and a former owner of Pacific Coach Lines, a Victoria-based bus company. These four plus a past president of Rogers' comprised the board of directors.

CURRENT OPERATIONS

Rogers' head office was located above its flagship store in the Inner Harbour area of Victoria, near the world-famous Empress Hotel. The head office consisted of a board room and offices for the management team. Those involved in production worked out of the factory about eight kilometers away, and the national wholesale sales manager worked in Kitchener, Ontario.

Rogers' main products were high-quality, hand-wrapped chocolates including its premiere line, the Victoria Creams, along with truffles, nuts and chews, almond bark, nutcorn, and various assortments. In addition to pure milk chocolate, dark chocolate, and white chocolate bars, and baking/fondue chocolate blocks, Rogers' also produced specialty items, such as chocolate-covered ginger, truffles, caramels, brittles, and orange peel. Rogers' also produced no-sugar-added chocolates. Select Rogers' products are shown in Exhibit 1. The company also produced and sold a line of premium ice cream novelty items through its retail stores. Rogers' chocolates were of the highest quality, and the company had many loyal customers around the world. In 2006, the company won a prestigious 2006 Superior Taste Award from the International Taste & Quality Institute (ITQI), an independent organization of leading sommeliers, beverage experts, and gourmet chefs, based in Brussels, Belgium. A company press release stated:

> "Classy, refined and elegant," were just a few of the words used to describe the 120-year-old company's chocolate line. The discerning panel of European chefs also identified the Rogers' assortment as a "top-of-the-range-product," filled with "abundant and rich chocolate aromas."[6]

PRODUCTION

Rogers' chocolates were produced in a 24,000-square-foot manufacturing facility on the outskirts of Victoria. There were about 110 non-unionized retail and production employees, with about 35 in production and the remainder in retail. Twenty employees worked seasonally in the two departments for the Christmas season. An additional 20 employees worked in management, administration, and sales, as shown in the organization chart in Exhibit 2. Production, which took place on a one-shift operation (day shift), was labor-intensive, since most chocolates were handmade, then hand-packed. Since there were so many different product offerings, most production consisted of batch processing, utilizing technology that had been used in the chocolate business for decades. Set-up times and equipment cleaning times were a significant component of costs, especially since they were required at the beginning and end of each eight-hour shift. To date, there had been no meaningful measures of productivity or efficiency in the plant, and thus no way of telling on a day to day basis if the plant was doing a good job.

Demand forecasting was difficult due to the seasonality of sales, but a long product shelf life (approximately six months) and a monthly sales forecast allowed Rogers' to deal with the ups and downs of sales patterns through healthy inventories kept on site. Nevertheless, the complicated nature of seasonal production created problems with out-of-stocks: souvenir items and ice cream were required in the spring and summer, then core Rogers' products and seasonal items were required for the fall and Christmas. The Christmas season was particularly chaotic, with 24 percent of annual sales occurring in the eight-week run up to Christmas. Valentine's and spring items were required for early January, which overlapped with the end of Christmas production. The wholesale business required early production for seasonal needs, whereas the online and retail business required late production. Art tins used for chocolate assortments came from China, and some were season-specific. The Chinese supplier was sometimes unable to produce tins in a timely way due to lack of electricity. As soon as there were out-of-stocks for one product, the back-order production of that product would throw the schedule off for the next product.

Exhibit 1 Rogers' Products

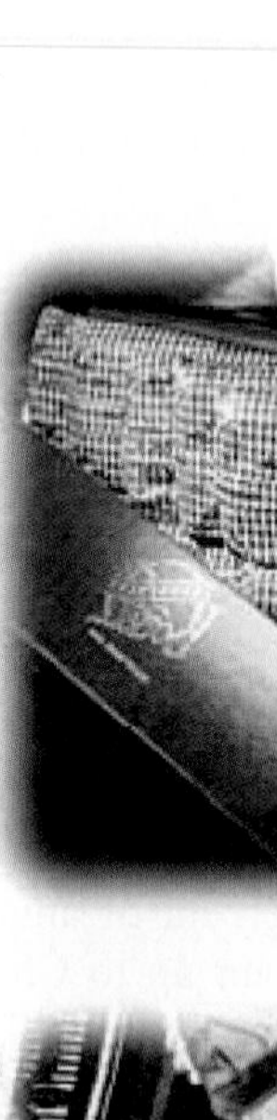

Empress Squares

Dark Chocolate Almond Brittle

Marquis Assortment

Collectible Gift Tins

Fruit & Nut Collection

Ice Cream and Ice Cream Bars

Exhibit 2 Organization Chart

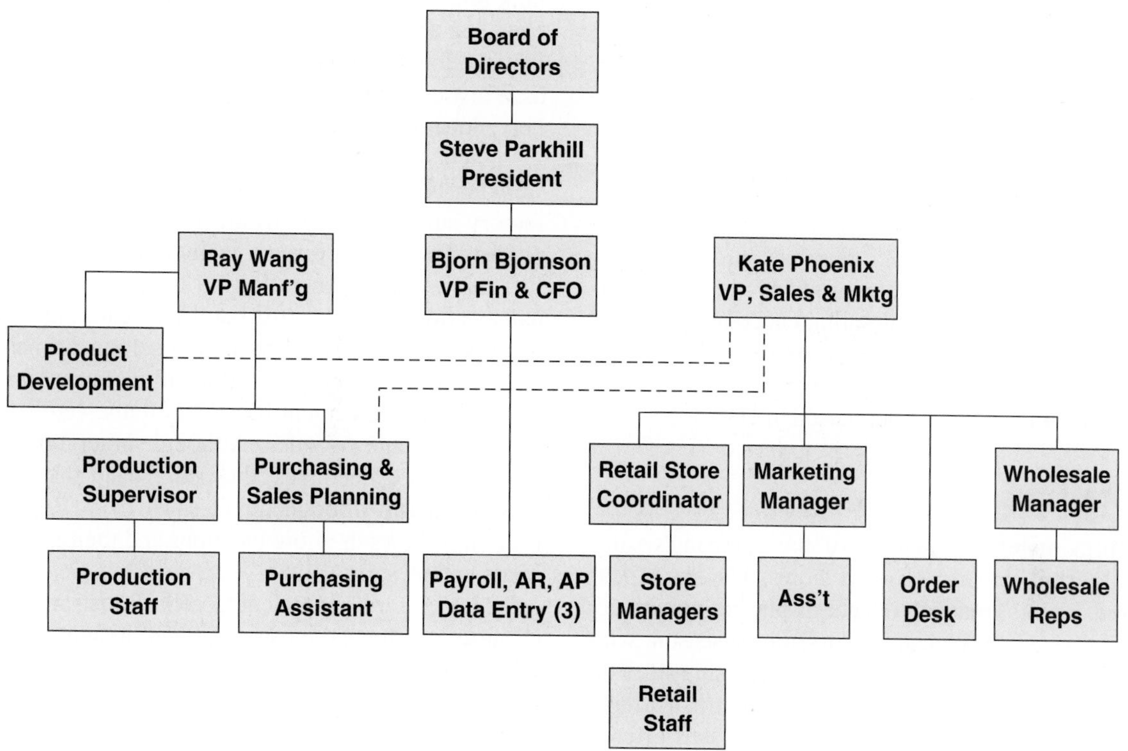

Production planning was made even more complicated by the impact of out-of-stocks on the historical information that was used to plan the following year's sales. For example, when an item was out of stock for a month, and the back orders were filled in a short period of time, the sales graph would be distorted with unnatural spikes; yet these spikes would be used for production planning for the following year. When there were overstock problems on an item, the retail stores would push the items, sometimes discounting them, again creating distortions in the sales data, which would be replicated over time since that data would be used for production planning. Because the same process recurred for hundreds of items, these issues created significant havoc for production planning and inventory management. Ice cream presented a problem in that it was a new item (two years old), and it was difficult to predict sales volume accurately.

The out-of-stock issue was a major one for the company. Each week, numerous products were shorted. Because out-of-stocks in the wholesale channel created problems with customers, and because the previous president had favored the wholesale channel, short supplies were diverted from the company's own stores and delivered to wholesalers. Furthermore, when a special order arrived in wholesale, it was not uncommon for the president to tell the plant to put production plans on hold to focus on the special order.

The plant was non-union, which was a direct reflection of the company's long history and strong family values. Some production workers were third-generation Rogers' employees. Employees were quite proud of the Rogers' heritage and commitment to quality and were quite passionate about the company. This passion sometimes created resistance to change: anything new caused concern that the company was compromising its values and its heritage. Employees learned multiple job functions and enjoyed a variety of work and tasks. Employees took great care in hand-wrapping chocolates, folding the traditional gingham packaging "just so," and hand-ribboning boxes, tins, and bags. Several disabled people were employed in the plant, and Rogers' supported a local social service agency by allowing a group of brain-damaged individuals in every Friday to help with production. Turnover was low, and wages were competitive. Permanent employees were on a first-name basis with all of the senior leaders, including the president.

MARKETS

Rogers' currently earned revenues in four major areas: retailing chocolate products through company-owned stores, wholesaling chocolate products, online/mail order sales of chocolate products, and sales from Sam's Deli, a well-known eatery in Victoria, which Rogers' had purchased in 2004.

Retail

Approximately 50 percent of the company's sales came from Rogers' 11 retail stores. The stores featured Rogers' many products displayed attractively in glass cases, merchandised to suit the season, with an overall Victorian theme. Rogers' flagship store on government street had been designated a Heritage Site by Parks Canada. Uniformed sales staff offered chocolate samples to customers, and the aromas and images in the store contributed to an excellent retail experience. In 2000, Rogers' had won the Retail Council of Canada's Innovative Retailer of the Year award in the small business category, for demonstrating "outstanding market leadership and innovative approaches to customer and employee relations. Through creative ideas and strong delivery, the winning retailer has taken their brand to the top of their class."[7] Each of Rogers' retail stores, other than the factory store itself, was located in a tourist area, such as Whistler, Granville Island, and Gastown, or at BC Ferry locations.[8]

Each store was wholly owned by Rogers'. Most were leased, with a minimum of a 10-year lease. The factory store and the downtown Victoria store were owned. The stores were typically about 500 square feet in size, with the exception of the ferry terminal locations, which were booths or catering wagons open on a seasonal basis and selling primarily ice cream. The ferry terminal locations were leased on an annual agreement basis, and rents were fixed as a percentage of sales. Although other retailers sold Rogers' Chocolates, they purchased the products wholesale through direct sales from Rogers'. Exhibit 3 shows the store locations and their approximate annual sales.

The Victoria stores could sell almost anything because of Rogers' positive brand image on the island. They were often used to clear inventory problems. The two newest stores, Gastown and Granville Island in Vancouver, were showing steady sales growth in their first two years of operations, but significantly shy of expectations. The Granville Island store was located next to the popular Arts Club Theatre, but it was, unfortunately, also behind several large metal refuse bins. Rogers' had waited a number of years for a location to open up on Granville Island, so although the present location wasn't perfect, it was

Exhibit 3 Retail Stores Sales in Fiscal 2007 (rounded to nearest thousand)

Store	Date Acquired	Approximate Annual Sales	Contribution Margin
Downtown Victoria	1885	$2,775,000	45.3%
Sam's Deli	2004	1,598,000	8.9*
Factory	1985	726,000	36.7
Granville Island	Dec. 2005	686,000	(11.5)
Whistler	1995	639,000	8.2
Tudor Sweet Shoppe	1983	517,000	22.86
Sidney	2003	401,000	29.1
Gastown	April 2006	138,000	(22.3)
Swartz Bay—BC Ferries	2000	60,000 (Mostly ice cream)	15.5
Departure Bay—BC Ferries	2006	42,000 (All ice cream; summer only)	18.2
Duke Point—BC Ferries	2005	35,000 (All ice cream; summer only)	21.1

*Reflects full cost of expenses to refurbish the store.

the best that could be obtained. The Gastown store was in a good location, likely to attract considerable cruise ship business.

Wholesale

Approximately 30 percent of sales came from wholesale accounts in five categories: (1) independent gift/souvenir shops; (2) large retail chains; (3) tourist retailers, such as duty-free stores, airport or train station stores, and hotel gift shops; (4) corporate accounts that purchased Rogers' products for gifts for customers or employees; and (5) a new segment, specialty high-end food retailers such as Thrifty Foods on Vancouver Island, Sobeys in Western Canada, Sunterra in Alberta, and Whole Foods in Toronto, Oakville, and Vancouver. Some large accounts, such as the Bay, Crabtree & Evelyn, and Second Cup, had been significant Rogers' customers, but had recently changed their purchasing to focus either on their own products or on less expensive lines. As a result, Rogers' wholesale sales had dropped over the last two years. Sales were strongest in BC, followed by Ontario. Sales in Alberta, Manitoba, and Saskatchewan had increased very recently due to the Sobeys roll-out, but sales were weak in Quebec and the Maritimes.

The wholesale business was supported by a sales structure that included a salaried national sales manager based in Ontario, who had been with the company for eight years, and nine sales reps across Canada, of which eight were sales agents. The one salaried rep, who had been with the company for 10 years, was located on Vancouver Island. Currently, sales agents were in place in the following territories: Vancouver/Lower Mainland; Interior BC and Alberta; Saskatchewan and Manitoba; Northern Ontario; Niagara Falls and Metro Toronto; east of Toronto to Ottawa area; Quebec and the Maritimes.

Sales agents maintained independent businesses but made agreements with Rogers' to have exclusive rights to sell Rogers' products within a certain geographical territory. These agreements were not contracted, and thus they were open to review at any time. Generally, terminations were given 90 days' notice by either party. Many had been with the company as long as the previous president, who had established the wholesale division nearly two decades earlier. Rogers' sales agents typically carried several non-competing lines, such as maple syrup, gourmet condiments, plush toys, smoked salmon, and kitchenware. A couple of sales agents were also customers as they also operated independent retail outlets that carried Rogers' Chocolates. Marketing vice president Kate Phoenix had the following to say about sales agents and the sales rep on Vancouver Island:

> Some perform very well. They cite many challenges with our brand—niche market, high prices, inadequate shelf life, old fashioned ("not glitzy or fashionable enough") packaging, and an unknown brand in many areas of Canada. We intend to introduce a "Tastes of Canada" product this year that we hope will play well to our wholesale and souvenir buyers.
>
> Some reps have other, much stronger lines and just carry Rogers' as an add-on to their existing accounts, which can be effective as their existing relationships with buyers gives us an "in" that a new salesperson would not have. The salaried rep on Vancouver Island receives a constant series of requests for our products, as it is our "home turf" and we do extensive advertising in our local market for our own stores. The brand is very well established and seen as a desirable product. In the Victoria area, some accounts will say they are honored to carry Rogers'. In other parts of Canada they have not heard of us and are dismissive of the products and their price points as they do not understand the brand and the value of the product. If the remote reps are not well trained, they just cannot present the brand adequately and sell it.

Similar to most gift products, retailers typically marked items up by about 100 percent. Rogers' earned about half the gross margins on wholesale sales as it did on retail and online sales and the company paid its sales agents approximately 10 percent commission. The salaried sales rep on the island earned a 1 percent commission on sales above her salary but benefited significantly from Rogers' high profile in Victoria and the extensive advertising the company did there.

There were 585 active wholesale customers in 2006. Of those, 346 purchased less than $2,000 per year. Of the 346, 221 purchased less than $1,000 per year. Rogers' provided these smaller customers with the same level of service as other retailers, sometimes crediting them for stale stock, and paying the shipping expenses on orders of more than $350. There had been problems in the past with smaller accounts selling stock past its expiration date.

Some of the wholesale accounts ordered custom products, such as logo bars for special events. Rogers' would custom-produce molds, then chocolate bars for the customers featuring their logos. In the past, some regular customers had created problems by ordering with too little lead time, so the plant typically kept some logo bars in inventory for customers in anticipation of their orders.

Online, Phone, and Mail Orders

A further 10 percent of sales came from the company's online (approximately 4 percent) and mail order (approximately 6 percent) business. Sixty percent of all orders were from regular customers. The average sale per phone or mail order was $138, while the average sale per website order was $91. Parkhill felt that online orders could be increased, since 30 percent of men and 18 percent of women in Canada were shopping online in 2006—these tended to be people in the 18–34 age group (44 percent), while only 20 percent of online purchasers were in the 35–54 age group.

Orders received by phone, mail, or online were generally processed within three to four days, wrapped in attractive packaging, then shipped via FedEx in a sturdy outer box. In addition to the order, a separate thank-you and confirmation letter from Rogers' was sent with a cataloge. In the summer, orders were shipped in insulated containers and packed with frozen ice packs. Shipping charges ranged from $10 for three- to five-day delivery within Canada and $15 to the United States for five-day shipping, to $42 for international air shipping, on products up to a $27 value. As the value of the product increased, shipping charges also increased: with product approaching $500, the costs were $18.50 within Canada for three- to five-day shipping, $37.50 to the United States, and $122 internationally. For orders over $500, Rogers' paid the shipping charges.

Approximately 60 percent of phone, mail, and online sales were shipped to Canadian destinations, while 35 percent went to the United States and 5 percent shipped to 50 countries internationally. Many of the mail-order sales came from rural locations in Canada, where the mail-order tradition was strong. Rogers' chocolates were delivered to the far North, sometimes via dogsled, and were shipped to lighthouses on both coasts. Many of the rural mail-order customers placed very large orders.

Products ordered through the online and mail-order business were given priority for inventory allocation and thus could usually be shipped within one or two working days. If there was a shortage of a particular product, its stock would be transferred back to the factory from the retail stores to meet mail-order commitments. The next priority for shipping was wholesale accounts, since wholesale back orders had to be shipped at Rogers' expense, and many accounts would not accept back orders. Yet, given that Rogers' margins on wholesale sales were much lower than in the retail business, this policy meant that sometimes a high-margin retail sale would be foregone for the much lower margins at wholesale.

Sam's Deli

The remaining sales were generated from Sam's Deli, a cafeteria-style restaurant on the Inner Harbour in Victoria, between the Rogers' head office store and the Empress Hotel. Sam's Deli featured made-to-order sandwiches, soups and salads, desserts (many featuring Rogers' chocolate) baked on the premises or at the Rogers' chocolate factory, and wine and beer. Sam's had strong sales of ice cream as well. At lunchtime in the summer, the line regularly extended out the door.

Sam's Deli had been a Victoria institution for many years. Since Rogers' purchased it, most of the long-term staff had turned over, and recruiting new employees was difficult in Victoria's tight labor market. Sam's had had to curtail its evening hours of operations due to staff recruiting problems. Although Sam's had a liquor license, the volume of alcohol sold was very small. Parkhill felt that Sam's wasn't living up to its potential.

MARKETING

Target Market

Since Rogers' chocolates were fairly expensive relative to others in the market (due to their quality ingredients and their hand-packaging processes), the company targeted affluent customers looking for a luxury experience with a superior taste, or an elegant, prestigious, and uncommon gift item. Many were cruise ship visitors and general tourists, though many locals were frequent visitors to the store and loyal to the brand. Some were huge spenders. Many local businesses also saw Rogers' as their corporate gift of choice. According to Phoenix:

> Our best and most loyal client base comes from customers (in all three sales channels) that have an emotional connection to Rogers'. For example, they were in the Victoria store on a holiday or a honeymoon, etc., or it was a traditional gift in their family. By tending this market carefully, it has grown. Many of those people then give Rogers' as a corporate gift or a personal gift to a substantial list and some of those recipients then become loyal customers. It's classic viral marketing.
>
> Other customers are affluent people who want to give something unique. They've found us on the Internet or in their travels and see us as an obscure but classic gift. What do rich people give each other as a present in this society of indulgence and privilege? Unique wines, flowers, a handmade cake or cookies from a remote little shop, or Rogers'!
>
> But how do you reach these people to promote to them? Advertising to this target is so expensive and they are scattered across Canada and USA predominantly, and of course they are courted by every advertiser around so are ceasing to respond to advertising. The best way in our experience to sell to them is not to make mistakes or disappoint them in any way. If you do, apologize and replace the product immediately—good old-fashioned service. This segment continues to grow for us.

Tourists often became mail-order or online customers—especially American tourists, since there were no American resellers. Happy customers from resellers often became mail-order or online customers as well, since information about Web and mail-order sales was available in all packaging. Rogers' also had an easy-to-navigate website and a superior search engine ranking that attracted Web shoppers.

Brand

The Rogers' brand had both significant strengths and some weaknesses. The brand was established around Rogers' long history, with traditional packaging, including pink or brown gingham-wrapped Victoria Creams, Chocolate Almond Brittle, and Empress Squares. Chocolates were packed in Rogers' traditional burgundy box, a new gold box, or tins. Some tins featured old-fashioned scenes such as English roses, cornucopias, or floral arrangements, while others featured Canadian art, particularly from the west coast. Chocolate and candy bars were also available, with a mixed variety of packaging. In the retail stores, individual chocolates could be purchased for immediate consumption or custom-packed into gift boxes to suit the buyers' tastes. Rogers' was a classic premium brand, Canadian and of high perceived value. Ingredients were mostly natural.

The brand had a very loyal following, particularly in the Victoria area. Parkhill described the brand perception:

> When I first began investigating Rogers', I asked everyone I knew what they thought of the brand. I received one of two reactions. People either said, "I've never heard of it," or they said "Oooooh, Rogers'. That is the best chocolate I've ever tasted." People would tell me stories about what Rogers' meant to them.
>
> It's become clear to me that the retail experience is key in creating the memories that lead to repeat sales. Through our store décor, sampling, aromas, taste, and service, I think we are delivering "chocolate orgasms" to our customers.

If the company wanted to grow, it needed to become known more broadly. The challenge would be to increase awareness without diluting the brand with weak messaging or presentation to wholesale accounts, or without cheapening the product. The premium price scared some consumers and wholesale accounts away. Although those who knew the brand were willing to pay for the product, those who didn't know the brand were often unwilling to try it. Discounting the product, or developing cheaper products to piggyback on the brand, would risk destroying brand integrity.

An additional problem was associated with the traditional image of the brand. As Rogers' loyal customers aged, who would take their place? Younger buyers were less likely to be attracted by the traditional image of Rogers' brand. Developing an organic or fair trade product might be a possibility, but Rogers' chocolate supplier did not yet have organic or fair trade capabilities, and Rogers' was not large enough to pressure its supplier to change. Rogers' would also have to source organic versions of all the other ingredients. Phoenix identified with brands such as Chanel and Lancome, which had developed classic images and refused to compromise the brand, and brands such as Jaguar, Cadillac, BMW and Volvo, which had developed a younger, sexier image while maintaining core design elements to keep the integrity of the brand.

Advertising

Rogers' used several types of advertising. To reach tourists, the company advertised in guide magazines such as *WHERE,* in flyers available on the ferry boat brochure rack, in hotel magazines, and in the *Enroute* magazine available on Air Canada flights. Seasonal print advertising, radio spots, and a small amount of TV advertising (in Victoria only) were also used. Rogers' also donated product extensively to charitable events in its markets, and participated in promotional events; for example, Rogers' was the headline sponsor for the Arts Club Theatre, next door to the Granville Island store. Rogers' had also purchased a delivery truck for Victoria last year and covered it with advertising. Rogers' preferred to use advertising that served each of the three major channels; for example, the *Enroute* magazine advertisements promoted Rogers' stores, its wholesale accounts, and its website to Air Canada flyers, a demographic with a large number of online shoppers. Direct mail and solid search engine rankings promoted the online business.

Website

Rogers' website was the key point of contact for the online business. It featured beauty shots of the different chocolate assortments, an easy ordering facility, a reminder service that e-mailed customers when a special occasion they had entered was upcoming, frequently updated online links, and optimized search engine placement. The website also had links to resellers, which provided added value to those retailers and helped customers find the nearest location that carried Rogers' chocolates. However, the sales agents had not been prompt about responding to requests to provide links for their top accounts, as they did not seem to understand the value provided by such links.

FINANCIALS[9]

Rogers' was in a strong financial position. As a privately held firm, Rogers' was under less pressure than a public firm to manage shareholders' expectations. Therefore, many of its financial strategies were designed to minimize taxable earnings. Assets were depreciated as quickly as possible under the Canada Revenue Agency's guidelines.

Although Rogers' had gone through a period of significant growth just after the current shareholders acquired the company, growth had slowed considerably in the past few years. In part, this decline had resulted from the slowdown in tourism from the United States since September 11, 2001, and the subsequent decline in the U.S. dollar. In fact, chocolate sales had declined since 2004, though the company's revenues had grown slightly, due to the contributions of Sam's Deli. Margins remained strong, however, at about 50 percent of sales on average. Financial statements are shown in Exhibits 4 to 7.

LEADERSHIP

Jim Ralph had been president and general manager of Rogers' from 1989 until 2007. It was his impending retirement that had launched the search for a new president. Ralph had been a well-networked sales manager in the gift business prior to his appointment as president, and as a result he had grown Rogers' wholesale business during his tenure. Ralph arrived every morning at 5 a.m. and oversaw Rogers' operations closely.

When Ralph announced his intention to retire in 2005, the controlling shareholders (and board of directors) considered selling Rogers'. It was a healthy company with significant assets, great cash flow, and good margins. Yet the board felt that Rogers' had significant potential to grow even more. They decided to hold onto the company and seek a leader who could take the company to the next level. They retained an executive recruitment firm, and the job ad shown in Exhibit 8 was posted on www.workopolis.com. In the two years during the search, managers were aware that Ralph was retiring, and significant decisions were put off until a new leader could be found.

A friend of Steve Parkhill saw the ad and thought it fitted Parkhill perfectly. Parkhill agreed. At the time, he was vice president of operations for Maple Leaf Foods, in charge of six plants and approximately 2,300 employees. Previously, Parkhill had been president of a seafood company and general manager of a meat processing subsidiary. His career had involved stints in marketing and sales in addition to operations, and he had an MBA from the Richard Ivey School of Business. Parkhill was known as an exceptional leader with an empowering style and significant personal integrity. He missed the strategy involved in his general management days and was looking for a smaller company to settle into: the west coast was very appealing. After several rounds of interviews, Parkhill was offered the position, and he accepted with excitement. Both Parkhill and the board of directors agreed that the position was intended to be a long-term one—10 years or more. To that end, the offer had a provision requiring Parkhill to purchase a significant number of shares in the company each year for the first three years, with an option to increase his holdings further after that.

The senior management team included three others. Kate Phoenix, vice president of Sales and Marketing, a Rogers' employee since 1994, managed the retail outlets, developed marketing plans, and oversaw the online and wholesale businesses, as well as Sam's Deli. She was also responsible for the ice cream business. She supervised the wholesale sales manager, the retail operations manager, a communications manager, and the order desk staff. The product development person and purchasing and sales planning person also reported indirectly to Phoenix, though they worked more directly with Ray Wong. Phoenix worked long hours at the office, had regularly helped out at Sam's Deli during short staff situations, and often drove product around to stores on the weekends when they ran out or were short-shipped by the factory. Before coming to Rogers', Phoenix had been an independent systems consultant, and had served as director, information systems and distribution, and assistant divisional manager, retail operations for Gidden Industries. Phoenix was a shareholder in the company.

Ray Wong, vice president of production, oversaw production and worked at the factory. Wong had completed a Bachelor of Food Science from the

Exhibit 4 Rogers' Chocolates Ltd., Consolidated Statement of Earnings and Retained Earnings

	Year Ended March 31	
	2006	2005
Sales	$11,850,480	$11,991,558
Cost of sales		
Amortization of property and equipment	135,385	108,759
Direct labor	1,545,794	1,677,247
Direct materials	1,770,603	2,745,995
Overhead	1,933,306	846,186
	5,385,088	5,378,187
Gross profit	6,465,392	6,613,371
Interest income	664	1,610
	6,466,056	6,614,981
Expenses		
Interest on long-term debt	91,465	86,943
Selling and administrative	5,221,520	5,007,145
	5,312,985	5,094,088
Earnings before income taxes	1,153,071	1,520,893
Income taxes	261,989	451,567
Net earnings	$ 891,082	$ 1,069,326
Retained earnings, beginning of year	$ 4,748,611	4,381,155
Net earnings	891,081	1,069,326
Dividends	—	(701,870)
Retained earnings, end of year	$ 5,639,692	$ 4,748,611

Exhibit 5 Rogers' Chocolates Ltd.—Schedule of Selling and Administrative Expenses

		Year Ended March 31	
		2006	2005
Selling	Advertising & Promotion	$ 489,345	$ 536,886
	Bad debts	23,000	12,796
	Credit card charges	125,198	125,544
	Mail order	118,606	133,081
	Office & Telephone	29,975	27,274
	Postage and freight	483,003	476,724
	Stores:		
	Factory Store	112,885	122,897
	Sam's Deli	572,495	323,995
	Sidney	75,854	84,047
	Swartz Bay	42,709	38,592
	The Bay Vancouver (closed in 2006)	3,938	4,058
	The Bay Victoria (closed in 2006)	4,236	2,759
	Tsawwassen	—	24,179
	Tudor Sweet Shoppe	87,103	119,058
	Whistler	168,157	182,939
	Royalties	29,862	31,099
	Salaries & benefits	812,269	715,325
	Travel	68,364	46,830
	Total	3,246,999	3,013,658
	Less: postage and freight recoveries	343,116	369,823
		2,903,883	2,638,260
Administrative	Amortization	196,970	135,267
	Automotive	28,658	24,404
	Bank charges and interest	22,533	20,882
	Consulting	102,241	107,379
	Foreign exchange	−6,272	
	Insurance	80,704	78,777
	Management fees	191,226	183,627
	Office supplies and postage	134,159	118,582
	Professional fees	42,872	67,952
	Rent, property taxes and utilities	61,211	56,815
	Repairs and maintenance	18,378	21,105
	Stores:		
	Sam's Deli	326,901	179,834
	Sidney	26,559	28,159
	Swartz Bay	22,038	26,927
	The Bay Vancouver	10,082	18,251
	The Bay Victoria	32,123	37,939
	Tsawwassen		14,647
	Tudor Sweet Shoppe	49,849	45,002
	Whistler	112,450	105,720
	Salaries and benefits	810,049	1,030,336
	Telecommunications	27,824	32,588
	Travel and promotion	27,082	34,692
Total Admin Expenses		$2,317,637	$2,368,885
TOTAL S, G, & A Expenses		$5,221,520	$5,007,145

Exhibit 6 Rogers' Chocolates Ltd.—Consolidated Balance Sheet

	March 31 2006	March 31 2005
Assets		
Current		
Cash	$ 112,185	$ 750,948
Receivables	358,969	461,874
Inventories		
Packaging materials	620,452	576,287
Raw materials	169,235	179,119
Work in progress	89,146	66,467
Manufactured finished goods	643,105	692,517
Finished goods for resale	21,878	36,241
	1,543,816	1,550,631
Investments	103,136	76,822
Income taxes receivable	127,515	—
Prepaids	84,620	56,566
	2,330,241	2,896,842
Property and equipment (see Note 1)	4,364,527	3,922,183
Intangible assets		
Goodwill	916,999	916,999
Trademarks	783,596	783,596
Total intangible assets	1,700,595	1,700,595
Total assets	$8,395,363	$8,519,620
Liabilities		
Current		
Bank indebtedness	$ 186,929	$ 599,146
Payables and accruals	1,098,232	1,226,570
Income taxes payable	—	127,845
Current portion of long term debt	419,971	373,405
	1,705,132	2,326,966
Long-term debt	1,017,679	1,411,184
Total liabilities	2,722,811	3,738,150
Shareholders' Equity		
Capital stock	32,860	32,860
Retained earnings	5,639,691	4,748,611
Total equity	5,672,551	4,781,471
Total liabilities & equity	$8,395,362	$8,519,621

Note 1

Property and Equipment	Cost	Accumulated Amortization	2006 Net Book Value	2005 Net Book Value
Land	1,219,819.20	—	1,219,819.20	1,219,819.20
Buildings	2,799,181.35	1,099,926.90	1,699,254.45	1,770,056.19
Manufacturing equipment	1,693,140.69	1,375,596.00	317,544.69	231,858.99
Furniture and fixtures	749,496.78	385,684.35	363,812.43	249,376.83
Office equipment	108,352.86	90,299.22	18,053.64	24,020.76
Computer equipment	250,683.90	225,157.26	25,526.64	53,214.81
Leasehold improvements	914,332.83	193,817.19	720,515.64	373,836.12
	7,735,007.61	3,370,480.92	4,364,526.69	3,922,182.90

Exhibit 7 Rogers' Chocolates Ltd.—Consolidated Statements of Cash Flows

	Year Ended March 31	
	2006	2005
Increase (decrease) in cash and cash equivalents		
Operating		
Net earnings	$891,081	$1,069,326
Amortization	332,355	244,026
	1,223,436	1,313,352
Change in non-cash oper. working capital	(328,344)	350,045
	895,092	1,663,397
Financing		
(Repayments of) advances from LT debt	(349,168)	661,806
Dividends paid	—	(701,870)
	(349,168)	(40,064)
Investing		
Purchase of assets of Sam's Deli	—	(1,198,500)
Purchase of property and equipment	(772,470)	(419,307)
	(772,470)	(1,617,807)
Net (decrease) increase in cash and cash equivalents	(226,546)	5,526
Cash and cash equivalents, beginning of year	151,802	146,276
Cash and cash equivalents, end of year	$ 74,744	$ 151,802
Comprised of:		
Cash	$112,185	$ 750,948
Bank indebtedness	(186,929)	(599,146)
	$ 74,744	$ 151,802

University of Alberta in 1978, and later took courses in material requirements planning, candy-making, ice-cream making, and management. He had worked in progressively responsible operations positions in a variety of food and beverage companies prior to joining Rogers' in 1990. Wong did not own shares in the company. Wong was especially interested in computer programming, and he had developed all of Rogers' internal production planning systems himself.

Bjorn Bjornson, vice president of Finance and chief financial officer, had retired as chief financial officer of Pacific Coach Lines in 1991, but joined Rogers' in 1997 at the urging of his former partner, who was on Rogers' board. Previously, Bjornson had worked in financial management in manufacturing and retail after articling as a chartered accountant with Price Waterhouse. Bjornson's expertise was in reorganizations, acquisitions, and dispositions. He maintained Rogers' books by hand, as he had never learned accounting or spreadsheet software programs. Bjornson owned shares in the company.

Phoenix and Bjornson were a cohesive team. In the past, there had been conflict between marketing and production, as marketing sought to reduce out-of-stocks and launch new products, while production sought to retain control of its own scheduling and production processes. Conflict between Phoenix and Wong had escalated to the board level during the past two years of uncertainty. Furthermore, because the wholesale division was favored by the past president, the wholesale manager in Kitchener had regularly gone over Phoenix's head to have the president overturn her decisions. Phoenix had indicated significant frustration with her job.

Exhibit 8 Workopolis Job Ad

A unique company . . . a unique location . . . a unique opportunity.

Our client, one of Canada's oldest and respected confectionery companies, is seeking a **PRESIDENT** to oversee the entire business on a day-to-day basis, and provide the vision and guidance for long-term success and profitable growth.

Reporting to the Board of Directors, the President will:

- Deliver superior results and guide the organization to improve.
- Develop formal planning systems and ongoing personnel development.
- Oversee the development of business and marketing strategies to maintain market leadership.
- Provide the necessary leadership to motivate and transform the organization to meet growth expectations.
- Leads, protects and reinforces the positive corporate culture, and is the overseer of the ethics and values in the organization.

An executive level compensation plan commensurate with the importance of this role is offered.

An opportunity that blends an executive level position with the lifestyle only Victoria can offer.

CANDIDATE PROFILE:
Given the high levels of autonomy and accountability, the President must display considerable maturity and business experience.

From a personal perspective, the ideal candidate will be:

- A strong non-authoritative team builder.
- A highly motivated and results oriented self-starter.
- Extremely customer, quality and safety oriented.
- People oriented with the innate ability to establish a high degree of credibility.
- Capable of providing objective insight in a non-confrontational manner.

The successful candidate will likely be or have been in one of the following positions in a manufacturing environment:

- President or General Manager
- At a VP level in operations/finance/marketing looking to rise to the next level

While food manufacturing experience would be a clear asset, it is not a pre-requisite.

GROWTH OPPORTUNITIES

During the recruitment process, and in his first few months on the job, Parkhill had been probing the managers and board members to get their perspectives on growth options. There was a dizzying array of options. One board member, who was very well connected in the tourism business in Victoria, had said Rogers' approach to cruise ship traffic needed to be reconsidered. Although for years Rogers' had counted on cruise ship passengers for business, representatives from Victoria's Butchart Gardens now boarded the cruise ships in San Francisco, and promoted bus tours from the ship north to Butchart Gardens in Victoria. Many of the passengers were thus no longer going downtown.

The idea of franchising Rogers' outlets had been discussed but not truly investigated, because the board was concerned about giving up control of the brand and pricing. Parkhill had visited a store in Banff that had a Rogers' chocolate store attached to a larger gift store. Yet the store was not owned or franchised by Rogers': the gift store had merely displayed the Rogers' chocolates in a separate area for their own purposes. Others who purchased Rogers' chocolates wholesale merely displayed Rogers' merchandise along with their regular merchandise.

For example, the Kingsmill's department store in London, Ontario, carried Rogers' chocolates in its food section. Of course, it might also be possible to franchise Sam's Deli.

The online business also appeared exciting. With low costs of sales and no intermediaries, the profits on the online business were exceptional. With such a high reorder rate, the chance to build a loyal following of online customers seemed like a sure winner.

The corporate gift market also seemed promising. Offering discounts of 25 percent to corporate purchasers enabled Rogers' to still earn stronger margins than wholesale, without the costs of retail. Furthermore, corporate gifting expanded trial of the product.

There were many other possibilities for growth. The Olympics were coming to Vancouver and Whistler in 2010, promising a huge boon for BC tourism. Although Rogers' wasn't big enough to gain official Olympic status, it needed a strategy to take advantage of the crowds. With two stores in Vancouver, and one in Whistler, Rogers' should be able to generate increased sales. Should Rogers' obtain more stores in Vancouver? Or should Rogers' extend its product line to take advantage of its strong franchise in British Columbia? Although ice cream had not been the runaway success the company had hoped, its sales were still building. Rogers' had a sugar-free chocolate line that served a small but growing market.

Another option might be for Rogers' to concentrate its efforts outside of BC. If American tourists had stopped coming to Victoria, due to the decline in the American dollar, should Rogers' go to them? Should Rogers' attempt to increase its penetration in Ontario or other parts of Canada? Should Rogers' attempt to extend its wholesale distribution outside of British Columbia? Would the current sales agency structure be appropriate for increased penetration? Should Rogers' consider an acquisition of another niche chocolate company or a joint venture with another firm to increase its geographical reach? Were there opportunities to pair Rogers' chocolates with other high-end products or brands for mutual benefit?

There was also the issue of the brand image. While Rogers' traditional image was treasured by loyal customers and employees alike, it didn't seem to play as well outside of Victoria. The packaging had been described as homey or dowdy by some, yet others were adamant that it should not be changed. Parkhill had spoken to a brand image consultant that had won numerous awards in the wine industry for the spunky brands he had designed. The consultant had suggested that the only dangerous thing in today's market was to play it safe—consumers loved edgy brands. Should Rogers' throw off tradition and try to reinvent itself?

Of course, if sales were to be increased, Rogers' would need more internal capacity to produce products and fill orders. Should more capacity be added in Victoria, with its expensive real estate and significant shipping costs to get product off the island, or should it be placed somewhere with lower costs and easier access to markets?

As Parkhill pondered all these options, he also knew that he had to take into consideration the culture of the organization and the desires of the board of directors and owners. Would the current managers and employees be willing and able to grow the organization? Would the board endorse a growth strategy that would increase the risk profile of the company? And with all these options, what should Rogers' do first?

Endnotes

[1] P. M. Parker, "The World Outlook for Chocolate and Chocolate Type Confectionery," INSEAD, http://www.marketresearch.com/, February 20, 2007.

[2] David Sprinkle, *The U.S. Chocolate Market, Packaged Facts.* New Orleans: MarketResearch.com, 2005.

[3] Company insider citing a presentation by Neilson at the Confectionery Manufacturer's Association of Canada conference, 2007.

[4] Rogers' was one of the first chocolate companies to announce a trans-fat-free product line.

[5] Note that Bernard Callebaut was not the same as the international chocolatier Callebaut.

[6] "Canadian Chocolate Legend Receives Taste Award from Top European Chefs," Press Release, May 9, 2006, available at www.rogerschocolates.com/archives (accessed December 21, 2006).

[7] From www.retailcouncil.org/awards/rcc/innovative (accessed December 7, 2006).

[8] The Whistler store was at the world-class Whistler ski area. Gastown and Granville Island were tourist attractions in Vancouver.

[9] Since Rogers' is a privately held company, all financial figures in the case are disguised.

Nucor Corporation: Competing against Low-Cost Steel Imports

CASE 10

Arthur A. Thompson
The University of Alabama

In the 1950s and early 1960s, Nuclear Corporation of America was involved in the nuclear instrument and electronics business. After suffering through several money-losing years and facing bankruptcy in 1964, the company's board of directors opted for new leadership and appointed F. Kenneth Iverson as president and CEO. Shortly thereafter, Iverson concluded that the best way to put the company on sound footing was to exit the nuclear instrument and electronics business and rebuild the company around its profitable South Carolina–based Vulcraft subsidiary, which was in the steel joist business—Iverson had been the head of Vulcraft prior to being named president. Iverson moved the company's headquarters from Phoenix, Arizona, to Charlotte, North Carolina, in 1966 and proceeded to expand the joist business with new operations in Texas and Alabama. Then, in 1968, management decided to integrate backward into steelmaking, partly because of the benefits of supplying its own steel requirements and partly because Iverson saw opportunities to capitalize on newly emerging technologies to produce steel more cheaply. The company adopted the name Nucor Corporation in 1972, and Iverson initiated a long-term strategy to grow Nucor into a major player in the U.S. steel industry.

By 1985, Nucor had become the seventh largest steel company in America, with revenues of $758 million, six joist plants, and four state-of-the-art steel mills that used electric arc furnaces to produce new steel products from recycled scrap steel. Nucor was regarded as an excellently managed company, an accomplished low-cost producer, and one of the most competitively successful manufacturing companies in the country.[1] A series of articles in the *New Yorker* related how Nucor, a relatively small American steel company, had built an enterprise that led the whole world into a new era of making steel with recycled scrap steel. NBC did a business documentary that used Nucor to make the point that American manufacturers could be successful in competing against low-cost foreign manufacturers.

At the turn of the century, Nucor was the second largest steel producer in the United States and charging to overtake longtime leader U.S. Steel. Nucor's sales in 2000 exceeded 11 million tons, and revenues were nearly $4.8 billion. Several years thereafter, Nucor surpassed U.S. Steel as the largest steelmaker in North America, but Nucor fell back into second place in 2006 when a global steel company in Europe made a series of acquisitions in the United States to create a U.S.-based subsidiary (Mittal Steel USA) with greater production capacity than Nucor. (However, Nucor shipped more tons of steel to customers in 2005 than did Mittal Steel.) At the end of 2006, Nucor was solidly entrenched as the second largest steel producer in North America based on total production capacity, with 18 plants having the capacity to produce 25 million tons of steel annually, 2006 revenues of $14.8 billion, and net profits of $1.8 billion. It was the most profitable steel producer in North America in both 2005 and 2006. The company was regarded as the low-cost steel producer in the United States and one of the most efficient and technologically innovative steel producers in the world. Nucor had earned a profit in every quarter and

Exhibit 1 Nucor's Growth in the Steel Business, 1970–2006

Year	Tons Sold to Outside Customers	Average Price per Ton	Net Sales (in millions)	Earnings before Taxes (in millions)	Pretax Earnings per Ton	Net Earnings (in millions)
1970	207,000	$245	$50.8	$2.2	$10	$1.1
1975	387,000	314	121.5	11.7	30	7.6
1980	1,159,000	416	482.4	76.1	66	45.1
1985	1,902,000	399	758.5	106.2	56	58.5
1990	3,648,000	406	1,481.6	111.2	35	75.1
1995	7,943,000	436	3,462.0	432.3	62	274.5
2000	11,189,000	425	4,756.5	478.3	48	310.9
2001	12,237,000	354	4,333.7	179.4	16	113.0
2002	13,442,000	357	4,801.7	230.1	19	162.1
2003	17,473,000	359	6,265.8	66.9	4	62.8
2004	19,109,000	595	11,376.8	1,731.3	96	1,121.5
2005	20,465,000	621	12,701.0	2,016.4	104	1,310.3
2006	22,118,000	667	14,751.3	2,693.8	129	1,757.7

Source: Company records posted at www.nucor.com (accessed October 3, 2006, and January 31, 2007).

every year since 1966—a truly remarkable accomplishment in a mature and cyclical industry where it was common for companies to post losses when demand for steel sagged. Going into 2007, Nucor had paid a dividend for 135 consecutive quarters. Exhibit 1 provides highlights of Nucor's growth since 1970.

NUCOR IN 2007

Ken Iverson, the architect of Nucor's climb from obscurity to prominence in the steel industry, was regarded by many as a "model company president." Under Iverson, who served as CEO until late 1998, Nucor was known for its aggressive pursuit of innovation and technical excellence, rigorous quality systems, strong emphasis on employee relations and workforce productivity, cost-conscious corporate culture, and ability to achieve low costs per ton produced. The company had a streamlined organizational structure, incentive-based compensation systems, and steel mills that were among the most modern and efficient in the United States. Iverson proved himself as a master in crafting and executing a low-cost leadership strategy, and he made a point of making sure that he practiced what he preached when it came to holding down costs. The offices of executives and division general managers were simply furnished. There were no company planes and no company cars, and executives were not provided with company-paid country club memberships, reserved parking spaces, executive dining facilities, or other perks. To save money on his own business expenses and set an example for other Nucor managers, Iverson flew coach class and took the subway when he was in New York City.

When Iverson left the company in 1998 following disagreements with the board of directors, he was succeeded briefly by John Correnti and then Dave Aycock, both of whom had worked in various roles under Iverson for a number of years. In 2000, Daniel R. DiMicco, who had joined Nucor in 1982 and risen up through the ranks to executive vice president, was named president and CEO. Under DiMicco, Nucor continued to pursue a rapid-growth strategy, expanding capacity via both acquisition and new plant construction and boosting tons sold from 11.2 million in 2000 to 22.1 million in 2006. Exhibit 2 provides a summary of Nucor's financial and operating performance for 2000–2006.

Product Line

Over the years, Nucor had expanded progressively into the manufacture of a wider and wider range of steel products, enabling it in 2006 to offer steel users one of the broadest product lineups in the industry.

Exhibit 2 Seven-Year Financial and Operating Summary, Nucor Corporation, 2000–2006 ($ in millions, except per share data and sales per employee)

	2006	2005	2004	2003	2002	2001	2000
For the Year							
Net sales	$14,751.3	$12,701.0	$11,376.9	$6,265.8	$4,801.8	$4,333.7	$4,756.5
Costs, expenses and other:							
Cost of products sold	11,283.1	10,085.4	9,128.9	5,996.5	4,332.3	3,914.3	3,929.2
Marketing, administrative and other expenses	592.5	493.6	415.0	165.4	175.6	150.7	183.2
Interest expense (income), net	(37.4)	4.2	22.4	24.6	14.3	6.5	(.8)
Minority interests	219.2	110.7	80.9	24.0	79.5	103.1	151.5
Other income	—	(9,200)	(1,596)	(11.6)	(29.9)	(20.2)	—
Total	12,057.5	10,684.6	9,645.6	6,199.0	4,571.7	4,154.3	4,263.0
Earnings before income taxes	2,693.8	2,016.4	1,731.3	66.9	230.1	179.4	493.5
Provision for income taxes	936.1	706.1	609.8	4.1	68.0	66.4	182.6
Net earnings	$ 1,757.7	$ 1,310.3	$ 1,121.5	$ 62.8	$ 162.1	$ 113.0	$ 310.9
Net earnings per share:							
Basic	$ 5.73	$4.17	$3.54	$ 0.20	$ 0.52	$ 0.37	$ 0.95
Diluted	5.68	4.13	3.51	0.20	0.52	0.37	0.95
Dividends declared per share	$ 0.90	$ 0.925	$ 0.235	$ 0.20	$ 0.19	$ 0.17	$ 0.15
Percentage of net earnings to net sales	11.9%	10.3%	9.9%	1.0%	3.4%	2.6%	6.5%
Return on average equity	38.6%	33.9%	38.7%	2.7%	7.2%	5.2%	14.2%
Capital expenditures	$ 338.4	$ 331.5	$ 285.9	$ 215.4	$ 243.6	$ 261.1	$ 415.4
Depreciation	363.9	375.1	383.3	364.1	307.1	289.1	259.4
Sales per employee (000s)	1,273	1,159	1,107	637	528	531	619
At Year End							
Current assets	$ 4,675.0	$ 4,071.6	$ 3,174.9	$1,620.7	$1,415.4	$1,373.7	$1,379.5
Current liabilities	1,450.0	1,255.7	1,065.8	629.6	591.5	484.2	558.1
Working capital	3,225.0	2,815.9	2,109.2	991.0	823.8	889.5	821.5
Cash provided by operating activities	2,251.2	2,136.6	1,024.8	493.8	497.2	495.1	820.8
Current ratio	3.2	3.2	3.0	2.6	2.4	2.8	2.5
Property, plant and equipment	$ 2,856.4	$ 2,855.7	$ 2,818.3	$2,817.1	$2,932.1	$2,365.7	$2,329.4
Total assets	7,885.0	7,138.8	6,133.2	4,492.4	4,381.1	3,759.3	3,710.9
Long-term debt	922.3	923.6	923.6	903.6	894.6	460.5	460.5
Stockholders' equity	4,826.0	4,279.8	3,456.0	2,342.1	2,323.0	2,201.5	2,131.0
Shares outstanding (000s)	301.2	310.2	319.0	314.4	312.8	311.2	310.4
Employees	11,900	11,300	10,600	9,900	9,800	8,400	7,900

Source: 2005 and 2006 10-K reports and company press release, January 25, 2007.

Steel products were considered commodities. While some steelmakers had plants where production quality was sometimes inconsistent or on occasions failed to meet customer-specified metallurgical characteristics, most steel plants turned out products of comparable metallurgical quality—one producer's reinforcing bar was essentially the same as another producer's reinforcing bar, a particular grade of sheet steel made at one plant was essentially identical to the same grade of sheet steel made at another plant. The commodity nature of steel products forced steel producers to be price-competitive, with the market price of each particular steel product being driven by demand–supply conditions for that product.

Steel Products Nucor's first venture into steel in the late 1960s, via its Vulcraft division, was principally one of fabricating steel joists and joist girders from steel that was purchased from various steelmakers; the joists and girders were sold mainly to construction contractors. Vulcraft expanded into the fabrication of steel decking in 1977, most of which was also sold to construction-related customers. Vulcraft's joist, girder, and decking products were used mainly for roof and floor support systems in retail stores, shopping centers, warehouses, manufacturing facilities, schools, churches, hospitals, and, to a lesser extent, multistory buildings and apartments.

In 1979, Nucor began fabricating cold finished steel products. These consisted mainly of cold drawn and turned, ground, and polished steel bars or rods of various shapes—rounds, hexagons, flats, channels, and squares—and were made of carbon, alloy, and leaded steels as per customer specifications or end-use requirements. Cold finished steel of one type or another was used in tens of thousands of products, including anchor bolts, farm machinery, ceiling fan motors, garage door openers, air conditioner compressors, and lawn mowers. Nucor sold cold finished steel directly to large customers in the automotive, farm machinery, hydraulic, appliance, and electric motor industries and to independent steel distributors (usually referred to as steel service centers) that supplied manufacturers buying steel products in relatively small quantities. The total market for cold finished products in the United States was an estimated 2 million tons annually. In 2006, Nucor Cold Finish was the largest producer of cold finished bars in the United States, with a market share of about 17 percent; its 4 cold finish facilities (in Nebraska, South Carolina, Utah, and Wisconsin) had annual capacity of 490,000 tons. Nucor Cold Finish obtained virtually all of the steel needed to produce cold finished bars from Nucor's bar mills.

Nucor's line of steel products also included metal building systems, light-gauge steel framing, and steel fasteners (bolts, nuts, washers, screws, and bolt assemblies). These were produced by the company's building system and fasteners divisions. Nucor Building Systems began operations in 1987 and had four manufacturing facilities (Indiana, South Carolina, Texas, and Utah) in 2007; its wall and roof systems were mainly used for industrial and commercial buildings, including distribution centers, automobile dealerships, retail centers, aircraft hangars, churches, office buildings, warehouses, and manufacturing facilities. Complete metal building packages could be customized and combined with other materials such as glass, wood, and masonry to produce a cost-effective, aesthetically sound building of up to 1 million square feet. The buildings were sold through a builder distribution network. Nucor Building Systems obtained a significant portion of its steel requirements from Nucor's bar and sheet mills.

The fastener division, located in Indiana, began operations in 1986 with the construction of a $25 million plant. At the time, imported steel fasteners accounted for 90 percent of the U.S. market because U.S. manufacturers were not competitive on cost and price. Iverson said, "We're going to bring that business back; we can make bolts as cheaply as foreign producers." Nucor built a second fastener plant in 1995, giving it the capacity to supply about 20 percent of the U.S. market for steel fasteners.

Steelmaking In 1968 Nucor got into basic steelmaking, building a mill in Darlington, South Carolina, to manufacture steel bars. The Darlington mill was one of the first plants of major size in the United States to use electric arc furnace technology to melt scrap steel and cast molten metal into various shapes. Electric arc furnace technology was particularly appealing because the labor and capital requirements to melt steel scrap and produce crude steel were far lower than those at conventional integrated steel mills, where raw steel was produced using coke ovens, basic oxygen blast furnaces, ingot casters, and multiple types of finishing facilities to make crude steel from iron ore, coke, limestone, oxygen, scrap steel, and other ingredients. By 1981, Nucor had four bar mills making carbon and alloy steels in bars, angles, and light structural shapes; in 2006, Nucor had 10 such plants with a total annual capacity of approximately 7.7 million tons. The products of bar mills were widely used in metal buildings, farm equipment, automotive products, furniture, and recreational equipment; many types of construction required the use of steel reinforcing rods, or rebar.

In the late 1980s, Nucor entered into the production of sheet steel at a newly constructed plant in Crawfordsville, Indiana. Flat-rolled sheet steel was used in the production of motor vehicles, appliances, steel pipes and tubes, and other durable goods. The Crawfordsville plant was the first in the world to employ a revolutionary thin-slab casting process that substantially reduced the capital investment and costs to produce flat-rolled sheet steel. Thin-slab casting machines had a funnel-shaped mold to squeeze molten steel down to a thickness of 1.5–2.0 inches, compared to the typical 8- to 10-inch-thick slabs produced by conventional casters. It was much cheaper to then build and operate facilities to roll thin-gauge sheet steel from 1.5- to 2-inch-thick slabs than from 8- to 10-inch-thick slabs. The Crawfordsville plant's costs were said to be $50 to $75 per ton below the costs of traditional sheet steel plants, a highly significant cost advantage in a commodity market where the going price at the time was $400 per ton. *Forbes* magazine described Nucor's pioneering use of thin-slab casting as the most substantial technological/ industrial innovation in the past 50 years.[2] By 1996, two additional sheet steel mills that employed thin-slab casting technology were constructed and a fourth mill was acquired in 2002, giving Nucor the capacity to produce 10.8 million tons of sheet steel products annually as of 2006.

Also in the late 1980s, Nucor added wide-flange steel beams, pilings, and heavy structural steel products to its lineup of product offerings. Structural steel products were used in buildings, bridges, overpasses, and similar such projects where strong weight-bearing support was needed. Customers included construction companies, steel fabricators, manufacturers, and steel service centers. To gain entry to the structural steel segment, in 1988 Nucor entered into a joint venture with Yamato-Kogyo, one of Japan's major producers of wide-flange beams, to build a new structural steel mill in Arkansas; a second mill was built on the same site in the 1990s that made the Nucor-Yamato venture in Arkansas the largest structural beam facility in the Western Hemisphere. In 1999, Nucor began production at a third structural steel mill in South Carolina. All three mills used a special continuous casting method that was quite cost-effective. As of 2006, Nucor had the capacity to make 3.7 million tons of structural steel products annually.

Starting in 2000, Nucor began producing steel plate of various thicknesses and lengths that was sold to manufacturers of heavy equipment, ships, barges, rail cars, refinery tanks, pressure vessels, pipes and tubes, and similar products. Steel plate was made at mills in Alabama and North Carolina that had combined capacity of about 2.8 million tons.

Exhibit 3 shows Nucor's sales by product category for 1990–2006. The breadth of its product line made Nucor the most diversified steel producer in North America. The company had market leadership in several product categories—it was the largest U.S. producer of steel bars, structural steel, steel joist, steel deck, and cold-rolled bars. Nucor had an overall market share of shipments to U.S.-based steel customers (including imports) of about 17 percent in both 2005 and 2006.

Strategy

Starting in 2000, Nucor embarked on a four-part growth strategy that involved new acquisitions, new plant construction, continued plant upgrades and cost reduction efforts, and joint ventures.

Strategic Acquisitions The first element of the four-part strategy was to make acquisitions that would strengthen Nucor's customer base, geographic coverage, and lineup of product offerings. Beginning in the late 1990s, Nucor management concluded that growth-minded companies like Nucor might well be better off purchasing existing plant capacity rather than building new capacity, provided the acquired plants could be bought at bargain prices, economically retrofitted with new equipment if need be, and then operated at costs comparable to (or even below) those of newly constructed state-of-the-art plants. At the time, the steel industry worldwide had far more production capacity than was needed to meet market demand, forcing many companies to operate in the red. Nucor had not made any acquisitions since about 1990, and a team of five people was assembled in 1998 to explore acquisition possibilities.

For almost three years, no acquisitions were made. But then the economic recession that hit Asia and Europe in the late 1990s reached the United States in full force in 2000–2001. The September 11, 2001, terrorist attacks further weakened steel purchases by such major steel-consuming industries as construction, automobiles, and farm equipment. Many steel companies in the United States and other parts of the world were operating in the red. Market conditions in the United States were particularly grim. Between October 2000 and October 2001,

Exhibit 3 Nucor's Sales of Steel Products, by Product Category, 1990–2006

Year	Tons Sold to Outside Customers (in thousands)									
	Steel									
	Sheet (2006 capacity of ~10.8 million tons)	Bars (2006 capacity of ~7.7 million tons)	Structural (2006 capacity of ~3.7 million tons)	Plate (2006 capacity of ~2.8 million tons)	Total (2006 capacity of ~25 million tons)	Steel Joists (2006 capacity of ~715,000 tons)	Steel Deck (2006 capacity of ~435,000 tons)	Cold Finished Steel (2006 capacity of ~490,000 tons)	Other Steel Products*	Total Tons
2006	8,495	6,513	3,209	2,432	20,649	570	398	327	174	22,118
2005	8,026	5,983	2,866	2,145	19,020	554	380	342	169	20,465
2004	8,078	5,244	2,760	1,705	17,787	522	364	271	165	19,109
2003	6,954	5,530	2,780	999	16,263	503	353	237	117	17,473
2002	5,806	2,947	2,689	872	12,314	462	330	226	110	13,442
2001	5,074	2,687	2,749	522	11,032	532	344	203	126	12,237
2000	4,456	2,209	3,094	20	9,779	613	353	250	194	11,189
1995	2,994	1,799	1,952	—	6,745	552	234	234	178	7,943
1990	420	1,382	1,002	—	2,804	443	134	163	104	3,648

*Includes steel fasteners (steel screws, nuts, bolts, washers, and bolt assemblies), metal building systems, and light-gauge steel framing.

Source: Company records posted at www.nucor.com (accessed October 3, 2006, and January 31, 2007).

29 steel companies in the United States, including Bethlehem Steel Corporation and LTV Corporation, the nation's third and fourth largest steel producers, respectively, filed for bankruptcy protection. Bankrupt steel companies accounted for about 25 percent of U.S. capacity. The *Economist* noted that of the 14 steel companies tracked by Standard & Poor's, only Nucor was indisputably healthy. Some experts believed that close to half of the U.S. steel industry's production capacity might be forced to close before conditions improved; about 47,000 jobs in the U.S. steel industry had vanished since 1997.

One of the principal reasons for the distressed market conditions in the United States was a surge in imports of low-priced steel from foreign countries. Outside the United States, weak demand and a glut of capacity had driven commodity steel prices to 20-year lows in 1998. Globally, the industry had about 1 billion tons of annual capacity, but puny demand had kept production levels in the 750 to 800 million tons per year range during 1998–2000. A number of foreign steel producers, anxious to keep their mills running and finding few good market opportunities elsewhere, had begun selling steel in the U.S. market at cut-rate prices in 1997–1999. Nucor and other U.S. companies reduced prices to better compete and several filed unfair trade complaints against foreign steelmakers. The U.S. Department of Commerce concluded in March 1999 that steel companies in six countries (Canada, South Korea, Taiwan, Italy, Belgium, and South Africa) had illegally dumped stainless steel in the United States, and the governments of Belgium, Italy, and South Africa further facilitated the dumping by giving their steel producers unfair subsidies that at least partially made up for the revenues lost by selling at below-market prices. Congress and the Clinton administration opted to not impose tariffs or quotas on imported steel, which helped precipitate the number of bankruptcy filings. However, the Bush administration was more receptive to protecting the U.S. steel industry from the dumping practices of foreign steel companies. In October 2001, the U.S. International Trade Commission (ITC) ruled that increased steel imports of semifinished steel, plate, hot-rolled sheet, strip and coils, cold-rolled sheet and strip, and corrosion-resistant and coated sheet and strip were a substantial cause of serious injury, or threat of serious injury, to the U.S. industry. In March 2002, the Bush administration imposed tariffs of up to 30 percent on imports of selected steel products to help provide relief from Asian and European companies dumping steel in the United States at ultra-low prices.

Even though market conditions were tough for Nucor in 2001–2003, management concluded that oversupplied steel industry conditions and the number of beleaguered U.S. companies made it attractive to expand Nucor's production capacity via acquisition. The company proceeded to make a series of acquisitions:

- In 2001, Nucor paid \$115 million to acquire substantially all of the assets of Auburn Steel Company's 400,000-ton steel bar facility in Auburn, New York. This acquisition gave Nucor expanded market presence in the Northeast and was seen as a good source of supply for a new Vulcraft joist plant being constructed in Chemung, New York.
- In November 2001, Nucor announced the acquisition of ITEC Steel Inc. for a purchase price of \$9 million. ITEC Steel had annual revenues of \$10 million and produced load-bearing light-gauge steel framing for the residential and commercial market at facilities in Texas and Georgia. Nucor was impressed with ITEC's dedication to continuous improvement and intended to grow ITEC's business via geographic and product line expansion. ITEC Steel's name was changed to Nucon Steel Commercial Corporation in 2002.
- In July 2002, Nucor paid \$120 million to purchase Trico Steel Company, which had a 2.2-million-ton sheet steel mill in Decatur, Alabama. Trico Steel was a joint venture of LTV (which owned a 50 percent interest), and two leading international steel companies—Sumitomo Metal Industries and British Steel. The joint venture partners had built the mill in 1997 at a cost of \$465 million, but Trico was in Chapter 11 bankruptcy proceedings at the time of the acquisition and the mill was shut down. The Trico mill's capability to make thin sheet steel with a superior surface quality added competitive strength to Nucor's strategy to gain sales and market share in the flat-rolled sheet segment. By October 2002, two months ahead of schedule, Nucor had restarted operations at the Decatur mill and was shipping products to customers.
- In December 2002, Nucor paid \$615 million to purchase substantially all of the assets of

Birmingham Steel Corporation, which included four bar mills in Alabama, Illinois, Washington, and Mississippi. The four plants had capacity of approximately 2 million tons annually. The purchase price also included approximately $120 million in inventory and receivables, the assets of Port Everglade Steel Corporation, the assets of Klean Steel, Birmingham Steel's ownership interest in Richmond Steel Recycling, and a mill in Memphis, Tennessee, that was not currently in operation. Top executives believed that the Birmingham Steel acquisition would broaden Nucor's customer base and build profitable market share in bar steel products.

- In August 2004, Nucor acquired a cold-rolling mill in Decatur, Alabama, from Worthington Industries for $80 million. This 1-million-ton mill, which opened in 1998, was located adjacent to the previously acquired Trico mill and gave Nucor added ability to service the needs of sheet steel buyers located in the southeastern United States.
- In June 2004, Nucor paid a cash price of $80 million to acquire a plate mill owned by Britain-based Corus Steel that was located in Tuscaloosa, Alabama. The Tuscaloosa mill, which currently had capacity of 700,000 tons that Nucor management believed was expandable to 1 million tons, was the first U.S. mill to employ a special technology that enabled high-quality wide steel plate to be produced from coiled steel plate. The mill produced coiled steel plate and plate products that were cut to customer-specified lengths. Nucor intended to offer these niche products to its commodity plate and coiled sheet customers.
- In February 2005, Nucor completed the purchase of Fort Howard Steel's operations in Oak Creek, Wisconsin; the Oak Creek facility produced cold finished bars in size ranges up to six-inch rounds and had approximately 140,000 tons of annual capacity.
- In June 2005, Nucor purchased Marion Steel Company located in Marion, Ohio, for a cash price of $110 million. Marion operated a bar mill with annual capacity of about 400,000 tons; the Marion location was in proximity to 60 percent of the steel consumption in the United States.
- In May 2006, Nucor acquired Connecticut Steel Corporation for $43 million in cash. Connecticut Steel's bar products mill in Wallingford had annual capacity to make 300,000 tons of wire rod and rebar and approximately 85,000 tons of wire mesh fabrication and structural mesh fabrication, products that complemented Nucor's present lineup of steel bar products provided to construction customers.
- In late 2006, Nucor purchased Verco Manufacturing Company for approximately $180 million; Verco produced steel floor and roof decking at one location in Arizona and two locations in California. The Verco acquisition further solidified Vulcraft's market leading position in steel decking, giving it total annual capacity of 530,000 tons.
- In January 2007, Nucor announced plans to acquire all of the shares of Canada-based Harris Steel for a total cash purchase price of about $1.07 billion. Harris Steel had 2005 sales of Cdn$1.0 billion and earnings of Cdn$64 million. The company's operations consisted of (1) Harris Rebar, which was involved in the fabrication and placing of concrete reinforcing steel and the design and installation of concrete post-tensioning systems; (2) Laurel Steel, which manufactured and distributed wire and wire products, welded wire mesh, and cold finished bar; and (3) Fisher & Ludlow, which manufactured and distributed heavy industrial steel grating, aluminum grating, and expanded metal. In Canada, Harris Steel had 24 reinforcing steel fabricating plants, two steel grating distribution centers, and one cold finished bar and wire processing plant; in the United States, it had 10 reinforcing steel fabricating plants, two steel grating manufacturing plants, and three steel grating manufacturing plants. Harris had customers throughout Canada and the United States and employed about 3,000 people. For the past three years, Harris had purchased a big percentage of its steel requirements from Nucor. Nucor planned to operate Harris Steel as an independent subsidiary.

By 2005–2006, steel industry conditions worldwide had improved markedly. Prices in the United States were about 50 percent higher than in 2000 and Nucor's sales and earnings were at all-time highs (see Exhibits 1 and 3). But dumping of foreign-made steel into the U.S. market at below-market prices was still a problem. In April 2005, the

U.S. International Trade Commission extended the antidumping and countervailing duty orders and suspension agreement covering imports of hot-rolled steel from Brazil, Japan, and the Russian Federation for an additional five years.

The Commercialization of New Technologies and New Plant Construction The second element of Nucor's growth strategy was to continue to be a technology leader and to be aggressive in constructing new plant capacity, particularly when such construction offered the opportunity to be first-to-market with new steelmaking technologies. Nucor management made a conscious effort to focus on the introduction of disruptive technologies (those that would give Nucor a commanding market advantage and thus be disruptive to the efforts of competitors in matching Nucor's cost competitiveness and/or product quality) and leapfrog technologies (those that would allow Nucor to overtake competitors in terms of product quality, cost per ton, or market share).

One of Nucor's biggest and most recent successes in pioneering new technology had been at its Crawfordsville facilities, where Nucor had the world's first installation of direct strip casting of carbon sheet steel—a process called Castrip. After several years of testing and process refinement at Crawfordsville, Nucor announced in 2005 that the Castrip process was ready for commercialization; Nucor had exclusive rights to Castrip technology in the United States and Brazil. The process, which had proved to be quite difficult to bring to commercial reality, was a major technological breakthrough for producing flat-rolled, carbon, and stainless steels in very thin gauges; it involved far fewer process steps to cast metal at or very near customer-desired thicknesses and shapes. The Castrip process drastically reduced capital outlays for equipment and produced savings on operating expenses as well—major expense savings included ability to use lower quality scrap steel and requiring 90 percent less energy to process liquid metal into hot-rolled steel sheets. A big environmental benefit of the Castrip process was cutting greenhouse gas emissions by up to 80 percent. Nucor's Castrip facility at Crawfordsville had the capacity to produce 500,000 tons annually and employed 55 people. In 2006, Nucor was building its second Castrip facility on the site of the Nucor-Yamato beam mill in Arkansas.

Nucor's growth strategy also included investing in the construction of new plant capacity whenever management spotted opportunities to strengthen its market presence:

- In 2006, Nucor announced that it would construct a new facility to produce metal buildings systems in Brigham City, Utah. The new plant, Nucor's fourth building systems plant, was to have capacity of 45,000 tons, employ over 200 people, and cost about $27 million; operations were expected to begin in the first quarter of 2008. The new plant gave Nucor national market reach in building systems products and total annual capacity of more than 190,000 tons.
- In 2006, Nucor announced plans to construct a state-of-the-art steel mill in Memphis, Tennessee, to produce special quality steel bars; the mill was expected to cost $230 million, employ more than 200 people, and have annual capacity of 850,000 tons. Management believed the mill would not only give Nucor one of the industry's most diverse lineups of special quality steel bar products but also provide a significantly better cost structure compared to both foreign and domestic competitors in the special quality steel bar segment. Nucor already had special quality bar mills in Nebraska and South Carolina.

The Drive for Plant Efficiency and Low-Cost Production A key part of Nucor's strategy was to continue making capital investments to improve plant efficiency and keep production costs low. From its earliest days in the steel business, Nucor had built state-of-the-art facilities in the most economical fashion possible and then made it standard company practice to invest aggressively in plant modernization and efficiency improvements as technology advanced and new cost-saving opportunities emerged. Nucor management made a point of staying on top of the latest advances in steelmaking around the world, diligently searching for emerging cost-effective technologies it could adopt or adapt in its facilities. Executives at Nucor had a long-standing commitment to provide the company's workforce with the best technology available to get the job done right in a safe working environment.

Nucor management also stressed continual improvement in product quality and cost at each one of its production facilities. Many Nucor locations were ISO 9000 and ISO 14001 certified. The company had a program called BESTmarking aimed at being the industrywide best performer on a variety of production and efficiency measures. Managers at all Nucor plants were accountable for demonstrating that their operations were competitive on both product quality and cost vis-à-vis the plants of rival companies. One trait of Nucor's corporate culture was the expectation that plant-level managers would be aggressive in implementing methods to improve product quality and keep costs per ton low relative to rival plants.

The company's latest initiative involved investments to upgrade and fully modernize the operations of its production facilities. Examples included a three-year bar mill modernization program and the addition of vacuum degassers to its four sheet steel mills. Adding the vacuum degassers not only improved Nucor's ability to produce some of the highest-quality sheet steel available but also resulted in expanded capacity at low incremental cost. Nucor's capital expenditures for new technology, plant improvements, and equipment upgrades totaled $415 million in 2000, $261 million in 2001, $244 million in 2002, $215 million in 2003, $286 million in 2004, $331 million in 2005, and $338 million in 2006. Capital expenditures for 2007 were projected to be $930 million; the big increase over 2006 capital spending was intended to ensure that Nucor plants were kept in state-of-the-art condition and globally competitive on cost. Top executives expected that all of Nucor's plants would have ISO 14001 certified Environmental Management Systems in place by the end of 2007.

Global Growth via Joint Ventures The fourth component of Nucor's strategy was to grow globally with joint ventures and the licensing of new technologies. Nucor had recently entered into a joint venture with Companhia Vale do Rio Doce (CVRD) to construct and operate an environmentally friendly pig iron project in northern Brazil. Production began in the fourth quarter of 2005. The joint venture at the Brazilian plant involved using fast-growing eucalyptus trees as fuel.[3] Eucalyptus trees reached a mature height of 70 feet in seven years and immediately began to grow back when harvested the first two times, after which they had to be replanted. The project appealed to Nucor because it counteracted global warming. As eucalyptus trees grow, they take in carbon dioxide from the atmosphere and sequester it in their biomass; some goes back into the soil as leaves and twigs fall to the ground, with the remainder being stored in the wood of the tree. While burning the eucalyptus wood to create the charcoal fuel on which this project depended resulted in the release of some of the stored carbon dioxide to the atmosphere and still more was released when the charcoal was combined with iron ore in a mini blast furnace to create pig iron, some of the carbon dioxide was locked up in the pig iron. But the net effect on any global warming due to the release of carbon dioxide was overwhelmingly positive, given that about 500,000 tons of pig iron were being produced and that over 200,000 acres, or about 312 square miles, of eucalyptus forest were being restored or protected. In the overall scheme, the production of pig iron at the Brazilian plant removed about 2,400 pounds of carbon dioxide from the atmosphere for every ton of pig iron produced; this compared quite favorably with the conventional method of producing pig iron, which increased the carbon dioxide in the atmosphere by 4,180 pounds for every ton of pig iron produced.

Nucor had recently partnered with the Rio Tinto Group, Mitsubishi Corporation, and Chinese steelmaker Shougang Corporation to pioneer Rio Tinto's HIsmelt technology at a new plant located in Kwinana, Western Australia. The HIsmelt plant converted iron ore to liquid metal or pig iron and was both a replacement for traditional blast furnace technology and a hot metal source for electric arc furnaces. Rio Tinto had been developing the HIsmelt technology for 10 years and believed that it had the potential to revolutionize iron making and provide low-cost, high-quality iron for making steel. Nucor had a 25 percent ownership in the venture and had a joint global marketing agreement with Rio Tinto to license the technology to other interested steel companies. The Australian plant represented the world's first commercial application of the HIsmelt technology. Production started in January 2006; the plant had a capacity of over 800,000 metric tons and was expandable to 1.5 million metric tons at an attractive capital cost per incremental ton. Nucor viewed the Australian plant as a future royalty stream and raw material source. The technology had also been licensed to a Chinese steelmaker that planned to construct an 800,000-ton steel plant in China using the HIsmelt process for its iron source.

Nucor's third principal international project involved a raw materials strategy initiative to develop a low-cost substitute for scrap steel. Nucor was already the largest purchaser of scrap steel in North America, and the company's rapid growth strategy made it vulnerable to rising prices for scrap steel. In an effort to curtail its dependence on scrap steel as a raw material input, Nucor acquired an idled direct reduced iron plant in Louisiana in September 2004, relocated its operation to Trinidad (an island off the coast of South America near Venezuela), and expanded the project to a capacity of 1.8 million metric tons. Nucor was currently purchasing 6 to 7 million tons of iron annually to use in making higher-quality grades of sheet steel; integrating backward into supplying 25 to 30 percent of its own iron requirements held promise of raw material savings and less reliance on outside iron suppliers. The Trinidad site was chosen because it had a long-term and very cost-attractive supply of natural gas, along with favorable logistics for receiving iron ore and shipping direct reduced iron to Nucor's sheet steel mills in the United States. Production began in January 2007.

Nucor was looking for other opportunities globally. But so far, Nucor's strategy to participate in foreign steel markets was via joint ventures involving pioneering use of new steelmaking technologies. The company did not currently have any plans to build and operate its own steel mills outside the United States—its only company-operated foreign facility was the one in Trinidad.

Operations

Nucor had 49 facilities in 17 states and was the largest recycler of scrap steel in North America. The company recycled over 23 million tons of scrap in 2005 and over 21 million tons in 2006. At Nucor's steel mills, scrap steel and other metals were melted in electric arc furnaces and poured into continuous casting systems. Sophisticated rolling mills converted the billets, blooms, and slabs produced by various casting equipment into rebar, angles, rounds, channels, flats, sheet, beams, plate, and other finished steel products. Nucor's steel mill operations were highly automated, typically requiring fewer operating employees per ton produced than the mills of rival companies. High worker productivity at all Nucor steel mills resulted in labor costs equal to about 8 percent of revenues in 2005–2006—a considerably lower percentage than the labor costs at the integrated mills of companies using union labor and conventional blast furnace technology. Nucor's value chain (anchored in using electric arc furnace technology to recycle scrap steel) involved far fewer production steps, far less capital investment, and considerably less labor than the value chains of companies with integrated steel mills that made crude steel from iron ore.

Nucor's two big cost components at its steel plants were scrap steel and energy. Scrap steel prices were driven by market demand–supply conditions and could fluctuate significantly—see Exhibit 4. Nucor implemented a raw material surcharge in 2004 to cope with sharply increasing scrap steel prices in 2004 and help protect operating profit margins. Total energy costs increased by approximately $7 per ton from 2004 to 2005 as natural gas prices increased by approximately 31 percent and electricity prices increased by approximately 19 percent; energy costs rose another $1 per ton in 2006. Due to the efficiency of Nucor's steel mills, however, energy costs remained less than 10 percent of revenues in 2004, 2005, and 2006. In 2006, Nucor hedged a portion of its exposure to natural gas prices out into 2007 and also entered into contracts with natural gas suppliers to purchase natural gas in amounts needed to operate

Exhibit 4 **Nucor's Costs for Scrap Steel and Scrap Substitute, 2005–2006**

Period	Average Scrap and Scrap Substitute Cost per Ton Used
2000	$120
2001	101
2002	110
2003	137
2004	238
2005	
Quarter 1	272
Quarter 2	246
Quarter 3	217
Quarter 4	240
2006	
Quarter 1	237
Quarter 2	247
Quarter 3	257
Quarter 4	243

Source: Nucor's 10-K reports and information posted at www.nucor.com (accessed October 25, 2006, and January 31, 2007).

its direct reduced iron facility in Trinidad from 2006 through 2028.

Nucor plants were linked electronically to each other's production schedules, and each plant strived to operate in a just-in-time inventory mode. Virtually all tons produced were shipped out very quickly to customers; consequently, finished goods inventories at Nucor plants were relatively small.

Organization and Management Philosophy

Nucor had a simple, streamlined organization structure to allow employees to innovate and make quick decisions. The company was highly decentralized, with most day-to-day operating decisions made by division or plant-level general managers and their staff. The three building systems plants and the four cold-rolled products plants were headed by a group manager, but otherwise each plant operated independently as a profit center and was headed by a general manager, who in most cases also had the title of vice president. The group manager or plant general manager had control of the day-to-day decisions that affected the group or plant's profitability.

The organizational structure at a typical plant had three management layers:

- General Manager
- Department Manager
- Supervisor/Professional
- Hourly Employee

Group managers and plant managers reported to one of four executive vice presidents at corporate headquarters. Nucor's corporate staff was exceptionally small, consisting of only 66 people in 2006, the philosophy being that corporate headquarters should consist of a small cadre of executives who would guide a decentralized operation where liberal authority was delegated to managers in the field. Each plant had a sales manager who was responsible for selling the products made at that particular plant; such staff functions as engineering, accounting, and personnel management were performed at the group/plant level. There was a minimum of paperwork and bureaucratic systems. Each group/plant was expected to earn about a 25 percent return on total assets before corporate expenses, taxes, interest, or profit sharing. As long as plant managers met their profit targets, they were allowed to operate with minimal restrictions and interference from corporate headquarters. There was a very friendly spirit of competition from one plant to the next to see which facility could be the best performer, but since all of the vice presidents and general managers shared the same bonus systems, they functioned pretty much as a team despite operating their facilities individually. Top executives did not hesitate to replace group or plant managers who consistently struggled to achieve profitability and operating targets.

Workforce Compensation Practices

Nucor was a nonunion "pay for performance" company with an incentive compensation system that rewarded goal-oriented individuals and did not put a maximum on what they could earn. All employees were covered under one of four basic compensation plans, each featuring incentives related to meeting specific goals and targets:

1. *Production Incentive Plan*—Production line jobs were rated on degree of responsibility required and assigned a base wage comparable to the wages paid by other manufacturing plants in the area where a Nucor plant was located. But in addition to their base wage, operating and maintenance employees were paid weekly bonuses based on the number of tons by which the output of their production team or work group exceeded the standard number of tons. All operating and maintenance employees were members of a production team that included the team's production supervisor, and the tonnage produced by each work team was measured for each work shift and then totaled for all shifts during a given week. If a production team's weekly output beat the weekly standard, team members (including the team's production supervisor) earned a specified percentage bonus for each ton produced above the standard—production bonuses were paid weekly (rather than quarterly or annually) so that workers and supervisors would be rewarded immediately for their efforts. The standard rate was calculated based on the capabilities of the equipment employed (typically at the time plant operations began), and no bonus was paid if the equipment was not operating (which gave maintenance workers a big incentive to keep a plant's equipment in

good working condition)—Nucor's philosophy was that everybody suffered when equipment was not operating and the bonus for downtime ought to be zero. Production standards at Nucor plants were seldom raised unless a plant underwent significant modernization or important new pieces of equipment were installed that greatly boosted labor productivity. It was common for production incentive bonuses to run from 50 to 150 percent of an employee's base pay, thereby pushing their compensation levels up well above those at other nearby manufacturing plants. Worker efforts to exceed the standard and get a bonus involved not so much working harder as practicing good teamwork and close collaboration in resolving problems and figuring out how best to exceed the production standards.

2. *Department Manager Incentive Plan*—Department managers earned annual incentive bonuses based primarily on the percentage of net income to dollars of assets employed for their division. These bonuses could be as much as 80 percent of a department manager's base pay.

3. *Professional and Clerical Bonus Plan*—A bonus based on a division's net income return on assets was paid to employees that were not on the production worker or department manager plan.

4. *Senior Officers Incentive Plan*—Nucor's senior officers did not have employment contracts and did not participate in any pension or retirement plans. Their base salaries were set at approximately 90 percent of the median base salary for comparable positions in other manufacturing companies with comparable assets, sales, and capital. The remainder of their compensation was based on Nucor's annual overall percentage of net income to stockholder's equity (i.e., return on equity, or ROE) and was paid out in cash and stock. Once Nucor's ROE reached a threshold of not less than 3 percent or more than 7 percent (as determined annually by the compensation committee of the board of directors), senior officers earned a bonus equal to 20 percent of their base salary. If Nucor's annual ROE exceeded 20 percent, senior officers earned a bonus equal to the 225 percent of their base salary. Officers could earn an additional bonus of up to 75 percent of their base salary based on a comparison of Nucor's net sales growth with the net sales growth of members of a steel industry peer group. There was also a long-term incentive plan that provided for stock awards and stock options; this incentive covered a three-year performance period and was linked to Nucor's return on average invested capital relative to that of other steel industry competitors. The structure of these officer incentives was such that Nucor officers could find their bonus compensation swinging widely—from close to zero (in years like 2003 when industry conditions were bad and Nucor's performance was subpar) to 400 percent (or more) of their base salaries (when Nucor's performance was excellent, as had been the case in 2004–2006).

Nucor management had designed the company's incentive plans for employees so that bonus calculations involved no discretion on the part of a plant/division manager or top executives. This was done to eliminate any concerns on the part of workers that managers or executives might show favoritism or otherwise be unfair in calculating or awarding bonuses. Based on labor costs equal to about 8 percent of revenues, a typical Nucor employee earned close to $91,300 in 2005 in base pay and bonuses. (The average in 2000–2002, when the steel market was in the doldrums, was about $60,000 per employee.)[4] Total worker compensation at Nucor could run double the average earned by workers at other manufacturing companies in the states where Nucor's plants were located. At Nucor's new $450 million plant in Hertford County, North Carolina, where jobs were scarce and poverty was common, Nucor employees earned three times the local average manufacturing wage. Nucor management philosophy was that workers ought to be excellently compensated because the production jobs were strenuous and the work environment in a steel mill was relatively dangerous.

Employee turnover in Nucor mills was extremely low; absenteeism and tardiness were minimal. Each employee was allowed four days of absences and could also miss work for jury duty, military leave, or the death of close relatives. After this, a day's absence cost a worker the entire performance bonus pay for that week, and being more than a half-hour late to work on a given day resulted in no bonus payment for the day. When job vacancies did occur, Nucor was flooded with applications; plant personnel screened job candidates very carefully, seeking people with initiative and a strong work ethic.

Employee Relations and Human Resources

Employee relations at Nucor were based on four clear-cut principles:

1. Management is obligated to manage Nucor in such a way that employees will have the opportunity to earn according to their productivity.
2. Employees should be able to feel confident that if they do their jobs properly, they will have a job tomorrow.
3. Employees have the right to be treated fairly and must believe that they will be.
4. Employees must have an avenue of appeal when they believe they are being treated unfairly.

The hallmarks of Nucor's human resources strategy were its incentive pay plan for production exceeding the standard and the job security provided to production workers—despite being in an industry with strong down cycles, Nucor had made it a practice not to lay off workers.

Nucor took an egalitarian approach to providing fringe benefits to its employees; employees had the same insurance programs, vacation schedules, and holidays as upper level management. However, certain benefits were not available to Nucor's officers. The fringe benefit package at Nucor included:

- *Profit sharing*—Each year, Nucor allocated 10 percent of its operating profits to profit-sharing bonuses for all employees (except senior officers). Depending on company performance, the bonuses could run anywhere from 1 percent to over 20 percent of pay. Twenty percent of the bonus amount was paid to employees in the following March as a cash bonus, and the remaining 80 percent was put into a trust for each employee, with each employee's share being proportional to his or her earnings as a percent of total earnings by all workers covered by the plan. An employee's share of the profits became vested after one full year of employment. Employees received a quarterly statement of their balance in profit sharing.
- *401(k) plan*—Both officers and employees participated in a 401(k) plan, in which the company matched from 5 percent to 25 percent of each employee's first 7 percent of contributions; the amount of the match was based on how well the company was doing.
- *Medical and dental plan*—The company had a flexible and comprehensive health benefit program for officers and employees that included wellness and health care spending accounts.
- *Tuition reimbursement*—Nucor reimbursed up to $2,750 of an employee's approved educational expenses each year and up to $1,250 of a spouse's educational expenses.
- *Employee stock purchase plan*—Nucor had a monthly stock investment plan for employees whereby Nucor added 10 percent to the amount an employee contributed toward the purchase of Nucor shares; Nucor paid the commission on all share purchases.
- *Service awards*—After each five years of service with the company, Nucor employees received a service award consisting of five shares of Nucor stock.
- *Scholarships*—Nucor provided the children of employees (except senior officers) up to $2,750 worth of scholarship funding each year to be used at accredited academic institutions.
- *Other benefits*—Long-term disability, life insurance, vacation. In 2004, 2005, and 2006 Nucor paid each employee (excluding officers) a special year-end bonus of $2,000; this was in addition to record profit-sharing bonuses and 401(k) matching contributions of $272.6 million in 2006, $206.0 million in 2005, and $172.3 million in 2004 (versus only $8.9 million in 2003). The extra $2,000 bonuses resulted in additional profit-sharing costs of approximately $23.8 million in 2006, $22.6 million in 2005, and $21.0 million in 2004.

Most of the changes Nucor made in work procedures and in equipment came from employees. The prevailing view at Nucor was that the employees knew the problems of their jobs better than anyone else and were thus in the best position to identify ways to improve how things were done. Most plant-level managers spent considerable time in the plant, talking and meeting with frontline employees and listening carefully to suggestions. Promising ideas and suggestions were typically acted on quickly and implemented—management was willing to take risks to try worker suggestions for doing things better and to accept the occasional failure when the results were disappointing. Teamwork, a vibrant team spirit, and a close worker–management partnership were much in evidence at Nucor plants.

Nucor plants did not use job descriptions. Management believed job descriptions caused more problems than they solved, given the teamwork atmosphere and the close collaboration among work group members. The company saw formal performance appraisal systems as added paperwork and a waste of time. If a Nucor employee was not performing well, the problem was dealt with directly by supervisory personnel and the peer pressure of work group members (whose bonuses were adversely affected).

Employees were kept informed about company and division performance. Charts showing the division's results in return on assets and bonus payoff were posted in prominent places in the plant. Most all employees were quite aware of the level of profits in their plant or division. Nucor had a formal grievance procedure, but grievances were few and far between. The corporate office sent all news releases to each division, where they were posted on bulletin boards. Each employee received a copy of Nucor's annual report; it was company practice for the cover of the annual report to consist of the names of all Nucor employees.

All of these practices had created an egalitarian culture and a highly motivated workforce that grew out of former CEO Ken Iverson's radical insight: that employees, even hourly clock punchers, would put forth extraordinary effort and be exceptionally productive if they were richly rewarded, treated with respect, and given real power to do their jobs as best they saw fit.[5] There were countless stories of occasions when managers and workers had gone beyond the call of duty to expedite equipment repairs (in many instances even blowing their weekends to go help personnel at other Nucor plants solve a crisis); the company's workforce was known for displaying unusual passion and company loyalty even when no personal financial stake was involved. As one Nucor worker put it, "At Nucor, we're not 'you guys' and 'us guys.' It's all of us guys. Wherever the bottleneck is, we go there, and everyone works on it."[6]

It was standard procedure for a team of Nucor veterans, including people who worked on the plant floor, to visit with their counterparts as part of the process of screening candidates for acquisition.[7] One of the purposes of such visits was to explain the Nucor compensation system and culture face-to-face, gauge reactions, and judge whether the plant would fit into "the Nucor way of doing things" if it was acquired. Shortly after making an acquisition, Nucor management moved swiftly to institute its pay-for-performance incentive system and to begin instilling the egalitarian Nucor culture and idea sharing. Top priority was given to looking for ways to boost plant production using fewer people and without making substantial capital investments; the take-home pay of workers at newly-acquired plants typically went up dramatically. At the Auburn Steel plant, acquired in 2001, it took Nucor about six months to convince workers that they would be better off under Nucor's pay system; during that time, Nucor paid people under the old Auburn Steel system but posted what they would have earned under Nucor's system. Pretty soon, workers were convinced to make the changeover—one worker saw his pay climb from \$53,000 in the year prior to the acquisition to \$67,000 in 2001 and to \$92,000 in 2005.[8]

New Employees Each plant/division had a "consul" responsible for providing new employees with general advice about becoming a Nucor teammate and serving as a resource for inquiries about how things were done at Nucor, how to navigate the division and company, and how to resolve issues that might come up. Nucor provided new employees with a personalized plan that set forth who would give them feedback about how well they were doing and when and how this feedback would be given; from time to time, new employees met with the plant manager for feedback and coaching. In addition, there was a new employee orientation session that provided a hands-on look at the plant/division operations; new employees also participated in product group meetings to provide exposure to broader business and technical issues. Each year, Nucor brought all recent college hires to the Charlotte headquarters for a forum intended to give the new hires a chance to network and provide senior management with guidance on how best to leverage their talent.

Pricing and Marketing

The commodity nature of steel products meant that the prices a company could command were driven by market demand–supply conditions that changed more or less continually. As a consequence, Nucor's average sales prices per ton varied considerably from quarter to quarter—see Exhibit 5. Nucor's pricing strategy was to quote the same price and sales terms to all customers, with the customer paying all shipping charges. Its prices were customarily the lowest or close to the lowest in the U.S. market for

Exhibit 5 Nucor's Average Sales Prices (per ton) for Steel Products, by Product Category, 2005–2006

Period	Sheet	Bars	Structural	Plate	Steel Joists	Steel Deck	Cold Finished Steel	Overall Price per Ton
2005								
Qtr 1	$675	$514	$605	$763	$1,102	$1,020	$1,012	$663
Qtr 2	609	499	574	708	1,084	972	1,067	621
Qtr 3	523	496	561	625	1,056	935	1,003	571
Qtr 4	583	542	634	684	1,077	931	1,069	630
2006								
Qtr 1	594	543	649	698	1,104	938	1,010	631
Qtr 2	625	567	667	712	1,092	930	1,033	654
Qtr 3	673	601	703	746	1,122	946	1,067	702
Qtr 4	624	576	727	732	1,175	1,031	998	683

Source: Company records posted at www.nucor.com (accessed October 23, 2006, and January 31, 2007).

steel. Nucor's status as a low-cost producer with reliably low prices had resulted in numerous customers entering into noncancelable 6- to 12-month contracts to purchase steel mill products from Nucor. These contracts contained a pricing formula tied to raw material costs (with the cost of scrap steel being the primary driver of price adjustments during the contact period). In 2005–2006, about 45 percent of Nucor's steel mill production was committed to contract customers. All of Nucor's steel mills planned to pursue profitable contract business in the future.

Nucor had recently begun developing its plant sites with the expectation of having several customer companies co-locate nearby to save shipping costs on their steel purchases. In order to gain the advantage of low shipping costs, two tube manufacturers, two steel service centers, and a cold-rolling facility had located adjacent to Nucor's Arkansas plant. Four companies had announced plans to locate close to a new Nucor plant in North Carolina.

Approximately 92 percent of the production of Nucor's steel mills was sold to outside customers in 2005–2006; the balance was used internally by Nucor's Vulcraft, Cold Finish, Building Systems, and Fasteners divisions. Steel joists and joist girder sales were obtained by competitive bidding. Vulcraft supplied price quotes to contractors on a significant percentage of the domestic buildings that had steel joists and joist girders as part of their support systems. Nucor's pricing for steel joists, girders, and decking included delivery to the job site. Vulcraft maintained a fleet of trucks to ensure and control on-time delivery; freight costs for deliveries were less than 10 percent of revenues in 2005–2006. In 2005, Vulcraft had a 40 percent share of the U.S. market for of steel joists. Steel deck was specified in the majority of buildings using steel joists and joist girders. In 2005 and 2006, Vulcraft supplied more than 30 percent of total domestic sales of steel deck; the 2006 Verco acquisition gave Nucor the capability to substantially increase its sales and market share of steel deck in 2007.

COMPETITION IN THE STEEL INDUSTRY

The global marketplace for steel was considered to be relatively mature and highly cyclical as a result of ongoing ups and downs in the world economy or the economies of particular countries. In general, competition within the steel industry, both in the United States and globally, was intense and expected to remain so. Numerous steel companies had declared bankruptcy during the past 10 years, either ceasing production altogether or more usually continuing to operate after being acquired and undergoing restructuring to become more cost-competitive.

Worldwide demand had grown by about 6 percent annually since 2000 (well above the 1.1 percent

Exhibit 6 Estimated Worldwide Production of Crude Steel, with Compound Average Growth Rates, 1975–2005

			Compound Average Growth Rates in Steel Production	
Year	Estimated Value of World Steel Production (in billions of $)	World Crude Steel Production (millions of tons)	Period	Percentage Rate
1975	n.a.	710	1975–1980	2.2%
1980	n.a.	790	1980–1985	0.1
1985	$250	792	1985–1990	1.4
1990	415	849	1990–1995	−0.5
1995	470	828	1995–2000	2.4
2000	385	934	2000–2005	6.0
2001	270	937		
2002	330	996		
2003	465	1,068		
2004	790	1,176		
2005	770	1,247		

n.a. = not available

Source: International Iron and Steel Institute, *World Steel in Figures, 2006,* www.worldsteel.org (accessed November 6, 2006).

Exhibit 7 Estimated Consumption of Steel Products, by Geographic Region, 2000–2005 (in millions of tons)

Region	2000	2001	2002	2003	2004	2005
European Union (25 countries)	177.6	174.6	173.2	176.0	185.2	176.8
Other European countries, Russia, and Ukraine	60.8	64.1	63.0	71.8	75.6	80.1
North America	161.6	145.6	145.9	143.5	164.2	149.7
Central and South America	31.0	31.8	30.4	30.4	36.0	35.8
Africa	17.0	18.4	20.3	21.0	22.6	24.7
Middle East	21.7	25.5	27.9	33.3	33.7	38.2
Asia	353.0	382.7	432.8	496.2	546.7	602.8
Australia, New Zealand	7.4	6.9	7.9	8.3	8.8	8.7
World total	830.2	849.6	901.5	980.6	1,072.9	1,116.8

Source: International iron and Steel Institute, *World Steel in Figures, 2006,* www.worldsteel.org (accessed November 6, 2006).

growth rate from 1975 to 2000), but there had been periods of both strong and weak demand during 2000–2006 (see Exhibit 6). Prices for steel products were near record levels throughout most of 2004–2006, driven by strong global demand for steel products (see Exhibit 7). Worldwide sales of steel products were in the $770 to $790 billion range in 2004–2005; prior to 2004, global sales had never exceeded $500 billion in any one year, according to data compiled by the International Iron and Steel Institute..

Nonetheless, steelmaking capacity worldwide still exceeded global demand in 2005–2006. Many foreign steelmakers, looking to operate their plants as close to capacity as possible or seeking to take advantage of favorable foreign currency fluctuations, had begun exporting steel products to the U.S. market, where strong demand and tight domestic supplies had pushed steel prices to highly profitable levels. According to U.S. Department of Commerce data, steel imports into the United States rose by over 70 percent between November 2005 and September 2006 and were expected to reach a record level of over 45 million tons in 2006 (see Exhibit 8); companies in China, Russia, Korea, Turkey, Taiwan, Japan, India, Australia, and Brazil were particularly aggressive in exporting their production to the U.S. market.[9] Steel imports from China, for example, jumped from 139,300 tons in November 2005 to a monthly average of over 575,000 tons in July, August, and September 2006. Steel imports from Taiwan rose from 48,400 tons in November 2005 to nearly 265,000 tons in September 2006. Steel imports from Russia were 121,300 tons in November 2005 and 517,000 tons in August 2006. Steel imports from Korea were about 115,700 tons in November 2005 and over 260,000 tons in September 2006; imports from Australia were 60,000 tons in November 2005 and 162,000 tons in September 2006. In 2005, foreign steelmakers captured a 22.8 percent share of the U.S. market for steel products (based on tons); foreign steelmakers were expected to achieve close to a 30 percent share of the U.S. market in 2006. Many non-U.S. steel producers were owned and/or subsidized by their governments, a condition that often meant their production and sales decisions were driven by political and economic policy considerations rather than by prevailing market conditions. Steel supplies in the United States (and other countries) were also subject to shifting foreign exchange rates, with more imports pouring in when the local currency was strong and more exports flowing out when the local currency was weak.

In February 2007, Nucor CEO Dan DiMicco applauded the announcement that the U.S. government had requested World Trade Organization (WTO) dispute settlement consultations with China regarding claims that China was violating WTO rules by providing subsidies to Chinese steel exporters.[10] Under the WTO dispute settlement procedures, a request for consultations was the first step in resolving the U.S. claim that the Chinese government was violating WTO rules. If a WTO panel found that China was indeed breaking WTO rules, it could order China to provide compensation to the United States by allowing the United States to impose higher tariffs on Chinese goods or take similar measures. Under U.S. countervailing duty law, if a U.S. Department of Commerce investigation confirmed that foreign plants exporting steel to the United States were being subsidized by their government and if the U.S. International Trade Commission determined that the subsidized imports had injured the domestic steel industry, then the United States could apply countervailing duties to offset the subsidies. While the U.S. government had not previously applied countervailing duties when authorized to do so, the Commerce Department was currently considering whether to

Exhibit 8 The U.S. Market for Steel Products, 1995–2005 (in millions of tons)

Year	U.S. Shipments of Steel Products	U.S. Exports of Steel Mill Products	U.S. Imports of Steel Mill Products	Apparent U.S. Consumption of Steel Mill Products*
1995	97.5	7.1	24.4	114.8
1996	100.9	5.0	29.2	125.0
1997	105.9	6.0	31.2	131.0
1998	102.4	5.5	41.5	138.4
1999	106.2	5.4	35.7	136.5
2000	109.1	6.5	38.0	140.5
2001	98.9	6.1	30.1	122.9
2002	100.0	6.0	32.7	126.7
2003	106.0	8.2	23.1	120.9
2004	111.4	7.9	35.8	139.3
2005	105.0	9.4	32.1	127.7

*Apparent U.S. consumption equals total shipments minus exports plus imports.

Source: American Iron and Steel Institute, as reported in Standard & Poor's Industry Surveys.

change this practice. DiMicco saw the U.S. government's request for WTO settlement consultations as only a first step toward leveling the playing field for U.S. steel producers; he said:

> This request does not cover the vast majority of the massive domestic subsidies China provides to its steel industry and other manufacturers. Nor does it address China's gross manipulation of its currency, which provides Chinese exports with a huge advantage in international trade. Free trade is possible only if everyone follows the rules—and China hasn't.[11]

Exhibit 8 shows steel production, steel exports, and steel imports for the U.S. market for 1995–2005. Exhibit 9 shows the value of steel mill shipments by U.S.-based steelmakers for 2004–2005, broken down by product category. Exhibit 10 shows data for the top 20 countries worldwide as concerns total steel production, steel exports, and steel imports; Exhibit 11 shows the 20 largest steel companies worldwide as of 2005.

STEEL PRODUCTION

Steel was produced by either integrated steel facilities or minimills that employed electric arc furnaces. Integrated mills used blast furnaces to produce hot metal typically from iron ore pellets, limestone, scrap steel, oxygen, assorted other metals, and coke. (Coke was produced by firing coal in large coke ovens and was the major fuel used in blast furnaces to produce hot metal.) Hot metal from the blast furnace process was then run through the basic oxygen process to produce liquid steel. To make flat-rolled steel products, liquid steel was either fed into a continuous caster machine and cast into slabs or else cooled in slab form for later processing. Slabs were further shaped or rolled at a plate mill or hot strip mill. In making certain sheet steel products, the hot strip mill process was followed by various finishing processes, including pickling, cold-rolling, annealing, tempering, or galvanizing. These various processes for converting raw steel into finished steel products were often distinct steps undertaken at different times and in different on-site or off-site facilities rather than being done in a continuous process in a single plant facility—an integrated mill was thus one that had multiple facilities at a single plant site and could therefore not only produce crude (or raw) steel but also run the crude steel through various facilities and finishing processes to make hot-rolled and cold-rolled sheet steel products, steel bars and beams, stainless steel, steel wire and nails, steel pipes and tubes, and other finished steel products. The steel produced by integrated mills tended to be purer than steel produced by electric arc furnaces since less scrap was used in the production process. (Scrap steel often contained nonferrous elements that could adversely affect metallurgical properties.) Some steel customers required purer steel products for their applications.

Exhibit 9 Dollar Value of Shipments of Steel Mill Products by U.S.-Based Steelmakers, by Product Category, 2004–2005 ($ in billions)

Product Category	2004	2005
Steel ingot and semifinished shapes	$ 4.9	$ 5.7
Hot-rolled sheet and strip, including tin mill products	25.2	24.8
Hot-rolled bars and shapes, plates, structural shapes, and pilings	14.9	17.1
Steel pipe and tube	9.5	10.9
Cold-rolled sheet steel and strip	12.2	13.5
Cold finished steel bars and steel shapes	2.0	2.1
Steel wire	2.3	2.3
All other steel mill products	1.3	1.3
Total	$72.7	$78.3

Source: U.S. Department of Commerce, "Current Industrial Reports, Steel Mill Products, 2005," www.census.gov/mcd (accessed November 2, 2006).

Exhibit 10 Top 20 Countries: Total Steel Production, Steel Exports, and Steel Imports, 2004–2005 (in millions of tons)

Rank	Total Steel Production, 2005		Steel Exports, 2004		Steel Imports, 2004	
1	China	385.0	Japan	38.3	China	36.6
2	Japan	124.0	Russia	33.5	United States	36.4
3	United States	104.6	Ukraine	31.1	Germany	21.9
4	Russia	72.8	Germany	30.1	Italy	21.4
5	South Korea	52.7	Belgium	25.9	South Korea	19.5
6	Germany	49.0	China	22.2	France	18.2
7	Ukraine	42.5	France	20.6	Belgium	16.4
8	India	42.0	South Korea	16.5	Taiwan, China	15.1
9	Brazil	34.8	Italy	14.7	Spain	13.0
10	Italy	32.3	Turkey	14.5	Thailand	12.2
11	Turkey	23.1	Brazil	13.2	Canada	10.2
12	France	21.5	Taiwan, China	10.4	United Kingdom	9.6
13	Taiwan, China	20.5	Netherlands	9.9	Turkey	9.0
14	Spain	19.6	United Kingdom	8.6	Iran	8.7
15	Mexico	17.9	United States	8.0	Malaysia	8.3
16	Canada	16.9	Spain	7.1	Netherlands	7.2
17	United Kingdom	14.5	Austria	6.4	Hong Kong	6.9
18	Belgium	11.0	Mexico	6.1	Mexico	6.4
19	South Africa	10.5	India	6.1	Vietnam	6.0
20	Iran	10.4	Canada	6.0	United Arab Emirates	5.1

Source: International Iron and Steel Institute, *World Steel in Figures, 2006,* www.worldsteel.org (accessed November 6, 2006).

Minimills used an electric arc furnace to melt steel scrap or scrap substitutes into molten metal which was then cast into crude steel slabs, billets or blooms in a continuous casting process; as was the case at integrated mills, the crude steel was then run through various facilities and finishing processes to make hot-rolled and cold-rolled sheet steel products, steel bars and beams, stainless steel, steel wire and nails, steel pipes and tubes, and other finished steel products. Minimills could accommodate short production runs and had relatively fast product change-over time. Minimills typically were able to produce a narrower range of steel products than integrated producers, and their products tended to be more commodity-like. The electric arc technology employed by minimills offered two primary competitive advantages: capital investment requirements that were 75 percent lower than those of integrated mills, and a smaller workforce (which translated into lower labor costs per ton shipped).

GLOBAL STEEL INDUSTRY TRENDS

Over the past five decades, changes in steelmaking technology had revolutionized the world's steel industry. Up until the 1960, steel was produced in large-scale plants using capital-intensive basic oxygen blast furnace technology and open hearth furnace technology where steel was made from scratch using iron ore, coke, scrap steel, limestone, and other raw materials—such companies were referred to as integrated producers because the value chains at such plants involved a number of production steps and processes to convert the raw materials into finished steel products. But starting in the 1960s, the advent of electric arc furnace technology spurred new start-up companies to enter the steelmaking business. These new companies, called minimills because their plants produced steel on a much smaller scale than did the

Exhibit 11 Top 20 Steel Companies Worldwide, Based on Crude Steel Production, 2005

		Crude Steel Production (in millions of tons)	
2005 Rank	Company (Headquarters)	2005	2004
1	Mittal Steel* (Netherlands)	69.4	47.2
2	Arcelor* (Luxembourg)	51.5	51.7
3	Nippon Steel (Japan)	35.3	35.7
4	POSCO (South Korea)	33.6	33.3
5	JFE (Japan)	32.9	34.8
6	Baosteel (China)	25.0	23.6
7	US Steel (USA)	21.3	22.9
8	Nucor (USA)	20.3	19.7
9	Corus Group† (Great Britain)	20.1	20.9
10	Riva (Italy)	19.3	18.4
11	ThyssenKrupp (Germany)	18.2	19.4
12	Tangshan (China)	17.7	7.8
13	Evraz (Russia)	15.3	15.1
14	Gerdau (Brazil)	15.1	16.1
15	Severstal (Russia)	15.0	14.1
16	Sumitomo (Japan)	14.9	14.3
17	SAIL (India)	14.8	13.3
18	Wuhan (China)	14.3	10.2
19	Anshan (China)	13.1	12.5
20	Magnitogorsk (Russia)	12.6	12.5

*Mittal Steel and Arcelor merged in 2006.

†Corus Group was acquired by Tata Steel (India) in 2006; Tata Steel was the world's 56th largest producer of steel in 2005.

Source: International Iron and Steel Institute, *World Steel in Figures, 2006,* www.worldsteel.org (accessed November 6, 2006).

integrated mills, used low-cost electric arc furnaces to melt scrap steel and cast the molten metal directly into a variety of steel products at costs substantially below those of integrated steel producers.

Initially, minimills were able to only make low-end steel products (such as reinforcing rods and steel bars) using electric arc furnace technology. But when thin-slab casting technology came on the scene in the 1980s, minimills were able to compete in the market for flat-rolled carbon sheet and strip products; these products sold at substantially higher prices per ton and thus were attractive market segments for minimill companies. Carbon sheet and strip steel products accounted for about 50–60 percent of total steel production and represented the last big market category controlled by the producers employing basic oxygen furnace and blast furnace technologies. Thin-slab casting technology, which had been developed by SMS Schloemann-Siemag AG of Germany, was pioneered in the United States by Nucor at its plants in Indiana and elsewhere. Other minimill companies in the United States and other countries were quick to adopt thin-slab casting technology because the low capital costs of thin-slab casting facilities, often coupled with the lower labor costs per ton, gave minimill companies a cost and pricing advantage over integrated steel producers, enabling them to grab a growing share of the global market for flat-rolled sheet steel and other carbon steel products. Many integrated producers also switched to thin-slab casting as a defensive measure to protect their profit margins and market shares.

By 2005, electric arc furnace technology was being used to produce about 33 percent of the world's steel; basic oxygen furnace technology was used to produce about 65 percent of the all steel products.

Limited supplies of scrap steel and upward-trending prices for scrap steel were said to be the main factors constraining greater use of electric arc technology across the world. Open hearth technology had largely been abandoned as of 2005 and was used only at plants in Russia, the Ukraine, India, and a few other Eastern European countries. In 2003–2006, about 90 percent of the world's production of steel involved the use of continuous-casting technology.

Industry Consolidation In both the United States and across the world, the last two industry downturns had resulted in numerous mergers and acquisitions. Some of the mergers/acquisitions were the result of a financially and managerially strong company seeking to acquire a high-cost or struggling steel company at a bargain price and then pursue cost reduction initiatives to make newly acquired steel mill operations more cost competitive. Other mergers/acquisitions reflected the strategies of growth-minded steel companies looking to expand both their production capacity and their geographic market presence.

In 2006, the world's two largest steel producers, Mittal Steel and Arcelor, both headquartered in Europe but with operations in various parts of the world, merged to form a giant company with total steel production of over 116 million tons (equal to about a 10 percent market share worldwide). Prior to its merger with Arcelor, Mittal Steel in 2005 had acquired International Steel Group, the second largest steel producer in the United States, with 13 major plants in eight states, and Inland Steel, another struggling U.S. steel producer. In 2006, Arcelor Mittal had total production capacity of nearly 125 million tons, annual revenues of $77 billion, earnings of $13.3 billion, plants in 27 countries on five continents (North America, South America, Europe, Asia, and Africa), and 330,000 employees.

Also in 2006, Tata Steel in India acquired Corus Steel (Great Britain), the world's eighth largest steel company; the new company produced over 27 million tons in 2005. Tata Steel was one of the lowest-cost steel producers in the world, with access to low-cost iron ore deposits, and was adding new production capacity at three sites in India, a plant in Iran, and a plant in Bangladesh; Corus was regarded as a relatively high-cost producer but had been profitable in 2004–2005 after posting huge losses in 2000–2003. Corus had a 50 percent share of the steel market in Great Britain and substantial sales in parts of Europe; it was formed in 1999 as the result of a merger between troubled British Steel and Koninklijke Hoogovens, a well-regarded steel company based in the Netherlands.

Jinan Iron and Steel and Laiwu Steel, the 6th and 7th largest steel producers in China and the 23rd and 24th largest producers in the world, merged in October 2006 to form a company with total sales of almost 23 million tons in 2005; the merged company was named Shandong Iron and Steel. Industry observers believed the Jinan-Laiwu merger was an attempt by Chinese steelmakers to better compete with Arcelor Mittal and other foreign rivals.

In the United States, United States Steel, headquartered in Pittsburgh, had acquired National Steel in 2003, giving it steelmaking capability of 26.8 million tons annually as of 2006. In 2006, U.S. Steel had 12 steelmaking facilities in the United States, one in Slovakia, and two in Serbia. U.S. Steel had a labor-cost disadvantage versus Nucor and Mittal Steel USA (the U.S.-based operations of Arcelor Mittal), partly due to the lower productivity of its unionized workforce and partly due to its pension costs. While Mittal Steel USA also had a union workforce, it had recently downsized the labor force at some of its plants by close to 75 percent and now operated many of its U.S. plants with a very lean workforce in a manner akin to Nucor. Arcelor Mittal's recent acquisitions of Inland Steel and International Steel Group in the United States had transformed Mittal Steel USA into North America's largest steel producer, with operations in 12 states and annual raw steel production capability of about 31 million tons. Mittal Steel USA's principal products included a broad range of hot-rolled, cold-rolled, and coated sheets; tin mill products; carbon and alloy plates; wire rod; rail products; bars and semifinished shapes to serve the automotive, construction, pipe and tube, appliance, container, and machinery markets. All of these products are available in standard carbon grades as well as high-strength, low-alloy grades for more demanding applications.

NUCOR'S CHIEF DOMESTIC COMPETITORS

Consolidation of the industry into a smaller number of larger and more efficient steel producers had heightened competitive pressures for Nucor and most other steelmakers. Nucor had three major rivals headquartered in the United States—Mittal Steel USA, U.S. Steel, and AK Steel. Mittal Steel USA competed only in carbon steel product categories; it had seven integrated mills, three plants that used electric arc furnaces, and four rolling and finishing facilities. About 17,200 of its approximately 20,500 employees were represented by unions. U.S. Steel had mostly integrated steel mills, a unionized workforce, worldwide annual raw steel production capacity of 26.8 million tons, and worldwide raw steel production of 21.2 million tons in 2005. AK Steel had seven steel mills and finishing plants in four states; about 6,300 of its approximately 8,000 employees were represented by unions. It sold much of its output to automotive companies—its two biggest customers were General Motors and Ford. Exhibit 12 presents selected financial and operating data for these three competitors.

Exhibit 12 Selected Financial and Operating Data for Nucor's Three Largest U.S.-based Competitors

Company	2005	2004	2003
Mittal Steel USA			
Net sales	$ 12,237	$ 12,174	
Cost of goods sold	10,617	10,315	
Selling, general, and administrative expenses	371	301	
Net income	$ 491	$ 1,286	
Net income as a percent of net sales	4.0%	10.6%	
Shipments of finished steel products (millions of tons)	18.8	21.1	
Raw steel production (millions of tons)	20.0	23.9	
U.S. Steel			
Net sales	$ 14,039	$ 13,975	$ 9,328
Cost of sales	11,601	11,368	8,458
Selling, general, and administrative expenses	698	739	673
Income (loss) from operations	1,439	1,625	(719)
Net income	$ 892	$ 1,117	$ (436)
Net income as a % of net sales	10.3%	8.0%	(4.7)%
Shipments of steel products (millions of tons)	19.7	21.8	19.2
Raw steel production (millions of tons)	21.2	23.0	19.8
Domestic	15.3	17.3	14.9
Foreign	5.9	5.7	4.9
Production as a % of total capability			
Domestic	79.1%	89.0%	90.1%
Foreign	79.5	76.8	87.9
AK Steel Group			
Net sales	$5,647.4	$5,217.3	$4,041.7
Cost of products sold	4,996.8	4,553.6	3,886.9
Selling and administrative expenses	208.4	206.4	243.6
Operating profit (loss)	113.1	(79.7)	(651.8)
Net income (loss)	$ (2.3)	$ 38.4	$ (560.4)
Operating profit as a % of net sales	2.0%	(1.5)%	6.0%
Net income as a % of net sales	(0.04)%	4.6%	(13.9)%
Shipments of finished steel products (millions of tons)	6.4	6.3	5.8

Source: Company 10-K reports.

In addition to the three major domestic rivals, there were a number of lesser-sized U.S.-based steelmakers with plants that competed directly against Nucor plants. However, Nucor's most formidable competitive threat in the U.S. market consisted of Mittal Steel USA and foreign steelmakers that were intent on exporting some of their production to the United States; there were many foreign steel producers that had costs on a par with or even below those of Nucor, although their competitiveness in the U.S. market varied significantly according to the prevailing strength of their local currencies versus the U.S. dollar.

Endnotes

[1] Tom Peters and Nancy Austin, *A Passion for Excellence: The Leadership Difference* (New York: Random House, 1985), and "Other Low-Cost Champions," *Fortune,* June 24, 1985.
[2] According to information posted at www.nucor.com (accessed October 11, 2006).
[3] This discussion is based on information posted at www.nucor.com (accessed October 17, 2006).
[4] Nanette Byrnes, "The Art of Motivation," *BusinessWeek,* May 1, 2006, p. 59.
[5] Ibid., p. 57.
[6] Ibid., p. 60.
[7] Ibid.
[8] Ibid.
[9] Based on information in the STAT-USA data base, U.S. Department of Commerce, http://ia.ita.doc.gov/steel/license/SMP/Census/GDESC52/MMT_ALL_ALL_12M.htm (accessed October 27, 2006).
[10] Company press release, February 2, 2007.
[11] Ibid.

Competition in Video Game Consoles: The State of the Battle for Supremacy in 2008

CASE 11

John E. Gamble
University of South Alabama

The video game industry, which grew in prominence with the 1985 introduction of the Nintendo Entertainment System (NES), was well into the battle for supremacy among third-generation consoles in 2008. Whereas the first-generation NES console had limited processing capabilities and offered rudimentary graphics, the game consoles launched by Microsoft in November 2005 and by Nintendo and Sony in November 2006 not only were equipped with powerful microprocessors, hard drives, and Internet connectivity but also offered high-definition graphics resolution. Video game industry analysts and consumers alike were quite impressed by the capabilities of third-generation video games. Both Microsoft's Xbox 360 and Sony's PlayStation 3 (PS3) allowed users to play highly sophisticated and lifelike games with others in their homes or with Internet-connected gamers from around the world. The Nintendo Wii also allowed users to play games online, but its unique wand controller was the key to its success in the marketplace. The Wii controller took more than one year to develop and was able to respond to hand motions that were used in throwing a ball, casting a fishing line, swinging a baseball bat, pointing a gun, or playing a musical instrument.

The Sony PS3, Microsoft Xbox 360, and the Nintendo Wii proved to be "must have" gifts during the 2006 and 2007 holiday retail seasons, with production at none of the three companies being able to keep up with demand. When January 2008 arrived, Nintendo proved to be the surprising early winner of the next-generation console war, with Wii sales exceeding 20 million units. Microsoft's Xbox 360 installed base had grown to more than 17 million units, while Sony's installed base in January 2008 stood at just over 10 million. Market observers had been shocked by Nintendo's climb to market leader, after its GameCube console had been a distant third in head-to-head competition against the PlayStation 2 (PS2) and Xbox; they were likewise shocked by Sony's dramatic decline from dominant market leader with the PS2 to also-ran with the PS3.

To make things even more interesting, Nintendo had also captured a solid lead in the handheld game category, with the Nintendo DS selling more than 8.5 million units in the United States alone during 2007. Sony's PlayStation Portable (PSP) was a distant runner up in the handheld game segment, with 2007 U.S. sales of 3.8 million units. To make matters worse, Sony was said to have lost as much as $300 on the sale of each PS3, and its older-generation PS2 outsold the PS3 by nearly 400,000 units during the 2007 holiday shopping period.

Going into the 2008 holiday retail season, industry analysts were awaiting signs that the PS3 would match the success of the PS2, which had sold nearly 120 million units since its October 2000 launch. The conventional wisdom had been that PS2 users would migrate to the PS3, but sales of the PS3 had been surprisingly small as of fall 2008. Graphics-oriented gamers seemed to prefer Microsoft's Xbox 360. When the Wii was launched in November 2006, analysts had predicted that avid gamers (who purchased the largest percentage of the industry's game software) would soon tire of the Wii's wand controller and that the appeal of Nintendo's Wii and handheld DS in both the youth and adult market segments would fade rapidly. So far, their predictions had been wrong, but there was opportunity for sales percentages of the Wii, PS3, and Xbox 360 to shift significantly during the 2008 fourth-quarter holiday season. Full-year 2008 sales data scheduled for release in January 2009 would likely provide telling indication of how well Microsoft, Nintendo, and Sony would fare in the market for current-generation video game consoles.

HISTORY OF VIDEO GAME SYSTEMS

The development of video games began as early as 1947, when engineers working on television projects began to tinker with programs to play simple games on cathode ray tubes. Two noteworthy developments were the creation of Tennis for Two by Brookhaven National Laboratory researcher William A. Higinbotham in 1958 and the invention of Spacewar by a trio of MIT graduate students in 1962. Ralph Baer, an engineer at Loral, filed the first patent for a video game in 1968, which led to the development of the Magnavox Odyssey. The Odyssey video game system, introduced to U.S. consumers in 1972, allowed users to play such games as table tennis, hockey, shooting gallery, and football on their black-and-white televisions. The graphics were limited to white lines, dots, and dashes projected on the picture tube, so Magnavox provided users with color transparencies to place on their TV screens to provide the appropriate background for each game.

The introduction of Pong, an arcade game produced by Atari, was another key video game launch that occurred in 1972. Atari developed a Pong system for televisions in 1975, but its 1977 launch of the Atari 2600 was the first home game system to achieve success in the marketplace. The Atari 2600 offered full-color output, sound, and cartridge-based games such as Space Invaders. Atari eventually sold more than 30 million of its 2600 game systems.

By 1983, consumers had tired of simple arcade-type games and for all practical purposes the industry was dying. Nintendo rescued the video game industry in 1985 with its introduction of its Nintendo Entertainment System (NES), which was bundled with the soon-to-be ubiquitous Super Mario Brothers video game. Nintendo sold 61.9 million NES systems before its 1991 introduction of the Super NES. Nintendo built on the success of the NES with the launch of the Game Boy, a handheld model that allowed users to take their games outside the home. Nearly 120 million Game Boy units were sold by 2001. Nintendo's ability to resurrect the industry with innovative game systems created a competitive, technology-driven industry environment that remained prevalent into 2008. Exhibit 1 presents a brief description of key video game systems, along with their launch prices and number of units sold.

OVERVIEW OF THE GLOBAL MARKET FOR VIDEO GAME CONSOLES

In 2008, about 300 million people worldwide played video games on console systems, handheld devices, PCs, and mobile phones. The majority of video game players were preteens, teenagers, and young adults (between the ages of 20 and 40). The average age of game players was rising, as people who became game players as a preteen or teenager continued to play in their adult years—in 2005 the average game player age in the United States was 33, and 25 percent of gamers were over 50.[1] Worldwide, video game enthusiasts spent 6 or more hours per week playing video games; the average American was said to spend 75 hours annually playing video games in 2003, more than double the amount spent gaming in 1997.[2] Exhibit 2 provides game-player demographics and other video-game-related statistics.

The dramatic increase in the amount of time consumers spent playing video games during the late 1990s and early 2000s was primarily attributable to the improved capabilities of game consoles launched at the turn of the 21st century. The processing capabilities of the Sony PlayStation 2, in particular, allowed game developers to create complex games that were presented at a high screen resolution. Sports games such as NCAA Football, racing games such as Need for Speed, and shooter games like Call of Duty provided game players with high levels of interaction and backgrounds that were surprisingly realistic compared to early video game systems.

The sale of game systems and software tended to decline as the installed base grew and consumers

Exhibit 1 Selected Information for Best-Selling Video Game Hardware Systems, 1972–2008

Launch Date	Manufacturer	System Name	Launch Price	Key Features	Units Sold
1972	Magnavox	Odyssey	$100	Black-and-white display, color overlays	350,000
November 1977	Atari	Atari 2600	$200	Color output, sound, cartridge-based games	30 million
October 1985	Nintendo	NES	$199	8-bit processor	61.9 million
August 1989	Sega Enterprises	Sega Genesis	$200	16-bit processor	13 million
August 1989	Nintendo	Game Boy	$109	Handheld system	118.7 million
August 1991	Nintendo	Super NES	$199	16-bit processor	49.1 million
April 1995	Sega Enterprises	Sega Saturn	$399	32-bit processor	1.4 million
September 1995	Sony Computer Entertainment	PlayStation	$299	32-bit processor	102.5 million
September 1996	Nintendo	Nintendo 64	$199	64-bit processor	32.9 million
September 1999	Sega Enterprises	Sega Dreamcast	$199	200 MHz processor, 3D graphics	8.2 million
October 2000	Sony Computer Entertainment	PlayStation 2	$299	294 MHz processor, DVD, backward compatibility with PS One	118 million as of Dec. 2007
June 2001	Nintendo	Game Boy Advance	$100	Handheld system, 32-bit processor, 32,000 color video resolution	81.1 million as of March 2008
November 2001	Microsoft	Xbox	$299	733 MHz processor, hard drive, Ethernet port	24 million
November 2001	Nintendo	GameCube	$199	485 MHz processor	21.7 million as of March 2008
November 2004	Nintendo	Nintendo DS	$199	Handheld system, Wi-Fi connection, touchpad	77.5 million as of July 2008
March 2005	Sony	PlayStation Portable	$249	Handheld system, 333 MHz processor, 3D graphics, music and movie playback	41 million as of July 2008
November 2005	Microsoft	Xbox 360	$299–$399	3.2 GHz processor, 500 MHz graphics card, Wi-Fi, 1080p HD resolution, 12x DVD, wireless controllers ($399 version only), 20 GB hard drive ($399 version only)	20 million as of July 2008
November 2006	Sony	PlayStation 3	$499–$599	3.2 GHz processor, 550 MHz graphics card, Wi-Fi ($599 version only), 1080p HD resolution, Blu-ray optical drive, wireless controllers, 20 or 60 GB hard drive	15 million as of July 2008
November 2006	Nintendo	Wii	$249	729 MHz processor, 243 MHz graphics card, Wi-Fi, 512 MB embedded flash memory, motion sensitive wireless controllers	29.6 million as of July 2008

Source: www.businessweek.com; company Web sites and annual reports; Mark Schilling and Ben Fritz, "Consoling Nintendo," *Daily Variety,* July 31, 2008, p. 6.

Exhibit 2 Video Game Statistics, U.S. Households, 2001–2005

- The average player spent about 6.8 hours per week playing games.
- In 2005, 31% of all game players were under 18, 44% were in the 1–49 age group, and 25% were over age 50 (up from 13% in 2000).
- The average game player in 2003 was 33 years old.
- 62% of gamers were male.
- The average age of the most frequent game purchaser was 40.
- 89% of the time parents were present when games were purchased or rented for children.
- The top 4 reasons parents played video games with their children:
  Because they were asked to—79%
  It's fun for the entire family—75%
  It's a good opportunity to socialize with the child—71%
  It's a good time to monitor game content—62%
- 44% of most frequent game players played games online, up from 19% in 2000.
- Best-selling video games by type of genre, 2002 and 2005:

	2002		2005	
Game Categories	PC Games	PC Games	PC Games	Console Games
Sports	6.3%	19.5%	3.7%	17.3%
Action	—	25.1	4.7	30.1
Strategy/role-playing	35.4	7.4	43.2	—
Racing	4.4	16.6	—	11.1
Fighting	0.1	6.4	—	4.7
Shooting	11.5	5.5	14.4	8.7
Family/child	25.6	—	19.8	9.3
Adventure	—	5.1	5.8	—
Edutainment	—	7.6	—	—

Note: The categories were "redefined" between 2002 and 2005.

- Computer and video game sales by rating, 2001 and 2005:

	2001	2005
Everyone	62.3%	49.0%
Teen	24.6	32.0
Mature	9.9	15.0
Everyone 10+	2.1	4.0

- In 2005, 16 of the top 20 best-selling console games and 16 of the top 20 best-selling PC games were rated Everyone or Teen.

Source: Interactive Digital Software Association, "Essential Facts about the Computer and Video Game Industry," 2002, www.idsa.com (accessed November 12, 2003), and Entertainment Software Association, "Essential Facts about the Computer and Video Game Industry," 2006, www.theESA.com (accessed September 7, 2006).

had purchased most "must have" titles. Industry sales slowed considerably between 2003 and 2005 as gamers postponed purchases until the eagerly awaited next generation of consoles became available. The launch of next-generation video game consoles, which offered unparalleled computing power and high-definition (HD) graphics, was expected to allow the global market for video game consoles to increase from approximately $3.9 billion in 2005 to nearly $5.8 billion by 2010. The value of the entire industry,

Exhibit 3 Size of the Global Video Games Market, by Sector, 2000, 2003, and 2005, with Projections for 2010 ($ in millions)

	2000	2003	2005	2010
Console hardware	$ 4,791	$ 6,047	$ 3,894	$ 5,771
Console software (both sales and rentals)	9,451	16,449	13,055	17,164
Handheld hardware	1,945	1,501	3,855	1,715
Handheld software (both sales and rentals)	2,872	2,238	4,829	3,113
PC software (both sales and rentals)	5,077	3,806	4,313	2,955
Broadband	70	497	1,944	6,352
Interactive TV	81	249	786	3,037
Mobile	65	587	2,572	11,186
Total	$24,352	$31,370	$35,248	$51,292

Source: Informa Telecoms & Media, "Games Market to Score Big in 2007," press release, October 24, 2005, and "Game Industry Boom Continues," press release July 24, 2003, both at www.informamedia.com (accessed September 8, 2006).

which included game software, hardware accessories, and online games, was expected to grow from approximately $35 billion in 2005 to more than $51 billion in 2010. The growth in video game sales had allowed it to account for a larger share of U.S. consumers' entertainment dollars than the motion picture industry. In 2005, sales of video game equipment in the United States exceeded $10 billion, while Americans spent approximately $9 billion at movie theater box offices. The size of the global market for video games by sector in 2000, 2003, and 2005 is presented in Exhibit 3. The exhibit also includes industry sales projections for 2010.

Competition in the Industry

Technological leadership in computing power and graphics rendering were critical competitive capabilities needed in the console segment of the video game industry. However, such capabilities did not guarantee success in the industry. Sega consistently beat Nintendo and Sony to the market with next-generation computing capabilities but was unable to achieve success and eventually withdrew from the console market in 2001. Sonic the Hedgehog had been Sega's only legitimate hit game title, which was not enough incentive for gamers to abandon their Nintendo or Sony systems. With Sega's installed base failing to grow, game software developers focused their efforts on Nintendo and Sony. The small number of new game titles becoming available for Sega's systems further compounded its problems in the marketplace. A survey of 16,670 video game players conducted by the NPD Group found that appealing game titles was the most important feature in choosing a game system for 87 percent of survey respondents.[3]

With the availability of intriguing games so important to gaining sales and increasing the installed base, Nintendo and, to a lesser extent, Microsoft had established internal game development capabilities. In fact, Nintendo's most popular game titles, including Mario Brothers, Pokémon, and Donkey Kong, had been developed by the company's own software development teams. Software operating profit margins that ranged from 35 to 40 percent had been a consistent contributor to Nintendo's profitability. Independent game publishers such as Electronic Arts, Activision, Take Two Interactive, THQ, Square Enix, Capcom, Atari, and Sega paid console makers royalties on each software copy sold. Independent game publishers made the greatest investments in new games for systems with a large installed base and continuing sales growth.

In addition to cooperative relationships with independent game publishers, makers of video game consoles were also required to collaborate with microprocessor and graphics accelerator producers to develop next-generation game systems. None of the established console manufacturers had the capability to produce all components needed for the assembly of game consoles—especially technologically advanced core components. In developing next-generation systems launched in 2005 and 2006, Microsoft, Nintendo, and Sony each allied with IBM in the development of the console microprocessor. In all three cases, IBM and the console maker began with standard PowerPC microprocessor technology but customized the microprocessor to perform the complex calculations needed to run game software. The processing tasks needed to run video game software were much different from those executed when running productivity software. All three companies maintained similar relationships with makers of graphics processing units (GPUs) to develop the technological capabilities to display HD quality graphics and 3D effects. Companies such as Nvidia frequently co-developed graphics chips for more than one of the three console makers.

PC manufacturers also collaborated with microprocessor and GPU manufacturers to build computers capable of running 3D and HD video games. AMD's four core, or "brain," microprocessors were developed to perform tasks similar to what the nine-brain PowerPC chip used in the PlayStation 3 could do. In 2006, Intel released its Core 2 Extreme microprocessor, which allowed gamers to play processing-intense games on PCs. In 2008, AMD was developing an eight-core microprocessor that would allow extreme gamers to play the most graphically intense video game, burn a DVD, download an HD movie, and make a Voice over Internet Protocol (VoIP) telephone call—all simultaneously. The Mach V PC, marketed by boutique computer maker Falcon Northwest, used eight gigabytes of memory, an Intel Core 2 Quad Extreme CPU, and an Nvidia GeForce 9800 GX2 GPU to perform such multiple tasks. The Mach V sold for $17,000 and included four Intel X25 solid-state hard drives, two 30-inch LCD displays and a Falcon Northwest T-shirt. Hewlett-Packard and Dell, the world's two largest manufacturers of desktop and laptop computers in 2008, had broadened product lines to include PC models with advanced graphics, wide-screen displays, and multiple processors that greatly enhanced the online gaming experience.

Competition in the industry also mandated that game console manufacturers establish relationships with such value chain allies as discounters, electronics retailers, and toy stores. Big-box retailers such as Wal-Mart, Target, Best Buy, Circuit City, and Toys "R" Us, along with specialty retailers like Gamestop, dedicated ample square footage to video game systems, accessories, and software. There was little price competition among retailers in the sale of video game consoles and software. More price competition at the retail level was found with video game accessories—especially accessories manufactured and marketed by third parties. Sony, Nintendo, or Microsoft accessories tended to sell at comparable price points across retailers.

Changes in the Competitive Landscape

Console Technology Future generations of game systems would undoubtedly include even more impressive technological capabilities than the next-generation consoles launched in 2005 and 2006. Jen-Hsun Huang, CEO of graphic accelerator maker Nvidia, believed there was ample opportunity for higher levels of photorealism in video games since no console was yet able to deliver the industry's aspirational "*Toy Story* standard."[4] Huang believed the industry was still "a good solid 10 years away from photorealism" and summarized the industry's innovation focus by commenting:

> In the next several years, we will still just be learning to do the basics of film, like motion, blur, depth of field—all of that stuff alone chews up a lot of graphics processing. We're pretty excited about moving to high-dynamic range where the color system has the fidelity of what we see in real life. The images don't seem realistic yet. Articulating a human form and human animation, the subtleties of humans and nature, are still quite a ways away for us.[5]

Online Gaming The manner in which video game software would be delivered to gamers was in the midst of a major change. The addition of Ethernet ports and Wi-Fi cards to video game consoles, coupled with the increased percentage of homes with broadband access, had given rise to online games. Web-enabled video game players could go online to play massively multiplayer online games (MMOGs) or console games with others; to download software, movies, and music; and to purchase software add-ons through various microtransactions. In 2007, 62 percent of all gamers played video games online, with 76 percent of Wii users playing games online and 70 percent of Xbox owners and PlayStation 3 owners going online to play games. At an average of 7.6 hours per week, Xbox owners spent the most time playing games online. PlayStation 3 users and PC users were next in line, with averages of 6.1 and 5.8 hours per week spent playing video games online, respectively. As presented in Exhibit 4, online game playing via broadband connections was expected to constitute a $6.4 billion market worldwide by 2010, up from $1.9 billion in 2005.

Mobile Gaming Historically, Nintendo's handheld devices had been the dominant leaders in the mobile video game player market segment. The company sold nearly 120 million Game Boy systems between 1989 and 2001. Nintendo introduced the Game Boy Advance in 2001, which was succeeded by the Nintendo DS. Nintendo sold more than 75 million Game Boy Advance players, 330 million Game Boy Advance game cartridges, and, by 2008, 77 million Nintendo DS devices and nearly 100 million games for Nintendo DS models. Sony entered the handheld/mobile gaming segment in 2005 with its PlayStation Portable (PSP), quickly becoming an important market contender, with worldwide sales exceeding 40 million units by mid-2008. Despite the historical popularity of traditional handheld devices for game playing (Game Boy, Nintendo DS, and PSP), the market for game software for such devices was expected to be stagnant, with projected sales of only $3.1 billion for gaming software on handheld sets in 2010 versus $4.8 billion in 2005.

However, mobile gaming on cellular phones and other wireless devices was expected to explode from a $2.6 billion market in 2005 to an $11.2 billion market in 2010 (see Exhibit 4). Mobile gaming was

Exhibit 4 Key Features of Microsoft Xbox 360, Sony PlayStation 3, and Nintendo Wii in 2008

	Xbox 360	PlayStation 3	Wii
U.S. launch date	May 12, 2005	November 17, 2006	November 19, 2006
Price	$200—core system $260—premium system $300—pro system	$400	$250
Microprocessor	3.2 GHz IBM PowerPC	3.2 GHz IBM PowerPC	729 MHz IBM PowerPC
Graphics processor	ATI 500 MHZ	RSX 550 MHz	ATI 243 MHz
Video resolution	1080p	1080p	480p
System memory	512 MB (shared with video)	256 MB dedicated	64 MB (shared with video)
Video memory	512 MB (shared with system)	256 MB dedicated	64 MB (shared with system)
Optical drive	12x DVD	Blu-ray HD	None
Storage/hard drive	256 MB memory card with core system; 20 GB hard drive with premium system; 60 GB hard drive with pro system	80 GB hard drive	512 MB embedded flash memory
Ethernet port	Yes	Yes	No
Wireless networking	Wi-Fi	Wi-Fi	Wi-Fi
Controllers	Wired controller with core system; wireless with premium system	Bluetooth wireless controller w/limited motion-sensing capabilities	Bluetooth wireless full motion-sensing controller
Online services	Free Xbox Live Silver service including online gaming and voice chat and text messaging; Premium Xbox Live service at $49/year; downloadable full-length movies and television programming starting at $2 per download	Web browser; free PlayStation online gaming network service providing game demos and game add-ons; online Sony store	Wii Network includes online shopping, weather, news, Web browsing, e-mail, and instant messaging
Game prices	$40–$60	$50–$60	$30–$50
Compatibility with previous generations	Compatible with approximately 300 Xbox titles	Compatible with most PlayStation 2 and PlayStation titles	Compatible with all GameCube titles; online access to titles originally released for Nintendo 64, SNES, NES, Sega Genesis, and TurboGrafx consoles

Sources: Product information published at www.gamestop.com, www.circuitcity.com, www.bestbuy.com, www.amazon.com, www.maxconsole.com, www.zdnet.com, and biz.gamedaily.com.

a fast-developing market segment because advancing technology made it possible to incorporate high-resolution color displays, greater processing power, and improved audio capabilities on cellular handsets, iPods and other brands of digital music players, and other sophisticated handheld devices (including those designed just for playing video games). There were more than 1.5 billion cell phones (about 35 percent of which were game-enabled) in active operation across the world, and new models with enhanced game-playing capability were selling briskly—most cell phone users, intrigued by the new features of next-generation models, upgraded their phones every few years. While playing video games on handheld devices had historically been a favorite pastime of preteens and teenagers, the popularity of game-capable cell phones, iPods, and other sophisticated handheld devices was expected to spur increases in mobile gaming among the young adult population worldwide in the years ahead.

PRODUCERS OF VIDEO GAME CONSOLES IN 2008

In 2008, video consoles that consumers might consider included those manufactured and marketed by Nintendo, Microsoft, and Sony. Each company's history in the video game industry differed, as did their approach to competing in the industry.

Microsoft

In the 30 years since its founding in 1976, Microsoft had become the most important software company in the world through the development and sale of such omnipresent software packages as Windows, Word, Excel, PowerPoint, and Internet Explorer. In 2008, Microsoft's software business, software consulting services business, online services, and entertainment and devices division contributed to total revenues of $60.4 billion and net earnings of $17.7 billion. Microsoft spent almost 15 percent of its revenues on research and development activities in 2008 to ensure that its future products offered levels of innovation and functionality necessary to sustain its advantage in the technology sector.

Microsoft's Entertainment and Devices Division Microsoft entered the video console industry in November 2001 with the introduction of the Xbox system, which was the industry's most technologically advanced game console until the November 2005 launch of the Xbox 360. The original Xbox sold 24 million units during its lifetime and its franchise software title, Halo 2, recorded sales of more than $125 million before the launch of Halo 3. The company's entertainment and devices division included the Xbox 360 business and other such products and services as Xbox Live, video game software, PC keyboards and mice, Zune digital music and media player, and Mediaroom Internet Protocol Television (IPTV). Microsoft's IPTV venture sought to change the delivery of television programming in a way that viewers could use broadband access and their home computers (or an Xbox 360) to watch TV broadcasts, on-demand programming, or archived episodes of classic TV series.

Revenues and operating losses for the division between 2004 and 2008 are shown in the following table:

Year	Revenue (in millions)	Operating profit (loss) (in millions)
2004	$2,737	$(1,337)
2005	3,515	(539)
2006	4,756	(1,284)
2007	6,069	(1,969)
2008	8,140	426

Source: Microsoft annual reports, various years.

Microsoft's entertainment and devices division earned its first operating profit in 2008 as its revenues increased by 41 percent and it gained economies of scale in the production of Xbox 360 game consoles. The division's revenue gains were attributable to increased sales of Xbox 360 game consoles and accessories, greater video game sales, and Xbox live subscription fees and download fees.

Xbox 360 Microsoft contracted its manufacturing activities for its game consoles and video game disks to third parties in Asia. The company had multiple sources for commodity-like components used in the production of the Xbox 360, but it chose to use single sources for core components. The company purchased all microprocessors from IBM, all GPUs from Taiwan Semiconductor Manufacturing Company, and all memory chips from NEC Corporation. Microsoft expected the life cycle for the Xbox 360 to reach five to seven years.

Video game industry analysts were quite satisfied with the Xbox 360's capabilities upon its release. The Xbox 360's HD graphics impressed many, as did its ease of use. Reviewers were also pleased with game titles that accompanied the Xbox 360 launch and Microsoft's Xbox Live Arcade games that could be played over the Internet. Analysts were particularly struck by Xbox 360 games that had been co-developed by Microsoft Game Studios and proven Hollywood screenwriters, directors, and producers. A full list of Xbox 360 features is presented in Exhibit 4.

The November 2005 Xbox 360 launch came one year earlier than the release of next-generation consoles by Sony and Nintendo. The one-year first-mover lead in game console technology gave Microsoft a temporary advantage in building Xbox's installed base and variety of video games. By year-end 2006, more than 160 game titles were available for the Xbox 360. With more than 5 million Xbox 360s installed prior to the launch of the PlayStation 3 or Wii, third-party game developers had little choice but to develop games for the Xbox 360. Gamers were unlikely to buy new software for current-generation consoles once they began to anticipate the launch of a new system. With the exception of annually updated games like Tiger Woods 2007, there was little point in developing new games for the PlayStation 2 or GameCube in 2005 and 2006.

Xbox Live Microsoft's one-year head start in making its next-generation console available also helped it build traffic to its Xbox Live Web site. Xbox Live provided Xbox users who had broadband access the capability to play online games, chat, watch game trailers, demo new game titles, maintain a profile, participate in forums, download television programming and movies, and access MMOGs. Xbox Live generated revenue from advertising, subscription fees to its premium-level Xbox Live Gold, movie and television program download fees, and download fees charged to Xbox Silver members. Counting the complimentary Xbox Silver memberships, Xbox Live had approximately 10 million registered users by January 2008. The company found that approximately 25 percent of Xbox Silver members purchased the full version of free demo versions of new games.

The addition of downloadable television programs and motion pictures to Xbox Live had the potential to change how Xbox 360 consoles were used. Xbox 360 owners could download TV shows and movies onto their hard drives from Xbox Live's 1,000-hour library of programming for on-demand viewing at a later time. Xbox Live offered movie downloads from MGM, Paramount, Lionsgate, and Warner Bros. as well as television programming from ABC, Disney Channel, Toon Disney, and other major networks and cable channels. Programming pricing was based on usage of points purchased online at Xbox Live or through Xbox 360 retailers. In August 2008, a 1,600-point card sold for $20. The price of a standard-definition television program download was 160 points. HD programs sold for 240 points. Microsoft charged Xbox Live users 320 points for standard-definition movie downloads and 480 points for downloads of HD movies.

The Xbox 360's 20-gigabyte hard drive could store 16 hours of standard definition programs or about 4½ hours of HD programming. Users who deleted programs to free hard drive space were allowed to download previously purchased programs at no charge. Standard-definition programming could be downloaded in minutes, while an HD movie might take hours to download. There was speculation among industry analysts that Microsoft and Netflix were in negotiations in 2008 to develop a new video streaming service that would allow Xbox users to rent movies included in Netflix's vast library of films. Peter Moore, a Microsoft vice president, explained to the *Wall Street Journal* that gaming was the primary selling point for the Xbox 360, but he added, "We look at the console as an entertainment amplifier for the living room."[6]

Marketing Microsoft used a variety of approaches to market the Xbox 360 and Xbox Live to consumers. The company supported the Xbox 360 with a $150 million ad campaign in fiscal 2007 and regularly entered into co-op advertising with its retail partners. Microsoft had also developed highly innovative viral marketing campaigns for the Xbox 360 and its game titles. Viral marketing had proved to be important with gamers since many young consumers did not respond to, and even resented, traditional advertising. One such campaign involved Perfect Dark Zero, an Xbox Live game that relied on users sending links to friends asking them to join in to expand its subscriber base. The viral marketing campaign for Viva Piñata was highly sophisticated. Viva Piñata was Microsoft's attempt at developing a game that might have the same level of appeal with young children that was achieved by Nintendo's Super Mario Bros. and Donkey Kong. The campaign included a new Saturday-morning cartoon based on Viva Piñata characters that aired on Fox Television and a line of electronic action figures produced by Playmates Toys. The Viva Piñata toy could interact with Xbox Live by allowing users to download and upload "special powers" that added to the experience of playing with the toy or playing the video game.

Xbox 360's First-Mover Advantage Microsoft's early launch of its next-generation console had allowed it quickly to build an installed base and economies of scale in production. By year-end 2006, Microsoft had sold more than 10.4 million Xbox 360 units, with more than 1.1 million units selling in December alone. By comparison, Sony sold 491,000 PlayStation 3 units in December 2006, while Nintendo sold 604,000 Wii systems. The large number of sales prior to the launch of the PS3 and Wii had allowed Microsoft to lower production costs for the Xbox 360 to $306 per unit by year-end 2006. An NPD Group analyst believed that the Xbox 360's early launch date allowed Microsoft "to really take advantage of its lead in this generation's race, provided they (and third-party supporters) keep bringing the games to market that keep consumers wanting to play on that system."[7]

Sony

The Sony Corporation was the world's leading manufacturer and marketer of audio, video, communications, and information technology products, with fiscal 2008 revenues of $83.5 billion and net income of $3.5 billion. Sony's video game business contributed $12.2 billion to the company's 2008 total revenues, but had recorded operating losses of $2.2 billion in fiscal 2007 and $1.2 billion in fiscal 2008. The division had been Sony's most profitable business unit as recently as 2004, but the sluggish sales of the PlayStation 3, along with its high development and production costs, had made the once profitable business unit a money loser. Sony's production cost for the PlayStation 3 in fiscal 2007 was estimated at $805 for the 20 GB version and $840 for the 60 GB version. Sony management believed that it would begin earning profits on the sale of each PS3 after cumulative production of the PS3 reached 20 million units. The division's operating loss in fiscal 2008 was directly attributable to the increased sales of PS3 game consoles in fiscal 2008. Revenues and operating profits for Sony's game division for fiscal 2004 through fiscal 2008 are presented in the following table:

Year	Revenues (in millions)	Operating profit (loss) (in millions)
2004	$ 7,412	$ 642
2005	6,936	410
2006	9,109	82.6
2007	9,664	(2,207)
2008	12,200	(1,183)

Source: Sony Corporation annual reports, various years.

Sony's PlayStation and PlayStation 2 When the Sony PlayStation was introduced in 1995, it was an instant success: more than 100,000 PlayStations were sold in North America during the first weekend the game console was on store shelves. More than 1 million units had been sold in North America by the PlayStation's six-month anniversary, and the company hit the 4 million mark in North America in just over two years. The PlayStation's cutting-edge graphics, CD optical drive, 32-bit processor, and variety of game titles made it much more appealing to adolescents and young adults than Nintendo's Super NES system. More than 100 million PlayStation consoles were eventually sold, which was more than twice the number of Nintendo SNES units sold.

By 2001, one in three U.S. households had purchased a PlayStation game console.

Nintendo launched its 64-bit Nintendo 64 console a year after the PlayStation was introduced, but it failed to take a considerable number of sales away from the PlayStation because of Nintendo's limited game categories. While Sony's third-party game developers were creating games that would be appealing to preteens, teenagers, and young adults, Nintendo's game development focus was on smaller children. Because Sony targeted older gamers, it was able to add features to the PlayStation 2 that might be difficult for young children to operate. The PS2 was able to play DVDs and could be connected to the Internet with an Ethernet adapter. The $299 PS2 was powered by a 294 MHz microprocessor, which was the most powerful game processor until the introduction of the Xbox.

As with the PlayStation, Sony's third-party game developers took advantage of the massive installed base and directed their resources toward developing blockbuster game titles for Sony consoles. Third-party developed games like Gran Turismo, Final Fantasy, Grand Theft Auto, Madden NFL, Medal of Honor, and Need for Speed were games likely to be found in most game collections. The Sony PS2 was also backward-compatible with the game titles that had made the PlayStation a marketplace success. The combination of technological superiority and large number of hit game titles allowed Sony to achieve a 70 percent worldwide market share in game consoles. Even though Sony introduced the PS3 in November 2006, it continued producing the PS2 as a lower-priced alternative to the PS3. Sony lowered the retail price of the PS2 to $130 in the United States once it began shipping PS3 consoles. With the PS2 outselling the PS3 by nearly 400,000 units during the 2007 holiday shopping period, a video game analyst suggested that the PS2's "breadth of available content and price point [would make it] an important part of the games ecosystem for several years."[8]

Sony PSP In 2005, Sony challenged Nintendo's dominance in handheld systems with the introduction of the $249 PlayStation Portable (PSP). The PSP utilized a 333 MHz microprocessor and a 4.3-inch LCD screen to allow gamers to play 3D games, watch television programs recorded with TiVo, connect to wireless Internet networks, review pictures from digital cameras, listen to MP3s, and watch full-length movies. In addition, up to 16 PSP players in proximity to one another could connect wirelessly to play multiplayer games. Sony sold 41 million PSP handheld game consoles between its March 2005 launch and July 2008.

Sony PlayStation 3 Sony hoped to replicate the success of the PlayStation 2 with the PlayStation 3 by following a similar strategy. The PS3 was packed with technological features that would allow game developers to create 3D and HD game titles that could exploit the processing power of its 3.2 GHz nine-brain processor and Nvidia GPU (a full list of PS3 features is presented in Exhibit 4). The PS3 also had the opportunity to become the central component of a home entertainment system since it included a state-of-the-art Blu-ray HD optical drive and Internet connectivity.

One of the few flaws evident in Sony's strategy in the first months after the November 2006 launch of the PS3 was the pricing of the console. The PS3 sold at either $499 or $599, depending on hard drive size. The company justified its PS3 pricing by noting that the retail price of a Blu-ray player was $1,000. Sony hoped that consumers would make the determination that a PS3 was at least $400 less expensive than a Blu-ray player and offered all of the video game capabilities of the PS3 as an added bonus.

In some ways, the November 2006 launch of the PS3 was a deviation from Sony's intended strategy. Sony had not planned to launch the PS3 when it did, but it was forced into an early launch date because of the November 2005 launch of the Xbox 360 by Microsoft. The PS3 was designed to be backward-compatible with more than 16,000 PlayStation and PS2 game titles, but the launch of the system was accompanied by only 24 PS3 game titles. The PS3 had tremendous graphics and processing capabilities, but all of this was not needed to play PS2 games. A PlayStation or PS2 video game was not going to look any better played on a PS3. In addition, the 24 HD games that accompanied the launch did not fully use the capabilities of the PS3 since third-party software developers had been forced to shorten their planned development times. Consumers would also have to own an HDTV before upgrading to a PS3.

Sony was barely able to get the PS3 to market in time for 2006 holiday shopping because of a variety of production problems. Some of its production problems centered on the use of the Blu-ray optical drive. An initial holdup involved the development of copy-protection technology for the Blu-ray drive, which was followed by a problem producing the laser component needed in the assembly of Blu-ray drives. Production problems also affected the PS3's backward-compatibility capacity, with many PS2 game titles not working on the PS3 when it was first launched. The cumulative effect of Sony's supply chain and production problems allowed it to ship only an estimated 125,000 to 175,000 units for its North American launch. The company had planned to support the launch with 400,000 units. Sony was eventually able to ship nearly 500,000 units before the 2006 holiday season ended. However, the production problems continued into 2007, with Sony delaying its European launch of the PS3 until March 2007.

Another factor that might hinder the sales of PS3 units for some time was the tremendous video game development costs necessary to produce games that could fully make use of the console's capabilities. Even with the PS2, game development costs typically ran $2 million to $7 million. Game developers were willing to make such an investment to develop games for the PS2 since a hit game could easily sell 5 million to 10 million units at $50 per unit. Analysts had projected that game development costs for the PS3 would average $20 million, with some titles requiring much higher investments. Many game developers had chosen to delay the development of new games for the PS3 until its installed base grew significantly beyond the 15 million units that had been sold by July 2008.

Sony expected that its Internet-based PlayStation Network might satisfy the gaming expectations of consumers until new PS3 games came to market. The PlayStation Network offered users free access to a limited number of multiplayer online games and text, voice, and video chat. Sony introduced a video delivery service on the PlayStation Network in 2008 that allowed members to download and watch nearly 300 movies and 1,200 television episodes in either standard definition (SD) or HD. PS3 users could rent SD movies from the PlayStation Network for $2.99 to $3.99 and rent HD movies for $5.99. PlayStation Network members could also purchase movies at prices ranging from $9.99 to $14.99. Movies downloaded onto a PS3 could be transferred to the Sony PSP handheld console.

Sony also released a Life with PlayStation feature at the PlayStation Network that would provide users with news headlines, weather updates, and live camera images for 60 cities around the world. Most video game industry analysts found the site's online games and content to be very limited and no match for Xbox Live. However, the PlayStation Network had 9.8 million registered accounts in 2008. Sony was also working to develop a social networking site similar to Second Life that could be used by PS3 users. The proposed PlayStation Home feature would allow PS3 users to create avatars to meet, chat, and play online games with other PS3 users in a 3D virtual world.

Nintendo

A playing card manufacturer founded in 1889 in Kyoto, Japan, eventually became known as the Nintendo Company Ltd. in 1963 when it expanded outside playing cards to other types of games. The company had produced electronic toys as early as 1970, but its 1981 introduction of a coin-operated video game called Donkey Kong transformed the company into a household name in North America, Asia, and Europe. By 2008, Nintendo had sold more than 470 million game consoles and 2.7 billion video games worldwide. In the United States, one in four households had a Nintendo game system of one generation or another.

The company's sales slowed between 2004 and 2006 as video game users waited for the introduction of next-generation consoles, but the popularity of its Wii and the PSP video game systems had allowed its revenues and net income to grow at compounded annual rates of 86 percent and 66 percent, respectively, between fiscal 2006 and fiscal 2008. The following table illustrates the dramatic impact of the Wii and DS on Nintendo's financial performance:

Year	Revenues (in millions)	Operating income (in millions)	Net income (in millions)
2004	$ 4,858	$1,016	$ 313
2005	4,867	1,049	821
2006	4,811	853	929
2007	9,134	2,136	1,647
2008	16,724	4,872	2,573

Source: Nintendo annual reports, various years.

Nintendo's Strategy in the Video Game Industry With the company's business limited to the sale of game consoles, handheld game systems, and game software, the company pursued a different strategic approach than that used by Sony and Microsoft. The company focused on earning profits from the sale of game consoles as well as from game software sales. A company senior VP commented, "We don't have other sister divisions that can underwrite big losses in our area. So we have to be able to get to breakeven, or profitability, pretty quickly on the hardware and then the software-tie ratio becomes the icing on that."[9]

Based on that business model, Nintendo had never held a technological advantage in the industry and didn't attempt to battle Sony and Microsoft for the allegiance of hard-core gamers. It had succeeded by developing game systems that were intuitive and easy to operate. Its video games were fun to play but didn't offer a cinematic experience. Nintendo's strategy was well matched to the interests of children and casual gamers. Nintendo's president, Satoru Iwata, explained in the company's annual report, "Nintendo has implemented a strategy which encourages people around the world to play video games regardless of their age, gender or cultural background. Our goal is to expand the gaming population."[10]

Nintendo's Handheld Game Systems Few in the video game industry anticipated the runaway success of Nintendo's Game Boy handheld system when it was introduced in 1989. In 1996, Nintendo paired the Game Boy with its new Pokémon video game, which was accompanied by an animated series and a line of trading cards. With the help of Pokémon, the low-screen-resolution Game Boy player sold nearly 120 million units. Even though the Game Boy had a life cycle of more than a decade, Nintendo kept its appearance fresh by making the handheld game in different colors and eventually adding a color display. Such cosmetic changes to handheld games were critical to sustaining sales, since many children thought of the Game Boy as a fashion accessory. Nintendo's next-generation successor to the Game Boy was the Game Boy Advance, which allowed users to play Pokémon and other games on a larger, higher-resolution screen. Nintendo sold more than 81 million Game Boy Advance units between its launch in June 2001 and December 2007.

The Nintendo DS replaced the Game Boy Advance and was developed to appeal to Nintendo's core youth market as well as such historically nongamers as women in general and both men and women over age 35. The system included dual screens, a stylus-operated touchpad, voice recognition, and Wi-Fi capabilities to make operation of the system intuitive rather than an exercise in dexterity. The company developed innovative new games for the DS that would appeal to those who were uninterested in first-person-shooter games or other genres preferred by the PlayStation aficionados. Nintendo DS games such as Nintendogs (which allowed gamers to play with a virtual pet) and Brain Training for Adults (which asked gamers to solve arithmetic puzzles) weren't very popular with 18–30-year-old males, but were a huge hit with people who had never before shown an interest in video games. Nintendo introduced several new game titles during 2007 and 2008 to appeal to the interest of new gamers and the child market. Hanna Montana, High School Musical, and Imagine Figure Skater were Nintendo DS games specifically designed for girls. Nintendo's popular games developed for adults included the memory-training games Brain Boost, Brain Age, and Big Brain Academy, as well as Flash Focus, which was a game designed to improve visual acuity. At year-end 2007, there were nearly 450 game titles available for the DS handheld system.

The retail price of the DS was also an aspect of Nintendo's handheld systems that was attractive to casual gamers. In October 2008, the retail price of the Nintendo DS was $130 compared to a retail price of $170 for the Sony PSP. The Nintendo DS had been the top-selling video game system during the 2006 and 2007 holiday retail seasons, with more than 1 million units sold in November 2006 and 1.53 million units sold in November 2007. Near the conclusion of the 2007 holidays, Nintendo of America's vice president of marketing and corporate communications emphatically stated, "There's no letup in sight [for the] Nintendo DS."[11]

Nintendo Wii Nintendo followed its game plan used with the Nintendo DS in developing the Wii. As with the DS, Nintendo attempted to develop a game system that would appeal to nongamers—especially moms. Shigeru Miyamoto, a key Wii developer, explained this key consideration to *BusinessWeek* writers in 2006:

> Our goal was to come up with a machine that moms would want—easy to use, quick to start up, not a huge energy drain, and quiet while it was running.

> Rather than just picking new technology, we thought seriously about what a game console should be. [CEO Satoru] Iwata wanted a console that would play every Nintendo game ever made. Moms would hate it if they had to have several consoles lying around.[12]

Miyamoto's colleague on the development team, Ken'ichiro Ashida, added, "We didn't want wires all over the place, which might anger moms because of the mess."[13]

The development team considered a variety of controller types that could be wireless and intuitive. Nintendo rejected such design inspirations as cell phones, car navigation remotes, and touch panels for a wireless wand. The wand took more than a year to develop and was able to respond to hand motions that were used in throwing a ball, casting a fishing line, swinging a baseball bat, pointing a gun, or playing a musical instrument. A separate "nunchuk" device allowed the user to create motion necessary to play games needing two hands. A Wedbush Morgan Securities analyst commented on the brilliance of the design by pointing out, "With the Wii remote, the learning curve for most games is 15 minutes or less. I think that will eliminate the intimidation factor and will attract a broader audience."[14]

Although Nintendo executives knew early during the development of the Wii that it would be unable to compete with the next-generation consoles soon to be launched by Microsoft and Sony, they believed the wireless wand controller would have appeal with the masses. Reggie Fils-Aime, the president of Nintendo of America, explained:

> What makes the Wii so special is obviously the Wii Remote: the ability to play tennis with a flick of the wrist, to play baseball like you do it on the ball field. That allows the consumer to get more in the game by having a totally different type of interface, plus it allows game developers to create all new different types of games. We have everything from a game like "Trauma Center" from Atlas, where you're the doctor, and you're using the precision of the Wii remote to stitch up a patient and take shards of glass out of their arm—things of that nature. The new way to play "Madden Football," a brand new Madden where you act like the quarterback, where you hike the ball, pass. All of that allows for totally unique game play.[15]

Another consideration was creating a game console that would easily fit within the family budget. Miyamoto explained, "Originally, I wanted a machine that would cost $100. My idea was to spend nothing on the console technology so all the money could be spent on improving the interface and software."[16] As a result, Nintendo wound up using a microprocessor, that although twice as fast as that used in the GameCube, was less powerful than what Microsoft had used in the original Xbox. Also, instead of a hard drive, the Wii contained only a 512 MB flash memory card to store data and could not play DVDs. The Wii could connect to the Internet through a wireless home network but not with an Ethernet cable. A full list of Wii features is presented in Exhibit 4. Analysts believed that, at launch, Nintendo would earn a profit on every Wii console sold because of its modest components costs.

One additional benefit of Nintendo's low-tech approach to a next-generation console was the low relative development costs needed for Wii video games. Analysts expected that on average the development cost for a Wii video game would be less than half of that necessary to develop games for the Xbox 360 or PS3. A video game analyst believed developers saw more opportunity for immediate profits from Wii games than those for PS3 and were "holding off on creating games for Sony" until its installed base grew.[17] At year-end 2007, the library of Wii games included more than 140 titles. In addition to new games, Wii users could also access all older games on Nintendo's Wii Connect24 online gaming site. Wii Connect24 also offered a weather channel, news channel, shopping channel, and Web browser. The Wii console also allowed users to view digital pictures stored on an SD memory card and create personalized "Mii" interfaces for each member of the family.

Nintendo and third-party developers created expected software titles such as Guitar Hero III, Mario Kart Wii, and Madden NFL 09, but also developed games unlike those published for Xbox 360 or the PlayStation 3 like Wii Music and Wii Fit. The Wii Fit fitness game allowed users to evaluate their posture, balance, and body mass index and to participate in more than 40 exercises and fitness activities. Wii Fit also allowed users to set fitness goals and track their progress with easy-to-interpret charts and graphs. A video game analyst commented that Wii Fit would help Nintendo further expand the market for video games since it was "definitely aimed at the Oprah crowd."[18] The company expected to sell more than 3 million Wii Fit games and $90 wireless Balance Boards needed to play the game by the end of 2008.

Wii Fit and other active games such as bowling, golf, tennis, and baseball had made the Wii an intergenerational hit. The company had discovered that a large number of nursing homes had purchased Wii units to use in recreational programs for residents. A marketing director of a Tampa, Florida, nursing home commented that Weinberg Village's Wii games and activities for residents had "quickly become one of our most popular programs."[19] The success of the Wii and its unique controller was phenomenal. In 2008, a video game industry analyst stated, "The Wii does not appear to be a fad and it has the chance to be one of the best selling systems of all time."[20] A downside to Nintendo's growing emphasis on non-traditional gamers was that such gamers were less likely than core gamers to purchase a wide array of video games. In 2008, the average Wii owner purchased 3.7 games per year, compared to 4.7 games per year for Xbox 360 owners and 4.6 games per year for PS3 owners.

GOING INTO THE 2008 HOLIDAY RETAIL SEASON

Even though some industry analysts had suggested that the Wii would be humbled in the marketplace by the more advanced PlayStation 3, and perhaps by the Xbox 360, the Wii had proved to be the early winner of the next-generation console battle. Predictions that the Wii would sell fewer than 25 million units by 2012 clearly had been wrong. More than 25 million Wii consoles had been sold by July 2008, and the Wii seemed to be on many Christmas wish lists that year. When asked about the success of the Wii at the end of the 2007 holiday season, a Nintendo executive stated, "We don't feel like we've made any mistakes."[21]

Going into the 2008 holiday retail season, Sony had lowered the price of the PlayStation 3 and had given it a larger hard drive (80 GB) to avoid a repeat of the 2007 holiday period, when it sold only 1.3 million units compared to 2.3 million units for the Wii and 2 million units for Microsoft's Xbox. Similarly, Microsoft had lowered the price of its base Xbox 360 model to $200 and its 20 GB version to $260 to better compete against the $250 Wii on price. However, Nintendo's biggest threat in the marketplace was expected to be its inability to meet demand. The company had been unable to meet holiday demand in 2007, and Best Buy and Circuit City had no inventory of Wii consoles in October 2008. Wal-Mart did have the Wii in stock, but it was available only as part of $500-plus bundles that included a Wii console and various combinations of accessories and game software. Analysts believed that Nintendo may have given up $1 billion or more in sales in 2007 because of its inability to meet demand. Retailers were anxious as well to determine whether their inventories of Nintendo DS handheld models and software would quickly be depleted from store shelves and eventually replace the Game Boy and PS2 as the best-selling game system in the industry's history.

Endnotes

[1] Entertainment Software association, "Essential Facts about the Computer and Video Game Industry," 2006, www.theesa.com (accessed September 7, 2006).

[2] Peter Lewis, "The Biggest Game in Town," *Fortune,* September 15, 2003, p. 135.

[3] "Report from the NPD Group Provides Insight into Consumer Purchase Intent of Next Generation Video Game Consoles," *Business Wire,* November 13, 2006.

[4] As quoted in "Nvidia CEO Talks Console War," *BusinessWeek* online, July 26, 2006.

[5] Ibid.

[6] As quoted in "Coming to Xbox 360: Films and TV," *Wall Street Journal* online, November 7, 2006, p. B3.

[7] As quoted in "Report: Sony Sold 490,700 PS3s in U.S.," *AFX International Focus,* January 13, 2007.

[8] As quoted in "Microsoft's Xbox 360 Came in Second to Nintendo Console Wii," *Seattle Post-Intelligencer,* January 18, 2008, p. E1.

[9] As quoted in "Nintendo Wii Enters Video Game Fray," *Investor's Business Daily,* November 20, 2006, p. A4.

[10] As quoted in Nintendo's 2006 annual report.

[11] As quoted in "Nintendo of America Press Release," PR Newswire, December 11, 2007.

[12] As quoted in "The Big Ideas behind Nintendo's Wii," *BusinessWeek* online, November 16, 2006.

[13] Ibid.

[14] As quoted in "Nintendo Brings the Games to the People," *Business-Week* online, October 31, 2006.

[15] As quoted in "Nintendo's U.S. Head: We're Doing Things Right with the New Console," Associated Press State & Local Wire, November 17, 2006.

[16] As quoted in "The Big ideas behind Nintendo's Wii."

[17] As quoted in "Will Sony's Pricey PS3 Pay Off?" *BusinessWeek* online, July 20, 2006.

[18] As quoted in "Wii a Hit, but Games Don't Sell Well," *Grand Rapids Press,* April 27, 2008.

[19] As quoted in "Guess Who Got a Wii?" *Tampa Tribune,* June 3, 2008.

[20] As quoted in "DFC Intelligence Press Release," *Business Wire,* June 30, 2008.

[21] As quoted in "A Year Later, the Same Scene: Long Lines for the Elusive Wii," *New York Times,* December 14, 2007, p. C1.

Nintendo's Strategy for the Wii: Good Enough to Beat Xbox 360 and PlayStation 3?

CASE 12

Lou Marino
The University of Alabama

Sally Sarrett
The University of Alabama

The battle for market supremacy in third-generation video game consoles began in earnest during the 2006 holiday season. Sony started selling its PlayStation 3 (PS3) on November 17, 2006, in head-on competition against Microsoft's first-to-market Xbox 360, which had been released a full year earlier, in November 2005. The media hype surrounding the PS3 launch overshadowed the introduction of Nintendo's Wii system two days later. Many hardcore gamers viewed the Wii as a toy, deriding the system for its weak graphics, lack of DVD playback, and childish name. Some video game industry analysts viewed the Wii as the last-ditch effort of a struggling company that had once dominated the global video game landscape and then become increasingly irrelevant when Sony entered the market with its first PlayStation, followed by Microsoft's entry into video gaming with the Xbox. Analysts acknowledged that the Wii system would fit well strategically with Nintendo's popular DS handheld video game player, but they expected that Nintendo's new Wii would appeal to a relatively small number of people who played video games, given the Wii's lack of technological sophistication relative to the PS3 and Xbox 360 and the limited availability of action-oriented titles designed to play on Wii consoles.

Interestingly enough, Nintendo did not disagree that the Wii would likely have limited market appeal. In fact, while the Wii was in the developmental stage, Nintendo's CEO Satoru Iwata preferred not to speak of the Wii as a "next-generation" video game console, since this implied it would be an evolutionary improvement over the Game Cube, which had achieved a small global market share against the wildly popular PlayStation 2 and the modestly popular Xbox.[1] Given Nintendo's declining sales and market share in the video game console segment since 2000, Iwata wanted to totally change the market's perception of the Wii by providing an entirely different video game playing experience that would be less intimidating to casual gamers and to people who had not previously played video games. The concept underlying the Wii—with its innovative and distinctively different controller—was to build on the company's success with the innovative user interface on the popular handheld Nintendo DS video game player.

While Nintendo's strategy for the Wii of concentrating on pioneering a daringly different video game controller (as opposed to building a raft of new graphics features and technological capability into the console itself—as had been done for the Xbox 360 and PS3) was viewed as very risky, it so far had proved spectacularly successful. Indeed, Nintendo quickly sold out of Wiis in the 2006 holiday season, sold all the Wiis it could produce throughout 2007, and was expected to have still higher sales in 2008. As of mid-2008, Nintendo's cumulative sales of the Wii far surpassed those of the PS3 and the Xbox 360. Nintendo's Wii, to the surprise of most everyone, was the market leader in sales of third-generation video game consoles.

Initially, both Microsoft and Sony were taken aback by the Wii's apparently broad appeal and resounding market success. During 2007, they initiated a series of efforts to attract more buyers for the Xbox and PS3, calling attention to an assortment of technological capabilities and graphic features built into their consoles and promoting the release of new games for their consoles. Their counterattack was only modestly successful. However, heading into the holiday season of 2008, Sony and Microsoft were launching a fresh attack on multiple fronts, including software designed for casual gamers, new controllers that allowed gamers to play in ways similar to Nintendo's controllers, and price cuts. Additionally, there was a patent infringement case in the United States on the core technology Nintendo used to develop its Wii remote (nicknamed the Wiimote), the popular controller that was one of the main factors that differentiated the Wii from its competitors.

COMPANY BACKGROUND

In 2008, Nintendo was a multinational corporation with a long history in the video gaming marketplace. From humble beginnings as a manufacturer of Japanese card games, the company had over the years gained a reputation for product innovation and introduced some of the industry's most astoundingly inventive and financially lucrative gaming products.

The Nintendo Company Ltd. was founded in 1889 by Fusajiro Yamauchi and began operations as a manufacturing company with a single product, Hanafuda cards. Yamauchi's company was the first Japanese company to produce Hanafuda playing cards, and most of its production was exported. However, Hanafuda quickly became extremely popular within Japan, and Yamauchi was forced to hire assistants in order to boost production and meet increasing demand. Yamauchi did not have a son to take over the family business when he was ready to retire. In keeping with Japanese custom, he adopted his son-in-law, Sekiryo Kaneda (Yamauchi after the marriage), in 1929 in order to preserve family ownership and control.

Sekiryo Yamauchi continued developing the playing card company in his father-in-law's footsteps, and in 1933 he established an unlimited partnership with another company to form Nintendo Playing Card Company Ltd. In 1953, Nintendo became the first playing card company to begin mass production of the product in plastic, which became a huge hit and allowed Nintendo to secure its hold over the playing card market. Hiroshi Yamauchi, who took over the company as the third president of Nintendo after Sekiryo passed away in 1949, traveled to the United States in 1959 to engage in talks with the dominant U.S. playing card manufacturer at the time, the United States Playing Card Company. Shocked by the small size of the office that the United States Playing Card Company was operating out of, considering it was the world's biggest company within his market, Yamauchi for the first time saw the limited growth potential of the playing card business and began considering alternatives to expand his company.

In 1959, Nintendo entered into an agreement with the Walt Disney Company to produce Disney's playing cards (all of which had recognizable Disney characters on them). The revenue and profit gains associated with being a producer of Disney playing cards encouraged Hiroshi to take the Nintendo Playing Card Company public; the company's stock was subsequently traded on the Osaka Stock Exchange. In 1963, the company's name was changed to Nintendo Company Ltd. and the company began to manufacture games as well as playing cards. While the Japanese economy boomed in 1964, in part due to the Olympics being held in Tokyo, the playing card market reached its saturation point, precipitating a decline in Nintendo's stock price from 900 yen to 60 yen. Gunpei Yokoi, a game designer who later created the Nintendo Game Boy, was hired in 1965, and in 1969 the company expanded and reinforced its gaming division while building a production plant in Uji City, a suburb of Kyoto.

The company moved into the Japanese toy industry in 1966 with its introduction of the Ultra Hand, an extending arm toy developed by Gunpei Yokoi; the Ultra Hand proved to be a market success, selling more than a million units. In 1970, the company introduced electronic technology into the toy industry in Japan with its Beam Gun series of toys that used opto-electronics. However, despite several successes in the Japanese toy market, Nintendo struggled to meet production demands and fast turnaround times between toy orders and deliveries to retailers, putting Nintendo at a competitive disadvantage versus well-established toy producers such as Bandai and Tomy.

In 1974, new product developers at Nintendo created an image projection system for amusement arcades and began exporting units to both Europe and America. That same year Nintendo secured a contract to distribute the Magnavox Odyssey, the world's first video gaming console. The prototype was completed by Ralph Baer in 1968 and first appeared in 1972, predating the Atari Pong console by several years.

Nintendo developed its first Nintendo-branded home video gaming system, the Color TV Game, in

1977 in cooperation with Mitsubishi Electric. Subsequently, four different versions of this system were produced, each playing variations on a single game. In 1978, Nintendo created and began selling coin-operated video games that utilized microcomputers, a move that established the company as a competitor in the video arcade gaming. In 1981, when Donkey Kong was released and quickly became the single hottest-selling individual coin-operated machine on the market, Nintendo's financial fortune changed for the better. Nintendo of America Inc., a wholly owned subsidiary with capital of $600,000 and headquartered in Seattle, Washington, was formed in 1982. In 1983, Nintendo began work on a new plant, also in Uji City, to increase production capabilities and allow for future business expansion. Also in 1983, Nintendo launched the Family Computer home video gaming system in Japan along with adaptations of many of its most popular arcade titles. The Family Computer employed a central processing unit (CPU) and a picture processing unit (PPU). In 1985, the Family Computer home video gaming system was released in the United States as the Nintendo Entertainment System (NES); one of the video games available for play on the new NES system was Super Mario Brothers, a title that now ranks as one of Nintendo's top-selling games of all time.

Nintendo introduced a handheld Game Boy device in 1989 that quickly became one of the world's best-selling video game playing systems. In 1991, Nintendo introduced the Super Nintendo Entertainment System (SNES); it had better graphics and stereo sound and was accompanied by a bigger selection and variety of games. The Nintendo 64 gaming system, a third-generation gaming system, was introduced in 1996; the N64's immense popularity drove Nintendo's revenues to record highs. It was followed by the also successful Game Boy Advance (2001) and a fourth-generation console system called GameCube (2001); while worldwide sales of the GameCube totaled 21.7 million units, it was considered by most video game enthusiasts as inferior to Sony's wildly popular PlayStation and PlayStation 2 and Microsoft's new Xbox.

In 2002, Satoru Iwata became Nintendo's fourth president, replacing Hiroshi Yamauchi, the great-grandson of Fusajiro Yamauchi and becoming the company's first president not related to its founder. To combat increasing competition within the handheld video gaming console market segment, Nintendo introduced the Nintendo Dual Screen (DS) in 2004.[2] Sales of the DS quickly took off, with sales surpassing 50 million units worldwide by September 2007 (a sales volume that made it the fastest-selling handheld video game console of all time). A successor—the DS Lite—was introduced in 2006; it, too, was a market success. As of September 30, 2008, cumulative worldwide sales of video game software for the DS and DS Lite had surpassed 400 million units. But Nintendo's major new product introduction in 2006 was the Wii, with its highly innovative wireless remote controller.

NINTENDO'S PRODUCT PORTFOLIO FROM 1983 TO 2008

Nintendo's product portfolio since 1983 has been dominated by video game consoles and handheld systems. Within the video game console segment of Nintendo's portfolio, the Wii was the company's fifth modern gaming console. The first was the Nintendo Entertainment System, followed by the Super Nintendo Entertainment System, the Nintendo 64, and the Nintendo GameCube. The second key element of Nintendo's product portfolio was handheld gaming systems. The first systems were the Game Boy and the Game Boy Color, followed by the Game Boy Advance, the Game Boy Advance SP, the Game Boy Micro, the Nintendo DS, and the Nintendo DS Lite. The release dates and total units sold of each of these console and handheld systems are shown in Exhibit 1.

NINTENDO'S HANDHELD GAME SYSTEMS

Handheld game systems were portable, lightweight electronic devices that included built-in speakers and displays designed largely for playing video games. The first handheld systems were introduced in the 1970s and 1980s, but the market had been largely dominated by Nintendo since its release of the Game Boy in 1989. The two main competitors in handheld game players in 2008 were the Nintendo DS and the Sony PlayStation Portable (PSP).

Exhibit 1 Estimated Total Sales of Nintendo Video Game Systems as of October 2008

Gaming System	Date First Released	Cumulative Units Sold (in millions)
Video Game Consoles		
Nintendo Entertainment System (NES)	July 15, 1983	61.90
Super Nintendo Entertainment System (SNES)	November 21, 1990	49.10
Nintendo 64 (N64)	June 23, 1996	32.90
Nintendo GameCube (GCN)	September 14, 2001	21.74
Nintendo Wii	November 19, 2006	34.50
Handheld Game Systems		
Game Boy and Game Boy Color	April 21, 1989 and October 21, 1998	118.70
Game Boy Advance	March 21, 2001	81.06
Game Boy Advance SP	February 14, 2003	43.23
Game Boy Micro	September 13, 2005	2.50
Nintendo DS	November 21, 2004	70.60
Nintendo DS Lite	March 2, 2006	51.78 million

Source: Compiled by the case researchers from a variety of sources.

Nintendo Game Boy

The Nintendo Game Boy was Nintendo's first handheld video gaming device; it was conceptualized and developed by Gunpei Yokoi, a longtime Nintendo employee. Yokoi's goal was to create a product (1) that was lightweight, durable, inexpensive, and small in overall size and (2) that had its own spectrum of recognizable games. The Game Boy could be powered with either disposable or rechargeable batteries. Nintendo's Tetris game—specially designed for the Game Boy—proved quite popular and was a factor in making the Game Boy a resounding market success. Game Boy's success in the handheld market soon led Nintendo to introduce many new versions: Game Boy Pocket (a smaller, lighter unit requiring fewer batteries); Game Boy Light (with a backlight); Game Boy Color (with a color screen); Game Boy Advance (with a higher-resolution screen and improved visual technology); Game Boy Advance SP (with backlighting, a flip-up screen, and rechargeable batteries as well as other solutions to problems with the original Game Boy Advance model); and Game Boy Micro (the third version of the Game Boy Advance system, the smallest Game Boy created, with the same resolution but higher visual quality).

Nintendo DS

In 2004, Nintendo released the Nintendo DS, a handheld video gaming system with a clamshell casing similar to that of the Game Boy Advance. The Nintendo DS had "dueling" screens on the top and bottom of the shell, and the bottom display was an LCD touch screen. The lower screen of the Nintendo DS was a touch-sensitive LCD designed to be pressed with a stylus, a user's finger, or a special thumb pad (a small plastic pad attached to the console's wrist strap that could be affixed to the thumb to simulate an analog stick). The DS was also equipped with a built-in microphone and Wi-Fi capability, which allowed its players to connectively network with one another's handheld systems to create a more interactive gaming experience.

Nintendo viewed the DS as a "third pillar" product with features that set it apart from the Game Boy Advance and the GameCube and that provided players with a unique entertainment experience. Nintendo President Satoru Iwata said:

> We believe that the Nintendo DS will change the way people play video games and our mission remains to expand the game play experience. Nintendo DS caters for the needs of all gamers whether for more dedicated gamers who want the real challenge they

expect, or the more casual gamers who want quick, pick up and play fun.[3]

After its launch in November 2004, the Nintendo DS did remarkably well due to superior marketing and growing demand for the product, significantly boosting the company's overall revenues and profits.[4] In recent years, the Nintendo DS system achieved about a 70 percent market share of all handheld video game players. According to one video game tracking researcher, as of October 2008, the Nintendo DS had sold more than 82 million units since its introduction, including 23.82 million in Japan, 26.03 million in America, and 32.06 million in other markets. These sales were especially impressive compared to Sony's PSP sales of 10.51 million units in Japan, 13.89 million in America, and 14.32 million in other markets, for a total of 38.72 million since its introduction.[5] Additionally, Nintendo had sold more than 400 million copies of video games for its DS and DS Lite systems.

NINTENDO'S VIDEO GAME CONSOLES

A video game console was an electronic device designed to be used with an external display device (e.g., a television or a monitor) that enabled people to play a variety of games stored on external media (e.g., cartridges or discs). The most recent consoles included on-board memory that could be used to download and store games. Consoles were larger and more powerful than handheld systems. Personal computers could also be used to play video games, as could arcade machines designed for commercial use. Over the years, Nintendo had introduced five generations of consoles: the The Nintendo Entertainment System (NES), the Super Nintendo Entertainment System (SNES), Nintendo 64 (N64), the Nintendo GameCube (GCN), and the Nintendo Wii.

Nintendo Entertainment System (NES)

The Nintendo Entertainment System (NES) was the most successful gaming system of its time, selling almost 62 million NES units worldwide (see Exhibit 1). The system proved a tremendous success for the Nintendo Corporation while simultaneously revitalizing the video gaming industry, which had taken a serious downturn in the early 1980s. The NES system was Nintendo's first cartridge-based home gaming console, although the company had developed several models of successful arcade gaming systems.

Super Nintendo Entertainment System (SNES)

The Super Nintendo Entertainment System (SNES) was Nintendo's second home gaming console and appeared on the market as part of the fourth generation of video game consoles that various companies had introduced throughout the industry's history. SNES, with its vastly upgraded graphics and sound capabilities, was the most successful 16-bit gaming console manufactured in its generation, selling over 49 million units worldwide despite having a relatively slow central processing unit (CPU) in comparison to rival game-playing systems.

Nintendo 64 (N64)

The video game industry's fifth-generation home game consoles included the Sega's Saturn, Sony's PlayStation, and the Nintendo 64 (N64). In terms of the number of units sold, the N64 with cumulative sales of nearly 33 million units ranked second in its generation behind the PlayStation with cumulative sales of 102.5 million units (Exhibit 1). Nintendo's developers struggled with the question of whether the N64 should have a cartridge-based memory or a disc-based memory. Their choice of sticking with a traditional cartridge-based system was said to be one of the major reasons why the N64 was unable to compete effectively with Sony's highly popular PlayStation.

Nintendo GameCube (GCN)

Nintendo's GameCube console gaming system was first introduced in Japan in September 2001. It was less expensive and more compact than Microsoft's Xbox and Sony's PlayStation 2, but lacked many of the graphics capabilities that attracted gamers to the Xbox and PS 2.The GameCube was Nintendo's first system that did not use a cartridge storage method—instead it used optical discs. But it had disappointing global sales of only 21.72 million units.

Nintendo Wii

The Wii was the Nintendo's latest gaming console system. Sales of the Wii exceeded all expectations. As of December 2008, market researcher VGChartz estimated that Nintendo had sold a total of 43.8 million Wiis, including 7.4 million in Japan, 20.0 million in America, and 16.4 in other markets.[6] Sales of the Wii were well above the Xbox 360's cumulative sales of 26.5 million units (of which 0.86 million were in Japan, 15.33 million in the United States, and 10.3 million in the rest of the world) and the PlayStation 3's cumulative sales of 18.8 million (of which 2.6 million were in Japan, 7.6 million in the United States, and 8.9 million in the rest of the world). Nintendo's sales of games for the Wii exceeded 150 million units.

Conception and design for the Wii gaming system began in 2001, the same year that Nintendo introduced the GameCube. Originally referred to by its code name of Revolution, the Wii gaming system quickly became the benchmark for the Nintendo product line, bringing together research, innovation, technology, and functionality to create a revolutionary Bluetooth-activated wireless controller that provided a wide range of motion possibilities and allowed game players to control a game's characters through comparable movements of their own. Thus, players playing tennis imagined that the controller was their racket and the swinging motion with their arm triggered the character to act simultaneously. Indeed, the driving concept for the development of the Wii was to allow users to get up, move around the room, interact, and become a physical part of the game they were playing. "By giving players the ability to physically interact with a virtual world, Nintendo has significantly changed the experience of video gaming. It's suddenly more immersive, more compelling and potentially more appealing to consumers who have never considered buying a videogame console before," said David M. Ewalt, a writer who reviewed the Wii after its release. The inspiration and capabilities for Nintendo's new user interface came, at least partially, from Nintendo's success with the DS; the company's successes with games such as Nintendo Duck Hunt, which used a gun controller; and Track and Field, which employed an exercise mat to allow users to participate in athletic events on their SNES consoles.

Nintendo developers chose the name *Wii* for the gaming system because it was a phonic allegory that linked the name of the system to its intended user. One member of the development team for the Wii system was quoted as saying, "Wii sounds like 'we,' which emphasizes this console is for everyone. People around the world can easily remember Wii no matter what language they speak. No confusion. Wii has a distinctive 'ii' spelling that symbolizes both the unique controllers and the image of people gathering to play." The two *i*'s in *Wii* were also a visual representation meant to resemble the system's controller design, as well as two people standing side by side, insinuating interaction and play together.

Nintendo marketers carefully analyzed rival products, trends in the video game marketplace, and their targeted segments of the population. Several characteristics stood out. As competition had increased and the market for video game products had become more saturated, Nintendo marketers paid particular attention to the fact that the concept, design, and functionality of rival video game consoles had become increasingly similar and offered increasingly similar game-playing experiences. As a consequence of weakening differentiation among new game playing devices, marketing strategies for gaining sales and market share became price-oriented. The penetration pricing strategies of the major rivals took on a "price war" character that squeezed profit margins and limited the potential for market share gains. When any particular company announced a new product and market entry strategy, it could expect a competitor to release a relatively similar product, usually within several months. In order to significantly grow the company's market share, Nintendo's executives believed that it had to focus on creating product differentiation advantages over competitors—typically by assessing what competitors were doing and generating ways to accomplish the same thing "better." The gaming market had become an arena for companies to "try to outperform their rivals to grab a greater share of existing demand."[7]

Thus, the marketers with Nintendo began developing a new strategy for the Wii system, and when the development of the Wii gaming system began, Nintendo designers had a new market in mind to appeal to. According to Shugery Miyamoto, a member of Nintendo's Wii development team, "We started with the idea that we wanted to come up with a unique game interface. The consensus was that power isn't everything for a console. Too many powerful consoles can't coexist. It's like having only ferocious dinosaurs. They might fight and hasten their own extinction."[8] Accordingly, the team decided to develop a system to attract people who generally did not play video games. This new market segment included populations of people who had been disregarded by gaming efforts: the elderly, women, and so on. According to Nintendo's CEO Iwata, "Women are the most prized targets but this untapped market spans a vast swath of the population—everybody, actually, bar fast-thumbed teenaged boys."[9] The view was that by marketing to segments of the consumer population currently not reached, Nintendo could create for itself infinite possibilities for profitable growth. Ultimately by taking its product outside the realms of the established demand, Nintendo intended to become its sole competitor. Mr. Iwata insisted that "having a unique product is more important than an attractive price point."[10]

By appealing to "ordinary" consumers, developers of the gaming console were able to simplify its design, focusing less on hyperrealistic graphics and more on artistic elements. Because of the intense competition within the gaming market, gaming systems had become extremely technologically complex. This factor alone was the cause for the large quantity of uncontested consumers who were either unable to learn or uninterested in learning to use such advanced systems for recreational entertainment. By simplifying the design and use of the Wii system, the developers created the perfect entry strategy for their new target market. The success and the challenges associated with this strategy were reflected by two comments that appeared on a blog in response to an article published by *Fortune* on CNNMoney.com in October 2008. One of the bloggers, representative of the hard-core gaming segment identified as "Former Nintendo Fan," commented:

> As a gamer, I have never disliked a console more than the Wii. How it continues to dominate in sales is beyond me when there's very little quality games to play on it. I guess Nostalgia (outdated graphics, simple gameplay etc.) really does sell.[11]

However, in response to this comment, a blogger who identified herself as Cheryl from Pittsburgh, Pennsylvania, and was more consistent with Nintendo's new target market replied:

> See, that's what nobody gets—it's not the gamers that are buying Wii. It's moms, families, grandparents. They're after an interactive game that anyone can figure out in a few minutes, not intricate games with awesome graphics.[12]

Nintendo personnel believed that by creating an innovative product that would appeal to an entirely new demographic and engage new players of video games with its innovative remote controllers, the company could avoid a protracted battle with Sony and Microsoft to win added sales and market share for the Wii. Moreover, Nintendo decided to introduce the Wii with an innovative marketing strategy. The strategy called for using commercials featuring the slogan "Wii would like to play" and exhibiting a varied collection of people as users of the gaming system (grandparents, teens, urban families, etc.).

Nintendo sourced components for the Wii from a number of manufacturers, but to ensure product quality and to control distribution. Nintendo originally engaged a single manufacturer, Taiwan-based Foxconn Precision Components, which also manufactured the Apple iPhone, Sony's PlayStation 3, and personal computers. However, as the company's inability to keep up with demand continued, in July 2007 Nintendo announced that it would continue to diversify its manufacturing base and formed additional partnerships for the manufacturing and supply of key components, such as controller chips, and for assembly of the Wii systems. While these tactics did help increase the supply of Wiis, the systems were still hard to find and retail outlets often sold out of them. Heading into the 2008 holiday season, it was predicted that there would once again be a global shortage of the Wii.

NINTENDO'S SITUATION IN 2008

In 2008, Nintendo's headquarters for the Western hemisphere were located in Redmond, Washington. The company's revenues were generated primarily through the sales and distribution of hardware, including the Nintendo DS and the Nintendo Wii, and software, including licensing agreements with third-party game developers. For the first quarter of the fiscal year that ended June 30, 2008, Nintendo saw a slight decline of unit sales of its Nintendo DS units from the same quarter in 2007, but it saw an increase of 2.33 million units in sales of Nintendo DS software. For the same quarter, sales of Wii hardware increased 1.74 million from the previous year. Software sales for the Wii saw an even greater increase, of 24.42 million units, from the same quarter in 2007. Nintendo attributed these sales to titles such as Mario Kart Wii, which used the Wii Wheel to allow users to feel like they were driving, and the overseas release Wii Fit, which used a balance board to help users exercise by combining fun and fitness.

Nintendo's four primary geographic operating segments were Japan, the Americas (the United States and Canada), Europe, and Other (including countries such as Korea and Australia). For the quarter ending June 30, 2008, Japan accounted for approximately 11.1 percent of Nintendo's net sales, the Americas accounted for 39.6 percent of net sales, Europe accounted for 42.8 percent, and the Other segment accounted for the remaining 6.5 percent. Nintendo had been so successful in the United States that it was estimated that more than 40 percent of American households were owners of at least one type of Nintendo video gaming system.

In the first quarter of 2008, Nintendo's net sales were up more than 20 percent from the same quarter the previous year and Wii was outselling its seventh-generation home system rivals, the Sony PlayStation 3 and the Xbox 360. Nintendo's net income in the same quarter was up more than 30 percent from the same quarter the previous year due to the continued strength of Wii and Nintendo DS hardware and software sales. A summary of Nintendo's recent financial performance is shown in Exhibits 2, 3 and 4.

VIDEO GAME CONSOLE INDUSTRY

The video gaming industry was established almost three decades ago. The Entertainment Software Association stated that, as of 2006, video game revenues contributed about $3.8 billion to the gross domestic product of the United States and the industry employed more than 25,000 people in the United States alone. Growth in the industry had fluctuated significantly over the past few decades and had been driven by technological advancements and societal trends, among other factors. The industry had also been impacted by the increase in the number of competitors, consolidation, and the continuous development of new products as competitors fought to capture a larger share of the core gamers in the market. Despite the increasing intensity of competition, the video gaming industry as a whole had continued to grow even in the face of the downturn in the general world economy.

The video gaming industry had responded so well, despite the economic strains of 2007 and 2008, that some industry experts suggested that it was possible that the industry was resistant to recession. The president of the North American branch of Nintendo, Reggie Fils-Aime, said in November 2007 that he thought the video gaming sector, and particularly Nintendo, would weather the coming economic storm well. NPD analyst Anita Frazier also noted that in general the population still desired to be entertained in times of economic trouble—which accounted for the industry's apparent resilience.

Since the inception of the video gaming industry, companies producing video gaming consoles had attempted to win market share by developing products that were technologically superior and more powerful than the offerings of rivals. Companies fought over bits and pieces of market share, tossing the majority control of shares from competitor to competitor and from console to console. Seemingly, companies continued to turn profits from their new products but never gained a significant edge over one another.

Technologically, significant advances had been made within the video gaming industry in the 21st century. Sixth-generation consoles such as Nintendo's GameCube, Sega's Dreamcast, Sony's PlayStation 2, and Microsoft's Xbox began the century with considerable developments in the realm of home video gaming technology (see Exhibit 5). Nintendo became the first to use optical discs rather than game cartridges for gaming storage. Sega's Dreamcast, the first console of the sixth generation, introduced Internet gaming as a standard feature through its built-in modem and a corresponding Web browser. The Dreamcast was also the first home gaming console to fully display in standard definition (SD) resolution. With the PlayStation 2, consumers were able to play DVDs through their console, which was also

Exhibit 2 Nintendo Income Statement 2005–2008

	(Millions of U.S. Dollars)			
	3/31/2005	3/31/2006	3/31/2007	3/31/2008
Revenues	$5,098.40	$5,041.60	$9,568.70	$16,557.00
Total Revenues	5,098.40	5,041.60	9,568.70	16,557.00
Cost of Goods Sold	2,946.40	2,911.90	5,630.30	9,626.40
Gross Profit	2,152.00	2,129.60	3,938.30	6,930.60
Total Selling General & Admin Expenses	1,028.80	905.3	1,297.70	1,705.40
R&D Expenses	—	302.8	373.3	366.3
Depreciation & Amortization, Total	—	17.5	26.4	33.7
Other Operating Expenses	1,028.80	1,225.60	1,697.30	2,105.40
Operating Income	1,123.20	904.1	2,241.00	4,825.20
Interest Expense	—	0	—	—
Interest and Investment Income	133.8	222.7	336.5	437.2
Net Interest Expense	133.8	222.7	336.5	437.2
Currency Exchange Gains (Loss)	216.3	450.6	254.8	−914.2
Other Non-Operating Income (Expenses)	−17.8	23.7	30.5	17.5
EBT, Excluding Unusual Items	1,455.50	1,601.10	2,862.80	4,365.70
Gain (Loss) on Sale of Investments	−16	35	5.5	−107.7
Gain (Loss) on Sale of Assets	—	−0.2	−1.3	36.3
Other Unusual Items, Total	—	12.2	—	—
EBT, Including Unusual Items	1,439.50	1,648.10	2,867.00	4,294.40
Income Tax Expenses	573.8	674.6	1,141.90	1,747.70
Minority Interest in Earnings	−0.2	0.5	0.4	1
Earnings from Continuing Operations	865.4	973.9	1,725.50	2,547.70
Net Income	865.4	973.9	1,725.50	2,547.70

backward-compatible[13] with games made for its predecessor, PlayStation. Microsoft's Xbox continued Dreamcast's idea of online game playing by including a feature called Xbox Live, Microsoft's online gaming community that became a success because of the utilization of PC-style features such as a broadband connection and a hard disk drive available for memory storage, which connected Xbox players all over the world together in one place.

The seventh generation of home video gaming consoles (Exhibit 5), which was the current generation in 2008, contributed significantly to advancement in video gaming technology. Each new console introduced a new type of breakthrough technology. For example, Microsoft's Xbox 360 and Sony's PlayStation 3 offered the first ever high-definition graphics. The Nintendo Wii offered the integration of controllers and motion sensors to create a completely new arena of player control based on the individual player's own movements. Additionally, all three of the seventh-generation consoles employed wireless controllers. With regard to handheld gaming systems, the seventh-generation Nintendo DS perfected the use of Wi-Fi wireless technology. Sony developed the PlayStation Portable with great multimedia capabilities, connectivity with the PlayStation 3, and other PlayStation Portable consoles through Internet connectivity.

While overall technology had continued to advance as companies built on one another's progress, the current generation of consoles had leveraged advances in both technology and social trends in an attempt to establish a competitive advantage over rivals. Developers of video gaming consoles looked to changes in social trends in order to better target an appropriate market and capture considerable market share. As the focus on social trends had grown,

Exhibit 3 Nintendo Balance Sheet 2005–2008

	(Millions of U.S. Dollars)			
	3/31/2005	3/31/2006	3/31/2007	3/31/2008
Assets				
Cash and Equivalents	7,848.00	6,109.70	6,818.50	10,925.10
Short-Term Investments	538.7	2,566.20	3,855.40	1,472.90
Total Cash and Short Term	8,386.70	8,675.90	10,673.90	12,398.00
Accounts Receivable	487.7	418.9	869	1,441.50
Total Receivables	487.7	418.9	869	1,441.50
Inventory	492.6	305.3	877.2	1,037.90
Deferred Tax Assets, Current	193.2	239.3	352.7	376.5
Other Current Assets	279.3	446.1	1,034.40	1,049.70
Total Current Assets	9,839.50	10,085.40	13,807.30	16,303.70
Gross Property Plant and Equipment	903.7	937.2	998.6	1,010.60
Accumulated Depreciation	−365	−383.1	−428.3	−464.6
Net Property Plant and Equipment	538.8	554.1	570.2	546
Long-Term Investments	726.6	596.1	914.9	730.2
Deferred Tax Assets, Long Term	100.5	102.1	142.7	233.1
Other Intangibles	—	3.2	5	19.9
Other Long-Term Assets	6.2	150.1	158.3	11.9
Total Assets	11,211.70	11,491.00	15,598.40	17,844.70
Liabilities & Equity				
Accounts Payable	1,271.50	829.8	2,980.70	3,324.60
Accured Expenses	—	17.1	17.6	18.3
Current Income Taxes Payable	514.3	525.1	891.1	1,113.30
Other Current Liabilities, Total	248.2	432.5	748.1	1,159.30
Total Current Liabilities	2,034.00	1,804.50	4,637.50	5,615.50
Minority Interest	2.2	1.7	1.4	1
Pension & Other Post-Retirement Benefits	48.4	32.7	44	44.6
Other Non-Current Liabilities	4.6	8.6	6.9	7.8
Total Liabilities	2,089.10	1,847.50	4,689.80	5,668.90
Common Stock	99.6	99.6	99.6	99.6
Additional Paid in Capital	114.7	114.7	114.7	115.2
Retained Earnings	10,225.10	10,851.10	12,080.90	13,666.30
Treasury Stock	−1,286.00	−1,535.60	−1,538.40	−1,546.20
Comprehensive Income and Other	−30.9	113.6	151.8	−159.2
Total Common Equity	9,122.50	9,643.50	10,908.60	12,175.80
Total Equity	9,122.50	9,643.50	10,908.60	12,175.80
Total Liabilities and Equity	11,211.70	11,491.00	15,598.40	17,844.70

developers such as Nintendo had shifted their focus to attempting to target *new* customers rather than fighting with competitors over the *old* customers. Competitors were actively seeking to develop new ways of attracting first-time video gaming consumers to their particular product but did not want to forget or neglect their loyal fan base.

When Nintendo released the Wii gaming console on September 14, 2006, the company was already facing significant competition from Microsoft's

Exhibit 4 Cash Flow Statement 2005–2008

	(Millions of U.S. Dollars)			
	3/31/2005	3/31/2006	3/31/2007	3/31/2008
Net Income	865.4	973.9	1,725.50	2,547.70
Depreciation & Amortization	29	35.6	59.1	72.9
(Gain) Loss on Sale of Investment	16	−22.5	−5.5	107.7
Other Operating Activities	−241.1	−527.5	−39.4	759.3
(Income) Loss on Equity Investments	—	−2.6	−7.9	−13.2
Provision & Write-off of Bad Debts	−12.1	—	—	—
Change in Accounts Receivable	−208.5	90.5	−422.6	−693.3
Change in Inventories	−175.6	213.4	−541.2	−242.7
Change in Accounts Payable	482	−283.9	1,663.90	339
Change in Income Taxes	398.8	—	—	—
Change in Other Working Capital	0.2	−17.7	287	413.3
Cash from Operations	1,154.10	459.2	2,718.90	3,290.50
Capital Expenditure	−20.4	−41	−60.8	−79.1
Sale of Property, Plant, and Equipment	0.1	0.9	3.7	50.8
Divestitures	10.6	—	—	—
Investments in Marketable & Equity	−127.6	−2,041.20	−1,656.70	2,342.20
Cash from Investing	−116	−2,067.20	−1,728.60	2,308.70
Repurchase of Common Stock	−425.7	−249.7	−2.8	−7.9
Common Dividends Paid	−182.7	−345.9	−493.6	−961.4
Total Dividend Paid	−182.7	−345.9	−493.6	−961.4
Other Financing Activities	0	0	0	0.7
Cash from Financing	−608.3	−595.6	−496.4	−968.7
Foreign Exchange Rate Adjustments	289.1	465.3	214.9	−524.1
Miscellaneous Cash Flow Adjustments	—	—	0	0
Net Change in Cash	718.9	−1,738.30	708.8	4,106.60

Xbox 360, which was released on November 22, 2005. Due to its early launch, the Xbox 360 had a one-year lead over both the Nintendo Wii and the Sony PlayStation 3; however, because of its new gaming concept, developers at Nintendo did not consider this a major setback. The target market they were aiming to pursue was completely different from that of Sony or Microsoft.

When launched, the Xbox 360 retailed at $279.99, PlayStation 3 at $499, and the Wii at $249.99. The Wii had generated monthly sales higher than those of competing products across the globe. According to the National Purchase Diary, a leading global market research company, in the first half of 2007, the Nintendo Wii sold more units in the United States than the Xbox 360 and PlayStation 3, fellow seventh-generation gaming consoles.[14] This lead was even larger in the Japanese market, where the Wii led in total sales, having outsold both consoles by factors of 2:1[15] and 6:1[16] nearly every week from its launch until November 2007.

Over the long term, both Microsoft and Sony had traditionally been operating at a loss in hopes of making significant profit gain in software and game sales, especially when the systems were first launched. For example, it was estimated that PlayStation 3 in particular was generating a $250 loss with each unit sold. According to the *Financial Times,* however, the Wii was earning a profit per console sold estimated at around $13 in Japan, $50 in the United States, and $79 in parts of Europe.[17] The differences in gains and loss were attributed to the Wii's low cost of production and the extensive amount of money and resources Nintendo's competitors

Exhibit 5 Evolution of the Home Gaming Console Industry

First generation	Magnavox Odyssey
	Philips Odyssey
	Pong
	Coleco Telstar
Second generation	Atari 2600
	Arcadia 2001
	Atari 5200
	ColecoVision
	Vectrex
Third generation	Nintendo Entertainment System
	Master System
	Atari 7800
Fourth generation	Genesis/Mega Drive
	Neo Geo
	Super Nintendo Entertainment System
Fifth generation	SDO
	Jaguar
	PlayStation
	NEC PC-FX
	Nintendo 64
Sixth generation	Dreamcast
	PlayStation 2
	GameCube
	Xbox
Seventh generation	PlayStation 3
	Nintendo Wii
	Xbox 360

expended upon development. However, by October 2008, it was estimated that Microsoft had reduced its production costs on some of its Xbox models so that the company was making a profit on some of these models, and that Sony was also taking steps to reduce its production costs.

Another one-up for the Wii—neither Sony nor Microsoft had made any significant developments with regard to their controller, which was one of the main differentiating features of the Wii gaming system. "Microsoft and Sony spend a lot of time developing cutting-edge technology. Nintendo is not a technology company—it is a toy company. It is not interested in bleeding-edge electronics and graphics," said In-Stat video game analyst Brian O'Rourke.[18] Even considering this, comparing the three consoles was very difficult. Both the Xbox 360 and the PlayStation 3 were high-definition (HD) consoles with quality graphics and games specifically designed for HD output, while the Wii was an experimental, next-generation technology gaming console. Wii's total sales since its launch are shown in Exhibit 6.

Exhibit 6 Total Nintendo Wii Unit Sales as of October 1, 2008

Region	Total Units Sold (in millions)	First available
Europe	10.56	December 8, 2006
Japan	6.86	December 2, 2006
America	14.61	November 19, 2006
Other regions	1.02	December 8, 2006
Worldwide	33.05	

*Based on data from www.vgchartz.com (accessed October 12, 2008).

SONY PLAYSTATION 3

Sony's seventh-generation video gaming console was the PlayStation 3. This model followed its similar predecessors—the PlayStation (fifth generation) and the PlayStation 2 (sixth generation). The PlayStation 3 separated itself from the previous systems through its unique feature of unified online gaming via the PlayStation Network.[19] Other distinguishing features of the PlayStation 3 system included connectivity with the PlayStation Portable,[20] the use of a high-definition Blu-ray disc as the primary storage solution, and various aggressive multimedia capabilities. Additionally, PlayStation 3 was the first gaming system on the market compliant Blu-ray 2.0. Two initial versions of the PlayStation 3 were backward-compatible with many of the PlayStation and PlayStation 2 games. However, in August 2008, in an effort to reduce production costs, Sony announced that new versions of the console would no longer be backward-compatible with the PlayStation and PlayStation 2 discs, although many of the most popular titles would be available for download at the PlayStation Store.

Exhibit 7 Total Sony PlayStation 3 Unit Sales as of October 1, 2008

Region	Total Units Sold (in millions)	First Available
Europe	6.31	March 23, 2007
Japan	2.4	November 11, 2006
America	6.00	November 17, 2006
Worldwide	15.77	

*Based on data from www.vgchartz.com (accessed October 12, 2008).

First released on November 11, 2006, the PlayStation 3 proved relatively unprofitable for Sony despite its sales of 15.77 million units worldwide as of October 1, 2008 (see Exhibit 7). The production cost for the PlayStation 3 was said to be $805.85. However, when introduced to the market, the units were priced between $499 and $599, giving Sony an average $250 loss per unit sold. Subsequently, Sony's games division posted an operating loss of ¥232.3 billion (U.S.$1.97 billion) in the fiscal year ending March 2007, a mere four months after its introduction. The PlayStation 3's outlook with regard to its consumer reception wasn't much better than its financial portfolio. Initially, the PlayStation 3 received generally critical reviews from customers, with many noting its unreasonably high retail price and the lack of games equivalent in quality to those of its competitors. However, after Sony made several cuts in the retail price and developed a handful of successful games, the console proceeded to receive more positive reviews.

Sony PlayStation 3 users with broadband Internet access had free access to the online PlayStation Network. The PlayStation Network provided users with an Internet browser, video and voice chat, and access to the PlayStation Store. The PlayStation Store allowed users to download both free and premium content, including full games, game demos, additional game content, and movies and television shows from major producers such as Sony Pictures, MGM, and Disney. Sony also planned to formally launch a new service named PlayStation Home by the end of 2008. PlayStation Home was designed to allow users to join a 3D virtual community in which they could create an avatar that would have its own home space that could be decorated with items that players could either acquire in games or purchase. Users in this virtual world could interact with others in a number of ways, including playing games.

MICROSOFT XBOX 360

At its launch, Nintendo Wii's other main competitor was Microsoft's Xbox 360. This seventh-generation console was the second system manufactured by Microsoft following its predecessor Xbox (released in 2001). A distinguishing feature of the Xbox 360 was the ability to access its online multiplayer gaming network, Xbox Live. Microsoft's online gaming community became a success because of the utilization of PC-style features such as a broadband connection and a hard drive disk available for memory storage, which connected Xbox players all over the world. Inside, the Xbox 360 used the triple-core Xenon, designed by IBM, as its central processing unit (CPU). However, the Xbox 360 had suffered from a higher than average number of technical issues, which had resulted in Microsoft extending the warranty to three years for "general hardware failures."

When released, the Xbox 360 was available in four different variations: (1) the entry-level option named the Xbox 360 Core, which had since been discontinued and replaced by the Xbox 360 Arcade, which featured a wireless controller, a 256 MB memory unit, a composite AV cable, HDMI 1.2 output, and five Xbox Live Arcade titles; (2) the Xbox 360 Premium, which included all the features of the Arcade as well as a hybrid composite and component cable with optional optical out instead of a composite cable; (3) the Xbox 360 Premium, which also included a detachable 20 GB hard disk drive to store downloaded content; and (4) the Xbox 360 Elite, the most expensive variation of the console, priced at $449.99, which included a 120 GB hard drive and a matte black finish. The Elite retail package also included an HDMI 1.2 cable and a controller and headset that matched the console's black finish.

A key component of Microsoft's strategy involved its Xbox Live service. This service allowed users to access a number of features depending on their choice of the free Silver level of service or the Gold level, which cost approximately $50.00 per year. Services at the Silver level included online voice chat; the opportunity to download new content for video games such as new levels; and access to

Exhibit 8 Total Microsoft Xbox 360 Unit Sales as of October 1, 2008

Region	Total Units Sold	First Available
Europe	5.98 million	November 22, 2005
Japan	746,392	December 10, 2005
United States	12.75 million	November 22, 2005
Worldwide	21.30 million	

the Xbox Live Marketplace, which had both free and premium content, including Xbox games, new game demos, and Xbox Live Arcade titles. Users who opted for the Gold level of service could play multiplayer games, had early access to downloadable content, and could use live video chat. In November 2008, Microsoft planned to expand Xbox Live with the New Xbox Experience, which would allow users to stream television shows and movies from Netflix, an online distributor of movies and television shows, with enhanced multiplayer gaming capabilities, and scheduled online programming that would allow Xbox live users to play against one another in Game Show Experience with a live host and prizes. Microsoft announced in October 2008 that it intended to leverage these enhanced services to aggressively target Japan in an effort to win market share from Nintendo and Sony in this key market.

THE FUTURE

As of October 2008, the primary challenges facing Nintendo were how Nintendo could continue to expand its customer base and defend its market from its rivals. Both Microsoft and Sony had announced intentions to create a broader variety of ways for users to interact with games on their respective systems. However, analysts who closely monitored the progression of the Wii noted that the only limitations of the system were the limitations of the designer and the user—leading most to believe they considered the possibilities endless. With that in mind, analysts predicted that Nintendo would continue to launch innovative products such as the Wii Fit to add to the company's already expansive repertoire of gaming possibilities with the console.

Despite Nintendo's success with the Wii, there were still some significant challenges facing the company. One challenge was the patent infringement lawsuits filed by multiple companies against Nintendo. These lawsuits by companies such as Copper Innovation and Hillcrest Labs claimed that the Nintendo's technologies, including the Wii Remote, infringed on U.S. patents that were issued as early as 1996. While most analysts believe that Nintendo could settle these cases without any significant issues, there was the possibility that these settlements would involve Nintendo having to license some of the patents, which would result in increased production costs.

However, most industry experts agreed that the most significant challenge facing Nintendo was identifying and investing in innovations that would allow Nintendo to continue expanding the video game market. In developing the Wii, Nintendo opened a new chapter on competition in the video game console industry by leveraging creativity and innovation as the basis of their competitive advantage rather than adhering to the predictable race toward more advanced technology. However, some analysts were concerned about how far the gaming market could realistically be expanded and doubted that the possibilities were as limitless as Nintendo portrayed. Further, industry experts were also concerned as to whether Nintendo could resist a significant attack by Microsoft and Sony on the growing casual gaming market. This was especially troubling given the Wii's relatively poor reputation with the core gaming market, which was generally more profitable than the casual gaming market. According to Brian Crecente, managing editor of gaming blog Kotaku, "That's a big issue with Nintendo. They seem totally focused right now on getting those new gamers. The risk there is that in not focusing on current gamers they could lose them for this generation and perhaps even future consoles."[21]

Endnotes

[1] N. Asami and H. Yomogita, "Regaining What We Have Lost: Nintendo CEO Iwata's Ambitions for the 'Wii,'" http://techon.nikkeibp.co.jp/english/NEWS_EN/20060525/117498/?P=1 (accessed on September 1, 2008).

[2] "Nintendo Announces Dual-Screen Portable Game System," January 20, 2004, accessed at www.gamesnews.yahoo.com on October 1, 2008.

[3] Craig Harris, "Europe DS Launch Title Details," January 27, 2007, accessed at www.subgamers.com on October 1, 2008.

[4] Daemon Hartfield, "DS Improves Nintendo's Forecast," October 3, 2006, accessed at http://ds.ign.com on September 23, 2008.
[5] Sourced from VGChartz, www.vgchartz.com (accessed October 12, 2008).
[6] Ibid., accessed on December 28, 2008.
[7] "A Conversation with W. Chan Kim and Renee Mauborgne, authors of Blue Ocean Strategy," accessed at http://www.insead.edu on September 22, 2008.
[8] Kenjii Hall, "The Big Ideas Behind Nintendo's Wii," *BusinessWeek,* November 16, 2006, www.businessweek.com/technology/content/nov2006/tc20061116_750580.htm (accessed October 10, 2008).
[9] Rhys Blakely, "Wii Are Swimming in a Clear Blue Ocean: Nintendo President Talks About Reinventing the Gaming Industry," July 12, 2007, accessed at http://business.timesonline.co.uk/tol/business/industry_sectors/technology/article2063714.ece?token=null&offset=0 on September 24, 2008.
[10] Ibid.
[11] Posted at http://techland.blogs.fortune.cnn.com/2008/10/06/no-slowdown-for-wii-and-ds-says-nintendo-prez/ in response to "No Slowdown for Wii and DS, Says Nintendo Prez," October 6, 2008, accessed September 18, 2008.
[12] Ibid.
[13] A product is said to be backward-compatible if it is able to take the place of an older model product by interoperating with products that were designed specifically for the older product.
[14] Ben Kuchera, "Nintendo the Big Winner, PS3 Dead Last for the First Half of 2007," Ars Technica, July 24, 2007 (accessed at www.arstechnica.com on July 31, 2007).
[15] "Xbox 360 Trumps PS3 in Japan," (accessed at www.edge-online.com on November 27, 2007).
[16] S. Nicolo, "Media Create Sales Stats (July 9–15): Nintendo Continues Domination," QJ.net, July 21, 2007.
[17] James Brightman, "Report: Nintendo Makes About $49 Per Wii Sold in U.S.," GamingDaily.BIZ, September 17, 2007.
[18] "Nintendo Chief Confident in Wii's Long Term Success," TechNewsWorld.com, July 6, 2006.
[19] PlayStation Network, which is often abbreviated to PSN in the gaming community, is the free online service provided by Sony for players to use with their PlayStation 3 (PS3) and PlayStation Portable (PSP) video game consoles in order to interact with one another.
[20] PlayStation Portable is the handheld gaming console developed by Sony Computer Entertainment. The system was released in December 2004 and was the first handheld video game console to use as its primary storage media, an optical disc format, Universal Media Disc (UMD).
[21] Michael Lee, "Will Wii Sink Nintendo?" October 3, 2008, www.redherring.com/Home/25150 (accessed October 12, 2008).

CASE 13 Corona Beer: From a Local Mexican Player to a Global Brand

Ashok Som
ESSEC Business School

It's a typical Friday afternoon in 2007, and Carlos Fernandez, chairman of Grupo Modelo's board since 1997, was making an unexpected stop at one of his company's brewing facilities in Zacatecas, Mexico, where the plant was going through major renovations to increase capacity. Grupo Modelo S.A. de C.V. (Modelo) was Mexico's largest beer producer and distributor. It was expanding production capabilities across the board. Among the company's many brands was Corona Extra, which had been the world's fourth best selling beer in terms of volume (see Exhibit 1 for world ranking). With an investment of more than $300 million to renovate its facilities, Modelo aimed to increase production to face growing international demand. Carlos Fernandez clarified his ambition soon after his appointment as CEO in 1997:

> [I want] Modelo to leapfrog the competition and catapult itself into the ranks of the world's top five brewers.

And they did that when Grupo Modelo surpassed Heineken for bragging rights as the number one selling import in the United States in 1997. Yet competitors did not let that happen without reacting, and Grupo Modelo soon faced tough times both in its domestic market and abroad.

How did Modelo build up its domestic power? How did it consider the attack on the U.S. market? Could the company sustain its success trend against competition? Those were some of the questions analysts asked at the time.

Exhibit 1 World's Top 10 Beer Brands, 2005 and 2006 (Millions of barrels—shipments)

Brands	2005	2006	2006 Market Share
1. Bud Light	39.3	41.1	3.0%
2. Budweiser	34.6	33.7	2.5
3. Skol	27.9	28.6	2.1
4. Snow	13.5	25.9	1.9
5. Corona	24.5	25.6	1.9
6. Brahma Chopp	20.6	21.6	1.6
7. Heineken	20.0	21.4	1.6
8. Miller Lite	18.2	18.2	1.3
9. Coors Light	16.5	16.8	1.2
10. Asahi Super Dry	15.0	14.8	1.1
Total top 10	229.9	247.6	18.2%

Source: Grupo Modelo annual report, 2007.

THE GRUPO MODELO STORY: BUILT TO BE A LOCAL LEADER

Cervecería Modelo S.A. was formed on March 8, 1922, and officially opened its first brewery three years later, with a strategic aim to focus on Mexico City and the surrounding areas. Modelo was the first brand to be produced by the group, followed a month later by Corona.

Headed in the early days by Pablo Diez Fernandez, Braulio Iriarte, and Martin Oyamburu, the company was soon controlled by Diez and Oyamburu after Iriarte died in 1932. Under the operational direction of Diez, Cervecia Modelo started producing Corona in clear quarter bottles in response to consumers' preference for clear glasses. Diez oversaw the expansion of the group's brewing capabilities that would turn it into Mexico's largest and most modern producer.

The 1930s were trying years for Modelo. After surviving the prohibition policy and the death of the company's president during the early 1930s, Diez bought Oyamburu's shares and became sole owner of the company in 1936, with financial help from Banco Nacional de Mexico. The company has remained under the majority ownership of the Fernandez family ever since.

In 1935, once financial stability was restored to the company, Cerveceria Modelo bought the brands and assets of the Toluca y México Brewery. From then on, Victoria, the country's oldest established brand of beer, would spearhead the company's fight to dominate the popular market. With these acquisitions, the 1940s proved to be a period of strong growth for the company, with production sky-rocketing as did its popularity. While most Mexican companies were focusing on selling beer to the American army for WWII efforts, Diez decided to concentrate domestically and improve distribution methods and production facilities within Mexico.

As Mexico became industrialized, the country's infrastructure allowed for large scale distribution. The key element behind the rapid growth domestically during the post-WWII era was a new way of distribution: direct with profit sharing.

> Modelo's sales were revolutionized by the idea of direct distribution with the executive in charge getting a share of profits. A key element of this second stage was specialized concessions. In other words, splitting beer from groceries and making it an exclusive business gave rise to direct distributors—sometimes run by the concessionaire or his successors, or sometimes by a person sent from head office, a traveling agent, supervisor, or manager who would be moved from area to area.

In 1971, Antonino Fernandez was appointed CEO of Modelo. He was the husband of Pablo's niece. Under his control, Corona was listed on the Mexican Stock exchange in 1994. At that time, Anheuser-Busch acquired 17.7 percent of the equity and had an option to increase its ownership to 50.2 percent over time. The 50.2 percent represented only 43.9 percent of voting rights in order to preserve the ownership of the Diez family over Grupo Modelo S.A.

A LOCAL LEADER GOING ABROAD

Modelo's first entry into the U.S. beer market came in 1979 with Corona distributed by Amalgamated Distillery Products Inc. (later renamed Barton Beers Ltd.). Due to its nonrefundable policy, its clear and unique bottle, and different marketing, Corona quickly distinguished itself from the competition and gained popularity in southern states. Corona's sales experienced rapid growth throughout the 1980s and by 1988 it had become the second most popular imported beer in the United States. It wasn't until late 1991, with the doubling of federal excise tax on beer, that Corona's rise to the top of America's import beer market was slowed considerably (a decrease of 15 percent). An important change in the pricing strategy by Corona's distributor, namely to absorb the tax rather than pass it on to consumers, in 1992 rectified the downward trend, and Modelo has experience increasing sales of Corona ever since.

In 1997, with his grandfather still chairman of the board and taking over for his uncle, Carlos Fernandez was appointed the new chief executive office of the company. At the young age of 29, Carlos encompassed all the attributes needed to take the company into the new millennium. Not only had the young man dedicated himself to the family business since he was 13, when he first started working at the company, but he carried with him a vision of an international business model—one that had the company expand internationally in order to capitalize on the newly introduced North American Free Trade Agreement (NAFTA) and streamline the company's focus. In just 12 years since his appointment, Carlos accomplished one of his more ambitious goals of leapfrogging his international competitors to become one of the top five beer companies in the world.

In 1997, at 37 years of age, Carlos Fernandez was named chairman when his grandfather stepped aside. In 2007, Grupo Modelo was exporting five kinds of beer to the United States: Corona Extra,

Exhibit 2 Total Imported Beers in the United States, 2006–2007 (thousands of cases)

Brand	2006	2007*
1. Corona Extra	116,155	115,060
2. Heineken	68,790	68,100
3. Modelo	19,605	22,404
4. Tecate	17,480	19,050
5. Guinness	12,725	13,360
6. Corona Light	11,055	12,207
7. Labatt Blue	12,500	12,000
8. Heineken Light	7,520	9,775
9. Stella Artois	6,175	8,335
10. Amstel Light	8,900	8,188
Total top 10	280,905	288,479

*Estimate.
Source: Grupo Modelo's annual report, 2007.

Corona Light, Modelo Especial, Pacifico Clara, and Negra Modelo. These exports represented 131 million cases in 2005 and three Grupo Modelo brands ranked among eight firsts in the United States (see Exhibit 2 for detailed rankings).

THE BEER MARKET, A PROGRESSIVE CONSOLIDATION

Modern beer was first brewed in Europe in the 14th century. The industry developed differently in every country in order to address local tastes and specific recipes. This resulted in a clustered industry with many local breweries. The lack of a transportation network made exportation impossible for centuries and brewing remained a local and then a national domain for a long time. The first steps of national consolidation were carried out in the 19th century in the United Kingdom and the United States to achieve economies of scale. In other, smaller countries, with several mid-size players, the consolidation process was lighter and local breweries survived and became specialists. One determining factor behind the type of domestic beer was the national taste of the particular country. Some countries have distinct cultural tastes, where beer is not the alcoholic drink of preference. In countries such as Italy and France, wine outperforms beer for consumption per capita, whereas in countries like Germany and Ireland, the reverse is true. Whereas Italy and France have a few national beer brands, Germany and Ireland both have numerous medium brewing companies that are well respected domestically and internationally.

In the 1990s, a new phenomenon appeared whereby national leaders began expanding abroad. For example, the Belgian company Interbrew acquired breweries in 20 countries and expanded its sales to 110 countries, leaving local managers controlling the local brands while enjoying their presence to develop sales of its flagship brand: Stella Artois. This trend also might be due to the fact that initial startup costs of a brewery have always been extremely high and the need for a constant cash flow for maintenance and the fluctuating price of resources. That structure of the industry supported concentration.

Other companies followed the same strategy and the consolidation process led to a small number of global players. On March 3, 2004, the world's third largest brewery company, Belgium-based Interbrew, and the world's fifth largest brewery, Brazil-based AmBev, announced plans to merge their operations. In a deal valued at $12.8 billion, the merger created the world's largest brewing company in terms of volume. In 2007, the panorama of the brewing industry was clear, showing the top players as Inbev, Anheuser-Bush, SABMiller, and Heineken ranking as the market leaders. See Exhibit 3 for the top six global producers as of 2005.

KEY WORLD MARKETS

The United States had the largest beer market in the world until China surpassed it in 2003. Yet the consumption per capita remained almost six times higher in the United States than it was in China at the time (see Exhibit 4 for global beer consumption). The growth expectations were significantly reduced in the United States, but performance was not consistent across the clusters.

The top three breweries controlled almost 80 percent of the U.S. market, with 45 percent for Anheuser-Busch, 23 percent for Miller Brew and 10 percent for Adolph Coors. That being said, 300 breweries

Exhibit 3 Top Brewing Companies (in millions of hectaliters)

In 2000	In 2005
1. Anheuser-Busch—121	1. InBev—233.5
2. Heineken—74	2. Anheuser-Busch—152
3. Ambev—63	3. SABMiller—135
4. Miller Brewing—53	4. Heineken—107
5. SAB (South Africa Breweries)—43	5. Carlsberg—78
6. Interbrew—87	6. Scottish & Newcastle—52

Exhibit 4 Beer Consumption around the World

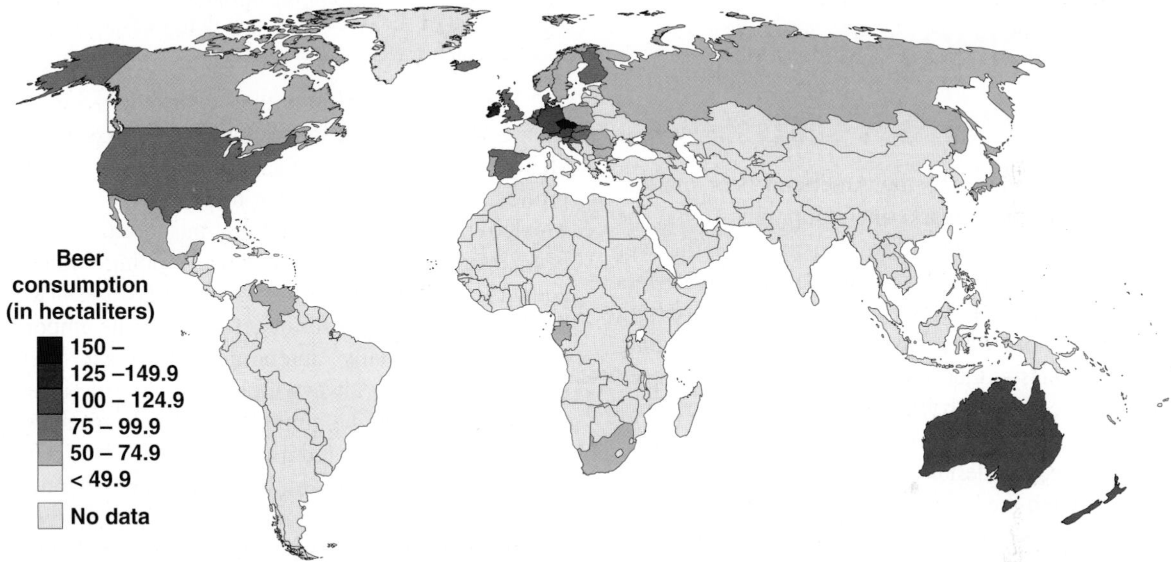

Source: http://upload.wikimedia.org/wikipedia/commons/9/99/Map_of_world_by_world_by_beer_consumption.png.
Note: Chinese beer consumption was allegedly 16 liters in 2003.

remained in the country thanks to a dense network of regional craft brewing. These companies struggled to find profitability since vertical integration and economies of scale were the main drivers to operating margins. The fact that Anheuser-Bush could capture 75 percent of the industry's total operating profits emphasized the volume effect in the industry.

Mexico, the world's 11th most populated country, was one of the largest beer markets in the world. This is impressive considering that Mexico is the birthplace and still home of the most affluent tequila market in the world. For a country that has a large proportion of its alcoholic industry split between beer and another beverage, Mexico is an anomaly considering the variety of beers it has to offer. Mexico has a large variety of brands with a vast array of tastes, from the darker and more sophisticated tastes of Dos Equis to the light and citrus flavor of Corona. However, even with this diversity, the market is essentially a duopoly split among two producers with very few microbreweries. Those two companies are Grupo Modelo and FEMSA. In 2007, Grupo Modelo captured 62.8 percent of the Mexican market (compared with 50 percent in 1989) and FEMSA owned the rest of the market.

In addition to owning the main beer brands of the domestic market (Corona, Dos Equis, and Sol) FEMSA and Grupo Modelo had built up strategic alliances with some major distributors that were enjoying the NAFTA environment. Grupo Modelo could enjoy the link with Anheuser-Busch to broaden its international impact, while FEMSA was distributing Coca-Cola products in Mexico and decided to have a partnership with Heineken to attack the

U.S. market. To sum it up, the two Mexican players decided to attack the U.S. market but could not do it alone considering entrance barriers. FEMSA's CEO presented it this way in 2006:

> It was an exceptional year for exports. We continued to attract new consumers, and our volume growth exceeded expectations, up to 15.3 percent. Through our distribution agreement with Heineken USA, we significantly expanded our brands' availability and developed our brands' value across our U.S. market territories.

GRUPO MODELO EXPANDING ABROAD

Corona and the Early Successes

Since its entrance into the American beer market, Corona had built a marketing campaign around the idea of "fun in the sun." A myth surrounding the beer was that it was discovered by Californian surfers while traveling the Mexican Pacific coast looking for the next big wave. Amid mixed reviews among beer enthusiasts, Corona's ascent to stardom could be attributed to its brilliant and unique marketing campaign which was a direct result of the international strategy undertaken by Grupo Modelo when it expanded into the United States. While continuing to produce the beer domestically, Modelo entered into distribution contracts with companies that had local knowledge of the market and gave them autonomy to market the product fittingly, yet maintained an active involvement in the decision making. The result was the rise of Corona from a beer sold primarily in the states bordering Mexico, to the number one imported beer in America. An analyst underlined:

> In recognition of the outstanding performance of Corona, Modelo Especial, and Negra Modelo in the U.S. import segment, they have been included in the *Impact Magazine* "Hot Brands" list. This happened 10 times in the last 11 years.

International Expansion through Competitive Distribution Channels

When Corona first entered the American beer market, it chose Chicago-based Barton Beers Ltd. as its distributor. According to Modelo executives, the choice to align itself with Barton Beers was an easy one because it was the largest beer importer in the 25 western states and was experienced in the marketing and sales of imported, premium beers. It was through Barton that the marketing image of "fun in the sun" was born. In 1986, to continue its growth within the United States and to supply the eastern states, Modelo decided to select a second distributor, Gambrinus Inc., which was headed by a former Modelo executive. Each company was responsible for its own 25 states and, according to Valentin Diez, Modelo's vice chairman and chief sales officer:

> There was a healthy competition that existed between the two of them, even if they didn't cover the same geographic area.

Modelo's agreement with its distributors was that each importer would be responsible for essentially all activities involving the sale of the beer, except its production, which took place in Modelo factories in Mexico. Everything—including transportation of the beer, insurance, custom clearance, pricing strategy, and creativity of the advertising campaigns—was the importers' responsibility. Although the importers were essentially autonomous to make these decisions, Modelo always took an active role in the decision making and maintained the final say on anything involving the brand image of its beers. In order to oversee all operations in the United States, Modelo set up Procermex Inc., a subsidiary whose purpose was to coordinate, support, and supervise the two distributors. The strength of the relationship between the importers and Modelo was very strong, as evidenced with the tax increase in 1991. After talks with Modelo, Grambrinus, followed shortly by Barton Beers, decided to absorb the increase instead of passing it on to customers (while all other imported beers did) after being reassured by the Mexican producer that they would be subsidized.

Marketing, the Other Key Leading to Success

Ironically, the key to Modelo's success had been foreseen by the main casualty of that success story when Michael Foley, Heineken's president, said in 1993:

> There's no mystery about brewing beer. Everyone can do it . . . Beer is all marketing. People don't drink beer, they drink marketing.

Corona's ingenious marketing philosophy, which was born out of Modelo's international expansion strategy of giving autonomous control to experienced, local distributors, focused on "fun in the sun" and quickly saw Corona in an ever-increasing number of bars and restaurants in the United States. The marketing campaign's distinguishing feature was that it did not focus on the classical target market for beer drinkers, which were males between the ages of 25 and 45. Campaigns geared toward this target market had historically been testosterone driven, focused on attractive women and party scenes. Premium imported beers differed slightly as they focused on the beers' distinguished quality, usually as a result of superior brewing and rich heritage.

Corona did away with this status quo. It needed to develop an image of a beer that would attract everyone, yet position itself as a premium import, necessary due to the import taxes and resultant higher price paid for the beer. With the "fun in the sun" campaigns, it sold the idea of escape and the idea of leaving behind everyday life for one that is relaxing. Whereas taste and quality are subjective and different for each consumer, general guidelines and surveys consistently and accurately show quality brewing standards. Undeniably, images of escape, enjoyment and relaxation are even more free-form, allowing the customers to make what they will about the image of the brand.

From the beginning, Corona's advertising accented this image as it focused on minimalist and often humorous, scenes of escape. Common to all advertisements was that these scenes of escape come in the form of relaxing on the beach. The advertisements never had a lot of action (in fact, most had little to no human action), and if there were people enjoying their time at the beach, their faces were never shown. The Corona bottle was always in the center of the screen, with no soundtrack other then the sounds of the sea and surrounding nature.

The most recent advertising slogan ("Miles away from ordinary") associated with Corona continues to conjure ideas of removing oneself from daily activities. In one advertisement, the scene shows a person relaxing by the beach on a slightly rainy day. In order to protect his Corona, he places his cellular phone above the bottle's neck so as not to allow water to drip in. By focusing on this image of escape, and not following the trend of testosterone-driven campaigns, Corona found a following like no other beer before it. Coupled with the fact that it had an unobtrusive or bland taste (a fact that beer enthusiasts continue to laud), Corona was able to get the non-beer-drinking population to drink beer, specifically, females. Eager to please the new market for beer drinkers, bars and restaurants decided to sell the beer, increasing its consumer reach. And because of its availability, it became a dependable second choice for beer drinkers who were frustrated with not having their favorite beer sold at the current establishment.

A good advertisement is not enough without the budgets to broadcast it widely. In 1996, Modelo spent $5.1 million in the United States, compared with $600,000 in 1985. Yet the same year Heineken spent $15.1 million and Anheuser-Busch spent $192 million. It must be précised that in the case of imported beers, advertising costs are shared by the producer and its distributors, the repartition being negotiated according to the campaign. Considering the performances of Heineken and Corona in 1996, the impact of the message was able to overcome a relative financial weakness.

THE 21ST-CENTURY CHALLENGES

Grupo Modelo had rarely played the role of the established brewery, or having one of its brands define a category. Even from its entrance into the Mexican beer market in 1925, it was a startup company that sought to focus on Mexico City and the surrounding areas, competing against the already established breweries for market share. When Corona was introduced into the international market, more specifically the U.S. beer market, it paled in comparison to the then-established import leader, Heineken. However, this status as the beer industry's underdog soon shifted.

Since 1997, Corona has been the best-selling import beer in the United States. In 2004, Corona outsold the former number one by about 50 percent. And with a 56 percent market share of the domestic Mexican market, Grupo Modelo is the undisputed leader in one of the world's largest beer markets. And this success can be seen worldwide as well. Not only is Corono Extra the fourth best-selling beer in the world (by quantity) but Grupo Modelo is one of the top 10 biggest breweries in the world.

Remain Mexican Leader . . .

According to surveys, the top seven best-tasting beers in Mexico are produced by a subsidiary of FEMSA, Mexico's second largest beer company in terms of market share (see Exhibit 5 for details). Until recently, FEMSA had been a distant second in the duopoly that is the Mexican beer industry.

In an industry so heavily dependent on distribution channels, FEMSA decided it wanted to control its beer from production to point of purchase. Not only did FEMSA produce all its beer domestically in Mexico, but it also owns Oxxo, Central America's largest chain of convenient stores (and one of the biggest in North America). Supplementing its beverage portfolio is the fact that FEMSA is the exclusive distributor of Coca-Cola products in Mexico and Central America.

The investment in a quality beer product, associated with the ownership of the complete distribution channel, has paid off with respect to the Mexican beer market. From 1997 to 2004, FEMSA continuously took more of the domestic beer market for Grupo Modelo. More significant is the fact

Exhibit 5 Taste Test Results for Mexican Beers

The following are the highest rated beers brewed in Mexico as they appear in the ranks at RateBeer.com. A minimum of 10 ratings is required to make the list. Beer scores are weighted means so that more ratings for a beer increase the score's tendency to the beer's actual mean.

	Name	Brewer	Ratings	Score
1	Casta Unica	Especialidades Cerveceras (FEMSA)	29	3.61
2	Casta Milenia	Especialidades Cerveceras (FEMSA)	73	3.59
3	Casta Urilca Castana	Especialidades Cerveceras (FEMSA)	17	3.48
4	Casta Morena	Especialidades Cerveceras (FEMSA)	142	3.45
5	Casta Dorade	Especialidades Cerveceras (FEMSA)	80	3.13
6	Casta Bruna	Especialidades Cerveceras (FEMSA)	105	3.12
7	Potro	Cerveceria Mexicana S.A. De C.V	18	3.09
8	Iodio	Femsa	18	2.86
9	Casta Triguera	Especialidades Cerveceras (FEMSA)	89	2.83
10	Noche Buena	Femsa	24	2.83
11	Negra Modelo	Grupo Modelo (Corona)	618	2.82
12	Dos Equis XX Amber	Femsa	616	2.55
13	Leon Negra	Grupo Modelo (Corona)	21	2.55
14	Victoria	Grupo Modelo (Corona)	23	2.42
15	Bohemia (Mexico)	Femsa	252	2.41
16	Dos Equis XX Special Lager	Femsa	405	2.24
17	Superior	Femsa	25	2.15
18	Pacifico Clara	Grupo Modelo (Corona)	350	2.13
19	Montejo	Grupo Modelo (Corona)	19	2.10
20	Modelo Especial	Grupo Modelo (Corona)	226	2.01
21	Carta Blanca	Femsa	154	2.01
22	Tecate	Femsa	369	1.86
23	Corona Extra	Grupo Modelo (Corona)	1245	1.72
24	Sol	Femsa	318	1.67
25	Chihuahua	Femsa	17	1.65
26	Tecate Light	Femsa	12	1.49
27	Corona Light	Grupo Modelo (Corona)	300	1.35

Source: www.ratebeer.com/Ratings/TopBeersByCountry.asp?CountryID=133.

that while domestic sales were decreasing for Modelo, FEMSA continued to experience steady growth which was in line with industry averages.

However, despite FEMSA's strength in the domestic market, it did not experience the same in the international arena. FEMSA beers are not nearly as popular as Modelo's in the United States. It launched a large marketing campaign in the mid-1990s, but failed to capture the imagination of the American customers and barely made an impact on the market. However, as economic conditions of the company improved, FEMSA decided to re-attempt to mass-market its beers north of the Mexican border. FEMSA recently entered into a marketing agreement with Heineken USA. With the expertise of one of the largest and most recognizable brands in the market leading the charge, FEMSA (and Heineken) hoped to dethrone Corona as the best-selling import in the United States. So far, exports for FEMSA's top three beers have greatly improved; in the 3rd quarter of 2005, the company realized an 18.7 percent growth in exports mainly driven by the U.S. market's demand.

Although Mexico's domestic beer market is one of the largest in the world, Carlos Fernandez knew that the future of Grupo Modelo was to go international. Mexico had the most trade agreements than any other country in the world, and the introduction of NAFTA in 1994 further reinforced the vision for Mexican companies that they had to have a global focus. However, with the opening of the international markets for Mexican companies comes the fact that the Mexican markets are also open to international companies. Specifically, with NAFTA and the beer market in Mexico, the newly introduced agreement opened the door for Canadian and American beer companies to operate in a previously highly protected market. Although their domestic market was now threatened by international companies, the years following 1994 showed that imported beer accounted for only 1 percent of beer sales in Mexico. Of that, half were sales from Anheuser-Busch products, which is distributed by Modelo. (Although the Fernandez family is still the primary stock holder of the company, Anheuser-Busch has a significant stake in the company, owning 50.6 percent of the available stock.)

The volatility of the Mexican economy was another reason to seek international markets for stability. With the devaluation of the Mexican peso in 1995, exporting became increasingly expensive, which led to a large decrease in sales. By having more operations internationally, Modelo would be able to rid itself of the dependency on the unstable peso for its profits. The proximity to the world's largest economy and the size of its beer market offered an opportunity for Modelo to create a beachhead for further international expansion.

Whereas Modelo sought to hedge its risk against the devaluating peso by pursuing international revenues, FEMSA went about doing the same by focusing on its core competency within Mexico. With the failed attempt to gain American market share in the 1990s, FEMSA realized it had a competitive advantage in Mexico through its distribution channel, namely OXXO, its chain of convenient stores. By owning the complete distribution channel for its different brands (therefore not having to exchange currency to transport or sell its products), coupled with the fact that its beers were made domestically, FEMSA's profits would not be significantly affected by a devaluated currency. Helping to stabilizing the company was the fact that it had the exclusive rights to Coca-Cola in Mexico. By distributing one of the most desired brands in the world, FEMSA held in its portfolio a brand that would not be susceptible to economic conditions.

. . . to Be a Global Player

Since the end of prohibition in the United States in 1935 and the introduction of imported beers shortly thereafter, the Dutch import Heineken was the undisputed best-selling import in the United States, which was consistent with its reputation for being among the top-selling beers in the world. Heineken did not see the introduction of Modelo's Corona in the United States in 1979 as threatening to its market share, nor did it see that Corona could eventually compete with it for pole position as the best-selling import. In fact, Heineken executives mocked the golden beer, saying it was nothing more than a novelty drink.

Like Modelo, Heineken decided that it would produce all its beer domestically in Holland and export to foreign markets. In contrast, Anheuser-Busch produced its beers in the foreign markets. Heineken did invest locally in its distribution channels as contracts were signed with local distributors for functions such as importing, distribution, and marketing. However, even here, Heineken headquarters remained in control as the companies that had the contracts were owned and operated by the Heineken parent company. This was the case in the United States, where Heineken USA (formerly known as Van Munching & Company) had the distribution contract for the Dutch beer but was owned and ultimately operated by executives from Holland.

Heineken's reputation throughout the years was built around marketing campaigns developed on positioning the beer as a premium import with superior taste. Because imports were subject to import taxes, distributors usually passed this tax on to their consumers to protect their profit margins, necessitating the need for the image of a premium product. To create this premium image, advertising for Heineken almost always focused on its superior quality, with little attention devoted to any other aspect of its brand.

However, this narrow-sighted vision of the beer eventually opened the door to other competitors, such as Corona, to create innovative campaigns that created more intangible myths surrounding their beers. By 1996, Corona had reached an import volume that was almost equal to Heineken's. Its "fun in the sun" advertising campaign paid no attention to taste.

Even Heineken's executives realized this issue. In reference to their declining sales in the 1990s, the new head of Heineken USA decided the company needed a new approach to marketing. Foley said:

> There aren't many brands with myths in any segment of business. I think Heineken has a myth . . . that's almost intangible.

He continued to say that all that was needed was for Heineken to market that myth differently than they had in the past in order to turn the tide of decreasing sales. Over the next few years, Heineken repositioned its image through its marketing. After a few failed attempts at harnessing what they thought were their strengths in their brand image, i.e., focusing on the red star as the focal point of the brand, market share continued to decline, and in 1997 Corona surpassed Heineken as America's top imported beer. This trend continued with Corona's import volume through 2003 growing at a double-digit pace, and in 2004 it outsold Heineken by 50 percent. However, Heineken was determined to become number one again with respect to the U.S. market and had approved a new marketing budget that would see an aggressive campaign in the United States. Results came soon, and in 2006 the CEO could assert:

> In particular, our growth has been driven by the USA, where the introduction of Heineken Premium Light has made a major contribution to overall performance.

FUTURE CHALLENGES

In 2007, Corona was Mexico's best-selling beer, the top-selling imported beer in the United States, and the world's fourth best-selling beer. It propelled Modelo into the elite class of being among the top 10 beer producers in the world. Grupo Modelo's CEO could proudly claim in the annual report (see Exhibit 6 for financials of Grupo Modelo):

> Grupo Modelo is a growth company. Net sales have risen 7.8 percent on a compounded basis over the last 10 years, demonstrating solid performance in the domestic market and the growing export market year after year . . . The total volume of beer sold in 2005 was 45.5 million hectoliters, an increase of 6.4 percent compared with the previous year. This reflected growth of 4.0 percent in the domestic market and 12.3 percent in the export market. Export sales comprised 30.2 percent of total volume for the year, compared to 28.6 percent in 2004.

This feat was accomplished by Modelo as it sought to expand internationally through smart strategic partnerships with experienced distributors that knew the local market, and wisely differentiated Corona from other imported beers through its marketing. But faced with increasing competition domestically and internationally as other top international brands gained momentum by spending more on media budgets, Corona's sales were decreasing domestically and in the United States. Corona's position as the world's most recognizable Mexican beer was becoming threatened.

Yet organic growth seemed to have limits, and global players aimed at more spectacular moves, as the *Financial Times* revealed on April 2:

> There was one question on everyone's mind when Carlos Brito, InBev's chief executive, presented the brewer's annual earnings last month—was the group in preliminary merger talks with U.S. rival

Exhibit 6 Grupo Modelo's Financial Highlights, 2004–2005

Grupo Modelo, S.A. de C.V. and Subsidiaries Figures in millions of constant Mexican pesos as of December 31, 2005 except sales of beer, per share data and employees.

	Year ended December		
	2005	2004	Change
Sales of Beer (millions of hectaliters)			
Domestic market	31.80	30.59	4.0%
Export market	13.74	12.23	12.3%
Total market	45.54	62.82	6.4%
Net sales	49,551	46,307	7.0%
Gross profit	26,776	26,082	2.7%
Operating income	13,773	13,588	1.4%
Net majority income	7,291	6,389	14.1%
Total assets	80,281	75,914	5.8%
Total liabilities	12,169	13,075	-6.9%
Majority stockholders' equity	52,365	48,283	8.5%
Funds provided by operating activities	10,292	10,486	-1.9%
EBITDA	15,817	15,418	2.6%
Capital expenditures	4,027	4,444	-9.4%
Return on equity	13.9%	13.2%	
Outstanding shares at year end (millions)	3,252	3,252	0.0%
Earnings per share	2.24	1.96	14.1%
Dividend per common share	1.07	0.91	17.8%
Closing stock price	38.50	30.66	25.6%
Number of employees and workers	40,617	44,591	-8.9%

> Anheuser-Busch? Such an alliance would form a brewing colossus with more than one-fifth of the world beer market by volume and could transform the sector.
>
> Rumors of mergers and acquisitions deals in the beer industry are a dime a dozen at present amid speculation that mid-tier brewers such as Anheuser, Scottish & Newcastle, Carlsberg, Heineken, and Molson Coors will all be forced to consolidate to compete with industry behemoths InBev and SAB Miller, which have been expanding globally.

Hence, many expectations and challenges were in store for Grupo Modelo, which had to face its new status on the market in order to make its success story a sustainable one.

References

"Mexico: 'Distrust' in Light Beers." Probrewery.com. Sept. 17, 2004. http://probrewery.com/news/news-002325.pho.

"U.S. Free-Trade Law Seen Aiding Mexican Beers; Cinqo de Mayo Highlights Popularity of South-of-the-Border Brews." MSNBC.com. May 5, 2005. http://msnbc.msn.com/id/7746223.

http://www.baramerica.com/bsreview/lager/014.html.

Beamish, Raul, and Goerzen, Anthony. "The Global Branding of Stella Artois." Ivey Management Services (Ivey Publishing), London. Reference #: 9B00A019.

CIA Fact book: Mexico. http://www.ciafactbook.com.

Herrero, Gustavo. "Corona Beers (A)." Harvard Business School. Harvard Business School Publishing, Boston, Jan. 23, 2003. Reference #: 9-502-023.

FEMSA.com. www.femsa.com Annual and Quarterly reports.

Gard, Lauren, Smith, G., and Weber, J. "Life's a Beach for Corona—Or Is It? Sales Growth Is Slowing in the U.S., So Grupo Modelo Is Searching for Better Margins and New Customers." *BusinessWeek Online.* Feb. 7, 2005. http://www.businessweek.com/magazine/content/05_06/b3919098_mz058.htm.

www.heineken.com Annual report.

http://www.anheuser-busch.com/ Annual report.

http://www.inbev.com Annual report.

http://www.ratebeer.com/Ratings/TopBeersByCountry.asp?CountryID=133.

Scheinman, Marc N. "Beer Baron: Grupo Modelo CEO Carlos Fernandez Sets a Deadline for Catapulting His Company into the World's Top 5 Beer Brewers—2004." Find Articles, Jan.–Feb. 2000. http://www.findarticles.com/p/articles/mi_m0OQC/is_2_1/ai_100541553.

"InBev May Slake the Thirst for Consolidation; Sarah Laitner, Jenny Wiggins and Jonathan Wheatley Examine the Options Facing the World's Largest Brewer in a Sector Ripe for Change." *Financial Times,* April 2, 2007.

CASE

14

Google's Strategy in 2008

John E. Gamble
University of South Alabama

The number of people worldwide accessing the Internet to read breaking news, conduct library research, make consumer e-commerce transactions, use Web-based business applications, and perform other online tasks had grown at an astronomic rate since the 1994 introduction of the Netscape Navigator browser. The number of Internet users worldwide had increased from about 360 million in 2000 to nearly 1.5 billion in 2008. North America had the world's highest Internet penetration rate, with 73.6 percent of the population having Internet access. About 220 million of the 248 million Internet users in North America resided in the United States. Even though only 15.3 percent of Asians had Internet access in 2008, Asia's 578.5 million Internet users made it the world's largest and fastest-growing geographic region for Internet usage.

The growth in the number of Internet users worldwide and in the United States had caused a shift in how advertisers communicated with consumers and had allowed Internet advertising to become the second most common form of advertising used in the United States in 2007. Only newspaper, with 2007 advertising revenues of $48.6 billion, controlled a larger share of U.S. advertising dollars. Cable television, radio, and network television each accounted for about $20 billion each in advertising revenues during 2007. The prospects for Internet advertisers looked strong in 2008, with Internet advertising expected to grow from $21 billion in 2007 to $36.5 billion in 2011. Search-based ads accounted for the largest portion of Internet advertisements in the United States during 2007—amounting to nearly $9 billion in industry revenues. Video ads shown on YouTube and other Web sites accounted for only $505 million in 2007 but were expected to grow to a $5.8 billion market by 2013. Mobile search was another rapidly growing advertising media format, which was projected to increase from worldwide revenues of $813 million in 2007 to $5 billion by 2013.

Advertisers believed search-based ads were particularly effective because they were highly targeted to what Internet users were immediately searching for. In 2008, Google was the worldwide leader in Internet and mobile search advertising because of consumers' faith in the search engine. Internet users trusted Google's results because its paid search results were not interspersed with other search results and were clearly marked as Sponsor Links. Perhaps Google's most important feature was its capability to retrieve highly relevant results to search queries that was made possible by its innovative text-matching techniques and PageRank technology.

When an Internet user entered a search query at Google.com, from a Google toolbar or deskbar, or requested a search at a Web site that licensed Google's search appliance, the search engine performed a computation of an equation involving 500 million variables and 2 billion terms to generate a list of best-matching search results. The results were generated in a fraction of a second and pulled from an index of 1 trillion Web sites that were constantly downloaded onto Google's PC and server farms located around the world. Many Internet users found Google's search results more relevant than results generated by competing search engines because of the company's equation that assessed how well the search terms matched and, most important, how many other Web sites pointed to a site. Google cofounder Larry Page suggested that the Google technology that counted the number of "votes" for various potential matches was superior to other search technologies: "You're asking the whole Web who's the greatest site to ask about this subject."[1]

Internet users' preference for Google's search results produced 2007 revenues of nearly $16.5 billion and profits of more than $4.2 billion. The highly scalable business model added relatively little additional fixed cost as volume increased, which helped boost the company's cash, cash equivalents, and marketable securities to $14.2 billion at the end of 2007. Google's stellar growth rate in revenues and net income was destined to continue into 2008, since its revenues and net income for the first nine months of the fiscal year stood at $16.1 billion and $3.8 billion, respectively. Neither Microsoft's Live Search nor Yahoo, which were the industry's second and third most popular search engines, seemed capable of slowing Google's growth in 2008.

With Google controlling the market for search-based ads, much of the company's attention was focused on new initiatives that might allow the company to sustain its extraordinary growth in revenues, earnings, and net cash provided by operations. Google launched its Android operating system for mobile phones in 2008, which would allow wireless phone manufacturers such as LG and Nokia to produce Internet enabled phones boasting features similar to what were available on Apple's iPhone. Widespread use of the Internet-enabled Android phones would not only help Google solidify its 2008 mobile search market share of 63 percent but also allow it to increase its share of banner ads and video ads displayed on mobile phones. Perhaps the company's most ambitious strategic initiative in 2008 was its desire to change the market for commonly used business productivity applications such as word processing, spreadsheets, and presentation software from the desktop to the Internet. Google Apps' "cloud computing" software would allow corporate software users to access Google's data centers to run software applications and store files that might be needed by other users engaged in collaborative projects. Information technology analysts believed that the market for cloud computing applications could grow to $95 billion by 2013. Other strategic issues confronting Google's chief managers in 2008 included how to best capitalize on such recent acquisitions as its DoubleClick banner ad management program, dMark media auctioning system, and YouTube video sharing network and how to increase its share of search-based ads in emerging markets.

COMPANY HISTORY

The development of Google's search technology began in January 1996 when Stanford University computer science graduate students Larry Page and Sergey Brin collaborated to develop a new search engine, which they named BackRub because of its ability to rate Web sites for relevancy by examining the number of back links pointing to the Web site. The approach for assessing the relevancy of Web sites to a particular search query used by other Web sites at the time was based on examining and counting metatags and keywords included on various Web sites. By 1997, the search accuracy of BackRub had allowed it to gain a loyal following among Silicon Valley Internet users. Yahoo cofounder David Filo was among the converted, and in 1998 Filo convinced Brin and Page to leave Stanford to focus on making their search technology the backbone of a new Internet company.

BackRub would be renamed Google, which was a play on the word *googol*—a mathematical term for a number represented by the numeral 1 followed by 100 zeros. Brin and Page's adoption of the new name reflected their mission to organize a seemingly infinite amount of information on the Internet. In August 1998, a Stanford professor arranged for Brin and Page to meet at his home with a potential angel investor to demonstrate the Google search engine. The investor, who had been a founder of Sun Microsystems, was immediately impressed with Google's search capabilities but was too pressed for time to hear much of their informal presentation. The investor stopped the two during the presentation and suggested, "Instead of us discussing all the details, why don't I just write you a check?"[2] The two partners held the investor's $100,000 check, made payable to Google Inc., for two weeks while they scrambled to set up a corporation named Google Inc. and open a corporate bank account. The two officers of the freshly incorporated company went on to raise a total of $1 million in venture capital from family, friends, and other angel investors by the end of September 1998.

Even with a cash reserve of $1 million, the two partners ran Google on a shoestring budget with its main servers built by Brin and Page from discounted computer components and its four employees operating out of a garage owned by a friend of the founders. By year-end 1998, Google's beta version was handling 10,000 search queries per day and *PC Magazine* had named the company to its list of "Top 100 Web Sites and Search Engines for 1998."

The new company recorded successes at a lightning-fast pace, with the search kernel answering more than 500,000 queries per day and Red Hat agreeing to become the company's first search customer in early 1999. Google attracted an additional $25 million in funding from two leading Silicon Valley venture capital firms by mid-year 1999 to support further growth and enhancements to Google's search technology. The company's innovations in 2000 included wireless search technology, search capabilities in 10 languages, and a Google Toolbar browser plug-in that allowed computer users to search the Internet without first visiting a Google-affiliated Web portal or Google's home page. Features added through 2004 included Google News, Google Product Search, Google Scholar, and Google Local. The company also expanded its index of Web pages to more than 8 billion and increased its country domains to more than 150 by 2004. Google also further expanded its products for mobile phones with a short message service (SMS) feature that allowed mobile phone users to send a search request to Google as a text message. After submitting the search request to 466453 (google), mobile phone users would receive a text message from Google providing results to the user's query.

The Initial Public Offering

Google's April 29, 2004, initial public offering (IPO) registration became the most talked-about planned offering involving an Internet company since the dot-com bust of 2000. The registration announced Google's intention to raise as much as $3.6 billion from the issue of 25.7 million shares through an unusual Dutch auction. Among the 10 key tenets of Google's philosophy, presented in Exhibit 1 (pages C-262 and C-263), was "You can make money without doing evil."[3] The choice of a Dutch auction stemmed from this philosophy since Dutch auctions allowed potential investors, regardless of size, to place bids for shares. The choice of a Dutch auction was also favorable to Google since it involved considerably lower investment banking and underwriting fees and little or no commissions for brokers.

At the conclusion of the first day of trading, Google's shares had appreciated by 18 percent, to make Brin and Page each worth approximately $3.8 billion. Also, an estimated 900 to 1,000 Google employees were worth at least $1 million, with 600 to 700 holding at least $2 million in Google stock. On average, each of Google's 2,292 staff members held approximately $1.7 million in company stock, excluding the holdings of the top five executives. Stanford University also enjoyed a $179.5 million windfall from its stock holdings granted for its early investment in Brin and Page's search engine. Some of Google's early contractors and consultants also profited handsomely from forgoing fees in return for stock options in the company. One such contractor was Abbe Patterson, who took options for 4,000 shares rather than a $5,000 fee for preparing a PowerPoint presentation and speaking notes for one of Brin and Page's first presentations to venture capitalists. After two splits and four days of trading, her 16,000 shares were worth $1.7 million.[4] The company executed a second public offering of 14,159,265 shares of common stock in September 2005. The number of shares issued represented the first eight digits to the right of the decimal point for the value pi. The issue added more than $4 billion to Google's liquid assets. Exhibit 2 tracks the performance of Google's common shares between August 19, 2004, and November 2008.

Google Feature Additions Between 2005 and 2008

Google used its vast cash reserves to make strategic acquisitions that might lead to the development of new Internet applications offering advertising opportunities. Google Earth was launched in 2005 after the company acquired Keyhole, a digital mapping company, in 2004. Google Earth and its companion software, Google Maps, allowed Internet users to view satellite images of any location in the world. The feature could give users close-up aerial views of the Eiffel Tower, the Taj Mahal, the Grand Canyon, or their own residence. The images were not real-time images but had been taken by commercial satellites within the past few years. The feature

Exhibit 1 The 10 Principles of Google's Corporate Philosophy

1. Focus on the user and all else will follow.

From its inception, Google has focused on providing the best user experience possible. While many companies claim to put their customers first, few are able to resist the temptation to make small sacrifices to increase shareholder value. Google has steadfastly refused to make any change that does not offer a benefit to the users who come to the site:

- The interface is clear and simple.
- Pages load instantly.
- Placement in search results is never sold to anyone.
- Advertising on the site must offer relevant content and not be a distraction.

By always placing the interests of the user first, Google has built the most loyal audience on the Web. And that growth has come not through TV ad campaigns, but through word of mouth from one satisfied user to another.

2. It's best to do one thing really, really well.

Google does search. With one of the world's largest research groups focused exclusively on solving search problems, we know what we do well, and how we could do it better. Through continued iteration on difficult problems, we've been able to solve complex issues and provide continuous improvements to a service already considered the best on the Web at making finding information a fast and seamless experience for millions of users. Our dedication to improving search has also allowed us to apply what we've learned to new products, including Gmail, Google Desktop, and Google Maps.

3. Fast is better than slow.

Google believes in instant gratification. You want answers and you want them right now. Who are we to argue? Google may be the only company in the world whose stated goal is to have users leave its website as quickly as possible. By fanatically obsessing on shaving every excess bit and byte from our pages and increasing the efficiency of our serving environment, Google has broken its own speed records time and again.

4. Democracy on the web works.

Google works because it relies on the millions of individuals posting websites to determine which other sites offer content of value. Instead of relying on a group of editors or solely on the frequency with which certain terms appear, Google ranks every web page using a breakthrough technique called PageRank™. PageRank evaluates all of the sites linking to a web page and assigns them a value, based in part on the sites linking to them. By analyzing the full structure of the web, Google is able to determine which sites have been "voted" the best sources of information by those most interested in the information they offer.

5. You don't need to be at your desk to need an answer.

The world is increasingly mobile and unwilling to be constrained to a fixed location. Whether it's through their PDAs, their wireless phones or even their automobiles, people want information to come to them.

6. You can make money without doing evil.

Google is a business. The revenue the company generates is derived from offering its search technology to companies and from the sale of advertising displayed on Google and on other sites across the web. However, you may have never seen an ad on Google. That's because Google does not allow ads to be displayed on our results pages unless they're relevant to the results page on which they're shown. So, only certain searches produce sponsored links above or to the right of the results. Google firmly believes that ads can provide useful information if, and only if, they are relevant to what you wish to find.

Advertising on Google is always clearly identified as a "Sponsored Link." It is a core value for Google that there be no compromising of the integrity of our results. We never manipulate rankings to put our partners higher in our search results. No one can buy better PageRank. Our users trust Google's objectivity and no short-term gain could ever justify breaching that trust.

7. There's always more information out there.

Once Google had indexed more of the HTML pages on the Internet than any other search service, our engineers turned their attention to information that was not as readily accessible. Sometimes it was just a matter of integrating

(*Continued*)

Exhibit 1 (Continued)

new databases, such as adding a phone number and address lookup and a business directory. Other efforts required a bit more creativity, like adding the ability to search billions of images and a way to view pages that were originally created as PDF files. The popularity of PDF results led us to expand the list of file types searched to include documents produced in a dozen formats such as Microsoft Word, Excel and PowerPoint. For wireless users, Google developed a unique way to translate HTML formatted files into a format that could be read by mobile devices. The list is not likely to end there as Google's researchers continue looking into ways to bring all the world's information to users seeking answers.

8. The need for information crosses all borders.

Though Google is headquartered in California, our mission is to facilitate access to information for the entire world, so we have offices around the globe. To that end we maintain dozens of Internet domains and serve more than half of our results to users living outside the United States. Google search results can be restricted to pages written in more than 35 languages according to a user's preference. We also offer a translation feature to make content available to users regardless of their native tongue and for those who prefer not to search in English, Google's interface can be customized into more than 100 languages.

9. You can be serious without a suit.

Google's founders have often stated that the company is not serious about anything but search. They built a company around the idea that work should be challenging and the challenge should be fun. To that end, Google's culture is unlike any in corporate America, and it's not because of the ubiquitous lava lamps and large rubber balls, or the fact that the company's chef used to cook for the Grateful Dead. In the same way Google puts users first when it comes to our online service, Google Inc. puts employees first when it comes to daily life in our Googleplex headquarters. There is an emphasis on team achievements and pride in individual accomplishments that contribute to the company's overall success. Ideas are traded, tested and put into practice with an alacrity that can be dizzying. Meetings that would take hours elsewhere are frequently little more than a conversation in line for lunch and few walls separate those who write the code from those who write the checks. This highly communicative environment fosters a productivity and camaraderie fueled by the realization that millions of people rely on Google results. Give the proper tools to a group of people who like to make a difference, and they will.

10. Great just isn't good enough.

Always deliver more than expected. Google does not accept being the best as an endpoint, but a starting point. Through innovation and iteration, Google takes something that works well and improves upon it in unexpected ways. Google's point of distinction however, is anticipating needs not yet articulated by our global audience, then meeting them with products and services that set new standards. This constant dissatisfaction with the way things are is ultimately the driving force behind the world's best search engine.

Source: Google.com.

was enhanced with street-view images that allowed users to upload pictures linked to any location in the world. Other search features added to Google between 2005 and 2008 that users found particularly useful included Book Search and the expansion of Google News to include archived news articles dating to 1900.

Google also expanded its Web site features beyond search functionality to include its Gmail e-mail software, a Web-based calendar, Web-based document and spreadsheet applications, Picasa Web photo albums, and a translation feature that accommodated 28 languages. Google Talk was a Google feature launched in 2005 that provided instant messaging services to Google users, along with free PC-to-PC local and long-distance voice calls. The company also released services for mobile phone uses such as Mobile Web Search, Blogger Mobile, Gmail, Google News, and Maps for Mobile.

The company used some proceeds of its IPO to make acquisitions that would expand its business model. The 2006 acquisition of dMark allowed Google advertisers to bid on radio advertising spots as well as search-based ads. Google's Web-based document and spreadsheet software resulted from the company's acquisition of Writely in 2006. Google was able to attract millions of new users

Exhibit 2 Performance of Google Inc.'s Stock Price, August 19, 2004, to November 2008

(a) Trend in Google Inc.'s Common Stock Price

(b) Performance of Google Inc.'s Stock Price Versus the S&P 500 Index

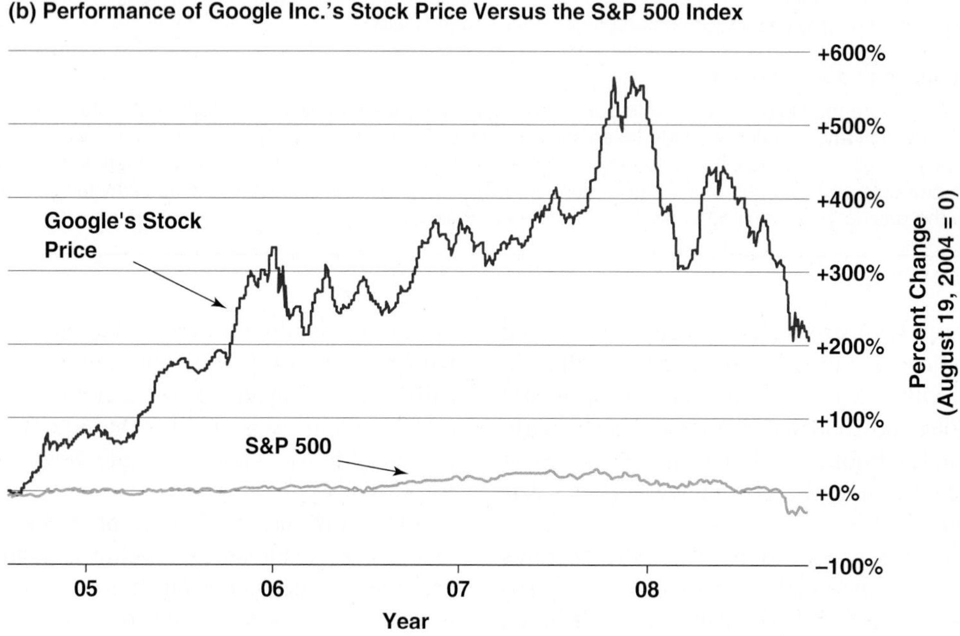

through its acquisition of YouTube in 2006, and its 2008 acquisition of DoubleClick allowed the company to generate advertising revenues through banner ad and in-stream video advertising management services. A complete list of Google services and tools for computers and mobile phones in 2008 is presented in Exhibit 3.

GOOGLE'S BUSINESS MODEL

Google's business model had evolved since the company's inception to include revenue beyond licensing fees charged to corporations needing search

Exhibit 3 List of Google Services and Tools in 2008

Search Features
Alerts Get email updates on the topics of your choice
Blog Search Find blogs on your favorite topics
Book Search Search the full text of books
Checkout Complete online purchases more quickly and securely
Google Chrome A browser built for speed, stability and security
Desktop Search and personalize your computer
Earth Explore the world from your computer
Finance Business info, news, and interactive charts
GOOG-411 Find and connect with businesses from your phone, for free
Google Health Organize your medical records online
iGoogle Add news, games and more to the Google homepage
Images Search for images on the Web
Maps View maps and directions

(*Continued*)

Exhibit 3 (Continued)

News — now with archive search
Search thousands of news stories

Notebook
Clip and collect information as you surf the Web

Patent Search
Search the full text of US Patents

Product Search
Search for stuff to buy

Scholar
Search scholarly papers

Special Searches
Search within specific topics

Toolbar
Add a search box to your browser

Video
Search for videos on Google Video and YouTube

Web Search
Search over billions of Web pages

Web Search Features
Find movies, music, stocks, books, and more

Google Tools and Web Applications

Blogger
Share your life online with a blog — it's fast, easy, and free

Calendar
Organize your schedule and share events with friends

Docs
Create and share your online documents, presentations, and spreadsheets

Gmail
Fast, searchable email with less spam

Groups
Create mailing lists and discussion groups

Knol
Share what you know

orkut

Orkut
Meet new people and stay in touch with friends

(Continued)

Exhibit 3 (Continued)

	Picasa Find, edit and share your photos
	Reader Get all your blogs and news feeds fast
	Sites Create Websites and secure group wikis
	SketchUp Build 3D models quickly and easily
talk	Talk IM and call your friends through your computer
	Translate View Web pages in other languages
YouTube	YouTube Watch, upload and share videos
Google Mobile Applications	
	Maps for mobile View maps and get directions on your phone
	Mobile Use Google on your mobile phone
SMS	SMS Use text messaging for quick info

Source: Google.com

capabilities on company intranets or Web sites. The 2000 development of keyword-targeted advertising expanded its business model to include revenues from the placement of highly targeted text-only sponsor ads adjacent to its search results. Google was able to target its ads to specific users based on the user's browsing history. The addition of advertising-based revenue allowed Google to increase annual revenues from $220,000 in 1999 to more than $86 million in 2001.

Beginning in 2005, Google charged fees to advertisers who were successful bidders for magazine, newspaper, radio, and television ads placed with its 650-plus traditional media partners. The company's 2006 acquisition of YouTube also allowed it to receive advertising revenues for ads displayed during Internet videos. The company's 2008 launch of Google Checkout allowed it to receive a fee of as much as 2 percent of the transaction amount for purchased made at participating e-retailer sites. A summary of Google's financial performance between 2001 and 2007 is presented in Exhibit 4. The company's balance sheets for 2006 and 2007 are presented in Exhibit 5.

Google Search Appliance

Google's search technology could be integrated into a third party's Web site or intranet if search functionality was important to the customer. Google's

Exhibit 4 Financial Summary for Google Inc., 2001–2007 ($ in thousands, except per share amounts)

	Fiscal Year End						
	2007	2006	2005	2004	2003	2002	2001
Revenues	$16,593,986	$10,604,917	$ 6,138,560	$3,189,223	$1,465,934	$ 439,508	$ 86,426
Costs and expenses:							
Cost of revenues	6,649,085	4,225,027	2,577,088	1,457,653	625,854	131,510	14,228
Research and development	2,119,985	1,228,589	599,510	225,632	91,228	31,748	16,500
Sales and marketing	1,461,266	849,518	468,152	246,300	120,328	43,849	20,076
General and administrative	410,604	293,687	185,823	139,700	56,699	24,300	12,275
Stock-based compensation	868,646	458,100	200,709	278,746	229,361	21,635	12,383
Contribution to Google Foundation	—	—	90,000	—	—	—	—
Nonrecurring portion of settlement of disputes with Yahoo	—	—	—	201,000	—	—	—
Total costs and expenses	11,509,586	7,054,921	4,121,282	2,549,031	1,123,470	253,042	75,462
Income (loss) from operations	5,084,400	3,549,996	2,017,278	640,192	342,464	186,466	10,964
Interest income (expense) and other, net	589,580	461,044	124,399	10,042	4,190	−1,551	−896
Income (loss) before income taxes	5,673,980	4,011,040	2,141,677	650,234	346,654	184,915	10,068
Provision for income taxes	1,470,260	933,594	676,280	251,115	241,006	85,259	3,083
Net income (loss)	$ 4,203,720	$ 3,077,446	$ 1,465,397	$ 399,119	$ 105,648	$ 99,656	$ 6,985
Net income (loss) per share:							
Basic	$13.53	$10.21	$5.31	$2.07	$0.77	$0.86	$0.07
Diluted	$13.29	$ 9.94	$5.02	$1.46	$0.41	$0.45	$0.04
Number of shares used in per share calculations:							
Basic	310,806	301,403	275,844	193,176	137,697	115,242	94,523
Diluted	316,210	309,548	291,874	272,781	256,638	220,633	186,776
Net cash provided by operating activities	$ 5,775,410	$ 3,580,508	$ 2,459,422	$ 977,044	$ 395,445	$ 155,265	N/A
Net proceeds from public offerings	—	2,063,549	4,287,229	1,161,466	—	—	—
Cash, cash equivalents, and marketable securities	14,218,613	11,243,914	8,034,247	2,132,297	334,718	146,331	N/A
Total assets	25,335,806	18,473,351	10,271,813	3,313,351	871,458	286,892	N/A
Total long-term liabilities	610,525	128,924	107,472	43,927	33,365	N/A	N/A
Total stockholders' equity	22,689,679	17,039,840	9,418,957	2,929,056	588,770	173,953	N/A

Source: Google Inc. Form S-1 filed April 29, 2004; Google Inc. 2007 10-K report.

Exhibit 5 Google Inc.'s Balance Sheets, 2006–2007 ($ in thousands, except per share amounts)

	As of December 31,	
	2007	2006
Assets		
Current assets:		
Cash and cash equivalents	$ 6,081,593	$ 3,544,671
Marketable securities	8,137,020	7,699,243
Accounts receivable, net of allowance of $16,914 and $32,887	2,162,521	1,322,340
Deferred income taxes, net	68,538	29,713
Income taxes receivable	145,253	—
Prepaid revenue share, expenses and other assets	694,213	443,880
Total current assets	17,289,138	13,039,847
Prepaid revenue share, expenses and other assets, non-current	168,530	114,455
Deferred income taxes, net, non-current	33,219	—
Non-marketable equity securities	1,059,694	1,031,850
Property and equipment, net	4,039,261	2,395,239
Intangible assets, net	446,596	346,841
Goodwill	2,299,368	1,545,119
Total assets	$25,335,806	$18,473,351
Liabilities and Stockholders' Equity		
Current liabilities:		
Accounts payable	$ 282,106	$ 211,169
Accrued compensation and benefits	588,390	351,671
Accrued expenses and other current liabilities	465,032	266,247
Accrued revenue share	522,001	370,364
Deferred revenue	178,073	105,136
Total current liabilities	2,035,602	1,304,587
Deferred revenue, long-term	30,249	20,006
Deferred income taxes, net	—	40,421
Income taxes payable, long-term	478,372	—
Other long-term liabilities	101,904	68,497
Stockholders' equity:		
Convertible preferred stock, $0.001 par value, 100,000 shares authorized; no shares issued and outstanding	—	—
Class A and Class B common stock, $0.001 par value per share: 9,000,000 shares authorized; 308,997 (Class A 227,670, Class B 81,327) and par value of $309 (Class A $228, Class B $81) and 312,917 (Class A 236,097, Class B 76,820) and par value of $313 (Class A $236, Class B $77) shares issued and outstanding, excluding 1,296 (Class A 1,045 Class B 251) and 361 (Class A 336, Class B 25) shares subject to repurchase at December 31, 2006 and 2007	313	309
Additional paid-in capital	13,241,221	11,882,906
Accumulated other comprehensive income	113,373	23,311
Retained earnings	9,334,772	5,133,314
Total stockholders' equity	22,689,679	17,039,840
Total liabilities and stockholders' equity	$25,335,806	$18,473,351

Source: Google Inc. 2007 10-K report.

Site Search allowed enterprises ranging from small businesses to public companies to license Google's search appliance for use on their Web sites for as little as $100 per year. The Google Search Appliance was designed for use on corporate intranets to allow employees to search company documents. The Search Appliance included a variety of security features to ensure that only employees with proper authority were able to view restricted documents. The Google Mini Search Appliance was designed for small businesses, with 50,000 to 300,000 documents stored on local PCs and servers. The Google Mini hardware and software package could be licensed online at www.google.com/enterprise/mini at prices ranging from $2,990 to $9,900, depending on document count capability. Google's more robust search appliance had a document count capability of up to 30 million documents and was designed for midsized to global businesses. Licensing fees for the Google Search appliance ranged from $30,000 to $600,000, depending on document count capability.

AdWords

Google AdWords allowed advertisers to, either independently through Google's automated tools or with the assistance of Google's marketing teams, create text-based ads that would appear alongside Google search results. AdWords users could evaluate the effectiveness of their advertising expenditures with Google through the use of performance reports that tracked the effectiveness of each ad. Google also offered a keyword targeting program that suggested synonyms for keywords entered by advertisers, a traffic estimator that helped potential advertisers anticipate charges, and multiple payment options that included charges to credit cards, debit cards, and monthly invoicing.

Larger advertisers were offered additional services to help run large, dynamic advertising campaigns. Such assistance included the availability of specialists with expertise in various industries to offer suggestions for targeting potential customers and identifying relevant keywords. Google's advertising specialists also helped develop ads for customers that would increase click-through rates and purchase rates. Google also offered its large advertising customers bulk posting services that helped launch and manage campaigns including ads using hundreds or thousands of keywords.

Google's search-based ads were priced using an auction system that allowed advertisers to bid on keywords that would describe their product or service. Bids could be made on a cost-per-impression (CPI) or cost-per-click (CPC) basis. Most Google advertisers placed bids based on CPC frequency rather than how many times an ad was displayed by Google. Google's auction pricing model assigned a Quality Score to each bidder that was determined by the advertiser's past keyword click-through rate and the relevance of the ad text. Advertisers with higher Quality Scores were offered lower minimum bids than advertisers with poor quality scores.

Google allowed users to pay a CPC rate lower than their bid price if their bid was considerably more than the next highest bid. For example, an advertiser who bid $0.75 per click for a particular keyword would only be charged $0.51 per click if the next highest bid was only $0.50. The AdWords discounter ensured that advertisers paid only one cent more than the next highest bid, regardless of the actual amount of their bid.

AdSense

Google's AdSense program allowed Web publishers to share in the advertising revenues generated by Google's text ads. The AdSense program served content-relevant Google text ads to pages on Google Network Web sites. For example, an Internet user reading an article about the 2008 global economic slowdown at Reuters.com would see Google text ads by investment magazines and companies specializing in home business opportunities. Google Network members shared in the advertising revenue whenever a site visitor clicked on a Google ad displayed on their sites. The 1 million–plus Google Network members did not pay a fee to participate in the program and received about 60 percent of advertising dollars generated from the ads. Google's AdSense program also allowed mobile phone operators to share in Google revenues if text and image ads were displayed on mobile handsets. Also, owners of dormant domain names and news feed services could also participate in the AdSense program.

The breakdown of Google's revenues by source is presented in the following table:

Advertising revenues (in $ thousands):	2007	2006	2005	2004	2003
Google Web sites	$10,624,705	$ 6,332,797	$3,377,060	$1,589,032	$ 792,063
Google Network Web sites	5,787,938	4,159,831	2,687,942	1,554,256	628,600
Total advertising revenues	16,412,643	10,492,628	6,065,002	3,143,288	1,420,663
Licensing and other revenues	181,343	112,289	73,558	45,935	45,271
Net revenues	$16,593,986	$10,604,917	$6,138,560	$3,189,223	$1,465,934

Source: Google Inc., Form S-1, filed April 29, 2004; Google 2007 10-K report.

Google's search-based ads could be delivered to Internet users in 41 different languages. In 2007, more than 50 percent of the company's revenues were generated from advertising sales within the United States. However, more than one-half of its traffic was generated from Internet users outside the United States. Growth in Internet use in rapidly emerging markets such as Russia, India, and China had allowed a larger percentage of Google's revenues to come from advertisers outside the United States. Between 2006 and 2007, Google's advertising revenues in the United States grew by 44 percent, while advertising revenues in the United Kingdom grew by 58 percent and rest of world revenues grew by 81 percent. A breakdown of Google's revenues and long-lived assets by geographic region is presented in the following table:

	Year Ended December 31,	
Revenues (in $ millions)	**2007**	**2006**
United States	$ 8,698,021	$ 6,030,140
United Kingdom	2,530,916	1,603,842
Rest of the world	5,365,049	2,970,935
Total revenues	$16,593,986	$10,604,917

	As of December 31,	
Long-Lived Assets	**2007**	**2006**
United States	$7,334,877	$5,070,694
Rest of the world	711,791	362,810
Total long-lived assets	$8,046,668	$5,433,504

Source: Google Inc. 2007 10-K report.

GOOGLE'S STRATEGY AND COMPETITIVE POSITION IN 2008

Google's Strategies to Dominate Internet Advertising

Google's multiple acquisitions since its 2004 IPO and the focus of its research and development activities were directed at increasing the company's dominance in Internet advertising. The addition of Google Maps, local search, airline travel information, weather, Book Search, Gmail, Blogger, and other features increased traffic to Google sites and gave the company more opportunities to serve ads to Internet users. Also, the acquisition of Double Click in 2008 allowed Google to diversify its Internet advertising beyond search ads to include banner ads. However, not all of Google's acquisitions and innovations had resulted in a meaningful contribution to the company's revenues. Even though more than 5 billion videos were watched on YouTube each month, the online video site recorded revenues of less than $200 million in 2007. Also, the company's internally developed social networking site, orkut.com, had failed to match the success of competing social networking sites, Facebook.com or MySpace.com.

Google's strategy to dominate search-based advertising on mobile devices had been very successful. In 2008, Google accounted for 63 percent of searches performed on Internet-enabled phones. The company's introduction of its Android operating system for mobile phones was expected to allow it to increase its share of mobile searches and expand the market for other types of Internet ads delivered on mobile devices. Android was not a phone, but an operating system that Google made available to any phone manufacturer wishing to market mobile devices with Internet capability. Android's core applications included Wi-Fi capability, e-mail, a Web-based calendar, Google Earth maps, a browser, and global positioning system (GPS) software. T-Mobile was the first wireless provider to market an Android phone. Its $179 G1 was launched in September 2008 and included essentially the same features found on the more expensive Apple iPhone. Reviews comparing the G1 to the iPhone found that the major advantage of the G1 was that its QWERTY keyboard was preferred by many users over the iPhone's virtual keyboard, which required users to type on a video image of a keyboard. The group of reviewers commented that the overall thicker design of the G1 might not be as appealing as the iPhone design for some mobile phone users. Nokia and LG planned to launch Android phones by 2009.

Google's Strategic Offensive to Control the Desktop

Google's chief managers believed that, in the very near future, most computer software programs used by businesses would move from local hard drives or intranets to the Internet. Many information technology analysts agreed that "cloud computing" would become a common software platform and could grow to a $95 billion market by 2013. Moving software applications to "the cloud" offered many possible benefits to corporate users, including lower software acquisition costs, lower computing support costs, and easier collaboration among employees in different locations. The beta version of Google Apps was launched in 2006 as a free word processing and spreadsheet package for individuals, but was relaunched in 2008 as a competing product to Microsoft Office. Google Apps was hosted on computers in Google's data centers and included Gmail, a calendar, instant messaging, word processing, spreadsheets, presentation software, and file storage space. Google Apps could be licensed by corporate customers at $50 per user per year. The licensing fee for the Microsoft Office and Outlook package was typically $350 per user per year.

Google's Chrome browser, launched in September 2008, was developed specifically to accommodate cloud computing applications. The bare-bones browser was built on a multiprocessor design that would allow users to operate spreadsheets, word processing, video editing, and other applications on separate tabs that could be run simultaneously. Each tab operated independently so that if one tab crashed, other applications running from Google's data centers were not affected. Chrome also provided Google with a defense against moves by Microsoft to make it more difficult for Google to deliver relevant search-based ads to Internet users. Microsoft's Internet Explorer 8 allowed users to hide their Internet address and viewing history, which prevented Google from collecting user-specific information needed for ad targeting. Mozilla's Firefox browser employed a similar feature that prevented third parties from tracking a user's viewing habits. In 2008, Microsoft Internet Explorer and Mozilla Firefox held browser market shares of 72 percent and 20 percent, respectively. As of late 2008, Google's revenues related to the sale of Google Apps to corporate customers stood at just $4 million. Microsoft Office's fiscal 2008 sales of approximately $17 billion gave Microsoft a 98 percent share of the market for office productivity software.

Google's Internet Rivals

Google's ability to sustain its competitive advantage among search companies was a function of its ability to maintain strong relationships with Internet users, advertisers, and Web sites. In 2008, Internet users went to Google to search for information more often than any other site with search capabilities. Google management believed its primary competitors to be Microsoft and Yahoo. A comparison of the percentage of Internet searches among Web sites offering search capabilities in July 2006 and April 2008 is shown in the following table:

	Percent of Searches	
Search Entity	**July 2006**	**April 2008**
Google sites	43.7%	61.6%
Yahoo sites	28.8	20.4
Microsoft sites	12.8	9.1
AOL	5.9	4.6
Ask	5.4	4.3
Others	3.4	n.m.
Total	100.0%	100.0%

n.m. = not material.

Source: ComScore.com.

Yahoo Yahoo, founded in 1994, was the second leading Internet destination worldwide in 2008, with 142 million unique visitors each month. Almost any information available on the Internet could be accessed through Yahoo's Web portal. Visitors could access content categorized by Yahoo or set up an account with Yahoo to maintain a personal calendar and e-mail account, check the latest news, check local weather, obtain maps, check TV listings, watch a movie trailer, track a stock portfolio, maintain a golf handicap, keep an online photo album, or search personal ads or job listings.

Yahoo also hosted Websites for small businesses and Internet retailers and had entered into strategic partnerships with 20 mobile phone operators in the United States and Europe to provide mobile search and display ads to their customers. By 2008, Yahoo accounted for 35 percent of searches performed on mobile phones. Yahoo's broad range of services allowed it to generate revenues from numerous sources—it received fees for banner ads displayed at Yahoo.com, Yahoo! Messenger, Yahoo! Mail, Flickr, or mobile phone customers; it received listing fees at Yahoo! Autos, Cars.com, and Yahoo! Real Estate; it received revenues from paid search results at Yahoo! Search; it shared in travel agency booking fees made at Yahoo! Travel; and it received subscription fees from its registered users at Rivals.com, Yahoo! Games, Yahoo! Music, and Yahoo! Personals.

In 2007, Yahoo entered into a strategic alliance with Intel and executed the acquisition of Right Media to expand its business model beyond Internet advertising and subscription fees charged to Internet users. Its alliance with Intel involved the development of a set-top box that would provide an interactive experience for television viewers. Under the terms of the agreement, Intel would develop the system hardware, while Yahoo would develop widget applications that would allow television viewers to connect to the Internet to keep track of such information as sports scores and breaking news or to watch an item listed on an eBay auction. Its Right Media acquisition allowed advertisers to bid for ads offered by Yahoo's partner newspapers and magazines.

Yahoo's relationship with Google dated to 2000 and, since that time, had oscillated between cooperative and adversarial. Yahoo was among Google's earliest customers for its search appliance, but Yahoo began to distance itself from Google in 2002 when it began acquiring companies with developed search technologies. Yahoo replaced Google with its own search capabilities in February 2004. Yahoo later levied a patent infringement charge against Google that resulted in a settlement that gave Google ownership of the technology rights in return for 2.7 million shares of Google stock. Yahoo attempted to renew its relationship with Google in 2008 in hopes of reversing a decline in profitability and liquidity that began in 2006. After averting a hostile takeover by Microsoft in June 2008, Yahoo reached an agreement with Google that would allow Yahoo to host Google search ads. The partnership would provide Yahoo with an estimated $800 million in additional revenues annually, most of which would go directly to its bottom line. However, Google withdrew from the agreement in November 2008 after receiving notification from the U.S. Justice Department that the alliance would possibly violate antitrust statutes. Shortly after being notified that Google was withdrawing from the deal, Yahoo's chief managers told business reporters that the company was "disappointed that Google has elected to withdraw from the agreement rather than defend it in court."[5] Technology analysts believed that it was in Yahoo's best interest to engage Microsoft in a friendly takeover of the company, albeit at a significantly lower buyout price than what was offered earlier in the year. A summary of the company's financial performance between 2003 and 2007 is presented in Exhibit 6.

Microsoft Online Services Microsoft Corporation recorded fiscal 2008 revenues and net income of approximately $60.4 billion and $17.7 billion, respectively, through the sales of computer software, consulting services, video game hardware, and online services. Windows Vista and Microsoft Office 2007 accounted for more than one-half of the company's 2008 revenues and nearly all of its operating profit. The company's online services business recorded sales of $3.2 billion and an operating loss of $1.2 billion during fiscal 2008. Microsoft's online services business generated revenues from banner ads displayed at the company's MSN Web portal and its affiliated Web sites, search-based ads displayed with Live Search results, and subscription fees from its MSN dial-up service. Revenues and operating profit for the division between fiscal 2006 and fiscal 2008 are shown in the following table.

Revenues and Operating Income (Loss) for Microsoft's Online Services Business, 2006–2008 (in millions)

	2008	2007	2006
Revenue	$3,214	$2,441	$2,296
Operating income (loss)	(1,233)	(617)	5

Source: Microsoft Corporation 2008 annual report.

A financial summary for Microsoft Corporation is provided in Exhibit 7.

Microsoft's Live Search was launched in November 2004 to compete directly with Google and slow whatever intentions it might have to threaten Microsoft in its core operating system and productivity software businesses. Microsoft's concern with threats posed by Google arose shortly after its IPO when Bill Gates noticed that many of the Google job postings on its site were nearly identical to Microsoft job specifications. Recognizing that the position announcements had more to do with operating-system design than search, Gates e-mailed key Microsoft executives, warning, "We have to watch these guys. It looks like they are building something to compete with us."[6] Gates later commented that Google was "more like us than anyone else we have ever competed with."[7]

Gates speculated that Google's long-term strategy involved the development of Web-based software applications comparable to Word, Excel, PowerPoint, and other Microsoft products.

Exhibit 6 Financial Summary for Yahoo, Inc., 2003–2007 (in thousands)

	2007	2006	2005	2004	2003
Revenues	$6,969,274	$6,425,679	$5,257,668	$3,574,517	$1,625,097
Income from operations	695,413	940,966	1,107,725	688,581	295,666
Net income	660,000	751,391	1,896,230	839,553	237,879
Cash and cash equivalents	$1,513,930	$1,569,871	$1,429,693	$ 823,723	$ 415,892
Marketable debt securities	849,542	1,967,414	2,570,155	2,918,539	2,150,323
Working capital	937,274	2,276,148	2,245,481	2,909,768	1,013,913
Total assets	12,229,741	11,513,608	10,831,834	9,178,201	5,931,654
Long-term liabilities	384,208	870,948	1,061,367	851,782	822,890
Total stockholders' equity	9,532,831	9,160,610	8,566,415	7,101,446	4,363,490

Source: Yahoo Inc. 2007 10-K report.

Exhibit 7 Financial Summary for Microsoft Corporation, 2004–2008 (in millions)

	Fiscal Year Ended June 30,				
	2008	2007	2006	2005	2004
Revenue	$60,420	$51,122	$44,282	$39,788	$36,835
Operating income	22,492	18,524	16,472	14,561	9,034
Net income	17,681	14,065	12,599	12,254	8,168
Cash, cash equivalents, and short-term investments	$23,662	$23,411	$34,161	$37,751	$60,592
Total assets	72,793	63,171	69,597	70,815	94,368
Long-term obligations	6,621	8,320	7,051	5,823	4,574
Stockholders' equity	36,286	31,097	40,104	48,115	74,825

Source: Microsoft Corporation 2008 Annual Report.

Microsoft's strategy to compete with Google was keyed to making Live Search more effective than Google at providing highly relevant search results. Microsoft believed that any conversion of Google users to Live Search would reduce the number of PC users who might ultimately adopt Google's Web-based word processing, spreadsheet, and presentation software packages. In 2008, Microsoft paid more than $100 million to acquire Powerset, which was the developer of a semantic search engine. Semantic search technology offered the opportunity to surpass the relevancy of Google's search results since semantic search evaluated the meaning of a word or phrase and considered its context when returning search results. Even though semantic search had the capability to answer questions stated in common language, it took several seconds to return results. The amount of time necessary to conduct a search had caused Microsoft to limit Powerset's search index only to articles listed in Wikipedia. Microsoft's developers were focused on increasing the speed of its semantic search capabilities so that its search index could be expanded to a greater number of Internet pages.

Microsoft's hostile bid for Yahoo was engineered to allow the company to increase its Internet search market share and achieve advertising scale necessary to make its online services business profitable. The addition of Yahoo's 142 million unique monthly users was expected to double exposure for Microsoft's banner ads to 240 million unique monthly users. Banner ads comprised the bulk of Microsoft's online advertising revenues, since Live Search accounted for less than 15 percent of online searches in 2008. After the rejection of its bid by Yahoo shareholders, Microsoft agreed to a $500 million agreement with Viacom that would place its banner ads on such Viacom Web sites as MTV.com, Nickelodeon.com, BET.com, CMT.com, Rhapsody.com, and Paramount.com. Even though the $7 billion market for display ads was only about one-third the size of the search ad market in 2008, the advertising spending on banner ads was expected to double by 2012, to reach $15 billion

Microsoft was also moving forward with its own approach to cloud computing. The company's 2008 launch of Windows Live allowed Internet users to store files online at its password-protected SkyDrive site. SkyDrive's online file storage allowed users to access and edit files from multiple locations, share files with co-workers who might need editing privileges, or make files available in a public folder for wide distribution. Azure was Microsoft's most ambitious cloud computing initiative in 2008 and was intended to allow businesses to reduce computing costs by allowing Microsoft to host its operating programs and data files. In addition to reducing capital expenditures for software upgrades and added server capacity, Azure's offsite hosting provided data security in the event of natural disasters such as fires or hurricanes.

GOOGLE'S PERFORMANCE GOING INTO 2009

Google's 41 percent growth AdWords revenues during the first nine months of 2008 made it evident that Google would again set annual revenue and net income records for the entire year. The company's revenues had increased to $16.1 billion by the end of its third quarter, while net income for the nine-month period had increased to $3.9 billion. In addition to expanding its applications for mobile phone users with the launch of Android and pushing forward with its plan to become the dominant provider of cloud computing solutions, Google also undertook efforts to increase international search revenues with the $140 million acquisition of ZAO Begun, a leading context advertising service in Russia. Going into 2009, Google had also reached an agreement with the U.S. Federal Communications Commission to open unused television frequencies for the development of large-area Wi-Fi zones. Under the terms of the agreement, Google, Microsoft, Motorola, and other technology firms could begin developing devices capable of accepting and transmitting data over unused television airwaves. Some analysts preferred that Google focus on activities related to its core business, such as developing semantic search capabilities for its Google search appliance. Some analysts also pointed to the company's weakness in

China, where it was a distant number two to local search-based ad provider Baidu. In 2008, 63 percent of Internet searches in China were performed by Baidu, while Google held a 26 percent share of searches in that country. China's 253 million Internet users were the most for any country and made China one of the world's fastest-growing markets for search-based advertising in 2008.

Endnotes

1. As quoted in "High-Tech Search Engine Google Won't Talk About Business Plan," *Wall Street Journal Online,* June 14, 1999.
2. As quoted in Google's Corporate Information, www.google.com/corporate/history.html.
3. As listed under "Our Philosophy," Google Corporate Information, www.google.com/corporate/tenthings.html.
4. As reported in "For Some Who Passed on Google Long Ago, Wistful Thinking," *Wall Street Journal Online,* August 23, 2004.
5. As quoted in "With Google Gone, Will Microsoft Come Back to Yahoo?" *Fortune,* November 5, 2008.
6. As quoted in "Gates vs. Google," *Fortune,* April 18, 2005.
7. Ibid.

The Challenges Facing eBay in 2008: Time for a Change in Strategy?

CASE 15

Louis Marino
The University of Alabama

Patrick Kreiser
Ohio University

On January 23, 2008, eBay announced that Meg Whitman would step down as president and CEO as of March 31, 2008. When Whitman joined eBay in 1998, the company had revenues of $86 million and employed just 30 people. After a decade of impressive growth fueled by international expansion, acquisition of new businesses, and internal growth, by 2008 eBay employed 15,000 people and had revenues of over $5.9 billion. Despite this growth, eBay's new president and CEO, John Donahoe, faced several significant challenges.

The most significant challenge facing Donahoe was the slowing growth in eBay's core business of online auctions. Donahoe had served as president of eBay Marketplaces, the division that includes online auctions and eBay's other e-commerce businesses, since 2005. In that time, despite several acquisitions such as StubHub.com, an online ticket marketplace, that diversified eBay's revenues in its Marketplaces division, the percentage of eBay's total revenues that came from this key division fell from 72 to 56 percent. This slowing growth in the company's core division was highlighted by a 1 percent decrease in gross merchandise volume, a measure of total sales, in the third quarter of 2008 as compared to sales in the third quarter of 2007 and a declining growth rate in the number of registered users, as can be seen in Exhibit 1.

There was also a significant concern that eBay's 2006 acquisition of Skype, an online communications service, had not produced the intended results. Specifically, although Skype's considerable revenue growth had contributed to eBay's ability to reach its revenue targets, eBay had never been able to meaningfully integrate Skype into is core operations and to capture the synergies that had provided the original justification for acquisition. Additionally, in late 2007 eBay had to take a $900 million writedown in the value of Skype, indicating that the company had significantly overpaid in the 2005 acquisition. When asked about Skype's fit with eBay's business model, eBay's newly appointed president, John Donahoe, said, "What we're about this year are the synergies. If the synergies are strong, we'll keep it in our portfolio, if not, we'll reassess it."[1]

Finally, heading into the holiday season of 2008, traditionally eBay's strongest quarter, net transaction revenues in eBay's core Marketplaces division, which included online auctions, were down 6 percent from the second quarter of 2007. Company executives predicted that this weakness would continue and that the fourth quarter of 2008 was likely to be the weakest quarter of the year. Donahoe attributed this poor performance to weakness in key economies across the globe, but some analysts and eBay customers believed it was indicative of deeper problems, including an erosion of eBay's core customer base and a loss of the company's innovative capabilities. In response to a series of changes eBay made between 2007 and 2008, one seller who had been with eBay since 2001 stated, "They've forgotten the base of their operation—the sellers. . . . It's not a fair selling venue anymore."[2] Additionally, analysts were concerned that the company's innovative culture, one of the keys to the company's early success, had eroded to the extent that some eBay employees were referring to the company as "the IBM of Silicon Valley"—an uncomplimentary reference to the stifling bureaucracy that now permeated the company. In describing how eBay would go about sustaining its growth and profitability, Donahoe said, "We will continue to stay focused on connecting consumers on our various e-commerce platforms, maintaining

Exhibit 1 Selected Indicators of eBay's Growth, 1998–2007 (all figures are in millions)

	2000	2001	2002	2003	2004	2005	2006	2007	2008 Partial Year†
Registered users	22.0	42.4	61.7	94.9	135.5	180.6	221.6	276.3	370.2
Active users*	NA	18.0	27.7	41.2	56.1	71.8	81.8	83.2	85.7
Gross merchandise sales	$5,400	$9,300	$14,900	$24,000	$34,200	$44,299	$52,474	$59,353	$46,004
Number of auctions listed	264	423	638	971	1,412.6	1,876.8	2,365.3	2,340.5	2,015

*Defined as a user who has bid on, bought, or listed an item during the most recent 12-month period.
†Totals as of September 30, 2008, based on third-quarter results, as posted in third-quarter report.

financial discipline, and capitalizing on new opportunities for growth."

However, analysts were not convinced that eBay could recover its dominance in the online auction industry given the projected weakness in the global economy. Further, a report by David Joseph, an investment analyst from Morgan Stanley, reported that eBay's share of the U.S. e-commerce market had fallen from 19 to 17 percent between 2006 and 2008, while Amazon.com's share rose from 3.7 to 5.3 percent over the same time period. As a reflection of these concerns, between November 2007 and November 2008, eBay's stock price dropped by more than 50 percent from its 52-week high of $35.98 to close at $15.01 on November 3, 2008. Additionally, there were significant concerns as to whether Donahoe was suited to lead eBay's turnaround. Following an announcement that eBay would lay off 10 percent of its workforce, Donahoe's CEO approval rating on Glassdoor.com, a Web site that allows employees to rate their CEOs, fell to 22 percent. Whitman's was 75 percent when she retired, with one employee saying, "Donahoe has made eBay a miserable debacle and it's getting worse every day. . . . I never thought I would say this, but I miss Meg! Come back Meg!!!!!"[3]

THE GROWTH OF E-COMMERCE AND ONLINE AUCTIONS

The fundamental concepts underlying the Internet were first conceived in the 1960s, but it wasn't until the 1990s that the Internet garnered widespread use and became a part of everyday life. The International Data Corporation (IDC), a leading Internet analysis firm, estimated that in 2008 there were approximately 1.4 billion Internet users worldwide and that that number would grow to 1.9 billion users worldwide by 2012. Additionally, it was predicted that almost half of Internet users would make online purchases in 2008. Internationally, Asia had the most Internet users, with more than 550 million in 2008, followed by Europe with more than 380 million, and North America with approximately 250 million. It was estimated that the United States alone accounted for approximately 220 million Internet users and that over 70 percent of the U.S. population used the Internet. However, the highest areas of Internet usage growth were expected to be in developing countries where Internet penetration was currently low, such as Asia, Latin America, and Eastern Europe due to increasing access through new technologies such as Web-enabled cell phones. Further, IDC predicted that by 2012 the number of users accessing the Internet from mobile devices such as phones would surpass the number accessing it from personal computers.

In 2007, according to Forrester Research, online retail sales in the United States increased by 21 percent over 2006, to $175 billion. Forrester predicted that the growth rate in online retail sales would continue to slow, dropping from 17 percent in 2008 to 11 percent in 2012; Forrester's forecast called for online sales in the U.S. to grow about $30 billion annually and reach a total of $335 billion by 2012. Internationally, IDC estimated that roughly 1.4 billion people used the Internet regularly, and the number of Internet users was expected to grow to 30 percent of the world's population, or 1.9 billion, by 2012. Further, IDC predicted that nearly 1 billion of these users would make purchases online in 2012 for a total of $1.2 trillion. However, it was estimated that business-to-business e-commerce would be 10 times larger, for a total of $12.4 trillion in 2012.

KEY SUCCESS FACTORS IN ONLINE RETAILING

While it was relatively easy to create a Web site that functioned like a retail store, the more significant challenge was for an online retailer to generate traffic to the site in the form of both new and returning customers. To reach new customers some online retailers partnered with shopping search engines (such as www.google.com, www.mysimon.com, or www.streetprices.com) that allowed customers to compare prices for a given product from many retailers. Other tactics employed to build traffic included direct e-mail, online advertising at portals and content-related sites, and some traditional advertising such as print and television. Most online retailers endeavored to set up their Web site so as to provide customers with extensive product information, include pictures of the merchandise, make the site easily navigable, and have enough new things happening at the site to keep customers coming back. (A site's ability to generate repeat visitors was known as "stickiness.") Retailers also had to overcome new Internet users' nervousness about using the Internet itself to shop for items they generally bought in stores. Web sites had to appease concerns regarding entering credit card numbers over the Internet and the possible sale of personal information to marketing firms. Online retailing had severe limitations in the case of those goods and services people wanted to see in person to verify their quality. From the retailer's perspective, there was the issue of collecting payment from buyers who wanted to use checks or money orders instead of credit cards.

ONLINE AUCTIONS

The first known auctions in history were held in Babylon around 500 BC. In AD 193, the entire Roman Empire was put up for auction after the emperor Pertinax was executed. Didius Julianus bid 6,250 drachmas per royal guard and was immediately named emperor of Rome. However, Julianus was executed only two months later, suggesting that he may have been the first-ever victim of the winner's curse (bidding more than the good would cost in a non-auction setting).

Auctions have endured throughout history for several reasons. First, they give sellers a convenient way to find a buyer for something they would like to dispose of. Second, auctions are an excellent way for people to collect difficult-to-find items, such as Beanie Babies or historical memorabilia that have a high value to them personally. Finally, auctions are one of the "purest" markets that exist for goods, in that they bring buyers and sellers into contact to arrive at a mutually agreeable price. As technological advances led to the advent and widespread adoption of the Internet, this ancient form of trade found a new medium.

Online auctions worked in essentially the same way as traditional auctions, the difference being that the auction process occurred over the Internet rather than at a specific geographic location with buyers and sellers physically present. There were three basic categories of online auctions:

1. Business-to-business auctions, typically involving equipment and surplus merchandise.
2. Business-to-consumer auctions, in which businesses sold goods and services to consumers via the Internet. Many such auctions involved companies interested in selling used or discontinued goods, or liquidating unwanted inventory.
3. Person-to-person auctions, which gave interested sellers and buyers the opportunity to engage in competitive bidding.

Online auction operators could generate revenue in four principal ways:

1. Charging sellers for listing their good or service.
2. Charging a commission on all sales.
3. Selling advertising on their Web sites.
4. Selling their own new or used merchandise via the online auction format.

More recently, however, the new revenue-generation option that was growing the most quickly was one that allowed buyers to purchase the desired good without waiting for an auction to close:

5. Selling their own goods or allowing other sellers to offer their goods in a fixed-price format.

Most sites charged sellers either a fee or a commission and sold advertising to companies interested in promoting their goods or services to users of the auction site.

Online Auction Users

Participants in online auctions could be grouped into six categories: (1) bargain hunters, (2) hobbyist/collector buyers, (3) professional buyers, (4) casual sellers, (5) hobbyist/collector sellers, and (6) corporate and power sellers.

Bargain Hunters Bargain hunters viewed online auctions primarily as a form of entertainment; their objective usually was to find a great deal. Bargain hunters were thought to make up only 8 percent of active online users but 52 percent of eBay visitors. To attract repeat visits from bargain hunters, industry observers said sites must appeal to them on both rational and emotional levels, satisfying their need for competitive pricing, the excitement of the search, and the desire for community.

Hobbyist/Collector Buyers Hobbyists and collectors used auctions to search for specific goods that had a high value to them personally. They were very concerned with both price and quality. Collectors prized eBay for its wide variety of product offerings.

Professional Buyers As the legitimacy of online auctions grew, a new type of buyer began to emerge: the professional buyer. Professional buyers covered a broad range of purchasers, from purchasing managers acquiring office supplies to antique and gun dealers purchasing inventory. Like bargain hunters, professional buyers were looking for a way to help contain costs; also, like hobbyists and collectors, some professional buyers were seeking unique items to supplement their inventory. The primary difference between professional buyers and other types, however, was their affiliation with commercial enterprises. With the growth of online auction sites dedicated to business-to-business auctions, professional buyers were becoming an increasingly important element of the online auction landscape.

Casual Sellers Casual sellers included individuals who used eBay as a substitute for a classified ad listing or a garage sale to dispose of items they no longer wanted. While many casual sellers listed only a few items, some used eBay to raise money for some new project.

Hobbyist/Collector Sellers Sellers who were hobbyists or collectors typically dealt in a limited category of goods and looked to eBay as a way to sell selected items in their collections to others who might want them. Items ranged from classic television collectibles, to hand-sewn dolls, to coins and stamps. The hobbyists and collectors used a range of traditional and online outlets to reach their target markets. A number of the sellers used auctions to supplement their retail operations, while others sold exclusively through online auctions and on fixed-price sites such as Half.com.

Corporate and Power Sellers Corporate and power sellers were typically individuals and small to medium-sized businesses that favored eBay as a primary distribution channel for their goods and often sold tens of thousands of dollars' worth of goods every month on the site. To achieve "PowerSeller" status on eBay, an individual had to meet minimum average sales requirements ($1,000 a month for 3 months or 100 items a month, or $12,000 a year or 1,200 items for the prior 12 months), have a feedback rating of at least 100 (98 percent of which had to be positive), and continue to maintain the minimum average monthly sales volume requirements. Some estimates indicated that PowerSellers accounted for over 80 percent of eBay's total business. Individuals who were PowerSellers could often make a full-time job of the endeavor.

As with the evolution of buyers, commercial enterprises were becoming an increasingly important part of the online auction industry. These commercial enterprises generally achieved PowerSeller status relatively rapidly. On eBay, for example, some of the new PowerSellers were familiar names such as IBM, Compaq, and the U.S. Post Office (which sells undeliverable items on eBay under the user name "usps-mrc").

PIERRE OMIDYAR AND THE FOUNDING OF EBAY

Pierre Omidyar was born in Paris, France, to parents who had left Iran decades earlier. The family emigrated to the United States when Pierre's father began a residency at Johns Hopkins University Medical Center. Pierre Omidyar attended Tufts University, where he met his future wife, Pamela Wesley, who came to Tufts from Hawaii to get a degree in biology. Upon graduating in 1988, the couple moved to California, where Omidyar, who had earned a bachelor's degree in computer science, joined Claris, an Apple Computer subsidiary in Silicon Valley, and wrote a widely used graphics application, MacDraw. In 1991, Omidyar left Claris and co-founded Ink Development (later renamed eShop), which became a pioneer in online shopping and was eventually sold to Microsoft in 1996. In 1994, Omidyar joined General Magic as a developer services engineer and remained there until mid-1996, when he left to pursue full-time development of eBay.

Internet folklore has it that eBay was founded solely to allow Pamela to trade Pez dispensers with other collectors. While Pamela was certainly a driving force in launching the initial Web site, Pierre had long been interested in how one could establish a marketplace to bring together a fragmented market. In 1995, he launched the first online auction under the name of Auctionwatch at the domain name of www.eBay.com with the intention of creating a person-to-person trading community based on a democratized, efficient market where everyone could have equal access through the same medium, the Internet. The name *eBay* stood for "electronic Bay area," coined because Pierre's initial concept was to attract neighbors and other interested San Francisco Bay area residents to the site to buy and sell items of mutual interest. The first auctions charged no fees to either buyers or sellers and contained mostly computer equipment (and no Pez dispensers). Pierre's fledgling venture generated $1,000 in revenue the first month and an additional $2,000 the second. Traffic grew rapidly, however, as word about the site spread in the Bay area, a community of collectors emerged, using the site to trade and chat—there were even some marriages that resulted from exchanges in eBay chat rooms.[4]

By February 1996, the traffic at Pierre Omidyar's site had grown so much that his Internet service provider informed him that he would have to upgrade his service. When Omidyar compensated for this by charging a listing fee for the auction, and saw no decrease in the number of items listed, he knew he was on to something. Although he was still working out of his home, Omidyar began looking for a partner and in May asked his friend Jeffrey Skoll to join him in the venture. While Skoll had never cared much about money, his Stanford MBA degree provided the firm with the business background that Omidyar lacked. With Omidyar as the visionary and Skoll as the strategist, the company embarked on a mission to "help people trade practically anything on earth." Their concept for eBay was to "create a place where people could do business just like in the old days—when everyone got to know each other personally, and we all felt we were dealing on a one-to-one basis with individuals we could trust."

In eBay's early days, Pierre Omidyar and Jeff Skoll ran the operation alone, using a single computer to serve all of the pages. Omidyar served as CEO, chief financial officer, and president, while Skoll functioned as co-president and director. It was not long until the partners grew the company to a size that forced them to move out of Pierre's living room, due to the objections of Pamela, and into Jeff's living room. Shortly thereafter, the operations moved into the facilities of a Silicon Valley business incubator for a time until the company settled in its current facilities in San Jose, California. Exhibits 2 and 3 present eBay's recent financial statements.

EBAY'S TRANSITION TO PROFESSIONAL MANAGEMENT

From the beginning, Pierre Omidyar intended to hire a professional manager to serve as the president of eBay: "[I would] let him or her run the company so . . . [I could] go play."[5] In 1997, both Omidyar and Skoll agreed that it was time to locate an experienced professional to function as CEO and president. In late 1997, eBay's headhunters came up with a candidate for the job: Margaret (Meg) Whitman, then general manager for Hasbro Inc.'s preschool division. Whitman had received her BA in economics from Princeton and her MBA from the Harvard Business School; her first job was in brand management at Procter & Gamble. Her experience also included serving as the president and CEO of FTD, as the president of Stride Rite Corporation's Stride Rite Division, and as the senior vice president of marketing for the Walt Disney Company's consumer products division.

When first approached by eBay, Whitman was not especially interested in joining a company that

Exhibit 2 eBay's Income Statements, 2000–2007 ($ in thousands, except per share figures)

	2000	2001	2002	2003	2004	2005	2006	2007
Net revenues	$ 431,424	$ 748,821	$ 1,214,100	$ 2,165,096	$ 3,271,309	$ 4,552,401	$5,969,741	$7,672,329
Cost of net revenues	95,453	134,816	213,876	416,058	614,415	818,104	1,256,792	1,762,972
Gross profit	335,971	614,005	1,000,224	1,749,038	2,656,894	3,734,297	4,712,949	5,909,357
Operating expenses:								
Sales and marketing	166,767	253,474	349,650	567,565	857,874	1,185,929	1,619,857	1,925,393
Product development	55,863	75,288	104,636	159,315	240,647	328,191	494,695	619,727
General and administrative	73,027	105,784	171,785	304,703	415,725	649,529	978,363	1,156,015
Patent litigation expense	—	—	—	29,965	—	—	—	—
Payroll taxes on stock options	2,337	2,442	4,015	9,590	17,479	—	—	—
Amortization of acquired intangibles	1,443	36,591	15,941	50,659	65,927	128,941	197,078	204,104
Impairment of goodwill	—	—	—	—	—	—	—	1,390,938
Merger related costs	1,550	—	—	—	—	—	—	—
Total operating expenses	300,977	473,579	646,027	1,119,797	1,597,652	2,292,590	3,289,993	5,296,177
Income (loss) from operations	34,994	140,426	354,197	629,241	1,059,242	1,441,707	1,422,956	613,180
Interest and other income (expense), net	46,337	41,613	49,209	37,803	77,867	111,099	130,017	154,271
Interest expense	(3,374)	(2,851)	(1,492)	(4,314)	(8,879)	(3,478)	(5,916)	(16,600)
Impairment of certain equity investments	0	(16,245)	(3,781)	(1,230)	—	—	—	—
Income before income taxes and minority interest	77,957	162,943	398,133	661,500	1,128,230	1,549,328	1,547,057	750,851
Provision for income taxes	(32,725)	(80,009)	(145,946)	(206,738)	(343,885)	(467,285)	(421,418)	(402,600)
Minority interests in consolidated companies	3,062	7,514	(2,296)	(7,578)	(6,122)	—	—	—
Net income	$ 48,294	$ 90,448	$ 249,891	$ 447,184	$ 778,223	$ 1,082,043	$1,125,639	$ 348,251
Net income per share:								
Basic	$0.19	$0.34	$0.43	$0.69	$0.59	$0.79	$0.80	$0.26
Diluted	$0.17	0.32	$0.43	$0.67	$0.57	$0.78	$0.79	$0.25
Weighted average shares:								
Basic	251,776	268,971	574,992	638,288	1,319,458	1,361,708	1,399,251	1,358,797
Diluted	280,346	280,595	585,640	656,657	1,367,720	1,393,875	1,425,472	1,376,174

Source: Company financial documents.

Fees and Procedures for Sellers

Buyers on eBay were not charged a fee for bidding on items on the site, but the total fee paid by sellers included an insertion fee and a "final value" fee; sellers could also elect to pay additional fees to promote their listing. Listing, or insertion, fees differed depending on the selling format (auction or fixed-price) and the type of merchandise being sold; fees were lower for books, music, DVDs and movies, and video games than for other items. Insertion fees ranged from $0.10 for auctions with opening bids, minimum values, or reserve prices of between $0.01 and $0.99, to $4.00 for auctions with opening bids, minimum values, or reserve prices of $500 and up.

Final value fees were computed according to a graduated fee schedule in which the percentage fell as the final sales price rose:

Value of Auction	Final Value Fee
Below $25.00	8.75 percent
Between $25.01 and $1,000	8.75 percent of the first $25.00 plus 3.5 percent of the amount between $25.01 and $1,000.00
Over $1,000	8.75 percent of the first $25.00, plus 3.5 percent of the amount between $25.01 and $1,000 plus 1.5 percent of the amount over $1,000

As an example, in a basic auction with no promotion, if the item had a starting price of $500.00 and eventually sold for $1,500, the total fee paid by the seller would be $47.81—the $4.00 insertion fee plus $43.81. This amount was based on a fee structure of 8.75 percent of the first $25 (or $2.19), 3.5 percent of the additional amount between $25.01 and $1,000 (or $34.12), and 1.5 percent of the additional amount between $1,000.01 and $1,500 (or $7.50).

Auction fees varied for special categories of goods. For example, passenger vehicles in eBay Motors were charged a $125 transaction fee when the first successful bid was placed but only $10.00 for power sports vehicles under 50 cc, and a $100 insertion fee for residential and commercial vehicles. In real estate, timeshare properties were charged an insertion fee of $35.00 for auction-style listings or fixed-price listings of up to 10 days and a final value fee of $35.00, while residential and commercial real estate was charged an insertion fee of between $100 and $300 based on the auction style and duration, but no final value fee was charged. For fixed-price sales, a format that allowed sellers to set a specific price for their goods similar to a more traditional retail format, the insertion fees were lower than those for the auction format, capping out at $0.35, but the percentages for final value fees were generally higher, ranging from 6 percent for the first $50 of computers and networking equipment to 15 percent for the first $50 of books, music, DVDs, and video games.

Sellers could also customize items by adding photographs and featuring their item in a gallery. Sellers could upload a photograph to include in the item's description, and items could be showcased in the Gallery section with a catalog of pictures rather than text. Sellers could either include a Gallery picture at no cost, pay an additional $24.95 to ensure that their auction would be listed on the first page of search results, or have their auction featured on eBay's home page for $59.95. The cost to list real estate on the Real Estate home page was also $59.95, but listing a vehicle on eBay Motors' home page cost $99.95.

To make doing business on eBay more attractive to potential sellers, eBay introduced several features. To ensure receiving a minimum price for an auction, the seller could specify an opening bid or set a reserve price. If the bidding did not top the reserve price, the seller was under no obligation to sell the item to the highest bidder and could relist the item free. For items with a reserve price between $0.01 and $199.99, the fee was $2.00; for items over $200, the fee was 1 percent of the reserve price, up to $50. If sellers wished, they could also set a "Buy It Now" price that allowed bidders to pay a set amount for a listed item. The fee for this service ranged from $0.05 for goods with a Buy It Now price for $1.00–$9.99 to $0.25 for a Buy It Now price of over $50. If the Buy It Now price was met, the auction would end immediately.

To register at eBay, sellers were required to provide both a credit card number and bank account information. While eBay acknowledged that these requirements were extreme, the company argued that they helped protect everyone in the community against fraudulent sellers and ensured that sellers were of legal age and were serious about listing the item on eBay.

Fostering Community Affinity

From its founding, eBay considered developing a loyal, vivacious trading community to be a cornerstone of its business model. This community was nurtured through open and honest communication and was built on five basic values that eBay expected its members to honor:

> We believe people are basically good.
>
> We believe everyone has something to contribute.
>
> We believe that an honest, open environment can bring out the best in people.
>
> We recognize and respect everyone as a unique individual.
>
> We encourage you to treat others the way that you want to be treated.[8]

The company recognized that these values could not be imposed by fiat. According to Omidyar, "As much as we at eBay talk about the values and encourage people to live by those values, that's not going to work unless people actually adopt those values. The values are communicated not because somebody reads the Web site and says, 'Hey, this is how we want to treat each other, so I'll just start treating people that way.' The values are communicated because that's how they're treated when they first arrive. Each member is passing those values on to the next member. It's little things, like you receive a note that says, 'Thanks for your business.'"[9] Consistent with eBay's desire to stay in touch with its customers and be responsive to their needs, the company flies in 10 new sellers every few months to hold group meetings known as Voice of the Customer. Another indication of eBay's responsiveness is that 75–80 percent of new features are originally suggested by community members.

To foster a sense of community among eBay users, the company employed tools and tactics designed to promote both business and personal interactions between consumers, to foster trust between bidders and sellers, and to instill a sense of security among traders. Interactions between community members were facilitated through the creation of chat rooms based on personal interests. These chat rooms allowed individuals to learn about their chosen collectibles and to exchange information about items they collected.

To manage the flow of information in the chat rooms, eBay employees went to trade shows and conventions to seek out individuals who had knowledge about and a passion for either a specific collectible or a category of goods. These enthusiasts would act as group leaders or ambassadors.

Feedback Forum

Although personal communication between members fostered a sense of community, as eBay's community grew from "the size of a small village to a large city" additional measures were necessary to ensure a continued sense of trust and honesty among users.[10] One of eBay's primary trust-building mechanisms was the Feedback Forum. The Feedback Forum was designed to build trust among buyers and sellers and to facilitate the establishment of reputations within its community. Feedback Forum encouraged individuals to record comments about their trading partners. From the time the Feedback Forum was originally implemented in 1996 until May 2008, both the buyer and seller were allowed to leave positive, negative, or neutral comments about each other. Individuals could dispute feedback left about them by annotating comments in question, or buyers and sellers could negotiate with each other to resolve problems and to have negative feedback removed from an account.

Users who received a sufficiently negative net feedback rating (typically a −4) had their registrations suspended and were thus unable to bid on or list items for sale. Users could review a person's feedback profile before deciding to bid on an item listed by that person or before choosing payment and delivery methods. Sellers with the highest positive feedback ratings could receive discounts on selling fees. As of November 2008, the seller with the highest feedback rating was Eforcity, which had a feedback rating of over 1 million.

The company believed its Feedback Forum was extremely useful in overcoming users' initial hesitancy about trading over the Internet, since it reduced the uncertainty of dealing with an unknown trading partner. However, there was growing concern among sellers and bidders that feedback could be positively skewed, as many eBayers were afraid to leave negative feedback for fear of unfounded retribution that could damage their carefully built reputations. This concern was heightened by the fact that buyers and sellers could agree to mutually withdraw negative feedback and thus expunge evidence of a failed transaction as if it never occurred.

In response to concerns about the feedback system, in May 2008, in a somewhat controversial move, Donahoe made a significant change to the feedback system so that sellers could no longer leave negative or neutral feedback for buyers. According to Donahoe, the change was intended to enhance honesty in the feedback system and to increase buyer participation on eBay since internal research indicated that receiving negative feedback discouraged buyers from purchasing goods on eBay. However, some smaller sellers felt that this change had essentially robbed them of their voice and made them more vulnerable to buyer fraud. One disgruntled eBay seller voiced these concerns by writing, "I am now open to threats and extortion and unethical pressure from buyers. I have absolutely no viable recourse if a buyer chooses to give me negative feedback and it is unjustified. The feedback system worked when it went both ways, there were mutual pressures to work out any difficulties. Now it is totally one-sided, and the seller can be targeted with unethical behavior by unscrupulous buyers."[11]

Unfortunately, eBay's Feedback Forum was not always sufficient to ensure honesty and integrity among traders. The company estimated that far less than 1 percent of the millions of auctions completed on the site involved some sort of fraud or illegal activity but some users, like Clay Monroe, disagreed. Monroe, a Seattle-area trader of computer equipment, estimated that "ninety percent of the time everybody is on the up and up [but] . . . ten percent of the time you get some jerk who wants to cheat you." Fraudulent or illegal acts perpetrated by sellers included misrepresentation of goods; trading in counterfeit goods or pirated goods that infringed on others' intellectual property rights; failure to deliver goods paid for by buyers; and shill bidding, whereby sellers would use a false bidder to artificially drive up the price of a good. Buyers could manipulate bids by placing an unrealistically high bid on a good to discourage other bidders and then withdraw their bid at the last moment to allow an ally to win the auction at a bargain price. Buyers could also fail to deliver payment on a completed auction.

EBAY'S BUSINESS MODEL

According to eBay's former CEO, Meg Whitman, the company could best be described as a dynamic, self-regulating economy. Its business model was based on creating and maintaining a person-to-person trading community where buyers and sellers from around the globe could readily and conveniently exchange information and goods. The Web site functioned as a value-added facilitator of buyer-seller transactions by providing a supportive infrastructure that enabled buyers and sellers to come together in an efficient and effective manner. Success depended not only on the quality of eBay's infrastructure but also on the quality and quantity of buyers and sellers attracted to the site; in management's view, this entailed maintaining a compelling trading environment, a number of trust and safety programs, a cost-effective and convenient trading experience, and strong community affinity. By developing the eBay brand name and increasing the customer base, eBay endeavored to attract a sufficient number of high-quality buyers and sellers necessary to meet the organization's goals. Each of the segments in eBay's business model was designed to carry zero inventories and could thus operate a marketplace without the need for a traditional sales force.

The eBay business model was built around three operating segments: Marketplaces, Payments, and Communications. As of December 31, 2007, the Marketplaces segment, representing 69.91 percent of eBay's net revenues, was focused on online commerce platforms: eBay.com, considered the core platform of the Marketplaces segment; Rent.com; Shopping.com; StubHub.com; and classified ad Web sites Kijiji, Gumtree.com, LoQUo.com, OpusForum, Marktplaats.nl, and Mobile.de. The Payments segment consisted of eBay's PayPal operations and represented 25.11 percent of eBay's total net revenues. Finally, eBay's Communications segment was comprised of Skype and represented 6.78 percent of eBay's total net revenue (see Exhibit 4). In terms of geography, as of December 31, 2007, only 48.78 percent of eBay's net revenues were derived from the United States (see Exhibit 5).

Marketplaces

The Marketplaces segment was comprised of a diverse set of online commerce platforms that were designed to bring together buyers and sellers on a local, national, and international basis. The largest platform in this segment was the one most people thought of when they heard the name *eBay:* eBay.com. This segment operated with localized Web

Exhibit 4 eBay's Net Revenues by Segment (in thousands)

	2005	2006	2007
Marketplaces	$3,499,137	$4,334,290	$5,363,891
Payments	1,028,455	1,440,530	1,926,616
Communications	24,809	194,921	381,822
Total	$4,552,401	$5,969,741	$7,672,329

Exhibit 5 eBay's Net Revenues by Geography (in thousands)

	2005	2006	2007
U.S.	$2,471,273	$3,108,968	$3,742,670
International	2,081,128	2,860,773	3,929,659
	$4,552,401	$5,969,741	$7,672,329

sites in 28 countries and included both auction-style listings, which represented 60 percent of gross merchandise value in 2007, as well as fixed-price formats including Buy It Now and eBay Stores.

In the second quarter of 2008, 667 million new listings were added to eBay.com worldwide, with more than 7 million listings added each day. Users could trade in more than 50,0000 categories. In the second quarter of 2008, the 10 largest categories and their annualized gross merchandise value totals were as follows:

Category	Annualized Gross Merchandise Value ($ in billions)
eBay Motors	$18.9
Clothing & Accessories	5.3
Consumer Electronics	5.2
Home & Garden	4.2
Computers	3.7
Sports	3.2
Books/Music/Movies	3.0
Collectibles	2.5
Business & Industrial	2.5
Jewelry & Watches	2.2

Despite impressive statistics regarding the sheer size of eBay's online commerce platform, there was evidence to suggest that growth in this key business unit was slowing. In the third quarter of 2008, one key metric, gross merchandise volume, fell for the first time in eBay's history, down 1 percent from the same quarter in 2007 and down 9 percent from the second quarter of 2008. Additionally, while eBay's net transaction revenues, excluding revenues from marketing services and other revenues, in the third quarter were up 1 percent to $1.16 billion from the same quarter in the previous year, this represented a 3 percent decline from the second quarter of 2008. Finally, while the number of eBay stores increased 3 percent, to 534,000, from the third quarter of 2007, this was a decrease of 3 percent from the second quarter of 2008.

Company executives had recognized the eventual maturation of their core segment as early as 2004, when they began expanding the variety of online commerce platforms within the Marketplaces segment. Accordingly the company expanded its offerings to include other classified ad Web sites, Rent.com, Shopping.com, and StubHub.

- *Other classified ad Web sites*—eBay realized that the classifieds market was a potential source of revenue generation for the company. In August 2004, eBay acquired a minority share in Craigslist, a leading provider of online classifieds and forums. However, eBay was particularly concerned about penetrating international markets with classified listings. In February 2005, eBay launched online classified ad Web sites in select international markets. The international Web site was launched under the brand name *Kijiji,* which means "village" in Swahili. As of March 2005, Kijiji was available in more than 50 cities in Canada, China, France, Germany, Italy, and

Japan. Other acquisitions eBay made to supplement the global reach of its online classified operations included Gumtree.com, LoQUo.com, OpusForum, Marktplaats.nl, and Mobile.de.

- *Rent.com*—eBay acquired Rent.com, a leader in the online listing of apartment and rental houses, in the first quarter of 2005. The company viewed this acquisition as a natural extension of its online real estate market. It earned its revenues in this segment from landlords who paid eBay a fee for renters who located their apartments through Rent.com.
- *Shopping.com*—In the second quarter of 2005, eBay completed the acquisition of Shopping.com. Shopping.com, which had more than 50 million unique visitors per month in the United States, the United Kingdom, and France, was the world's third largest Internet shopping destination. In 2008, Shopping.com was a leading company in online comparison shopping and consumer reviews. Retailers paid a fee to eBay for shoppers that were directed to their sites from Shopping.com.
- StubHub—In 2007, eBay acquired StubHub, a leading online marketplace for tickets and concerts. StubHub was seen as a strong fit with eBay's existing tickets business.

These businesses had proved to be successful additions to eBay's Marketplaces segment and were recognized as key to the company's future growth. The growth strategy for the Marketplaces segment was focused on increasing the gross merchandise value on eBay.com and expanding into additional adjacent markets as had been done with the acquisition of StubHub.com. Executives planned to increase traffic to the site through advertising and promotions while investing in the site to enhance the buyer experience and seller economics; improve customer support and the company's Trust and Safety initiatives; expand product offerings into new geographies, formats, and categories; and test new buyer retention and seller pricing strategies.

Payments

The Payments segment included PayPal and Bill Me Later. Acquired in 2002 to facilitate person-to-person credit card payments, PayPal allowed eBay to make credit card payment a "seamless and integrated part of the trading experience."[12] By 2008, PayPal had expanded its original business model to include payments throughout the businesses in eBay's Marketplaces division, as well as facilitating payments for any online merchant, and had more than 57 million active, registered accounts, up from 41 million accounts in 2005. In expanding its business model, PayPal also expanded its geographic reach: individuals and businesses in more than 190 markets worldwide could make and receive payments through the service.

PayPal offered three types of accounts—Personal, Business, and Premier. Buyers benefited from PayPal as it allowed them to make payments without disclosing personal financial information to individual online merchants. Additionally, PayPal offered a Buyer Protection Program for certain qualified purchases on eBay that would reimburse buyers who were victims of fraudulent transactions. Sellers benefited from PayPal by having the ability to process online transactions without having to make a significant investment in software and by paying lower fees relative to other merchant accounts. Also, PayPal's Seller Protection Program could reduce the risks associated with unauthorized credit card use and fraudulent chargebacks.

PayPal earned revenue in several ways, including receiving fees from business and premier account holders who received funds, merchants who used PayPal's online payment processing services, users who withdrew money to non-U.S. bank accounts, and users who converted funds to foreign currencies. Additionally PayPal generated revenues through the PayPal Buyer Credit Program, operated in conjunction with GE Money Bank; PayPal ATM/debit cards; and the PayPal Plus credit card and eBay MasterCard issued by GE Money Bank. As of the third quarter of 2008, the majority of PayPal revenues were earned from payments associated with eBay Marketplaces transactions, but PayPal president Scott Thompson estimated that by the end of 2009, the company would derive more of its total payment volume from its merchant services than from eBay transactions.

The revenue growth in the Payments segment had been strong from 2005 to 2007, with the unit experiencing 40 percent growth from 2005 to 2006 and an additional 34 percent from 2006 to 2007. The merchant services operations within the Payments segment were especially rapidly growing, experiencing 59 percent growth from 2006 to 2007 and growing from 35 percent of the Payments segment's total payment volume in 2006 to 42 percent in 2007. The percentage of segment revenues derived from international sources was growing as well, with an increase from 36 percent of total net transaction revenues in 2005 to 42 percent in 2007. The company planned to continue to grow PayPal's user base and revenues by continuing to expand the usage of PayPal on Marketplaces transactions, including those on eBay and in adjacent markets; continuing to build a global network of merchants who used PayPal for the payment processing; and expanding the breadth of financial products offered.

Recognizing the growing potential of the financial services and payment processing operations, eBay expanded its presence in this market by purchasing Bill Me Later, a provider of instant credit to e-commerce customers, for $945 million in October 2008. Interestingly, one of the early investors in Bill Me Later was Amazon.com, one of eBay's primary rivals. Bill Me Later used a proprietary credit algorithm based on criteria including an individual's credit score, credit outstanding, and status with credit agencies to determine, in less than three seconds, whether to grant credit to that individual for a specific purchase. The purchase of Bill Me Later allowed eBay to expand its operations into consumer credit, rather than merely offering credit through partners. In 2008, Bill Me Later had more than 4 million customers, serving a diverse range of stores from Amazon.com to the Apple Store online to Zappos.com and was expected to finance over $1 billion in online purchases, resulting in $125 million in revenues, with a projected growth rate of 20 percent in 2009. However, Bill Me Later was not expected to be profitable on a net income basis until the end of 2009, at the earliest.

Despite the rapid growth of PayPal, some of the company's safety policies had been drawing increasing criticism from eBay and PayPal users. One of the policies announced in February 2008 that sellers found particularly troubling was that eBay would hold payments associated with high-risk transactions for up to 21 days. The factors that would determine whether a transaction was high-risk included the length of time a seller had been on eBay, the seller's feedback score, and the amount of the transaction. The company felt that its transaction hold policy would enhance security by making it easier for the company to issue refunds in case of fraudulent transactions. PayPal estimated that this new policy would affect less than 5 percent of eBay transactions and that the impact would largely be on new or untested sellers. Specifically, PayPal stated that sellers with a dissatisfied buyer rate of less than 5 percent who had been on eBay for more than six months and had a feedback score of higher than 100 would never have their funds held. If PayPal did freeze a transaction, the funds would be released after the buyer left positive feedback, three days after the item's confirmed delivery, or 21 days after the transaction if there were no disputes filed. Another policy that was troubling to sellers was that eBay required new sellers in some categories to have a PayPal account or a merchant credit card account to sell on eBay. While many eBay sellers understood these policies, some, such as Bob Lee, who ran PowerSellersUnite, felt that the new policies were helpful for buyers but not sellers. Lee said, "A seller is at risk of being taken advantage of by the buyer. Not having access to revenue, and having to wait for a buyer to leave positive feedback, leaves sellers in the lurch. PayPal and eBay are not allowing sellers to play on a level playing field."[13]

Communications

The Communications segment was based on Skype. In September 2005, eBay had acquired Skype Technologies, a global Internet communications company, for $3.1 billion in an effort to increase the company's global presence and, according to Meg Whitman, to facilitate communication between buyers and sellers on the eBay.com platform. Skype allowed users to make free Skype-to-Skype voice and video calls and to send instant messages. Skype earned revenues by charging users to place calls from Skype to landline and mobile phones, and by charging for services such as text messaging, voice mail, and call forwarding. Users could purchase a subscription plan that would provide them with an unlimited number of calls.

At the time of the acquisition, Skype had 54 million members in more than 225 countries and eBay believed that this move would allow the company to develop an enhanced global marketplace and payments platform.[14] In 2007, Skype sought to expand its user base by forming an agreement with Wal-Mart stores in the United States to sell Skype-certified handsets and prepaid cards, forming an agreement with MySpace, a popular social networking site, and further integrating Skype with PayPal by launching Skype Send Money, which allowed users to send and receive funds using PayPal through the Skype platform. These growth initiatives proved successful. In the third quarter of 2008, Skype added 32 million registered users, for a global total of 370 million users, and reported revenue growth of 46 percent over the same quarter the previous year.

The growth strategy eBay planned for Skype was keyed on securing new users and encouraging users to upgrade to premium services and subscriptions. The company also intended to continue to encourage users of the eBay.com marketplace to use Skype for communicating between buyers and sellers in an effort to enhance the speed of communication between these parties and thereby reduce friction in online shopping.

Despite Skype's impressive growth and the potential benefits that eBay felt could be gained through further integration of Skype and the eBay trading platform, Skype's future with eBay was unclear heading into 2009. A number of analysts felt that eBay had never been able to capture the synergies Whitman hoped Skype would generate with eBay and pointed to eBay's 2007 writedown of $1.4 billion of the value of Skype as evidence of the company's inability to maximize Skype's potential. When Donahoe replaced Whitman in 2008, he added additional fuel to the speculation regarding Skype's future when he stated that the company's ownership of Skype would be evaluated. Analysts who supported the potential sale of Skype speculated that Microsoft or Google would be likely buyers.

HOW EBAY COMPARED WITH RIVALS

Auction sites varied in a number of respects, including their inventory, the bidding process, extra services and fees, technical support, functionality, and sense of community. Since its inception, eBay had gone to great lengths to make its Web site intuitive, easy to use by both buyers and sellers, and reliable. Efforts to ensure ease of use ranged from narrowly defining categories (to allow users to quickly locate desired products) to introducing services designed to personalize a user's eBay experience, such as My eBay. My eBay gave users centralized access to confidential, current information regarding their trading activities. From their My eBay page, users could view information pertaining to their current account balances with eBay, their feedback rating, the status of any auctions in which they were participating (as either buyer or seller), and auctions in favorite categories.

Among the most important competitive factors in both the online auction and the general e-commerce industries were the ability to attract buyers, the volume of transactions, the selection of goods, customer service and security, and brand recognition. In positioning its offerings vis-à-vis competitors, eBay's advertising campaigns ranged from focusing on the expansive amount of product variety offered by the company to the thrill shoppers could get from winning an auction for a hard-to-find item. In addition to factors such as variety and brand image, eBay was also attempting to differentiate itself from its competition along several other dimensions: sense of community, system reliability, reliability of delivery and payment, Web site convenience and accessibility, low levels of service fees, and efficient information exchange.

Early in its history, eBay's main rivals could be considered classified ads in newspapers, garage sales, flea markets, collectibles shows, local auction houses, and liquidators. As eBay's product mix and selling techniques evolved, the company's range of competitors did as well. The broadening of eBay's product mix beyond collectibles to include practical household items, office equipment, toys, and so on brought the company into more direct competition with brick-and-mortar retailers, import/export companies, and catalog and mail order companies. Further, with the acquisition of Half.com, the introduction of eBay stores, and the growing percentage of fixed-price and Buy it Now sales as a percentage of eBay's revenue, eBay considered itself to be competing in a broad sense with a number of other online retailers, such as Wal-Mart, Kmart, Target, Sears, JCPenney, and Office Depot. In competing with these larger sellers, eBay began to adopt some of their tools, such as the use of gift certificates. The company also felt that it was competing with a number of specialty retailers, such as Christie's (antiques), KB Toys (toys), Blockbuster (movies), Dell (computers), Foot Locker (sporting goods), Ticketmaster (tickets), and Home Depot (tools).[15] Exhibit 6 displays eBay's customer service rankings as compared to a variety of rivals.

Exhibit 6 Comparative Customer Service Rankings, Selected Web Sites (scores out of 100)

Company/Sector	2000	2001	2002	2003	2004	2005	2006	2007
Internet retail	**78**	**77**	**83**	**84**	**80**	**81**	**83**	**83**
1-800-Flowers.com	69	76	78	76	79	77	77	NA
Amazon.com	84	84	88	88	84	87	87	88
Barnesandnoble.com	77	82	87	86	87	87	87	88
Buy.com	78	78	80	80	80	81	80	81
eBay	80	82	82	84	80	81	80	81
Priceline.com*	66	69	71	71	73	72	72	73
uBid.com	NM	67	69	70	73	73	73	74
Department and discount stores	**72**	**75**	**74**	**76**	**74**	**75**	**74**	**73**
Dillards	72	75	75	75	77	76	75	76
Kmart	67	74	70	70	67	70	70	NA
Macy's	69	69	71	71	74	74	71	75
Sears	71	73	76	75	73	74	73	73
Target	73	77	78	77	75	75	78	77
Wal-Mart	73	75	74	75	73	72	72	68
Specialty retail stores	**76**	**73**	**74**	**74**	**75**	**74**	**75**	**75**
Best Buy	NM	NM	NM	72	72	71	76	74
Circuit City	NM	NM	NM	73	72	70	69	71

*Priceline.com is included in the ACSI in the Internet Travel industry.

Source: American Customer Satisfaction Index, www.theacsi.org.

Management at eBay saw traditional brick-and-mortar competitors as inefficient because their fragmented local and regional nature made it expensive and time-consuming for buyers and sellers to meet, exchange information, and complete transactions. Moreover, they suffered from three other deficiencies: (1) they tended to offer limited variety and breadth of selection as compared to the millions of items available on eBay, (2) they often had high transactions costs, and (3) they were information-inefficient in the sense that buyers and sellers lacked a reliable and convenient means of setting prices for sales or purchases. Management saw eBay's online auction format as competitively superior to these rivals because (1) it facilitated buyers and sellers meeting, exchanging information, and conducting transactions; (2) it allowed buyers and sellers to bypass traditional intermediaries and trade directly, thus lowering costs; (3) eBay provided global reach to a greater selection and a broader base of participants; (4) the eBay format permitted trading at all hours and provided continuously updated information; and (5) it fostered a sense of community among individuals with mutual interests.

Competitors for eBay's services ranged from brick-and-mortar discount retailers such as Wal-Mart to auction houses such as Christie's; however, many analysts agreed that the most significant competitors to eBay included e-tailers such as Amazon.com and Overstock.com as well as auction sites such as uBid.com

Amazon.com

Amazon.com's business strategy was to "Offer Earth's Biggest Selection and seek to be Earth's most customer-centric company for three primary customer sets: consumer customers, seller customers and developer customers."[16] With its customer base of 35 million users in more than 220 countries and a very well-known brand name, Amazon.com was considered the closest overall competitive threat to eBay, especially as eBay expanded its business model beyond its traditional auction services. Amazon was created in July 1995 as an online bookseller and rapidly transitioned into a full-line, one-stop-shopping retailer with a product offering that included books, music, toys, electronics, tools and hardware, lawn and

Exhibit 7 Amazon.com's Income Statement, 2005–2007 ($ in millions)

	2005	2006	2007
Net sales	$8,490	$10,711	$14,835
Cost of sales	6,451	8,255	11,482
Gross profit	2,039	2,456	3,353
Operating expenses:			
Fulfillment	745	937	1,292
Marketing	198	263	344
Technology and content	451	662	818
General and administrative	166	195	235
Other operating expense, net	47	10	9
Total operating expenses	1,607	2,067	2,698
Income from operations	432	389	655
Interest income	44	59	90
Interest expense	(92)	(78)	(77)
Other income (expense), net	2	(4)	(1)
Remeasurements and other	42	11	(7)
Total non-operating income (expense)	(4)	(12)	5
Income before income taxes	428	377	660
Provision for income taxes	95	187	184
Income before cumulative effect of change in accounting principle	333	190	476
Cumulative effect of change in accounting principle	26	—	—
Net income	$ 359	$ 190	$ 476

Source: Amazon.com, 2007 annual report, p. 11.

patio products, video games, software, and a mall of boutiques (called z-shops). Amazon was the Internet's number one music, video, and book retailer; as of the third quarter of 2008, media represented 62 percent of Amazon's sales. Additionally, in 2008 Amazon had Web sites in seven countries, including the United States, the United Kingdom, Germany, Canada, France, Japan, and China, with international revenues representing approximately 45 percent of the company's net sales in 2007, a percentage that had been relatively stable since 2005. One of the distinctive features customers appreciated about Amazon.com was the extensive reviews available for each item. These product reviews were written both by professionals and by regular users who had purchased a specific product. The company's 2007 net income was more than $476 million, which was an increase of over 250 percent from 2006 (as seen in Exhibit 7). Exhibit 8 shows Amazon's balance sheet data.

Amazon's strategy was centered on servicing customers by providing them with a broad selection of merchandise, low prices, and convenience. While many companies made similar claims, Amazon consistently invested in developing new products, partnerships, and service offerings to support the basic tenets of its strategy. To increase the selection of products available to customers, Amazon offered merchandise in a broad array of categories, hosted Web stores for sellers such as Target, operated specialty Web sites such as Shopbop.com and Endless.com (fashion Web sites) and operated the Amazon Marketplace. To help keep prices low, Amazon regularly offered free or low-cost shipping deals; allowed customers to use Amazon Prime, which provided free two-day shipping on millions of items in the United States, for a nominal fee of $79 annually; and allowed sellers to offer used merchandise through the Marketplace. Finally, to expand its product offerings

Exhibit 8 Amazon.com's Balance Sheet, 2005–2007 ($ in millions)

	2006	2007
Assets		
Current assets:		
Cash and cash equivalents	$1,022	$2,539
Marketable securities	997	573
Inventories	877	1,200
Accounts receivable, net and other	399	705
Deferred tax assets	78	147
Total current assets	3,373	5,164
Fixed assets, net	457	543
Deferred tax assets	199	260
Goodwill	195	222
Other assets	139	296
Total assets	$4,363	$6,485
Liabilities and Stockholders' Equity		
Current liabilities:		
Accounts payable	$1,816	$2,795
Accrued expenses and other	716	919
Total current liabilities	2,532	3,714
Long-term debt	1,247	1,282
Other long-term liabilities	153	292
Outstanding shares 416 and 414	4	4
Treasury stock, at cost	(252)	(500)
Additional paid-in capital	2,517	3,063
Accumulated other comprehensive income (loss)	(1)	5
Accumulated deficit	(1,837)	(1,375)
Total stockholders' equity	431	1,197
Total liabilities and stockholders' equity	$4,363	$6,485

Source: Amazon.com, 2007 annual report, p. 11.

and enhance customer convenience, Amazon had developed a number of service offerings, including the ability for customers to download books through Amazon's Kindle device or Audible.com (acquired in 2008), as well as music and videos.

Amazon's Marketplace was the most direct competitor to eBay, as it allowed individuals and companies to list their new and used goods alongside those offered by Amazon for any given product; customers could choose to buy new from Amazon or to buy new or used from another seller. Amazon did not charge sellers a listing fee but did charge a transaction fee that ranged from $0.80 to $1.35, which was waived for Pro Merchant Subscribers, who paid $39.99 a month, and a commission called a referral fee based on the type of good sold. Referral fees ranged from 6 percent for computers to 20 percent for jewelry and other items. In return for these relatively high commissions, Amazon took care of order and payment processing and after-sale service. If sellers chose, they could even store their merchandise in one of Amazon's 19 fulfillment centers located worldwide, and, for a fee, Amazon would pack and ship their orders directly to their customers. As on eBay, buyers were able to rate sellers. Sellers who did not maintain a sufficient rating, and those who had customer service problems (e.g., having to issue an excessive amount of refunds) or who had guarantee claims filed against them, could be charged higher fees or no longer allowed to sell on Amazon. Despite these higher fees, there was evidence that Amazon was luring sellers away from eBay, especially in the wake of increasing seller dissatisfaction with changes in eBay's policies and fees. In August 2008, Gene Munster, an analyst for Piper Jaffray, estimated that third parties had sold $6 billion in goods on Amazon over the last 12 months. While this was only one-tenth the value of goods sold on eBay, Munster predicted that if Amazon was willing to cut its fees, it could capture more market share from eBay.[17]

Overstock.com

Overstock.com was another competitor that was beginning to compete more directly with eBay, especially as the latter increasingly focused on fixed-price selling. Founded in 1999 in Salt Lake City, the company was conceived as an online outlet mall where customers could find brand-name merchandise at deep discounts and sellers could liquidate their excess inventory. In 1999, Overstock offered fewer than 100 products, but by 2008 the company offered a total of 783,000 products (720,000 in the books, music, movies, and games [BMMG] category and 63,000 in non-BMMG). Over 99 percent of the company's sales were made in the United States, and Overstock earned revenues from two main sources: direct sales (those fulfilled from Overstock's own warehouse) and fulfillment partner sales (which involved third parties selling their merchandise on Overstock's Web sites). As can be seen in Exhibit 9, despite the company's growth efforts, total revenue had declined from 2005–2007 as the company struggled with its net income.

In an attempt to build revenue growth, Overstock had expanded its business model several times. In 2004, Overstock launched an auction site to compete with eBay. As on eBay, sellers listed the opening bid price, the duration of the auction, and the Make It Mine price (which was optional) and were charged a listing fee (ranging from $0.10 to $3.15) and a closing fee (3 percent for $0.01–$25.00, $0.75 plus 2 percent of the value over $25.01 for auctions closing with a value of between $25.01 and $1,000, and $20.25 plus 1 percent of the value over $1,000.01 for auctions closing with a value over $1,000). Sellers could pay additional fees if they wanted a reserve price auction or could upgrade their listing with options such as a bold or highlighted font.

In 2007, the company launched an automobile marketplace named Overstock Cars. Overstock Cars served as an intermediary that connected customers to local dealers and provided them with a fixed, no-haggle price. The site also used a proprietary search function named Clearance Lot, to help bargain hunters identify cars offered at the greatest discount. In 2008, Overstock expanded this business model to real estate; like Overstock Cars, Overstock Real Estate connected potential buyers with realtors in their local areas and used a proprietary algorithm to

Exhibit 9 Overstock.com's Income Statement, 2005–2007 ($ in thousands)

	2005	2006	2007
Revenue			
Direct revenue	$324,875	$ 303,202	$195,622
Fulfillment partner revenue	474,441	484,948	564,539
Total revenue	799,316	788,150	760,161
Cost of goods sold			
Direct	282,383	284,943	164,368
Fulfillment partner	400,057	408,407	468,222
Total cost of goods sold	682,440	693,350	632,590
Gross profit	$116,876	$ 94,800	$127,571
Operating expenses			
Sales and marketing	$ 77,155	$ 70,897	$ 55,458
Technology	27,901	65,158	59,453
General and administrative	33,043	46,837	41,976
Restructuring	—	5,674	12,283
Total operating expenses	138,099	188,566	169,170
Operating loss	(21,223)	(93,766)	(41,599)
Interest income, net	(270)	3,566	4,788
Interest expense	(5,582)	(4,765)	(4,188)
Other (expense) income, net	4,728	81	(92)
Loss from continuing operations	(22,347)	(94,884)	(41,091)
Discontinued operations:			
Loss from discontinued operations	(2,571)	(6,882)	(3,924)
Net loss	$ (24,918)	$(101,766)	$ (45,015)

Source: Overstock.com, 2007 annual report.

Exhibit 10 Overstock.com's Balance Sheet, 2006–2007 ($ in thousands)

	2006	2007
Assets		
Current assets:		
Cash and cash equivalents	$126,965	$101,394
Marketable securities	—	46,000
Cash, cash equivalents and marketable securities	126,965	147,394
Accounts receivable, net	11,638	12,304
Note receivable	6,702	1,506
Inventories, net	20,274	25,933
Prepaid inventory	2,241	3,572
Prepaid expense	7,473	7,572
Current assets of held for sale subsidiary	4,718	—
Total current assets	180,011	198,281
Property and equipment, net	56,198	27,197
Goodwill	2,784	2,784
Other long-term assets, net	578	86
Notes receivable	—	4,181
Long-term assets of held for sale subsidiary	16,594	—
Total assets	$256,165	$232,529
Liabilities and Stockholders' Equity		
Current liabilities:		
Accounts payable	$ 66,039	$ 70,648
Accrued liabilities	40,142	52,598
Capital lease obligations, current	5,074	3,796
Current liabilities of held for sale subsidiary	3,684	—
Total current liabilities	114,939	127,042
Capital lease obligations, non-current	3,983	—
Other long-term liabilities	—	3,034
Convertible senior notes	75,279	75,623
Total liabilities	194,201	205,699
Total stockholders' equity	61,964	26,830
Total liabilities and stockholders' equity	$256,165	$232,529

Source: Overstock.com, 2007 annual report.

help buyers locate properties that might represent an especially good value.

uBid.com

Founded in April 1997, uBid.com launched an initial public offering on the NASDAQ in December 1998. The company's mission statement was to "be the most recognized and trusted business-to-consumer marketplace, consistently delivering exceptional value and service to its customers and supplier partners."[18] As of 2005, uBid believed that its core values of integrity, agility, execution, caring, and innovation would allow the company to deliver competitive success in the online auction industry and to build valuable relationships with its customers, employees, and suppliers.[19] As such, uBid considered itself to be in direct competition with eBay, although the company had difficulty denting the portion of eBay's business that was derived from large corporations and smaller companies wanting to sell their products through an auction format. As a company, uBid had experienced increased revenues almost every year since its inception, but it had never captured the share of the auction market that its founders hoped was possible, although it at one time had a 14.7 percent share of revenues in the online auction market. In mid-2000, uBid was sold to CGMI Networks, and then it was sold again to Petters Group Worldwide in 2003. With each sale, the number of workers employed by uBid fell and the product mix was changed in an attempt to find a niche market that would insulate the company from the competitive power of eBay.

Despite the company's challenges, in 2007 uBid claimed to have more than 3,500 certified merchants who sold to more than 6 million registered uBid users. The company's business model centered on offering brand-name merchandise (often refurbished and closeout goods) at a deep discount in a relatively broad range of categories from leading brand-name manufacturers such as Sony, Hewlett-Packard, IBM, Compaq, AMD, Minolta, and 1,000-plus additional suppliers. Categories included Computer and Office; Consumer Electronics; Music, Movies & Games; Jewelry & Gifts; Travel & Events; Home & Garden; Sports; Toys & Hobbies; Apparel; Collectibles; and Everything Else. The merchandise was offered in both an online auction format (in which prices started at $1.00) and through uBid's fixed-price superstore. The merchandise was sourced from corporate partners and from uBid's own operations, which included a 400,000-square-foot warehouse and refurbishment center; from parent company Petters Group Worldwide; and from small and medium-sized companies that were members of uBid's Certified Merchant Program.

In 2008, uBid.com launched a site to compete directly with Overstock.com. Similar to Overstock.com, uBid's site, named RedTag.com, worked with manufacturers, distributors, and retailers of brand-name products to provide an outlet for their excess merchandise. RedTag planned to distinguish its offerings from rivals by offering $1.95 shipping and by providing a 30-day money back guarantee on purchases.

EBAY'S NEW CHALLENGES

Throughout its history, eBay faced each new challenge with an eye on its founding values and an ear for community members. As Pierre Omidyar stated in 2001, "What we do have to be cautious of, as we grow, is that our core is the personal trade, because the values are communicated person-to-person. It can be easy for a big company to start to believe that it's responsible for its success. Our success is really based on our members' success. They're the ones who have created this, and they're the ones who will create it in the future. If we lose sight of that, then we're in big trouble."[20] The company had historically applied this perspective in response to significant customer concerns regarding the growing presence of corporate sellers on eBay.

Omidyar and Whitman recognized the importance of eBay's culture and were aware of the potential impact rapid growth and the evolution of the product line could have on this valued asset. When asked about the importance of the culture, Omidyar said, "If we lose that, we've pretty much lost everything."[21] Whitman agreed with the importance of eBay's culture, but she did not see the influx of larger retailers and liquidators as a significant problem. Even as these sellers grew to account for 5 percent of eBay's total business in 2004 (from 1 percent in 2001), these large sellers received no favorable treatment; Whitman stated, "There are no special deals. I am passionate about creating this level playing field."[22]

However, there was significant doubt among the eBay community as to whether eBay's newest CEO, John Donahoe, shared these values or whether he would focus on improving internal efficiencies at the expense of the company's culture. One eBay staffer admitted that employees feared for eBay's culture since, when Meg Whitman was leading the company, employees regularly bought and sold products on eBay and discussed this as a badge of honor. However, in the holiday season of 2007, eBay's mailroom was reportedly receiving a dismaying number of packages from Amazon.com.

Heading into the 2008 holiday season, eBay faced two fundamental questions:

1. As eBay's business model evolved to include more fixed-price sales in an effort to combat the saturation of its domestic market, how could the

Exhibit 11 eBay's Stock Price Performance, December 2007–November 2008

Source: www.bigcharts.com, November 14, 2008.

company transfer its competitive advantage in the online auction industry to the more general area of online retail?

2. How could the company reinvigorate growth in its core market, especially in the face of a global economic slowdown and growing dissatisfaction among smaller eBay sellers? Given the slowing growth in the company's core market, should the company be concerned with the growing dissatisfaction among smaller eBay sellers? If so, what could it do to remedy this without alienating the larger sellers?

Downgrades of eBay's stock seemed to indicate that analysts were not as optimistic about eBay's future growth potential as they once had been, and some questioned whether eBay could extend its dominance to the general online retailing segment. While some industry experts predicted that eBay could make the transition, others suggested that eBay might consider selling its online auction operations and focusing its attentions on PayPal. Donahoe emphatically rejected this potential course of action, but when the company announced that it would lay off more than 1,000 employees in 2008, it was becoming increasingly clear that something had to change. These concerns were clearly reflected in eBay's stock price, as can be seen in Exhibit 11.

Endnotes

1 Richard Waters, "eBay Ready to Sell Skype If Strong Synergies Prove Elusive," *Financial Times,* April 18, 2008, www.ft.com/cms/s/0/13482a26-0ce1-11dd-86df-0000779fd2ac.html?nclick_check=1 (accessed November 1, 2008).

2 E. Maltby, "Has eBay Hit Its Twilight?" Money.cnn.com, October 17, 2008 (accessed October 28, 2008).

3 Blog poster "Software Engineer in San Jose," GlassDoor.com, http://blog.glassdoor.com/2008/10/07/ebay-layoffs-%e2%80%93-is-donahoe-next/ (accessed on November 4, 2008).

4 Quentin Hardy, "The Radical Philanthropist," *Forbes,* May 1, 2000, p. 118.

5 "Billionaires of the Web," *Business 2.0,* June 1999.

[6] eBay press release, May 7, 1998.
[7] Brad Stone, "Ebay President Is 'A Big Fan of Breaking Patterns,'" *International Herald Tribune,* February 20, 2007.
[8] eBay.com, http://pages.ebay.com/community/people/values.html, November, 11, 2008.
[9] "Q&A with eBay's Meg Whitman," *BusinessWeek E.Biz,* December 3, 2001.
[10] Claire Tristram, "'Amazoning' Amazon," Contextmag.com, November 1999.
[11] Ed Foster, "Negative Feedback on eBay's Feedback Changes," www.gripe2ed.com/scoop/story/2008/5/23/91215/5053 (accessed November 11, 2008).
[12] Company press release, May 18, 1999.
[13] Kathleen Ryan O'Connor, "eBay's PayPal Funds Freeze Plan Draws Fire," Money.com, February 11, 2008 (accessed November 13, 2008).
[14] Company press release, September 12, 2005.
[15] eBay, 2001 annual report.
[16] Amazon.com, 2007 annual report, p. 11.
[17] Larry Dignan, "Amazon: Still Trailing eBay in Third Party Sales, But . . . ," www.zdnet.com, August 11, 2008 (accessed November 5, 2008).
[18] uBid.com, www.ubid.com/about/companyinfo.asp, December 18, 2005.
[19] Ibid.
[20] "Q&A with eBay's Pierre Omidyar," *BusinessWeek E.Biz,* December 3, 2001.
[21] "The People's Company," *BusinessWeek E.Biz,* December 3, 2001.
[22] "Queen of the Online Flea Market," Economist.com, December 30, 2003.

CASE 16 Loblaw Companies Limited: Preparing for Wal-Mart Supercenters[1]

Kenneth G. Hardy
University of Western Ontario

Veronika Papyrina
University of Western Ontario

In early February of 2007, Loblaw Companies Limited (Loblaw), the market share leader among Canadian supermarket operators, announced that it would write down its earnings by about $900 million. This revaluation was related to the company's decision to close 19 of its Provigo grocery stores in Quebec in 2007. Retail analysts suggested that poor operations at Provigo stores as well as stiff competition from Metro Inc. and Sobeys had negatively affected Loblaw's performance. These analysts also speculated that Loblaw's executives had diverted their attention from problems at Provigo because they were concerned with competition from three Wal-Mart Supercenters that had opened in Ontario in the fall of 2006. "Fundamentally, there is a structural weakness in the profitability of our business in Quebec, and the impairment reflects that," said Loblaw's executive chairman, Galen Weston Jr.[2]

As a result of the Provigo write-down, Loblaw expected to report a loss of up to $503 million for the fourth quarter of 2006. It was the first quarterly loss reported by Loblaw in 19 years, and its first annual loss in more than 20 years. In the fourth quarter of 2006, revenue was $6.8 billion but operating income before the expected write-down had decreased by $289 million from the previous year to $105 million. Operating margin before the write-down declined from 6 percent to 1.5 percent in the comparable period of 2005, because of increased labor costs, higher markdowns as the company liquidated excess inventory and other costs, such as information technology investments. One of the retail analysts noted that Loblaw's write-down was the largest that a retailer in Canada had ever taken, and he downgraded its stock even though Loblaw's sales for the full year were $28.6 billion, or 3.7 percent ahead of its 2005 sales (see Exhibit 1).

Loblaw's difficulties seemed to go beyond the closure of the unprofitable Provigo stores and soft financial results. In a conference call with analysts just a few hours after reporting the write-down of Provigo's assets, executive chairman Galen Weston Jr. acknowledged other problems. He said that the company's research showed that consumers were not satisfied with the offering of The Real Canadian Superstores and thought that its prices were too high. Weston also added that the store employees were not able to handle customer matters properly because they were occupied with stocking issues and getting products from the backrooms. Inventory problems, such as stale-dated food and empty shelves, had apparently become common in The Real Canadian Superstores since Loblaw had started a reorganization of its distribution system in 2004. Loblaw had also undertaken a significant repositioning of The Real Canadian Superstores and Loblaws food stores in anticipation of Wal-Mart Canada's entry into food retailing. Indeed, in the fall of 2006 Wal-Mart had built a large retail food Supercenter in three test cities in Ontario—and it appeared to be prepared for rapid expansion.

Exhibit 1 Loblaw's Annual Financials for the Period of 2002–2006 ($ millions except where otherwise indicated)

	2006	2005	2004	2003	2002
Operating Results					
Sales	**28,640**	27,627	26,030	25,066	22,953
Sales excluding the impact of VIEs[1]	**28,257**	27,212	26,030	25,066	22,953
Adjusted EBITDA[2]	**1,892**	2,132	2,125	1,881	1,671
Operating income	**289**	1,401	1,652	1,467	1,303
Adjusted operating income	**1,326**	1,600	1,652	1,488	1,317
Interest expense	**259**	252	239	196	161
Net (loss) earnings	**(219)**	746	968	845	728
Financial Position					
Working capital	**675**	539	290	356	320
Fixed assets	**8,055**	7,785	7,113	6,390	5,557
Goodwill	**794**	1,587	1,621	1,607	1,599
Total assets	**13,486**	13,761	12,949	12,113	11,047
Net debt	**3,891**	3,901	3,828	3,707	2,932
Shareholders' equity	**5,441**	5,886	5,414	4,690	4,082
Cash Flow					
Cash flows from operating activities	**1,180**	1,489	1,443	1,032	998
Free cash flow	**70**	103	(24)	(437)	(208)
Capital investment	**937**	1,156	1,258	1,271	1,079
Per Common Share ($)					
Basic net (loss) earnings	**(0.80)**	2.72	3.53	3.07	2.64
Adjusted basic net earnings	**2.72**	3.35	3.48	3.10	2.68
Dividend rate at year end	**0.84**	0.84	0.76	0.60	0.48
Cash flows from operating activities	**4.31**	5.43	5.26	3.75	3.61
Capital investment	**3.42**	4.22	4.59	4.62	3.91
Book value	**19.85**	21.48	19.74	17.07	14.79
Market price at year end	**48.79**	56.37	72.02	67.85	54.00
Financial Ratios					
Adjusted EBITDA margin (%)	**6.70**	7.80	8.20	7.50	7.30
Operating margin (%)	**1.00**	5.10	6.30	5.90	5.70
Adjusted operating margin (%)	**4.70**	5.90	6.30	5.90	5.70
Return on average total assets (%)	**2.30**	11.20	14.20	13.90	13.80
Return on average shareholders' equity (%)	**(3.90)**	13.20	19.20	19.30	19.00
Interest coverage	**1.00**	5.10	6.40	6.40	6.80
Net debt to equity	**0.72**	0.66	0.71	0.79	0.72
Cash flows from operating activities to net debt	**0.30**	0.38	0.38	0.28	0.34
Price/net earnings ratio at year end	**(61.00)**	20.70	20.40	22.10	20.50
Market/book ratio at year end	**2.50**	2.60	3.60	4.00	3.70

[1]Variable interest entity (VIE)—an entity that either does not have sufficient equity at risk to finance its activities without subordinated financial support or where the holders of the equity at risk lack the characteristics of a controlling financial interest.

[2]Adjusted EBITDA—Adjusted operating income before depreciation and amortization.

Source: "Financial Sections: Five Year Summary," http://www.loblaw.ca/en/lcl_ar06e/fin_fiveyear.html (accessed May 30, 2007).

Overall, Weston admitted that The Real Canadian Superstores were performing sub-optimally and the new management team was highly focused on improving its performance. Earlier, a Loblaw spokesperson made a statement that the company was "committed to a strategy developed under three core themes: Simplify, Innovate and Grow." The company also announced that it was striving to become more "consumer focused, cost effective and agile, with the goal of achieving long term growth for its many stakeholders."[3] The new management team said that it would need three to five years to turn around the business, but they were not specific or detailed about what exactly should be done.

COMPANY HISTORY

In 1953, Garfield Weston was chief executive officer (CEO) of George Weston Ltd., a company that specialized in bakery goods and was named after his father. Garfield Weston acquired a majority interest in a Chicago-based food distributor named Loblaws Groceterias. Three years later, he incorporated the company as Loblaw Companies Limited, and on this foundation the Weston family built a food empire by purchasing other grocery manufacturers, retailers, and wholesalers across Canada and the Midwestern United States. In the early 1970s, Garfield Weston had undertaken a major-restructuring of George Weston Ltd.'s various holdings, and his son Galen persuaded him to keep Loblaw Companies Limited.

Upon the death of his father in 1978, Galen left the University of Western Ontario in order to become chairman of both George Weston and Loblaw. In the 1980s, he acquired Golden Dawn Foods, Star Supermarkets, and Wittington Leaseholds. By 1996, Loblaw had sold all its assets in the United States and focused on Canadian expansion by adding about 50 new Loblaws retail food store locations. In 1998, it bought Montreal-based grocery chain Provigo for $1.1 billion. Following that purchase, Loblaw acquired three warehouses in eastern Canada from The Oshawa Group and the 80-outlet Agora Foods stores that operated mostly under the IGA banner.

In the 1970s, Loblaw had faced many difficulties both in its internal and external environments. In particular, its corporate structure had become complicated from the many acquisitions, and some analysts believed that the company had tolerated weak management. At the same time, Loblaw was facing intense competition with Dominion Stores and was dogged by major union problems. To cope with these challenges, Galen hired his former college roommate and Richard Ivey School of Business graduate Dave Nichol to assume marketing responsibilities, and Richard Currie, Harvard MBA, to take a strategic management role.

The team had started with standard measures, such as closing unprofitable stores and firing underperforming employees. In addition, they invited food retail store design expert Don Watt, who brought modern style to Loblaw's stores and moved the higher-margin fresh produce to the front of the stores. They also hung posters on the walls with appetizing pictures of food and developed distinctive yellow packaging for the new, higher-margin No Name private brand.

By the 1980s, Nichol had developed the President's Choice private-label line and launched a promotional campaign for this brand's merchandise on television and in the company's Insider's Report flyers. At the time, grocers had frequently hired suppliers to make less expensive and lower quality versions of manufacturer's premium brands, and these in-store brands were not a novel offering. However, making high-quality retailer-branded products and charging for them accordingly was certainly a cutting-edge concept. Nichol demonstrated that consumers were changing from their past habits of buying national brands to preferring the quality and value of in-store brands, and he was credited by many for inventing the premium category of private brands in North America.

The private labels seemed to give Loblaw a distinctive edge over its competitors. It helped develop Loblaw into a multibillion-dollar company and the largest supermarket chain in Canada. By 2007, Loblaw operated more than 1,500 corporate, franchised, and associated stores throughout the country under different banners, such as Loblaws, Atlantic Superstores, The Real Canadian Superstores, Zehrs Markets, and others (see Exhibit 2). Its stores offered more than 7,000 private-label products, including No Name and President's Choice brands. In 2001, Loblaw also launched a new President's Choice Organics product line. Unlike many retailers, Loblaw owned most of its real estate and, in addition to traditional and organic groceries, offered financial services. Its President's Choice bank was

Exhibit 2 Loblaw's Corporate Stores in 2005 by Banner

Banner	Number of Stores
1. Maxi	97
2. Loblaws	95
3. The Real Canadian Superstore	88
4. Provigo	81
5. Extra Foods	78
6. Cash & Carry & Presto	57
7. Zehrs Markets	52
8. Atlantic Superstore	51
9. The Real Canadian Wholesale Club	37
10. Maxi & Cie	15
11. Dominion (in Newfoundland & Labrador)	14
12. Other corporate banners	5
Total	670

Source: http://www.hoovers.com.

Exhibit 3 Loblaw's Corporate Stores in 2005, by Province

Province	Number
1. Quebec	252
2. Ontario	169
3. Alberta	67
4. British Columbia	41
5. Nova Scotia	36
6. Saskatchewan	34
7. Manitoba	24
8. New Brunswick	22
9. Newfoundland & Labrador	16
10. Prince Edward Island	5
11. Northwest Territories	3
12. Yukon	1
Total	670

Source: http://www.hoovers.com.

popular and drew customers back to the stores with its loyalty program. In 2007, Loblaw was also the largest wholesale food distributor in Canada. About 63 percent of Loblaw was owned by its parent company, George Weston Ltd., and, in turn, more than 62 percent of George Weston Ltd. was owned by Loblaw's former chairman, Galen Weston Sr.

In 2004, Loblaw generated about 50 percent of its sales from discount formats, and John Lederer, the president of Loblaw at the time, said that the company considered the possibility that this share could rise to 75 percent during the next several years. He went on to say that the company was trying to change the retail landscape by giving customers what it thought they wanted, and that the discount segment of Loblaw's business would be its fastest-growing segment.

After the annual meeting in May 2004, Lederer announced that the company's goal was to become the low-price leader in all its markets. In accordance with this strategy, Loblaw stopped investing in its conventional supermarkets and focused on building its major discount format, The Real Canadian Superstores, mostly in Ontario. In 2003, the company spent Cdn$25 million to motivate 635 older workers to retire early as it closed traditional grocery stores or converted them into superstores. In 2004, Loblaw spent Cdn$1.4 billion on new stores and conversions, and a similar amount in 2005, up from Cdn$1.27 billion in 2003 and Cdn$1.08 billion in 2002. By 2005, Loblaw had created 88 The Real Canadian Superstores across Canada, and the company planned to increase the number of superstore outlets in subsequent years. Retail analysts expected that in 2005, 50 percent of all Loblaw's sales would be generated by megastores. See Exhibit 3 for a 2005 overview of Loblaw corporate stores by province.

INDUSTRY OVERVIEW

In 2006, Canada's supermarket industry was valued at about $73 billion annually (see Exhibit 4). Compared to 2005, total grocery sales had increased by 2.49 percent but this percentage change was lower than a traditional year-over-year increase of approximately 4.8 percent. By contrast to the United States, the grocery business in Canada was less fragmented, more competitive and dominated by companies that were strong on a national level. The province of Ontario was the biggest market for Loblaw and the key market in Canada overall, although in 2006, for the first time in years, Ontario's total grocery sales had declined by 4.3 percent.

In 2005, with an estimated market share of 34.9 percent, Loblaws was the largest supermarket chain in Canada, with Nova Scotia–based Sobeys and

Exhibit 4 Canadian Grocery Industry in 2005 and 2006

Region	Sales in 2006	Number of Stores in 2006	Sales in 2005	Number of Stores in 2005
1. Atlantic	$ 6,462,126,000	3,428	$ 6,350,101,000	3,413
2. Quebec	18,443,378,000	6,801	17,334,555,000	6,875
3. Ontario	22,718,607,000	6,515	23,533,672,000	6,652
4. Manitoba and Saskatchewan	5,403,421,000	2,451	5,032,329,000	2,396
5. Alberta	9,924,693,000	2,387	9,077,685,000	2,420
6. British Columbia (including Yukon, Northwest Territories and Nunavut)	10,389,388,000	2,230	10,232,794,000	2,250
Total	$73,341,613,000	23,812	$71,561,136,000	24,006

Source: Jerry Tutunjian, "Market Survey 2006," *Canadian Grocer,* February 2007, http://proquest.umi.com/pqdweb?index=16&did=1238623131&SrchMode=3&sid=1&Fmt=3&VInst=PROD&VType=PQD&RQT=309&VName=PQD&TS=1183258375&clientId=11263&aid=1 (accessed May 30, 2007).

Exhibit 5 Market Shares in Food Sales in Canada in 2005

Retailer	Market Share
1. CO-OP	3.4%
2. Costco*	5.2
3. Loblaw	34.9
4. Metro	13.1
5. Overwaitea	3.5
6. Safeway	7.1
7. Sobeys	16.0
8. Wal-Mart*	2.6
9. Others	14.3

*Food sales only.

Source: TD Newcrest, February 2007 *Report on Business.*

Montreal-based Metro Inc. being the second- and the third-ranked chains, respectively (see Exhibit 5). Sobeys and Metro Inc. had focused on bolstering their fresh food assortments, in response to Wal-Mart's anticipated diversification into the food category and changes occurring at Loblaws. The CEO of Sobeys, Bill McEwan, said that he was taking a food-first approach even as competition from Loblaw was hurting the financial performance of his company. "Others have lost their focus on food," he said. "We're not into towels, pipe wrenches and hammers."[4] Metro Inc. further strengthened its market position in 2005, when it acquired A&P and its subsidiary Dominion food retail chain in Ontario.

Commenting on Wal-Mart's expansion into the food business, retail analysts noted that expectations of grocery stores in Canada were higher compared to the United States and that "fresh" was the biggest buzzword in Canadian grocery retailing. "It's certainly a different market and environment that has kept Wal-Mart from trying to copy what they've done in the United States so far," said one analyst.[5] Another analyst agreed that if Wal-Mart wanted to succeed in the more competitive Canadian grocery market, it could not simply duplicate its United States operations. "The Canadian market is too sophisticated and too multicultural for that," he said, pointing out that Canada had a well-developed discount grocery sector, "with very high standards for produce, meat, deli, bakery and seafood."[6]

THE REAL CANADIAN SUPERSTORES

Until recently, Loblaw had positioned its conventional format supermarkets operating under the same banner as its upscale grocery stores, which offered a large assortment of fresh food. In 2004, in a preemptive move to defend its market share against Wal-Mart, Loblaw opened a series of The Real Canadian Superstores in Ontario, where it expected Wal-Mart to open its first food superstores. The Real Canadian Superstores were built as low-cost, one-stop-shopping destinations. They capitalized on Loblaw's decades-long experience with The Real Canadian Superstore's discount format in Western Canada. However, in that region, Loblaws had faced conventional Safeway supermarkets for a long time and little competition in the big-box segment. Commenting on the Loblaw's superstore strategy and Wal-Mart's Supercenter concept, one retail analyst commented that investors should prepare for fierce competition.

The Real Canadian Superstores were as big as the size of two football fields (up to 150,000 square feet) and sold a combination of groceries and non-food items. They also offered services such as a photo shop, dry cleaning, a bank, a medical clinic, and a women's-only fitness center. In line with a growing retail trend, Loblaw also added gas stations at some of The Real Canadian Superstore locations. The essence of the superstore strategy was to lower prices; to offer lower prices, however, the company needed to reduce costs. To improve cost-saving efficiencies, Loblaw had taken several actions in different areas:[7]

- *Delivery.* To minimize the time during which its trucks ran empty, Loblaw maximized the use of its own fleet instead of relying totally on manufacturers' trucks.
- *Uniform pricing strategy.* Loblaw wanted to pay the same price for any good at any of The Real Canadian Superstores across the country.
- *Use of information technology.* To determine how much product to stock, Loblaw installed new software for assessing patterns of consumer demand.
- *Consolidation:* Loblaw relocated facilities for distribution of general merchandise in Eastern Canada to Ontario and merged eight head office locations into one by 2005. It was also building a new food distribution center in Ajax, Ontario, which was scheduled to open in late 2007 or early 2008.
- *General merchandise.* To reduce overseas delivery times, Loblaw decided to eliminate as many intermediaries as possible. In 2004, Lederer said that the company could and should purchase general merchandise at significantly lower prices. The company's goal was to match the prices at Wal-Mart.
- *Design.* The partially enclosed glass boxes of The Real Canadian Superstores were judged to be more appealing than Wal-Mart Supercenters, according to a number of analysts. However, some elements of the interior design, such as the angled aisles, high ceilings, and attractive display cases, made the stores more expensive to build and operate. Don Watt, a retail consultant who had helped design Loblaw's superstores in Western Canada and Wal-Mart's Supercenters in the United States, suggested that Loblaw should follow the practice used by Wal-Mart and move to identical store layouts. Standardized models not only reduced architectural fees and other building costs but also facilitated stocking the stores.
- *Labor costs.* For an extensive period, Loblaw had been locked in union contracts that provided for higher wages and better benefit packages than those of the non-unionized Wal-Mart employees. In 2003, Loblaw won important wage concessions from the United Food and Commercial Workers International Union. Under this agreement, part-time workers in the superstores' general merchandise section were paid Cdn$10 an hour, compared to about Cdn$12 an hour for part-time grocery clerks. The Cdn$10-an-hour wage matched the top rates at Wal-Mart.

  In October 2006, Loblaw signed a four-year contract with union leaders, which allowed it to convert 44 of its conventional Loblaws and Zehrs stores to either lower cost The Real Canadian Superstores or into remodeled, more competitive food stores if it invested at least Cdn$3 million into each store's renovation. The company executives could decide which stores were least competitive and convert them to the new format with lower labor costs. One retail analyst noted that this four-year deal meant a substantial period of cost certainty and provided Loblaw with an opportunity to convert units that were located close to Wal-Mart Supercenters to a more competitive cost platform. Also, at the beginning of 2007, Loblaw announced that it planned to eliminate up to 1,000 administrative jobs, about 20 percent of its administrative workforce.

In 2004, one of Loblaw's former CEOs estimated that the company could reduce costs by $250 million over the next three years. In addition, he said that The Real Canadian Superstores faced the challenge of creating awareness about its general merchandise offering among customers in Eastern Canada. He added that at the conventional Loblaws, shoppers were accustomed to prices driven by regular sale promotions rather than to the deep discount pricing strategy that was implemented by The Real Canadian Superstores. Hence, The Real Canadian Superstores needed to educate their consumers about this strategy. Compared to Wal-Mart Supercenters, which practiced a strategy of everyday low pricing (EDLP), a deep discount pricing strategy required regular repricing and costly ads to feature the latest low-price products. Also, some shoppers, who were accustomed to traditional Loblaw supermarkets of smaller sizes, found The Real Canadian Superstores difficult to navigate.

DISTRIBUTION

Between 2004 and late 2006, Loblaw's president, John Lederer, had consolidated the company's distribution centers from 32 facilities to 26, in order to increase the efficiency of the supply system. At the same time as he was closing old warehouses and opening new ones, he moved the corporate headquarters to Brampton, Ontario. In 2005, approximately 2,000 employees moved to Brampton from a number of offices in Ontario and Alberta. Contrary to the company's expectations, however, only about 50 percent of the 150 general merchandise buyers, who had been based in Calgary, decided to relocate to Ontario; the others had chosen to leave the company. Buyers played a key role in a retail operation and represented a large part of its intellectual capital. Even for those buyers who moved to Ontario, finding homes and settling their families created a lot of distraction. The result was often disarrayed buyer–supplier relationships. "The guy that was buying last week isn't buying this week and may not be buying next week," one vendor, who asked not to be named, said at the time. "It's been very difficult."[8]

The problems in the distribution system extended beyond the uncertainty about who was responsible for purchasing transactions. In the summer of 2005, one supplier shipped general merchandise worth tens of thousands of dollars to Loblaw's Calgary warehouse, and the shipment was refused. According to the supplier, the boxes remained in containers in the warehouse's yard for three or four months before they were moved inside, and only then was the supplier finally paid.

By January 2006, Loblaw's president, Lederer, acknowledged that he had mishandled the reorganization of the supply system. "It has to be said that probably we—I—went a little bit too fast. And, obviously, you learn from that." A few weeks later, Lederer made another statement. "When you begin to take things for granted that you can just execute, you become a little bit careless. And so we are no longer careless."[9]

Since Loblaw had begun consolidation of its distribution centers, it had lost millions of dollars because of the delays in delivering goods to stores. First, when the products did not arrive at stores in time for a big flyer promotion, consumers might have been dissatisfied enough to switch stores. Second, because of the delays, Loblaw reduced the number of promotions, which, in turn, attracted fewer customers to the stores. Third, the merchandise that did not arrive at a store in a timely fashion was likely to miss its moment, and most of it would not be sold until it was marked down. For example, one of the vendors sent $15,000 worth of seasonal merchandise to a Loblaw warehouse in September 2005. The goods did not arrive at the stores before December. "By then, the season was already gone," the supplier said,[10] and the stores had to discount the goods to clear out the excess inventory. The supplier also added that he waited 10 months before he was paid, and that Loblaw still owed him $5,000. That season, other time-sensitive merchandise, such as Halloween and Christmas decorations, also had to be liquidated shortly after getting on the shelves because it did not arrive at stores on time.

One retail analyst provided another example of how harmful the effect of delays in product delivery could be. "The success of the cosmetics business depends to a large extent on launching new products at the right moment," he said. "Because Loblaw appears to have lost control of its inventory management, its shelves are still full of old products when new products are being launched," he said. "This ends up hurting both the company's revenues and margins."[11] While Loblaw was trying to clear out older merchandise at low margins just to make room on shelves for new items, competitors were gaining an advantage on product rollouts.

In addition, there were other indirect costs associated with reorganization of the distribution system. For example, in some cases, stores had hired crews to unpack boxes but the shipments never arrived. In other situations, suppliers shipped goods straight to the stores instead of sending them to the warehouses, which led to extra labor and transportation costs for Loblaw. One store manager described his staff receiving new shipments from the company's warehouse this way: "It's a little bit of a surprise sometimes when they open the trailers and find out what they're getting."[12] Although shelves in the stores were often empty, warehouses in Western Canada were so packed that Loblaw had to rent more space.

One of the vendors commented on disruptions in Loblaw's supply system:

> A lost sale is one thing, but even in your transportation network, you're sending out trailers that are not full, which is not an efficient situation. You lose on both sides. You don't make your margins, and it's going to cost you money because the trailer is going in with 900 cases—that's not as good as a trailer going at capacity with 1,200 cases.[13]

To help solve problems in its distribution system, in February 2006, Loblaw hired from Wal-Mart Peter McMahon as executive vice president of supply chain. At the end of 2006, McMahon left Loblaw; but before resigning, he introduced a system of penalties for suppliers, which was similar to the practice at Wal-Mart. McMahon targeted those who were "no shows" in their deliveries and those who were making other mistakes in shipping goods. In a letter to suppliers in September 2006, McMahon wrote:

> The no-show issue is of serious concern to our company and we expect that it will be for you as well. Our schedules for receiving dictate our labor and equipment resource allocation and drive our service level to customers. When loads no-show, our resources are wasted and our customers ultimately suffer from out-of-stocks and increased costs. Other vendor schedules are also negatively impacted.[14]

In October 2006, Loblaw started a two-part plan: imposing $1,000 fines on its suppliers each time they were late and refusing deliveries that arrived in improper condition. The penalties applied to shipments to Loblaw's distribution centers in Central and Eastern Canada, where it faced the most problems.

"Loblaw would like to look at this not as a revenue producer, but it will turn out to be that," said one of the suppliers after receiving a notice of the new fines.[15] "It's going to make it difficult for the suppliers," added another vendor. "If we don't make the dock time or if, for some reason, when we get there it's not to their liking, there's a whole fine system. The $1,000 fines could be a revenue generator for Loblaw, but will cut into suppliers' profit margins," he said.[16] "It's a very hard-nosed approach but it needs to be like this," commented one of the retail consultants. "We'll see a ripple effect if others aren't doing it . . . Tough love—that's what is needed."[17]

Loblaw's president, Lederer, expected that changes in the supply chain would absorb more than $90 million by the end of 2008. One retail analyst suggested that the costs associated with reorganization of the distribution system could increase by an additional $60 million by the end of 2007. For the fourth quarter of 2006, the company took a charge of about $120 million to liquidate excess general merchandise, even as store shelves often stood empty. Another charge of as much as $140 million was budgeted to close unprofitable stores and convert conventional stores to lower paying superstores or improved supermarkets under the new labor agreement. In addition, the new management team warned that it might undertake more restructuring of warehouses in the near future and began to backtrack on Lederer's promise that in the next three years the company would realize at least $100 million in supply-chain savings. In this regard, the former CEO of Loblaw, Richard Currie, opined that the write-downs could skyrocket by the time all the changes would be completed.

FOOD OFFERING

For most of its history, Loblaw had been positioned as a grocer with a large assortment and high-quality fresh food. It also had the highest ratio of store-brand items to total items among major North American supermarket chains. Beginning about 2004, it encountered some customer satisfaction issues in The Real Canadian Superstores.

"There is a Superstore across the street from my home," said one customer. "Whenever I go there, there are lots of empty shelves and the fruits and vegetables are generally in such bad shape I wouldn't feed them to a pet."[18] In the spring of 2006, another customer, who had been a long-time loyal Loblaws customer, could not find some of his favorite products on repeat visits to The Real Canadian Superstore near his home in Ottawa. He wrote a letter to Loblaw:

> You have a serious problem with your store. Product stock selection and/or inventory management issues with this location have seriously eroded the Loblaw image in my mind.[19]

He received a reply that the goods he inquired about had been delivered to the store, and, in fact, he started to notice some improvement in the store by the fall of 2006. However, similar cases became common in The Real Canadian Superstores. Other shoppers complained that the once-reliable retailer was often out of stock not only of delicacies but of staples, such as President's Choice diet soft drinks, fresh-baked bread, and good tomatoes.

Similarly, retail consultants also expressed their disappointment with Loblaw's performance in the food category. Don Watt, who had advised Loblaw for more than two decades and who had also participated in designing Wal-Mart's Supercenters in the United States, said that Loblaw's food offering "has just gone bland" and lacked innovation over the past few years. Although the store has had strong private labels, "they seem to be coasting with them," lacking smart promotion, he added. All told, the bond with customers was broken, Watt said. "Trust is a very difficult thing to get back. They have to prove themselves every day."[20] Another observer agreed, pointing out that "Loblaw is not doing fresh food as well as the others are right now, so Wal-Mart is trading on a weakness."[21] Another consultant echoed this sentiment, noting that Loblaw and Wal-Mart are "certainly much better at their core business than the other. However, whereas Wal-Mart has continually pushed its general merchandise dominance forward (while developing its food business), Loblaw has let its food business stagnate."

GENERAL MERCHANDISE OFFERING

Whereas Wal-Mart used its strong general merchandise traffic to introduce shoppers to its food offerings, Loblaw began using its food to introduce customers to its general merchandise offerings. To preempt competition from Wal-Mart, in 2004 Loblaw, began to expand its offering in The Real Canadian Superstores by adding lines of kitchenware, furniture, home supplies, hardware, electronics, office supplies, toys, clothing, and pharmaceuticals—all at relatively low prices. In 2004, about 17 percent of Loblaw's $26 billion in annual sales was generated by nonfood items. The task of managing general merchandise inventory, however, became a challenge for Loblaw because, compared to groceries, nonfood goods offered wider profit margins but inventory turned over less rapidly.

The reaction of both shoppers and retail consultants to the general merchandise launched in The Real Canadian Superstores was similar to their dissatisfaction with the stores' recent food offering. "I have to walk from one end to the other to get my groceries and pass junk that has nothing to do with food," complained one customer.[22] Similarly, Nichol, who had left Loblaw in 1993 and opened his own consulting firm, commented that the general merchandise carried by the retailer was substantially below the company's standards for style and quality. "You need products you can only buy at Loblaw that are fairly priced," he said.[23] His former colleague, Don Watt, agreed that the general merchandise in The Real Canadian Superstores "really doesn't reach out and make you want to buy it. It's not compelling."[24] Another retail consultant commented:

> There isn't quite enough general merchandise to make it a destination, except in kitchen goods—as you'd expect from a grocer—and electronics. The pickings are too slim in other areas. They must hope consumers will pick up these items on impulse.[25]

JOE FRESH STYLE FASHION CLOTHING LINE

In March 2006, one of the categories of general merchandise launched in The Real Canadian Superstores was a new line of designer fashions, named Joe Fresh Style, which seemed to complement Loblaw's positioning as a business that sells fresh fruit and vegetables. This line of apparel was designed by Joe Mimran, who had co-founded the Club Monaco chain and was also involved in developing the Caban label and upscale Holt Renfrew fashions. The company described the new clothing line as simple and elegant, with elements of an Asian style, influenced by Alfred Sung, a long-term associate of Mimran.

"Our goal with Joe Fresh Style was to create a line of clothing that is accessible and affordable to Canadians," said Mimran. "The level of style, quality and fit is extremely high and complemented by outstanding value," he added.[26] The new collection included more than 350 apparel items for men and women, which were priced at the lower end of the fashion spectrum. The maximum price for an item was $40, with an average price of $13. Fitting rooms in The Real Canadian Superstores were designed to be big enough for a stroller and shopping cart, with one-stop check-outs.

Louise Drouin, senior vice president in charge of the Hard & Soft Line department, commented:

> We are thrilled to offer our customers a wide selection of casual apparel items that fit today's lifestyle. We understand our customers lead busy and budget-conscious lives, and are committed to providing them with the convenience of a one-stop shop for all their daily needs.[27]

Some customers thought that Joe Fresh Style clothes were of inferior quality; however, most feedback had been positive. One retail analyst commented:

> The pieces are pretty trendy for that season, and priced really well. And that's the idea: something you wear for a season and toss, and then come back the next season for the next hot trend. It updates your wardrobe and doesn't break the bank.[28]

In 2006, sales of Joe Fresh Style clothing had met their revenue target, and the company believed that this line could become a draw for consumers on the nonfood side. Similar to groceries, fashion items entailed quick inventory turnarounds and required fast replenishment of shelves as goods were sold.

WAL-MART SUPERCENTERS

In 1994, Wal-Mart opened its first discount store in Canada after purchasing 122 Woolco general merchandise discount stores from the Woolworth retail chain; by 2006, it had more that 270 outlets across the country. In October 2006, Wal-Mart entered Canadian food retailing by opening its first two Supercenters: one in Ancaster, about 70 kilometers southwest of Toronto, and another in London, Ontario, about 200 kilometers southwest of Toronto. Both cities had existing Wal-Mart general merchandise stores that were expanded to include a full line of groceries. A third Wal-Mart Supercenter was opened in Stouffville, north of Toronto, in early November of 2006. Another four Supercenters were scheduled to open in Ontario in 2007: one in Vaughan and one in Brampton (both north of Toronto), another in Scarborough (east Toronto) and still another in Sarnia, 300 kilometers southwest of Toronto.

Wal-Mart had not announced any further expansion plans in Canada, but retail analysts expected that the company would continue opening new Supercenters and converting existing outlets to the Supercenter format. They estimated that by 2010, between 55 and 180 Supercenters could be located in Canada and predicted that if Wal-Mart could maintain its existing low prices and high product standards, Loblaws and other supermarkets could start losing sales to "this strong new competitor, with its unique position, built-in traffic and deep pockets."[29]

Industry analysts commented that Wal-Mart's entry into Canadian food markets posed a serious threat to other grocers. Over the course of the 1990s, Wal-Mart had grown from the biggest general merchant into the largest grocery retailer in the United States. Dozens of American grocers had gone bankrupt because they were not able to match Wal-Mart's economies of scale and scope, low costs, and influence on suppliers. By 2005, Wal-Mart surpassed Kroger and Safeway Co., which had been the top grocery retailers in the United States; Wal-Mart had gained 38 percent of the U.S. food business.

In 2007, Wal-Mart was the world's largest retailer; it had 6,779 stores, including 1,075 discount outlets and 2,256 stores that offered a combination of groceries and general merchandise. These latter stores were called Wal-Mart Supercenters in the United States and Canada, and operated under the banner of Asda in the United Kingdom. Exhibit 6 shows Wal-Mart's financial success from 2002 to 2006, from its worldwide operations.

In the late 1980s, Wal-Mart had begun to experiment in the United States with the concept of selling food and nonfood items in the same store. At the time, it was unclear whether consumers would embrace the idea of buying milk and automotive oil at the same place, and the common complaint was that these stores were too big to navigate. One customer, for example, said that he was so frustrated with the size of a Supercenter that he just wanted to "stand in the middle of the store and scream."[30] By 2007, sales in the category of groceries, candy, and tobacco accounted for 31 percent of Wal-Mart's total sales.

Exhibit 6 Wal-Mart's Annual Financial Highlights for the Period of 2002–2006 Worldwide

Year	2006	2005	2004	2003	2002
Net sales (in millions)	$312,427	$285,222	$256,329	$229,616	$204,011
Cost of sales (in millions)	$240,391	$219,793	$198,747	$178,299	$159,097
Net income (in millions)	$11,231	$10,267	$9,054	$7,955	$6,592
Diluted earnings per share (in millions)	$2.68	$2.41	$2.01	$1.79	$1.47
Long-term debt (in millions)	$26,429	$20,087	$17,102	$16,597	$15,676
Return on assets	8.9%	9.3%	9.2%	9.2%	8.4%
Return on shareholders' equity	22.5%	22.6%	21.3%	20.9%	19.4%

Source: "Shareholder Information: 2007 Annual Report," http://walmartstores.com/Files/2006_annual_report.pdf (accessed June 12, 2007).

Retail analysts attributed Wal-Mart's success to a variety of factors. One contributing factor was its information technology system, called Electronic Data Interchange (EDI). This technology implemented item-by-item inventory control, which allowed the company to collect data about store activities on a continuous basis and facilitated prompt delivery of purchase orders. EDI operated via the company's satellite communication system, which was the largest two-way, fully integrated, privately owned satellite network in the world. At each cash register in all stores, Wal-Mart installed a laser scanning system that read the bar code of every product sold. This data was then transmitted through EDI to the head office, distribution centers, and suppliers. In the database, vendors could view information on sales, in-stock levels and shipments of their products. Such information-sharing allowed Wal-Mart to put most responsibility for inventory control on its suppliers. Some of them delivered goods to the company's distribution centers, whereas others drop-shipped directly to Wal-Mart stores. In return, the company often guaranteed vendors both a certain amount of orders and better payment terms than other retailers.

Wal-Mart also regularly used information collected via EDI to determine sales trends, forecast consumer demand, and decide on the optimal merchandising mix for different stores. Other applications of EDI included automatic invoicing, electronic remitting, packing slip printing, and other features. The satellite system also provided two-way interactive voice and video capability, which allowed the company to broadcast communications to all its stores simultaneously.

Another source of Wal-Mart's competitive advantage was its distribution system. A typical Wal-Mart distribution center was approximately 1 million square feet (the size of 23 American football fields). Each regional facility was designed to support about 150 stores. The accuracy of shipments was more than 99 percent. To ensure efficient delivery of merchandise, as much as possible, the company located its stores no farther than a one-day's drive from its distribution centers. The stores were serviced by a fleet of company-owned trucks that made deliveries to all stores at least twice per week. For the majority of stores, however, deliveries were made on a daily basis. As a result, Wal-Mart was rarely out of stock on any item. In addition, frequent deliveries reduced the need to warehouse merchandise in stores, which allowed stores to utilize most of their available space for selling. A typical Supercenter carried up to 65,000 stock-keeping units (SKUs). Compared to many other retailers, Wal-Mart usually had fewer SKUs per product category, which meant that it offered a broad but relatively shallow assortment. The company also tended both to choose SKUs with high rates of turnover and to purchase large volumes of SKUs in order to keep the costs low.

Commenting on the new Wal-Mart Supercenter in Ancaster, Ontario, one of the Canadian retail analysts commented that it was "a formidable grocery entry" and a "serious, impressive effort by Wal-Mart," unlike anything it had attempted in the United States "except experimentally."[31] This Supercenter, which the analyst described as a "discount plus" format, featured a 30,000-square-foot grocery section called Your Fresh Market. This name distinguished the grocery section from the general merchandise section, which was called Home and Living—and located next door.

Your Fresh Market offered a wider selection of perishables than most competing discount food retailers and, unlike its rivals, featured a bakery, a deli counter, and a Ready-to-Go Meals area. The produce and the meat departments were also a little bigger than a typical Canadian discount box store. In addition, Your Fresh Market carried international (ethnic) items as well as natural and organic food, which made it a more upscale store than its U.S. counterpart. As noted by one retail consultant, "The fresh strategy and Wal-Mart's recent commitment to organic products and to the environment really follows along a more up-market vein."[32]

In Ancaster, Your Fresh Market competed with a nearby 30,000-square-foot Food Basics, owned by Metro Inc., and a 75,000-square-foot Fortinos, the Loblaw's franchise operation. In 2007, Fortinos had approximately 20 stores in Ontario. It called itself a "Supermarket with a Heart" and was positioned as a grocery chain that offered its customers "fresh, quality foods, competitive prices and unsurpassed customer service."[33]

Based on their observations in this Supercenter, retail analysts concluded that Wal-Mart appeared to have introduced a regional, rather than a national, pricing strategy to its Canadian operations. One analyst suggested that Wal-Mart would likely match the discount box store's prices on 200 to 400 core items, go lower in price on a few selected categories that it believed were more important to its shoppers and try to undercut more conventional grocers by at least 10 percent. The analyst commented:

> This places it [Wal-Mart] clearly as a discounter, but not quite as low (overall) as Food Basics. The added service and wider selection is better than at Basics, but not nearly on the level of the Fortino's. It [Wal-Mart] will therefore be staking out a market position between the two players, but closer to the Basics.[34]

The analyst further predicted that, as a result of the Wal-Mart's pricing strategy, Food Basics in Ancaster, which he estimated earned $360,000 in sales weekly, would lose 5 to 7 percent of its business to Your Fresh Market, whereas Fortinos, which he estimated grossed $850,000 weekly, would lose between 8 and 10 percent of its business to the new Supercenter.

Similar to its U.S. counterparts, Canadian Supercenters were implementing Wal-Mart's new customization and segmentation strategy. In this strategy, characteristics of the ethnic and demographic community around each store were used to determine product assortment. Retail analysts also speculated that Wal-Mart's Canadian Supercenters might relaunch Wal-Mart's 500-item Great Value in-house packaged goods brand and add a premium tier to compete with Loblaw's premium private label, President's Choice.

LOBLAW'S MANAGEMENT TEAM

Following September 2006, several major changes occurred in Loblaw's executive ranks. Galen Weston Sr., who had been in charge of Loblaw since 1978, stepped down, and his son, 34-year-old Galen Weston Jr., took over his position of executive chairman of Loblaw.[35]Galen Jr. had earned his MBA at Columbia University and had begun working at Loblaw in 1998. He started by managing a pilot online grocery business in Mississauga, Ontario, and then joined a team that was introducing President's Choice financial services at Loblaws stores. In his next job, Galen Jr. was responsible for managing operations at the No Frills chain. Before assuming his executive chairman position, he was involved in market analysis as Loblaw's senior vice president of corporate development. After meeting Galen Jr. in person, one of the financial analysts said that he was impressed with both his depth of knowledge about the U.S. grocery industry, which was unusual in Canada, and his ability to relate to people. Nichol, who had known Galen Jr. since infancy, also expressed confidence in him. He had "tremendous potential," Nichol said, and simply "needs strong mentoring."[36]

At the same time as Galen Jr. was appointed executive chairman of Loblaw, Lederer, who had been president of Loblaw since 2001, left the company. In April 2006, he was succeeded by Mark Foote, who had worked for Canadian Tire Corporation Ltd. for 27 years. At Canadian Tire, he had been one of the leaders who had decided to meet competition from Wal-Mart by focusing on goods that it offered exclusively and by investing in its core strengths of car parts, sporting goods, and housewares. Commenting on this appointment, one retail analyst said that Foote had extensive expertise with general merchandise, which was much needed at Loblaw, and that "he just seems universally respected."[37] The analyst also mentioned that he knew a manager who had decided to quit Loblaw because he was disappointed with its performance but changed his mind when he learned that Foote was coming.

Also recruited to play a crucial role in developing Loblaw's strategy was Allan Leighton. After Lederer left Loblaw, Allan Leighton was appointed to a newly created position of the company's deputy chairman. Since 2000, Allan Leighton had been a trusted advisor for a number of Weston businesses. He also sat on the board of George Weston Ltd., the parent of Loblaw, and was deputy chairman of Selfridges and two other Weston family-owned luxury goods companies. In Great Britain, Leighton had started his career at Mars Inc., as a salesman for the subdivision manufacturing confectionary, earned several promotions in a few years, and eventually was involved in the company's pet care business. He then moved to a supermarket chain, Asda Group PLC, and was later credited with helping improve its performance. In 1999, Asda was acquired by Wal-Mart, and Leighton spent a year as CEO of the discounter's European division. Subsequently, Leighton set up a website to provide consulting services to different organizations, which he referred to as "going plural."[38] In the United Kingdom, Leighton was known for his uncompromising position in labor-related issues and his strong belief in staff input. He had a reputation as a person who did not hesitate to cut thousands of jobs or bypass union leaders to communicate directly with employees.

In January 2007, Dalton Phillips, a former executive with Irish department-store chain Brown Thomas, was named chief operating officer of Loblaw. He replaced Dave Jeffs, who had been with Loblaw for 28 years. Regarding this appointment, one analyst remarked that "notwithstanding the talents of Phillips," it was unusual, as it added to the ranks "yet another senior executive lacking solid North American food distribution experience at a time when we see it as sorely needed."[39] Another analyst noted that Loblaw was interested in Dalton's experience with Wal-Mart in Germany, which was one of the divisions that Wal-Mart recently shuttered because its performance had not measured up to expectations. Commenting on the management changes at Loblaw, Richard Currie said that they added up to a lot of uncertainty. In his opinion, the company created a tangled management structure at just the wrong moment, and he doubted that all replacements in the head office were necessary. "I think the delineation of responsibilities could at best be described as fuzzy," he added.[40]

FEBRUARY 2007

Loblaw's new executive team had completed a 100-day review of the company's performance and had outlined a new business plan. "We are not delivering the right value for money and we are not getting the credit with the customer for the investments that we do make," executive chairman Galen Weston Jr. acknowledged in a meeting with analysts. "We have insufficient distinctive formats, with poor availability and, in relative terms, we are still overpriced," he added.[41]

Galen Jr. said that the company's goal was to increase sales by 5 percent. He also said that Loblaw was aiming to increase earnings by 10 percent by cutting prices, offering more products, and improving customer service. Following this announcement, Loblaw's share price dropped $0.29 to $48.13 in Toronto trading. The management team estimated that three to five years were needed to reach the company's announced goals. "That's just ridiculous," said Richard Currie, regarding this time frame.[42] He argued that the hardest part of reorganization had already been done, and that the remaining changes should be completed within 18 months; otherwise, the competition might start surpassing Loblaw. Although at the beginning of 2007, Loblaw remained the leading supermarket chain in Canada, its rivals "are getting better, and they're not standing still," Currie said.[43]

As the new executive team was working through the company's issues, different options were being considered:

- Loblaw's spokesperson made a statement that the company would clear out excess inventory and improve stocking so that neither groceries nor general merchandise would become "stale-dated." He said that the company would continue to "manage inventory levels down to more desirable levels in store backrooms, outside storage as well as in distribution centres."[44]

- When Loblaw announced the signing of a four-year contract with unionized employees in October 2006, it emphasized its intention to "vastly improve"[45] the food offering. Retail analysts predicted that Loblaw would continue the strong offering of private labels, de-emphasize national brands, and eliminate redundant sizes and ineffective promotions.
- New president Mark Foote told analysts that The Real Canadian Superstores allocated too much space to general merchandise. He said that the company would either rearrange the space and devote more area to food, or reduce the size of stores. He also said that the company would narrow the assortment of general merchandise. Specifically, the plan was to eliminate furniture, shrink electronics and hardware, and sell toys only during holiday seasons. Instead, the retailer intended to strengthen its focus on drugstore products, housewares, and the in-house Joe Fresh Style fashion line. One retail analyst mentioned that Galen Jr. was very supportive of Mimran's collection and wanted to expand it. He believed that its low prices fit well with the overall positioning of The Real Canadian Superstores and could give Loblaw an advantage over Wal-Mart, which had difficulties in promoting its fashion business.
- One retail analyst predicted that Loblaw would lower prices for selected items to retain its customers. "The pricing actions will be serious and lengthy and, despite better labor economics, will take a toll on Loblaw's bottom line," he said. "Investors should prepare for a pricing bloodbath" between Loblaw and Wal-Mart, the analyst added.[46] Another consultant commented that the strategy of one-stop shopping destination worked effectively for Wal-Mart because of economies of scale and scope, which allowed the discounter to maintain low prices and broad assortment. "We strongly advise retailers, especially ones that are already known in consumers' minds for quality and specialty products, not to try to be all things to all people," he said. "You're just competing on price, and you're unlikely to succeed."[47] Thus, the question for the new executive team was whether it would be possible for Loblaw to be competitive with Wal-Mart, which had lower labor costs, a refined logistics system, and significantly fewer SKUs as well as experience with a fundamental merchandising strategy of EDLP.
- The new management team said that the company needed to clearly differentiate between the smaller conventional Loblaw supermarkets and the larger discount outlets, The Real Canadian Superstores. The company's intention was to use both brands simultaneously to defeat a threat from Wal-Mart.
- In February 2007, the company made a formal announcement to investors that it would reconstruct the famous Maple Leaf Gardens in downtown Toronto, the former home of the Toronto Maple Leafs hockey team, into a grocery store. "This is an icon, just like Loblaw is an icon. I think it represents a huge evolution of what's happening to Loblaw, as well as what's happening in Toronto," said Galen Weston Sr.[48] The arena had been empty since the Toronto Maple Leafs hockey club moved to the Air Canada Centre in 1999. Galen Weston Jr. said that the company would begin to clean up the building in the summer of 2007, and planned to open the store in 22 months.
- Finally, some observers speculated that the Weston family might be preparing to sell its controlling stake in Loblaw Companies Limited. Galen Sr. refuted this suggestion and said that Loblaw was "core for the family." However, he also acknowledged that there were some situations in which he decided to divest weak assets:

> My history, wherever it is in the world, is: You buy things or you inherit things and you keep them fresh and you keep them vital. And where it doesn't work, like our fishing business or our pulp and paper business or our cookie business, we've decided to exit those businesses.[49]

Endnotes

[1] This case has been written on the basis of published sources only. Consequently, the interpretation and perspectives presented in this case are not necessarily those of Loblaw Companies Limited or any of its employees.
[2] "Loblaw Writing Down Provigo amid Structural Weakness in Profitability," *CBC News,* February 8, 2007, http://www.cbc.ca/cp/business/070208/b020885A.html (accessed June 7, 2007).
[3] "About Us: Company Profile," http://www.loblaw.ca/en/abt_corprof.html (accessed February 27, 2007).
[4] Reg Curren, "Canada's Loblaw Expands in a 'Pre-Emptive Strike' at Wal-Mart," *Bloomberg News,* November 18, 2004, http://www.bloomberg.com/apps/news?pid=10000082&sid=a_b7RJp5cJ5E&refer=canada (accessed February 27, 2007).
[5] "Rumours Loblaw May Be Sold to Wal-Mart," *CTV News,* February 15, 2002, http://www.ctv.ca/servlet/ArticleNews/story/CTVNews/1024895338527_20304538/ (accessed February 27, 2007).
[6] Perry Caicco and Mark Petrie, "Loblaw Companies Limited. First Look at the Wal-Mart Supercenter: Trouble Brewing," CIBC World Markets: Equity Research Change in Recommendation, October 17, 2006, http://www.yorku.ca/pshum/Loblaw%20Highlight%20Oct%2017%2006.pdf (accessed February 27, 2007).
[7] Marina Strauss, "Loblaw Strikes Back," *The Globe and Mail,* May 29, 2004, http://www.theglobeandmail.com/servlet/Page/document/v4/sub/MarketingPage?user_URL=http://www.theglobeandmail.com%2Fservlet%2Fstory%2FRTGAM.20040529.wxloblaw0529%2FBNStory%2FBusiness%2F&ord=1145748148892&brand=theglobeandmail&force/_login=true (accessed February 27, 2007).
[8] Marina Strauss, "Memories of Excellence," *The Globe and Mail,* January 26, 2007, http://www.theglobeandmail.com/servlet/story/RTGAM.20070125.rmloblaw0125/BNStory/specialComment (accessed February 15, 2007).
[9] Ibid.
[10] Ibid.
[11] Ibid.
[12] Ibid.
[13] Ibid.
[14] Marina Strauss, "Loblaw to Levy Fines in Crackdown on Suppliers," *The Globe and Mail,* October 16, 2006, http://globeandmail.workopolis.com/servlet/Content/fasttrack/20061016/RLOBLAW16?section=Retail (accessed February 27, 2007).
[15] Ibid.
[16] Ibid.
[17] Ibid.
[18] "Marina Strauss Took Your Questions on Loblaw," *The Globe and Mail Update,* January 26, 2007, http://www.theglobeandmail.com/servlet/story/RTGAM.20070125.wloblaw-discussion/BNStory/specialComment/home (accessed February 15, 2007).
[19] Marina Strauss, "Memories of Excellence," *The Globe and Mail,* January 26, 2007, http://www.theglobeandmail.com/servlet/story/RTGAM.20070125.rmloblaw0125/BNStory/specialComment (accessed February 15, 2007).
[20] Ibid.
[21] Hollie Shaw, "Wal-Mart Launches Fresh Attack on Loblaw," *Financial Post,* October 18, 2006, http://www.canada.com/nationalpost/financialpost/story.html?id=a8345c2a-acdc-467a-822c-f110a800695d&k=12242 (accessed February 27, 2007).
[22] Marina Strauss, "Memories of Excellence," *The Globe and Mail,* January 26, 2007, http://www.theglobeandmail.com/servlet/story/RTGAM.20070125.rmloblaw0125/BNStory/specialComment (accessed February 15, 2007).
[23] Ibid.
[24] Ibid.
[25] Ibid.
[26] "Loblaw Launches New Fashion Line," *CBC News,* March 13, 2006, http://www.cbc.ca/money/story/2006/03/13/loblaw-060313.html?ref=rss (accessed February 27, 2007).
[27] Ibid.
[28] "Marina Strauss Took Your Questions on Loblaw," *The Globe and Mail Update,* January 26, 2007, http://www.theglobeandmail.com/servlet/story/RTGAM.20070125.wloblaw-discussion/BNStory/specialComment/home (accessed February 15, 2007).
[29] Perry Caicco and Mark Petrie, "Loblaw Companies Limited. First Look at the Wal-Mart Supercenter: Trouble Brewing," CIBC World Markets: Equity Research Change in Recommendation, October 17, 2006, http://www.yorku.ca/pshum/Loblaw%20Highlight%20Oct%2017%2006.pdf (accessed February 27, 2007).
[30] Steve Weiner, "Golf Balls, Motor Oil and Tomatoes," *Forbes,* October 30, 1989, p. 134.
[31] Perry Caicco and Mark Petrie, "Loblaw Companies Limited. First Look at the Wal-Mart Supercenter: Trouble Brewing," CIBC World Markets: Equity Research Change in Recommendation, October 17, 2006, http://www.yorku.ca/pshum/Loblaw%20Highlight%20Oct%2017%2006.pdf, (accessed February 27, 2007).
[32] Hollie Shaw, "Wal-Mart Launches Fresh Attack on Loblaw," *Financial Post,* October 18, 2006, http://www.canada.com/nationalpost/financialpost/story.html?id=a8345c2a-acdc-467a-822c-f110a800695d&k=12242 (accessed February 27, 2007).
[33] "Who We Are: History of Fortinos," http://www.fortinos.ca/about_us.asp (accessed June 7, 2007).
[34] Perry Caicco and Mark Petrie, "Loblaw Companies Limited. First Look at the Wal-Mart Supercenter: Trouble Brewing," CIBC World Markets: Equity Research Change in Recommendation, October 17, 2006, http://www.yorku.ca/pshum/Loblaw%20Highlight%20Oct%2017%2006.pdf (accessed February 27, 2007).
[35] Galen Weston Sr. remained chairman of Loblaw's parent company, George Weston Ltd.
[36] Marina Strauss, "Memories of Excellence," *The Globe and Mail,* January 26, 2007, http://www.theglobeandmail.com/servlet/story/RTGAM.20070125.rmloblaw0125/BNStory/specialComment (accessed February 15, 2007).
[37] Ibid.
[38] Ibid.
[39] Zena Olijnyk, Erin Pooley, Jeff Sanford, and Andrew Wahl, "Deal or No Deal?" *Canadian Business Magazine,* January 15, 2007, http://www.canadianbusiness.com/markets/stocks/article.jsp?content=20070115_84597_84597 (accessed May 23, 2007).
[40] Marina Strauss, "Memories of Excellence," *The Globe and Mail,* January 26, 2007, http://www.theglobeandmail.com/servlet/story/RTGAM.20070125.rmloblaw0125/BNStory/specialComment (accessed February 15, 2007).
[41] "Loblaw Unveils New Business Plan, Will Revamp Maple Leaf Gardens," *CBC News,* February 21, 2007, http://www.cbc.ca/money/story/2007/02/21/loblaw.html (accessed February 27, 2007).
[42] Marina Strauss, "Memories of Excellence," *The Globe and Mail,* January 26, 2007, http://www.theglobeandmail.com/servlet/story/RTGAM.20070125.rmloblaw0125/BNStory/specialComment (accessed February 15, 2007).
[43] Ibid.
[44] Virginia Galt, "First Loss in 10 Years Looms for Loblaw," *The Globe and Mail Update,* February 8, 2007, http://www.theglobeandmail.com/servlet/Page/document/v5/content/subscribe?user_URL=http://www.theglobeandmail.com%2Fservlet%2Fstory%2FRTGAM.20070208.wloblaw0208%2FCommentStory%2FBusiness%2Fhome&ord=8816676&brand=theglobeandmail&force_login=true (accessed February 27, 2007).

[45] Perry Caicco and Mark Petrie, "Loblaw Companies Limited. First Look at the Wal-Mart Supercenter: Trouble Brewing," CIBC World Markets: Equity Research Change in Recommendation, October 17, 2006, http://www.yorku.ca/pshum/Loblaw%20Highlight%20Oct%2017%2006.pdf (accessed February 27, 2007).

[46] Ibid.

[47] Marina Strauss, "Memories of Excellence," *The Globe and Mail,* January 26, 2007, http://www.theglobeandmail.com/servlet/story/RTGAM.20070125.rmloblaw0125/BNStory/specialComment (accessed February 15, 2007).

[48] "Loblaw Unveils New Business Plan, Will Revamp Maple Leaf Gardens," *CBC News,* February 21, 2007, http://www.cbc.ca/money/story/2007/02/21/loblaw.html (accessed February 27, 2007).

[49] "Marina Strauss Took Your Questions on Loblaw," *The Globe and Mail Update,* January 26, 2007, http://www.theglobeandmail.com/servlet/story/RTGAM.20070125.wloblaw-discussion/BNStory/specialComment/home (accessed February 15, 2007).

CASE 17 Research In Motion: Managing Explosive Growth

Rod White
University of Western Ontario

Paul Beamish
University of Western Ontario

Daina Mazutis
University of Western Ontario

In early January 2008, David Yach, chief technology officer for software at Research In Motion (RIM), had just come back from Christmas break. Returning to his desk in Waterloo, Ontario, relaxed and refreshed, he noted that his executive assistant had placed the preliminary holiday sales figures for BlackBerry on top of his in-box with a note that read "Meeting with Mike tomorrow." Knowing 2007 had been an extraordinarily good year, with the number of BlackBerry units sold doubling, Dave was curious: Why did Mike Lazaridis, RIM's visionary founder and co–chief executive officer, want a meeting? A sticky note on page three flagged the issue. Mike wanted to discuss Dave's research and development (R&D) plans—even though R&D spending was up $124 million from the prior year, it had dropped significantly as a percentage of sales. In an industry driven by engineering innovations and evaluated on technological advances, this was an issue.

Ivey
Richard Ivey School of Business
The University of Western Ontario

Daina Mazutis wrote this case under the supervision of Professors Rod White and Paul W. Beamish solely to provide material for class discussion. The authors do not intend to illustrate either effective or ineffective handling of a managerial situation. The authors may have disguised certain names and other identifying information to protect confidentiality.

Version: (A) 2008-05-13.

R&D was the core of the BlackBerry's success—but success, Dave knew, could be a double-edged sword. Although RIM's engineers were continually delivering award-winning products, explosive growth and increased competition were creating pressures on his team to develop new solutions to keep up with changes in the global smartphone marketplace. With 2007 revenue up 98 percent from the previous year, his team of approximately 1,400 software engineers should also have doubled—but both talent and space were getting increasingly scarce. The current model of "organic" growth was not keeping pace, and his engineers were feeling the strain. As the day progressed, Dave considered how he should manage this expansion on top of meeting existing commitments, thinking: "How do you change the engine, while you're speeding along at 200 kilometers per hour?" As his BlackBerry notified him of dozens of other urgent messages, he wondered how to present his growth and implementation plan to Mike the next morning.

RESEARCH IN MOTION LTD. (RIM)

RIM was a world leader in the mobile communications market. Founded in 1984 by 23-year-old University of Waterloo student Mike Lazaridis, RIM designed, manufactured, and marketed the very popular line of BlackBerry products that had recently reached 14 million subscribers worldwide and had just over $6 billion in revenue (see Exhibits 1 and 2).

Exhibit 1 BlackBerry Subscriber Account Base (in millions)

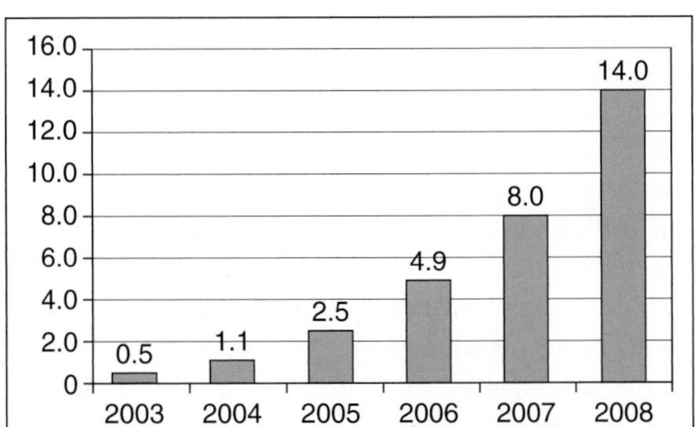

RIM Annual Revenue (in millions of U.S. dollars)

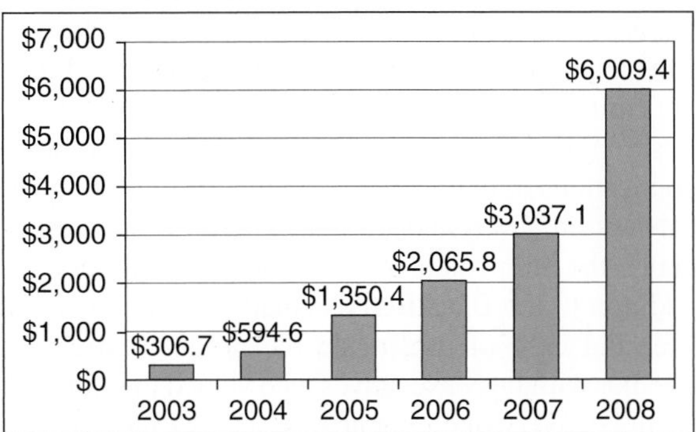

Note: RIM Fiscal year ends in March (Fiscal 2008 is the year ending March 31, 2008).
Source: RIM Fiscal 2007 annual report and Fiscal 2008 press release (April 2, 2008).

Exhibit 2 Consolidated Statement of Operations, Research in Motion, Ltd., 2004–2008 (in thousands of U.S. dollars, except per share data)

	For the year ended				
	Mar. 1, 2008 (Projected)	Mar. 3, 2007	Mar. 4, 2006	Feb. 26, 2005	Feb. 28, 2004
Revenue	$6,009,395	$3,037,103	$2,065,845	$1,350,447	$594,616
Cost of sales	2,928,814	1,379,301	925,598	636,310	323,365
Gross margin	3,080,581	1,657,802	1,140,247	714,137	271,251
Gross margin %	51.30%	54.60%	55.20%	52.88%	45.62%
Expenses					
Research and development	359,828	236,173	158,887	102,665	62,638
Selling, marketing, & admin.	881,482	537,922	314,317	193,838	108,492
Amortization	108,112	76,879	49,951	35,941	27,911
Litigation			201,791	352,628	35,187
	1,349,422	850,974	724,946	685,072	234,228
Income from operations	1,731,159	806,828	415,301	29,065	37,023
Investment income	79,361	52,117	66,218	37,107	10,606
Income before income taxes	1,810,520	858,945	481,519	66,172	47,629
Provision for income taxes					
Current	587,845	123,552	14,515	1,425	
Deferred	(71,192)	103,820	92,348	(140,865)	
	516,653	227,373	106,863	(139,440)	−4,200
Net Income	$1,293,867	$ 631,572	$ 374,656	$ 205,612	$ 51,829
Earnings per share					
Basic	$2.31	$1.14	$1.98	$1.10	$0.33
Diluted	$2.26	$1.10	$1.91	$1.04	$0.31

Source: Company annual reports; fiscal 2008 form; press release, April 2, 2008, "Research in Motion Reports Fourth Quarter and Year-End Results for Fiscal 2003," http://www.rim.com/news/press/2008/pr-02_04_2008-01.shtml.

In early 2008, RIM was one of Canada's largest companies with a market capitalization of $69.4 billion.[1]

The BlackBerry wireless platform and line of handhelds could integrate e-mail, phone, Instant Messaging (IM), Short Message Service (SMS), Internet, music, camera, video, radio, organizer, Global Positioning System (GPS), and a variety of other applications in one wireless solution that was dubbed "always on, always connected." These features, especially the immediate pushed message delivery, in addition to the BlackBerry's small size, long battery life, and ease of use, made the product extremely popular with busy executives who valued the safe and secure delivery of corporate mail and seamless extension of other enterprise and Internet services.

In particular, organizations that relied on sensitive information, such as the U.S. government and large financial institutions, were early and loyal adopters of BlackBerry and RIM's largest customers. RIM's enterprise e-mail servers, which were attached to the customer's e-mail and IM servers behind company firewalls, encrypted and redirected e-mail and other data before forwarding the information to end consumers through wireless service providers (see Exhibit 3). Having been the first to market with a "push" e-mail architecture and a value proposition built on security, RIM had more than 100,000 enterprise customers and an estimated 42 percent market share of converged devices, and significantly higher market share of data-only devices, in North America.[2]

RIM generated revenue through the "complete BlackBerry wireless solution," which included wireless devices, software, and services. Revenues, however, were heavily skewed to handheld sales (73 percent), followed by service (18 percent), software (6 percent) and other revenues (3 percent). In handhelds, RIM had recently introduced the award-winning BlackBerry Pearl and BlackBerry Curve, which were a significant design departure from previous models and for the first time targeted both consumer and business professionals (see Exhibit 4). RIM had accumulated a wide range of product design and innovation awards, including recognition from Computerworld as one of the Top 10 Products of the Past 40 Years.[3]Analysts and technophiles eagerly awaited the next-generation BlackBerry series expected for release in 2008.

Although originally built for busy professionals, BlackBerry had made considerable headway in the consumer market and had become something of a social phenomenon. Celebrity sightings put the BlackBerry in the hands of Madonna and Paris Hilton among others. The term "crackberry," used to describe the addictive or obsessive use of the BlackBerry, was added to Webster's New Millennium dictionary. Just six months after launching Facebook for BlackBerry, downloads of the popular social networking software application had topped one million, indicating that younger consumers were gravitating toward the popular handhelds.[4] RIM also actively sought partnerships with software developers to bring popular games such as Guitar Hero III to the BlackBerry mobile platform,[5] suggesting a more aggressive move to the consumer, or at least prosumer,[6] smartphone space.

Wireless carriers, such as Rogers in Canada and Verizon in the United States, were RIM's primary direct customers. These carriers bundled BlackBerry handhelds and software with airtime and sold the complete solution to end users. In 2007, RIM had over 270 carrier partnerships in more than 110 countries around the world. Through the BlackBerry Connect licensing program other leading device manufacturers such as Motorola, Nokia, Samsung, and Sony Ericsson could also equip their handsets with BlackBerry functionality, including push technology to automatically deliver e-mail and other data. Expanding the global reach of BlackBerry solutions was therefore a fundamental part of RIM's strategy. In 2007, 57.9 percent of RIM's revenues were derived from the United States, 7.3 percent from Canada and the remaining 34.8 percent from other countries. To date, RIM had offices in North America, Europe, and Asia Pacific; however, it had only three wholly owned subsidiaries—two in Delaware and one in England.

THE WIRELESS COMMUNICATIONS MARKET AND SMARTPHONES

Mobile wireless communication involved the transmission of signals using radio frequencies between wireless networks and mobile access devices. Although RIM was one of the first to market with

Exhibit 3 Blackberry Enterprise Solution Architecture

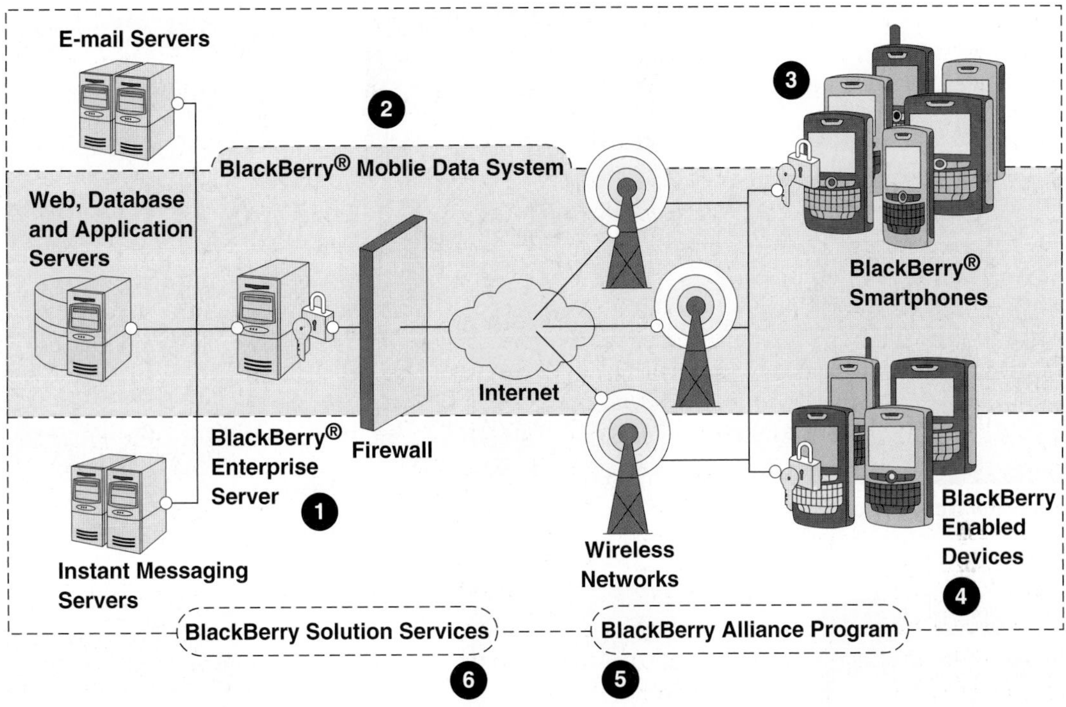

1. BlackBerry® Enterprise Server: Robust software that acts as the centralized link between wireless devices, wireless networks, and enterprise applications. The server integrates with enterprise messaging and collaboration systems to provide mobile users with access to e-mail, enterprise instant messaging and personal information management tools. All data between applications and BlackBerry® smartphones flows centrally through the server.

2. BlackBerry® Mobile Data System (BlackBerry MDS): An optimized framework for creating, deploying and managing applications for the BlackBerry Enterprise Solution. It provides essential components that enable applications beyond e-mail to be deployed to mobile users, including developer tools, administrative services, and BlackBerry® Device Software. It also uses the same proven BlackBerry push delivery model and advanced security features used for BlackBerry e-mail.

3. BlackBerry® Smartphones: Integrated wireless voice and data devices that are optimized to work with the BlackBerry Enterprise Solution. They provide push-based access to e-mail and data from enterprise applications and systems in addition to web, MMS, SMS, and organizer applications.

4. BlackBerry® Connect™ Devices: Devices available from leading manufacturers that feature BlackBerry push delivery technology and connect to the BlackBerry Enterprise Server.

5. BlackBerry® Alliance Program: A large community of independent software vendors, system integrators, and solution providers that offer applications, services, and solutions for the BlackBerry Enterprise Solution. It is designed to help organizations make the most of the BlackBerry Enterprise Solution when mobilizing their enterprises.

6. BlackBerry Solution Services: A group of services that include: BlackBerry® Technical Support Services, BlackBerry® Training, RIM® Professional Services, and the Corporate Development Program. These tools and programs are designed to help organizations deploy, manage, and extend their wireless solution.

Source: http://na.blackberry.com/eng/ataglance/solutions/architecture.jsp.

Exhibit 4 The Evolution of the BlackBerry Product Line (Select Models)

RIM Inter@ctive Pager 850

RIM 957

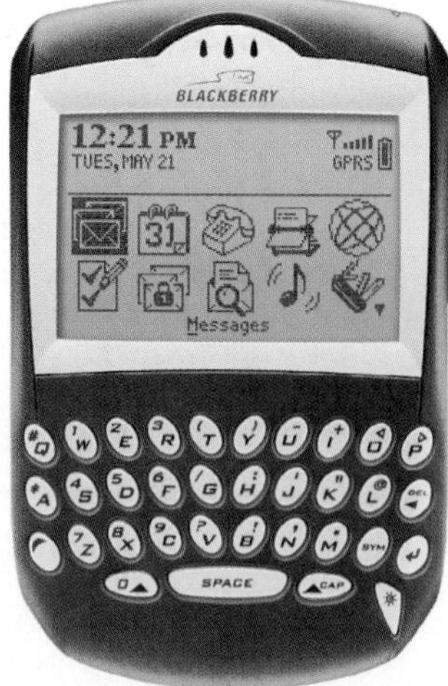

BlackBerry 6200

BlackBerry 8820

BlackBerry Pearl 8110

BlackBerry Curve 8330

Source: http://www.rim.com/newsroom/media/gallery/index.shtml and Jon Fortt, "BlackBerry: Evolution of an Icon," *Fortune,* Sept. 21, 2007 (accessed April 7, 2008), http://bigtech.blogs.fortune.cnn.com/blackberry-evolution-of-an-icon-photos-610/.

two-way messaging, recent technological developments had encouraged numerous handheld and handset vendors to go beyond traditional "telephony" and release new "converged"[7] devices including smartphones, Personal Digital Assistants (PDA), phone/PDA hybrids, converged voice and data devices, and other end-to-end integrated wireless solutions. A shift in the telecommunication industry was moving demand beyond just cellphones to smartphones—complete communications tools that marry all the functions of mobile phones with fully integrated e-mail, browser, and organizer applications. In 2007, key competitors to RIM's BlackBerry line-up included the Palm Treo 700 and 750, Sony Ericsson P900 Series, the Nokia E62, Motorola Q, and the Apple iPhone.

Exhibit 5 **Mobile Telephone Users Worldwide (in millions)**

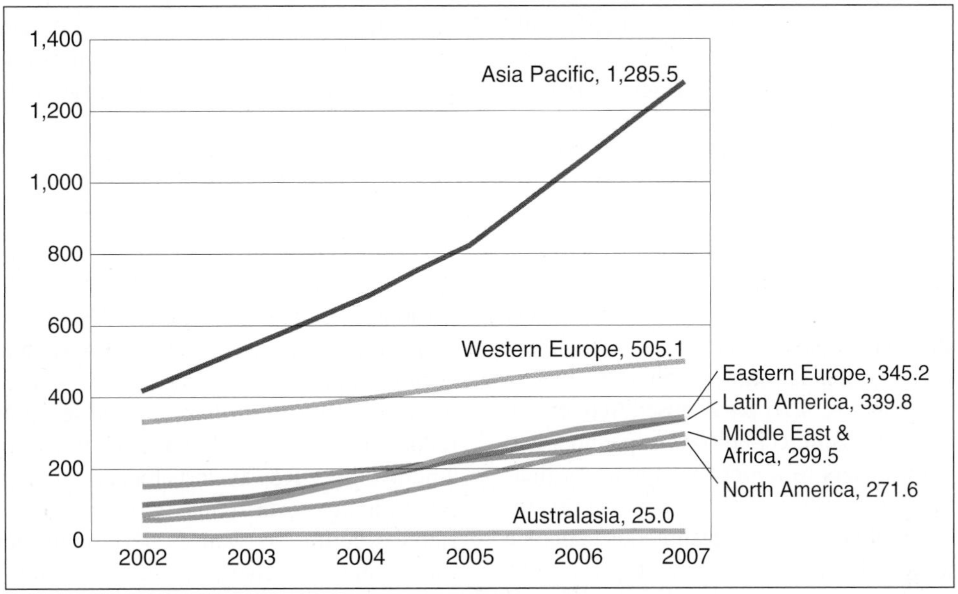

1,400
1,200
1,000
800
600
400
200
0
2002 2003 2004 2005 2006 2007
Asia Pacific, 1,285.5
Western Europe, 505.1
Eastern Europe, 345.2
Latin America, 339.8
Middle East & Africa, 299.5
North America, 271.6
Australasia, 25.0

Source: Created from data accessed from the Global Market Information Database, April 4, 2008, http://www.donal.suromonitor.com.proxy1lb.uo.ca.2048/portal/server.pt?control=SetCommunity&CommunityID=207&PageID=720&cached=false&space=CommunityPage.

The number of wireless subscriber connections worldwide had reached 3 billion by the end of 2007. China led with over 524 million subscribers, followed by the United States at 254 million, and India with 237 million (see Exhibit 5). Year over year growth in the United States, however, was only 9.5 percent, with an already high market penetration rate (87 percent). In contrast, China's growth was 18.3 percent with only 39 percent penetration. In sheer numbers, India was experiencing the fastest growth rate with a 60 percent increase and room to grow with 21 percent market penetration. To put that into context, in late 2007 there were almost 300,000 new wireless network subscribers in India every day.[8]

Since the launch of Apple's iPhone in June 2007, competition in the smartphone segment of the mobile telecommunications industry had intensified. The iPhone "set a new standard for usability."[9] In 2007, smartphones represented only 10 percent of the global mobile phone market in units. However, this segment was projected to reach over 30 percent market share within five years.[10] In the U.S. the number of smartphone users had doubled in 2007 to about 14.6 million[11] while global shipments of smartphones rose by 53 percent worldwide, hitting 118 million in 2007.[12] Some analysts saw the opportunity for smart phones as "immense," predicting that during 2008 and 2009, 500 million smart devices would be sold globally and cumulative global shipments would pass the one billion mark by 2012.[13]

Worldwide demand for wireless handhelds had been fueled by several global trends, including the commercial availability of high-speed wireless networks, the emergence of mobile access to corporate intranets, and the broad acceptance of e-mail and text messaging as reliable, secure, and indispensable means of communication. Coupled with the growth of instant messaging as both a business and personal communications tool, the demand for wireless handhelds and smartphones was robust.

COMPETING PLATFORMS

Symbian, a proprietary Operating System (OS) designed for mobile devices and jointly owned by Nokia, Ericsson, Sony Ericsson, Panasonic, Siemens AG, and Samsung, held an estimated

65 percent worldwide share of the converged devices, shipping 77.3 million smartphones in 2007 (up 50 percent from 2006).[14] This was significantly ahead of Microsoft's Windows Mobile OS (12 percent) and RIM's BlackBerry OS (11 percent). However, in North America, RIM led with 42 percent of shipments, ahead of Apple (27 percent), Microsoft (21 percent) and Palm (less than 9 percent and shrinking).[15]

However, RIM could not afford to rest on its laurels. In the North American marketplace, Apple had recently announced that it would be actively pursuing the business segment. Conceding that push e-mail and calendar integration were key to securing enterprise users, Apple licensed ActiveSync Direct Push, a Microsoft technology. Apple hoped to entice corporate users to adopt the iPhone as their converged device of choice.[16] Similarly, Microsoft, which had struggled to gain widespread acceptance for its Windows Mobile OS, had recently revamped its marketing efforts and announced an end-to-end solution for enterprise customers as well as desktop-grade web browsing for Windows Mobile enabled phones.[17] Even Google had entered the fray with Android, an open and free mobile platform which included an OS, middleware and key applications. Rivalry, it seemed, was intensifying.

In early 2008, an analyst commented about the increasing competition in the converged device (smartphone and wireless handheld) segment:

> Apple's innovation in its mobile phone user interface has prompted a lot of design activity among competitors. We saw the beginnings of that in 2007, but we will see a lot more in 2008 as other smart phone vendors try to catch up and then get back in front. Experience shows that a vendor with only one smart phone design, no matter how good that design is, will soon struggle. A broad, continually refreshed portfolio is needed to retain and grow share in this dynamic market. This race is a marathon, but you pretty much have to sprint every lap.[18]

Another analyst observed:

> The good news for RIM? There still aren't many trusted alternatives for business-class mobile e-mail. This company could be one of the world's biggest handset manufacturers one day. It's hard for me to believe there won't be e-mail on every phone in the world. RIM is going to be a major force in this market.[19]

Given the rapid advances in the mobile communications industry, no technological platform had become the industry standard. In light of the dynamic market situation, RIM needed to ensure that its investment in R&D kept up with the pace of change in the industry.

R&D AT RIM

R&D and engineering were the heart and soul of RIM. In March 2007, RIM employed just over 2,100 people with different R&D areas of expertise: radio frequency engineering, hardware and software design, audio and display improvement, antenna design, circuit board design, power management, industrial design, and manufacturing engineering, among others. R&D efforts focused on improving the functionality, security, and performance of the BlackBerry solution, as well as developing new devices for current and emerging network technologies and market segments. The ratio of software to hardware developers was approximately 2:1, and about 40 percent of the software engineers were involved in core design work while another 40 percent were engaged in testing and documentation (the remaining 20 percent were in management, and support functions like documentation and project management).

R&D had increased significantly both in terms of the total number of employees as well as the geographic scope of its operations. Since 2000, the R&D group had grown more than tenfold, from 200 to 2,100 people and expanded to two more locations in Canada (Ottawa and Mississauga), several in the United States (Dallas, Chicago, Atlanta, Seattle, and Palo Alto) and one in England. Waterloo was still the principal location—home to a vibrant and collaborative culture of young and talented engineers.

RIM's cryptographic and software source code played a key role in the success of the company, delivering the safe and secure voice and data transmission on which the BlackBerry reputation was built. Chris Wormald, vice president of strategic alliances, who was responsible for acquisitions, licensing, and partnerships, described the challenge as follows:

> At the end of the day, our source code is really among our few enduring technical assets. We have gone through extraordinary measures to protect it.

Exhibit 6 Competitive R&D Spend, Select Competitors (in millions of US$)

Nokia		Dec. 31/04	Dec. 31/05	Dec. 31/06	Dec. 31/07
Revenue		$46,606	$54,022	$64,971	$80,672
R&D		$ 5,784	$ 6,020	$ 6,157	$ 8,229
% of Revenue		12.41%	11.14%	9.48%	10.20%
Microsoft	**June 30/03**	**June 30/04**	**June 30/05**	**June 30/06**	**June 30/07**
Revenue	$32,187	$ 36,835	$39,788	$44,282	$51,122
R&D	$ 6,595	$ 7,735	$ 6,097	$ 6,584	$ 7,121
% of Revenue	20.49%	21.00%	15.32%	14.87%	13.93%
Motorola	**Dec. 31/03**	**Dec. 31/04**	**Dec. 31/05**	**Dec. 31/06**	**Dec. 31/07**
Revenue	$23,155	$29,663	$35,310	$42,847	$36,622
R&D	$ 2,979	$ 3,316	$ 3,600	$ 4,106	$ 4,429
% of Revenue	12.87%	11.18%	10.20%	9.58%	12.09%
Apple	**Sept. 27/03**	**Sept. 25/04**	**Sept. 24/05**	**Sept. 30/06**	**Sept. 29/07**
Revenue	$6,207	$8,279	$13,931	$19,315	$24,006
R&D	$ 471	$ 491	$ 535	$ 712	$ 782
% of Revenue	7.59%	5.93%	3.84%	3.69%	3.26%
RIM	**Feb. 28/04**	**Feb. 26/05**	**Mar. 4/06**	**Mar. 3/07**	**Proj. Mar./08**
Revenue	$ 595	$1,350	$2,066	$3,037	$6,009
R&D	$ 63	$ 103	$ 159	$ 236	$ 360
% of Revenue	10.59%	7.63%	7.70%	7.77%	5.99%
Palm	**May 31/03**	**May 31/04**	**May 31/05**	**May 31/06**	**May 31/07**
Revenue	$ 838	$ 950	$ 1,270	$ 1,578	$ 1,561
R&D	$ 70	$ 69	$ 90	$ 136	$ 191
% of Revenue	8.35%	7.26%	7.09%	8.62%	12.24%

Note: Nokia 2007 includes Nokia Siemens.
Source: Company annual reports.

> Extraordinary is probably still too shallow of a word. We don't give anyone any access under any circumstances. RIM was founded on a principle of "we can do it better ourselves"—it is a philosophy that is embedded in our DNA. This vertical integration of technology makes geographic expansion and outsourcing of software development very difficult.

Intellectual property rights were thus diligently guarded through a combination of patent, copyright, and contractual agreements. It was also strategically managed through a geography strategy that divided core platform development from product and technology development, with most of the core work (on the chip sets, software source code, product design) still occurring in Waterloo. However, the exponential growth in sales, competition, and industry changes was placing tremendous pressures on the R&D teams at the Canadian headquarters.

Similar to other players in the telecommunications industry (see Exhibit 6), it was RIM's policy to maintain its R&D spending as a consistent percentage of total sales. Investment analysts often looked to this number to gauge the sustainability of revenue growth. R&D expenses were seen as a proxy for new product or service development and therefore used as a key indicator of future revenue potential. Human capital represented the bulk of R&D dollars, and the organizational development team in charge of hiring at RIM was working overtime to try to keep up with the growing demand for the qualified

Exhibit 7 Employee Growth at RIM

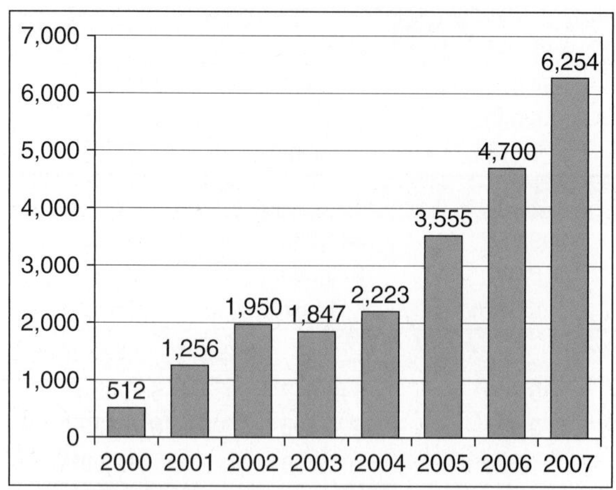

Source: RIM annual reports.

engineers needed to deliver on both customer and investor expectations.

ORGANIZATIONAL DEVELOPMENT FOR R&D AT RIM

The 2,100 R&D employees made up about 35 percent of RIM's 6,254 employees.[20] Total headcount had also been growing in double digits over the last five years (see Exhibit 7). However, if investment analysts were correct and sales grew by almost 70 percent again in 2008,[21] the large numbers involved could hinder RIM's ability to rely on its historic growth strategy: sourcing from the local talent pool, through employee referrals and new graduate recruitment, and making selective acquisitions of small technology companies. It needed to find upwards of 1,400 new software developers just to maintain the status quo in R&D. And not only did they have to find large numbers of talented individuals, they also had to figure out where they would be located and how to integrate them into RIM's culture.

The culture at RIM headquarters was seen as one of its differentiators and was a key factor in RIM's low employee turnover rate. In fact, the company had recently been recognized as one of "Canada's 10 Most Admired Corporate Cultures."[22] In describing the way things worked in the software development group at RIM, Dayna Perry, director of organizational development for R&D, commented:

> What we have here is flexibility, adaptability, and the ability to work collaboratively and collegially. We haven't had a lot of process or the kind of bureaucracy that you may see in other larger organizations. . . . It is what has allowed us to be very responsive to market opportunities. It is sort of the "magic" or the "secret sauce" of how things just work and we get things done.

A software developer leading a team working on BlackBerry's many multilingual devices agreed, saying:

> RIM, in comparison to some of its competitors, is a nice and dynamic environment . . . RIM is a place engineers like to work. Some of our competitors treat their engineers as something unimportant. They don't participate in decisions. They are interchangeable. There is a very very strong bureaucracy . . . it's crazy. RIM is very different.

Maintaining its unique culture was a priority for RIM. Remaining centered in Waterloo nurtured this ability. But it was becoming clear that growing mostly in Waterloo was going to become increasingly difficult. Not only did RIM already employ most of the best developers in the area, it already attracted the best and brightest of the nearby University of Waterloo's engineering and computer science graduates. About 300 students came on board every semester through the company's coveted co-op program and many were asked to remain with RIM after graduation. In fact, the talent at the University of Waterloo was so widely recognized that even Bill Gates made frequent visits to the university to court the best students[23] and Google had recently opened facilities there, acknowledging that "Waterloo is an incredible pool of talent"[24] and that it was ready to start hiring the best and the brightest "as quickly as possible."[25]

Attracting outside talent to Waterloo was difficult given the competitive nature of the global software development industry. Most of the big players in the smartphone space were also ramping up. For example, Sony Ericsson had posted 230 design and engineering jobs in Sweden, China, and the United States. Nokia was looking for 375 R&D employees in Finland, the United States, India, and Germany, among other development sites. In California's Silicon Valley, Apple and Google had scooped up many of the top mobile browser developers in a technology cluster famous for its exaggerated employee benefits and unbeatable climate. Motorola could be the exception to the rule, having announced layoffs of engineers. Although Waterloo, Ontario, had recently been named ICF's "Intelligent Community of the Year," the city of 115,000 people[26] might not be perceived by some candidates to be as attractive as other high tech centers which were more cosmopolitan, for example: Silicon Valley, or previous winners of the ICF, Taipei (2006), Mitaka (2005), or Glasgow (2004).[27]

Compounding the problem was a shortage of physical space at RIM's Waterloo campus that was a running joke around headquarters. Even company founder Mike Lazaridis had to laugh about it—responding to a reporter's question about his most embarrassing moment, Lazaridis replied: "Scraping my Aston Martin in RIM's driveway. I was leaving a space and a car came from nowhere. The scratches have been fixed, but not the too-busy parking lot. It's a hazard of a growing company."[28]

On top of it all, RIM was looking to hire a very particular mix of engineers. Although new graduates were essential, to be ahead of the game a good proportion of the incoming employees was going to have to be senior hires. RIM needed people who could fit with the culture and hit the ground running. Dayna noted: "We just don't have the luxury of time to grow all our own talent. We do that in parallel and do a lot of internal promotion, but that is an investment you make in the future, it is not going to help you solve your problem today." And it wasn't just a question of the number of engineers. In software, breakthrough innovations often came from small teams led by a visionary. Many at RIM believed that "software is as much about art as it is about engineering." And in the dynamic wireless communications market, exceptional software developers were scarce.

MANAGING EXPLOSIVE GROWTH

The approach to growth used by RIM in the past would not deliver the scale and scope of R&D resources required to maintain its technical superiority. RIM had several options.

Do What We Do Now, Only More of It

RIM had been very successful in its local recruiting strategy as well as nationwide campus recruitment drives. It relied heavily on the personal and professional networks of existing employees as an ear-on-the-ground approach to finding new talent. One option was to expand co-op programs to other universities as well as increase the frequency and intensity of its new graduate recruitment efforts. Microsoft's intern program, for example, included subsidized housing and transportation (car rental or bike purchase plan), paid travel to Redmond, health club memberships, and even subsidized housecleaning![29]

Likewise, RIM could follow Microsoft's lead and form a global scouting group dedicated to finding the best talent worldwide and bringing them into RIM. Canada ranked as one of the best countries in the world to live in terms of life expectancy, literacy, education, and other standards of living.[30] These and other benefits could attract young developers particularly from emerging markets. As well, the stronger dollar made Canada more attractive.

Similar to other players in the industry (e.g., Apple, Motorola, Sony Ericson, Nokia), RIM posted many of its job openings online and potential employees searched and applied for the positions best suited for their skills and interests. However, with over 800 worldwide job postings, finding the right job was often a daunting task. RIM also had no formal way to manage qualified candidates that may have simply applied to the wrong team and hence good leads were potentially lost. Some competitors allowed candidates to build an open application (similar to Monster or Workopolis) that could then be viewed by anyone in the organization looking for talent. Revamping the careers website and being more creative in the way in which they structured recruiting was being considered.

Some competitors had also formalized hiring and the onboarding processes of computer scientists by hiring in "waves." Rather than posting individual job openings, Symbian, for example, solicited résumés once a year, which were then reviewed, and successful candidates invited to the London, U.K.-based head office to attend one of nine Assessment Days. If the attendees passed a series of tests and interviews, they were then inducted into the company during a formal "bootcamp" training session that lasted five weeks.[31] Symbian had also set up extensive collaborations with 44 universities in 17 countries including China, Russia, and India as well as Ethiopia, Kuwait, Lebanon, Thailand, and the United States. Dubbed The Symbian Academy, this network allowed partners and licensees to post jobs for Symbian Academy students and for professors to collaborate on the research and development of innovative applications such as pollution monitors on GPS-enabled Symbian smartphones.[32] Although RIM enjoyed an excellent relationship with the University of Waterloo, it did not currently have a recruiting strategy of this scope.

Grow and Expand Existing Geographies

RIM had established R&D operations beyond Waterloo, in Ottawa, Mississauga, Dallas, and Chicago over the last five years. It was also expanding the number of product and technology development facilities in locations such as Fort Lauderdale by recruiting through general job fairs. This strategy, however, had to be balanced with a number of trade-offs. First, RIM wanted to ensure that its geographic expansion was not haphazard, but rather strategically executed. Second, the cost of talent in various locations had to be considered. Software engineers in Palo Alto, for example, commanded much higher wages than in Waterloo and the competition there was even more intense, with high turnover costs incurred when employees were wooed away by the many other high tech companies in the area.

There was also some internal resistance to expanding R&D to locations outside of Waterloo. Although there was a growing realization that RIM could no longer continue to grow locally, one senior executive commented:

> There are people here, even leaders and senior people, who have said: "What? Products being built elsewhere? No! We can't do that! Then we won't have any control!" So some of it is a cultural shift and a mind shift for the people that have been here and it is hard for them to let go and to be part of a really big company. And RIM is getting to be a big company now. And for some people, from an organizational culture perspective, it just doesn't resonate well with them.

This sentiment was not uncommon among software-centric organizations. Despite some geographic expansion, Microsoft, for example, had recently recommitted to its Redmond, Washington campus, spending over $1 billion on new and upgraded facilities there with room to house an additional 12,000 employees.[33] Google was also strongly committed to maintaining its Mountain View, California, headquarters, with only a few satellite offices. Its unique company culture, built on attracting and keeping the best talent in a young and fun environment was part of Google's incredible success story, and helped it achieve the status of the number one company to work for, according to *Fortune* magazine.[34] Other large software companies such as Oracle and Apple also kept their software developers in one location to foster innovation. In some ways, RIM was already more geographically distributed than many larger software organizations.

Although establishing a geographic expansion plan posed difficulties, RIM had nevertheless laid out several criteria for selecting new locations for product and technology development sites. First, the area had to already have a pool of talent that housed a mature skill set; the city or region had be home to an existing base of software or hardware companies, thus ensuring that a critical mass of highly skilled employees was available. RIM's strategic expansion into Ottawa, for example, was influenced by the availability of talented software engineers in the area in the wake of Nortel's massive layoffs.[35] Lastly, the city or region had to have universities with strong technical programs. This allowed RIM to expand on its successful co-op programs and graduate recruitment initiatives. Once a satellite development site was set up, however, there was still the issue of how to transfer RIM's young and dynamic corporate culture to these locations.

Increase Acquisitions

RIM had success in bringing people on board through acquisition. Several years earlier, RIM had acquired Slangsoft, a high tech start-up in Israel that was developing code which allowed for the ability to display and input Chinese characters—key to tailoring BlackBerry for Asian and other foreign markets. As part of the acquisition, RIM worked with Immigration Canada to relocate 11 of the engineers to Waterloo, 10 of whom were still with RIM more than six years later.

Growth by acquisition was a common practice in the high tech and telecommunications sectors. Google had made its initial move to Waterloo in 2006, for example, through the acquisition of a small wireless software company, subsequently discontinuing the company's web browser product, making it a purchase of talent and intellectual property.[36] Other companies had also made strategic acquisitions of technology. In 2002, Apple, for example, purchased EMagic, a small German company whose software was then used in the development of the popular Mac program Garage Band.[37] In larger and more public acquisitions, Nokia and Motorola had both recently acquired software companies in the hopes of gaining faster access to the growing smartphone market. In 2006, Nokia purchased Intellisync Corporation, a wireless messaging and mobile-software developer, for $430 million, creating Nokia's "business mobility solutions" group.[38] Also in 2006, Motorola purchased Good Technology for a rumored $500 million and released Good 5.0, allowing for secure access to corporate intranets so enterprise users could download, edit, and send documents remotely.[39]

Given the depressed economic climate in the United States in early 2008, many smaller firms and technology start-ups were struggling financially, as were some larger competitors. There were persistent rumors that Palm, for example, was in severe financial trouble.[40] Further, growth by acquisition could also allow for the tactical expansion in other strategic markets.

The European mobile telecommunications market, in particular, was highly "nationalistic," with end users favoring home-grown companies over foreign solutions. Establishing a presence there through acquisition could buy RIM goodwill and serve as a portal to this lucrative market. The economic downturn in the United States and recent competitor plant closures in Europe presented RIM with the potential for opportunistic acquisitions, either of technology or of software engineering talent.

Go Global

In early 2008, most of the R&D was still done in Waterloo, with some core work also being done in Ottawa and product and technology sites throughout the United States and in the United Kingdom. RIM was exploring a broader global expansion. It already had customer service operations in Singapore and sales & marketing representative offices in France, Germany, Italy, Spain, China, Australia, Hong Kong, and Japan. Yet it had stopped short of establishing core research and development sites outside of Canada. Nonetheless, despite a strong desire to keep R&D close to home, RIM estimated that of all the new hires in 2008, likely half would have to be outside of Canada. In addition to the United States, it was looking to Europe, the Middle East, and Africa (EMEA) and Eastern Europe. The same selection criteria of a mature skill set and strong technological universities applied to choosing R&D sites outside North America.

Some of RIM's key competitors had a long history of global expansion of their R&D activities. Symbian, for example, opened an R&D center in Beijing in August 2007, already having three others in the United Kingdom and India.[41] Motorola, had been present in China since 1993 when it established its first R&D center there as part of its Global Software Group (GSG). It had since set up R&D activities in Beijing, Tianjin, Shanghai, Nanjing, Chengdu, and Hangzhou, investing an estimated US $800 million and employing more than 3,000 R&D staff in China. In 2007, Motorola added R&D sites in Vietnam and South Korea[42] and announced it would open an additional R&D complex in Wangjing, China, with another 3,000 employees.[43]

China in particular was beginning to gain worldwide recognition as a center for innovation. The number of patent applications was doubling every two years and the R&D to GDP ratio had also doubled in the last decade. In addition to Motorola, Nokia had set up a number of research bases in China.[44] In 2005, Nokia had five R&D units there, employing more than 600 people; an estimated 40 percent of its global Mobile Phones Business Group handsets were designed and developed in the Beijing Product Creation Center.[45] The company had also recently announced a long-term joint research program with Tsinghua University in Beijing that would see 20 Nokia researchers working alongside 30 professors and associates and up to 50 students.[46] Globally, Nokia Research Centers (NRC) described its R&D strategy as follows:

> NRC has a two-fold approach to achieving its mandate of leading Nokia into the future. The work for core technology breakthroughs supporting Nokia's existing businesses takes place in the Core Technology Centers, the CTCs. More visionary, exploratory systems research that goes well beyond any current business model is conducted at the many System Research Centers, the SRCs.[47]

Nokia's core technology centers were in Finland, with the SRCs in China, Germany, the United Kingdom, the United States, Finland, and Japan. The company employed 112,262 people, of which 30,415, or 27 percent, were in R&D.[48]

The Motorola Global Software Group (GSG) was more decentralized. In addition to China it had R&D centers in Australia, Singapore, Mexico, Argentina, the United Kingdom, Poland, Russia, Italy, Canada, and India, among others, and employed approximately 27,000 R&D employees worldwide. The Motorola GSG in India had nearly 3,500 engineers and was responsible for designing 40 percent of the software used in Motorola phones worldwide, including the MOTORAZR and MOTO Q. However, Motorola was not noted for having world-class smartphone software. The GSG structure was speculated to have contributed to Motorola's inability to deliver a successful follow-up product to the RAZR as well as to have precipitated the company's recent financial downturn.[49]

Nonetheless, partnering with major research institutes to source top talent appeared to be a fairly common strategy. Motorola India collaborated with six of the seven Indian Institutes of Technology (IIT), as well as the Indian Institute of Science (IISC) and the Indian Institute of Information Technology (IIIT).[50] Other technology firms were also partnering with emerging market governmental and educational institutions to secure a foothold in future markets. Cisco Systems, for example, a leading manufacturer of network equipment, had recently announced a US$16 billion expansion plan into China, including investments in manufacturing, venture capital and education. Working with China's Ministry of Education, Cisco had established 200 "Networking Academies" in 70 cities in China and had trained more than 90,000 students.[51]

These types of collaborations and international research consortiums, however, raised not only logistical but also legal issues. Source code loss, software piracy, and product imitations were more common in developing countries where IP protection laws (or enforcement) lagged the United States or Canada, leading to both explicit and tacit knowledge "leakage." For example, despite its strong commitment to China, Nokia was recently forced to file suit against two Beijing firms for manufacturing and selling mobile phones that were a direct copy of its proprietary and legally protected industrial designs.[52] Other large high tech companies such as Cisco and Microsoft had also suffered source code breaches. In late 2006, China Unicom, the state-run telecommunications company, had launched its own wireless e-mail service, which it boldly named the Redberry, announcing that their Redberry brand not only continued the already familiar "BlackBerry" image and name, it also fully reflected the symbolic meaning of China Unicom's new red corporate logo.[53] For much of East Asia, reverse engineering and copying foreign products were important sources of learning, helping to transition these markets from imitators of technology to innovators and competitive threats.[54]

Wormald described the difficulties with emerging market dynamics as follows:

> I was just talking to a Fortune 500 CEO the other day who is closing up shop in India. This company had a 45 percent employee turnover rate. They just walk down the street and go work for his competitor and he was tired of his source code just walking out the door.

For RIM, going global was therefore problematic on a number of fronts, most notably because the BlackBerry source code had to be protected. In addition, expanding to emerging markets was also complicated by restrictions regarding cryptographic software. Most governments, including those of Canada and the United States, along with Russia and China, regulated the import and export of encryption products due to national security issues. Encryption was seen as a "dual-use technology" which could have both commercial and military value and was thus carefully monitored. The U.S. government would not purchase any product that had not passed the Federal Information Processing Standard (FIPS) certification tests. This would preclude any product that had encrypted data in China because "if you encrypt data in China, you have to provide the Chinese government with the ability to access the keys."[55] India had also recently notified RIM that it planned to eavesdrop on BlackBerry users, claiming that terrorists may be hiding behind the encrypted messages to avoid detection.[56]

Even if these hurdles could be overcome, going global also brought with it additional challenges of organizational design, communication, and integration between head office and other geographically dispersed locations. Some competitors had chosen to expand globally by product line, while others had outsourced less sensitive functions such as testing and documentation. Eastern European countries such as Poland and Hungary, for example, were emerging as strong contenders for quality assurance testing. The lower cost of labor in developing and transitional economies, however, was showing signs of inflationary pressures in some locales and any planned savings might be somewhat offset by the increased monitoring, coordination, and integration costs. Furthermore, RIM was not set up to manage a multicountry research consortium and the mindset in Waterloo was still very much such that core engineers needed to be seen to be perceived as valuable. On the other hand, the potential could not be ignored. In China, where the penetration rate was only 38 percent, the Symbian OS system used in Nokia, Samsung, Sony Ericsson, and LG smartphones enjoyed a 68.7 percent share, and iPhone sales had reached 400,000 "unlocked" units.[57] In India, where the penetration rate stood at 21 percent, Virgin Mobile had recently struck a brand franchise agreement with Tata Teleservices, announcing plans to gain at least 50 million young subscribers to its mobile services, generating estimated revenues of US$350 billion.[58] The sheer number of potential new users was overwhelming.

CONCLUSION

Looking at the holiday sales numbers and the projected growth for 2008, Yach took a minute to think about the path he was on. He knew that first-quarter revenue projections alone were estimated at $2.2 billion to $2.3 billion and that RIM was expecting to add another 2.2 million BlackBerry subscribers by the end of May 2008.[59] At that rate, analysts projected that 2008 would bring at least another 70 percent growth in sales.[60] Furthermore, Mike Lazaridis had recently said in an interview:

> If you really want to build something sustainable and innovative you have to invest in R&D. If you build the right culture and invest in the right facilities and you encourage and motivate and inspire both young and seasoned people and put them all in the right environment—then it really performs for you. It's what I call sustainable innovation. And it's very different from the idea that you come up with something and then maximize value by reducing its costs. But building a sustainable innovation cycle requires an enormous investment in R&D. You have to understand all the technologies involved.[61]

Yach knew that his software developers were key to RIM's continued success; he was committed to delivering on the expectations for continued and sustainable growth in 2008 and beyond. Although he wanted to keep growing organically, sourcing talent locally and bringing his engineers into the cultural fold of RIM in Waterloo, he suspected this era was ending. In light of the unprecedented and exponential growth of the last year, coupled with the increasing competition and untapped global opportunities, he needed a plan.

Leaving the office after a hectic and frenetic first day back, Yach thought to himself: "How can I plan for this growth when it is just one of 10 burning issues on my agenda? We can't take a time-out to decide how to execute the growth." Grabbing the sales numbers to prepare for tomorrow's meeting, Yach knew he had the evening to consider the way ahead. The vacation was definitely over.

Endnotes

[1] D. George-Cosh, "Analysts cheer RIM results, hike targets," *Financial Post,* April 4, 2008, http://www.nationalpost.com/scripts/story.html?id=420318 (accessed April 22, 2008).
[2] Of converged device shipments (smartphones and wireless handhelds). Canalys Smart Mobile Device Analysis service, Press Release, February 5, 2008, http://www.canalys.com/pr/2008/r2008021.htm (accessed April 2, 2008).
[3] http://www.rim.com/newsroom/news/awards/index.shtml.
[4] AFX International Focus, "RIM: Facebook for BlackBerry downloads top 1M," April 1, 2008, http://global.factiva.com (accessed April 1, 2008).
[5] Business Wire, "Guitar Hero II Mobile will rock your BlackBerry Smartphone," April 1, 2008, http://global.factiva.com (accessed April 1, 2008).
[6] Prosumer refers to "professional consumers," customers that use their mobile devices for both business and personal communications.
[7] "Converged" refers to the convergence of the digital wireless communication industry (cellular telephony) and information technology industries, signaled by the arrival of 2G networks which merged voice and data transmissions.
[8] GSMA 20 year factsheet, http://www.gsmworld.com/documents/20_year_factsheet.pdf (accessed April 5, 2008).
[9] P. Svensson, "Microsoft Upgrades Windows Mobile," Associated Press Newswire, April 1, 2008, http://global.factiva.com (accessed April 1, 2008).
[10] Esmerk Finish News, "Global: Survey: Nokia has best innovation strategy," March 25, 2008, http://global.factiva.com (accessed April 1, 2008).
[11] N. Gohring, "Smartphones on the rise? Thank the iPhone, panel says," *Washington Post,* March 31, 2008, http://www.washingtonpost.com/wp-dyn/content/article/2008/03/31/AR2008033102392.html (accessed April 1, 2008).
[12] Canalys Smart Mobile Device Analysis service, Press Release, February 5, 2008, http://www.canalys.com/pr/2008/r2008021.htm (accessed April 2, 2008).
[13] Chris Ambrosio, Strategy Analytics, January 2008 and Pete Cunningham, Canalys, as quoted on www.symbian.com (accessed April 3, 2008).
[14] www.symbian.com (accessed April 3, 2008).
[15] Canalys Smart Mobile Device Analysis service, Press Release, February 5, 2008, http://www.canalys.com/pr/2008/r2008021.htm (accessed April 2, 2008).
[16] A. Hesseldahl, "How the iPhone is suiting up for work," *BusinessWeek,* March 6, 2008, www.businessweek.com (accessed March 21, 2008).
[17] "Microsoft unveils smartphone advancements to im-prove ability to work and play with one phone," April 1, 2008, Press Release; and "Microsoft announces enterprise-class mobile solution," April 1, 2008, Press Release, www.microsoft.com/prespass/press/2008/apr08.
[18] Canalys Smart Mobile Device Analysis service, Press Release, February 5, 2008, http://www.canalys.com/pr/2008/r2008021.htm (accessed April 2, 2008).
[19] Ken Dulaney of Gartner, as quoted in A. Hesseldahl, "RIM: Growth rules the day," February 22, 2008, www.businessweek.com.
[20] The remaining groups included 836 in sales, marketing and business development; 1,098 in customer care and technical support; 1,158 in manufacturing; and 1,002 in administration, which included information technology, BlackBerry network operations and service development, finance, legal, facilities, and corporate administration.
[21] http://finance.yahoo.com/q/ae?s=RIMM.
[22] Canada's 10 Most Admired Corporate Cultures for 2006, www.waterstonehc.com (accessed April 5, 2008).
[23] D. Friend, "Microsoft hunting IT grads," *London Free Press,* March 22, 2008.
[24] "Google expands Waterloo base," http://atuw.ca/feature-google-expands-waterloo-base/, (accessed April 11, 2008).
[25] A. Petroff, "A Recruiter's Waterloo?" http://www.financialpost.com/trading_desk/technology/story.html?id=389305, (accessed April 11, 2008).
[26] The greater Kitchener-Waterloo area had approximately 450,000 inhabitants.
[27] Intelligent Community Forum, 2007 Intelligent Community of the Year Awards, press release May 18, 2007, http://www.intelligentcommunity.org/displaycommon.cfm?an=1&subarticlenbr=221, (accessed April 5, 2008).
[28] J. Shillingford, "A life run by BlackBerry," *Financial Times,* March 19, 2008, http://global.factiva.com, (accessed on April 1, 2008).
[29] http://www.microsoft.com/college/ip_overview.mspx.
[30] United Nations Human Development Index 2007/2008.
[31] http://www.symbian.com/about/careers/graduate%20program/index.html (accessed April 3, 2008).
[32] www.symbian.com (accessed April 3, 2008).
[33] B. Romano, "Microsoft campus expands, transforms, inside out," *Seattle Times,* November 23, 2007, http://seattletimes.nwsource.com/cgi-bin/PrintStory.pl?document_id=2004007121&zsection_id=2003750725&slug=microsoft11&date=20071111 (accessed April 22, 2008).
[34] http://money.cnn.com/magazines/fortune/bestcompanies/2007/snapshots/1.html (accessed April 22, 2008).
[35] Estimated at over 15,000 total jobs in the last eight years; B. Hill, "Nortel to keep Ottawa as main R&D centre," April 4, 2008, *The Montreal Gazette,* http://www.canada.com/montrealgazette/news/business/story.html?id=24aa8d53-154a-4d88-aa9d-593ce9794e10 (accessed April 11, 2008).
[36] M. Evans, "Waterloo gets Googled," January 6, 2006, http://www.financialpost.com/story.html?id=c4f6f084-d72f-43ea-8a82-affe38df3830&k=58579 (accessed April 11, 2008).
[37] A. Hesseldahl, "What to do with Apple's cash," *BusinessWeek,* March 1, 2007, http://www.businessweek.com/technology/content/mar2007/tc20070301_402290.htm (accessed April 11, 2008).
[38] TelecomWeb News Digest, "Nokia completes Intellisync purchase," February 10, 2006, http://global.factiva.com (accessed April 11, 2008).
[39] RCR Wireless News, "Motorola set to leverage Good in competitive e-mail market," June 25, 2007, http://global.factiva.com (accessed April 11, 2008).
[40] S. Weinberg, "Palm acquisition not considered threat to RIM," Dow Jones Newswire, http://global.factiva.com (accessed April 11, 2008).
[41] Business Monitor International, Asia Pacific Telecommunications Insight, April 2008, Issue 24.
[42] Business Monitor International, Asia Pacific Telecommunications Insight, January 2008, Issue 21.
[43] Press Release, "Twenty years' commitment ensures a more successful future," November 8, 2007, http://www.motorola.com/mediacenter/news/detail.jsp?globalObjectId=8923_8852_23&page=archive.
[44] Business Monitor International, Asia Pacific Telecommunications Insight, November 2007, Issue 19.
[45] Press Release, May 21, 2004, "Nokia Expands R&D in China," http://press.nokia.com/PR/200405/946603_5.html.
[46] Press Release, May 28, 2007, "Nokia and Tsinghua University announce new research framework," http://www.nokia.com/A4136001?newsid=1129236.
[47] http://research.nokia.com/centers/index.html.
[48] Nokia annual report 2007.
[49] "What's on Motorola's agenda?" *BusinessWeek,* January 9, 2008, http://www.businessweek.com/innovate/content/jan2008/id20080114_304911_page_2.htm (accessed April 16, 2008).
[50] Motorola 2007 10-K and http://www.motorola.com/mot/doc/6/6294_MotDoc.pdf.
[51] Business Monitor International, Asia Pacific Telecommunications Insight, January 2008, Issue 21.
[52] "Nokia files suit over alleged copy of model," *Shanghai Daily,* June 29, 2006, http://global.factiva.com (accessed April 16, 2008).
[53] A. Hesseldahl, "BlackBerry vs. Redberry in China," *BusinessWeek,* September 25, 2006, http://www.businessweek.com/technology/content/apr2006/tc20060413_266291.htm?chan=search (accessed April 16, 2008).

[54] United Nations World Investment Report 2005, "Transnational Corporations and the Internationalization of R&D," New York and Geneva, 2005, p. 165.
[55] E. Messmer, "Encryption restrictions" and "Federal encryption purchasing requirements," *Network World,* March 15, 2004, http://www.networkworld.com/careers/2004/0315man.html?page=1 (accessed April 22, 2008).
[56] N. Lakshman, "India wants to eavesdrop on BlackBerrys," *BusinessWeek,* April 1, 2008, http://global.factiva.com (accessed April 7, 2008).
[57] Business Monitor International, Asia Pacific Telecommunications Insight, April 2008, Issue 24.
[58] Ibid.
[59] Press Release, April 2, 2008: http://www.rim.com/news/press/2008/pr-02_04_2008-01.shtml
[60] http://finance.yahoo.com/q/ae?s=RIMM
[61] A. Hesseldahl, "BlackBerry: Innovation Behind the Icon," *Business Week*, April 4, 2008, http://www.businessweek.com/innovate/content/apr2008/id2008044_416784.htm?chan=search (accessed April 6, 2008).

CASE 18 Adidas in 2008: Has Corporate Restructuring Increased Shareholder Value?

John E. Gamble
University of South Alabama

For more than a decade, adidas AG's corporate strategy had been focused on making acquisitions that would allow it to surpass Nike as the leader of the global sporting goods industry. The company's 1998 acquisition of French sporting goods manufacturer and marketer Salomon SA diversified it beyond footwear and apparel and into ski equipment, golf clubs, bicycle components, and winter sports apparel. The €1.5 billion acquisition allowed adidas to surpass Reebok to become the world's second largest sporting goods company, with 1998 sales of nearly €5.1 billion. However, almost as soon as the deal was consummated, it looked doubtful that the acquisition would help adidas achieve its strategic intent of becoming the world's largest seller of sporting goods. Chief concerns with the acquisition were the declining attractiveness of the winter sports industry and integration problems between the adidas footwear and apparel business and Salomon's business units. Not until 2003, five years after the acquisition, had adidas's earnings per share returned to the level that shareholders enjoyed in 1997. In addition, the company's stock price failed to return to its 1998 trading range until 2004.

Adidas management divested all of Salomon's winter sports and bicycle components brands in 2005 to Amer Sports Corporation for €485 million. The divestiture of Salomon's winter sports and bicycle components business made TaylorMade Golf the lone business retained from the company's 1998 acquisition of Salomon SA. Adidas management followed the divestiture of Salomon business units with the €3.1 billion acquisition of Reebok International Ltd. in 2006. In addition to Reebok-branded athletic footwear and apparel, Reebok International also designed, marketed, and sold Rockport footwear, Greg Norman apparel, and CCM hockey equipment.

The Reebok acquisition increased the company's revenues from €5.8 billion in 2005 to €10.1 (approximately $13.3 billion) in 2006 and brought it closer to Nike, which ended fiscal 2006 with total revenues of $14.9 billion. Adidas revenues had grown to €10.3 billion by year-end 2007, and adidas management expected that the Reebok acquisition would boost 2008 revenues by an additional €250 million. The integration of adidas and Reebok supply chain activities was expected to result in cost savings of €105 million by year-end 2008 and contribute to improvements in both the company's gross margins and bottom line. However, Nike's continued to hold a substantial lead over adidas in the U.S. athletic footwear market, with a 36 percent market share compared to a combined 21 percent market share for adidas and Reebok branded footwear in 2008. Evidence seemed to be mounting to support the thesis of New Balance's CEO, Jim Davis, who upon hearing of adidas management's latest round of corporate restructuring in 2005 and 2006 concluded, "You can try to take on Nike, but . . . Nike is Nike and will continue to be Nike.[1] A summary of

Exhibit 1 Financial Summary for adidas AG, 1998–2007 (€ in millions, except per share data)

	2007	2006	2005	2004	2003	2002	2001	2000	1999	1998
Net sales	€10,299	€10,084	€6,636	€5,860	€6,267	€6,523	€6,112	€5,835	€5,354	€5,065
Cost of sales	5,417	5,589	3,439	3,047	3,453	3,704	3,511	3,307	3,002	2,941
Gross profit	4,882	4,495	3,197	2,813	2,814	2,819	2,601	2,528	2,352	2,124
Royalty and commission income	102	90	47	42	42	46	42	43	35	45
Operating expenses	4,035	3,704	2,537	2,236	2,324	2,343	2,126	2,091	1,870	1,698
Operating profit	949	881	707	584	490	477	475	437	482	416
Financial expenses, net	135	158	52	59	49	87	102	94	84	115
Income before taxes	815	723	655	526	438	390	376	347	398	319
Income taxes	260	227	221	193	167	148	147	140	153	105
Minority interests	4	13	8	7	11	14	21	25	18	9
Net income	€ 551	€ 483	€ 426	€ 326	€ 260	€ 228	€ 208	€ 182	€ 227	205 €
Basic earnings per share	€ 2.71	€ 2.37	€ 2.05	€ 1.72	€ 1.43	€ 1.26	€ 1.15	€ 1.00	€ 1.26	€ 1.13
Diluted earnings per share	€ 2.57	€ 2.25	€ 1.93	€ 1.64	€ 1.43	€ 1.26	€ 1.15	€ 1.00	€ 1.26	€ 1.16
Dividends per share	€ 0.50	€ 0.42	€ 0.33	€ 0.33	€ 0.25	€ 0.25	€ 0.23	€ 0.23	€ 0.23	€ 0.21
Number of shares outstanding at year-end	203,629	203,537	203,047	183,436	181,816	181,692	181,396	181,396	181,396	181,396

Source: adidas AG, 2007 annual report.

adidas's financial performance for 1998 through 2007 is presented in Exhibit 1. The performance of the company's common shares between October 1999 and October 2008 is provided in Exhibit 2. Exhibit 3 presents balance sheets for adidas for 2006 and 2007.

COMPANY HISTORY

The history of adidas can be traced to 1920, when German baker Adolph "Adi" Dassler, began trying his hand at designing and producing footwear for athletes competing in soccer, tennis, and track-and-field events. In 1924, Adi Dassler's brother, Rudolph "Rudi" Dassler, joined him in the shoemaking venture to establish Gebrüder Dassler Schuhfabrik (Dassler Brothers Shoe Factory) in Herzogenaurach, Bavaria. The Dassler brothers made their first major innovation in athletic shoe design in 1925, when they integrated studs and spikes into the soles of track-and-field shoes. The Dassler brothers continued to develop key innovations in athletic footwear such as the arch support. Many of the standard features of today's athletic footwear were developed by Dassler brothers, with Adi Dassler alone accumulating 700 patents and property rights worldwide by the time of his death in 1978.

The Dasslers were also innovators in the field of marketing—giving away their shoes to German athletes competing in the 1928 Olympic Games in Amsterdam. By the 1936 Olympic Games in Berlin, most athletes would compete only in Gebrüder Dassler shoes, including Jesse Owens, who won four gold medals in the Berlin games. By 1937, the company was making 30 different styles of shoes for athletes in eleven sports. All of the company's styles were distinguished from other brands by two stripes applied to each side of the shoe.

The Dassler brothers' sports shoe production ceased during World War II when Gebrüder Dassler Schuhfabrik was directed to produce boots for the armed forces of Nazi Germany. Adi Dassler was allowed to remain in Herzogenaurach to run the factory, but Rudi Dassler was drafted into the army and spent a year in an Allied prisoner-of-war camp after being captured. Upon the conclusion of the war, Rudi Dassler was released by the Allies and returned to Herzogenaurach to rejoin his family. The Dassler brothers returned to production of athletic shoes in

Exhibit 2 Performance of adidas AG's Stock Price, October 1999–October 2008

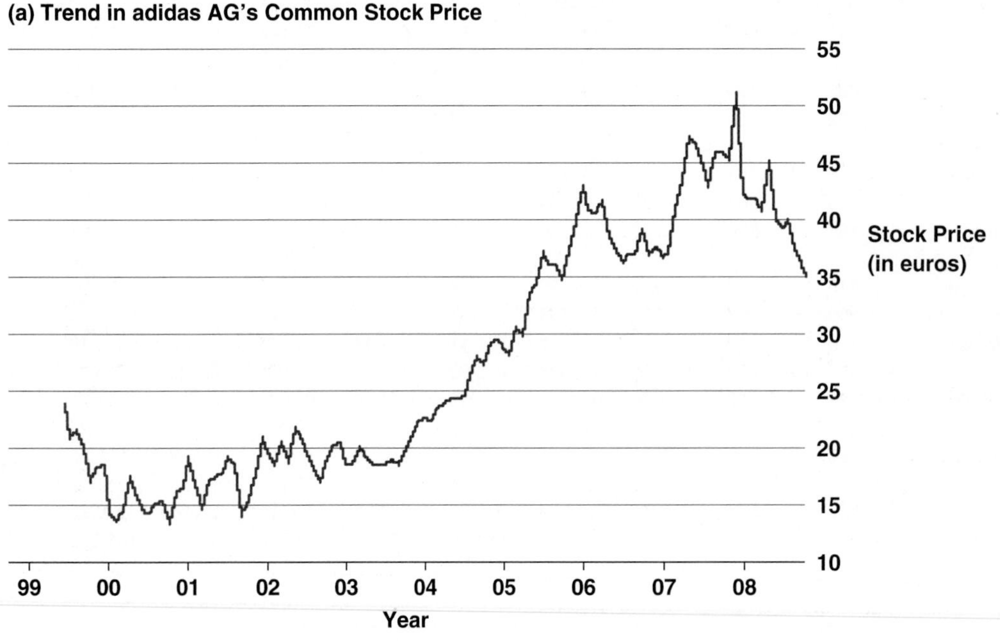

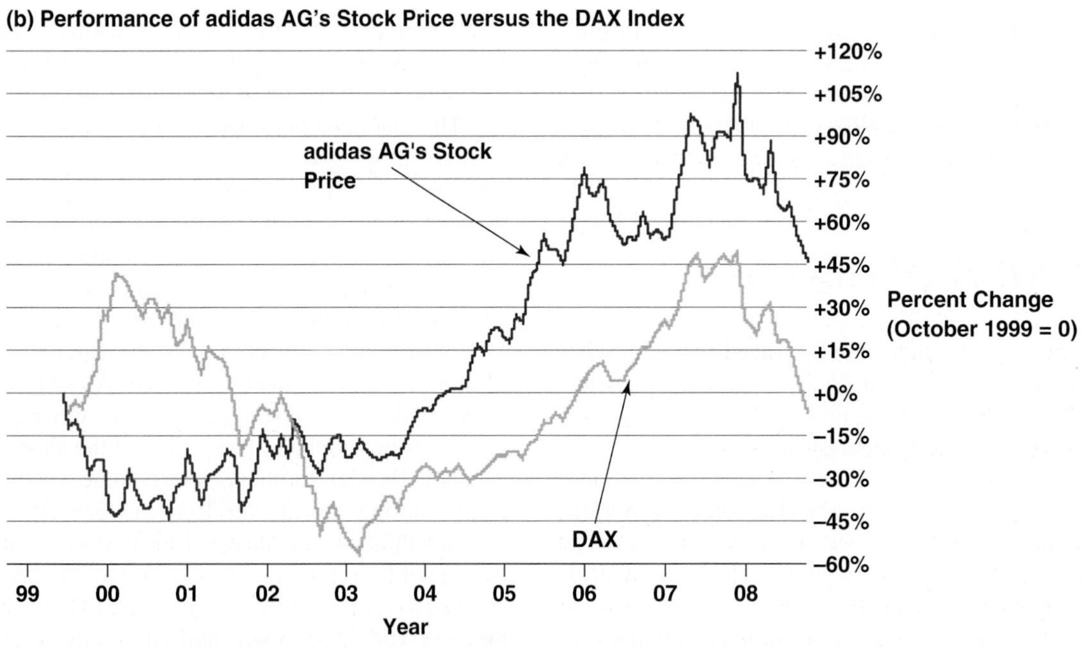

Exhibit 3 Adidas AG Balance Sheets, 2006–2007 (€ in millions)

	December 31,	
	2007	2006
Assets		
Cash and cash equivalents	€ 295	€ 311
Short-term financial assets	86	36
Accounts receivable	1,459	1,415
Inventories	1,629	1,607
Other current assets	669	556
Total current assets	4,138	3,925
Property, plant, and equipment, net	702	689
Goodwill, net	1,436	1,516
Trademarks	1,291	1,545
Other intangible assets, net	194	223
Long-term financial assets	103	106
Deferred tax assets	315	332
Other noncurrent assets	147	134
Total noncurrent assets	4,188	4,454
Total assets	€8,325	€8,379
Liabilities, Minority Interests, and Shareholders' Equity		
Short-term borrowings		
Accounts payable	€ 849	€ 752
Income taxes	285	283
Accrued liabilities and provisions	1,025	921
Other current liabilities	270	236
Total current liabilities	2,429	2,192
Long-term borrowings	2,146	2,578
Pensions and similar obligations	124	134
Deferred tax liabilities	450	522
Other noncurrent liabilities	142	117
Total noncurrent liabilities	2,862	3,351
Minority interests	11	8
Shareholders' equity	3,023	2,828
Total liabilities, minority interests, and shareholders' equity	€8,325	€8,379

Source: adidas AG, 2007 annual report.

1947, but the company was dissolved in 1948 after Adi and Rudi Dassler entered into a bitter feud. Rudi Dassler moved to the other side of the small village to establish his own shoe company, Puma Schuhfabrik Rudolph Dassler. With the departure of Rudi, Adi renamed the company adidas—a combination of his first and last names. Adi Dassler applied a third stripe to the sides of adidas shoes and registered the three-stripe trademark in 1949.

The nature of the disagreement between the two brothers was never known for certain, but the two never spoke again after their split and the feud became the foundation of both organizations' cultures while the two brothers were alive. The two rival companies were highly competitive, and both discouraged employees from fraternizing with cross-town rivals. An adidas spokesperson described the seriousness of the feud by stating, "Puma employees wouldn't be caught dead with adidas employees. . . . It wouldn't be allowed that an adidas employee would fall in love with a Puma employee."[2]

Adi Dassler kept up his string of innovations with molded rubber cleats in 1949, and in 1952 he developed track shoes with screw-in spikes. He expanded the concept to soccer shoes in 1954 with screw-in studs, which has been partially credited for Germany's World Cup Championship that year. By 1960, adidas was the clear favorite among athletic footwear brands with 75 percent of all track-and-field athletes competing in the Olympic Games in Rome wearing adidas shoes. The company began producing soccer balls in 1963 and athletic apparel in 1967. The company's dominance in the athletic footwear industry continued through the early 1970s with 1,164 of the 1,490 athletes competing in the 1972 Olympic Games in Munich wearing adidas shoes. As jogging developed into a popular recreational activity in the early 1970s, adidas became the leading brand of consumer jogging shoe in the United States. Also, T-shirts and other apparel bearing adidas's three-lobed trefoil logo were popular wardrobe items for U.S. teenagers during the 1970s.

At the time of Adi Dassler's death in 1978, adidas remained the worldwide leader in athletic footwear, but the company was rapidly losing market share in the United States to industry newcomer Nike. The first Nike shoes appeared in the 1972 U.S. Olympic Trials in Eugene, Oregon, and had become the best-selling training shoe in the United States by 1974. Both Adi Dassler and his son, Horst Dassler, who took over as adidas's chief manager after Adi Dassler's death, severely underestimated the threat of Nike. With adidas perhaps more concerned with cross-town adversary Puma, Nike pulled ahead of its European rivals in the U.S. athletic footwear market by launching new styles in a variety of colors and by signing recognizable sports figures to endorsement contracts. Even though Nike was becoming the market leader in U.S. athletic footwear market, adidas was able to retain its number one ranking among competitive athletes, with 259 gold medal winners in the 1984 Olympic Summer Games in Los Angeles wearing adidas products. Only 65 Olympic athletes wore Nike shoes during the 1984 Summer Games, but the company signed up-and-coming NBA star Michael Jordan to a $2.5 million endorsement contract after adidas passed on the opportunity earlier in the year. At the time of Horst Dassler's unexpected death in 1987, Nike was the undisputed leader in the U.S. athletic footwear market, with more than $1 billion in annual sales.

Adidas's performance spiraled downward after the death of Horst Dassler, with no clear direction from the top and quality and innovation rapidly deteriorating. By 1990, adidas had fallen to a number eight ranking in the U.S. athletic footwear market and held only a 2 percent share of the market. A number of management and ownership changes occurred between Horst Dassler's death in 1987 and 1993, when a controlling interest in the company was acquired by a group of investors led by French advertising executive Robert Louis-Dreyfus. Louis-Dreyfus launched a dramatic turnaround of the company—cutting costs, improving styling, launching new models, and signing endorsement contracts with popular athletes such as Kobe Bryant, Anna Kournikova, and David Beckham. At year-end 1994, adidas had increased its annual sales in the United States by 75 percent from the prior year and improved its market share enough to become the third largest seller of athletic footwear in the United States, trailing only Nike and Reebok.

The 1998 Salomon SA Acquisition

Even though the company's turnaround had produced outstanding results with sales and earnings growing at annual rates of 38.3 percent and 37.5 percent, respectively, in 1995 and 1997, the company was a distant number three in the worldwide athletic footwear and apparel industry. Nike's 1997 revenues of $9.2 billion were nearly three times greater than those of adidas, and Nike continued to grow at a fast pace as it expanded into more international markets. In late 1997, Louis-Dreyfus and the family owners of Salomon SA, a French sports equipment manufacturer, agreed to a €1.5 billion merger that would diversify adidas beyond footwear and apparel and into ski equipment, golf clubs, bicycle components, and winter sports apparel. Salomon's business lineup contained a large number of strong businesses—its Salomon ski division was the leading producer of ski equipment; TaylorMade Golf was the second largest seller of golf equipment; and Mavic was the leading producer of high-performance bicycle wheels and rims. Other Salomon businesses included Bonfire snowboard apparel and Cliché skateboard equipment.

Adidas's €1.5 billion acquisition of Salomon SA allowed it to surpass Reebok to become the world's second largest sporting goods company, with 1998 sales of nearly €5.1 billion. The price of adidas's shares fell upon the announcement of the acquisition over concerns about the high price adidas agreed to pay for Salomon and how the company might finance the acquisition. There was also some concern among investors that adidas did not have expertise in manufacturing sports equipment since its apparel and footwear were produced by contract manufacturers. A Merrill Lynch analyst suggested the Salomon acquisition might prove troublesome for adidas since other athletic shoe companies had "dabbled in the hard goods segment, but they have been unsuccessful to date in making inroads."[3]

Louis-Dreyfus expected the Salomon acquisition to boost the company's pretax profits by 20–25 percent annually through 2000. However, Louis-Dreyfus's projections never materialized, with adidas taking control of Salomon just as the winter sports equipment and golf equipment industries were becoming less attractive. The poor performance of Salomon and TaylorMade in 1998 led to a net loss of $164 million for adidas-Salomon during the first nine months of its fiscal year. To make matters worse, the integration of Salomon's bicycle components, skateboard, winter sports, and golf equipment businesses did not go as smoothly as Louis-Dreyfus and adidas's shareholders had expected.

By the summer of 1999, adidas-Salomon's share price had declined by more than a third from its early-1998 high, and most large investors believed that adidas had bitten off more than it could chew with the acquisition.[4] Robert Louis-Dreyfus announced in early 2000 that he would step down from adidas-Salomon and rejoin his family's business in France in early 2001. Herbert Hainer, the company's head of marketing in Europe and Asia, was tapped as his replacement to run the diversified sporting goods company. Under Hainer's leadership, the company cut costs, introduced new apparel and footwear products, increased the company's advertising, signed additional athletes to endorsement contracts, and opened extended retail distribution to company-owned stores.

Adidas's Broad Corporate Restructuring Plan

Adidas's 1998 acquisition of diversified sporting goods producer Salomon was expected to allow the athletic footwear company to vault over Nike to become the leader of the global sporting goods industry. But almost as soon as the deal was consummated, it looked doubtful that the €1.5 billion acquisition of Salomon would help adidas achieve its strategic intent. Chief concerns with the acquisition were the declining attractiveness of the winter sports industry and integration problems between the adidas footwear and apparel business and Salomon's business units. Not until 2003, five years after the acquisition, had adidas's earnings per share returned to the level that shareholders enjoyed in 1997. In addition, the company's stock price failed to return to its 1998 trading range until 2004. The Salomon winter sports business had contributed very little operating profit to the company's overall financial performance since its acquisition and the TaylorMade-adidas Golf division had struggled at various times to deliver good earnings. However, TaylorMade seemed to have turned the corner in 2005, with sales and operating earnings finally improving after a three-year decline.

The 2005 Divestiture of Salomon Business Units The company divested all of its winter sports brands and Mavic bicycle components business in October 2005 to Amer Sports Corporation for €485 million. Amer Sports was the maker of Atomic skis and Wilson sporting goods. The divestiture of Salomon's winter sports and bicycle components business would make TaylorMade Golf the lone business retained from the company's 1998 acquisition of Salomon SA. Upon the completion of the Salomon divestiture, adidas-Salomon's shareholders approved a resolution to change the company's name to adidas AG.

The 2006 Acquisition of Reebok International Ltd. With the Salomon divestiture to Amer Sports all but consummated, adidas management announced in August 2005 that it would acquire Reebok International Ltd. for €3.1 billion. The acquisition of Reebok would be the final component of a restructuring initiative that would focus the company's business lineup primarily on athletic footwear and apparel and golf equipment by 2006. In addition to Reebok-branded athletic footwear and apparel, Reebok International also designed, marketed, and sold Rockport footwear, Greg Norman apparel, and CCM hockey equipment. In 2004, Rockport and Reebok's hockey brands contributed

$377.6 million and $146.0 million, respectively, to the company's total sales of nearly $3.8 billion. The company's sales of Greg Norman golf apparel approximated $50 million in 2004. Exhibit 4 provides Reebok International's sales by product line and by geographic region for 2002 through 2004.

The Reebok acquisition, finalized in 2006, increased the company's revenues from €5.8 billion in 2005 to €10.1 in 2006 and allowed sales in North America to more than double between 2005 and 2006. In addition, adidas expected to capture annual cost-sharing benefits of approximately €125 million within three years of the closing date. The company's postmerger branding strategy would position adidas as a technologically superior shoe designed for serious athletes, while Reebok would be positioned as leisure shoe that would sell at middle price points. Adidas divested the Greg Norman golf apparel line shortly after the completion of the Reebok acquisition.

Performance Expectations for Adidas's Restructured Business Lineup

Even though the restructured lineup of businesses offered adidas an improved chance of catching Nike in its race to be the world's largest sporting goods company, some observers were not convinced the move would prove to be any more successful than the company's 1998 acquisition of Salomon. The president of a sports marketing firm doubted that adidas's "German mentality of control, engineering, and production" would prove to be compatible with Reebok's "U.S. marketing-driven culture" and added, "In reality, I don't think [the merged company] is going to dent the market, because Nike is already too far ahead."[5] A Goldman Sachs analyst added, "We fail to see how this combo will erode Nike's franchise as the global brand leader."[6]

ADIDAS'S CORPORATE STRATEGY IN 2008

In 2008, adidas's businesses were organized under three units based around the company's core brands—adidas, Reebok, and TaylorMade-adidas Golf. The company's corporate strategy was focused on extending its leadership in product innovation, creating a differentiated image for the products offered by each of its three business segments, expanding controlled retail space through its network of company-owned stores, and achieving efficiencies in its global supply chain processes and activities. The relative performance of adidas's business units during 1998 through 2007 is presented in Exhibit 5.

Exhibit 4 Net Sales by Product Type and Geographic Region for Reebok International, 2002–2004 (in thousands of $)

Reebok International's Net Sales by Product Type			
	2004	2003	2002
Footwear	$2,430,311	$2,226,712	$2,060,725
Apparel	1,354,973	1,258,604	1,067,147
Total	$3,785,284	$3,485,316	$3,127,872
Reebok International's Net Sales by Geographic Region			
	2004	2003	2002
United States	$2,069,055	$2,021,396	$1,807,657
United Kingdom	474,704	444,693	416,775
Europe	810,418	692,400	607,381
Other countries	431,107	326,827	296,059
Total	$3,785,284	$3,485,316	$3,127,872

Source: Reebok International Ltd., 2004 10-K report.

Exhibit 5 Adidas AG Financial Data by Operating Segment, 1998–2007, (€ in millions)

	2007	2006	2005	2004	2003	2002	2001	2000	1999	1998
Adidas										
Sales	€7,133	€6,626	€5,861	€5,174	€4,950	€5,105	€4,825	€4,672	€4,427	€4,316
Gross profit	3,370	3,059	2,654	2,284	2,008	2,004	1,845	1,907	1,827	1,818
Operating profit	920	788	693	564	365	343	352	391	431	412
Operating assets	3,329	3,211	2,526	2,089	2,172	2,294	1,954	2,286	1,987	1,730
Capital expenditures	150	135	138	85	63	84	113	93	105	102
Amortization and depreciation	104	91	69	56	56	63	57	52	45	48
Reebok*										
Sales	€2,333	€2,473	—	—	—	—	—	—	—	—
Gross profit	902	863	—	—	—	—	—	—	—	—
Operating profit	109	86	—	—	—	—	—	—	—	—
Operating assets	2,913	3,217	—	—	—	—	—	—	—	—
Capital expenditures	57	72	—	—	—	—	—	—	—	—
Amortization and depreciation	60	53	—	—	—	—	—	—	—	—
TaylorMade-adidas Golf										
Sales	€804	€856	€709	€633	€637	€707	€545	€441	€327	€263
Gross profit	360	376	312	298	290	345	281	221	160	118
Operating profit	65	73	50	48	67	74	63	44	30	20
Operating assets	629	656	692	619	391	433	316	219	156	99
Capital expenditures	12	13	17	9	12	49	16	12	10	16
Amortization and depreciation	12	13	13	11	9	7	6	4	4	2
Salomon										
Net sales	—	—	—	€653	€658	€684	€714	€703	€587	€487
Gross profit	—	—	—	259	264	279	313	296	233	188
Operating profit	—	—	—	9	35	39	63	61	32	6
Operating assets	—	—	—	505	521	581	679	566	533	598
Capital expenditures	—	—	—	19	18	18	38	24	17	20
Amortization and depreciation	—	—	—	7	7	7	7	7	5	7
Corporate/Consolidation										
Sales	€ 49	€ 129	€ 66	€ 53	€ 22	€ 27	€ 28	€ 19	€ 10	—
Gross profit	250	195	232	232	252	191	162	104	—	—
Operating profit	(145)	(66)	(36)	(27)	23	21	(3)	(59)	(14)	(22)
Operating assets	1,454	1,295	2,532	1,072	1,104	953	1,234	947	903	782
Capital expenditures	70	57	45	27	29	22	20	16	—	—
Amortization and depreciation	25	25	30	28	17	26	25	23	6	6

*2006 financial data is for an 11-month period because of the closing date of the Reebok International acquisition by adidas AG.

Source: adidas AG, 2005 and 2007 annual reports.

Adidas's corporate focus on product design and innovation contributed to the differentiation strategies employed in each of its businesses. Each business unit was expected to develop at least one major product innovation per year in each product category. In 2008, TaylorMade Golf introduced its r7 CGB Max Limited driver, which incorporated nine movable weights and three interchangeable shafts. The movable weights and interchangeable shafts allowed golfers to make adjustments to the club that could produce more than 1,000 different ball flight trajectories. In 2007, the adidas athletic footwear and apparel division introduced its innovative SuperNova and Response running shoe families and a Stella McCartney gym and yoga apparel collection. Reebok's major product launches in 2007 included its Trinity KFS III running shoes and Rbk Edge uniform systems for hockey. The company also improved the comfort of its Rockport footwear collection in 2007 by incorporating its Torsion system developed for adidas running shoes.

Adidas also relied heavily on ongoing brand-building activities to further differentiate adidas, Reebok, and TaylorMade from competing brands of sporting goods. Partnerships with major sporting events around the world and with notable athletes competing in winter sports, track-and-field, soccer, basketball, tennis, and golf were critical to creating a distinctive image with consumers. The company also attempted to provide its retailers with superior customer service, including on-time deliveries, since retailer activities were such important elements of the sporting goods industry value chain.

Adidas management believed that controlled retail space would provide customers with a thorough understanding of product features and offer consumers a rewarding point-of-sale experience. In 2008, the company's controlled space included mono-branded retail stores, shop-in-shop locations, factory outlet stores, team apparel stores located in stadiums and arenas, and e-commerce sites. Adidas had opened company-owned retail stores in the United States and Europe and such emerging markets as Russia and China. Adidas management expected its company-owned retail stores to generate at least 30 percent of its revenues by 2010. The following table presents the number of adidas and Reebok locations in 2006 and 2007.

	2007	2006
Company-owned adidas retail stores		
Sport performance stores	459	356
Originals stores	83	58
Factory outlets	317	256
Concession sales locations	142	203
Consumer e-commerce sites	2	2
Total U.S. retail locations	1,003	875
Company-owned Reebok retail stores		
Factory outlets	288	236
Concept stores	142	47
	430	283

Efficient supply chain management was critical to adidas's profitability because of the importance of getting new styles to market quickly and because of the importance of low cost manufacturing. Adidas kept its production costs low by outsourcing more than 95 percent of its production requirements to contract manufacturers located throughout Asia. In 2005, the company launched an initiative called World Class Supply Chain to improve coordination with its contract manufacturers, get new products to market more quickly, and lower costs. The initiative allowed adidas to reduce its number of contract manufacturers from 547 in 2005 to 377 in 2007, thereby reducing complexities in its procurement planning. The reduced number of suppliers also allowed the company to better respond to rapid changes in the marketplace that called for certain styles to be discontinued or production of others to be increased. The fewer number of contract manufacturers also allowed Adidas to speed its product design-to-market cycle times. Adidas management also reengineered replenishment activities to improve product availability to retailers without substantially boosting its inventories of footwear, apparel, and sporting goods hardware.

Adidas management expected its supply chain initiatives and other operating practices to produce visible improvements in operating margins each year. Company managers anticipated that the company's strategies would allow it to improve gross profit margins from 47 percent in 2007 to 48 percent in 2008 and allow its operating margins to improve from 9.2 percent in 2007 to 9.5 percent in 2008.

Anticipated profitability improvements in Europe, strong top-line and bottom-line growth in Asia, and synergies from the Reebok integration in North America were expected to deliver sought-after gains in operating profit margins. The company's chief managers believed operational efficiency coupled with product innovation would allow it to attain number one or number two positions in each sporting goods segment where it competed.

Adidas Footwear and Apparel

Adidas footwear and apparel was organized under two categories, which were based on the clothing needs of the consumer. The adidas Sport Performance group developed sports shoes and attire suitable for use by athletes in four key sports categories—running, soccer, basketball, and general training. The Sport Style product line was marketed to those who enjoyed the comfort of athletic apparel. The worldwide sales of athletic apparel and footwear for athletes and those drawn to sports-inspired products totaled nearly $125 billion in 2007. The annual growth rate for the global athletic footwear and apparel industry had slowed from 6.8 percent in 2005 to 3.3 percent in 2007. At about $42.5 billion, North America was the largest market for athletic apparel and footwear, but its 3 percent annual growth rate was greater than only Europe's 2 percent annual growth rate among all developed and emerging markets for athletic apparel and footwear. Markets in Eastern Europe, South and Central Asia, and China grew at rates of 20 percent, 13 percent, and 15 percent, respectively, between 2006 and 2007.

Adidas's strongest product category was soccer, where it held market shares greater than 50 percent in Europe and North America. Adidas was runner-up to Nike in most other athletic categories in which it competed. It maintained its advantage over other sporting attire and footwear producers primarily through innovations like its AdiSTAR cushion system for running shoes and its TECHFIT athletic apparel designed to increase blood flow during athletic activity and through endorsements by individual athletes or league sponsorships. Kevin Garnett, Dwight Howard, and Tracy McGrady were among the latest NBA athletes to endorse adidas footwear and apparel. In soccer, players such as David Beckham and Lionel Messi and entire clubs endorsed adidas soccer shoes and clothing. Adidas was the official sponsor for the German national women's team and UEFA soccer league teams in Munich, Amsterdam, Milan, and Madrid. Also, the adidas Roteiro was the "official match ball" for all UEFA games. Adidas was also the official sportswear partner of the 2008 Beijing Olympics and the London Olympics set for 2012. The Sport Performance group accounted for 80 percent of adidas-branded apparel and footwear sales in 2007. Sport Performance sales increased by 10 percent during 2007.

The company's Sport Style streetwear and lifestyle fashion group represented a relatively small fraction of adidas's overall apparel and footwear sales but offered high profit margins because of the small research and development budget needed to design such items. Another attractive aspect of adidas's lifestyle apparel group was that the market for sports lifestyle apparel and footwear was growing at a faster rate than the market for actual sports products. The Sport Style group included two segments—adidas Originals and Y-3. Adidas Originals targeted consumers in three distinct categories—hip-hop fans, surfers and skateboarders, and young metropolitan consumers. Adidas Originals products designed for the hip-hop and surfer/skater lifestyle included items such as warmup suits, T-shirts, and updated versions of classic adidas court shoes. The company's products targeted to young metropolitan consumers included a jeans line developed in collaboration with Diesel and its Grün footwear collection made from recycled materials. Adidas Y-3 ready-to-wear fashion collection was developed in collaboration with designer Yohji Yamamoto. Y-3 line included apparel items such as women's tights, skirts, blouses, and leather jackets. Y-3 apparel for men included jeans, coats, leather jackets, polo shirts, and stretch pants. The Sport Style group accounted for 20 percent of adidas-branded apparel and footwear sales in 2007. Sport Style sales declined by 1 percent between 2006 and 2007.

Europe accounted for 50 percent of adidas-branded sales of footwear and apparel in 2007. Sales in Europe increased by 8 percent during 2007, with Russia accounting for the majority of the sales increase in Europe. Adidas sales increased by 5 percent in North America in 2007 and accounted for 18 percent of adidas's total sales of athletic gear. Asia accounted for 24 percent of adidas-branded apparel and footwear sales and grew by 17 percent during 2007, with China accounting for much of the overall growth. Latin America grew by 39 percent in 2007 to account for 8 percent of adidas apparel and footwear sales.

Adidas had long held the title of market share leader in Europe's developed country markets for athletic footwear and apparel, but the company was also intent on holding leading positions in emerging markets in Eastern Europe and Asia. Sales had grown by as much as 50 percent annually in Russia and other former Soviet states such the Ukraine, Armenia, and Belarus to give it a 2-to-1 margin over runner-up Nike. Adidas management expected Russia to become its largest and most profitable market in Europe by 2010.

Asia was projected to become adidas's largest market overall within the near term because of the strong demand for athletic footwear and apparel in Asia and the vast numbers of consumers living in Asian country markets. Asia made up more than two-thirds of the world's population in 2008 and was projected to grow from 3.2 billion people in 2008 to 3.6 billion people by 2028. Adidas's emphasis on emerging markets had made it the largest seller of athletic gear in Asia in 2008, and the company expected to displace Nike as market leader in Latin America by 2010. The company's acquisition of Reebok had allowed it to double its sales in North America since 2005, but it still trailed Nike's 36 percent market share in North America by a 15-point margin in 2008. Exhibit 6 presents a summary of adidas AG's geographic financial performance for 1998 through 2007.

Reebok

The Reebok brand was acquired by adidas AG in 2006 to boost the company's sales in North America. Approximately $2 billion of Reebok International's 2004 sales of $3.7 were generated in North America from the sale of Reebok athletic footwear and apparel; Rbk and CCM hockey skates, uniforms, and gear; Rockport men's shoes; and Greg Norman golf apparel. Adidas divested the Greg Norman apparel line soon after the completion of the 2006 acquisition of Reebok International.

At the time of its acquisition by adidas, the Reebok brand suffered from a poor reputation for quality, innovation, and styling. Reebok did, however, have a loyal following among women participating in general fitness training, walking, and aerobics. In 2008, adidas management had chosen to use the Reebok brand of athletic footwear to focus on beginning and recreational runners and women athletes participating in running, aerobics, walking, and training. Reebok athletic shoes were also frequently purchased by women looking for comfortable casual shoes. The company developed a variety of new styles and color combinations that were intended to appeal to women and developed a partnership with the Avon Walk Around the World for Breast Cancer charitable organization to increase awareness of the Reebok brand among women.

Adidas management had also undertaken efforts to improve Reebok's image in men's sports with endorsements from such professional athletes as Peyton and Eli Manning, Allen Iverson, Yao Ming, David Ortiz, and Vince Young. Reebok was also the official outfitter of the National Football League and was an apparel partner with Major League Baseball. Its relationship with the National Hockey League, the American Hockey League, and the Canadian Hockey League helped solidify Reebok-CCM as the number one seller of hockey skates and gear. Reebok and CCM both offered complete head-to-toe product lines for hockey, but in 2008 the company had begun to position CCM as a premium skate brand and Rbk as general hockey equipment and apparel brand. Adidas's strategic priority for the Rockport line of casual men's shoes was to increase the brand's sales outside of North America. Adidas management expected that more than 50 percent of Rockport's sales would be generated in Europe, Asia, and Latin America by 2010.

Adidas management had also expanded Reebok's distribution beyond its historical focus on specialty athletic footwear stores and discount family footwear retailers to both improve its image and make Reebok shoes available to a wider range of consumers. Beginning in 2008, the company increased Reebok's distribution network to include a greater number of large sporting goods stores and department stores. Distribution was also improved by the addition of 95 additional concept stores and 52 additional factory outlet stores during 2008. Adidas also moved to control distribution of Reebok in emerging markets by purchasing distribution rights in Russia and China, which had been sold to third parties by Reebok International management. Adidas also began purchasing distribution rights for Rockport in emerging markets, which too had been sold to third parties by Reebok International management.

Exhibit 6 Adidas AG Financial Data by Geographic Region, 1998–2007, (€ in millions)

	2007	2006	2005	2004	2003	2002	2001	2000	1999	1998
Europe										
Net sales	€4,369	€4,162	€3,166	€3,068	€3,365	€3,200	€3,066	€2,860	€2,723	€2,774
Operating assets	1,819	1,808	1,376	1,461	1,428	1,396	1,419	1,107	1,167	1,114
Capital expenditures	105	84	57	46	44	56	74	55	40	35
North America										
Net sales	€2,929	€3,234	€1,561	€1,332	€1,562	€1,960	€1,818	€1,907	€1,826	€1,784
Operating assets	1,489	1,564	325	768	778	969	945	862	848	666
Capital expenditures	34	49	51	27	22	82	68	54	26	29
Asia										
Net sales	€2,254	€2,020	€1,523	€1,192	€1,116	€1,166	€1,010	€ 875	€ 663	€ 383
Operating assets	772	719	617	480	447	505	743	455	390	201
Capital expenditures	49	74	37	23	12	16	15	17	18	9
Latin America										
Net sales	€ 657	€ 499	€ 319	€ 224	€ 179	€ 163	€ 178	€ 171	€ 126	€ 112
Operating assets	285	217	176	56	93	79	98	109	75	66
Capital expenditures	10	7	5	1	1	1	2	3	3	2
Headquarters/consolidation										
Net sales	€ 89	€ 169	€ 66	€ 47	€ 45	€ 34	€ 40	€ 23	€ 34	€ 12
Operating assets	3,960	4,071	3,256	1,601	1,442	1,312	978	1,485	1,108	1,162
Capital expenditures	91	63	50	43	43	15	28	16	45	63

Source: adidas AG, 2005 and 2007 annual reports.

Reebok's net sales declined by 6 percent between 2006 and 2007. However, the February 1, 2006, closing date of the Reebok International acquisition disguised the business unit's true net sales decline, since Reebok's 2006 fiscal year included only 11 months under adidas ownership. The company's gross margin improved by 3.7 percentage points during 2007 as adidas management gained greater economies of scope in sourcing activities. The higher gross margins allowed operating margin for the Reebok business unit to improve from 3.5 percent in 2006 to 4.7 percent in 2007. When examining only the last 11 months of both fiscal years, the sales of Reebok-branded athletic footwear and apparel declined by 7 percent during 2007, sales of hockey equipment increased by 3 percent during 2007, and Rockport sales improved by 1 percent between 2006 and 2007. Net sales during the 2007 fiscal year were also negatively affected by the divestiture of its Greg Norman apparel line, which had 2006 net sales of approximately $50 million. Reebok's sales in North America and Europe declined by 5 percent and 1 percent, respectively, during 2007. The business unit's strongest growth during 2007 was in Latin America and Asia, where net sales increased by 32 percent and 24 percent, respectively.

TaylorMade-adidas Golf

TaylorMade Golf was the third largest producer of golf equipment in the $3.8 billion industry. Sales in the golf equipment industry had declined by about 5 percent between 2000 and 2007 as a variety of forces converged to decrease industry attractiveness. One factor contributing to the decline in industry sales was a reduction in the number of golfers in the United States from 27.5 million in 1998 to 22.7 million in 2007. Also, the number of rounds of golf played in the United States had not grown appreciably since 2000 and had declined by 2.2 percent during the first six months of 2008. In addition, golf equipment manufacturers had become stifled in their abilities to pursue innovation-based strategies directed at making golf easier to play for those of modest talent. Beginning in 1998, golf's governing organizations, the United States Golf Association (USGA) and the Royal & Ancient Golf Club (R&A), put a series of new rules in place that limited technological innovation in golf equipment that they believed might pose a threat to the game.

TaylorMade-adidas Golf management expected to increase sales primarily through market share gains since they had concluded that it would be unwise to count on growth of the game. TaylorMade believed it could increase market share through endorsement contracts with touring professionals on the PGA Tour and other professional tours and through new product innovations like the moveable weight system used in its r7 driver. TaylorMade management also wished to achieve revenue growth by increasing sales in Asia. The company had successfully increased its sales in Asia from 13 percent of sales in 1999 to 35 percent of sales in 2007 and the United States accounted for only 52 percent of sales in 2007 versus 69 percent of sales in 1999.

In 2008, TaylorMade was the largest seller of drivers, fairway woods, and hybrid clubs. Although technological innovation had been limited by the USGA and R&A, TaylorMade maintained its lead in the driver category of the golf equipment industry with updated models of the r7 that were launched at 12- to 18-month intervals. In 2008, the company's flagship r7 driver was sold in four basic configurations that ranged in price from $400 to $600. The price of each model depended on the shaft option selected and the number of extra weights included with the driver. The r7 CGB Max Limited carried a retail price of $1,000 and came with an r7 clubhead, three interchangeable shafts, and nine weight plugs. The three shaft options and 9 weights allow golfers to create more than 1,000 different ball flight paths by choosing different shaft and weight combinations.

Even though TaylorMade held achieved the number one ranking in metalwoods, its market share in irons was about one-half that of industry leader, Callaway Golf Company, and its market share in wedges and putters was negligible. TaylorMade also produced and marketed a line of golf balls but had not achieved any significant market success in the product category.

The sales of TaylorMade's adidas-branded golf apparel and golf shoes had grown at compounded annual rates of 28 percent and 18 percent, respectively, between 2004 and 2007 through the continued introduction of new styles and exposure on the professional tours by such well-known golfers as Sergio Garcia, Natalie Gulbis, Paula Creamer, and Retief Goosen. In all, TaylorMade-adidas Golf had signed endorsement contracts with 70 golfers on the men's and women's professional tours. The heavy reliance on endorsements by touring professionals made adidas the most widely worn apparel brand on the professional tours. Some of its touring staff was also compensated to use TaylorMade's TP Red or TP Black golf balls during tournaments. TaylorMade also had limited contracts with an additional 40 golfers to use TaylorMade drivers during professional tournaments. The following table presents the TaylorMade-adidas Golf division's sales by product category for 2004–2007.

TaylorMade-adidas Golf Sales by Product Line (€ in millions)

	2007	2006	2005	2004
Metalwoods	€338	€325	€319	€304
Apparel	145	197	99	70
Footwear	72	60	50	44
Other hardware*	249	274	255	215

*Other hardware includes irons, putters, golf balls, golf bags, gloves, and other accessories.

Source: adidas AG annual reports, various years.

ADIDAS AG'S PERFORMANCE GOING INTO 2009

Going into 2009, there were signs that adidas AG's corporate strategies were bringing about the hoped-for improvement in the company's financial performance. During the first six months of 2008, corporate revenues increased by 12 percent, with sales for the adidas business unit growing by 16 percent and sales at TaylorMade-adidas Golf growing by 11 percent. Sales at Reebok declined by 2 percent during the first six months of 2008. The revenue growth and cost savings resulting from the Reebok integration allowed adidas AG's gross margins and operating margins to improve by 2.5 percentage points and 1.1 percentage points, respectively, during the first half of 2008. Earnings per share increased by 25 percent during the first half of 2008, and the company's improvement in free cash flow allowed the company to buy back nearly 7.7 million shares at an average price of €41.35 per share.

Adidas AG management expected the company's integration efforts between the Reebok and the adidas business units to result in revenue growth of €250 million and cost savings of €105 million by year-end 2008. In addition, the company's revenue growth in China was expected to allow China to become the company's second largest market after the United States by the end of 2008. The company also expected that its October 2008 acquisition of Ashworth Inc. would lead to growth in apparel sales for its TaylorMade-adidas Golf division. The $72.8 million acquisition of the traditionally styled Ashworth clothing line would broaden adidas's golf apparel beyond the athletically cut adidas Golf apparel items. Although adidas had achieved a number of significant strategic goals during 2008, it had lost market share in the North American athletic footwear market to Nike through the first nine months of the year.

Endnotes

[1] As quoted in "Reebok and Adidas: A Good Fit," *BusinessWeek Online,* August 4, 2005.

[2] As quoted in "The Brothers Dassler Fight On," *Deutsche Welle,* dw-world.de.

[3] As quoted in "Sporting Goods Consolidation Off to the Races," *Mergers & Acquisitions Report,* November 10, 1997.

[4] As quoted in "Sports Goods/Shareholders Criticize Salomon Takeover," *Handelsblatt,* May 21, 1999.

[5] As quoted in "Reebok and Adidas: A Good Fit."

[6] Ibid.

CASE

19 PepsiCo's Diversification Strategy in 2008

John E. Gamble
University of South Alabama

PepsiCo was the world's largest snack and beverage company, with 2007 net revenues of approximately $39.5 billion. The company's portfolio of businesses in 2008 included Frito-Lay salty snacks, Quaker Chewy granola bars, Pepsi soft drink products, Tropicana orange juice, Lipton Brisk tea, Gatorade, Propel, SoBe, Quaker Oatmeal, Cap'n Crunch, Aquafina, Rice-A-Roni, Aunt Jemima pancake mix, and many other regularly consumed products. Gatorade, Propel, Rice-A-Roni, Aunt Jemima, and Quaker Oats products had been added to PepsiCo's arsenal of brands through the $13.9 billion acquisition of Quaker Oats in 2001. The acquisition was the final component of a major portfolio restructuring initiative that began in 1997. Since the restructuring, the company had increased revenues and net income at annual rates of 7 percent and 12 percent, respectively. A summary of PepsiCo's financial performance is shown in Exhibit 1.

Through 2007, the company's top managers were focused on sustaining the impressive performance that had been achieved since its restructuring through strategies keyed to product innovation, close relationships with distribution allies, international expansion, and strategic acquisitions. Newly introduced products such as Gatorade G2, Tiger Woods signature sports drinks, and Quaker Simple Harvest multigrain hot cereal had accounted for 15–20 percent of all new growth in recent years. New product innovations that addressed consumer health and wellness concerns were the greatest contributors to the company's growth, with PepsiCo's better-for-you and good-for-you products accounting for 16 percent of its 2007 snack sales in North America, 70 percent of net beverage revenues in North America during 2007, and more than 50 percent of its 2007 sales of Quaker Oats products in North America. The company also increased the percentage of healthy snacks in markets outside North America since consumers in most developed countries wished to reduce their consumption of saturated fats, cholesterol, trans fats, and simple carbohydrates.

The company's Power of One retailer alliance strategy had been in effect for more than 10 years and was continuing to help boost PepsiCo's volume and identify new product formulations desired by consumers. Under the Power of One strategy, PepsiCo marketers and retailers collaborated in stores and during offsite summits to devise tactics to increase consumers' tendency to purchase more than one product offered by PepsiCo during a store visit. In addition, some of PepsiCo's most successful new products had been recommended by retailers.

PepsiCo's international sales had grown by 22 percent during 2007, but the company had many additional opportunities to increase sales in markets outside North America. The company held large market shares in many international markets for beverages and salty snacks, but it had been relatively unsuccessful in making Quaker branded products available outside the United States. In 2006, 75 percent of Quaker Oats' international sales of $500 million was accounted for by just six countries. In addition, PepsiCo's international operations were much less profitable than its businesses operating in North America. While the operating profit margins of PepsiCo's international division had ranged from 13.4 to 15.6 percent between 2004 and 2007, operating profit margins for its Frito-Lay and North American beverage business ranged from 21.3 to 25 percent during

Exhibit 1 Financial Summary for PepsiCo Inc., 1998–2007 ($ in millions, except per share amounts)

	2007	2006	2005	2004	2003	2002	2001	2000	1999	1998
Net revenue	$39,474	$35,137	$32,562	$29,261	$26,971	$25,112	$23,512	$20,438	$20,367	$22,348
Net income	5,599	5,065	4,078	4,212	3,568	3,000	2,400	2,183	2,050	1,993
Income per common share—basic, continuing operations	$3.38	$ 3.00	$2.43	$2.45	$2.07	$1.69	$1.35	$1.51	$1.40	$1.35
Cash dividends declared per common share	$1.42	$1.16	$1.01	$0.85	$0.63	$0.60	$0.58	$0.56	$0.54	$0.52
Total assets	$34,628	$29,930	$31,727	$27,987	$25,327	$23,474	$21,695	$18,339	$17,551	$22,660
Long-term debt	4,203	2,550	2,313	2,397	1,702	2,187	2,651	2,346	2,812	4,028

Source: PepsiCo 10-Ks, various years.

the same time period. Quaker Foods' sales of Cap'n Crunch, Life cereal, Quaker oatmeal, Chewy granola bars, Aunt Jemima, and Rice-A-Roni produced the highest profit margins among all PepsiCo brands, with operating profits exceeding 30 percent each year between 2004 and 2007.

PepsiCo management developed a new organizational structure in 2008 to address the low relative profitability of its international operations and to produce even faster growth in international markets. The new structure that would place all brands sold in the United Kingdom, Europe, Asia, the Middle East, and Africa into a common division was expected to aid the company in its ability to capture strategic fits between its various brands and products. It was also quite possible that PepsiCo management needed to consider restructuring its lineup of snack and beverage businesses to improve overall profitability and reverse the downturn in its stock price that began in 2008. Exhibit 2 tracks PepsiCo's market performance between 1998 and October 2008.

COMPANY HISTORY

PepsiCo Inc. was established in 1965 when Pepsi-Cola and Frito-Lay shareholders agreed to a merger between the salty snack icon and soft drink giant. The new company was founded with annual revenues of $510 million and such well-known brands as Pepsi-Cola, Mountain Dew, Fritos, Lay's, Cheetos, Ruffles, and Rold Gold. PepsiCo's roots can be traced to 1898, when New Bern, North Carolina, pharmacist Caleb Bradham created the formula for a carbonated beverage he named Pepsi-Cola. The company's salty-snack business began in 1932 when Elmer Doolin of San Antonio, Texas, began manufacturing and marketing Fritos corn chips and Herman Lay started a potato chip distribution business in Nashville, Tennessee. In 1961, Doolin and Lay agreed to a merger between their businesses to establish the Frito-Lay Company.

During its first five years as a snack and beverage company, PepsiCo introduced new products such as Doritos and Funyuns; entered markets in Japan and Eastern Europe; and opened, on average, one new snack food plant per year. By 1971, PepsiCo had more than doubled its revenues to reach $1 billion. The company began to pursue growth through acquisitions outside snacks and beverages as early as 1968, but its 1977 acquisition of Pizza Hut significantly shaped the strategic direction of PepsiCo for the next 20 years. The acquisitions of Taco Bell in 1978 and Kentucky Fried Chicken in 1986 created a business portfolio described by Wayne Calloway (PepsiCo's CEO between 1986 and 1996) as a balanced three-legged stool. Calloway believed the combination of snack foods, soft drinks, and fast food offered considerable cost-sharing and skills-transfer opportunities, and he routinely shifted managers between

Exhibit 2 Monthly Performance of PepsiCo Inc.'s Stock Price, 1998 to March 2008

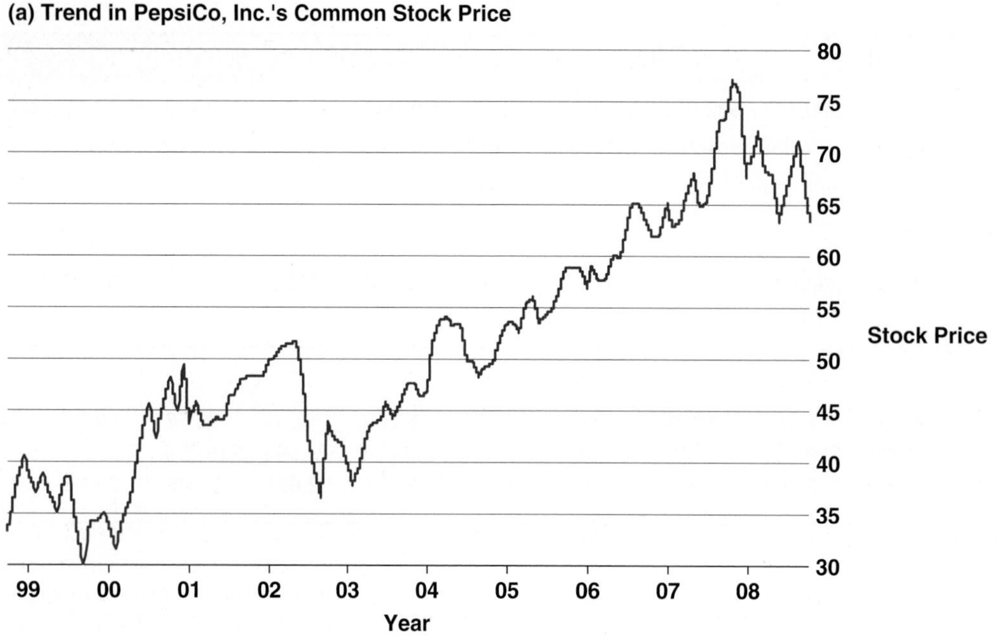

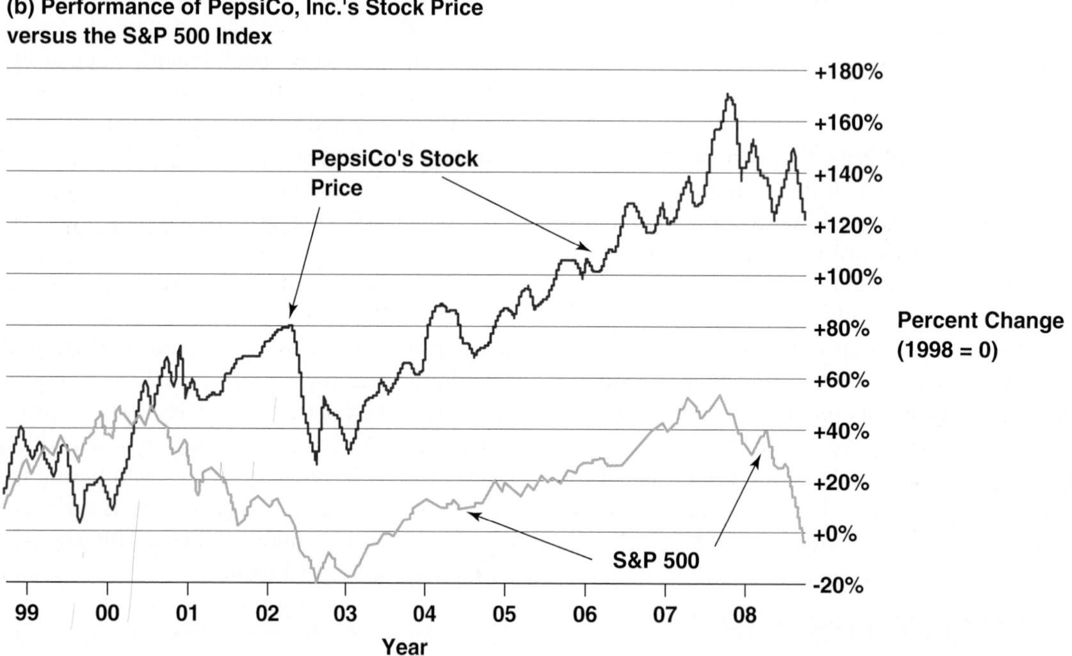

the company's three divisions as part of the company's management development efforts.

PepsiCo also strengthened its portfolio of snack foods and beverages during the 1980s and 1990s with acquisitions of Mug root beer, 7UP International, Smartfood ready-to-eat popcorn, Walker's Crisps (UK), Smith's Crisps (UK), Mexican cookie company, Gamesa, and SunChips. Calloway also added quick-service restaurants Hot-n-Now in 1990, California Pizza Kitchens in 1992, and East Side Mario's, D'Angelo Sandwich Shops, and Chevy's Mexican Restaurants in 1993. The company expanded beyond carbonated beverages with a 1992 agreement with Ocean Spray to distribute single-serving juices, the introduction of Lipton ready-to-drink teas in 1993, and the introduction of Aquafina bottled water and Frappuccino ready-to-drink coffees in 1994.

By 1996, it had become clear to PepsiCo management that the potential strategic-fit benefits existing between restaurants and PepsiCo's core beverage and snack businesses were difficult to capture. In addition, any synergistic benefits achieved were more than offset by the fast-food industry's fierce price competition and low profit margins. In 1997, CEO Roger Enrico spun off the company's restaurants as an independent, publicly traded company to focus PepsiCo on food and beverages. Soon after the spin-off of PepsiCo's fast-food restaurants was completed, Enrico acquired Cracker Jack, Tropicana, Smith's Snackfood Company in Australia, SoBe teas and alternative beverages, Tasali Snack Foods (the leader in the Saudi Arabian salty snack market), and the Quaker Oats Company.

The Quaker Oats Acquisition

At $13.9 billion, Quaker Oats was PepsiCo's largest acquisition and gave it the number one brand of oatmeal in the United States, with a 60+ percent category share; the leading brand of rice cakes and granola snack bars; and other well-known grocery brands such as Cap'n Crunch, Rice-A-Roni, and Aunt Jemima. However, Quaker's most valuable asset in its arsenal of brands was Gatorade.

Gatorade was developed by University of Florida researchers in 1965 but was not marketed commercially until the formula was sold to Stokely–Van Camp in 1967. When Quaker Oats acquired the brand from Stokely–Van Camp in 1983, Gatorade gradually made a transformation from a regionally distributed product with annual sales of $90 million to a $2 billion powerhouse. Gatorade was able to increase sales by more than 10 percent annually during the 1990s, with no new entrant to the isotonic beverage category posing a serious threat to the brand's dominance. PepsiCo, Coca-Cola, France's Danone Group, and Swiss food giant Nestlé all were attracted to Gatorade because of its commanding market share and because of the expected growth in the isotonic sports beverage category. PepsiCo became the successful bidder for Quaker Oats and Gatorade with an agreement struck in December 2000 but would not receive U.S. Federal Trade Commission (FTC) approval until August 2001. The FTC's primary concern over the merger was that Gatorade's inclusion in PepsiCo's portfolio of snacks and beverages might give the company too much leverage in negotiations with convenience stores and ultimately force smaller snack food and beverage companies out of convenience store channels. In its approval of the merger, the FTC stipulated that Gatorade could not be jointly distributed with PepsiCo's soft drinks for 10 years.

Acquisitions after 2001

After the completion of the Quaker Oats acquisition in August 2001, the company focused on integration of Quaker Oats' food, snack, and beverage brands into the PepsiCo portfolio. The company made a number of "tuck-in" acquisitions of small, fast-growing food and beverage companies in the United States and internationally to broaden its portfolio of brands. Tuck-in acquisitions in 2006 included Stacy's bagel and pita chips, Izze carbonated beverages, Duyvis nuts (Netherlands), and Star Foods (Poland). Acquisitions made during 2007 included Naked Juice fruit beverages, Sandora juices (Ukraine), Bluebird snacks (New Zealand), Penelopa nuts and seeds (Bulgaria), and Lucky snacks (Brazil). The company also entered into a joint venture with the Strauss Group in 2007 to market Sabra, the top-selling and fastest-growing brand of hummus in the United States and Canada.

PepsiCo's acquisitions in 2007 totaled $1.3 billion, whereas the company had made acquisitions totaling $522 million in 2006 and $1.1 billion in 2005. The combination of acquisitions and the strength of PepsiCo's core snacks and beverages business allowed the company's revenues to increase from approximately $20 billion in 2000 to more than

Exhibit 3 PepsiCo Inc.'s Consolidated Statements of Income, 2005–2007 ($ in millions, except per share amounts)

	2007	2006	2005
Net revenue	$39,474	$35,137	$32,562
Cost of sales	18,038	15,762	14,176
Selling, general, and administrative expenses	14,208	12,774	12,314
Amortization of intangible assets	58	162	150
Operating profit	7,170	6,439	5,922
Bottling equity income	560	616	557
Interest expense	(224)	(239)	(256)
Interest income	125	173	159
Income before income taxes	7,631	6,989	6,382
Provision for income taxes	1,973	1,347	2,304
Net income	$ 5,658	$ 5,642	$ 4,078
Net income per common share—basic	$3.48	$3.42	$2.43
Net income per common share—diluted	$3.41	$3.34	$2.39

Source: PepsiCo Inc., 2007 10-K report

$39.5 billion in 2007. Exhibit 3 presents PepsiCo's consolidated statements of income for 2005–2007. The company's balance sheets for 2005–2007 are provided in Exhibit 4. The company's calculation of management operating cash flow for 2004–2007 is shown in Exhibit 5.

BUILDING SHAREHOLDER VALUE IN 2008

Three people had held the position of CEO since the company began its portfolio restructuring in 1997. Even though Roger Enrico was the chief architect of the business lineup as it stood in 2007, his successor, Steve Reinemund, and the company's CEO in 2007, Indra Nooyi, were both critically involved in the restructuring. Nooyi joined PepsiCo in 1994 and developed a reputation as a tough negotiator who engineered the 1997 spin-off of Pepsi's restaurants, spearheaded the 1998 acquisition of Tropicana, and played a critical role in the 1999 initial public offering of Pepsi's bottling operations. After being promoted to chief financial officer, Nooyi was also highly involved in the 2001 acquisition of Quaker Oats. Nooyi was selected as the company's CEO upon Reinemund's retirement in October 2006. Nooyi had emigrated to the United States in 1978 to attend Yale's Graduate School of Business and worked with Boston Consulting Group, Motorola, and Asea Brown Boveri before arriving at PepsiCo in 1994.

In 2008, PepsiCo's corporate strategy had diversified the company into salty and sweet snacks, soft drinks, orange juice, bottled water, ready-to-drink teas and coffees, purified and functional waters, isotonic beverages, hot and ready-to-eat breakfast cereals, grain-based products, and breakfast condiments. Most PepsiCo brands had achieved number one or number two positions in their respective food and beverage categories through strategies keyed to product innovation, close relationships with distribution allies, international expansion, and strategic acquisitions. A relatively new element of PepsiCo's corporate strategy was product reformulations to make snack foods and beverages less unhealthy. The company believed that its efforts to develop "good-for-you" or "better-for-you" products would create growth opportunities from the intersection of business and public interests.

The company was organized into four business divisions, which all followed the corporation's general strategic approach. Frito-Lay North America manufactured, marketed, and distributed such snack foods as Lay's potato chips, Doritos tortilla chips,

Exhibit 4 PepsiCo Inc.'s Consolidated Balance Sheets, 2005–2007 ($ in millions, except per share amounts)

	December 29, 2007	December 30, 2006	December 31, 2005
Assets			
Current assets			
Cash and cash equivalents	$ 910	$ 1,651	$ 1,716
Short-term investments	1,571	1,171	3,166
Accounts and notes receivable, net	4,389	3,725	3,261
Inventories	2,290	1,926	1,693
Prepaid expenses and other current assets	991	657	618
Total current assets	$10,151	$ 9,130	$10,454
Property, plant and equipment, net	11,228	9,687	8,681
Amortizable intangible assets, net	796	637	530
Goodwill	5,169	4,594	4,088
Other nonamortizable intangible assets	1,248	1,212	1,086
Nonamortizable intangible assets	6,417	5,806	5,174
Investments in noncontrolled affiliates	4,354	3,690	3,485
Other assets	1,682	980	3,403
Total assets	$34,628	$29,930	$31,727
Liabilities and Shareholders' Equity			
Current liabilities			
Short-term obligations	—	$ 274	$ 2,889
Accounts payable and other current liabilities	7,602	6,496	5,971
Income taxes payable	151	90	546
Total current liabilities	7,753	6,860	9,406
Long-term debt obligations	4,203	2,550	2,313
Other liabilities	4,792	4,624	4,323
Deferred income taxes	646	528	1,434
Total liabilities	$17,394	$14,562	$17,476
Commitments and contingencies			
Preferred stock, no par value	41	41	41
Repurchased preferred stock	(132)	(120)	(110)
Common shareholders' equity			
Common stock, par value 1⅔¢ per share (issued 1,782 shares)	30	30	30
Capital in excess of par value	450	584	614
Retained earnings	28,184	24,837	21,116
Accumulated other comprehensive loss	(952)	(2,246)	(1,053)
	27,712	23,205	20,707
Less: repurchased common stock, at cost (144 and 126 shares, respectively)	(10,387)	(7,758)	(6,387)
Total common shareholders' equity	$17,325	$15,447	$14,320
Total liabilities and shareholders' equity	$34,628	$29,930	$31,727

Source: PepsiCo Inc., 2007 10-K report.

Exhibit 5 Net Cash Provided by PepsiCo's Operating Activities, 2004–2007 ($ in millions)

	2007	2006	2005	2004
Net cash provided by operating activities	$6,934	$6,084	$5,852	$5,054
Capital spending	(2,430)	(2,068)	(1,736)	(1,387)
Sales of property, plant and equipment	47	49	88	38
Management operating cash flow	$4,551	$4,065	$4,204	$3,705

Source: PepsiCo Inc., 2007 10-K report.

Cheetos cheese snacks, Fritos corn chips, Quaker Chewy granola bars, Grandma's cookies, and Smartfood popcorn. The PepsiCo Beverages North America beverage business manufactured, marketed, and sold beverage concentrates, fountain syrups, and finished goods under such brands as Pepsi, Gatorade, Tropicana, Lipton, Dole, and SoBe. PepsiCo International manufactured, marketed, and sold snacks and beverages in approximately 200 countries outside the United States. Quaker Foods North America manufactured and marketed cereals, rice and pasta dishes, and other food items that were sold in supermarkets. A full listing of Frito-Lay snacks, PepsiCo beverages, and Quaker Oats products is presented in Exhibit 6. Selected financial information for PepsiCo's four divisions is presented in Exhibit 7.

Exhibit 6 PepsiCo Inc.'s Snack, Beverage, and Quaker Oats Brands, 2008

Frito-Lay Brands	PepsiCo Beverage Brands	Quaker Oats Brands
• Lay's potato chips	• Pepsi-Cola	• Quaker Oatmeal
• Maui Style potato chips	• Mountain Dew	• Cap'n Crunch cereal
• Ruffles potato chips	• Mountain Dew AMP energy drink	• Life cereal
• Doritos tortilla chips	• Mug root beer	• Quaker 100% Natural cereal
• Tostitos tortilla chips	• Sierra Mist	• Quaker Squares cereal
• Santitas tortilla chips	• Slice	• Quisp cereal
• Fritos corn chips	• Lipton Brisk (partnership)	• King Vitaman cereal
• Cheetos cheese flavored snacks	• Lipton Iced Tea (partnership)	• Quaker Oh's! Cereal
• Rold Gold pretzels and snack mix	• Dole juices and juice drinks (license)	• Mother's cereal
• Funyuns onion flavored rings	• FruitWorks juice drinks	• Quaker grits
• Go Snacks	• Aquafina purified drinking water	• Quaker Oatmeal-to-Go
• SunChips multigrain snacks	• Frappuccino ready-to-drink coffee (partnership)	• Aunt Jemima mixes & syrups
• Sabritones puffed wheat snacks	• Starbucks DoubleShot (partnership)	• Quaker rice cakes
• Cracker Jack candy-coated popcorn	• SoBe juice drinks, dairy, and teas	• Quaker rice snacks (Quakes)
• Chester's popcorn	• SoBe energy drinks (No Fear and Adrenaline Rush)	• Quaker Chewy granola bars
• Grandma's cookies	• Gatorade	• Quaker Dipps granola bars
• Munchos potato crisps	• Propel	• Rice-A-Roni side dishes
• Smartfood popcorn	• Tropicana	• PastaRoni side dishes
• Baken-ets fried pork skins	• Tropicana Twister	• Near East side dishes
• Oberto meat snacks	• Tropicana Smoothie	• Puffed Wheat

(Continued)

Exhibit 6 (Continued)

Frito-Lay Brands	PepsiCo Beverage Brands	Quaker Oats Brands
• Rustler's meat snacks	• Izze soft drinks	• Harvest Crunch cereal
• Churrumais fried corn strips	• Naked Juice	• Quaker Baking Mixes
• Frito-Lay nuts	**Outside North America**	• Spudz snacks
• Frito-Lay, Ruffles, Fritos, and Tostitos dips and salsas	• Mirinda	• Crisp'ums baked crisps
• Frito-Lay, Doritos, and Cheetos snack crackers	• 7UP	• Quaker Fruit & Oatmeal bars
• Fritos, Tostitos, Ruffles, and Doritos snack kits	• Pepsi	• Quaker Fruit & Oatmeal Bites
• Hickory Sticks	• Kas	• Quaker Fruit and Oatmeal Toastables
• Hostess Potato	• Teem	• Quaker Soy Crisps
• Lay's Stax potato crisps	• Manzanita Sol	• Quaker Bakeries
• Miss Vickie's potato chips	• Paso de los Toros	**Outside North America**
• Munchies snack mix	• Fruko	• FrescAvena beverage powder
• Stacy's pita chips	• Evervess	• Toddy chocolate powder
• Flat Earth Fruit and Vegetable Chips	• Yedigun	• Toddynho chocolate drink
• Sabra hummus	• Shani	• Coqueiro canned fish
Outside North America	• Fiesta	• Sugar Puffs cereal
• Bocabits wheat snacks	• D&G (license)	• Puffed Wheat
• Crujitos corn snacks	• Mandarin (license)	• Cruesli cereal
• Fandangos corn snacks	• Radical Fruit	• Hot Oat Crunch cereal
• Hamka's snacks	• Tropicana Touche de Lait	• Quaker Oatso Simple hot cereal
• Niknaks cheese snacks	• Alvalle gazpacho fruit juices and vegetable juices	• Scott's Porage Oats
• Quavers potato snacks	• Tropicana Season's Best juices and juice drinks	• Scott's So Easy Oats
• Sabritas potato chips	• Loóza juices and nectars	• Quaker bagged cereals
• Smiths potato chips	• Copella juices	• Quaker Mais Sabor
• Walkers potato crisps	• Frui'Vita juices	• Quaker Oats
• Gamesa cookies	• Sandora juices	• Quaker oat flour
• Doritos Dippas		• Quaker Meu Mingau
• Sonric's sweet snacks		• Quaker cereal bars
• Wotsits corn snacks		• Quaker Oatbran
• Red Rock Deli		• Corn goods
• Kurkure		• Magico chocolate powder
• Smiths Sensations		• Quaker Vitaly Cookies
• Cheetos Shots		• 3 Minutos Mixed Cereal
• Quavers Snacks		• Quaker Mágica
• Bluebird Snacks		• Quaker Mágica con Soja
• Duyvis Nuts		• Quaker Pastas
• Lucky snacks		• Quaker Frut
• Penelopa nuts and seeds		

Source: Pepsico.com.

Exhibit 7 Selected Financial Data for PepsiCo Inc.'s Business Segments, 2004–2007 ($ in millions)

	2007	2006	2005	2004
Net Revenues				
Frito-Lay North America	$11,586	$10,844	$10,322	$ 9,560
PepsiCo Beverages North America	10,230	9,565	9,146	8,313
Pepsi International	15,798	12,959	11,376	9,862
Quaker Foods North America	1,860	1,769	1,718	1,526
Total division	39,474	35,137	32,562	29,261
Corporate	—	—	—	—
Total	$39,474	$35,137	$32,562	$29,261
Operating Profit				
Frito-Lay North America	$2,845	$2,615	$2,529	$2,389
PepsiCo Beverages North America	2,188	2,055	2,037	1,911
Pepsi International	2,322	2,016	1,661	1,323
Quarker Foods North America	568	554	537	475
Total division	7,923	7,240	6,764	6,098
Corporate	(753)	(738)	(780)	(689)
Total	$7,170	$6,502	$5,984	$5,409
Capital Expenditures				
Frito-Lay North America	$ 624	$ 499	$ 512	$ 469
PepsiCo Beverages North America	430	492	320	265
Pepsi International	1,108	835	667	537
Quaker Foods North America	41	31	31	33
Total division	2,203	1,857	1,530	1,304
Corporate	227	211	206	83
Total	$2,430	$2,068	$1,736	$1,387
Total Assets				
Frito-Lay North America	$ 6,270	$ 5,969	$ 5,948	$ 5,476
PepsiCo Beverages North America	7,130	6,567	6,316	6,048
Pepsi International	14,747	11,274	9,983	8,921
Quaker Foods North America	1,002	1,003	989	978
Total division	29,149	25,110	23,482	21,423
Corporate	2,124	1,739	5,331	3,569
Investments in bottling affiliates	3,355	3,378	3,160	2,995
Total	$34,628	$29,930	$31,727	$27,987
Depreciation and Other Amortization				
Frito-Lay North America	$ 437	$ 432	$ 419	$ 420
PepsiCo Beverages North America	302	282	264	258
Pepsi International	564	478	420	382
Quaker Foods North America	34	33	34	36
Total division	1,337	1,225	1,137	1,096
Corporate	31	19	21	21
Total	$1,368	$1,244	$1,158	$1,117

(*Continued*)

Exhibit 7 (Continued)

	2007	2006	2005	2004
Amortization of Other Intangible Assets				
Frito-Lay North America	$ 9	$ 9	$ 3	$ 3
PepsiCo Beverages North America	11	77	76	75
Pepsi International	38	76	71	68
Quaker Foods North America	—	—	—	1
Total division	58	162	150	147
Corporate	—	—	—	—
Total	$58	$162	$150	$147

Source: PepsiCo Inc., 2007 10-K report.

Frito-Lay North America

In 2007, Frito-Lay brands accounted for 29 percent of the PepsiCo's total revenues and 36 percent of the company's operating profits. Frito-Lay also accounted for more than 70 percent of the salty snack food industry's total sales in the United States, which had grown at low single-digit rates annually since 2000 to reach $15.9 billion in 2008. Three key trends that were shaping the industry were convenience, a growing awareness of nutritional content of snack foods, and indulgent snacking. A product manager for a regional snack producer explained, "Many consumers want to reward themselves with great-tasting, gourmet flavors and styles. . . . The indulgent theme carries into seasonings as well. Overall, upscale, restaurant-influenced flavor trends are emerging to fill consumers' desires to escape from the norm and taste snacks from a wider, often global, palate."[1] Most manufacturers had developed new flavors of salty snacks such as jalapeno and cheddar tortilla chips and pepper jack potato chips to attract the interest of indulgent snackers. Manufacturers had also begun using healthier oils when processing chips and had expanded lines of baked and natural salty snacks to satisfy the demands of health-conscious consumers. Snacks packaged in smaller bags also addressed overeating concerns and were additionally convenient to take along on an outing. In 2008 Frito-Lay owned the top-selling chip brand in each U.S. salty snack category and held more than a two-to-one lead over the next largest snack food maker in the United States. The following table presents shares of the U.S. convenience food market for leading manufacturers in 2006. Convenience foods included both salty and sweet snacks such as chips, pretzels, ready-to-eat popcorn, crackers, dips, snack nuts and seeds, candy bars, and cookies.

Manufacturer	Market Share
PepsiCo	21%
Kraft Foods	12
Hershey	9
Kellogg	6
Master Foods	5
General Mills	2
Procter & Gamble	1
Private label	7
Others	37
Total	100%

Note: The share information shown above excludes data from certain retailers such as Wal-Mart that do not report data to Information Resources Inc. and ACNielsen Corporation.

Source: PepsiCo Inc., 2006 10-K report.

Frito-Lay North America's (FLNA) revenues increased 7 percent during 2007 as a result of double-digit growth in sales of SunChips, Quaker rice cakes, and multipacks of other products. FLNA's better-for-you and good-for-you snacks also grew at double-digit rates during 2007 and represented 16 percent of the division's total revenue. In 2008, improving the performance of the division's core salty brands and further developing health and wellness products were key strategic initiatives. The company had eliminated trans fats from all Lay's, Fritos, Ruffles, Cheetos, Tostitos, and Doritos varieties and was looking for further innovations to make its salty snacks more healthy. The company had introduced Lay's Classic potato chips, which were cooked in sunflower oil and retained Lay's traditional flavor but contained 50 percent less saturated fat. The company had also developed new multigrain and flour tortilla Tostitos varieties that appealed to indulgent snackers and were healthier than traditional Tostitos. Other new indulgent Doritos flavors included Fiery Habanero and Blazin' Buffalo & Ranch. FLNA had also expanded the number of flavors of SunChips to sustain the brand's double-digit growth. New SunChips flavors included Garden Salsa and Cinnamon Crunch. SunChips were also introduced in 100-calorie minipacks and 20-bag multipacks.

PepsiCo's 2006 acquisition of Flat Earth fruit and vegetable snacks offered an opportunity for the company to exploit consumers' desires for healthier snacks and address a deficiency in most diets. Americans, on average, consumed only about 50 percent of the U.S. Department of Agriculture's recommended daily diet of fruits and vegetables. Flat Earth's baked vegetable crisps (Farmland Cheddar, Tangy Tomato Ranch, Garlic & Herb Field) and baked fruit crisps (Peach Mango Paradise, Apple Cinnamon Grove, and Wild Berry Patch) were launched in 2007. Other good-for-you snacks included Stacy's pita chips, which was also acquired in 2006, and Quaker Chewy granola bars. In 2008, Stacy's pita chips came in 15 varieties, including Multigrain, Soy Thin Sticky Bun, Cinnamon Sugar, Whole Wheat, and Texarkana Hot. Quaker Chewy granola bars had achieved a number two rank in the segment, with a 25 percent market share in 2006. Some of the success of Quaker Chewy granola products was related to product innovations such as reduced-calorie oatmeal-and-raisin bars. PepsiCo Beverages North America also distributed Quaker rice cakes, which had added chocolate-drizzled and multigrain varieties in 2007.

PepsiCo Beverages North America

PepsiCo was the largest seller of liquid refreshments in the United States, with a 26 percent share of the market in 2006. Coca-Cola was the second largest nonalcoholic beverage producer, with a 23 percent market share. Cadbury Schweppes and Nestlé were the third and fourth largest beverage sellers in 2006, with market shares of 10 percent and 8 percent, respectively. Like Frito-Lay, PepsiCo's beverage business contributed greatly to the corporation's overall profitability and free cash flows. In 2007, PepsiCo Beverages North America (PBNA) accounted for 28 percent of the corporation's total revenues and 31 percent of its profits. Revenues for PBNA had increased by 7 percent annually between 2006 and 2007 as the company broadened its line of noncarbonated beverages like Gatorade, Tropicana fruit juices, Lipton ready-to-drink tea, Propel, Aquafina, Dole fruit drinks, Starbucks cold coffee drinks, and SoBe. Carbonated soft drinks were the most-consumed type of beverage in the United States, with a 48 percent of share of the total beverage market, but carbonated soft drink volume declined by 2.6 percent in 2007 as consumers searched for healthier beverage choices. In contrast, flavored and enhanced water products grew by 30.6 percent, energy drinks grew by 24.7 percent, ready-to-drink tea grew by 15 percent, and bottled water grew by 6.9 percent between 2006 and 2007. The size and volume share of the U.S. beverage industry by beverage category for 2005 through 2007 is presented in Exhibit 8.

PepsiCo's Carbonated Soft Drinks Business

During the mid-1990s, it looked as if Coca-Cola would dominate the soft drink industry, with every Pepsi-Cola brand except Mountain Dew losing market share to Coca-Cola's brands. Coca-Cola's CEO at the time, Roberto Goizueta, had stated that the company's strategic intent was to control 50 percent of the U.S. cola market by 2000 and seemed convinced PepsiCo could do little to stop the industry leader. Goizueta summed up his lack of concern about Pepsi as a key rival in an October 28, 1996, *Fortune* article entitled "How Coke Is Kicking Pepsi's Can" by saying, "As they've become less relevant, I don't need to look at them very much anymore."

PepsiCo's management engineered a comeback in the late 1990s and early 2000s by launching new brands like Sierra Mist and focusing on strategies to improve local distribution. Among Pepsi's most successful strategies to build volume and share in soft drinks was its "Power of One" strategy, which attempted to achieve the synergistic benefits of a combined Pepsi-Cola and Frito-Lay envisioned by shareholders of the two companies in 1965. The Power of One strategy called for supermarkets to place Pepsi and Frito-Lay products side by side on shelves. In 2006, PepsiCo added "Innovation Summits" to its Power of One program whereby retailers could share their views on consumer shopping and

Exhibit 8 Volume Size and Share of the U.S. Liquid Refreshment Beverage Market by Segment, 2005–2007

	Volume by Beverage Category (Millions of Gallons)			Volume Share		
Beverage Category	2005	2006	2007	2005	2006	2007
Carbonated soft drinks	15,271.6	15,103.6	14,707.4	52.9%	50.1%	48.1%
Bottled water*	7,537.1	8,253.1	8,822.4	26.1	27.4	28.9
Fruit beverages	4,119.0	4,020.1	3,899.5	14.3	13.3	12.8
Isotonic sports drinks	1,207.5	1,322.0	1,355.1	4.2	4.4	4.4
Ready-to-drink tea	555.9	760.9	875.1	1.9	2.5	2.9
Flavored and enhanced water	—	418.5	546.5	—	1.4	1.8
Energy drinks	152.5	242.7	302.6	0.5	0.8	1.0
Ready-to-drink coffee	38.9	44.5	45.1	0.1	0.1	0.1
Total	28,882.5	30,165.8	30,553.7	100.0%	100.0%	100.0%

*Excludes flavored and enhanced water after 2005.
Source: Beverage Marketing Corporation.

eating habits. PepsiCo used the information gleaned from the summits in developing new products like SoBe Life Water and Lay's potato chips cooked in sunflower oil. The summits, which continued into 2007, also helped identify PepsiCo supply chain inefficiencies that affected retailers. PepsiCo managers and retailers collaborated during one Innovation Summit to develop new shipping procedures that reduced stock-outs in retailers' stores.

PepsiCo's primary focus in soft drink innovation was directed toward improving the nutritional properties of soft drinks. The company was attempting to develop new types of sweeteners that would lower the calorie content of nondiet drinks. The company also hoped its 2006 acquisition of Izze lightly carbonated sparkling fruit drinks would prove popular with health-conscious consumers. Tava was an additional calorie-free, caffeine-free, better-for-you carbonated beverage that PBNA launched in the United States in 2007. Even though PepsiCo strengthened its position in the U.S. carbonated soft drink industry, its 31.1 percent market share during 2007 was considerably less than Coca-Cola's 2007 market share of 41.6 percent.

PepsiCo's Noncarbonated Beverage Brands

Although carbonated beverages made up the largest percentage of PBNA's total beverage volume, much of the division's growth was attributable to the success of its noncarbonated beverages. In 2007, total revenue for the division increased by 7 percent, which was driven by a 5 percent increase in noncarbonated beverages and the contribution of new acquisitions. Carbonated soft drink volume declined by 3 percent during 2007.

Aquafina was the number one brand of bottled water in the United States and grew by 6.9 percent between 2006 and 2007. Bottled water was a particularly attractive segment for PepsiCo since bottled water consumption in the United States had increased from 4.6 billion gallons in 1999 to 8.8 billion gallons in 2007. PepsiCo's Frappuccino ready-to-drink (RTD) coffee and Lipton RTD teas made it the leader in the RTD tea and RTD coffee categories as well. The RTD tea category grew by 15 percent between 2006 and 2007, while RTD coffees grew by just over 1 percent during 2007. PepsiCo's SoBe Essential Energy and SoBe Adrenaline Rush drinks held a negligible share of the energy drink market, with Red Bull accounting for 40 percent of industry sales in 2007. Red Bull was produced and marketed by the privately held Red Bull GmbH, of Austria. Hansen Natural Corporation's Monster energy drink and Coca-Cola's Full Throttle energy drink accounted for approximately 30 percent of industry sales in 2007.

In 2008, PBNA's Propel Fitness Water was the leading brand of functional water. In 2006, the company had also introduced SoBe Life Water and functional versions of Aquafina. The product lines for its water business were developed around customer type and lifestyle. Propel was a flavor- and vitamin-enriched water marketed to physically active consumers, while Life Water was a vitamin-enhanced water marketed to image-driven consumers. The company targeted mainstream water consumers with unflavored Aquafina, Aquafina FlavorSplash (offered in four flavors), and Aquafina Sparkling (a zero-calorie, lightly carbonated citrus- or berry-flavored water). Aquafina Alive, launched in 2007, included vitamins and natural fruit juices. The company's strategy involved offering a continuum of healthy beverages from unflavored Aquafina to nutrient-rich Gatorade. In 2007, Gatorade, Propel, and Aquafina were all number one in their categories, with market shares of 76 percent, 40 percent, and approximately 15 percent, respectively.

Gatorade's volume had grown by 21 percent in 2005 and by 12 percent in 2006 to reach sales of over $3 billion. Gatorade's impressive growth had come about through the introduction of new flavors and formulations such as the lower-calorie G2 and the Tiger Woods signature Gatorade sub-brand. Volume growth was also attributable to new container sizes and designs, new multipacks, world-class advertising, and added points of distribution. Analysts believed that Gatorade could achieve even stronger performance once the U.S. Federal Trade Commission's 10-year prohibition on bundled beverage contracts with retailers and joint Gatorade/soft drink distribution came to an end. Gatorade's broker-distribution system also allowed Tropicana and Lipton RTD teas to double sales volume between the 2001 acquisition of Quaker Oats and year-end 2006. PepsiCo's 39.5 percent market share in RTD teas in 2007 was nearly four times greater than the 10.7 percent share held by Coca-Cola's Nestea RTD tea. Tropicana was the number one brand in the $3 billion orange juice industry, with an approximate 30 percent market share in 2007. Coca-Cola's Minute Maid brand of orange juice held a 25 percent market share in 2007. The combined sales of PBNA's better-for-you and good-for-you beverages made up 70 percent of the division's net revenue in both 2006 and 2007.

PepsiCo International

All PepsiCo snacks, beverages, and food items sold outside North America were included in the company's PepsiCo International division. International snack volume grew by 9 percent in 2007, with double-digit growth in emerging markets such as Russia, the Middle East, and Turkey. Beverage volume in international markets increased by 8 percent during 2007, with the fastest growth occurring in the Middle East, China, and Pakistan. Volume gains, along with acquisitions in Europe, the Middle East, Africa, New Zealand, and Brazil, allowed the division's revenues and operating profits to increase by 22 percent and 15 percent, respectively, between 2006 and 2007. PepsiCo's 2007 acquisitions in international markets were expected to boost 2008 revenues by more than $1 billion.

PepsiCo's Sale of Beverages in International Markets PepsiCo also found that it could grow international sales through its Power of One strategy. A PepsiCo executive explained how the company's soft drink business could gain shelf space through the strength of Frito-Lay's brands: "You go to Chile, where Frito-Lay has over 90 percent of the market, but Pepsi is in lousy shape. Frito-Lay can help Pepsi change that."[2] PepsiCo's market share in carbonated soft drinks in its strongest international markets during 2006 is presented in the following table:

Country/Region	PepsiCo's Carbonated Soft Drink Market Share
Middle East	75% +
India	49
Thailand	49
Egypt	47
Venezuela	42
Nigeria	38
China	36
Russia	24

Source: PepsiCo Investor Presentation by Mike White, CEO PepsiCo International, 2006.

PepsiCo International management believed further opportunities in other international markets existed. In 2007, the average consumption of carbonated soft drinks in the United States was 60 servings per month, while the average consumption of carbonated soft drinks in other developed countries was 23 servings per month and in developing countries was 6 servings per month. The company also saw a vast opportunity for sales growth in the $70 billion market for noncarbonated beverages in international markets. In 2006, PepsiCo International recorded less than $1 billion in noncarbonated beverage sales outside North America. The company was rapidly rolling out Tropicana to international markets and had acquired two international juice brands to capture a larger share of the $37 billion international markets for juice drinks. Also, PepsiCo was making Gatorade available in more international markets to capture a share of the $5 billion isotonic sports drink market outside the United States. Sales of Gatorade in Latin America more than doubled between 2001 and 2006, giving the sports drink a 72 percent market share in the entire Latin American region in 2006. PepsiCo International was also moving into new markets with Lipton RTD tea, gaining a share of the $15 billion international RTD tea market. In 2007, Gatorade was available in 42 international markets, Tropicana was in 27 country markets outside North America, and Lipton was sold in 27 international markets. Tropicana was the number one juice brand in Europe and had achieved a 100 percent increase in sales in the region between 2001 and 2006. By 2012, PepsiCo planned to launch Gatorade in 15 additional country markets, Tropicana in 20 new markets, and Lipton in 5 new international markets.

PepsiCo had moved somewhat slowly into international bottled water markets, with its most notable effort occurring in Mexico. In 2002, PepsiCo's bottling operations acquired Mexico's largest Pepsi bottler, Pepsi-Gemex SA de CV, for $1.26 billion. Gemex not only bottled and distributed Pepsi soft drinks in Mexico but was also Mexico's number one producer of purified water. After its acquisition of Gemex, PepsiCo shifted its international expansion efforts to bringing Aquafina to selected emerging markets in Eastern Europe, the Middle East, and Asia. In 2006, Aquafina was the number one brand of bottled water in Russia and Vietnam, and the number two brand in Kuwait.

PepsiCo's Sales of Snack Foods in International Markets Frito-Lay was the largest snack chip company in the world, with sales of approximately $7 billion outside the United States and a 40+ percent share of the international salty snack industry in 2006. Frito-Lay held commanding shares of the market for salty snacks in many country markets. The following table presents PepsiCo's salty snack market share in selected countries in 2006:

Country	PepsiCo's Salty Snack Market Share
Mexico	75%
Holland	59
South Africa	57
Australia	55
Brazil	46
India	46
United Kingdom	44
Russia	43
Spain	41
China	16

Source: PepsiCo Investor Presentation by Mike White, CEO PepsiCo International, 2006.

PepsiCo management believed international markets offered the company's greatest opportunity for growth since per capita consumption of snacks in the United States averaged 6.6 servings per month, while per capita consumption in other developed countries averaged 4.0 servings per month and per capita consumption in developing countries averaged 0.4 servings per month. PepsiCo executives expected that, by 2010, China and Brazil would be the two largest international markets for snacks. The United Kingdom was projected to be the third largest international market for snacks, while developing markets Mexico and Russia would be the fourth and fifth largest international markets, respectively.

Developing an understanding of consumer taste preferences was a key to expanding into international markets. Taste preferences for salty snacks were more similar from country to country than many other food items, which allowed PepsiCo to make only modest modifications to its snacks in most countries. For example, classic varieties of Lay's, Doritos, and Cheetos snacks were sold in Latin America. However, the company supplemented its global brands with varieties spiced to local preferences such as the seaweed-flavored Atesanas chips sold in Thailand and Lay's White Mushroom potato chips sold in Russia. In addition, consumer characteristics in the United States that had forced snack food makers to adopt better-for-you or good-for-you snacks applied in most other developed countries as well. In 2007, PepsiCo was eliminating trans fats from its snacks and expanding the nutritional credentials of its snacks sold in Europe, since demand for health and wellness products in Europe was growing by 10–13 percent per year. The annual revenue growth for core salty snacks in Europe was growing at a modest 4–6 percent per year. Among PepsiCo's fastest-growing snacks in the United Kingdom was Walker's baked potato chips, which had 70 percent less saturated fat and 25 percent less salt than regular Walker's chips. Walker's baked potato chips was named Britain's best new product of 2007 by *Marketing Week* magazine.

International Sales of Quaker Oats Products

PepsiCo International also manufactured and distributed Quaker Oats oatmeal and cereal in international markets. In 2006, 75 percent of Quaker Oats' international sales of $500 million was accounted for by just six countries. The United Kingdom was Quakers largest market outside the United States, where it held more than a 50 percent market share in oatmeal. The company had launched new oatmeal products in the United Kingdom, including Organic Oats, OatSo Simple microwaveable oatmeal and oatmeal bars, and Oat Granola and Oat Muesli cereals. PepsiCo also added new varieties of Quaker oatmeal products in Latin America to double the brand's sales in the region. Exhibit 9 presents a breakdown of PepsiCo's net revenues and long-lived assets by geographic region.

Quaker Foods North America

Quaker Oats produced, marketed, and distributed hot and ready-to-eat cereals, pancake mixes and syrups, and rice and pasta side dishes in the United States and Canada. The division recorded sales of approximately $1.8 billion in 2007. Sales volume of Quaker Foods products increased by 2 percent during 2007, with Quaker Oatmeal, Life cereal, and Cap'n Crunch cereal volumes increasing at mid-single-digit rates. Sales of Aunt Jemima syrup and pancake mix declined slightly, while sales of Rice-A-Roni and PastaRoni kits declined at a double-digit rate during 2007. Quaker Oats was the star product of the division, with a 58 percent market share in North America in 2006. Rice-A-Roni held a 33 percent market share in the rice and pasta side dish segment of the consumer food industry. Quaker Foods was the third largest ready-to-eat cereal maker, with a 14 percent market share in 2005. In 2005, Kellogg's held a 30 percent share of the $6 billion ready-to-eat cereal market and General Mills held a 26 percent market share. Quaker grits and Aunt Jemima pancake mix and syrup competed in mature categories, and all enjoyed market leading positions. More than half of Quaker Foods' 2007 revenues were generated by better-for-you and good-for-you products.

Exhibit 9 PepsiCo Inc.'s U.S. and International Sales and Long-Lived Assets, 2004–2006 ($ in millions)

	2007	2006	2005	2004
Net Revenues				
United States	$21,978	$20,788	$19,937	$18,329
Mexico	3,498	3,228	3,095	2,724
United Kingdom	1,987	1,839	1,821	1,692
Canada	1,961	1,702	1,509	1,309
All other countries	10,050	7,580	6,200	5,207
Total	$39,474	$35,137	$32,562	$29,261
Long-Lived Assets				
United States	$12,498	$11,515	$10,723	$10,212
Mexico	1,067	996	902	878
United Kingdom	2,090	1,995	1,715	1,896
Canada	699	589	582	548
All other countries	6,441	4,725	3,948	3,339
Total	$22,795	$19,820	$17,870	$16,873

Source: PepsiCo Inc., 2006 10-K report.

Value Chain Alignment Between PepsiCo Brands and Products

PepsiCo's management team was dedicated to capturing strategic fit benefits within the business lineup throughout the value chain. The company's procurement activities were coordinated globally to achieve the greatest possible economies of scale, and best practices were routinely transferred between its 230 plants, 3,600 distribution systems, and 120,000 service routes around the world. PepsiCo also shared marketed research information to better enable each division to develop new products likely to be hits with consumers and coordinated its Power of One activities across product lines.

PepsiCo management had a proven ability to capture strategic fits between the operations of new acquisitions and its other businesses. The Quaker Oats integration produced a number of noteworthy successes, including $160 million in cost savings resulting from corporate-wide procurement of product ingredients and packaging materials and an estimated $40 million in cost savings attributed to the joint distribution of Quaker snacks and Frito-Lay products. Also, the combination of Gatorade and Tropicana hot fill operations saved an estimated $120 million annually by 2005.

PEPSICO'S STRATEGIC REALIGNMENT IN 2008

For the most part, PepsiCo's strategies seemed to be firing on all cylinders in 2007. PepsiCo's chief managers expected the company's lineup of snack, beverage, and grocery items to generate operating cash flows sufficient to reinvest in its core businesses, provide cash dividends to shareholders, fund an $8 billion share buyback plan, and pursue acquisitions that would provide attractive returns. Nevertheless, the low relative profit margins of PepsiCo's international businesses created the need for a new organizational structure that might better exploit strategic fits between the company's international operations.

Beginning in 2008, PepsiCo's former Frito-Lay North America, Quaker Foods North America and all of its food and snack businesses in Latin America would be combined into a common PepsiCo Americas Foods division. The Latin American beverage businesses would be pulled from the PepsiCo International division and combined with PepsiCo Beverages North America to form the PepsiCo Americas Beverages division. PepsiCo International would include all of the company's snack and beverage businesses outside of North America and Latin America. The new three-division structure would include six reporting segments: Frito-Lay North America, Quaker Foods North America, Latin American Foods, PepsiCo Americas Beverages, United Kingdom & Europe, and Middle East, Africa & Asia. Some food and beverage industry analysts had speculated that corporate strategy changes might also be required to improve the profitability of PepsiCo's international operations and to help restore share price appreciation. Possible actions might include a reprioritization of internal uses of cash, new acquisitions, further efforts to capture strategic fits existing between the company's various businesses, or the divestiture of businesses with poor prospects of future growth and minimal strategic fit with PepsiCo's other businesses.

Endnotes

[1] As quoted in "Snack Attack," *Private Label Buyer,* August 2006, p. 26.

[2] "PepsiCo's New Formula," *BusinessWeek Online,* April 10, 2000.

CASE

20 Robin Hood

Joseph Lampel
New York University

It was in the spring of the second year of his insurrection against the High Sheriff of Nottingham that Robin Hood took a walk in Sherwood Forest. As he walked he pondered the progress of the campaign, the disposition of his forces, the Sheriff's recent moves, and the options that confronted him.

The revolt against the Sheriff had begun as a personal crusade. It erupted out of Robin's conflict with the Sheriff and his administration. However, alone Robin Hood could do little. He therefore sought allies, men with grievances and a deep sense of justice. Later he welcomed all who came, asking few questions and demanding only a willingness to serve. Strength, he believed, lay in numbers.

He spent the first year forging the group into a disciplined band, united in enmity against the Sheriff and willing to live outside the law. The band's organization was simple. Robin ruled supreme, making all important decisions. He delegated specific tasks to his lieutenants. Will Scarlett was in charge of intelligence and scouting. His main job was to shadow the Sheriff and his men, always alert to their next move. He also collected information on the travel plans of rich merchants and tax collectors. Little John kept discipline among the men and saw to it that their archery was at the high peak that their profession demanded. Scarlock took care of the finances, converting loot to cash, paying shares of the take, and finding suitable hiding places for the surplus. Finally, Much the Miller's son had the difficult task of provisioning the ever-increasing band of Merrymen.

The increasing size of the band was a source of satisfaction for Robin, but also a source of concern. The fame of his Merrymen was spreading, and new recruits were pouring in from every corner of England. As the band grew larger, their small bivouac became a major encampment. Between raids the men milled about, talking and playing games. Vigilance was in decline, and discipline was becoming harder to enforce. "Why," Robin reflected, "I don't know half the men I run into these days."

The growing band was also beginning to exceed the food capacity of the forest. Game was becoming scarce, and supplies had to be obtained from outlying villages. The cost of buying food was beginning to drain the band's financial reserves at the very moment when revenues were in decline. Travelers, especially those with the most to lose, were now giving the forest a wide berth. This was costly and inconvenient to them, but it was preferable to having all their goods confiscated.

Robin believed that the time had come for the Merrymen to change their policy of outright confiscation of goods to one of a fixed transit tax. His lieutenants strongly resisted this idea. They were proud of the Merrymen's famous motto: "Rob the rich and give to the poor." "The farmers and the townspeople," they argued, "are our most important allies. How can we tax them, and still hope for their help in our fight against the Sheriff?"

Robin wondered how long the Merrymen could keep to the ways and methods of their early days. The Sheriff was growing stronger and becoming better organized. He now had the money and the men and was beginning to harass the band, probing for its weaknesses. The tide of events was beginning to turn against the Merrymen. Robin felt that the campaign must be decisively concluded before the Sheriff had a chance to deliver a mortal blow. "But how," he wondered, "could this be done?"

Robin had often entertained the possibility of killing the Sheriff, but the chances for this seemed increasingly remote. Besides, killing the Sheriff might satisfy his personal thirst for revenge, but it would not improve the situation. Robin had hoped that the perpetual state of unrest, and the Sheriff's failure to collect taxes, would lead to his removal from office. Instead, the Sheriff used his political connections to obtain reinforcement. He had powerful friends at court and was well regarded by the regent, Prince John.

Prince John was vicious and volatile. He was consumed by his unpopularity among the people, who wanted the imprisoned King Richard back. He also lived in constant fear of the barons, who had first given him the regency but were now beginning to dispute his claim to the throne. Several of these barons had set out to collect the ransom that would release King Richard the Lionheart from his jail in Austria. Robin was invited to join the conspiracy in return for future amnesty. It was a dangerous proposition. Provincial banditry was one thing, court intrigue another. Prince John had spies everywhere, and he was known for his vindictiveness. If the conspirators' plan failed, the pursuit would be relentless, and retributions swift.

The sound of the supper horn startled Robin from his thoughts. There was the smell of roasting venison in the air. Nothing was resolved or settled. Robin headed for camp promising himself that he would give these problems his utmost attention after tomorrow's raid.

CASE

21 Dilemma at Devil's Den

Allan R. Cohen
Babson College

Kim Johnson
Babson College

My name is Susan, and I'm a business student at Mt. Eagle College. Let me tell you about one of my worst experiences. I had a part-time job in the campus snack bar, The Devil's Den. At the time, I was 21 years old and a junior with a concentration in finance. I originally started working at the Den in order to earn some extra spending money. I had been working there for one semester and became upset with some of the happenings. The Den was managed by contract with an external company, College Food Services (CFS). What bothered me was that many employees were allowing their friends to take free food, and the employees themselves were also taking food in large quantities when leaving their shifts. The policy was that employees could eat whatever they liked free of charge while they were working, but it had become common for employees to leave with food and not to be charged for their snacks while off duty as well.

I felt these problems were occurring for several reasons. For example, employee wages were low, there was easy access to the unlocked storage room door, and inventory was poorly controlled. Also, there was weak supervision by the student managers and no written rules or strict guidelines. It seemed that most of the employees were enjoying freebies, and it had been going on for so long that it was taken for granted. The problem got so far out of hand that customers who had seen others do it felt free to do it whether they knew the workers or not. The employees who witnessed this never challenged anyone because, in my opinion, they did not care and they feared the loss of friendship or being frowned upon by others. Apparently, speaking up was more costly to the employees than the loss of money to CFS for the unpaid food items. It seemed obvious to me that the employees felt too secure in their jobs and did not feel that their jobs were in jeopardy.

The employees involved were those who worked the night shifts and on the weekends. They were students at the college and were under the supervision of another student, who held the position of manager. There were approximately 30 student employees and 6 student managers on the staff. During the day there were no student managers; instead, a full-time manager was employed by CFS to supervise the Den. The employees and student managers were mostly freshmen and sophomores, probably because of the low wages, inconvenient hours (late weeknights and weekends), and the duties of the job itself. Employees were hard to come by; the high rate of employee turnover indicated that the job qualifications and the selection process were minimal.

The student managers were previous employees chosen by other student managers and the full-time CFS day manager on the basis of their ability to work and on their length of employment. They received no further formal training or written rules beyond what they had already learned by working there. The student managers were briefed on how to close the snack bar at night but still did not get the job done properly. They received authority and responsibility

over events occurring during their shifts as manager, although they were never actually taught how and when to enforce it! Their increase in pay was small, from a starting pay of just over minimum wage to an additional 15 percent for student managers. Regular employees received an additional nickel for each semester of employment.

Although I only worked seven hours per week, I was in the Den often as a customer and saw the problem frequently. I felt the problem was on a large enough scale that action should have been taken, not only to correct any financial loss that the Den might have experienced but also to help give the student employees a true sense of their responsibilities, the limits of their freedom, respect for rules, and pride in their jobs. The issues at hand bothered my conscience, although I was not directly involved. I felt that the employees and customers were taking advantage of the situation whereby they could "steal" food almost whenever they wanted. I believed that I had been brought up correctly and knew right from wrong, and I felt that the happenings in the Den were wrong. It wasn't fair that CFS paid for others' greediness or urges to show what they could get away with in front of their friends.

I was also bothered by the lack of responsibility of the managers to get the employees to do their work. I had seen the morning employees work very hard trying to do their jobs, in addition to the jobs the closing shift should have done. I assumed the night managers did not care or think about who worked the next day. It bothered me to think that the morning employees were suffering because of careless employees and student managers from the night before.

I had never heard of CFS mentioning any problems or taking any corrective action; therefore, I wasn't sure whether they knew what was going on, or if they were ignoring it. I was speaking to a close friend, Mack, a student manager at the Den, and I mentioned the fact that the frequently unlocked door to the storage room was an easy exit through which I had seen different quantities of unpaid goods taken out. I told him about some specific instances and said that I believed that it happened rather frequently. Nothing was ever said to other employees about this, and the only corrective action was that the door was locked more often, yet the key to the lock was still available upon request to all employees during their shifts.

Another lack of strong corrective action I remembered was when an employee was caught pocketing cash from the register. The student was neither suspended nor threatened with losing his job (nor was the event even mentioned). Instead, he was just told to stay away from the register. I felt that this weak punishment happened not because he was a good worker but because he worked so many hours and it would be difficult to find someone who would work all those hours and remain working for more than a few months. Although a customer reported the incident, I still felt that management should have taken more corrective action.

The attitudes of the student managers seemed to vary. I had noticed that one in particular, Bill, always got the job done. He made a list of each small duty that needed to be done, such as restocking, and he made sure the jobs were divided among the employees and finished before his shift was over. Bill also stared down employees who allowed thefts by their friends or who took freebies themselves; yet I had never heard of an employee being challenged verbally, nor had anyone ever been fired for these actions. My friend Mack was concerned about theft, or so I assumed, because he had taken some action about locking the doors, but he didn't really get after employees to work if they were slacking off.

I didn't think the rest of the student managers were good motivators. I noticed that they did little work themselves and did not show much control over the employees. The student managers allowed their friends to take food for free, thereby setting bad examples for the other workers, and allowed the employees to take what they wanted even when they were not working. I thought their attitudes were shared by most of the other employees: not caring about their jobs or working hard, as long as they got paid and their jobs were not threatened.

I had let the "thefts" continue without mention because I felt that no one else really cared and may even have frowned upon me for trying to take action. Management thus far had not reported significant losses to the employees so as to encourage them to watch for theft and prevent it. Management did not threaten employees with job loss, nor did they provide employees with supervision. I felt it was not my place to report the theft to management, because I was just an employee and I would be overstepping the student managers. Also, I was unsure whether management would do anything about it anyway—maybe they did not care. I felt that talking to the student managers or other employees would be useless, because they were either abusing the rules themselves or were clearly aware of what was going on and just ignored it. I felt that others may have frowned upon me and made it uncomfortable for me to continue working there. This would be very difficult for me, because I wanted to become a student manager the next semester and did not want to create any waves that might have prevented me from doing so. I recognized the student manager position as a chance to gain some managerial and leadership skills, while at the same time adding a great plus to my résumé when I graduated. Besides, as a student manager, I would be in a better position to do something about all the problems at the Den that bothered me so much.

What could I do in the meantime to clear my conscience of the freebies, favors to friends, and employee snacks? What could I do without ruining my chances of becoming a student manager myself someday? I hated just keeping quiet, but I didn't want to make a fool of myself. I was really stuck.

Wal-Mart Stores Inc. in 2008: Management's Initiatives to Transform the Company and Curtail Wal-Mart Bashing

CASE

22

Arthur A. Thompson
The University of Alabama

In June 2008, Wal-Mart's CEO, H. Lee Scott, presented a glowing report to the estimated 16,000 shareholders attending the company's annual shareholder meeting held at the 19,000-seat Bud Walton Arena on the University of Arkansas campus, located a few miles from Wal-Mart's headquarters in Bentonville, Arkansas. In the tradition of prior annual meetings of Wal-Mart shareholders, the 2008 meeting was an elaborate event lasting most of the day; the meeting included not only a series of presentations by company executives but also entertainment by Tim McGraw, David Cook (who had been named the 2008 American Idol a few weeks earlier), British singer Joss Stone, and Oscar winner and Idol finalist Jennifer Hudson. Scott said he was quite pleased with the results of the transformation process that top management had initiated in 2006 to provide customers with a more satisfying shopping experience, better fulfill the company's new mission, and do a better job of getting Wal-Mart's 2.1 million employees worldwide to understand and practice the cultural values and business principles espoused by the company's esteemed founder, Sam Walton.

Scott explained to shareholders why transformation had become essential to the company's continued growth and success even though in 2006 Wal-Mart's traditional business model of driving costs out of its supply chain, constantly implementing ways to operate more cost-efficiently, offering customers worldwide a broad range of merchandise at appealingly low prices, and opening stores in more and more places to serve an ever-growing customer base had served the company well:

> It would be easy to take comfort in the success we have had in our business. . . . If you know that something works, why not just replicate it and replicate it and replicate it? Well, we have done that before. For several years, we did what we knew worked. And we did it very well. We grew beyond expectations. Our stock price went up. And we felt good about it. And we had every right to.
>
> But, in time, the world changed. People's expectations of us—and of corporations in general—changed. And we found ourselves playing catch-up. We can never let that happen again. Not only must we never fall behind . . . we must always push ourselves to stay ahead.
>
> We must continue to ask fundamental questions that alter perspectives and ultimately behavior. Questions like: How do you persuade someone in a successful organization that real change is needed and can be achieved in a way that is consistent with their core beliefs? How do you get a leadership team to step back and ask what success means not just in their own business, but in the larger context of the company as a whole? How do you take the trends of the future and put them into the business, so a company is relevant to today's consumers and well positioned for tomorrow's consumers?

These are not easy questions to ask. They are not easy questions to answer. But we have to keep asking them. And when necessary make difficult decisions.

Your Wal-Mart has an opportunity to be a leader in the retail industry for more ethical and environmentally friendly sourcing. Your Wal-Mart can play a role in reducing the world's dependence on oil and other high-carbon sources of energy. Your Wal-Mart can bring even greater value to customers who need and deserve to save on everyday needs.

And there are things we need to do inside our company—such as making your Wal-Mart more diverse and creating a more inclusive environment. I am confident that if we put diversity and inclusion into our business and really commit to it, we can make real progress. I am determined Wal-Mart will do this. It is essential to attracting and keeping the best possible people and staying relevant to our customers. [In 2008, as Scott delivered his remarks, Wal-Mart was already a decidedly diverse employer. Its workforce included more than 154,000 Hispanics; 237,000 African Americans; 41,000 Asian Americans; 15,000 Native Americans; 826,000 women; and 256,000 people age 55 or older.]

But I also urge you to think about what we can do—and what the world will expect us to do in the future. There are very clear trends that the retail industry and the world will have to confront—the aging of the global population, a multi-polar balance of power, income inequality, the disruptive power of technology, increased demand for energy, to name a few.

Think about these trends, the strengths of your Wal-Mart and our model of "Saving Money" and "Living Better." We have the best global footprint to serve millions worldwide who will want the opportunity to lift themselves up into the middle class. Our leadership in sustainability will give customers and suppliers everywhere the ability to be more energy efficient and therefore more energy independent. An older global population will need us to help them stretch their money and maintain their quality of life while living on a fixed income. Here's the bottom line for our business and the larger role we can play. . . . Your Wal-Mart is uniquely positioned to succeed not just in this economy, but in these times. And among retailers, we are the best positioned to lead in the world of tomorrow.

So how do we continue to turn our position of strength into leadership for the future? I want to repeat a quote from Sam [Walton] that I shared on this stage two years ago: "You can't just keep doing what works one time. Everything around you is always changing. To succeed, stay out in front of that change."

The world has become too complex and changes too rapidly for a company of our size to just replicate. I am not saying that we have to constantly reinvent ourselves. We do not. And we should not. We have a culture, a mission, and core values that are timeless and universal. But we have to constantly look at how we apply those things to the changing world around us. The challenge ahead is that we must continue to challenge ourselves.

I am confident that your Wal-Mart will continue to transform. And I am confident we will continue to succeed.[1]

Scott's leadership of the transformation process under way at Wal-Mart included a number of initiatives:

- *Recasting the company's mission as one of "Saving People Money So They Can Live Better."* "Saving money" had always been a fundamental component of what Wal-Mart was all about—for decades, the front of every Wal-Mart store had signage touting "We Sell for Less" and its everyday low prices were unmatched by any other retailer. But the new "Live Better" piece of Wal-Mart's mission was, in Scott's view, a way to "unlock the full potential of Wal-Mart" and "strengthen our ability not only to do well as a business . . . but also to do good in the world."[2]
- *Revising Wal-Mart's logo* to better mirror the company's shift in emphasis away from "Always low prices. Always." and "We Sell for Less" to the broader mission of "Saving People Money So They Can Live Better."
- *Making a special effort to convince Wal-Mart's 2.1 million associates why the company's new mission was more than a hollow statement* and a reflection of the company's new marketing campaign tied to the theme "Save Money. Live Better." Scott and Wal-Mart's other senior executives believed the new mission would not have the desired transformational effect unless it led to better operating practices and a cultural energy that actually delivered added value to customers and touched the communities in which Wal-Mart operated.
- *Broadening Wal-Mart's appeal to existing customers and attracting new customers to shop at Wal-Mart, updating merchandise offerings, instituting faster checkout procedures, and revising the layout and decor of Wal-Mart stores*

to enhance store ambience and better present merchandise offerings in a manner calculated to spur sales. A sizable number of the company's apparel lines were upgraded to better appeal to shoppers looking for a bit more upscale and stylish clothing. Stores were redecorated, aisles were widened, skylights were added to improve lighting, clutter was reduced, cleanliness was improved, and inventory on shelving that was out of reach to shoppers was eliminated. Store managers and regional managers were given more authority to stock their stores with merchandise that was particularly appealing to the local population—the objective was for each store's merchandise offerings to be "locally and regionally correct." For instance, most Wal-Mart stores stocked sports apparel and merchandise of locally popular teams, along with products that were made locally or had local appeal. Numerous Wal-Mart Supercenters began stocking locally grown produce. According to Scott, who along with other Wal-Mart executives toured Wal-Mart stores every week, in 2008 the company's 6,800 stores "look better . . . . they feel better and are friendlier too."

- *Initiating a flat $4 price for the generic versions of some 200 common prescription drugs.* In 2008, this program was extended to provide a 90-day supply of certain prescription medicines for $10. Wal-Mart estimated that its $4 prescription program had saved customers $1.1 billion in the first 20 months of the program's existence. The company also lowered the prices of some 1,000 over-the-counter drugs.
- *Increasing "green" merchandise offerings and promoting their use to customers.* One such effort entailed helping customers live better by promoting the use of superefficient compact fluorescent light bulbs. When the program was initiated in November 2006, Wal-Mart announced a goal of selling 100 million bulbs; by early 2008, it had sold 192 million bulbs, estimated to save customers $6 billion in electricity costs and eliminate the need to build the equivalent of 3 power plants (which in turn promoted a cleaner environment and reduced carbon dioxide emissions that were said to contribute to global warming). Another effort involved stocking a wider selection of organic foods, which were all grown using sustainable agricultural methods that did not include the use of pesticides and chemical fertilizers. Wal-Mart's tracking of customers' decisions to purchase five key eco-friendly products showed that sales increased 66 percent between April 2007 and April 2008.[3] These and other "green" initiatives being pursued by Wal-Mart were follow-ons to Scott's public commitment in October 2005 that Wal-Mart would henceforth take a leadership position in promoting environmental sustainability via efforts to operate all aspects of its business in a manner calculated to promote sustainability and make the earth a better place. To make the sustainability commitment a reality, Scott had appointed several new top executives to spearhead Wal-Mart's campaign to be a good steward of the environment
- *Launching a multifaceted "Zero Waste" campaign.* Through its Kids Recycling Challenge, Wal-Mart worked with elementary schools in 12 states to begin recycling plastic bags—each school received $5 for each 60-gallon collection bag that students brought to their local Wal-Mart store. In October 2007, Wal-Mart introduced reusable shopping bags inscribed with "Paper or Plastic? Neither"; management estimated that a reusable bag could eliminate the use of 100 disposable plastic bags and, by May 2008, Wal-Mart had sold enough of the reusable shopping bags to eliminate the need for 400 million plastic bags. In April 2008, as part of Earth Month, Wal-Mart gave away 1 million reusable bags. Wal-Mart partnered with its laundry detergent suppliers to introduce concentrated liquid laundry detergents in smaller containers and thereby save on packaging; in May 2008, Wal-Mart announced that it had achieved its goal of selling only concentrated detergents in its U.S. and Canadian stores, estimating that over a three-year period its actions would save more than 400 million gallons of water, more than 95 million pounds of plastic resin, and more than 125 million pounds of cardboard—approximately 25 percent of the liquid laundry detergent sold in the United States was at Wal-Mart stores. Wal-Mart began pushing its suppliers to use biodegradable packaging; it made the use of biodegradable packaging a part of its standards

for suppliers and actively began working with its 66,000 suppliers to develop more eco-friendly packaging. Wal-Mart was engaged in both internal efforts and efforts with the trucking industry to double the fuel efficiency of its fleet of 7,200 trucks, which logged some 850 million miles annually—since 2005, efficiency had been improved by 20 percent.

- *Instituting ways to make Wal-Mart stores both more energy efficient and supplied by 100 percent renewable energy.* Wal-Mart began working with architects, engineers, contractors, and landscape designers to begin a long-term effort to build new stores that would reduce energy usage, reduce pollution, and conserve natural resources. Two experimental stores were built to serve as living laboratories for testing new technologies and products—in 2008, one such new technology, LED lighting, was in the process of being incorporated in Wal-Mart stores across the United States. In 2007, Wal-Mart opened three high-efficiency stores that used 20 percent less energy than a typical Supercenter, were constructed with recycled building materials, and had motion-sensing LED lighting, low-flow bathroom faucets, reflective white roofs, and a100-percent integrated water-source heating, cooling, and refrigeration system. In January 2008, the first of four ultra-high-efficiency stores with additional energy-saving and environmentally friendly building features was opened. Pilot projects for solar-powered stores were under way at 22 stores in California and Hawaii. In March 2008, Wal-Mart announced that it would begin building a series of still more efficient prototype stores that were designed for specific climates and that could make use of energy-saving innovations specific to those climates. Wal-Mart was open to sharing its learning and experiences with all its new energy-saving stores so as to help drive energy-saving innovations in building design worldwide.
- *Making Wal-Mart an even better place to work.* Efforts here included making every full-time and part-time Wal-Mart associate (and their children) eligible for health insurance, improving the affordability of the various health insurance options (in terms of both monthly premiums and co-pay amounts), and revising the health insurance coverage to include security from catastrophic medical expenses (after one year of eligibility, there was no lifetime maximum for most types of expenses). Going into 2008, some 92.7 percent of Wal-Mart's associates had some form of health insurance, up from 90.4 percent in 2006. Senior management was sensitive to the importance of providing good jobs with competitive pay and benefits. The average hourly wage for full-time Wal-Mart associates was \$10.83 in early 2008; the hourly averages were in the \$11–\$12 range in urban areas and states like California. A sizable fraction of the jobs at Wal-Mart, particularly those in its retail stores, were considered entry-level jobs that required minimal skills and education. While the majority of Wal-Mart's associates were full-time employees (defined as working 34–40 hours per week), many were students who wanted work experience and seniors looking for part-time jobs to supplement their retirement income. In January 2006, some 25,000 people applied for 325 available jobs at a new store in the Chicago area; in March 2007, there were more than 11,000 applicants for 300 job openings at a new store in Maryland; and in March 2008, there were more than 12,000 applications for 450 jobs at a new store in Decatur, Georgia. For decades, Wal-Mart had offered company personnel good opportunities for advancement owing to an ongoing stream of new store openings and a policy of promoting from within—more than 75 percent of the managerial personnel at Wal-Mart's stores had joined the company as hourly associates.
- *Driving growth in the company's international operations via both acquisitions of foreign retailers* (whose operations could later be converted to Wal-Mart stores) and opening newly constructed stores. This strategic thrust was aimed at transforming Wal-Mart into an increasingly global retailer with more and more stores in more and more countries.
- *Making a positive contribution to the quality of life in every community in which the company conducted business.* Following the Katrina disaster, the company established nine disaster distribution centers strategically located across the United States that were stocked with relief supplies needed to assist communities recover in the event of a disaster. Health clinics to treat

common ailments were opened in numerous Wal-Mart stores as a means of helping bring affordable and accessible health care to low-income people—between 30 and 40 percent of the patients at these clinics were uninsured. Wal-Mart expected to have 400 "Clinic at Wal-Mart" outlets by 2010; all the clinics were leased to and operated by local, certified health care professionals, not Wal-Mart personnel. Wal-Mart was the biggest corporate cash donor in the United States, giving some $296 million to 4,000+ communities in 2007. It donated $1 million or more annually to such charitable organizations as the National Fish and Wildlife Foundation, the Special Olympics, Boys & Girls Clubs of America, the United Negro College Fund, and the Muscular Dystrophy Association.

RECENT WAL-MART BASHING: THE REASON FOR SCOTT'S TRANSFORMATION INITIATIVES

H. Lee Scott's sweeping effort to transform Wal-Mart was, to a large degree, a thoughtfully and carefully crafted response to a loud and growing chorus of Wal-Mart critics and a series of embarrassing incidents. During the 2003–2005 period, numerous journalists, union leaders, community activists, and so-called cultural progressives had united in a campaign to bash Wal-Mart on a variety of fronts and turn public opinion against Wal-Mart and its seemingly virtuous business model of relentlessly wringing cost efficiencies out of its supply chain and providing customers with everyday low prices. At the center of the crusade to cast Wal-Mart in a bad light were Wal-Mart Watch and Wake Up Wal-Mart.[4] Wal-Mart Watch was founded by Andrew Stern, president of the Service Employees International Union (SEIU). Wake Up Wal-Mart was a project of the United Food and Commercial Workers International Union (UFCW). Wal-Mart Watch had an e-mail utility that visitors could use to direct the recipient to anti-Wal-Mart stories; the e-mail carried a prewritten header: "I thought you might enjoy this story from Wal-Mart Watch, a group who is starting to expose Wal-Mart for their bad labor standards, political corruptness and overall bad citizenship. It's getting a lot of attention in the press. Take a look."[5] The SEIU and the UFCW, along with most other unions, had for decades voiced their displeasure with Wal-Mart's conduct on a variety of fronts.

The biggest complaint of critics was that Wal-Mart's zealous pursuit of low costs had resulted in substandard wages and insufficient medical benefits for Wal-Mart's U.S. employees. Others complained that Wal-Mart sourced too much of its merchandise from Chinese suppliers, thus costing jobs for American workers and hastening the decline of the U.S. manufacturing sector. Some said the "Beast of Bentonville" was too big and too powerful. Community activists in California, New York, Vermont, Massachusetts, and several other areas were vigorously opposing the company's attempts to open big-box stores in their locales, claiming that they were unsightly and detracted from the small merchant atmosphere they wanted to preserve. Wal-Mart's low prices tended to attract customers away from locally owned apparel shops, general stores, pharmacies, sporting goods stores, shoe stores, hardware stores, supermarkets, and convenience stores. It was common for a number of local businesses that carried merchandise similar to Wal-Mart's lines to fail within a year or two of Wal-Mart's arrival—this phenomenon, known as the "Wal-Mart effect," was so potent that it had spawned sometimes fierce local resistance to the entry of a new Wal-Mart among both local merchants and area residents wanting to preserve the economic vitality of their downtown areas.

Union leaders at the UFCW, which represented workers at many supermarket chains, were adamant in their opposition to the opening of Wal-Mart Supercenters that had a full-sized supermarket in addition to the usual merchandise selection. The UFCW and its Wake Up Wal-Mart organization were exerting all the pressure they could to force Wal-Mart to raise its wages and benefits for associates to levels that would be comparable to union wages and benefits at unionized supermarket chains. A UFCW spokesperson said:

> Their productivity is becoming a model for taking advantage of workers, and our society is doomed if we think the answer is to lower our standards to Wal-Mart's level. What we need to do is to raise Wal-Mart to the standard we have set using the supermarket

> industry as an example so that Wal-Mart does not destroy our society community by community.[6]

Wal-Mart's labor costs were said to be 20 percent less than those at unionized supermarkets.[7] In Dallas, 20 supermarkets had closed once Wal-Mart had saturated the area with its Supercenters. According to one source, for every Wal-Mart Supercenter opened in the next five years, two other supermarkets would be forced to close.[8] A trade publication had estimated that Wal-Mart's opening of more than 1,000 Supercenters in the United States in the 2004–2008 period would boost Wal-Mart's grocery and related revenues from $82 billion to $162 billion, thus increasing its market share in groceries from 19 to 35 percent and its share of pharmacy and drugstore-related sales from 15 to 25 percent.[9]

Wal-Mart's public image took a hit in late 2003 when federal agents arrested nearly 250 illegal immigrants who worked for companies that had contracts to clean some 61 Wal-Mart stores in 21 states. Agents had searched a manager's office at Wal-Mart's Bentonville headquarters and taken 18 boxes of documents relating to cleaning contractors dating back to March 2000.[10] Federal officials reportedly had wiretaps showing that Wal-Mart officials knew the company's janitorial contractors were using illegal cleaning crews. Wal-Mart, however, was indignant about the charges, saying that its managers had cooperated with federal authorities in the investigations for almost three years, helped agents tape conversations between some of its store managers and employees of the cleaning contractors suspected of using illegal immigrants, and revised its cleaning contracts in 2002 to include language that janitorial contractors comply with all federal, state, and local employment laws (because of the information developed in 2001), and begun bringing all janitorial work in-house because outsourcing was more expensive—at the time of the arrests, fewer than 700 Wal-Mart stores used outside cleaning contractors, down from almost half in 2000. In March 2005, Wal-Mart settled the charges with the Justice Department.

But Wal-Mart was battling a class action discrimination lawsuit filed in 2003 by six female employees claiming that management systematically discriminated against women in pay, promotions, training, and job assignments at Wal-Mart's U.S. stores. According to data from various sources, while two-thirds of Wal-Mart's hourly employees were women, less than 15 percent of management positions were held by women. There were also indications of pay gaps of 5–6 percent between male and female employees doing similar jobs and with similar experience levels; the pay gap allegedly widened higher up the management ladder. Female management trainees allegedly made an average of $22,371 a year, compared with $23,175 for male trainees. A second lawsuit claimed that some Wal-Mart store managers forced employees to work beyond their shifts without pay whenever employees were unable to complete assigned tasks.

And there had been several other incidents that had resulted in unflattering publicity and hits to Wal-Mart's public persona:

- In December 2005, Wal-Mart became the subject of a criminal investigation in Los Angeles over how it handled merchandise classified as hazardous waste. Wal-Mart apparently transported the materials from stores in California via a return center in Las Vegas before dumping them at a disposal site. But federal prosecutors said that violated the U.S. Resource Conservation and Recovery Act. Instead of stopping by the return center in Vegas, the materials should have gone straight to the disposal site.
- Wal-Mart was ordered to compensate a number of former employees in Canada after it was ruled that the retail giant closed a store as a reprisal against unionization attempts. In Colorado, the UFCW had accused Wal-Mart of harassing workers to keep them from joining its local in Denver and elsewhere; the number of such complaints had grown in recent years.
- A Wal-Mart board member, a high-level executive, and two Wal-Mart associates were dismissed following an internal investigation of improper expense account charges, improper payment of third-party invoices, and improper use of gift cards (some of which, according to critics, entailed efforts to finance anti-union activities and defeat unionization efforts at various Wal-Mart stores).
- Wal-Mart had to temporarily stop selling guns at its 118 stores across California following what California's attorney general said were hundreds of violations of state laws. Investigations by California authorities revealed that six

Wal-Mart stores had released guns before the required 10-day waiting period, failed to verify buyers' identity properly, sold illegally to felons, and allowed other violations. Wal-Mart cooperated with government officials and agreed to immediately suspend firearm sales until correction action could be taken and store associates properly trained on state firearms laws.

- In New York State, Wal-Mart had run afoul of a 1988 toy weapons law. The toy guns Wal-Mart sold had an orange cap at the end of the barrel but otherwise looked real, thus violating New York laws banning toy guns with realistic colors such as black or aluminum and not complying with New York's requirement that toy guns have unremovable orange stripes along the barrel. Investigators from the state attorney general's office shopped 10 Wal-Marts in New York state from Buffalo to Long Island and purchased toy guns that violated the law at each of them. Wal-Mart had sold more than 42,000 toy guns in the state.
- Critics had slammed the company for refusing to stock CDs or DVDs with parental warning stickers (mostly profanity-laced hip-hop music) and for either pulling certain racy magazines (*Maxim, Stuff,* and *FHM*) from its shelves or obscuring their covers. They contended that Wal-Mart made no effort to survey shoppers about how they felt about such products but rather that it responded in ad hoc fashion to complaints lodged by a relative handful of customers and by conservative outside groups.[11] Wal-Mart had also been the only one of the top 10 drugstore chains to refuse to stock Preven, a morning-after contraceptive introduced in 1999, because company executives did not want its pharmacists to have to grapple with the moral dilemma of abortion. Moreover, Wal-Mart's high profile had made it a lightning rod for lawsuits, including one that it discriminated against female employees and another that claimed Wal-Mart.
- A 98-minute feature-length documentary entitled *Wal-Mart: The High Cost of Low Price* premiered in November 2005 and bashed the company for destroying once-thriving downtowns, running local merchants out of business, paying meager wages, selling goods produced in sweatshops in third world countries, and assorted other corporate sins. The film included testimony from ex-employees describing seedy practices as well as clips of individuals, families, and communities that had struggled to fight the company on various issues. Canadian unions had urged their 340,000 members to take time to see the documentary and, where possible, to arrange screenings at local meetings and other union events. Anti-Wal-Mart journalists had praised the documentary. The *San Francisco Bay Guardian* said the movie "will make you fear and loathe it even more. The unscrupulous megaretailer is exposed from every angle: its devastating effect on small businesses and communities; its inadequate health care plans; its rabid antiunion stance; the racism and sexism sprinkled throughout its ranks; its blatant disregard for environmental issues; its practice of importing nearly all of its goods (churned from company sweatshops in countries like China, Bangladesh, and Honduras); and—perhaps most offensively—its faux-homespun television advertisements, which cast a golden glow on a corporation that clearly cares not for human beings, but for cold, hard cash."[12]

Initially, H. Lee Scott and other top Wal-Mart executives shrugged off the bad publicity and criticism and concentrated their full attention on running the business and expanding the company's operations into more countries and more communities—as Scott put it, "We would put up the sandbags and get out the machine guns."[13] But in 2004–2005, Scott started to see that all the Wal-Mart bashing was taking a toll on the company's sales growth and throwing up roadblocks to its expansion plans. He initiated an in-depth review of the company's legal and public relations woes and concluded that Wal-Mart ought to reach out to its critics, examine whether their concerns had merit, and seriously consider whether Wal-Mart ought to alter some of its practices without abandoning doing things that were the keys to its success.[14] Over the next several months, he met with an assortment of environmentalists and company critics to better understand their views, learn how companies could promote environmental sustainability, and solicit their suggestions about how the company could improve. The comprehensive transformation program initiated by Scott in 2005–2006 was his response.

COMPANY BACKGROUND

Wal-Mart's journey from humble beginnings in the 1960s as a folksy discount retailer in the boondocks of Arkansas to a global retailing juggernaut in 2008 was unprecedented among the companies of the world:

Fiscal Year	Sales	Profits	Stores
1962	$1.4 million	$112,000	9
1970	$31 million	$1.2 million	32
1980	$1.2 billion	$41 million	276
1990	$26 billion	$1 billion	1,528
2000	$153 billion	$5.3 billion	3,884
2008	$375 billion	$12.7 billion	7,262

Sales were expected to exceed $400 billion in fiscal 2009. Wal-Mart was the largest retailer in the United States, Canada, and Mexico, as well as the world as a whole. In 2007, Wal-Mart's sales revenues were bigger than the combined revenues of The Home Depot, Kroger, Costco, Target, and Sears and about 2.7 times the revenues of the world's second biggest retailer, France-based Carrefour. In calendar year 2006–2007, Wal-Mart's sales grew by more than Target's total 2007 sales. A 2003 report by the prominent Boston Consulting Group concluded that "the world has never known a company with such ambition, capability, and momentum."

Just as unprecedented was Wal-Mart's impact on general merchandise retailing and the attraction its stores had to shoppers in locations where it had stores. In 2008, nearly 180 million people per week shopped Wal-Mart's stores in 14 countries; in the United States, the numbers averaged 127 million per week. Since the early 1990s, the company had gone from dabbling in supermarket sales to being number one in grocery retailing worldwide. In the United States, Wal-Mart was the biggest employer in 21 states. As of June 2008, the company employed about 2.1 million people worldwide and was expanding its workforce by about 120,000 members annually.[15]

Wal-Mart's performance and prominence in the retailing industry had resulted in numerous awards. It had been named "Retailer of the Century" by *Discount Store News,* made the *Fortune* magazine lists of "Most Admired Companies in America" (it was ranked first in 2003 and 2004 and fourth in 2005) and "100 Best Companies to Work for in America," and been included on *Financial Times*' "Most Respected in the World" list. In 2005, Wal-Mart was ranked second on *Fortune*'s "Global Most Admired Companies" list. Wal-Mart was number one on both the Fortune 500 list of the largest U.S. corporations and *Fortune*'s Global 500 list every year from 2002 through 2007. Wal-Mart received the 2002 Ron Brown Award, the highest presidential award recognizing outstanding achievement in employee relations and community initiatives. In 2003, American Veterans Awards gave Wal-Mart its Corporate Patriotism Award. Three Wal-Mart executives were named to *Fortune*'s 2006 "50 Most Powerful Women in Business" list.

Exhibit 1 provides a summary of Wal-Mart's financial and operating performance for the 2000–2008 fiscal years. Wal-Mart's success had made the Walton family (Sam Walton's heirs and relatives) exceptionally wealthy—in 2008, various family members controlled more than 1.7 billion shares of Wal-Mart stock worth over $100 billion. Increases in the value of Wal-Mart's stock over the years had made hundreds of Wal-Mart employees, retirees, and shareholders millionaires or multimillionaires. Since 1970, when Wal-Mart shares were first issued to the public, the company's stock had split 11 times. A 100-share investment in Wal-Mart stock in 1970 at the initial offer price of $16.50 equated to 204,800 shares worth $12.1 million as of June 2008.

Sam Walton, Founder of Wal-Mart

Sam Walton graduated from the University of Missouri in 1940 with a degree in economics and took a job as a management trainee at J. C. Penney Co. His career with Penney's ended with a call to military duty in World War II. When the war was over, Walton decided to purchase a franchise and open a Ben Franklin retail variety store in Newport, Arkansas, rather than return to Penney's. Five years later, when the lease on the Newport building was lost, Walton decided to relocate his business to Bentonville, Arkansas, where he bought a building and opened Walton's 5 & 10 as a Ben Franklin–affiliated store. By 1960 Walton was the largest Ben Franklin franchisee, with nine stores. But Walton was becoming concerned about the long-term competitive threat to variety stores posed by

Exhibit 1 Financial and Operating Summary, Wal-Mart Stores, Fiscal Years 2000–2008 ($ in billions, except earnings per share data)

	Fiscal Years Ending January 31					
	2008	2007	2006	2004	2002	2000
Financial and Operating Data						
Net sales	$374.5	$345.0	$308.9	$252.8	$202.2	$156.2
Net sales increase	8.6%	11.7%	9.8%	11.6%	13.0%	18.7%
Comparable store sales increase in the United States*	2%	2%	3%	4%	6%	8%
Cost of sales	286.5	264.2	237.6	195.9	156.8	119.5
Operating, selling, general, and administrative expenses	70.3	64.0	55.7	43.9	34.3	25.2
Interest costs, net	1.8	1.5	1.2	.8	1.2	.8
Net income	12.7	11.3	11.2	9.1	6.6	5.3
Earnings per share of common stock (diluted)	$ 3.13	$ 2.71	$ 2.68	$ 2.07	$ 1.47	$ 1.19
Balance Sheet Data						
Current assets	$ 47.6	$ 47.0	$ 43.8	$ 34.2	$ 25.9	$ 23.0
Net property, plant, equipment, and capital leases	97.0	88.4	77.9	55.2	44.2	34.6
Total assets	163.5	151.6	136.2	104.9	79.3	67.3
Current liabilities	58.5	52.1	49.0	37.4	26.3	25.1
Long-term debt	29.8	27.2	26.4	17.5	15.6	13.7
Long-term obligations under capital leases	3.6	3.5	3.7	3.0	3.0	2.9
Shareholders' equity	64.6	61.6	53.2	43.6	35.2	25.9
Financial Ratios						
Current ratio	0.8	0.9	0.9	0.9	1.0	0.9
Return on assets	8.4%	8.8%	9.3%	9.7%	9.0%	10.1%
Return on shareholders' equity	21.1%	22.0%	22.9%	22.4%	20.7%	24.5%
Other Year-End Data						
Number of Wal-Mart discount stores in the United States	971	1,075	1,209	1,478	1,647	1,801
Number of Wal-Mart Supercenters in the United States	2,447	2,256	1,980	1,471	1,066	721
Number of Sam's Clubs in the United States	591	579	567	538	500	463
Number of Neighborhood Markets in the Untied States	132	112	100	64	31	7
Number of stores outside the United States	3,121	2,757	2,181	1,248	1,050	892

*Based on sales at stores open a full year that have not been expanded or relocated in the past 12 months.

Source: Wal-Mart annual report for 2008.

the emerging popularity of giant supermarkets and discounters. An avid pilot, he took off in his plane on a cross-country tour studying the changes in stores and retailing trends, then put together a plan for a discount store of his own because he believed deeply in the retailing concept of offering significant price discounts to expand sales volumes and increase overall profits. Walton went to Chicago to try to interest Ben Franklin executives in expanding into discount retailing; when they turned him down, he decided to go forward on his own.

The first Wal-Mart Discount City opened July 2, 1962, in Rogers, Arkansas. The store was successful, and Walton quickly began to look for opportunities to open stores in other small towns and to attract talented people with retailing experience to help him grow the business. Although he started out as a seat-of-the-pants merchant, he had great instincts, was quick to learn from other retailers' successes and failures, and was adept at garnering ideas for improvements from employees and promptly trying them out. Sam Walton incorporated his business as Wal-Mart Stores in 1969, with headquarters in obscure Bentonville, Arkansas—in 2005, the Wal-Mart-related traffic into and out of Bentonville was sufficient to support daily nonstop flights from New York City and Chicago. When the company went public in 1970, it had 38 stores and sales of $44.2 million. In 1979, with 276 stores, 21,000 employees, and operations in 11 states, Wal-Mart became the first company to reach $1 billion in sales in such a short time.

As the company grew, Sam Walton proved an effective and visionary leader. His folksy demeanor, and his talent for motivating people, combined with a very hands-on management style and an obvious talent for discount retailing, produced a culture and a set of values and beliefs that kept Wal-Mart on a path of continuous innovation and rapid expansion. Moreover, Wal-Mart's success and Walton's personable style of leadership generated numerous stories in the media that cast the company and its founder in a positive light. As Wal-Mart emerged as the premier discount retailer in the United States in the 1980s, an uncommonly large cross-section of the American public came to know who Sam Walton was and to associate his name with Wal-Mart. Regarded by many as "the entrepreneur of the century" and "a genuine American folk hero," he enjoyed a reputation as being community-spirited, a devoted family man who showed concern for his employees, demonstrated the virtues of hard work, and epitomized the American Dream. People inside and outside the company held him in high esteem.

Just before Walton's death in 1992, his vision was for Wal-Mart to become a $125 billion company by 2000. But his handpicked successor, David D. Glass, beat that target by almost two years. Under Glass's leadership (1988–2000), Wal-Mart's sales grew at an average annual compound rate of 19 percent, pushing revenues up from $20.6 billion to $156 billion. When Glass retired in January 2000, H. Lee Scott was chosen as Wal-Mart's third president and CEO. In the eight years that Scott had been CEO, Wal-Mart's sales had grown to $218 billion, more than double the revenue level the company achieved in its first 30 years.

WAL-MART'S STRATEGY

The hallmarks of Wal-Mart's strategy were a deeply ingrained dedication to cost-efficient operations, everyday low prices, multiple store formats, wide selection, a mix of both name-brand and private-label merchandise, a customer-friendly store environment, astute merchandising, limited advertising, customer satisfaction, disciplined expansion into new geographic markets, and the use of acquisitions to enter foreign country markets. Several of these elements merit further discussion.

Cost-Efficient Operations and Everyday Low Prices

From its earliest days and continuing to the present, top executives at Wal-Mart had vigorously and successfully pursued a low-cost leadership strategy. None of the world's major retailers could match Wal-Mart's zeal and competence in ferreting out cost savings and finding new and better ways to operate cost-efficiently. Wal-Mart's emphasis on achieving low costs extended to each and every value chain activity—starting with all the activities related to obtaining the desired merchandise from suppliers and then proceeding to all the logistical and distribution-related activities associated with managing inventory levels and stocking the shelves of its retail stores, all the activities involving the construction and operation of its retail stores, and keeping a tight rein on the costs of selling, general, and administrative activities. The company's competencies and capabilities in keeping its costs low allowed it to sell its merchandise at or near rock-bottom prices.

While Wal-Mart had not invented the concept of everyday low pricing, it had done a better job than any other discount retailer in executing the concept. The company was widely seen by consumers as being the general merchandise retailer with the lowest everyday prices, and its pricing strategy spilled over to cause other discount retailers to keep their prices lower than they otherwise might when one of their stores had to compete with a nearby Wal-Mart store. An independently certified study showed that Wal-Mart saved the average U.S. household more than $2,500 annually, counting both the direct effect on the purchases made by Wal-Mart shoppers and the indirect effect stemming from lower prices on the part of nearby retailers to better compete with Wal-Mart.[16] A second independent study showed that prices of grocery items at Wal-Mart Supercenters were 5 to 48 percent below such leading supermarket chain competitors as Kroger (which used the City Market brand in the states west of the Mississippi), Safeway, and Albertson's, after making allowances for specials and loyalty cards.[17] On average, Wal-Mart offered many identical food items at prices averaging 15 to 25 percent lower than traditional supermarkets. Warren Buffet said, "You add it all up and they have contributed to the financial well-being of the American public more than any other institution I can think of."[18]

Multiple Store Formats

In 2008, Wal-Mart employed four different retail concepts in the United States and Canada to attract and satisfy customers' needs: Wal-Mart discount stores, Supercenters, Neighborhood Markets, and Sam's Clubs:

- *Discount stores*—These stores ranged from 30,000 to 224,000 square feet (the average was 108,000 square feet), employed an average of 150 people, and offered as many as 80,000 different items, including family apparel, automotive products, health and beauty aids, home furnishings, electronics, hardware, toys, sporting goods, lawn and garden items, pet supplies, jewelry, housewares, prescription drugs, and packaged grocery items. Annual sales at a Wal-Mart discount store normally ran in the $40 to $60 million range. Wal-Mart was phasing down the number of discount stores; since 2000, the company had expanded or relocated and converted anywhere from 100 to 170 of its discount stores to the Supercenter format annually.
- *Supercenters*—Supercenters, which Wal-Mart started opening in 1988 to meet a demand for one-stop family shopping, joined the concept of a general merchandise discount store with that of a full-line supermarket. They ranged from 98,000 to 246,000 square feet (the average was 187,000 square feet), employed between 200 and 500 associates, had about 36 general merchandise departments, and offered up to 150,000 different items, at least 30,000 of which were grocery products. In addition to the value-priced merchandise offered at discount stores and a large supermarket section with 30,000+ items, Supercenters contained such specialty shops as vision centers, tire and lube express centers, a fast-food restaurant, portrait studios, one-hour photo centers, hair salons, banking, and employment agencies. Typical Supercenters had annual sales in the $70–$100 million range.
- *Sam's Clubs*—A store format that Wal-Mart launched in 1983, Sam's was a cash-and-carry, members-only warehouse that carried about 4,000 frequently used, mostly brand-name items in bulk quantities along with some big-ticket merchandise. The product lineup included fresh, frozen, and canned food products; candy and snack items; office supplies; janitorial and household cleaning supplies and paper products; apparel; CDs and DVDs; and an assortment of big-ticket items (TVs, tires, large and small appliances, watches, jewelry, computers, camcorders, and other electronic equipment). Stores ranged from 71,000 to 190,000 square feet (the average was 132,000 square feet), with most goods displayed in the original cartons stacked in wooden racks or on wooden pallets. Many items stocked were sold in bulk (five-gallon containers, bundles of a dozen or more, and economy-size boxes). Prices tended to be 10–15 percent below the prices of the company's discount stores and Supercenters since merchandising costs and store operation costs were lower. Sam's was intended to serve small businesses, churches and religious organizations, beauty salons and barber shops, motels, restaurants, offices, schools, families, and individuals looking for great prices on large-volume quantities or big-ticket items. Annual member fees were $35 for businesses and $40 for individuals—there were more than 47 million members in 2008. Sam's stores employed about 125 people and had annual sales averaging $75 million. A number of Sam's stores were located adjacent to a Supercenter or discount store.
- *Neighborhood Markets*—Neighborhood markets, the company's newest store format, launched in 1998, were designed to appeal to customers who just needed groceries, pharmaceuticals, and general merchandise. They were always located in markets with Wal-Mart Supercenters so as to be readily accessible to Wal-Mart's food

distribution network. Neighborhood Markets ranged from 37,000 to 56,000 square feet (the average was 42,000 square feet), employed 80–120 people, and had a full-line supermarket and a limited assortment of general merchandise.

U.S. and Canadian customers could also purchase a broad assortment of merchandise and services online at www.walmart.com.

During 2008 and 2009, Wal-Mart expected to open about 310 new Supercenters, 50 new Neighborhood Markets, and 50 new Sam's Clubs in the United States. Internationally, Wal-Mart planned to spend more than $10 billion to add about 50 million square feet of retail space in 2008 and 2009. A major initiative to enter the retailing market in India was under way. Wal-Mart expected that its international growth would outpace its domestic growth in the years to come.

Exhibit 2 shows the number of Wal-Mart stores by country as of January 31, 2008. A number of locations in the United States were underserved by Wal-Mart stores. Inner-city sections of New York City had no Wal-Mart stores of any kind because

Exhibit 2 Wal-Mart's Store Count, January 31, 2008

Country	Discount Stores	Supercenters	Sam's Clubs	Neighborhood Markets
United States	971 (all states except Nebraska, South Dakota, and Wyoming)	2,447 (all states except Hawaii and Vermont)	591 (all states except Oregon and Vermont)	132 (in 15 states)

	Number of Stores	Store Formats and Brand Names
Argentina	21	20 Supercenters and 1 combination discount and grocery store (Changomas)
Brazil	313	29 Supercenters; 21 Sam's Clubs; 70 hypermarkets (Hiper Bompreco, Big); 158 supermarkets (Bompreco, Mercadorama, Nacional): 13 cash-and-carry stores (Maxxi Alacado): 21 combination discount and grocery stores (Todo Dia): and 1 general merchandise store (Magazine)
Canada	305	31 Supercenters, 268 discount stores, 6 Sam's Clubs
China	202	96 Supercenters, 2 Neighborhood Markets, 3 Sam's Clubs, 101 hypermarkets (Trust-Mart)
Costa Rica	154	6 hypermarkets (Hiper Mas), 28 supermarkets (Más por Menos), 9 warehouse stores, (maxi Bodega), and 111 discount stores (Despensa Familiar)
El Salvador	70	2 hypermarkets (Hiper Piaz), 32 supermarkets (La Despensa de Don Juan), and 36 discount stores (Despensa Familiar)
Guatemala	145	6 hypermarkets (Hiper Piaz), 28 supermarkets (Piaz), 12 warehouse stores (Maxi Bodega), 2 membership clubs (Club Co), and 97 discount stores (Despensa Familiar)
Honduras	47	1 hypermarket (Hiper Piaz), 7 supermarkets (Piaz), 7 warehouse stores (Maxi Bodega), and 32 discount stores (Despensa Familiar)
Japan	394	114 hypermarkets (Livin, Seiyu), 276 supermarkets (Seiyu, Sunny), and 4 general merchandise stores (Seiyu)
Mexico	1,023	136 Supercenters; 83 Sam's Clubs; 129 supermarkets (Superama, Mi Bodega); 246 combination discount and grocery stores (Bodega); 76 department stores (Suburbia); 349 restaurants; and 4 discount stores (Mi Bodega Express)
Nicaragua	46	6 supermarkets (La Unión) and 40 discount stores (Pali)
Puerto Rico	54	6 Supercenters, 8 discount stores, 9 Sam's Clubs, and 31 supermarkets (Amigo)
United Kingdom	352	29 Supercenters (Asda); 298 supermarkets (Asda, Asda Small Town); 13 general merchandise stores (Asda Living); and 12 apparel stores (George)—the apparel stores were scheduled to be closed in 2008

Source: Wal-Mart's 2008 annual report., p.51.

ample space with plenty of parking was unavailable at a reasonable price. Wal-Mart's first Supercenter in all of California opened in March 2004, and the whole state had just 31 Supercenters in early 2008. There were only 6 Supercenters in Massachusetts, 1 in New Jersey, and 5 in Connecticut (versus 289 in Texas, 152 in Florida, 119 in Georgia, 99 in Tennessee, 87 in Alabama, and 86 in Missouri).

Wide Product Selection and a Mix of Name-Brand and Private-Label Merchandise

A core element of Wal-Mart's strategy was to provide customers with such a wide assortment of products that they could obtain much of what they needed at affordable prices in one convenient place. Supercenters, which carried a broad lineup of general merchandise as well as a full selection of supermarket items, were very much a one-stop shopping experience for many consumers.

A significant portion of the merchandise that Wal-Mart stocked consisted of name-brand, nationally advertised products. But it also marketed merchandise under some 20 private-label brands and, in addition, such licensed brands as General Electric, Disney, McDonald's, and Better Homes and Gardens.

Customer-Friendly Store Environment

In all Wal-Mart stores, efforts were made to present merchandise in easy-to-shop shelving and displays. Floors in the apparel section were carpeted to make the department feel homier and to make shopping seem easier on customers' feet. Lighting was designed to create a soft, warm impression. Signage indicating the location of various departments was prominent. Store layouts were constantly scrutinized to improve shopping convenience and make it easier for customers to find items. Store associates wore blue vests with the tag line "How May I Help You?" on the back to make it easier for customers to pick them out from a distance. Yet nothing about the decor conflicted with Wal-Mart's low-price image; retailing consultants considered Wal-Mart as being adept at sending out an effective mix of vibes and signals concerning customer service, low prices, quality merchandise, and friendly shopping environment. Wal-Mart's management believed that the attention paid to all the details of making the stores more user-friendly and inviting caused shoppers to view Wal-Mart in a more positive light.

Astute Merchandising

Wal-Mart was unusually active in testing and experimenting with new merchandising techniques. From the beginning, Sam Walton had been quick to imitate good ideas and merchandising practices employed by other retailers. According to the founder of Kmart, Sam Walton "not only copied our concepts; he strengthened them. Sam just took the ball and ran with it."[19] Wal-Mart prided itself on its "low threshold for change," and much of management's time was spent talking to vendors, employees, and customers to get ideas for how Wal-Mart could improve. Suggestions were actively solicited from employees. Most any reasonable idea was tried; if it worked well in stores where it was first tested, then it was quickly implemented in other stores. Experiments in store layout, merchandise displays, store color schemes, merchandise selection (whether to add more upscale lines or shift to a different mix of items), and sales promotion techniques were always under way. Wal-Mart was regarded as an industry leader in testing, adapting, and applying a wide range of cutting-edge merchandising approaches. In 2005–2006, Wal-Mart began upgrading the caliber of the merchandise it stocked in certain departments so as to be more competitive with Target, its major rival in discount retailing.

Limited Advertising

Wal-Mart relied less on advertising than most other discount chains. The company distributed only one or two circulars per month and ran occasional TV ads, relying primarily on its widely known reputation and word of mouth to generate store traffic. Wal-Mart's advertising expenditures ran about 0.3 percent of sales revenues, versus around 1.5 percent for Kmart and 2.3 percent for Target. Wal-Mart's spending for radio and TV advertising was said to be so low that it didn't register on national ratings scales. Most Wal-Mart broadcast ads appeared on local TV and local cable channels. The company often allowed charities to use its parking lots for their fund-raising activities. Wal-Mart did little or no advertising for its Sam's

Club stores; however, in 2008, Wal-Mart did put a four-page color brochure insert in local newspapers that included a printed invitation giving anyone (including nonmembers) the ability to shop at their local Sam's Club during Sam's special 25th Anniversary Open House celebration on April 18–20.

Disciplined Expansion into New Geographic Markets

One of the most distinctive features of Wal-Mart's domestic strategy in its early years was the manner in which it expanded into new geographic areas. Whereas many chain retailers achieved regional and national coverage quickly by entering the largest metropolitan centers before trying to penetrate less populated markets, Wal-Mart always expanded into adjoining geographic areas, saturating each area with stores before moving into new territory. New stores were usually clustered within 200 miles of an existing distribution center so that deliveries could be made cost-effectively on a daily basis; new distribution centers were added as needed to support store expansion into additional areas. In the United States, the really unique feature of Wal-Mart's geographic strategy had involved opening stores in small towns surrounding a targeted metropolitan area before moving into the metropolitan area itself—an approach Sam Walton had termed "backward expansion." Wal-Mart management believed that any town with a shopping area population of 15,000 or more was big enough to support a Wal-Mart discount store and that towns of 25,000 could support a Supercenter. Once stores were opened in towns around the most populous city, Wal-Mart would locate one or more stores in the metropolitan area and begin major market advertising. By clustering new stores in a relatively small geographic area, the company's advertising expenses for breaking into a new market could be shared across all the area stores, a tactic Wal-Mart used to keep its advertising costs under 1 percent of sales.

The Use of Acquisitions to Expand into Foreign Markets

In recent years, Wal-Mart had been driving hard to expand its geographic base of stores outside the United States largely through acquisition and partly through new store construction. Wal-Mart's entry into Canada, Mexico, Brazil, Japan, Puerto Rico, China, Germany, South Korea, and Great Britain had been accomplished by acquiring existing general merchandise or supermarket chains. Many of the acquired stores still operated under their former names (see Exhibit 2), and in most countries Wal-Mart was being cautious in rebranding them as Wal-Mart stores. In August 2007, Wal-Mart and India-based Bharti Enterprises announced a joint venture to conduct wholesale cash-and carry and back-end supply chain management operations in India, the world's second most populous country; the first wholesale facility was scheduled to open in late 2008. Wal-Mart's international strategy was to "remain local" in terms of the goods it merchandised, its use of local suppliers where feasible, and in some of the ways it operated. Management strived to adapt Wal-Mart's "standard" operating practices to be responsive to local communities and cultures, the needs and merchandise preferences of local customers, and local suppliers. Most store managers and senior managers in its foreign operations were natives of the countries where Wal-Mart operated; many had begun their careers as hourly employees. Wal-Mart did, however, have a program where stores in different countries exchanged best practices.

Wal-Mart's international division had fiscal 2008 sales of $90.6 billion (up 17.5 percent over fiscal 2007) and operating profits of $4.8 billion (up 21.7 percent). International sales accounted for 24.2 percent of total sales—this percentage had been rising steadily since 2000 and was expected to continue to rise in coming years. Sales at Wal-Mart's international stores averaged about $29 million in sales per store in fiscal 2008; Wal-Mart had more than 620,000 employees in its international operations.

WAL-MART'S COMPETITORS

Discount retailing was an intensely competitive business. Competition among discount retailers centered around pricing, store location, variations in store format and merchandise mix, store size, shopping atmosphere, and image with shoppers. Wal-Mart's primary competitors were Kmart and Target. Like Wal-Mart, Kmart and Target had stores that stocked only general merchandise as well as superstores

(Super Target and Super Kmart) that included a full-line supermarket on one side of the store. Wal-Mart also competed against category retailers like Best Buy and Circuit City in electronics; Toy "R" Us in toys; Kohl's and Goody's in apparel; and Bed, Bath, and Beyond in household goods.

Wal-Mart's rapid climb to become the largest supermarket retailer via its Supercenters had intensified competition in the supermarket industry in the United States and Canada. Virtually all supermarkets located in communities with a Supercenter were scrambling to cut costs, narrow the price gap with Wal-Mart, and otherwise differentiate themselves so as to retain their customer base and grow revenues. Continuing increases in the number of Wal-Mart Supercenters meant that the majority of rival supermarkets in the United States would be within 10 miles of a Supercenter by 2010. Wal-Mart had recently concluded that it took fewer area residents to support a Supercenter than originally thought—sales data indicated that Supercenters in sizable urban areas could be as little as four miles apart and still attract sufficient store traffic.

The two largest competitors in the warehouse club segment were Costco Wholesale and Sam's Clubs; BJ's Wholesale Club, a smaller East Coast chain, was the only other major U.S. player in this segment. In 2007, Costco had sales of $63.1 billion at 499 stores versus $44.4 billion at 591 stores for Sam's. The average Costco store generated annual revenues of $126 million, about 68 percent more than the $75 million average at Sam's. Costco, which had 52.6 million members as of May 2008, catered to affluent households with upscale tastes and located its stores in mostly urban areas. Costco was the United States' biggest retailer of fine wines ($500 million annually) and roasted chickens (100,000 a day). While its product line included food and household items, sporting goods, vitamins, and various other merchandise, its main attraction was big-ticket luxury items (diamonds and big-screen TVs) and the latest gadgets at bargain prices (Costco capped its markups at 14 percent). Costco had beaten Sam's in being the first to sell fresh meat and produce (1986 versus 1989), to introduce private-label items (1995 versus 1998), and to sell gasoline (1995 versus 1997).[20] Costco offered its workers good wages and fringe benefits: full-time hourly workers made about $40,000 a year after four years.

Internationally, Wal-Mart's biggest competitor was Carrefour, a France-based retailer with 2007 sales of €92.2 million and nearly 15,000 stores of varying formats and sizes across much of Europe and in such emerging markets as Argentina, Brazil, Colombia, China, Indonesia, South Korea, and Taiwan. Both Wal-Mart and Carrefour were expanding aggressively in Brazil and China, going head-to-head in an increasing number of locations. Going into 2008, Carrefour had 1,615 stores (500 of which were hypermarkets) in Asia and Latin America, with sales approximating €15.8 million.

WAL-MART'S APPROACHES TO STRATEGY EXECUTION

To profitably execute its everyday low price strategy, Wal-Mart put heavy emphasis on getting the lowest possible prices from its suppliers, forging close working relationships with key suppliers in order to capture win–win cost savings throughout its supply chain, keeping its internal operations lean and efficient, paying attention to even the tiniest details in store layouts and merchandising, making efficient use of state-of-the art technology, and nurturing a culture that thrived on pleasing customers, hard work, constant improvement, and passing cost-savings on to customers in the form of low prices.

Relationships with Suppliers

Wal-Mart was far and away the biggest customer of virtually all of its 66,000 suppliers. Wal-Mart's scale of operation (see Exhibit 3) allowed it to bargain hard with suppliers and get their bottom prices. In 2005, Wal-Mart's requirements for personal computers for the holiday sales season were so big that Hewlett-Packard devoted 3 of its 10 plants operated by contract manufacturers to turning out products solely for Wal-Mart. Wal-Mart looked for suppliers who were dominant in their category (thus providing strong brand-name recognition), who could grow with the company, who had full product lines (so that Wal-Mart buyers could both cherry-pick and get some sort of limited exclusivity on the products it chose to carry), who had the long-term commitment to R&D

Exhibit 3 The Scale of Wal-Mart's Purchases from Selected Suppliers and Its Market Shares in Selected Product Categories, 2002–2003

Supplier	Percent of Total Sales to Wal-Mart	Product Category	Wal-Mart's U.S. Market Share*
Tandy Brands Accessories	39%	Dog food	36%
Dial	28	Disposable diapers	32
Del Monte Foods	24	Photographic film	30
Clorox	23	Shampoo	30
Revlon	20–23	Paper towels	30
RJR Tobacco	20	Toothpaste	26
Procter & Gamble	17	Pain remedies	21
		CDs, DVDs, and videos	15–20
		Single-copy sales of magazines	15
Although sales percentages were not available, Wal-Mart was also the biggest customer of Disney, Campbell Soup, Kraft, and Gillette		Although market shares were not available, Wal-Mart was also the biggest seller of toys, guns, detergent, video games, socks, and bedding.	

*Based on sales through food, drug, and mass merchandisers.

Sources: Jerry Useem, "One Nation Under Wal-Mart," *Fortune,* March 3, 2003, p. 66, and Anthony Bianco and Wendy Zellner, "Is Wal-Mart Too Powerful?" *BusinessWeek,* October 6, 2003, p. 102.

to bring new and better products to retail shelves, and who had the ability to become more efficient in producing and delivering what they supplied. But it also dealt with thousands of small suppliers (mom-and-pop companies, small farmers, and minority businesses) who could furnish particular items for stores in a certain geographical area. Many Wal-Mart stores had a "Store of the Community" section that showcased local products from local producers; in addition, Wal-Mart had set up an export office in the United States to help small and medium-sized businesses export their American-made products (especially to Wal-Mart stores in foreign countries).

Wal-Mart buyers literally shopped the world for merchandise suitable for the company's stores—it purchased from 61,000 U.S. suppliers and some 5,000 foreign suppliers in 40 countries in 2007; purchases from U.S. suppliers totaled $200 billion in 2005 and supported more than 3 million American jobs. Procurement personnel spent a lot of time meeting with vendors and understanding their cost structure. By making the negotiation process transparent, Wal-Mart buyers soon learned whether a vendor was doing all it could to cut down its costs and quote Wal-Mart an attractively low price. Wal-Mart's purchasing agents were dedicated to getting the lowest prices they could, and they did not accept invitations to be wined or dined by suppliers. The marketing vice president of a major vendor told *Fortune* magazine:

> They are very, very focused people, and they use their buying power more forcefully than anybody else in America. All the normal mating rituals are verboten. Their highest priority is making sure everybody at all times in all cases knows who's in charge, and it's Wal-Mart. They talk softly, but they have piranha hearts, and if you aren't totally prepared when you go in there, you'll have your ass handed to you.[21]

All vendors were expected to offer their best price without exception; one consultant that helped manufacturers sell to retailers observed, "No one would dare come in with a half-ass price."[22]

Even though Wal-Mart was tough in negotiating for absolute rock-bottom prices, the price quotes it got were still typically high enough to allow suppliers to earn a profit. Being a Wal-Mart supplier generally meant having a stable, dependable sales base that allowed the supplier to operate production facilities cost-effectively. Moreover, once it decided to source from a vendor, then Wal-Mart worked closely with the vendor to find *mutually beneficial* ways to squeeze costs out of the supply chain. Every aspect of a supplier's operation got scrutinized—how products got developed, what they were made of, how costs might be reduced, what data Wal-Mart could supply that would be useful, how sharing of data online could prove beneficial, and so on. Nearly always, as they went through the process with Wal-Mart personnel, suppliers saw ways to prune costs or otherwise streamline operations to enhance profit margins.

In 1989, Wal-Mart became the first major retailer to embark on a program urging vendors to develop products and packaging that would not harm the environment. In addition, Wal-Mart expected its vendors to contribute ideas about how to make its stores more fun insofar as their products were concerned. Those suppliers that were selected as "category managers" for such product groupings as lingerie, pet food, and school supplies were expected to educate Wal-Mart on everything that was happening in their respective product category.

Some 200 vendors had established offices in Bentonville to work closely with Wal-Mart on a continuing basis—most were in an area referred to locally as "Vendorville." Vendors were encouraged to voice any problems in their relationship with Wal-Mart and to become involved in Wal-Mart's future plans. Top-priority projects ranged from using more recyclable packaging to working with Wal-Mart on merchandise displays and product mix to tweaking the just-in-time ordering and delivery system to instituting automatic reordering arrangements to coming up with new products with high customer appeal. Most recently, one of Wal-Mart's priorities was working with vendors to figure out how to localize the items carried in particular stores and thereby accommodate varying tastes and preferences of shoppers in different areas where Wal-Mart had stores. Most vendor personnel based in Bentonville spent considerable time focusing on which items in their product line were best for Wal-Mart, where they ought to be placed in the stores, how they could be better displayed, what new products ought to be introduced, and which ones ought to be rotated out.

A 2007 survey conducted by Cannondale Associates found that manufacturers believed Wal-Mart was the overall best retailer with which to do business—the ninth straight year in which Wal-Mart was ranked number one.[23] Target was ranked second, and Costco was ranked third. The criteria for the ranking included such factors as clearest company strategy, store branding, best buying teams, most innovative consumer marketing/merchandising, best supply chain management practices, overall business fundamentals, and best practice management of individual product categories. One retailing consultant said, "I think most [suppliers] would say Wal-Mart is their most profitable account."[24] While this might seem surprising because of Wal-Mart's enormous bargaining clout, the potentially greater profitability of selling to Wal-Mart stemmed from the practices of most other retailers to demand that suppliers pay sometimes steep slotting fees to win shelf space and their frequent insistence on supplier payment of such "extras" as in-store displays, damage allowances, handling charges, penalties for late deliveries, rebates of one kind or another, allowances for advertising, and special allowances on slow-moving merchandise that had to be cleared out with deep price discounts. Further, most major retailers expected to be courted with Super Bowl tickets, trips to the Masters Golf tournament, fancy dinners at conventions and trade shows, or other perks in return for their business. All of these extras represented costs that suppliers had to build into their prices. At Wal-Mart, everything was boiled down to one price number and no "funny-money" extras ever entered into the deal.[25]

Most suppliers viewed Wal-Mart's single bottom-line price and its expectation of close coordination as a win–win proposition, not only because of the benefits of cutting out all the funny-money costs and solidifying their relationship with a major customer but also because what they learned from the collaborative efforts and mutual data sharing often had considerable benefit in the rest of their operations. Many suppliers, including Procter & Gamble, liked Wal-Mart's supply chain business model so well that they had pushed their other customers to adopt similar practices.[26]

Wal-Mart's Standards for Suppliers

In 1992 Wal-Mart began establishing standards for its suppliers, with particular emphasis on suppliers located in foreign countries that had a history of problematic wages and working conditions. Management believed that the manner in which suppliers conducted their business regarding the hours of work required of workers daily and weekly, the use of child labor, discrimination based on race or religion or other factors, and workplace safety and whether suppliers complied with local laws and regulations could be attributed to Wal-Mart and affect its reputation with customers and shareholders. To mitigate the potential for Wal-Mart to be adversely affected by the manner in which its suppliers conducted their business, Wal-Mart had established a set of supplier standards and set up an internal group to see that suppliers were conforming to the ethical standards and business practices stated in its published standards. The company's supplier standards had been through a number of changes as the concerns of Wal-Mart management evolved over time.

In February 2003, Wal-Mart took direct control of foreign factory audits; factory certification teams based in China, Singapore, India, United Arab Emirates, and Honduras were staffed with more than 200 Wal-Mart employees dedicated to monitoring foreign factory compliance with the company's supplier standards. Training and compliance sessions were held regularly with foreign suppliers at various locations around the world. All suppliers were asked to sign a document certifying their compliance with the standards and were required to post a version of the supplier standards in both English and the local language in each production facility servicing Wal-Mart. In 2006, Wal-Mart conducted 16,700 audits at 8,873 plants of suppliers; 26 percent of the audits conducted were unannounced. Wal-Mart worked closely with suppliers to correct any violations; supplier factories that failed to correct serious violations were permanently banned from producing merchandise sold by Wal-Mart (0.2 percent of the foreign factories failed Wal-Mart's auditing of their operations in both 2005 and 2006 and were permanently banned; an additional 2.1 percent in 2006 and 0.1 percent in 2005 were banned for one year after re-audits found insufficient progress in correcting prior audit violations that were deemed significant).

Wal-Mart's Use of Cutting-Edge Technology

Wal-Mart's approach to technology was to be on the offense—probing, testing, and then deploying the newest equipment, retailing techniques, computer software programs, and related technological advances to increase productivity and drive costs down. Wal-Mart was typically a first-mover among retailers in upgrading and improving its capabilities as new technology was introduced. The company's technological goal was to provide employees with the tools to do their jobs more efficiently and to make better decisions.

Wal-Mart began using computers to maintain inventory control on an item basis in distribution centers and in its stores in 1974. In 1981, Wal-Mart began testing point-of-sale scanners and then committed to systemwide use of scanning bar codes in 1983—a move that resulted in 25–30 percent faster checkout of customers. In 1984, Wal-Mart developed a computer-assisted merchandising system that allowed the product mix in each store to be tailored to its own market circumstances and sales patterns. Between 1985 and 1987, Wal-Mart installed the nation's largest private satellite communication network, which allowed two-way voice and data transmission between headquarters, the distribution centers, and the stores and one-way video transmission from Bentonville's corporate offices to distribution centers and to the stores; the system was less expensive than the previously used telephone network. The video system was used regularly by company officials to speak directly to all employees at once.

In 1989, Wal-Mart established direct satellite links with about 1,700 vendors supplying close to 80 percent of the goods sold by Wal-Mart; this link-up allowed the use of electronic purchase orders and instant data exchanges. Wal-Mart had also used the satellite system's capabilities to develop a credit card authorization procedure that took 5 seconds, on average, to authorize a purchase, speeding up credit checkout by 25 percent compared to the prior manual system. In the early 1990s, through pioneering collaboration with Procter & Gamble, it instituted an automated reordering system that notified suppliers as their items moved though store checkout lanes; this allowed suppliers to track sales and inventories of their products (so they could plan production and schedule shipments accordingly).

By 2003, the company had developed and deployed sophisticated information technology (IT) systems and online capability that not only gave it real-time access to detailed figures on most any aspect of its operations but also made it a leader in cost-effective supply chain management. It could track the movement of goods through its entire value chain—from the sale of items at the cash register backward to stock on store shelves, in-store backup inventory, distribution center inventory, and shipments en route. Moreover, Wal-Mart had collaborated with its suppliers to develop data-sharing capabilities aimed at streamlining the supply of its stores, avoiding both stock-outs and excess inventories, identifying slow-selling items that might warrant replacement, and spotting ways to squeeze costs out of the supply chain. The company's Retail Link system allowed 30,000 suppliers to track their wares through Wal-Mart's value chain, get hourly sales figures for each item, and monitor gross margins on each of their products (Wal-Mart's actual selling price less what it paid the supplier).

In mid-2003, in another of its trend-setting moves, Wal-Mart informed its suppliers that they had to convert to electronic product code (EPC) technology based on radio frequency identification (RFID) systems. Electronic product codes involved embedding every single item that rolled off a manufacturing line with an electronic tag containing a unique number. EPC tags could be read by radio frequency scanners when brought into range of a tag reader, thus providing the ability to locate and track items throughout the supply chain in real time. With EPC and RFID capability, every single can of soup or DVD or screwdriver in Wal-Mart's supply chain network or on its store shelves could be traced back to when it was made, where and when a case or pallet of goods arrived, and where and when an item was sold or turned up missing. Further, EPC codes linked to an online database provided a secure way of sharing product-specific information with supply chain partners. Wal-Mart management believed EPC technology, in conjunction with the expanding production of RFID capable printers/encoders, had the potential to revolutionize the supply chain by providing more accurate information about product movement, stock rotation, and inventory levels; it was also seen as a significant tool for preventing theft and dealing with product recalls. An IBM study indicated that EPC tagging would reduce out-of-stocks by 33 percent, while an Accenture study showed that EPC/RFID technology could boost worker productivity by 5 percent and shrink working capital and fixed capital requirements by 5 to 30 percent. In 2005, EPC/RFID technology implementation was under way for Wal-Mart's top 200 suppliers, with some 20,000 suppliers to be involved in some way by the end of 2006 and virtually all suppliers to have RFID capabilities by 2010.

In 2008, Wal-Mart's data center was tracking more than 700 million stock-keeping units (SKUs) weekly. The company had more than 88,000 associates engaged in logistics and information systems activities. The attention Wal-Mart management placed on using cutting-edge technology and the astuteness with which it deployed this technology along its value chain to enhance store operations and continuously drive down costs had, over the years, resulted in Wal-Mart being widely regarded as having the most cost-effective, data-rich IT systems of any major retailer in the world. It spent less than 1 percent of revenues on IT (far less than other retailers) and had stronger capabilities. According to Linda Dillman, Wal-Mart's chief information officer, "The strength of this division is, we are doers and do things faster than lightning. We can implement things faster than anyone could with a third party. We run the entire world out of facilities in this area [Bentonville] at a cost that no one can touch. We'd be nuts to outsource."[27] Wal-Mart rarely used commercial software, preferring to develop its own IT systems. So powerful had Wal-Mart's influence been on retail supply chain efficiency that its competitors (and many other retailers as well) had found it essential to follow Wal-Mart's lead and pursue "Wal-Martification" of their retail supply chains.[28]

Distribution Center Operations

In 2008, Wal-Mart had 112 distribution centers. A distribution center served 75–100 stores (usually within a 250-mile radius) and employed anywhere from 500 to 1,000 associates. Distribution centers had as much as five miles of conveyor belts and the capability to move hundreds of thousands of cases through the center each day.

Over the past three decades, Wal-Mart had pursued a host of efficiency-increasing actions at its distribution centers. It had been a global leader in adopting the latest technology to automate most all of the labor-intensive tasks at its distribution centers, gradually creating an ever-more-sophisticated and cost-efficient system of conveyors, bar coders, handheld computers, and other devices with the capability to quickly sort incoming shipments from manufacturers into smaller, store-specific quantities and route them to waiting trucks to be sent to stores to replenish sold merchandise. Prior to automation, bulk cases received from manufacturers had to be opened by distribution center employees and perhaps stored in bins, then picked and repacked in quantities needed for specific stores and loaded onto trucks for delivery to Wal-Mart stores—a manual process that was error-prone and sometimes slow in filling store orders. Often, incoming goods from manufacturers being unloaded at one section of the warehouse were immediately sorted into store-specific amounts and conveyed directly onto waiting Wal-Mart trucks headed for those particular stores—a large portion of the incoming inventory was in a Wal-Mart distribution center an average of only 12 hours. Distribution center employees had access to real-time information regarding the inventory levels of all items in the center and used the different barcodes for pallets, bins, and shelves to pick up items for store orders. Hand-held computers also enabled the packaging department to get accurate information about which items to pack for which store and what loading dock to have packages conveyed. Wal-Mart's trendsetting use of cutting-edge retailing technologies and its best-practices leadership in logistical activities had given it operating advantages and raised the bar for not only its competitors but most other retailers as well.

The company's latest initiatives to enhance distribution and logistical efficiency were to (1) achieve full implementation of RFID systems from suppliers to distribution systems to store operations and (2) double the fuel efficiency of its truck fleet. In early 2008, because some 15,000 suppliers were deemed to be dragging their heels in implementing RFID, Wal-Mart announced it would begin charging its Sam's Club suppliers a $2 fee for each pallet delivered without RFID tagging to select distribution centers, with the fee applying to progressively more distribution centers in upcoming periods; Wal-Mart also said the $2 fee would gradually be increased to $3 and that RFID tagging would in upcoming months begin applying to cases and selling-unit packages on pallets.

Truck Fleet Operations Wal-Mart had a fleet of 7,200+ company-owned trucks and a force of 8,000+ drivers that it used to transport goods from its 112 distribution centers to its stores. Wal-Mart hired only experienced drivers who had driven more than 300,000 accident-free miles with no major traffic violations. Distribution centers had facilities where drivers could shower, sleep, eat, or do personal business while waiting for their truck to be loaded. A truck dispatch coordinator scheduled the dispatch of all trucks based on the available time of drivers and estimated driving time between the distribution center and the designated store. Drivers were expected to pull their truck up to the store dock at the scheduled time (usually late afternoon or early evening) even if they arrived early; trucks were unloaded by store personnel during nighttime hours, with a two-hour gap between each new truck delivery (if more than one was scheduled for the same night).

In instances where it was economical, Wal-Mart trucks were dispatched directly to a manufacturer's facilities, picked up goods for one or more stores, and delivered them directly, bypassing the distribution center entirely. Manufacturers that supplied certain high-volume items or even a number of different items sometimes delivered their products in truckload lots directly to some or many of Wal-Mart's stores.

Store Construction and Maintenance

Wal-Mart management worked at getting more mileage out of its capital expenditures for new stores, store renovations, and store fixtures. Ideas and suggestions were solicited from vendors regarding store layout, aisle width, the design of fixtures, and space needed for effective displays. Wal-Mart's store designs had open-air offices for management personnel that could be furnished economically and featured a maximum of display space that could be rearranged and refurbished easily. Because Wal-Mart insisted on a high degree of uniformity in the new stores it built, the architectural firm Wal-Mart employed was able to use computer modeling techniques to turn out complete specifications for 12 or more new stores a week. Moreover, the stores were designed to permit quick, inexpensive construction as well as to allow for high energy efficiency and low-cost maintenance and renovation. All stores were renovated and redecorated at least once every seven years. If a given store location was rendered obsolete by the construction of new roads and highways and the opening of new shopping locations, then the old store was abandoned in favor of a new store at a more desirable site.

In keeping with the low-cost theme for facilities, Wal-Mart's distribution centers and corporate offices were also built economically and furnished simply. The offices of top executives were modest and unpretentious. The lighting, heating, and air-conditioning controls at all Wal-Mart stores were connected via computer to Bentonville headquarters, allowing cost-saving energy management practices to be implemented centrally and freeing store managers from the time and worry of trying to hold down utility costs. Wal-Mart mass-produced a lot of its displays in-house, not only saving money but also cutting the time to roll out a new display concept to as little as 30 days. It also had a group that disposed of used fixtures and equipment that could not be used at other stores via auctions at the store sites where the surplus existed—a calendar of upcoming auctions was posted on the company's Web site.

Wal-Mart's Approach to Customer Service and Creating a Pleasant Shopping Experience

Wal-Mart tried to put some organization muscle behind its pledge of "Satisfaction Guaranteed" and do things that would make customers' shopping experience at Wal-Mart pleasant. Store managers challenged store associates to practice what Sam Walton called "aggressive hospitality." A "greeter" was stationed at store entrances to welcome customers with a smile, thank them for shopping at Wal-Mart, assist them in getting a shopping cart, and answer questions about where items were located. Clerks and checkout workers were trained to be courteous and helpful to customers and to exhibit a "friendly, folksy attitude." Store associates were expected to adhere to the "10-foot rule": "I promise that when I come within 10 feet of a customer, I will look them in the eye, greet them, and ask if I can be of help." Wal-Mart management believed that friendly, helpful store associates were a strong contributor to getting customers to shop frequently at Wal-Mart.

At the same time, Wal-Mart worked at continuously improving customers' shopping experience. H. Lee Scott's transformation program featured a major initiative to boost the appeal of shopping at Wal-Mart's stores. In 2005, Scott appointed Eduardo Castro-Wright, the head of Wal-Mart Mexico, as the new chief executive of Wal-Mart's U.S. stores division and charged him with upgrading the customer experience. Castro-Wright immediately put together a three-year plan to improve store atmosphere and make shopping at Wal-Mart more appealing. He was particularly concerned about slow checkout lines and what he saw as cluttered merchandising tactics. His campaign included replacing high shelves to reduce shelf clutter and improve sight lines throughout the stores, widening the aisles, improving navigational signs in the stores so shoppers could find things more easily, boosting efforts to keep the store environment clean and attractive (which included a more upscale store decor), and investing in technology that speeded the checkout process. Castro-Wright, together with Wal-Mart's buyers, also shifted their thinking about customer choice, concluding that good customer choice went beyond just providing low prices and broad selection; the new theme was to place more attention on carefully selecting products and brands that shoppers cared about. Three of the biggest merchandising mix and product choice changes involved stocking more items in faster-growing categories such as consumer electronics, including more of the biggest and best brand names in select product categories (to broaden Wal-Mart's appeal to more upscale customers), and localizing product selection to better accommodate variations in shopper tastes and preferences from one area to another.

The Culture at Wal-Mart in 2008

Wal-Mart's culture in 2008 continued to be deeply rooted in Sam Walton's business philosophy and leadership style. Mr. Sam, as he was fondly referred to, was not only Wal-Mart's founder and patriarch but also its spiritual leader—and still was in many respects. Four key core values and business principles underpinned Sam Walton's approach to managing:[29]

- Treat employees as partners, sharing both the good and bad about the company so they will strive to excel and participate in the rewards. (Wal-Mart fostered the concept of partnership by referring to all employees as "associates," a term Sam Walton had insisted upon from the company's beginnings because it denoted a partner-like relationship.)
- Build for the future, rather than just immediate gains, by continuing to study the changing concepts that are a mark of the retailing industry and be ready to test and experiment with new ideas.
- Recognize that the road to success includes failing, which is part of the learning process rather than a personal or corporate defect or failing. Always challenge the obvious.

- Involve associates at all levels in the total decision making process.

Walton practiced these principles diligently in his own actions and insisted that other Wal-Mart managers do the same. Up until his health failed badly in 1991, he spent several days a week visiting the stores, gauging the moods of shoppers, listening to employees discuss what was on their minds, learning what was or was not selling, gathering ideas about how things could be done better, complimenting workers on their efforts, and challenging them to come up with good ideas.

The values, beliefs, and practices that Sam Walton instilled in Wal-Mart's culture and that still carried over in 2008 were reflected in statements made in his autobiography:

> Everytime Wal-Mart spends one dollar foolishly, it comes right out of our customers' pockets. Everytime we save a dollar, that puts us one more step ahead of the competition—which is where we always plan to be.
>
> One person seeking glory doesn't accomplish much; at Wal-Mart, everything we've done has been the result of people pulling together to meet one common goal. . . .
>
> I have always been driven to buck the system, to innovate, to take things beyond where they've been.
>
> We paid absolutely no attention whatsoever to the way things were supposed to be done, you know, the way the rules of retail said it had to be done.
>
> . . . I'm more of a manager by walking and flying around, and in the process I stick my fingers into everything I can to see how it's coming along. . . . My appreciation for numbers has kept me close to our operational statements, and to all the other information we have pouring in from so many different places. . . .
>
> . . . The more you share profit with your associates—whether it's in salaries or incentives or bonuses or stock discounts—the more profit will accrue to your company. Why? Because the way management treats the associates is exactly how the associates will then treat the customers. And if the associates treat the customers well, the customers will return again and again. . . .
>
> . . . There's no better way to keep someone doing things the right way than by letting him or her know how much you appreciate their performance.
>
> The bigger we get as a company, the more important it becomes for us to shift responsibility and authority toward the front lines, toward that department manager who's stocking the shelves and talking to the customer.
>
> We give our department heads the opportunity to become real merchants at a very early stage of the game. . . . We make our department heads the managers of their own businesses. . . . We share everything with them: the costs of their goods, the freight costs, the profit margins. We let them see how their store ranks with every other store in the company on a constant, running basis, and we give them incentives to want to win.
>
> We're always looking for new ways to encourage our associates out in the stores to push their ideas up through the system. . . . Great ideas come from everywhere if you just listen and look for them. You never know who's going to have a great idea.
>
> . . . A lot of bureaucracy is really the product of some empire builder's ego. . . . We don't need any of that at Wal-Mart. If you're not serving the customers, or supporting the folks who do, we don't need you.
>
> You can't just keep doing what works one time, because everything around you is always changing. To succeed, you have to stay out in front of that change.[30]

Walton's success flowed from his cheerleading management style, his ability to instill the principles and management philosophies he preached into Wal-Mart's culture, the close watch he kept on costs, his relentless insistence on continuous improvement, and his habit of staying in close touch with both shoppers and associates. It was common practice for Walton to lead cheers at annual shareholder meetings, store visits, managers' meetings, and company events. His favorite was the Wal-Mart cheer:

> *Give me a W!*
>
> *Give me an A!*
>
> *Give me an L!*
>
> *Give me a squiggly! (Here, everybody sort of does the twist.)*
>
> *Give me an M!*
>
> *Give me an A!*
>
> *Give me an R!*
>
> *Give me a T!*
>
> *What's that spell?*
>
> *Wal-Mart!*
>
> *Whose Wal-Mart is it?*
>
> *My Wal-Mart!*

Who's number one?

The customer! Always!

In 2008, the Wal-Mart cheer was still a core part of the Wal-Mart culture and was used throughout the company at meetings of store employees, managers, and corporate gatherings in Bentonville to create a "whistle while you work" atmosphere, loosen everyone up, inject fun and enthusiasm, and get sessions started on a stimulating note. While the cheer seemed corny to outsiders, once they saw the cheer in action at Wal-Mart they came to realize its cultural power and significance. And much of Sam Walton's cultural legacy remained intact in 2008, most especially among the company's top decision makers and longtime managers. As a *Fortune* writer put it:

> Spend enough time inside the company—where nothing backs up a point better than a quotation from Walton scripture—and it's easy to get the impression that the founder is orchestrating his creation from the beyond.[31]

The Three Basic Beliefs Underlying the Wal-Mart Culture in 2008 Wal-Mart top management stressed three basic beliefs that Sam Walton had preached since 1962:[32]

1. *Respect for the individual*—Management consistently drummed the theme that dedicated, hardworking, ordinary people who teamed together and who treated each other with respect and dignity could accomplish extraordinary things. Throughout company literature, comments could be found referring to Wal-Mart's "concern for the individual." Such expressions as "Our people make the difference," "We care about people," and "People helping people" were used repeatedly by Wal-Mart executives and store managers to create and nurture a family-oriented atmosphere among store associates.
2. *Service to our customers*—Management always stressed that the company was nothing without its customers. To satisfy customers and keep them coming back again and again, management emphasized that the company had to offer quality merchandise at the lowest prices and do it with the best customer service possible. Customers had to trust in Wal-Mart's pricing philosophy and to always be able to find the lowest prices with the best possible service. One of the standard Wal-Mart mantras preached to all associates was that the customer was number one and that the customer was boss. Associates in stores were urged to observe the "10-foot rule."
3. *Strive for excellence*—The concept of striving for excellence stemmed from Sam Walton's conviction that prices were seldom as low as they needed to be and that product quality was seldom as high as customers deserved and expected. The thesis at Wal-Mart was that new ideas and ambitious goals made the company reach further and try harder—the process of finding new and innovative ways to push boundaries and constantly improve made the company better at what it did and contributed to higher levels of customer satisfaction. Wal-Mart managers at all levels spent much time and effort motivating associates to offer ideas for improvement, and to function as partners. It was reiterated that every cost counted and that every worker had a responsibility to be involved.

Wal-Mart's culture had unusually deep roots at the headquarters complex in Bentonville and mirrored Sam Walton's 10 rules for building a business—see Exhibit 4. The numerous journalists and business executives who had been to Bentonville and spent much time at Wal-Mart's corporate offices uniformly reported being impressed with the breadth, depth, and pervasive power of the company's culture. Jack Welch, former CEO of General Electric and a potent culture builder in his own right, noted that "the place vibrated" with cultural energy. There was little evidence that the culture in Bentonville was any weaker in 2008 than it had been 17 years earlier when Sam Walton personally led the culture-building, culture-nurturing effort and infused the company with unparalleled dedication to frugality, wringing every penny out of costs, and passing the savings on to customers in the form of low prices. Not only were there tireless efforts to achieve cost savings in product design, materials, packaging, labor, transportation, store construction, and store operations but Wal-Mart associates, including executives, also flew coach, shared hotel rooms, and emptied their own trash. The philosophy was expressed as follows: "If we can go without something to save money, we do. It's the cornerstone of our culture to pass on our savings. Every penny we save is a penny in our customers' pockets."[33] But in 2008, a new cultural

Exhibit 4 Sam Walton's Rules for Building a Business

Rule 1: Commit to your business. Believe in it more than anybody else. I think I overcame every single one of my personal shortcomings by the sheer passion I brought to my work. I don't know if you're born with this kind of passion, or if you can learn it. But I do know you need it. If you love your work, you'll be out there every day trying to do it the best you possibly can, and pretty soon everybody around will catch the passion from you—like a fever.

Rule 2: Share your profits with all your Associates, and treat them as partners. In turn, they will treat you as a partner, and together you will all perform beyond your wildest expectations. Remain a corporation and retain control if you like, but behave as a servant leader in a partnership. Encourage your Associates to hold a stake in the company. Offer discounted stock, and grant them stock for their retirement. It's the single best thing we ever did.

Rule 3: Motivate your partners. Money and ownership alone aren't enough. Constantly, day-by-day, think of new and more interesting ways to motivate and challenge your partners. Set high goals, encourage competition, and then keep score. Make bets with outrageous payoffs. If things get stale, cross-pollinate; have managers switch jobs with one another to stay challenged. Keep everybody guessing as to what your next trick is going to be. Don't become too predictable.

Rule 4: Communicate everything you possibly can to your partners. The more they know, the more they'll understand. The more they understand, the more they'll care. Once they care, there's no stopping them. If you don't trust your Associates to know what's going on, they'll know you don't really consider them partners. Information is power, and the gain you get from empowering your Associates more than offsets the risk of informing your competitors.

Rule 5: Appreciate everything your Associates do for the business. A paycheck and a stock option will buy one kind of loyalty. But all of us like to be told how much somebody appreciates what we do for them. We like to hear it often, and especially when we have done something we're really proud of. Nothing else can quite substitute for a few well-chosen, well-timed, sincere words of praise. They're absolutely free—and worth a fortune.

Rule 6: Celebrate your successes. Find some humor in your failures. Don't take yourself so seriously. Loosen up, and everybody around you will loosen up. Have fun. Show enthusiasm—always. When all else fails, put on a costume and sing a silly song. Then make everybody else sing with you. Don't do a hula on Wall Street. It's been done. Think up your own stunt. All of this is more important, and more fun, than you think, and it really fools the competition. "Why should we take those cornballs at Wal-Mart seriously?"

Rule 7: Listen to everyone in your company. And figure out ways to get them talking. The folks on the front lines—the ones who actually talk to the customer—are the only ones who really know what's going on out there. You'd better find out what they know. This really is what total quality is all about. To push responsibility down in your organization, and to force good ideas to bubble up within it, you must listen to what your Associates are trying to tell you.

Rule 8: Exceed your customers' expectations. If you do, they'll come back over and over. Give them what they want—and a little more. Let them know you appreciate them. Make good on all your mistakes, and don't make excuses—apologize. Stand behind everything you do. The two most important words I ever wrote were on that first Wal-Mart sign, "Satisfaction Guaranteed." They're still up there, and they have made all the difference.

Rule 9: Control your expenses better than your competition. This is where you can always find the competitive advantage. For 25 years running—long before Wal-Mart was known as the nation's largest retailer—we ranked No. 1 in our industry for the lowest ratio of expenses to sales. You can make a lot of different mistakes and still recover if you run an efficient operation. Or you can be brilliant and still go out of business if you're too inefficient.

Rule 10: Swim upstream. Go the other way. Ignore the conventional wisdom. If everybody else is doing it one way, there's a good chance you can find your niche by going in exactly the opposite direction. But be prepared for a lot of folks to wave you down and tell you you're headed the wrong way. I guess in all my years, what I heard more often than anything was: a town of less than 50,000 population cannot support a discount store for very long.

Source: www.walmartstores.com (accessed December 19, 2005).

trait was evident in the Bentonville headquarters: the "Living Better" element of the company's new mission statement was fast becoming a core value at Wal-Mart and an integral part of its culture and operating practices. While saving money was still the dominant value and a pervasive cultural trait, much energy and effort at headquarters was being devoted to modifying Wal-Mart's priorities and conducting the company's business in a manner that produced "Living Better" outcomes.

But Wal-Mart executives nonetheless were currently facing a formidable challenge in instilling a vibrant, resourceful, and dedicated Bentonville-like culture in the company's distribution centers and most especially in its stores. Annual turnover rates at Wal-Mart stores ran as high as 40 percent in 2002–2008 and had run as high as 70 percent in 1999, when the economy was booming and the labor market was tight. Such high rates of turnover in a workforce that numbered 2.1 million people in 2008, coupled with net workforce increases of about 120,000 associates annually, made it a Herculean task to maintain a deeply ingrained, values-driven culture—indeed, no other company in all of business history had been confronted with having to culturally indoctrinate so many new employees in so many locations in such a relatively short time. Even though Wal-Mart's distribution centers had lower turnover and fewer new employees to culturally train and absorb annually than the company's retail stores, Wal-Mart's culture was much less deeply rooted in its distribution centers than in Bentonville. And the cultural traits so evident in Bentonville were shared by relatively few of the associates at Wal-Mart's retail stores, partly or even mostly because so many store associates chose not to make a career of working at Wal-Mart.

Soliciting Ideas from Associates

Associates at all levels were expected to be an integral part of the process of making the company better. Wal-Mart store managers usually spent a portion of each day walking around the store checking on how well things were going in each department, listening to associates, soliciting suggestions and discussing how improvements could be made, and praising associates who were doing a good job. Store managers frequently asked associates what needed to be done better in their department and what could be changed to improve store operations. Associates who believed a policy or procedure detracted from operations were encouraged to challenge and change it. Task forces to evaluate ideas and plan out future actions to implement them were common, and it was not unusual for the person who developed the idea to be appointed the leader of the group.

Listening to employees was a very important part of each manager's job. All of Wal-Mart's top executives relied on management by walking around (MBWA); they visited stores, distribution centers, and support facilities regularly, staying on top of what was happening and listening to what employees had to say about how things were going. Senior managers at Wal-Mart's Bentonville headquarters believed that visiting stores and listening to associates was time well spent because a number of the company's best ideas had come from Wal-Mart associates—Wal-Mart's use of people greeters at store entrances was one of those ideas.

Compensation and Benefits

In 2007, Wal-Mart's average hourly wage for regular full-time associates in the United States was $10.83, up from $9.68 an hour in 2005 (the federal minimum wage was raised from $5.15 to $5.85 beginning July 24, 2007; existing legislation called for the hourly minimum to increase to $6.55 beginning July 24, 2008, and to $7.25 beginning July 24, 2009). Wal-Mart's average pay was higher in certain urban areas; for example, average hourly wages in Chicago were $11.18; in Atlanta, $11.27; and in Boston, $11.98.[34] Store clerks generally earned the lowest wage; workers who unloaded trucks and stocked store shelves could earn anywhere from $25,000 to $50,000. Part-time jobs at Wal-Mart were most common among sales clerks and checkout personnel in the stores where customer traffic varied appreciably during days of the week and months of the year.

New hourly associates in the United States were paid anywhere from $1 to $6 above the minimum wage, depending on the type of job, and could expect to receive a raise within the first year at one or both of the semiannual job evaluations. Typically, at least one raise was guaranteed in the first year if Wal-Mart planned to keep the individual on the staff. The other raise depended on how well the associate worked and improved during the year. In addition, every store associate was eligible to receive performance bonuses based on the performance of their store, and every hourly associate with 20 or more years of service was awarded an extra week of pay—in fiscal 2008, Wal-Mart awarded more than $636 million in performance bonuses to its U.S. hourly associates. At the store level, only the store manager and assistant manager were salaried; all other associates, including the department managers, were considered hourly employees. Store managers generally had six-figure incomes.

A majority of Wal-Mart's hourly store associates in the United States worked full-time—at most U.S. retailers, the percentage of employees that worked full-time ranged between 20 and 40 percent.

Improving Health Care Benefits In 2005, about 48 percent of Wal-Mart's associates in the United States had signed up for health insurance coverage in a Wal-Mart-sponsored plan (compared with an average of 72 percent for the whole retailing industry). Many Wal-Mart associates did not sign up for health coverage because another household member already had family coverage at his or her place of employment. New full-time and part-time associates became eligible for health care benefits, after a six-month wait and a one-year exclusion for preexisting conditions. Worker premiums for coverage were as little $11 per month for individuals and 30 cents per day for children (no matter how many children an associate had). There were several plans that workers could choose from; usually, the lower the premium, the higher the annual deductible. There were no lifetime maximums for most expenses (a feature offered by fewer than 50 percent of employers). The health benefit package covered 100 percent of most major medical expenses above $1,750 in employee out-of-pocket expenses and entailed no lifetime cap on medical cost coverage (a feature offered by fewer than 50 percent of employers).[35] The company's health benefits in 2005 also included dental coverage, short- and long-term disability, an illness protection plan, and business travel accident insurance. But to help control its health costs for associates, Wal-Mart's health care plan did not pay for flu shots, eye exams, child vaccinations, chiropractic services, and certain other treatments allowed in the plans of many companies; further, Wal-Mart did not pay any health care costs for retirees.

However, during 2004–2006, critics assailed Wal-Mart's health care offering on grounds that the coverage was skimpier than that of many employers and that far too few Wal-Mart employees were eligible for coverage. For example, until 2005, Wal-Mart's health insurance plan did not cover the cost of vaccinations for routine childhood diseases and part-time employees had to work for two years before becoming eligible for coverage for themselves (family coverage was not available to part-time employees). According to 2005 data, 5 percent of Wal-Mart associates were on Medicaid, compared to an average for national employers of 4 percent, and 27 percent of associates' children were on such programs, compared to a national average of 22 percent. In total, 46 percent of associates' children were either on Medicaid or were uninsured.[36]

Wal-Mart recognized that its critics had made valid points regarding the shortcomings of the company's health care offering. Starting in January 2006, Wal-Mart began providing health insurance to more than 1 million of its 1.7 million associates and offering up to 18 different plans. As of 2008, further improvements had been made in Wal-Mart's health care benefits. Every associate who worked in the United States could become eligible for individual health coverage costing as little as $5 per month in some areas and as little as $8 per month nationwide; full-time employees were eligible for coverage after 6 months, and the two-year waiting period for part-time associates was reduced to one year. As soon as an associate became eligible for benefits, his or her spouse and children became eligible too. Associates had more than 50 ways to customize their health coverage. In the $5-per-month plan, Wal-Mart gave each employee or family a grant of $100 to $500 to defray health expenses; an $8-per-month plan entailed a $100 health care credit and a deductible of $2,000 before medical expense coverage kicked in. In still another plan, an associate paid premiums of up to $79 a month, received a health care credit of $100, and paid a deductible of $500. Most options paid for 80 percent of eligible medical expenses incurred after the deductible was reached; however, once an associate's out-of-pocket medical expenses reached $5,000, the plans paid 100 percent of eligible charges. Some 2,400 generic drugs were available for $4; brand-name drugs cost $30 to $50. There were no lifetime maximums on most health care expenses.

Other Benefits Wal-Mart's package of fringe benefits for full-time employees (and some part-time employees) also included the following:

- Vacation and personal time.
- Holiday pay.
- Jury duty pay.
- Medical and bereavement leave.
- Military leave.
- Maternity/paternity leave.
- Confidential counseling services for associates and their families.

- Child care discounts for associates with children (through four national providers).
- GED reimbursement/scholarships for associates and their spouses.
- 10 percent discounts on regularly priced merchandise, fresh fruits and vegetables, and eyewear purchased at Wal-Mart Vision Centers. (Sam's Club associates received a Sam's membership card at no cost. In fiscal 2008, Wal-Mart contributed $420 million in discounted merchandise to hourly associates and family members.)

Profit-Sharing and Retirement Plans Wal-Mart maintained a profit-sharing plan for full-time and part-time associates in the United States; individuals were eligible after one year and 1,000 hours of service. Annual contributions to the plan were tied to the company's profitability and were made at the sole discretion of management and the board of directors. Employees could contribute up to 15 percent of their earnings to their 401(k) accounts. Wal-Mart's contribution to each associate's profit-sharing account became vested at the rate of 20 percent per year beginning the third year of participation in the plan. After seven years of continuous employment the company's contribution became fully vested; however, if the associate left the company prior to that time, the unvested portions were redistributed to all remaining employees.

The plan was funded entirely by Wal-Mart and most of the profit-sharing contributions were invested in Wal-Mart's common stock. In recent years, the company's contribution to profit sharing and the 401(k) plan had averaged 4 percent of a U.S. associate's eligible pay, with total contributions amounting to $945 million in fiscal 2008, $890 million in fiscal 2007, and $827 million in fiscal 2006. Wal-Mart's contributions to the profit-sharing and retirement plans of foreign associates totaled $267 million in fiscal 2008, $274 million in fiscal 2007, and $244 million in fiscal 2006. Associates could begin withdrawals from their account upon retirement or disability, with the balance paid to family members upon death.

Stock Purchase and Stock Option Plans A stock purchase plan was adopted in 1972 to allow eligible employees a means of purchasing shares of common stock through regular payroll deduction or annual lump-sum contribution. Prior to 1990, the yearly maximum under this program was $1,500 per eligible employee; starting in 1990, the maximum was increased to $1,800 annually. The company contributed an amount equal to 15 percent of each participating associate's contribution. Long-time employees who had started participating in the early years of the program had accumulated stock worth over $100,000. About one-fourth of Wal-Mart's employees participated in the stock purchase plan in 1993, but this percentage had since declined, as many new employees opted not to participate. In fiscal 2008, Wal-Mart contributed $50.1 million to the stock purchases of some 764,000 associates.

In addition to regular stock purchases, certain employees qualified to participate in stock option plans; options expired 10 years from the date of the grant and could be exercised in nine annual installments. Share-based compensation of executives and associates totaled $276 million in fiscal 2008 and $271 million in fiscal 2007.

Overall Benefit Costs In fiscal 2005, Wal-Mart spent $4.2 billion on benefits for its associates (equal to 1.9 percent of revenues), up from $2.8 billion in 2002 (1.5 percent of revenues). The company's benefit expenses were growing 15 percent annually due to a combination of factors: growing workforce size, increased age and average tenure of associates, and rising cost trends for benefits, particularly health care. Top management and the board of directors were actively looking at strategies to contain the rising costs of the company's fringe benefit package, while at the same time preserving employee satisfaction with the benefit package and avoiding outcries from critics. Recent surveys of associates indicated overall satisfaction with the current benefit package (although this varied by benefit and associate demographics), but there was opposition to higher deductibles. Interestingly, the least healthy, least productive employees tended to be the most satisfied with their benefits and expressed interest in longer careers with Wal-Mart.

Training

Top management was committed to providing all associates state-of-the-art training resources and development time to help achieve career objectives. The company had a number of training tools in place, including classroom courses, computer-based learning, distance learning, corporate intranet sites, mentor programs, satellite broadcasts, and skills assessments. In November 1985, the Walton Institute of Retailing was opened in affiliation with the University of Arkansas. Within a year of its inception, every Wal-Mart manager from the stores, the distribution facilities, and the general office were expected to take part in special programs at the Walton Institute to strengthen and develop the company's managerial capabilities.

Management Training Wal-Mart store managers were hired in one of three ways. Hourly associates could move up through the ranks from sales to department manager to manager of the checkout lanes to store manager—more than 65 percent of Wal-Mart's managers had started out as hourly associates. Second, people with outstanding merchandising skills at other retail companies were recruited to join the ranks of Wal-Mart managers. And third, Wal-Mart recruited college graduates to enter the company's training program. Store management trainees went through an intensive on-the-job training program of almost 20 weeks and then were given responsibility for an area of the store. Trainees who progressed satisfactorily and showed leadership and job knowledge were promoted to an assistant manager, which included further training in various aspects of retailing and store operations. Given Wal-Mart's continued store growth, above-average trainees could progress to store manager within five years. Through bonuses for sales increases above projected amounts and company stock options, the highest-performing store managers earned well into six figures annually.

Associate Training Wal-Mart did not provide a specialized training course for its hourly associates. Upon being hired, an associate was immediately placed in a position for on-the-job training. From time to time, training films were shown in associates' meetings. Store managers and department managers were expected to train and supervise the associates under them in whatever ways were needed. As one associate put it, "Mostly you learn by doing. They tell you a lot; but you learn your job every day."

Special programs had been put in place to ensure that the company had an adequate talent pool of women and minorities who were well prepared for management positions. If company officers did not meet their individual diversity goals, their bonuses were cut 15 percent.

Wal-Mart's Use of Meetings: A Time for Rapid Action

The company used meetings both as a communication device and as a culture-building exercise. Store managers had several regularly scheduled meetings with store associates daily. In Bentonville, there were Thursday-afternoon meetings dealing with store operations, Friday-morning management meetings, Friday-noon merchandising meetings, and Saturday-morning meetings covering a range of topics. Most every meeting began and ended with the Wal-Mart cheer.

Store and Distribution Center Meetings Each Wal-Mart store had a 15-minute shift-change meeting when a new group of cashiers, stockers, and supervisors arrived. Managers reviewed sales numbers for the previous day, making a point to single out (1) displays that were effective and those that needed attention and (2) products that were selling particularly well and those whose sales were lagging.[37] An assistant department manager who reported big sales of particular items was likely to receive supportive applause and cheering. Associates were nearly always asked for their suggestions about how to spur sales and improve customers' shopping experience. They quickly learned that a key to advancement at Wal-Mart was to be a frequent and thoughtful contributor of ideas and suggestions at these meetings (as well as in conversations with their department manager and when assistant store managers and the store manager were touring their part of the store). Good ideas and suggestions were acted on immediately, with the associate responsible for the suggestion having a lead implementation role when it involved something he or she could undertake. When appropriate, store managers relayed the best ideas and suggestions on up the chain to regional vice presidents (VPs), who had responsibility over 100 or so stores and who visited each store about 6 times annually. The regional VPs decided which ideas and suggestions bubbling up from the stores to bring up at one of the weekly meetings in Bentonville.

The same kind of meeting cycles and solicitation of ideas from associates occurred in Wal-Mart's 110 + distribution centers, in the Sam's

Club division, and in Wal-Mart's stores in countries outside the United States.

The Meetings in Bentonville The weekly Thursday-afternoon store operations meeting, attended by about 70 people, dealt with the nuts and bolts of making the stores operate smoothly. Attendees remained standing—a tactic that kept the meeting from dragging on and prompted those speaking to make their point quickly; topics ranged from inventory management to store staffing issues to new-store real estate planning.[38] The weekly management meetings held at 7:00 a.m. on Fridays included the top 200 people in the company; outsiders were not permitted to attend, since the sometimes spirited discussions and debates involved sensitive strategic and competitive issues.[39] At both meetings, the information sharing and the ensuing discussions led to decisions about what actions needed to be taken; very rarely were issues left open for further debate and resolution at an upcoming meeting.

The weekly Friday merchandising meeting was an hour-and-a-half noontime session involving about 300 people—Wal-Mart's buyers and merchandising staff headquartered in Bentonville and the regional vice presidents who directed store operations and were fresh back from tours of Wal-Mart stores and, frequently, visits to the stores of the company's two closest competitors, Kmart and Target, earlier in the week. The merchandising meeting had two purposes: (1) to give the buyers a direct sense of what was and was not selling well in the stores and why and (2) to give the regional VPs a means to get instant action to resolve merchandising issues in their stores.[40] Considerable time was usually devoted to merchandising errors—having too much of a product (which prompted markdowns) and not having enough of a hot-selling item. It was also normal for the regional VPs to report on instances when they found that Wal-Mart's prices for particular items were higher that those at either Kmart or Target and when they believed that Wal-Mart was missing out on a hot-selling product. On one occasion, a regional VP reported that a Kmart store he had just visited was selling a $9.99 poker table cover and chip set that was a much better value than a comparable item Wal-Mart was selling—he pulled the poker set Kmart was selling out of a Kmart bag and showed it to the group.[41] Wal-Mart's divisional merchandising manager responded by saying, "We've got a pretty nice poker set in our stores, but I will check with our sources and get back to you." The discussion then moved to another regional VP complaining about a series of shortages of bedding and kitchen items at her stores. Then the divisional merchandising manager reported to the group that he had arranged for the poker sets sold at Kmart to be acquired and that they would be on Wal-Mart trucks for delivery to stores the upcoming week—attendees cheered. David Glass, Wal-Mart's former CEO, recalled what took place at the Friday merchandise meetings during his tenure:

> In retailing, there has always been a traditional, head-to-head confrontation between operations and merchandising. You know, the operations guys say, "Why in the world would anybody buy this? It's a dog, and we'll never sell it." Then the merchandising folks say, "There's nothing wrong with that item. If you guys were smart enough to display it well and promote it properly, it would blow out the doors." So we sit all these folks down together every Friday at the same table and just have at it.
>
> We get into some of the doggonedest, knock-down drag-outs you have ever seen. But we have a rule. We never leave an item hanging. We will make a decision in that meeting even if it's wrong, and sometimes it is. But when the people come out of that room, you would be hard-pressed to tell which ones oppose it and which ones are for it. And once we've made that decision on Friday, we expect it to be acted on in all the stores on Saturday. What we guard against around here is people saying, "Let's think about it." We make a decision. Then we act on it.[42]

Shortly after the conclusion of the Friday merchandise meetings, the "priorities were culled from the meeting, and buyers and regional VPs were sent a priority e-mail outlining perhaps a dozen follow-on assignments to complete by the end of the day."[43]

The Saturday-morning meetings, a Wal-Mart ritual since 1961, were held 52 weeks a year at 7:00 a.m. sharp. Top officers and as many as 600 other people (including relatives of Wal-Mart personnel attending the meeting and special VIP guests, frequently including celebrities with a role on the program) gathered in a 400-seat stageless auditorium and an adjoining cafeteria for a two-and-a-half-hour session that was a combination pep rally, talk show, financial report, town-hall forum, gripe session, idea exchange, business update, merchandising lesson, decision-making meeting, and morale booster.[44] Each week's agenda was deliberately designed to be interesting and important enough to cause attendees to want to be there despite the early hour. Typically, the meeting began with CEO H. Lee Scott or honored guests leading the Wal-Mart cheer, with other attendees standing, clapping their hands, and joining in enthusiastically. The business part of the meeting featured presentations concerning how well things were going, a new company initiative, a review of the week's sales, ideas and suggestions that originated in the stores and distribution centers, new product launches and special promotion items, store construction and new store openings, distribution centers, transportation, supply chain activities, and the like. Management described the nature and purpose of the Saturday meetings as follows:

> Created with a sense of the unpredictable and intended to entertain as well as inform, the Saturday morning meeting lets everyone know what the rest of the company is up to.
>
> The agenda constantly changes, so each meeting has an element of spontaneity. Sometimes we'll bring associates from the field in to Bentonville to praise them in front of the whole meeting. Other mornings, an associate may get a standing ovation as he receives a 20-year service award.
>
> On any given Saturday, we may invite special guests to promote product launches or just to share insights. We've had CEOs of other Fortune 500 companies, musicians, actors, journalists, authors, athletes, politicians, and children's characters. . . . That kind of unpredictability keeps things interesting.
>
> But beyond focusing on giving good news, entertaining special guests, and having a good time, we use that valuable time to critique our business. We review what we could do better and encourage suggestions about correcting those weaknesses. If the solution is obvious, we can order changes right then and carry them out over the weekend, while almost everyone else in retail business is off.
>
> The meeting is where we discuss and debate management philosophy and strategy. It's the focal point of our communication efforts, where we share ideas. We look at what our competition is doing well and look for ways to improve upon their successes in our own business. Often, it's the place where we decide to try things that seem unattainable, and instead of shooting those ideas down, we try to figure out how to make them work.
>
> The Saturday morning meeting remains the pulse of our culture.

As at the Friday merchandise meetings, decisions were made at the Saturday-morning meetings about what actions needed to be taken. According to former CEO David Glass, "The rule of thumb was that by noon we wanted all the corrections made in the stores. Noon on Saturday."[45]

The store meetings and the Thursday-Friday-Saturday meetings in Bentonville, along with the in-the-field visits by Wal-Mart management, created a strong bias for action. A *Fortune* reporter observed, "Managers suck in information from Monday to Thursday, exchange ideas on Friday and Saturday, and implement decisions in the stores on Monday."[46]

Wal-Mart's Environmental Sustainability Campaign

In 2008, Wal-Mart was fast emerging as the world's greenest retailer and a model of how companies could promote environmental sustainability by conducting their business in an eco-friendly manner. The environmental commitment at Wal-Mart was a byproduct of H. Lee Scott's efforts to combat the bad press the company was receiving in 2004–2005. In June 2004, Scott had an informal meeting with two officials from Conservation International with whom he had recently become acquainted and another environmentally oriented individual; all three argued that Wal-Mart could improve its image, motivate employees, and save money by going green. Scott was intrigued. Shortly thereafter, he decided to hire Conservation International to measure Wal-Mart's environmental impact. Rather quickly, Conservation International spotted ways that Wal-Mart could cut waste, reduce excessive packaging, and improve energy efficiency—and save tens of millions of dollars in the process. Another influential consulting firm that advocated green operating practices was brought in to study how Wal-Mart could wring more energy efficiency out of its trucking fleet. Because going green held the promise of reducing Wal-Mart's operating costs—something always cherished at Wal-Mart—Scott and other senior executives very quickly began pulling eco-friendly ideas from everywhere, including prominent environmental advocates, suppliers, regulators, and other eco-friendly companies like Starbucks, Patagonia, and Whole Foods.[47] Wal-Mart set up meetings with suppliers, environmental groups, and regulators every few months to share ideas, set goals, and monitor progress. Al Gore was invited to speak at a Saturday-morning meeting, following the showing of his movie *An Inconvenient Truth;* Gore's parting thought was that there need not be any conflict between the environment and the economy.[48]

Over a period of 12–14 months, Scott came to the conclusion that Wal-Mart should be an engaged, difference-making contributor to environmental sustainability. He told a *Fortune* reporter:

> To me, there can't be anything good about putting all these chemicals in the air. There can't be anything good about the smog you see in cities. There can't be anything good about putting chemicals in these rivers in Third World countries so that somebody can buy something for less money in a developed country. Those things are just inherently wrong whether you are an environmentalist or not.
>
> Some people say this is foreign to what Sam Walton believed. . . . What people forget is that there was nobody more willing to change. Sam Walton did what was right for his time. Sam loved the outdoors. And he loved the idea of building a company that would endure. I think Sam Walton would, in fact, embrace Wal-Mart's efforts to improve the quality of life for our customers and our associates by doing what we need to do in sustainability.[49]

In October 2005, Scott gave a speech titled "Twenty-First Century Leadership" in which he committed Wal-Mart to achieving three long-term objectives:

1. To be 100 percent supplied by renewable energy.
2. To create zero waste.
3. To sell products that sustained natural resources and the environment.

Then in a speech broadcast to all Wal-Mart facilities in November 2005, Scott announced that Wal-Mart would be pursuing three specific short-term objectives:

- Increase the efficiency of its truck fleet by 25 percent within three years and by 100 percent in 10 years.
- Reduce solid waste in U.S. stores by 25 percent in three years.
- Reduce energy usage in stores by 30 percent.

Scott also said the company would invest $500 million in sustainability projects. A senior vice president for sustainability was appointed to spearhead and oversee Wal-Mart's environmental sustainability strategies. A number of Wal-Mart's critics—union leaders, environmental extremists, and ideological elites—were unimpressed. The union-funded Wal-Mart Watch labeled Wal-Mart's environmental push as a "high-priced green-washing campaign."[50]

But Scott's resolve was unshaken. What began as a defensive strategy soon became something of a crusade. Pursuing ways to save money was a company strength. And Wal-Mart was adept at getting suppliers to do things that served the company's long-term interests. Company personnel warmed quickly to the idea of being a far better steward of the environment, and ideas for how Wal-Mart could further the cause of environmental sustainability began to blossom and take root across the company. Wal-Mart's buyers, already responding to growing buyer interest in organic food products, began contracting to buy the products of organic foods producers. In many instances, Wal-Mart made a point of buying organic produce locally, which had the effect of increasing freshness, reducing the shipping costs of food products, and providing local organic farmers with a market for their crops. In February 2006, Wal-Mart announced that over the next three to five years it would purchase all of its wild-caught seafood from fisheries that had been certified as sustainable by the Marine Stewardship Council, an independent nonprofit organization.

After a ladies' apparel buyer for Sam's Club ordered 190,000 units of a yoga outfit made of organic cotton that quickly sold in 10 weeks, Wal-Mart buyers visited organic cotton farms, learned about the environmental benefits of organically grown cotton as opposed to conventionally grown cotton, and began purchasing a range of organic cotton products for Wal-Mart and Sam's Club stores, despite their higher cost.[51] Going into 2007, Wal-Mart was the organic cotton industry's biggest customer, using more than 8 million metric tons; the company made a verbal commitment to buy organic cotton for at least five years, giving organic cotton farmers assurance of a market for their crops.

Wal-Mart began working with suppliers to explore ways to cut packaging costs, promote recycling, and boost energy efficiency. H. Lee Scott spoke personally with the CEO at General Electric about superefficient LED lighting for Wal-Mart stores and a campaign to promote compact fluorescent bulbs, with the CEO of Kimberly-Clark about compressing toilet paper and paper towels into package-saving megarolls, with the CEO of PepsiCo about a contest to recycle plastic bottles of Aquafina water and other PepsiCo beverages, and with the CEOs at Procter & Gamble and Unilever about selling concentrated laundry detergent in slimmed-down plastic bottles. In all these instances, Scott indicated that Wal-Mart would put its marketing muscle behind the efforts to win greater consumer acceptance of green products. Scott's efforts had paid off. As of May 2008, all laundry detergent sold at Wal-Mart was concentrated and packaged in smaller containers. Also in 2008, Wal-Mart was selling packs of 6 Charmin megarolls that contained the same amount of toilet paper as a regular Charmin 24-roll pack—selling twice as many packs of Charmin allowed Wal-Mart to ship twice as many units on its trucks, eliminate 89.5 million cardboard roll cores, eliminate 360,087 pounds of plastic wrapping, and reduce diesel fuel consumption by 53,966 gallons.

In 2007 and 2008, Wal-Mart's environmental sustainability campaign became increasingly sweeping and comprehensive. This was mirrored by a statement on the company's Web site: "Our opportunity is to become a better company by looking at every facet of our business—from the products we offer to the energy we use—through the lens of sustainability."[52] Eighteen environmental sustainability initiatives were launched, including those relating to reduction of greenhouse gases, alternative fuels, protection of wildlife habitat, the use of chemical intensive products, sustainable agriculture and seafood, reusable bags, and eco-friendly textiles and apparel. In November 2007, Wal-Mart issued a comprehensive report detailing its sustainability initiatives and the results being achieved.

WAL-MART'S FUTURE

Sam Walton had engineered the development and rapid ascendancy of Wal-Mart to the forefront of the retailing industry—the discount stores and Sam's Clubs were strategic moves that he directed. His handpicked successor, David Glass, had directed the hugely successful move into Supercenters and grocery retailing, as well as presiding over the company's growth into the world's largest retailing enterprise; the Neighborhood Market store format also came into being during his tenure as CEO. H. Lee Scott, Wal-Mart's third CEO, had the challenge of sustaining the company's growth, globalizing Wal-Mart operations, continuing the long-term process of saturating the U.S. market with Supercenters, overseeing Wal-Mart's ever-larger business operations, and, most recently, figuring out how to counteract the efforts of the company's critics and adversaries to portray Wal-Mart as a corporate villain.

In 2008, Scott had reason to believe that his transformation plan was producing the desired results. Company morale was decidedly improved, partly because Wal-Mart's far-reaching efforts to adopt business practices that were better for the environment had energized company personnel, triggered a burst of innovative thinking, and made associates feel good about their jobs and the company. There had been a noticeable falloff in the Wal-Mart bashing that had taken place in 2004–2006. Time would tell whether Scott's transformation initiatives would eventually restore the luster to Wal-Mart's image, spur the company's sales revenues, and reduce community resistance to opening new Supercenters.

But Wal-Mart was beginning to fight back. It had hired a public relations firm, which had put a staff of seven professionals in Bentonville to assist Wal-Mart's own public relations staff to get the company's story out and respond within hours to any new blast of criticism.[53] Since mid-2004, Lee Scott had done nine interviews on TV, met with the editorial boards of the *Wall Street Journal* and the *Washington Post,* been interviewed by numerous newspaper journalists, and spoken to business and community leaders in Chicago, Los Angeles, Istanbul, and Paris. The company was striving to build relationships with congressional delegations, governors, mayors, community leaders, and activists in key locations. It had run ads in more than 100 newspapers. And it created a Web site (www.walmartfacts.com) to help set the record straight about what Wal-Mart did and did not do.

Wal-Mart had received favorable publicity in the media following hurricane Katrina, when its quick response with food, supplies, and cash assistance was praised for being faster than the U.S. government's effort; Wal-Mart had also donated $15 million to the Katrina relief effort. And there was growing interest on the part of academic researchers over whether Wal-Mart had a positive or negative effect on the economy. A New York University economist reported that a Wal-Mart store opening in Glendale, Arizona, received 8,000 applicants for 525 jobs. A University of Missouri economist in an article published in the prestigious *Review of Economics and Statistics* found that the entry of a Wal-Mart store increased a county's retail employment by 100 jobs in the first year and over time led to the elimination of 50 jobs at less-efficient retailers. Studies also showed that new businesses quickly sprang up near Wal-Mart stores; both new and existing stores along the routes leading to a Wal-Mart tended to flourish because of the heavy traffic flow to and from the company's stores.

But heading into 2009, there continued to be occasional stories in the media that were critical of Wal-Mart's operating practices and of the company in general. It was unclear whether the company's transformation initiatives were having the desired impact on public opinion and whether Wal-Mart's growth and profitability would be adversely affected by its critics and adversaries.

Nonetheless, the economic slowdown that began in early 2008, followed by the global financial crisis and even sharper economic downturn that transpired in Fall 2008, had resulted in significant increases in customer traffic and purchases at Wal-Mart's stores. Many consumers—already feeling the pinch of recessionary forces or else anxious about the prospects of being laid off—were shopping at Wal-Mart more frequently and Wal-Mart's average sales per customer checkout were above prior-year levels, due in part to steep declines in gasoline prices in September–November 2008 which made a trip to Wal-Mart cheaper and gave consumers more discretionary income to spend at Wal-Mart. Sales at Wal-Mart stores open at least a year rose a robust 3.4 percent for the 43-week period ending November 28, 2008 (versus just 1.4 percent for the same period in 2007). Wal-Mart executives believed that in tough economic times Wal-Mart was the best destination for shoppers to save money.

Endnotes

[1.] Presentation to attendees at the 2008 annual meeting of Wal-Mart shareholders on June 6, 2008; Scott's remarks were posted in the news section at www.walmart.com (accessed June 9, 2008).
[2.] H. Lee Scott's remarks at Wal-Mart's 2008 shareholders meeting, www.wal-mart.com (accessed on June 9, 2008).
[3.] "Wal-Mart Live Better Index Shows Improvement in Acceptance of Green Products," Datamonitor NewsWire, April 22, 2008, www.walmart.com (accessed June 10, 2008).
[4.] Kevin Haslett, "Unions Wage Vicious, Misguided War on Wal-Mart," December 19, 2005, www.bloomberg.com (accessed December 20, 2005).
[5.] www.walmartwatch.com (accessed December 20, 2005).
[6.] As quoted in Lorrie Grant, "Retail Giant Wal-Mart Faces Challenges on Many Fronts," *USA Today,* November 11, 2003, p. B2.
[7.] Anthony Bianco and Wendy Zellner, "Is Wal-Mart Too Powerful?" *BusinessWeek,* October 6, 2003, p. 103.
[8.] Ibid.
[9.] Ibid., p. 108.
[10.] Ann Zimmerman, "After Huge Raid on Illegals, Wal-Mart Fires back at U.S.," *Wall Street Journal,* December 19, 2003, pp. A1, A10.
[11.] Bianco and Zellner, "Is Wal-Mart Too Powerful?" pp. 104, 106.
[12.] *San Francisco Bay Guardian* 40, no. 8 (November 23–29, 2005), www.sfbg.com (accessed December 20, 2005).
[13.] As quoted in Marc Gunter, "The Green Machine," *Fortune,* August 7, 2006, p. 48.
[14.] As quoted in "Can Wal-Mart Fit into a White Hat?" *BusinessWeek,* October 3, 2005, p. 94.
[15.] Jerry Useem, "One Nation Under Wal-Mart," *Fortune,* March 3, 2003, p. 66.
[16.] Business Planning Solutions, Global Insight Advisory Services Division, "The Price Impact of Wal-Mart: An Update Through 2006," September 4, 2007, www.livebetterindex.com (accessed June 11, 2008).
[17.] See Jerry Hausman and Ephraim Leibtag, "Consumer Benefits from Increased Competition in Shopping Outlets: Measuring the Effect of Wal-Mart" paper presented at the Economic Impact Research Conference: An In-Depth Look at Wal-Mart and Society, held in Washington, D.C., on November 4, 2005.
[18.] As quoted in Useem, "One Nation Under Wal-Mart," p. 68.
[19.] As quoted in Bill Saporito, "What Sam Walton Taught America," *Fortune,* May 4, 1992, p. 105.
[20.] John Helyar, "The Only Company Wal-Mart Fears," *Fortune,* November 24, 2003, pp. 158–166.
[21.] As quoted in *Fortune,* January 30, 1989, p. 53.
[22.] As quoted in Useem, "One Nation Under Wal-Mart," p. 68.
[23.] Cannondale Associates, "2005 PoweRanking Results," press release, November 2, 2005, www.cannondaleassoc.com (accessed December 15, 2005).
[24.] As quoted in Useem, "One Nation Under Wal-Mart," p. 74.
[25.] Ibid.
[26.] Ibid.
[27.] As quoted in "Wal-Mart's Way," *Information Week,* September 27, 2004,
[28.] Paul Lightfoot, "Wal-Martification," *Operations and Fulfillment,* June 1, 2003, www.opsandfulfillment.com.
[29.] Sam Walton with John Huey, *Sam Walton: Made in America* (New York: Doubleday, 1992), p. 12.
[30.] Ibid., pp. 10, 12, 47, 63, 115, 128, 135, 140, 213, 226–29, 233, 246, 249–54, and 256.
[31.] Useem, "One Nation Under Wal-Mart," p. 72.
[32.] Information posted at www.walmartstores.com (accessed June 18, 2008).
[33.] Quote taken from the section on Wal-Mart Culture, www.walmartstores.com (accessed December 19, 2005).
[34.] Information posted at www.walmartstores.com (accessed June 10, 2008).
35.Bernard Wysocki and Ann Zimmerman, "Wal-Mart Cost-Cutting Finds Big Target in Health Benefits," *Wall Street Journal,* September 30, 2003, pp. A1, A16.
[36.] Based on an internal memo by Susan Chambers to Wal-Mart's board of directors that was leaked to Wal-Mart Watch and posted at www.walmartwatch.com (accessed December 20, 2005).

[37] Brent Schlender, "Wal-Mart's $288 Billion Meeting," *Fortune,* April 18, 2005, p. 102.
[38] Ibid.
[39] Ibid.
[40] Ibid.
[41] Ibid.
[42] Walton with Huey, *Sam Walton,* pp. 225–26.
[43] Schlender, "Wal-Mart's $288 Billion Meeting," pp. 102, 104.
[44] Ibid.
[45] Ibid.
[46] Saporito, "What Sam Walton Taught America," p. 105.
[47] Gunter, "The Green Machine," p. 48.
[48] Ibid, p. 44.
[49] Ibid.
[50] Ibid., p. 45.
[51] Ibid., p. 54.
[52] Information posted at www.walmart.com (accessed August 18, 2008).
[53] Robert Berner, "Can Wal-Mart Fit into a White Hat?" *BusinessWeek,* October 3, 2005, p. 94.

Southwest Airlines in 2008: Culture, Values, and Operating Practices

CASE 23

Arthur A. Thompson
The University of Alabama

John E. Gamble
University of South Alabama

In 2008, more people were flying Southwest Airlines than any other U.S. airline, and Southwest had the enviable distinction of being the only major U.S. air carrier that was consistently profitable. After losing more than $35 billion during 2001–2005, U.S. commercial airlines earned a combined $3.1 billion in 2006 and $5.0 billion in 2007; but sharply higher costs for jet fuel in 2008 were expected to result in another money-losing year for most major U.S. airlines, with the notable exception of Southwest. In August 2008, analysts were projecting combined 2008 losses of $5 to $8 billion for the U.S. airline industry as a whole, depending on what happened to crude oil prices and jet fuel prices for the remainder of the year. However, the U.S. airline industry's profit outlook brightened considerably when crude oil prices dropped below $100 per barrel in September, prompting revised 2008 profit projections for the industry somewhere near breakeven point—the difference between buying jet fuel when crude oil was $147 per barrel (as it was in portions of July 2008) versus when crude oil was $100 per barrel (as in a portion of September 2008) equated to a fuel cost savings industry-wide of $15 billion.

The U.S. airline industry had lost money in 14 of the 28 years from 1980 through 2007, with combined annual losses exceeding combined annual profits by $15 billion. Yet in July 2008, Southwest reported record quarterly revenues, its 69th consecutive quarter of profitability, rising passenger traffic on its flights, and a record load factor (percentage of available seats sold). The company had reported a profit every year since 1973. During 1990–1994, when the airline industry had five straight money-losing years, laid off 120,000 employees, and lost a cumulative $13 billion, Southwest earned a profit every quarter of every year. It had weathered industry downturns, economy-wide recessions, fare wars and other attempts by rivals to undercut its business, energy crises, and cataclysmic falloffs in airline traffic due to terrorist attacks. It had contended successfully with a series of industry problems and business pressures—air-traffic congestion, mergers of rivals, stricter government regulations regarding aircraft safety and maintenance, and mounting customer dissatisfaction with airline service.

Once regarded as little more than a scrappy underdog with quirky practices that flew mainly to "secondary" airports (rather than high-traffic airports like Chicago's O'Hare, Dallas–Fort Worth, Atlanta's Hartsfield, and New York's LaGuardia and Kennedy airports), Southwest had proved it was a major competitive force in the U.S. airline industry. It had the lowest operating cost structure in the domestic airline industry and consistently offered the lowest and simplest fares. Not only was it the market share leader in terms of passengers carried, but its market share was climbing at a time when passenger traffic on other major U.S. airlines was stagnant—see Exhibit 1.

COMPANY BACKGROUND

In late 1966, Rollin King, a San Antonio entrepreneur who owned a small commuter air service, marched into Herb Kelleher's law office with a plan to start a low-cost/low-fare airline that would shuttle passengers between San Antonio, Dallas, and Houston.[1]

Exhibit 1 Number of Domestic and International Passengers by Air Carrier, 1998–First Quarter 2008 (in thousands)

Carrier	1998	1999	2000	2001	2002	2003	2004	2005	2006	2007	First Quarter 2008
America West*											
Domestic	17,305	18,265	19,467	19,013	18,799	19,187	20,151	20,868	19,956	14,674	n.a.
International	475	427	478	565	640	861	982	1,262	1,234	991	n.a.
Total	17,780	18,692	19,945	19,578	19,439	20,048	21,133	22,130	21,190	15,665	n.a.
American Airlines											
Domestic	63,987	63,893	68,319	61,704	77,489	72,202	72,648	77,297	76,813	76,581	17,724
International	17,372	17,516	17,951	16,370	16,580	16,560	18,858	20,710	21,313	21,562	n.a.
Total	81,359	81,409	86,270	78,074	94,069	88,762	91,506	98,007	98,126	98,143	n.a.
Continental Air Lines											
Domestic	34,985	36,130	36,591	34,635	31,653	30,853	31,529	32,971	35,795	37,117	8,713
International	6,611	7,814	8,747	8,058	8,247	7,926	9,146	9,795	10,994	11,859	n.a.
Total	41,596	43,944	45,338	42,693	39,900	38,779	40,675	42,766	46,789	48,976	n.a.
Delta Air Lines											
Domestic	97,879	98,212	97,965	86,888	83,747	77,793	79,374	77,581	63,496	61,599	14,307
International	7,259	7,158	7,596	7,150	7,036	6,335	7,416	8,359	10,020	11,435	n.a.
Total	105,138	105,370	105,561	94,038	90,783	84,128	86,790	85,940	73,516	73,034	n.a.
JetBlue Airways											
Domestic	n.a.	n.a.	1,128	3,056	5,672	8,950	11,616	14,463	18,098	20,528	7,024
International	n.a.	n.a.	n.a.	n.a.	n.a.	n.a.	116	218	408	777	n.a.
Total	n.a.	n.a.	1,128	3,056	5,672	8,950	11,732	14,681	18,506	21,305	n.a.
Northwest Airlines											
Domestic	41,931	46,666	48,462	44,786	43,314	43,310	45,959	46,690	45,141	43,812	9,685
International	6,914	7,575	8,228	7,418	7,454	6,871	7,576	7,912	7,831	8,042	n.a.
Total	48,845	54,241	56,690	52,204	50,768	50,181	53,535	54,602	52,972	51,854	n.a.
Southwest Airlines											
Domestic only	59,053	65,288	72,568	73,629	72,459	74,768	81,121	88,436	96,330	101,948	24,724
United Air Lines											
Domestic	75,058	75,436	72,450	63,947	57,830	56,308	60,081	55,173	57,229	56,402	12,369
International	9,912	9,969	10,625	9,996	9,532	8,541	9,490	10,355	10,770	11,011	n.a.
Total	84,970	85,405	83,075	73,943	67,362	64,849	69,571	65,528	67,999	67,413	n.a.
US Airways*											
Domestic	55,603	53,272	56,667	52,658	43,480	37,302	37,810	37,040	31,886	51,895	12,000
International	2,384	2,539	3,105	3,455	3,679	3,954	4,598	4,829	4,609	4,978	n.a.
Total	57,987	55,811	59,772	56,113	47,159	41,256	42,408	41,869	36,495	56,873	n.a.

*US Airways and America West merged in September 2005. US Airways numbers prior to 2007 include only US Airways. America West data is included in US Airways numbers starting in 2007.

n.a. = not applicable.

Source: U.S. Department of Transportation, Bureau of Transportation Statistics, Air Carrier Statistics Form T-100.

Over the years, King had heard many Texas businessmen complain about the length of time it took to drive between the three cities and the expense of flying the airlines currently serving these cities. His business concept for the airline was simple: attract passengers by flying convenient schedules, get passengers to their destination on time, make sure they have a good experience, and charge fares competitive with travel by automobile. Kelleher, skeptical that King's business idea was viable, dug into the possibilities during the next few weeks and concluded a new airline was feasible; he agreed to handle the necessary legal work and also to invest $10,000 of his own funds in the venture.

In 1967, Kelleher filed papers to incorporate the new airline and submitted an application to the Texas Aeronautics Commission for the new company to begin serving Dallas, Houston, and San Antonio.[2] But rival airlines in Texas pulled every string they could to block the new airline from commencing operations, precipitating a contentious four-year parade of legal and regulatory proceedings. Herb Kelleher led the fight on the company's behalf, eventually prevailing in June 1971 after winning two appeals to the Texas Supreme Court and a favorable ruling from U.S. Supreme Court. Kelleher recalled, "The constant proceedings had gradually come to enrage me. There was no merit to our competitors' legal assertions. They were simply trying to use their superior economic power to squeeze us dry so we would collapse before we ever got into business. I was bound and determined to show that Southwest Airlines was going to survive and was going into operation."[3]

In January 1971, Lamar Muse was brought in as the CEO to get operations under way. Muse was an aggressive and self-confident airline veteran who knew the business well and who had the entrepreneurial skills to tackle the challenges of building the airline from scratch and then competing head-on with the major carriers. Through private investors and an initial public offering of stock in June 1971, Muse raised $7 million in new capital to purchase planes and equipment and provide cash for start-up. Boeing agreed to supply three new 737s from its inventory, discounting its price from $5 million to $4 million and financing 90 percent of the $12 million deal.

Because the airline industry was in the throes of a slump in the early 1970s, Muse was able to recruit a talented senior staff that included a number of veteran executives from other carriers. He particularly sought out people who were innovative, wouldn't shirk from doing things differently or unconventionally, and were motivated by the challenge of building an airline from scratch. Muse wanted his executive team to be willing to think like mavericks and not be lulled into instituting practices at Southwest that were largely imitative of those at other airlines. According to Rollin King, "It was our one opportunity to do it right. . . . We all understood that this was our opportunity to decide how to do it our way. Our philosophy was, and still is, we do whatever we have to do to get the job done."[4]

SOUTHWEST'S STRUGGLE TO GAIN A MARKET FOOTHOLD

In June 1971, Southwest initiated its first flights with a schedule that soon included 6 round-trips between Dallas and San Antonio and 12 round-trips between Houston and Dallas. The introductory $20 one-way fares to fly the Golden Triangle, well below the $27 and $28 fares charged by rivals, attracted disappointingly small numbers of passengers—some days the total for all 18 flights would be less than 250 people. Southwest's financial resources were stretched so thin that the company bought fuel for several months on Lamar Muse's personal credit card. The company was short of ground equipment, and most of what it had was used and in worn condition. Money for parts and tools was so tight that, on occasion, company personnel got on the phone with acquaintances at rival airlines operating at the terminal and arranged to borrow what was needed. Nonetheless, morale and enthusiasm remained high; company personnel displayed can-do attitudes and adeptness at getting by on whatever resources were available.

To try to gain market visibility and drum up more passengers, Southwest decided it had to do more than just run ads in the media:

- Southwest decided to have its flight hostesses dress in colorful hot pants and white knee-high boots with high heels. Recruiting ads for Southwest's first group of hostesses were headlined "Attention, Raquel Welch: You can have a job if you measure up." Two thousand applicants responded, and those selected for interviews were asked to come dressed in hot pants to show off their legs—the company wanted to hire long-legged beauties with sparkling personalities. More than 30 of Southwest's first graduating class of 40 flight attendants consisted of young women who had been cheerleaders or majorettes in high school and thus had experience performing in front of people while skimpily dressed.

- A second attention-getting action was to give passengers free alcoholic beverages during daytime flights. Most passengers on these flights were business travelers. Management's thinking was that many passengers did not drink during the daytime and that with most flights being less than an hour's duration it would be cheaper to simply give the drinks away rather than collect the money.
- Taking a cue from being based at Dallas's Love Field, Southwest began using the tag line "Now There's Somebody Else Up There Who Loves You." The routes between Houston, Dallas, and San Antonio became known as the Love Triangle. Southwest's planes were referred to as Love Birds, drinks became Love Potions, peanuts were called Love Bites, drink coupons were Love Stamps, and tickets were printed on Love Machines. The "Love" campaign set the tone for Southwest's approach to its customers and company efforts to make flying Southwest an enjoyable, fun, and differentiating experience. (Later, when the company went public, it chose LUV as its stock-trading symbol.)
- In order to add more flights without buying more planes, the head of Southwest's ground operations came up with a plan for ground crews to off-load passengers and baggage, refuel the plane, clean the cabin and restock the galley, on-load passengers and baggage, do the necessary preflight checks and paperwork, and push away from the gate in 10 minutes. The 10-minute turn became one of Southwest's signatures during the 1970s and 1980s. (In later years, as passenger volume grew and many flights were filled to capacity, the turnaround time gradually expanded to 25 minutes—because it took more time to unload and load a full plane with 125 passengers, as compared to a half-full plane with just 60–65 passengers. Even so, the 25-minute average turnaround time at Southwest in 2002 was still shorter than the 40- to 60-minute turnaround times typical at other major airlines.)
- In late November 1971, Lamar Muse came up with the idea of offering a $10 fare to passengers on the Friday-night Houston–Dallas flight. With no advertising, the 112-seat flight sold out. This led Muse to realize that Southwest was serving two quite distinct types of travelers in the Golden Triangle market: (1) business travelers who were more time-sensitive than price-sensitive and wanted weekday flights at times suitable for conducting business and (2) price-sensitive leisure travelers who wanted lower fares and had more flexibility about when to fly.[5] He came up with a two-tier on-peak and off-peak pricing structure in which all seats on weekday flights departing before 7:00 p.m. were priced at $26 and all seats on other flights were priced at $13. Passenger traffic increased significantly—and systemwide on-peak and off-peak pricing soon became standard across the whole airline industry.
- In 1972, the company decided to move its flights in Houston from the newly opened Houston Intercontinental Airport (where it was losing money and where it took 45 minutes to get to downtown) to the abandoned Houston Hobby Airport located much closer to downtown Houston. Despite being the only carrier to fly into Houston Hobby, the results were spectacular—business travelers that flew to Houston frequently from Dallas and San Antonio found the Houston Hobby location far more convenient and passenger traffic doubled almost immediately.
- In early 1973, in an attempt to fill empty seats on its San Antonio–Dallas flights, Southwest cut its regular $26 fare to $13 for all seats, all days, and all times. When Braniff International, at that time one of Southwest's major rivals, announced $13 fares of its own, Southwest retaliated with a two-page ad, run in the Dallas newspapers, headlined "Nobody Is Going to Shoot Southwest Airlines Out of the Sky for a Lousy $13" and containing copy saying Braniff was trying to run Southwest out of business. The ad announced that Southwest would not only match Braniff's $13 fare but that it would also give passengers the choice of buying a regular-priced ticket for $26 and receiving

> a complimentary fifth of Chivas Regal scotch, Crown Royal Canadian whiskey, or Smirnoff vodka (or, for nondrinkers, a leather ice bucket). Over 75 percent of Southwest's Dallas–Houston passengers opted for the $26 fare, although the percentage dropped as the two-month promotion wore on and corporate controllers began insisting that company employees use the $13 fare. The local and national media picked up the story of Southwest's offer, proclaiming the battle as a David-versus-Goliath struggle in which the upstart Southwest did not stand much of a chance against the much larger and well-established Braniff; grassroots sentiment in Texas swung to Southwest's side.

Southwest reported its first-ever annual profit in 1973.

MORE LEGAL AND REGULATORY HURDLES

During the rest of the 1970s, Southwest found itself embroiled in another round of legal and regulatory battles. One involved Southwest's refusal to move its flights from Dallas Love Field, located 10 minutes from downtown, out to the newly opened Dallas–Fort Worth Regional Airport, which was 30 minutes from downtown Dallas. Local officials were furious because they were counting on fees from Southwest's flights in and out of DFW to help service the debt on the bonds issued to finance the construction of DFW. Southwest's position was that it was not required to move because it had not agreed to do so nor had it been ordered to do so by the Texas Aeronautics Commission—moreover, the company's headquarters were located at Love Field. The courts eventually ruled that Southwest's operations could remain at Love Field.

A second battle ensued when rival airlines protested Southwest's application to begin serving several smaller cities in Texas; their protest was based on arguments that these markets were already well served and that Southwest's entry would result in costly overcapacity. Southwest countered that its low fares would allow more people to fly and grow the market. Again, Southwest prevailed and its views about low fares expanding the market proved accurate. In the year before Southwest initiated service, 123,000 passengers flew from Harlingen Airport in the Rio Grande Valley to Houston, Dallas, or San Antonio; in the 11 months following Southwest's initial flights, 325,000 passengers flew to the same three cities.

Believing that Braniff and Texas International were deliberately engaging in tactics to harass Southwest's operations, Southwest convinced the U.S. government to investigate what it considered predatory tactics by its chief rivals. In February 1975, Braniff and Texas International were indicted by a federal grand jury for conspiring to put Southwest out of business—a violation of the Sherman Antitrust Act. The two airlines pleaded "no contest" to the charges, signed cease-and-desist agreements, and were fined a modest $100,000 each.

When Congress passed the Airline Deregulation Act in 1978, Southwest applied to the Civil Aeronautics Board (now the Federal Aviation Agency) to fly between Houston and New Orleans. The application was vehemently opposed by local government officials and airlines operating out of Dallas–Fort Worth (DFW) because of the potential for passenger traffic to be siphoned away from DFW. The opponents solicited the aid of Fort Worth congressman Jim Wright, the majority leader of the U.S. House of Representatives, who took the matter to the floor of the House of Representatives; a rash of lobbying and maneuvering ensued. What emerged came to be known as the Wright Amendment of 1979: no airline could provide nonstop or through-plane service from Dallas Love Field to any city in any state except for locations in states bordering Texas. The amendment, which continued in effect as of 2003, meant that Southwest could not advertise, publish schedules or fares, or check baggage for travel from Dallas's Love Field to any city it served outside Texas, Louisiana, Arkansas, Oklahoma, and New Mexico.

The Battles to Survive Breed a Warrior Mentality

The legal, regulatory, and competitive battles that Southwest fought in its early years produced a strong esprit de corps among Southwest personnel and a drive to survive and prosper despite the odds. With newspaper and TV stories reporting Southwest's difficulties regularly, employees were fully aware that the airline's existence was constantly on the line.

Had the company been forced to move from Love Field, it would most likely have gone under, an outcome that employees, Southwest's rivals, and local government officials understood well. According to Southwest's president, Colleen Barrett, the obstacles thrown in Southwest's path by competitors and local officials were instrumental in building Herb Kelleher's passion for Southwest Airlines and ingraining a combative, can-do spirit into the corporate culture:

> They would put twelve to fifteen lawyers on a case and on our side there was Herb. They almost wore him to the ground. But the more arrogant they were, the more determined Herb got that this airline was going to go into the air—and stay there.
>
> The warrior mentality, the very fight to survive, is truly what created our culture.[6]

THE START OF THE HERB KELLEHER ERA

When Lamar Muse resigned in 1978, Southwest's board wanted Herb Kelleher to take over as chairman and CEO. But Kelleher enjoyed practicing law and, while he agreed to become chairman of the board, he insisted that someone else be CEO. Southwest's board appointed Howard Putnam, a group vice president of marketing services at United Airlines, as Southwest's president and CEO in July 1978. Putnam asked Kelleher to become more involved in Southwest's day-to-day operations, and over the next three years, Kelleher got to know many of the company's personnel and observe them in action. Putnam announced his resignation in the fall of 1981 to become president and chief operating officer at Braniff International. This time, Southwest's board succeeded in persuading Kelleher to take on the additional duties of CEO and president.

When Kelleher took over in 1981, Southwest had 27 planes, $270 million in revenues, 2,100 employees, and 14 destination cities. Over the next 26 years, Southwest Airlines prospered, racking up many industry firsts and expanding into more geographic areas—see Exhibit 2. In 2008, Southwest was the largest U.S. commercial airline in terms of passengers flown and the sixth largest in terms of revenues. It had 2007 revenues of $9.9 billion annually and 34,000 employees, and its 527 jets flew 3,400 flights to 64 cities in 32 states. Southwest had been profitable every year since 1973—in an industry noted for its vulnerability to economic cycles and feast-or-famine profitability. During 1990–1994, when the airline industry had five straight money-losing years, laid off 120,000 employees, and lost a cumulative $13 billion, Southwest earned a profit every quarter of every year.

Exhibit 3 provides a five-year summary of Southwest's financial and operating performance. Exhibits 4 and 5 provide industry-wide data on airline travel for 1995–2008.

HERB KELLEHER: COFOUNDER OF SOUTHWEST AND LONGTIME CEO

Herb Kelleher majored in philosophy at Wesleyan University in Middletown, Connecticut, graduating with honors. He earned his law degree at New York University, again graduating with honors and also serving as a member of the law review. After graduation, he clerked for a New Jersey Supreme Court justice for two years and then joined a law firm in Newark. Upon marrying a woman from Texas and becoming enamored with Texas, he moved to San Antonio, where he became a successful lawyer and came to represent Rollin King's small aviation company.

When Kelleher took on the role of Southwest's CEO in 1981, he made a point of visiting with maintenance personnel to check on how well the planes were running and talking with the flight attendants. Kelleher did not do much managing from his office, preferring instead to be out among the troops as much as he could. His style was to listen and observe and to offer encouragement. Kelleher attended most graduation ceremonies of flight attendant classes, and he often appeared to help load bags on Black Wednesday, the busy travel day before Thanksgiving. He knew the names of thousands of Southwest employees and was held in the highest regard by Southwest employees. When he attended a Southwest employee function, he was swarmed like a celebrity.

Kelleher had an affinity for bold-print Hawaiian shirts, owned a tricked-out motorcycle, and made no secret of his love for smoking cigarettes and drinking Wild Turkey whiskey. He loved to make jokes and

Exhibit 2 Milestones at Southwest Airlines, 1983–2007

1983	Three additional Boeing 737s are purchased; Southwest flies more than 9.5 million passengers.
1984	Southwest is ranked first in customer satisfaction among the U.S. airlines for the fourth straight year.
1985	Service begins to St. Louis and Chicago Midway airports. Southwest names the Ronald McDonald House as its primary charity—the tie-in was the result of an effort by a Southwest pilot who lost a daughter to leukemia and who believed that Ronald McDonald Houses were a worthy way to demonstrate Southwest's community spirit.
1986	Southwest flies more than 13 million passengers.
1988	Southwest becomes the first U.S. airline to win the Triple Crown (best on-time record, fewest reports of mishandled baggage, and fewest complaints per 100,000 passengers) for a single month.
1990	Revenues reach $1 billion; Southwest was the only major U.S. airline to record both an operating profit and a net profit.
1992	Southwest wins its first annual Triple Crown for best on-time record, best baggage handling, and fewest customer complaints; for the second year running, Southwest was the only major U.S. airline to record both an operating profit and a net profit.
1993	Southwest begins operations on the East Coast and wins its second annual Triple Crown; revenues exceed $2 billion and profits exceed $100 million. For the third consecutive year, Southwest is the only major U.S. airline to record both an operating profit and a net profit.
1994	Southwest leads the industry by introducing ticketless travel in four cities; Southwest wins its third Triple Crown and acquires Morris Air, based in Salt Lake City.
1995	Ticketless travel becomes available systemwide; Southwest wins fourth consecutive Triple Crown.
1996	Service to Florida begins; Southwest wins fifth consecutive Triple Crown. Southwest and its employees contribute almost $740,000 to help support Ronald McDonald Houses, including $34,000 in cash donations from the company and $302,500 in free air travel for families staying at Ronald McDonald Houses in cities served by Southwest.
1997	Service begins to Southwest's 50th city; more than 50 million people fly Southwest.
1998	Southwest is named by *Fortune* as the best company to work for in America.
1999	Service is added to three more cities.
2000	The number of passengers on Southwest flights exceeds 60 million, and revenues surpass the $5 billion mark; the company records its 28th consecutive year of profitability and 9th consecutive year of increased profits. Southwest becomes the 4th largest U.S. airline in terms of passengers carried.
2001	Southwest is profitable for the 30th consecutive year and the only U.S. airline to report a profit for 2001; a record 64.5 million passengers fly Southwest.
2002	Southwest ranks second among companies across all industry groups, and first in the airline industry on *Fortune*'s 2002 list of America's most admired companies.
2005	Southwest becomes the 2nd largest U.S. airline in terms of passengers carried.
2006	A record 96.3 million passengers fly Southwest.
2007	Southwest becomes the largest U.S. airline in terms of passengers carried and is profitable for the 35th consecutive year. Southwest Airlines is named to *BusinessWeek*'s first ever "Customer Service Champs" list and is voted "Overall Best Airline" in the United States by Frost & Sullivan's CEO Leadership Forum.

engage in pranks and corporate antics, prompting some people to refer to him as the "clown prince" of the airline industry. He once appeared at a company gathering dressed in an Elvis costume and had arm-wrestled a South Carolina company executive at a public event in Dallas for rights to use "Just Plane Smart" as an advertising slogan.[7] Kelleher was well-known inside and outside the company for his combativeness, particularly when it came to beating back competitors. On one occasion, he reportedly told a group of veteran employees, "If someone says they're going to smack us in the face—knock them out, stomp them out, boot them in the ditch, cover them over, and move on to the next thing. That's the Southwest spirit at work."[8] On another occasion, he said, "I love battles. I think it's part of the Irish in me. It's like what Patton said, 'War is hell and I love it so.' That's how I feel. I've never gotten tired of fighting."[9]

Exhibit 3 Summary of Southwest Airlines' Financial and Operating Performance, 2003–2007

	Years Ended December 31				
	2007	2006	2005	2004	2003
Financial Data ($ in millions, except per share data)					
Operating revenues	$9,861	$9,086	$7,584	$6,530	$5,937
Operating expenses	9,070	8,152	6,859	6,126	5,558
Operating income	791	934	725	404	379
Other expenses (income) net	(267)	144	(54)	65	(225)
Income before taxes	1,058	790	779	339	604
Provision for income taxes	413	291	295	124	232
Net Income	$ 645	$ 499	$ 484	$ 215	$ 372
Net income per share, basic	$0.85	$0.63	$0.61	$0.27	$0.48
Net income per share, diluted	.84	.61	.60	.27	.46
Cash dividends per common share	$0.018	$0.018	$0.018	$0.018	$0.018
Total assets at period-end	$16,772	$13,460	$14,003	$11,137	$9,693
Long-term obligations at period-end	$2,050	$1,567	$1,394	$1,700	$1,332
Stockholders' equity at period-end	$6,941	$6,449	$6,675	$5,527	$5,029
Operating Data					
Revenue passengers carried	88,713,472	83,814,823	77,693,875	70,902,773	65,673,945
Enplaned passengers	101,910,809	96,276,907	88,379,900	81,066,038	74,719,340
Revenue passenger miles (RPMs) (000s)	72,318,812	67,691,289	60,223,100	53,418,353	47,943,066
Available seat miles (ASMs) (000s)	99,635,967	92,663,023	85,172,795	76,861,296	71,790,425
Load factor*	72.6	73.1	70.7	69.5	66.8
Average length of passenger haul (miles)	815	808	775	753	730
Average aircraft stage length (miles)	629	622	607	576	558
Trips flown	1,160,699	1,092,331	1,028,639	981,591	949,882
Average passenger fare	$106.60	$104.40	$93.68	$88.57	$87.42
Passenger revenue yield per RPM	13.08¢	12.93¢	12.09¢	11.76¢	11.97¢
Operating revenue yield per ASM	9.90¢	9.81¢	8.90¢	8.50¢	8.27¢
Operating expenses per ASM	9.10¢	8.80¢	8.05¢	7.97¢	7.74¢
Fuel costs per gallon (average)	$1.70	$1.53	$1.03	$0.83	$0.72
Fuel consumed, in gallons (millions)	1,489	1,389	1,287	1,201	1,143
Full-time equivalent employees at year-end	34,378	32,664	31,729	31,011	32,847
Size of fleet at year-end†	520	481	445	417	388

*Revenue passenger miles divided by available seat miles.

†Includes leased aircraft.

Source: 2007 10-K report.

While Southwest was deliberately combative and flamboyant in some aspects of its operations, when it came to the financial side of the business Kelleher insisted on fiscal conservatism, a strong balance sheet, comparatively low levels of debt, and zealous attention to bottom-line profitability. While believing strongly in being prepared for adversity, Kelleher had an aversion to Southwest personnel spending time drawing up all kinds of formal strategic plans; he once said, "Reality is chaotic; planning

Exhibit 4 Selected Operating and Financial Data for Major U.S. Airline Carriers, 1995–First Quarter 2008

	1995	2000	2005	2006	2007	First Quarter 2008
Passengers (in millions)	559.0	666.2	738.3	744.2	769.2	181.1
Flights (in thousands)	8,062.0	9,035.0	11,558.0	11,264.0	11,365.0	2,529.7
Revenue passenger miles (in billions)	603.4	692.8	778.6	796.8	829.0	190.3
Available seat miles (in billions)	807.1	987.9	1,016.4	1,006.3	1,037.6	247.7
Load factor	67.0	72.3	77.5	79.2	79.9	77.2
Passenger revenues (in millions)	$69,470	$93,622	$93,500	$101,419	$107,011	$25,527
Average domestic fare (4th quarter)	$ 288	$ 340	$ 315	$ 318	$ 331	n.a.
Operating profit (loss) (in millions)	$ 5,852	$ 6,999	$ 427	$ 7,514	$ 9,210	n.a.
Net profit (loss) (in millions)	$ 2,283	$ 2,486	($ 5,782)	$ 3,126	$ 4,998	n.a.
Fuel cost (in millions)	$ 9,696	$16,447	$33,150	$ 38,548	$ 41,580	$12,824
Total employees	546,987	679,967	562,467	545,695	560,997	n.a.

Sources: Air Transport Association, *2008 Economic Report,* p. 7; Air Transport Association, *2005 Economic Report,* p. 7; and U.S. Department of Transportation, Bureau of Transportation Statistics, airline traffic data press releases, various years.

is ordered and logical. The meticulous nit-picking that goes on in most strategic planning processes creates a mental straitjacket that becomes disabling in an industry where things change radically from one day to the next." Kelleher wanted Southwest managers to think ahead, have contingency plans, and be ready to act when it appeared that the future held significant risks or when new conditions suddenly appeared and demanded prompt responses.

Kelleher was a strong believer in the principle that employees—not customers—came first:

> You have to treat your employees like your customers. When you treat them right, then they will treat your outside customers right. That has been a very powerful competitive weapon for us. You've got to take the time to listen to people's ideas. If you just tell somebody no, that's an act of power and, in my opinion, an abuse of power. You don't want to constrain people in their thinking.[10]

Another indication of the importance that Kelleher placed on employees was the message he had penned in 1990 that was prominently displayed in the lobby of Southwest's headquarters in Dallas:

> The people of Southwest Airlines are "the creators" of what we have become—and of what we will be.

Exhibit 5 Operating Revenues of Selected U.S. Airlines, 2000–2007 ($ in billions)

Airline	2007	2006	2005	2004	2003	2002	2001	2000
American	$22.9	$22.5	$20.6	$18.6	$17.4	$15.9	$15.6	$18.1
United	20.1	19.3	17.3	15.7	13.4	13.9	16.1	19.3
Delta	19.2	17.5	16.5	15.2	14.3	12.4	13.2	15.3
Continental	14.2	13.1	11.1	9.9	7.3	7.4	8.2	9.4
Northwest	12.5	12.6	12.3	11.3	10.1	9.2	9.6	11.0
US Airways	11.7	11.6	7.2	7.1	6.8	6.9	8.3	9.2
Southwest	9.9	9.1	7.6	6.5	5.9	5.5	5.6	5.7
America West	*	*	3.4	2.5	2.2	2.0	2.0	2.3

*Merged with US Airways in 2005; revenues included in US Airways for 2006 and 2007.
Sources: Bureau of Transportation Statistics, *Air Carrier Financial Reports,* Schedule P-12 and company annual reports for 2007.

> Our people transformed an idea into a legend. That legend will continue to grow only so long as it is nourished—by our people's indomitable spirit, boundless energy, immense goodwill, and burning desire to excel.
>
> Our thanks—and our love—to the people of Southwest Airlines for creating a marvelous family and a wondrous airline.

In June 2001, Herb Kelleher stepped down as CEO but continued on in his role as chairman of Southwest's board of directors and the head of the board's executive committee; as chairman, he played a lead role in Southwest's strategy, expansion to new cities and aircraft scheduling, and governmental and industry affairs. In May 2008, after more than 40 years of leadership at Southwest, Kelleher retired as chairman of the board (but he was scheduled to remain a full-time Southwest employee until July 2013).

NEW EXECUTIVE LEADERSHIP AT SOUTHWEST: 2001–2008

In June 2001, Southwest Airlines, responding to anxious investor concerns about the company's leadership succession plans, began an orderly transfer of power and responsibilities from Herb Kelleher, age 70, to two of his most trusted protégés. James F. Parker, 54, Southwest's general counsel and one of Kelleher's most trusted protégés, succeeded Kelleher as Southwest's CEO. Another of Kelleher's trusted protégés, Colleen Barrett, 56, Southwest's executive vice president–customers and self-described keeper of Southwest's pep rally corporate culture, became president and chief operating officer.

James Parker: CEO, 2001–2004

James Parker's association with Herb Kelleher went back 23 years, to the time when they were colleagues at Kelleher's old law firm. Parker moved over to Southwest from the law firm in February 1986. Parker's profile inside the company as Southwest's vice president and general counsel had been relatively low, but he was Southwest's chief labor negotiator and much of the credit for Southwest's good relations with employee unions belonged to Parker. Prior to his appointment as CEO, Parker had been a member of the company's executive planning committee; his experiences ranged from properties and facilities to technical services to the company's alliances with vendors and partners. Parker and Kelleher were said to think much alike, and Parker was regarded as having a good sense of humor, although he did not have as colorful and flamboyant a personality as Kelleher. Parker was seen as an honest, straight-arrow kind of person who had a strong grasp of Southwest's culture and market niche and who could be nice or tough, depending on the situation. When his appointment was announced, Parker said:

> There is going to be no change of course insofar as Southwest is concerned. We have a very experienced leadership team. We've all worked together for a long time. There will be evolutionary changes in Southwest, just as there have always been in our history. We're going to stay true to our business model of being a low-cost, low-fare airline.[11]

Parker retired unexpectedly, for personal reasons, in July 2004, stepping down as CEO and vice chairman of the board and also resigning from the company's board of directors. He was succeeded by Gary C. Kelly.

Colleen Barrett: Southwest's President, 2001–2008

Colleen Barrett began working as Herb Kelleher's legal secretary in 1967 and had been with Southwest since 1978. As executive vice president–customers, Barrett had a high profile among Southwest employees and spent most of her time on culture building, morale building, and customer service; her goal was to ensure that employees felt good about what they were doing and felt empowered to serve the cause of Southwest Airlines.[12] She and Kelleher were regarded as Southwest's guiding lights, and some analysts said she was essentially functioning as the company's chief operating officer prior to her formal appointment as president. Much of the credit for the company's strong record of customer service and its strong-culture work climate belonged to Barrett.

Barrett had been the driving force behind lining the hallways at Southwest's headquarters with photos of company events and trying to create a family atmosphere at the company. Believing it was important to make employees feel cared about and important, Barrett had put together a network of contacts across the company to help her stay in touch with what was happening with employees and their families. When network members learned about events that were worthy of acknowledgment, the word quickly got to Barrett—the information went into a database and an appropriate greeting card or gift was sent. Barrett had a remarkable ability to give gifts that were individualized and connected her to the recipient.[13]

Barrett was the first woman appointed as president and chief operating officer of a major U.S. airline. In October 2001, *Fortune* included Barrett on its list of the 50 most powerful women in American business (she was ranked number 20). Barrett retired as Southwest's president in July 2008 but was scheduled to remain as a full-time Southwest employee until 2013.

Gary C. Kelly: Southwest's CEO, 2004–Present

Gary Kelly was appointed vice chairman of the board of directors and CEO of Southwest effective July 15, 2004. Prior to that time, Kelly was executive vice president and chief financial officer from 2001 to 2004, and vice president–finance and chief financial officer from 1989 to 2001. He joined Southwest in 1986 as its controller. In 2008, effective with the retirement of Kelleher and Barrett, Kelly assumed the titles of chairman of the board, CEO, and president.

When he was named CEO in 2004, Herb Kelleher said:

> Gary Kelly is one of our brightest stars, well respected throughout the industry and well known, over more than a decade, to the media, analyst, and investor communities for his excellence. As part of our Board's succession planning, we had already focused on Gary as Jim Parker's successor, and that process has simply been accelerated by Jim's personal decision to retire. Under Gary's leadership, Southwest has achieved the strongest balance sheet in the American airline industry; the best fuel hedging position in our industry; and tremendous progress in technology.[14]

During his tenure as CEO, Kelly had worked with other top-level Southwest executives to sharpen and fine-tune Southwest's strategy in a number of areas, continued to expand operations (adding both more flights and initiating service to new airports), and strived to maintain the company's low-cost advantage over its domestic rivals.

Kelly saw four factors as keys to Southwest's recipe for success:

- Hire great people, treat 'em like family.
- Care for our Customers warmly and personally, like they're guests in our home.
- Keep fares and operating costs lower than anybody else by being safe, efficient, and operationally excellent.
- Stay prepared for bad times with a strong balance sheet, lots of cash, and a stout fuel hedge.[15]

To help Southwest be a standout performer on these four key success factors, Kelly had established five strategic objectives:

- Be the best place to work.
- Be the safest, most efficient, and most reliable airline in the world.
- Offer Customers a convenient flight schedule with lots of flights to lots of places they want to go.
- Offer Customers the best overall travel experience.
- Do all of these things in a way that maintains a low cost structure and the ability to offer low fares.[16]

SOUTHWEST AIRLINES' STRATEGY

From day one, Southwest had pursued a low-cost/low-price/no-frills strategy. Its signature low fares made air travel affordable to a wide segment of the U.S. population—giving substance to the company's tag line "The Freedom to Fly." It employed a relatively simple fare structure featuring low, unrestricted, unlimited, everyday coach fares, as well as even lower fares available on a restricted basis. All of Southwest's different fare options could easily be perused at the company's Web site, and the company's restrictions on tickets were more lenient than those of its rivals. In 2008, its highest one-way unrestricted walkup fare was $399 (a fare charged for its longest flights); substantially lower fares were available for short- and medium-distance flights. Many flights had some seats available at deeply discounted fares, provided they were purchased via the company's Web site. In November 2007,

Southwest introduced a new Business Select fare to attract economy-minded business travelers; Business Select customers had early boarding privileges, received extra Rapid Rewards (frequent-flyer credits), and a free cocktail. In 2008, when rival airlines instituted a series of add-on fees—including a fuel surcharge for each flight, fees for checking bags, fees for processing frequent-flyer travel awards, fees for buying a ticket in person at the airport, and fees for in-flight beverages—in order to cover skyrocketing costs for jet fuel (which had climbed from about 15 percent of operating expenses in 2000 to 40 percent of operating expenses in mid-2008), Southwest chose to forgo à la carte pricing and stuck with an all-inclusive fare price.

From time to time, Southwest ran special fare promotions. To celebrate its 30th anniversary in 2001, Southwest announced special $30 one-way fares to 30 destinations from 35 cities for a four-month travel period; its car rental and hotel partners participated in the promotion, offering $30-per-day rentals, $30-off discounts, and $30-per-day hotel rooms at some locations. The 30-year celebration also included decorations in gate areas, prize giveaways, and employees playing games in the gate areas so that customers could share in the "Southwest Spirit."

Southwest was a shrewd practitioner of the concept of price elasticity, proving in one market after another that the revenue gains from increased ticket sales and the volume of passenger traffic would more than compensate for the revenue erosion associated with low fares. When Southwest entered the Florida market with an introductory $17 fare from Tampa to Fort Lauderdale, the number of annual passengers flying the Tampa–Fort Lauderdale route jumped 50 percent, to more than 330,000. In Manchester, New Hampshire, passenger counts went from 1.1 million in 1997, the year prior to Southwest's entry, to 3.5 million in 2000 and average one-way fares dropped from just over $300 to $129. Southwest's success in stimulating higher passenger traffic at airports across the United States via low fares and frequent flights had been dubbed the "Southwest effect" by personnel at the U.S. Department of Transportation. Exhibit 6 shows the cities and airports Southwest served in mid-2008; Southwest had sizable market shares at the five airports where its passenger counts were highest: Oakland (65 percent), Baltimore (55 percent), Las Vegas (38 percent), Phoenix (31 percent), and Chicago Midway (18 percent).

Unlike the hub-and-spoke route systems of rival airlines (where operations were concentrated at a limited number of hub cities and most destinations were served via connections through the hub), Southwest's route system had been carefully designed to concentrate on flights between pairs of cities 150 to 700 miles apart where there was enough passenger traffic that Southwest could offer a sizable number of daily flights. As a general rule, Southwest did not initiate service to an airport unless it envisioned the potential for originating at least 8 flights a day there and saw opportunities to add more flights over time—in Denver, for example, Southwest had boosted the number of daily departures from 13 in January 2006 (the month in which service to and from Denver was initiated) to 79 in May 2008. Southwest's point-to-point route system minimized connections, delays, and total trip time—its emphasis on nonstop flights between about 410 pairs of cities in 2008 allowed about 75 percent of Southwest's passengers to fly nonstop to their destination. While a majority of Southwest's flights involved actual in-air flight times of less than 90 minutes, in recent years the company had added a significant number of nonstop flights to more distant destinations at those airports where its classic low fares could generate profitable amounts of passenger traffic.

Southwest's frequent-flyer program, Rapid Rewards, was based on trips flown rather than mileage. Rapid Rewards customers received one credit for each one-way trip or two credits for each round-trip flown and could also earn credits by using the services of Southwest's car rental, hotel, and credit card partners. There were two types of travel awards: (1) one free round-trip after the accumulation of 16 credits within 24 months and (2) a companion pass for travelers who accumulated 100 credits within a 12-month period—the companion pass was for unlimited free round-trip travel, provided the Rapid Rewards member purchased a ticket or used a free award ticket and the companion Rapid Rewards member flew on the same flight. Award tickets were automatically generated when earned, valid for 12 months after issuance, and subject to a limited number of blackout dates around major holidays. Rapid Rewards members who flew 32 qualifying flights within a 12-month period received priority boarding privileges for a year. In 2007, Southwest customers redeemed approximately 2.8 million award tickets and flights on companion passes, accounting for about 6.2 percent of the passengers on Southwest flights.

Exhibit 6 Airports and Cities Served by Southwest Airlines, May 2008

Southwest's Top 10 Airports	Daily Departures	Number of Gates	Nonstop Cities Served
Las Vegas	240	21	55
Chicago Midway	225	29	47
Phoenix	198	24	43
Baltimore/Washington	166	26	38
Oakland	134	13	21
Houston Hobby	145	17	29
Dallas (Love Field)	140	14	16
Los Angeles	127	11	19
Orlando	112	14	37
San Diego	108	10	19

Other Airports Served by Southwest Airlines			
Albany	El Paso	Manchester, NH	Reno/Tahoe
Albuquerque	Fort Lauderdale	Midland/Odessa	Sacramento
Amarillo	Fort Myers/Naples	New Orleans	St. Louis
Austin	Harlingen/South Padre Island	Norfolk	Salt Lake City
Birmingham	Hartford/Springfield	Oklahoma City	San Antonio
Boise	Indianapolis	Omaha	San Jose
Buffalo	Long Island/Islip	Ontario, CA	Seattle
Burbank	Jackson, MS	Orange County, CA	Spokane
Cleveland	Jacksonville	Philadelphia	Tampa
Columbus, OH	Kansas City	Pittsburgh	Tucson
Corpus Christi	Little Rock	Portland OR	Tulsa
Denver	Louisville	Providence	Washington, DC (Dulles)
Detroit Metro	Lubbock	Raleigh-Durham	West Palm Beach

Source: Southwest Airlines.

Customer Service and Customer Satisfaction

Southwest's approach to delivering good customer service and creating customer satisfaction was predicated on presenting a happy face to passengers, displaying a fun-loving attitude, and doing things in a manner calculated to make sure passengers had a positive flying experience. The company made a special effort to employ gate personnel who enjoyed interacting with customers, had good interpersonal skills, and displayed cheery, outgoing personalities. A number of Southwest's gate personnel let their wit and sense of humor show by sometimes entertaining those in the gate area with trivia questions or contests such as "Who has the biggest hole in their sock?" Apart from greeting passengers coming onto planes and assisting them in finding open seats and stowing baggage, flight attendants were encouraged to be engaging, converse and joke with passengers, and go about their tasks in ways that made passengers smile. On some flights, attendants sang announcements to passengers on takeoff and landing. On one flight while passengers were boarding, an attendant with bunny ears popped out of an overhead bin exclaiming "Surprise!" The repertoires used to amuse passengers varied from flight crew to flight crew.

Both Herb Kelleher and Colleen Barrett had made a point of sending congratulatory notes to employees when the company received letters from customers complimenting particular Southwest employees; complaint letters were seen as learning opportunities for employees and reasons to consider making adjustments. Barrett provided the following policy guidelines to employees regarding how far to go in trying to please customers:

> No Employee will ever be punished for using good judgment and good old common sense when trying to accommodate a Customer—no matter what our rules are.[17]
>
> When you empower People to make a positive difference every day, you allow them to decide. Most guidelines are written to be broken as long as the Employee is leaning toward the Customer. We follow the Golden Rule and try to do the right thing and think about our Customer.[18]

Southwest executives believed that conveying a friendly, fun-loving spirit to customers was the key to competitive advantage. As one Southwest manager put it, "Our fares can be matched; our airplanes and routes can be copied. But we pride ourselves on our customer service."[19] The company's mission statement, revised in 2008, highlighted its customer service commitment:

> The mission of Southwest Airlines is dedication to the highest quality of Customer Service delivered with a sense of warmth, friendliness, individual pride, and Company Spirit.

In 2007, Southwest did an "extreme gate makeover" to improve the airport experience of customers. The makeover included adding (1) a business-focused area with padded seats, tables with power outlets, power stations with stools, and a flat-screen TV with news programming and (2) a family-focused area with smaller tables and chairs, power stations for charging electrical devices, and kid-friendly programming on a flat screen TV.

Marketing and Promotion

Southwest was continually on the lookout for novel ways to tell its story, make its distinctive persona come alive, and strike a chord in the minds of air travelers. Many of its print ads and billboards were deliberately unconventional and attention-getting so as to create and reinforce the company's maverick, fun-loving, and combative image. Some previous campaigns had included such tag lines as "*The* Low-Fare Airline" and "The All-Time On-Time Airline"; others touted the company's Triple Crown awards. One of the company's billboard campaigns promoted the frequency of the company's flights with such phrases as "Austin Auften," "Phoenix Phrequently," and "L.A. A.S.A.P." Each holiday season since 1985 Southwest had run a "Christmas card" ad on TV featuring children and their families from the Ronald McDonald Houses and Southwest employees. Fresh advertising campaigns were launched periodically—Exhibit 7 shows four representative ads.

In 2002, Southwest began changing the look of its planes, updating its somewhat drab gold/orange/red scheme to a much fresher and brighter canyon blue/red/gold/orange scheme—see Exhibit 8.

Other Strategy Elements

Southwest's strategy included several other elements:

- *Gradual expansion into new geographic markets*—Southwest generally added one or two new cities to its route schedule annually, preferring to saturate the market for daily flights to the cities/airports it currently served before entering new markets. In selecting new cities, Southwest looked for city pairs that could generate substantial amounts of both business and leisure traffic. Management believed that having numerous flights flying the same routes appealed to business travelers looking for convenient flight times and the ability to catch another flight if they unexpectedly ran late.
- *Adding flights in areas where rivals were cutting back service*—When rivals cut back flights to cities that Southwest served, Southwest often moved in with more flights of its own, believing its lower fares would attract more passengers. When Midway Airlines ceased operations in November 1990, Southwest moved in overnight and quickly instituted flights to Chicago's Midway Airport. Southwest was a first-mover in adding flights on routes where rivals had cut their offerings following the September 11, 2001, terrorist attacks. When American Airlines closed its hubs in Nashville and San Jose, Southwest immediately increased the number of its flights into and out of both locations. When US Airways trimmed its flight schedule for Philadelphia and Pittsburgh, Southwest promptly boosted its flights into and out of those airports. Southwest initiated service to Denver when United, beset

Exhibit 7 Four Samples of Southwest's Ads

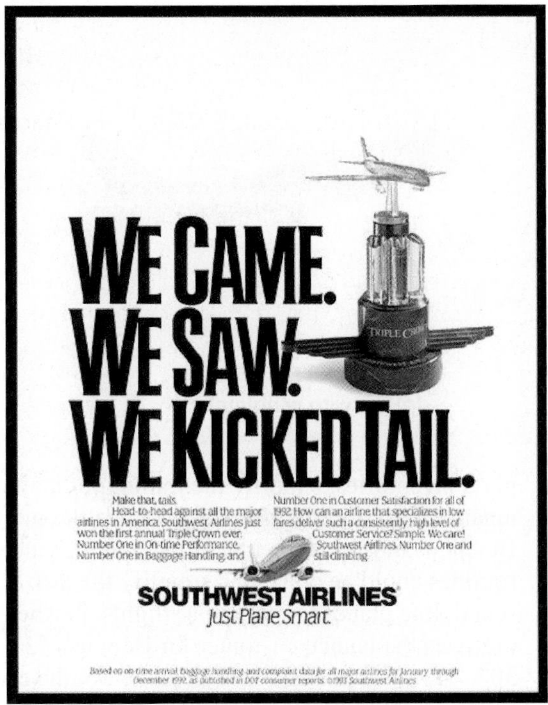

No matter what the competition may come up with, Southwest Airlines' everyday low unrestricted fares are still lower than the Big Three. That's a fact that can save you a lot of money every day.

And unlike our competitors, with our low unrestricted fares, we don't charge you a penalty when your plans change. Which makes our fares the smart choice for you and your company. Always have been. Always will be.

SOUTHWEST AIRLINES
Just Plane Smart.
1-800-I-FLY-SWA
(1-800-435-9792)

CAN YOU NAME
THE AIRLINE
WITH LOW FARES
ON EVERY SEAT
OF EVERY FLIGHT,
EVERYWHERE
IT FLIES?

Exhibit 8 Southwest's New Look and Aircraft Equipped with Winglets

Old Color Scheme (plane without winglets)

New Color Scheme (plane with winglets)

with financial difficulties, cut back operations at its big Denver hub.

- *Curtailing flights on marginally profitable routes where numerous seats often went unfilled and shifting planes to routes with good growth opportunities*—Management was attracted to this strategy element because it enabled Southwest to grow revenues and profits without having to add so many new planes to its fleet.
- *Putting strong emphasis on safety, high-quality maintenance, and reliable operations.*

Southwest management believed the company's low-fare strategy, coupled with frequent flights and friendly service, delivered "more value for less money" to customers rather than "less value for less money." Kelleher said, "Everybody values a very good service provided at a very reasonable price."[20]

SOUTHWEST'S EFFORTS TO EXECUTE ITS LOW-FARE STRATEGY

Southwest management fully understood that low fares necessitated zealous pursuit of low operating costs and had, over the years, instituted a number of practices to keep its costs below those of rival carriers:

- The company operated only one type of aircraft—the Boeing 737—to minimize the size of spare parts inventories, simplify the training of maintenance and repair personnel, improve the proficiency and speed with which maintenance routines could be done, and simplify the task of scheduling planes for particular flights. Furthermore, as the launch customer for Boeing's 737-300, 737-500, and 737-700 models, Southwest acquired its new aircraft at favorable prices. See Exhibit 9 for statistics on Southwest's aircraft fleet.
- Southwest was the first major airline to introduce ticketless travel (eliminating the need to print and process paper tickets) and also the first to allow customers to make reservations and purchase tickets at the company's Web site (thus bypassing the need to pay commissions to travel agents for handling the ticketing process and reducing staffing requirements at Southwest's reservation centers). Selling a ticket on its Web site cost Southwest roughly $1, versus $3–$4 for a ticket booked through its own internal reservation system and as much as $15 for tickets for business travelers purchased through travel agents and professional business travel partners. Ticketless travel accounted for more than 95 percent of all sales in 2007, and nearly 74 percent of Southwest's revenues were generated through sales at its Web site.
- The company de-emphasized flights to congested airports, stressing instead serving airports near major metropolitan areas and in medium-sized cities. This helped produce better-than-average on-time performance and reduce the fuel costs

Exhibit 9 Southwest's Aircraft Fleet as of May 2008

Type of Aircraft *	Number	Seats
Boeing 737-300	189	137
Boeing 737-500	25	122
Boeing 737-700	313	137

Other Statistical Facts

Average age of aircraft fleet—close to 9 years

Average aircraft trip length—631 miles and an average duration of 1 hour and 51 minutes

Average aircraft utilization in 2008—7 flights per day and about 13 hours of flight time

Fleet size—1990: 106, 1995: 224, 2000: 344, 2008: 527

Firm orders for new aircraft—2008: 29, 2009: 20, 2010: 10, 2011–2014: 49

*In each case, Southwest was Boeing's launch customer for this model.

associated with planes sitting in line on crowded taxiways or circling airports waiting for clearance to land; in addition, it allowed the company to avoid paying the higher landing fees and terminal gate costs at such high-traffic airports as Atlanta's Hartsfield International, Chicago's O'Hare, and Dallas–Fort Worth (DFW) where landing slots were controlled and rationed to those airlines willing to pay the high fees. In several cases, Southwest was able to compete on the perimeters of several big metropolitan areas by flying into nearby airports with less congested air space. For example, Southwest drew some Boston-area passengers away from Boston's Logan International by initiating service into nearby Providence, Rhode Island, and Manchester, New Hampshire. Southwest's preference for less congested airports also helped minimize total travel time for passengers—driving to the airport, parking, ticketing, boarding, and flight time.

- Southwest's point-to-point scheduling of flights was more cost-efficient than the hub-and-spoke systems used by rival airlines. Hub-and-spoke systems involved passengers on many different flights coming in from spoke locations (or perhaps another hub) to a central airport or hub within a short span of time and then connecting to an outgoing flight to their destination (a spoke location or another hub). Most flights arrived and departed a hub across a two-hour window, creating big peak-valley swings in airport personnel workloads and gate utilization—airport personnel and gate areas were very busy when hub operations were in full swing and then were underutilized in the interval awaiting the next round of inbound/outbound flights. In contrast, Southwest's point-to-point routes permitted scheduling aircraft so as to minimize the time aircraft were at the gate, currently approximately 25 minutes, thereby reducing the number of aircraft and gate facilities that would otherwise be required. Furthermore, with a relatively even flow of incoming/outgoing flights and gate traffic, Southwest could staff its terminal operations to handle a fairly steady workload across a day, whereas hub-and-spoke operators had to staff their operations to serve three or four daily peak periods.
- To economize on the amount of time it took terminal personnel to check passengers in and to simplify the whole task of making reservations, Southwest dispensed with the practice of assigning each passenger a reserved seat. Instead, for many years, passengers were given color-coded plastic cards with the letters A, B, or C when they checked in at the boarding gate. Passengers then boarded in groups, according to the color/letter on their card, sitting in whatever seat was open when they got on the plane—a procedure described by some as a "cattle call." Passengers who were particular about where they sat had to arrive at the gate early to get boarding cards and then had to make sure to be up front when it was their group's turn to board. In 2002, Southwest abandoned the use of plastic cards and began printing a big, bold A, B, or C on the boarding pass when the passenger checked in at the ticket counter; passengers then boarded in groups according to the letter on their boarding pass. In 2007–2008, in order to significantly reduce the time that passengers spent standing in line waiting for their group to board, Southwest introduced an enhanced boarding method that automatically assigned each passenger a specific number within the passenger's boarding group at the time of check-in; passengers then boarded the aircraft in that numerical order. All

passengers could check in online up to 24 hours before departure time and print out a boarding pass, thus bypassing counter check-in (unless they wished to check baggage).

- Southwest flight attendants were responsible for cleaning up trash left by deplaning passengers and otherwise getting the plane presentable for passengers to board for the next flight. (Until recently, other carriers had cleaning crews come on board to perform this function; however, recurring losses at many airlines in 2001–2005 forced stringent cost-cutting measures, prompting most all airlines to cut out the use of cleaning crews and copy Southwest's practice.)
- Southwest did not have a first-class section in any of its planes and had no fancy clubs for its frequent flyers to relax in at terminals. No meals had ever been served on Southwest flights; passengers were offered beverages and snacks (a practice that made reprovisioning planes simple and quick). During 2001–2005, virtually all airlines discontinued meal service on domestic flights (except for first-class passengers) as a way to cut expenses; a few of Southwest's rivals had begun charging passengers $2 for coffee, soft drinks, and bottled water served during flights.
- Southwest offered passengers no baggage transfer services to other carriers—passengers with checked baggage who were connecting to other carriers to reach their destination were responsible for picking up their luggage at Southwest's baggage claim and then getting it to the check-in facilities of the connecting carrier. (Southwest only booked tickets involving its own flights; customers connecting to flights on other carriers had to book such tickets either through travel agents or the connecting airline.) Starting in 2008, Southwest's airline rivals began charging $25 to $50 for a second checked bag, and a few had instituted fees for the first checked bag.
- In mid-2001 Southwest implemented use of new software that significantly decreased the time required to generate optimal crew schedules and help improve on-time performance.
- Starting in 2001, Southwest began converting from cloth to leather seats; the team of Southwest employees that investigated the economics of the conversion concluded that an all-leather interior would be more durable and easier to maintain, more than justifying the higher initial costs.
- Southwest was a first-mover among major U.S. airlines in employing fuel hedging and derivative contracts to counteract rising prices for crude oil and jet fuel. Since 1998, the company's aggressive fuel hedging strategy had produced fuel savings of about $3.5 billion over what it would have spent had it paid the industry's average price for jet fuel. These savings had been a huge contributor to the company's ongoing profitability; for example, in the second quarter of 2008, Southwest realized $511 million in favorable cash settlements from derivative contracts and reported net earnings of $321 million. (By comparison, Delta had hedged 49 percent of its fuel requirements and realized gains of $313 million on its fuel hedge contracts in the 2008 second quarter.) Southwest had derivative contracts for approximately 80 percent of its third-quarter 2008 estimated fuel consumption at an average crude-equivalent price of approximately $61 per barrel (compared to approximately 90 percent at approximately $51 per barrel for third-quarter 2007); crude oil prices were in the $110–$130 range in July–August 2008, but fell to the $90–$95 range in September 2008. Moreover, Southwest had derivative contracts in place for approximately 80 percent of its estimated fuel consumption for the fourth quarter of 2008 at an average crude-equivalent price of approximately $58 per barrel; approximately 70 percent in 2009 at an average crude-equivalent price of $66 per barrel; approximately 40 percent in 2010 at an average crude-equivalent price of approximately $81 per barrel; and over 20 percent in 2011 and 2012 at an average crude-equivalent price of approximately $77 and $76 per barrel, respectively.
- To enhance the performance and efficiency of its aircraft fleet, Southwest had recently added vertical winglets on the wing tips of most all its planes and had begun ordering new planes equipped with winglets (see Exhibit 8). These winglets reduced lift drag, allowed aircraft to climb more steeply and reach higher flight levels quicker, improved cruising performance, helped extend engine life and reduce maintenance costs, and reduced fuel burn. In 2007, Southwest partnered with Naverus, an aviation consulting firm, to develop new flight systems and procedures that would result in its planes being able to reduce fuel consumption, lower

emissions, and curtail noise while simultaneously taking better advantage of the high-performance characteristics of its aircraft.

- In 2007–2008, Southwest began investing in technology and software to replace its ticketless system and its back-office accounting, payroll, and human resource information systems, so as to enhance data flow, operational efficiency, and customer service capability.

Southwest's operating costs were consistently the lowest of the major U.S. airline carriers—see Exhibit 10. Exhibit 11 shows a detailed breakdown of Southwest's operating costs for the period 1995–2007.

SOUTHWEST'S PEOPLE MANAGEMENT PRACTICES AND CULTURE

Whereas the litany at many companies was that customers come first, at Southwest the operative principle was that "employees come first and customers come second." The high strategic priority placed on employees reflected management's belief that delivering superior service required employees who not only were passionate about their jobs but also knew the company was genuinely concerned for their well-being and committed to providing them with job security. Southwest's thesis was simple: Keep employees happy—then they will keep customers happy. (The company changed the personnel department's name to the People Department in 1989.)

In Southwest's 2000 annual report, senior management explained why employees were the company's greatest asset:

> Our people are warm, caring and compassionate and willing to do whatever it takes to bring the Freedom to Fly to their fellow Americans. They take pride in doing well for themselves by doing good for others. They have built a unique and powerful culture that demonstrates that the only way to accomplish our mission to make air travel affordable for others, while ensuring ample profitability, job security, and plentiful Profitsharing for ourselves, is to keep our costs low and Customer Service quality high.
>
> At Southwest, our People are our greatest assets, which is why we devote so much time and energy to hiring great People with winning attitudes. Because we are well known as an excellent place to work with great career opportunities and a secure future, lots of People want to work for Southwest. . . . Once hired, we provide a nurturing and supportive work environment that gives our Employees the freedom to be creative, have fun, and make a positive difference. Although we offer competitive compensation packages, it's our Employees' sense of ownership, pride in team accomplishments, and enhanced job satisfaction that keep our Culture and Southwest Spirit alive and why we continue to produce winning seasons.

CEO Gary Kelly echoed the views of his predecessors: "Our People are our single greatest strength and our most enduring long term competitive advantage."[21]

Recruiting, Screening, and Hiring

Southwest hired employees for attitude and trained for skills. Kelleher explained:

> We can train people to do things where skills are concerned. But there is one capability we do not have and that is to change a person's attitude. So we prefer an unskilled person with a good attitude . . . [to] a highly skilled person with a bad attitude.[22]

Management believed that delivering superior service came from having employees who treated customers warmly and courteously; the company wanted employees who genuinely believed that customers were important, not employees who had merely been trained to *act* like customers were important. The belief at Southwest was that superior, hospitable service and a fun-loving spirit flowed from the heart and soul of employees who themselves were fun-loving and spirited, who liked their jobs and the company they worked for, and who were also confident and empowered to do their jobs as they saw fit (rather than being governed by strict rules and procedures).

Southwest recruited employees by means of newspaper ads, career fairs, and Internet job listings; a number of candidates applied because of Southwest's reputation as one of the best companies to work for in America and because they were impressed by their experiences as a customer on Southwest flights. Recruitment ads were designed to capture the attention of people thought to possess Southwest's "personality profile." For instance, one ad showed Herb Kelleher impersonating Elvis Presley and had the following headline: "Work In A

Exhibit 10 Comparative Operating Cost Statistics, Major U.S. Airlines, 1995, 2000, and 2005—First Quarter 2008 (in cents per passenger seat mile)

		Costs Incurred per Passenger Revenue Mile*									
		Salaries and Fringe Benefits									
	Year	Pilots and Copilots	All Employees	Fuel and Oil	Maintenance	Rentals	Landing Fees	Advertising	General and Administrative	Other Operating Expenses	Total Operating Expenses
America West[†]	**1995**	0.64¢	3.01¢	1.40¢	0.94¢	1.30¢	0.23¢	0.23¢	0.84¢	2.62¢	10.57¢
	2000	0.81	3.14	2.18	1.82	1.73	0.18	0.14	0.55	2.41	12.15
	2005	0.77	3.06	3.32	1.46	0.44	0.23	0.04	0.82	5.13	14.50
	2006	0.76	3.32	3.85	1.41	0.47	0.23	0.05	1.27	5.57	16.15
	2007	0.76	3.28	3.87	1.55	0.55	0.23	0.03	0.43	5.65	15.58
	Q1 2008	—	—	—	—	—	—	—	—	—	—
American Airlines	**1995**	0.94¢	5.59¢	1.53¢	1.34¢	0.59¢	0.22¢	0.19¢	1.14¢	3.65¢	14.25¢
	2000	1.16	5.77	2.04	1.90	0.48	0.23	0.18	0.58	3.30	14.48
	2005	0.90	4.65	3.67	1.42	0.41	0.32	0.10	0.95	3.66	15.18
	2006	0.85	4.64	4.15	1.46	0.42	0.31	0.11	0.80	3.64	15.55
	2007	0.84	4.63	4.34	1.48	0.42	0.30	0.12	0.91	3.78	15.98
	Q1 2008	0.90	4.79	5.72	1.75	0.38	0.32	0.13	0.85	4.24	18.18
Continental Air Lines	**1995**	0.95¢	3.69¢	1.67¢	1.50¢	1.25¢	0.27¢	0.25¢	0.56¢	3.68¢	12.87¢
	2000	1.25	4.43	2.18	1.42	1.17	0.24	0.09	0.59	3.57	13.70
	2005	0.79	3.85	3.42	1.18	0.91	0.34	0.13	0.82	5.74	16.38
	2006	0.71	3.76	3.82	1.20	0.87	0.33	0.12	1.03	5.38	16.51
	2007	0.75	3.85	3.97	1.24	0.81	0.30	0.13	1.09	5.17	16.56
	Q1 2008	0.79	3.82	5.26	1.34	0.85	0.33	0.14	0.92	6.15	18.81
Delta Air Lines	**1995**	1.27¢	4.97¢	1.70¢	1.16¢	0.71¢	0.30¢	0.18¢	0.43¢	4.07¢	13.53¢
	2000	1.27	5.08	1.73	1.41	0.54	0.22	0.12	0.74	3.03	12.85
	2005	0.93	4.31	3.68	1.10	0.38	0.22	0.16	0.84	6.01	16.68
	2006	0.73	3.81	4.18	1.15	0.21	0.20	0.15	0.94	6.87	17.50
	2007	0.73	3.64	4.32	1.21	0.15	0.20	0.17	1.18	6.75	17.63
	Q1 2008	0.83	3.95	5.67	1.27	0.21	0.21	0.12	1.07	8.45	20.95

Northwest Airlines	**1995**	1.21¢	4.84¢	1.73¢	1.39¢	0.58¢	0.37¢	0.20¢	0.52¢	3.14¢	12.77¢
	2000	1.01	4.76	2.35	1.55	0.53	0.31	0.17	0.55	2.77	12.99
	2005	0.94	5.07	4.01	1.54	0.57	0.38	0.12	0.58	5.13	17.40
	2006	0.73	3.83	4.56	1.38	0.31	0.48	0.10	0.51	5.02	16.20
	2007	0.78	3.60	4.47	1.32	0.28	0.33	0.09	0.71	5.09	15.90
	Q1 2008	0.74	3.79	5.94	1.48	0.26	0.31	0.08	0.85	6.54	19.25
Southwest Airlines	**1995**	0.92¢	3.94¢	1.56¢	1.21¢	0.79¢	0.35¢	0.41¢	1.09¢	1.56¢	10.91¢
	2000	0.86	4.22	1.95	1.22	0.48	0.31	0.35	1.42	0.96	10.91
	2005	1.18	4.70	2.44	1.17	0.31	0.34	0.29	0.73	1.23	11.21
	2006	1.19	4.72	3.37	1.13	0.27	0.33	0.27	0.70	1.24	12.03
	2007	1.22	4.67	3.71	1.27	0.26	0.34	0.26	0.80	1.20	12.53
	Q1 2008	1.28	4.80	4.54	1.26	0.27	0.43	0.31	0.90	1.35	13.85
United Air Lines	**1995**	0.86¢	4.73¢	1.51¢	1.51¢	0.90¢	0.29¢	0.17¢	0.53¢	2.92¢	12.58¢
	2000	1.15	5.75	1.98	1.84	0.73	0.28	0.21	0.76	3.09	14.65
	2005	0.62	3.72	3.53	1.60	0.35	0.30	0.16	0.60	5.09	15.35
	2006	0.61	3.84	4.11	1.71	0.35	0.30	0.09	0.92	4.76	16.07
	2007	0.62	3.86	4.26	1.87	0.35	0.29	0.07	0.91	4.65	16.27
	Q1 2008	0.69	4.16	5.85	2.13	0.34	0.32	0.07	1.00	5.26	19.13
US Airways‡	**1995**	1.55¢	7.53¢	1.59¢	2.09¢	1.05¢	0.29¢	0.13¢	0.73¢	4.32¢	17.73¢
	2000	1.36	7.59	2.44	2.30	0.97	0.28	0.19	1.10	4.81	19.68
	2005	0.78	3.74	3.89	1.50	1.06	0.31	0.06	0.66	7.27	18.49
	2006	0.73	3.85	4.30	1.62	1.08	0.28	0.05	1.04	7.82	20.03
	2007	0.71	4.25	4.45	1.71	1.12	0.26	0.04	0.86	7.46	20.14
	Q1 2008	0.83	4.13	5.63	2.11	1.26	0.24	0.03	0.25	7.81	21.45

*Costs per passenger revenue mile represent the costs per ticketed passenger per mile flown; it is derived by dividing the company's total expenses in each of the cost categories by the total number of miles flown by all ticketed passengers—thus if there are 100 ticketed passengers on a flight that travels 500 miles, the number of passenger revenue miles for that flight is 100 x 500 (or 50,000).

†Merged with US Airways in 2005; combined reporting began in October 2007.

‡Merged with America West in September 2005; combined reporting began in October 2007.

Source: U.S. Department of Transportation, Bureau of Transportation Statistics, Air Carrier Statistics Form 298C Summary Data and Form 41, Schedules P-6, P-12, P-51, and P-52.

Exhibit 11 Trends in Southwest Airline's Operating Expenses per Average Seat Mile, 1995–2007

	Costs per Available Seat Mile								
Expense Category	2007	2006	2005	2004	2003	2002	2001	2000	1995
Salaries, wages, bonuses, and benefits	3.22¢	3.29¢	3.27¢	3.18¢	3.10¢	2.89¢	2.84¢	2.81¢	2.40¢
Fuel and oil	2.55	2.31	1.58	1.30	1.16	1.11	1.18	1.34	1.01
Maintenance materials and repairs	0.62	0.51	0 .52	0.60	0.60	0.57	0.61	0.63	0.60
Aircraft rentals	0.16	0.17	0.19	0.23	0.25	0.27	0.29	0.33	0.47
Landing fees and other rentals	0.56	0.53	0.53	0.53	0.52	0.50	0.48	0.44	0.44
Depreciation	0.56	0.56	0.55	0.56	0.53	0.52	0.49	0.47	0.43
Other expenses	1.43	1.43	1.41	1.37	1.44	1.55	1.65	1.71	1.72
Total	9.10¢	8.80¢	8.05¢	7.70¢	7.60¢	7.41¢	7.54¢	7.73¢	7.07¢

Note: Figures in this exhibit differ from those for Southwest in Exhibit 9 because the cost figures in Exhibit 9 are based on *cost per passenger revenue mile,* whereas the cost figures in this exhibit are based on *costs per available seat mile.* Costs per revenue passenger mile represent the costs per ticketed passenger per mile flown, whereas costs per available seat mile are the *costs per seat per mile flown (irrespective of whether the seat was occupied or not).*

Source: Company 10-K reports and annual reports.

Place Where Elvis Has Been Spotted." The body of the ad read:

> The qualifications? It helps to be outgoing. Maybe even a bit off center. And be prepared to stay for a while. After all, we have the lowest employee turnover rate in the industry. If this sounds good to you, just phone our jobline or send your resume. Attention Elvis.[23]

Colleen Barrett elaborated on what the company looked for in screening candidates for job openings:

> We hire People to live the Southwest Way [see Exhibit 12]. They must possess a Warrior Spirit, lead with a Servant's Heart, and have a Fun-LUVing attitude. We hire People who fight to win, work hard, are dedicated, and have a passion for Customer Service. We won't hire People if something about their behavior won't be a Cultural fit. We hire the best. When our new hires walk through the door, our message to them is you are starting the flight of your life.[24]

All job applications were processed through the People and Leadership Development Department.

Screening Candidates In hiring for jobs that involved personal contact with passengers, the company looked for people-oriented applicants who were extroverted and had a good sense of humor. It tried to identify candidates with a knack for reading peoples' emotions and responding in a genuinely caring, empathetic manner. Southwest wanted employees to deliver the kind of service that showed they truly enjoyed meeting people, being around passengers, and doing their job, as opposed to delivering the kind of service that came across as being forced or taught. According to Kelleher, "We are interested in people who externalize, who focus on other people, who are motivated to help other people. We are not interested in navel gazers."[25] Southwest was drawn to candidates who not only presented a "whistle while you work" attitude but also appeared likely to exercise initiative, work harmoniously with fellow employees, and be community-spirited.

Southwest did not use personality tests to screen job applicants, nor did it ask applicants what they would or should do in certain hypothetical situations. Rather, the hiring staff at Southwest analyzed each job category to determine the specific behaviors, knowledge, and motivations that job holders needed and then tried to find candidates with the desired traits—a process called targeted selection. A trait common to all job categories was teamwork; a trait deemed critical for pilots and flight attendants was judgment. In exploring an applicant's aptitude for teamwork, interviewers often asked applicants to tell them about a time in a prior job when they went out of their way to help a coworker or to explain how they had handled conflict with a coworker. Another frequent question was "What was your most embarrassing moment?" The thesis here was that having applicants talk about their past behaviors provided good clues about their future behaviors.

To test for unselfishness, Southwest interviewing teams typically gave a group of potential employees ample time to prepare five-minute presentations about themselves; during the presentations in an informal conversational setting, interviewers watched the audience to see who was absorbed in polishing their presentations and who was listening attentively, enjoying the stories being told, and applauding the efforts of the presenters. Those who were emotionally engaged in hearing the presenters and giving encouragement were deemed more apt to be team players than those who were focused on looking good themselves. All applicants for flight attendant positions were put through such a presentation exercise before an interview panel consisting of customers, experienced flight attendants, and members of the People Department. Flight attendant candidates who got through the group presentation interviews then had to complete a three-on-one interview conducted by a recruiter, a supervisor from the hiring section of the People Department, and a Southwest flight attendant; following this interview, the three-person panel tried to reach a consensus on whether to recommend or drop the candidate.

In 2007, Southwest received 329,200 résumés and hired 4,200 new employees.

Training

Apart from the FAA-mandated training for certain employees, training activities at Southwest were designed and conducted by Southwest's University for People. The curriculum included courses for new recruits, employees, and managers. Learning was viewed as a never-ending process for all company personnel; the expectation was that each employee should be an "intentional learner," looking to grow and develop not just from occasional classes taken at Southwest's festive University for People learning center but also from their everyday on-the-job experiences.

Southwest's University for People conducted courses on safety, communications, stress management, career development, performance appraisal, decision making, leadership, corporate culture, and employee relations. Leadership courses for managers emphasized a management style based on coaching, empowering, and encouraging, rather than supervising or enforcing rules and regulations. One of the keystone course offerings for managers was Leadership Southwest Style, which made extensive use of the Myers-Briggs personality assessment to help managers understand the "why" behind coworkers' behaviors and to learn how to build trust, empathize, resolve conflicts, and do a better job of communicating. From time to time supervisors and executives attended courses on corporate culture, intended to help instill, ingrain, and nurture such cultural themes as teamwork, trust, harmony, and diversity. All employees who came into contact with customers, including pilots, received customer care training.

Orientation for new employees included videos on Southwest's history, an overview of the airline industry and the competitive challenges that Southwest faced, and an introduction to Southwest's culture and management practices. The culture introduction included a video called *The Southwest Shuffle* that featured hundreds of Southwest employees rapping about the fun they had on their jobs. (At many Southwest gatherings, it was common for a group of employees to do the Southwest Shuffle, with the remaining attendees cheering and clapping.) There were also exercises that demonstrated the role of creativity and teamwork and a scavenger hunt in which new hires were given a time line with specific dates in Southwest's history and asked to fill in the missing details by viewing the memorabilia decorating the corridors of the Dallas headquarters and getting information from people working in various offices. Much of the indoctrination of new employees into the company's culture was done by coworkers and the employee's supervisor. Southwest made active use of a one-year probationary employment period to help ensure that new employees fit in with its culture and adequately embraced the company's cultural values.

The OnBoarding Program for Newly Hired Employees Southwest had an employee orientation program called OnBoarding designed to provide new hires with information and assistance from the time they were selected until the end of their first year. During their first 30 days at Southwest, new employees could access an interactive online tool—OnBoarding Online Orientation—to learn about the company.

Promotion

Approximately 80 to 90 percent of Southwest's supervisory positions were filled internally, reflecting management's belief that people who had "been there and done that" would be more likely to appreciate and understand the demands that people under them were experiencing and also be more likely to enjoy the respect of their peers and higher-level managers. Employees could either apply for supervisory positions or be recommended by their present supervisor. New appointees for low-level management positions attended a three-day class called Leading with Integrity, aimed at developing leadership and communication skills. Employees being considered for managerial positions of large operations (deemed "Up and Coming Leaders") received training in every department of the company over a six-month period in which they continued to perform their current job. At the end of the six-month period, candidates were provided with 360-degree feedback from department heads, peers, and subordinates; representatives of the People Department analyzed the feedback in deciding on the specific assignment of each candidate.[26]

Compensation

Southwest's pay scales tended to be above the industry average—sometimes even at or near the top of the industry, and the company offered good benefit packages relative to other airlines. In 2008, median hourly pay at Southwest was in the neighborhood of $31 for flight attendants, $40 for aircraft mechanics and service technicians, $24 for customer service representatives and baggage handlers, $20 for cargo and freight agents, $95 for flight engineers and copilots, and $135 for commercial pilots.[27] Pay scales for the company's 6,800 ramp agents, operations agents, provision agents, and freight agents—all of whom were represented by the Transport Workers Union—were said to be the highest in U.S. airline industry.[28] Southwest was also an industry leader in total compensation of pilots and flight attendants.

Southwest introduced a profit-sharing plan for senior employees in 1973, the first such plan in the airline industry. By the mid-1990s the plan had been extended to cover most Southwest employees. As of 2008, Southwest had stock option programs for various employee groups, a 401(k) employee savings plans that included company-matching contributions, and a profit-sharing plan covering virtually all employees that consisted of a money purchase defined contribution plan and an employee stock purchase plan. Company contributions to employee 410(k) and profit-sharing plans totaled $241.5 million in 2000, $264 million in 2005, $301 million in 2006, and $279 million in 2007; in recent years, these payments had represented 8 to 12 percent of base pay. Employees participating in stock purchases via payroll deduction bought 677,000 shares in 1998, 686,000 shares in 2000, 1.5 million shares in 2005, and 1.3 million shares in 2007 at prices equal to 90 percent of the market value at the end of each monthly purchase period. Southwest employees owned about 10 percent of Southwest's outstanding shares and held options to buy some 28.5 million additional shares.

Employee Relations

About 80 percent of Southwest's 34,300 employees belonged to a union, making it one of the most highly unionized U.S. airlines. The Teamsters Union represented Southwest's airline mechanics, stock clerks, and aircraft cleaners; the Transport Workers Union represented flight attendants; Local 555 of the Transport Workers Union represented baggage handlers, ground crews, and provisioning employees; and the International Association of Machinists represented the customer service and reservation employees. There was one in-house union—the Southwest Airline Pilots Association that represented the company's 5,400 pilots. Despite having sometimes spirited disagreements over particular issues, Southwest and the unions representing its employee groups had harmonious and non-adversarial relationships for the most part—the company had experienced only one brief strike by machinists in the early 1980s.

Management encouraged union members and negotiators to research their pressing issues and to conduct employee surveys before each contract negotiation. Southwest's contracts with the unions representing its employees were relatively free of restrictive work rules and narrow job classifications that might impede worker productivity. All of the contracts allowed any qualified employee to perform any function—thus, pilots, ticket agents, and gate personnel could help load and unload baggage when needed and flight attendants could pick up trash and make flight cabins more presentable for passengers boarding the next flight.

In 2000–2001, the company had contentious negotiations with Local 555 of the Transport Workers Union (representing about 5,300 Southwest employees) over a new wage and benefits package; the previous contract had become open for renegotiation in December 1999 and a tentative agreement reached at the end of 2000 was rejected by 64 percent of the union members who voted. A memo from Kelleher to TWU representatives said, "The cost and structure of the TWU 555 negotiating committee's proposal would seriously undermine the competitive strength of Southwest Airlines; endanger our ability to grow; threaten the value of our employees' profit-sharing; require us to contract out work in order to remain competitive; and threaten our 29-year history of job security for our employees." In a union newsletter in early 2001, the president of the TWU said, "We asked for a decent living wage and benefits to support our families, and were told of how unworthy and how greedy we were." The ongoing dispute resulted in informational picket lines in March 2001 at several Southwest locations, the first picketing since 1980. Later in 2001, with the help of the National Mediation Board, Southwest and the TWU reached an agreement covering Southwest's ramp, operations, and provisioning employees.

Prior to the September 11, 2001, terrorist attacks, Southwest's pilots were somewhat restive about their base pay relative to pilots at other U.S. airlines. The maximum pay for Southwest's 3,700-plus pilots (before profit-sharing bonuses) was $148,000, versus maximums of $290,000 for United's pilots, $262,000 for Delta's pilots, $206,000 for American's pilots, and $199,000 for Continental's pilots.[29] Moreover, some veteran Southwest employees were grumbling about staff shortages in certain locations (to hold down labor costs) and cracks in the company's close-knit family culture due to the influx of so many new employees over the past several years. A number of employees who had accepted lower pay because of Southwest's underdog status were said to feel entitled to "big airline" pay now that Southwest had emerged as a major U.S. carrier.[30] However, when airline traffic dropped precipitously following 9/11, airlines won big wage and salary concessions from unions representing pilots and other airline workers; moreover, about 1 in 5 airline jobs—some 120,000 in all—were eliminated. In 2006, a senior Boeing 737 pilot at Delta Air Lines working a normal 65-hour month made $116,200 annually, down 26 percent from pre-9/11 wages. A comparable pilot at United Airlines earned $102,200, down 34 percent from before 9/11 and at American Airlines, such a pilot made $122,500, 18 percent less than the days before 9/11. As of 2006–2007, Southwest pilots were quite well paid compared to their counterparts at most other airlines, earning about 45 percent more than pilots at United Airlines and 18 percent more than pilots at American Airlines. In 2007–2008, Southwest and its pilots' union were in the process of negotiating a new agreement.

In 2004 and 2007, in an attempt to contain rising labor costs, Southwest offered voluntary buyout packages to approximately 8,700 flight attendants, ramp workers, customer service employees, and those in reservations, operations, and freight who had reached a specific pay scale; the buyout consisted of a $25,000 payment and medical and dental benefits for a specified period. About 1,000 employees accepted the 2004 buyout offer. In some cases, the employees who accepted the buyout were not replaced; in cases where replacements were needed, Southwest was able to hire new employees for lesser pay than the departing employees were earning (because only employees who were at or near the top of their pay grade—due to good job performance and length of service with the company—were offered buyouts).

The No-Layoff Policy

Southwest Airlines had never laid off or furloughed any of its employees since the company began operations in 1971. The no-layoff policy was seen as integral to how the company treated its employees and to management efforts to sustain and nurture the culture. According to Kelleher:

> Nothing kills your company's culture like layoffs. Nobody has ever been furloughed here, and that is unprecedented in the airline industry. It's been a huge strength of ours. It's certainly helped negotiate our union contracts. . . . We could have furloughed at various times and been more profitable, but I always thought that was shortsighted. You want to show your people you value them and you're not going to hurt them just to get a little more money in the short term. Not furloughing people breeds loyalty. It breeds a sense of security. It breeds a sense of trust.[31]

Southwest had built up considerable goodwill with its employees and unions over the years by avoiding layoffs. Both senior management and Southwest employees regarded the two recent buyout offers as a better approach to workforce reduction than involuntary layoffs.

Operation Kick Tail

In 2007, Southwest management launched an internal initiative called Operation Kick Tail, a multiyear call to action for employees to focus even more attention on providing high-quality customer service, maintaining low costs, and nurturing the Southwest culture. One component of Operation Kick Tail involved singling out employees for special recognition when they did something to make a positive difference in a customer's travel experience or in the life of a coworker.

CEO Gary Kelly saw this aspect of Operation Kick Tail as a way to foster the employee attitudes and commitment needed to fulfill Southwest's promise of "Positively Outrageous Customer Service"; he explained:

> One of Southwest's rituals is finding and developing People who are "built to serve." That allows us to provide a personal, warm level of service that is unmatched in the airline industry.

Management Style

At Southwest, management strived to do things in a manner that would make Southwest employees proud of the company they worked for. Managers were expected to spend at least one-third of their time out of the office, walking around the facilities under their supervision, observing firsthand what was going on, listening to employees, and being responsive to their concerns. A former director of people development at Southwest told of a conversation he had with one of Southwest's terminal managers:

> While I was out in the field visiting one of our stations, one of our managers mentioned to me that he wanted to put up a suggestion box. I responded by saying that, "Sure—why don't you put up a suggestion box right here on this wall and then admit you are a failure as a manager?" Our theory is, if you have to put up a box so people can write down their ideas and toss them in, it means you are not doing what you are supposed to be doing. You are supposed to be setting your people up to be winners. To do that, you should be there listening to them and available to them in person, not via a suggestion box. For the most part, I think we have a very good sense of this at Southwest. I think that most people employed here know that they can call any one of our vice presidents on the telephone and get heard, almost immediately.
>
> The suggestion box gives managers an out; it relinquishes their responsibility to be accessible to their people, and that's when we have gotten in trouble at Southwest—when we can no longer be responsive to our flight attendants or customer service agents, when they can't gain access to somebody who can give them resources and answers.[32]

Company executives were very approachable, insisting on being called by their first names. At new employee orientations, people were told, "We do not call the company chairman and CEO Mr. Kelly; we call him Gary." Managers and executives had an open-door policy, actively listening to employee concerns, opinions, and suggestions for reducing costs and improving efficiency.

Employee-led initiatives were common. Southwest's pilots had been instrumental in developing new protocols for takeoffs and landings that conserved fuel. Another frontline employee had suggested not putting the company logos on trash bags, saving an estimated $250,000 annually. Rather than buy 800 computers for a new reservations center in Albuquerque, company employees determined that they could buy the parts and assemble the computers themselves for half the price of new ones, saving the company $1 million. It was Southwest clerks who came up with the idea of doing away with paper tickets and shifting to e-tickets.

There were only four layers of management between a frontline supervisor and the CEO. Southwest's employees enjoyed substantial authority and decision-making power. According to Kelleher:

> We've tried to create an environment where people are able to, in effect, bypass even the fairly lean structures that we have so that they don't have to convene a meeting of the sages in order to get something done. In many cases, they can just go ahead and do it on their own. They can take individual responsibility for it and know they will not be crucified if it doesn't work out. Our leanness requires people to be comfortable in making their own decisions and undertaking their own efforts.[33]

From time to time, there were candid meetings of frontline employees and managers where operating problems and issues among workers and departments were acknowledged, openly discussed, and resolved.[34] Informal problem avoidance and rapid problem resolution were seen as managerial virtues.

Southwest's Core Values

Two core values—LUV and fun—permeated the work environment at Southwest. LUV was much more than the company's ticker symbol and a recurring theme in Southwest's advertising campaigns. Over the years, LUV grew into Southwest's code word for treating individuals—fellow employees and customers—with dignity and respect and demonstrating a caring, loving attitude. LUV and red hearts commonly appeared on banners and posters at company facilities, as reminders of the compassion that was expected toward customers and other employees. Practicing the Golden Rule, internally and externally, was expected of all employees. Employees who struggled to live up to these expectations were subjected to considerable peer pressure and usually were asked to seek employment elsewhere if they did not soon leave on their own volition.

Fun at Southwest was exactly what the word implies. Throughout the company, fun appeared in the form of the generally entertaining behavior of employees in performing their jobs, the ongoing pranks and jokes, and frequent company-sponsored parties and celebrations (which typically included the Southwest Shuffle). On holidays, employees were encouraged to dress in costumes. There were charity benefit games, chili cook-offs, Halloween parties, new Ronald McDonald House dedications, and other special events of one kind or another at one location or another almost every week. According to one manager, "We're kind of a big family here, and family members have fun together."

Culture-Building

Southwest executives believed that the company's growth was primarily a function of the rate at which it could hire and train people to fit into its culture, to mirror the Southwest Spirit, and to consistently display the traits that comprised the Southwest Way (see Exhibit 12). CEO Gary Kelly said, "Some things at Southwest won't change. We will continue to expect our people to live what we describe as the 'Southwest Way,' which is to have a Warrior Spirit, Servant's Heart, and Fun-Loving Attitude. Those three things have defined our culture for 36 years."[35]

The Culture Committee Southwest formed a Culture Committee in 1990 to promote "Positively Outrageous Service" and devise tributes, contests, and celebrations intended to nurture and perpetuate the Southwest Spirit. The committee, chaired by Colleen Barrett until mid-2008, was composed of 100 employees who had demonstrated their commitment to Southwest's mission and values and zeal in exhibiting the Southwest Spirit. Members came from a cross-section of departments and locations and functioned as cultural ambassadors, missionaries, and storytellers during their two-year term.

The Culture Committee had four all-day meetings annually; ad hoc subcommittees formed throughout the year met more frequently. Over the years, the committee had sponsored and supported hundreds of ways to promote and ingrain the Southwest Spirit—examples included promoting the use of red hearts and LUV to embody the spirit of caring, serving

Exhibit 12 Personal Traits, Attitudes, and Behaviors That Southwest Wanted Employees to Possess and Display

Live the Southwest Way		
Warrior Spirit	**Servant's Heart**	**Fun-LUVing Attitude**
• Work hard • Desire to be the best • Be courageous • Display a sense of urgency • Persevere • Innovate	• Follow the Golden Rule • Adhere to the Basic Principles • Treat others with respect • Put others first • Be egalitarian • Demonstrate proactive Customer Service • Embrace the SWA Family	• Have FUN • Don't take yourself too seriously • Maintain perspective (balance) • Celebrate successes • Enjoy your work • Be a passionate team player

Source: www.southwest.com (accessed September 5, 2008).

pizza or ice cream to employees, or remodeling an employee break room. Kelleher indicated, "We're not big on committees at Southwest, but of the committees we do have, the Culture Committee is the most important."[36]

Efforts to Nurture and Sustain the Southwest Culture Apart from the efforts of the Culture Committee, Southwest management had sought to reinforce the company's core values and culture via an annual Heroes of the Heart Award, a mentoring program called CoHearts, an event called Day in the Field during which employees spent time working in another area of the company's operations, a program called Helping Hands that gathered volunteers from around the system to work two weekend shifts at other Southwest facilities that were temporarily shorthanded or experiencing heavy workloads, and periodic meetings called Culture Exchange to celebrate the Southwest Spirit and company milestones. Almost every event at Southwest was videotaped, which provided footage for creating such multipurpose videos as *Keepin' the Spirit Alive* that could be shown at company events all over the system and used in training courses. The concepts of LUV and fun were spotlighted in all of the company's training manuals and videos.

Southwest's monthly newsletter, *LUV Lines,* often spotlighted the experiences and deeds of particular employees, reprinted letters of praise from customers, and reported company celebrations of milestones. A quarterly news video, *As the Plane Turns,* was sent to all facilities to keep employees up to date on company happenings, provide clips of special events, and share messages from customers, employees, and executives. The company had published a book for employees describing "outrageous" acts of service. Sometimes important information was circulated to employees in "fun" packages such as Cracker Jack boxes.

Employee Productivity

Management was convinced the company's strategy, culture, esprit de corps, and people management practices fostered high labor productivity and contributed to Southwest having very low labor costs compared to other airlines (as shown in Exhibit 10). When a Southwest flight pulled up to the gate, ground crews, gate personnel, and flight attendants hustled to perform all the tasks requisite to turn the plane quickly—employees took pride in doing their part to achieve good on-time performance. Southwest's turnaround times were in the 25- to 30-minute range, versus an industry average of around 45 minutes. In 2007, Southwest's labor productivity compared favorably with the U.S. airline average:

Productivity Measure	Southwest	U.S. Airline Industry Average
Passengers enplaned per employee, 2007	2,964	1,371
Employees per plane, 2007	65.2	71.8

System Operations

Under Herb Kelleher, instituting practices and support systems that promoted operating excellence had become a tradition and a source of company pride. Much time and effort over the years had gone into finding the most effective ways to do aircraft maintenance, to operate safely, to make baggage handling more efficient and baggage transfers more accurate, and to improve the percentage of on-time arrivals and departures. Believing that air travelers were more likely to fly Southwest if its flights were reliable and on time, Southwest's managers constantly monitored on-time arrivals and departures, making inquiries when many flights ran behind and searching for ways to improve on-time performance. One initiative to help minimize weather and operational delays involved the development of a state-of-the-art flight dispatch system. CEO Gary Kelly had followed Kelleher's lead in pushing for operational excellence. One of Kelly's strategic objectives was for Southwest "to be the safest, most efficient, and most reliable airline in the world." Southwest managers and employees in all positions and ranks were proactive in offering suggestions for improving Southwest's practices and procedures; those with merit were quickly implemented. Southwest was considered to have one of the most competent and thorough aircraft maintenance programs in the commercial airline industry and, going into 2008, was widely regarded as the best operator among U.S. airlines. Its recent record vis-à-vis rival airlines on four important measures of operating performance was commendable—see Exhibit 13.

Exhibit 13 Comparative Statistics on On-Time Flights, Mishandled Baggage, Oversales, and Passenger Complaints for Seven Major U.S. Airlines, 2000 through Quarter 1 of 2008

Percentage of Scheduled Flights Arriving within 15 Minutes of Scheduled Time (previous 12 months ending in May of each year)					
Airline	**2000**	**2005**	**2006**	**2007**	**Q1 2008**
American Airlines	75.8 %	78.0 %	75.6 %	72.4 %	66.9 %
Continental Air Lines	76.7	78.7	74.8	73.5	74.1
Delta Air Lines	78.3	76.4	76.2	76.6	75.7
Northwest Airlines	80.7	79.3	75.1	71.4	71.1
Southwest Airlines	78.7	79.9	80.3	80.7	78.5
United Air Lines	71.6	79.8	75.7	73.0	69.1
US Airways	72.7	76.0	78.9	69.7	75.5

Mishandled Baggage Reports per 1,000 Passengers (in May of each year)					
Airline	**2000**	**2005**	**2006**	**2007**	**Q1 2008**
American Airlines	5.44	4.58	4.91	6.40	5.82
Continental Air Lines	4.11	3.30	3.85	5.02	3.78
Delta Air Lines	3.64	6.21	4.75	5.26	3.81
Northwest Airlines	4.98	3.58	3.11	3.80	2.97
Southwest Airlines	4.14	3.46	3.66	5.54	4.41
United Air Lines	6.71	4.00	3.89	4.83	4.76
US Airways	4.57	9.73	5.69	7.17	3.86

Involuntary Denied Boardings per 10,000 Passengers Due to Oversold Flights (January through March of each year)					
Airline	**2000**	**2005**	**2006**	**2007**	**Q1 2008**
American Airlines	0.59	0.72	1.16	1.06	0.98
Continental Air Lines	0.50	3.01	2.60	1.93	1.57
Delta Air Lines	0.44	1.06	2.68	3.47	1.80
Northwest Airlines	0.12	1.70	1.00	1.25	1.15
Southwest Airlines	1.70	0.74	1.81	1.25	1.68
United Air Lines	1.61	0.42	0.88	0.40	0.89
US Airways	0.80	1.01	1.07	1.68	2.01

Complaints per 100,000 Passengers Boarded (in May of each year)					
Airline	**2000**	**2005**	**2006**	**2007**	**Q1 2008**
American Airlines	2.77	1.01	1.22	1.44	1.30
Continental Air Lines	2.25	0.89	0.85	0.75	1.03
Delta Air Lines	1.60	0.91	0.93	1.50	2.14
Northwest Airlines	2.17	0.83	0.69	1.13	0.92
Southwest Airlines	0.41	0.17	0.18	0.19	0.32
United Air Lines	5.07	0.87	1.19	2.00	1.61
US Airways	1.63	0.99	1.22	2.65	1.94

Source: Office of Aviation Enforcement and Proceedings, Air Travel Consumer Report, various years.

The First Significant Blemish on Southwest's Safety Record While no Southwest plane had ever crashed and there had never been a passenger fatality, there was an incident in 2005 in which a Southwest plane landing in a snow storm with a strong tailwind at Chicago's Midway airport was unable to stop before overrunning a shorter-than-usual runway, rolling onto a highway, crashing into a car, killing one of the occupants, and injuring 22 of the passengers on the plane. A National Traffic Safety Board investigation concluded that "the pilot's failure to use available reverse thrust in a timely manner to safely slow or stop the airplane after landing" was the probable cause.

Belated Aircraft Inspections Further Tarnish Southwest's Reputation In early 2008, various media reported that Southwest Airlines over a period of several months in 2006 and 2007 had knowingly failed to conduct required inspections for early detection of fuselage fatigue cracking on 46 of its older Boeing 737-300 jets. The company had voluntarily notified the Federal Aviation Administration (FAA) about the lapse in checks for fuselage cracks but continued to fly the planes until the work was done—about eight days. The belated inspections revealed tiny cracks in the bodies of six planes, with the largest measuring four inches; none impaired flight safety. According to Gary Kelly, "Southwest Airlines discovered the missed inspection area, disclosed it to the FAA, and promptly re-inspected all potentially affected aircraft in March 2007. The FAA approved our actions and considered the matter closed as of April 2007." Nonetheless, on March 12, 2008, shortly after the reports in the media surfaced about Southwest not meeting inspection deadlines, Southwest canceled 4 percent of its flights and grounded 44 of its Boeing 737-300s until it verified that the aircraft had undergone required inspections. Kelly then initiated an internal review of the company's maintenance practices; the investigation raised concerns about the company's aircraft maintenance procedures, prompting Southwest to put three employees on leave. The FAA subsequently fined Southwest $10.2 million for its transgressions. In an effort to help restore customer confidence, Kelly publicly apologized for the company's wrongdoing, promised that it would not occur again, and reasserted the company's commitment to safety; he said:

> From our inception, Southwest Airlines has maintained a rigorous Culture of Safety—and has maintained that same dedication for more than 37 years. It is and always has been our number one priority to ensure safety.
>
> We've got a 37-year history of very safe operations, one of the safest operations in the world, and we're safer today than we've ever been.

In the days following the public revelation of Southwest's maintenance lapse and the tarnishing of its reputation, an industry-wide audit by the FAA revealed similar failures to conduct timely inspections for early signs of fuselage fatigue at five other airlines—American, Continental, Delta, United, and Northwest. An air travel snafu ensued, with more than 1,000 flights subsequently being canceled due to FAA-mandated grounding of the affected aircraft while the overdue safety inspections were performed. Further public scrutiny, including a congressional investigation, turned up documents indicating that in some cases planes flew for 30 months after the inspection deadlines had passed. Moreover, high-level FAA officials were apparently aware of the failure of Southwest and other airlines to perform the inspections for fuselage skin cracking at the scheduled times and chose not to strictly enforce the inspection deadlines—according to some commentators, because of allegedly cozy relationships with personnel at Southwest and the other affected airlines. Disgruntled FAA safety supervisors in charge of monitoring the inspections conducted by airline carriers testified before Congress that senior FAA officials frequently ignored their reports that certain routine safety inspections were not being conducted in accordance with prescribed FAA procedures. Shortly thereafter, the FAA issued more stringent procedures to ensure that aircraft safety inspections were properly conducted.

Endnotes

[1] Kevin and Jackie Freiberg, *NUTS! Southwest Airlines' Crazy Recipe for Business and Personal Success* (New York: Broadway Books, 1998), p.15.
[2] Ibid., pp. 16–18.
[3] Katrina Brooker, "The Chairman of the Board Looks Back," *Fortune,* May 28, 2001, p. 66.
[4] Freiberg and Freiberg, *NUTS!,* p. 41.
[5] Ibid., p. 31.
[6] Ibid., pp. 26–27.
[7] Ibid., pp. 246–47.
[8] As quoted in the *Dallas Morning News,* March 20, 2001.
[9] Brooker, "The Chairman of the Board Looks Back," p. 64.

[10] As quoted in ibid., p. 72.
[11] As quoted in *Seattle Times,* March 20, 2001, p. C3.
[12] Speech at Texas Christian University, September 13, 2007; www.southwest.com (accessed September 8, 2008).
[13] Freiberg and Freiberg, *NUTS!,* p. 163.
[14] Company press release, July 15, 2004.
[15] Speech to Greater Boston Chamber of Commerce, April 23, 2008, www.southwest.com (accessed September 5, 2008).
[16] Speech to Business Today International Conference, November 20, 2007, www.southwest.com (accessed September 8, 2008).
[17] As cited in Freiberg and Freiberg, *NUTS!,* p. 288.
[18] Colleen Barrett, speech, January 22, 2007, www.southwest.com (accessed on September 5, 2008).
[19] Brenda Paik Sunoo, "How Fun Flies at Southwest Airlines," *Personnel Journal* 74, no. 6 (June 1995), p. 70.
[20] Statement made in a 1993 Harvard Business School video and quoted in Roger Hallowell, "Southwest Airlines: A Case Study Linking Employee Needs Satisfaction and Organizational Capabilities to Competitive Advantage," *Human Resource Management* 35, no. 4 (Winter 1996), p. 517.
[21] Statement posted in the Careers section, www.southwest.com (accessed September 8, 2008).
[22] As quoted in James Campbell Quick, "Crafting an Organizational Structure: Herb's Hand at Southwest Airlines," *Organizational Dynamics* 21, no. 2 (Autumn 1992), p. 51.
[23] Southwest, advertisement, "Work in a Place Where Elvis Has Been Spotted," and Sunoo, "How Fun Flies at Southwest Airlines," pp. 64–65.
[24] Speech to the Paso Del Norte Group in El Paso, Texas, January 22, 2007, www.southwest.com (accessed September 5, 2008).
[25] Quick, "Crafting an Organizational Structure," p. 52.
[26] Sunoo, "How Fun Flies at Southwest Airlines," p. 72.
[27] Based on pay scale data for Southwest Airlines, www.payscales.com (accessed September 8, 2008).
[28] Terry Maxon, "Southwest Airlines Begins Contract Talks with Ground Workers," *Dallas Morning News,* January 23, 2008, www.dallasnews.com (accessed September 8, 2008).
[29] Shawn Tully, "From Bad to Worse," *Fortune,* October 15, 2001, p. 124.
[30] Melanie Trottman, "Amid Crippled Rivals, Southwest Tries to Spread Its Wings," *Wall Street Journal,* October 11, 2001, p. A10.
[31] Brooker, "The Chairman of the Board Looks Back," p. 72.
[32] Freiberg and Freiberg, *NUTS!,* p. 273.
[33] Ibid., p. 76.
[34] Hallowell, "Southwest Airlines: A Case Study," p. 524.
[35] Speech to Business Today International Conference.
[36] Freiberg and Freiberg, *NUTS!,* p. 165.

CASE

24 Shangri-La Hotels

Dennis Campbell
Harvard Business School

Brent Kazan
Harvard Business School

In November 2006, Symon Bridle, the newly appointed chief operating officer of Shangri-La Hotels and Resorts, was reviewing the progress the Hong Kong–based company had made over the previous 10 years as it grew from a regionally focused business into a rapidly expanding international deluxe hotel group. With 18,400 employees, 50 hotels, and $842 million in revenues, Shangri-La Hotels and Resorts (Shangri-La) was a leading player in the luxury hotel industry. The company was growing rapidly to satisfy increased demand for deluxe hotels and resorts in Asia, Europe, and North America and Bridle was in charge of ensuring that Shangri-La's signature standards of "Shangri-La Hospitality," a service model based on traditional Asian hospitality, were maintained during this expansion.

For the past two weeks, Bridle and a task force of his top managers had been discussing a number of organizational issues that presented challenges to Shangri-La's rapid expansion strategy. There were three major issues at hand: (1) the company was expanding into high-wage economies in Europe and North America; (2) the company was expanding its presence in China—a country where front-line employees were not used to exercising decision-making authority; and (3) newcomers in the Chinese hotel market were poaching Shangri-La's staff and driving up wages in historically low-wage markets.

All of these issues weighed on Bridle's mind as he wondered what he should do next. "How do you still articulate your brand in tight labor markets with these pressure points?" he pondered.

HARVARD | BUSINESS | SCHOOL
9-108-006

CORPORATE BACKGROUND

Shangri-La Hotels and Resorts, a deluxe Asian hotel chain, was founded in 1971 in Singapore by the Malaysian-Chinese tycoon Robert Kuok. Inspired by British author James Hilton's legendary novel *Lost Horizon,* the name "Shangri-La" meant "eternal youth, peace and tranquility" and embodied the serenity and service for which the hotel chain was renowned throughout the world.

With its first and flagship hotel in Singapore, the company quickly differentiated itself from the competition and provided distinctive Asian standards of hospitality and service. Within a decade, Hong Kong–based Shangri-La established a world-class reputation and became one of the world's finest hotel management companies, garnering international awards and recognition from prestigious publications and industry partners—"Best Business Hotel Chain in Asia Pacific" by *Business Traveler* (U.K. and Germany) and "Best Hotel Chain" by *Chinese Hurun Report* (China)[1]—along the way.

As of 2006, Shangri-La had four main business segments: hotel ownership and operations, property development including commercial buildings and serviced apartments, hotel management services to group-owned and third-party hotels, and spas.

Expansion History

In the early 1980s, Shangri-La went through a period of rapid expansion in Asia and built 29 hotels over the next decade. The hotel chain continued to prosper throughout the 1990s, in step with Asia's economic boom. By 1999, Shangri-La had a total of 35 hotels and resorts located in Asia's most sought-after leisure destinations. In the following years, the company continued to grow. To raise funds for expansion, Shangri-La subsidiaries in various countries, including Malaysia and Thailand, were incorporated and listed on local stock exchanges between 1982 and 2002, under Shangri-La Asia.

In the early 2000s, Shangri-La began expanding beyond its core Asian markets through both management contracts and owner/operator developments. The Shangri-La Dubai, in the United Arab Emirates, opened in July 2003, followed a year later by the Traders Hotel Dubai, and a destination Shangri-La & Spa Resort in Muscat, Oman. Opportunities were also taken in Sydney (2003) and Cairns (2004) in Australia, while contracts were signed for upcoming properties in North America (Vancouver, Chicago, Las Vegas, Toronto, Miami, New York) and Europe (London, Paris, Vienna).

As of 2006, Shangri-La was the largest Asian-based deluxe hotel group in Southeast Asia. The company managed a total of 50 hotels under two brands: the five-star Shangri-La and the four-star Traders—a sister brand established in 1989 to deliver high value, mid-range, quality accommodation to the business traveler—with total inventory of over 23,000 rooms across 39 locations (see Exhibit 1 for locations).[2] As of November 2006, the company still had over 40 projects under development worldwide (see Exhibit 2).

Despite its aggressive expansion elsewhere, the company remained focused on business and capital investments in the Asia-Pacific region, in particular China. The primary reason for this decision was the fact that China's successive relaxation of travel restrictions dating back to the late 1980s, coupled with rising urban incomes, had created a boom in Chinese domestic and outbound travel. In addition, inbound international travel was also increasing. The country had recently entered into the World Trade Organization and its capital, Beijing, was selected as the host of the 2008 Olympics. With an additional role as the host of the World Expo

Exhibit 1 Shangri-La Hotels and Resorts Growth Timeline

1971	April	Shangri-La Hotel, Singapore, opens (managed by Westin until January 1983)
1979		Kuok Hotels established to manage three properties:
		Rasa Sayang (2004 November) temporarily closed for re-development and re-opened in September 2006
		Golden Sands
		The Fijian
1981	April	Kowloon Shangri-La opens (managed by Westin until April 1991)
1983	January	Shangri-La International Hotel Management Limited (management takeover of Shangri-La Hotel, Singapore)
1984	November	Shangri-La Hotel, Hangzhou (management takeover of Hangzhou Hotel)
1985	April	Shangri-La Hotel, Kuala Lumpur opens
1986	March	Shangri-La Hotel, Bangkok opens
	April	Shangri-La Hotel, Penang opens
	October	Shangri-La Hotel, Beijing opens
1988	December	Shangri-La's Tanjung Aru Resort, Kota Kinabalu (management takeover)

(*Continued*)

Exhibit 1 (Continued)

1989	December	Traders Hotel, Beijing opens
1990	July	China World Hotel, Beijing opens
1991	March	Island Shangri-La, Hong Kong opens
	April	Kowloon Shangri-La, Hong Kong (Shangri-La assumes management)
1992	August	Edsa Shangri-La, Manila opens
	September	Shangri-La Hotel, Shenzhen opens
1993	March	Rasa Sentosa Resort, Singapore opens
	April	Makati Shangri-La, Manila opens
	June	Shangri-La Golden Flower, Xian (management takeover)
	October	Shangri-La's Mactan Island Resort & Spa, Cebu opens
1994	March	Shangri-La Hotel, Jakarta opens
	March	Shangri-La's Far Eastern Plaza Hotel, Taipei opens
1995	January	Rebranding of Traders Hotel, Manila
	January	Shangri-La Hotel, Surabaya opens
	April	Traders Hotel, Singapore opens
1996	April	Shangri-La Hotel, Beihai opens
	June	Shangri-La's Rasa Ria Resort, Kota Kinabalu opens
	August	Traders Hotel, Shenyang opens
	August	Shangri-La Hotel, Changchun opens
	November	Traders Hotel, Yangon opens
1997	August	Shangri-La Hotel, Qingdao opens
	December	Shangri-La Hotel, Dalian opens
1998	August	Pudong Shangri-La, Shanghai opens
1999	April	Shangri-La Hotel, Wuhan opens
	April	Shangri-La Hotel, Harbin opens
	August	The Kerry Centre Hotel, Beijing opens
2003	February	Putrajaya Shangri-La Hotel opens
	July	ANA Harbour Grand Hotel rebrands as Shangri-La Hotel, Sydney, Australia
	July	Shangri-La Hotel, Dubai opens
2004	January	Shangri-La Hotel, Zhongshan opens
	July	Traders Hotel, Dubai opens
	August	Shangri-La Hotel, The Marina, Cairns re-branding
2005	January	Traders Hotel, Changzhou opens
	January	Shangri-La Hotel, Fuzhou opens
	September	Shangri-La Hotel, New Delhi opens
	October	Traders Hotel, Kunshan opens
2006	February	Shangri-La's Barr Al Jissah Resort and Spa, Muscat opens
	July	Traders Hotel, Kuala Lumpur opens
	July	Shangri-La Hotel, Suzhou opens
2007	January	Shangri-La Hotel, Guangzhou opens

Source: Shangri-La Hotels and Resorts, http://www.shangri-la.com/en/home.aspx (accessed February 5, 2007).

Exhibit 2 Ongoing Shangri-La Developments

Hotel Name	Hotel Location	Expected Opening Date
Shangri-La Hotel, Chiang Mai	Chiang Mai, Thailand	2007
Shangri-La Hotel, Xian	Xian, China	2007
Shangri-La Hotel, Baotou	Baotou, China	2007
Futian Shangri-La, Shenzhen	Futian, China	2008
Shangri-La Hotel, Huhhot	Huhhot, China	2007
Shangri-La Hotel, Chengdu	Chengdu, China	2007
Shangri-La Hotel, Qaryat Al Beri, Abu Dhabi	Abu Dhabi, UAE	2007
Shangri-La Hotel, Bangalore	Bangalore, India	2008
Traders Hotel, Bangalore	Bangalore, India	2009
Shangri-La's Phuket Resort and Spa, Thailand	Phuket, Thailand	2009
Shangri-La Hotel, Manzhouli	Manzhouli, China	2008
Shangri-La Hotel, Doha	Doha, Qatar	2008
Palm Retreat Shangri-La, Bangalore	Bangalore, India	2008
Shangri-La Hotel, Ningbo	Ningbo, China	2008
Shangri-La Hotel, Vancouver	Vancouver, Canada	2009
Shangri-La Hotel, Wenzhou	Wenzhou, China	2008
Shangri-La Hotel, Macau	Macau	2009
Traders Hotel, Macau	Macau	2009
Shangri-La's Villingili Resort and Spa, Maldives	Villingili Island, Maldives	2008
Traders Hotel, Urumqi	Urumqi, China	2009
Shangri-La's Boracay Resort and Spa, Philippines	Boracay, Philippines	2008
Shangri-La Hotel, Palais d'lena, Paris	Paris, France	2009
Shangri-La Resort and Spa, Seychelles	Mahe, Seychelles	2009
Shangri-La Hotel, Chicago	Chicago, U.S.	2009
Shangri-La Hotel, Guilin	Guilin, China	2009
Shangri-La Hotel, Tokyo	Tokyo, Japan	2009
Shangri-La Hotel, Miami	Miami, U.S.	2010
Shangri-La Hotel, Dongguan	Dongguan, China	2009
Shangri-La Hotel, Las Vegas	Las Vegas, U.S.	2010
Shangri-La West, Jingan, Shanghai	Jingan, China	2010
Shangri-La Hotel, at London Bridge Tower, London	London, United Kingdom	2011
Shangri-La Vienna	Vienna, Austria	2010

Source: Shangri-La Hotels and Resorts, http://www.shangri-la.com/en/home.aspx, accessed February 5, 2007.

2010, Shangri-La planned to capitalize on China's economic advancement and expand its hotels in China from 17 to over 30 by 2008.[3]

Financials

Shangri-La's early focus on the Chinese market helped the company shield itself from the worst of the Asian economic crisis of 1997–98, which hit Southeast Asia hard but left China relatively unscathed. In 2005, the company benefited from continuing robust travel demand in Hong Kong and China to post revenues of $842 million (see Exhibit 3 and Exhibit 4 for financials). Both room and food and beverage revenues continued to improve and occupancy rates of Shangri-La hotels increased to 73 percent in 2005,

Exhibit 3 Shangri-La Asia Ltd., Annual Income Statements, 2002–2006* (in USD millions)

	2006	2005	2004	2003	2002
Filed currency	USD	USD	USD	USD	USD
Net sales	$1,002.9	$ 842	$725.5	$540.4	$600.5
Revenue	1,002.9	842	725.5	540.4	600.5
Total revenue	1,002.9	842	725.5	540.4	600.5
Cost of revenue	408.8	345.6	308.5	234.4	248.8
Cost of revenue, total	408.8	345.6	308.5	234.4	248.8
Gross profit	594.1	496.4	417	306	351.8
Selling/general/ administrative expense	121.3	114.3	90.5	77.4	80.1
Total selling/general/ administrative expenses	121.3	114.3	90.5	77.4	80.1
Other operating expense	279.8	238.4	209.9	116.3	155.8
Other, net	−80.3	−44.7	−26	−23.7	−6.9
Other operating expenses, total	199.5	193.7	183.8	92.6	149.0
Total operating expense	729.6	653.6	582.8	404.4	477.8
Operating income	273.3	188.4	142.7	136	122.8
Interest expense—non-operating	−32.5	−39.9	−52.7	−48.6	−43.8
Interest capitalized—non-operating	—	7	4.4	2.3	1.7
Interest expense, Net non-operating	−32.5	−32.9	−48.3	−46.4	−42.1
Investment income—non-operating	42.0	64.3	41.0	38.8	41.7
Interest/investment income—non-operating	42.0	64.3	41.0	38.8	41.7
Interest income (expense)—net non-operating	9.5	31.5	−7.3	−7.6	−0.4
Income before tax	282.8	219.8	135.4	128.4	122.4
Total income tax	63.5	52.3	12.9	46.4	49.7
Income after tax	219.3	167.5	122.5	82	72.7
Minority interest	−17.2	−16.5	−9.0	−9.3	−9.3
Net income before extraord items	202.2	151.0	113.5	72.7	63.4
Net income	$ 202.2	$151.0	$113.5	$ 72.7	$ 63.4

*2006 projected.

Source: Shangri-La Asia Ltd. Financial Report (Reuters), via OneSource, accessed February 26, 2008.

compared with 71 percent for 2004 (see Exhibit 5 for hotel operating statistics). While hotel operating costs were market-specific, labor, utilities, and maintenance costs together accounted for approximately 32 percent of gross operating revenue in a typical Shangri-La property in Asia with 20 percent due to labor costs and the remaining 12 percent due to utilities (7 percent) and maintenance (5 percent) costs.

Exhibit 4 **Shangri-La Asia Ltd., Summary of Balance Sheet, 2002–2006* (in USD millions)**

	2006	2005	2004	2003	2002
Cash and short term investments	$ 380.3	$ 313.8	$ 223.9	$ 199.1	$ 164.8
Total receivables, net	112.0	126.9	157.4	152.9	166
Total inventory	22.0	20.7	18.9	17.4	15.7
Total current assets	627.6	492.1	417.2	369.4	346.4
Property/plant/equipment—net	3045	2,508.6	2,393.7	3,761.6	3,605.1
Goodwill, net	75.8	76.8	−109.0	−116.3	−122.1
Intangibles, net	393.1	385.0	379.5	—	—
Long-term investments	925.7	790.5	626.4	723.4	725.5
Other long-term assets, total	4.6	6.6	7.6	4.3	4.6
Total assets	5,075.7	4,263.1	3,720.1	4,742.5	4,559.5
Accounts Payable	107.1	213.2	150.9	331.5	266.5
Other current liabilities, total	248.3	205.2	169.1	1.7	4.9
Total current liabilities	355.4	418.4	320.0	333.2	271.4
Long-term debt	1,506.4	990.4	952.7	1,037.2	1,010.9
Total long-term debt	1,506.4	990.4	952.7	1,037.2	1,010.9
Total debt	1,549.3	1,143.3	1,056.6	1,215.2	1141.0
Deferred income tax	211.9	202.2	189.5	356.6	339.8
Other liabilities, total	26.6	21.8	92.5	—	—
Total liabilities	2,376.5	1882.0	1,742.4	2,118.5	2,004.4
Common stock	330.7	326.4	310.6	282.0	281.8
Other equity, total	108.6	−39.6	−43.9	56.5	27.1
Total equity	2,699.2	2381.0	1,977.7	2624.0	2,555.1
Total liabilities and shareholders' equity	5,075.7	4,263.1	3,720.1	4,742.5	4,559.5
Total common shares outstanding	2,560.8	2,527.4	2,404.3	2,181.3	2,179.7

*2006 projected.

Source: Shangri-La Asia Ltd. Financial Report (Reuters), via OneSource (accessed February 26, 2008).

SERVICE MODEL: "SHANGRI-LA HOSPITALITY"

Starting with its first hotel, Shangri-La Hotel-Singapore, Shangri-La built its brand on service excellence with a stated mission to "delight customers each and every time" (see Exhibit 6). The core of the Shangri-La brand was steeped in offering customers an unforgettable experience by blending local cultures, exotic art, and lively ambience.

With its Asian foundations, Shangri-La's service model of "Shangri-La Hospitality" was built around five core principles: respect, humility, courtesy, helpfulness, and sincerity. With properties spanning geographic and cultural boundaries, implementing these principles consistently was challenging and affected everything from staffing and amenities to customer–employee interactions. For example, certain service principles (i.e., respect) meant different things to different customers in different markets.

Greg Dogan, regional vice president, explained:

> Shangri-La Hospitality basically covers what we do in Asia. Within each country, you need to adapt to the local requirements whether it is Myanmar, Philippines, or Indonesia. In Thailand it is very normal for a service employee to serve you tea or coffee on one knee. In the Philippines, this is a big no-no. Similarly, in most countries, staff would normally walk in, serve the tea, and walk out facing the guest. It is the little things like that you need to pick up from each culture. In each country there is a different expectation and we adapt to

Exhibit 5 Shangri-La Asia Limited Occupancy and Rates Statistics (June 2006)

Hotel	Current Month Rooms Available		Occupancy				Average Room Rates				Revenue per Available Room			
			YTD June			INC/(DEC)	YTD June			INC/(DEC)	YTD June			INC/(DEC)
	2006	2005	2006		2005	06 vs 05	2006		2005	06 vs 05	2006		2005	06 vs 05
	Actual	Actual	Actual %	Budget %	L-Year %	%	Actual US$	Budget US$	L-Year US$	%	Actual US$	Budget US$	L-Year US$	%
1. Kowloon Shangri-La Hotel	700	700	78%	76%	73%	5%	$236	$238	$214	10%	$180	$176	$151	19%
2. Island Shangri-La Hotel	565	565	83	79	76	7	324	311	273	19	263	240	224	17
Total Hong Kong average (1–2)	1,265	1,265	80	77	74	6	277	271	241	15	217	204	182	19
3. Shangri-La Hotel, Beijing	528	528	73	76	69	4	117	114	102	15	82	83	67	22
4. China World Hotel, Beijing	716	716	75	80	81	(6)	196	188	164	19	147	149	132	11
5. Traders Hotel, Beijing	570	570	84	86	86	(2)	104	95	91	14	87	81	78	12
6. Portman Ritz Carlton Hotel, Shanghai	506	488	77	80	81	(4)	220	221	204	8	169	178	165	2
7. Shangri-La Hotel, Hongzhou	383	383	71	73	74	(2)	120	122	117	2	80	84	81	(0)
8. Shangri-La Hotel, Shenzhen	522	522	74	72	67	8	101	98	91	10	74	67	60	25
9. Shangri-La Golden Flower Hotel, Xian	416	416	65	73	75	(10)	69	65	62	11	44	46	45	(1)
10. Shangri-La Hotel Changchun	458	458	71	72	71	0	83	85	77	8	56	60	58	(5)
11. Traders Hotel Shenyang	588	588	60	64	62	(2)	44	46	42	5	25	28	25	1
12. Shangri-La Hotel Beihai	362	362	31	34	32	(1)	50	48	44	13	15	16	14	12
13. Shangri-La Hotel, Qingdoo	501	501	70	78	77	(7)	103	99	87	19	78	85	67	16
14. Shangri-La Hotel, Dalian	562	562	63	68	71	(8)	92	98	85	8	56	65	59	(5)
15. Shangri-La Hotel, Pudong	957	606	68	73	78	(10)	225	231	187	20	148	165	139	6
16. Shangri-La Hotel, Wuhan	448	468	75	68	66	9	72	70	66	9	52	49	42	24
17. Shangri-La Hotel, Harbin	340	342	66	66	64	2	80	80	73	9	52	52	59	(12)
18. Beijing Kerry Centre Hotel	487	487	75	79	80	(5)	170	167	138	23	126	131	109	15
19. Shangri-La Hotel, Zhongshan	458	426	50	59	58	(7)	83	81	69	21	41	47	39	6
20. Shangri-La Hotel, Fuzhou	414	367	64	64	63	2	80	78	67	20	50	49	39	27
Total China average (3–20)	9,217	8,790	68	71	71	(3)	125	124	108	16	84	87	75	11
21. Shangri-La Hotel, Makati, Manila	697	693	89	86	84	5	136	128	121	12	118	106	98	20
22. Shangri-La's Edsa Plaza Hotel, Manila	620	651	69	76	71	(2)	87	76	72	21	67	62	49	36
23. Shangri-La's Moctan Island Resort, Cebu	543	543	65	62	79	(14)	137	134	126	8	117	109	96	21
Total Philippines average (21–23)	1,860	1,887	75	75	78	(3)	121	112	107	13	101	92	81	25

Hotel	Current Month Rooms Available		Occupancy				Average Room Rates				Revenue per Available Room			
			YTD June			INC/(DEC)	YTD June			INC/(DEC)	YTD June			INC/(DEC)
	2006	2005	2006		2005	06 vs 05	2006		2005	06 vs 05	2006		2005	06 vs 05
	Actual	Actual	Actual %	Budget %	L-Year %	%	Actual US$	Budget US$	L-Year US$	%	Actual US$	Budget US$	L-Year US$	%
24. Shangri-La Hotel, Jakarta	668	668	52%	63%	55%	(3)%	$109	$114	$103	6%	$51	$ 70	$ 49	4%
25. Fijian Resort	436	436	71	71	63	8	144	132	133	9	101	92	116	(13)
Total Philippines, Jakarta & Fiji average (21–25)	2,964	2,991	69	72	71	(1)	123	116	110	12	89	87	77	16
Original group average (1–25)	13,446	13,046	70	72	71	(1)	142	137	122	16	98	99	86	14
26. Shangri-La Hotel, Singapore	750	750	78	80	80	(1)	198	174	162	23	153	138	127	21
27. Shangri-La's Rosa Sentosa Resort	459	459	82	80	81	1	114	101	99	16	92	79	77	19
28. Traders Hotel, Singapore	546	546	77	85	83	(6)	115	97	87	33	88	82	71	24
Total Singapore average (26–28)	1,755	1,755	79	82	81	(2)	150	130	121	24	117	105	96	21
29. Shangri-La Hotel, Bangkok	799	799	80	79	77	3	130	124	118	11	101	95	87	17
30. Traders Hotel, Yangon	385	403	51	49	47	4	35	36	33	8	18	17	15	20
31. Shangri-La Hotel, Kuala Lumpur	694	695	69	73	68	1	94	93	87	9	63	66	56	11
32. Traders Hotel, Penang	441	441	79	71	67	13	49	48	43	14	38	33	29	31
33. Shangri-La's Golden Sands Resort, Penang	395	395	78	76	64	14	82	80	71	14	62	59	45	40
34. Shangri-La's Tanjung Aru Resort	495	495	84	81	80	4	90	87	74	22	72	68	56	29
35. Shangri-La's Rasa Ria Resort	330	328	80	76	72	8	80	78	64	25	63	58	54	16
Total Malaysia average (31–35)	2,355	2,354	77	75	70	7	80	79	70	14	60	58	49	23
Total other area average (21–35)	8,258	8,302	74	75	72	2	115	107	100	14	85	80	71	19
Total group average (1–35)	18,740	18,357	72%	73%	72%	(0)%	$132	$127	$114	16%	$93	$ 92	$ 81	16%

Note: Portman Ritz-Carlton is undergoing major renovation. Available rooms, occupancy %, average room rates, and revenue per available room are based on saleable rooms. Rasa Sayang Resort ceased operations in Dec 04 for redevelopment. Fiji Mocambo was disposed in Dec 05.

*Decrease in RevPar due to renovation in 2005, i.e. lower saleable roomnights.

Source: Shangri-La Investors Relations, http://www.ir.shangri-la.com/en/hoteloperatingstatistics/ (accessed January 31, 2008).

Exhibit 6 Shangri-La Mission Statement

Our Philosophy

Shangri-La hospitality from caring people

Our Vision

The first choice for customers, employees, shareholders and business partners

Our Mission

Delighting customers each and every time

Our Guiding Principles (Core Values)

We will ensure leadership drives for results.

We will make customer loyalty a key driver of our business.

We will enable decision making at customer contact point.

We will be committed to the financial success of our own unit and of our company.

We will create an environment where our colleagues may achieve their personal and career goals.

We will demonstrate honesty, care and integrity in all our relationships.

We will ensure our policies and processes are customer and employee friendly.

We will be environmentally conscientious and provide safety and security for our customers and our colleagues.

Source: Shangri-La Hotels and Resorts, http://www.shangri-la.com/en/home.aspx (accessed February 6, 2007).

> those countries. The danger is to become a cookie-cutter company and we cannot be. We have to be individualistic in each of our cities but still maintain our strong brand integrity.

For many years personalized guest service remained Shangri-La's main competitive advantage. By the early 2000s, as more and more Asian hotel groups such as Mandarin Oriental, Banyan Tree, and others expanded around the world, creating a strong brand and a tangible differentiation became even more important for the company.

DELEGATION OF AUTHORITY

To achieve exceptional customer service, Shangri-La used a five-level organizational design. The company grouped its employees into five tiers: Level 1 (divisional managers), Level 2 (departmental managers), Level 3 (sectional managers), Level 4 (front-line supervisors), and Level 5 (front-line employees). Each level had separate guidelines, discretion, and a dollar amount they could use (Level 1–3: HK$500; Level 4–5: HK$100) without management's approval in handling customer requests that were outside of normal operational guidelines.

Bridle explained:

> To deliver superior results, we believed in giving all front-line personnel decision-making power with respect to guest requests. For example, we allowed cashiers to waive amounts up to HK$100 without manager approval. Operationally, the system looked great. Then we realized, regardless of the amount, it was not always easy to get some Asian cultures to actually accept that they could make these decisions, on the spot, and exercise authority.

Bridle had just discovered a new problem. Giving decision-making power to the front-line employees was not always effective in Shangri-La's hotels in China. Although fully authorized to address guest requests, front-line employees in Shangri-La's China hotels appeared uncomfortable making decisions, especially those involving small monetary issues.

Chinese employees were very good at performing their duties in strict accordance with operational guidelines. However, the cultural predilection was not to take initiative but to be told by a superior how to handle a given situation. Once an order was given to do a specific task, most Chinese workers followed the instructions to the letter. While this was an advantage in getting many operational steps completed in the right order, it also meant that small problems encountered by guests took a long time to be corrected.

Bridle quickly found out that while the task-related skills such as making a reservation could be taught easily, it took time and practice to acquire judgment skills such as letting a mini bar expense go. "Decisions did not always involve money," he added. "The issue could be as simple as a guest forgetting her passport at the airport. Our front-line employee would think 'It could be expensive to take staff off duty to help the customer. What should I do?' They would also think about operational implications, as in who is going to cover me when I am gone. And that made the decision-making even harder for them." "Even when they knew they had the decision-making authority, they were not using it effectively," Dogan echoed Bridle's concern. "I remember, in the very early days, there was a situation where we had a guest who had a very small problem during check-in. The front-desk was so eager to get rid of the problem, they gave away a bottle of Dom Perignon to the guest."

In some cases, Chinese employees hesitated because they were simply not used to taking initiative. In others, local Chinese managers were unwilling to delegate and give up their perceived authority. "All it took was for one person further up the chain to say 'don't do that' and our front-line employees would not take another bite at the apple," recalled Tan Eng-Leong, Shangri-La's group director of human resources. Dogan agreed: "We introduced the delegation of authority a number of years ago and the culture that was being developed by us over the years was to empower people. Easily said, but very hard to implement. We tried to give our staff the confidence to make decisions, without any kickbacks or punishment. It was important that we developed a management culture and philosophy that brought that out."

Bridle continued:

> We knew that we could not deliver the desired standards of service if our front-office personnel in China were hesitant to take initiative. We had to instill a level of confidence in the employee that they could make those decisions. That required a great deal of communication and a need for continual training support to get the concepts across.

TRAINING AND THE SHANGRI-LA ACADEMY

Despite Shangri-La's commitment to highly personalized guest service, performance still varied considerably from hotel to hotel. Much of this variation was tied to hotel location and economics, but some was also tied to hotel management capability, leadership, and culture. In addition, the company's research reports showed that Shangri-La's aggressive expansion in China required the company's current workforce to grow from nearly 10,000 to approximately 19,000 employees—all of whom needed to meet Shangri-La's customer service standards. Shangri-La had to think bigger.

Bridle explained:

> Another one of our challenges was to ensure that there are enough qualified people to fill growing needs. This concerned all staff levels, from frontline staff and mid-level managers to senior leaders. We decided to invest heavily in training, both onsite in hotels and also at a brand new training academy near Beijing.

In 2004, the company opened its first training facility in China, the Shangri-La Academy, in efforts at standardizing the delivery of its brand promise throughout its network of hotels worldwide. While the academy was primarily set up to train employees in China to maintain consistent service delivery across Shangri-La's China hotels, all other Shangri-La hotels were also asked to allocate budget for this training and to send their high-potential employees to undergo the training modules offered by the Academy.

The training facility had six training rooms, a library, a computer lab, training and demonstration kitchens, a training restaurant, a training lounge, and a housekeeping practice suite. The Academy offered five-week to three-month training programs in western service operations, culinary arts (western cuisine), housekeeping operations, front office operations, and advanced hospitality management. The goal was to develop a new breed of hospitality professionals with enhanced skills and a strong service orientation equipped to adopt innovative approaches in tackling challenges at work. The academy's broad curriculum ensured that learners left the academy with the breadth and depth of knowledge and skill to thrive in their careers and advance global hospitality trends. After the training programs, participants were awarded certificates in F&B service, Housekeeping operations, Front Office operations, Culinary Arts and the Diploma in Hotel Management for the Advanced Hospitality Management Course.

The training programs focused heavily on preparing employees to more effectively utilize decision-making authority through the use of progressive and interactive instructional methodologies, such as role playing, to create the circumstances employees would face. "In our training facility we tried to simulate interaction with customers. For instance, in our training lounge—used as a restaurant in our restaurant simulation—we would have people pose as customers. They would come as guests, order food and beverages, and go through the whole service sequence. And our employees would get a chance to interact with them and practice what they learned in the classroom," said Perry, Director of the Room programs at the Shangri-La Academy.

In these interactive modules, a work situation scenario was taught with emphasis on common mistakes and best practices, so that trainees would learn to examine and question why "things were done in a certain way." Classes were often videotaped and analyzed for employee body language and manner with "customers." "What was their body language? Did they smile? Was the hand in the pocket when they served the customers? We would look at things like that," added Perry.

Tay Beng Koon, Director of Academic Development, added:

> One of our challenges was that our employees could see the immediate costs, as in I am giving up this room, but could not easily see the long-term implications. The issue was very tangible on one side and intangible on the other. To emphasize the future benefits, we developed and focused on company-wide guiding principles.

SHANGRI-LA CARE

Shangri-La's employee philosophy was to develop local talent to world class expectations. The company had already launched its culture training program, Shangri-La Care, in 1996 to ensure that each global employee delivered service "the Shangri-La Way" (see Exhibit 7). Shangri-La Care 1 focused on the five core values of Shangri-La Hospitality: respect, humility, courtesy, helpfulness and sincerity. The program was strongly supported by the top management and continuously cascaded through the organization. All hotels were required to allocate a specific budget for training and development, and the general manager of each hotel was personally responsible for ensuring that all the allocated funds were spent year after year.

As the company grew, Shangri-La added new modules to its culture program. In 1998, Shangri-La Care 2 was launched. In Module 2, the company focused on retention and guest loyalty. Going the extra mile, pleasing guests not just the first time but every single time, being flexible and never saying no, anticipating and responding quickly to customer requests, and recognizing the guest's individual needs were emphasized.

In 2003, the company launched Shangri-La Care 3 to emphasize the importance of recovery when a mistake was made. In Module 3, the company focused on the five steps to recovery—Listen, Apologize, Fix the Problem, Go the Extra Mile, and Follow Up.

Exhibit 7 The Shangri-La Care (also known as the Shangri-La Way)

Care Module 1: Shangri-La Hospitality from Caring People (Launched in 1996)

Addresses how to make our guests feel special and important by focusing on the five core values of Shangri-La Hospitality: Respect, Humility, Courtesy, Helpfulness and Sincerity. It also imbues the value of "Pride Without Arrogance" as the service hallmark.

Care Module 2: Delighting Customers (Launched in 1998)

Focuses on the importance of guest loyalty and how it can only be achieved by delighting our guests not just the first time but every single time. Employees must be guest obsessed, doing more for guests by "going the extra mile," being flexible and never saying no, anticipating and responding quickly, and recognizing the guest's individual needs.

Care Module 3: Recover to Gain Loyalty (Launched in 2003)

Highlights the importance of recovery when a mistake is made. When recovery is done well, it may be an opportunity to gain further commitment and loyalty but if there is no or poor recovery the lifetime value of the guest is lost in addition to at least 25 others who may hear of the incident through word of mouth. The module teaches the five steps to recovery—Listen, Apologize, Fix the Problem, Go the Extra Mile and Follow Up.

Care Module 4: Take Ownership (Launched in 2005)

Addresses the importance of our employees taking ownership—to show care for our customers, colleagues and company. The driver of ownership is "SELF," which means S—Show commitment, E—Eager to take initiative, L—Lead ourselves and F—Filled with passion. This module attempts to create in our employees the mind-set to live in an environment that is filled with Care for guests, Compassion for colleagues and Pride in our Company.

Source: Shangri-La Hotels and Resorts, http://www.shangri-la.com/en/home.aspx (accessed February 5, 2007).

In 2005, Shangri-La announced its fourth Shangri-La Care module, addressing the need of employees to take responsibility for customer satisfaction.

COMPENSATION AND CAREER GROWTH

By investing heavily in employee development, the company was not only making its employees valuable to Shangri-La but also to its competitors. "Retention became a big problem," said Tan Eng-Leong. "Traditionally, our turnover had always been low, 19–20 percent, compared to the industry norm, 27–28 percent, but the competition was offering 35 to 50 percent higher salaries."

Shangri-La had a three-tier compensation system. The company's level 1 employee—typically division heads and hotel general managers (GMs)—were paid a base salary and a bonus based on the hotel's overall performance. Overall, GM compensation was heavily geared towards the financial results (Gross Operating Profit and Gross Operating Revenue attainment).* Compensation for level 2 and 3 employees (e.g., property line managers) was similar to the level 1 structure—salary and bonus pay—with the exception that factors such as customer loyalty and employee satisfaction scores were also linked to employees' bonus awards. Employees at levels 4 and 5 typically enjoyed a common bonus incentive which was linked to property overall performance, but not to individual goals.

Bridle explained Shangri-La's compensation structure:

> We almost have a three-tier type of approach to it. We award our GMs very much based on the financial results: against budget and last year's financial performance. And there is a discretionary element based on their leadership competency. Level 2–3 compensation is also linked directly to GM's financial goals—everyone's compensation is—but at that level bonus numbers start breaking down to additional goals that reflect customer loyalty and employee satisfaction. All these things come in below the GM level. So, if you are at a level 3, you have more of directly measurable items like customer loyalty, quality standards, and audit standards. As you move up to Level 1 and 2, the compensation becomes more financial results oriented. However, even though our GM compensation doesn't have a direct link to customer satisfaction, they still have incentives to make sure that those goals are met. I think our senior management, as in level 1 and 2, sees this. They see that the performance is bottom-up; they know without customer satisfaction they would not achieve financial results.

He continued:

> It is becoming more transparent now. I think the important step for us is to move customer satisfaction, employee satisfaction and some compliance goals into the performance review scoring system, still with its key emphasis on financial results, to allow bonus/incentive numbers to move up and down. And indirectly it may influence your salary increment potential as well.

At individual properties, incentive pay did not typically vary across employees within each level. Increasingly, Shangri-La corporate executives moved to standardize pay practices across properties.

Dogan elaborated:

> In our old system, we had a lot of variation in compensation across properties. For instance, when people moved from one property to another, sometimes their compensation went down. That was not fair. We realized that we needed to reform our incentive pay model immediately.

To retain its workforce, the company also focused on creating transparent, well-defined career paths (see Exhibit 8). "Employees felt that an opportunity for professional growth was a key motivator," said Tan Eng-Leong. "So we created a lot of opportunities for our staff. We were expanding and we promoted from within. Our expansion gave huge opportunities to a lot of young people. People frequently got promoted to another property. We wanted to give our employees career paths and opportunities outside of their areas that other companies could not provide." Shangri-La's growth created a lot of opportunities for advancement. Within one to two years, most Shangri-La Service Associates were promoted to be Service Leaders. Another two years on the job would get them a managerial position and if they worked four years as a Senior Service Manager they became Service Executives.

Shangri-La staff could also move laterally from property to property. "Our expansion gave huge opportunities for our employees. Not only were there opportunities to move up within the property, there

*RevPar (Revenue Per Available Room) = A (Average Price Per Room) × O% (Rate of Occupancy)

Exhibit 8 Career Path in Shangri-La

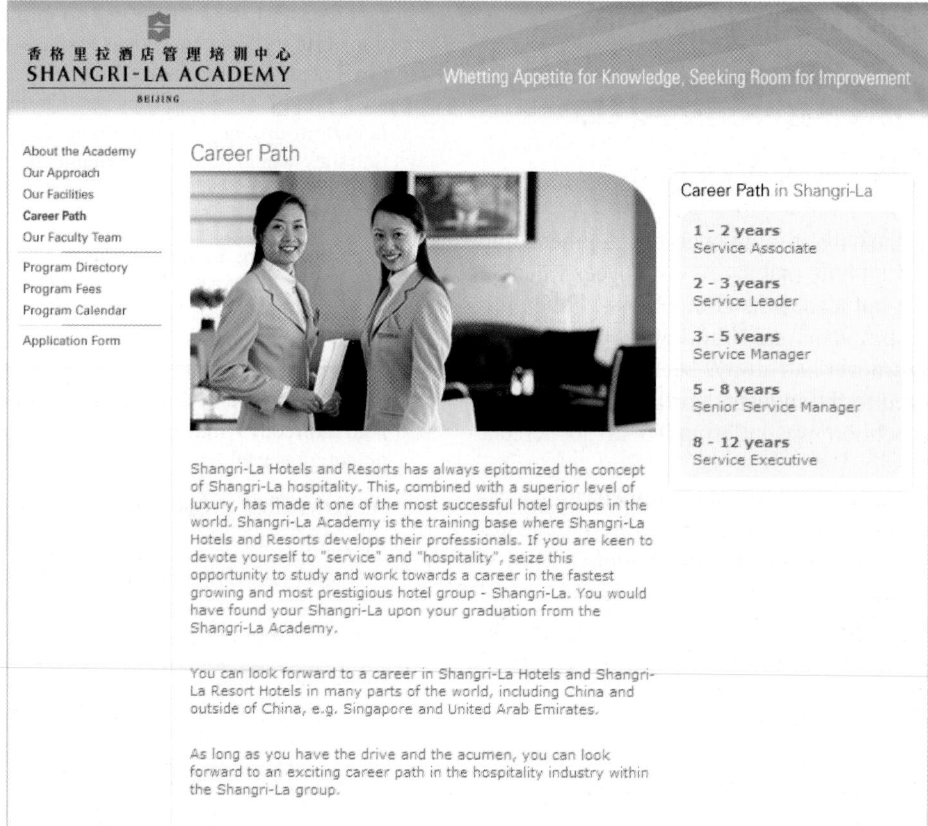

Source: Shangri-La Academy Beijing, http://www.shangri-la-academy.com/careerpath/en/index.aspx (accessed January 21, 2008).

were also opportunities to transfer to other Shangri-La properties in exotic locations like Dubai. Basically, if our staff decided to stay with our company, we gave them a future," Dogan added.

The company also tried alternative methods, including non-pay recognition (i.e., contests, awards, etc.) to motivate employees. Dogan recalled: "When I had the staff assembly with 2,000 people in the ballroom, I used to get out there with a $100 bill and say 'Anybody who has the guts to come up here, from each department, and recite the guiding principle and tell me what it means, come up here.' People would storm the stage. It was a lot of fun, everyone was cheering for their department, and it was a simple, non-stressful way of getting them to make sure that they knew it, understood it, and practiced it. It became a real culture."

EXPANSION TO THE EAST: CHINA'S HOTEL MARKET

As Shangri-La trained its employees, fixed cultural issues, and expanded its operations in China, the company faced additional challenges. After 20 years of rapid economic growth, China in 2006 had become the world's fourth largest economy and one of the world's most attractive destinations for tourists, which meant significant opportunities for hotel development.[4] According to industry analysts, China would be Asia's hottest spot for hotel development in 2006, accounting for nearly half of all new projects in the region.[5] Of the 386 hotels actively in development throughout Asia in 2006, 188 were in China, and 134 of those were rated four- or five-star.[6]

Competition

With growth slowing in Europe and North America, hotel chains were targeting Asia—China in particular—for their new growth. Soon after the International Olympic Committee announced Beijing as the 2008 Olympics' host, premium hotels started to pop up all over Shanghai, Beijing and other Chinese cities as Regent, Ritz-Carlton, Hyatt, Sheraton and others poured billions of dollars into expansion.[7]

By 2001, the U.K.-based InterContinental Hotel Group (IHG), which also operated the Crowne Plaza and Holiday Inn chains, was the most ambitious player in the Chinese market. IHG had a portfolio of 51 hotels in China and planned to develop an additional 74 by 2008.[8] The U.S.-based Marriott chain, which operated the Ritz-Carlton, Renaissance, and Courtyard brands, had 26 hotels in China and planned to expand its portfolio to 100 by 2010. France's Accor had 30 hotels under development in China, all scheduled to open before 2008.[9] Wyndham Hotel Group, which also owned the Ramada and Wingate Inn brands, had a portfolio of 60 hotels in China in 2006 and planned to expand its China business at an annual rate of 40 percent in anticipation of the 2008 Olympics.[10]

Local Hotels

Local hotels had poor brand recognition relative to their overseas rivals. Some thought that the influx of foreign capital and brands would force the local hotels to improve their establishments and services. However, none of the Chinese hotel chains could match the name recognition and service standards of Hilton, Hyatt, InterContinental, or Marriott. Some local hotel groups considered forming alliances with international brands, in which the local partner would be responsible for funding the construction of the hotel, while the foreign partner took on the management and operation of the business.

Pressure on Wages

Asia's low labor costs boosted hotel gross profits significantly. In 2001, China's average cost of manual labor averaged less than $1 per hour, while the U.S. averaged $16 per hour (see Exhibit 9). As a result, the hotel industry was more profitable in Asia than in the West. A typical four- or five-star luxury hotel in Asia achieved gross profit margins of 35 to 45 percent, compared with 20 to 25 percent in the West.[11]

Exhibit 9 Hourly Wages by Country

Country	Dollars per Hour
Japan	$16.46
United States	16.14
Europe	14.13
Singapore	6.72
Korea	5.69
Taiwan	5.18
Mexico	2.08
Brazil	2.04
China	0.61

Source: Bureau of Labor Statistics; China Statistical Yearbook, http://www.bls.gov/opub/cwc/content/articles.stm (accessed March 28, 2007).

In 2001, several major international hotel chains entered the Chinese deluxe (four- and five-star) hotel market, creating sudden demand for skilled hotel workers. Newcomers either poached Shangri-La's trained staff or offered higher than average industry wages to attract their own. Shangri-La, the only major player in China up until that point, found it difficult to keep up with the competition. "Consider Beijing," Bridle said. "A half-dozen five-star hotels coming into the market . . . Our reservation managers are being offered 35 percent higher salary by our competitors. Our security managers are being offered 50 percent higher!" Shangri-La's low annual turnover rates of 19 to 20 percent—versus 27 to 28 percent for the industry as a whole—were under threat.

Dogan commented:

> With China coming onto the world stage, what I am finding out is that some of our staff is like "gold dust" to outside industry. Our trained, English speaking front office staff is whisked away when the multinationals come in to set up their company. That is our biggest challenge.

EXPANSION TO THE WEST

China was not Shangri-La's only focus. The company was about to launch multiple hotels in Europe, Australia, and North America. These countries had relatively more expensive labor markets, where trained hotel staff was in short supply. In Sydney, for instance, the typical staff-to-guest ratio was 0.8 (compared to Shangri-La's 1.5). Chicago, Miami, Las Vegas, Vancouver, and Toronto—some of the locations Shangri-La targeted for expansion—all had similar labor markets. The only exception was Paris, with a staff-to-guest ratio of 2.1 or higher, but this was driven by Paris' comparatively high hotel prices. A typical five-star hotel room in Paris usually went for €600 or €700. "Unfortunately, this pricing strategy cannot necessarily be translated into other markets where new Shangri-La's were coming," Bridle said. "Charging more for rooms could not really be considered as an option in new high-wage markets, since pricing is dictated by the market."

He continued:

> During our expansion, our main concern is to maintain worldwide service quality standards and deliver excellent service to customers. An immediate, and long-term, challenge is to ensure that signature Shangri-La quality and service standards are translated to new hotels in new markets. It's been said that you only have one chance to make a first impression and guests must know they will experience the essence of Shangri-La hospitality wherever one of its hotels opens its doors. And when loyal Shangri-La guests travel outside the region, they must experience the same level and style of service they have come to expect at Shangri-La hotels and resorts in Asia-Pacific and the Middle East. We need to maintain control and translate our Asian service model into tighter labor markets in the western world.

Superior customer care was typical of many luxury Asian hotels and was definitely a standard at Shangri-La and to deliver a consistent experience of Asian grace, warmth, and care—what Shangri-La called "Shangri-La Hospitality"—all of its hotels maintained a high staff-to-guest ratio. In Hong Kong and Singapore, for example, this ratio was close to 1.25 to 1.5 staff per guest. In developing countries it could be as high as 2.5 to 3.0 staff per guest.[12] Keeping a high ratio of staff-to-guests, which ensured better service and attention to detail, had never been an issue for Shangri-La in low-wage countries like Malaysia or China; however, the practice was not easily transferable to high-wage countries such as the U.S., Australia, or Canada—at least not without creating unacceptably high payroll costs.

LOOKING AHEAD

As Bridle grabbed the phone to call his assistant to schedule another executive meeting, a stream of questions rushed through his mind. Did Shangri-La need to alter its strategy? Could they maintain their unique brand of Shangri-La Hospitality as they moved into tighter labor markets? They were battling high-end Western hotel chains at home and abroad and needed to overcome wage and cultural issues in their properties across the globe.

Bridle wanted to ensure that Shangri-La maintained its service model as they continued to expand. "We need to have a consistent platform and consistent service quality," thought Bridle. With the first of the new slate of hotels scheduled to open in 2007, time was running out.

Endnotes

[1] "Shangri-La Hotels and Resorts," http://www.shangri-la.com/en/home.aspx (accessed February 5, 2007).

[2] "Tej Company Profile—Shangri-La Asia Ltd," *Taiwan Economic Journal,* available via Factiva (accessed February 2, 2007).

[3] "Shangri-La Hotels Opens The Shangri-La Academy to Provide Chinese Students Hospitality Tools and Training," http://www.hotel-online.com/News/PR2004_4th/Dec04_ShangriLaAcademy.html (accessed April 18, 2007).

[4] "China, India to Drive Strong Growth in Emerging Asia: IMF," *Agence France Presse,* April 11, 2007, available via Factiva (accessed April 11, 2007).

[5] "First-ever Lodging Development Pipeline for Asia Reveals China as Having the World's Largest Development Activity Outside the U.S.," *Lodging Econometrics,* June 2, 2006 (accessed April 18, 2007).

[6] "InterContinental Ramps Up China Growth Pace," *Reuters News,* October 17, 2006, available via Factiva (accessed March 12, 2007).

[7] "China Hotel and Tourism News," http://www.chinaeconomicreview.com/hotels/2006/08/ (accessed April 10, 2007).
[8] "Intercontinental Hotels Transcript of Preliminary Results Conference," http://www.ihgplc.com/files/presentations/prelims05/conference_call_transcription.pdf (accessed April 18, 2007).
[9] "Competition Heats Up in Hotel Market," *China Daily,* September 27, 2006, available via Factiva (accessed March 12, 2007).
[10] "Wyndham Plans Rapid China Hotel Growth, Eyes India," *New Zealand Press Association,* October 12, 2006, available via Factiva (accessed March 29, 2007).
[11] "A Tasteful Host," *Forbes,* July 28, 1997, available via ProQuest (accessed April 10, 2007).
[12] "Shangri-La Hotels to Spread Their Allure to Vancouver," *Sun,* September 24, 2004 (accessed April 12, 2007).

CASE

25 E. & J. Gallo Winery

Marion Armstrong
The University of Alabama

A. J. Strickland
The University of Alabama

Taylor Green
The University of Alabama

In 2006, wine in the United States represented a $28 billion industry, with 716 million gallons sold, of which about 92 million gallons were dessert wines.[1,2] Included within the dessert wine category was a group of cheap, low-grade, and highly controversial high-proof, or "fortified," wines that contained added alcohol to increase their potency and additional sugar or sweetener to enhance their taste—see Exhibit 1. Most natural wine products had only about 8 to 12 percent alcohol by volume, since the yeasts that were used in the fermentation process were killed by higher alcohol concentrations. Many of the cheap fortified wine products were deliberately made and sold at the highest potency because they were the low-cost alcoholic beverage favored by people with low incomes and budget-constrained teenagers and college students who were looking for something "relatively strong, inexpensive, and pleasant tasting."[3]

Wild Irish Rose and Cisco were two fortified wines that together made their parent company, Canandaigua, the number one seller in the fortified wine market, with about 70 percent of the industry's business in 1996,[4] followed by Gallo's Thunderbird brand and Mogen David Wine's MD 20/20. Canandaigua's Cisco wine cooler, known as "liquid cocaine" on the streets, had the fourth leading market share in the dessert wine segment. For several decades, low-end dessert and fortified wines had been a profitable, high-volume market segment that winemakers had targeted. *The Wall Street Journal* reported in 1988 that, of all the wine brands sold in America, Richard's Wild Irish Rose (named after the founder's son, Richard Sands, who had been Canandaigua's president until 1999) was 6th in volume of sales, Thunderbird was 10th, and MD 20/20 was 16th.

Originally, fortified wines were made by adding brandy (distilled wine) to wine to raise the alcohol content so as to help prevent spoilage during shipping and to extend the shelf life—the higher alcohol content killed off bacteria and other organisms. Port and sherry wines were good examples of high-quality fortified wines. However, the makers of low-grade fortified wines often used cheaper grain alcohol to raise the alcohol content to 14 to 20 percent and thus make their products more appealing to buyers looking to get drunk cheap. Low-grade fortified wines like Richard's Wild Irish Rose, Thunderbird, Night Train (another Gallo product), and Boone's Farm are generally sold for less than $3.50 per 750 ml bottle and for between $1 and $2 per 375 ml bottle (about 12.5 ounces). These low prices made them a favorite of low-income drinkers, skid-row alcoholics, and young adults since they produced more intoxication for less money than just about any other type of alcoholic beverage. The dose of alcohol in a typical 12.5-ounce Cisco wine cooler or a pint of Thunderbird was five times the dose of alcohol in a 12-ounce can of beer, a 4- to 5-ounce serving of wine, or a 1.25-ounce shot of bourbon—see Exhibit 2.

Typical of the critics of fortified wines was Mark Dalton, a social worker for Washington State's Division of Alcohol and Substance Abuse; Dalton said,

Exhibit 1 Examples of Low-end Fortified Wines That Had Attracted Criticism

"Fortified wines and cheap strong beer are packaged and marketed to alcoholics, and the corner stores who sell them are making profits while contributing to a cycle of addiction as well as a public nuisance."[5] Addiction professionals had dubbed cheap fortified wine "the most seriously abused drug in this country."[6] It was common for people who were charged with trying to help the chronic alcoholics who drank cheap fortified wines to express the view that manufacturing and selling such products was unethical, even bordering on being criminal; they often charged that the providers (wineries and licensed retail stores) had no conscience and that their actions were repulsive. A drug and alcohol counselor from Mountain View Hospital in Gadsden, Alabama, told of crack addicts' stories about buying Mad Dog (the street name for MD 20/20) to help them come off their crack high; according to the counselor, addicts said they chose Mad Dog because it was "cheap and strong." The president of one winery said, "Fortified wines lack any socially redeeming values." In a 1988 *Wall Street Journal* article, Paul Gillette, publisher of *Wine Investor*, said, "Makers of skid-row wines are the dope-pushers of the wine industry. And these companies are the largest producers and appear the most successful wineries."[7]

In many states, fortified wines were effectively limited to a maximum of 20 percent alcohol content by tax and licensing laws. For example, Indiana law defined *wine* as a beverage "that does not contain 21% or more alcohol." This meant that a wine with higher alcohol content could not be sold in grocery and convenience stores (which were typically licensed to sell only beer and wine); wines with more than the legal alcohol content limit were taxed at the much higher rates for distilled spirits. Federal taxes also jumped up for wines with alcohol content above 20 percent.

The major producers and marketers of low-end dessert and fortified wines defended their products and disputed the critics' characterization of the buyers of fortified wines. Sid Abrams of the Wine Institute, which represented California vintners, said, "There are a lot of people who just like the flavor. And some older people buy inexpensive sherry because they can't afford the more expensive product."[8] The problem of street alcoholics presents a dilemma, Abrams said, "but I don't think you can blame the manufacturers." Another defense was that since it was legal to produce and market cheap fortified wines, there was nothing wrong with winemakers and store retailers pursuing the market opportunities that existed. However, the producers of the top-selling fortified wines distanced themselves from their fortified wine

Exhibit 2 Alcohol Content of Selected Alcoholic Beverages

Alcoholic Beverage	Alcohol Content
12 ounces of 4% beer	0.48 ounces
5 ounces of 10% wine	0.50 ounces
1.25 ounces of 40% vodka (80 proof)	0.50 ounces
1.25 ounces of 43% whiskey (86 proof)	0.52 ounces
40 ounce bottle of 8% malt liquor	3.20 ounces
1.25 ounce shot of 151 proof rum	0.94 ounces
12.5 ounce bottle of 6% wine cooler	0.75 ounces
12.5 ounce bottle of 20% fortified wine cooler	2.50 ounces

Examples of high-potency alcoholic beverages

- Fortified wines (most low-cost brands were sold at or near 20% alcohol by volume)
- Wine coolers (most were about 6% alcohol by volume, 1.5 times more potent than typical beer)
- Specialty wine coolers, such as Cisco (up to 20% alcohol by volume)
- Malt liquors (up to 8% alcohol by volume, nearly twice the potency of typical American beer)
- Neutral grain spirits, such as Everclear (95% alcohol by volume)
- High-proof liquors, such as 151 Rum (75.5% alcohol by volume, about twice the potency of other rums)

Source: William J. Bailey, "Factline on High Potency Alcoholic Beverages," Indiana Prevention Resource Center, Indiana University, www.drugs.indiana.edu/publications/iprc/factline/high_potency.html.

product offerings by leaving their corporate names off the labels—an omission that critics interpreted as being deliberately intended to obscure the producer's link to these brands. While vintners claimed that "indistinct labeling is a common industry practice that reserves a vintner's name only for its most expensive products," critics of the industry segment were not convinced, claiming hypocrisy on the part of the manufacturers. Gallo manufactured wines for a number of different price ranges under various labels and listed all of those wines as a part of its family of brands. But while this list included Gallo's lower-end labels such as Boone's Farm and Bartles & Jaymes, noticeably absent from the list was Thunderbird, even though it was still sold in low-income areas across the United States.

THE E. & J. GALLO WINERY

The Early Years

The E. & J. Gallo Winery, the largest wine producer in the world, was founded by Ernest and Julio Gallo in 1933. The Gallo brothers got their start in the wine business working during their spare time in their father's vineyard near Modesto, California. Their father, Joseph Gallo Sr., had immigrated from the Piedmont region in northwest Italy and was a small-time grape grower and shipper of California wine. He survived Prohibition because the government permitted the personal production of no more than 100 gallons of wine per year; many Californians made wine in amounts under this limit if they could get the grapes. This loophole allowed the elder Gallo to sell grapes in bulk shipments to private brewers. But the Depression was tough, and Gallo's company almost went under and during the spring of 1933 the family was scarred by tragedy when Joseph Gallo Sr. and his wife were found dead in an apparent murder/suicide.

Following his parents' deaths, Ernest Gallo became head of the family and the business. The Gallo brothers, both in their early 20s, decided it would be a good idea to integrate forward into making wine even though neither knew anything about the process. Ernest and Julio found two thin pamphlets on winemaking in the Modesto Public Library and, with $5,900 to their names, began to invest in winemaking capability. Julio oversaw the vineyards and the winemaking operation, while Ernest handled marketing and distribution; their youngest brother, Joseph Gallo Jr., was an employee. Ernest pushed to build the company, aiming at a broad national market and envisioning E. & J. Gallo as becoming the "Campbell Soup company of the wine industry." He drove himself and his employees hard, sometimes working 16-hour days and taking long trips around the country by car to make sales calls and learn about consumers' wine-drinking preferences and habits. It was his practice to study the company's markets and customers very carefully and base the winery's marketing strategy on detailed market research concerning buyer behavior and preferences.

With the end of Prohibition, the Gallo brothers set out to become market leaders in what was then a relatively small and mostly downscale American wine market. Ernest effectively marketed cheap, fortified wines like White Port and lemon-flavored Thunderbird in inner-city markets. There were stories, which Gallo denied, that the winery got the idea for citrus-flavored Thunderbird from reports that liquor stores in Oakland, California, were catering to the tastes of certain customers by attaching packages of lemon Kool-Aid to bottles of white wine to be mixed at home. Thunderbird, introduced in the late 1950s and named after the ritzy Thunderbird Hotel in Las Vegas, Nevada, became Gallo's first phenomenal success. A catchy radio jingle helped send Thunderbird to the top of the sales charts in many inner-city and low-income neighborhoods across the United States:

What's the word?

Thunderbird

How's it sold?

Good and cold

What's the jive?

Bird's alive

What's the price?

Thirty twice.

According to author Ellen Hawkes, who wrote an unauthorized history of the Gallo family called *Blood and Wine,* Ernest later delighted in telling the story of driving through a tough inner-city neighborhood and, upon seeing a man walking down the sidewalk, pulling alongside, rolling down his window, and calling out, "What's the word?" The man's immediate answer was "Thunderbird."

The Gallos began researching varietal grapes in 1946, planting more than 400 varieties in experimental vineyards during the 1950s and 1960s and testing each variety in the different grape-growing regions of California for its ability to produce fine table wines. Their greatest difficulty was to persuade growers to convert from common grape varieties to the delicate, thin-skinned varietals because it took at least four years for a vine to begin bearing and perhaps two more years to develop typical varietal characteristics. As an incentive, in 1967, Gallo offered long-term contracts to growers, guaranteeing the prices for their grapes every year, provided they met Gallo quality standards. With a guaranteed long-term buyer for their crops, growers were able to borrow the needed capital to finance the costly replanting, and the winery's staff of skilled viticulturists provided technical assistance to aid contract growers.

While most California wineries concentrated on production and sold their wines through wholesale distributors, Gallo pursued a vertical integration strategy and participated in every aspect from growing grapes to making wine to sales and marketing to owning and operating its wine distributorships. E. & J. Gallo Winery owned the wholesale distributors of Gallo wines in about 10 geographic markets and probably would have bought many of the more than 300 independent distributors handling its wines if laws in most states had not prohibited it. The entrepreneurial freedom that came with private ownership, the wise stewardship of Ernest and Julio Gallo, low-cost mass production, and strong distribution were the major competitive advantages contributing to Gallo's success. Since the company was family-owned, the Gallo brothers could use low prices and paper-thin margins to win market share from higher-cost rivals and could absorb occasional losses in introducing new brands and widening the winery's geographic reach, whereas wineries that were publicly held had to appease earnings-minded stockholders. While Gallo bought about 95 percent of its grapes, it virtually controlled its 1,500 growers through long-term contracts. Gallo's trucking company, Fairbanks, hauled wine out of Modesto and brought raw materials in. Gallo was the only winery that manufactured its own bottles (2 million a day) and screw-top caps.

Gallo's Gradual Shift to More Upscale Wines

Gallo's major competitive weakness over the years had always been its reputation as a maker of low-end wines in screw-top bottles—an image that flowed partly from its Thunderbird and Night Train brands. This was not so much a liability in the company's early days, when wine sales in the United States were heavily concentrated in the low end of the market, but Gallo's low-end image became an increasing liability in the 1980s as wine consumers began to purchase better-quality table wines in increasing numbers and as wine became a favored beverage at cocktail parties. As the company grew over the years, first becoming the largest winemaker in the United States and then the largest in the world, the Gallo brothers initiated a series of moves to shed the winery's image as a maker of low-end wines sold in screw-top bottles and jugs. Gallo's new strategy was to distance itself from the Thunderbird and Night Train brands and begin the long-range task of repositioning itself as a maker of better quality, moderately priced table wines and then later as a maker of truly fine wines.

From 1985 to 2000, the company spent hundreds of millions in advertising aimed at boosting consumer perceptions of Gallo wines and cultivating a clientele for its new, more upscale wines.[9] At the same time, the company invested in production facilities to make more upscale table wines under a variety of labels, some of which were created internally and some of which were acquired. Ernest Gallo studied the markets the company targeted and the tastes and wine-drinking habits of consumers very carefully—from the high end to the low end of the price/quality scale. Under his watchful eye, Gallo's marketing strategy was always based on detailed market research concerning buyer behavior and preferences. By the mid-1990s, the company had been reasonably successful in attracting more upscale wine drinkers to try its newly introduced wines and wine brands. In 1998, one of the company's estate-bottled premium Chardonnay wines was rated 94 points on *Wine Spectator*'s 100-point scale.[10] In 1998 and again in 2001, Gallo won the Premio Gran VinItaly at the International Wine and Distilled Fair in Verona, Italy, making Gallo the only foreign winery to win twice in the history of the award. As of 2001, the company had more than 75 brands in its product lineup and was exporting wines to countries all over the world.

While Ernest and Julio Gallo were pouring their money and efforts into introducing new, higher quality wines with the goal of improving the company's overall image, they not only tried to distance themselves from their earlier all-star labels but also began to phase out the production of these products altogether. In 1993, Gallo was selling roughly 3 million cases of Thunderbird a year. The company had quit advertising the product altogether by 2003 and sold only 300,000 cases that year.[11] This decrease in focus on Thunderbird was more than likely a result of the changing tastes of American wine consumers as well as the social pressures the company began to face in the late 1980s. In August 1989, Gallo stopped distributing its two lower-end wines (Thunderbird and Night Train) and instructed retailers not to sell these brands anymore. Whatever good intentions it demonstrated, this ban didn't last: Thunderbird returned to inner cities and skid-row areas less than six months later.[12]

Ernest and Julio Gallo were active contributors to political campaigns, with Ernest contributing largely to Democrats and Julio giving more to Republicans. Over the years, the Gallos reportedly contributed $381,000 to Senator Robert Dole and about $900,000 to foundations with which Dole was connected.[13] In 1998, Ernest Gallo helped bring in $100,000 for a Bill Clinton fund-raising lunch in San Francisco only weeks after the *Los Angeles Times* reported that he had met privately with President Clinton to discuss Chilean wine imports (which had recently been gaining market share in the low-priced end of the U.S. wine market). Shortly after Ernest's meeting with the president, Congress delayed any action to authorize increases in Chilean wine imports and also passed increased funding for a wine promotion program that funneled millions of dollars to Gallo to promote its wines overseas. A bipartisan group of senators included this program in a 1998 listing of a "dirty dozen" examples of corporate welfare.

E. & J. Gallo Winery in 2007

In 2007, the E. & J. Gallo Winery was continuing to operate as a privately owned and family-operated corporation. Second-generation family members Joseph and Robert Gallo, along with Julio's son-in-law James Coleman, were serving as co-presidents of the company in 2007. Julio died in a 1993 car accident, and Ernest passed away in 2007 in his Modesto home at the age of 97. Julio's grandchildren Matt and Gina had by this time become important members of the company's winemaking team. Gina Gallo studied winemaking at the University of California–Davis and crafted her first wine in 1993.[14] Her views on winemaking were featured at the company's Web site:

> For me, wine is a pleasure. It has to be beautiful to look at and smell and astonishing to taste. But I don't want to make obvious wines. I want depth and a little

mystery, and I want some "wow" in there too. Along with the rest of my family, I was very proud when Gallo of Sonoma was named Winery of the Year in 1996, 1998 and again in 2001. As a winemaker, however, I've never forgotten a secret that my grandpa once told me. The true test of a wine, he said, happens in the face of someone when they drink it for the first time. If they smile before their eyes meet yours, then the wine is a success. They have already told you so, without ever saying a word.[15]

At another point, Gina Gallo wrote:

> Our guiding principle remains the same as it was for our grandparents: Make each vintage better than the last. This philosophy has helped us create wines that continue to receive international recognition.[16]

Matt Gallo commented on the company's grape-growing practices and technological advances in how Gallo's vineyards in California's Sonoma wine region were now being managed:

> Many of the vineyards I look after today were planted by my grandfather, Julio. He was an early pioneer of sustainable agriculture in this county. At a time when farmers took what they could get from the land, Julio was conserving the soil, the water and the natural environment. Only half of the property we own in Sonoma is actually cultivated, thanks to the 50/50 Give Back Program he created. Julio didn't just believe in the land—he showed people that redwoods and vineyards could thrive together.
>
> From my father, Bob Gallo, I learned how to focus my efforts on the fruit. He was forever experimenting with new rootstock, trellising techniques and better ways of harvesting the grapes. As a result, every vine at Gallo of Sonoma is "touched" at least six times prior to harvest to ensure the growing conditions are optimal.
>
> Fortunately, I have access to new technologies—tools Dad and Grandpa didn't have—that can help. For instance, I can pinpoint weather conditions in a certain section of a vineyard using the latest technology. The accuracy is unbelievable, especially when you cross-reference it with soil and crop data. Does that mean less time in the vine rows, tasting grapes and touching the soil? Not by a long shot. Computers have memory, but farmers have a feeling for the land—a feeling that someday I hope to hand down to my kids.

In April 2001, Ernest Gallo received the Lifetime Achievement Award from the prestigious James Beard Foundation; in presenting the award, Charles Osgood spoke about "the power and persistence of the Gallo mission to make not just the most, but the best wines possible."[17] John Deluca, chairman of the Wine Institute, further elaborated on Ernest Gallo and the Gallo legacy: "He has really created the modern wine industry in America. . . . The Gallo brothers have been the most important force in the positive transformation of the California wine industry this last century." Marvin Shanken, publisher of *Wine Spectator,* said, "All Americans who drink wine at their dinner table today are in his debt." But what always seemed to go unsaid was that, despite the company's industry prominence and the growing market success and quality of Gallo table wines, the cheap bottles of Thunderbird and Night Train still continued to be among the best-selling and most notorious wines that E. & J. Gallo Winery produced and marketed. In 2008, the company's Web site featured many of its award-winning wines and highlighted the care and attention paid by the company's winemakers to making quality wines—but there was no mention of Thunderbird.

Exhibit 3 shows the 10 largest U.S. wineries. In 2006, the E. & J. Gallo Winery produced more than one-fifth of the total volume of wine in the United States (20.6 percent).[18] The company sold about 70 million cases of wine in domestic and international markets in 2007, resulting in about 3.5 billion in sales revenues.[19] Constellation, the second leading winery based on volume, produced 20.5 percent of U.S. wine. Constellation was the parent company of Canandaigua, a New York–based winery and producer of Richard's Wild Irish Rose. Constellation showed approximately $4.6 billion in 2007 sales revenues, but that figure included the sale of beer and spirits.[20]

As E. & J. Gallo approached its 75th anniversary, the company had a lot of things to be proud of. Gallo had more than 60 different wine brands visible in many segments of the industry, in 90 different countries, and they were growing. In 2007, Gallo purchased more than 325 acres in the Napa Valley reportedly to "keep pace with growing consumer demand worldwide."[21] Gallo also recently appointed the Swedish company Spendrups Vin as a new importer to handle the distribution of its products in Sweden.[22]

In addition to its expansive growth, E. & J. Gallo Winery continued to position itself as a maker of high-end fine wines. According to *Wine Spectator,* Gallo was the "largest-selling global brand."

Exhibit 3 The 10 Largest U.S. Wineries Based on Sales Volume, 2006

Winery	Brands	Sales Volume (cases)
E. & J. Gallo	Gallo, Turning Leaf, Carlo Rossi, Thunderbird, Red Bicyclette, Sonoma County, Barelli Creek, Stefani, Laguna, Frei, New Russian River, Reserve, and others	62,000,000
Constellation Brands	Includes labels under Canandaigua (Wild Irish Rose), Franciscan Estates, Hardy Wine Company, Nobilo Wine Group, Pacific Wine Partners, and others	57,000,000
The Wine Group	Franzia Bros., Mogen David, Tribuno, Edgewood Estate, Monthaven, Summerfield, The Big House, bulk wines, and others	42,000,000
Bronco Wine Company	Forestville, Estrella, Charles Shaw, Montpellier, Grand Cru, Silver Ridge, Rutherford Vintners, Fox Hollow, Napa Ridge, and others	22,000,000
Foster's Wine Estates	Lindemans, Rosemount, Little Penguin, Beringer, Etude, Stags' Leap, St. Clement, Jean, Asti, Meridian, and others	16,000,000
Trinchero Family Estates	Sutter Home, alcohol-free Fre, Trinchero, Montevina, Trinity Oaks, Ménage a Trois, and others	10,000,000
Brown-Forman Wines	Virgin Wines, Gala Rouge, Little Black Dress, Fetzer, and others	6,600,000
Diageo Chateau & Estate Wines	Beaulieu Vineyard, Sterling Vineyards, Sterling Vintner's Collection, Solaris, Century Cellars, Monterey Vineyard, and others	5,500,000
Jackson Family Wines	Kendall-Jackson, White Rocket, Vintner's Reserve, Cambria, Hartford Family Wines, and others	5,000,000
St. Michelle Wine Estates	Chateau Ste. Michelle, Columbia Crest, Snoqualmie, NorthStar, Stimson Estate Cellars, Red Diamond, and others	4,200,000

Source: The Wine Institute; Gomberg, Fredrikson & Associates.

Gallo produced the top-selling (by unit volume) red and white table wines in the United States. Its Blush Chablis became the best-selling blush-style wine within the first year of its national introduction. Gallo's award-winning vertical wines were among the top sellers in their classification. During 1999 and 2000, Gallo's Carlo Rossi and Livingston Cellars brands outsold all other popular-priced wines except Franzia. Gallo's Andre Champagne brand was by far the best-selling champagne in the United States, and E&J Brandy outsold the number two and three brands combined. Gallo's line of wine coolers, produced under the brand name of Bartles & Jaymes, had been a leader in the wine cooler segment since its introduction in the 1980s and was the top-ranking seller in 2000. VinItaly named Gallo of Sonoma the International Winery of the year in 1998, 2001, and 2002, making Gallo the first (and to date only) American company to win three times. In 2006, Gallo received the Gold and Best of Class awards at the San Francisco Wine Competition and won individual awards for its cabernet sauvignon and its chardonnay. In 2007, Gallo partnered with Martha Stewart to market a special edition premium wine.[23]

So why, after winning so many awards and apparently having done so well in other parts of the wine market, did Gallo still produce the skid-row wines?

THE U.S. WINE INDUSTRY

Sales of all types of wines sales in the United States grew from about 90 million gallons in 1940 to 587 million gallons in 1986. Over the next 7 years, wine sales declined annually and totaled on 449 million gallons in 1993. But a resurgence of consumer interest in wine began, pushing wine sales up steadily each year. Total sales reached 745 million gallons in 2007—see Exhibit 4. Exhibit 5 shows trends in per capita wine consumption in the United States. In 2006, wine accounted for 16.6 percent of the total alcohol consumed in United States, up from 15.7 in 2000.[24] The United States was the world's fourth leading wine producer, in terms of volume, behind France, Italy, and Spain. Retail wine sales in the United States exceeded $28 billion in 2006.

Per capita consumption of wine in the United States was relatively low prior to the 1970s because wine was perceived as a drink either for the very wealthy or for skid-row winos. Fortified dessert wines were the top-selling wines of the 1935–1970 period. The first surge in wine consumption in the late 1960s was the result of the introduction of inexpensive "pop" wines such as Boone's Farm, Cold Duck, and various brands of sangria. These wines were bought by baby boomers, who were then college-aged young adults; sweet pop wines with a kick were better suited to the high-energy party atmosphere in which they were consumed than were the more pricy table wines. By the mid-1970s, pop wine drinkers began moving up to Lambrusco and trendy wine spritzers. The introduction of wine coolers helped drive several years of rising consumption in the 1984–1988 period; by 1987 sales of wine coolers totaled 72.6 million nine-liter cases, with Gallo's Bartles & Jaymes brand rising quickly to a market-leading position. Some of the slowdown in wine consumption in the 1985–1995 period was attributed to the national obsession with fitness, increases in the legal drinking age from 18 to 21, and crackdowns on drunk driving.

During the 1990s, consumer interest in the United States began to grow in better-quality and premium-quality table wines; interest in red wines had increased considerably because of medical reports that a glass of red wine was healthy owing to its ability to reduce the risk of heart disease. In addition, the booming stock market of the 1990s and busy lifestyles contributed to more dining out and,

Exhibit 4 Wine Consumption in the United States, 1940–2007

Year	Total Consumption, All Types of Wines* (in millions of gallons)	Total Consumption, Table Wines Only (in millions of gallons)
2007	745	650
2006	717	628
2005	692	609
2004	665	589
2003	639	570
2002	617	552
2001	574	512
2000	568	507
1995	464	404
1990	509	423
1985	580	478
1980	480	360
1970	267	133
1960	163	53
1950	140	36
1940	90	27

*Includes table wines, sparkling wines, dessert wines, vermouth, and all other still wines not over 14 percent alcohol.

Source: The Wine Institute, Gomberg, Fredrikson & Associates.

Exhibit 5 Per Capita Wine Consumption in the United States, 1935–2007

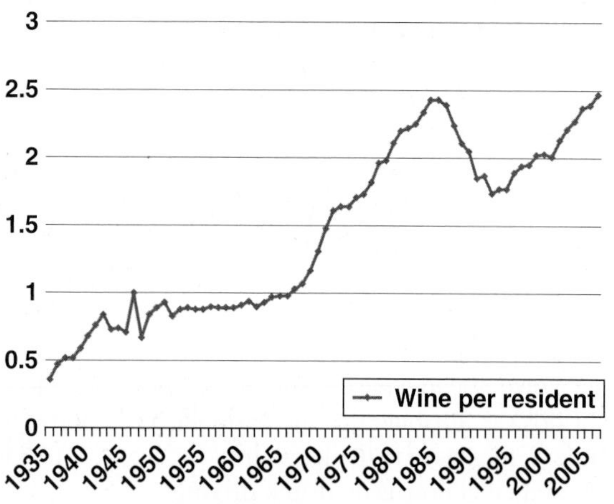

Note: Based upon Bureau of the Census estimated resident population. Per capita consumption is higher when based only on legal drinking age population.
Source: The Wine Institute Gomberg; Fredrikson & Associates.

thus, an increase in the sale of wine in restaurants. Although more than half of the U.S. adult population enjoyed wine occasionally in 2007, research indicated that by global standards most Americans were still infrequent wine drinkers. Per capita consumption in the United States was only about 2.5 gallons per year in 2007, compared to about 18 gallons in France and Italy, where drinking wine with meals was part of the local culture.

The Dessert and Fortified Wine Segment

During the 1980s, dessert wine sales totaled about 55 million gallons annually (about 10 percent of total wine sales based on volume); sales of low-end brands accounted for 43 million gallons (nearly 80 percent of all dessert wines). Approximately 50 percent of the low-end fortified dessert wines were sold in half pints; buyers of high-proof dessert wines were said to like half-pint bottles because they fit well in the back pocket of a pair of pants and gave skid-row drinkers a more secure feeling. However, dessert wine volume had trended down in the 1990s, to around 32 million gallons in 2000 (Exhibit 4), the majority of which continued to be low-end fortified wines. Whereas dessert wines accounted for almost 10 percent of total wine sales (based on volume) in the late 1980s, by 2000 the dessert wine category accounted for just 5.7 percent of total volume—the percentage drop was chiefly attributable to a decline in the popularity of wine coolers. By 2005, fortified dessert wines accounted for only 7.03 percent of the wine sold in the United States (see Exhibit 6).

The dessert wine category was typically a profitable market segment for low-end wine producers to pursue because many of the wines in this category were made with less expensive ingredients, packaged in less expensive containers, and could be sold with little or no marketing and promotion. Canandaigua estimated that profit margins in this category were as much as 10 percent higher than those of ordinary table wines. Gallo said this was not true for its products, but did not reveal its figures.

According wine industry analysts, local wine distributors were anxious to handle the low-end dessert and fortified wines because the margins were relatively large and it was generally easy to convince food retailers in low-income neighborhoods to stock them. As one distributor said, "All you have to do is to put it on the shelf in the right zip codes and it sells itself." Little or no advertising or sales promotion was needed—although in 1988 one magazine reported that Gallo sales representatives, in attempting to gain customers in newly entered markets, had on occasion gone so far as to trash the streets with empty bottles of Thunderbird and Night Train as a way to advertise to winos. Since distributors owned by Gallo were restricted by law from handling spirits (bourbon, vodka, scotch, gin, etc.), they were anxious to stock and distribute low-end wines because the sizable volumes and good profit margins were a major contributor to covering fixed costs and ensuring decent profitability.

A sales representative for an Alabama distributor of Gallo wines indicated that his company

Exhibit 6 Wine Sales, by Category, 2005

Category	Millions of Gallons	Percentage of Sales
Table wine	591	88.47%
Dessert wine	47	7.03
Sparkling wine	30	4.49

Sources: www.commerce.gov, www.ita.doc.gov/td/ocg/outlook05_wine.pdf.

Exhibit 7 Consumer Wine Purchases by Price Category, 2006

Price Category	Volume Share
Up to $3	12.0%
$3 to $6	25.1%
$6 up to $9	24.6%
$9 up to $15	27.2%
$15 and over	10.8%

Source: Goliath Business Knowledge on Demand, http://goliath.ecnext.com/comsite5/bin/comsite5.pl.

distributed Thunderbird and other high-proof wines to retail outlets in ethnic and low-income neighborhoods, with bottle sizes varying according to the time of the month. The representative indicated that it was the distributor's practice at the first of the month, when many people in poorer ethnic neighborhoods were cashing their government checks, to stock area retailers' shelves with larger containers of wines (jugs and 1.5-liter bottles). Then toward the middle and end of the month, when customers were likely to have less cash in their pockets, the wine distributor made sure that retailers' shelves were amply stocked with pint bottles that retailed anywhere from $0.99 to $1.49 per bottle.

Low-End Fortified Wines and Pop Culture

Cheap fortified wines had, over the years, found their way into the pop culture in the United States, often coming to symbolize the plight of the poor and less fortunate. Such wines were what people drank when they were sad, miserable, or just wanted to get drunk. Gallo's Night Train Express, an apple-flavored wine known as the Pocket Rocket and popular with both street alcoholics and teenagers, was alluded to in Guns N' Roses' debut album, *Appetite for Destruction,* on which Axl Rose sang "Nightrain":

Loaded like a freight train

flying like an aeroplane

Speeding like a space brain

one more time tonight

I'm on a Nightrain

bottoms up

I'm on a Nightrain

fill my cup

I'm on the Nightrain

I love that stuff,

I'm on the Nightrain

I can never get enough.

Wild Irish Rose was the inspiration for a song written and sung by Neil Diamond. On a 1970 trip to an Indian reservation in Canada where there were many more men than women, Diamond observed men leaving without a date on Saturday night and making wine their "woman for the night." He decided to compose "Cracklin' Rosie" to characterize the relationship of a lonely wine drinker and his bottle of Richard's Wild Irish Rose:

Cracklin' Rosie, make me a smile

God if it lasts for an hour, that's alright

We got all night

To set the world right

Find us a dream that don't ask no questions, yeah

Oh, I love my Rosie child

You got the way to make me happy

You and me, we go in style

Cracklin Rosie, you're a store-bought woman

You make me sing like a guitar hummin'

So hang on to me, girl

Our song keeps runnin' on.

Product Reviews of Low-End Fortified Wines

By and large, low-end fortified wines did not fare well in product reviews, even when the reviewers were members of the target clientele and experienced drinkers. Adam Martin, a college-age writer for a Web site in California called West Oakland Wine Tasting, offered his take on the appeal of low-end wines to the college crowd and presented colorful ratings of five brands:

> We live in one of the great wine producing regions of the world and it's a crying shame that nobody around here gives a #@&%. I know I don't. We could be in France, taking all kinds of wine baths and I would still

be craving Pabst Blue Ribbon and Milwaukee's Best. As a young, unrefined student on a budget, I simply can't afford to be a wine aficionado. I couldn't, that is, until last Friday, when, along with a panel of experts (namely Wrath and the Reverend, my good-for-nothing-except-drinking-cheap-wine-when-I-buy-it roommates), I ventured out into my neighborhood to see what good old Grand Foods had to offer for the sacred palate. The following review focuses on five wines popular in West Oakland and the surrounding areas (North Oakland and East Oakland). Wines are rated on packaging, taste, alcohol content, and some other stuff.

Night Train Express 17.5% apv, $3.49 for 750 ml.

This bottle looks foreboding at first because of the spooky-ass train on the front. It's all dark, done in deep maroons and yellows. There's a heavy fog and the train is probably loaded with all kinds of dangerous cargo and people. Wrath points out, however, that although it's scary at first, if you look close you can see how the windows on the front of the engine make bright little eyes, the single headlight a perfect button nose, and the rim of the tank right above the cow-catcher a wide, welcoming grin. "I'm not nearly as afraid to drink it any more," he proclaimed, and fell to it. We also liked the ornate cursive writing at the bottom of the label explaining how it's a product of Modesto, and the instruction to "serve very cold."

Night Train is thick, heavy, syrupy stuff, but for some reason it still tastes pretty bad. It's sort of like sucking on a rotten lollipop or something. We decided that, while Brussels sprouts taste good, and chocolate tastes good, you wouldn't want a chocolate Brussels sprout, and that's what this is. It's strong, though, and one bottle will get you very drunk. Night Train is the classic hobo wine, celebrated in story and song, so get a bottle if for no other reason than to celebrate our American heritage.

Thunderbird 17.5% apv, $3.49 for 750 ml.

Thunderbird is by far the burliest wine we tasted, and we are still afraid to say anything bad about it for fear it will come hunt us down and kill us in our sleep. I dare you to drink a whole bottle. Seriously, I dare you. Even looking at it makes me shiver. The word "Thunderbird" is written in a boldly slanted, straight lined typeface in white on a red background with a gold border. Directly under that word is the instruction to "Serve Cold," and under that is written "The American Classic." Then there is this . . . logo of an eagle wearing a crown. It looks like a state seal or something—the state of being all drunk and mean.

Wrath thought this was the most likely to give you whiskey face, and once we finished it I agreed with all three of him. Drink this wine if you want to get in a fight. But make sure the other person has also drunk a bottle of T-bird, too, or you'll get beat up. Thunderbird doesn't help you once you're in the fight. It just helps you get started. Even though it has the same amount of alcohol as Night Train and slightly less than Wild Irish Rose, it will still kick both of their asses and then yours. Watch it, punk.

Carlo Rossi California Sangria 10% apv, $4.00 per 1.5 liter bottle

While Burgundy is generally the favorite in Carlo Rossi's circles, the California Sangria definitely wins, as far as we were concerned. For starters, it has that classic "moonshine jug" shape that can't be beat, with the round bottle, and little finger loop on the neck. The proper way to take a slug of Carlo Rossi is to hook your finger through the loop and rest the bottle on the outside of your elbow while you drink it over your shoulder. . . .

The flavor of Carlo Rossi is better than the others because it's spicy as well as sweet. It has a nice light flavor with a little kick to it, and you can definitely nurse it for a while. Sure, you could nurse a bottle of the burgundy for a while too, but the sangria won't turn your mouth all purple and make you throw up. Compared to the other wines we tasted, this is the easiest to drink. It also has the most pretensions toward serious winehood, although this may be a strike against its image.

Wild Irish Rose 18% apv, $3.49 for 750 ml.

Wild Irish Rose has a simple, understated bottle with a picture of a rose above its name, and the accurate (if vague) description "100% pure grape wine." What's nice about this bottle is that it kind of knows it's being treated more like a liquor than a wine. The bottle is flat on the sides and kind of rectangular which makes it look more like a bottle of gin. This may be why it needs to say the word "wine" at least three times on the bottle. For a fun party game, see who can find all three the fastest. If you're drinking alone, see how fast you can find them and then try to break that record.

Taste wise, Wild Irish Rose is surprisingly agreeable. . . . We thought it was the best value for the money because it was the strongest and still really cheap. Also, even though it still had the same "death" aftertaste as Night Train and Thunderbird, it wasn't as prominent. We licked our lips and howled at the moon after Wild Irish Rose. Try it. It's a winner.

> **Boone's Farm Kiwi-Strawberry 8% apv, $2.90 for 750 ml.**
>
> This crap needs to stay on the store shelf. It's weak, bubbly and sweet in just the wrong ways. Both bottle and drink are bland as hell. The label just has this boring old picture of some farm-house (presumably Boone's) and nothing else really eye-catching. It tastes like weak strawberry soda, but . . . you could drink Vintage soda for about a third of the price and still get just as loaded. Unless you're a sixteen-year-old girl, don't bother with the stuff.[25]

Brian Gnatt, another college reviewer writing for the *Michigan Daily Online* at the University of Michigan, had the following to say about low-end fortified wines and their appeal to younger consumers of alcoholic beverages:

> For those who don't care for the taste of beer or hard alcohol, those who can't afford to buy quality alcohol, or for those who simply like the taste and effects of drinking cheap wine, usually out of a bottle with a screw-off cap, there's a line of alcoholic beverages just for you that adds a splash of color to liquor store shelves everywhere. Best of all, the bottles come in various shapes, sizes and colors; the wine comes in different flavors and most important, various strengths so everyone can find one to their liking.
>
> From the bright rainbow colors of MD 20/20 (a.k.a. Mad Dog) to the lighter, pastels of Boone's, ghetto wines look quite similar to wine coolers or even Kool-Aid. But don't be deceived—their punch is stronger than Bartles & Jaymes or the Kool-Aid Man. Ranging from about 5 percent alcohol (similar to beer) to 18 percent (about half of hard alcohol), cheap wines offer easy, economical and colorful ways to get drunk.
>
> The fact that the wines are cheap, easy and appealing are some of the reasons many young people enjoy drinking the less-than-tasty beverages. When I first started drinking, Mad Dog was my drink of choice. And I thought it was great; memories of skipping high school and watching reruns of "Alf" with friends and a bottle of Wild Berry 20/20—life didn't get much better. But as I got older, and my taste buds refined a bit, I realized Mad Dog and Thunderbird weren't the best drinks in the world, but that they're not all that bad either.
>
> Years later, the occasional bottle of wine still hits the spot. Now, however, it usually includes ridicule by friends and other onlookers who respond with the customary "Mad Dog? Yuck!" Nevertheless, cheap wine will always have a place in my heart, even though I have moved on to some finer forms of fermented fruit drinks, like Franzia, a.k.a. "wine in a box."
>
> While all wino-wines may get a bad rap for being a little pungent, there still are better cheap wines. The Michigan Daily taste-tested a number of the area's top-selling rot-gut wines to find which ones are the best bargains in the cheap wine market.
>
> **The Test**
>
> Finding cheap wine isn't a problem in Ann Arbor. Just about every beer, wine and liquor store sells some variation of the drink, most for less than $4. While all of our selections aren't available at every store, they are all available within walking distance of campus. . . .
>
> For the taste test, we gathered 11 different bottles of wine: five of Mad Dog (Hawaiian Blue, Lightning Creek, Pink Grapefruit, Red Grape Wine and Wild Berry), two Boone's (Snow Creek Berry and Strawberry Hill), two Wild Irish Rose varieties (regular and White Label), a bottle of Thunderbird and a bottle of Night Train. Then we tasted. Here's the findings:
>
> Out of the 11 samples, Boone's Snow Creek Berry was the best tasting of all the samples, but to no surprise. The lightly carbonated drink is only about five percent alcohol, while many of the other samples had more than three times that amount. It was sweet, fruity and fresh, and the taste of alcohol was almost non-existent.
>
> Boone's Strawberry Hill variety ranked No. 2 on the list, weighing in at 7.5 percent alcohol. The alcohol was a bit more prevalent and the wine had a bit of a sharp taste—drinkable, yet not as enjoyable as the Snow Creek Berry. Again though, the relatively small amount of alcohol almost nullifies Boone's from the contest, and forces it to stand alone in its own lightweight wine category.
>
> The Mad Dog flavors were the next most successful in the taste test, with the Pink Grapefruit flavor ranking No. 3, after the weaker Boone's. At 13.5 percent alcohol, Pink Grapefruit was fairly smooth and had less of a church-wine taste than the rest of the MD 20/20 flavors. It was tangy and not too sweet, for a somewhat refreshing flavor.
>
> Wild Berry Mad Dog (13.5 percent alcohol) was the next best, but was quite sweet and sharp and had a lasting aftertaste. Mad Dog's Red Grape Wine (18 percent alcohol) followed at No. 5, the first drink to ever make me hurl. The wine was quite sweet, a bit dry and very grapey, but still drinkable. At No. 6 was Lightning Creek (17 percent alcohol), the clear variety of Mad Dog for all of you who don't like artificial

colors in your food. The smell of rubbing alcohol and a taste of watered-down alcohol made this selection the turning point in the tasting, and the wines went downhill from here.

Next in line was the potent Thunderbird (18 percent alcohol)—with "An American Classic" as the slogan on the bottle. With its strong alcohol flavor, Thunderbird is strong at first taste, but it doesn't linger on the palate as much as some of the other selections, mainly the Wild Irish Rose and the Hawaiian Blue Mad Dog, which followed Thunderbird for a No. 8 ranking. With its 2,000 Flushes aqua blue color, alcohol flavor and a hint of coconut, Hawaiian Blue coats your system like a good bathtub scum, with its only redeeming quality being it's a pretty color.

Wild Irish Rose Wine (18 percent) ranked in at No. 9, with its red color, hint of grape flavor and plain taste. Not very tasty, to say the least. The infamous Night Train (18 percent) pulled into the station at No. 10, pushing a train wreck for anyone who could top off the entire bottle of wine. It had a rather nasty, pungent and incarcerating taste and side effects to back up its poor reputation.

Coming in last was Wild Irish Rose's White Label (18 percent alcohol), a harsh, sharp and brutal wine without any flavor whatsoever. The White Label produced breath of fire, and left nothing to be desired.

For all it's worth, cheap wine still has its virtues, even if it doesn't have a very desirable taste. All but the Boone's could probably get you drunk for less than the price of the average beer at the average bar. So if drunk's what you want, and $3 is all you've got, a not-so-good bottle of wine is all you need to cure those sobriety blues.[26]

ATTEMPTS TO CONTROL EXCESSIVE CONSUMPTION OF HIGH-PROOF WINES

Public drunkenness in inner cities and low-income neighborhoods, alcoholism, and binge drinking on college campuses had provoked concerns among various citizens groups, community organizations, churches, government agencies, makers of alcoholic beverages, and wine companies. In June 1989, Gallo conducted an experiment whereby it stopped distributing Thunderbird and Night Train wines in the Tenderloin District of San Francisco for six months. Canandaigua Wine Company indicated it would cooperate in the experiment by pulling Wild Irish Rose from the shelves, but it failed to follow through during the trial period because it said the ultimate decision to halt sales was up to its local distributors. But there was reportedly little beneficial impact; as local winos said, "You can't get it in one store, you get it in another . . .or you just drink something else." The minimal impact of pulling Gallo's Thunderbird and Night Train wines off retailer shelves in San Francisco was taken as validation of the oft-stated views within the wine industry (and elsewhere as well) that alcoholics, if deprived of one source, would simply seek out alternatives to satisfy their desires for alcohol.

In addition to Gallo's mostly independent effort in San Francisco, several cities had experimented with ways to remove cheap fortified wines from inner-city stores as a means of defeating the efforts of people looking for a cheap way to get drunk. Salt Lake City and Portland tried imposing bans on the sales of such wines, with somewhat conflicting results. Both cities reported substitute alcohol sales up. However, while Salt Lake City reported a decline in public drunkenness, in Portland the conclusion was that winos just drank something else.

Banning Cisco, one of the most potent fortified wine coolers, became a cause célèbre during the early 1990s, because its packaging was deceptively similar to that of normal wine coolers and because it was shelved in the same beverage cases in convenience stores and supermarkets. Cisco's very sweet flavorings made it a favorite target of adolescent shoplifters. Former U.S. surgeon general Antonio Novello referred to heavily fortified wine coolers as "wine foolers"—innocent-looking bottles of wine and sugared fruit juices that looked like a regular wine cooler but packed more than three times the punch (Exhibit 2).

One defense of winemakers who were profiting from producing and marketing cheap, fortified wines to skid-row alcoholics was offered by Professor Edward Freeman, a nationally prominent ethicist at the University of Virginia's Darden Graduate School of Business Administration: "There is a long tradition of freedom of contract in our country. People are free to make their own mistakes."[27] Freeman emphasized that the problem of street alcoholics was far more complex than just the sale of the products. The root issue, he claimed, was the underlying social conditions that helped push alcoholics into their disease. "Not selling this stuff is like moving the deck chairs on the *Titanic,*" he said. "The question is, do you really want to be a company associated with these products that are so abused? In our system, we let the companies decide."

Endnotes

1. Wine Institute, "Wine Consumption in the U.S.," www.wineinstitute.org/resources/statistics/article86.
2. National Association for Business Economics, "Economics of the U.S. Wine Industry," www.nabe.com/publib/news/07/10/05.html.
3. American Alcohol & Drug Information Foundation, "High Potency and Other Alcoholic Beverage Consumption Among Adolescents," 2005, www.thefreelibrary.com/High+potency+and+other+alcoholic+beverage+consumption+among. . .-a0142871709.
4. "The Bottom of the Barrel," *San Francisco Chronicle,* www.sfgate.com/cgi-bin/article.cgi?f=/c/a/1996/07/07/sc22167.dtl&hw=Thunderbird+Wine&sn=002&sc=926.
5. Kelly Payne, "Drying Up the Square," www.realchangenews.org/pastarticles/features/articles/new_dec_Boozeban.html.
6. "Banning the Saturday Night Special of Booze," *Newsweek,* March 10, 1986.
7. Alix Freedman, "Market Misery—Winos and Thunderbird Are a Subject Gallo Doesn't Like to Discuss," *Wall Street Journal,* February 25, 1988, pp. 1, 18.
8. As quoted in Warren King, "Ethics of Manufacturing Profits from Drunks," *Seattle Times,* January 20, 1998.
9. *Standard Directory of Advertisers,* 2000.
10. Jeff Morgan, "Gallo of Sonoma," *Wine Spectator Online,* June 30, 1999.
11. "Last Call for Thunderbird," *L.A. Times,* http://pqasb.pqarchiver.com/latimes/access/275328361.html?dids=275328361:275328361&FMT=ABS&FMTS=ABS:FT&type=current&date=Jan+8%2C+2003&author=Corie+Brown&pub=Los+Angeles+Times&edition+&startpage=F.7&desc=Last+call+for+Thunderbird.
12. "Cheap Wine Returns to the Tenderloin," *San Francisco Chronicle,* www.winefiles.org/results.cgi?boolean=thunderbird+wine&f=simple&start=1.
13. "So You Want to Buy a President," *Frontline,* www.pbs.org/wgbh/pages/frontline/president/players/gallo.html.
14. California Farm Bureau Federation, "Growing Up Gallo," www.cfbf.com/magazine/MagazineStory.cfm?ID=42&ck=A1D0C6E83F027327D8461063F4AC58A6.
15. Posted at www.gallo.com, December 11, 2001.
16. Posted at www.gallosonoma.com, April 8, 2008.
17. www.gallo.com/UK/html/ernestaward.htm.
18. "Wine Industry Market Share Summary," Goliath Business Knowledge on Demand, http://goliath.ecnext.com/comsite5/bin/comsite5.pl.
19. "At 75, Wine Giant Gallo Is Refining Its Palate," *L.A. Times,* www.latimes.com/business/la-fi-gallo4apr04,1,3429722.story.
20. Constellation annual reports, www.cbrands.com/CBI/constellationbrands/AboutUs/AnnualReport/FY06_Annual_Report.pdf.
21. E. & J. Gallo press release, www.gallo.com/PDFs/WilliamHillNewsRelease.pdf.
22. "E & J Gallo Winery," *BusinessWeek,* http://investing.businessweek.com/research/stocks/private/snapshot.asp?privcapId=162756.
23. E. & J. Gallo press release, www.gallo.com/PDFs/MarthaStewartVintageRelease.pdf.
24. "Wine Industry Table Database Articles," Goliath Business Knowledge on Demand, http://goliath.ecnext.com/comsite5/bin/comsite5.pl.
25. Adam Martin, "What to Do When You've Only Got $5.22 and a Serious Liquor Monkey on Your Back," West Oakland Wine Tasting, www.readsatellite.com/culture/2.4/wine.martin.2.4.1.htm.
26. Brian A. Gnatt, "A Touch of Underclass: Cheap Wine, an Alternative, Proletariat Potable," *Michigan Daily Online,* www.pub.umich.edu/daily/1997/apr/04-10-97/arts/art3.html.
27. As quoted in Warren King, "Ethics of Manufacturing Profits from Drunks," *Seattle Times,* January 20, 1998.

CASE 26 Detecting Unethical Practices at Supplier Factories: The Monitoring and Compliance Challenges

Arthur A. Thompson
The University of Alabama

Importers of goods from Bangladesh, Cambodia, China, the Dominican Republic, Honduras, India, Indonesia, Korea, Malaysia, Pakistan, Peru, the Philippines, Sri Lanka, Tunisia, Vietnam, and several other countries in Latin America, Eastern Europe, the Middle East, and Africa have long had to contend with accusations by human rights activists that they sourced goods from sweatshop manufacturers who paid substandard wages, required unusually long work hours, used child labor, exposed workers to toxic chemicals and other safety hazards, failed to provide even minimal fringe benefits, and habitually engaged in assorted other unsavory practices. Exhibit 1 provides a sample of the problems in eight countries. Factories in China were particularly in the spotlight because of China's prominence as the largest single source of goods imported into both the United States and the 25 countries comprising the European Union; U.S. imports from Chinese manufacturers amounted to about $320 billion in 2007. Political support in many countries for growing trade ties with countries where low-cost manufacturers were located, especially China, often hinged on the ability of companies with global sourcing strategies to convince domestic governmental officials, human rights groups, and concerned citizens that they were doing all they could do to police working conditions in the plants of suppliers in low-wage, poverty-stricken countries where sweatshop practices were concentrated.

Starting in the 1990s, companies began countering these criticisms by instituting elaborate codes of conduct for suppliers and by periodically inspecting supplier facilities to try to eliminate abuses and promote improved working conditions. A strong program of auditing labor practices and working conditions in supplier factories was a way for a company to cover itself and negate accusations that it was unfairly exploiting workers in less-developed countries. By 2008, hundreds of companies that sourced goods from factories in less-developed parts of the world had instituted strict codes for suppliers and either had an internal staff to conduct audits of supplier factories or used the services of recognized third parties with auditing expertise to inspect supplier factories. Most companies focused their efforts on improving working conditions at supplier factories, preferring to help suppliers comply with the expected standards rather than to impose penalties for violations and perhaps abruptly and/or permanently cutting off purchases.

However, in November 2006, *BusinessWeek* ran a cover story detailing how shady foreign manufacturers were deliberately deceiving inspection teams and concealing violations of supplier codes of conduct.[1] According to the *BusinessWeek* special report, Ningbo Beifa Group—a top Chinese supplier of pens, mechanical pens, and highlighters to Wal-Mart, Staples, Woolworth, and some 400 other retailers in 100 countries—was alerted in late 2005 that a Wal-Mart inspection team would soon be visiting the company's factory in the coastal city of Ningbo. Wal-Mart was Beifa's largest customer, and on three previous occasions Wal-Mart inspectors

Exhibit 1 Comparative Labor and Workplace Conditions in Eight Countries, 2006

Country	Labor and Workplace Overview
Brazil	The primary problems in the manufacturing workplace are forced labor, inadequate occupational safety (work accidents are common in several industries), and wage discrimination (wages paid to females are 54% to 64% of those paid to males).
China	Factories are most prone to ignore minimum-wage requirements, underpay for overtime work, subject workers to unsafe and unhealthy working conditions, and suppress worker attempts to join independent unions.
India	The most common issues concern underpayment of minimum wages, overtime pay violations, use of child labor (according to one estimate some 100 million children ages 5 to 14 work and at least 12.6 million work full-time), the use of forced labor (perhaps as many as 65 million people), and inattention to occupational safety.
Indonesia	The stand-out issues concern weak enforcement of minimum-wage rules and work hours in factories, overtime pay violations in factories, subpar occupational safety (especially in mining and fishing), and use of underage labor (particularly in domestic service, mining, construction, and fishing industries).
Mexico	Problem areas include sweatshop conditions in many assembly plants near U.S. border and elsewhere, fierce opposition to unions, insistence on pregnancy tests for female job applicants of child-bearing age, and use of child labor in non-export economic sectors.
Peru	The worst workplace conditions relate to lack of enforcement of wage and overtime provisions in factories, mandatory overtime requirements for many workers, and inattention to occupational safety.
South Africa	The most frequent offenses entail failure to observe minimum-wage and overtime pay rules (particularly in the garment industry), use of child labor, occupational safety violations (especially in non-export sectors where outside monitoring is nonexistent), and low pay for women.
Sri Lanka	The most frequent violations relate to underpayment of wages, forced overtime requirements, compulsory work on Sundays and holidays, and inattention to worker health and safety (such as excessive noise, blocked exits, and disregard for worker safety—one study found 60% of grain and spice mill workers lost fingers in work-related accidents and/or contracted skin diseases).

Source: Compiled by the author from information in "How China's Labor Conditions Stack Up Against Those of Other Low-Cost Nations," *BusinessWeek Online,* November 27, 2006, www.businessweek.com (accessed January 26, 2007). The information was provided to *BusinessWeek* by Verité, a Massachusetts-based nonprofit social auditing and research organization with expertise in human rights and labor abuses in supplier factories around the world.

had caught Beifa paying its 3,000 workers less than the Chinese minimum-wage and violating overtime rules. A fourth offense would end Wal-Mart's purchases from Beifa. But weeks prior to the audit, an administrator at Beifa's factory in Ningbo got a call from representatives of Shanghai Corporate Responsibility Management & Consulting Company offering to help the Beifa factory pass the Wal-Mart inspection.[2] The Beifa administrator agreed to pay the requested fee of $5,000. The consultant advised management at the Beifa factory in Ningbo to create fake but authentic-looking records regarding pay scales and overtime work and make sure to get any workers with grievances out of the plant on the day of the audit. Beifa managers at the factory were also coached on how to answer questions that the auditors would likely ask. Beifa's Ningbo factory reportedly passed the Wal-Mart inspection in early 2006 without altering any of its practices.[3] A lawyer for Beifa confirmed that the company had indeed employed the Shanghai consulting firm but said that factory personnel engaged in no dishonest actions to pass the audit; the lawyer indicated that the factory passed the audit because it had taken steps to correct the problems found in Wal-Mart's prior audits.

WAGE AND EMPLOYMENT PRACTICES IN CHINA

Minimum-wage rules in China were specified by local or provincial governments and in 2007 ranged from $36 to $105 per month, which equated to hourly rates of $0.21 to $0.61 based on a 40-hour workweek.[4] In recent years, governments in most Chinese locales had boosted minimum-wage requirements annually so as to preserve worker purchasing power in light of the 5–7 percent annual rates of inflation experienced in China. A comprehensive study involving 57 million employees of larger Chinese manufacturing enterprises revealed average hourly compensation of $0.98 as of 2004, but there were big variations from sector to sector (in textiles and apparel wages averaged about $0.70 per hour, whereas the hourly average was $1.35 in transportation equipment and $1.59 in petroleum processing).[5] Using more recent but somewhat sketchy Chinese government income data compiled by the U.S. Bureau of Labor Statistics and a Beijing consulting firm, another study showed the average manufacturing wage in China in 2005 was $0.64 per hour (again assuming a 40-hour workweek). While the standard workweek in Chinese provinces officially ranged from 40 to 44 hours, there were said to be numerous instances where plant personnel worked 60 to 100 hours per week, sometimes with only one or two days off per month. Such long work hours meant that the actual average manufacturing wage in China was likely well below the levels based on a 40-hour workweek. According to estimates made by a veteran inspector of Chinese factories, employees at garment, electronics, and other plants making goods for export typically worked more than 80 hours per week and earned an average of $0.42 per hour.[6]

Overtime pay rules in Chinese provinces officially called for time-and-a-half pay for all work over eight hours per day and between double and triple pay for work on Saturdays, Sundays, and holidays. However, it was commonplace for Chinese employers to disregard overtime pay rules, and governmental enforcement of minimum-wage and overtime requirements by both Beijing officials and officials in local Chinese provinces was often minimal to nonexistent. At a Hong Kong garment plant where 2,000 employees put in many overtime hours operating sewing and stitching machines, worker pay averaged about $125 per month—an amount which the owner acknowledged did not meet Chinese overtime pay requirements. The owner said the overtime rules were "a fantasy" and added: "Maybe in two or three decades we can meet them."[7] Many young Chinese factory workers were tolerant of long hours and less than full overtime pay because they wanted to earn as much as possible, the idea being to save enough of their income to return to their homes in the countryside after a few years of factory employment.

Chinese export manufacturing was said to be rife with tales of deception to frustrate plant monitoring and escape compliance with local minimum-wage and overtime rules and supplier codes of conduct. Indeed, a new breed of consultants had sprung up in China to aid local manufacturers in passing audits conducted both by customer companies and industry alliance groups.[8]

GROWING USE OF STRATEGIES TO DELIBERATELY DECEIVE PLANT INSPECTORS

The efforts of unscrupulous manufacturers in China and other parts of the world to game the plant-monitoring system and use whatever deceptive practices it took to successfully pass plant audits had four chief elements:

1. *Maintaining two sets of books*—Factories generated a set of bogus payroll records and time sheets to show audit teams that their workers were properly paid and received the appropriate overtime pay; the genuine records were kept secret. For example, at an onsite audit of a Chinese maker of lamps for Home Depot, Sears, and other retailers, plant managers provided inspectors with payroll records and time sheets showing that employees worked a five-day week from 8:00 a.m. to 5:30 p.m. with a 30-minute lunch break and no overtime hours; during interviews, managers at the plant said the records were accurate. But other records auditors found at the site, along with interviews with workers, indicated that employees worked an extra three to five hours daily with one or two days off per month during peak production periods; inspectors were unable to verify whether workers at the plant received overtime pay.[9] According to a compliance manager at a major multinational company who had overseen many factory audits, the percentage of Chinese employers submitting false payroll records had

risen from 46 percent to 75 percent during the past four years; the manager also estimated that only 20 percent of Chinese suppliers complied with local minimum-wage rules and that just 5 percent obeyed hour limitations.[10]

2. *Hiding the use of underage workers and unsafe work practices*—In some instances, factories in China, parts of Africa, and select other countries in Asia, Eastern Europe, and the Middle East employed underage workers. This was disguised either by falsifying the personnel records of underage employees, by adeptly getting underage employees off the premises when audit teams arrived, or by putting underage employees in back rooms concealed from auditors. A memo distributed in one Chinese factory instructed managers to "notify underage trainees, underage full-time workers, and workers without identification to leave the manufacturing workshop through the back door. Order them not to loiter near the dormitory area. Secondly, immediately order the receptionist to gather all relevant documents and papers."[11] At a toy plant in China, a compliance inspector, upon smelling strong fumes in a poorly ventilated building, found young female employees on a production line using spray guns to paint figurines; in a locked back room that a factory official initially refused to open, an apparently underage worker was found hiding behind coworkers.[12]

3. *Meeting requirements by secretly shifting production to subcontractors*—On occasion, suppliers met the standards set by customers by secretly shifting some production to subcontractors who failed to observe pay standards, skirted worker safety procedures, or otherwise engaged in abuses of various kinds.

4. *Coaching managers and employees on answering questions posed by audit team members*—Both managers and workers were tutored on what to tell inspectors should they be interviewed. Scripting responses about wages and overtime pay, hours worked, safety procedures, training, and other aspects related to working conditions was a common tactic for thwarting what inspectors could learn from interviews. However, in instances where plant inspectors were able to speak confidentially with employees away from the worksite, they often got information at variance with what they were told during onsite interviews—plant personnel were more inclined to be truthful and forthcoming about actual working conditions and pay practices when top-level plant management could not trace the information given to inspectors back to them.

There was a growing awareness among companies attempting to enforce supplier codes of conduct that all factories across the world with substandard working conditions and reasons to hide their practices from outside view played cat-and-mouse games with plant inspectors. In many less-developed countries struggling to build a manufacturing base and provide jobs for their citizens, factory managers considered deceptive practices a necessary evil to survive, principally because improving wages and working conditions to comply with labor codes and customers' codes of conduct for suppliers raised costs and imperiled already thin profit margins. Violations were said to be most prevalent at factories making apparel, but more violations were surfacing in factories making furniture, appliances, toys, and electronics.

However, large global corporations such as General Electric, Motorola, Dell, Nestlé, and Toyota that owned and operated their own offshore manufacturing plants in China and other low-wage countries had not been accused of mistreating their employees or having poor working conditions. The offshore factories of well-known global and multinational companies were seldom subject to monitoring by outsiders because the workplace environments in their foreign plants were relatively good in comparison to those of local manufacturing enterprises that made a business of supplying low-cost components and finished goods to companies and retailers in affluent, industrialized nations.

Corporate sensitivity to charges of being socially irresponsible in their sourcing of goods from foreign manufacturers had prompted hundreds of companies to establish supplier codes of conduct and to engage in compliance monitoring efforts of one kind or another. The clothing retailer Gap had an internal compliance team of more than 90 people to audit approximately 2,000 factories of its garment suppliers; Gap's team conducted 4,316 inspections in 2005.[13] The retailing giant Target had 40 full-time compliance employees, including more than

20 foreign-based auditing staff, and conducted 100 percent of its factory audits unannounced. Hewlett-Packard had a program to monitor conduct at some 550 supplier factories. Moreover, an increasing number of companies, many with common suppliers, had begun collaborating to establish standards for suppliers and to conduct factory audits. For example, in 2004, Hewlett-Packard, Dell, IBM, and five other electronics companies that relied heavily on outside manufacturers to supply components or assemble products had created the Electronics Industry Code of Conduct; the new code replaced individual codes used by these companies and sought to establish industrywide standards for supplier factories regarding labor and employment practices, worker health and safety, ethics, and environmental protection. Other electronics companies were invited to voluntarily adopt the same standards, because it was simpler for supplier factories to comply with a single set of standards as opposed to scrambling to satisfy the different code requirements of different companies.

FOREIGN SUPPLIER COMPLIANCE PROGRAMS AT NIKE AND WAL-MART

Nike and Wal-Mart were two companies with supplier codes of conduct and rather extensive programs to monitor whether suppliers in low-wage, low-cost manufacturing locations across the world are complying with those codes. Both companies initiated such efforts in the 1990s because they came under fire from human rights activist groups for allegedly sourcing goods from sweatshop factories in China and elsewhere.

Nike's Supplier Code of Conduct and Compliance Monitoring Program

Nike was the world's leading designer, distributor, and marketer of athletic footwear, sports apparel, sports equipment and accessories, but it did no manufacturing. All of Nike products were sourced from contract manufacturers. In 2007, Nike reported that it had almost 700 factories in 52 countries actively engaged in manufacturing its products; of these, about 148 were in China (including Hong Kong and Macau); 63 in Thailand, 35 in Indonesia, 29 in Korea, 35 in Vietnam, 34 in Malaysia, 18 in Sri Lanka, 18 in India, 26 in Brazil, and 9 in Honduras.[14] Nike's contract factories employed roughly 800,000 workers, an estimated 80 percent of whom were women ages 18 to 24 performing entry-level, low-skill jobs. In fiscal year 2006, Nike approved 81 new contract factories for the Nike brand, down from 83 in 2005 and 122 in 2004. Of the new contract factories, 11 were in the Americas, 6 in the Europe/Middle East/Africa region, and 64 in Asia.

Nike drafted a code of conduct for its contract factories in 1991, distributed the code to all of its contract factories in 1992, and directed them to post the code in a visible place and in the appropriate local language. The code had been modified and updated over the years, and in 2007 also included a set of leadership standards that was adopted in 2002. Nike's code of conduct is presented in Exhibit 2. In 1998, in a move to strengthen its opposition to the use of child labor in factories, Nike directed its contract factories to set age standards for employment at 16 for apparel and 18 for footwear; these age standards were more demanding than those set in 1991 and exceeded the International Labor Organization's age minimum of 15.

Nike's System for Monitoring Contract Manufacturers During 2003–2006, Nike used four approaches to plant monitoring:[15]

- *Basic monitoring or SHAPE inspections:* SHAPE inspections, used since 1997, sought to gauge a factory's overall compliance performance, including environment, safety, and health. They were typically performed by Nike's field-based production staff and could be completed in one day or less. Nike's stated goal was to conduct two SHAPE audits on each active factory each year, but the actual number of such audits had fallen short of that target.
- *In-depth M-Audits:* The M-Audit was designed to provide a deeper measure of the working conditions within contract factories. As a general rule, Nike focused its plant inspection efforts on factories where noncompliance

Exhibit 2 Nike's Code of Conduct for Its Suppliers and Contract Manufacturers, 2006

Nike, Inc. Was Founded on a Handshake

Implicit in that act was the determination that we would build our business with all of our partners based on trust, teamwork, honesty and mutual respect. We expect all of our business partners to operate on the same principles.

At the core of the NIKE corporate ethic is the belief that we are a company comprised of many different kinds of people, appreciating individual diversity, and dedicated to equal opportunity for each individual.

NIKE designs, manufactures, and markets products for sports and fitness consumers. At every step in that process, we are driven to do not only what is required by law, but what is expected of a leader. We expect our business partners to do the same. NIKE partners with contractors who share our commitment to best practices and continuous improvement in:

1. Management practices that respect the rights of all employees, including the right to free association and collective bargaining
2. Minimizing our impact on the environment
3. Providing a safe and healthy work place
4. Promoting the health and well-being of all employees

Contractors must recognize the dignity of each employee, and the right to a work place free of harassment, abuse or corporal punishment. Decisions on hiring, salary, benefits, advancement, termination or retirement must be based solely on the employee's ability to do the job. There shall be no discrimination based on race, creed, gender, marital or maternity status, religious or political beliefs, age or sexual orientation.

Wherever NIKE operates around the globe we are guided by this Code of Conduct and we bind our contractors to these principles. Contractors must post this Code in all major workspaces, translated into the language of the employee, and must train employees on their rights and obligations as defined by this Code and applicable local laws.

While these principles establish the spirit of our partnerships, we also bind our partners to specific standards of conduct. The core standards are set forth below.

Forced Labor

The contractor does not use forced labor in any form—prison, indentured, bonded or otherwise.

Child Labor

The contractor does not employ any person below the age of 18 to produce footwear. The contractor does not employ any person below the age of 16 to produce apparel, accessories or equipment. If at the time Nike production begins, the contractor employs people of the legal working age who are at least 15, that employment may continue, but the contractor will not hire any person going forward who is younger than the Nike or legal age limit, whichever is higher. To further ensure these age standards are complied with, the contractor does not use any form of homework for Nike production.

Compensation

The contractor provides each employee at least the minimum wage, or the prevailing industry wage, whichever is higher; provides each employee a clear, written accounting for every pay period; and does not deduct from employee pay for disciplinary infractions.

Benefits

The contractor provides each employee all legally mandated benefits.

Hours of Work/Overtime

The contractor complies with legally mandated work hours; uses overtime only when each employee is fully compensated according to local law; informs each employee at the time of hiring if mandatory overtime is a condition of employment; and on a regularly scheduled basis provides one day off in seven, and requires no more than 60 hours of work per week on a regularly scheduled basis, or complies with local limits if they are lower.

Environment, Safety and Health (ES&H)

The contractor has written environmental, safety and health policies and standards, and implements a system to minimize negative impacts on the environment, reduce work-related injury and illness, and promote the general health of employees.

Documentation and Inspection

The contractor maintains on file all documentation needed to demonstrate compliance with this Code of Conduct and required laws; agrees to make these documents available for Nike or its designated monitor; and agrees to submit to inspections with or without prior notice.

Source: www.nike.com (accessed January 25, 2007).

was most likely to occur. Factories located in highly regulated countries where workers were more informed about their rights and workplace laws and regulations were enforced were deemed less likely to be out of compliance. In 2003, Nike focused its M-Audits on factories presumed to have the highest risk of noncompliance and the greatest size (as measured by worker population). In 2004, M-Audits were focused on factories believed to be of medium risk for noncompliance. Nike's stated goal was to conduct M-Audits for approximately 25–33 percent of its active factory base each year. The M-Audit included four major categories of inquiry (hiring practices, worker treatment, worker-management communications, and compensation) and covered more than 80 labor-management issues.

In 2004 Nike had 46 employees who regularly conducted M-Audits. The typical M-Auditor was under the age of 30, and 74 percent were women. Nike tried to hire auditors who were local nationals and understood the local language and culture. In 2003–2004, more than 9,200 factory workers were individually interviewed as part of the M-Audit process. Each interview took approximately 30 minutes. The typical M-Audit took an average of 48 hours to complete, including travel to and from the factory—travel hours accounted for between 25 and 30 percent of total M-Audit time.

- *MAV Audits:* Starting in fiscal year 2006, Nike introduced a new audit focused on finding root causes of noncompliance issues that most impacted workers, specifically work hours, wages/benefits, grievance systems, and freedom of associations. Prior audit experience had led Nike's staff to believe that root cause identification would help supplier factories remediate the problems that were identified. Nike conducted 42 MAV audits through fiscal year 2006.
- *Independent external monitoring:* Beginning in 2003, Nike became a member of the Fair Labor Association (FLA), an organization that conducted independent audits of factories that provided goods to members. The FLA applied a common set of compliance standards in all of its factory audits.

In 2004, Nike's compliance team consisted of 90 people based in 24 offices in 21 countries. The typical Nike compliance team in each country spent about one-third of their time on monitoring and auditing activities, about half their time assisting and tracking factory remediation activities, and the remainder of their time on troubleshooting and collaboration/outreach work.[16] In its 2004 Corporate Responsibility Report, Nike said:

> With an average of one compliance staff for more than 10 factories—some of which are remote and some of which are large and complex businesses with 10,000 or more employees—tracking and assisting factory remediation is at times an overwhelming and incomplete body of work.[17]

Nike's 2003–2004 factory audits were announced rather than unannounced because "much of the information we require in our evaluation of a factory is dependent upon access to relevant records and individuals within factory management."[18] When a factory was found to be out of compliance with the code of conduct, Nike's compliance team worked with factory management and the Nike business unit for which products were being manufactured to develop a master action plan (MAP) that specified the factory's needed remediation efforts. The Nike production manager responsible for the business relationship with the contract factory monitored MAP progress and exchanged information about progress or obstacles with Nike's country compliance team. The Nike general manager for production monitored the progress of all factories within his or her purview and weighed in when factory remediation progress was too slow.

To further facilitate factory compliance with Nike's code of conduct for suppliers, the company conducted or sponsored training and education programs for factory personnel. In 2004, more than 16,500 factory managers and workers attended programs relating to labor issues, worker health and safety, and environmental protection.[19]

Nike's Compliance Rating System Nike's factory ratings for SHAPE and M-Audits resulted in numeric scores ranging from 0 to 100 (a score of 100 indicated full compliance); these numeric scores were then converted to one of four overall grades (see table below):[20]

Exhibit 3 presents a summary of Nike's factory ratings for fiscal years 2003–2004. Exhibit 4 shows the ratings for fiscal years 2005 and 2006.

Grade	Criteria
A	Isolated violations of standards, but none considered serious or critical; no more than 5 minor issues outstanding on a factory's master action plan (MAP) for improving working conditions and achieving higher levels of compliance with Nike's code of conduct
B	Isolated violations of standards, but none considered serious or critical; more than 5 minor issues outstanding on the MAP, but none considered serious or critical
C	Noncompliant with serious failures and making little progress in remedying them. Examples of C-level issues include: • Factory does not provide basic terms of employment (contracts, documented training on terms, equal pay, discriminatory employment screening). • More than 10 percent of employees work between 60 and 72 hours each week. • More than 10 percent of employees exceed annual legal limits. • More than 10 percent of employees work seven or more consecutive days without a break. • Factory violates local migrant labor laws. • Non-income-related benefits fall short of legal provisions. • Some evidence of verbal or psychological harassment or abuse. • One or more serious issues on MAP, but none considered critical.
D	Noncompliant; general disregard for Nike's code of conduct; and evidence of deliberately misleading auditors. Examples of D-level issues and problems include: • Management refuses or continues to demonstrate unwillingness to comply with Nike standards. • Management provides false information (statements, documents or demonstrates coaching). • Factory fails to provide verifiable timekeeping system to accurately record work hours. • Factory fails to pay legally mandated minimum wage. • More than 10 percent of employees work more than 72 hours each week. • More than 10 percent of employees exceed daily work hour limits. • More than 10 percent of employees work 14 or more consecutive days without a break. • Factory requires pregnancy testing as condition of employment. • Factory uses workers under the minimum legal age. • Factory uses bonded, indentured or prison labor. • Factory uses force to compel illegal work hours. • Audit finds confirmed evidence of physical or sexual abuse. • Factory management denies access to authorized compliance inspectors. • Factory denies freedom of association for workers, including demotion or dismissal of workers seeking to exercise their rights. • Factory provides no benefits tied to security (workers' compensation, medical coverage, social security, retirement funds). • Factory outsources to unauthorized facilities or issues homework to employees.
E	Not enough information to measure compliance

Exhibit 3 Summary of Nike's Audits of Supplier Factories, Fiscal Years 2003 and 2004

	Geographic Region				
	Americas	Europe, Middle East, Africa	Northern Asia	Southern Asia	Worldwide Total
Number of SHAPE* audits in 2004	178	157	378	303	1,016
Number of M-Audits† in 2003 and 2004	148	56	198	167	569
M-Audit numeric scores in 2003–2004					
Lowest score	46	49	25	20	20
Average score	78	70	58	58	65
Highest score	94	96	95	95	99
Compliance ratings for contact factories as of June 2004					
Grade of A	32	15	34	25	106 (15%)
Grade of B	64	40	147	76	327 (44%)
Grade of C	18	7	33	65	123 (17%)
Grade of D	5	35	14	8	62 (8%)
Grade of E	18	7	22	70	117 (16%)

*SHAPE audits were a monitoring tool used by Nike since 1997 and provided a basic gauge of a factory's compliance performance.

†M-Audits, Nike's main auditing tool in 2003–2004, provided a deeper assessment of a factory's management practices. Worker population in M-Audited factories was 375,000 in fiscal year 2003 and 213,000 in fiscal year 2004.

Source: Nike's 2004 Corporate Responsibility Report, pp. 20, 34, and 35.

Nike's Corrective Actions to Deal with Noncomplying or Nonperforming Suppliers

A factory was cut from Nike's supplier base when, over a period of time, Nike management determined that factory management lacked the capacity or the will to correct serious issues of noncompliance. One supplier in China, for example, was cited for repeated violations of overtime standards and falsification of records. The compliance team established action plans, which three different Nike business units worked with the factory to implement. After six months of continuous efforts and no improvement, the factory was dropped. In November 2006, Nike severed its business relationship with a Pakistani supplier of soccer balls that failed to correct serious code of conduct violations.

More typically, Nike's decisions to end a business relationship with problem suppliers was based on a "balanced scorecard" of factory performance that took into account labor code compliance along with such measures such as price, quality, and delivery time. For example, a manufacturing group in South Asia had performed poorly on a range of issues, from overtime and worker–management communication to the quality of product and shipping dates. After a series of performance reviews, Nike management informed the factory group that it would not be placing orders for the next season. Nike did not report on factories dropped solely from noncompliance reasons related to its code of conduct because management said "it is often difficult to isolate poor performance on compliance as the sole reason for terminating a business relationship."[21]

To give its contract manufacturers greater incentive to comply with Nike's workplace standards and expectations, during crunch production periods Nike management and plant auditors had given some factories latitude to institute long workweeks (above 72 hours) and not hold them to a strict standard of 1 day off out of every 14 days if the employer gave workers more days off during slack production periods. Nike was also working to streamline its methods of designing shoes and placing orders with key suppliers and helping foreign factories develop more efficient

Exhibit 4 Summary Results of Nike's Audit Grades for Contract Factories, Fiscal Years 2005–2006

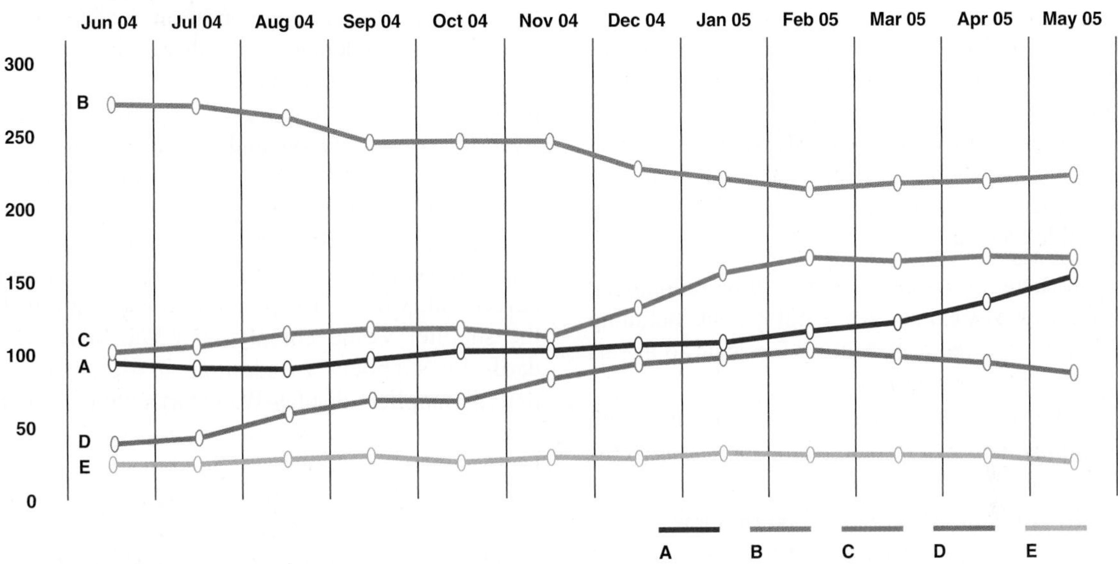

Factory Rating Trends FY2006

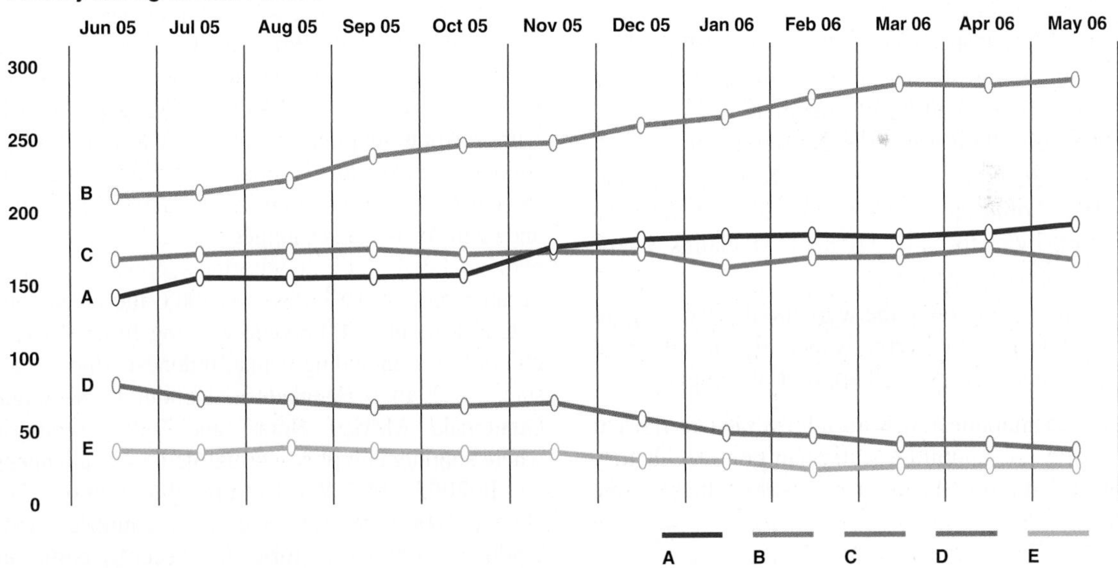

Note: Of the 42 M-Audits that Nike conducted through fiscal year 2006, 7 supplier factories received a grade of A and 13 factories received a D rating; Nike found the two big drivers of noncompliance were ignorance of the law or Nike standards and a lack of systems to manage people and processes.

Source: Nike fiscal year 2005–2006 Corporate Responsibility Report, pp. 30 and 31.

production techniques, so as to help contract factories eliminate the need to institute long workweeks and excessive overtime. According to Nike's vice president for global footwear operations, "If you improve efficiency and innovation, it changes the cost equation" for factories.[22]

In 2008, Nike discovered serious breaches of conduct involving unacceptable living conditions, withholding of worker passports, and garnishing of wages at a contract factory in Malaysia. To correct the problem, Nike announced that it was requiring the supplier to immediately make the following non-negotiable changes:[23]

1. All current migrant workers will be reimbursed for fees associated with employment including but not limited to recruiting fees paid to agents and worker permit fees.
2. Going forward, any and all fees associated with employment will be paid by the factory as a cost of doing business.
3. Any worker who wishes to return home will be provided with return airfare, irrespective of their contract requirements.
4. The majority of housing has been found to be unacceptable. All workers will be transitioned into new Nike-inspected and approved housing within 30 days. This transition has already begun.
5. All workers will have immediate and total free access to their passports. No restrictions.
6. Workers will have access to a 24-hour Nike hotline should they be denied access to their passports by factory management. All claims will be promptly investigated.
7. Communication to the workers of these changes will be delivered verbally as well as posted in all communal areas in all appropriate languages.

Nike also announced that during the next 10 days, it would review its entire Malaysian contract factory base and require factories to institute these same policies.

Wal-Mart's Supplier Code of Conduct and Compliance Monitoring Program

In 1992 Wal-Mart established a set of standards for its suppliers and put in place an ethical standards program to monitor supplier compliance with these standards.[24] Since then, Wal-Mart's standards for suppliers had been periodically evaluated and modified based on experience and feedback from the ethical sourcing community. The company's standards for suppliers covered compensation, working hours, forced labor, underage labor, discrimination, compliance with applicable national laws and regulation, health and safety practices, environmental abuse, freedom of association and collective bargaining, rights concerning foreign contract workers, and the right of audit by Wal-Mart.

Prior to contracting with any supplier, Wal-Mart required suppliers to review and sign a supplier agreement, which incorporated an expectation that the supplier would comply with Wal-Mart's standards for suppliers. In addition, it was mandatory that all suppliers display Wal-Mart's "Standards for Suppliers" poster in all of the suppliers' factories. Factory management was required to sign that it had read and fully understood the "Standards for Suppliers" poster, and a copy of the poster in the relevant language had to be posted in a public place within the factory. Wal-Mart's "Standards for Suppliers" poster was available in 25 languages.

In February 2002, Wal-Mart created an entity called the Global Procurement Services Group (GPSG), which was charged with identifying new suppliers, sourcing new products, building partnerships with existing suppliers, managing Wal-Mart's global supply chain of direct imports, providing workplace standards training to suppliers, and enforcing compliance with Wal-Mart's supplier standards. All Wal-Mart personnel engaged in monitoring supplier compliance became part of the GPSG. In 2008, the GPSG consisted of about 1,700 people working from offices in 25 countries, including China, Indonesia, India, Pakistan, Sri Lanka, Bangladesh, Honduras, Nicaragua, Guatemala, Mexico, Brazil, and Turkey (countries where supplier compliance presented big challenges).

In 2005–2007, Wal-Mart purchased goods from close to 9,000 factories in some 60 countries; about 2,500 of the 9,000 factories had recently come into Wal-Mart's compliance and factory audit system due to mergers, acquisitions, and new factory construction. About 200 Wal-Mart personnel scattered across the GPSG's offices in all 25 countries were engaged in monitoring suppliers for compliance with Wal-Mart's standards for suppliers. Suppliers covered by Wal-Mart ethical standards program had to disclose the factory (or factories) used to fulfill each order placed by Wal-Mart.

Wal-Mart's Supplier Auditing Program and Compliance Rating System During 2006, Wal-Mart audited more factories than any other company in the world, performing 16,700 initial and follow-up audits of 8,873 factories. In 2005, Wal-Mart conducted 13,700 initial and follow-up audits of 7,200 supplier factories; in 2004, Wal-Mart conducted 12,561 initial and follow-up audits at 7,600 factories. The company's audit methodology and factory rating system is described in Exhibit 5. A summary of Wal-Mart's audit findings for 2004–2006 is contained in Exhibit 6. According to Wal-Mart management, the lower number of disapproved factories in 2005 and 2006 relative to 2004 was chiefly due to extending the disapproval period from 90 days to one year for factories receiving four Orange ratings within a two-year period; other contributing factors were a revision of the ratings and Wal-Mart's public announcement that it was expanding the percentage of unannounced audits to 20 percent in 2005 and as many as 30 percent in 2006. Also, starting in 2004, more rigorous supplier standards were instituted, certain types of violations were reclassified to increase their severity, and audits were conducted by two-person teams instead of just a single individual. Increases in the number of audits had also resulted in Wal-Mart's auditors becoming more familiar with the factories and their workers. About 52 percent of the supplier factories audited in 2005 were not included in the 2006 audit program because of supplier turnover, disapproved factories, permanently banned factories receiving Red ratings, and the two-year re-audit cycle for supplier factories receiving a Green Rating. Rather than promptly banning the placement of orders at supplier factories receiving Yellow and Orange ratings, Wal-Mart's policy was to work with supplier factories to reduce violations and achieve steady improvement of workplace conditions, a position widely endorsed by most human rights activists, concerned citizens groups, and nongovernmental agencies striving for better factory conditions for low-wage workers. To help promote higher levels of supplier compliance, Wal-Mart trained more than 8,000 supplier personnel in 2004, 11,000 suppliers and members of factory management in 2005, and 5,000 suppliers and members of factory management in 2006. The training focused on increasing supplier familiarity with Wal-Mart's standards for suppliers and encouraging an exchange of information about factory operating practices. Wal-Mart actively worked with its foreign suppliers on ways to do better production planning, enhance plant efficiency, better educate and train workers, make supply chain improvements, and adopt better factory operating practices. Wal-Mart also consulted with knowledgeable outside experts and organizations on ways to accelerate ethical compliance and the achievement of better working conditions in supplier factories.

Upon learning of the incident in the *BusinessWeek* report cited in the opening of this case, Wal-Mart began an investigation of the Beifa factory in Ningbo. Wal-Mart acknowledged that some of its suppliers were trying to deceive plant monitors and avoid complying with Wal-Mart's standards for suppliers.

Audit Fatigue on the Part of Supplier Factories In 2008, supplier monitoring had become a standard practice for many retailers and brand owners that sourced their goods from factories in foreign locations where working conditions were often less than satisfactory. It was not uncommon for the audit teams of different companies to be in some supplier factories as often as 10 times each month, leading not only to duplication of audit efforts but also to audit fatigue and frustration on the part of factory managers. While the supplier codes of conduct of various retailers and brand owners tended to be similar, the interpretation of standards and local laws frequently varied by company, thus resulting in situations where factory managers were asked to comply with a variety of interpretations.

Wal-Mart recognized that multiple audits by multiple companies with varying standards and interpretations needed to be addressed. Its response had been to increase its collaboration with other companies and organizations that were engaged in monitoring to work toward a convergence of supplier codes of conduct and common interpretation of standards and local laws; Wal-Mart's goal was to develop a unified and credible certification program for factories that would both facilitate compliance and reduce audit fatigue.

Toward this end, Wal-Mart had begun working closely with the International Council of Toy Industries (ICTI) CARE Process and the Global Social Compliance Program. ICTI consisted of toy trade

Exhibit 5 Wal-Mart's Factory Audit Methodology and Factory Ratings System, 2006

- **Opening Meeting**—The Opening Meeting consisted of (1) confirmation of the factory and its information, (2) an introduction by the Wal-Mart auditors to factory management and supplier representatives, (3) a presentation and signing of the Wal-Mart Gifts & Gratuity Policy (which forbids any offer or receipt of gifts or bribes by the factory or the auditor), and (4) a request by the auditors of factory documentation related to personnel, production, time and pay records.
- **Factory Tour**—The auditors conducted a factory walk-through to examine factory conditions. The walk-through had minimal factory managers present because auditors asked production employees questions about machinery operation and other working conditions. Auditors also followed up with workers interviewed in previous audits about conditions since the last audit. The tour lasted up to three hours, depending on the size of the factory.
- **Worker Interviews**—During factory tours, auditors typically choose workers off the shop floor to interview, although additional workers could be requested to verify factory records during the documentation review process. Factory management had provide a private location for interviews, and under no circumstances were interviews conducted with factory management or supplier representatives present. Workers were interviewed in same-sex groups. The objectives of the interviews were to discover what interviewees had to say relevant to the audit, verify findings and observations made by the auditors, and ensure that workers understood their rights. A minimum of 15 workers were interviewed. The number of workers interviewed depended on the size of the factory.
- **Factory Documentation Review**—Auditors conducted an on-site inspection of payroll records, time cards, personnel files, and other pertinent production documents. For Initial and Annual audits, document review required records dating back at least three months and up to one year. Follow-up audits not only included reviewing findings from the previous audit, but also always included review of hours and compensation. Any factory that failed or refused to comply with this requirement was subject to immediate cancellation of any and all outstanding orders.
- **Closing Meeting**—Auditors summarized the audit findings, described any violations found, made recommendations to remedy the violations, and gave factory management a chance to ask any questions about the audit. Factory management and the auditor both signed the on-site audit report. Auditors left a copy of the signed audit findings and recommendations. Factory management was expected to act on all the recommendations in the on-site report and to present a completed action plan to the auditor during the follow-up audit opening meeting so auditors could validate that the actions were taken. Suppliers and factory management were encouraged to contact the regional Wal-Mart Ethical Standards office to discuss any concerns or questions about the on-site report and recommendations.
- **Factory Ratings**—Factories were rated Green, Yellow, Orange, or Red.

  A Green rating was assigned for factories having no or only minor violations

  A Yellow rating signified medium-risk violations.

  An Orange rating entailed high-risk violations (an Orange-Age rating was automatic for factories where the use of one or two underage workers was discovered). Factories receiving four Orange ratings within a two-year period were disapproved for producing goods for Wal-Mart for one year; after a year, the factory could be approved to supply Wal-Mart if it achieved a Yellow or Green rating.

  A Red rating indicated failure to pass the audit because of such egregious violations as use of prison or forced labor, extremely unsafe working conditions, employing more than two underage workers, serious worker abuse, or exceptionally long work hours. Red-rated factories were immediately and permanently banned from producing merchandise for Wal-Mart.

Starting in 2006, Green-rated factories had re-audits every two years instead of annually. Yellow- and Orange-rated factories had follow-up audits after 120 days to allow time for corrections and verification that corrective actions had been implemented. Factories rated Orange with underage labor violations for only one or two workers were an exception to the timeline for re-audits; such factories were re-audited within 30 days. If the follow-up audit for these factories indicated that the use of underage labor had been corrected, the factory could continue production for Wal-Mart; a failure on the follow-up 30-day audit resulted in a Red rating and a permanent order ban. A factory receiving an Orange assessment four times in a two-year period was banned from producing for Wal-Mart for up to one year (the ban on orders for such factories was extended from 90 days to one year starting January 1, 2005, in order to strengthen the seriousness of program noncompliance).

- **Use of Outside Auditors**—When Wal-Mart sourced goods for its foreign stores from suppliers in the same country in which the foreign stores were located, it used outside auditors to check supplier compliance. In 2005–2007, the outside auditing firms performing audits for some supplier factories included Accordia, Bureau Veritas, Cal Safety Compliance Corporation (CSCC), Global Social Compliance, Intertek Testing Services, and Société Générale de Surveillance.

Source: Wal-Mart's Report on Ethical Sourcing, 2005 and 2006, posted at www.walmart.com (accessed January 25, 2007, and September 18, 2008).

Exhibit 6 Comparison of Wal-Mart's Factory Audit Results for 2004, 2005, and 2006

	2004	2005	2006
Total number of factory audits	12,561 (8% were unannounced)	13,600 (20% were unannounced)	16,700 (26% were unannounced)
Number of factories audited	7,600	7,200	8,873
Audits resulting in Green ratings (re-audited after 2 years)	19.1%	9.6%	5.4%
Audits resulting in Yellow ratings (re-audited after 120 days*)	38.8%	37.0%	51.6%
Audits resulting in Orange ratings (re-audited after 120 days)	32.5%	52.3%	40.3%
Audits resulting in Orange-Age ratings (re-audited after 30 days)	—	0.8%	0.4%
Factories disapproved for producing for one year—four Orange assessments in a two-year period	8.8%	0.1%	2.1%
Audits resulting in Red ratings—factories permanently banned from receiving orders	0.8%	164 (141 of these related to the use of underage labor)	0.2%

*In 2007, the re-audit period for Yellow-rated factories was changed to 180 days.

Source: Wal-Mart's Report on Ethical Sourcing, 2005 and 2006, www.walmart.com (accessed January 25, 2007, and September 18, 2008).

associations from 21 countries and was engaged in promoting toy safety standards, fair labor treatment and safe working conditions in toy factories, and a responsible approach in advertising and marketing toys to children. ICTI had developed a code of business practices that included high standards for labor practices and employee health and safety. Its CARE Process was aimed at providing a single, thorough, and consistent audit program for monitoring toy factories compliance with the code; most of ICTI's auditing activities were concentrated in China, where 70 percent of the world's toy volume was manufactured. Wal-Mart had begun accepting ICTI's audit results in lieu of conducting its own audits.

Wal-Mart was a cofounder of the Global Social Compliance Program (GSCP). The GSCP was an initiative to promote uniform global standards for supplier conduct and acceptable factory working conditions, particularly as concerned health and safety, child labor, discrimination, and compensation. Factory monitoring was an important component of the program. Although much of the work to put the program in place was being done by CIES, an international association of food retailers and suppliers, the scope of the GSCP covered both food and nonfood production. While the current members of GSCP were companies, it was envisioned that there would be extensive collaboration with trade unions, governmental organizations, and nongovernmental organizations.

In July 2008, Wal-Mart announced that Intertek Group, PLC, an independent supplier monitoring organization with 25 offices in China, would begin conducting audit of Wal-Mart's supplier factories in China. Intertek was among the several outside groups that Wal-Mart used to help conduct audits of its supplier factories.

COMPLIANCE EFFORTS OF INDUSTRY GROUPS AND NONGOVERNMENTAL ORGANIZATIONS

Some companies, rather than conducting their own supplier monitoring and compliance effort, had banded together in industry groups or multi-industry coalitions to establish a common code of supplier conduct and to organize a joint program of factory inspections and compliance efforts. For example, Hewlett-Packard, Dell, and other electronics companies that relied heavily on Asian-based manufacturers to supply components or else assemble digital cameras, handheld devices, and PCs had entered into an alliance to combat worker abuse and poor working conditions in the factories of their suppliers.

The Fair Labor Association

One of the most prominent and best organized coalitions was the Fair Labor Association (FLA), whose members and affiliates included 194 colleges and universities, a number of concerned nongovernmental organizations, and a group of 35 companies that included Nike, the Adidas Group (the owner of both Reebok and Adidas brands), Puma, Eddie Bauer, Liz Claiborne, Patagonia, Cutter & Buck, Russell Corporation, and Nordstrom. As part of its broad-based campaign to eliminate human rights abuses and improve global workplace conditions, the FLA had established its Workplace Code of Conduct, a document to which all members and affiliates had subscribed. To aid in winning supplier compliance with the Workplace Code of Conduct, the FLA conducted unannounced audits of factories across the world that supplied its members and affiliates.

In 2006, FLA's teams of independent plant monitors conducted inspections at 147 factories in 18 countries, the results of which were published in FLA's 2007 annual public report. The audits, all of which involved factories that were supplying goods to one or more FLA members, revealed 2,511 instances of noncompliance with FLA's Workplace Code of Conduct, an average of 18.2 violations per factory (versus averages of 15.1 per factory in 2003 and 18.2 per factory in 2004).[25] The violations included excessive work hours, underpayment of wages and overtime, failure to observe legal holidays and grant vacations (27.5 percent); health and safety problems (44 percent); and worker harassment (5.1 percent). The FLA concluded that the actual violations relating to underpayment of wages, hours of work, and overtime compensation were probably higher than those discovered because "factory personnel have become sophisticated in concealing noncompliance relating to wages. They often hide original documents and show monitors falsified books."[26]

In its 2006 public annual report, the FLA said that accredited independent monitors conducted unannounced audits of 99 factories in 18 countries in 2005; the audited factories employed some 77,800 workers.[27] The audited factories were but a small sample of the 3,753 factories employing some 2.9 million people from which the FLA's 35 affiliated companies sourced goods in 2005; however, 34 of the 99 audited factories involved facilities providing goods to 2 or more of FLA's 35 affiliated companies. The 99 audits during 2005 revealed 1,587 violations, an average of 15.9 per audit. The greatest incidence of violations was found in Southeast Asia (chiefly factories located in China, Indonesia, Thailand, and India), where violations averaged about 22 violations per factory audit. As was the case with the audits conducted in 2004, most of the violations related to health and safety (45 percent); wages, benefits, hours of work, and overtime compensation (28 percent); and worker harassment and abuse (7 percent). The FLA stated in its 2006 report that the violations relating to compensation and benefits were likely higher than those detected in its 2005 audits: "Factory personnel have become accustomed to concealing real wage documentation and providing falsified records at the time of compliance audits, making any noncompliances difficult to detect."[28]

In its 2007 public annual report, the FLA said that accredited independent monitors conducted unannounced audits of 147 factories in 30 countries in 2006; the audited factories employed some 110,000 workers.[29] The audited factories were but a small sample of the 5,178 factories employing some 3.8 million people from which the FLA's affiliated companies sourced goods in 2006; however, 24 of the audited factories involved facilities providing goods to 2 or more of FLA's affiliated companies. The 147 audits during 2006 revealed 2,511 violations, an average of 17.1 per audit. Over 80 percent of all the reported violations were in Asian countries; there was an average of 37.4 violations per factory visited in South Asia. Most of the 2006 violations related to health and safety (46 percent); wages, benefits, hours of work, and overtime compensation (30 percent); and code awareness (9 percent). Once again, the FLA stated in its report that the violations relating to compensation and benefits were likely higher than those detected in its prior-year audits because "Factory personnel have become accustomed to concealing real wage documentation and providing falsified records at the time of compliance audits, making noncompliances difficult to detect."[30]

The Fair Factories Clearinghouse

The Fair Factories Clearinghouse (FFC), formed in 2004, was a collaborative effort to create a system for managing and sharing factory audit information that would facilitate detecting and eliminating sweatshops and abusive workplace conditions in foreign factories. Members as of 2008 included ASICS America, L. L. Bean, Timberland, Hudson's Bay Company, Levi Strauss & Co., Macy's Merchandising Group, Mark's Work Wearhouse, Nike Inc., Patagonia, Starbucks Coffee Company, and VF Corporation. Membership fees were based on a company's annual revenues, with annual fees ranging from as little as $5,000 to as much as $75,000 (not including one-time initiation fees of $2,500 to $11,500). The idea underlying the FFC was that members would pool their audit information on offshore factories, creating a database on thousands of manufacturing plants. As of October 2007, FFC's database included 25,000 audits of 13,000 factories. Once a plant was certified by a member company or organization, other members could accept the results without having to do an audit of their own. One benefit of collaborative audit-sharing via an organization like FFC was that members sourcing goods from the same factories could band together and apply added pressure on a supplier to improve its working conditions and comply with buyers' codes of supplier conduct.[31]

Aside from the audit-sharing appeal of making factory audit programs less expensive, audit-sharing had the additional appeal of lessening the time that factory managers had to spend dealing with the audit teams of many different customer companies that conducted their own audits, thereby reducing "audit fatigue." Some large plants with big customer bases were said to undergo audits as often as weekly and occasionally even daily; in addition, they were pressured into having to comply with varying provisions and requirements of each auditing company's code of supplier conduct—being subject to varying and conflicting codes of conduct was a factor that induced cheating.

THE OBSTACLES TO ACHIEVING SUPPLIER COMPLIANCE WITH CODES OF CONDUCT IN LOW-WAGE, LOW-COST COUNTRIES

Factory managers subject to inspections and audits of their plants and work practices complained that strong pressures from their customers to keep prices low gave them a big incentive to cheat on their compliance with labor standards. As the general manager of a factory in China that supplied goods to Nike said, "Any improvement you make costs more money. The price [Nike pays] never increases one penny but compliance with labor codes definitely raises costs."[32]

The pricing pressures from companies sourcing components or finished goods from offshore factories in China, India, and other low-wage, low-cost locations were acute. Since 1996, the prices paid for men's shirts and sweaters sourced in China were said to have dropped by 14 percent, while the prices of clocks and lamps had dropped 40 percent and the prices of toys and games had fallen 30 percent.[33] Such downward pressure on prices made it financially difficult for foreign manufacturers to improve worker compensation and benefits, make their workplaces safer and more pleasant, introduce more efficient production methods, and overhaul inefficient plant layouts. Many factory managers believed that if they paid workers a higher wage, incurred other compliance costs, and then raised their prices to cover the higher costs that their customers would quickly cut and run to other suppliers charging lower prices. Hence the penalties and disincentives for compliance significantly outweighed any rewards.

The CEO of the Fair Labor Association, Auret van Heerden, in a 2006 interview with *BusinessWeek,* offered a number of reasons why underpayment of wages and excessive overtime in supplier factories in China were such difficult problems to resolve:

> The brands book and confirm orders really late. And they often change their orders after booking. The brands want to order later and they don't want to hold

product. Then you add price pressures into that and it is really tough for the supplier [to not overwork its workers].

But the factory often doesn't order the materials until too late and they are often delivered late [to the factory], too. The factory production layout is often a mess, so the supplier gets behind schedule and over budget even before they know it. Then they have to catch up. And to save money, they extend hours, but don't pay overtime premiums. And the suppliers also lack proper training. The styles [of clothing and footwear] are becoming more complicated and are changing more frequently.

Multiple codes are a big problem. The classic example is the height that a fire extinguisher should be kept off the ground—how high varies according to different codes. Companies like McDonald's, Disney, and Wal-Mart are doing thousands of audits a year that are not harmonized. That's where audit fatigue comes in.

And auditing in itself tells you a little about the problem, but not enough, and not why there is a problem. So you have an overtime problem, but you don't know why. Is it because of electricity shortages, labor shortages, or a shorter order turnaround time? You don't know.[34]

Endnotes

1. Dexter Roberts and Pete Engardio, "Secrets, Lies, and Sweatshops," *BusinessWeek,* November 27, 2006, pp. 50–58.
2. Ibid., p. 50.
3. Ibid.
4. www.chinatownconnection.com(accessed September 17, 2008).
5. Judith Bannister, "Manufacturing in China Today: Employment and Labor Compensation," *Conference Board,* November 2007, p. 22.
6. Roberts and Engardio, "Secrets, Lies, and Sweatshops," p. 54.
7. Ibid., p. 54.
8. Ibid., p. 50.
9. Ibid., p. 55.
10. Ibid., p. 53.
11. Ibid., pp. 55–56.
12. Ibid., p. 53.
13. Lisa Roner, "Wal-Mart's Ethical Sourcing: Green Does Not Mean Ethical," October 19, 2007, www.ethicalcorp.com (accessed September 22, 2008).
14. Nike FY2005-06 Corporate Responsibility Report, www.nike.com/nikebiz (accessed September 19, 2008), p. 28.
15. Information posted at www.nikebiz.com (accessed on January 26, 2007); Nike's 2004 Fiscal Year Corporate Responsibility Report, pp. 21–24.
16. Nike's 2004 Fiscal Year Corporate Responsibility Report, p. 28.
17. Ibid., p. 29.
18. Ibid., p. 20.
19. Ibid., p. 30.
20. Ibid., p. 25.
21. Ibid., p. 26.
22. Pete Engardio and Dexter Roberts, "How to Make Factories Play Fair," *BusinessWeek,* November 27, 2007, p. 58.
23. Company press release, August 1, 2008.
24. The content of this section was developed by the case author from information posted in the supplier section at www.walmartstores.com (accessed January 25, 2007).
25. Fair Labor Association, 2005 annual public report, www.fairlabor.org (accessed January 23, 2007).
26. Ibid., p. 38; also quoted in Roberts and Engardio, "Secrets, Lies, and Sweatshops," p. 54.
27. Fair Labor Association, 2006 annual public report, www.fairlabor.org (accessed January 23, 2007).
28. Ibid., p. 40.
29. Fair Labor Association, 2007 annual public report, www.fairlabor.org (accessed September 19, 2008).
30. Ibid., p. 48.
31. Roberts and Engardio, "Secrets, Lies, and Sweatshops," p. 58.
32. As quoted in ibid., p. 53.
33. Ibid., p. 58.
34. As quoted in Dexter Roberts, "A Lion for Worker Rights," *BusinessWeek* Online Extra, November 27, 2006, www.businessweek.com (accessed on January 23, 2007).

Endnotes

Chapter 1

1. Costas Markides, "What Is Strategy and How Do You Know If You Have One?" *Business Strategy Review* 15, no. 2 (Summer 2004), pp. 5–6.
2. For a discussion of the different ways that companies can position themselves in the marketplace, see Michael E. Porter, "What Is Strategy?" *Harvard Business Review* 74, no. 6 (November–December 1996), pp. 65–67.
3. For an excellent treatment of the strategic challenges posed by rapid industry change, see Shona L. Brown and Kathleen M. Eisenhardt, *Competing on the Edge: Strategy as Structured Chaos* (Boston, MA: Harvard Business School Press, 1998), Chapter 1.
4. See Henry Mintzberg and Joseph Lampel, "Reflecting on the Strategy Process," *Sloan Management Review* 40, no. 3 (Spring 1999), pp. 21–30; Henry Mintzberg and J. A. Waters, "Of Strategies, Deliberate and Emergent," *Strategic Management Journal* 6 (1985), pp. 257–72; Costas Markides, "Strategy as Balance: From 'Either-Or' to 'And,'" *Business Strategy Review* 12, no. 3 (September 2001), pp. 1–10; Henry Mintzberg, Bruce Ahlstrand, and Joseph Lampel, *Strategy Safari: A Guided Tour through the Wilds of Strategic Management* (New York: Free Press, 1998), Chapters 2, 5, and 7; and C. K. Prahalad and Gary Hamel. "The Core Competence of the Corporation." *Harvard Business Review* 70, no. 3 (May–June 1990), pp. 79–93.
5. Joseph L. Badaracco, "The Discipline of Building Character," *Harvard Business Review* 76, no. 2 (March–April 1998), pp. 115–24.
6. Joan Magretta, "Why Business Models Matter," *Harvard Business Review* 80, no. 5 (May 2002), p. 87.

Chapter 2

1. For a more in-depth discussion of the challenges of developing a well-conceived vision, as well as some good examples, see Hugh Davidson, *The Committed Enterprise: How to Make Vision and Values Work* (Oxford: Butterworth-Heinemann, 2002), Chapter 2; W. Chan Kim and Renée Mauborgne, "Charting Your Company's Future," *Harvard Business Review* 80, no. 6 (June 2002), pp. 77–83; James C. Collins and Jerry I. Porras, "Building Your Company's Vision," *Harvard Business Review* 74, no. 5 (September–October 1996), pp. 65–77; Jim Collins and Jerry Porras, *Built to Last: Successful Habits of Visionary Companies* (New York: HarperCollins, 1994), Chapter 11; and Michel Robert, *Strategy Pure and Simple II: How Winning Companies Dominate Their Competitors* (New York: McGraw-Hill, 1998), Chapters 2, 3 and 6.
2. Davidson, *The Committed Enterprise,* pp. 20, 54.
3. Jeffrey K. Liker, *The Toyota Way* (New York: McGraw-Hill, 2004); and Steve Hamm, "Taking a Page from Toyota's Playbook," *BusinessWeek*, August 22–29, 2005, p. 72.
4. Davidson, *The Committed Enterprise,* pp. 36, 54.
5. As quoted in Charles H. House and Raymond L. Price, "The Return Map: Tracking Product Teams," *Harvard Business Review* 60, no. 1 (January–February 1991), p. 93.
6. Mark Gottfredson, Steve Schaubert, and Hernan Saenz, "The New Leader's Guide to Diagnosing the Business, *Harvard Business Review* 86, no. 2 (February 2008), p. 73.
7. Robert S. Kaplan and David P. Norton, *The Strategy-Focused Organization* (Boston: Harvard Business School Press, 2001), p. 3.
8. Ibid., p. 7. Also, see Robert S. Kaplan and David P. Norton, *The Balanced Scorecard: Translating Strategy into Action* (Boston: Harvard Business School Press, 1996), p. 10; Kevin B. Hendricks, Larry Menor, and Christine Wiedman, "The Balanced Scorecard: To Adopt or Not to Adopt," *Ivey Business Journal* 69, no. 2 (November–December 2004), pp. 1–7; and Sandy Richardson, "The Key Elements of Balanced Scorecard Success," *Ivey Business Journal* 69, no. 2 (November–December 2004), pp. 7–9.
9. Information posted on the Web site of Bain and Company, www.bain.com (accessed March 27, 2008).
10. Information posted on the Web site of Balanced Scorecard Institute, www.balancedscorecard.org (accessed March 27, 2008).
11. The concept of strategic intent is described in more detail in Gary Hamel and C. K. Prahalad, "Strategic Intent," *Harvard Business Review* 89, no. 3 (May–June 1989), pp. 63–76; this section draws on their pioneering discussion. See also Michael A. Hitt, Beverly B. Tyler, Camilla Hardee, and Daewoo Park, "Understanding Strategic Intent in the Global Marketplace," *Academy of Management Executive* 9, no. 2 (May 1995), pp. 12–19.
12. As reported in "We Called It: Toyota Tops GM in '07," *Automotive News,* January 28, 2008, p. 6.
13. As described in "Honda Is Expected to State Plans to Break into U.S. Jet Market," *The Wall Street Journal Online,* July 24, 2006.
14. For a fuller discussion of strategy as an entrepreneurial process, see Henry Mintzberg, Bruce Ahlstrand, and Joseph Lampel, *Strategy Safari: A Guided Tour through the Wilds of Strategic Management* (New York: Free Press, 1998), Chapter 5. Also, see Bruce Barringer and Allen C. Bluedorn, "The Relationship Between Corporate Entrepreneurship and Strategic Management," *Strategic Management Journal* 20 (1999), pp. 421–44; Jeffrey G. Covin and Morgan P. Miles, "Corporate Entrepreneurship and the Pursuit of Competitive Advantage," *Entrepreneurship: Theory and Practice* 23, no. 3 (Spring 1999), pp. 47–63; and David A. Garvin and Lynned C. Levesque, "Meeting the Challenge of Corporate Entrepreneurship," *Harvard Business Review* 84, no. 10 (October 2006), pp. 102–12.
15. For an excellent discussion of why a strategic plan needs to be more than a list of bullet points and should in fact tell an engaging, insightful, stage-setting story that lays out the industry and competitive situation as well as the vision, objectives, and strategy, see Gordon Shaw, Robert Brown, and Philip Bromiley, "Strategic Stories: How 3M Is Rewriting Business Planning," *Harvard Business Review* 76, no. 3 (May–June 1998), pp. 41–50. For a valuable discussion of the role of mission, values, vision, objectives, and strategy statements in providing organizational direction, see David J. Collins and Michael G. Rukstad, "Can You Say What Your Strategy Is?" *Harvard Business Review* 86, no. 4 (April 2008), pp. 82–90.
16. Fred Vogelstein, "Winning the Amazon Way," *Fortune,* May 26, 2003, p. 64.
17. As discussed in Garvin and Levesque, "Meeting the Challenge," pp. 110–12.
18. For a more in-depth discussion of the leader's role in creating a results-oriented culture that nurtures success, see Benjamin Schneider, Sarah K. Gunnarson, and Kathryn Niles-Jolly, "Creating the Climate and Culture of Success," *Organizational Dynamics* 23, no. 1 (Summer 1994), pp. 17–29.
19. For an excellent discussion of strategy as a dynamic process involving continuous, unending creation and recreation of strategy, see Cynthia A. Montgomery, "Putting Leadership Back into Strategy," *Harvard Business Review* 86, no. 1 (January 2008), pp. 54–60.
20. James Brian Quinn, *Strategies for Change: Logical Incrementalism* (Homewood, IL: Richard D. Irwin, 1980), pp. 20–22.
21. For discussions of what it takes for the corporate governance system to function properly, see David A. Nadler, "Building Better Boards," *Harvard Business Review* 82,

no. 5 (May 2004), pp. 102–5; Cynthia A. Montgomery and Rhonda Kaufman, "The Board's Missing Link," *Harvard Business Review* 81, no. 3 (March 2003), pp. 86–93; and John Carver, "What Continues to Be Wrong with Corporate Governance and How to Fix It," *Ivey Business Journal* 68, no. 1 (September/October 2003), pp. 1–5. See also Gordon Donaldson, "A New Tool for Boards: The Strategic Audit," *Harvard Business Review* 73, no. 4 (July–August 1995), pp. 99–107.

Chapter 3

1. There are a large number of studies of the size of the cost reductions associated with experience; the median cost reduction associated with a doubling of cumulative production volume is approximately 15 percent, but there is a wide variation from industry to industry. For a good discussion of the economies of experience and learning, see Pankaj Ghemawat, "Building Strategy on the Experience Curve," *Harvard Business Review* 64, no. 2 (March–April 1985), pp. 143–49.
2. The five-forces model of competition is the creation of Professor Michael E. Porter of the Harvard Business School. For his original presentation of the model, see Michael E. Porter, "How Competitive Forces Shape Strategy," *Harvard Business Review* 57, no. 2 (March–April 1979), pp. 137–45. A more thorough discussion can be found in Michael E. Porter, *Competitive Strategy: Techniques for Analyzing Industries and Competitors* (New York: Free Press, 1980), Chapter 1. Porter's five-forces model of competition is reaffirmed and extended in Michael E. Porter, "The Five Competitive Forces That Shape Strategy," *Harvard Business Review* 86, no. 1 (January 2008), pp. 78–93.
3. The tendency of firms to counter competitive moves of rival firms tends to cause escalating competitive pressures that affect the profitability of rivals; see Pamela J. Derfus, Patrick G. Maggitti, Curtis M. Grimm, and Ken G. Smith, "The Red Queen Effect: Competitive Actions and Firm Performance," *Academy of Management Journal* 51, no. 1, (February 2008), pp. 61–80.
4. Many of these indicators of whether rivalry produces intense competitive pressures are based on Porter, *Competitive Strategy,* pp. 17–21; and Porter, "The Five Competitive Forces That Shape Strategy," pp. 85–86.
5. The role of entry barriers in shaping the strength of competition in a particular market has long been a standard topic in the literature of microeconomics. For a discussion of how entry barriers affect competitive pressures associated with potential entry, see J. S. Bain, *Barriers to New Competition* (Cambridge, MA: Harvard University Press, 1956); F. M. Scherer, *Industrial Market Structure and Economic Performance* (Chicago: Rand McNally & Co., 1971), pp. 216–20, 226–33; and Porter, *Competitive Strategy,* pp. 7–17; and Porter, "The Five Competitive Forces That Shape Strategy," pp. 80–82.
6. Michael E. Porter, "How Competitive Forces Shape Strategy," *Harvard Business Review* 57, no. 2 (March–April 1979), p. 140; Porter, *Competitive Strategy,* pp. 14–15; and Porter, "The Five Competitive Forces That Shape Strategy," p. 82.
7. For a good discussion of this point, see George S. Yip, "Gateways to Entry," *Harvard Business Review* 60, no. 5 (September–October 1982), pp. 85–93.
8. Porter, "How Competitive Forces Shape Strategy," p. 142; Porter, *Competitive Strategy,* pp. 23–24; and Porter, "The Five Competitive Forces That Shape Strategy," pp. 82–83.
9. Porter, *Competitive Strategy,* p. 10; and Porter, "The Five Competitive Forces That Shape Strategy," p. 85.
10. Porter, *Competitive Strategy,* pp. 27–28; and Porter, "The Five Competitive Forces That Shape Strategy," pp. 82–83.
11. Porter, *Competitive Strategy,* pp. 24–27; and Porter, "The Five Competitive Forces That Shape Strategy," pp. 83–84.
12. For a more extended discussion of the problems with the life-cycle hypothesis, see Porter, *Competitive Strategy,* pp. 157–62.
13. Ibid., p. 162.
14. Most of the candidate driving forces described here are based on the discussion in ibid., pp. 164–83.
15. Ibid., Chapter 7.
16. Ibid., pp.129–30.
17. For an excellent discussion of how to identify the factors that define strategic groups, see Mary Ellen Gordon and George R. Milne, "Selecting the Dimensions that Define Strategic Groups: A Novel Market-Driven Approach," *Journal of Managerial Issues* 11, no. 2 (Summer 1999), pp. 213–33.
18. Porter, *Competitive Strategy,* pp. 152–54.
19. Strategic groups act as good reference points for predicting the evolution of an industry's competitive structure. See Avi Fiegenbaum and Howard Thomas, "Strategic Groups as Reference Groups: Theory, Modeling and Empirical Examination of Industry and Competitive Strategy," *Strategic Management Journal* 16 (1995), pp. 461–76. For a study of how strategic group analysis helps identify the variables that lead to sustainable competitive advantage, see S. Ade Olusoga, Michael P. Mokwa, and Charles H. Noble, "Strategic Groups, Mobility Barriers, and Competitive Advantage," *Journal of Business Research* 33 (1995), pp. 153–64.
20. Porter, *Competitive Strategy,* pp.130, 132–38, and 154–55.
21. For a discussion of legal and ethical ways of gathering competitive intelligence on rival companies, see Larry Kahaner, *Competitive Intelligence* (New York: Simon & Schuster, 1996).
22. Ibid., pp. 84–85.
23. Some experts dispute the strategy-making value of key success factors. Professor Pankaj Ghemawat has claimed that the "whole idea of identifying a success factor and then chasing it seems to have something in common with the ill-considered medieval hunt for the *philosopher's stone,* a substance which would transmute everything it touched into gold." Pankaj Ghemawat, *Commitment: The Dynamic of Strategy* (New York: Free Press, 1991), p. 11.

Chapter 4

1. Many business organizations are coming to view cutting-edge knowledge and intellectual resources of company personnel as a valuable competitive asset and have concluded that explicitly managing these assets is an essential part of their strategy. See Michael H. Zack, "Developing a Knowledge Strategy," *California Management Review* 41, no. 3 (Spring 1999), pp. 125–45; and Shaker A. Zahra, Anders P. Nielsen, and William C. Bogner, "Corporate Entrepreneurship, Knowledge, and Competence Development," *Entrepreneurship Theory and Practice,* Spring 1999, pp. 169–89.
2. In the past decade, there's been considerable research into the role a company's resources and competitive capabilities play in crafting strategy and in determining company profitability. The findings and conclusions have coalesced into what is called the resource-based view of the firm. Among the most insightful publications on the topic are Birger Wernerfelt, "A Resource-Based View of the Firm," *Strategic Management Journal,* September–October 1984, pp. 171–80; Jay Barney, "Firm Resources and Sustained Competitive Advantage," *Journal of Management* 17, no. 1 (1991), pp. 99–120; Margaret A. Peteraf, "The Cornerstones of Competitive Advantage: A Resource-Based View," *Strategic Management Journal,* March 1993, pp. 179–91; Birger Wernerfelt, "The Resource-Based View of the Firm: Ten Years After," *Strategic Management Journal* 16 (1995), pp. 171–74; Jay B. Barney, "Looking Inside for Competitive Advantage," *Academy of Management Executive* 9, no. 4 (November 1995), pp. 49–61; Christopher A. Bartlett and Sumantra Ghoshal, "Building Competitive Advantage through People," *MIT Sloan Management Review* 43, no 2 (Winter 2002), pp. 34–41; Danny Miller, Russell Eisenstat, and Nathaniel Foote, "Strategy from the Inside Out: Building Capability-Creating Organizations," *California Management Review* 44, no. 3 (Spring 2002), pp. 37–54; and Jay B. Barney and Delwyn N. Clark, *Resource-Based Theory: Creating*

and Sustaining Competitive Advantage (New York: Oxford University Press, 2007).

3. George Stalk Jr. and Rob Lachenauer, "Hardball: Five Killer Strategies for Trouncing the Competition," *Harvard Business Review* 82, no. 4 (April 2004), p. 65.
4. For a more extensive discussion of how to identify and evaluate the competitive power of a company's capabilities, see David W. Birchall and George Tovstiga, "The Strategic Potential of a Firm's Knowledge Portfolio," *Journal of General Management* 25, no. 1 (Autumn 1999), pp. 1–16; and Nick Bontis, Nicola C. Dragonetti, Kristine Jacobsen, and Goran Roos, "The Knowledge Toolbox: A Review of the Tools Available to Measure and Manage Intangible Resources," *European Management Journal* 17, no. 4 (August 1999), pp. 391–401. Also see David Teece, "Capturing Value from Knowledge Assets: The New Economy, Markets for Know-How, and Intangible Assets," *California Management Review* 40, no. 3 (Spring 1998), pp. 55–79.
5. See Barney, "Firm Resources and Sustained Competitive Advantage," *Journal of Management* 17, no. 1 (1991), pp. 105–9; and Jay B. Barney and Delwyn N. Clark, *Resource-Based Theory: Creating and Sustaining Competitive Advantage* (New York: Oxford University Press, 2007). Also, see M. A. Peteraf, "The Cornerstones of Competitive Advantage: A Resource-Based View," *Strategic Management Journal* 14, (1993), pp. 179–91; and David J. Collis and Cynthia A. Montgomery, "Competing on Resources: Strategy in the 1990s," *Harvard Business Review* 73, no. 4 (July–August 1995), pp. 120–23.
6. For a more detailed discussion, see George Stalk, Philip Evans, and Lawrence E. Schulman, "Competing on Capabilities: The New Rules of Corporate Strategy," *Harvard Business Review* 70, no. 2 (March–April 1992), pp. 57–69.
7. Donald Sull, "Strategy as Active Waiting," *Harvard Business Review* 83, no. 9 (September 2005), pp. 121–22.
8. Ibid., p. 122.
9. Ibid., pp. 124–26.
10. See Jack W. Duncan, Peter Ginter, and Linda E. Swayne, "Competitive Advantage and Internal Organizational Assessment," *Academy of Management Executive* 12, no. 3 (August 1998), pp. 6–16.
11. The value chain concept was developed and articulated by professor Michael E. Porter at the Harvard Business School and is described at greater length in Michael E. Porter, *Competitive Advantage* (New York: Free Press, 1985), Chapters 2 and 3.
12. Porter, *Competitive Advantage,* p. 36.
13. Ibid., p. 34.
14. The strategic importance of effective supply chain management is discussed in Hau L. Lee, "The Triple-A Supply Chain," *Harvard Business Review* 82, no. 10 (October 2004), pp. 102–12.
15. M. Hegert and D. Morris, "Accounting Data for Value Chain Analysis," *Strategic Management Journal* 10 (1989), p. 180; Robin Cooper and Robert S. Kaplan, "Measure Costs Right: Make the Right Decisions," *Harvard Business Review* 66, no. 5 (September–October, 1988), pp. 96–103; and John K. Shank and Vijay Govindarajan, *Strategic Cost Management* (New York: Free Press, 1993), especially Chapters 2–6, 10.
16. For more on how and why the clustering of suppliers and other support organizations matter to a company's costs and competitiveness, see Michael E. Porter, "Clusters and the New Economics of Competition," *Harvard Business Review* 76, no. 6 (November–December 1998), pp. 77–90.
17. For discussions of the accounting challenges in calculating the costs of value chain activities, see John K. Shank and Vijay Govindarajan, *Strategic Cost Management* (New York: Free Press, 1993), especially Chapters 2–6, 10, and 11; Robin Cooper and Robert S. Kaplan, "Measure Costs Right: Make the Right Decisions," *Harvard Business Review* 66, no. 5 (September–October, 1988), pp. 96–103; and Joseph A. Ness and Thomas G. Cucuzza, "Tapping the Full Potential of ABC," *Harvard Business Review* 73, no. 4 (July–August 1995), pp. 130–38.
18. For more details, see Gregory H. Watson, *Strategic Benchmarking: How to Rate Your Company's Performance Against the World's Best* (New York: John Wiley, 1993); and Robert C. Camp, *Benchmarking: The Search for Industry Best Practices That Lead to Superior Performance* (Milwaukee: ASQC Quality Press, 1989); Christopher E. Bogan and Michael J. English, *Benchmarking for Best Practices: Winning through Innovative Adaptation* (New York: McGraw-Hill, 1994); and Dawn Iacobucci and Christie Nordhielm, "Creative Benchmarking," *Harvard Business Review* 78, no. 6 (November–December 2000), pp. 24–25.
19. Jeremy Main, "How to Steal the Best Ideas Around," *Fortune*, October 19, 1992, pp. 102–3.
20. Shank and Govindarajan, *Strategic Cost Management,* p. 50.
21. Some of these options are discussed in more detail in Porter, *Competitive Advantage,* Chapter 3.
22. An example of how Whirlpool Corporation transformed its supply chain from a competitive liability to a competitive asset is discussed in Reuben E. Stone, "Leading a Supply Chain Turnaround," *Harvard Business Review* 82, no. 10 (October 2004), pp. 114–21.
23. James Brian Quinn, *Intelligent Enterprise* (New York: Free Press, 1993), p. 54.
24. Ibid., p. 34.

Chapter 5

1. This classification scheme is an adaptation of a narrower three-strategy classification presented in Michael E. Porter, *Competitive Strategy: Techniques for Analyzing Industries and Competitors* (New York: Free Press, 1980), Chapter 2, especially pp. 35–40 and 44–46. For a discussion of the different ways that companies can position themselves in the marketplace, see Michael E. Porter, "What Is Strategy?" *Harvard Business Review* 74, no. 6 (November–December 1996), pp. 65–67.
2. Michael E. Porter, *Competitive Advantage* (New York: Free Press, 1985), p. 97.
3. For a discussion of how unique industry positioning and resource combinations are linked to consumer perspectives of value and their willingness to pay more for differentiated products or services, see Richard L. Priem, "A Consumer Perspective on Value Creation," *Academy of Management Review* 32, no. 1 (2007), pp. 219–35.
4. Ibid., pp. 135–38.
5. For a more detailed discussion, see George Stalk, Philip Evans, and Lawrence E. Schulman, "Competing on Capabilities: The New Rules of Corporate Strategy," *Harvard Business Review* 70, no. 2 (March–April 1992), pp. 57–69.
6. The relevance of perceived value and signaling is discussed in more detail in Porter, *Competitive Advantage,* pp. 138–42.
7. Ibid., pp. 160–62.

Chapter 6

1. Yves L. Doz and Gary Hamel, *Alliance Advantage: The Art of Creating Value through Partnering* (Boston: Harvard Business School Press, 1998), pp. xiii, xiv.
2. Jason Wakeam, "The Five Factors of a Strategic Alliance," *Ivey Business Journal* 68, no. 3 (May–June 2003), pp. 1–4.
3. Jeffrey H. Dyer, Prashant Kale, and Harbir Singh, "When to Ally and When to Acquire," *Harvard Business Review* 82, no. 7/8 (July–August 2004), p. 109.
4. Salvatore Parise and Lisa Sasson, "Leveraging Knowledge Management across Strategic Alliances," *Ivey Business Journal* 66, no. 4 (March–April 2002), p. 42.
5. David Ernst and James Bamford, "Your Alliances Are Too Stable," *Harvard Business Review* 83, no. 6 (June 2005), p.133.
6. An excellent discussion of the portfolio approach to managing multiple alliances and how to restructure a faltering alliance is presented in ibid., pp. 133–41.
7. Michael E. Porter, *The Competitive Advantage of Nations* (New York: Free Press, 1990), p. 66. For a discussion of how to realize the advantages of strategic partnerships, see Nancy J. Kaplan and Jonathan Hurd,

"Realizing the Promise of Partnerships," *Journal of Business Strategy* 23, no. 3 (May–June 2002), pp. 38–42; Parise and Sasson, "Leveraging Knowledge Management," pp. 41–47; and Ernst and Bamford, "Your Alliances Are Too Stable," pp. 133–41.

8. For a discussion of how to raise the chances that a strategic alliance will produce strategically important outcomes, see M. Koza and A. Lewin, "Managing Partnerships and Strategic Alliances: Raising the Odds of Success," *European Management Journal* 18, no. 2 (April 2000), pp. 146–51.
9. A. Inkpen, "Learning, Knowledge Acquisition, and Strategic Alliances," *European Management Journal* 16, no. 2 (April 1998), pp. 223–29.
10. Doz and Hamel, *Alliance Advantage,* Chapters 4–8; Patricia Anslinger and Justin Jenk, "Creating Successful Alliances," *Journal of Business Strategy* 25, no. 2 (2004), pp. 18–23; Rosabeth Moss Kanter, "Collaborative Advantage: The Art of the Alliance," *Harvard Business Review* 72, no. 4 (July–August 1994), pp. 96–108; Joel Bleeke and David Ernst, "The Way to Win in Cross-Border Alliances," *Harvard Business Review* 69, no. 6 (November–December 1991), pp. 127–35; Gary Hamel, Yves L. Doz, and C. K. Prahalad, "Collaborate with Your Competitors—and Win," *Harvard Business Review* 67, no. 1 (January–February 1989), pp. 133–39; and Jonathan Hughes and Jeff Weiss, "Simple Rules for Making Alliances Work," *Harvard Business Review* 85, no. 11 (November 2007), pp. 122–31.
11. Hughes and Weiss, "Simple Rules for Making Alliances Work," p. 122.
12. Doz and Hamel, *Alliance Advantage,* pp. 16–18.
13. Denis K. Berman, "Merger Frenzy Winds Down after 6 years," *The Wall Street Journal,* October 1, 2007, p. C5.
14. For an excellent discussion of the pros and cons of alliances versus acquisitions, see Dyer, Kale, and Singh, "When to Ally and When to Acquire," pp. 109–15.
15. For an excellent review of the strategic objectives of various types of mergers and acquisitions and the managerial challenges that different kinds of mergers and acquisition present, see Joseph L. Bower, "Not All M&As Are Alike—and That Matters," *Harvard Business Review* 79, no. 3 (March 2001), pp. 93–101.
16. For a more expansive discussion, see Dyer, Kale, and Singh, "When to Ally and When to Acquire," pp. 109–10.
17. See Kathryn R. Harrigan, "Matching Vertical Integration Strategies to Competitive Conditions," *Strategic Management Journal* 7, no. 6 (November–December 1986), pp. 535–56; for a more extensive discussion of the advantages and disadvantages of vertical integration, see John Stuckey and David White, "When and When Not to Vertically Integrate," *Sloan Management Review* (Spring 1993), pp. 71–83.
18. The resilience of vertical integration strategies despite the disadvantages is discussed in Thomas Osegowitsch and Anoop Madhok, "Vertical Integration Is Dead or Is It?" *Business Horizons* 46, no. 2 (March–April 2003), pp. 25–35.
19. This point is explored in greater detail in James Brian Quinn, "Strategic Outsourcing: Leveraging Knowledge Capabilities," *Sloan Management Review* 40, no. 4 (Summer 1999), pp. 9–21.
20. For a good discussion of the problems that can arise from outsourcing, see Jérôme Barthélemy, "The Seven Deadly Sins of Outsourcing," *Academy of Management Executive* 17, no. 2 (May 2003), pp. 87–100.
21. Michael E. Porter, *Competitive Strategy* (New York: Free Press, 1980), pp. 216–23.
22. Phillip Kotler, *Marketing Management,* 5th ed. (Englewood Cliffs, NJ: Prentice Hall, 1984), p. 366; and Porter, *Competitive Strategy,* Chapter 10.
23. Several of these were pinpointed and discussed in Charles W. Hofer and Dan Schendel, *Strategy Formulation: Analytical Concepts* (St. Paul, MN: West Publishing, 1978), pp. 164–65.
24. Ibid., pp. 164–65.
25. Porter, *Competitive Strategy,* pp. 238–40.
26. The following discussion draws on ibid., pp. 241–46.
27. An in-depth analysis of 500 companies experiencing slowing growth since 1955 indicates that about 13 percent of revenue stalls result from external factors. For a discussion of strategic factors affecting slowing revenue growth, see Matthew S. Olson, Derek van Bever, and Seth Verry, "When Growth Stalls," *Harvard Business Review* 86, no. 3 (March 2008), pp. 50–61.
28. Kathryn R. Harrigan and Michael E. Porter, "End-Game Strategies for Declining Industries" *Harvard Business Review* 61, no. 4 (July–August 1983), pp. 112–13.
29. R. G. Hamermesh and S. B. Silk, "How to Compete in Stagnant Industries," *Harvard Business Review* 57, no. 5 (September–October 1979), p. 161; and Kathryn R. Harrigan, *Strategies for Declining Businesses* (Lexington, MA: D. C. Heath, 1980).
30. Hamermesh and Silk, "How to Compete in Stagnant Industries," p. 162; Harrigan and Porter, "End-Game Strategies for Declining Industries," p. 118.
31. Hamermesh and Silk, "How to Compete in Stagnant Industries," p. 165.
32. Harrigan and Porter, "End Game Strategies for Declining Industries," pp. 111–21; Harrigan, *Strategies for Declining Businesses;* and Phillip Kotler, "Harvesting Strategies for Weak Products," *Business Horizons* 21, no. 5 (August 1978), pp. 17–18.
33. The strategic issues companies must address in fast-changing market environments are thoroughly explored in Gary Hamel and Liisa Välikangas, "The Quest for Resilence," *Harvard Business Review* 81, no. 9 (September 2003), pp. 52–63; Shona L. Brown and Kathleen M. Eisenhardt, *Competing on the Edge: Strategy as Structured Chaos* (Boston: Harvard Business School Press, 1998); and Richard A. D'Aveni, *Hyper-Competition: Managing the Dynamics of Strategic Maneuvering* (New York: Free Press, 1994). See also Richard A. D'Aveni, "Coping with Hypercompetition: Utilizing the New 7S's Framework," *Academy of Management Executive* 9, no. 3 (August 1995), pp. 45–56; and Bala Chakravarthy, "A New Strategy Framework for Coping with Turbulence," *Sloan Management Review* (Winter 1997), pp. 69–82.
34. Brown and Eisenhardt, *Competing on the Edge,* pp. 4–5.
35. Ibid., p. 4.
36. For deeper insight into building competitive advantage through R&D and technological innovation, see Shaker A. Zahra, Sarah Nash, and Deborah J. Bickford, "Transforming Technological Pioneering into Competitive Advantage," *Academy of Management Executive* 9, no. 1 (February 1995), pp. 32–41.
37. Brown and Eisenhardt, *Competing on the Edge,* pp. 14–15. See also Kathleen M. Eisenhardt and Shona L. Brown, "Time Pacing: Competing in Markets That Won't Stand Still," *Harvard Business Review* 76, no. 2 (March–April 1998), pp. 59–69.
38. The circumstances of competing in a fragmented marketplace are discussed at length in Porter, *Competitive Strategy,* Chapter 9; this section draws on Porter's treatment.
39. Porter, *Competitive Advantage,* pp. 232–33.
40. For research evidence on the effects of pioneering versus following, see Jeffrey G. Covin, Dennis P. Slevin, and Michael B. Heeley, "Pioneers and Followers: Competitive Tactics, Environment, and Growth," *Journal of Business Venturing* 15, no. 2 (March 1999), pp. 175–210; Christopher A. Bartlett and Sumantra Ghoshal, "Going Global: Lessons from Late-Movers," *Harvard Business Review* 78, no. 2 (March–April 2000), pp. 132–45; and Fernando Suarez and Guianvito Lanzolla, "The Role of Environmental Dynamics in Building a First Mover Advantage Theory," *Academy of Management Review* 32, no. 2 (April 2007), pp. 377–92.
41. For a more extensive discussion of this point, see Fernando Suarez and Gianvito Lanzolla, "The Half-Truth of First-Mover Advantage," *Harvard Business Review* 83, no. 4 (April 2005), pp. 121–27.
42. Gary Hamel, "Smart Mover, Dumb Mover," *Fortune,* September 3, 2001, p. 195.
43. W. Chan Kim and Renée Mauborgne, "Blue Ocean Strategy," *Harvard Business Review* 82, no. 10 (October 2004), pp. 76–84.
44. Porter, *Competitive Advantage,* pp.232–33.
45. Costas Markides and Paul A. Geroski," Racing to be 2nd: Conquering the Industries of the Future," *Business Strategy Review* 15, no. 4 (Winter 2004), pp. 25–31.

Chapter 7

1. For an insightful discussion of how much significance these kinds of demographic and market differences have, see C. K. Prahalad and Kenneth Lieberthal, "The End of Corporate Imperialism," *Harvard Business Review* 76, no. 4 (July–August 1998), pp. 68–79.
2. Joseph Caron, "The Business of Doing Business with China: An Ambassador Reflects," *Ivey Business Journal* 69, no. 5 (May–June 2005), p. 2.
3. U.S. Department of Labor, "International Comparisons of Hourly Compensation Costs in Manufacturing, 2006," *Bureau of Labor Statistics Newsletter,* January 25, 2008.
4. Michael E. Porter, *The Competitive Advantage of Nations* (New York: Free Press, 1990), pp. 53–54.
5. Ibid., p. 61.
6. For two especially insightful studies of company experiences with cross-border alliances, see Joel Bleeke and David Ernst, "The Way to Win in Cross-Border Alliances," *Harvard Business Review* 69, no. 6 (November–December 1991), pp. 127–35; and Gary Hamel, Yves L. Doz, and C. K. Prahalad, "Collaborate with Your Competitors—and Win," *Harvard Business Review* 67, no. 1 (January–February 1989), pp. 133–39.
7. Jan Borgonjon and David J. Hoffmann, "The Re-emergence of the Joint Venture?" *China Business Review,* May–June 2008, p. 34.
8. See Yves L. Doz and Gary Hamel, *Alliance Advantage: The Art of Creating Value through Partnering* (Boston: Harvard Business School Press, 1998), especially Chapters 2–4; Bleeke and Ernst, "The Way to Win in Cross-Border Alliances," pp. 127–33; Hamel, Doz, and Prahalad, "Collaborate with Your Competitors," pp. 134–35; and Porter, *Competitive Advantage of Nations,* p. 66;
9. H. Kurt Christensen, "Corporate Strategy: Managing a Set of Businesses," in *The Portable MBA in Strategy,* ed. Liam Fahey and Robert M. Randall (New York: Wiley, 2001), p. 43.
10. For an excellent presentation on the pros and cons of alliances versus acquisitions, see Jeffrey H. Dyer, Prashant Kale, and Harbir Singh, "When to Ally and When to Acquire," *Harvard Business Review* 82, no. 7/8 (July–August 2004), pp. 109–15.
11. For additional discussion of company experiences with alliances and partnerships, see Doz and Hamel, *Alliance Advantage,* Chapters 2–7; and Rosabeth Moss Kanter, "Collaborative Advantage: The Art of the Alliance," *Harvard Business Review* 72, no. 4 (July–August 1994), pp. 96–108.
12. Details are reported in Shawn Tully, "The Alliance from Hell," *Fortune,* June 24, 1996, pp. 64–72.
13. Jeremy Main, "Making Global Alliances Work," *Fortune,* December 19, 1990, p. 125.
14. Pralahad and Lieberthal, "The End of Corporate Imperialism," p. 77.
15. Ibid.
16. For more details on the merits of and opportunities for cross-border transfer of successful strategy experiments, see C. A. Bartlett and S. Ghoshal, *Managing Across Borders: The Transnational Solution,* 2nd ed. (Boston: Harvard Business School Press, 1998), pp. 79–80 and Chapter 9.
17. Approaches to improving a company's local relevance through adaptation of products and services to match local preferences are discussed in Pankaj Ghemawat, "Managing Differences: The Central Challenge of Global Strategy," *Harvard Business Review* 85, no. 3 (March 2007), pp. 58–68.
18. The benefits of static and dynamic arbitrage that may accompany global strategies are discussed in ibid.
19. The ability for global companies to achieve economies of scale and/or scope through aggregation is discussed in ibid., p. 65.
20. Porter, *Competitive Advantage of Nations,* pp. 53–55.
21. Arbitrage strategies that exploit cultural, governmental policy, geographic, and economic differences between countries are discussed in Pankaj Ghemawat, "The Forgotten Strategy," *Harvard Business Review* 81, no. 11 (November 2003), pp. 76–84.
22. Porter, *Competitive Advantage of Nations,* pp. 55–58.
23. C. K. Prahalad and Yves L. Doz, *The Multinational Mission* (New York: Free Press, 1987), pp. 58–60; and Ghemawat, "Managing Differences," pp. 58–68.
24. This point is discussed at greater length in Prahalad and Lieberthal, "The End of Corporate Imperialism," pp. 68–79; also see David J. Arnold and John A. Quelch, "New Strategies in Emerging Markets," *Sloan Management Review* 40, no. 1 (Fall 1998), pp. 7–20. For a more extensive discussion of strategy in emerging markets, see C. K. Prahalad, *The Fortune at the Bottom of the Pyramid: Eradicating Poverty through Profits* (Upper Saddle River, NJ: Wharton, 2005), especially Chapters 1–3.
25. Brenda Cherry, "What China Eats (and Drinks and . . .)," *Fortune,* October 4, 2004, pp. 152–53; "A Ravenous Dragon," *Economist* 386, no. 8571 (March 15, 2008), online edition; and "China: Just the Facts," *Journal of Commerce,* June 2, 2008, p. 24.
26. Prahalad and Lieberthal, "The End of Corporate Imperialism," pp. 72–73.
27. Tarun Khanna, Krishna G. Palepu, and Jayant Sinha, "Strategies That Fit Emerging Markets," *Harvard Business Review* 83, no. 6 (June 2005), p. 63; and Arindam K. Bhattacharya and David C. Michael, "How Local Companies Keep Multinationals at Bay," *Harvard Business Review* 86, no. 3 (March 2008), pp. 94–95.
28. Prahalad and Lieberthal, "The End of Corporate Imperialism," p. 72.
29. Khanna, Palepu, and Sinha, "Strategies That Fit Emerging Markets," pp. 73–74.
30. Ibid., p. 74.
31. Ibid., p. 76.
32. The results and conclusions from a study of 134 local companies in 10 emerging markets are presented in Tarun Khanna and Krishna G. Palepu, "Emerging Giants: Building World-Class Companies in Developing Countries," *Harvard Business Review* 84, no. 10 (October 2006), pp. 60–69; also, an examination of strategies used by 50 local companies in emerging markets is discussed in Bhattacharya and Michael, "How Local Companies Keep Multinationals at Bay," pp. 85–95.
33. Steve Hamm, "Tech's Future," *BusinessWeek,* September 27, 2004, p. 88.
34. Niroj Dawar and Tony Frost, "Competing with Giants: Survival Strategies for Local Companies in Emerging Markets," *Harvard Business Review* 77, no. 1 (January–February 1999), p. 122; see also Guitz Ger, "Localizing in the Global Village: Local Firms Competing in Global Markets," *California Management Review* 41, no. 4 (Summer 1999), pp. 64–84; and Khanna and Palepu, "Emerging Giants," pp. 63–66.
35. Dawar and Frost, "Competing with Giants," p. 124.
36. Ibid., p. 126; and Khanna and Palepu, "Emerging Giants," pp. 60–69.

Chapter 8

1. For a further discussion of when diversification makes good strategic sense, see Constantinos C. Markides, "To Diversify or Not to Diversify," *Harvard Business Review* 75, no. 6 (November–December 1997), pp. 93–99. For a discussion of how hidden opportunities within a corporation's existing asset base may offer growth to corporations with declining core businesses, see Chris Zook, "Finding Your Next Core Business," *Harvard Business Review* 85, no. 4 (April 2007), pp. 66–75.
2. Michael E. Porter, "From Competitive Advantage to Corporate Strategy," *Harvard Business Review* 45, no. 3 (May–June 1987), pp. 46–49.
3. Michael E. Porter, *Competitive Strategy: Techniques for Analyzing Industries and Competitors* (New York: Free Press, 1980), pp. 354–55.
4. Ibid., pp. 344–45.
5. Yves L. Doz and Gary Hamel, *Alliance Advantage: The Art of Creating Value through Partnering* (Boston: Harvard Business School Press, 1998), Chapters 1 and 2.
6. Michael E. Porter, *Competitive Advantage* (New York: Free Press, 1985), pp. 318–19 and pp. 337–53; and Porter, "From Competitive Advantage to Corporate

Strategy," pp. 53–57. For an empirical study confirming that strategic fits are capable of enhancing performance (provided the resulting resource strengths are competitively valuable and difficult to duplicate by rivals), see Constantinos C. Markides and Peter J. Williamson, "Corporate Diversification and Organization Structure: A Resource-Based View," *Academy of Management Journal* 39, no. 2 (April 1996), pp. 340–67.

7. For a discussion of the strategic significance of cross-business coordination of value chain activities and insight into how the process works, see Jeanne M. Liedtka, "Collaboration across Lines of Business for Competitive Advantage," *Academy of Management Executive* 10, no. 2 (May 1996), pp. 20–34.
8. "Beyond Knowledge Management: How Companies Mobilize Experience," *Financial Times,* February 8, 1999, p. 5.
9. For a discussion of what is involved in actually capturing strategic fit benefits, see Kathleen M. Eisenhardt and D. Charles Galunic, "Coevolving: At Last, a Way to Make Synergies Work," *Harvard Business Review* 78, no. 1 (January–February 2000), pp. 91–101. Adeptness at capturing cross-business strategic fits positively impacts performance; see Constantinos C. Markides and Peter J. Williamson, "Related Diversification, Core Competences and Corporate Performance," *Strategic Management Journal* 15 (Summer 1994), pp. 149–65.
10. Peter Drucker, *Management: Tasks, Responsibilities, Practices* (New York: Harper & Row, 1974), pp. 692–93.
11. While arguments that unrelated diversification are a superior way to diversify financial risk have logical appeal, there is research showing that related diversification is less risky from a financial perspective than is unrelated diversification; see Michael Lubatkin and Sayan Chatterjee, "Extending Modern Portfolio Theory into the Domain of Corporate Diversification: Does It Apply?" *Academy of Management Journal* 37, no. 1 (February 1994), pp. 109–36.
12. For a review of the experiences of companies that have pursued unrelated diversification successfully, see Patricia L. Anslinger and Thomas E. Copeland, "Growth through Acquisitions: A Fresh Look," *Harvard Business Review* 74, no. 1 (January–February 1996), pp. 126–35.
13. Of course, management may be willing to assume the risk that trouble will not strike before it has had time to learn the business well enough to bail it out of almost any difficulty. But there is research that shows this is very risky from a financial perspective; see, for example, Lubatkin and Chatterjee, "Extending Modern Portfolio Theory," pp. 132–33.
14. For research evidence of the failure of broad diversification and trend of companies to focus their diversification efforts more narrowly, see Lawrence G. Franko, "The Death of Diversification? The Focusing of the World's Industrial Firms, 1980–2000," *Business Horizons* 47, no. 4 (July–August 2004), pp. 41–50.
15. For an excellent discussion of what to look for in assessing these fits, see Andrew Campbell, Michael Gould, and Marcus Alexander, "Corporate Strategy: The Quest for Parenting Advantage," *Harvard Business Review* 73, no. 2 (March–April 1995), pp. 120–32.
16. Ibid., p. 123.
17. A good discussion of the importance of having adequate resources, and also the importance of upgrading corporate resources and capabilities, can be found in David J. Collis and Cynthia A. Montgomery, "Competing on Resources: Strategy in the 90s," *Harvard Business Review* 73, no. 4 (July–August 1995), pp. 118–28.
18. Ibid., pp. 121–22.
19. Drucker, *Management,* p. 709.
20. See, for, example, Constantinos C. Markides, "Diversification, Restructuring, and Economic Performance," *Strategic Management Journal* 16 (February 1995), pp. 101–18.
21. For a discussion of why divestiture needs to be a standard part of any company's diversification strategy, see Lee Dranikoff, Tim Koller, and Antoon Schneider, "Divestiture: Strategy's Missing Link," *Harvard Business Review* 80, no. 5 (May 2002), pp. 74–83.
22. Drucker, *Management,* p. 94.
23. See David J. Collis and Cynthia A. Montgomery, "Creating Corporate Advantage," *Harvard Business Review* 76, no. 3 (May–June 1998), pp. 72–80.
24. Drucker, *Management,* p. 719.
25. Evidence that restructuring strategies tend to result in higher levels of performance is contained in Markides, "Diversification, Restructuring and Economic Performance," pp. 101–18.
26. Company press release, October 6, 2005.
27. Dranikoff, Koller, and Schneider, "Divestiture," p.76.
28. C. K. Prahalad and Yves L. Doz, *The Multinational Mission* (New York: Free Press, 1987), p. 2.
29. Ibid., p. 15.
30. Ibid., pp. 62–63.

Chapter 9

1. James E. Post, Anne T. Lawrence, and James Weber, *Business and Society: Corporate Strategy, Public Policy, Ethics,* 10th ed. (Burr Ridge, IL: McGraw-Hill/Irwin, 2002), p.103.
2. For an overview of widely endorsed guidelines for creating codes of conduct, see Lynn Paine, Rohit Deshpandé, Joshua D. Margolis, and Kim Eric Bettcher, "Up to Code: Does Your Company's Conduct Meet World-Class Standards?" *Harvard Business Review* 83, no. 12 (December 2005), pp. 122–33.
3. For research on what the universal moral values are (six are identified—trustworthiness, respect, responsibility, fairness, caring, and citizenship), see Mark S. Schwartz, "Universal Moral Values for Corporate Codes of Ethics," *Journal of Business Ethics* 59, no. 1 (June 2005), pp. 27–44.
4. See, for instance, Mark. S. Schwartz, "A Code of Ethics for Corporate Codes of Ethics," *Journal of Business Ethics* 41, nos.1–2 (November–December 2002), pp. 27–43.
5. For more discussion of this point, see ibid. pp. 29–30.
6 . T. L. Beauchamp and N. E. Bowie, *Ethical Theory and Business* (Upper Saddle River, NJ: Prentice-Hall, 2001), p. 8.
7. U.S. Department of Labor, "The Department of Labor's 2006 Findings on the Worst Forms of Child Labor," 2006, p. 17, www.dol.gov/ilab/programs/ocft/PDF/2006OCFTreport.pdf, accessed September 8, 2008.
8. This dilemma is presented in W. M. Greenfield, "In the Name of Corporate Social Responsibility," *Business Horizons* 47, no. 1 (January–February 2004), p. 22.
9. For a study of why low per capita income, lower disparities in income distribution, and various cultural factors are often associated with a higher incidence of bribery, see Rajib Sanyal, "Determinants of Bribery in International Business: The Cultural and Economic Factors," *Journal of Business Ethics* 59, no.1 (June 2005), pp. 139–45.
10. For a study of bribe-paying frequency by country, see Transparency International, *2003 Global Corruption Report,* p. 267, www.globalcorruptionreport.org, accessed September 9, 2008.
11. Roger Chen and Chia-Pei Chen, "Chinese Professional Managers and the Issue of Ethical Behavior," *Ivey Business Journal* 69, no, 5 (May/June 2005), p. 1.
12. Thomas Donaldson and Thomas W. Dunfee, "When Ethics Travel: The Promise and Peril of Global Business Ethics," *California Management Review* 41, no. 4 (Summer 1999), p. 53.
13. For a study of "facilitating" payments to obtain a favor (such as expediting an administrative process, obtaining a permit or license, or avoiding an abuse of authority) which are sometimes condoned as unavoidable or are excused on grounds of low wages and lack of professionalism among public officials, see Antonio Argandoña, "Corruption and Companies: The Use of Facilitating Payments," *Journal of Business Ethics* 60, no. 3 (September 2005), pp. 251–64.
14. Donaldson and Dunfee, "When Ethics Travel," p. 59.
15 . Thomas Donaldson and Thomas W. Dunfee, *Ties That Bind: A Social Contracts Approach to Business Ethics* (Boston: Harvard Business School Press, 1999), pp. 35, 83.
16. Based on a report in M. J. Satchell, "Deadly Trade in Toxics," *U.S. News and World Report,* March 7, 1994, p. 64, and cited in Donaldson and Dunfee, "When Ethics Travel," p. 46.

17. Chen and Chen, "Chinese Professional Managers," p. 1.
18. Two of the definitive treatments of integrated social contracts theory as applied to ethics are Thomas Donaldson and Thomas W. Dunfee, "Towards a Unified Conception of Business Ethics: Integrative Social Contracts Theory," *Academy of Management Review* 19, no. 2 (April 1994), pp. 252–84 and Donaldson and Dunfee, *Ties That Bind,* especially Chapters 3, 4, and 6. See also Andrew Spicer, Thomas W. Dunfee, and Wendy J. Bailey, "Does National Context Matter in Ethical Decision Making? An Empirical Test of Integrative Social Contracts Theory," *Academy of Management Journal* 47, no. 4 (August 2004), p. 610.
19. P. M. Nichols, "Outlawing Transnational Bribery through the World Trade Organization," *Law and Policy in International Business* 28, no. 2 (1997), pp. 321–22.
20. Donaldson and Dunfee, "When Ethics Travel," pp. 55–56.
21. Archie B. Carroll, "Models of Management Morality for the New Millennium," *Business Ethics Quarterly* 11, no. 2 (April 2001), pp. 367–69.
22. Ibid., pp. 369–70.
23. For survey data on what managers say about why they sometimes behave unethically, see John F. Veiga, Timothy D. Golden, and Kathleen Dechant, "Why Managers Bend Company Rules," *Academy of Management Executive* 18, no. 2 (May 2004), pp. 84–89.
24. For more details see Ronald R. Sims and Johannes Brinkmann, "Enron Ethics (Or: Culture Matters More Than Codes)," *Journal of Business Ethics* 45, no. 3 (July 2003), pp. 244–46.
25. As reported in Gardiner Harris, "At Bristol-Myers, Ex-Executives Tell of Numbers Games," *Wall Street Journal,* December 12, 2002, pp. A1, A13.
26. Ibid., p. A13.
27. Veiga, Golden, and Dechant, "Why Managers Bend the Rules," p. 36.
28. The following account is based largely on the discussion and analysis in Sims and Brinkmann, "Enron Ethics," pp. 245–52. Perhaps the definitive book-length account of the corrupt Enron culture is Kurt Eichenwald, *Conspiracy of Fools: A True Story* (New York: Broadway Books, 2005).
29. Chip Cummins and Almar Latour, "How Shell's Move to Revamp Culture Ended in Scandal," *Wall Street Journal,* November 2, 2004, p. A14.
30. Anna Wilde Mathews and Barbara Martinez, "E-Mails Suggest Merck Knew Vioxx's Dangers at Early Stage," *Wall Street Journal,* November 1, 2004, pp. A1, A10.
31. Archie B. Carroll, "The Four Faces of Corporate Citizenship," *Business and Society Review* 100/101 (September 1998), p. 6.
32. Gedeon J. Rossouw and Leon J. van Vuuren, "Modes of Managing Morality: A Descriptive Model of Strategies for Managing Ethics," *Journal of Business Ethics* 46, no. 4 (September 2003), pp. 389–400.
33. Empirical evidence that an ethical culture approach produces better results than the compliance approach is presented in Terry Thomas, John R. Schermerhorn, and John W. Dienhart, "Strategic Leadership of Ethical Behavior," *Academy of Management Executive* 18, no. 2 (May 2004), p. 64.
34. Business Roundtable, "Statement on Corporate Responsibility," New York, October 1981, p. 9.
35. Sarah Roberts, Justin Keeble, and David Brown, "The Business Case for Corporate Citizenship," a study for the World Economic Forum, p. 3, www.weforum.org/corporatecitizenship (accessed October 14, 2003),
36. Dirk Matten and Andrew Crane, "Corporate Citizenship: Toward an Extended Theoretical Conceptualization," *Academy of Management Review* 30, no. 1 (2005), pp. 166–79.
37. Gerald I. J. M. Zetsloot and Marcel N. A. van Marrewijk, "From Quality to Sustainability," *Journal of Business Ethics* 55 (2004), pp. 79–82.
38. BP's environmental record is discussed in "Beyond the Green Corporation," *BusinessWeek,* January 29, 2007, p. 50.
39. For an excellent discussion of crafting corporate social responsibility strategies capable of contributing to a company's competitive advantage, see Michael E. Porter and Mark R. Kramer, "Strategy & Society: The Link Between Competitive Advantage and Corporate Social Responsibility," *Harvard Business Review* 84, no. 12 (December 2006), pp. 78–92.
40. N. Craig Smith, "Corporate Responsibility: Whether and How," *California Management Review* 45, no. 4 (Summer 2003), p. 63.
41. Porter and Kramer, "Strategy & Society," p. 81.
42. World Business Council for Sustainable Development, "Corporate Social Responsibility: Making Good Business Sense," January 2000, p. 7, www.wbscd.ch (accessed October 10, 2003). For a discussion of how companies are connecting social initiatives to their core values, see David Hess, Nikolai Rogovsky, and Thomas W Dunfee, "The Next Wave of Corporate Community Involvement: Corporate Social Initiatives," *California Management Review* 44, no. 2 (Winter 2002), pp. 110–25. Also see Susan Ariel Aaronson, "Corporate Responsibility in the Global Village: The British Role Model and the American Laggard," *Business and Society Review* 108, no. 3 (September 2003), p. 323.
43. www.chick-fil-a.com (accessed November 4, 2005).
44. Smith, "Corporate Responsibility," p. 63; see also World Economic Forum, "Findings of a Survey on Global Corporate Leadership," www.weforum.org/corporatecitizenship (accessed October 11, 2003).
45. Roberts, Keeble, and Brown, "The Business Case for Corporate Citizenship," p. 6.
46. Ibid., p.3.
47. Wallace N. Davidson, Abuzar El-Jelly, and Dan L. Worrell, "Influencing Managers to Change Unpopular Corporate Behavior through Boycotts and Divestitures: A Stock Market Test," *Business and Society* 34, no. 2 (1995), pp. 171–96.
48. Tom McCawley, "Racing to Improve Its Reputation: Nike Has Fought to Shed Its Image as an Exploiter of Third-World Labor Yet It Is Still a Target of Activists," *Financial Times,* December 2000, p. 14, and Smith, "Corporate Social Responsibility," p. 61.
49. Based on data in Amy Aronson, "Corporate Diversity, Integration, and Market Penetration," *BusinessWeek,* October 20, 2003, pp. 138ff.
50. Smith, "Corporate Social Responsibility," p. 62.
51. See Social Investment Forum, *2001 Report on Socially Responsible Investing trends in the United States* (Washington, D.C.: Social Investment Forum, 2001).
52. Smith, "Corporate Social Responsibility," p. 63.
53. See James C. Collins and Jerry I. Porras, *Built to Last: Successful Habits of Visionary Companies,* 3rd ed. (London: HarperBusiness, 2002); Roberts, Keeble, and Brown, "The Business Case for Corporate Citizenship," p. 4; and Smith, "Corporate Social Responsibility," p. 63.
54. Roberts, Keeble, and Brown, "The Business Case for Corporate Citizenship," p. 4.
55. Smith, "Corporate Social Responsibility," p. 65; Lee E. Preston and Douglas P. O'Bannon, "The Corporate Social-Financial Performance Relationship," *Business and Society* 36, no. 4 (December 1997), pp. 419–29; Ronald M. Roman, Sefa Hayibor, and Bradley R. Agle, "The Relationship between Social and Financial Performance: Repainting a Portrait," *Business and Society* 38, no. 1 (March 1999), pp. 109–25; and Joshua D. Margolis and James P. Walsh, *People and Profits* (Mahwah, NJ: Lawrence Erlbaum, 2001).
56. Based on information in Edna Gundersen, "Rights Issue Rocks the Music World," *USA Today,* September 16, 2002, pp. D1, D2.

Chapter 10

1. As quoted in Steven W. Floyd and Bill Wooldridge, "Managing Strategic Consensus: The Foundation of Effective Implementation," *Academy of Management Executive* 6, no. 4 (November 1992), p. 27.
2. As cited in Gary L. Neilson, Karla L. Martin, and Elizabeth Powers, "The Secrets of Successful Strategy Execution," *Harvard Business Review* 86, no. 6 (June 2008), pp. 61–62.
3. Jack Welch with Suzy Welch, *Winning* (New York: HarperBusiness, 2005), p. 135.
4. For an excellent pragmatic discussion of this point, see Larry Bossidy and Ram Charan, *Execution: The Discipline of Getting Things*

Done (New York: Crown Business, 2002), Chapter 1.

5. For an insightful discussion of how important staffing an organization with the right people is, see Christopher A. Bartlett and Sumantra Ghoshal, "Building Competitive Advantage through People," *MIT Sloan Management Review* 43, no. 2 (Winter 2002), pp. 34–41.
6. The importance of assembling an executive team with exceptional ability to see what needs to be done and an instinctive talent for figuring out how to get it done is discussed in Justin Menkes, "Hiring for Smarts," *Harvard Business Review* 83, no. 11 (November 2005), pp. 100–109; and Justin Menkes, *Executive Intelligence* (New York: HarperCollins, 2005), especially Chapters 1–4.
7. Welch with Welch, *Winning,* p. 139.
8. See Bossidy and Charan, *Execution,* Chapter 1.
9. Menkes, *Executive Intelligence,* pp. 68, 76.
10. Bossidy and Charan, *Execution,* Chapter 5.
11. Welch with Welch, *Winning,* pp. 141–42.
12. Menkes, *Executive Intelligence,* pp. 65–71.
13. Jim Collins, *Good to Great* (New York: HarperBusiness, 2001), p. 44.
14. John Byrne, "The Search for the Young and Gifted," *BusinessWeek,* October 4, 1999, p. 108.
15. James Brian Quinn, *Intelligent Enterprise* (New York: Free Press, 1992), pp. 52–53, 55, 73–74, and 76. Also, see Christine Soo, Timothy Devinney, David Midgley, and Anne Deering, "Knowledge Management: Philosophy, Processes, and Pitfalls," *California Management Review* 44, no. 4 (Summer 2002), pp. 129–51; and Julian Birkinshaw, "Why Is Knowledge Management So Difficult*?" Business Strategy Review* 12, no. 1 (March 2001), pp. 11–18.
16. Robert H. Hayes, Gary P. Pisano, and David M. Upton, *Strategic Operations: Competing through Capabilities* (New York: Free Press, 1996), pp. 503–7. Also, see Jonas Ridderstråle, "Cashing in on Corporate Competencies," *Business Strategy Review* 14, no. 1 (Spring 2003), pp. 27–38; and Danny Miller, Russell Eisenstat, and Nathaniel Foote, "Strategy from the Inside Out: Building Capability-Creating Organizations," *California Management Review* 44, no. 3 (Spring 2002), pp. 37–55.
17. Quinn, *Intelligent Enterprise,* p. 43.
18. Ibid., pp. 33, 89; James Brian Quinn and Frederick G. Hilmer, "Strategic Outsourcing," *Sloan Management Review* 35, no. 4 (Summer 1994), pp. 43–55; Jussi Heikkilä and Carlos Cordon, "Outsourcing: A Core or Non-Core Strategic Management Decision," *Strategic Change* 11, no. 3 (June–July 2002), pp. 183–93; and James Brian Quinn, "Strategic Outsourcing: Leveraging Knowledge Capabilities," *Sloan Management Review* 40, no. 4 (Summer 1999), pp. 9–22. A strong case for outsourcing is presented in C. K. Prahalad, "The Art of Outsourcing," *Wall Street Journal,* June 8, 2005, p. A13. For a discussion of why outsourcing initiatives fall short of expectations, see Jérôme Barthélemy, "The Seven Deadly Sins of Outsourcing," *Academy of Management Executive* 17, no. 2 (May 2003), pp. 87–98.
19. Quinn, "Strategic Outsourcing," p. 17
20. For a more extensive discussion of the reasons for building cooperative, collaborative alliances and partnerships with other companies, see James F. Moore, *The Death of Competition* (New York: HarperBusiness, 1996), especially Chapter 3; Quinn and Hilmer, "Strategic Outsourcing," pp. 43–55; and Quinn, "Strategic Outsourcing," pp. 9–22.
21. Quinn, *Intelligent Enterprise,* pp. 39–40; also see Barthélemy, "The Seven Deadly Sins of Outsourcing," pp. 87–98.
22. The importance of matching organization design and structure to the particular needs of strategy was first brought to the forefront in a landmark study of 70 large corporations conducted by Professor Alfred Chandler of Harvard University. Chandler's research revealed that changes in an organization's strategy bring about new administrative problems that, in turn, require a new or refashioned structure for the new strategy to be successfully implemented. He found that structure tends to follow the growth strategy of the firm—but often not until inefficiency and internal operating problems provoke a structural adjustment. The experiences of these firms followed a consistent sequential pattern: new strategy creation, emergence of new administrative problems, a decline in profitability and performance, a shift to a more appropriate organizational structure, and then recovery to more profitable levels and improved strategy execution. See Alfred Chandler, *Strategy and Structure* (Cambridge, MA: MIT Press, 1962).
23. The importance of information flows in centralized organizational structures and the value of granting decision-making rights to those close in the field is discussed in Neilson, Martin, and Powers, "The Secrets to Successful Strategy Execution," pp. 61–70.
24. The importance of empowering workers in executing strategy and the value of creating a great working environment are discussed in Stanley E. Fawcett, Gary K. Rhoads, and Phillip Burnah, "People as the Bridge to Competitiveness: Benchmarking the 'ABCs' of an Empowered Workforce," *Benchmarking: An International Journal* 11, no. 4 (2004), pp. 346–60.
25. Iain Somerville and John Edward Mroz, "New Competencies for a New World," in *The Organization of the Future,* ed. Frances Hesselbein, Marshall Goldsmith, and Richard Beckard (San Francisco: Jossey-Bass, 1997), p. 70.
26. Exercising adequate control over empowered employees is a serious issue. For example, a prominent Wall Street securities firm lost $350 million when a trader allegedly booked fictitious profits; Sears took a $60 million write-off after admitting that employees in its automobile service departments recommended unnecessary repairs to customers. Several makers of memory chips paid fines of over $500 million when more than a dozen of their employees conspired to fix prices and operate a global cartel—some of the guilty employees were sentenced to jail. For a discussion of the problems and possible solutions, see Robert Simons, "Control in an Age of Empowerment," *Harvard Business Review* 73 (March–April 1995), pp. 80–88.
27. For a discussion of the importance of cross-business coordination, see Jeanne M. Liedtka, "Collaboration across Lines of Business for Competitive Advantage," *Academy of Management Executive* 10, no. 2 (May 1996), pp. 20–34.
28. Michael Hammer and James Champy, *Reengineering the Corporation* (New York: HarperBusiness, 1993), pp. 26–27.
29. Although functional organization incorporates Adam Smith's division-of-labor principle (every person/department involved has specific responsibility for performing a clearly defined task) and allows for tight management control (everyone in the process is accountable to a functional department head for efficiency and adherence to procedures), *no one oversees the whole process and its result.* Hammer and Champy, *Reengineering the Corporation,* pp. 26–27.
30. Rosabeth Moss Kanter, "Collaborative Advantage: The Art of the Alliance," *Harvard Business Review* 72, no. 4 (July–August 1994), pp. 105–6.
31. For an excellent review of ways to effectively manage the relationship between alliance partners, see ibid., pp. 96–108.

Chapter 11

1. For a discussion of the four types of tools that can be used by managers to bring about organizational change, see Clayton M. Christensen, Matt Marx, and Howard Stevenson, "The Tools of Cooperation and Change," *Harvard Business Review* 84, no. 10 (October 2006), pp. 73–80.
2. For a discussion of the value of benchmarking in implementing strategy, see Christopher E. Bogan and Michael J. English, *Benchmarking for Best Practices: Winning Through Innovative Adaptation* (New York: McGraw-Hill, 1994), Chapters 2, 6; Mustafa Ungan, "Factors Affecting the Adoption of Manufacturing Best Practices," *Benchmarking: An International Journal* 11, no. 5 (2004), pp. 504–20; and Paul Hyland and Ron Beckett, "Learning to Compete: The Value of Internal Benchmarking," *Benchmarking: An International* Journal 9, no. 3 (2002), pp. 293–304; and Yoshinobu Ohinata, "Benchmarking: The Japanese

Experience," *Long-Range Planning* 27, no. 4 (August 1994), pp. 48–53.

3. Michael Hammer and James Champy, *Reengineering the Corporation* (New York: HarperBusiness, 1993), pp. 26–27.
4. Gene Hall, Jim Rosenthal, and Judy Wade, "How to Make Reengineering Really Work," *Harvard Business Review* 71, no. 6 (November–December 1993), pp. 119–31.
5. For more information on business process reengineering and how well it has worked in various companies, see James Brian Quinn, *Intelligent Enterprise* (New York: Free Press, 1992), p. 162; Ann Majchrzak and Qianwei Wang, "Breaking the Functional Mind-Set in Process Organizations," *Harvard Business Review* 74, no. 5 (September–October 1996), pp. 93–99; Stephen L. Walston, Lawton. R. Burns, and John R. Kimberly, "Does Reengineering Really Work? An Examination of the Context and Outcomes of Hospital Reengineering Initiatives," *Health Services Research* 34, no. 6 (February 2000), pp. 1363–88; and Allessio Ascari, Melinda Rock, and Soumitra Dutta, "Reengineering and Organizational Change: Lessons from a Comparative Analysis of Company Experiences," *European Management Journal* 13, no. 1 (March 1995), pp. 1–13. For a review of why some company personnel embrace process reengineering and some don't, see Ronald J. Burke, "Process Reengineering: Who Embraces It and Why?" *The TQM Magazine* 16, no. 2 (2004), pp. 114–19.
6. For some of the seminal discussions of what TQM is and how it works written by ardent enthusiasts of the technique, see M. Walton, *The Deming Management Method* (New York: Pedigree, 1986); J. Juran, *Juran on Quality by Design* (New York: Free Press, 1992); Philip Crosby, *Quality Is Free: The Act of Making Quality Certain* (New York: McGraw-Hill, 1979); and S. George, *The Baldrige Quality System* (New York: Wiley, 1992). For a critique of TQM, see Mark J. Zbaracki, "The Rhetoric and Reality of Total Quality Management," *Administrative Science Quarterly* 43, no. 3 (September 1998), pp. 602–36.
7. For a discussion of the shift in work environment and culture that TQM entails, see Robert T. Amsden, Thomas W. Ferratt, and Davida M. Amsden, "TQM: Core Paradigm Changes," *Business Horizons* 39, no. 6 (November–December 1996), pp. 6–14.
8. For easy-to-understand overviews of what Six Sigma is all about, see Peter S. Pande and Larry Holpp, *What Is Six Sigma?* (New York: McGraw-Hill, 2002); Jiju Antony, "Some Pros and Cons of Six Sigma: An Academic Perspective," *TQM Magazine* 16, no. 4 (2004), pp. 303–6; Peter S. Pande, Robert P. Neuman, and Roland R. Cavanagh, *The Six Sigma Way: How GE, Motorola and Other Top Companies Are Honing Their Performance* (New York: McGraw-Hill, 2000); and Joseph Gordon and M. Joseph Gordon, Jr., *Six Sigma Quality for Business and Manufacture* (New York: Elsevier, 2002). For how Six Sigma can be used in smaller companies, see Godecke Wessel and Peter Burcher, "Six Sigma for Small and Medium-sized Enterprises," *TQM Magazine* 16, no. 4 (2004), pp. 264–72.
9. Based on information posted at www.isixsigma.com (accessed November 4, 2002).
10. Kennedy Smith, "Six Sigma for the Service Sector," *Quality Digest Magazine,* May 2003, posted at www.qualitydigest.com (accessed September 28, 2003).
11. Del Jones, "Taking the Six Sigma Approach," *USA Today,* October 31, 2002, p. 5B.
12. Pande, Neuman, and Cavanagh, *The Six Sigma Way,* pp. 5–6.
13. Smith, "Six Sigma for the Service Sector."
14. Jones, "Taking the Six Sigma Approach," p. 5B.
15. Brian Hindo, "At 3M, a Struggle Between Efficiency and Creativity," *BusinessWeek,* June 11, 2007, pp. 8–16.
16. For a discussion of approaches to pursuing radical or disruptive innovations while also seeking incremental gains in efficiency, see Charles A. O'Reilly and Michael L. Tushman, "The Ambidextrous Organization," *Harvard Business Review* 82, no. 4 (April 2004), pp. 74–81.
17. Terry Nels Lee, Stanley E. Fawcett, and Jason Briscoe, "Benchmarking the Challenge to Quality Program Implementation," *Benchmarking: An International Journal* 9, no. 4 (2002), pp. 374–87.
18. For a recent study documenting the imperatives of establishing a supportive culture, see Milan Ambrož, "Total Quality System as a Product of the Empowered Corporate Culture," *TQM Magazine* 16, no. 2 (2004), pp. 93–104. Research confirming the factors that are important in making TQM programs successful in both Europe and the United States is presented in Nick A. Dayton, "The Demise of Total Quality Management," *TQM Magazine* 15, no. 6 (2003), pp. 391–96.
19. Judy D. Olian and Sara L. Rynes, "Making Total Quality Work: Aligning Organizational Processes, Performance Measures, and Stakeholders," *Human Resource Management* 30, no. 3 (Fall 1991), pp. 310–11; and Paul S. Goodman and Eric D. Darr, "Exchanging Best Practices Information through Computer-Aided Systems," *Academy of Management Executive* 10, no. 2 (May 1996), p. 7.
20. Thomas C. Powell, "Total Quality Management as Competitive Advantage," *Strategic Management Journal* 16 (1995), pp. 15–37. See also Richard M. Hodgetts, "Quality Lessons from America's Baldrige Winners," *Business Horizons* 37, no. 4 (July–August 1994), pp. 74–79; and Richard Reed, David J. Lemak, and Joseph C. Montgomery, "Beyond Process: TQM Content and Firm Performance," *Academy of Management Review* 21, no. 1 (January 1996), pp. 173–202.
21. Based on information at www.utc.com and www.otiselevator.com (accessed November 14, 2005).
22. Fred Vogelstein, "Winning the Amazon Way," *Fortune,* May 26, 2003, pp. 70, 74.
23. "The Web Smart 50," *BusinessWeek,* November 21, 2005, pp. 87–88.
24. Such systems speed organizational learning by providing fast, efficient communication, creating an organizational memory for collecting and retaining best-practice information, and permitting people all across the organization to exchange information and updated solutions. See Goodman and Darr, "Exchanging Best Practices Information through Computer-Aided Systems," pp. 7–17.
25. "The Web Smart 50," *BusinessWeek,* November 21, 2005, pp. 85–90.
26. Vogelstein, "Winning the Amazon Way," p. 64.
27. For a discussion of the need for putting appropriate boundaries on the actions of empowered employees and possible control and monitoring systems that can be used, see Robert Simons, "Control in an Age of Empowerment," *Harvard Business Review* 73 (March–April 1995), pp. 80–88.
28. Ibid. Also see David C. Band and Gerald Scanlan, "Strategic Control through Core Competencies," *Long Range Planning* 28, no. 2 (April 1995), pp. 102–14.
29. The importance of motivating and empowering workers so as to create a working environment that is highly conducive to good strategy execution is discussed in Stanley E. Fawcett, Gary K. Rhoads, and Phillip Burnah, "People as the Bridge to Competitiveness: Benchmarking the 'ABCs' of an Empowered Workforce," *Benchmarking: An International Journal* 11 no. 4 (2004), pp. 346–60.
30. Pfeffer and Veiga, "Putting People First for Organizational Success," pp. 37–45; Linda K. Stroh and Paula M. Caligiuri, "Increasing Global Competitiveness through Effective People Management," *Journal of World Business* 33, no. 1 (Spring 1998), pp. 1–16; and articles in *Fortune* on the 100 best companies to work for (various issues).
31. As quoted in John P. Kotter and James L. Heskett, *Corporate Culture and Performance* (New York: Free Press, 1992), p. 91.
32. Clayton M. Christensen, Matt Marx, and Howard Stevenson, "The Tools of Cooperation and Change," pp. 74–77.
33. The effect of management decisions on employees' basic drives that underlie motiviation is discussed in Nitin Nohria, Boris Groysberg, and Linda-Eling Lee, "Employee Motivation: A Powerful New Model," *Harvard Business Review* 86, no. 7/8 (July–August 2008), pp. 78–84.
34. For a provocative discussion of why incentives and rewards are actually counterproductive, see Alfie Kohn, "Why Incentive Plans Cannot Work," *Harvard Business Review* 71, no. 6 (September–October 1993), pp. 54–63.

35. See Steven Kerr, "On the Folly of Rewarding A While Hoping for B," *Academy of Management Executive* 9, no. 1 (February 1995), pp. 7–14; Steven Kerr, "Risky Business: The New Pay Game," *Fortune,* July 22, 1996, pp. 93–96; and Doran Twer, "Linking Pay to Business Objectives," *Journal of Business Strategy* 15, no. 4 (July–August 1994), pp. 15–18.
36. Kerr, "Risky Business: The New Pay Game," p. 96.

Chapter 12

1. Joanne Reid and Victoria Hubbell, "Creating a Performance Culture," *Ivey Business Journal* 69, no. 4 (March/April 2005), p. 1.
2. John P. Kotter and James L. Heskett, *Corporate Culture and Performance* (New York: Free Press, 1992), p. 7. See also Robert Goffee and Gareth Jones. *The Character of a Corporation* (New York: HarperCollins, 1998).
3. Kotter and Heskett, *Corporate Culture and Performance,* pp. 7–8.
4. Ibid., p. 5.
5. John Alexander and Meena S. Wilson, "Leading across Cultures: Five Vital Capabilities," in *The Organization of the Future,* ed. Frances Hesselbein, Marshall Goldsmith, and Richard Beckard (San Francisco: Jossey-Bass, 1997), pp. 291–92.
6. For a discussion of the steps involved in conducting cultural diligence, see David Harding and Ted Rouse, "Human Due Diligence," *Harvard Business Review* 85, no. 4 (April 2007), pp. 124–31.
7. Terrence E. Deal and Allen A. Kennedy, *Corporate Cultures* (Reading, MA: Addison-Wesley, 1982), p. 22. See also Terrence E. Deal and Allen A. Kennedy, *The New Corporate Cultures: Revitalizing the Workplace after Downsizing, Mergers, and Reengineering* (Cambridge, MA: Perseus, 1999).
8. Vijay Sathe, *Culture and Related Corporate Realities* (Homewood, IL: Richard D. Irwin, 1985).
9. Kotter and Heskett, *Corporate Culture and Performance,* Chapter 6.
10. See Kurt Eichenwald, *Conspiracy of Fools: A True Story* (New York: Broadway Books, 2005).
11. Reid and Hubbell, "Creating a Performance Culture," pp. 2, 5.
12. This section draws heavily on the discussion of Kotter and Heskett, *Corporate Culture and Performance,* Chapter 4.
13. There's no inherent reason why new strategic initiatives should conflict with core values and business principles. While conflict is always possible, most strategy makers lean toward choosing strategic initiatives that are compatible with the company's character and culture and that don't go against ingrained values and beliefs. After all, the company's culture is usually something that strategy makers have had a hand in building and perpetuating, so they are not often anxious to undermine core values and business principles without serious soul-searching and compelling business reasons.
14. Kotter and Heskett, *Corporate Culture and Performance,* p. 52.
15. Ibid., p. 5.
16. Avan R. Jassawalla and Hemant C. Sashittal, "Cultures That Support Product-Innovation Processes," *Academy of Management Executive* 16, no. 3 (August 2002), pp. 42–54.
17. Kotter and Heskett, *Corporate Culture and Performance,* pp. 15–16. Also see Jennifer A. Chatham and Sandra E. Cha, "Leading by Leveraging Culture," *California Management Review* 45, no. 4 (Summer 2003), pp. 20–34.
18. Clayton M. Christensen, Matt Marx, and Howard H. Stevenson, "The Tools of Cooperation and Change," *Harvard Business Review* 84, no. 10 (October 2006), pp. 77–78.
19. John Humphreys and Hal Langford, "Managing a Corporate Culture Slide," *MIT Sloan Management Review* 49, Issue 3 (Spring 2008), pp. 25–27.
20. Judy D. Olian and Sara L. Rynes, "Making Total Quality Work: Aligning Organizational Processes, Performance Measures, and Stakeholders," *Human Resource Management* 30, no. 3 (Fall 1991), p. 324.
21. www.dardenrestaurants.com (accessed November 25, 2005); for more specifics, see Robert C. Ford, "Darden Restaurants' CEO Joe Lee on the Importance of Core Values: Integrity and Fairness," *Academy of Management Executive* 16, no. 1 (February 2002), pp. 31–36.
22. For several perspectives on the role and importance of core values and ethical behavior, see Joseph L. Badaracco, *Defining Moments: When Managers Must Choose between Right and Wrong* (Boston: Harvard Business School Press, 1997); Joe Badaracco and Allen P. Webb. "Business Ethics: A View from the Trenches." *California Management Review* 37, no. 2 (Winter 1995), pp. 8–28; Patrick E. Murphy, "Corporate Ethics Statements: Current Status and Future Prospects," *Journal of Business Ethics* 14 (1995), pp. 727–40; Lynn Sharp Paine, "Managing for Organizational Integrity," *Harvard Business Review* 72, no. 2 (March–April 1994), pp. 106–17; and Tom Tyler, John Dienhart, and Terry Thomas, "The Ethical Commitment to Compliance: Building Value-Based Cultures," *California Management Review* 50, no. 2 (February 2008), pp. 31–51.
23. For a study of the status of formal codes of ethics in large corporations, see Emily F. Carasco and Jang B. Singh, "The Content and Focus of the Codes of Ethics of the World's Largest Transnational Corporations," *Business and Society Review* 108, no. 1 (January 2003), pp. 71–94; and Patrick E. Murphy, "Corporate Ethics Statements: Current Status and Future Prospects," *Journal of Business Ethics* 14 (1995), pp. 727–40. For a discussion of the strategic benefits of formal statements of corporate values, see John Humble, David Jackson, and Alan Thomson, "The Strategic Power of Corporate Values," *Long Range Planning* 27, no. 6 (December 1994), pp. 28–42. An excellent discussion of whether one should assume that company codes of ethics are always ethical is presented in Mark S. Schwartz, "A Code of Ethics for Corporate Codes of Ethics," *Journal of Business Ethics* 41, nos. 1–2 (November–December 2002), pp. 27–43.
24. See Schwartz, "A Code of Ethics for Corporate Codes of Ethics," p. 27.
25. Ford, "Darden Restaurants' CEO Joe Lee on the Importance of Core Values," pp. 31–36.
26. Michael T. Kanazawa and Robert H. Miles, *Big Ideas to Big Results* (Upper Saddle River, NJ: FT Press, 2008), p. 96.
27. James Brian Quinn, *Strategies for Change: Logical Incrementalism* (Homewood, IL: Richard D. Irwin, 1980), pp. 20–22.
28. Ibid., p. 146.
29. For a good discussion of the challenges, see Daniel Goleman, "What Makes a Leader," *Harvard Business Review* 76, no. 6 (November–December 1998), pp. 92–102; Ronald A. Heifetz and Donald L. Laurie, "The Work of Leadership," *Harvard Business Review* 75, no. 1 (January–February 1997), pp. 124–34; and Charles M. Farkas and Suzy Wetlaufer, "The Ways Chief Executive Officers Lead," *Harvard Business Review* 74, no. 3 (May–June 1996), pp. 110–22. See also Michael E. Porter, Jay W. Lorsch, and Nitin Nohria, "Seven Surprises for New CEOs," *Harvard Business Review* 82, no. 10 (October 2004), pp. 62–72.
30. Joanne Reid and Victoria Hubbell, "Creating a Performance Culture," *Ivey Business Journal* 69, no.4 (March/April 2005), p. 1.

Organization Index

A

B

C

D

G

H

O

P

Q

R

T

U

X

Y

Z

Name Index

Page numbers followed by n refer to notes.

L

M

N

O

P

Q

R

S

T

U

V

W

Y

Z

Subject Index

D

E

G

H

J

K

L

M

N

Q

R

S

T

U

W